THE TEACHER'S
BIBLE COMMENTARY

THE TEACHER'S BIBLE COMMENTARY

Edited by

H. Franklin Paschall, Old Testament
Herschel H. Hobbs, New Testament

BROADMAN PRESS
Nashville, Tennessee

4211–16

ISBN: 0–8054–1116–X
Library of Congress catalog card number: 75–189505
Dewey decimal classification: 220.7
Printed in the United States of America

CONTRIBUTORS

Donald F. Ackland, author and former editor, Nashville, Tennessee, *Deuteronomy, Hosea through Malachi*

J. P. Allen, Radio and Television Commission (SBC), Fort Worth, Texas, *John*

James E. Carter, First Baptist Church, Natchitoches, Louisiana, *Isaiah 1–39*

Robert L. Cate, First Baptist Church, Aiken, South Carolina, *Leviticus*

William B. Coble, Midwestern Baptist Theological Seminary, Kansas City, Missouri, *Revelation*

Wayne Dehoney, Walnut Street Baptist Church, Louisville, Kentucky, *Acts*

Russell H. Dilday, Jr., Second-Ponce de Leon Baptist Church, Atlanta, Georgia, *Esther through Psalms 41*

W. C. Fields, Executive Committee, Southern Baptist Convention, Nashville, Tennessee, *Galatians through James*

Fred L. Fisher, Golden Gate Baptist Theological Seminary, Mill Valley, California, *Romans through 2 Corinthians*

Clyde T. Francisco, Southern Baptist Theological Seminary, Louisville, Kentucky, *Genesis*

J. Leo Green, Southeastern Baptist Theological Seminary, Wake Forest, North Carolina, *Jeremiah and Lamentations*

Herschel H. Hobbs, First Baptist Church, Oklahoma City, Oklahoma, *editor, New Testament*

J. Hardee Kennedy, New Orleans Baptist Theological Seminary, New Orleans, Louisiana, *Psalms 42–150*

Ralph H. Langley, Willow Meadows Baptist Church, Houston, Texas, *Exodus*

Landrum P. Leavell, First Baptist Church, Wichita Falls, Texas, *Mark*

Peter McLeod, First Baptist Church, Waco, Texas, *Isaiah 40–66*

H. Franklin Paschall, First Baptist Church, Nashville, Tennessee, *editor, Old Testament*

Ben F. Philbeck, Carson-Newman College, Jefferson City, Tennessee, *Joshua through 1 Samuel*

Billy E. Simmons, East Texas Baptist College, Marshall, Texas, *1 Chronicles through Nehemiah*

Scott L. Tatum, Broadmoor Baptist Church, Shreveport, Louisiana, *2 Samuel through 2 Kings*

Malcolm O. Tolbert, New Orleans Baptist Theological Seminary, New Orleans, Louisiana, *Luke*

Curtis Vaughan, Southwestern Baptist Theological Seminary, Fort Worth, Texas, *1 Peter through Jude*

Wayne E. Ward, Southern Baptist Theological Seminary, Louisville, Kentucky, *Matthew*

Conrad R. Willard, Central Baptist Church, Miami, Florida, *Proverbs through Song of Solomon*

Fred M. Wood, Eudora Baptist Church, Memphis, Tennessee, *Numbers, Ezekiel, Daniel*

PREFACE

So far as the editors can determine, *The Teacher's Bible Commentary* is the first book of its kind ever prepared with the direct help of Sunday School teachers. This is one of several features that make this a distinctive work. It seeks to answer the actual questions that lay readers have about the meaning of the Bible.

Writers worked with Sunday School teachers in two ways. First, they secured questions from teachers concerning the passages assigned. After this, they secured readings by teachers of their manuscripts for clarity and completeness.

Also distinctive is the choice exercised in the selection of writers. As is true of many commentaries, all writers are fully committed to the unique authority and reliability of the Bible as the Word of God. All are highly qualified by study and experience as interpreters of the Bible. In addition, however, all are widely known for their ability to teach biblical materials effectively to lay people.

Another feature, though not unique, should be of interest to most readers. Writers have used both the King James Version and more recent translations in their work. The continuing use of the King James Version requires that it be given serious attention. The growing place of recent translations, however, justifies and even demands that they also be considered.

As usual in commentaries, each writer has divided his biblical material into appropriate sections. These are often one chapter in length but may be longer or shorter as indicated by the nature of the material.

The approach to discussing these sections is unusual. For each there is first a brief summary of the main content or purpose of the passage. This enables the reader to grasp the meaning of the whole passage quickly. Usually following this is a discussion of special points—problems in the meaning of particular words, concepts, events, customs, and so forth. Finally, for many passages, there is an application to Christian living today.

The commentary attempts, then, to concentrate on highlights of the biblical message. Due to the spatial limits of a one-volume commentary, it does not attempt to explain many details that are of concern to advanced Bible scholars. For such study, readers are referred to multivolume works such as *The Broadman Bible Commentary*.

The Teacher's Bible Commentary has its origin in a request from the Southern Baptist Convention to its Sunday School Board (parent agency of Broadman Press) in 1965 to prepare a one-volume commentary on the Bible. Due to the publisher's work at the time on *The Broadman Bible Commentary*, detailed work on the new project could not be undertaken until 1969. Specific plans were completed in 1970 by an editorial advisory group that included, in addition to the editors, nine key personnel of the Board and two prospective writers. Joseph F. Green has worked with the editors from this time as Broadman Press's coordinator for the project.

The editors and publisher join in expressing their thanks to all twenty-three of the writers who have made this book possible. Special gratitude also must be expressed to two of these, Donald F. Ackland and Fred M. Wood, who stepped in to take up the assignment of one prospective writer who was unable to complete his work. These two men thus have made an unusually large contribution by the quantity as well as the quality of their work.

A further word of appreciation is due to the Foreign Mission Board of the Southern Baptist Convention and its audio-visual personnel under the leadership of Fon H. Scofield, Jr., for providing the many excellent pictures that illustrate the book. As credit lines with the pictures show, Mr. Scofield also deserves recognition as the principal photographer involved.

Four items in the concluding section on bible study aids are taken from the Broadman Films transparency sets "Bible Lands" and "Bible Maps." These have been prepared by W. Murray Severance and are copyrighted 1969 or 1971 by Broadman Films.

This book is issued with the prayer that it may aid many Christians in their understanding of, and loyalty to, the Bible as God's Word for us today. All of its writers are Southern Baptists, in line with the Convention request of 1965, but it is offered to the Christian world for the use of all who would grow in their understanding of Bible truth.

CONTENTS

GENESIS

Clyde T. Francisco

THE MYSTERIOUS WAYS OF GOD

When God finally appeared to Job in Job 38—41, he reminded him of the mysterious nature of creation. Yet in the midst of his hidden work he still spoke to his servant Job. There is much that perplexes us about the book of Genesis and the subjects it treats; yet God still speaks to us from its sacred pages with a sure and certain word.

Many people are disturbed by the apparent conflict between Genesis and science. Genesis says that the earth was created in six days while modern science claims that it is billions of years old. Genesis speaks of man as a special creation of God but many scientists contend that he has developed from lower forms of life. Yet the Bible does not say that the six days were 24 hours in length. They could have been 24 hours or millions of years, for a day is as a thousand years with God. Genesis does not really stress either the time or the manner of God's creation, but the certainty that all the universe, climaxed by man, is the creative work of God. "It is he that hath made us, and not we ourselves" (Ps. 101:3).

Equally shrouded in mystery is the history of the book of Genesis. The English title "The First Book of Moses Called Genesis" is an addition to the actual text of the Bible, which has no title at all, and represents the opinion of the translators. The book itself does not claim to be written by Moses, although it could have been; nor does any other passage in the Bible, Old Testament or New Testament, claim that he was the responsible author. Many scholars are convinced that the book of Genesis is composed of three basic sources which contain Hebrew tradition handed down for centuries.

Such source analysis is not accepted by many scholars. The most telling criticism of the prevalent position is made by Derek Kidner in his commentary on Genesis ("Tyndale Old Testament Commentaries"). Yet even he admits that traditional sources were used by the author of Genesis, call them what we may.

Amid all of the uncertainty concerning how the materials contained in the book of Genesis have come down to us, we need to realize that they have been used by the Spirit of God to proclaim to all men the assured word of God. We can believe in what they give witness. In the words of a perceptive writer centuries ago, "It matters not with what pen the king has written his letter as long as it be known that he writ it!"

Another problem is the relationship of the Old Testament accounts to similar ones in Babylon and Canaan, especially the Babylonian creation account (Enuma Elish) and flood story (Gilgamesh Epic). Their similarities, such as the dividing by the firmament of the waters above and below it, the serpent's robbing man of eternal life, the sending forth of the raven after the flood, can hardly be coincidental. Did the Hebrews borrow from the Babylonians? Or are the accounts derived from an older original source? The difference in personal names in the stories would indicate the latter. Abraham came from the same region where the Babylonian accounts were current. His family had preserved the old stories in the biblical form.

Further perplexity surrounds the problems of the literary form of the materials in Genesis. How much of the account is figurative and how much literal? Some would say that since the accounts are in the Bible, they are all to be interpreted literally. Yet it is apparent that the Bible does not always use literal language. When Jesus said that his followers must eat his flesh and drink his blood, he did not mean to be taken literally, but rather to be taken seriously. If the serpent in Genesis were only a serpent, then the statement in Genesis 3:15 would mean that there would be continual warfare between mankind and snakes, until all snakes were crushed! No one makes such an interpretation of the passage. The serpent symbolized the power of evil in the world, which the New Testament identifies as Satan. Adam is not symbolic man, but representative man. He was the first man, who is like us all, or rather the one whom we all resemble—our common ancestor.

The search for meaning in Genesis continues. We must make an honest attempt to recognize the true literary form of a passage. After we have interpreted it in this light, we are bound to the meaning it brings to us. Literal or figurative, it is truth to be believed. Often we may not agree upon the literal or figurative nature of a passage, but the basic meaning will still be the same. We should stress our common ground, not make a battleground of our differences, and thus obscure the truth we all possess.

The Creative Acts of God (Gen. 1:1—2:4a)

The passage.—This magnificent chapter is one of the most concise and dramatic sections of the Old Testament. It indeed covers a longer period of time than all of the rest of the Bible, yet with an overview that could only come from the perspective of divine revelation. Some have called it a creation hymn, but this cannot be true, for it is in prose. It shows every evidence of being intended for liturgical use, of being recited in public worship. It was not intended to be dissected by theologians, but to be listened to and proclaimed. It is clear that the passage has one major thrust—to declare that one Creator formed the natural world according to his own will and ordained it for his purpose.

Special points.—The Hebrew does not say "in the beginning" but rather "in beginning" or "when he began." There has been no beginning for God, for he has always been. Here the writer presents the beginning of the universe, not the beginning of all reality. When the scene unfolds, the earth has neither form nor content, but the deep is already there. Obviously God had already created it, but Genesis does not deal with that matter, since it is concerned with the creation of the present world and is not a theology textbook.

The verb translated "create" literally means "to cleave" or to "split" as a carpenter employs his trade. Yet in this particular form it is never used of man. Only God can create. Creation is what God can do that is impossible for man. Man, created in God's image, may, many years later, perform similar acts. If scientists one day produce life from inorganic compounds, they will not have proved that there is no God, but rather will affirm what Genesis has claimed all this time—that man is made in the image of God!

How long did it take God to create the heaven and the earth? The term "day" is used three different ways in

Genesis 1 and 2. In verse 5*a* it is used of light over against darkness, in 5*b* of the combination of evening and morning (darkness and light) and in 2:4*b* of the entire period of creation. It would be unwise, then, to limit the passage to six twenty-four-hour days. The sun, which determines the length of our days, was not in place until the fourth day!

Some expositors see a destruction of a previous earth and a new creation between Genesis 1:1 and 1:2, thus explaining the obvious age of the earth and its life-forms in this way. This view holds that scientists observe evidence from the old earth, not the more recent one. Yet this can hardly be true, for if the first earth ceased to have form or content, there would be nothing left to examine! Besides, Revelation 21:1 says that this present earth is the first one, not the second.

What is the image of God in man? Many volumes have been written on this matter, resulting in as many opinions. Yet most of them present impossible difficulties. This image must be something common to all men, yet not shared by the animals, which are not said to possess it. This immediately eliminates the physical aspect, which a casual visit to any zoo will verify. The suggestion that it is language which distinguishes man from animals must be rejected since many animals, even fish, have ways of communicating with each other. On the other hand, we always are discovering that human lines of communication constantly are breaking down. As for intelligence, some animals may be smarter than some people. Is the difference that man has a soul and lower animals do not? The Hebrew word for soul is *nephesh*. In 2:7 man becomes a living *nephesh*. But in 2:19 the identical phrase is applied to animals ("living creature," Hebrew—"living *nephesh*"). The difference between man and animals is not in the fact that one is a soul (personality) and the other is not, but in the kind of soul that man is. God gives to man his own breath (2:7), but that is not said of the animals.

What then, is the image of God? The simplest explanation is to notice how God is described in the first chapter of Genesis. Man is like that. God is pictured as freely creating. The Hebrew word *bara* ("create") is never used of man, but the fact that God summoned man to assume supervision over creation reveals that he gave him the ability to respond freely to the challenge. Animals can only adjust to their environment; man can create his own. To combat the cold, he has built furnaces. To alleviate the heat he has devised air-conditioners. When man adjusts meekly to an uncomfortable environment, he assumes the level of lower animals. Man was made for higher things.

What is the meaning of the plural, "Let us make man" in 1:26? Some say it speaks of the Trinity, others see in it the remnants of an old polytheism, the belief in many gods. The word "God" (*Elohim*) is plural, but it takes a singular verb except in 1:26. Genesis 1 teaches, therefore, that God is both singular and plural. In what sense it does not say. The doctrine of the Trinity will rightly develop later from these beginnings.

The Original State of Man (Gen. 2:4b–25)

The passage.—It is obvious that this passage presents creation from a different perspective from Genesis chapter 1. Yet these chapters do not contradict each other. Rather they are complementary. As in the Gospels the difference in perspective enriches our understanding of Jesus, so the diversity of the Genesis accounts strengthens their witness. Genesis 1:1 to 2:4*a* pictures God as transcendent, creating by speaking. Genesis

2:4*b*–25 describes his shaping man as a potter would shape his clay and speaks of his walking in the garden in the cool of the day. Are not both pictures necessary? God is both holy and accessible, speaking from afar yet dwelling close to man.

In Genesis 1:1 to 2:4*a* God moves in creation from lower to higher forms. In 2:4*b*-25, man makes his appearance before the animals. Again, there is no contradiction. The first account clearly presents creation in chronological order, whereas the second mentions each form of life as the need arises in the story.

In the first account the name for deity is "God" (Hebrew, *Elohim*), while the divine name in the second account is "the Lord God" (Hebrew, *Yahweh Elohim*). *Elohim* is the general name for deity; *Yahweh* is the personal and covenant name of Israel's God. Placed together the two passages say *"Yahweh is Elohim*. It is the God of Israel who brought the world into existence."

The thrust of Genesis 1:1 to 2:4*a* is comprehensive. It stresses how God brought the universe into being. This universe is the home for man who was made like God and commissioned to attain mastery over the world his Lord had created. However, Genesis 2:4*b*-25 is more detailed. Where the first passage speaks in generalities, the second becomes more specific. One section has a more commanding overview; the other has more intriguing insights along the way. However, they serve the same purposes of God for man. In one instance man is to serve him in a garden, in the other the whole earth. Clearly man has been created to realize the purposes of God.

Special points.—The word "Eden" means a pleasant place. The word "garden" in Hebrew is the usual word for garden. However, when the scholars who

translated the Old Testament into the Greek around 200 B.C. made their choice, they selected a Persian word, *Paradise.* Since that time the home of Adam and Eve has been known as the "Paradise of Eden" or simply "Paradise."

Where was the Garden of Eden? Three of the four rivers mentioned are the Tigris (Hiddekel), Euphrates, and the Nile (Gihon). The fourth could be the Indus (Pishon). These rivers do not touch one another now. Some scholars would explain this by saying that the rivers have changed their courses because of the great Flood. If this is true, the Flood must have been much earlier than is commonly supposed. Certainly the location described is in the general area known as the Fertile Crescent of the Near East.

Other expositors believe that the Garden of Eden tradition preserves the memory of the original cradles of civilization in Africa, Arabia, and Mesopotamia. They are said to branch from one source because originally all men came from one place.

The tree of life represents everlasting life. It should be noted that man was not given everlasting life in creation. He is not naturally immortal, as the Greeks believed. The Hebrews believed that all men continued to exist after they died, but that this afterlife was a shadowy, meaningless existence (Job 10:21–22; Isa. 38:18–19). Meaningful everlasting life is a gift of God, given only to his children.

The tree of knowledge represents the knowledge possible to man by the use of his own reason. The phrase should be translated "the tree of knowledge, good and evil." It is both good and evil, depending upon the use made of it. God himself possesses this knowledge (3:22). In all probability, he would have one day let Adam eat of it. In Genesis 1:29,

Adam was told that he could eat of every tree (no exceptions). This is the ideal: He must not eat of it *now,* for he was not yet ready. First of all, he must learn to trust God's word. Then, he would know what to do with the knowledge.

The problem confronting the world today is not that we have too much knowledge, for knowledge is good. Our dilemma is that we do not have the faith to give the knowledge meaning and direction. To substitute knowledge for faith is to destroy ourselves. To let faith interpret and direct our knowledge is to fulfil the will of God.

When God created Adam, he made him innocent but not virtuous. Innocence is man's condition before he knows the difference between right and wrong. He is innocent because he does not know what evil is. A person is virtuous when he comes face to face with temptation and rejects the evil in favor of the good.

What connection did the tree of knowledge have with sex? The popular view is that it was physical sex between the two. However, this could not be true, for God had commanded them to be fruitful and multiply. It would not be a sin to follow his directions. Besides, Eve committed the sin by herself and then Adam sinned. Their sin was not the first physical relationship. A relationship that was wholesome and sacred was distorted. Their new knowledge made them see evil where before there had only been good. Sex became shameful because their minds were evil. In this passage there is also a clear protest against the perverse use of sex in Canaanite religion. The Canaanites were turning good into evil. Still today distorted minds see in the sex relationship only the possibility for the realization of selfish lust or an unpleasant submission to a marriage

vow. It was meant to be a natural and wholesome expression of love and of the urge to continue the creative work of God.

The Fall of Man (Gen. 3:1–7)

The passage.—The "fall" was a failure as well as a fall. Throughout the Bible, whether in the Old Testament or the New, the word "sin" means missing the mark, or failure. Man's failure to be what God intends is sin. If there is anything in one's life that should not be there, or if at any time one falls short of what God wants him to be, he has sinned. As the New Testament puts it, "All have sinned and come short of the glory of God" (Rom. 3:23). A person is a sinner whenever he fails to become the very best that God intends for him, whenever he fails to accomplish God's original purpose—to reveal his glory. Adam not only fell—he failed; he came short; he sinned.

When God created Adam, he created him innocent but not virtuous. There is a difference. Innocence is one's condition before he knows the difference between right and wrong. He is innocent because he is not aware of evil. A person is virtuous when he comes face to face with temptation and rejects the evil in favor of the good. Adam had not yet become virtuous; he was innocent. God intended that Adam should progress to the point where he could overcome all temptations; then he would become virtuous, or righteous. However, he fell short, and we have been following his example ever since.

The scene in the third chapter of Genesis is not only something that happened to Adam and Eve thousands of years ago. It takes place in the life of every person. Individuals today have similar experiences and yield just as Adam and Eve did. Eve's threefold temptation (v. 6) was in the area of strong human drives.

John clearly describes it in 1 John 2:16: "the lust of the flesh, and the lust of the eyes, and the pride of life." This is the threefold temptation that came to Jesus, for just as the first Adam fell, the Second Adam must triumph.

Special points.—In Genesis the serpent is both literal and figurative. He is not called Satan, although the New Testament later identifies him as such (Rev. 12:9). An ancient story of why snakes crawl on their bellies is used to picture the invasion of the human realm by demonic power. Genesis 3:15 clearly describes the conflict between the human race and evil forces, not simply hostility between people and snakes! The serpent is a "creature" formed by God. Whatever trouble exists in the universe has happened within it. God's world is not challenged by rival forces outside it (as in dualistic polytheism) but from within, and subject to his control. Later Satan is always described as a fallen angel, never a rival god.

Genesis 2:23–24 says that Adam, in his delight, broke into poetry at the sight of Eve. But what did Eve think about Adam? On an occasion like this it is strange that she said nothing.

Apparently Eve was more interested in something else. The most wonderful person that Eve knew was not Adam; it was God. The serpent came to her and said, "Now if you want to be like God, you must eat of this tree." Is there anything wrong with a desire to be like God? Surely such an ambition is the highest that a man or woman can have. But there are no shortcuts to its fulfilment. To be like God, man must have righteousness as well as knowledge.

Truth for today.—Eve fell because she ignored what God said: "In the day that thou eatest thereof, thou shalt surely die." Satan said, "You shall not surely die." She preferred the word of Satan to the word of God.

This decision continues to confront us. Time and time again we come face to face with an act which the Word of God condemns. Yet we, ignoring the word of God, decide to do it. Temptation is overcome by believing and obeying the word of God. Jesus knew the Scripture well enough to apply its truth to overcome every temptation. Now he uses it as he helps us in our struggles.

Consequences of the Fall (Gen. 3:8–24)

The passage.—Adam and Eve probably feared that they would be struck dead by a blow from God when they ate the forbidden fruit, but his wrath, as so often it does, took an unexpected turn. They were overcome with a deep sense of guilt that made them aware of their nakedness. Man cannot sin against God without experiencing a profound sense of alienation and shame.

Yet God did not leave them alone in their fallen condition. He sought them out in the twilight of that tragic day. His clearest word to them was one of condemnation, but the encounter was not without hope, for God is love in the Old Testament as well as the New.

Eve is told that she must endure the pain of travail and submission to her husband, and Adam must toil for his living in a hostile environment. Men and women alike must struggle desperately with the serpent's seed as he pours his venom into their lives.

Yet the serpent's head will one day be crushed and evil conquered by woman's seed, born of her travail. And man amid his toil, and condemned to return to dust, will one day rise above it, for the gate to the tree of life is not locked forever, but guarded by the angelic cherubim (cf. Ezek. 1,10), who will turn their flaming swords aside when the True man arrives before that gate. Else the gate would not be guarded, but rather the tree of life would have been uprooted, the wall torn down, and the garden destroyed, as in Isaiah 5. It is kept in its pristine condition for the benefit of another more perfect generation (Rev. 2:7; 22:1 ff.).

In spite of the fallen state of man which necessitated his removal from paradise, there is still hope for him in the grace of God. His nakedness is covered by God himself, an act which symbolizes God's forgiveness. To be forgiven by God does not spare men or their descendants the consequences of their sins upon the earth. Yet by the grace of God they may find forgiveness even while they are paying the penalty for their thoughtlessness. The use of animal skins in clothing Adam and Eve implies the death of the animals, perhaps even an animal sacrifice.

Special point.—Genesis 3:15 is known as the Protevangelium (first gospel). In its original context it speaks of the mortal conflict between mankind (seed of woman) and evil (seed of the serpent). As man "crushes" the head of the serpent, the fangs of the serpent "crush" his heel. Some expositors feel there is no certain note of victory here, for the blows shared prove fatal on both sides! However, it is certain that the serpent will die, but by a miracle man may survive. Yet it will clearly take a miracle. The victory implied in this passage is not to be found in the one verse, but in the context of hope pervading the entire story. Man deserves to die, but God will surely not allow evil to defeat his good purpose for man. A way will be found to get man back into that garden. Genesis 3:15 does not tell us how. It remains for the New Testament to declare that

Jesus has fulfilled this passage. In him man has finally conquered Satan (Rev. 12:9).

East of Eden (Gen. 4:1–26)

The passage.—It might appear that Satan was right in saying that Adam and Eve would not die when they ate of the forbidden fruit. To be true they were forced to leave the bliss of Eden, but life still went on, as laborious as it was. Eve rejoiced in the birth of their first son, calling him Cain ("possession"). In an alien world she at last had something "all her own" by the grace of God. Then, for some mysterious reason, she named her second son Abel ("vanity"). Had stubborn Cain already been more than she could handle? However, some expositors suggest that the boys were twins, since conception is mentioned only once, and bearing a son, twice! If this was true, Abel's name reflected her dismay over the continuing travail of giving birth.

It is to be noted that the first murder occurred because of a disagreement among brothers concerning how God should be worshiped. No controversies breed more hostility than religious ones. When Adam and Eve discovered the dead body of Abel, they had their first encounter with human death. They saw the divinely declared consequences of their sin in the lives of their children before they experienced death themselves. Too late they understood the death about which God had warned them.

The mark that was put on Cain was not placed there as punishment, but in order to protect him. It was not a curse but a blessing. The curse was that the farmer would be forced from his land, to become a wanderer on the face of the earth. His descendants, seeking to compensate for their restlessness, were the founders of civilization, domesticating animals, and pioneering in music and industry. Lamech, boasting in his pride of achievement, exclaimed that he did not need God to protect him, as did Cain, but could defend himself with the sword made by his skilled son Tubal-Cain. Only the line of Seth, Adam's third son, turned to God. Enosh ("weakness") felt his need of God's strength.

Special points.—What was the sin of Cain? Some suggest that he was rejected for not bringing an animal sacrifice. However, since he was a farmer, what was more natural than for him to bring his produce? Of course, the blood offering was the principal offering in the Old Testament;. this passage accentuates that. However, in the later Mosaic system produce was quite acceptable to God as a thank offering, which this probably was. The "meat" offering of Leviticus 2:1 ff. was a cereal or produce offering. At the time of the King James Version "meat" meant food of any sort, not just flesh.

Cain and his offering were rejected because he did not bring his best produce. Abel brought his firstlings, his best sheep. Cain did not bring his firstfruits, his best, but only some of his crop. His gift expressed his gratitude to God for helping him have a good crop. God had served him well. Abel's gift expressed his total dependence upon God. Symbolically his life was poured out before God. It is not the purpose of religion to get God to help man become successful, to do man's will (as in Canaanite religion), but to help man discover and carry out the will of God for him.

Where did Cain get his wife? Adam and Eve had other sons and daughters (Gen. 5:4). He probably married (in later years) a sister or a more distant relative. Yet the passage seems to assume the existence of other people besides his family. Cain is afraid of being killed by other people. His marriage is mentioned so matter-of-factly that the writer seems to see no problem in it.

It is possible that other men were created after Adam and Eve, and the Bible does not mention it except here. If such men were created, their posterity were destroyed in the flood. All men living today are descendants of Adam through Noah, because only Noah and his family survived the flood.

The Antediluvian Patriarchs (Gen. 5:1–32)

The passage.—This chapter presents the descendants of Adam until the great flood. The average life was nine hundred years. Methuselah, who lived the longest, died in the year of the flood. The pathetic refrain, "he lived . . . he begat . . . he died" is unbroken except in the case of Enoch, who "was not, for God took him." This statement is all the more remarkable because it occurs in this context. One man from this long list did not share the fate common to all men since the fall of Adam. Death as we know it did not come to him. There was no "corpus delecti," for he was taken directly to be with God. Why was this possible? Because he walked with God. Later writers came to the conclusion that if this could happen to Enoch, they too had hope for the afterlife if they walked with God (cf. Ps. 73:24).

Special point.—How can the long life of these patriarchs be explained? Did they have a different way of keeping time then? Their method was not that different. A year in any culture has transpired when the seasons return. Does the writer simply make them live longer in order to teach that sin has shortened the life span? Old Testament writers do not deal that carelessly with history.

It is obvious that the ages of the patriarchs listed here were the ages attributed to them in Hebrew tradition. It is significant to note that the ages given in the Greek Septuagint and the Samaritan Pentateuch differ from these and from one another. When traditions are handed down, changes sometimes occur which are similar to those that happen when texts are copied.

Did these patriarchs actually live this long, or did the inspired writer simply use the expanded traditions as they came to him? There is no way to prove either position, but biblical statements stand until disproved. The burden of proof rests with those who question the historicity of the tradition.

Truth for today.—The refrain that pervades this chapter, "He lived . . . he begat . . . he died," is not simply a résumé of life before the flood. It also sums up the average life today. The usual obituary will give only the date of birth, the names of the children, and the date of death. The person is simply a link between the generations; the world is no better and no worse for his having been here. Surely more is intended for man than that. We are placed here to make the world a better place in which to live. It should be a little more pleasant because our lives have touched others. The travail of the universe should be somewhat eased by the birth of God's children.

The Great Flood (Gen. 6:1—8:19)

The passage.—Many scholars find two sources in this section. The earlier, more popular one says that two of every kind of unclean animal was taken on the ark, but seven pairs of every clean animal were taken. The later account, the priestly one, has only two of every kind whether clean or unclean, for this source does not mention sacrifice until the time of Moses, when God ordained the He-

brew sacrificial system. In the earlier source the flood lasted only a little over two months. In the later one it prevailed for more than a year.

This view necessitates the slicing of verses into fragments and independent segments. There is a growing tendency today to distrust such arbitrary "scissors and paste" methods. If two sources exist, they only show occasional traces of their independence, and rather than contradicting one another, reinforce the validity of the original event to which they give independent witness.

In the view of the biblical writer the flood was necessary because man had become so evil that there was no hope for civilization. The situation was so bad that God "repented" that he had made man. This does not mean that God was taken by surprise. The literal meaning of the verb "repent" is "to sigh." The verb expresses his heartache over the sad state of man, not his failure to anticipate it.

One reason why man had become so wretched was the strange behavior of the "sons of God." Traditional expositors identify them with the sons of Seth ("godly sons") who married the daughters of Cain, thus completely corrupting the human race. Yet the idiom "sons of God" occurs elsewhere only three times, in the book of Job (1:6; 2:1; 38:7). There they plainly are angels. Thus, according to another view, the Genesis passage seems to be saying that angels married women. The Old Testament view would permit this interpretation. Angels always looked like men. In fact, the men of Sodom tried to sin with them; from this comes our word "sodomy." Jesus said that in the afterlife we would be like the angels in heaven, but what about the angels *in hell* for their misdeeds in Genesis 6?

Other scholars suggest that the writer

of Genesis took an old story that told how giants sprang from the union of angels and women, and used it to explain the invasion of the human realm by the demonic. God revealed to the writer that if it had not been for the presence of the demonic in society, man's condition would have been less hopeless. He used a story at hand to illustrate this sobering truth.

Whether man had brought himself into such a hopeless condition or whether the presence of the demonic explains it, there was no recourse but to destroy society. The flood is variously identified today. Some find evidence for it in the silt left by Mesopotamian rivers. Others are suggesting that it was a devastating typhoon roaring in from the Indian Ocean. However, it is more likely that the deluge came in primeval times, and extensive traces of its presence have been erased by subsequent sands of time.

Special points.—Was the great flood universal? There is no question but that the traditions used by the writer of Genesis contains such a view. The world known to the Hebrews was covered by water. There is also the possibility that the flood covered all the earth where human and animal life existed, all the earth known to the family of Noah. The essentials of the biblical story do not demand that the water cover every inch of the earth's surface but that it destroy all life where man was then living.

Some scholars believe that archaeology has proven a universal flood. To be sure it has not disproved it. What it has done is to show that there is evidence that every part of the earth was at one time covered with water. The evidence is not clear that it happened at the same time in one flood. The flood may have covered all the earth, but it can not be proven by archaeology, nor does science have to prove it for us to believe it.

What bearing do the flood stories of other peoples have upon an understanding of the biblical accounts? Every nation has a flood story, a fact which reinforces the biblical claim of a flood experienced by the ancestors of us all. The accounts most similar to the Hebrew are from Babylonia, particularly the Gilgamesh Epic. Here the correspondences are verbal and hardly coincidental. Descriptive details are often identical. It is in the picture of the kind of God who sends the flood that the stories are so different. It would appear then that the God of Israel led an inspired writer to speak of his wrath and grace toward sinful man. The story of the flood, preserved faithfully by the Hebrew forefathers, was used to illustrate this timeless reality.

Aftermath of the Flood (Gen. 8:20—9:28)

The passage.—As soon as Noah was once again on dry land, God proceeded to correct any misconceptions he or later generations might have imagined because of the deluge. Since God had so quickly destroyed the human race, some might have concluded that human life was cheap. Therefore God warned Noah that this was not the case. Any man who took another's life must pay with his own. It was also likely, every time a heavy rain began to fall, that men would fear another flood. Noah was assured that the regular cycles of nature would occur as long as the earth stood. God's mercy would triumph over his wrath even if man still deserved to die (8:20–22).

The command to Adam to multiply was repeated to Noah, but the order to have dominion was changed to an assurance of dominion (9:1–2). Man, for the first time, was given the right to eat flesh, since the animals owed their very existence to Noah's care of them during the flood.

Never did a man have a better chance to build a brave new world. All evil men and power structures were destroyed. At long last the kind of society God had first intended was possible. But what happened? Noah was found drunk in his tent. Would that men strove in times of peace with the same heroism they exhibit in days of peril!

Special points.—It is not said in Genesis 9:13 that this was the first time a rainbow had appeared, any more than the silence of Genesis teaches that it did not rain until the flood. Surely life would have had more trouble surviving in those times of draught than during the flood. Every schoolchild knows what causes a rainbow. Surely such atmospheric conditions had prevailed before the deluge. The meaning is that what was formerly only a phenomenon of nature had taken on a new significance every time it appeared. Its beauty would henceforth remind both God and man of his promises.

What was the sin of Ham? Some expositors suggest that it was a homosexual act, for carnal knowledge is sometimes referred to in the Old Testament as "uncovering the nakedness" of someone (cf. Lev. 18:6–18; 20:17). In this passage, however, Ham does not uncover his father but finds him in that condition. If his had been a sexual act, he probably would not have told his brothers; had he told them, they probably would have stoned him! This passage reflects the Hebrew view that nakedness was related to shame (cf. Gen. 3:7), a concept the Greeks did not share.

Neither was Ham blamed for stumbling upon his drunken father. What he is censored for is his failure to cover up his father's shame, and his gossip to his brothers. If, after seeing his father, he had covered Noah's nakedness and kept the matter to himself, he would have been totally exonerated.

The greatest problem in the passage, however, is the fact that a curse is not pronounced upon Ham, but rather upon Canaan, his son. Why would Canaan be cursed because of the sin of his father? Some scholars support a corrupt text here and suggest either that it was originally Ham who was cursed, or that it was Canaan who actually committed the sin. It is more likely, however, that Noah was making a prediction than that he was pronouncing a curse on an innocent man. There is no verb "to be" in 9:25. Literally it reads, "Cursed Canaan." With a father like Ham, Canaan's future is dark indeed!

Truth for today.—Noah's sin is taken seriously. Genesis 6:9 says that Noah "walked with God" even as Enoch. One would suppose that God would "take" him also to be with him, for he is no respecter of persons. But afterward Noah sinned, and it is simply said that "he died." Yet the sin of Ham is viewed even more seriously here. Drunkenness is morally inexcusable, but idle gossip about such an error is even worse.

The opinion that "A Negro is all right in his own place" (second to the white man) is derived from this passage. Canaan is to be the slave of the Indo-Europeans (Japheth). However, Negroes are not descendants of Canaan, who was white, but are descended from Ham. The curse was not predicted upon all of Ham's descendants, but only upon the Canaanites. This passage was written to explain the Hebrews' right to enslave the Canaanites. It has nothing to do with the white-black issue.

The Human Family (Gen. 10:1–32)

The passage.—This chapter arranges all the people known to the biblical writers among the descendants of the three

sons of Noah. The offspring of Ham settled primarily in Africa and Arabia, the
descendants of Japheth in Asia Minor
and Europe, and the Semites (Shemites)
in Mesopotamia, Syria, and Palestine.
The arrangement here is more geographical than racial, however. If a people
dwelt in the territory commonly ascribed
to Ham, they were considered Hamite,
for they became adopted sons of that
culture.

Special points.—Many of the names
in the chapter cannot be identified with
certainty. For instance, Cushites can be
either Arabians or Ethiopians (10:7), and
Tarshish may be either Crete, Italy, or
Spain. Other names have modern deriva-
tives such as Gomer and Germany,
Meshech and Moscow, Tiras and Tyre.
Javan is Greece; Kittim is Cyprus; Aram
is Syria; Mizraim is Egypt.

These genealogical lists are occasionally broken by interesting personal nota-
tions. One of the most significant is the
reference to Nimrod (9:8–10). Even
God regarded him as a great hunter ("the
mighty hunter before the Lord"). This
description does not mark him as a godly
man, but rather accentuates his strength.
Not only was Nimrod the founder of the
sport of hunting, but he also became the
symbol of the anti-God forces of the
world. His association with Babel, and
the later experiences of Israel with
Babylon, place him at the heart of the
anti-Messiah ideology.

The other person of particular interest
is Eber ("Heber," 10:21–25; 11:14–
17). Some scholars believe that it was he
who gave his name to the people of God
(Hebrews, "descendants of Heber"). The
importance of his name in chapters 10
and 11 would give credence to this (the
life-span suddenly shortened after he
died, Gen. 11:16–18), although others
would derive the name "Hebrew" from
the verb "to pass over," "those who

passed over the Euphrates" and migrated to Palestine.

Truth for today.—In spite of the many
difficulties of identification in Genesis 10,
there is one fact that is evident: all races
of men are descended from the three
sons of Noah (v. 32). Therefore, we all
belong to one family. If this is true, we
should be able to live together in peace.
The problem is how to move from where
we are to where we ought to be. If we
could see that our present hostile stances
are unrealistic and irrational, then we
would find a way to correct them. Genesis 10 must not be ignored by the Christian.

The Tower of Babel (Gen. 11:1–9)

The passage.—According to the biblical tradition, the first migrations after
the expulsion from the Garden of Eden
were eastward. Genesis 11:2 says that
after the flood the migration was westward. Finding an ideal spot, men began
to build a tall tower or ziggurat ("high-
rise temple") that would win them universal acclaim. God heard of their efforts and "came down" to see what they
were doing. This type of language illustrates the dilemma of biblical writers.
How do you speak of God, who is utterly
unlike us, so that men can understand?
One uses words that must not be taken
too literally. In order to emphasize the
diminutive nature of man's undertaking,
it was said that God "came down." They
were building a tower "unto heaven" but
it was so far short of that objective that
God had to come down before he could
see it!

As small as the beginnings were, however, God observed that if left alone,
men would reach their objective. This is
the highest compliment ever paid the ingenuity of man; and it still applies. Left
alone, brilliant men will achieve the objectives they set for themselves. But the

question is, will God leave them alone? The answer here is, "Only if they are working in the context of his will."

Special points.—What was so wrong about the effort to build the tower of Babel? Some say they were trying to work their way into heaven, but the expression "unto heaven" is surely an idiom meaning "a tall tower." A "skyscraper" does not scrape the sky, nor did their tower reach unto heaven. From the ground it would look as if it reached the sky.

Others say that it was an attempt to build above the possible level of another flood, but they could not have hoped to build it higher than Mount Ararat. The most likely fault of their purpose was that they were building a tall, conspicuous tower that could be seen for miles around (making a name for themselves) so that men would migrate to the city and not scatter to regions beyond. We have seen nothing wrong in this because most of our cities and churches have been doing similar things. Yet this is obviously contrary to God's purpose. We are to live to the glory of his name, not our own, and our concern should be for the whole world. "Be fruitful and multiply and replenish the earth and subdue it" (Gen. 1:28).

Anyone who has been working in a cause contrary to the will of God will understand how the "confusion of tongues" came about. Selfish, ambitious men soon lost all means of communication with one another. No parent who has suddenly discovered that he and his thirteen-year-old can no longer speak the same language will find this passage difficult to understand. God brings about the alienation both by letting matters take their natural course and by giving an occasional extra push of his own.

Truth for today.—The builders at Babel clearly stated that they were making their mighty effort in order to avoid being scattered abroad (11:6). Then it is twice stated that God scattered them abroad anyway (11:8–9). If we are absorbed only with our little circle of concern, he will force us to become aware of world needs. Either we will go into all the world voluntarily or against our will. Go we must! How many more "world wars" must be fought before we truly pursue world peace?

Abraham's Ancestors (Gen. 11:10–32)

The passage.—This section is obviously placed here to prepare for the call of Abram in chapter 12. We learn that he was a direct descendant of Shem and Eber, that his father was Terah, and that Sarai his wife was barren. The family lived in Ur of the Chaldees, one of the most progressive cities of the ancient world, but where idolatry was a way of life. The family had left Ur after the death of Haran, which might have influenced their departure. Their intention was to go to Canaan, but they settled short of their objective, in Haran, where Terah died.

Special points.—When the genealogies in this passage are compared with those in Genesis 5, there are many similarities, but the differences are even more noteworthy. Shem lives less than half as long as the antediluvian patriarchs (*ca.* 500 years), and the life-span quickly drops to about four hundred for the next three patriarchs. After Eber it is cut in half, continuing in the two hundreds until and including Terah. Abraham lives even fewer years, but more than the 120 years of Genesis 6:3 which clearly apply to the years of grace before the flood. Had sin been shortening the length of life? Scientific evidence indicates that the life-span of early man was less than today, but obviously they have not exhumed every man's body.

Another difference in the genealogies is an omission in the formula of chapter 5, "He lived . . . he begat . . . he died." In chapter 11 "he died" is omitted until Haran's decease (which is not in a formula), but returns in the usual pattern at the death of Terah (11:32). The two occurrences of the verb are obviously emphatic in this chapter. The death of Haran influenced the family's exodus from Ur. Were they a godly family who had become too absorbed in Ur's exciting pagan culture? And did the death of Haran shock them back to reality?

The death of Terah obviously did not occasion Abraham's determination to go on to Canaan, for he did not die until long after Abraham had left Haran. Since Abraham was 75 when he left (Gen. 12:4), his father was about 145 at the time (Gen. 11:26). Terah lived to be 205 (11:32). Apparently the death of Terah in Haran is mentioned in order to show that he did not go with Abraham. Abraham had to leave his father behind when he followed God's call. When they left Ur, Terah took Abraham (11:31). Now Abraham was on his own.

The Call of Abraham (Gen. 12:1–20)

The passage.—The call of Abraham and his response to it form one of the most momentous events in history. In this account the tension between divine promise and fulfilment is especially evident. At the time of the call Abram was living in a land where heathen gods were worshiped and might have participated in the worship himself before his experience with the true God. Immediately upon his call he set out for the Land of Promise although he did not know what it would be. All he had was the right sense of direction. He knew enough to head toward the West. Not until he was actually in Canaan was he told that this was the land of which God had spoken. No sooner had he arrived than a famine struck the land. A famine in the Land of Promise? Abram was no better prepared for that than we are today. With his faith in complete disarray he "went down" into Egypt and acted as if he had never known God, even jeopardizing the promise of a glorious seed by giving Sarah to Pharaoh as his wife. This was the lowest moment in Abraham's life, and the Bible does not spare him, for it clearly illustrates that man's only hope, even for Abraham, is in the grace of God.

Special point.—Where did Abraham's call take place, in Ur or Haran? The Old Testament accounts seem to place it in Haran (cf. 11:31 with 12:1). However, Stephen in Acts 7:1 ff. clearly asserts that it came in Ur. Although it should not appear strange that a good deacon was confused about the Old Testament, the most likely explanation is that God first appeared to Abram in Ur, and that he influenced his father to leave for Canaan (11:31*b*); when he saw that Terah had no desire to go farther, he went on without him.

The tendency of the Jews in later times was to think that God had called Abraham simply because he wanted to lavish his favors upon him and his descendants. The promise to Abraham clearly involves God's concern for the entire world. The purpose of Abraham's call was that he might be a blessing to all men, even as God has chosen us to be a help to others.

Abraham and Lot (Gen. 13:1–18)

The passage.—From 12:1 it appears that Abraham was to separate himself from all of his kindred and that it was a mistake for him to take Lot with him at all. Apparently he was unable to make a clean break when he first left Haran.

1. Excavation at Ai (Deir Dibwan) showing American archaeologists Furman Hewitt and Joseph Callaway (see Gen. 12:8)

This inevitably spelled trouble for both men, for Lot did not share Abraham's sense of mission. As they both became more prosperous (based upon the tainted dowry given Abraham when he deceived Pharaoh!), Lot's servants began to clash with those of Abraham, who soon saw that he and Lot could no longer live together in harmony. He considerately suggested that they go their separate ways, Lot having first choice of a place to settle. When Lot chose the plain of Sodom, his decision might not have been entirely selfish, for though the land was desirable, it was not what Abraham most wanted. He had shown interest only in the pasturage of the highlands. Abraham's unselfish offer to Lot, and his clear decision to separate from him, which

must have been reached with considerable reluctance, was rewarded by God with a new assurance that the land of Canaan was surely to be his, even toward the East where Lot now sojourned. Even what he had given away would come back to him (cf. 13:11 with 13:14).

Truth for today.--Abraham's words to Lot, "Let there be no strife, I pray thee, between me and thee . . . for we are brethren," are most perceptive. Nothing is to be gained by family quarrels either domestically or religiously. The more privileged party (Abraham) makes the necessary concession to the less privileged (Lot). The more devout moves aside for the more ambitious. The great man refuses to fight with the

25

lesser. The God-called man is too involved in his mission to spend his ener-
gies in minor skirmishes. What he
relinquishes he does not really lose. What
men like Lot gain is not really theirs.

Abraham and Melchizedek (Gen. 14:1–24)

The passage.—This is one of the most
unusual passages in Genesis. It cannot
be assigned to any of the tradition
groups commonly recognized by scholars. It stands alone, presenting Abraham
in a light unseen elsewhere, as a fierce
warrior. Where his own interests were
at stake, as it was with Lot's servants,
Abraham was conciliatory, a peacemaker; but where the welfare of another
was involved, he was a fierce antagonist,
defeating by the use of surprise strategy
an army vastly superior in numbers to
his own. Upon his triumphant return he
was met by both the king of Sodom and
the priest-king of Salem (probably Jerusalem), Melchizedek, whose name
means "king of righteousness." Abraham
treated the king of Sodom with disdain,
refusing to accept any favors from him,
"Lest thou shouldst say, 'I have made
Abram rich.'" Toward Melchizedek his
behavior was quite the opposite. Abraham partook of a meal with him, and
gave him a tithe of all his booty. The
most significant statement of all is his
identification of the God of Melchizedek
with his own God. Melchizedek called
his God "the most high God" (Hebrew,
El Elyon), and Abraham knew God as
"the Lord" (JAHWEH). In 14:22 he
asserts that "the Lord" and "the most
high God" are the same God. In other
words, Melchizedek and Abraham call
God by different names, but they worship the same God.

Special points.—The two most important questions that arise with this
chapter concern the identity of the King
of Shinar, Amraphel (14:1) and the
mysterious Melchizedek. At one time it
was thought that Amraphel was the
famous Hammurabi of the eighteen
century B.C., but there is no scholarly
concensus on this. Abraham must have
lived about this time, for the conditions
described in the patriarchal stories best
agree with this period. Although the
basic historicity of the traditions concerning the patriarchs is confirmed by
the findings of archaeology, the evidence
concerning an actual contact between
Hammurabi and Abraham is negligible.

At face value Melchizedek appears
simply to be a priest-king of the Jerusalem region whom Abraham respected as
serving the same God he worshiped
under another name, and through whom
he offered tithes because he was a priest.
However, the description of Melchizedek
in Hebrews 7:3 ff. presents other possibilities: "Without father, without mother,
without descent, having neither beginning of days, nor end of life; but
made like unto the Son of God, abideth
a priest continually."

Some expositors equate him with
Shem, who by biblical chronology could
still have been living, but Shem had a
mother and father. Others suggest that it
was the Son of God himself, preincarnate, for he alone had no beginning or
end of life. Yet Hebrews clearly says
that he was 'like unto" the Son of God,
not the Son of God himself. The most
likely explanation is that the writer of
Hebrews is using a literary analogy
rather than a genealogical one. Just as
in the book of Genesis Melchizedek had
no mother and father, beginning or end,
just so Jesus actually is eternal. *In the
book of Genesis* Melchizedek suddenly
appears without antecedents, and with
no account of his death. *In that record*

he is always a priest, for we are not told of his successor. His historical uniqueness is that he served as priest both of Gentiles and of Hebrews. Thus Jesus was "after his order" as a priest of all mankind.

Saved by Faith (Gen. 15:1–21)

The passage.—In this chapter God assures Abraham that the promise of a seed will be fulfilled through his actual son. Abraham accepted this word and was thereby found acceptable by God. Yet Abraham deserved to have more than a promise. In response to his request God instructed him to provide sacrificial animals in preparation for a covenant ceremony, in which each animal was cut asunder. Usually in such a covenant scene the men involved walked between the halves (cf. Jer. 34:18–19), but here Abraham was not called upon to do so; rather, God caused a burning oven, such as Sarah used for cooking, to pass between the parts. Thus God himself guaranteed "to keep Israel's home fires burning" through the centuries. Although here God gave Abraham visible assurance of his purpose, yet in the last analysis the future of Abraham's family was still rooted in the determination of God to keep his promise. This continued to be Abraham's only basis of hope, even as it is for the Christian.

Special point.—The question is often asked, "How were people saved during Old Testament times?" Some interpreters suggest that they were saved by believing that the Messiah would die for their sins. There is in Genesis no indication that Abraham knew that much. When Jesus said that Abraham saw his day and was glad (John 8:56), he based his statement upon what his Scriptures said: That Abraham believed that God would one day bless the whole world

through his descendants. Now that promise was being fulfilled by Jesus in a way beyond anything Abraham could have seen. Abraham would recognize its legitimacy, and if the Pharisees had possessed his kind of faith, they too would have seen Jesus as the fulfilment of the promise.

Abraham was received by God because he "believed in him" (Hebrew, "leaned upon him," "trusted him"). Because of his trust God gave him credit for being righteous, for such assent to God's will would produce righteousness since God could work through him. We know more about God's plan of salvation today, but Abraham's faith remains the unchallenged standard for us all (cf. Rom. 4:1 ff.). How was Abraham saved, and Moses, and Jeremiah? By faith in God, even as we. We have received more revelation and are responsible to it, but the faith required is still the same. In Old Testament times God received men by faith in light of the future sacrifice of Christ. He knew what must be done, although they did not. What was expected of them was that they assent to what God revealed to them at the time. Like us, they were not saved by knowledge, but by faith.

It should be noted that it is said in this chapter that God did not give Abram full possession of the land during his day, because the iniquity of the Amorites was not yet full (15:16). God would not arbitrarily dispossess one people for another, even to fulfil his purpose. Later, when the Canaanites were conquered, it was because they had lost the right to the land by their own sinfulness. Later the Jews were expelled for the same reason. God's laws have never changed. The earth is still his to give to whomever he desires. No government based upon injustice and characterized by unethical practices can long endure.

Sarah and Hagar (Gen. 16:1–16)

The passage.—Since Hagar was an Egyptian, she probably was given to Sarah by Pharaoh in his dowry. Sarah's suggestion that Abraham go to Hagar for a child was an acceptable custom of the day, for a slave woman could provide an heir for a man if his wife was barren. The child, then, would be regarded as the legal son of the mistress as well. As soon as the slave conceived, she made life difficult for Sarah, who placed the blame on Abraham for an arrangement that she had suggested. Discreetly he stayed out of the argument and let the women settle it. It is not to Sarah's credit that she made Hagar's life so intolerable that she preferred the possibility of death in the wilderness.

Mistreated by Sarah and unprotected by Abraham, Hagar was not forgotten by God. The questions put to her by the angel are still primary ones for every life today: (1) Where have you come from? (2) Where are you going? The Latin for the second question is the familiar *Quo Vadis*. Also the angel reminds Hagar that she is Sarah's slave (16:8*a*) and somehow must perform her role, regardless of its difficulty. If she will hold on, God will reward her with a son, Ishmael, who as a fierce warrior will be able, unlike her, to maintain his independence in the clan of Abraham (16:12).

Hagar described God as "the God who sees." She had thought that no one cared what happened to her, but now she knew that God was concerned.

Truth for today.—When in disgrace Abraham left Egypt, perhaps he found some satisfaction in that he still possessed the wealth that Pharaoh had bestowed upon him. Yet among the presents was Hagar, who was to occasion such grief for his later years. Even until today the hostility between Ishmael and Isaac persists in the Israeli-Arab tensions. Frequently the consequences of sin extend beyond the third and fourth generations.

The Covenant of Circumcision (Gen. 17: 1–27)

The passage.—In chapter 15 God acted to seal his side of the covenant. In chapter 17 Abraham is told what he must do on his part. He must inaugurate and perpetuate the rite of circumcision for every male in every Hebrew household. The penalty for noncompliance would be excommunication (17:14).

It was made evident, however, that circumcision itself was not sufficient. Abraham (and his descendants) must walk perfectly (maturely) before God at all times (17:1). The rite of circumcision was essential as the ritualistic confirmation of a determination to walk maturely before God (17:11). It was no substitute for it.

God further assured Abraham that he would have an actual son of his own to circumcise, although the patriarch was willing to settle upon Ishmael, whom as his son he had come to love, and who was now thirteen years old. In light of this God changed Abram's name to Abraham and Sarai's to Sarah, to mark the new era.

With characteristic obedience Abraham immediately proceeded to circumcise his household, performing the rite upon every male that same day. Thus began the historic Hebrew custom. Why was circumcision used as the token of covenant? It emphasized the perpetual nature of the covenant for it was passed from father to son to be renewed with each generation.

Special point.—The fact that the covenant was to be perpetual through all
their generations occasioned a great deal
of tension among early Jewish Christians. How could a Gentile convert become a true believer in Israel's God
unless he was circumcised? Circumcision
was necessary for both Hebrews an !
Gentiles in the Hebrew community of
worship. Apparently the position of Paul
in Colossians 2:11–12 is that baptism
has taken the place of circumcision as
the initiation rite among the people of
God. It is the fulfilment of the old custom, but is administered when a person
is born into the kingdom rather than
when he is physically born.

Entertaining Angels (Gen. 18:1–33)

The passage.—Some expositors, especially the early Christian fathers, believed
that this chapter speaks of the Trinity.
Verse 1 says that the Lord visited Abraham, and yet in verse 2 he appeared as
three men. However, Abraham addressed one of them as the obvious
leader (18:3) and continued to talk with
the Lord after the two angels departed
(18:16; 18:22; 19:1). It is more likely
therefore that one of the three was the
angel of the Lord (God manifesting himself), and the other two were the angels
who had come to assist in the investi-
gation of Sodom.

Did Abraham know whom he was
entertaining? His eager preparations suggest it, but this might have been the
usual hospitality of his home. Sarah
certainly did not recognize them, or she
would not have laughed. When her
thoughts were read, however, she knew
then who it was.

The response of God to Sarah, "Is
there anything too hard for the Lord?"
(18:14), is a reminder to all of us. To
deny God the miraculous is to deny his
existence. If he is God, he can do as he
wills, even in performing acts unknown
to the experience of man. The chapter
ends with the lonely prayer of Abraham
before God as he desperately pleads for
Lot.

Special points.—This chapter is typical
of the way angels are described in the
Old Testament. They are not feminine,
nor do they have wings. They have the
appearance of men and even share a
meal with Abraham. They must personally investigate Sodom before God
knows for certain the true condition
(18:21). Are these angels simply the
ancient writer's symbolic way of talking
about the activities of God, or did they
really appear in the flesh? If they did,
the gulf between the worlds of spirit and
flesh is more easily bridged than men
may think. The fact that in the flesh man
cannot invade the realm of the spirit
does not mean that the reverse is untrue.
Before a passage such as this, we must
always remain humble and receptive,
realizing the limitations of our knowledge but willing to believe all that God
reveals to us.

Is Abraham trying, in 18:23–33, to
change the mind of God? Is his concern
for the people of Sodom greater than
that of God? Obviously not. He is attempting to discover the mind of God.
When he asks enough questions to learn
that God will save as many as he can, he
is satisfied, for he feels certain that he
will rescue Lot. In this great prayer he
discovers the mysteries of God's grace.
The most momentous experiences of
prayer do not occur when we talk to
God but when he makes his revelation
to us. However, if we do not ask the
right questions, we will not get the best
answers. Abraham asked the right
questions.

The Destruction of Sodom (Gen. 19:1–38)

The passage.—This story clearly tells of Lot's entertaining angels unawares. He obviously believed them to be strangers in the town and was both fearful for their safety and desirous of their company. Apparently he had few friends in that wicked city. When the men of Sodom demanded that they be allowed "to know" the guests, they spoke of sexual aberrations, hence our word "sodomy." Lot's offer to give them his daughters instead is incomprehensible to us but it was done both in the light of the demands of hospitality in the ancient world and the comparatively lesser place of women in the household. Yet his lack of concern for their welfare might have influenced the callous behavior of his daughters recorded in 19:30 ff.

His daughters are said to be virgins (19:8), yet they were married (19:14). The Hebrew expression in verse 14 should be translated, "who were about to marry his daughters." Being already betrothed and so close to marriage, the daughters were even more frustrated by the turn of events.

Lot's love for Sodom (19:16*a*) and his fear of the mountains (v. 19) mark him as an urban type and probably explain his original choice of Sodom. Neither he nor his wife ever adjusted to leaving Ur or Haran. Yet after the fall of Sodom, he was afraid to stay in the small town of Zoar although he was given permission. He fled to the mountains anyway, without any thought about the loneliness of his daughters. Even so fear makes cowards of us all.

Special point.—Some expositors are surprised that Lot's daughters are not condemned for their sin with their father. We are simply told the story. Perhaps the biblical writer understood the intolerable position into which their father had taken them. However, it is more likely that he leaves the conclusion to his readers. From this union came no end of trouble for Israel.

Truth for today.—Nowhere do we find the inadequacies of a merely righteous man's way more clearly revealed. Although Lot was a righteous man (2 Pet. 2:6–8), his righteousness was of little value in the turbulent times in which he lived. Beyond such righteousness, his troubled life required the sort of faith manifested by Abraham. Lot, his wife, and his daughters loved the world too much. By seeking the opportunities and security of a settled city they lost all they had. Abraham looked for a city eternal in the heavens and is still receiving dividends.

Sarah and Abimelech (Gen. 20:1–18)

The passage.—The resemblance between this chapter and Genesis 12:10–20 is obvious. In both stories Abraham says that Sarai is his sister and permits her to be married to a king. In both, his deception is discovered and he is reprimanded by the offended sovereign, yet he ends up richer in possessions.

Is this another way of telling the same story, or did Abraham intend to practice this deception wherever he went? The statement in 20:13 would indicate this, but if he was prepared to pursue such a course habitually, his integrity was considerably lessened. Some scholars prefer to take 20:13 as a later scribal comment seeking to explain how we could have such similar accounts. They argue that Abraham practiced this deception only once. The original tradition was preserved in separate accounts, one attaching it to Pharaoh and the other to Abimelech. However, as the story now stands in the Bible, it is a separate event.

Special point.—As we compare 12:10 ff. with this passage, it should be noted that a different name for God occurs in the two chapters ("the LORD" in chap. 12 and "God" in chap. 20). Whereas chapter 12 simply tells the story, chapter 20 is careful to explain that Abraham is not a total scoundrel, for Sarah was really his sister (the daughter of his father by another wife), and that he was still a prophet (20:7) and had the ear of God (20:17). The promise of a seed by Sarah was not jeopardized because Abimelech was prevented from ever approaching Sarah. This is not clear in chapter 12.

This passage is obviously from another source, even if it is regarded as a separate event in Abraham's life. It views him from a different perspective, but is just as valid as the earlier account.

Truth for today.—In chapter 12 Pharaoh gave Abraham his wealth before the marriage to Sarah. In chapter 20, Abimelech bestowed gifts upon them when he restored Sarah to Abraham. Rather than forcing Abraham to leave in disgrace, he offered him free access to his territory. In addition, he reminded Sarah of his generosity to her "brother." The best way to expose unkindness is to be kind; the most effective way to reprove hate is to perform deeds of love; the strongest protest against selfishness is to be generous in return.

Hagar and Ishmael (Gen. 21:1–21)

The passage.—This passage should be studied in relationship to chapter 16, for a comparison between the two reveals a situation similar to that existing between chapter 20 and chapter 12. In chapter 16 "the LORD" is used for deity, but in chapter 21 he is "God." In both, an angel appears to Hagar, but in chapter 16 he is "the angel of the LORD" and in chapter 21 "the angel of God." In each passage Hagar flees into the wilderness because of Sarah's hostility. In chapter 16 as in chapter 21 the desert scene occurs in the vicinity of a well, and Hagar is assured of God's care for her son.

In the first story, however, Hagar has just conceived, while in this one Ishmael is about sixteen years old, for he was thirteen when Isaac was conceived (Gen. 17:25). Obviously Hagar was not carrying him. In verse 15 she "pushed" the lad under the desert bush rather than "cast" him. In the earlier chapter she had already found the water before the angel appeared. Just as in chapter 20, this passage, which also uses the term "God," seeks to present Abraham in a more favorable light. In chapter 16 he lets Sarah do whatever she wants without interference. Here he struggles with the decision and only allows Hagar to go when instructed by God, nor does he let her leave without essential provisions.

Some expositors feel that these two chapters represent different traditions that have been developed from the same event, one told in Judah (chap. 16) and the other (chap. 21) in North Israel. Rather than being contradictory, they give witness to the historicity of the basic event. Courtroom testimony is more reliable where witnesses come together at essential points than when they agree in every particular.

Others are just as convinced that the accounts represent two separate incidents in the life of Hagar. In either case the two chapters come from different sources and are invaluable aids for our understanding of Israel's early history.

The Covenant with Abimelech (Gen. 21: 22–34)

The passage.—This story illustrates anew the friendly relationship between the Philistines and Abraham. Again Abimelech is presented in a favorable light. He initiated the covenant. Upset over the report of friction between his servants and those of Abraham over the well, he was most desirous of Abraham's welfare. The patriarch reinforced his claim to the well at Beer-sheba ("well of the oath") by presenting Abimelech with seven ewe lambs as an act of good faith. All was at peace between Hebrew and Philistine.

Special point.—Abimelech is portrayed as a most remarkable man. In chapter 20 he returned good for evil. He lived by the Golden Rule, for he did to Abraham what he would have liked Abraham to do to him (21:23). Could these accounts have influenced the teachings of Jesus? Certainly they are advanced ideas, and for these virtues to be found in a Philistine king is even more unusual.

The Sacrifice of Isaac (Gen. 22:1–24)

The passage.—Here is one of the greatest chapters in the Old Testament. Not only did Abraham pass the supreme test of his faith, but God made clear to Israel that he would not allow human sacrifice. Abraham must be willing to sacrifice Isaac, but God did not ultimately require the offering—only the willingness. We are not told how God impressed Abraham with his desire for his son, but the passage is exceptional in perceiving that such demands are the ultimate test of our relationship to God. He is always calling upon us to make decisions that seem to shatter the fulfilment of his promises. Yet here is where faith is most essential.

When Abraham and Isaac walked alone up the mountain, it seemed to be the end of all that God had ever promised the patriarch. Yet this great man knew two things that appeared to be contradictory and by faith held on to both. God was surely asking him for Isaac, and to sacrifice him meant the end of all hope for a seed through him. Somehow God would keep that promise, even if it necessitated the return of Isaac from the dead.

Special points.—This chapter cannot be read without an awareness of its implications for the Christian. What God would not permit Abraham to do, he has done for us. He has sacrificed his Son upon the altar of Calvary. Surely the heartache of Abraham on this occasion provides a sobering glimpse into the grieving heart of God who knew even then what one day he must do.

What is meant by the statement of the angel of the Lord, "Now I know that thou fearest God, since thou hast not withheld thy son, thine only son, from me?" Did God not know beforehand what Abraham would do? Obviously he would have known whatever was true of Abraham. If it was not known, it did not exist. The writer is saying that not until Abraham acted upon his faith did that faith come to fruition. Until he lifted the knife upon his son, his ultimate surrender to God had not occurred. Faith is not just a nice attitude toward God; it is submission to his will. To will it in the heart is not enough. The act is the ultimate test.

Truth for today.—It should be noted that Abraham's supreme test of faith did not come when he left Haran, but rather when he offered Isaac. Faith can easily be confused with imagination. That is not necessarily faith which makes us believe that God will do all sorts of wonderful things for us. That is faith which enables us to give up what we love the most, believing that we can trust God.

The Family Burial Ground (Gen. 23:1–20)

The passage.—Sarah is the only woman in the Bible whose age is given. Evidently, she often mentioned her ad-

2. Hittite city gate in Turkey, about 1400 B.C. (see Gen. 23:1–20)

vanced age at Isaac's birth. The account of Abraham's burial arrangements for her is given emphasis because it was imperative that he have a family cemetery. The living could be content with sojourning but the dead must lie in their own land. Abraham's title to Canaan was sealed when the body of Sarah was laid to rest in the Cave of Machpelah.

The Hittites mentioned in this chapter are of uncertain origin. We can only be sure that they were not Canaanites. This was probably the reason for Abraham's desire to buy from them, for he would have no more wanted to make the Canaanites rich than the king of Sodom (14:23). Nor would they have been likely to be disposed to sell to him, thus giving a foothold to an alien family.

The account recorded here gives a vivid picture of the method of sale common at the time. Ephron politely suggests that he will give Abraham the field, but he knew Abraham was determined to have legal title to it. His casual mention of the price (23:15) did not disguise the fact that he was asking an exorbitant amount. An entire village could have been bought for 400 shekels of silver. When Abraham paid his price, he owned the only property he possessed in his lifetime. He knew that his descendants would be given the rest by God.

Special point.—It is sad to notice that although Abraham and Sarah were together most of their lives, apparently she died in Hebron while he was still in Beersheba (22:19). When he came to mourn for her, he demonstrated a remarkable clarity of mind, bargaining with the sons of Heth with an alertness uncommon in such a situation. Faith not only enabled him to walk with God; it gave him dignity among his neighbors, whose respect he had already won.

Providing a Wife for Isaac (Gen. 24: 1–67)

The passage.—This, the longest chapter in the book of Genesis, is a beautiful story, delightfully told. The servant whom Abraham commissioned to find a wife for Isaac was Eliezer (15:2) who would have been his heir had Isaac died without a son. To undertake this mission was to deny any personal ambition of his own. Thus he represents the dedicated servant of God in any age.

In 22:23 we learn that Abraham was still in contact with his family. His desire for Isaac to marry a kinswoman was not based upon family loyalty but upon the fact that they had a similar cultic and religious heritage. Laban is said to have worshiped the same God as Abraham (24:50).

Rebekah's decision to go with Eliezer to become Isaac's wife took courage and ambition. Yet she bravely set her face to go to a man and a country she did not know. Such qualities characterized our pioneer women of America. Some ambition was mixed with her other qualities, but it took more than that to beckon her.

When she met Isaac, she was clearly in charge of the situation, alighting from her camel lest she look down upon him at the outset, and put on her veil according to custom.

Special point.—It is quite evident that Isaac was closely attached to his mother (24:63,67). If Abraham had not taken the initiative, Isaac might never have married at all. Rebekah is said to have taken the place of his mother. That is not the last time that a wife has had to serve in that capacity. In fact, to a certain extent, it is usually so.

Truth for today.—It was no coincidence that Eliezer chose to identify the prospective wife for Isaac by her offer to water the camels also (24:14). Not only was it necessary for the wife of unassuming Isaac to do more than he asked of her, but it is a virtue to be desired in everyone. It is the second mile of Jesus. The person who does only what is expected of him will never make a significant contribution to life. Success comes to those who do more than is required, whether they are wives, husbands, students, teachers, or church members.

The Last Days of Abraham (Gen. 25: 1–18)

The passage.—It is surprising after Abraham and Sarah were so close that he would marry again at his advanced age. Most of his descendants by Keturah became enemies of the descendants of Isaac. Although Abraham at the time of his death tried to prevent friction by sending them away with the inheritance, it did not prevent trouble in the centuries that followed.

Abraham was said to have had "a good old age" (25:28), which is never an accident. It was his reward for a life well lived. His old age was a good one not just because of his length of life, but because of its quality. At his funeral both Isaac and Ishmael were present. Why is it that a father's death will unite estranged brothers when it would mean so much more while he lives?

In this last summary of Abraham's

life the genealogy of Ishmael is also given. God kept his promise to Hagar, for Ishmael's tribe multiplied in Arabia. Although there was no fellowship between him and Isaac, he found a welcome among his other relatives. One could wish that the circle of friends might have been wider.

The greater part of this chapter deals with the birth and youth of Esau and Jacob. Although the twins were delayed in arriving, the world has never since been the same. Esau was a typical outdoorsman, hunting, fishing and finding no interest in the ways of civilization. Jacob was thoroughly domesticated, a man who lived by his brain rather than his brawn. The parents unfortunately played favorites, Isaac preferring Esau because the lad was his opposite and what he must have secretly wanted to be, and Rebekah favoring Jacob because he was so much like her. When it is said that Jacob was a "plain" man, the word is one that is translated "perfect" elsewhere (Gen. 6:9; Job 1:1). It literally means "mature." Jacob was a mature man who knew what he wanted and how to discipline himself to get it. The word carries no necessary ethical connotation but it is reserved for only a few select men in the Old Testament.

The deal made between Jacob and Esau over the pottage was seen by the biblical writer as not so much unfairness by Jacob as stupidity by Esau. His birthright was worth only "a mess of pottage." Esau had been carrying the price tag for his birthright all the time. Jacob bought it for what he knew Esau thought it was worth. This does not excuse Jacob's behavior, nor does it mark him worse than the average man. Rather it reveals him as quite typical. Rare is the man who will pay more than another asks for his merchandise.

Special point.—What was the birthright in question in this passage? It usually included both property and family superiority. The reason why Jacob still wanted Isaac's blessing, which was the final conveyance of the birthright, was to secure his purchased rights. Esau, after his father's death, might not honor the agreement made here. It is interesting to note that Jacob never received the property in question here and never mentioned it again to Esau. With his father's blessing he did not need it.

Truth for today.—Jacob was doing all this in spite of the fact that God had already told Rebekah that the birthright belonged to him (25:23). Surely she had told him, since she so obviously favored him. How much better it would have been if he had waited in faith for God's will to work itself out. Far too often men run ahead of God and mar his good purpose for them.

Isaac and Abimelech (Gen. 26:1–35)

The passage.—The chapter pictures Isaac as imitating his father's example both in vices and achievement. As Abraham had done before him, he lied to Abimelech about his wife, Rebekah, who by no stretch of imagination was even his half-sister. Not only did he dig again the same wells his father had dug but he also gave them the same names (26:18).

Isaac is portrayed as lacking the competitive spirit of Abraham, avoiding any conflicts with the servants of Abimelech, and settling only where the water supply was not contested (26:19–22). Yet he was blessed beyond Abraham in possessions and outlived him by five years (35:28). Such prosperity and long life was viewed by the ancient Hebrews as a mark of God's favor. What some might interpret as weakness in Isaac, others might understand as strength.

The picture in Genesis 22 of Isaac on

the altar, submissive to Abraham even in the hour of death, is the one that we still see in this chapter. Because he honored his father he called the wells the names given by Abraham. Why should he arbitrarily change them simply because the patriarch was no longer alive? His reluctance to war with Abimelech may be interpreted as reflecting the ideal characteristic, taught by Jesus in the Sermon on the Mount, of turning the other cheek. Abraham had the faith it takes to reach a new goal; Isaac had the faith that is necessary for survival in a land already reached by another generation. The one is more exciting, but the other just as necessary.

Special point.—Many scholars see the story of Isaac's deception concerning his wife as a variant of the one about Abraham and Sarah (chap. 20). Abimelech should have suspected trickery from Isaac since Abraham had tried the same thing. In fact, Abraham and Abimelech were such close acquaintances that the Philistine king should have known Isaac had no sister. However, the differences in the stories are significant. Neither Abimelech nor his men actually approached Rebekah (perhaps they were suspicious), and as one would expect when the possessions of the Hebrew family increased (26:16), there was far more tension between Abimelech and Isaac than there had been with Abraham. What would be more natural than for the son to feel that if the sister ruse worked for his father, it would work for him.

The Blessing of Isaac (Gen. 27:1–46)

The passage.—It is not a pretty sight to see Isaac and Rebekah by their petty favoritism encouraging their sons in their rivalry. Isaac surely already knew that God had told Rebekah that Jacob should receive the birthright, for she would certainly have tried to encourage him to favor Jacob (Gen 25:23). Yet he took the initiative to bless Esau. It was when she learned of Isaac's premature move that she sought to counteract his intention. It should be noted that Jacob was reluctant to follow her suggestion, not because it was wrong, but because he might be detected. Not until she said, "Upon me by thy curse, my son" (27:13), did he proceed.

Although the blessing was given by mistake to Jacob, it was nevertheless binding (27:33). All Isaac could do was to mitigate the assertion that Jacob would "be lord of the brethren" (27:29) to an assurance to Esau that "thou shalt break his yoke from off thy neck" (27:40).

Rebekah probably thought that Esau, absorbed in his hunting expeditions, would soon forget the deception of his brother, but she soon learned otherwise. The treachery had struck a blow to Esau's heart, and he was biding his time for vengeance. She suggested to Isaac that Jacob should be sent back to the home country to secure a wife. They sent him away for what she thought would be only a brief period of time during which Esau's wrath would surely cool. Little did she realize that her death would come before he could return. Indeed the curse did fall upon her.

Truth for today.—It is tragic for parents to encourage children to become rivals in the home. Frequently such conflicts result from the inability of the mother and father to relate properly to each other. Rivalry between marriage partners will be reflected in the children. Each child must be given the individual attention he requires, for no two children are alike. Yet each must be treated with the same fairness. By their favoritism Isaac and Rebekah not only brought their sons into conflict, but initiated a long history of hostility between their descendants, Edom and Israel. God has provided a last judgment day because the ultimate consequences of what we have done, good and bad, will not be determined until the end of time.

Jacob at Bethel (Gen. 28:1–22)

The passage.—As he blessed Jacob in this chapter, Isaac revealed his genuine goodness. He had put aside all personal preference and graciously conferred upon him the promise to Abraham. On the other hand Esau was pathetic in his attempt to please his father by marrying a daughter of Ishmael, a maneuver that surely met with little enthusiasm from his parents, especially since he was already married to two Hittite women (Gen. 26:34). It is to his credit, however, that he did not callously divorce them in his play for recognition.

The dream of Jacob featured a passageway (rather than ladder, 28:12) from earth to heaven. The fact that the angels were ascending and descending (the reverse would be the expected order) symbolizes the promise that the ministering angels would carry Jacob's needs to God, returning with the help that was required.

His vow was indeed in the form of a bargain with God, but what he requested is worth attention. All he wanted was to keep alive until he could return home. This was the first time he had ever been away from home, and he was overcome with loneliness. His promise to tithe precedes the requirements of the law and represents the natural response of a man to the blessings of God. Should our gratitude be expressed in lesser offerings?

Truth for today.—Two expressions that Jacob used in response to his dream are significant: (1) "Surely the Lord is in this place; and I knew it not" (28:16) and (2) "This is none other than the house of God, and this is the gate of heaven" (28:17). His first confession warns us that we may also fail to recognize the presence of God in unexpected places. The second alerts us to the fact that we may think the place where we met God is the only avenue for meeting him. The way to heaven was open wherever Jacob went although he, like us, did not always discover it.

Rachel and Leah (Gen. 29:1–30)

The passage.—The story of Jacob and Rachel is one of the most charming of all time. When at the community well he first inquired concerning his relatives, he was informed that his cousin Rachel, the daughter of Laban, was even now approaching. When he urged the shepherds to water their flocks and go on their way (so he could be alone with Rachel), they replied that such was not the custom for they always waited until all the shepherds had arrived before they removed the stone from the mouth of the well. (It was easier to move with everyone helping.) At first sight of the beautiful, bright-eyed Rachel, Jacob himself, with a super-human effort born of love at first sight, removed the heavy stone from the well. The weeping that followed the kiss he gave Rachel was joyous, obviously. Soon he met the rest of the family, especially Leah with her dull eyes (rather than tender or weak). The trick of Laban when he substituted Leah for Rachel could not have been possible without Rachel's consent. Evidently she did not fear any competition from her less-favored sister, and welcomed the thought of her company back to Canaan. It is a certainty that Jacob did not wait another seven years before he was given Rachel. Rather he waited a week, the customary time of the honeymoon, and then was given Rachel, for whom he had yet to work the additional time. As Rachel had anticipated, Jacob's love for her, in spite of all the scheming, never waned.

Special points.—This passage reveals Jacob as a young man passionately in love rather than a scheming, ambitious man. The seven years "seemed unto him but a few days, for the love he had for her" (29:20). He worked for Laban a month without discussing wages, and his uncle later was the first one to bring up the subject. Jacob's suggestion that he work seven years for Rachel was hardly a hard-nosed business deal, but more the mark of a romantic idealist. He had the potential of greatness, for not many men are capable of such unselfish devotion.

The exploitation and deception practiced by Laban should be seen in light of Jacob's earlier dealing with Esau and Isaac. Now he was on the receiving end of the maneuvering, and it must have given him a different view of such behavior. In Laban Jacob almost met his match.

The Sons of Jacob (Gen. 29:31—30:24)

The passage.—Events now took a turn that Rachel had not anticipated. Leah was blessed with children and she was barren. Leah mistakenly thought that she could win Jacob's affection by presenting him with children (29:34), but Rachel, who had no fear of losing Jacob, was sensitive to public disgrace for her inability to bear children. In desperation she sent Jacob to her handmaiden, as Sarah had appointed Hagar, which was an accepted custom at that time. One writer has suggested that the race for children that continued between Rachel and Leah was like a chess game in which two women were the pawns, but actually the most helpless person in the affair was Jacob, who seemed to be the victim of their manipulation (30:16).

The names given the children expressed the conditions under which they were born. This was the ancient custom. They did not commonly confer upon a child a name that merely struck the parents' fancy, unrelated to the life situation into which he was born. Naming children is a more serious business than most people realize. A name can inspire or intimidate a child.

Special point.—Mandrakes were plants that were thought to produce fertility in a woman. Rachel bargained for them in her desperation to have a child. How pathetic is the scene where she doled out to Leah one night with Jacob (who was hers to dispose) for the right to the magic herbs. Apparently it did Rachel little good. Later she tried a more effective method. She asked God to help her, and her firstborn finally lay in her arms (30:22–24).

Jacob and His Wages (Gen. 30:25–43)

The passage.—When Jacob prepared to leave Laban with his wives and children as his only possessions after more than 14 years of labor, Laban was reluctant to release such a hard worker. He was more than pleased when Jacob suggested that if he stayed his only wages would be the odd-colored sheep, cattle, and goats. Suspecting some trickery from Jacob, Laban separated the regular animals from the odd ones, letting Jacob care for the regulars. Jacob, however, was not to be outdone. In light of a belief that has persisted even to this day, that what a female witnessed at the time of pregnancy would affect the nature of the offspring, at mating time he placed before the females odd-colored branches, with the bark stripped off in spots to add to the motley array. Strangely, it happened just as he had anticipated: the young that were born were speckled and spotted. However, Jacob was later told by God that it was not his scheming after all but God's arrangement that the right males mated with the females to assure the desired results (31:10–12). God's promises at Bethel were being kept. Had Jacob forgotten about his?

The Flight from Laban (Gen. 31:1–55)

The passage.—After twenty years in Padan-Aram (Haran) Jacob decided to return home. Aware that Laban might try to prevent him from taking with him his possessions, all of which had at one time belonged to Laban (v. 43), Jacob gathered his willing wives, who showed little natural affection for their father (vv. 15–16), and fled toward Canaan. Although Laban had been told by God in a dream that he should not speak to Jacob "either good or bad" (v. 24), this was more than he could bear. Because he respected the warning from God he was determined not to harm Jacob, yet he could not endure being silent about what was happening, particularly since his images (Hebrew, *teraphim,* "household gods") had been stolen. These were regarded in Near Eastern cultures as tokens of family property rights.

Jacob foolishly told Laban that if the gods could be found on anyone in his household, that person would pay with his life. The fact that Laban searched the women's tents shows that they were the likely culprits, especially since these teraphim were thought to guarantee fertility and the general welfare of the home. Jacob should have known by now that his women were capable of questionable behavior in this area, particularly Rachel. Her shrewdness in dealing with Laban, pretending to be in her menstrual period (v. 35), proved her to be a true daughter of the scheming Syrian.

Jacob's response to Laban after his unsuccessful search is a classic. All the frustration and resentment of twenty years' toil came welling up (vv. 36–42). The rightness of what the son-in-law was saying even impressed the older man. Meekly he suggested a reconciliation without any further demands of restitution. The famous Mizpah benediction (v. 49), however, still contained overtones of mistrust. "The Lord keep his eye on you," he was saying, "when I cannot see what you are doing."

Special point.—This section gives a significant description of the religious situation in Laban's household. He worshiped the same God that Jacob did, for he respected the warning given to him. Laban asserted that both his father Nahor and Abraham worshiped the same God that their father Terah served (v. 53). Yet this family worship of the true God was mixed with idolatry, such as the use of the teraphim. Apparently when Abraham was called it was not necessary to leave the God of his fathers, but rather to follow him, and to purify his worship.

Jacob at Peniel (Gen. 32:1–32)

The passage.—The encounter with the angels at Mahanaim ("two bands") was reminiscent of the angel band at Bethel except that there only one band existed, that of the angels. Now Jacob had a company of his own. The presence of the angel band assured Jacob of God's approval of his return to Canaan and of his continued presence with him. In spite of the evidence of God's care for him, Jacob was terrified by the news that Esau was coming to meet him with four hundred armed men, for an offended brother would not commonly behave this way unless he intended to do harm. Using his best acumen, the younger brother sent numerous presents ahead of the company to assure Esau of his desire for reconciliation, but he stayed behind to think and to pray concerning the outcome of such a potentially disastrous encounter.

Suddenly a man jumped him in the darkness, and for all he knew it was Esau. Desperately he fought for his life, not knowing he wrestled with more than flesh and blood, until his thigh went out of joint at a touch, and the angel pled to be released at the approach of dawn. Even when he knew this was no mortal, Jacob still clung to him, pleading for a blessing, which was not long in coming. A new name, "prince of God," was given him to replace the old one, "the heel snatcher," "the selfishly ambitious." The conqueror of men would become the representative of God. Instead of seeing himself as over against other men, now he would view himself as under God.

Special point.—Why does the angel say that he must go when the day breaks? Do not angels function during the day as well as night? This remark has caused some expositors to feel that originally there was a belief that a night demon guarded the Jabbok, and that Jacob was thought to have wrestled victoriously with him. Later generations perceived that such an encounter was unlikely, and in reality he was wrestling with the angel of God. Regardless of the history, the present form of the story is a reliable picture of Jacob's meeting with God.

Truth for today.—The thrust of the story is Jacob's realization that prevailing with God is not achieved in the same way he disposed of Esau and Laban, by outmaneuvering them and asserting his superiority. God could never be forced to yield to Jacob. The only hope for a blessing from him was to hold desperately to him and beg for it. Jesus spoke of an unwilling judge who nevertheless aided an importunate widow because she would not let him rest. God is not unwilling to bless us, but his help awaits our humble pleas. It is not that he enjoys seeing us abjectly prostrate before him, but that in such a desperate condition we realize both who we are and how much we need him.

The Meeting with Esau (Gen. 33:1–20)

The passage.—Whatever Esau's original intention, when he actually met Jacob, the encounter was a friendly one, with all past offenses forgotten. Had Esau had a change of mind during the night while Jacob was wrestling with the angel? Or had Jacob's abundant gifts swayed him? However it occurred, it is obvious that God had been working with him as well as with Jacob, whether he was aware of it or not. Such forgiveness as that offered by Esau is hardly a possible virtue without the providence of God.

Without much hesitation Esau accepted the gifts from Jacob. The ensuing conversation revealed that although Esau had apparently forgiven Jacob, the younger man was still uncertain that all was well. When Esau suggested that Jacob follow him to his home, Jacob answered that the slow progress of his family would delay his arrival for some while. He suggested that Esau return, and he would later follow him to Seir. Obviously, he had no such intention, which was apparent even to Esau when he refused a token guard to accompany him. As soon as Esau departed, Jacob moved off in the opposite direction. They would not meet again until Isaac's death (Gen. 37:29).

Special point.—Jacob had called the place where he wrestled with the angel Peniel, "the face of God." On meeting Esau he remarked that, when he looked at him, he was reminded of the face of God. Who would ever have thought, on looking at Esau, that he was looking upon God? The resemblance noticed by

3. Jacob's
well at
Sychar, near
Shechem (see
Gen. 33:18–20
and John 4:5)

Jacob must have been the look of mercy and forgiveness upon his brother's face. We often say that for men to see God in us, we should live the right kind of lives before them. This is true, but they are far more likely to see God in us when we express concern and forgiveness toward them.

Jacob's purchase of the field from the Hivites was the second purchase of land for the patriarchs (cf. Gen. 23). It had become necessary because of the size of Jacob's family. Abraham with his small company could easily move about, but Jacob felt the need to settle down. The monetary value of the one hundred

Kesitahs mentioned here is unknown. It was a smaller coin than the shekel, or its value would have been preserved in the tradition. In typical fashion Jacob made a shrewder deal than Abraham.

The Dinah Affair (Gen. 34:1–31)

The passage.—This story is apparently recorded in order to show that although Jacob intended to settle down and acquire property like any other prosperous sojourner, this was not to be. There could be no compromise with the Canaanites. Israel must remain a sojourner until the whole land became theirs. To settle down too soon would be to lose all

41

sense of destiny and to become just like the Canaanites.

The events in this chapter do not favor the hostile acts of Simeon and Levi. Their treacherous behavior is pictured in contrast with the attempt of Shechem to act in good faith. The author recognizes that the brothers had reason enough for their resentment over the treatment of Dinah (vv. 14,31). Yet he clearly feels that Shechem, who could not be excused for violating Dinah, was trying with unusual integrity to make honest atonement for an act of passion. He mentions that Shechem "was more honorable than all the house of his father" (v. 19). In describing the cruel behavior of Simeon and Levi, he seems to be implying that Shechem may be even more honorable than all of Jacob's family as well. However, he seems also to be saying, "God's will be done." It was not to be that the Canaanites and Israel should live at peace.

Special point.—The later history of Simeon and Levi needs to be understood in light of this chapter. Jacob's curse fell on them even in the midst of his blessing upon his other sons (Gen. 49:5–7). They that lived by the sword eventually died by it. Neither Simeon nor Levi continued to exist as a separate tribe in the councils of Israel. Simeon was absorbed into Judah, and Levi was assigned the priestly role. In the case of Simeon the militant spirit ultimately led to division and loss of identity. Levi took the better way. His warlike character was exercised in the defense of the law of God, and the Torah became his sword.

Back to Bethel (Gen. 35:1–29)

The passage.—Over twenty years had passed since Jacob had met God at Bethel. As he felt God calling him to return, he suddenly realized that preparations had to be made. His family had

been practicing idolatry, and this must be abandoned. They must also appear before God with clean bodies and clothes. (Is this the origin of our custom of wearing our "Sunday best"?) The fact that they gave him the earrings probably meant that they were pagan symbols. We wonder why he "hid" ("buried") them rather than destroying them. Perhaps the women were too superstitious to let him become an iconoclast! Since the items were probably metal (certainly the earrings), they could only have been melted down, not destroyed. Burial might have been customary. Regardless of the reason, it still was true that they could be recovered after the visit to Bethel. Were some of Jacob's family relying upon that?

The giving of the new name to Jacob in 35:9–15 repeats the act of 32:28, and the account is in the same style as Gen. 1. It also again explains the name of Bethel (v. 15). This is an obvious example of the fact that historical materials in Genesis came from different sources, but are not therefore any less reliable.

Special points.—The return to Bethel marked the inauguration of a new period in Jacob's life. After a long sojourn in the far country, this was a return to the dedication that characterized his first experience there. It was surely a high moment for him. Yet the shadow of death hung all about Bethel. First Deborah, Rebecca's nurse, died. She must have meant much to Jacob since his mother was no longer living. She had accompanied Rebekah when she first left Haran (24:59) and had probably nursed Jacob as well and become a sort of grandmother to him. This first encounter with the actual death of a loved one prepared Jacob for the saddest hour of his life, the loss of Rachel. Dying in childbirth, she left behind the memories of what might have been and the comforting presence of the new son, Benjamin. The prodigal's return to God was sealed by the death of the one he loved most. This time Jacob was not likely to forget the vows at Bethel.

The Esau Genealogy (Gen. 36:1–43)

The passage—Just as upon the death of Abraham the genealogy of Ishmael was given (25:12), the family of Esau is presented after the death of Isaac (35:27–29). These records represent ancient authentic materials and come from a time before the Edomites were regarded with that hostility which marked most of Israel's relationship with their kinsmen. We learn in this chapter that it was Esau who voluntarily left the country west of the Jordan valley where his forefathers had lived, lest his presence cause trouble between him and Jacob (vv. 6–8). The "dukes" mentioned in this chapter are contemporary terms applied to Edomite officials by the translators of the King James Version. The word is the common one for "chief."

Special points.—The modern reader finds little material of interest in this chapter. At the time when it was finally included in the book of Genesis, it probably held little interest in Israel. Yet the writer has included it in the Scripture. There are probably two reasons for this. He wanted to be fair to Esau, who in spite of his shortcomings contributed substantially to both patriarchal and later Hebrew history. In addition, a break was needed to give proper emphasis to the new principal character about to be introduced. As the reader is treated to an Edomite interlude, Jacob will give way to Joseph.

The word translated "mules" in verse 24 is an enigmatic one. Older versions render the object of discovery as hot springs or even "giants." Mules were probably not running wild in the Edomite

wilderness in that period of history. It is most likely that the translation should be conjectured as simply "water." To find a fresh water supply by chance in those barren hills would be an event worth remembering.

It should be noted in the list of the Edomite kings that not a single one was succeeded by his son (36:31–39). Even the anarchy characteristic of the reigns in North Israel was not that disastrous. This stands in contrast to the history of Judah in which every king came from the royal house of David. Secular Edom lacked a common bond of unity. Perhaps it stemmed largely from a lack of any set goal or purpose for the people. Because there was no vision, Edom was perishing.

Joseph and His Brothers (Gen. 37:1–36)

The passage.—It is tragic, after all the trouble caused between him and Esau by their parents' favoritism, that Jacob should make a similar mistake. Indeed his preference for Joseph was carried to an absurd extreme when he gave him a coat that set him apart from his brothers. The coat is described by a word that can mean either "extremities" or "diversities." The King James Version favored the latter, "coat of many colors." More recent translations prefer the former, "long coat with sleeves," which would have been a long-sleeved white garment worn by royal youths of those times. This would have been a galling offense to Joseph's brothers.

The dreams that Joseph related to his brothers were valid evidence of his special destiny, but he was most naive in thinking that they would be as impressed by them as was his proud father. Their hostile reaction certainly is not surprising. We wonder why Jacob did not anticipate it. Certainly if he had been a schemer at heart, he would have thought of it. However, he apparently sent Joseph to them without any awareness of their bristling resentment.

Many scholars find evidence in the Joseph story of two narratives, one told in Judah and the other in North Israel, both based upon the same original events but giving separate and essentially reliable witness to those events. According to this view the North Israel account reports that he was stolen by Midianites (v. 28*a*), while the Judean account says that he was sold by his brothers to the Ishmaelites (v. 28*b*). They agree that his brothers' treachery resulted in his enslavement in Egypt. The possible existence of the former account is attested by the statement of Joseph, "I was stolen away out of the land of the Hebrews" (40:15), and the latter account may be reflected in his statement to his brothers, "I am Joseph your brother, whom ye sold into Egypt" (45:4).

Other interpreters insist that these sources exist only in the imagination of scholars. The Ishmaelites and the Midianites in the passage are the same people, they say. When Joseph said he was sold by his brothers, he correctly blamed them for his enslavement though they did not do the actual selling.

Truth for today.—Sometimes the deepest wounds are given by those who are not aware that they are causing hurt. Jacob did not seem to be conscious of the hostility that his treatment of Joseph aroused in his other sons. Joseph was totally unconscious of the adverse effect that the recital of his dreams would have upon his brothers. He naively expected them to rejoice with him over the prospects. The alienated and hurt men described here warn us of our responsibility to cultivate a sensitivity to the responses of those around us. Most of us are so confined to our own small world that we cannot imagine how others must

be thinking. Some of us do not even care how they feel.

Genuine Christian concern is evidenced not only in the good we do others, but in the care with which we refrain from doing those unnecessary and irritating things that will so alienate them from us that they are not open even to our most sincere overtures. Should it matter to us what people think about us? Indeed it does if our vanity is responsible for their lack of understanding, for we have first of all not understood them.

Judah and Tamar (Gen. 38:1–30)

The passage.—This strange chapter is unlike any other in the Old Testament. The primitive life pictured here is true to the times. The story is told with accurate detail. Without restraint or criticism the lustful behavior of Judah is told just as it occurred. In the light of later Old Testament law his indiscretions were strongly condemned, but he lived in an earlier time. Certainly he should not be used as a proper example for the youth of today. The story is inserted at this point in order to furnish a more complete picture of Judah at a time when Joseph had momentarily disappeared from the scene. What more appropriate moment could another character be on the stage? In spite of Judah's sexual carelessness, he showed real nobility when confronted by Tamar. He confessed, "She hath been more righteous than I" (v. 26). He still had far to go, but he had the stuff out of which men are made.

The sin of Onan has occasioned considerable comment. It should be observed that he was condemned, not just for spilling his seed, but for doing it in an attempt to avoid his marital responsibilities. God's wrath upon him accentuates the lessons to be drawn from this clear context.

When the writer says God "slew" the sons of Judah, this does not necessarily mean that he struck them down with a sudden wrathful blow. There could have been many ways in which they died. Whatever the manner of death, the wrath of God lay behind it.

Special point.—Through Mary, Jesus was a descendant of Perez (Pharez, v. 29), as his genealogy in the New Testament clearly states (Luke 3:33). Surely the passions we struggle against surged through his veins. As we see Judah yielding to the desires of the flesh, we are reminded all the more of the significance of Jesus' triumph over every temptation common to man.

Joseph and Potiphar (Gen. 39:1–23)

The passage.—Joseph was the kind of man who excelled at anything he undertook. Soon he was the principal servant in the household of Potiphar, his master. He attracted not only the attention of his master but also the eyes of Potiphar's wife. Her overtures to him failed, not because he was not tempted, but because of his respect for the demands of God and his refusal to betray Potiphar's trust in him (39:9).

There is some evidence in the chapter that Potiphar did not believe the story told him by his wife but had to act to halt her busy tongue. He put Joseph into a prison where important persons were held (v. 20), a sentence which was hardly to be expected for a slave taken for attempted rape of a man's wife. It would have been more natural that he be executed or certainly thrown into the darkest dungeon. Furthermore, Potiphar is said to be the captain of the guard (39:1), and later it is "the captain of the guard" who charged Joseph with the care of the other prisoners (40:4).

Special points.—It is significant that the story of Joseph's resolute chastity is placed alongside the lustful behavior of Judah in chapter 38. There could not be a stronger contrast. In the former chapter we see a nobleman reflecting the moral customs of his own culture. The other portrays a man who is true to his convictions even in a foreign land. Judah lives by his inadequate conscience, whereas Joseph by sheer determination remains true to God. Of the two, Joseph is obviously presented as the ideal to be followed.

In Egyptian literature there is a story similar to that of Potiphar's wife, "The Tale of the Two Brothers." Some have attempted to trace the biblical story back to this source but with insufficient reason. Stories of marital difficulties such as this are common in any culture. It is the behavior of Joseph that is so uncommon, not the behavior of Potiphar's wife. His was the temptation of a young slave in his mistress' household, not that of a man in his brother's house, as in the Egyptian story.

Joseph in Prison (Gen. 40:1–23)

The passage.—Even in prison Joseph could not be kept down. Soon he was the most responsible man in the compound, in charge of the two most important men in the jail. One was the king's butler (cupbearer) and the other the royal baker. Both were responsible positions, for a favorite way to assassinate kings was by poisoning their food. Each had apparently been accused of a plot to assassinate the Pharaoh. From their dreams Joseph predicted that the cupbearer would be restored (Pharaoh drank from his cup again) but that the baker would be beheaded and impaled (rather than beheaded and hanged, an unlikely procedure). The clue to the different fate of the baker was that the birds and not Pharaoh ate his pastries.

Special point.—The fact that Joseph

was so adept at interpreting the dreams of others was certainly due in part to the fact that he had not given up his own dreams. Obviously it was due also to the insight given him by God (v. 8). Yet such ability would not be sought by a man who no longer believed in the validity of his own dreams, for he would have had no interest in such illusions. If we are to understand the dreams of others, we must guard a few of our own.

Truth for today.—Just as the cupbearer gave no thought to Joseph whom he left languishing in prison, we find it easy to forget our indebtedness to others. The restored official did not intend to slight Joseph, but staying in the confidence of Pharaoh was such a responsibility that the young Hebrew soon drifted out of his consciousness. If we are permitting someone for whom we are responsible to remain in intolerable circumstances although we may be able to alleviate his suffering, the story of the absent-minded cupbearer should shock us back to consciousness. To forget such a person is kin to murder, for to us he has already ceased to exist.

Joseph and Pharaoh (Gen. 41:1–57)

The passage.—When Pharaoh dreamed a dream that no one could interpret, suddenly the cupbearer remembered how Joseph had interpreted his dream while in prison. It is to his credit that he told Pharaoh of his experience while he was there, although it would remind the monarch of an episode better forgotten. When Joseph was summoned into Pharoah's presence, he first of all shaved himself. We now know that the pharaohs of this era were clean-shaven and expected the same appearance in those who appeared at court. The biblical writer's knowledge of this fact attests to the authenticity of the account.

The corn mentioned in this chapter was simply grain, probably wheat. American corn or maize was unknown to the rest of the world until after the discovery of America. The word "corn" in England, unlike America, means grain of any kind.

When Joseph described the kind of man needed to supervise the agricultural program necessary to offset the coming famine, Pharaoh immediately perceived that Joseph was better qualified than anyone else to do it. It would appear that Pharaoh might have been a little hasty, in reasoning that just because Joseph could interpret dreams and present a plausible program he would be able to supervise it. Often dreamers and practical men live in entirely different worlds, and qualities necessary to both activities are seldom found in the same man. Fortunately for him, Joseph did possess that rare combination.

Special points.—At first glance it is difficult to see why the wise men of Egypt could not interpret Pharaoh's dreams, since they were specialists in that area. It seems simple to us that seven lean cattle devouring seven fat ones would mean famine swallowing up prosperity. The solution often seems simple after we know the answer. Perhaps they suspected what it meant but were afraid to risk being wrong. Many people never succeed because they are too afraid of failure.

Joseph's marriage to Asenath, daughter of the priest of On, was disastrous in its ultimate consequences. The lines of Ephraim and Manasseh were later the leaders in Israel's idolatry, continuing the pagan tendencies stemming from this marriage. It might have seemed an honor to Joseph to receive her as his wife, but it was a tragic mistake. In compromising his faith by a marriage of convenience, he was doing what his ancestors had scrupulously avoided.

The Brothers in Egypt (Gen. 42:1–38)

The passage.—When the famine became so severe that Joseph's brothers were forced to come to Egypt for grain, he recognized them, but they had no idea who he was, for he was only seventeen when taken to Egypt and was at least thirty-seven now. As they bowed before him, he remembered his boyhood dream. God was not dead!

Insisting that the brothers bring back Benjamin to prove their good faith, Joseph forced them to leave Simeon behind as surety of their return. Was this his way of disciplining Simeon for his part in the Dinah affair? As the brothers left Egypt they discovered to their dismay that their money was in their sacks. They were filled with fear that such a blessing would result in some divinely instituted catastrophe (v. 28). Thus some men cannot enjoy the blessings of God for fear that these are a prelude to disaster. It was too good to be true.

Jacob too was convinced that life was turning against him. He had lost two sons, and now his youngest might have to go. Obviously the assurances of Reuben were no comfort to him (vv. 37–38). Why should a grandfather slay two grandsons because he has lost a son? Such well-meaning but foolish assurance from his eldest bode no good for any future venture into Egypt.

Truth for today.—Although there was no hint to them of any connection between their trouble with the Egyptian governor and their earlier treatment of Joseph, the brothers immediately declared that God had finally caught up with them (42:21). The human conscience acts in strange ways. It may be silent for years but suddenly come to life to haunt a man for the rest of his days. If a person has a good conscience, he will do well to heed it. It is easy to silence for a while, but almost impossible to kill.

The Brothers' Return to Egypt (Gen. 43: 1–34)

The passage.—The famine finally became so severe that Jacob was forced to permit the brothers to take Benjamin with them. The assurance of Judah was more helpful than that of Reuben, however. He accepted the blame if anything went wrong and asked for the consequences to fall upon him in whatever way providence might declare. Whereas Reuben had pledged his two sons, Judah promised himself and all that were his or ever would be. Jacob still took a fatalistic view of it all (v. 14).

The brothers were completely mystified by their royal reception in Egypt, particularly the special banquet provided for them. They probably feared they were being fattened for the kill. When the seating arrangement turned out to be from the eldest to the youngest, they still did not suspect who Joseph might be. When Benjamin was given five times more food than they, although he showed no reluctance to accept it, there were none of the jealous glances for which Joseph was so carefully watching. At this time Benjamin, who was born before Joseph's seventeenth birthday, must have been at least thirty years old, for Joseph was now about forty. A hungry man at thirty can eat as heartily as a younger lad in ordinary times.

Special point.—The Hebrews were segregated from the Egyptians at the meal, for they were regarded by them as second-class citizens. The Egyptian prejudice was not based upon color, but upon differences in culture. Every nation has the problem of differing cultural classes, and every country has seen it magnified in different forms. It is difficult for the upper classes to see the worth of those below them, for they do not have the opportunity of really knowing them. On the other hand the lower classes resent their subjugation. How can it be corrected? Either by sudden changes in the social structure (in Egypt by a change of dynasty from native to Hyksos), or by the determination of the enlightened ruling class to see that justice is done (which has seldom happened).

The Brothers on Trial (Gen. 44:1–34)

The passage.—Joseph was now ready to give the final test to the brothers, for they had passed all the others. When they were faced with the possible loss of Benjamin, whom Jacob had favored as much as he had Joseph (except for the special coat), would they be willing to sacrifice him to save their own lives?

The divining cup was used in determining the outcome of affairs by shaking the wine dregs in the bottom. Such practices were forbidden in later Hebrew law, and we cannot be certain that Joseph ever really used the cup for that purpose. As skilful as he was in foreseeing the future through his relationship with God, he had no need of the cup.

The speech of Judah is one of the greatest in the world's literature. It came from his very soul and revealed him as the proper ancestor for the suffering servant. He freely offered himself as a ransom for his brother Benjamin. His concern for his grieving father surpassed all personal anxieties. As Joseph listened, he could plainly see that the brothers had changed from selfish, ambitious men to concerned members of a united family.

Special point.—Why did Joseph put his brothers through such painful testing? Was he enjoying their discomfort? It is obvious that he was not doing it out of revenge. If they had not changed, it would be better for Joseph not to reveal himself to them, for they would use the

relationship for their own benefit so as to lead to future conflicts worse than the first. As difficult as it would be to keep his identity secret, Joseph would suffer less that way than if he allowed the brothers to break his heart again. This he could not endure.

But what about his father? If the brothers had failed the test, would Joseph have let Jacob die without revealing to him that he was alive? It is doubtful that Joseph himself had gone that far in his thoughts. The important thing is that they passed the test gloriously, and the family finally was joyously reunited.

A Family United (Gen. 45:1–28)

The passage.—This section was at first entitled "A Family Reunited," but it was obvious this was not a true description, for it was only after the reunion with Joseph that the family of Jacob became a unit for the first time. There is nothing like suffering either to bring a family together or to tear one apart. Which result will occur depends upon the real depth of loyalty that exists beneath the surface of petty rivalries and divisions.

It was decided that the family of Jacob would live in the land of Goshen, which possessed ideal pastureland but was not highly valued by the Egyptians, who were primarily farmers. It was also close to the northern border and near to Canaan when the time came to leave.

The delight of Pharaoh's house when they learned that a large new Hebrew family was coming to live in Egypt is in contrast to their segregation of the family at the meal in Joseph's home. Perhaps they rejoiced in the prosperity of the Hebrews as long as they did not have to associate intimately with them. It is more likely that the Pharaoh himself was not a native Egyptian, but a Hyksos king from a people kin to the Hebrews, and his views were different from those of the Egyptians who served under him in Joseph's home.

Special point.—It is important to note the difference in the reactions of the brothers and of Jacob to the announcement of Joseph's true identity. The brothers were troubled at the revelation (v. 3), for they feared it surely meant that they were in deep trouble. Their fears drowned out their natural inclination to rejoice. Jacob on the other hand almost fainted (v. 26) because he wanted so much to believe it, but was afraid to do so. Jacob feared to believe it, but his sons were afraid because they did believe it!

Truth for today.—Joseph's assurance to his brothers that "God did send me before you to preserve life" (v. 5) was surely a recent conclusion for him. When he was thrown into slavery or was languishing in jail, he must have wondered often what would become of his dreams. Yet his faith kept them alive. Now he was certain of God's providence in it all, for he was looking back. We must always remember that, present circumstances to the contrary, God does not forget his own.

Jacob's Move Down to Egypt (Gen. 46: 1–34)

The passage.—When he first heard that Joseph was in Egypt, Jacob immediately made his plans to head that way. As he came closer to the border of Canaan, however, he remembered the trouble into which Abraham had fallen, and the prohibition which God had given Isaac when he started toward Egypt (Gen. 26:2). Surely it would be better to get a word from God before going any farther. So he paused to offer sacrifice at Beer-sheba.

God's reply to him, "Fear not to go down into Egypt" (v. 27), reveals that Jacob had now become quite hesitant about going any farther. He had learned too well already the folly of leaving God out of his plans. He was assured at long last that God would let him do something he longed for, and would go with him into Egypt.

Before the family had settled in Egypt Joseph gave them instructions for their interview with Pharaoh. When he asked them what their occupation was, they were to reply that they were herdsmen, for then the sovereign would automatically assign them to Goshen, which for the Hebrews was the most desirable land in Egypt. The tension between farmers and shepherds in Egypt is reminiscent of the Cain and Abel story in Genesis 4. In Egypt also the farmers held resentment toward the shepherds.

Special point.—In the list of Jacob's seventy descendants is a man by the name of Job. Could he be the same as the one in the book of Job? That is quite possible. If so, he left Egypt before the sojourn was over. Other Hebrews may well have done the same thing during the years that followed. When Joshua led the Israelites into Canaan, they probably found relatives already there, particularly around Shechem where Jacob had bought property. Joshua is not said to have fought for Shechem, for the people were apparently friendly toward the invading army.

The Worsening of the Famine (Gen. 47: 1–26)

The passage.—Just as Joseph had anticipated, Pharaoh assigned the Hebrews to Goshen. (Of course, this probably resulted from a previous suggestion or two to the monarch.) After the land was assigned, Joseph brought Jacob into Pharaoh's presence. The first words the king addressed to the patriarch were, freely translated, "How old are you, old man?" Tersely and pathetically Jacob summed up his life: "Few and evil have the days of my life been, and have not attained to the days of the years of the life of my fathers" (v. 9). In other words, he was saying that he was not as old as he seemed to be. It was not his age but the mileage that was showing. What a contrast between this autobiographical statement and the eager young Jacob who first "lifted up his feet" to leave Bethel. The "grand old age" of Abraham could not be his. The fruit of his earlier sowing was now being harvested, but that was not the entire story. It had been his lot to suffer, and not all of it was from any fault of his. Jacob, bowed beneath the load, did not ask why.

While the Hebrews were prospering, the lot of the Egyptians was worsening. Soon they had delivered to Pharaoh, through Joseph, all their money, animals, land, and even themselves. Graciously Joseph worked out an agreement in which the Egyptians would give to Pharaoh 20 percent of the increase of the land. This is in sharp contrast to the tithe of the Jews to God for the use of the land of Palestine; it amounted only to 10 percent unless they added other tithes to the principal one. It appears that Joseph was taking advantage of the distress of the people of Egypt in order to increase the power of Pharaoh. Although the 20 percent allotment to the king was a generous arrangement for that time, it was considerably more austere than the lot of the Egyptians before the famine. Surely a man who had been a slave should have been more hesitant to enslave others.

The Last Days of Jacob (Gen. 47:27—48:22)

The passage.—As the time approached for Jacob to die, he summoned Joseph and made him swear in a manner like the charge of Abraham to Eliezer (chap. 24) that he would surely bury him in the family burying ground at Hebron.

Soon afterward Joseph brought his two sons, Manasseh being the firstborn, for their grandfather's blessing. Jacob, however, placed his right hand upon Ephraim's head. Thinking that his father's eyesight had failed him, Joseph tried to change the hands, but he was curtly informed that the old man knew what he was doing (48:19). Thus the prominent place of the Ephraim tribe in North Israel (it became the largest tribe) was traced back to Jacob's deathbed.

Special points.—Jacob's word to his grandsons is in sharp contrast to his words to Pharaoh (47:9): "The God which fed (Hebrew, shepherded) me all my life long unto this day, the Angel which redeemed me from all evil, bless the lads" (48:15b–16a). Before Pharaoh "few and evil" were his days. Now his life is a witness to the providence of God. How can this difference in viewpoint be explained? One reason is that he is speaking to young lads whom he would not discourage. Perhaps, however, the best explanation is that he has lived happily in Egypt with his family for the last seventeen years, and their rosy glow has colored all his reminiscing, or has helped him notice things he had not seen before.

Jacob's statement in verse 22 that he had conquered a portion (Hebrew, "mountain-slope") of Canaan with his sword and bow is mystifying, for there are no such references in the rest of Genesis. Perhaps he was speaking of Shechem, and the allusion is to his sons' capturing it in the Dinah episode.

The Blessing of Jacob (Gen. 49:1–27)

The passage.—This chapter should be studied alongside the Blessing of Moses in Deuteronomy 33 and the Song of Deborah in Judges 5. The tribal characteristics are summed up in the form of Jacob's blessing. Were future traits described beforehand by Jacob, or did Israel read its history back into his blessing? There is no reason to doubt that he pronounced such blessings on his sons. Later history might have led to an expansion of the earlier oracles, but the chapter is surely rooted in history.

Each tribe is described the way a father would understand his children. *Reuben,* unstable as water, was undisciplined and as a consequence would have a less rightful place of influence as the firstborn. *Simeon* and *Levi* are comrades in crime whose symbol is a sword, and who must be separated if either one ever would succeed. *Judah,* the lionhearted, must assume the military ascendancy and hence rule the tribes. *Zebulun* and *Issachar* are also pictured as partners, but their association was a helpful one. Zebulun's symbol was a ship and Issachar's a plow. The farmer and the sailor needed each other, the merchant relying upon the roots of the farmer, the home worker profiting from the other's vision. *Dan's* symbol was a serpent, and he would wisely judge in Israel. However, the tribe does not appear in the text of Revelation 7. Could this be due to the serpent figure in his history? *Gad* is the underdog who will eventually triumph, but *Asher,* whose symbol is the horn of plenty, will accomplish little because of his life of ease. The uninhibited hind, *Naphtali,* will furnish the poets in Israel. He will be the first to sound the call to freedom. *Joseph,* the fruitful bough, will be numerous but not necessarily profitable. Finally Benjamin, the wolf, will be the fighter. The apostle Paul truly represented his tribe.

Special point.—The prediction concerning Judah in 49:10 is the most important one in the chapter for messianic understanding. The expression "until Shiloh come" is quite troublesome, yet the heart of the verse. There is little likelihood that the translation "Shiloh" is correct, although it is an actual translation of the Hebrew word as it now stands. Towns do not "come," but the meaning of the word "peace" may be understood figuratively.

It is more likely that we have here an abbreviation for a longer expression, found in Ezekiel 21:27, which may be translated "until he comes to whom it belongs." Thus the verse is saying that the scepter shall not depart from Judah until the one arrives for whom it is destined, the messianic son of David.

The Death and Burial of Jacob (Gen. 49: 28—50:13)

The passage.—Just as he charged Joseph (47:29–31), Jacob now called upon his other sons to take his body back to Hebron. There Abraham and Sarah, Isaac and Rebekah were buried. Then Jacob uttered a surprising word, "There I buried Leah." His last request was to be buried beside Leah rather than beside Rachel, whose body rested near Bethlehem. Was this just because Leah happened to be buried at Hebron, or had he buried her there in preparation for his own last resting place? After the death of Rachel, Leah had Jacob alone for a number of years. Did she finally win his love, and did Jacob see that her love was far more meaningful than the fitful passion of the more beautiful Rachel? We cannot tell for certain, but this passage hints at Leah's ultimate victory over Rachel. This should be a great comfort to the majority of women who must temporarily surrender the center of the stage to the more glamorous exceptions.

The funeral procession into Canaan was composed of all the prominent officials of Egypt, except Pharaoh, and all the family of Jacob. Accompanying them were the chariots and horsemen of Egypt and all the paraphernalia of the royal court. Such a funeral was unrivaled in Hebrew history. Jacob's troubled life was ultimately crowned with glory. Yet all the pomp of that occasion would have dimmed before the angelic vision that Jacob first witnessed at Bethel.

The Return to Egypt (Gen. 50:14–26)

The passage.—The long journey back to Egypt gave abundant opportunity for reappraisal on the part of the brothers. They could not believe that Joseph's forgiveness of them was genuine, perhaps because they were not given to such emotions. Upon their return to Egypt they abjectly fell down before him, confessing themselves to be his slaves. Joseph wept at their lack of understanding of him (cf. Jesus weeping at the tomb of Lazarus, John 11). He no longer enjoyed seeing them prostrate before him as in his boyhood dreams, for now he knew himself to be a man like them, not God (v. 19). Perhaps earlier he had thought that he could one day become a super-man compelling their submission. Now he knew better.

Truth for today.—There has never been a more vivid picture of the providence of God than in the words of Joseph to his brothers, "Ye thought evil against me; but God meant it unto good" (v. 20). He was not saying that God caused them to think evil against him, for they were responsible for their own thoughts. In his wisdom and power, however, God used their evil purposes to achieve his will.

All of creation is destined to witness to his glory, for God is the ultimate alchemist. Only he can make gold from the baser metals, use evil men to achieve good. If we make such attempts, we will become as frustrated as the ancient chemists at their alchemy.

The book of Genesis begins with a burst of light and closes with a coffin in a tomb in Egypt. Yet this coffin was also truly a light shining in the darkness, for it held the body of a great man who believed that one day his remains would be carried back with the return of his people to their Promised Land. In Genesis 1:1 God created light. In Genesis 50: 25–26 Joseph turned his face toward it.

EXODUS

Ralph H. Langley

INTRODUCTION

Exodus is a book of faith. It proceeds on the bold assumption that Israel's escape from Egyptian slavery, and the victorious establishment as a free people and independent nation is the key event of their history and of God's revelation. Moreover, Exodus treats Israel's experience as the clue to the meaning of all history and existence. This is true of all the Old Testament. But the distinctive point in Exodus is this focus on emancipation from Egypt and establishment as the distinctive people of God.

The force of the book of Exodus comes across in such key words and ideas as power, freedom, and sovereignty. These are evident in the attributes and actions of God. Exodus is a book of power and deeds, the vivid, historic acts of God. The God of Exodus is a God with a purpose and a plan and most importantly the power to execute it. This God of Exodus is a righteous God, performing his actions with terrific moral force. Exodus profiles this God and his new community of chosen people by the social and moral standards of Israel's common life. It is also powerfully evident in the Ten Commandments, one of the great peaks of divine revelation. And again it is expressed in the great concepts of the Covenant Code, indicative of God's ethical and moral activity.

Exodus is not history in the usual sense of that word. More correctly it is theological and spiritual truth vividly and vitally expressed through real historic experiences. It combines remembered events from the painful and glorious pages of Israel's past with the throbbing chapters of Israel's present. The faith of the present is directly related to those roots of her history. So it was God's hand and God's power in and through those events that brought Israel not only out of bondage, but into nationhood as a unique instrument for the divine will.

The whole Bible insists with Exodus that creation's meaning is to be understood by the light of God's redemptive purpose. Our Jewish friends who prize Exodus so highly and for good reasons still cut their Bible off too soon and miss the greater revelation. They cut their Bible off by 27 books too soon!—27 books and one resurrection!

The place and function of the church looms large in Exodus. By church here we mean the community of faith. This body of believers was held together not only by its enemies, by its common life and principles, but most especially by its celebration of the *ex odos*—"the road out." In Exodus Israel is God's church—the "camp" of God in the wilderness—"a kingdom of priests and a holy nation" (19:6)—and all of this specifically in the thrilling experience that it was God that led this people out of Egypt.

I. MOSES PREPARED (EX. 1:1—7:13)

Israel in Bondage in Egypt (Ex. 1:1–22)

The passage.—The book of Exodus is written like a drama. The opening chapter reads like the introduction of a cast of characters. But it is a deadly serious drama, no mere stage show. Jacob's 70 descendents form the cast first to be played out in Egypt. That number "70" is symbolic: not just a census figure, but the sign of Israel's unity under God.

After Joseph's death the Jews in Egypt felt the awful sting of persecution. The new king of Egypt put them into labor camps—slaves of the Pharaoh. With this labor he built two of the great treasure-store cities of Egypt, Pithom and Raamses. But the heavier the persecution, the greater God's signs of "promise!"

Special points.—The aim of the Egyptian enslavement was more than slave labor. Beyond the economic exploitation the idea was to stop the population explosion of the Jews! But it did not work. The humaneness of the midwives (Egyptian women) took precedence over their national prejudice and interests. Thus the story echoes the hand of God in revealing himself through enemy hands. God can work anywhere and through any people. Here he is revealed universally in man's creation (both races are his) and most especially in man's redemption.

Truth for today.—Don't miss the humor reflected in this passage. The Jews are masters of wit and have the grace to laugh through the tears of torture and tyranny. Here they are laughing their way through the tough times of Egyptian slavery, a lesson for the sufferers of all ages. The midwives made clever use of wit and excuse. Pharaoh comes off as a ludicrous fathead: the joke is on the king! and everybody knows it but him! So while they laugh the king right out of his court, God wins another round and moves victoriously on.

Divine Provision of Leadership (Ex. 2: 1–25)

The passage.—This chapter features the birth and adoption of Moses. This story has always been loved by Jew and Christian alike, from children on up, and for good reason. It vividly portrays the hand of God in a warm human-interest story that sweeps us up in its simplicity and its grandeur.

Moses is the hero of the book of Exodus. And he is the mightiest name in all the Pantheon of Jewish heroes—above the likes of a David, or an Abraham or an Elijah. So the birth narrative of a nation's greatest son takes on an unusual interest value. Curiously the great man who is to captain Israel's ship of state and pilot her through not only a Red Sea, but other baffling "seas," himself baffles his enemies even in infancy when he is so little he's hidden by bulrushes!

Special points.—Every nation can recall sacred moments in its history when so much depended on so little. At this point Israel's destiny seems to hang breathlessly in the balance. Imagine that tiny ark among the river's reeds watched over by the loving eyes of one little sister. And God! And so it was to be centuries later when the doors of history would swing again on the tiny hinges of a baby's life, when his enemies would hound him and his family right into this same Egypt from his homeland (Matt. 2:13–23).

The Moses story heightens in climactic fashion as we see the king's daughter appear at precisely that spot on the Nile to bathe. And there it "just happened" that right at that place and moment she made the amazing discovery, a tiny ark with a precious cargo. And though her own father-king had ordered a halt to Jewish population growth, how could she resist that little baby so lovingly placed there by a mother's heart and hand?

Then comes the innocent question of that attentive sister: "Shall I go and call . . . a nurse of the Hebrews?" All of which was the working out of a divine scheme. Here is God taking warm human hearts and overriding sheer cruelty. For in all of this God was not only saving Moses' life, but providing him a king's education. As always, God was looking far into the future. He was preparing a leader. On the surface it all seems to hang on accident and circumstance. But woven into the theme is the unmistakable finger of God.

Moses' name, as most Jewish names, has special meaning. It must come from the Hebrew word "to draw out" or "the one who draws forth" as Pharaoh's daughter had precisely done with the baby Moses from the river Nile. Prophetically and wonderfully this was to be Moses' role under the Will Divine: the drawer forth of his people.

Very early Moses' life took on some heroic characteristics. He seemed always ready to sacrifice himself for his oppressed people. He had a deep sense of feeling against injustice. His temper was often hot in righteous wrath. He seemed almost reckless in audacity. His was a bold courage. And it quickly got him into trouble.

The Special Call and Appointment of Moses (Ex. 3:1–10)

The passage.—Moses was a prophet. The Bible says he was the greatest of the prophets (Deut. 34:10; Num. 12: 6–7). From this vocation he was called and commissioned to a place of authority and leadership. This came directly from God by angelic messenger in the incident of "the burning bush."

He is commanded to take off his shoes, for it is holy ground. It became even more hallowed ground later as Moses obediently responded to God's call and challenge. All ground where God meets man and life-changing decisions are made becomes consecrated.

Special points.—For Moses, and Israel, and all people this is a great moment: one of the truly significant watersheds of history. It is "the fullness of time." God is about to reveal himself as the Great Destroyer. (Exodus moves on the theme of God's power.) He is also to reveal himself as the Great Deliverer. And Moses is to be the human instrument of that mighty deliverance. God's plan in calling Moses (or using men any time) is to endow him with authority. Then God will harness to his purpose the natural gifts of the man: his audacity and daring, his courage and faith, and the terrific sense of justice, so passionately strong in this man Moses.

God's Careful Instructions to Moses (Ex. 3:11–22)

The passage.—God will not just call the man of his choosing. That man and God's plan must not be left to chance. God has a strategy always. Preparation must precede performance. Leave nothing to accident. That's always the case with our God. Now for Moses must come not only what to do in Egypt/but more basic still: his relationship to the Lord in his all-important mission. Otherwise it will remain mission impossible!

Truth for today.—Moses' modesty (the Bible calls him meek as later in the New Testament with Jesus) must be transformed into the power of humility through faith. So God says "I will be with you." That should galvanize any man against any foes and any fears. It was Moses' armor, inside and out. So can it be ours. The deliverance is to be God's doing.

The Power of Moses' Rod in God's Hands (Ex. 4:1–17)

The passage.—The rod in Moses' hands is only a cane. But Moses plus God is another matter—soon to be equal to all the might of an Egyptian Pharaoh. The rod is now to be an instrument of the divine will and power. But before that rod is to push Egypt's king against the wall, God uses it to draw forth the faith of Moses and convince him it will be adequate to impress and defeat the Egyptian priests and magicians.

All of this seems to make Moses look like a mere magician, against other magicians. But this contest is vastly more: it is part of the cosmic struggle of God against all the forces of evil. These signs given to Moses point up the always-needed, always-relevant insight: this God of biblical revelation and faith is the unquestioned Master in this world he himself created.

As the high drama unfolds, Moses still offers his alibi "O my Lord, I am not eloquent." He still talks and acts as if he assumes he is to deliver Israel in his own power and gifts. Never. He complains he cannot play the hero, not grasping the fact God has called him not to be a hero, but a servant.

God answers the alibi—"I will be thy mouth." God is not weak and in need of Moses' strength. Just the other way around. God is equal to his own purposes. And he knows how to accomplish his goals. The weakness of men—even men of the stature of Moses—presents a helpless-looking situation against the awful might of evil like an obstinate Pharaoh. But such weakness magnifies the power of God. It should be added this makes God (not Moses) the Hero and Mover in the book of Exodus.

Enter Aaron. The doubting and difficult Moses must yet be convinced. This angers God. So Aaron is to be called as Moses' voice of eloquence.

Special points.—Aaron is the representative of the priests and priestly line. And Moses is a prophet. Thus the two are to become vital and active instruments of the Lord in the function of the Covenant relationships from now on.

Moses Obeys—Returns to Egypt (Ex. 4: 18–31)

The passage.—Moses now takes his wife Zipporah and his sons and his rod (symbol of his power and commission) and reenters the land of Egypt, from which he had fled for his life 40 years before. The plot thickens as the author tells us it is God himself who hardens Pharaoh's heart. Thus the face-to-face conflict with Pharaoh is heightened.

Truth for today.—The hardening of Pharaoh's heart (necessitating extra wonders to convince him) is to stage God's power in a more dramatic fashion. These Egyptians must know God in all his power. Israel must know him as the great God who is able. This God must be Israel's God in all his freedom and power. This God can make even the stubbornness and wrath of man to praise him (Ps. 76:10).

Moses Faces Pharaoh and Fierce Opposition (Ex. 5:1–23)

The passage.—This chapter brings the combatants (Moses *vs.* Pharaoh) into open conflict. The issue is drawn and the fierce battle engaged. In the king's stubbornness and retaliation we get a taste of raw idolatry and despotic will. Surprisingly one of the deep lessons the Jewish slaves must learn is they too will suffer loss. They will have to pay a price for their freedom-to-be. It is not just a gift from God. Moses himself hardly seems to understand the burden of the mystery. But slowly he moves on, motivated by faith in God and yearning and pity for his people.

There stands Pharaoh asking the question of all pagan hearts: "Who is the Lord?" It seems an unthinkable exercise to release his profitable slaves to a god he does not even know! The irony of the unfolding drama reveals his progressive surrender to this omnipotent God he is learning to know in all his mighty power.

But first Pharaoh insultingly demands "Get you unto your burdens" (5:4). He assumes that Moses and Aaron are still his slaves and have simply deserted their slaving work. Maybe he senses a Jewish strike or work slowdown. He disdainfully supposes these two Jews to be agitators without either a cause or a following.

Predictably the king responds by making the slave-load heavier. He orders the straw removed from the brickmakers. But the production quotas remained. Even the taskmasters see these demands as capricious and unreasonable. They even appeal to the king in their behalf. But to no avail. Pharaoh is furious and unyielding.

Truth for today.—Moses learns by the things he suffers. This chapter ends on the difficult but important point of gaining God's victory through defeat. To all intents it seems Moses' first efforts have not only ended in miserable failure, but made the lot of his people wretchedly worse. But wait. Taking the longer look, God says in effect, "I will deliver the people in due course. This petty king shall not have the final say. Be patient. Our day will come."

God Unveils His Strategy (Ex. 6:1–9)

The passage.—Right from the start God reemphasizes his power—and the assurance it will be adequate. "I am the Lord" has the idea of Divine force capable of violence and destructive energy.

Moses' Inadequacy (Ex. 6:10–13, 28–30)

Special points.—This section seems a bit confusing. Part of the difficulty is in our grasping the Jewish concept of a vitally close relationship between the land, the race, and the religion of God's chosen people. Part of the problem is in the meaning of the word for God. Different names for God would likely be the writer's attempt to show us that the same God reveals himself in different ways at different times by differing names.

Moses still trembles over his seeming failure with his own people, and before Pharaoh. Despite God's names, and power, and covenant promises, Moses still repeats his fears and pleads his inadequacy. So Moses needs to have his heart and lips regalvanized by divine grace—to "get his courage in the sticking place"—before he can say again with fire and force "Let my people go!"

The Genealogy of Moses and Aaron (Ex. 6:14–27)

The passage.—The main emphasis in this "Family Tree" is the priestly line of the tribe of Levi. Aaron and Moses are exactly four generations removed from Jacob. It is striking that the line stops in Moses, but continues in Aaron. The author wants us to see the important place of the priestly line in the founding of the new nation. So, without eroding the present place of prophetic power in Moses, the list here asserts the high place of Aaron, the firstborn of Amram.

The Divine Choice of Aaron (Ex. 6:28— 7:7)

The passage.—The author tells us how God uses two men of very different talents (Moses and Aaron) to accomplish the will divine. Moses is to be "as God to Pharaoh" and Aaron is to be as prophet. Moses can't speak well, but represents the power-base and power-image of the two men who are the human instruments of the mission. Moses will possess the authority of God but leave the speaking to Aaron.

Special points.—Again, the hardened heart and stubborn will of Pharaoh is no surprise (3:19;4:21). The explanation by the author is in verse 5: to make the Egyptians know who is the Lord. The fall of Pharaoh will symbolize the downfall of all the gods of Egypt because he is their representative. The "signs" and "wonders" illustrate God's power, spelled out in the unmistakable language of doomsday: plagues and pestilence everywhere. And on the positive side these wonders will be victoriously manifested in Israel's emancipation.

The Moment of Truth—Can Moses and Aaron Match Pharaoh and His Men? (Ex. 7:8–13)

The passage.—God equips his men and commissions them for the showdown encounter. He even deigns to give them black magic. The rod-to-serpent magic is to match the enemy trick for trick. And more. When the magicians of Egypt seem equal to the challenge thrown down by God's men, making their rods also into serpents (the word means dragon like a primeval monster), Aaron's dragon eats theirs up! God will not be upstaged or defeated. All this is a dramatic power-play, but the reader knows God remains the central actor on and off stage. His power and sovereignty will be vindicated. And Israel's faith must be assured.

II. THE PLAGUES (EX. 7:14—12:51)

The Pollution of the Nile (Ex. 7:14–25)

The passage.—First the fish of the river are smitten. This caused a water-famine. The water was undrinkable. Then Moses touched the river and turned it to blood, not only in the Nile, but all the waters of the country. Then the magicians of Egypt brought the same curse on the streams (though it is not clear what waters they so cursed).

Special points.—One of the key points of this classic confrontation is the river itself. It was so vital to Egypt's life it had long since been revered and worshiped as a god in Egypt's pantheistic religions. In fact this same Pharaoh had no doubt acted as "High Priest" at the annual flood-time, to celebrate the "blessings" of that river of life. Thus the climactic confrontation here in cursing *this* river: in the presence of Pharaoh God smites Egypt's very god of life, the river Nile.

The Plague of Frogs (Ex. 8:1–15)

The passage.—Interestingly the frog is rare in Palestine (cf. Pss. 78:45;105:30). But it was a different story in Egypt: frogs were not only common, but like the river Nile became a religious symbol. The frog to the Egyptians was the embodiment of life-giving power. Also the Egyptians (of ancient and modern times) believed there was life-giving power in the slime left by the great river.

Thus the plague of the frogs has deep religious significance, as well as a natural pestilence. And as in the first plague every part of Egypt was affected. And again the magicians of Egypt also matched Moses' magic, deed for grisly deed. A slight change of attitude now appears in Pharaoh, however. He acknowledges Moses as the voice of a real deity. He no longer scoffs at God.

Here Moses tries a new approach. In daring faith and boldness he asks Pharaoh to set a specific time for the prayer that will signal the immediate stoppage of the scourge. The idea is to impress the king with God's power to stop as well as initiate a plague. Such a faith and concern over "coincidence" is common throughout the Bible (cf. Matt. 8:13; 15:28). The sad result, however, is Pharaoh's misinterpreting this sign-in-reverse. He reads it as God's softness. He remains drunk on his own power, rejoices in his relief, and promptly forgets his promise to let God's people go.

The Plague of Gnats (Ex. 8:16–19)

The passage.—Some translators feel this plague was one of mosquitoes (the word can be read as small insects, or gnats). The writer uses Oriental exaggeration to describe the awfulness and size of this third plague. "All the dust of the earth became gnats" is his way of describing the overwhelming number of those wretched insects. And this is the first plague the magicians could not duplicate. They have met their match. Yahweh (God) has beaten them.

The Plague of the Flies (Ex. 8:20–32)

The passage.—There may well be a graduation and causal effect in the sequence of the sufferings inflicted because of Pharaoh. From the poisoned river to the dead fish the frogs were driven ashore. Perhaps the insects were bred from the dead fish and frogs causing the infection of cattle and the plague of boils.

Flies may have been a common pest to the Egyptians. But this time the curse is magnified to unbearable proportions. And, as always, the fly is a disease bearer. Amazingly and providentially this scourge and its epidemic-dangers were held back from the northern region of Goshen, where the Jews were enslaved. This was to the Israelites a sure "sign" of God's wrath on the foe and his protecting hand on his own—a powerful evidence of divine sovereignty.

And the ruin was almost total for the land of Egypt. The effect on man and beast was fierce. At last Pharaoh bends and relents. But on two conditions: (1) the Jews were not to go far, and, (2) even exacted a promise to remember him in prayer!

The Plague on the Cattle (Ex. 9:1–7)

The passage.—Again another plague has natural and religious effects. For cattle had special sanctity in the superstitious religious life of Egypt. And the animals of the Jews were spared (not one died). This the writer again interprets as judgment on Israel's foe and sovereign power and protection for the chosen people.

The Plague of Boils on Man and Beast (Ex. 9:8–12)

The passage.—This ailment came in the form of violent skin eruptions affecting the bodies of people and animals. It might have been like leprosy or some malignancy. Even Pharaoh's magicians are themselves smitten and unable to stand before the king. So they not only cannot duplicate the marvel, they are helpless as its victims. The defeat is overwhelming, illustrating the unlimited power of Yahweh (God). God's sovereignty is so complete that he is here again credited as hardening the heart of Pharaoh who is himself a divine-king type.

The Plague of Hail (Ex. 9:13–35)

The passage.—This plague-story is the longest of all, and one of the most devastating. Its purpose again is a demonstration of God's power and his uniqueness. No other is "like to me in all the earth" (v. 14). Hailstorms must have been extremely rare in a tropical country like Egypt. It spelled havoc to the vital agriculture of this land.

Yet it took more time (as well as increased devastation) to soften the heart of Pharaoh. At last it seems to have worked. He confesses he is wrong (v. 27). He begs Moses to secure relief from God. Now he agrees to an "unconditional surrender." "I will let you go, and you shall stay no longer."

Truth for today.—So Moses is told of God to lift his arms toward heaven and the storm will be stopped. But notice that this nature-wonder is for the purpose of revelation, and not merely an end within itself. It is not Pharaoh in control of this earth, nor Pharaoh's gods—but Yahweh the God of Israel, he is the Lord of all (Ps. 24:1).

The Plague of Locusts (Ex. 10:1–20)

The passage.—Like another stanza in a bitter refrain Pharaoh goes back on his promise and must yet be convinced by more pestilence. This scourge is even more convincing in devastation. This re-play seems to point up again the shortness of memory as well as the stubbornness of spirit in Pharaoh. So God's furious punishment must be levied again on the man and the land.

This time there appears a slight progression on the release-theme. Pharaoh's servants are now convinced of God's power and appeal to their king. The offer of release this time is *before* the plague. And most amazingly Pharaoh seeks to be forgiven.

Special points.—As release-time approaches Pharaoh still tries to hedge and hold back at least the cattle and property of the Jews. But Moses matches his will and with resolute firmness demands total release of people and property. After all, in the theology of the Israelites all belongs to God.

The Plague of Darkness (Ex. 10:21–29)

The passage.—Darkness to Egyptians who worshiped the sun would be especially symbolic and significant. Once again this life-and-death struggle has deep theological overtones. Thus this ninth plague has a climactic force far more than might appear to casual western eyes. For three days the sun is blotted out in total and intense darkness. And a people who

hover in superstition and fear would be mortified. But once more the providential hand of God exempts the land of Goshen, slave-home of the Jews.

Now the author readies us for the final and climactic chapter of this classic spiritual struggle. It will be the plague to end all plagues. It will thereafter be impossible to stand before this God of might and majesty. His will and his terms must be accepted and obeyed. It is to be one of history's great moments.

The Plague of Death Announced (Ex. 11:1–10)

The passage.—This final climactic plague is God's doing alone. Moses and Aaron are not the instruments in this act. The writer seems to be suggesting that the situation had so deteriorated the Lord must intervene more directly himself. Moses' role in this plague was with his own people. He was to instruct Israel that the end was near and how to prepare.

Truth for today.—So there is "a great cry" through all the land. It sounds like the last judgment. Thus do the curtains come down on this much of the Exodus-drama. The acts of God in signs and demonstrations have accomplished the first phase of withdrawal. Now God will concentrate on possessing his chosen people.

God Takes Possession of Israel (Ex. 12: 1–51)

The passage.—Before the death-plague there is an interruption. The author, stressing the importance of law and organization, introduces three of Israel's rituals. The three are Passover, unleavened bread, and dedication of firstborn (ch. 13). All three have special connections with this fateful final plague. All three commemorate and celebrate the work of God in the exodus. In their deeper meanings they dramatize divine ownership.

Passover is the most sacred of all festivals to the Jews. It celebrates Israel's birth as a nation. As such it ushers in a whole new age for God's people.

Regulations for Passover were rigid and specific. The sacrificial lamb must be "perfect" as a first-year animal. The slaying was carefully prescribed and timed. The blood was the most significant and symbolic item. It must be carefully caught and applied to the doorposts and lintel. This was the central feature and meaning of the sacred observance. This dramatically captured and symbolized God's provision and protection. The Passover meal followed with every item rich in sacred symbolism, right down to the bitter herbs, as poignant reminders of Israel's hardships and bitter sufferings. It was first eaten in darkness and in haste consonant with the departure-readiness of the slaves being summoned from their slave-state in Goshen to their new home of promise and freedom in Canaan.

The permanence of Passover is also stressed. It is to be a "memorial" kept "throughout your generations," "an ordinance forever."

The Feast of Unleavened Bread was another major Jewish festival celebrating the annual barley harvest. But it soon came to be more than an agricultural thanksgiving. It was connected spiritually and historically to God's mighty deliverance from Egypt. Inevitably it came to be bound up with Passover. The central feature was a service of burnt offerings for seven successive days. Scrupulous observance was required. Anyone violating the regulation of "no leaven" would be "cut off" from the family of Israel and regarded as dead!

Special points.—The third of Israel's rituals (dedication of the firstborn) will come in chapter 13. First the writer must give us his account of the death of Egypt's firstborn, of human families and cattle also. It was like a "last judgment" (Ex. 12:29–30). The "great cry" of anguish reflects the crushing of human pride in the execution of God's wrath. It seals the vindication of God and signals his peoples' release.

So Israel is free at last, free to go. And before another sun shall rise these slaves hastily take their leave of the hated land of their bondage.

This motley band now hurried away, not stopping for the first twenty-five miles. Then they made their first stop at Succoth. Here they baked their unleavened bread (v. 34). After 430 years God's people were free at last. This was the night of independence. It was the night of Israel's birth, the birth of a nation. God was sovereign and he was Israel's deliverer and protector. Therefore Israel must ever cherish and guard the very memory of this night and its triumph.

III. THE PEOPLE DELIVERED (EX. 13:1—18:27)

Dedication of Firstborn and More Instructions on Passover (Ex. 13:1–16)

The passage.—This chapter opens with a brief summation of the law relating to the firstborn (of sons and animals.) The focal meaning of this rite is that Israel and her possessions belong to God. The beginning of this observance dates from the awful tenth plague in Egypt—the death of their firstborn. This ritual also reminds the Jew that all life is uniquely the gift of God. This would be memorably timed from Israel's birth-hour in nationhood.

These rites were meant to be more than symbols, more than memorials. They were to be vivid visual aids by which the older generation could instruct the younger in the ways of God. Man's memory is all too short, at best. Man needs reminders, especially in following faithfully a God unseen. Therefore the monuments left along God's mighty road of deliverance were to be teaching instruments perpetuating the life of God in the continuing life of Israel for all time to come. In this sense these rites were to be flames of remembrance, keeping God alive in the hearts of his people.

The Victorious Red Sea Crossing (Ex. 13:17—14:4)

This was one of the great moments of all history. It is celebrated throughout the rest of the Bible. It stands as the central event of the revelation of God in the Old Testament.

Special points.—The road out (Exodus literally means "the road out") is a surprise choice, ordered under divine guidance. The route selected was not the fortified, more travelled road to Philistia (the coastal road). It was toward Succoth and the edge of the wilderness of Paran and on toward Sinai. Moses knew this route better, and there would be spiritual dividends at the Sinai base. They marched out "equipped for battle"—at least in a semblance of order, perhaps as fives or fifties. These were the first signs of order and organization of these hitherto disorganized slave-people.

Truth for today.—As the people left Egypt they were charged to bring out the bones of Joseph. This would symbolize the totality of the Exodus. But it would do even more. It would underscore the faithfulness of God.

And the continuing sign of this divine faithfulness would be a pillar of cloud by day and a pillar of fire by night. This illustrates the uniqueness of God's protecting and providential hand. The presence of God is always a reassuring force to his pilgrim people through whatever hazards they must pass.

God's Triumph at the Red Sea (Ex. 14: 5–31)

The passage.—One more time Pharaoh reverses himself and tries to overtake the Hebrews. He would reenslave them. The horrible memory of the ten plagues must have been short-lived. The home-front burden of replacing all that Jewish slave-labor suddenly became the overriding factor. Why let this bunch of slave-hands just walk away? Maybe those plagues were only "bad luck" and not due after all to Israel's God? We've got an army haven't we? Why not use our soldiers to round up this rabble and bring them back to finish our treasure cities?

So off they ride—chariots and all— under Pharaoh's own hand. They figure on a quick capture and an easy return of "their slaves." How foolish and ill-advised to have yielded to Moses and let them go. But it should require only a modest display of military might to round them up and return them to their slave quarters in Goshen. Just a minor "police action," really.

But these Egyptians forgot something. They forgot about God. The Bible carefully points this up by describing the Hebrews' march as "defiantly" and "with a high hand" meaning the powerful act of God. These people, we are reassured, are under the providential protection of Almighty God.

Now the mood shifts as Pharaoh's hosts approach and God's people, also short on memory, tremble in fear. Their faith falters and wilts in the face of Egyptian force. But not Moses. His faith remains strong and steady in contrast to the frightened, panic-stricken people he shepherds. In great courage Moses orders them to "fear not, stand firm and see the salvation of the Lord."

Special points.—God reveals himself as Savior. In this crisis and his salvation God is going to give not only physical escape, but spiritual redemption. The two often go together throughout the Bible. These Egyptians are about to perish in the sea. And God's people will be delivered and saved. This historic victory will forever establish God's lordship beyond any dispute. So Moses says "Be silent" and see the superiority of God. Moses is not merely silencing a people of little faith and loud complaints. He is declaring the transcendence and superiority of God.

Now comes one of the dramatic moments of all time. Moses lifts his rod and the waters of the sea are divided. His people have a way of redemption opened. This moment of deliverance would be forever after interpreted as *the* redemptive event of Israel's history. It would hereafter be celebrated as the focal turning point of the nation of Israel. It would be a monument of historic value and abiding wonder. What the coming of Christ is for the New Testament (revealing, redeeming act of God) this crossing-of-the-sea-event is to the Old Testament.

Truth for today.—Moses commands his people to "go forward." They must go forward in faith and responsibility. Pull up all stakes and march on toward Canaan. This involves much more than physical advance. It is like a divine summons to follow God's will to a new way as well as to a new land.

God's hand of might and protection appears again. God's Angel stood in the vanguard and the rearguard. His people were surrounded by divine strength and protection. Then came the calamity on the hosts of Pharaoh. As they sought to follow they were utterly destroyed. Thus were God and his man Moses vindicated. Faith was restored and Israel was on her way toward nationhood and freedom. It would be a long, long road yet. But at least the beginnings had been made. And that victory at the Red Sea would never be blotted out. It was the birth of a nation.

The Song of Moses and the Song of Miriam (Ex. 15:1–21)

The passage.—Victories are often celebrated in song. So it was with the Jews at the Red Sea crossing. Both of these songs are really hymns of praise. They became fixtures in Jewish worship for centuries.

There are three basic ideas scored in the lyrics of these historic hymns. First, the songs are in praise to God for his marvelous acts and power (a key theme all through Exodus). Second is a rehearsing of the Red Sea victory. The third theme stressed is the ultimate goal of God's wondrous deeds, namely the realization of their national destiny in Canaan, a land of their own.

Special points.—How did this music get into the Exodus story? Its place and its point is exultant joy and celebration in God's mighty deliverance and vindication. It was placed in Exodus to stress the importance and meaning of one climactic event: crossing that Red Sea.

Truth for today.—That was cause for celebration not only on the day of that victory, but whenever and wherever his people needed to recelebrate the hand of God in their history. And so does God always put a song in the hearts of his people all through their history.

Every nation needs a song. All great movements have had their musicians. They captured the mood and spirit of victory in the notes of mighty music. This song of Moses (and of Miriam) came to be a sort of "national anthem" to the Jews. Many of the psalmists took the Red Sea triumph as their theme.

Later the young church of Jesus Christ was to have its song also. Indeed the Christian religion has rightly been called the singing religion. Christianity is one of the few religions of the world with a hymnbook as a companion volume to its Bible.

On the Road to Sinai (Ex. 15:22–27)

The passage.—The victory at the Red Sea was the climax-event of the exodus. But the full import and lasting value of that deliverance is yet to be interpreted. This is where Sinai comes into focus. Sinai will become "God's School" for the explanation and implementation of the faith and theology of the exodus.

Special points.—On the way to Sinai the story turns not so much on historical events and details as on the meaning of history's events. Both the geography and the history take on religious significance. The struggles in the wilderness come to illustrate the struggles of all men. Underlying the trials is the truth that God gives meaning and purpose to the struggle. This desert journey is therefore more than a trip. It is a pilgrimage with divine direction. With all its fears and problems it is a fulfilment of life and faith for all time. As such it becomes a trust, and Israel must live to share its lessons and make the more responsible contribution in history.

Many dangers yet surround the camp of Israel. Thirst and hunger and all kinds of other enemies are daily threats. The Bible does not gloss over these hardships. It honestly reports them. And God is portrayed as permitting them—for God is "testing" Israel to see if the Jews will really live under the faith which can give spiritual significance to their historical journey.

Truth for today.—The bitter waters of Marah proved to be one of God's "testing" places. Still short on memory of God's power and recent demonstrations, the people start to complain or murmur. Their fear and lack of faith is still very evident. But Moses does not rebuke them nor even show irritation (as he does in other places). As all through the Exodus God is here the central actor. It is He who "heals" the waters. And by direct spiritual applications the writer lifts up this God as the healer of all Israel.

The Heaven-sent Manna (Ex. 16:1–36)

The passage.—The feeble faith of the people is again the cause of murmuring. This time the complaint is hunger. They cry out for even the food of slaves. The wilderness overwhelms them. They wallow in self-pity. But right in the midst of their need and faithlessness God offers his strength and sustenance. For one day at a time, and just enough for that day only God provides his manna. Some think the line in the Lord's Prayer "Give us *this day* our daily bread . . ." comes from this experience and verse (16:4).

Truth for today.—The manna was not only life-saving food, it was another symbol of the divine presence and provision. Yet the people are not satisfied. The rigors of their desert march show up again and again in their complaints. They beg for more, and God supplements the manna with quail. This was also more than food. It was to reassure the people of God's power and strengthen their tender faith.

Notice how the supply was equal to the demand. God's provisions are always adequate, not indulgent, not a lack—just enough. There should be no wastage. Nor should we be surfeited with oversupply. That breeds self-sufficiency, not faith. The wonderful thing in the desert was that all the people were supplied. Those who were greedy and those who were timid enjoyed the same amount.

God is always fair.

One of Israel's most sacred and honored institutions is the sabbath. Its origin is datable to the wilderness period and in particular to the manna-miracle. The people were amazed that the manna gathered each day always amounted to just one omer. Even more astonishing was the fact that on Fridays it came to precisely two omers—just enough for two day's supply.

This would mean no gatherings would be necessary on Saturdays. Hence "the people rested on the seventh day." Originally in ancient cultures that seventh day was considered a day of bad omens —an evil day. The consecration of this day in Jewish life—and later the "first-day sabbath" of Christian culture—is a marvelous illustration of the transformation of pagan dates into God's purposes.

Water from the Rock (Ex. 17:1–6)

The passage.—Here we have the second of three episodes of murmuring caused by thirst. Those three are Marah-Massah, Massah-Meribah, and Meribah-Kadesh. In each instance the problem is faith versus disobedience and rebellion. And the transgression seems to grow progressively worse until in the third account Moses' own faith falters.

Day by day the Jewish pilgrims travel at the command of the Lord. They probably advanced by various divisions, or camps. One of the units moved up to a place called Rephidim. But, alas, they found no water and promptly blamed Moses. In turn Moses interpreted their quarrel with him as a quarrel with God.

Special points.—Some believe Moses struck a solid rock and water miraculously flowed therefrom. Others feel he smote a rock and uncovered a previously closed spring. Whatever one's view, the point is clear: God is the giver of life-giving water. This idea carries over into

the New Testament in portraying Jesus as the Water of life (John 4:10 ff).

Attack from the Amalekites (Ex. 17:8–16)

The passage.—Passing through the desert was made difficult not only for rations and water, but by active opposition from hostile peoples. Anti-Semitism was to be an agelong cross for these Jews and their descendents. Thus it should be no surprise that Amalek opposed their passage. But then maybe God's purpose in human history is not to give us easy blessings, but to give us opportunities to fight for those victories. Only then would they be cherished and valued.

Truth for today.—God raises up his men to meet the challenge. To assist Moses in battling the men of Amalek, God calls forth Joshua (17:9) who assumes the mantle of military leadership. It is a role he is prepared to discharge well, now and in later battles. Joshua is to be a "second Moses" and ultimately will lead Israel through the period of conquest in Canaan.

Jethro Pays a Visit (Ex. 18:1–27)

The passage.—Jethro has heard "how the Lord had brought Israel out of Egypt." Jethro has evidently been keeping Zipporah, Moses' wife, and their two sons, Gershom and Eliezer. Thus we have a kind of family reunion.

Special points.—Whether Jethro was a "believer" at this point is not quite clear. But in this review of the mighty acts of God it is reported he was "astonished." So if Jethro did not know God before this, he has now learned something decisively new about Yahweh, Moses' God and leader. Through this account of the insolence of Pharaoh and the marvelous deliverance of the Israelites Jethro seems convinced of the power of this their

God.

The people who so recently have been disorganized slaves need organization and administration. They will need laws and regulations. But first they will need leaders who can give guidance and administer justice. And real leadership always begins with the delegation and distribution of responsibility.

Truth for today.—Moses, caught up in the momumental task of emancipating his people, has been doing too much and delegating too little. An outsider can sometimes see this better. Jethro did, and tactfully suggested an organizational change to make for effective management and administering of justice. The father-in-law was concerned both for Moses' health and the dignity of his leadership under the burdens. Out of this modest family setting and concern was born the political organization of a new nation, God's Israel.

Jethro now makes his specific and highly constructive suggestion. "Choose" subordinate leaders who are men of faith who "fear God." They must be men of character and integrity. Then divide the people into units "of thousands, of hundreds, of fifties, and of tens."

IV. THE COVENANT GIVEN (EX. 19:1—24:18)

The Impact of Sinai (Ex. 19:1–25)

The passage.—Exodus now presents God as sovereign Lord over the whole life of man. It does this by emphasizing the covenant relationship and mutual responsibilities. Exodus also asserts Yahweh's lordship by the divinely inspired and authoritative character of the law.

Special points.—All of the book up to this point has prepared us for the events of Sinai. This is where the author has been leading us. Here is the mountain of God—the object of Moses'

dream. Sinai becomes the setting for the sealing of that covenant.

Truth for today.—Sinai would hold a sacred and special place in Moses' heart. It was here or near it that Moses himself met the Lord. He was commissioned from this very spot. He had taken off his shoes on this sacred soil. Now he wanted his people to feel something of this divine presence and power. As Moses ascends the holy mount, God calls out to him and offers the covenant. The guarantee of God's faithfulness in the contract is assured by the divine action already experienced by the deliverance from Egypt. Obedience was the responsibility from Israel's side of the covenant. There must be faith and loyalty. In plain language "to keep my covenant" would mean obeying the law. Israel is to be God's personal possession, his elect community. And this covenant is sealed with all the people, not just its leaders or priests.

Israel was intended of God to be "a holy nation." This meant she was set apart for a divine redemptive purpose in history. Israel was to be the church of God. This is the clear teaching in the Old and New Testaments (1 Pet. 2:5, 9).

God does not show his face, but he does speak. He verifies the authority and prophetic role of Moses. The cloud was the symbolic representation of God's presence—as indeed it had been on pilgrimage. The cloud would rest over the tabernacle when they moved on from Sinai.

The ceremonial cleansing implies the holiness of God and its opposite in men. The distance between man and God is illustrated by the three-day period of purification required for those approaching this God of holiness. This entire passage stresses an inherent and permanent distinction and difference of position between God and man.

And even after ceremonial purification the people do not have the same access as priests. The penalty for violating these sacred restrictions in the tabernacle (and later the Temple) was severe indeed. It was death.

The Ten Commandments (Ex. 20:1–20)

The passage.—In Hebrew the Ten Commandments are described as "The Ten Words" (Decalogue). In their original form they consisted of ten brief phrases, each just two words long. It seems (v. 21) these words were first spoken by God directly to the people. Later, for the valued purpose of continuing instruction, Moses was called to the summit of Sinai to receive them on tablets of stone. Apparently all other laws were given indirectly. That is, they were given through the mouth of Moses, not directly from God to the people. It should be added that in the Bible view of things all true laws are an extension of these. Indeed all righteous orders and laws are an extension of the will and character of God. Law by Bible definition is God himself in holy action. This should form the base and motivation of obedience to law—respect for the God who established the laws for a well-ordered society.

Special points.—Israel, and those who worship Israel's holy God must be holy because God is. This law is based upon God's righteousness. Since God out of goodness redeemed Israel from slavery, the law becomes a means for a mutual relationship in which faith responds to love. This lifts law into a channel for expressing gratitude.

The first four Commandments have a vertical reach. They are concerned with man's right relationship to the right God. The last six relate to man with his fellow man. All ten are grounded in the essential worth of God and those made in his image, as unique human beings. Right worship should also issue in right social relationships. The worship of Israel's God (and him alone) is based on the concept of his uniqueness and his worthiness. This God alone must be worshiped and in the right manner. That's what these Commandments are about and that's what makes this one of the truly great chapters of all the Bible.

"I am the Lord your God" is the opening line of the preamble. This covenant was original with God. He initiated it. It was not a joint "arrangement" between Israel and the Lord, as between equals in a marriage. God is Lord and his sovereignty was the ground and source of this covenant.

The command stresses the positive aspect of worship, insisting that Israel worship the Lord God and no other. This made Judaism a distinctive monotheistic religion. Some scholars believe the greatest contribution of the Jews to history and civilization was its ethical monotheism.

The First Commandment emphasizes the unity of God and his uniqueness. The second underscores the spirituality of God. Both these commands would protect Israel against idolatry. Man has always had the temptation to make a god, one he can manage and manipulate to do his will and make him successful. All images are forbidden. The Bible simply does not leave us a picture of God or his image. One of the important religious truths is thus emphasized in the ark. When one penetrates into the holy of holies he finds only the golden box containing the law tablets. And in the New Testament when men ask, "What does God look like?" (John 14; Heb. 1), the Bible answer is clear: "Look at Jesus the Christ; he is the express image of God, the Father.

The Third Commandment is a warning against profanity. It indicts the profanity of cursing, or prostituting the holy name of God into a blasphemous oath. Even more sinful would be professing to belong to God and then living as though we belong to Satan. This is the profanity of life, not just lips. This would indeed be taking God's name in vain, as so many modern church members have. In Old Testament times a name was understood to be an extension of one's personality. So the holy name of God expresses his power and character. To invoke that beautiful name in a vile curse is profanity the Bible here condemns as sheer blasphemy.

The Fourth Commandment concerns the sabbath and sets it apart as a distinct Jewish institution. For the Jew the sabbath was a symbol and sacred reminder of the covenant between God and his Chosen People (Ezek. 20:12,20). It was a day of rest in remembrance of God's rest after his labor of creation (Gen. 2:3; Ex. 31:17). It was in its Sinai context a weekly day of thanksgiving for the Egyptian deliverance. It was a day of sanctification. It was a prophetic day as noted in the grace with the sabbath meals. It was a day of joy and celebration of God's goodness. It was a day of worship, of special religious services, of the reading of God's Word, and later of other religious books. The keeping of the sabbath has long been viewed as a mark of differentiation between Jews and other races. And later it would take a resurrection to change the calendar for Christians from Saturday to Sunday for the sabbath rest and sacred celebrations.

The Fifth Commandment is concerned with the home and family. Family solidarity has long been one of the unique features of Jewish life. Underlying this law is the warning against the heathen habit of abandoning the aging when they can no longer support themselves. In some ancient cultures the "old folks" were put out to die of exposure or be eaten by wild beasts. This inhuman act is now sternly forbidden by God. Parents are to be respected and revered and protected. And the reward is plain: a stable society blessed by prosperity. Happily both Judaism and Christianity are family religions and this emphasis has contributed mightily to history's progress.

The Sixth Commandment recognizes the sacredness of human life. Life is a precious possession, and only God should say when it is to be ended. By this command members of the covenant community were protected from the threat of death by another individual. As it stands, this law does not speak to the issue of war, or suicide, or capital punishment. But by implication they could all be indirectly involved with the underlying principle of the sacredness of life. In a positive sense this law makes the community responsible for the safety and good of the individual. And community attitudes and actions should keep the spirit of this law. That means upholding the dignity and sanctity of each individual as one made in the image of God, and therefore of infinite worth.

The Seventh Commandment stresses the sacredness of marriage. This law became a kind of cornerstone of monogamous marriage. God's ideal was (and still is) one man for one woman for life. As it stands this command does not touch the whole range of sexual morality —except by implication. But those implications are important. Originally this prohibition (as so much Old Testament material) was slanted in favor of the male Jew. It might well have been paraphrased "My wife is my own property, and therefore forbidden to all other men." Still this law stands as a landmark in its concern for, and protection of, the home and its inviolability.

The Eighth Commandment gives us the foundation on which to base the concept of private property. It shields the wise and diligent against the lazy and careless. This rule not only forbids stealing, but was intended to free men in the covenant community from the anxiety and threat of crimes against their property. Property is sacred whether it's in a bank or a church. I have no right to take that which belongs to another, no matter how he got it or how much I need it. Even the Robin Hoods who magnanimously steal from the rich to reward the poor must be judged before this law.

The Ninth Commandment upholds the sacredness of the judicial process. Indirectly it emphasizes that basic and all-important virtue of honesty. A man summoned as a witness must not perjure himself. He is here called to tell the truth that justice may be served. This law frowns on talebearing and gossip that misrepresents. But the key idea is the maintenance of the integrity of the judicial system. In the famous Code of Hammurabi (of another Near Eastern culture in Moses' time) anyone guilty of false witness was given the punishment for the crime of which he had falsely charged someone else. It is interesting how often the Bible cries out for honesty —to the Jews in the Old Testament and the Christians in the New Testament. Wonder why? Is it so rare? Or is it so crucially important to a well-ordered society?

The Tenth Commandment stresses a right attitude. It warns against indulging a spirit which could lead to actions condemned in at least the four preceding commandments. The word "covet" means to set one's heart upon an object with the idea of possessing it. The intent of this Tenth Command is therefore to check grasping hearts that invariably lead to grasping actions. This warning is comprehensive. It includes the neighbor's house and wife and animals and possessions. This final and climactic word of the Decalogue lies in the realm of the inner man, his attitudes and thoughts. Later Jesus is to say, "Out of the heart are the issues of life." Could this Tenth Commandment have been his inspiration? The very inwardness of the last lines of the Decalogue make them a kind of prelude or threshold of New Testament truth. It's only a short step from here into the words of Jesus in his Sermon on the Mount.

Truth for today.—The people respectfully stand "afar off" keeping a reverent distance and attitude before the "Holy One of Israel." Moses as mediator drew near to the thick cloud where God was. There the Lord gave the remaining laws of the Sinai Code to Moses. He then delivered them to the people. The mood and impression of this revelation and experience is one of awe and mystery and the holy. God's transcendence and "otherness" is dominant. This God is separate and holy, and must be so worshiped and respected.

Laws of the Covenant (Ex. 20:21–26)

Exodus 20:21 begins a section of laws of the covenant that extends through 23:33. This section is sometimes known as the Book of the Covenant. Before examining these laws in some detail it is interesting to assume the kind of social and community life they reflect. The nomadic nature of their desert existence seems to have changed the village and city life. Their animals are the domesticated variety, not the camel and horse, but the ass, the cow, the sheep. Property laws now touch cattle-raising, farms, orchards, olive groves, and vineyards. Money is counted in gold and silver.

Loans are transacted and interest rates are regulated and for the needy no interest! Some slavery still existed among these Jews who were all so recently slaves themselves in Egypt. (Evil institutions die hard.) Vocations included priests, judges, doctors, artisans, and shepherds. Oddly there is no mention of shopkeepers, policemen, or soldiers. The rules reflect concern for the poor, the weak, the widows, and orphans and strangers.

The laws touching slavery are relatively mild (implying mild treatment in Egypt? or its opposite?). The rule of a father with his family was not so mild. He had absolute power. He could even sell his children into slavery. And the death sentence was possible for those offending parents by rebellion.

The old pagan law of an eye for an eye (*lex talionis*—tit for tat) was still upheld. But this book of the covenant was a definite advance. It attempted to improve conditions and brought advances in both justice and morality.

Specific regulations are given regarding the altar. All these prescriptions emphasize holiness. The warning against nakedness in this connection (20:26; Lev. 18:6) is also based on the idea of the holy, even more than on modesty. The mystery of life and its connection with man's sexuality gave to the sex organs a uniqueness—even a holiness. This concept is vitally significant for the Jews in their religious regard for circumcision.

The Civil and Criminal Laws (Ex. 21:1— 22:31)

The passage.—These rules pertain only to Jews as slaves of other Jews, not foreigners or prisoners of war. How would a Jew get himself in such a fix? Maybe in selling himself he hoped to get out of debt (2 Kings 4:1). He might have

been sold by his parents in their need for money (Neh. 5:2). He would serve six years, or until the year of jubilee, whichever came first. When freedom came he would have all the rights of free Jews. He was even helped along by his master with gifts of cattle, grain, and wine.

Special points.—Slavery was a grim business and it was always an inhuman practice. But these regulations at least sought to govern and mitigate some of its evils. To some extent these laws tended to make the slaves as members of the master's family. The fact that slaves were circumcised (Gen. 17:12) and joined in family worship (Deut. 12:18) made them brothers in religious experience.

Some of the offenses listed as deserving death (21:12–17) shock us today. Maybe our practices have swung too far in the other direction. Murder was considered a capital offense. But the same punishment for striking a parent? Or cursing a parent? The authority of parenthood was so sacred the ancient Jews felt it must be guarded jealously. Children simply must obey their parents, or expect the severest of penalties. Another capital offense grouped with these was kidnaping, or manstealing.

Some noncapital offenses are treated in 21:18–32. The law requiring payment for personal injury (from a quarrel) helped eventually to create today's important insurance industry. The laws affecting injury of slaves (by flogging) seem to reflect the spirit of barbarism. But actually the opposite was probably intended. Their humaneness is apparent when they are compared not with our time, but contemporary experience in the cultures of Moses' day. A woman with child (if injured and miscarries) must be compensated. If satisfaction is not obtained, the eye-for-an-eye (*lex talionis*) principle might be invoked. The point is the wicked must be made to suffer for his deeds. The cattle owner must be responsible for his animals and held liable for any damages they might inflict.

Several laws dealing with property are given in 21:33—22:17. A man should be held liable with regard to another's property loss on his land as with open pits, if negligence is evident. And he was liable if his animals or property caused damages to another. Severe penalties were levied on cattle rustlers.

If a man killed an intruder there was no penalty if it happened at night. In part this law lifted up human life as of greater worth than that of property values. Compensation must be paid for animals abusing another's fields or vineyard. A man was responsible for fire or its damages. Money or goods kept in trust by another made the latter responsible before the law. Shepherds and herdsmen were made responsible for the animals they were charged to keep. Borrowed property must be returned intact, or duly compensated. The seduction of a virgin daughter, considered of monetary value, must issue in compensation or marriage, or both.

Sorcery was condemned as punishable by death (22:18). It was believed witchcraft denied the very freedom and unity of God. As such it was blasphemous. The abnormal sex act of bestiality (sex with an animal) was also a capital offense, for both men and women. Anyone sacrificing to an alien god was also condemned.

Truth for today.—Israelite law sought to protect the stranger, the helpless, and the poor (22:21–31). The law pointedly reminds the Jews that they were themselves "strangers" not long ago in Egypt. There is a spirit of genuine compassion in this, reminding of God's compassion.

Inserted at this point are three regulations concerning offerings. There was to be an offering of the harvest, probably of grains and grapes. Then there was to be an offering of the firstborn. Thus both land and man are God's. This underscores his ownership (of all) and man's stewardship.

The Spirit of Justice Toward Enemies (Ex. 23:1–9)

The passage.—This is the last of the religious and moral laws in this section of the code. It is concerned with the issue of justice and duty regarding one's enemy. Verses 6–8 give protection to the poor, the innocent, and the righteous. Then come two warnings: (1) Let no one falsely charge another, maybe causing the death of innocent persons. (2) Reject all bribes in the interest of honor and justice.

Laws of Religious Institutions and Practices (Ex. 23:10–33)

The passage.—Inserted here are the laws of the sabbatical year, the sabbath, and the three annual feasts, with an addition of some ritual regulations. The year of the sabbatical emphasized God's ownership of all the land. Man is merely permitted to use it. God is still the owner, man is the steward, accountable and responsible to God. In the sabbath the stress is on worship and devotion. Both the land and time belong to God.

The three great festival feasts of Israel were designated in the covenant code. They are (1) The Feast of Unleavened Bread combined with Passover celebrated each spring (March or April). (2) The Feast of Harvest, also named Pentecost (50 days after Passover) was a day of thanksgiving celebrated in May or June. (3) The Feast of Ingathering (also called Feast of Tabernacles or Booths) lasted seven days and came in September or October. It was in remembrance of the desert wanderings in the wilderness. With each of these major festivals all the Jewish men were summoned to appear before God—a kind of call to spiritual renewal and rededication.

Special points.—The ritual prescriptions included laws on the holiness of the blood and the fat (cf. Lev. 3:17). The symbolism of offering God the firstfruits put priority on divine goodness and represented the divine purposes in the whole crop. True stewardship begins not only in the tithe—giving God the first tenth—but also the right use of all the rest—the nine tenths of crop or money.

Truth for today.—The last part of the Book of the Covenant (ending with chap. 23) reads like a farewell address. It is filled with appeals and promises, not laws. And they relate to the journey into the Promised Land. God's angel will go forth to do battle for Israel. If Israel will respond courageously, the conquest is assured. The angel represents God's leadership. The Lord offers guidance to all those who will follow his will.

But this farewell is also marked by warnings. Israel is here warned that her safety lies in obedience to God's will. Israel's enemies (including the Canaanites) could become God's instruments of judgment. It would remain for the prophets to explain this difficult lesson.

The "terror" of other nations over the approach of God and his people is drawn here (v. 27–29) in vivid metaphor. The word "hornets" would represent God's might to conquer and see his enemies flee as from a swarm of insects. God's power in Canaan would be just as great as it was in Egypt. This is Israel's God, the same yesterday, today, and forever.

The Covenant Is Ratified (Ex. 24:1–18)

The passage.—This is done by two ceremonies. With Moses still on Sinai, the directions of the second rite are given (vv. 1–2). Then occurs the first rite by

which Moses consecrates the people (vv. 3–8). Then follows the sacred meal between God and the leaders of Israel (vv. 9–11). Next comes the eventful receiving of the great stone tablets of the Law by Moses and Joshua from the hand of God (vv. 12–14).

Special points.—This chapter is memorable most of all by its report of Moses alone with God on the Mount. The important point is that Moses is close to God, not just in proximity, but in spirit. He is therefore more in tune with the divine will. This undergirds confidence and insures real leadership. The people will be better prepared to follow in the still-rugged days of march and conquest ahead.

V. REGULATIONS FOR WORSHIP (Ex. 25:1—31:18)

The Offering Required (Ex. 25:1–9)

The passage.—God's lordship is to be established further in the content of Israel's worship. Precise regulations must be made in the building and use of the sanctuary and the essentials of Israel's religious life. First, Moses must ask for an offering in order to build the tabernacle.

Special points.—Apparently it was a freewill offering from each "whose heart makes him willing." It was to be an expression of love and gratitude. All kinds of gifts are designated as acceptable "coin." Even woven goods along with skins and wood are welcome. Oil and stones would have their usage also. The wide range of acceptable donations would indicate the scope of participation involved. It might also imply that God wills the consecration of many more objects and vocations than we have traditionally called "religious."

Truth for today.—The word "sanctuary" (vv. 8–9) means the whole area dedicated as sacred. That would include the tabernacle and the court surrounding it. It is the place of God's abode. The design is according to the pattern given Moses on the Mount. This pattern is explicit for the ark of the covenant, the lampstand, the table, the tent, and the altar. Later the same was believed to be true of the divine pattern in the Temple (1 Chron. 28:19). If this was the physical shape of the first church it must have looked like a tent. More important than its appearance would be its characteristics of mobility and flexibility. Too often the churches of a later day, in buildings and in spirit, are lacking in these vital points of this divine pattern. Some critics have even observed sarcastically (but all too truly) that the church is the last institution in town to change, or react creatively to change. Is that my church they are describing? We proclaim that we are the light of the world. Too often we look more like the taillight.

The Ark (Ex. 25:10–22)

The passage.—The ark was to be built first; but in actual execution of the plans it was built after the tabernacle. It was a most sacred and mysterious medium, though in appearance it was a rather simple, even crude wooden box.

Special points.—The ark was open at the top with very little decoration. It measured forty-five inches long and twenty-seven inches wide and twenty-seven inches deep. It was mobile by virtue of poles attached for carrying. This implies the mobility of Israel's God. The function and role of the ark was most important, especially in Israel's early nomadic years. It led Israel on pilgrimage and also in battle. What the flag is to many nations this little box was to Israel. It was a spiritual and emotional symbol, a rallying point of the highest magnitude.

The ark was given a cover which was

known as the "mercy seat." It was the place where through blood the sins of the Israelites were to be "covered" or atoned for (Lev. 16:2,13–15). It thereby became the most sacred object in the most holy place; it was the very throne of the Lord God. Over this there were the guardian angels or cherubim. Their function, as in the Temple, was to overshadow the divine Presence.

The Table (Ex. 25:23–30)

The table of acacia wood was for the "Bread of the Presence." This bread (holy bread or showbread) was an eloquent reminder that man's food is the gift of God, and it should be consecrated to his service (Matt. 12:4; Mark 2:26).

The Lampstand (Ex. 25:31–40)

The function of the lamps was for illuminating the Holy Place. Natural light could come in from only one direction (East). The lamps may have added a note of needed aesthetics. But primarily they served a religious purpose. This was a sign of God's presence in their midst (Zech. 4:1–14).

The Tabernacle (Ex. 26:1–37)

The passage.—The tabernacle was to be adorned in colors of blue and purple and scarlet. Its beauty was designed to inspire reverence and worship.

Special points.—The tabernacle enclosed a rectangular area 15 by 45 feet. It stood 15 feet high. Inside it was partitioned into two rooms. The room to the rear (holy of holies) was 15 by 15 feet. The entry room (holy place) was 15 by 30 feet. The curtains were most impressive and formed a beautiful and symbolic wall (separateness to emphasize God's holiness over against man's sin).

The tentlike covering of the tabernacle was made of durable goat's hair. It was prepared and fitted to the frame.

The two pieces of the covering were held together by fifty clasps of bronze.

Truth for today.—The frame itself was of sturdy wood, but in keeping with its spirit of mobility, constructed so as to be easily dismantled for sudden transport. When the desert city of God needed to advance, this central edifice of the covenant community must be movable and indeed become the vanguard of that progress toward the Land of Promise.

The Brass Altar (Ex. 27:1–8)

The passage.—This altar is "the altar of burnt offering." It occupied the central place in the court on the east side of the tabernacle. Underneath its bronze top it was of acacia wood. It measured 4½ feet high and 7½ by 7½ feet across the top. The so-called "horns" of this altar were projections on its four corners. These were viewed as especially holy. A person could hold these horns and claim refuge from those who sought his very life (2 Kings 1:50 f; 2:28).

The Wall of the Court (Ex. 27:9–19)

This consisted of a series of curtains 7½ feet high. They encompassed a rectangular area 75 feet wide and 150 feet long. On the east side (the side of entry) the wall was 30 feet wide. It was woven of "blue and purple and scarlet stuff and fine twined linen, embroidered with needlework" (v. 16).

Oil for the Lamp (Ex. 27:20–21)

The passage.—This oil in keeping with the sacredness of the holy place had to be the purest. Everything reflected the presence of the Lord. Each object bore out the continuing presence of God— and also offered a reverent approach by the priests for each Israelite. The way of Israel in its tabernacle worship was the way of rich symbolism. The priest, representing every Jew, made his mean-

ingful ascent from altar to laver, to bread, to lamp, to incense, to law, to atonement, and gloriously to the ultimate presence of the Lord God.

The Priestly Garments (Ex. 28:1–43)

The passage.—The vestments of priests were full of symbolism like the tabernacle. To start with the emphasis was on cleanliness. The idea was to be pure and holy in approaching the God of holiness. The ephod was a vest-like garment made beautifully of rich colors, gold, blue, purple, and scarlet in a finely woven linen. This was suspended by shoulder straps. On each strap was an onyx inscribed with the 12 names of the sons of Israel. These were arranged in order of their birth. They were called stones of remembrance. It is impressive to imagine how as the priest served before the Lord he bore his people on his heart. That would be a fitting example for every minister and every follower of God as he ministers—laymen included.

Special points.—The breastplate of judgment contained sacred lots (Urim and Thummim). These were used to make decisions and render judgments. It was a pouch (9 inches square) overlaid with four rows of stones, 3 to a row, symbolizing the 12 tribes.

The robe of the priest was a blue garment of one piece, no sleeves, fitted with an opening for the head. At the skirt the robe had pomegranites. They were in colors of blue, purple, and scarlet and had bells of gold between them.

Truth for today.—The bells would serve the useful function of letting the people outside know of the priestly movements of intercession in the unseen holy places. And if in the awesome and solemn duties therein the bells ceased to ring the people would have the telegraphed message their priest was stricken. What an eloquent silence—

should those bells cease to ring! What else could the Scripture here mean in saying so solemnly "lest he die"?

For Aaron's sons (Nadah, Abibu, Eleazer, and Ithamar) the priestly dress was markedly simple compared to their father's. Theirs were coats, sashes, and caps, for glory and beauty. But they were not ornate as with those of the high priest, their father. Special religious words emphasize the sacredness of their calling: anoint, ordain, and consecrate.

This chapter closes by noting their linen breeches (v. 42). These were to insure the covering of the sex organs while they ministered. And more than modesty is implied. It was another way of protecting the holiness of God.

Consecration of Priests (Ex. 29:1–46)

The passage.—The consecration of the priests was taken very seriously. The real reason is the holiness of God. Thus the care with which a man progressively entered into the ceremonial cleansing, the robing and its symbolisms, and special sacrifices. There were three such sacrifices on behalf of the priests themselves. Then—but only then—would he be ready to go before God in ministry for his people.

Special points.—Ritual cleansings were important for physical and symbolic reasons. For the priests it is quite significant that the very first stage in ordination involved a washing away of the "unclean" in his life. Thus he would be a fit vessel while handling the holy things of his intercessory ministry.

Next came his sin offering (Lev. 4:1 ff.). It was a sacrifice through an animal substitute that secured his personal forgiveness. In making his offering the priest placed his hands on the body of the animal. This identified the animal as his and also suggested the transfer of his sins to the sacrifice. Purification and

dedication were the objectives in this solemn ritual.

Truth for today.—The burnt offering was a sacrifice of atonement. In this consecration service the entire animal was burned on the altar. The very smoke in ascent suggested the offering up to God of the man himself. The "wholeness" of this burnt offering represented the totality of committing oneself as a priest unto the Lord. Even the "laying on of hands" as the priest-to-be did with his sacrifice conveyed the idea of giving himself up to the Lord. This "laying on of hands" has carried over into most ordination services in Christendom, as for deacons and ministers.

A seven-day period was allotted for installing the priests. The number "seven" had a special sanctity and connoted completeness and perfection. So was implied the full-time service to God of these priests.

Even the altar was to be set apart by an anointing of "holy oil." Its uncleanness was thus purged away. It must be holy so that it, too, would be acceptable before this holy God of Israel.

Special Additional Instructions (Ex. 30: 1–38)

The passage.—This chapter presents a miscellaneous collection of extra rules for the worship area. The altar of incense was prescribed at 36 inches high, 18 inches square, and overlaid with gold. Incense was offered on it each morning and evening. Incense was probably a traditional association with the "pillar of cloud" reminding of the presence of God so remembered in the exodus.

Special points.—The poll tax was an authorized levy on each person over 20. It was half a shekel (cf. Matt. 17:24–27) and went for the support of the sanctuary and priestly system. The laver for washing was not detailed as to size. Its function was clear though, for ceremonial cleansings. In it the priests washed hands and feet (as compared to entire body in ordinations). The hands must be clean for handling holy objects, the feet to walk in sacred ways.

Truth for today.—The anointing oil was to be a blend of myrrh, cinnamon, aromatic cane, cassia, and olive oil. The tent of meeting was to be perfumed with this fragrance. Again it underscores the holiness associated with God. Anointing to the Jew held a specially symbolic meaning. It set apart objects and persons for the service of God. It was used in consecrating kings. And it even came to be the word for Messiah—"Mine Anointed."

Provisions for Constructing the Sanctuary and Other Guidelines (Ex. 31:1–18)

The passage.—For this important task God told Moses to appoint two craftsmen. One was Bezalel of the tribe of Judah, though originally his lineage was traceable to Caleb (later absorbed by Judah). The other was Oholiab of the tribe of Dan. Their skills were believed to be endowed by the Spirit of God. Just as there is beauty in holiness, this passage implies a holiness in beauty. The consecration of these workmen and their work would be an inspiration to all others who work to the glory of God. Not every man is called to build a Temple, but let the work of his hands be just as trained and just as dedicated. All work that is honorable can be brought into this spirit of art and handywork in the service of the Lord.

VI. THE COVENANT RENEWED (EX. 32:1—40:38)

The Golden Calf: Rebellion (Ex. 32:1–35)

The passage.—Chapters 32, 33, and 34 are a study in the sin of rebellion, the

apostasy (backsliding) of God's people, of Moses' mediation and the restoring of God's purpose in the covenant relationship. First came the idolatrous act of making a golden calf—in flagrant disregard of the Commandments so recently given.

Special points.—Why this idolatry by God's people? They could have been copying their pagan neighbors. Or it could have been a throwback to the idols of Egypt. More likely it was a reflection of the bull of Baalism. Their sin was compounded in that the sin was against Moses as well as against God. In essence they are repudiating Moses as God's representative leader. On top of this double-rebellion, there seems to have been open immorality associated with the calf-worship. The words "and rose up to play" probably imply sexual license and orgies. This would befit the fertility cults they were disobediently copying.

God's patience with the Jews seems exasperated and exhausted. He seems ready to let them go, or destroy them, unless Moses can assuage his wrath. Israel's sin in apostasy was threefold: a corruption of themselves, a turning aside in idolatry, and letting their worship degenerate into an end and object, rather than a means in adoration of their Holy God. Yet God relented and the people are spared. Moses was the mediator and happily his reconciling work brought the people back into a right relationship with God and the covenant.

Truth for today.—Forgiveness is not a trivial matter. Moses' wrath over these sins demanded an unusual expiation. The golden calf must be ground to powder, mixed with water, and then swallowed by the offenders! It is presumed such a prescription would teach a profound lesson. It would be like an acted parable.

But though the sin was great, God graciously granted atonement. Had God refused, Moses declares he would have wanted his own name blotted out. Clearly Moses was willing to offer up his own life for his people—the mark of true dedication and leadership. But not even Moses could bear the sins and guilt of Israel. That would all have to wait for a later covenant and a new Moses. This Mediator would by his own blood through the new covenant be able to do what the first Moses could not accomplish.

The Promise of God's Presence: Restoration (Ex. 33:1–23)

The passage.—God's presence would be forfeited if the Jews follow other gods, or trifle with idolatry as with the golden calf. His presence would be assured by renewal and rededication. Here God orders the removal of the "ornaments." These must have been religious trinkets or medallions. They suggest another form of compromise and God will have none of it.

Special points.—At this point, the story introduces "the tent of meeting." This was a simple tent structure and was quite different from the tabernacle. The important point and the important similarity is both tent and tabernacle represented the vital presence of God. The tent idea of God's presence also implies God's mobility. God will go on with Moses and the people—on through the wilderness, on to Canaan. He is a moving God and expects his people to move forward with him.

And God's promise includes not only his assured presence, but "I will give you rest." This rest would have deep and symbolic significance to a pilgrim people, always tired, but always being summoned to go on and on toward Canaan. The promise to Moses is this: the face of God will lead you and your men to that promised rest. In the New Testament the author of Hebrews interprets this "rest" in both historic (Ca-

naan) and spiritual dimensions (the City of God, regardless of history or geography).

Truth for today.—Moses, like all men, is curious to see God. But this longing can only be partially granted. The Lord does reveal himself: in his power and goodness, by his name and self-disclosure, by his grace and mercy. Yet there is a place and point where God stops our curiosity. He says "You cannot see my face; for man shall not see me and live." This is not just to prevent familiarity, and maintain a sense of awe and mystery. This deep insight means no man can know God fully, or apprehend him completely. In addition it means God will always be the God of the beyond.

In never seeing his face, we must be content to behold his back—at least in this life and pilgrimage. Whatever one may experience or understand of God, there is always more, much more. He is inexhaustible. This is why the Lord's glory is revealed, yet hidden. And for this same reason the human quest to see him and know him must ever remain an unending quest.

The Covenant and Its Renewal (Ex. 34: 1–35)

The passage.—The real "heart" of this chapter is "the ritual decalogue" (vv. 14–26). It gives us the true spiritual and religious position of Moses. It also presents the doctrine of the forgiveness of sins. This section of this chapter is considered extremely important by leading Bible scholars. They regard it as our primary source of Israel's early religious history. It may also represent the earliest written record of Israel's social and political history as well.

Special points.—This chapter should be read and compared closely with chapter 20 and chapter 24. Most authorities believe this chapter (34) is an older account of the Sinai code and covenant than either of the ones reported in 20 and 24. Three terms are employed to illustrate the wonderful nature of God's purposes for Israel. First the Lord will perform "marvels" (or miracles). Second other nations will see God's glory evidenced in the life of Israel. Thirdly, God's action will be "terrible" (or awe-inspiring) and thus elicit reverence and godly fear.

The covenant obligations will insure the purity of Israel's religious life. Even the harsh requirement of driving out the inhabitants from Canaan is to insure this same religious integrity and purity. This explains the important nickname the writer gives God in this context, "the Lord, whose name is Jealous, is a jealous God." This is plain language for God's demand of exclusive loyalty.

And Israel must never forget God's mighty deliverance from Egypt. Thus the feasts and rituals of that deliverance must be scrupulously observed. This explains how the feast of unleavened bread came to occupy a place of priority right alongside the commandments.

The connection between the covenant regulations of chapter 34 and the famous "ten words" and commandments of chapter 20 is rather complex. In essence it amounts to two distinct lists of ten commandments. And they each present a different and distinctive emphasis. The set in Exodus 20 might well be called an "ethical decalogue." The set of Exodus 34 could best be described as the "ritual decalogue." Of course there are close similarities, but the best scholars consistently view them as separate and distinct decalogues.

Truth for today.—This section portrays Moses as living the life of communion with God. This explains how he came to reflect the very glory of God. Even his face shone as reflecting the glory of the fiery burning presence of God. The light in Moses' countenance was the writer's picturesque way of expressing Moses' close relationship with the Lord. It also depicts the role of Moses in the faith of Israel.

The Fulfilment of the Religious Ordinances (Ex. 35:1—40:38)

The last six chapters of Exodus give the details and accomplishments of what God commanded in the previous instructions to Moses. Virtually no new material is introduced. These chapters are best understood in reading them alongside chapters 24–31.

This final section of Exodus describes the care in preparation and construction of the tabernacle. It also reviews the equipment for the tabernacle, and the special vestments for priests. It is climaxed with an account of the magnificence and glory of God filling the tabernacle.

LEVITICUS

Robert L. Cate

INTRODUCTION

For most Christians Leviticus is a dull, dry, uninteresting, and insignificant book. Its emphasis upon ritual and minute legal details becomes extremely boring if one sees nothing more. However, there is more here if one will look for it by approaching the book with an informed imagination.

The basic contents are legal in nature, with a few historical details thrown in as illustrations of the laws. The main divisions in the book are: 1. The Laws of Sacrifice (1:1—7:38) deal with the worship of the people. 2. The Laws Concerning the Priests (8:1—10:20) are concerned with the ministry and its relationship to the people and to God. 3. The Laws of Purity, including the Day of Atonement (11:1—16:34) relates to those things which make a man pure or impure. 4. The Laws of Holiness (17:1—26:46) expound the idea of a holy people in the presence of a holy God. 5. The book comes to its conclusion with an appendix relating to vows and tithes (27:1–34).

For the reader who approaches this only from the standpoint of the New Testament, it becomes quite frustrating since it falls so far short of the understanding of God which Christ reveals. However, as you seek to understand these laws in the light of their own time and of the religion of the surrounding nations, you see that they were a distinct advance over the cruel, inhuman practices of Israel's neighbors.

As to the religious value of the book, it primarily lies in the fact that its audience were to be a holy people because they belonged to a holy God ("ye shall be holy; for I am holy:" 11:44). The book deals with the horror of sin and with the grace of forgiveness. It is significant not only in the fact that the New Testament refers to it now and then, but also in that it provides in its language of Old Testament worship the framework which the New Testament uses to describe the ministry and mission of Jesus.

To really understand Leviticus, it must not be read alone, for it provides only the forms of Old Testament worship. You should read it side by side with the Psalms which provide the music and content of Old Testament worship. Then it comes to life as the celebration of the presence and activity of a holy God among his people and of their response to him. Perhaps its best commentary is the epistle to the Hebrews.

The authorship of the book is not indicated. Even though it is referred to as "The Third Book of Moses," the book nowhere claims to have been written by Moses, but only that it is God's revelation to Moses ("and the Lord spake unto Moses" 4:1, *et al*) and to others ("and the Lord spake unto Aaron" 10:8). Its ultimate author is clearly identified as God. Any claim to have identified its human author must be recognized as a theory based upon one's own understanding of both the internal and external evidence. Such theories may satisfy intellectual curiosity but add little, if anything, to understanding the book.

I. THE WORSHIP OF THE PEOPLE (LEV. 1:1—7:38)

The Burnt Offering (Lev. 1:1–17)

The passage.—With startling suddenness we are plunged into the midst of the sacrificial system. It seems archaic, brutal, and very out of date. But we cannot begin to understand this chapter, or the book itself, if we approach it as being primitive and childish.

Rather we have here the worship of a people dedicated to God. It is not their faith at its highest and best, but it does reveal their tremendous awe of, and dedication to, God.

The essence of this chapter is to be found, not in the details of the burnt offering, but in the fact that here was provided a way by which the worshiper committed himself to his God for cleansing from sin. This aimed at sin in general and not specific sins which were dealt with elsewhere (Lev. 4:1—5:13).

Furthermore, in this sacrifice, God provided for anyone regardless of his economic condition. Whether one had much or little, it was all one to God. He must come to God for the covering of sin.

Special points.—Regardless of whether the offering which was to be burnt was from "the herd" (cattle), from "the flocks" (sheep or goats), or from the "fowls" (turtle doves), it was to be "without blemish." The worshiper had to bring a sacrifice that was perfect.

He was to "put his hand upon the head" to identify himself with it. The phrase implies great force and indicated identification.

The slaughter of the victim, except for the fowls, was made by the worshiper. The blood, which was the seat of life (Lev. 17:11), was handled only by the priests, teaching that life was sacred. Due to the smallness of the fowls, they were handled in a somewhat different manner.

The Cereal Offering (Lev. 2:1–16)

The passage.—We move from the offerings of flesh to the offerings of grain (cereal). These offerings were intended to indicate the dedication and submission of both a man's income and his labor to God. As such, though the details are remote from us, the essential meaning is not.

Special points.—The term "meat offering" occurs in almost every verse of this chapter, but obviously indicated merely a cereal offering and not a flesh offering. In Genesis 4:3, it applies to both, but here it is limited to grain.

This cereal offering could have been brought raw as flour (Lev. 2:2), cooked in any one of several ways as cakes (vv. 4,5,7) or roasted as parched grain (v. 14). The point was that a person could offer the fruits of his labor in one of several ways, as long as it was offered with a proper ritual.

That which did not involve extra labor through baking, had to have incense added to it (vv. 1,15,16). An offering to God had to be extra special.

Furthermore, nothing that fermented was to be included, neither honey nor leaven (v. 11). Fermentation was always a biblical symbol of corruption.

Finally, all grain offerings were to include salt (v. 13). Salt was not only a preservative, it was also a symbol of fellowship. Those who had shared salt together were considered to be in a special relationship to each other by the peoples of the Ancient Near East.

The Peace Offering (Lev. 3:1–17)

The passage.—The "peace offering" has frequently been called the "thank offering." It is considered by most authorities to be the most ancient form of sacrifice practiced by men in their religions.

In the Old Testament it was a sign of good fellowship between a man, his fellow worshipers, and his God. This section gives specific instructions for the handling and disposal of the victim. Later we are told how the sacred meal was to be observed (Lev. 7:11–36).

This offering was the outward expression of an inner experience. To properly understand it, we must see it as an outgrowth of a worshiper's gratitude. It was the grateful offering of a choice and valued animal and his solemn identification with it. It included the proper handling of a sacred life, concluding with its sharing between the worshiper, the priests, and God (vv. 4–5; 7:15–17, 30–32), and the communion meal. The significance of the meal was that it showed that the worshiper and his God were in fellowship.

Special points.—The peace offering was similar to the burnt offering, with the exceptions that here only part of the victim was burned, and that both males and females were acceptable. Also, there was no provision for fowls here. The reason for this was that there would have been little left for a meal. The poor were probably included in the meals of those able to present larger sacrifices.

Apparently the intestinal fat was also considered sacred to life, since it was prohibited to the worshiper and reserved for God (v. 17).

The Sin Offering (Lev. 4:1—5:13)

The passage.—This section and the next (Lev. 5:14—6:7) deal with two special forms of burnt offering. The purpose of both was to atone for sin.

The sin offering was intended to make atonement for sins committed through ignorance or weakness (vv.

4:2,13,22,27). A better translation would be "unwitting sins." It is imperative to note that the sin dealt with here was not what we would normally term "sin." We must clearly understand that neither here nor anywhere else in the Old Testament was a sacrifice provided for deliberate sins, or sins "with a high hand" (Num. 15:30–31).

Finally, we should realize that there was no magic removal of guilt by the performance of this rite. Rather, here was a rite which God had ordained to accept. This ritual was based not upon man's magic but upon God's grace.

Special points.—The victim of the sin offering depended upon the rank of the one for whom atonement was sought. For the anointed priest (high priest) and the congregation it was a bullock (4:3,14), for a ruler it was a he-goat (v. 23, and for an ordinary person it was a she-goat (v. 28), a she-lamb (v. 32), two pigeons or doves (5:7), or some fine flour (v. 11), depending upon his ability to pay. Thus God provided a way of atonement for all men.

The handling of the sacrifice itself was primarily concerned with the blood and fat, the sacred seats of life, and the final disposal of the carcass, which had to be destroyed since it had been contaminated by the offender's sin. The need for two doves or pigeons was due to the fact they were too small to be handled in the usual way.

The last section identified three types of unwitting sin: the failure of a witness to testify (5:1), touching something unclean and forgetting to make a proper sacrifice (vv. 2–3), and making a vow, then forgetting to fulfil it (v. 5).

The Trespass Offering (Lev. 5:14—6:7)

The passage.—The trespass offering was another special form of the burnt offering. It dealt primarily with unwitting sins for which repayment was possible.

We must note that when a man had committed such a sin he was expected to offer sacrifice which was preceded by repayment with a 20 percent penalty added to it.

Special points.—Three types of sins which fell in this classification were: (1) keeping for one's own use some holy thing which belonged to the Lord (vv. 15–16); (2) an unwitting sin not covered by the sin offering (4:1—5:13) but for which no restitution was possible (5:17–19); (3) taking something which belonged to one's neighbor (6:2–7). It should be noted that a sin against one's neighbor was also considered a sin against God.

"The shekel of the sanctuary" (5:15) was a standard weight used to establish the value of silver. There were no coins in Palestine until the end of the sixth century B.C.

Instructions for Priests (Lev. 6:8–30)

The passage.—Part of this chapter and all of the next deal with instructions to the priests for the offering of sacrifices. The first part of this section addressed the worshipers (Lev. 1:2—6:7).

It is apparently of no significance that the sacrifices were dealt with in a different order than in the first section. In this chapter they are: the burnt offering (6:9–13), the cereal offering (vv. 14–23), and the sin offering (vv. 24–30).

Special points.—The burnt offering (v. 9) here was the twice-daily offering of a lamb for all Israel referred to in Exodus 29:38–42, rather than the private burnt offerings of Leviticus 1:2–17. In its observance the priest was to approach the altar in his official clothes (v. 10), but he was to put on ordinary clothes when he went outside the sacred area (v. 11). The continual fire was a symbol of uninterrupted worship.

The law of the cereal offering added new directions for the part which was the priests' (vv. 16–18). It also included new instructions for a perpetual cereal offering to be observed by Aaron and his successors to the high priesthood (vv. 20–23). It must be remembered that "meat" here refers to grain and not to flesh.

The part of the sin offering which belonged to the priest was "most holy" (vv. 25–29), and had to be handled in a special fashion. However, no part of the sin offering brought by the high priest or the congregation as a whole could be eaten (cf. Lev. 4:7,16; 6:30), but had to be entirely consumed by fire.

More Priestly Instructions (Lev. 7:1–38)

The passage.—The special instructions to the priests begun in 6:8 are concluded in this chapter. The detailed instructions indicated that it was (and is) important that those things offered to God must be offered properly.

Special points.—The trespass offering laws (vv. 1–10) review the material given in Leviticus 5:14—6:7 and add a few details. Also included in this section was an additional note concerning private burnt offerings (7:8).

The peace offerings of 3:1–17 were further classified into three kinds: thanksgiving (7:12–15), votive (vv. 16–18), and freewill. The difference between the first and the other two was in the time in which they could be eaten (vv. 15–17). The "abomination" (v. 18) is better translated as "spoiled."

The remainder of the chapter (vv. 22–36) contains miscellaneous instructions dealing with the blood and fat of the victims and with those special portions reserved for the priests, the "wave" and "heave offerings." This apparently refers to their having been moved or waved toward and away from the altar, indicating a gift to God and then that God had given those portions back to the priests.

Truth for today.—These archaic laws of sacrifice seem foreign to Christian worship, but there are lessons for us. Some have been pointed out already. In summary, worship is both a duty and a privilege which must not be taken lightly. It is effective, not because of the forms used but because God graciously makes it so. Finally, we must note that man is responsible to God for his actions —all of them.

II. THE MINISTRY OF THE PRIESTS (LEV. 8:1—10:20)

The Consecration Ceremony (Lev. 8: 1–36)

The passage.—We now move into a section which tells in a narrative the fulfilment of the laws of the consecration of the priests. Though there is no such service in the church today, yet the principles here are of permanent validity. The consecration to the priestly office is applicable to every church member who is a believer in Christ, while the Christian ministry must be understood as a special vocation within the universal priesthood of all believers.

The events described in this chapter were in fulfilment of Exodus 29.

Special points.—Moses was commanded to make proper preparations (vv. 1–3) and act as the priestly mediator, performing those functions which were later reserved to the priests (vv. 6–30). The "commandment" of verse 5 referred to Exodus 29.

The "Urim" and the "Thummim" (v. 8) were the sacred stones which the priest used in the casting of lots.

After Moses had dressed Aaron properly, he consecrated the tabernacle, the altar and its vessels, and finally Aaron himself (vv. 6–12). [A good Bible dictionary will help you identify the various items of this passage.] Then Moses dressed the sons of Aaron (v. 13). The anointing of Aaron with holy oil was apparently symbolic of his having been given spiritual power. The other priests were not anointed, this rite being reserved for the high priest.

Moses then sacrificed the sin offering (vv. 14–17), by which the new priests were shown that their position was not one of sinlessness. This was followed by the burnt offering (vv. 18–21), which showed the priests that they, like the victim, must be consumed in God's service.

The final sacrificial victim was the "ram of consecration" (v. 22), which is literally the "ram of the filling" and apparently meant that they were filled by God's gifts. The placing of the blood (v. 23) indicated that they were to hear God's word, to do his will, and to walk in his way. In short, their entire life was to be filled with God's service.

These rites of consecration were repeated daily for a week (v. 33).

The Installation Ceremony (Lev. 9:1–14)

The passage.—After the ordination (Lev. 8) came the installation (Lev. 9), when Aaron and his sons assumed the office of priests. Even after the elaborate consecration service, Aaron did not approach the altar to assume his priestly duties until Moses summoned him to this task (9:1–7; cf. Heb. 5:4–5). He did not presume upon his position.

He offered sacrifices for the first time for himself and his family (vv. 8–14), then for the people (vv. 15–21). This was followed by the priestly blessing (v. 22), the wording of which was recorded in Numbers 6:24–26.

After the blessing, Aaron and Moses went into the tabernacle to pray; then

returned for a final blessing (v. 23). At
this point the glory of God appeared in
the form of fire (cf. Ex. 3:2–4; 13:21;
19:18; *et al*) which completely consumed
the slowly burning sacrifice.

Special points.—The "elders of Israel"
(v. 1) were representative of the nation.
In the preceding chapter Moses had
acted as the representative of God. In
this chapter Aaron and his family assumed the responsibility of being the
representative of the people to God.

The "fire" from God may have come
from above or from the tabernacle. This
meant to the people that God had accepted both the sacrifices and the ordination of Aaron and his family. This
verse (24) explained how "the glory of
the Lord" (v. 23) appeared.

God's Holiness Ignored (Lev. 10:1–20)

The passage.—This chapter gives a
warning from history against presump-
tuousness by the priesthood.

Special points.—The precise meaning
of the "strange fire" of Nadab and Abihu
(v. 1) is uncertain. It is clear that they
were performing their priestly functions
in a manner contrary to God's command. While their punishment may not
seem just, it goes far deeper than that.
Their act indicated an inner lack of respect for the awesome holiness of God.
They simply ignored his holiness. Their
action may be compared with that of
Ananias and Sapphira (Acts 5:1–12).

Aaron and his sons were forbidden to
show the normal signs of mourning
(10:6–7), lest it should show dissatis-
faction with God's judgment. Verses
8–11 are an interlude in which Aaron
was instructed as to the need for an
absolute clarity of mind in fulfilling the
functions of priest as mediator and
teacher.

Lest they begin to become faint-
hearted, Moses then reminded Aaron
and his sons that privileges also came to
them with their awesome responsibilities.
(vv. 12–15).

Finally, Moses' indignation was
aroused by their failure to comply with
the letter of the law in regard to the sin
offering (vv. 16–18). Aaron's explanation
(v. 19) indicated that he felt defiled by
the actions and punishment of his sons.
Moses broad-mindedness was shown by
his acceptance of the explanation (v.
20).

Truth for today.—The basic lesson
from this section lies in an understanding of our position in the universal
priesthood of all believers. Though we
may enjoy our privileges, we dare not
forget our responsibilities, nor take them
lightly.

III. THE DEDICATION OF LIFE (LEV. 11:1—16:34)

Most of chapters in this section (Lev.
11–16) are, to the contemporary Christian, the most meaningless in the entire
Bible. At best, they appear dull and unprofitable; at worst, they are almost
repulsive.

Yet there are two real values in their
study. First, there is an underlying
principle which is applicable to modern
life; everything done in life must be
done to God's honor and glory. Second,
we can never understand the extreme
legalism which Jesus faced and from
which the early church sprang without
having some knowledge of these laws
and their meaning for Israel. The first
Christians believed in and obeyed these
laws. The first major controversy of the
church had to do with their obedience.
The Christian freedom which is so important to us was, in part, a deliverance
from such restrictions. They must be
studied with these ideas before us.

Clean and Unclean Animals (Lev. 11: 1–47)

The passage.—In order to understand this passage and those that follow, it is necessary to try to grasp the meaning of the word "unclean."

It must be admitted that this will be extremely difficult, for no single word can be used to translate the Hebrew. The basic reason for this problem is that the Hebrew word does not so much express an idea as an emotion. Unless we can in some way grasp the inner feeling, any word which we use will not be leading us to understanding but merely to covering over, and therefore compounding, our ignorance.

The word "unclean" is in some sense the opposite of "holy." Avoiding uncleanness is a part of the way to holiness. But this is not all.

We are another step toward understanding when we realize that any attempt to rationalize why certain things were unclean leads to a dead end. We may feel that certain things were unclean because they were unhealthy and that others were unclean because they were connected with idolatry. But they believed things were unclean because the Lord had said they were. It was as simple as that.

Another step toward understanding this idea may be found by recognizing that Hebrew religion was never thought of as the summation of religious ideas and experiences; it was always something that vitally involved public life. To the Hebrew, religion was action more than ideas, obedience more than orthodoxy, a way of life more than any system of theology. That which was unclean affected the public as well as the private life.

Therefore, that which was unclean was that which in some way violated God's holiness and man's holiness. The Hebrews were to be "different" from the surrounding peoples. They were to be special to God. That which kept them so was "clean." That which was "unclean" was thought of as sin and brought a sense of guilt. National life must have a pattern, some set of laws, restrictions and conventions. Their violation brought "uncleanness." Things or actions which were "unclean" brought a sense of horror, of revulsion, of unthinkableness to the hearts of the people. It was this emotion which the word describes.

Special points.—This set of regulations needs to be studied in relation to Deuteronomy 14:3–20.

"The coney" and 'the hare" (Lev. 11:5–6) do not really "chew the cud" but the constant movement of their jaws makes it appear so.

None of the animals which were beasts of prey were considered to be clean. Neither were shellfish or the many varieties of slick-skinned fish.

Since there was no good way of classifying unclean birds, they are listed by name (vv. 13–19).

Verse 21 might have been a little difficult to interpret without the accompanying identifications of verse 22. Technically, these insects have more than "four feet," but the expression is a figure of speech portraying the fact that they walked with their body horizontal to the earth.

The ritual for purification from uncleanness was specified (vv. 31–40) in each instance.

Finally, the motive for this intense preoccupation with "clean" and "unclean" was given. We must recognize that the underlying thought was not the fear of suffering or punishment but the honoring of God who had set them apart in history (vv. 44–45).

Purification Following Childbirth (Lev. 12:1–8)

The passage.—This chapter is particularly difficult to understand, but we must remember the ancient Hebrews were infinitely more concerned with obedience than with understanding. The underlying reasons for considering the woman unclean after childbirth are lost in antiquity. It was sufficient for the Hebrew that God said it.

Special points.—The child was not considered to be unclean, only the mother. "Circumcision" was an external sign indicating that the child had become a part of the covenant people and had entered into a covenant relationship with God (cf. Gen. 17:10–14).

The woman was considered to be "unclean" twice as long for a girl as for a boy (vv. 2,4–5).

When the woman was allowed back into society, her first duty was to worship. The sacrifice specified (vv. 6,8) took into account that the very poor could not afford a lamb for each child. It is of significance that it was the sacrifice of the poor which Mary brought after Jesus' birth (Luke 2:22–24).

Diagnosis of Leprosy (Lev. 13:1–59)

The passage.—This chapter and the next deal with the diagnosis and treatment of leprosy. We must grasp from the beginning that what was intended was not just the disease which we identify as leprosy, though it would certainly include this. What was included was a variety of skin diseases, as well as conditions which affected clothes and houses.

The prime significance of these verses for us lies in the fact that throughout the Bible leprosy is used as a figure of speech for sin. Because of its horror, its loathesome effects, its rapid spread, its contagion, and its isolation of its victims from fellowship, it is peculiarly appropriate for such.

Special points.—The victim of suspected leprosy was to be quarantined for sufficient time to enable a proper diagnosis to be made. If it turned out not to be leprosy, he could then return to society. But when the diagnosis was confirmed as leprosy, his condition was pitiable indeed. In such cases he had to assume the traditional forms of mourning (v. 45), for to all practical purposes he was dead to society.

The expression, "without the camp," was fitting for a nomadic people, wandering through the wilderness. After they had settled in cities, then the leper lived outside the city (2 Kings 6:3).

The leprosy of a garment (vv. 47–59) was apparently some form of mold or mildew. The requirements here were apparently to teach the Israelites to hate even the appearance of evil.

Since the priests were guardians of the holiness of the nation, it was their responsibility to determine uncleanness and to see that others were protected from it.

Treatment of Leprosy (Lev. 14:1–32)

The passage.—When a leper was cured, it was the responsibility of the priest to make the final determination. Lest there might be some mistake, the leper was examined outside the camp (v. 3). If he was really cured, his ritual of purification took three steps. The first of these is in verses 4–7, where a bird was sacrificed and another was released. Then followed a period of complete cleansing (vv. 8–9). Finally, the cured leper was required to bring a trespass offering, a sin offering, a burnt offering, and a cereal offering (vv. 10–20). A close examination of these verses reveal some slight differences from these rituals as described earlier (Lev. 1:1—2:16; 4:1—6:7), which differences were due to the special nature of these sacrifices here.

Special points.—The birds used in the first step (vv. 4–7) are unidentified. Later usage required sparrows. The one released (v. 7) was not a sacrifice, but was apparently symbolic of the leper's new freedom, in contrast to the sacrificed bird which apparently replaced the leper in his old condition of death.

In verses 21–32 (as elsewhere), special provisions were made for the poor. The ritual remained the same.

Leprosy in Houses (Lev. 14:33–57)

The passage.—It would appear that these verses have been displaced in the transmission of the text, for they seem logically to follow 13:59. Be that as it may, we can easily grasp their meaning regardless of their position in the book.

This section deals with "leprosy in a house" (v. 34). Exactly what is intended by this expression is somewhat difficult to determine. Apparently it was some form of lichen or mold. The identification again was the responsibility of the priests, and if there was any question, then a quarantine was called for.

Finally, procedures were outlined by which the house, when it was clean was made fit for habitation again.

Special points.—Apparently the concern here was that somehow such a growth represented evil. In the same manner in which the circumcision of the flesh represented a heart condition, so leprosy in the house represented spiritual evil, some form of corruption.

Anyone who came in contact with such a house was contaminated and made unclean, until proper cleansing procedures had been employed (vv. 46–47). If the house could not finally be cleansed, then it had to be destroyed (v. 45).

The purification ritual (vv. 48–53) was the same as that for a man (vv. 4–7).

Sexual Purity (Lev. 15:1–33)

The passage.—This chapter deals with sexual discharges, both normal and abnormal. The principle underlying these laws was that any such discharge from the sex organs rendered one ritually or ceremonially unclean.

Two abnormal discharges were dealt with, one for men (vv. 2–12) and one for women (vv. 25–27). It is obvious in both of these that they were dealing with a diseased condition. When the discharge was ended and the person was physically "cleansed," then there was a ritual washing so that he was ceremonially "clean" (vv. 13,28). Following this there was to be a sin offering and a burnt offering (vv. 14–15, 29–30).

Three normal discharges were dealt with; the first the involuntary ejaculation of a man (vv. 16–17), then ejaculation as a result of sexual intercourse (v. 18); and finally the normal menstrual cycle of a woman (vv. 19–24). In the second of these both the man and the woman were considered to be ceremonially unclean. In the other two only the person having the discharge was unclean unless he touched someone or something else, in which case it too was contaminated. Since these three were all normal, nothing more than a ceremonial bath was necessary.

Special points.—Verse 31 seems to sum up not only the laws in this chapter but in the entire section (Lev. 11–15). They were all designed to make the Hebrews a separated people; especially were they to have been separated from their uncleanness.

Truth for today.—In spite of the intrinsic difficulty of these chapters (11–

15) for the modern reader, there are two essential concepts taught here. The first is that all of life must be lived to God's honor and glory. The second is that sin is more than an act, it is a condition in which one lives and from which he must be delivered. The cleansing actions prescribed here were the means by which the restored person could resume his normal life.

The Ritual of Atonement (Lev. 16:1–34)

The passage.—In this chapter we come to what is rightly understood as the highest point of the Old Testament sacrificial system: the ritual of the Day of Atonement. The Christian is likely to miss the significance of it for New Testament theology unless he reads it together with Hebrews 9:6–28.

On the Day of Atonement all the sins, which had not been dealt with through the regular and occasional sacrifices throughout the year, were confessed and atoned for, so that a right relationship with God might be maintained by the people of Israel.

On this day, and only on this day, Aaron was to enter the "holy place within the veil" (vv. 2–3,30). He was to wear the simple garments of an ordinary priest rather than the colorful and ornate garb of the high priest (v. 4; for a full description see Ex. 28). His entrance into the holy of holies was to be as a humble priest rather than in the magnificence of his authority.

In preparation, he was to select the animals for the sacrifices (vv. 3,5). Further, he was to make himself ceremonially clean (v. 4).

When all was ready, he was to make his sin offering (vv. 6,11). Then he was to separate the two goats by lot (vv. 6–10). Next he entered the holy place "within the veil" with burning incense (vv. 12–13), which served two purposes.

It was symbolic of the prayers of himself and the nation but it also served to cover with a cloud of smoke the manifestation of God upon the mercy seat.

It is implied that he then went out for the blood of his sin offering, entering a second time into the holy place, where he placed it upon and near the mercy seat (v. 14). Again he left the holy place, this time to sacrifice the goat which had been designated by lot as a sin offering for the people. This done, he returned a third time to the mercy seat, where he sprinkled the blood in atonement for the sins of the people (vv. 15–16).

During the performance of this part of the ritual, no one else was to be in the "tabernacle of the congregation" (v. 17). When he left the holy place, he went out to cleanse the altar and the tabernacle itself (vv. 18–20). At this point he took the other goat, placed his hands upon it and confessed the sins of the people, thus symbolicly transferring to it their sins. Then a man who had been prepared led the goat into the wilderness (vv. 20–22).

Following this, Aaron cleansed himself again, resumed the normal garments of the high priest, and offered the burnt offerings for himself and the people (vv. 24–25). Others involved in this and the one who led the goat away also had to go through a ceremonial cleansing (vv. 26–28).

The Day of Atonement was established as a permanent celebration for Israel, to be observed by Aaron and his successors (vv. 29–34).

Special points.—The "mercy seat" (v. 2) was the lid of the ark of the covenant, which is described in Exodus 25:17–21.

The "scapegoat" (vv. 10,20–22) is better translated as the "goat for Azazel." But what does this mean? Apparently Azazel was the name of something that was the opposite of God. This would indicate that we should identify him as the chief of the forces of evil, hence as the devil. (He seems to have been so identified in the nonbiblical book of Enoch.) The significance of sending the goat to Azazel seems to have been that as one goat had served to cleanse the people from their sins, the other goat had carried those sins back to their author. Let us understand that there was no concept of magic here, at least not as it was originally intended. Rather these things happened only because God made it so.

"The testimony" in verse 13 refers to the two tablets of the law given to Moses.

This Day of Atonement was the only day of fasting set aside in the Old Testament. The expression, "afflict your souls" (vv. 29,31) refers to this and carries the idea of putting into subjugation one's bodily appetites in penitence for sin.

Of all the special days and seasons, this was the most significant. It was called a "sabbath of rest" (v. 31), which literally is a "sabbath of sabbaths." It was the highest and holiest of all the high and holy days.

Truth for today.—The Christian finds in this special ritual a foreglimmer of the ultimate atonement wrought by Jesus, our great High Priest. Also, we may see a picture of the fact that our sins have been carried away from us. Finally, we may rejoice in that ours is an atonement that was accomplished once for all time.

IV. LAWS OF HOLINESS (LEV. 17: 1—26:46)

This section of Leviticus (Lev. 17–26) has long been called the Holiness Code, for it is a collection of laws involving all areas of life and aimed at producing "holiness." It has three distinctive characteristics. (1) The phrase, "I am the Lord" occurs nearly fifty times in this section and not at all in the rest of the book. (2) The basis for the holiness of the people is established by the frequent phrase, "Ye shall be holy, for I, the Lord, your God, am holy." (3) This section seems to be more involved with life and less with ritual than the rest of the book.

At first glance, these are disorganized, mixed elements, but they were all bound together in the idea of a holy people serving a holy God in a holy land. To properly understand these laws, we must understand what "holiness" meant to a Hebrew. To them God was holy because he was separate and different from man. His majesty, righteousness, and power all entered into this idea. Israel was holy because it had been separated from other men by a holy God. It was to constantly demonstrate this "otherness" by religion and life. Finally, their land was holy because it had been set apart by God for his holy people. Thus they had always to live as if they were in a sacred place.

All this emphasis on holiness, on separateness, could lead to legalism; and it did, as we know from the Gospels. But the external signs of holiness were—and are—important. These should reflect the heart condition. Such was the admonition of Jesus, who said, "These ought ye to have done, and not to leave the other undone" (Luke 11:42).

Most of the laws in this section are easily understood and need little explanatory comment.

The Sacredness of Life (Lev. 17:1–16)

The passage.—This chapter deals with the proper slaughtering of animals from the standpoint that, to a holy people, all life was sacred.

Special points.—In the time of this prohibition, all killing of animals was considered to be sacrificial to some god. Lest the Israelites be misunderstood by their neighbors, all animals were to be brought to the door of the tabernacle as a peace offering to God. (vv. 3–7). This law was changed when the Hebrews went into Canaan, for it was impractical in a settled community (Deut. 12:15).

The eating of flesh from which the blood was not properly drained was also condemned, for the blood was the seat of life and thus was sacred to God.

The punishment for the violation of these laws was to have been "cut off" (vv. 4,9,10,14). Whether this meant excommunication or execution is not clear.

Unlawful Sexual Acts (Lev. 18:1–30)

The passage.—These laws governing sexual purity were aimed at keeping the people separate from pagans (v. 3), who practiced many immoral sex acts.

Special points.—The phrase "uncover the nakedness" obviously refers to sexual union. The prohibition against marrying sisters was confined to the lifetime of the first wife (v. 18).

Verse 21 seems to be out of place, unless the worship of Molech included some form of sexual license. Much pagan worship did so. The expression, "the fire," is not in the Hebrew, but was supplied by the translators. What was being prohibited was not only the worship of a pagan god, but also adopting pagan worship for the true God.

Holy Living (Lev. 19:1–37)

The passage.—This chapter exhibits some of the highest ethical standards of the Old Testament. Unfortunately, its interpretation by the Hebrews watered it down considerably in its application.

Special points.—The Ten Commandments were the basis for these laws. Jesus identified the last part of verse 18 as the second of the great commandments

(Matt. 19:19).

"She shall be scourged" (v. 20) should be translated as "an inquiry shall be made." Verses 23–28 were to avoid pagan practices, underscoring the holiness of Israel. The love of the stranger (v. 34) was the highest ethical teaching of the Old Testament. Unfortunately, it was seldom applied.

Pagan Practices Condemned (Lev. 20:1–27)

The passage.—The laws in this chapter were almost all given in other places in Leviticus or Exodus. The major difference was that here the punishments were also given.

Special points.—"If the people . . . hide their eyes" indicated that if they did not punish the sin, then God himself would see that the guilty man did not escape punishment (vv. 4–5). The emphasis was still upon holiness because of their relation to the holy God (v. 26).

Regulations for the Priests (Lev. 21:1–24)

The passage.—Here we have laws which set up a higher standard of holiness for the priests than for the ordinary Israelite (vv. 1–9, 17–24). An even higher standard was set for the high priest (vv. 10–15). Their ministry was more important than human relationships.

Special points.—The domestic life, the ceremonial life, and the physical body of the priest were all to be free of defects. "He shall eat the bread" (v. 22), indicated that, though a man with physical defects could not serve as a priest, he was not refused the sacred gifts provided for the support of the priesthood.

More Priestly Regulations (Lev. 22:1–33)

The passage.—Here is a continuation of the material in chapter 21, but the formula of verse 1 indicates that it was a new section. These laws refer more to the priest's actions than to his being. The underlying idea was a sense of reverence for all things sacred.

Special points.—"Until even" (v. 6) reflects the idea that the new day began at sunset. "Stranger" (v. 10), in this context, refers to a layman. The phrase "bruised, or crushed, or broken, or cut," (v. 24) was a technical expression referring to castrated animals. Each of these laws underscored the idea of a holy priest before a holy God (vv. 31–33).

Holy Times (Lev. 23:1–44)

The passage.—No religion can exist without sacred times for worship when men could rejoice in what their god had done. Such seasons were provided for the Hebrews. They furnished specific occasions for the assembling of the people to give outward form to what should have been regularly in their hearts.

Special points.—"Feast" literally means "an appointed time," and does not mean a banquet. The first of these sacred occasions was "the sabbath" (v. 3), the weekly day of rest.

The "passover" and "the feast of unleavened bread" (vv. 5–14) are given in detail in Exodus 12. They commemorated God's redemptive activity in history as well as indicating rejoicing at the beginning of the grain harvest. None of the harvest was to be eaten until the firstfruits were offered to God.

Fifty days after Passover came Pentecost (from the Greek word for "fifty"), celebrating the completion of the grain harvest (vv. 15–22). The two loaves offered (v. 17) were the only grain offering ever made with leaven. It probably was offered in this form as being that which was most useful to the people.

The Feast of Trumpets (vv. 23–25) was the civil New Year. The Day of Atonement (vv. 26–32) was given in de-

tail in chapter 16.

Finally came the Feast of Booths (vv. 33–44) which corresponds to our Thanksgiving, celebrating the conclusion of all the harvests and how God made provision for them in their wilderness wanderings.

Holy Behavior (Lev. 24:1–23)

The passage.—Here several unrelated acts are tied together by the idea of holy people acting in a holy manner.

Special points.—The holy worship (vv. 2–9) indicates continual prayers (the burning lamps) and continual Thanksgiving (the bread on the table).

An historical interlude raises the question as to how the laws of behavior related to non-Hebrews (vv. 10–23). In attitude toward God, all were judged equally responsible (v. 22). The law of retaliation (vv. 17–21) was a limitation of vengeance, permitting *no more* than equal indemnity. Though Jesus condemned the spirit of vengeance (Matt. 5:38 ff.), this limit in Leviticus was a significant advance over Genesis 4:23–24.

Holy Years (Lev. 25:1–55)

The passage.—Since life was sacred, time was sacred; but the sabbatical year and the Year of Jubilee were especially so. In these years the land was to lie fallow. Further, in the Jubilee Year special laws for persons and property were observed. These laws were based on the idea that the land belonged to God (v. 23).

Special points.—Verses 5–7 indicate that the uncultivated produce of the sabbath year could be eaten, though it could not be harvested and stored. The Year of Jubilee followed the seventh sabbatical year (vv. 8–12) and the same provision was made. In addition, all Hebrew slaves were to be freed and all property restored to its rightful owners. The only exceptions were urban houses (vv. 29–30) and property of the Levites (vv. 32–34). Also included in this section were laws regarding usury, which referred to Hebrews only, being confined to loans for personal need and not being applicable to loans for commercial purposes (vv. 35–37).

These laws put a check upon ambition and greed, seeking to adjust the social welfare of the community. Unfortunately, the prophets reveal that they were not always successful.

Exhortation to Holiness (Lev. 26:1–46)

The passage.—This section of the laws for holiness comes to a conclusion with a prophetic sermon, urging the nation to be faithful to the covenant. The first point gives the blessings of faithfulness (vv. 1–13), the second lists punishments for disobedience (vv. 14–39), and then there was the promise of forgiveness and restoration upon repentance (vv. 40–45).

Special points.—The promise of "rain" (v. 4) at the proper time was a necessary part of prosperity. The bringing "forth the old" (v. 10) was the result of an overabundant harvest. On the other hand, "seven times more" (v. 18) punishment is symbolic of intense punishment. "Iron" heavens would give no rain, so the earth would become as hard as "brass" (v. 19). "Ten women shall bake . . . in one oven" (v. 26) shows the scarcity of food.

God's punishment is always aimed at leading to repentance, so that he can bless his people (vv. 40–45). Even his punishment is loving punishment.

Truth for today.—This entire section aimed at getting God's people to be holy. If there was need for this then, there is much more so now. Through Christ, our understanding of holiness has been enlarged and through his Spirit our ability to be holy has been increased.

V. REGULATION OF VOWS AND TITHES (LEV. 27:1–34)

The passage.—This chapter deals with vows (freewill expressions of a worshiper), and tithes (a kind of rent paid by a man to God). Vows, common to all religions, are usually connected with a prayer to gain the object of the one praying. As such, they were not commanded, but had to be regulated. Further, a manner of redeeming vows was provided to prevent undue suffering as the result of a thoughtless or rash vow. Vows could not be ignored, and once made had to be fulfilled.

Tithes belonged to God, but they too could be redeemed—at a price. The cost at this point was designed to discourage this practice.

Special points.—Verses 2–8 cover vows of human life. The evaluation was apparently established by one's worth as a laborer, and varied with age and sex. The "shekel" was a certain weight of silver. There is no accurate way of establishing its value in modern terms. Special provisions were made for people too poor to pay the established price (v. 8).

Verses 9–13 deal with the redemption of vowed animals and verses 14–25 with vowed houses or land. The situation with the latter was further complicated by the requirements of the Jubilee Year (vv. 17–24). "According to the seed," indicated that a field was valued by the amount of seed required to sow it properly (v. 16).

Things which already belonged to the Lord could not be vowed to him (vv. 26–27). "The devoted thing" (vv. 28–29) is totally foreign to our concept of "devotion." This expression refers to things upon which special vows were made and which were permanently removed from human use or contact.

"Under the rod" (v. 32) refers to a manner of counting animals by making them walk under the owner's staff. Every tenth animal belonged to God.

Truth for life.—As we noted at the beginning, the details of this book are alien to us. On the other hand, here we have principles of worship of a holy God by a holy people. Form was stressed, and frequently in practice became more important than meaning. But it was never intended to be so. Rather, we have here a step, a giant step, forward in man's worship of God. Lest we too quickly condemn these ancients for failing to understand these ideas and ideals, look again at how far short we fall in observing the ideals of worship and life which Jesus established for us in another giant step forward. The underlying principle is still the same: "Be ye holy, for I am holy."

NUMBERS

Fred M. Wood

INTRODUCTION

Exodus closes with the erection of the tabernacle at Sinai. Leviticus consists of ritual and other regulations concerning worship. Numbers opens with further regulations and then narrates Israel's history from Sinai to the Plains of Moab opposite Jericho.

The first section (1:1—10:10) gives events at Sinai before leaving. This includes numbering the people, outlining their positions around the tabernacle, enumerating duties of the priests and regulations related to worship and service.

The second (10:11—22:1) records the journey from Sinai to the Plains of Moab. It gives most of the information we have about the wilderness wanderings of nearly forty years. Most of the time was spent in the neighborhood of Kadesh. The final (22:1—36:13) tells of Israel's activity while encamped in the Plains of Moab.

The title of the book (given to it in the Greek and Latin versions) was undoubtedly applied because of the two numberings of the people (chaps. 1 and 26). In most Hebrew Bibles it is called by its first distinctive word "in the wilderness."

Traditionally, Numbers has been considered the "fourth book of Moses." The material in it is associated with the days of Israel's great leader. Modern critical scholarship has divided the Pentateuch into four main documents and some lesser ones. There are, of course many variations within this school of thought. Unfortunately, the historical integrity of the accounts has been called in question by some of these scholars. It is not the purpose of this commentary to examine minutely the findings and contentions of those men. We will approach the book as Mosaic in content and will not spend time debating the historicity of the accounts. Certain problems may be pointed out but it will not be possible to give exhaustive treatment to them.

The Bible is a living book. Although part of Numbers is statistical and legalistic, it breathes the spirit of the divine Inspirer and is a vitally helpful book in understanding a crucial period in the life of Israel. Rather than attempt a critical dissection of the literary structure, we shall seek to discover spiritual truth for our growth in the knowledge of God's redemptive program.

The Military Census and General Outline of Levites' Duties (Num. 1:1–54)

The passage.—The purpose was not to discover possible revenue sources but to record the manpower capable of being utilized in battle. The worship structure for Israel had been outlined first. It was followed by a practical organization which would provide for security in time of war. Verse 3 seems to indicate there was already some type of protective system in effect by each tribe.

Moses was instructed to choose a census captain from each tribe to assist him. One was considered old enough for military service when he became twenty. The census revealed Judah had the largest fighting force (74,600), followed by

Dan (62,700), Simeon (59,300), Zebulon (57,400), Issachar (54,400), Naphtali (53,400), Reuben (46,500), Gad (45,-650), Asher (41,500), Ephraim (40,-500), Benjamin (35,400) and Manasseh (32,200). The total was 603,550.

Verses 47–54 outline the duties of the Levites. They were not included in the military census but were given the task of caring for the tabernacle and performing ministries related to its services.

Special points.—To keep the tribes at twelve, corresponding to the number of Jacob's sons, two changes were made. Levi dropped out to become the priestly tribe. Joseph dropped out and each of his sons, Ephraim and Manasseh, received an identification.

Truth for today.—Although a man's spiritual relationship to God is of first importance, it is also necessary to be practical minded. To ignore either the need for God in national security, or our own personal responsibility to provide a strong army is unwise.

The work of ministry demands one's entire devotion. Those rendering full-time service are worthy of high honor and should be supported by the religious community. They should be freed from involvement in secular affairs.

Positions of Tribes in Camp and in March (Num. 2:1–34)

The passage.—Three tribes were placed on each side of the camp. On the east, Judah was the middle tribe flanked by Issachar and Zebulun. On the south side, Reuben was flanked by Simeon and Gad. On the west Ephraim was flanked by Manasseh and Benjamin, while on the north Dan was flanked by Asher and Naphtali.

The Levites were excluded in this arrangement. They were given positions closer to the tabernacle on three sides of it.

Special points.—Some scholars have contended it is impossible to find any space around Sinai big enough to accommodate such a fantastic number of people. One should not be a purist. This was Moses' ideal in marching. This group of ignorant, newly-liberated slaves was a discipline problem many times. There is ample space in many areas in the peninsula as has been proved by scholars. These people moved slowly. There were many problems of day-to-day living but there is no need to doubt the historical integrity of these accounts.

Truth for today.—It is God's delight to do things in an orderly way. The sun, moon, and stars operate according to a fixed pattern. The tide ebbs and flows in the regular succession of seasons. Even comets are not erratic wanderers in space. They move with precision.

Although the entire army of Israel was a unit, there was room within it for each tribe and each family to have its own distinctive standards of identification. God does not glorify monotony.

The Number, Arrangement, and Duties of the Levites (Num. 3:1—4:49)

Moses and Aaron were Levites. Two of Aaron's sons (Nadab and Abihu) died without children. The other two (Eleazar and Ithmar) were given definite duties.

Levi had three sons (Gershon, Kohath, and Merari). Moses and Aaron were from the family of Kohath through Amram.

There were 7,500 Gershonites a month old or older. They were placed behind the tabernacle on the west side and were put in charge of the tabernacle, the Tent, the covering, and the screen for the door of the tent of meeting. Also, they were in charge of the hangings of the court, the screen for the door of the court which was by the tabernacle, and by the altar round about it, and for the cords of it for all the service pertaining to it.

There were 8,600 Kohathites (see section on special notes) one month or older. They were placed on the south side of the tabernacle and put in charge of the ark, table, candlestick, altars, vessels of the sanctuary, the screen, and all the services related to these items. Eleazar, the son of Aaron was in charge of them.

There were 6,200 Merarites, one month or older. They were placed on the north side of the tabernacle and put in charge of the boards of the tabernacle, the bars, the pillars, the sockets, the instruments, the services connected with these items, the pillars of the court, their sockets, their pins, and and their cords.

Moses, Aaron, and Aaron's sons were placed on the east side of the tabernacle. The total number of Levites was 22,000. God decreed they would be accepted in lieu of the 22,273 firstborn as dedicated to him in a special way. He ruled, however, that for the remaining 273 difference there must be payment made to Aaron and his sons.

In chapter 4 the duties of the Kohathites (vv. 4–16), Gershonites (vv. 21–28), and Merarites (vv. 29–33) are outlined. The remainder of the chapter gives the number of the Kohathites (2,750), Gershonites (2,630), and Merarites (3,200) who were between the ages of thirty to fifty. This was the age for service to be rendered by them.

Special points.—In 3:39 the number of Levites is given as 22,000. If we compare this with the total of the three groups (vv. 21–32), we have a discrepancy of 300. Most scholars believe the correct number of Kohathites (3:28) should be 8,300. Many texts read this way.

Truth for today.—Assignment of definite duties for definite people is necessary in order to implement the planning of a work load for any organization. Supervision and authority are important. People need to learn the importance of obedience to duty. When one is assigned a position of honor it means weightier responsibility.

Laws Concerning Camp Conduct (Num. 5:1–31)

The passage.—Instructions concerning defense were followed by practical suggestions for everyday living. Personal hygiene was important. The people were concentrated in a small geographical area. Those whose bodily impurities threatened the physical health of the camp must be separated from the people. Moses specified three—lepers, those having bodily discharges, and any who have had contact with a dead person (vv. 1–4).

Personal property must also be protected. Close living conditions made it difficult to secure one's possessions. A 20 percent penalty was invoked upon anyone who was found guilty of theft. In addition, he must also make atonement with God by bringing offering to the priests.

The procedure which a man was to take (vv. 11–31) if he suspected his wife of infidelity but could not prove it shows the distinct superiority of the man's position in society. It was virtually up to the woman to prove her innocence if she was even suspected of violating the marriage vows.

Special points.—The "trial by ordeal" seems cruel by modern standards. We should remember, however, that other civilizations of that day considered it a proper way of determining innocence or guilt.

Isolation of those who might defile the camp was considered essential. Modern medicine can cope with some diseases today without completely isolating the victim but the Israelites had neither the knowledge nor the facilities for such treatment.

Truth for today.—Personal hygiene and spiritual purity are closely connected. Cleanliness is still next to godliness. The permissiveness of our society toward wrongdoing and our "too easy attitude" in insisting upon restitution stands condemned in light of these ancient people. In our day, the pendulum has swung too far away from their stern measures.

Although woman has a higher place in society today than ever before, she still loses more when unfaithful than the man. Christianity has done much to elevate the woman but even an enlightened community expects more from the woman and holds her of greater guilt when she goes astray.

Laws Concerning Nazarites and Formula for Priestly Blessing (Num. 6:1–27)

The vow to become a Nazarite could be a lifelong commitment or a limited one. It seems to have come into existence at an early time in Israel's history. The word "Nazarite" means separate and the things to which he voluntarily subjected himself were indicative of the concept underlying the office.

First, from wine or strong drink. This went so far as to include any juice of grapes . . . fresh or dried. Second, from the razor. Many religions of that day had special religious customs involving the hair. In Semitic literature, hair was related to the presence of life.

Finally, from the vicinity of a dead body. He was even more restricted than the priests. He, like the high priest, was forbidden from approaching the dead body of even his nearest relative.

Verses 13–21 give the ritual requirements when he completed his vow. He must bring a burnt offering, sin offering, and peace offering. These must be accompanied by the usual meal offering and drink offering. All of these are outlined in Leviticus 1–7. The cutting of the hair followed and after that he was free to drink wine. It is significant that he was not released from other responsibilities because of his unique vow.

Special points.—Such Old Testament passages as these cannot be used by the Christian to justify social drinking of alcoholic beverages. The Old Testament is not our final authority for conduct. Our final authority is the lordship of Jesus Christ as interpreted by the Holy Spirit.

Nothing short of total abstinence from alcoholic beverages is wise when the subject is viewed against the teachings of the New Testament concerning both the body as the temple of God and the Christian life as a stewardship of influence.

Truth for today.—Those who seek positions of prestige and leadership in the Christian community must also be willing to bear special responsibilities. This is not a "double standard" but rather a price that one must pay if he is to serve in a unique capacity.

Description of Offerings to Consecrate the Altar (Num. 7:1–89)

This chapter (one of the longest in the Bible) describes those things given to be used in the service of the tabernacle. There were six wagons and twelve oxen brought to be used in transporting the tabernacle. In addition, there were identical gifts from each of the twelve tribes brought on twelve successive days. They consisted of gold and silver vessels to be used in the sanctuary service. Also, there were sacrificial animals and other materials for the ceremony of dedication.

In verses 12–83 there are twelve sections of six verses each which describe the gifts of the princes on successive days. These sections are almost identical. The chapter closes with a summary statement of the cumulative amount of the gifts (vv. 84–88). A closing verse describes the entrance of Moses into the tent of meeting to speak with God when he heard his voice from above the mercy seat.

Special points.—The redundant style of the Hebrews in describing the gifts should not constitute a problem for us. Although monotonous to the modern ear, the Hebrews seemingly took a delight in using this means to emphasize the liberality of the tribal princes.

Truth for today.—Although no one can "buy his way" into God's favor, God expects his people to bring their material possessions to be used in the work of his kingdom. A pastor is wise who teaches his people to give their money to support the work of the churches. No pastor ever contributes to the growth of his people when he keeps silent on the question of financial support.

Consecration of the Levites (Num. 8: 1–26)

The passage.—The Menorah (place of a lamp) has continued throughout history to be important to the Jews. The lampstand was placed on the south side of the holy place with the "spouts" pointing north. This was for the light to shine over the table of the shewbread.

The main body of this chapter (vv. 5–22) describes a ceremony in which Moses was to cleanse the Levites and "offer them for a wave offering." God had accepted the Levites as a substitute for all the firstborn of Israel. Since the Levites were to serve as a shield for the people, it was necessary that atonement be made first for them. In this way the people could be saved from the anger of God (which might be expressed by a

plague or some other calamity) caused by an improper worship action.

Special points.—The "wave offering" was a special contribution. In it, the symbolism was that of waving the sacrifice toward the altar and then away from the altar. It symbolized the fact that the people gave the offering to God and then received it back again. It is difficult to know exactly how this was done with reference to the Levites. They obviously could not be waved back and forth physically but, no doubt, in some way the symbolism was fulfilled in spirit if not literally.

Truth for today.—Although we as Christians interpret God as Spirit and recognize our service to him is spiritual, we also must recognize, as God did in the days of Moses, the practical aspects of both worship and everyday living. There were unique problems concerning sanitation among the Israelites during the experience of wilderness living. Although we are not required to obey legalistically every command Moses gave to the Israelites, we should recognize the close relationship of good hygiene and spiritual worship.

Proper division of manpower is also important. God gives different abilities to people and we must accept both ourselves and others as they are and seek to work from that point.

The Second Passover and Preparation for Leaving Sinai (Num. 9:1—10:10)

This Passover was not accompanied by the killing of the firstborn of Israel's enemies nor were the Jews required to sprinkle blood on the doorpost in order to immunize the home from death. It has been suggested that the sprinkling of the blood on the altar replaced the ceremony on the doorpost.

A new feature added to the Passover was the provision of a second observance a month later for those who were unavoidably and legitimately refrained from observing the feast at the regular time. It is interesting to note the stern punishment (v. 13) for one who, without excuse, failed to take part in the original observance.

When one studies 9:15–23, he should refer to Exodus 40:34–38. There is both a mystical and a practical element connected with the "cloud by day" and "pillar of fire by night" which guided the Israelites in their march. It was necessary to exercise extreme caution in traveling because of the scorching sun. People were trained to take advantage of every weather change. Today we listen to the explanation of meteorologists. The people of that day followed God's provision for shelter and interpreted God's provision as proof of his presence with them. They were not wrong! For the two million Jews to survive for nearly forty years under such conditions was indeed a miracle from God!

A way was needed to summons the people from time to time for march. The trumpets had another use. When the nation went to war, these trumpets would be blown to remind the Lord of their distress and urge him to deliver them.

Special points.—One might infer from Exodus 12:25 that regular observances of the Passover would begin when Israel was settled in the Promised Land. This command in Numbers, however, prevents that interpretation. If one is disturbed as to where all of the provisions came from to observe this feast, he should remember the Israelites had personal possessions while in Egypt and also Exodus 12:35–36 indicates they must have taken much Egyptian wealth with them.

Truth for today.—When God's people are working with him toward his redemptive purpose, he is with them in a unique way. God often uses what seems to us to be the natural elements to aid him in carrying out his plans and protecting his people. The miracle is often the fact that God made a certain natural phenomenon occur at the particular time that it was needed to meet the exigency of his people. God is not limited to working through his natural laws, but often it is the timing of an event that signifies his unique presence.

Departure from Sinai and Enlistment of Hobab as Guide (Num. 10:1–36)

The passage.—After remaining at Sinai for eleven months, the Israelites set forward. The marching was in accordance with previous instructions and the position around the camp. Judah led, followed by Issachar and Zebulun. Next came the tabernacle borne by the Gershonites and the Merarites. The tribes of Reuben, Simeon, and Gad followed. Then came the Kohathites bearing the sanctuary. The tribes of Ephraim, Manasseh, Benjamin, Dan, Asher, and Naphtali followed in order.

The dialogue of Moses and Hobab is interesting. Moses' first motivation was the Israelites would do Hobab good if he would come with them. This seemingly did not appeal to him and he indicated he was going back to his own people. Moses then pointed out to Hobab that he would be of much help to the people as a guide since he knew the land. This obviously was the point that persuaded Hobab to join the group.

As they set forward, the ark of the covenant went three days in advance to seek a good camp site. The section closes with a summary of the words for Moses for marching and another statement for resting.

Special points.—Who was the father-in-law of Moses? The Hebrew text (v.

29) could support either Hobab or Reuel. Other passages, however, make it clear Reuel is the father-in-law (Ex. 2:18) and Hobab is the brother-in-law (Judg. 4:11). Who was Jethro? Several passages indicate he was the father-in-law. Most scholars see the word "Jethro" as a title for the priest of Midian similar to the use of "pharaoh" for the kings of Egypt.

Truth for today.—Strong leaders need dependable help. Our complex world makes it impossible for one person to be an expert in all fields. A wise administrator chooses capable help and delegates as much work as possible. One must be careful and enlist those who are both qualified and trustworthy.

A Murmuring People and a Resourceful God (Num. 11:1–35)

At the beginning of the trip complaints began. It was necessary for God to be firm. This explains some of the drastic actions such as the sending of fire into camp.

Temporarily silenced, the Israelites were stirrred again by the "mixed multitude" who had joined themselves to the Israelites. The manna had at first (Ex. 16) been a lifesaver, but now it was a cause for complaint. The people wanted meat.

Moses was human and had his pressure points. This was one of them. When he prayed, he was told to enlist seventy spiritual leaders to help him. When he doubted God's ability to send meat, God gave him an object lesson in overabundance of divine resourcefulness.

Moses showed a beautiful spirit in failing to be jealous of the two "unofficial" prophesiers. These were difficult days for him, but he was wise enough to seek God's leadership continuously.

Special points.—The manna has been associated by some with the sweet juice of a desert tree. It forms small round white grains which drop to the ground. They melt early in the morning as the sun's rays come upon them. Josephus, a Jewish historian of the first century, says manna was still available in the Sinai Peninsula during his day. Even modern explorers tell of a product collected in this area which resembles the biblical description of manna. The miracle would be the tremendous availability. We do not know how voluminous the growth may have been in that day. The account of the quails is very reasonable for this was in the pathway of a migration which occurred regularly. Often, they flew low and it is very understandable that God could have arranged to have an abundance of quail there at the particular time needed. *The timing would be a miracle indeed!*

Truth for today.—It is not easy to listen to the complaints of people. A leader is tempted to "throw in the towel" and quit. Unless he has a strong personal relationship with God, he can literally go to pieces. The assistance of like-minded people can take a tremendous burden off of a leader. One must never doubt God's ability to provide for any emergency. Unless we believe in an unlimited God, we do not really believe in God at all!

Jealousy of Miriam and Aaron Against Moses (Num. 12:1–15)

The passage.—The Cushite woman whom Moses married was probably Zipporah. There was a time when she was not with Moses but her father brought her to join him again at Sinai. Up until this time Miriam, being an older sister, had a great influence on Moses' decisions. When his wife joined him, she probably took her place as the leading lady of the organizational team. In addition, her father offered advice to Moses which probably Miriam and Aaron resented.

The fact punishment was given to Miriam rather than Aaron implies she was the aggressor in the revolt. It was only when Moses pled for her to be spared that Jehovah agreed to lessen her punishment.

Special points.—It is not possible for us to be certain concerning the skin of the Cushite woman. It actually is a case of speculation and there is no real merit in pursuing the case.

Did Moses write the words in 12:3? In all probability he did not. Whatever our views concerning the authorship of the Pentateuch we certainly must have a concept of inspiration flexible enough to allow some man to insert this passage about Moses. Moses certainly did not write it about himself. Nothing is lost with reference to the authority of the Scripture if we admit that a scribe, either in the days of Moses, or as late as the time of the Exile, added this descriptive statement concerning Israel's great leader.

Truth for today.—Times have not changed. People still become jealous when their authority and prestige are threatened. God's leaders must constantly deal with followers who resent anyone "moving in on their territory" of being close to the leader. It is not easy to do it but we must follow the advice of Kipling who cautioned us that we should let "all men count with you but none too much."

Mission of the Spies and Its Sequel (Num. 12:16—14:45)

One spy was sent from each tribe but they are not the ones appointed as census takers in 1:5–15. They were not to fight any battles but merely to bring back a report about the land. Their forty-day trip over the entire land convinced them that it was desirable, but ten of the twelve felt it was impossible for the land to be conquered.

The minority report of Joshua and Caleb was refused, even though it was the optimistic recommendation and the one which should have spurred the people to action because of their faith in God as well as their desire for the "good land" that had been promised to them. There seems no doubt it was the descendants of Anak, the legendary giants who frightened the spies and even filled them with terror.

In spite of the pleas of Caleb and Joshua, the people refused to have faith. They began to murmur against Moses and Aaron. The Lord was displeased and threatened to disinherit the people and make of Moses' family a great nation to replace them. Moses interceded. God reconsidered, but the penalty was stern. No man over twenty years of age would be allowed to enter the Promised Land except the two spies who brought the favorable recommendation.

Alarmed by God's decree, the people then made an attempt to enter the land but it met with disaster. God was not with them. They were actually seeking to escape punishment instead of obeying God.

Special points.—Who were the Nephilim who are called the sons of Anak? Literally the word "Anak" means "sons of neck" which is a Hebrew idiom for the "long necked people." They lived in the South Country and were very tall and lanky. In 13:33 these sons of Anak are called the "Nephilim." This word is of uncertain meaning but is probably best translated "the giants" (Gen. 6:4). There are many extra biblical traditions concerning the enormous size and strength of a group of people that existed in this land and eventually settled in the vicinity of Hebron.

Truth for today.—The majority is not always right. Unless people are close to

God and disciplined by his word and will, the majority will seldom, if ever, be right. If our future is to be both secure and happy, we must base our choices on faith in the resources available to us because of our fellowship with God and our desire to let our life be a working out of his purpose.

Once a decision is made, the die is cast. An unstable multitude reacts emotionally rather than logically and can never be depended upon for rational action.

A leader must be strong or else he will be overpowered by "mob rule" and thwarted in his attempt to lead. He cannot be a despot or exploiter but he must stand firm with cool head and sweet spirit and insist people follow him even as he follows the Lord.

Laws Concerning Offerings, the Sabbath, and the Tassels (Num. 15:1–41)

The first thirty-one verses deal with laws concerning the offerings. They deal with the future—the time that the children of Israel will be in the land of Canaan. Two things are significant. First, there is a provision for unintentional sin. This was a real contingency because of the multitude of legal requirements. Second, the sojourner was on an equal basis with the regular Israelites both in privileges and in responsibilities.

Verses 32–35 seem severe when judged by modern standards. The sabbath breaker, even guilty of such a simple thing as gathering sticks, was to be stoned to death. Stern measures were necessary if the pure moral and ethical monotheism of Jehovah was to triumph over the type of worship which existed in Canaan.

The fringes on the garments were to remind the people constantly of God's commandments. Although the background of tassel wearing associated it

with magical charms, it was invested here with a valid religious significance.

Special points.—At first, it seems this chapter is out of place. It would be nearly forty years before these laws were relevant. But the Israelites had come through a traumatic experience. These laws would be a source of assurance the nation would not be destroyed in the wilderness. The day would come when they would be settled in their own land with their own culture and regulations from their God. This might bring only "small comfort" but it would be at least a hope for the future.

Truth for today.—God's redemptive love is in action even when days are dark. He is concerned with his people's hygienic customs as well as their religious ritual. Discipline is important. One should learn to wear its yoke early both in national and personal life. One can develop no better habit than that of being extremely "God-conscious" in every relationship and experience of life.

Rebellion Against Authority (Num. 16:1–50)

The people had already seen God deal with murmurings and uncooperative attitudes (11:1–3,4–35; 12:1–15). This feeling may have been building up among some of the Levites who resented being subordinate to Moses and Aaron. Korah was first cousin to Moses and Aaron. Their fathers were brothers.

When confronted with the problem, Moses fell on his face and appealed to God. He recognized the human ambition of Korah and his followers. It was not a matter of an open priesthood that Korah was seeking but rather he wished the position of Aaron. He desired "an exclusive dignity which he would gladly perpetuate and hold."

Moses took this matter very seriously. They blamed him for bringing them out of Egypt and also with the fact they had not gone immediately into the Promised Land. Moses defended himself but when the Lord stated his purpose to destroy the entire congregation he interceded for them.

When the plague broke out, Moses sent Aaron quickly to stand "between the dead and the living" and make atonement for them. In spite of the pressure against him, Moses maintained a sweet spirit in standing firm as Israel's leader.

Special points.—It may seem to us that God was unbearably cruel, but the issue was great. Frustration had set in among the people. They realized the decision they had made sentenced a whole generation to death in the wilderness. God realized he must not let his leadership bear the brunt because they were not to blame. The people must be shown that Moses and Aaron were leading with the approval of God and their authority must not be challenged.

Truth for today.—We live in a time when strong authority is questioned. There is, of course, a danger in investing mere human beings with too much authority. A person with a small spirit is intoxicated when he is given too much power but the other side is true also—little people resent authority over them.

God must have leaders. They must stay close to God and be very careful that they do not become filled with pride. On the other hand, "mass rule" is anarchy. Even within a democracy there are guidelines for authority. Leaders must be respected and obeyed.

Budding of Aaron's Rod (Num. 17:1–13)

The passage.—During the rebellion of Korah it took power to conquer the tumult and restore order. It was in a sense "negative truth" directed to the people that no one who is not of Aaron's seed could come near and burn incense before the Lord.

This section is a bit more "positive" in its teaching. The people must understand in a quiet but unquestionable way that God had chosen the Levites to be his ministers in a unique sense.

The vindication is actually twofold. Aaron's name, written on the rod representing the tribe of Levi, gave special recognition both to the tribe and also to Aaron. All Israel must recognize the unique function of the Levites, but the Levites, in turn, must recognize the unique position of Aaron.

Special points.—Verses 12–13 should not be considered as a misplaced fragment. They form a natural transition to the next chapter. The people recognized that unrestricted access to the Holy Place would be dangerous for them. The next chapter deals with the specific duties and responsibilities of the Levites. The two sections join together in a most natural manner.

Truth for today.—Religion is more than cringing before the power and majesty of God. It is life, beauty, and fruitfulness. The eradication of sin is not enough. Those who serve God must have thoughts that are holy and purposes that are noble. God's leaders are to lead people into fruit-bearing through spiritual ministries. There are various stages in the Christian life (budding, blossoming, and bearing of fruit) of growth in grace and in knowledge of the Lord.

Obligations and Revenues of the Priests and Levites (Num. 18:1–32)

The passage.—The first section (vv. 1–7) give the particular duties of priests and Levites. The priests are to have oversight of the sanctuary but the Levites are to help them. It is made clear that only the priests (family of Aaron) could come in contact with the sacred utensils of the altar. The Levites were to serve the Aaronites and were in a subordinate role. No one but the priests and Levites were permitted to approach the tent of meeting. Only the priests were permitted to approach the altar or the holy of holies.

Verses 8–21 deal with the provisions for supporting both the priests and the Levites. All of the "holy things" would be the property of the priests. This was, however, limited later by certain regulations. In verses 21–24 the tithes are given for the Levites but in verses 25–32 they are commanded to pay tithes of the tithes to the priests. This latter tithe was to be brought directly to Aaron.

Special points.—The "covenant of salt" in verse 19 was considered an unbreakable bond. The eating of salt, in ancient days, or any minute portion of food which belonged to another man constituted a sacred bond between them. It was an "irretrievable intermixture of themselves" and would, therefore, point to an unbreakable covenant. It may be that the fact that salt is a preservative and indicated durability might be at least in the background of this concept.

Truth for today.—God's work must be supported financially. Those who are dedicated in a specific way to carrying on the functions of worship must be cared for by the voluntary gifts of the people who worship. People respect things when they pay for them. They love God's work more when they contribute to it. An old cliche says, "Preaching that's not paid for is poor preaching."

Procedure for Purification (Num. 19:1–22)

The passage.—Verses 1–10 deal with the ritual concerning the red heifer. Two things are distinctive. First, offerings were customarily of male animals. Also, the priest has a limited participation in this ceremony. This priest (v. 7) and the

one who does the burning (v. 8) were considered unclean after performing their task. The gathering and storing of the ashes must be performed by a third person who then became unclean. There is a certain air of mystery about this passage and much we do not know about the local conditions but the constant emphasis is on purity. God considered it important enough to require strict regulations.

Verses 11–22 give details concerning purification of one who has had contact with the dead. Ancient people regarded leprosy, bodily discharges, and contact with a corpse as causing uncleanness. They were very cautious about any contagion because of physical contact.

Special points.—There is much we do not know even today concerning the mysteries of the body especially as related to birth and death. The ancient mind conceived of powerful and mysterious forces at work and felt the spirit of the dead round about the corpse to do harm to anyone nearby. A passage such as this one may seem entirely irrelevant to modern-day living and yet we should be cautious about "writing it off" completely as unrelated to our day. Much study is being done and new discovery is constantly being made within the realm of the spirit. We may some day find these ancient people, under inspiration of God, were guided in a strange and mysterious way to wisdom that was beneficial for them and their day.

Truth for today.—The modern world is coming to discover afresh the importance of environmental purity. All ecology must begin with personal standards of cleanliness. Although the particular method of purification used by the Hebrews may not be the most practical for today, we should, nevertheless, make an all-out effort for "clean living and high thinking." If these crude methods of the limited Hebrews could sustain them through forty years of wilderness living, how much more can we, with our modern technology, make our land a fit dwelling place for our millions.

Death of Miriam, Refusal of Edomites, Sin of Moses, and Death of Aaron (Num. 20:1–29)

The passage.—The decree that no one "twenty years old and upward" (14:29) could enter the Promised Land applied to Miriam, Aaron, and even to Moses. This section tells of the death of Miriam (v. 1) and Aaron (vv. 23–29) and the sin of Moses (vv. 10–13) which disqualified him from entering the Promised Land. The sin of Moses has been variously interpreted. The best explanation seems to be that Moses failed to exalt God and inferred that he (and perhaps Aaron also) were bringing the water through their own power.

The request of Moses to the king of Edom for passage through the land and the obstinate refusal (vv. 14–21) reveal the continuing bitter spirit that existed between these two nations descended from the two sons of Isaac. It seems there is no more bitter relationship than between brethren or near relations that are alienated.

Special points.—The chronology of the entire forty years wandering in the wilderness is difficult. In chapters 13 and 14 the people were at Kadesh. In 20:1 they are back again at Kadesh. We have no account of the time element between these two sojourns. Perhaps 20:1 is meant to be a summary and condensation of the entire time at Kadesh. The verse speaks of the "first month" but is silent as to which year it occurred. Most scholars believe Miriam died after the approximately thirty-eight years of wandering rather than at the beginning of it.

Truth for today.—Even God's leaders must abide by the rules for the people. From a human standpoint, it seems unfair that Miriam, Aaron, and Moses (especially Moses) could not share in the triumph of entering the Promised Land. Many times, however, this story has been repeated in history.

A leader cannot lead the people any farther in doing God's will than he is willing to do. It is not fair to blame Moses and Aaron with the people's disbelief, but we are all "bound together in a bundle of life" and must pay the price of living together. Innocent people suffer because bad people make decisions that affect the group. God buries his workmen but his work goes on.

Final Wanderings Preceding Arrival in Moab (Num. 21:1–35)

The passage.—This section records three battles fought by Israel while enroute to the Plains of Moab. It also tells how fiery serpents bit the people and they were spared through Moses' prayer and God's instructions to erect a brass serpent on a pole for the people to look at and be healed. One other section (vv. 10–20) gives in detail the camping places along the way.

The battle against the king of Arad was fought in the same general vicinity as the abortive attempt to enter the Promised Land nearly forty years earlier (14:40–45). The people in this vicinity could have remembered a generation earlier or the king of Edom could have sent word to beware of them. It was necessary, however, that these people be eliminated for Israel's security. The battle against Sihon, king of the Amorites (21:21–32) and Og, king of Bashan (21:33–35) was necessary in order to bring the Israelites along their way to the Plains of Moab from which they would enter Canaan. The Amorites had fought the Moabites earlier and taken some of their territory. Thus the Israelites in defeating the Amorites actually took territory that had formerly belonged to Moab.

The account of the fiery serpents is simple and rather obvious in interpretation. It has been made the basis for typologies concerning the plan of salvation in the New Testament. Jesus referred to it in his interview with Nicodemus.

Special points.—It is not fair to associate the story of the brazen serpent with traditions and superstitions of the neighboring nations. God can use any method he wishes to accomplish his purpose. If he wished to work through a current symbol and appropriate the significance of it to reinforce faith in himself, we can accept it as a part of God's redemptive activity. The image was not the end in itself. It stood for the one whose power was behind it.

Truth for today.—The most important message in the Old Testament is that God is at work through those he has chosen to bring redemption to the world. He protected Israel miraculously because he planned to use Israel in his divine plan of the ages. Since we do not know all of the geographical facts, we cannot explain in detail every event. It is reassuring, however, to know that God is "on the field when he seems most invisible" watching over his chosen people and bringing his purposes to fruition.

Account of Balak and Balaam (Num. 22: 1—24:25)

The passage.—The soothsayer from Pethor is one of the strangest and yet most interesting characters in the Old Testament. His relationship with Balak, king of Moab, covers the first three chapters of this third and last division of the

book of Numbers. The Israelites were encamped in the Plains of Moab east of Jericho and the Jordan River.

Balak was alarmed at the success of the Israelites against the neighboring countries. He decided to enlist the help of a prophet (more of a seer or soothsayer) who must have been of great reputation for he lived, according to the general verdict of scholarship, a traveling distance of nearly three hundred and fifty miles. Balak seems to have shared the general feeling of that day that a spoken word, either to bless or curse, by a prophet was the instrument of its own fulfilment.

The first group sent by Balak (22:1–6) was not successful (vv. 7–14) in persuading Balaam to come curse Israel. He, therefore, sent a second time (vv. 15–21) and met with success—at least Balaam agreed to come and visit the land of Balak and view the situation. Each time the emissaries came Balaam sought the will of God. The first time he was told definitely he should not go. The second time he was given limited permission. God told him to go with the men but warned him only to do what he was told by God.

The journey to Moab (vv. 22–35) was a trip fraught with difficulties. Although God told Balaam to go with the men, he was displeased with Balaam for going. It may be that Balaam misunderstood God or that he had convinced himself, since the material rewards were great, that God had told him to go. It has been suggested that perhaps God permitted him to go but since Balaam knew he could not curse the people and did not tell Balak's committee immediately, he was guilty of misrepresentation and, therefore, displeased the Lord.

Balaam's confrontation with "the angel of the Lord" was seemingly an

4. Jericho, excavation of old city (see Num. 22:1)

encounter with a temporary appearance of God in human form. We must be cautious as we read and not imagine the significant figure of the story is the animal. It is the presence of God and his words to Balaam.

The meeting of Balak and Balaam (vv. 36–41) revealed two different personalities. Balak chided the prophet for his delay in coming and received a "chilling assurance" that any oracle would be the will of God and not a word purchased by Balak. Balaam delivered three oracles concerning Israel. All of them were displeasing to Balak.

The first (23:1–12) caused Balak to complain bitterly. The second (vv. 13–26) called forth a plea from Balak, "Neither curse them at all, nor bless them at all." The third (23:27—24:13) aroused Balak's anger. Balaam then uttered short oracles concerning Moab and Edom (24:14–25), Amalek (v. 20), the Kenite (vv. 21–22), and the Kittim (vv. 23–25).

Balaam showed keen insight in his appreciation for the Israelites. It is quite significant that he, although not a Jewish prophet, was used of Jehovah in a definite way to further his redemptive program. Israel was God's people. No

107

power could block the determined will of the Lord to work out his purpose for the world through his chosen channel.

Special points.—Did Balaam's animal actually speak? Did Balaam actually see the angel of the Lord standing with his sword drawn? There have been reliably documented experiences of animals seeing that which was invisible to human eyes. There is no reason to doubt that this could have happened in Balaam's day.

Did God appear in human form? We should remember that God was working out his purpose in history for the redemption of the world. In the early stages of revelation a number of unusual events occurred. They are unexplainable except in terms of God speaking in a definite way to people in order to further his plan for mankind's salvation.

Truth for today.—God often uses people to accomplish his will who are not in the full and direct line of divine revelation. Paul spoke of those who "preach Christ of contention" (Phil. 1:16) and assured us that he rejoiced when Christ was lifted up and honored in any way. We should always be careful not to condemn those who are our "competitors" in preaching the gospel. Jesus reminded one of his disciples "he that is not against us is for us" (Luke 9:50).

There have always been plots and conspiracies to destroy the work of God. Times are different now but men are not. No combination of evil forces, however, can destroy God's purpose in the world. Base and desperate measures have been and still are being used but these attacks will not permanently succeed. Children of God find their safety in his power and his promises. Great dangers can become noble triumphs if we place our faith in the God whose methods may vary but whose essential character will never change.

Terrible Results of Idolatry and Immorality (Num. 25:1–18)

Although it was the Moabite women who led in enticing the Israelites into sexual impurity, the latter were not without blame. An Israelite was so bold as to bring one of the Midianitish women (who joined in the temptations and orgies) into plain sight of Moses and the tent of meeting (v. 6). Phinehas took strong measures to correct this abuse but he prevented the terrible plague that had begun from expanding any further.

Phinehas, the grandson of Aaron, pleased the Lord with his zeal for keeping both the people and the worship pure. We cannot be sure exactly how far Zimri (v. 14) took Cozbi into the worship place. Verse 6 speaks of the "tent of meeting" while verse 8 speaks of "the inner room." The Hebrew word in verse 8 may refer merely to the tent of meeting or to an inner part of it. The mere mention of these places, however, certainly sets the story in a religious framework and indicates the unblushing audacity of the people in their sin.

Special points.—One should always refer to 31:15–16 when reading chapter 25. The regular stories concerning Balaam tell nothing of his counseling the Moabites to lay temptation in front of the Israelites. This does not, however, mean the account in 31:16 is untrustworthy. There is every reason to believe this conniving prophet may have at least received some fee for his shrewd suggestion that though he could not curse the people he could suggest a way to lead them to sin and arouse God's wrath.

Truth for today.—The weakness of the flesh is real. No person should ever feel that he can relax his guard even briefly. One must not depend on the decision of the moment to remain pure. He should have a preconceived set of values and make a firm decision that he will not depart from this standard. If one depends on the whim of the moment, he is likely to give in at a weak time in his life.

The Second Census (Num. 26:1–65)

There was an additional reason for the second numbering of the people. It was not only to determine the number of fighting men but also to serve as a basis for dividing the land of Canaan. Territory must be allotted to each tribe and it was only fair that the size of the inheritance would be according to the number of people in the tribe. The location, however, would be "by lot" (vv. 55–56).

After forty years wandering in the wilderness, the number of men eligible for military service showed a decline of only 1,820. Five tribes (Reuben, Simeon, Gad, Ephraim, and Naphtali) showed a decrease while seven tribes (Judah, Issachar, Zebulon, Manasseh, Benjamin, Dan, and Asher showed an increase. The declines showed 61,020 while the increases showed 59,200. The tribes showing the greatest gains were Manasseh, Asher, and Benjamin. Simeon was the third largest in the first census but lost 37,000 and became the smallest of the twelve in the second census. The Levites showed an increase of 1,000. The Levites were included in the census if they were a month old or more rather than twenty years of age (the requirement for military service).

The ultimate purpose of counting the people was to preserve the purity of Jehovah worship. A special note at the end of the chapter points out that only two were left of the original adult population—Caleb and Joshua. These were the two who had faith in God forty years earlier and believed the Promised Land could have been taken at that time with God's help.

Special points.—All of the figures are in round numbers. It is quite inconceivable that every one of the tribes could have come out this way. We should note that the thought pattern of the Semitic-Hebrew people was often "general and non-specific" rather than meticulously technical in computer fashion. In other words, these figures are reliable but they are rounded off to the nearest point in some cases—perhaps in all.

Truth for today.—God is with his people and constantly watching over them for their good. He must keep worship pure in order for it to survive. A practical approach was to be aware of the fighting force and also have a systematic basis for settling the people in the new land. Organization is still important today—not to replace spirituality but to complement it and put it to the greatest possible use in extending its influence.

New Inheritance Laws and a New Leader (Num. 27:1–23)

The passage.—Verses 1–11 deal with the perpetually controversial matter of a woman's legal, social, and economic position. A parallel problem is the passing of land from a family because no heirs are present to receive it.

The daughters of Zelophehad insisted it was not fair for their father to have no heritage because he had no sons. Earlier law had held that only men could own property. A new law was proclaimed by Moses, after conference with God, which assured a man his inheritance could pass through his daughters and made even further provision if he had no children. The levirate marriage law (Deut. 25:5–10) made further provision. Numbers 36:1–12 should be noted in connection with this passage.

Verses 12–23 relates Moses' conversation with God. He is allowed to view the land which he cannot enter because of his disobedience. With a sweet spirit, he asked God to appoint his successor. Joshua is chosen, brought before Eleazar the priest and then before the congregation. The solemn act by which Moses placed his approval on Joshua may be compared in some ways to the Levites laying their hands on the animals. The Levites identified themselves with their sacrifice and Moses identified himself with his successor. Although Moses symbolically transferred his authority to Joshua, the latter was limited. God never talked "face to face" with him as he did with Moses.

Special points.—Israel was not a static community. There was a constant need for rethinking of laws because of the changing situations among the people. The basic principle concerning ownership was that the Lord wanted a continuation of landed property within a specific family.

Truth for today.—The clearer revelation of God and his will man has had, the kinder he has been to woman. The best friend woman has today is Jesus Christ. It is because of Jesus that she is no longer chattel or man's plaything but now his loving companion and partner in every sense of the word.

Regulations Concerning Worship and Sacrifice (Num. 28:1—29:39)

These two chapters set out the public sacrifices for the sacred year. It has been called a "cultic calendar."

There were three special offerings mentioned: The Daily Offering (vv. 3–8) required the bringing of a he lamb both as a morning and as an evening offering; The Sabbath Offering (vv. 9–10) required the bringing of seven he lambs, two young bullocks, one ram, and one

he goat as a sin offering.

The Feast of Unleavened Bread (vv. 16–25) was the Passover. It was related to the release from Egypt. Following the Passover on the fourteenth day of the first month, there was a seven-day feast of unleavened bread. In addition to the regular morning and evening offerings, there was to be a daily offering of seven he lambs, two young bullocks, one ram, and a he goat for a sin offering. The Feast of Weeks (vv. 26–31) called for the same meat offerings as the week of unleavened bread. It was a harvest festival.

The seventh month was important. The first day began their new year. The tenth day was a holy convocation known as the Day of Atonement. Each of these required seven he lambs, one young bullock, one ram, and one he goat as a sin offering.

The final feast, an eight-day festival, was the famous Feast of Tabernacles. There was a sliding scale of sacrifices downward over the eight-day period. The size of the offerings exceeded that of any other feast. Even after the Israelites settled in the Promised Land, they continued to dwell in booths to remind them of God's goodness in times of stress. This also was a harvest feast.

In addition to the animal sacrifices, there were required offerings of meal, oil, and wine to accompany the meat offerings. These were regular offerings and were not to take the place of free-will offerings or the offerings of any particular vow.

Special points.—These ritual requirements may seem irrelevant to us but there is a basic value in them. God did not want the public gatherings to become mechanical rituals nor a time of unbridled license and revelry. The people were reminded as they brought their offerings that they were subject to the lordship of the one who had redeemed them from slavery and who held a peculiar claim upon their lives.

Truth for today.—God's work is worthy of financial support. We need special seasons for special emphases and we need an organized plan of worship to help us plan our program. A "free lance" type of worship and giving of gifts does not develop strong stability in one's religious life. There was ample room for one to give "as he felt led" after he had fulfilled the minimum requirements of supporting the basic work of the Lord. So, today the structured institutions have a basic claim on our loyalty and financial support before we give our "freewill offerings" to those independent causes with which we identify because of their emotional appeal.

The Law of Vows for Men and Women (Num. 30:1–16)

The passage.—Only verse 2 concerns the vows and oaths of a man. He must observe all made without exception—both the promise to give something to God (vow) or a prohibition one lays upon himself to refrain from the doing of a deed (bond or pledge).

The remainder of the chapter deals with the responsibility of a woman. The chapter deals with the following situation: (1) An unmarried woman in her father's house (vv. 3–5); (2) a woman who carries a vow or pledge into a marriage (vv. 6–8); (3) a widow or divorcee (v. 9); (4) a married woman (vv. 10–15).

The basic principle is that the woman is subject to masculine authority. The man of the house may veto a woman's decision, but if he fails to do so when he learns of it, he forfeits his right to do it later. If he fails to veto the woman, losing his right to do so, then changes his mind and makes her vows or pledges

null and void, he will be guilty of breaking the vow and suffer the consequences himself. The new bridegroom has the privilege of voiding his wife's vow if he wishes, but must do so immediately. The widow or divorcee is the head of her own social unit.

Truth for today.—Promises are important! On the other hand, a woman is wise to have a definite understanding with her father or husband before obligating herself for a major responsibility in the Lord's service. A woman at home, whether single or married, has responsibilities that are uniquely feminine. We have seen some liberation of the woman but the basic policy of "checking with the man of the house" is still good common sense!

The Holy War Against Midian (Num. 31:1–54)

This was not merely a war to spread the faith. It was for the survival of moral monotheism. The corrupting influence of the enemy must be completely eradicated! Moses closed his public career with this significant event.

Since Phinehas was the leader in turning back God's wrath previously (25:11), he was chosen to go with the twelve thousand troops either as commander or chaplain. This protected his father, Eleazar, the high priest, from contact with the dead.

The victory was decisive! Not an Israelite was lost! Although they slew every male, the women and children were brought, along with the booty, to Moses, Eleazar, and the congregation. Moses commanded every male child and every woman, except the virgins, to be killed. A purifying process was established.

Half the booty went to the soldiers and half to the congregation. The soldiers paid one five hundredth to Eleazar, the priest, while the congregation paid one fiftieth to the Levites for their support. In addition, the army officers brought gifts to Moses and to Eleazar from the jewels and precious metals as an offering for atonement.

Special points.—The severe treatment of the enemy is, of course, sub-Christian but these people lived before the fulness of revelation in Jesus Christ. This passage cannot be used as justification for cruel treatment of prisoners of war today. We should remember, however, that God's redemptive plan depended on Israel being usable and contamination with the immorality of Baal worship would have meant her disqualification as God's unique channel.

The reason Israel won such a decisive victory and never lost a man is not difficult to explain. In all probability, it was a surprise attack and caught the enemy completely unaware.

Truth for today.—When the call of duty comes, all private interests must be subordinated. All the gains of life must be shared with God so his work may be carried on in the world.

Assignment of Transjordan to Reuben and Gad (Num. 32:1–42)

The passage.—The request of Reuben and Gad was not, at first, favorably received. Moses recognized the fading of pioneer spirit and the arising of schemes for success in the grazing and dairy business. He foresaw a dwindling of enthusiasm on the part of all twelve tribes and a fragmenting into individual interests. This could lead to a repetition of Kadesh-barnea.

Although the two tribes assured Moses of their willingness to help the others conquer the land west of the Jordan, it is doubtful they would have done so without his strong arraignment. Moses accepted their proposal and restated the

terms clearly so as to avoid misunderstanding.

In addition to constructing folds (rough enclosures of stone piled on each other) for their sheep, the two tribes reconstructed and fortified cities which had been destroyed. Some of these are mentioned in verse 3 as territory which motivated the desire for the land. It could be that some new cities were founded.

Special points.—The half tribe of Manasseh is not mentioned until verse 33. There is no reason, however, to consider these verses as an independent campaign of Manasseh later after the death of Moses as some radical scholars have done. In all probability the half tribe decided to join the group later and was accepted on the same basis.

Truth for today.—There is always the danger we shall forget the primary goals in life and begin to pursue "second-rate causes." It is important to keep our integrity by remaining faithful to promises that we make.

An Annotated Summary of Journey from Egypt to Plains of Moab and Instructions Concerning Inhabitants of Canaan (Num. 33:1–56)

The passage.—This review of Israel's route is one of the few passages in the Pentateuch attributed directly to Moses. Forty-two places are named. A large number of them are not mentioned elsewhere in the Pentateuch while several occurring in 21:12–20 are not included here. In spite of the omissions and difficulty of locating many places with certainty, the general route is clear because a few well-known places are mentioned. It is the general verdict of scholarship that verse 36 tells of the gathering of the tribes after the wilderness wanderings. The encampment along Jordan was probably about five miles long. This presented a formidable front and caused uneasiness to those across the Jordan.

Verses 50–56 make it clear the Israelites would not "receive" the inheritance unless they completely exterminated the enemy. Israel's God could not share this land with any other religious faith or concept.

Special points.—The same name sometimes indicates a city while at other times an area. According to Deuteronomy 10:6, Aaron died and was buried in Moserah which is another form of Moseroth (Num. 33:30). According to Numbers 33:38–40 and 20:27–28, Aaron died and was buried on Mount Horeb. In all probability Aaron died in the vicinity of Kadesh near the border of Edom.

Truth for today.—Records of past events are helpful. They remind us of God's blessings and also warn us concerning life's mistakes. The obstacles of life contribute to our growth. It is far more important to develop morally than have physical conveniences. We should be zealous in waging war against any sinful enticements that would lower our personal standards.

Boundaries of Canaan Established (Num. 34:1–29)

These boundaries were for territory west of Jordan. Two and one-half tribes had already been allocated land on the east side. The eastern and western boundaries are clearly stated as the River Jordan and the Great Sea (Mediterranean). The northern and southern limits are a little more difficult to establish with modern-day geography.

It was not until David's time that these boundaries actually became secure. At the height of Solomon's power he "reigned over all the kings from the river even unto the land of the Philistines and to the border of Egypt" (2

Chron. 9:26). This "river" was the Euphrates and included a much larger territory than was given to it in the day of Moses.

The land was divided according to population but also by lot. A man was chosen from each tribe to assist in the division. These men were appointed by Moses, upon instruction of God, rather than by the people. It is a safe assumption, however, that these were men who were respected as leaders by the tribes. This is the natural interpretation of verse 18.

Appointment of Levitical Cities and Special Ordinances (Num. 35:1–34)

The passage.—The Levites were to receive forty-eight cities. Six of them were to be cities of refuge. The dimensions of the pasture surrounding the city would be over two hundred acres.

The cities of refuge provided protection for a killer while the death was being investigated. The old tribal custom of blood revenge was dangerous. It could lead to a chain reaction. The cities were to be located in such a way that lengthy travel would not be necessary.

The ultimate authority concerning the fate of a killer was to be the congregation. The death sentence, however, could be decreed only if there was more than one witness. No one who was guilty of wilful murder could go free by the payment of a fine.

Special points.—Joshua made the actual assignment of the Levitical cities. He allocated four to each tribe with the exception of Naphtali who contributed three while the tribes of Judah and Simeon gave nine. Records are not available as to how soon the Levites began to actually dwell in these cities or how completely the orders were carried out. In the Period of Judges there were Levites living in places other than their cities. Moses was stating an ideal and we should not be disturbed to learn that the ideal did not come into existence automatically, if ever.

Truth for today.—God has a tender regard for human life. Even one who is guilty of a crime is entitled to a fair trial. Although the analogy is not complete in every respect, these "cities of refuge" symbolize the security of those who flee to Christ as a refuge from sin.

Law Concerning Marrying of Heiresses (Num. 36:1–12)

The passage.—This section should be studied in connection with 27:1–11. There seemed to be a "loophole" in the inheritance laws in the earlier section. Property could pass outside the tribe through the marriage of a woman who had inherited it. The solution was that no woman should marry one of another tribe. In this way no inheritance would pass from one tribe to another. The daughters of Zelophehad assured the property they controlled would stay as a part of Manasseh's portion by marrying their cousins.

Special points.—The solution offered seems to be very narrow and could be interpreted as fostering the "isolated clan spirit" but in this period of developing legislation and application it was necessary. The Jewish people emphasized purity in their religion and a dread of defilement. They were also "purists" in connection with land ownership. They were determined to hold tenaciously to a principle that had value for a developing nation.

Truth for today.—Marriage is an important thing. It not only unites a man and woman but also families. Careful consideration of the background of both should be given by a couple before entering into a relationship which should be lifelong.

Summary (Num. 36:13)

A similar verse concludes the book of Leviticus. This has led scholars to believe they may have been added reverently by a scribe when the Pentateuch was divided into its present five parts. Although this is only a theory, it can be accepted without doing violence to one's concept of revelation and inspiration. We do note, however, that the writer is careful to emphasize the important place of Moses in the giving of God's commandments to the Israelites.

DEUTERONOMY

Donald F. Ackland

INTRODUCTION

The fifth and last book of the Pentateuch is known as Deuteronomy, a word that means "second law-giving." Examination of the contents reveals that it is not merely a repetition of laws previously given, but a commentary on those laws given in spoken form.

Deuteronomy consists of three messages delivered by Moses to the Hebrew people as a preparation for their entry into the Promised Land. Two major reasons occasioned these messages: Moses' knowledge that he would not accompany the people across Jordan (4:21) and the changed circumstances that awaited them in the land of the Canaanites.

The generation of Israelites that left Egypt under Moses' command had perished in the wilderness. A new generation, with no personal memories of the Exodus or the giving of the law at Sinai, was about to begin a critical chapter in that young nation's history. They needed to be reminded of their past, prepared for a new life-style as they ceased to be wanderers and became settlers, and warned against their coming confrontation with idolatry.

Deuteronomy played an important part in the later history of Israel. It was the book that was found (in whole or in part) in the Temple during Josiah's reign, occasioning a national revival (2 Kings 22–23). Our Lord's familiarity with Deuteronomy is revealed by many references that he made to it. Notable among these was his use of the book in his replies to each of the three wilderness temptations (Matt. 4:1–11).

The book of Deuteronomy claims to preserve "the words which Moses spake" (1:1). While no specific claim is made that Moses himself recorded all these words, there are references in the book to the writing of "this law" (31:9) by Moses. Substantial parts of Deuteronomy would thereby seem to be attributed to him as author.

By whom and when the book was put into the form in which we have it now is a matter for scholarly inquiry. We have every reason to believe, however, that behind the book stands the historic figure of the man whose words it perpetuates.

I. MOSES' FIRST SPEECH (DEUT. 1:1—4:43)

The book begins with a brief statement of location (1:1–5). The RSV corrects *on this side of Jordan* to read "beyond the Jordan" (vv. 1,5), that is, east of the river in the land of Moab. This was the last camp ground of the Israelites before commencing the occupation of Canaan. Not all the places named can be identified, but they were obviously connected with the wilderness journey, which is summarized from Sinai (Horeb) to Kadesh-barnea.

Before confronting the people with their obligations to God, Moses rehearsed in 1:6—3:29 some of his undertakings in their behalf. Reviewing the wilderness journey in three stages, he

115

began with their experiences from Sinai to Kadesh-barnea.

Wilderness Journey: First Stage (1:6–46)

The passage.—After nearly a year at Sinai, God gave the command to march that Israel might possess its promised home. An early step by Moses was the organization of the people into units over which officers were appointed to administer the law and preserve order. Although the initiative in this matter is attributed to Jethro in Exodus 18:13–26, it was implemented by Moses, who clearly desired to give the credit to God.

Eleven days (1:2) after they left Sinai, the people reached Kadesh-barnea and the border of the territory God intended for their future home (vv. 19–21). There occurred the tragic demonstration of unbelief in God's ability to fulfil his promise that resulted in forty years of wilderness wandering (vv. 22–46). The full story of this act of faithlessness is told in Numbers 13–14. The considerable emphasis given by Moses to the incident was intended as a warning against future lapses into unbelief and disloyalty.

Special points.—The Israelites could have entered Canaan eleven days after leaving Sinai (1:2) if their faith had not failed. Instead, they wandered for forty years in the wilderness. Similarly, they were promised a territory (v. 7) far more extensive than they ever possessed. The reason why they came short of God's best is stated: *ye did not believe the Lord your God* (v. 32). *Caleb* (v. 36) and *Joshua* (v. 38; 3:21,28) were rewarded for their faith by being allowed to enter Canaan.

Truth for today.—The realization of God's purposes of blessing is for those who trust and obey. The attainment of God's best is dependent on courageous faith.

Wilderness Journey: Second Stage (2:1–37)

The passage.—Kadesh-barnea and Heshbon were the starting and concluding points of this stage. Moses recalled the passage through the lands of Moab and Ammon, occupied by the descendants of Esau (v. 4) and Lot (v. 19) respectively. The instruction given was, "Meddle not with them" (v. 5). God had given Moab and Ammon their lands of which he made himself protector. This did not apply, however, to the land of the Amorites (vv. 22–37). When Sihon, king of Heshbon, refused to sell provisions to the traveling Israelites and denied passage through his territory, his land was conquered.

Special points.—For the moral problem in the extermination of the Amorites see note on 7:2.

Truth for today.—God's sovereignty over all nations is indicated in his protection of Moab and Ammon as well as in the judgment of the Amorites. Because he had special purposes for Israel, he accorded that nation peculiar favors; but all peoples are his and are subjects of his mercy as well as his judgments.

Wilderness Journey: Third Stage (3:1–29)

The passage.—The final stage of the journey was from Heshbon to "the valley over against Beth-peor" (v. 29). Og, king of Bashan, offered armed resistance to the Israelites and suffered the same fate as Sihon (vv. 1–11). Moses divided this conquered territory, east of Jordan, between the tribes of Reuben and Gad and the half tribe of Manasseh (vv. 12–22). The condition was that they stay with the main force of Israel until Canaan was subdued.

Moses closed the opening part of his first message on an autobiographical note (vv. 21–29). He told how he had pleaded with God to be allowed to enter the Promised Land. For the reason he was denied this privilege see Numbers 20:7–12. Moses' plea was refused. He was told to appoint a new leader, Joshua, for the entry into the land (v. 28).

Special points.—Og was apparently the only survivor of a race of giants who are called Zamzummims in 2:20. It was people like these who scared the spies when they first explored the land (Num. 13:33). The size of Og's bedstead, which apparently still existed at the time the record was compiled (v. 11), was 13½ by 6 feet.

In saying, "The Lord was wroth with me for your sakes" (v. 26), Moses did not mean that he was punished for the people's sins but to furnish them a warning. They needed to learn that the God of deliverance is also the God of judgment and that he is no respecter of persons.

The Lord's Expectation (4:1–43)

The passage.—God's leadership blessings required response from those who received them. "Now therefore hearken" (v. 1) was Moses' introduction to an appeal for respect for and obedience to God-given laws (vv. 1–13). Knowledge of God and the possession of his law should be regarded as a precious national inheritance to be passed on from generation to generation (v. 9).

The greatest danger encountered in Canaan would be inducement to idolatry. The people of the land were notorious for their depraved forms of worship. Hence Moses appealed to the Israelites to remember how the Lord had brought them out of Egypt (v. 20) and the covenant into which they had entered (v. 23) and so avoid the contamination of idols (vv. 14–24). Not to do so would bring certain punishment (vv. 25–31). However, their loyalty to God should

not be based on fear but on gratitude for his great goodness (vv. 32–40). Few Old Testament passages more beautifully express God's blessings on Israel than this. The RSV effectively brings out its depth of meaning.

This section concludes with a reference to cities of refuge (vv. 41–43), more adequately described in 19:1–13 (see discussion).

Special points.—The word "cleave" (v. 4) belongs to a vocabulary of tenderness that is characteristic of Deuteronomy in describing the relationship of men to God. In Genesis 2:24 the word is used of the marriage relationship. Here it describes those who remained faithful in an apostasy recorded in Numbers 25:1–5.

An important Old Testament concept of God is contained in v. 12—"The Lord spoke to you out of the midst of the fire; you heard the sound of words, but saw no form; there was only a voice" (RSV). The very circumstances in which God entered into covenant with his people at Sinai forbade any attempt to reproduce him in visible form.

Truth for today.—Our experience of God's goodness is the ground on which we are enjoined to love and honor him. So the New Testament epistles invariably proceed from instruction on God's redemptive work to exhortation to appropriate response in holiness of life.

A New Testament counterpart of verse 12 is John 4:24 (RSV): "God is spirit, and those who worship him must worship in spirit and truth." Thus our Lord sustained and amplified the truth Moses stated.

II. MOSES' SECOND SPEECH (DEUT. 4:44—28:68)

The second and longest speech begins with a historical introduction similar to 1:1–5. Moses was approaching his restatement of the law, but to the end of chapter 11 continued to emphasize God's past dealings as reasons for future obedience.

The covenant with God is presented in 5:1—11:32. This is an important concept in Deuteronomy. At Sinai, the ex-slaves of Egypt pledged themselves to serve loyally the God who had delivered them. The test of their sincerity would be their response to divinely-given commandments. At their final camp before entering Palestine, Moses called on their children and grandchildren to renew this solemn contract (11:26–32).

The Ten Commandments (5:1–33)

The passage.—Moses restated the Ten Commandments (vv. 6–21) with minor, but significant, variations from the original version (Ex. 20). He recalled the reactions of the people to the awesome manifestations of God that accompanied the giving of the law (vv. 22–27). Fire is, throughout the Bible, a symbol of the divine presence. The people's acceptance of the covenant was indicated by their statement, "we will hear it, and do it" (v. 27). God, in turn, promised blessings for obedience (vv. 28–33). But the past conduct of the Israelites occasioned misgivings as to the ability of the people to fulfil their part of the covenant: "O that there were such an heart in them" (v. 29).

Special points.—Three modifications of the Ten Commandments are found here. The reason for keeping the sabbath was changed from God's seventh-day rest to the Exodus event (v. 15). Thus the way was prepared for the Christian adoption of the first day of the week for worship purposes, since this day commemorated the completion of Christ's work of deliverance in his resurrection.

Priority was given to "thy neighbour's wife" above his other possessions (v. 21).

Some think this marked progress in the status of women. It may, however, have been a warning against following the low sexual standards of the Canaanites. The addition of "his field" (v. 21) was necessitated by the change from a nomadic to an agricultural life-style.

The Faith of Israel (6:1–25)

The passage.—Summarizing the faith of Israel in a few impressive words (vv. 4–5), Moses enjoined the people to communicate their faith to their children by instruction and example (vv. 7–9), a theme resumed in verses 20–25. The intervening verses contain a warning against forgetting God and turning aside to idols (vv. 10–19).

Special points.—Verses 4–5 (the *Shema,* from the Hebrew for "Hear") are regarded by Jews as the essence of their faith. They are quoted in every synagogue service, are taught Jewish children at an early age, and are repeated twice daily by the orthodox. The commandments of verses 8–9 were taken literally by later generations of Jews who strapped phylacteries (small leather boxes containing these words) to their persons and fastened similar containers (mezuzahs) to their doorposts.

Truth for today.—Parents have a spiritual obligation to share their faith with their children by precept and practice. Instead of a literal interpretation of verses 8–9, we should see these instructions as a reminder of the need to make all of life bear witness to our faith. Our members (hands and eyes) should be both disciplined and directed so that they glorify God and serve others. Our homes should testify to our beliefs to all who enter them.

Relationships with Canaanites (7:1–26)

The passage.—The command to "utterly destroy them" (v. 2) raises moral problems that are partly answered by the need to protect Israel from the degrading religion of the Canaanites. Failure to do as they were ordered involved Israel in the very idolatry they were warned to avoid with its accompanying sexual perversions. The Israelites were not acting in vengeful fury against enemies but as the instrument of divine justice against people whose abominations were an offense to God.

The prohibition against marrying into these tribes was not based on race but religion (vv. 3–4). Israel must regard herself as "an holy people" (v. 6), not chosen for their goodness or greatness, but because of divine love (vv. 7–8). The fact of God's grace shines through his dealings with his people.

Lessons from History (8:1–20)

The passage.—The repetitions of Deuteronomy may seem unnecessary until we realize that, in spite of them, the people strayed away from God. Some truths are so important, and human memories are so weak, that they need to be stated over and over again.

In chapter 8 Moses went over ground previously traveled, reminding his listeners of God's past goodness and calling them to reciprocal loyalty and love. In this case, however, he described with new detail the character of the land to which they were going (vv. 7–10). With all these blessings they would still be in danger of forgetting God (v. 12) and giving themselves credit for their new-found prosperity (v. 17). Such ingratitude would not go unpunished (vv. 19–20).

Truth for today.—National achievement and success have their dangers. In times of prosperity it is easy to forget the true source of blessing and even assume that life's good things are the result of our own effort and the reward of our merit.

Remedy for Pride (9:1–29)

The passage.—Any tendency to pride was reproved in advance by Moses. The Israelites would possess Canaan "Not for thy righteousness, . . . but for the wickedness of these nations" (v. 5). Moses recalled the perverse behavior of Israel while he was receiving the law from God (vv. 7–21; Ex. 32). God would have destroyed them for worshiping the golden calf at that time, had not Moses effectively pleaded for them (vv. 18–19). Subsequently, at Kadesh-barnea, only the interceding of Moses turned back the Lord's wrath. Security in the future depended on remembering such things.

The Heart of Moses' Message (10:1–22)

The passage.—After rehearsing how, under God's instruction, he provided the ark to hold the tables of the law (vv. 1–5), and appointed the Levites as its custodians (vv. 8–11), Moses gave a summary of his total message (vv. 12–22). The chief concepts of Deuteronomy are all to be found in these verses. Divine grace is specially evident in verse 15. After extolling the greatness of the Lord, Moses continued: "Yet the Lord set his heart in love upon your fathers and chose his descendants after them, you above all peoples, as at this day" (RSV). They were chosen to be the instruments of his redemptive purpose toward all men.

The exhortation to reciprocal love (v. 12) introduces a new note into the Old Testament. God's love should induce a responsive love based on his greatness (v. 17) and mercy (v. 18). The expression of Godward love was also to include love for "the stranger" (v. 19).

Special points.—Here, as elsewhere, the exhortation to "fear the Lord" (vv. 12,20) must be understood in the sense of reverential awe. "The stranger" (vv. 18–19) was a non-Hebrew residing in their midst.

Truth for today.—The beautiful summary of Godward duty given in verse 12 is echoed throughout the Bible (Mic. 6:8) and became the basis for our Lord's statement (Matt. 22:37). If such completeness of dedication was expected from those who had received physical deliverance at God's hands, what level of devotion should we return who have known the blessing of Christ's atoning sacrifice?

Retrospect and Prospect (11:1–32)

The passage.—Again, in this chapter, Moses reviewed God's past deliverances (vv. 1–9), described the attractions of the Promised Land (vv. 10–12), and repeated the blessings of obedience and the penalties of disobedience (vv. 13–25).

The distinctive feature of this chapter is the provision of a ceremony of covenant renewal that was to take place after the land had been occupied (vv. 26–32). See 27:9–26 for a more detailed description of this occasion. For the historic record of the holding of this ceremony see Joshua 8:30–35.

Special points.—"Gerizim" and "Ebal" (v. 29) were adjoining peaks. "Gilgal," however, was not near them, unless the reference is to another place of this name. In the same verse, "champaign" is a term then used for the Jordan valley ("the Arabah," RSV).

Truth for today.—Each generation must determine its own relationship to God. The experience of earlier generations will not suffice for the new.

A Central Sanctuary (12:1–28)

Moses' preliminary statements were now over. At 12:1 he began his restatement of God's laws. His first subject was worship (12:1—16:17).

The passage.—God gave commandment for the provision of a central place of worship as soon as Canaan had been conquered and settled (v. 10). One purpose of this was disclosed in an introductory instruction to destroy completely all idols, altars, and shrines dedicated to the worship of pagan gods (vv. 2–3). There was danger that if these were allowed to survive the Israelites would adopt the degraded worship they fostered.

A central sanctuary was not provided until Solomon built the Temple (1 Kings 6). By then, many local shrines were in use and were permitted to survive. In later history, shrines competitive to the Temple in Jerusalem served to undermine the purity of Israel's faith (1 Kings 12:25–33).

All sacrifices were to be offered at the place where God would "cause his name to dwell" (vv. 11–14,17–18). There also the people would observe their religious festivals (chap. 16). Apparently they had followed a practice of eating only meat that had been killed at a sanctuary; so, with the anticipated restriction to a single sanctuary it was necessary to assure them that they could slaughter for food at home (vv. 15–16,20–24), provided they observed an earlier prohibition against eating "the blood" (vv. 16,23; Lev. 17:10–11).

Included in these laws was an injunction, "forsake not the Levite" (v. 19), a reminder that those who served in the Temple were entitled to adequate support.

Special points.—The Israelites were ordered to "destroy the names" (v. 3) of pagan deities and replace their shrines with one where God himself would "put his name" (v. 5). In Hebrew thinking, a name was intimately related to the person who bore it, justifying the later concept of the Temple as God's dwelling place (Kings 6:12–13).

The phrase, "whatsoever thy soul

5. Mount Gerizim (at left) and Mount Ebal
(see Deut. 11:29–30)

lusteth after" (v. 15), is better rendered, "as much as you desire" (RSV). In the same verse "roebuck" ("gazelle," RSV) and "hart" are probably mentioned as favorite delicacies that were in plentiful supply.

Truth for today.—There is strong emphasis in this chapter on happiness in the practice of religion (vv. 12,18). At the same time, the idea that we may worship God "any way we like" receives at least two reproofs (vv. 4,8). For worship to be worship it must conform to God's wishes and instructions.

Dealing with Idolatory (12:29—14:2)

The passage.—The degraded nature of Canaanitish religion has been confirmed by archaeological discovery. It permitted human sacrifice (12:31) and encouraged sexual immorality. As a fertility cult, this form of religion made a ritual of sex activity for which sacred prostitutes were housed at idol shrines. If the laws in this section appear harsh, they must be seen as expressing the Lord's concern that his people avoid the contagion of these perversions.

In 12:29–32 the danger of unbridled curiosity about false religions is indicated. Some things are so morally and spiritually corrosive that all contact with them is best avoided. Even after the physical aspects of paganism had been removed, there was risk that Israel might revive the forbidden cult by seeking answers to the question, "How did these nations serve their gods?" (v. 30).

121

False prophets are the subject of 13:1–5. Men would arise who would attempt to wean Israel away from the Lord by performing "a sign or a wonder" (v. 1). Such men were to be considered national enemies and put to death. Whatever powers they might profess, they were to be judged on their motives (v. 2).

The seriousness of forsaking the true God for idols is nowhere more vividly expressed than in 13:6–11. Even members of a man's family were to be put to death if they attempted to undermine his loyalty to God. We must bear in mind that Israel was at this time a theocracy. God was their king, and those who rebelled against him or encouraged others to do so were guilty of treason.

Furthermore, if apostate communities arose, they were to be exterminated after their guilt had been adequately determined (13:12–18). It would have made a mockery of divine justice if Canaanitish cities had been destroyed for their idolatries and such people spared. Moreover, if areas of contagion were tolerated in the new nation of Israel, they would eventually permeate the whole.

The last precaution against lapsing into paganism is obscure (14:1–2). Mutilation of the body and shaving of the head were apparently heathen mourning customs. These rites belonged to a veneration of the dead, or of death itself, and were therefore entirely inappropriate for the people of the living God. The prohibition against such practices took high ground, "For thou art a holy people unto the Lord thy God" (v. 2).

Truth for today.—Purposeful inquiry into other religions, both ancient and contemporary, for the purpose of ascertaining the truth about them, cannot be considered wrong. But we need warning against exposing ourselves, and

others, to the subtle influences of false faiths by contacts that have no better reason than undisciplined curiosity. Christian courtesy toward persons of all faiths, and none, should not lead to a tolerance that fails to recognize the difference between truth and error.

Rules of Diet (14:3–21)

The passage.—The reasons why some meats were considered unclean and others clean are not stated. Health reasons are probable, and there is validity for the suggestion that the distinctions relate to the fact that certain creatures were given idolatrous veneration. However, what matters is the purpose of these classifications: by the very food they ate, or abstained from eating, Israelites were to show themselves an holy people (v. 21), that is, a separated people.

Special points.—The distinguishing factors between clean and unclean animals were carefully spelled out. Only those that had cloven hooves and chewed the cud were permissible as food: both requirements were necessary (vv. 7–8).

The prohibition of v. 21, "Thou shalt not seethe a kid in his mother's milk," is variously interpreted. Some see this as a matter of humaneness; but more likely the forbidden practice had pagan associations.

Truth for today.—That dietary regulations were related to ritual rather than to hygiene seems probable from our Lord's pronouncements about them. Mark, commenting on his own quotation of Jesus in Mark 7:18–23, said, "Thus he declared all foods clean" (v. 19, RSV). Also Paul when discussing food said, "For every creature of God is good, and nothing to be refused, if it be received with thanksgiving" (1 Tim. 4:4).

Showing Gratitude and Mercy (14:22—15:18)

The passage.—It is surely not accidental that duties to God and to fellowmen are brought together here. Throughout the Bible our treatment of others is always presented as a test for our love for God.

The Old Testament law of the tithe is nowhere consolidated but is stated in a variety of places. There is room for doubt as to how precisely it operated. This statement relates to one aspect only (see also Lev. 27:30–33; Num. 18:21–24). The circumstance anticipated by Moses was the existence of a central sanctuary to which the people could bring tithes of their produce. They were to eat this tithe themselves "that thou mayest learn to fear the Lord thy God always" (v. 23). Thus the eating of the tithe was an act of obedience that both expressed and stimulated gratitude to God as the giver. Every third year this tithe was to be distributed among the needy at home (vv. 28–29).

A practical provision was made for those who lived too far from the central sanctuary to take their tithe in kind. They could turn their produce into cash and use the proceeds to buy food for the festival meal at the end of their pilgrimage (vv. 24–27).

Concern for the needy expressed in 14:29 is amplified in chapter 15 in instructions for the treatment of debtors (vv. 1–11) and slaves (vv. 12–18). The law of release provided that, every seventh year, outstanding debts were to be canceled. Questions have been raised as to whether this meant the interest or the capital; but concensus favors the latter. This was an early antipoverty measure instituted by God. It did not apply to non-Hebrews (v. 3) since its purpose was the establishment of domestic economic security.

There is reason to believe that this law was never fully implemented. The more moderate law of the year of jubilee (Lev. 25) may have taken its place. If so, this failure to live up to God's ideal may account for the frank acknowledgement, "the poor shall never cease out of the land" (v. 11).

The Mosaic law was more humanitarian at many points than those of other nations. Its provision for the release of slaves (vv. 12–18) is a case in point. A man might sell himself to another to pay a debt; but he could only be held in bondage for six years. In the seventh year he was to be freed and given means to sustain himself (v. 14). All this was required in light of God's deliverance of Israel from Egyptian bondage (v. 15). An interesting provision was made for a slave who did not desire freedom (vv. 16–17).

Concluding verses of chapter 15 are concerned with God's claim on the firstborn of sheep and oxen (vv. 19–22). Although these animals were to be eaten at the Temple festivals, by setting them apart the people were reminded of their obligation to God.

Special points.—The reference to strong drink (14:26) has obvious problems. Perhaps we should regard it as a reminder that the Old Testament is not the Christian's final guide to conduct. We must follow the higher ethic of the New Testament.

The human tendency to seek loopholes in our response to laws is rebuked in 15:9. The temptation to refuse help to the needy as the seventh year drew near was to be resisted. The spirit in which we should show kindness to others is stated in 15:18. We should not act under a sense of hardship but with openhandedness.

Truth for today.—God's care for the poor is expressed througout the Bible.

He does not regard poverty as desirable or inevitable, but lays on the well-provided the responsibility for relieving poverty and suffering wherever possible. His goodness to us should stimulate our generosity to others.

Three Religious Festivals (16:1–17)

The passage.—In Leviticus 23, six religious observances are described, three of which are repeated in this chapter. These are: the Passover (vv. 1–8), Pentecost (vv. 9–12), and Tabernacles (vv. 13–15).

The Hebrew calendar began with the month *Abib* (v. 1), in the spring of the year. After the Babylonian captivity this month was called Nisan. It was the month of the Exodus, annually commemorated by the observance of the Passover, or Feast of Unleavened Bread as it was later called. Moses reminded the people of the original circumstances and instructions for the keeping of this feast (Ex. 12). After possession of the land, they were to go up to the central sanctuary each year for this observance (v. 6).

Pentecost, from the Greek word for fiftieth, fell that number of days after Passover. It was a harvest celebration, lasting for one day only, and was originally called the Feast of Weeks (v. 10). Various sacrifices of thanksgiving were offered, including "a tribute of a free-will offering" (v. 10), that is, an adequate offering brought by individual worshipers as a token of gratitude for God's goodness: "according as the Lord thy God hath blessed thee" (v. 10; see 1 Cor. 16:2). Persons who had no harvest of their own were to share in the feasting (v. 11).

The Feast of Tabernacles (or Booths) coincided with the end of harvest. For its observance the people lived in rustic shelters, or arbors, reproducing the simple dwellings they used in their wilderness wanderings (Lev. 23:40–42). It was the most joyous of all the feasts for it contrasted what had been with what was. This memorialization of God's goodness (v. 15) was to be shared by everybody (v. 14).

Truth for today.—These three feasts have special significance for Christians. Each was a type of greater events to come. Passover anticipated the death of our Lord as the divinely-provided means for our escape from the penalty and power of sin (1 Cor. 5:7–8). The fact that the Passover coincided with the passion of Jesus (John 13:1), and that he instituted a new memorial meal, the Lord's Supper, to take its place, are meaningful facts to his redeemed people.

Fifty days after the crucifixion the Jews gathered in Jerusalem for the feast of Pentecost (Acts 2:1). The Holy Spirit was then poured upon the church, enduing it with power for effective witness. The day resulted in a great harvesting of souls as some three thousand people (Acts 2:41) responded to the preaching of Peter.

The third feast, that of Tabernacles, awaits fulfilment when the redeemed are gathered home. Then the memories of their earthly pilgrimage, and of God's never-failing goodness, together with the felicities of heaven, will inspire them to eternal thanksgiving.

Leadership Responsibilities (16:18—18:22)

The remainder of Moses' second message was devoted to various rules and regulations concerning the administration of justice, sanitation, slavery, sexual behavior, war, and other subjects. Moses did not make an immediate transition, however, from the subject of worship. After a message to judges (16:18–20), he voiced a prohibition of idolatry

(16:21–22), followed by instructions about sacrifices (17:1), penalties for religious apostasy (17:2–7), and the provision of a supreme court of law (17:8–13).

The passage.—A section that deals mainly with the appointment and responsibilities of national leadership begins with judges and court officers (16:18–20). These were to be appointed "in all your towns" (v. 18, RSV). Three principles of judicial integrity are stated: judges shall not "pervert justice," "show partiality," or "take a bribe" (v. 19, RSV). Absolute justice was essential to the survival of the nation: "Justice, and only justice, you shall follow" (v. 20, RSV).

In verses that deal with the penalty for religious apostasy (17:2–7), the legal function of witnesses is stated. Evidence must be given by "two witnesses, or three witnesses" (v. 6), the testimony of a single individual being rejected as inadequate.

Moses next made provision for a supreme court, as distinct from local courts, to be located at the central sanctuary (17:8–13). Cases too difficult for local decision were to be referred to this court—"any case . . . requiring decision between one kind of homicide and another, one kind of legal right and another, or one kind of assault and another" (v. 8, RSV).

The findings of this court, which was to be composed of priests and laity (17:9) were final (vv. 10–11). Refusal to accept its verdicts would be punishable by death (v. 12). Respect for the administration of law on the part of the people (v. 13) was contingent on the expectation that judges would act with integrity (16:18–20).

When the time came for Israel to have a king, guidelines for his selection and conduct were provided (17:14–20). He must be a man chosen of God and an Israelite (v. 15). He should not rely on military might or foreign alliances (v. 16), not indulge in sexual or material excesses (v. 17). His life, like the lives of his subjects, must be regulated by the laws of God (vv. 18–20).

Levites, members of the priestly tribe of Levi, had no territorial allotment in Israel and were therefore to be supported by the offerings of the people (18:1–8). When the establishment of a central sanctuary made it necessary for Levites to move from provincial cities to Jerusalem, they were to share in the priestly portion (vv. 6–8).

In seeking spiritual counsel the people of Israel were not to resort to magicians and practices of the occult (18:9–14). Other nations were under divine judgment because of these things (v. 12) which fostered such iniquities as child sacrifices (v. 10).

There would be no need for appeal to false prophets for God would provide his people with a succession of prophets like Moses himself (18:15–22). Such prophets would function under an obligation of truth, not attributing to God that which did not come from him, nor speaking in the name of other gods (v. 20). They would be recognized by the fulfilment of the things they foretold (v. 22).

This promise came to be identified with one particular Prophet whom Peter claimed to be the Lord Jesus Christ (Acts 3:22). His likeness to Moses as deliverer and teacher is recognizable, yet he is to be acknowledged as greater than Moses (Heb. 3:3).

Truth for today.—National strength and prosperity depend on the acceptance of appropriate responsibilities by both leadership and people. If law and order are to be upheld, they must be administered by men who command respect by the integrity of their lives. The prospect of ultimate truth and justice, however, depends on the activity of God who committed himself to send among men One who would speak and act on his behalf and who is not only Prophet but also Priest and King.

Administering Justice (19:1–21)

The passage.—The provision of cities of refuge (vv. 1–13) was necessary because of a primitive form of justice whereby "the avenger of the blood" (v. 6), a kinsman of a slain person, hunted down the killer and took his life. Recognizing a difference between premeditated and unpremeditated murder, cities were to be assigned to which a person might go for refuge until his defence could be heard and his guilt be cleared or confirmed.

Moses had ordered three such cities while the Israelites were still east of Jordan (4:41–43). Three more were to be assigned when Canaan was occupied, located in different parts of the country to make them readily accessible (v. 3). The implementation of this is recorded in Joshua 20. The provision for a third set of three cities (vv. 8–9) was probably never implemented since Israel failed to take possession of the total area assigned by the Lord.

A killer whose action was judged accidental (v. 5) was allowed to remain under the protection of the city of refuge until the death of the existing high priest (Josh. 20:6). A person judged guilty of deliberate murder, however, was delivered into the hands of the avenger of blood (vv. 11–13).

In a single-verse reference (v. 14) a law is stated against encroachments on a person's real estate. After the apportionment of the land between the tribes, property was regarded as an inheritance from God to be jealously protected and passed on from generation to generation. Any attempt to steal such property, by moving the stone fence (landmark) which defined its boundaries, was forbidden.

The concluding verses of this chapter (vv. 15–21) deal with the judicial function of witnesses already referred to in 17:6. Again it is stated that the testimony of one individual was not enough; there must be at least two or three witnesses to establish guilt. Severe penalties were threatened against persons who bore false witness. If such were discovered, they were to be punished with a sentence equivalent to that which they had sought to bring upon the innocent (v. 19).

Special points.—Three purposes may be recognized for these laws concerning the administration of justice. The first was the avoidance of shedding "innocent blood" (v. 10). These and other laws support the Old Testament's teaching on the value of human life as summed up in the Sixth Commandment (Ex. 20:13). A second purpose was the restraint of crime through respect for law (v. 20). A third is suggested by verse 21, namely, to insure that penalties would be matched to offences and be neither too light nor too severe.

Truth for today.—The fair administration of justice is essential to any nation's well-being. The innocent should have no reason to fear the courts and the guilty no cause to despise them. When the law falls into contempt through bad administration or interpretation, the moral foundations of a nation are endangered.

Waging Holy War (20:1–20)

The passage.—The concept of "holy war" is prominent in the book of Deuteronomy (see also 21:10–14; 23:9–14). Israel regarded itself as the instrument of divine justice in its campaigns against heathen enemies. This was particularly true of its wars with the Canaanites. The cause was God's, for the enemy was in conflict with God and under his judgment.

The rules under which such warfare was conducted were plainly stipulated. They may seem to us to be strangely contradictory; but we are at a loss to make any final judgment because at no time before nor since has one nation been specifically chosen by God as the arm of his vengeance.

The people were to go into battle with the encouragement of the priest (vv. 1–4) and in the assurance that, no matter how strong the enemy, God would give them the victory. Exemptions from military service were allowed on somewhat generous terms. Those to be excused were: the owner of a new house or vineyard (vv. 5,6), a man anticipating marriage (v. 7), and he who was just plain scared (v. 8).

Different treatments were to be given to enemies. Those who lived at a distance were to be given the opportunity to make a peaceful settlement (vv. 10–11). These would be non-Canaanitish tribes. If they refused to negotiate, the men were to be killed but women, children, and cattle spared (vv. 12–16). However, the tribes of Canaan (v. 17) were to be completely exterminated to remove forever their contaminating influence (v. 18).

The chapter concludes with a commandment about the treatment of trees in warfare (vv. 19–20). Fruit trees were not to be cut down and used as engines of war. They were to be spared for needed food. This regard for the resources of nature strikes an impressive contemporary note.

Special points.—For the Christian, the concept of "holy war" has many unresolved problems. Yet we should recognize that the rules for such warfare, while demanding extermination for the Canaanites, expressed a humaneness completely foreign to the prevailing practices of contemporary nations. In later centuries, the Jews themselves experienced the barbarism of other conquerors who showed mercy to none. The practices of modern conflict, particularly in their concept of "total war," show considerably less regard for enemy civilians than this early Hebrew code.

Truth for today.—The God who revealed himself as a God of judgment through Israel has revealed himself as a God of mercy through Jesus Christ. Our conduct toward others is to be based on the teaching and practice of our Lord who taught forgiveness of others, even of enemies, and said, "The Son of man is come not to destroy men's lives, but to save them" (Luke 9:56).

A Variety of Laws (21:1—23:14)

The passage.—The number and diversity of laws in this section of Moses' second speech makes classification impossible in a consecutive discussion of content such as this. Hence, each chapter will be reviewed individually.

Chapter 21.—To emphasize further the value of human life, instruction was given on a ceremony of expiation to be carried out if a dead body was found without clues as to the manner of death (vv. 1–9). The elders of the city nearest the point of discovery were to lead a heifer to a stream and here break (RSV) the heifer's neck. Priests would then preside over a ritual in which the elders would wash their hands over the heifer as they said, "Our hands have not shed this blood, neither have our eyes seen it" (v. 7). Then they would pray to God not to hold them responsible for the death (v. 8). How this reproves our ofttimes callous acceptance of death as a necessary accompaniment to technological progress!

The verses that follow (vv. 10–14) deal with the treatment of women captives and therefore relate to the subject of chapter 20. The men of Israel were called upon to demonstrate a chivalry rarely practiced in wars of that time, or since. A captured woman, presumably single, could be taken as wife but must first be given a month to make adjustment to her new circumstances (vv. 12–13). Should the marriage not work out, the woman was to be released unconditionally and not sold to another (v. 14).

Two cases of domestic dissension are next provided for. In the first (vv. 15–17), a polygamous situation is described in which two wives, one loved and one hated, bear children. If the son of the less-loved woman is born first, he is to be given the full legal rights of the firstborn, and not discriminated against on account of his mother. It should be noted that while polygamy is recognized in the Old Testament, it is frequently described in a context of family disruption. There is no attempt to make polygamy appear as a good thing.

The other family situation is that of a rebellious son (vv. 18–21). Not only is he undisciplined and disrespectful but also "a glutton, and a drunkard" (v. 20). Such a son is to be turned over to the elders of the city and, if proven guilty, put to death. If the treatment seems extreme, it should be noted that there is no record in the Bible of it being put into effect. Perhaps the law was intended more as a deterrent (see v. 21), for which there is still need.

Finally, chapter 21 gives instruction on disposing of the body of a criminal (vv. 22–23), presumably executed by stoning and then hanged on a tree as a warning. The body must be taken down

before midnight "that thy land be not defiled" (v. 23). The statement, "he that is hanged is accursed of God," is used by Paul in Galatians 3:13 in a discussion of the meaning of the cross of Christ.

Chapter 22.—A law about lost property begins this chapter (vv. 1–4). The prohibition, "Thou shalt not . . . hide thyself" (v. 1), forbids the avoidance of responsibility for the misfortunes of others. A persistent trait of selfish humanity is the desire not to become involved in another's troubles. This law, however, declares that a man must set the same value on his neighbor's property as he does on his own. When he is aware that his neighbor has sustained a loss, it is his duty to take active steps to restore the lost property to its owner.

Verse 5 should probably be interpreted as a prohibition against wearing the clothing of the opposite sex with immoral intentions. It may have had reference to condemned Canaanitish customs. The regulation is difficult to apply on any universal basis since styles of dress vary from culture to culture.

Verses 6–7 echo a constant concern of the Bible for the conservation and protection of nature. An early building code is found in verse 8. Eastern rooftops were used for recreation and rest and "a battlement" ("parapet," RSV) would afford protection against falling off.

Following several laws briefly stated comes a section dealing with relationships between the sexes. First (vv. 13–21) comes the case of a man who charges his new wife with not being a virgin. (His objection would be regarded as naive and amusing in many social circles today.) The matter is to be referred to the elders of the city by the girl's parents. If they can prove that their daughter has been falsely accused, a fine is to be paid to the father and the girl is to remain wedded to the man. On the other hand, if the charge is substantiated the girl is to be put to death.

After a statement of the penalty for adultery (v. 22), three possibilities of seduction are presented (vv. 23–29). In the first, a girl is assaulted in a populated area (vv. 23–24). The girl is to be considered a willing partner since she did not call for help. In the second, a similar assault takes place in a rural setting (vv. 25–27). The benefit of doubt goes to the girl who could not have obtained help even if she had called for it. Death for both parties is prescribed in the first instance; for the man only in the second. Lastly, the case is cited of an unbetrothed girl who is assaulted (vv. 28–29). The man involved must take her as his wife and pay the girl's father fifty shekels.

Chapter 23:1–14.—Persons to be excluded from the religious congregation of Israel are listed (vv. 1–6). Sexual mutilation, birth from unnatural unions, and membership of certain enemy nations were disqualifications from sharing the worship of Israel. On the other hand, Edomites and Egyptians (vv. 7–8) were to be admitted, the former as kinsmen, the latter as a gesture of kindness to former oppressors. This admixture of exclusion and concession would eventually give place to a gospel which says, "Whosoever will, let him take the water of life freely" (Rev. 22:17).

Verses 10–14 are concerned with sanitation in a military camp and belong to the subject of chapter 20. The camp was to be kept clean because "the Lord thy God walketh in the midst of thy camp" (v. 14).

Special points.—If many of these laws seem strange and irrelevant to us, we must nevertheless accept them as an expression of the divine wisdom for God's people in a learning stage of their de-

velopment. Certainly, some of the laws were temporary and have been superseded by the coming of the gospel: witness our Lord's dealings with the woman taken in adultery (John 8:1–11). He did not deal with her in judgment but mercy and warned against a condemnatory spirit on the part of persons who were themselves sinners, which includes us all.

A penetrating insight into the significance of these laws is provided in a surprising context. In a verse already quoted (23:14) sanitary practices are demanded among soldiers in camp because of the presence of the Lord among them. This affords a clue to the primary purpose of many of these laws. They were a reminder of the holiness of God, a warning against anything that would offend him, and a summons to special standards of behavior in view of Israel's relationship to him. "You shall be blameless before the Lord your God" (18:13, RSV).

Truth for today.—Present tendencies to discard all moral standards are a summons to Christians to acknowledge and exemplify the relationship between belief and behavior. God made high demands on Israel because they were his people. Though delivered from the bondage of law and inducted into a relationship of grace, it still behooves the Christian to heed the exhortation, "Let every one that nameth the name of Christ depart from iniquity" (2 Tim. 2:19).

Protecting Human Rights (23:15—25:19)

The passage.—The medley of laws continues, although most in this section are concerned with the protection of individual rights. We will consider them in their respective chapters.

Chapter 23:15–25.—A prohibition against surrendering an escaped slave to

his former master (vv. 15–16) presup-
poses that he has been the victim of
harsh treatment. God's abhorrence of
sexual perversion is further evidenced
by a forthright prohibition of harlotry
and sodomy (vv. 17–18). Proceeds of
immoral living were not to be offered as
gifts to God. It is probable that "a dog"
(v. 18) is a contemptuous reference to a
homosexual.

Hebrews were forbidden to lend
money for interest (usury) to fellow
Hebrews, although they might do so to
persons of other races (vv. 19–20). This
was probably a measure to preserve
economic stability in the nation. Persons
making vows (vv. 21–23) were required
to fulfil them. The law is here confined
to vows to God. A final provision of this
chapter gave permission to eat "grapes"
from another's vineyard, but not to
gather and remove them (vv. 24–25).
The same principle applied to "corn,"
a word which always means small grain
in the KJV.

Truth for today.—An alarming increase in illicit sexual relationships is a
sad feature of our times. When Christian
people tend to tolerance in these areas,
it is well for them to recognize that in
both Testaments the Bible states God's
disapproval of all types of sexual indulgence and perversion (Rom. 1:18–
32).

Chapter 24.—The Old Testament
makes no provision for divorce but recognizes the existence of the practice. The
law stated in verses 1–4 was apparently
given to control divorce. It provided that
no woman could be divorced without
good reason. She could not be summarily dismissed but should be legally separated from her husband and given a
document to this effect. She could marry
again but could not resume the original
partnership if her second husband died
or divorced her.

A happier note is struck in verse 5
where a new bridegroom is freed from
the obligation of military service for a
year. He may stay at home and *"cheer
up his wife!"* There follows a prohibition
against accepting "the nether or the upper millstone" as a pledge (v. 6). Either
would render a mill useless and prevent
the necessary daily grinding of meal.
Next come laws against forcing a fellow
Hebrew into slavery (v. 7) and summarizing earlier provisions for dealing with
leprosy (vv. 8–9, see Lev. 13:13–14).

The protection of the poor is the concern of the remaining enactments of this
chapter. A pledge was not to be publicly
collected in return for a loan (vv.
10–11). Out of consideration for the
debtor's feelings and reputation, he
must be allowed to bring the pledge
himself. Moreover, if the pledge was a
garment, which doubled as a blanket for
a poor person, it must not be kept
through the night (vv. 12–13).

Prompt payment of wages earned is
the subject of the next law (vv. 14–15).
These were to be paid on a daily basis so
that the worker could buy needed provisions. The responsibility of the individual
was recognized in verse 16. Exploitation
of the helpless was condemned (vv. 17–
19). The concluding provision (vv.
19–22) required that the crop owner
should deliberately leave a surplus in his
fields to be gathered by the poor.

Chapter 25.—Rights of condemned
persons are to be protected (vv. 1–3). A
man must not be beaten before trial.
The beating, when administered, shall
take place before the judge; and it shall
not exceed forty stripes. (It became the
practice to give only thirty-nine stripes
as a safeguard against transgressing this
law. See 2 Cor. 11:24.) These provisions
were made in view of the fact that a
convicted offender was still a fellow human being who should not be regarded

as vile (v. 3), literally, "made light," that is, less than a person.

Even an ox was to be allowed to eat as he worked (v. 4). Paul used this verse as an argument for the payment of preachers (1 Cor. 9:9)!

Provision for what is known as levirate marriage is given in verses 5–10. If a husband died, his brother should marry the widow. The purpose was to perpetuate a man's name and lineage (v. 6). It needs to be recognized that, lacking a clear hope of an afterlife, the Hebrews sought immortality through their children. A brother who would not render this service was to be held in contempt.

Honesty in trading is the theme of verses 13–16. Both weights and measures were to be accurate so that the purchaser was not defrauded. The chapter ends with a somber call, "Remember what Amalek did unto thee" (vv. 17–19). For Amalek's offence see Exodus 17: 8–16. Their treachery was to be avenged, a very human response to hurt, but one far below the requirements of the Christian gospel.

Special points.—Twice in chapter 24, acts of compassion toward others are enjoined on the ground of God's mercies to Israel (vv. 18,22). The Exodus was a perpetual reminder of divine deliverance and a spur to kindness to others. Other people's rights were to be respected and their needs met because Israel had been brought out of oppression and obscurity by the strong hand of a loving God.

Truth for today.—Paul lifted this principle a giant step higher when he wrote, "Be ye kind one to another, tenderhearted, forgiving one another, even as God for Christ's sake hath forgiven you" (Eph. 4:32).

Two Religious Ceremonies (26:1–19)

The passage.—This chapter concludes the statement of laws that began with chapter 12. It consists mainly of directions for two ceremonies, with appropriate liturgical confessions.

The first of these (vv. 1–11) is a ceremony of firstfruits. Each year, a basket containing first harvestings of the soil was to be brought to the central sanctuary and presented to God. In making this presentation the worshiper was to engage in a spoken confession of his faith (vv. 5–10). This confession rehearsed the mighty acts of God in the deliverance from Egypt and the occupation of Canaan. Thus the Lord's historic acts became the basis for thanksgiving and the foundation of faith. The opening words of this confession are better rendered: "A wandering Aramean was my father" (v. 5, RSV), wandering, that is, in the sense of being homeless and lost.

The second ceremony (vv. 12–15) was related to the third-year tithe (see 14: 28–29). This tithe was to be kept in the worshiper's home community, but later, probably at the Feast of Tabernacles, the tither was to appear at the central sanctuary and make a statement that the tithing had been carried out (vv. 13–15). Included in this were three declarations (v. 14): the tithe had not been defiled by contact with the dead, nor used for any other purpose that might be ceremonially unclean, nor as a sacrifice to the dead (see 14:1). The confession concluded with a prayer to God for blessing on the nation.

Chapter 26 ends with an exhortation (vv. 16–19) which may have been part of a ceremony of covenant renewal, but certainly forms an appropriate conclusion to Moses' restatement of God's laws. It begins with a reference to the reading of these laws (v. 16) which was followed by a pledge from the people to keep them (v. 17). The word "avouched" becomes "declared" in the RSV. As a consequence of this pledge, the Lord commits himself afresh to his people to whom he renews his promises (vv. 18–19).

Service of Covenant Renewal (27:1–26)

The passage.—Moses' second speech carries through to 28:68 and the contents of this chapter would logically follow, so that it may have become misplaced. It is clearly not part of Moses' speech but implements instructions given in 11:29 for a ceremony of covenant renewal.

God's laws were to be inscribed in plaster and displayed on Mount Ebal (vv. 2–4). Note the additional instruction of verse 8 that the laws be written "very plainly." An altar was to be built and sacrifices offered (vv. 6–7). Then the tribes were to be divided, six of them standing on Mount Gerizim and six on Mount Ebal (vv. 11–13). The Levites, apparently standing between the two groups, would recite the curses for disobedience, to each of which the people would respond, "Amen" (vv. 14–26), or, "So be it." What has happened to the corresponding blessings we cannot say. Some scholars think that chapter 28 continues this ceremony. However, that chapter is presented as the conclusion to Moses' speech.

Rewards and Punishments (28:1–68)

The passage.—Moses ended his second message by rehearsing the blessings and curses that would attend obedience or disobedience to God's laws. His statement must be considered in the context of the covenant into which Israel had entered. Divine promises of national prosperity and security were dependent on compliance to God's will as revealed in his commandments. Transgression of his will would bring penalties corresponding to the blessings. The fact that the blessings (vv. 1–14) are considerably

fewer than the curses (vv. 15–68) has led to the supposition that part of the original statement may be missing.

It was the solemn pronouncements of this chapter that brought alarm to Josiah after the finding of "the book of the law" in the Temple (2 Kings 22). He recognized that the nation had committed the very offences described by Moses. The circumstances of Israel's eventual decline and fall, and present condition, are here described with amazing accuracy.

III. MOSES' THIRD SPEECH (DEUT. 29:1—30:20)

We are taken back to the scene "beyond the Jordan, in the land of Moab" (1:5, RSV) where Moses addressed the assembled people. Not only did he provide for future ceremonies of covenant renewal (Deut. 27; 31:9–13) but also called for rededication then and there. Note the recurring phrase "this day" (29:4,10,12,15, etc.).

The passage.—Since repetition is a principle of learning, Moses did not hesitate to return once more to the theme of the deliverance from Egypt and God's subsequent care of his people (29:2–9). Of the Exodus Moses said, "Ye have seen" (v. 2), although actually the event took place before his listeners were born. However, they knew the facts as well as though they had been present, and in Hebrew thinking they were present in their forebears, for the concept of racial solidarity was strong. But they had not penetrated beyond these facts to acknowledge the response due from them in obedience to God (v. 4). The opportunity was therefore given them to make an act of commitment (v. 9).

Moses addressed himself not only to the representative audience before him (29:10–11) but also to future generations (vv. 14–15). Each in turn must make its own terms with the Lord, for no one can do this for another. Nevertheless, there was a reminder here of the importance of influence. In that solemn assembly there might be those who engaged hypocritically in the rite of covenant renewal (vv. 18–21). Such are quoted as saying, "I shall have peace, though I walk in the imagination of mine heart" (v. 19), that is, I shall escape the consequences even if I transgress God's laws. Persons who so behave would bring judgment on the entire nation (vv. 22–28). Was the phrase, "as it is this day" (v. 28), added by someone as a testimony to the fact that this is precisely what happened?

Moses is described as a prophet in 18:15 and 34:10. These next words (30: 1–10) are a remarkable description of what happened in the Babylonian exile and subsequent restoration. It would seem that the plea for loyalty to God was made not only on the basis of his past deliverances but also of mercies yet to come.

Paul borrowed 30:11–14 in Romans 10:6–8. In their original setting these verses state that God's laws were not unknown to Israel but had been revealed to them. Therefore there was no excuse for disobedience. A choice was before the people (vv. 15–20). Like the preacher of today, Moses gave his message and then added an invitation for decision.

Truth for today.—Some things are so important that they bear frequent repetition. Moses reminded Israel of God's past activities with special emphasis on the deliverance from Egypt. Today men need to be constantly reminded of the facts of the gospel—the incarnation, life, death, and resurrection of our Lord. These made possible the greatest of all deliverances—from sin and its consequences. They also contain the possibility of eternal life for all who believe and

obey. When the facts of the gospel have been presented, listeners need to be challenged to decision. The issues still are "life . . . and death" (30:15).

IV. BIOGRAPHICAL CONCLUSION (DEUT. 31:1—34:12)

Moses had known for a long time that he would not enter the Land of Promise (4:21–22). He had completed a major part of his mission by preparing the people for their new life through his three messages. There remained a few things he must do.

Israel's New Leader (31:1–30)

The passage.—Reference was made to Joshua as Moses' successor in the first speech (3:21,28). He was God's choice for this heavy responsibility (Num. 27: 18–23). He is described as the son of Nun and was chosen by Moses to lead the fight against the Amalekites, whom he successfully routed (Ex. 17:8–13). Joshua and Caleb were the only survivors of the original group that left Egypt who were permitted to enter Palestine. This was their reward for remaining loyal to the Lord at Kadesh-barnea (Num. 14:30).

Acknowledging himself as an hundred and twenty years old and with waning strength (v. 2), Moses spoke words of encouragement to the people (vv. 3–6) and then to Joshua (vv. 7–8). For the future instruction of the new leader and the people he put the law into writing (vv. 9–13,24–27), and gave orders for the scroll to be kept "by the side of the ark" (v. 26, RSV), not "in the side" as the KJV reads. Every seven years (v. 10) it was to be read to the people as the basis for a recurring act of covenant renewal.

Chapter 31 also contains the record of a divine summons to Moses to appear before the Lord in the company of

Joshua (vv. 14–21). In this confrontation Moses was commanded to write a song and teach it to the people (v. 19). The time would come (as Moses himself had warned) when Israel would go astray after idols and incur dire penalties (vv. 16–18). In their suffering they would question God's ways. The song Moses was to compose would be "a witness . . . against the children of Israel" (v. 19). It would remain in their memories as a testimony to God's activities in history in behalf of his people.

Special points.—How much of the present book of Deuteronomy was written by Moses we cannot tell. The concluding chapters contain material that must necessarily have been written by someone other, the record of his death, for example (chap. 33–34). But there are good reasons for believing that the book is substantially of Mosaic origin. Its historic basis is not in question.

Truth for today.—God uses various ways of communicating with people. He does it through chosen instruments, such as Moses and Joshua. He does it through the written word in which we are particularly rich since we have both Old and New Testaments. And he does it through memory. God's endorsement of the ministry of songs and poetry puts his approval on their use for worship and witness, as well as for growth in Christian living. The practice of memorization has divine commendation. Truth stored in the mind may become God's messenger of encouragement, comfort, or reproof when these are most needed.

The Song of Moses (32:1–52)

The passage.—The song Moses composed begins with ascription of praise to God (vv. 1–4). He describes his message as doctrine (v. 2) or "teaching" (RSV), literally "my taking," something received from God and then given to

others. The purpose was instruction and the theme him who is "the Rock, . . . a God of truth . . . , just and right" (v. 4).

Words of indictment against Israel follow (vv. 5–6). The transgressions of these people were a sorry response to one who was both Father and Creator. Then the purpose of the song emerges as the plea is made to "Remember the days of old" (vv. 7–14). God's dealings in mercy are described in exquisite language. He had trained, disciplined, and provided for his people. Yet they had forgotten him (vv. 15–18). They had turned to gods that were "no gods" (v. 17, RSV). The depth of their ingratitude is expressed in verse 18.

A long section of the song (vv. 19–30) recites the judgments that would follow upon such disloyalty. Because they had forsaken the Lord for "no god" they would be chastened by "no people" (v. 21, RSV), that is, by a nation unknown to them.

It seems probable that verses 31–42 refer to Israel's enemies: "their rock is not as our Rock" (v. 31) would seem to indicate this. If so, then the point is that although God would use a foreign, unbelieving people to punish Israel, they would themselves come under divine judgment.

The song ends with a doxology (v. 43) in which the nations are called on to sing praises to Israel: "Praise his people, O ye nations" (RSV). The reason, however, is what God has done for Israel and what he will yet do.

After Moses had given the song to Joshua and the people, and had exhorted them to commit it to memory (vv. 44–47), he was summoned by God to ascend Mount Nebo and prepare for his death (vv. 49–52).

Special points.—The use of *Jeshurun* as a synonym for Israel needs to be recognized here and in 33:5. The word may have been used ironically in this case since it means honest, or upright, and this was far from true of Israel in her times of defection.

As the RSV shows, this chapter is in verse form. Hebrew poetry did not depend on rhyming words but on rhythm and what is known as parallelism. The latter involves the repetition of an idea, a second line echoing the thought of the first. This may be seen in verses 2–3 (RSV) where lines 2, 4, and 6 repeat the ideas of lines 1, 3, and 5, using different words.

The Blessing of Moses (33:1–29)

The passage.—The dying blessing of heads of families and tribes was the equivalent of a last will and testament. The words here attributed to Moses may be compared with those of Jacob in similar circumstances (Gen. 49). One difference is that Moses began with the praise of God (vv. 1–5). He compared the Lord to the rising sun who comes, with a heavenly host, for the blessing of his people. The giving of the law is specially mentioned (v. 4) as evidence of God's goodness. As a result, God was acknowledged as "king in Jeshurun" (v. 5) as the people covenanted to obey him in response to his commandments. Thus the blessing recalls the unfulfilled intentions of the people of Israel while the song of Moses declares their default.

Tribe by tribe, with the exception of Simeon, Moses pronounced his blessings (vv. 6–25). Reuben, though apparently weak, was assured of survival. The Lord's help was sought for Judah against his enemies. The blessing of Levi, the priestly tribe, contains obscurities but gave praise for loyalty to God above the claims of family (v. 9, RSV). Benjamin was promised the special protection of the Lord. The longest blessing was for Joseph, to whom was promised economic and military strength. Zebulun and Issachar would be leaders in worship and would draw their resources from the sea. Gad was commended (although the text is difficult) for helping the other tribes in their settlement of the land. Brief blessings for Dan, Naphtali, and Asher, the three northern tribes, conclude Moses' dying pronouncement, each being assured of future prosperity.

The blessing ends as it began with an acknowledgement of the Lord's greatness (vv. 26–29). He is the strength and security of his people who are counted happy to have such a divine protector.

Special points.—As the RSV indicates, this chapter, like the previous one, is in poetic form. The writing is not attributed to Moses, who is referred to in the third person (vv. 1,4), but the blessing itself is claimed as his.

For "thy Thummim and thy Urim" (v. 9) see Exodus 28:30. These were precious stones, carried in the breastplate of the chief priest, and used to determine God's will. The procedure followed is not known. The prayer for Asher, "let him dip his foot in oil" (v. 24), refers to olive oil, a major product of Palestine. The RSV reads "bars" for "shoes" (v. 25) making this verse an assurance of defence against enemies.

Truth for today.—National prosperity and security are gifts from God. The natural resources which give economic stability to a people are also his provision. The continued enjoyment of such blessings depends on loyalty and obedience to the divine giver. Moses' final words were blessings, which he most earnestly desired for his people. But he was realist enough to know that unfaithfulness to the God of all goodness would bring disaster on the very people he desired to bless. This is a universal law as operative today as it was in Moses' time.

The Death of Moses (34:1–12)

The passage.—In obedience to the call of God, Moses ascended Mount Nebo, east of Jordan and facing Jericho (32:48–52). There he was given a panoramic view of the land which God had promised to Abraham and which was soon to be occupied by his descendants. Then, at the age of one hundred twenty, Moses died and was buried by God himself. The pronoun "he" (v. 6) must be so interpreted.

After thirty days of mourning, those whom Moses had led from Egypt to the borders of the Promised Land, moved forward under the leadership of Joshua. The record ends with a tribute to Moses as the greatest of all prophets. He had performed other important functions, but his most valuable and permanent contribution to Israel and the world was his interpretation of God's character and will through a covenant of law.

Special points.—While the graves of many of history's great men are known and venerated, it is expressly stated of Moses "that no man knoweth of his sepulchre unto this day" (v. 6). Could the Lord have kept this a secret as a pre-caution against the development of a superstitious Mosiac cult that would have threatened the purity of Israel's faith and become a competitor to that central sanctuary about which Moses himself gave instructions?

While the physical details of Moses' death are withheld, the rabbis of Israel beautifully said that he died "by the kiss of God."

Truth for today.—The greatness of Moses is universally acknowledged. Yet when his task was ended, God raised up another to carry his mission to completion. The ongoing purposes of God depend on dedicated personalities who, though differing in mental and spiritual stature, are responsive to his will.

Moses' own anticipation of "a Prophet . . . , like unto me" (Deut. 18:15) was realized in the coming of one whom the New Testament salutes as "counted worthy of more glory than Moses" (Heb. 3:3). His deliverance of God's people, the leadership he gave them, and the revelation of the divine mind and will that he transmitted at Sinai and after, are all eclipsed by the achievements of the Lord Jesus Christ. For as John the beloved disciple wrote, "The law was given by Moses, but grace and truth came by Jesus Christ" (John 1:17).

JOSHUA

Ben F. Philbeck

INTRODUCTION

The book of Joshua relates the story of Israel's reoccupation of the Promised Land. Her ancestors, there during the patriarchal period, had been dislodged in the unrest reflected in the stories about Joseph (Gen. 37–50). Small isolated pockets of people distantly related to Israel could probably be found, but most of the land was now controlled by Israel's enemies.

In bold sweeping strokes the book traces the occupation of Canaan (chap. 1–12), the assignment of each tribe's territory (chaps. 13–21), and the conclusion of Joshua's ministry (chaps. 22–24). Only the broad outlines of a very complex period have been preserved, however. Thus, the laborious occupation of tribal lands (13:1) was proleptically viewed as a completed event in the time of Joshua (11:23). Actually, the central message of Joshua is more concerned with the nature of Israel's God than with a description of her past. Israel's history merely provided the medium in which the character of her unseen God could be observed.

The central theme of Joshua, therefore, focuses on the Lord's pivotal role in the occupation of Canaan. It was he who would exalt Joshua (1:1–9;3:7), and by his hand the Israelites would be empowered to drive their enemies before them (3:10; 4:24; etc.). Those who were faithful to God's law were promised his blessing, but swift retribution awaited those who rejected his leadership (7: 1–26).

Commission of Joshua (1:1–18)

The passage.—At the death of Moses, Joshua became Israel's supreme political leader in his own right. In an apparent effort to avoid a power struggle when Moses died, Joshua had earlier been designated as his successor (Num. 27: 15–23). On numerous occasions Joshua had appeared before the people as Moses' servant or minister (Ex. 24:13; 33: 11; Num. 11:28). The way had thus been prepared for a smooth transfer of authority.

Assured of success as long as he was true to God's law (1:1–9), Joshua prepared to cross the Jordan. For the task that lay ahead, Israel had to be united. Even the trans-Jordan tribes (Reuben, Gad, and part of Manasseh) were expected to send troops. Eventually the lack of such unified action threatened Israel with extinction (cf. Judg. 4–5).

Special points.—The ideal boundaries of the Promised Land (v. 4) were never actually realized. Even Israel's largest kingdom under David only reached the southern extremities of the Hittite empire which extended westward into central Asia Minor. This reference to the land of the Hittites does not appear in the Septuagint or the Vulgate, however, and it may be a later addition to the text.

The book of the law (v. 8) was probably the core of our book of Deuteronomy. Early compilers sharing a similar outlook appear to have arranged Deuteronomy, Joshua, Judges, Samuel, and Kings.

Truth for today.—Note the point of view from which the story is told. No mention is made of severe practical problems involved in the process by which an unseen spiritual God revealed his will. It would be a mistake to assume that people in the ancient world were unusually receptive to divine leadership. The reader is repeatedly reminded that Israel had been rebellious in the past (Ex. 16:2 f.) and she would continue to be so in the future (Deut. 31:16–18).

The author is not attempting to give a history of Israel's government. He has instead abstracted that history to emphasize God's role in ordering the course of human events.

To many observers modern life seems devoid of clear examples of divine leadership. The problem, however, resides with man. He must again learn to perceive God's presence underlying the complexities of personal and national experience.

Rahab and the Spies (2:1–24)

The passage.—Joshua sent two men from the Israelite camp east of Jordan to reconnoiter the territory around Jericho. They made their way to the house of Rahab, a harlot, where the presence of strangers would be least likely to arouse suspicion. From her they learned of the low morale of the people of Jericho upon hearing of the advance of the Israelites (v. 11). In return for Rahab's collaboration, the spies promised that she and her family would be spared.

Upon learning of the spies' presence, the king of Jericho began a desperate search. Rahab hid the men on the flat roof of her house among the stalks of flax which were drying there. After dark the men escaped through Rahab's window which was located in the upper reaches of the city wall. The spies hid in the mountains to the west while they were being hunted in the land toward the Jordan in the east. When the search was ended, they reported to Joshua how the Lord had prepared the way for his people (v. 24).

Special points.—The story of Rahab became a favorite in Israel. It demonstrated that a foreigner, even a woman of ill repute, could rise to prominence because of her faith in God (cf. Matt. 5:6–7).

The relation of this story to the account of the fall of Jericho (6:1–27) is uncertain. In chapter 6 God's power overwhelmed the city and there was no need for intrigue (cf. 3:4). Apparently, the record was once more complex than it now stands.

Since flax was harvested in the early spring, these incidents perhaps occurred in late March or early April (v. 6).

Israel Crosses Jordan (3:1–17)

The passage.—Under Joshua's command Israel set out for the Jordan in a line of march reminiscent of the wilderness experience. The ark of the covenant, representing the very presence of God among his people (Num. 10:33 f.), was at the head of the column. When the feet of the priests bearing the ark reached the edge of the river, the Jordan was blocked off upstream and the people crossed on dry ground.

Israel's crossing of the Jordan under Joshua's leadership is comparable to her experience at the Red Sea under Moses. Again the form of the story calls attention to the Lord's support of Joshua and his intervention on behalf of his people.

Special points.—Ritual preparation for a military expedition (v. 5) was considered to be very important in ancient Israel. Sacrifices were offered (1 Sam. 7:9), the soldiers were to remain continent (1 Sam. 21:6), the camp was to be kept clean (Deut. 23:10–15), and the will of the Lord was to be discerned (Judg. 20:23). In this case, the people were to respect the holiness of the ark by separating themselves from it (cf. 1 Sam. 6:19). A cubit was the distance from the elbow to the tip of the middle finger, about eighteen inches.

The Jordan was swollen in the springtime as the melting snows on the Lebanon mountains added their water to the heavy winter rains. In the view of some interpreters the river may have been dammed up at Adam where high clay bluffs line its banks. On numerous occasions earthquakes have tumbled these cliffs, undermined by water currents, into the river. The flow of the Jordan was interrupted by such an occurrence in 1927 for 21 hours.

Monuments of the Crossing (4:1–24)

The passage.—As Israel completed the crossing of the Jordan, arrangements were made for the construction of two mounds of memorial stones. One was erected in the riverbed where the priests bearing the ark had stood and the other at Gilgal, their first night's camp. Each was made of 12 stones borne by representatives of the 12 tribes of Israel. The monuments were to stimulate the curiosity of children who would then be told the story (vv. 6–7, 21–24). The successful crossing of the Jordan further exalted Joshua in the eyes of the people.

Special points.—The chapter as it stands is very complex and perhaps was originally ordered somewhat differently. Most duplications (e.g. vv. 6–7 and 21–24) are avoided if the stories of the two monuments are separated. This results in reasonably consistent accounts of the memorial mounds in the Jordan (3:12; 4:5–7, 9–14) and at Gilgal (4:1–3, 8,15–24).

The statement that the ark passed over "in the presence of the people" (v. 11) indicates that the ark resumed its position at the head of the column of march.

The contributions of the eastern tribes were obviously important in Israel's conquest of Canaan (1:12–18; 22:1–34). Nevertheless, it is hardly likely that they provided 40,000 fighting men. Even Egypt was defeated on numerous occasions by armies of smaller size. The term translated "thousand" may also refer to a conscription unit or clan within a tribe. Ordinarily only a few soldiers were taken from each group. Possibly a total of less than five hundred troops were involved.

Purification for Battle (5:1–15)

The passage.—Here we encounter two of the rites of sanctification (cf. 3:5) preparing the people for the coming conquest. First they circumcised the males who had grown up during the wilderness period when proper consecration of the newborn had become lax. Then, after the men were healed, the entire nation observed the feast of the Passover in commemoration of the Lord's mighty acts in delivering Israel from Egypt. Such fidelity to the requirements of the law was essential if God's blessings in the conquest were to be secured (1:7–9).

In his own preparation for the battle at Jericho, Joshua was granted further assurances of divine support. The "captain of the Lord's host" (v. 15) and the army under his command represent the unseen forces of God who were fighting on Israel's behalf (3:10). The ancient Hebrews lacked our concept of natural causation growing out of certain "laws" established in the beginning by the creator. Instead they saw God working directly in nature and history through his normally unseen emissaries (Gen. 32:

1–2; 2 Kings 6:15–17; Ps. 103:20–21).
Apparently they conceived God as governing these forces in the way an earthly king presided over his court (Job 1–2).

Special points.—Circumcision was widely practiced in the ancient world, but its significance no doubt varied from one culture to another. It was common among the Egyptians but not among the Philistines, Assyrians, or Babylonians. In Israel circumcision was primarily conceived as a symbol of the covenant relationship between God and his people (Gen. 17:11).

The Fall of Jericho (6:1–27)

The passage.—For six days soldiers, seven priests blowing rams' horns, and the ark of the Lord made a single journey around Jericho. On the seventh day, the process was repeated seven times, and on the final circuit the people shouted as the city walls fell before them.

The Israelites were instructed to destroy everything within the city except for Rahab and her household (cf. 2: 1–21). The inhabitants were to be killed and their property destroyed. Implements of metal were to be added to the Lord's treasury. This procedure was a regular feature of the *herem* or holy war which was a common practice among Israel's neighbors. This was the supreme act of devotion designed to secure divine blessing since the participants realized no profit from victory. Rahab was excepted from the ban since, by her actions, she had won an enduring place in Israel's history (v. 25).

Special points.—The spectacular repetition of the number "seven" calls attention to its significance in the Old Testament. It represented a state of completion or fulfillment. Anything done seven times or a multiple thereof was done "just right."

Archaeological evidence concerning the fall of Jericho has been the subject of considerable discussion. On the basis of excavations at the site from 1929 through 1936, John Garstang concluded that he had uncovered the city destroyed by Joshua.

In the meantime, however, archaeological technique has been improved dramatically. Thus, Miss Kathleen Kenyon in her excavations from 1952 through 1958 showed Garstang's conclusions to be in error. No walls from Joshua's time have been found and most remains from that period were washed away by erosion long ago.

The Sin of Achan (7:1–26)

The passage.—Following the conquest of Jericho, Joshua prepared to move into the hill country of central Palestine. He chose to go against Ai, a modest town located at the head of a precipitous gorge leading up from the river valley. A favorable report by his spies encouraged him to send only a small company against Ai.

The expedition met with disaster, however, as the men of Ai killed 36 Israelites and put the rest to flight. If, as seems likely, the term translated "thousand" actually refers to a much smaller unit (cf. comments on 4:1–24), a majority of the force was destroyed.

The true significance of the disaster must be seen against its theological background. Since God had been responsible for Israel's victories (5:13—6:2), a defeat indicated that the Lord's favor had been lost.

Joshua learned that someone had violated the rules for holy war by taking spoils for himself (cf. comments on 6: 1–27). The guilt was successively traced until Achan was found to be at fault.

Achan's punishment was deemed particularly fitting by the Israelites. Since he had failed to carry out his obligation to destroy the enemy and all his property, his own family and all his holdings would be annihilated.

The Israelites' strong sense of community solidarity led them to see that the consequences of sin can never be restricted solely to the individual. At this time they held the family, tribe, and even the nation accountable for the sins of one of its members (cf. Ex. 20:5). Later, they recognized a much larger degree of individual responsibility (Deut. 24:16; Jer. 31:29–30).

The Destruction of Ai (8:1–29)

The passage.—With Achan's sin purged, Joshua was free to resume the attack with assurances of victory (8:1–2). The description of the action is rather complex, but the Israelite plan is clear. One group was hidden west of Ai while Joshua and the main force encamped in full view of the city a short distance to the north.

When the king of Ai attacked the following morning, Joshua's troops pretended to panic. Their headlong flight back toward the Jordan drew even the reserves within Ai into pursuit. With the gates undefended, the men in ambush had little difficulty in seizing the city and putting it to the torch. The trap now snapped shut. Joshua halted the flight of his troops, and the men of Ai were hopelessly caught in a battle on two fronts. All Canaanite resistance crumbled, and the city was totally destroyed.

Special points.—A special dispensation of the rules for holy war (cf. comments on 6:1–27) allowed the Israelites to keep the cattle and goods that they seized in battle in order to continue the conquest. The people of the city, however, remained under the ban (v. 2).

As it stands, the account of the battle for Ai is not consistent (cf. v. 3 and v. 12). It is less confusing if verses 11–13 are omitted. Apparently two separate accounts of the action have been combined.

The Altar on Mount Ebal (8:30–35)

The passage.—These verses describe how Joshua carried out the instructions of Moses in Deuteronomy 11:29–30. At the earliest opportunity, he established a place of worship and reacquainted the people with the law. Although it is not explicit here, this probably represents a renewal of the covenant between God and his people (cf. Josh. 24:1–28).

Special points.—This incident is set on Mount Ebal and Mount Gerizim near the city of Shechem. The Bible contains no records of Israelite conquests in this area. Since vigorous resistance was still encountered in other areas (9:1–2), Israel may have encountered friendly people here (cf. Introduction). They may even have been relatives since Israel was to destroy foreign cities in the Promised Land (Deut. 20:16–18).

Canaanite Coalitions Formed (9:1–27)

The passage.—The land of Canaan had no centralized government at this time, and the small city-states were no match for a moderately well-organized foe. As other cities learned the fate of Jericho and Ai, they formed alliances to protect themselves. Although a majority of these resisted Israel's advances (9:1–2; 10:1 f.), some were willing to become Israel's vassals in order to preserve their lives.

The tactics of the Gibeonite confederation are based on a rather precise knowledge of Israel's foreign policy. Distant cities were allowed to sue for peace (Deut. 20:10–11), but the major powers of central Palestine were to be utterly destroyed (Deut. 7:1–2). Understanding this, men from Gibeon used elaborate disguises to convince the Israelites that they had traveled great distances to seek their friendship. Finally, convinced of the truth of their story, Joshua granted a treaty guaranteeing the safety of the Gibeonites.

Ancient Israel took solemn vows very seriously. Although the Gibeonites had misrepresented their situation, their covenant could not be abrogated. The Israelites, however, were eager to exploit the inferior status of their deceitful neighbors (v. 27).

The four cities in the alliance led by the Gibeonites lie within a ten-mile radius from Jerusalem, northwest of the city.

Joshua's Southern Campaign (10:1–43)

The passage.—Following Israel's treaty with the Gibeonite confederation, Canaanite leaders in southern Palestine were even more concerned. From the strong Gibeonite cities, Joshua was in a position to isolate the south. The king of Jerusalem, therefore, quickly organized a coalition to force Gibeon back into the Canaanite camp.

As Israel's vassals (servants, v. 6), the Gibeonites appealed to Joshua for aid. He arranged a forced night march and surprised the king of Jerusalem and his allies as dawn broke. With divine assistance (vv. 11, 13–14), Israel inflicted heavy losses on the enemy and put them to flight.

Following a long disastrous retreat, the five Canaanite kings sought to save themselves by hiding in a cave near Makkedah. Their strategem failed, however. Joshua destroyed them at his leisure after completing his attack on their armies.

The remainder of the chapter (vv. 28–43) gives a summary of Joshua's victories over certain other southern cities. Little is known about the conditions un-

der which these events took place. The Bible, for example, elsewhere describes the fall of Hebron and Debir under circumstances which differ considerably from those given here (Josh. 15:14–19; Judg. 1:10–11).

Special points.—As has been the case formerly, Joshua's southern campaign stresses God's protective care and minimizes the role of Israelite arms (vv. 8, 11,25,42). While we can no longer reconstruct the phenomena involved in the Lord's intervention (vv. 11–14), we recognize that the Israelites were convinced that their God could, and would, use any means necessary to bring victory.

Joshua's return to Gilgal appears out of place in verse 15. The incidents which follow it seem to be immediate consequences of the rout at Gibeon. Perhaps the reference to Gilgal in verse 43 represents the proper sequence.

Joshua's Northern Campaign (11:1–23)

The passage.—As word of Israel's victories in the south spread, a defensive alliance was formed among the Canaanite cities of the north. This coalition, under the leadership of Jabin, king of Hazor, fielded a formidable army of both foot soldiers and chariotry. Seizing the initiative, Joshua struck swiftly and surprised the enemy by the waters of Merom, a stream flowing into the Sea of Galilee from the northwest.

The Canaanite coalition was put to flight, leaving their horses to be hamstrung and their chariots burned. Joshua pursued the enemy as far as the Phoenician Coast, pillaging the countryside and destroying its people (v. 14). Of the great walled cities, however, Joshua took only Hazor (v. 13). Archaeologists estimate that this great city of some 40,000 people fell to the Israelites during the latter half of the thirteenth century B.C.

The remainder of the chapter (vv.

6. Gibeon, present-day town over site of ancient ruins
(see Josh. 9:3–27)

16–23) provides a summary of the entire conquest. Joshua took all the land from Mount Halak in the south to Mount Hermon in the north, and "the land had rest from war" (v. 23, RSV).

Special points.—The biblical author was undoubtedly aware that much unconquered Canaanite territory remained in Palestine. The fortified cities of Galilee had not been taken (11:15), nor had the Philistine plain (13:2–3). Manasseh was unable to possess the fertile Plain of Esdraelon (17:11–13), and in Joshua's old age there were many unconquered areas (13:1; Judg. 1:1–36). The author is merely saying that under Joshua's leadership, Israel had won a lasting foothold in the Promised Land.

Verse 20 explains the bitter resistance of the Canaanites as the result of the Lord's hardening of their hearts (See also Ex. 9:12; 10:20). Such a view is an outgrowth of efforts to understand the sovereignty of God. In keeping with this conviction, some Old Testament passages portray God as the author of all things, the evil as well as the good (1 Sam. 16:14; Isa. 45:7). Elsewhere, however, man is depicted as a free and morally responsible creature (Gen. 2–3; Ex. 8:15,32). As a whole, the Bible takes into account both God's sovereignty and man's freedom.

Summary of Defeated Kings (12:1–24)

The passage.—The story of the conquest is recreated here in a list of the kings Israel defeated under the leader-

143

ship of Moses and Joshua. The eastern campaigns (vv. 1–6) are given a prominent position here to add weight to the author's stress on the unity within Israel's tribal structure at this time (1:12–18; 22:1–34).

Most of this information is drawn from other known biblical sources. Deuteronomy 2:16—3:17 and Numbers 21 f., for example, provide a much broader knowledge of the conquest east of Jordan. In the western campaign, the kings listed in verses 7–13 are drawn directly from Joshua 6–10. Only a few of the remaining kings (vv. 13–24) are drawn from some source other than Joshua 10–11.

Special points.—Not all of the cities whose kings are listed here were destroyed. The kings may have participated in unsuccessful coalitions against the Hebrews by providing troops for battlefield engagements. Joshua avoided prolonged sieges of many of the larger fortified cities.

Conditions of the Allotment (13:1–33)

The passage.—Now that the author's story of the conquest was complete, he turned his attention to the division of the land (chaps. 13–21). Substantial areas were still beyond Israelite control, but the entire land was to be apportioned to the tribes. The Philistines and the Phoenicians along the coast as well as the Canaanites north of Mount Hermon would be driven out by the Lord himself (vv. 1–6). This optimistic forecast was never fully realized in ancient Israel.

Again special attention is devoted to the eastern tribes whose land had been granted them by Moses (12:1–6; Deut. 2–3). Reuben's territory lay east of the Dead Sea between the Arnon River and Wadi Husban (Hesbon) which flows into the Jordan just south of Jericho (vv. 15–23).

Gad claimed the land from the Wadi Husban on the south to Mahanaim (located somewhere near the Jabbok River) on the north. Apparently this included a narrow section of the Jordan valley extending up to the southern tip of the Sea of Chinnereth (Galilee). God's holdings were bordered on the east by the Ammonites, who provided a lasting threat to their holdings. Gad survived, however, and gradually absorbed Reuben's lands (cf. Num. 32:34–38).

The half-tribe of Manasseh settled in the territory running northward from Gad's boundary near Mahanaim to an undisclosed frontier north and east of the Sea of Galilee (vv. 29–31). The term Machir was later used to designate the eastern segment of Manasseh (cf. Judg. 5:14).

Levi, as a priestly tribe, was not granted a territorial inheritance. Certain cities throughout the country, however, were turned over to her people to provide them with homes and sustenance.

Hebron Granted to Caleb (14:1–15)

The passage.—Almost as if chapter 13 were not present, we are given an introduction setting the stage for the allotment itself. The major contribution of this passage seems to lie in its explanation of a direct grant of Hebron and its environs to Caleb, a Kenizzite (vv. 6–15).

Caleb, along with Joshua, had returned a report encouraging Israel to enter Canaan from the south (Num. 13–14; Deut. 1:35–36). His absolute fidelity to the Lord's instructions brought him undiminished powers into his eighty-fifth year (vv. 10–11) and a legitimate claim on the land he had surveyed. Although the struggle for Hebron was not yet over (v. 12), he and his descendants were given it as their inheritance.

Caleb's identification as a Kenizzite suggests that he may have come from a

FON H. SCOFIELD, JR.

7. Lachish, ruins of the governor's palace at top
(see Josh. 10:3–5)

foreign background. As a matter of fact, Kenaz, for whom the Kenizzites were named, is listed as a descendant of Esau, the father of the Edomites (Gen. 36: 9–11). Elsewhere, Caleb is recognized as a member of the tribe of Judah (Num. 13:6; 34:6). Apparently this is another illustration of the inclusion of foreigners among the heroes of Israel (cf. also Rahab and Ruth).

Special points.—We are not told here how the lots were used to divide the land. The lots themselves appear to have been used as one today would flip a coin. The ancient Israelite believed that God revealed his will by controlling the lots to give a positive or negative response. The questions had to be worded very carefully by the priest so that only

yes or no answers were required.

The term "lot" was then extended to refer to the conclusion reached by such means (cf. 15:1).

Judah's Territory (15:1–63)

The passage.—Here the author finally gives his account of the distribution of the western lands. Judah's territory is described in three segments. Two statistical records (vv. 1–12 and 20–63) are separated by a narrative concerning Caleb's occupations of Hebron and Debir (vv. 13–19).

Caleb had been given a land grant in the southern hill country with the understanding that he would have to make his own arrangements for conquering it (14:6–15). After seizing Hebron himself,

145

Caleb promised his daughter in marriage to the person who would take Debir. Othniel, leader of another Kenizzite clan, was successful in capturing the city; thus another foreign group was adopted into Judah.

The ideal limits of Judah's territory are given (vv. 1–12). Roughly, Judah's southern border ran from the lower tip of the Dead Sea southwest to Kadesh-barnea and thence northwest to the sea. The northern border approximately followed the route a traveler would have taken from the northern tip of the Dead Sea to the Mediterranean. Since Judah's territory included all the land between these two seas, it also embraced the Philistine plain which was independent until David's time. Jerusalem, however, was excluded (v. 63).

The second statistical list in this section surveys the towns in Judah, grouped according to their geographical location (vv. 20–63). The number of these groups and the systematic manner in which they are presented suggest that the list reflects the administrative districts within the kingdom of Judah. Judean territory is, therefore, presented as it was known during the tenth-ninth century B.C.

Special points.—Hebron and Debir were also destroyed by Joshua (10: 36–39). Neither passage takes note of the other, however. One of the campaigns, possibly the one by the Kenizzites, was considerably earlier than this context indicates.

Ephraim's Territory (16:1–10)

The passage.—In contrast with the detailed records for Judah, the materials for reconstructing Ephraim's boundaries are sparse and ambiguous. Fortunately, it can be supplemented by descriptions of the borders of Ephraim's neighboring tribes.

On the south, Ephraim shared a common border with Benjamin (18:11–28) and Dan (19:40–48). This boundary ran from a point on the Jordan River just north of Jericho, to Bethel, through the valley near Beth-horon, and thence to the Mediterranean. The northern border, shared with Manasseh, followed a line just below Shechem running east and west from the river to the sea.

In verse 10 the author indicates that the Canaanites remained in Gezer as Israel's servants until his own time. In the ancient world a well-fortified city could maintain itself for years even in the midst of a hostile countryside. Gezer was destroyed and the population enslaved in the time of Solomon (1 Kings 9:15–21).

Special points.—Bethel and Luz in verse 2 are elsewhere explained as variant names for the same place (18:13).

Manasseh's Territory (17:1–18)

The passage.—Asher and Michmethath (v. 7) represent the northern and southern extremities of Manasseh's territory and not a boundary as such. In the south Manasseh adjoined Ephraim near Shechem at Michmethath. From that point the border ran eastward to the Jordan and westward to the sea. In the north, Manasseh shared the plain of Esdraelon (Jezreel) with Asher, Zebulun, and Issachar.

In the coastal plain and in Esdraelon, strong Canaanite settlements thwarted Manasseh's attempts to possess her territory (vv. 11–12). In that terrain, foot soldiers were no match for the armored chariots of the Canaanites (v. 16). The more simply equipped Israelite troops were much more effective in the hill country where the chariots had difficulty maneuvering. Unable to expel the Canaanites from the lowlands, Manasseh was forced to exploit the forested slopes of her mountains (vv. 14–15).

Assembly Shifts to Shiloh (18:1–10)

The passage.—The complexity of the Israelite conquest and settlement is reflected by the delay in establishing each tribe's territory. Clearly, the unity reflected in Joshua's early campaigns (chaps. 1–11) was more ideal than real. With seven of the tribes still without permanent homes (v. 2), interest in the allotment lagged, and the process was finally halted. We are not told where these people lived nor why their interests were neglected, but a careful reading of the biblical record indicates that the occupation of Canaan was a long, complicated process.

When the allotment was resumed, Israel's base camp had been shifted from Gilgal to Shiloh. The central sanctuary remained there until about 1050 B.C. when the ark was captured by the Philistines (1 Sam. 4). After rebuking the people for their delay, Joshua arranged for a detailed survey of the land and then divided it according to the decision of the lot (cf. comments on 14:1–15).

Territory of Benjamin (18:11–28)

The passage.—Benjamin's holdings are given in considerable detail. Bounded by Ephraim on the north and Judah on the south, Benjamin's land extended from the Jordan River on the east to Lower Beth-horon and Kiriath-jearim on the west. This represents a maximum distance of 25 miles east to west and ten miles north to south.

Within this limited area lay some of the best known cities in Israel: Jericho, Bethel, Gibeon, Ramah, and Jerusalem. Most of these were small according to modern standards, but they were of historic importance to the Hebrews and often to the Canaanites before them.

Special points.—Benjamin's cities are listed in a fashion shared only by Judah (15:20–63) and Simeon (19:1–9). The groupings of the towns in these lists probably represent administrative districts within the kingdom of Judah (which later included the territories of all three tribes).

Remaining Territory Allotted (19:1–51)

The passage.—The holdings of the remaining tribes are given in considerably less detail than has been the case formerly. Apparently official documents were available only for the territory within the kingdom of Judah.

The inheritance of Simeon lies wholly within the borders of Judah (vv. 1–9). Simeon seems to have been on the verge of disappearing as an independent tribe at a very early time (cf. Deut. 33). Only a few cities in the southwestern desert of Judah remained for her people.

The holdings of the four Galilean tribes are very difficult to reconstruct. Asher, Zebulun, and Issachar adjoined Manasseh on the south in the plain of Esdraelon. Asher (vv. 24–31) claimed the coastal plain from Mount Carmel to the Phoenician city of Tyre. Her control of this territory was always tenuous at best.

Issachar occupied the rolling hills rising out of the eastern half of Esdraelon (vv. 17–23). From the base of Mount Gilboa in the south and including Mount Tabor in the north her territory ran eastward to the Jordan River south of the Sea of Galilee.

Zebulun (vv. 10–16) claimed a narrow strip of land about ten miles wide between Asher and Issachar. It extended about 20 miles northward from Esdraelon.

Naphtali settled in a broad section along the Jordan from the foot of Mount Lebanon to the southern tip of the Sea of Galilee (vv. 32–39). Although this region was still dominated by Canaanite influences (Judg. 1:33;

4:2), the tribe of Dan later migrated in this direction when the Philistines drove them from their allotment between Judah, Benjamin, and Ephraim (vv. 40–48; cf. Judg. 17–18).

Cities of Refuge (20:1–9)

The passage.—During the conquest, Israel still had not developed an effective central government. With each tribe pursuing its own interests, little could be done to establish equitable law enforcement. Primarily each family or clan had to protect its own members in accordance with the law of retaliation (i.e. "an eye for an eye"; cf. Lev. 24:17–21).

A distinction was rarely made between murder and manslaughter. Blood feuds often resulted when a bereaved family executed a man who had unintentionally killed one of its members.

In an effort to curb such excesses, three cities of refuge were established on each side of the Jordan. An accused man could find sanctuary there if he could convince its elders that he was not guilty of premeditated murder.

Levitical Cities (21:1–45)

The passage.—While the Levites as a priestly group were not granted a territorial allotment, they were given certain cities scattered throughout the land. According to the commandment of Moses (Num. 35:1–8), they were given 48 cities, normally four from each tribe. A slightly variant list of Levitical cities is found in 1 Chronicles 6:54–81. Apparently the priestly holdings were altered from time to time as historical circumstances demanded.

The final paragraphs of this chapter provide a theological conclusion for Israel's conquest of Canaan. The Lord had fulfilled the promises he made to Joshua at the beginning of his ministry

(1:2–6). The tribes had taken possession of their allotments (v. 43), and the land lay subdued before them (v. 44). With Joshua's major objectives accomplished, the author can now draw his story to a close.

Special points.—Here again (cf. 11: 23) at the end of Joshua's ministry, the conquest is portrayed as a completed event. Not one of Israel's enemies had been able to withstand them (v. 44). This is obviously a generalization designed to make a theological point. God does fulfil his promises, but at the death of Joshua, many Canaanites remained in Israel (Judg. 1–2).

Eastern Tribes Dismissed (22:1–34)

The passage.—At the end of the united campaign for control of the Promised Land, Joshua dismissed the eastern tribes to return to their homes. As the troops from Manasseh, Gad, and Reuben withdrew, they built a replica of the altar of the Lord on the western bank of the Jordan (v. 11, RSV).

A misinterpretation of the purpose of the altar almost led to civil war. A monument, intended to bind the eastern and western tribes together (vv. 24–28), was interpreted as an effort to establish a rival religious center (v. 19).

Israel's central sanctuary was of pivotal importance. In addition to its religious function, it served as the focal point of her government as well. Only in their worship of the Lord were the independent tribes of Israel united in any real sense. To build a rival altar was to violate the covenant by seceding from the nation.

Special points.—In a political sense, the withdrawal of the eastern tribes could bring destruction upon the whole nation. Shorn of her inner unity, Israel would be easy prey for her enemies. The biblical author saw God underlying all human history. Rebellion by a portion of Israel one day would bring the Lord's anger on the whole congregation the next (v. 18).

Joshua's Farewell Address (23:1–16)

The passage.—Joshua's farewell message to the leaders of Israel gives a clear insight into the theological premise of the whole history from Deuteronomy through Kings. Israel is promised the Lord's blessings if she faithfully keeps the covenant and his wrath if she departs from his instructions. Since Israel had been steadfastly loyal to God, not one of his promises had been broken (v. 14). The Lord gave Israel victory in the conquest by multiplying the effectiveness of her soldiers a thousandfold (v. 10). Should Israel prove faithless in the future, however, disaster would certainly follow (vv. 12–13,16).

Joshua's warnings provided an ominous foreshadowing of the period following his death. Israel was threatened with virtual extinction (v. 15). This was not the result of any impotence on the Lord's part. Rather such reverses represent God's judgment on the rebelliousness of his people.

Special points.—The theological principle expressed by Joshua is called the doctrine of divine retribution. It is based on the realization that righteous people *tend* to be blessed in life, and the unrighteous *tend* to be brought low. Later Old Testament thought, however, recognized that not all prosperity is the result of godliness and not all suffering is the result of sin (see Job 1–2; Isa.

52:13—53:12). Overall biblical thought takes into account both these views.

The Covenant at Shechem (24:1–33)

The passage.—The book of Joshua concludes with an account of the covenant renewal ceremony at Shechem. After recounting glorious instances of God's deliverance of Israel (vv. 2–13), Joshua calls on the people to declare their loyalty to the Lord alone (vv. 14–16). They are cautioned against hasty commitment (vv. 19–20), for the Lord will tolerate absolutely no division of loyalties. Fully aware of the consequences of their decision, the people pledge their allegiance to God. In commemoration of the event, Joshua erected a monument in the sanctuary at Shechem.

The chapter ends with brief notices concerning the tombs of Joshua, Joseph, and Eleazar in the territory of the Joseph tribes. Under these leaders Israel had remained true to the Lord (v. 31).

Special points.—No reason is given for the shift from Shiloh which is presumed to have been Israel's central sanctuary at this time (22:12; see also 18:1; 21:1). Perhaps the covenant at Shechem actually occurred earlier in the life of Joshua in connection with the events described in 8:30–35 (see also Deut. 27–28).

Verse 19 should be read in context and not overgeneralized. God does forgive sin, but he also takes covenant violations very seriously (v. 20). Idolatry will not be tolerated.

JUDGES

Ben F. Philbeck

INTRODUCTION

In Hebrew memory the death of Joshua marked a turning point in the occupation of the Promised Land. During his lifetime the conquest had gone well, and the nation was able to gain a foothold in Canaan against overwhelming odds. After his death, however, regional isolation and local self-interests undermined national unity. Civil wars broke out (Judg. 12:1–6; 20:1–48), some tribes were unable to occupy their allotments (Judg. 18:1–31), and others virtually ceased functioning as independent units (such as Simeon, see Josh. 19:1–9). By the time of Samuel, the last of the judges, Israel had been nearly destroyed by the Philistines (1 Sam. 4–6; 13:19–23), and her tribal government was giving way to a monarchy.

Israel's historians explained this change in national fortunes on theological grounds. Under Joshua the people had been faithful unto God (Josh. 23:8; 24:31), thus ensuring themselves of the Lord's protection. The failure of Israel's cause under the judges was seen to be the consequence of her violation of the covenant. Israelites intermarried with the local population and began worshiping foreign gods (Judg. 2:1–13). Such actions were certain to bring disaster (2:14–15).

This premise of divine causation in human history, called the doctrine of divine retribution (see comments on Josh. 23), is clearly demonstrated in the core of the book of Judges (2:6—16:

31). The story of each major judge is presented in a precise formula involving sin, judgment, repentance, and deliverance. When the people sin, God sends punishment in the form of a foreign conqueror who oppresses Israel for a number of years. When adversity ultimately causes the nation to repent, the Lord sends a judge who throws off the yoke of the oppressor. Unfortunately a restoration of prosperity regularly entices Israel to return to her sinful ways, and the cycle begins again.

Unconquered Lands (Judg. 1:1–36)

The passage.—The phrase "after the death of Joshua" is probably best regarded as the ancient title of the book. In Jewish practice, the name of each scroll was derived from the first words which appeared in it. Much of the material contained in the first chapter has been reported earlier (Josh. 10:1 f.). In the present account the role of the southern tribes is stressed (Judg. 1:1), and otherwise only the unconquered territories are given.

Special points.—The similarity of the names and fates of Adonibezek and Adonizedek (Josh. 10:1–27) suggests variant accounts of a single attack on Jerusalem. The broader Old Testament record shows that Israel was unable to gain permanent control over the city (Josh. 15:63; 2 Sam. 5:6). The Judeans may have captured the city except for a strongly fortified garrison on the heights of Zion. Following the initial wave of Israelite devastation, the Jebusites were able to regain control of the city.

Israelite power was restricted primarily to the hill country and smaller towns (vv. 19–36 and commentary on Josh. 21:43–45). The larger walled cities of the Canaanites and Philistines were too strong to be taken by the Hebrews. Thus the Septuagint indicates that Judah did *not* take Gaza, Ashkelon, and Ekron, cities of the coastal plain of Palestine.

Failures of Israel Explained (Judg. 2:1–23)

The passage.—The author clearly sets forth the theological framework of his history (see Introduction to Judges). He was convinced that the conquest was successful because the people served the Lord during Joshua's whole generation (v. 7). Likewise, the nation faltered during the following period because the people adopted the false gods of the people among whom they settled (vv. 11–14).

Understandably this framework is something of a generalization. Even Joshua was not completely successful in driving out the enemy (v. 23). Nevertheless, the impact of the author's theological perspective is quite clear. God was at work on behalf of his people, and their affairs would *tend* to go smoothly when they were faithful unto him. Conversely, lack of fidelity would undermine Israel's unity, and the nation would become increasingly open to foreign domination.

The book of Judges provides valuable insights into the pressures and problems which threatened to destroy the nation (see chaps. 5 and 19–21). The very desperation of Israel's predicament, however, also serves to highlight the stature of the leadership during this period. Indeed without God's provision

of the judges, the nation might have died aborning.

Othniel, Ehud, and Shamgar (Judg. 3:1–31)

The passage.—As Israel became established in Palestine, her existence was threatened by hostile neighbors. Our author was convinced of the Lord's sovereignty over human history (see Introduction). He, therefore, sought to explain why God did not use his power to overthrow the enemies of his people (see Josh. 23:9–10). He offered several answers. (1) Because of Israel's infidelity, the Lord was punishing them (2:11–15). (2) Enemies were allowed to remain so that those who had not experienced the conquest might know the discipline of war (3:2). (3) Foreign nations with enticing ways were left to test Israel's ability to withstand temptation (v. 4).

These should probably be considered tentative rather than final answers. Experience indicates that each has a place in practical reality, but God's motives are not always perfectly understood. Later biblical thought, for example, repudiates the idea that God tempts or tests men in this sense (the Septuagint uses the same word in 3:4 that is used in James 1:13–14).

Special points.—The reference to Cushan-rishathaim, king of Mesopotamia (Aram), is obscure. Extensions of Mesopotamian power into Palestine are unknown during this period. Since Othniel and Caleb were members of Judean clans, a southern enemy may be involved. Cushan is elsewhere associated with Edom and Midian (Hab. 3:7), and the terms "Aram" and "Edom" are easily confused in Hebrew.

Another crisis for the southern tribes was precipitated when the city of palms (Jericho) fell to a coalition of Ammonites, Moabites, and Amalekites. The coalition collapsed, however, when Ehud treacherously assassinated its leader Eglon, king of Moab, in his own palace. Such deception was apparently not condemned since success in warfare was considered a gift of God (v. 28).

Little is known about Shamgar who is also mentioned in the Song of Deborah (5:6). The Philistines were not known to have posed a threat until the time of Samson.

Israel Defeats Hazor (Judg. 4:1–24)

The passage.—Judges 4 and 5 represent prose and poetic accounts respectively of Israel's struggle with Jabin, king of Hazor. This important Canaanite stronghold apparently had recovered from an earlier Israelite defeat (Josh. 11:1–15). The city, located about eight miles north of the Sea of Galilee, is estimated to have had a population of about 40,000 at one time. The pre-Israelite occupation ended about 1250 B.C.

Deborah's role in public affairs is unusual in ancient Israel, but not unique. The Decalogue listed a man's wife along with his other possessions (Ex. 20:17), but a woman could also rule over the nation (2 Kings 11) or serve as an advisor to the king (2 Kings 22:14).

Sisera, commander of the army from Hazor, depended heavily on a large force of horse-drawn chariotry. In the lowlands around Mount Tabor, the Canaanite war machines provided a marked advantage over the Israelite foot soldiers. The Lord, perhaps with an untimely flood (5:21), immobilized the chariots, however, and Israel's enemies were put to flight. Sisera sought sanctuary in the tent of a Kenite only to be killed in his sleep by a woman.

Special points.—The Kenites were nomadic metalsmiths who were generally on friendly terms with the people among whom they settled. From Moses until the time of David (1 Sam. 30:29), however, they were especially regarded as allies to Israel.

Song of Deborah (Judg. 5:1–31)

The passage.—This great victory song is one of the oldest examples of Hebrew poetry in existence. Roughly contemporary with the events it describes, this work is of pivotal importance in the study of premonarchic Israel. In addition to the story of Deborah, we learn of the religion, history, and culture of Israel in the early twelfth century B.C.

The song combines the exultant mood of a victory celebration with a reflective expression of thanksgiving to the Lord. Israel's down-to-earth faith was based on the conviction that her destiny was guided by God. From the time of Moses' encounter on Sinai (v. 5), the Lord had been engaged in history protecting his people. In the battle against Sisera, even the forces of nature conspired to bring about the downfall of Hazor (vv. 4,20–21).

Internally, however, Israel is shown to be on the verge of collapse. While six tribes were commended for responding to the call to arms, four were rebuked for their failure to participate, and Judah and Simeon are not even mentioned. Apparently Zebulun and Naphtali bore the brunt of the struggle (4:6,10), as regional interests weakened Israel's resolve to function as a united people.

While the nation may have been reeling under the impact of growing isolationism, her people were still the recipients of a rich cultural heritage.

8. Wine press (see Judg. 6:11)

FON H. SCOFIELD, JR.

The literary quality of the Song of Deborah marks it as an outstanding example of Semitic poetic forms in the late second millennium B.C. The author's portrayal of the oppression under Jabin (vv. 6–9), her sarcastic rebuke of Israel's reluctant warriors (vv. 15–17), and her account of the battle (vv. 19–27) attest her creative genius. Her portrayal of a distraught mother awaiting the return of her dead son (vv. 28–30) evokes the sympathy of the reader and serves to balance triumphal glee of the remainder of the poem. This successful combination of reflective thought, emo-

tional impact, and artistic form truly mark this work as one of the notable literary creations of all times.

Call of Gideon (Judg. 6:1–40)

The passage.—Israel faced another grave political crisis in the attacks of a coalition of nomadic groups from the East. Prior to this time the desert provided an effective barrier against invaders dependent on donkeys. By using the newly-domesticated camel (v. 5), these marauders gained the element of surprise. They abandoned the customary travel routes and bypassed fortified

153

outposts, robbing the peasants of their produce in the harvest season. Extensive military campaigns by the Israelites were foredoomed since the raiders would soon mount their camels and melt back into the vast deserts.

Israel was poorly equipped to deal with a crisis of such magnitude. The ability of her tribal leaders (Josh. 22: 30; 23:2; etc.) to unite the nation was limited at best, and their efforts were now being undercut by religious differences. Even prominent Israelite families possessed Baalistic altars, and the people were prepared to kill in the name of religious zeal (Judg. 6:25–32). A population thus divided was ripe for foreign exploitation.

Clearly the nation needed a resolute man of faith and a dynamic, courageous leader. Gideon, a member of a small clan of Manasseh, was just such a man. Cautious (v. 11), skeptical (v. 13), and apologetic (v. 15), he sought and received confirmation of his commission from God. First, a spectacular fire consuming a sacrificial meal (vv. 19–24) and then the test of the fleece (vv. 36–40) attested the Lord's support of his cause. Thus reassured, he called Israel to arms to resist the Midianites and the Amalekites who encamped in the Valley of Jezreel (vv. 33–35).

Gideon Selects His Men (Judg. 7:1–25)

The passage.—Gideon's attack on the Midianite camp is, on the whole, quite straightforward. Over 30,000 men from Manasseh, Asher, Zebulun, and Naphtali responded to Gideon's call to arms. Three hundred of these were selected for a surprise night attack on the marauder's camp, and the Midianites were put to flight.

The logic of Gideon's plan is variously explained. The theological impact of a small band winning an important victory over a formidable foe is quite clear. Israel would be encouraged to acknowledge the Lord's hand in the whole affair (v. 2).

A strategic justification for Gideon's actions is less apparent, but it may be no less real. He faced an enemy who depended on the mobility of their camels to carry on a guerrilla-type warfare. Although the Midianites' morale was apparently at a low ebb (vv. 9–14), surprise was essential. Gideon, therefore, used a small select group to arrange a night ambush. The noise and confusion of the attack routed the Midianites who were unaccustomed to fighting at night. Gideon then called on his reserves to pursue the fleeing enemy (vv. 23–25). However Gideon's strategy is explained, the Midianite nomads were never again able to threaten Israel.

Special points.—The test by which Gideon's men were selected is variously interpreted. While the drinker's stance may suggest alertness, the text itself offers no clues. The stress seems to fall on the restricted number who remained to assist Gideon.

Gideon's Men Pursue Midianites (Judg. 8:1–35)

The passage.—As the Midianites retreated east of the Jordan, the fragile nature of Israel's control over her own territory became more apparent. Two Israelite towns, Succoth and Penuel, refused to give provisions to Gideon and his weary men. They feared repraisals from the Midianites whose leaders were still free. After making an end of the Midianites, Gideon returned and exacted revenge for the affront offered by these two cities (vv. 13–17). The brutality of his actions must be understood against the background of his own day.

The ancient author apparently regarded the outcome as quite appropriate.

Gideon also slew the Midianite kings, Zebah and Zalmunna, for their treatment of Israelite prisoners of war. They had killed Gideon's brothers who had been captured in the battle at Mount Tabor. Gideon, therefore, exacted the ancient law of blood guilt (Num. 35:16–21) in avenging the death of his own kin.

When the magnitude of Gideon's victory became apparent, the leaders of Israel sought to make him their king. Thus the nation would be drawn together and a trained leadership would be assured to meet future emergencies. Gideon firmly declined, however, on the grounds that the Lord was Israel's true ruler (v. 23). The heritage of the past was too deeply ingrained to be set aside without difficulty.

Special points.—From the spoils of war, Gideon constructed a golden ephod which, in this context, seems to have been some kind of idol (v. 27). This object must be distinguished from the linen ephod which was a vestment worn by a priest (1 Sam. 2:28).

Abimelech Seeks Kingship (Judg. 9:1–57)

The passage.—The story of Abimelech's abortive kingship at Shechem speaks eloquently of the disastrous conditions in Israel during this period. Shechem was apparently still a Canaanite city although it was nominally a part of Israel. The Bible does not include it as a part of Israel's wars of conquest, but the city is portrayed as the site of Joshua's farewell address (Josh. 23–24). Gideon had a Shechemite concubine, the mother of Abimelech, but she never became assimilated into Israel. Abimelech was later very aware of the distinction between his mother's and his father's people (v. 2).

Religious tensions also probably played an important role in the attempt to establish an independent kingdom at Shechem. Gideon had earlier come into conflict with Baalism (6:25–32), and now funds to hire assassins for his sons come from the house of Baalberith (v. 4). Abimelech hired "worthless and reckless fellows" to murder 70 of his brothers, missing only the youngest, Jotham.

After Abimelech's treachery, Jotham proclaimed a fable in which the king and his people brought disaster to each other (vv. 7–21). Jotham condemned Abimelech as a bramble trying to rule over the majestic cedars of Lebanon, but his greatest wrath was reserved for the people of Shechem. When their lack of good faith became known, all involved in the dubious venture would be destroyed (v. 15).

Surely enough, the Shechemites were soon enticed to follow Gaal the son of Ebed, and they plotted to overthrow their new king. Abimelech attacked the city, razing its buildings and destroying its people. The last section of the city to fall was the citadel. The survivors barricaded themselves in the stronghold of El-berith which was burned down around them. Jotham's fable was coming true.

Abimelech was finally killed in an attack on Thebez which had also rebelled against his rule. Already mortally wounded by a millstone thrown from the ramparts by a woman, Abimelech called on his armor bearer to strike the final blow. So ended the life of one who had killed 70 of his brothers to become king.

Special points.—Abimelech's kingdom appears to have included only the central area of Palestine. Aside from the general statement in verse 22, the story itself only involved Shechem, Arunah, Thebez, and perhaps Ophrah.

Israel Oppressed by Ammonites (Judg. 10:1–18)

The passage.—The longer stories of Israel's judges are presented in recurrent cycles of sin, punishment, repentance, and deliverance (see Introduction). The book of Judges also contains shorter notices of leaders who are presented apart from this framework. Six of these so-called minor judges are listed: Shamgar (3:31), Tola (10:1–2), Jair (10:3–5), Ibzan (12:8–10), Elon (12:11–12), and Abdon (12:13–15). Little is known of their carrers or influence.

The standard introductory formula, in a slightly expanded form, is included as a preface to the stories of Jephthah (11:1—12:6) and Samson (13:1—16:31). Again the root of Israel's problem lay in her lack of fidelity to the Lord. The people tended to take on the ways, and the gods, of the people among whom they settled (v. 6). As a consequence they lost their identity as the people of God and became an easy prey for foreign oppressors.

The Ammonites were the specific foe in question at this time. Since the Philistines do not figure in the Jephthah story which follows, they are presumably introduced here in anticipation of the Samson episodes. The Ammonite pressure seems to have been largely directed against Gilead. Although some raids had been directed against Ephraim, Benjamin, and Judah (v. 9), the leaders of Gilead were left to face the struggle against Ammon alone (v. 18; see also 12:1–6).

Jephthah Delivers Israel (Judg. 11:1–40)

The passage.—The elders of Gilead recognized the necessity of locating a man with sufficient leadership qualities and enough practical experience to unite the people against the foe. Unfortunately the one man who satisfied these requirements was an outcast from their society.

Jephthah was the son of a harlot and as such without social position or right of inheritance. Recognizing that he was without future among his own people, he withdrew to form a society of his own. With a band of men of dubious character about him, he became a desert raider. His brigands thus became the nucleus of the trained army that his people so desperately needed. His experiences may well have served as a pattern for David whose destiny as an outcast followed a similar course (1 Sam. 22:1–2). Contacted by the elders of Gilead, Jephthah extracted a promise of permanent leadership among them. Never again would he be an outcast from his people.

Jephthah first tried diplomacy in dealing with the invaders. The Ammonites were seeking to occupy the lowlands along the Jordan which belonged to Israel by right of conquest. Jephthah argued that the Lord had won this territory for Israel by driving the Amorites out before them (v. 23). He then urged the Ammonites to be content with the highlands which their god Chemosh had won for them. Whether he recognized Chemosh as a legitimate deity or was using this line of reasoning for his own convenience is uncertain. In any case the Ammonites persisted in their ambitions for conquest.

As Jephthah moved under the Lord's leadership to meet the enemy, however, he made a disastrous vow. In return for victory he promised to offer as a burnt sacrifice the first person who came to greet him as he returned home (v. 31). Unfortunately, he was met by his only daughter. Obviously the horrors of human sacrifice had not yet been expunged from Israel's religion. Indeed Saul only narrowly escaped a similar experience with his son Jonathan (1 Sam. 24:14–46).

Civil War Erupts (Judg. 12:1–15)

The passage.—Surprisingly, Jephthah's stunning victory brought his people little relief. Foreign oppression was ended, but intense tribal jealousies precipitated another costly war. Ephraim took offense at Gilead's single-handed action against the Ammonites. The motivating factors behind the complaint are not altogether clear. Ephraim may have acted out of disappointment at being unable to share the spoils of war. The real issue, however, seems to have involved a decline in Israel's tribal structure. Individual tribes or groups of tribes were acting where the whole nation should have been involved.

In the eyes of Ephraim, Jephthah's supporters had committed a twofold offense. First, Gilead, as a mere geographical territory, lacked the authority to act as an independent tribe. The people who settled there should have sought redress of their problems through their original tribal organizations (v. 4). The people then compounded their error by a further departure from the old tribal system. Rather than awaiting a decision by the old, slow-moving council of elders, the Gileadites granted broad powers to Jephthah who proposed immediate, if solitary, action (v. 3).

Ephraim had earlier raised similar charges against Gideon (8:1–3). But where Gideon had used flattery to allay Ephraim's fears, Jephthah met the issue head-on. If Ephraim would not understand his dilemma, he was prepared to fight. As if to dramatize Israel's problems with her tribal government, Ephraim, the champion of the old ways was soundly defeated.

The minor judges listed here (Ibzan,

Elon, and Abdon) have no connection with the events just described. Little is known about them other than that given here.

Birth of Samson (Judg. 13:1–25)

The passage.—As grave as Israel's earlier crises under the judges may have been, her most serious challenge lay yet ahead. About 1188 B.C. bands of Aegean adventurers attacked Egypt and after fighting that nation to a draw moved northward to the lower coast of Canaan. These people, called Philistines, were a part of the larger migrations of the "Sea Peoples" who wrought havoc in the eastern Mediterranean during this time.

The Philistines enjoyed a number of advantages over their more loosely organized neighbors. They were a well-organized group composed of five cooperating city states, each under the leadership of a single ruler. Their people were good soldiers, and their weapons were the finest since they held a monopoly on iron manufacturing during this period. Their first occupation of coastal towns had little impact on Israel, but their expansionist ambitions soon became clear to their neighbors.

Israel again found herself in need of a leader who could unite the people in resisting the growing Philistine menace. The stories about Samson (chaps. 13–16) clearly portray him as God's man for this critical hour. Through the Lord's graciousness he is born to a couple long childless. His forthcoming birth is announced by a heavenly messenger, and his parents are given special instructions as to his proper care. In short, he is to be a Nazirite ("one consecrated") from before his birth. Thus his mother was to avoid strong drink and unclean food, and when the boy was born, his hair was not to be cut (Num. 6:2 f.). As an indication of his approval,

God blessed him and sent his spirit upon him while he was still a youth.

Samson Betrayed by His Wife (Judg. 14: 1–20)

The passage.—In striking contrast with the divine influence which surrounded his youth, Samson's exploits as an adult are described in strangely human terms. He resembles the anti-hero of modern literature. Fully subject to the limitations and weaknesses of ordinary men, he almost inadvertently realized his destiny by striking out at the enemies of his people.

At this time hostilities between Israel and the Philistines had not yet broken out into the open. Free travel and communication existed between the two groups and intermarriage, though not favored by the Israelites, was not uncommon.

Prejudices and tensions were undoubtedly running high, but Samson's first struggles with the Philistines grew out of personal, not national, motives. He was infuriated that his Philistine wife had revealed the solution to his riddle to her own people. Apparently he either did not know or did not care that she had been intimidated into revealing his secret (v. 15). In retaliation, Samson killed 30 Philistines in Ashkelon some 20 miles away and used their clothes to pay his wager (vv. 12–13).

Special points.—Samson's attraction to a Philistine woman is explained as the result of God's planning (v. 4). For discussions of the author's understanding of God's autonomy in human affairs see the Introduction and comments on 3:1–31.

Samson Seeks Vengeance (Judg. 15:1–20)

The passage.—The early unrest between Israelite and Philistine gradually escalated into conflicts of national scope.

While our attention is focused on Samson's exploits, it must be understood that acts of provocation were no doubt being committed by both sides.

Samson's next outburst against the Philistines was again the result of his rage over a family matter. After storming out of the wedding feast before his marriage was consummated, Samson retreated from his attack on the Philistines at Ashkelon to take refuge among his own people (14:19). When he finally returned to possess his intended bride, he learned she had married his best man! Not to be placated, he struck out against all Philistines. He tied torches to foxes' tails and freed them to spread fire through the ripening grain of his enemy. When the Philistines discovered the reasons for their holocaust, they held Samson's wife and her family accountable for his deeds (cf. Israel's treatment of Achan in Josh. 7). In spite of his own dispute with his in-laws, Samson vowed to avenge their deaths.

By this time, Samson had become an outlaw among the Philistines and an embarrassment to his own people. When he sought to hide in Judean territory, their fear of Philistine retaliation prompted them to seek his surrender. As they presented him bound to their overlords, he burst his bonds and inflicted a fearful slaughter upon the Philistines at Lehi. The Lord was responsible for Samson's enormous strength, and it was really he who was delivering Israel (v. 14).

Samson and Delilah (Judg. 16:1–31)

The passage.—Samson is noted for weakness when dealing with women. his strength in fighting men and his The present episodes reflect both qualities. Perhaps in an effort to spare his own people further reprisals (15:9–12), Samson sought refuge among the Philistines. At Gaza, he very narrowly avoided being captured in the company of his harlot companion. He escaped during the night by breaking down the portals in the city gates and carrying them some 30 miles to Hebron!

The Philistine leaders were by this time almost desperate to bring their elusive enemy to bay. When they learned of Samson's affection for another Philistine woman, they envisioned a means to bring about his downfall. Upon the promise of an enormous bribe, Delilah agreed to uncover the secret of Samson's prodigious strength. After three successive failures, she discovered the key —his hair. Shorn of that he was easily captured and abused by the Philistines (v. 21).

Samson's hair represents his last remaining contact with Nazirite vows (see Num. 6:2–12). Laws concerning abstention from wine and from contact with the dead had long ago been broken. When the last vestige of his commitment to God was stripped from him, his divinely appointed strength was no longer his to command. Blind and abused, Israel's former champion provided sport for his captors.

As Samson served at the mill, however, his hair grew and his strength returned. In one last crushing victory, he demolished the temple of Dagon and again destroyed an enormous number of his enemies. Thus ended the life of one of the great tragic heroes. His weaknesses brought about his own downfall, but God nevertheless used his life to serve his people.

Micah's Priest (Judg. 17:1–13)

The passage.—With the end of Samson's story, the ancient document about Israel's leaders between the conquest and the kingdom came to an end (2:6—16:31). The chapters which follow form an appendix to this older book. They give important information about this period, but no judges emerge as God's appointed leaders in times of crisis. Moreover, the literary framework and the point of view have shifted. The cycles of sin, punishment, repentance, and deliverance are no longer used to demonstrate God's autonomy in history (see the Introduction). The remaining chapters show the debased conditions before Israel had a king (17:6; 18:1; 19:1; 21:25). Thus, the sentiments reflected here counterbalance the anti-monarchic attitudes in 8:23 and 1 Samuel 8:5–22 and 12:11 f.

Chapters 17 and 18 are concerned with an indictment of the shrine at Dan. Worship there was focused around an image which originally belonged to an Ephraimite named Micah. The image was made by a silversmith in direct violation of the Lord's commandment (v. 4, see Ex. 20:4). Even the material out of which the image was made was tainted. It had been stolen and possibly even bore a curse as well (v. 2).

Leadership at the shrine was also suspect since the worship started out in the hands of a thief and ended under the control of an unknown, rootless Levite (vv. 5,9).

This derogatory assessment of the shrine at Dan may reflect a southern viewpoint. After the division of the monarchy (1 Kings 12:25–31), Judeans condemned the sanctuaries at Bethel and Dan which rivaled the Temple in Jerusalem. The passage appears to have been written after 734 B.C. when Dan fell to the Assyrians (18:30).

Danite Migration (Judg. 18:1–31)

The passage.—The Danites are further ridiculed because they had been unable to win a lasting foothold in the territory allotted to them. Their entire relationship to God was called into question. Where was the divine power which gave Joshua victory at Jericho or even the tragic strength of Samson at Gaza? Unaided by legitimate contact with the Lord, the impotent Danites simply looked for less formidable foes.

The land to which the Danites were moving was in the far north above the Sea of Galilee. The people there were related to the Phoenicians of Tyre and Sidon but were too far removed from these cities to expect assistance. The city of Dan became the traditional northern extremity of Israel's territory (1 Sam. 3:20).

As the Danites began the long march to their new home, they came into contact with the shrine which would be established in their capital city. Passing through the hill country of Ephraim, they simply used 600 fighting men to take the images and a willing priest from Micah. Not only was the shrine at Dan of dubious ancestry (17:1–13), it was also stolen!

Outrage at Gibeah (Judg. 19:1–30)

The passage.—The three remaining chapters of Judges describe the circumstances surrounding Israel's civil war against Benjamin. As with the earlier appendix (17:1—18:31), this material is included to illustrate the degenerate conditions which existed before Israel had a king (19:1; 21:25).

The first segment of the story (chap. 19) describes the incidents which precipitated the declarations of war. The story is not a pretty one, but its implications are quite clear. Israel's tribal structure had degenerated to such a point that law, order, and morality were hopelessly broken down. A traveler was no safer among his fellow Israelites than he would be among foreigners and heathen (v. 12).

The abysmal moral conditions emerge as classic examples of the storyteller's artistic skill. The infidelity of the Levite's wife is offset by his own intemperate drinking (vv. 4–9). The lack of hospitality by the people of Gibeah and the immoral demands of the rascals there differ only in degree from the Levite's cowardly treatment of his concubine. The dead woman's hands on the doorstep served as an indictment of all who were involved in the affair at Gibeah (v. 27). She died with hands outstretched for help that would be too late in coming.

War Against Benjamin (Judg. 20:1–48)

The passage.—The grim spectacle of the concubine's dismembered corpse finally moved Israel to take action. The elders of each tribe gathered at Mizpah to hear the charges against the men of Gibeah and to consider an appropriate course of action. They were of one accord. This atrocity had to be avenged lest Israel's whole corporate structure be similarly torn asunder. In keeping with the old ways, the militia was called out. One man in ten throughout Israel would be conscripted to exercise judgment on Gibeah.

Again the lack of unity in Israel became apparent. Not even Gibeah's obvious guilt could shake Benjamin's determination to defend her own people. Once more blind tribal loyalty was placed above a commitment to broader national goals. Recognizing that no effective central government was possible as long as such defiance was allowed to persist, Israel prepared for war.

The battles which ensued were bitter and costly for both sides. Rugged warriors were to be found in both armies, but divine leadership (vv. 18,28) and superior numbers finally brought victory to the central government's forces. After two calamitous defeats, Israel finally captured Gibeah and completely routed its forces. Except for a small contingent of 600 men who escaped to Rimmon, the flower of Benjamin's manhood was destroyed. Israel had maintained the integrity of its central government but had almost lost one of its important tribes in the process.

Benjaminites Seek Wives (Judg. 21:1–25)

The passage.—Israel's fearful decimation of Benjamin's territory (20:48) left the tribe's future in doubt. When the passions of battle cooled somewhat, Israel realized that the complete loss of Benjamin would also work against the national interest. Israel sought to heal the breaches within her community, but efforts to restore Benjamin to the mainstream of corporate life were complicated by resolutions passed during the civil war.

At Mizpah Israel had sworn to withhold its daughters from marriage to the men of Benjamin (vv. 1,7,18). Since marital relations outside the nation were usually frowned upon (14:3), this amounted to an excommunication from the tribal federation. After the war, Israel wanted to welcome Benjamin back, but oaths once pronounced were not easily recalled. They decided, therefore, to keep the letter of the law, but to break its spirit. They would provide the Benjaminites with suitable wives without giving them any of their own daughters.

One group of wives was provided as Israel punished those who had "dodged the draft" during the Benjaminite war. Jabesh-gilead, which had not been represented at the muster at Mizpah, was destroyed and its people killed. Four hundred maidens were spared as brides for the Benjaminites. Thus an amnesty ending the war was announced.

The elders of Israel further provided that additional wives could be found during the annual religious festival at Shiloh. While the wartime oath still prohibited Israelites from giving daughters in marriage to their former enemies, the Benjaminites could capture wives from the young women at the dances there. Presumably only those looking for husbands participated in the festivities.

RUTH

Ben F. Philbeck

INTRODUCTION

The story of Ruth is another superb literary work of the Old Testament. It is a simple story, well told, in which the best elements of Old Testament religion and life are portrayed. Naomi and Ruth represent the noblest qualities of Israelite womanhood: fidelity, industry, practicality, and faith (Prov. 31:10–31). Boaz likewise exhibits the characteristics of an ideal Hebrew man: wealthy, generous, amorous, cunning, and wise.

The ancient author pursued his task with an openness seldom found in modern literature. The story is obviously told to condemn national prejudice and to encourage faith in God. At the same time, it is told with an earthy humor which would embarrass the modern church member. Nevertheless, the plot is well-balanced and the characters fairly vibrate with life.

The action is placed in the period of the judges which probably accounts for the present position of the book before Samuel. In Hebrew manuscripts it is a part of the third section of the canon called the Writings. Modern versions follow the order of early Greek translations which placed it after Judges.

Since a good short story is seldom improved by elaboration, explanatory notes will be included only where modern readers might otherwise miss a point of the story.

Ruth Comes to Judah (Ruth 1:1–22)

Special points.—Marriages between Israelites and foreigners are generally frowned upon in the Old Testament (Deut. 7:1–4; Neh. 13:23–25). Ruth's marriages to two successive Israelites are never questioned, however, and she is proudly included as one of David's ancestors. This book, along with Jonah, Amos 9:7–10, etc., takes a more liberal view toward foreigners than do other Old Testament passages.

Naomi returned to Judah because widows had little protection in ancient Near Eastern societies. As a foreigner, she was even more vulnerable in Moab. For the same reason, she encouraged her daughters-in-law to stay among their own people. Ruth's decision to accompany Naomi to Judah required great faith and stamina. This was especially true since the deaths of Elimelech, Mahlon, and Chilion were taken as an evidence of the Lord's displeasure (vv. 20–21).

Orpah's return to her own people was assumed to be a return to her former worship (v. 15). In the ancient world each nation presumably had its own god. Against this background the stature of Israel's God was even more remarkable. The Lord guided the destiny of his people wherever they might be.

Ruth Pleases Boaz (Ruth 2:1–23)

Special points.—Some grain was to be left during harvesting as a means of providing for the poor. Sometimes, however, the gleanings were scarce (Isa. 17:5–6), and dangers to the gleaners were many (vv. 9,22). Apparently not all the poor were allowed to work in the fields, and special concessions may have been demanded by some landowners for permission to do so (v. 2). Boaz' treatment of Ruth was notably generous and gentlemanly.

Ruth Approaches Boaz (Ruth 3:1–18)

The passage.—Naomi's earthly tactics to capture Boaz must have drawn chuckles of appreciation from ancient readers. How typically female she and Ruth turned out to be! Although Boaz had demonstrated an active concern for Ruth's well-being, he made no moves toward providing her with a permanent home. Recognizing that a man could refuse to function in the role of a kinsman (4:6), Naomi told Ruth to use her most seductive ways to secure a marriage proposal from Boaz (vv. 3–4).

Such a plan could be foolhardy if the man were of low character, but Boaz had already proven himself to be above reproach. Again during the night at the threshing floor he conducted himself with dignity and consideration for Ruth's reputation (v. 14). As a responsible man, he was prepared to wait until the legal technicalities regarding his relationship to Ruth were resolved (vv. 12–14).

Special points.—The role of the kinsman was of fundamental importance in maintaining social stability in ancient Israel. It was the duty of each family to provide for the welfare of all of its members, and the lines of responsibility were carefully established. The nearer the relationship, the more pressing was the obligation. Since, as in Ruth's case (4:3), these obligations could also carry some property rights, the proper legal steps had to be taken. Boaz recognized this and acted accordingly.

Truth for today.—Society still seeks to protect itself and the persons involved by establishing strict laws concerning marriage. Unless the lines of responsibility are clearly understood and fairly enforced, unscrupulous persons will inevitably abuse the rights of the weak, the innocent, and the naive.

Boaz Redeems Ruth (Ruth 4:1–22)

Private ownership of land was a jealously guarded privilege in ancient Israel, a right which was proudly handed down within the family. Women were normally excluded from inheritance rights, however, and in no known circumstances were women allowed to inherit their husband's estates. Naomi may have received income from the sale of Elimelech's estate, but she probably was not allowed to retain title to the land. The nearest surviving male member of the family would inherit the first option of purchase (Num. 27:7–11).

Elimelech's unnamed kinsman was eager to buy additional land, but he was unwilling to assume the responsibilities which went with it. Boaz argued that the nearest kinsman had a moral obligation to keep Elimelech's line alive. This would involve marrying Ruth and raising a family under his name. In such a case title to the land would eventually revert to Ruth's children. Under such circumstances, the kinsman hastily renounced his rights as next of kin.

Boaz and Ruth were, therefore, free to pursue their own destiny. The story ends happily for the major characters. Naomi had a grandson to care for her in her old age, and Boaz and Ruth became known as the ancestors of David. Through it all is seen the hand of the Lord who works continually for those who trust in him (2:20; 4:11,14).

1 SAMUEL

Ben F. Philbeck

INTRODUCTION

At the beginning of the twelfth century B.C., Israel's fortunes had reached a dangerously low ebb. Her resources were depleted by repeated attacks from hostile neighbors, and her internal structure was weakened by civil war and regional self-interests. Theoretically, the judges were able to deliver Israel from adversity (see Judg. 2:1–23), but even under Deborah's leadership, a majority of the tribes failed to cooperate (Judg. 5).

By about 1050 B.C. Israel was in dire straits. The Philistines, who had captured a foothold on the southern coast of Canaan more than a century earlier, began an aggressive campaign to control their neighbors to the east. In this struggle, the Philistines enjoyed many tactical advantages. Their forces were more united, their troops were better trained, and their iron weapons were among the first commonly used in Palestine. Under this new threat, Israel's national existence was gravely endangered.

Against this background Israel changed her system of government. This first book of Samuel describes the transition from a loose tribal federation under Samuel to the beginnings of a typical Oriental monarchy under David. This process was fraught with both political and religious dangers, but in the end Israel survived with the basic elements of her faith in the Lord intact.

The story is told from a purely theological perspective. The author was not concerned with modern interests in social or political causation. He saw God directly at work in human history, rewarding goodness and punishing evil (see Introduction to Judges). The books of Samuel face squarely the twofold theological problem precipitated by Israel's grave political crisis. Israel's defeats at the hands of the Philistines were the result of the people's violation of the Lord's will rather than an indication of his weakness. Similarly, Israel's shift in governmental structure was brought about by the people's persistent cry for a king, not by inherent weaknesses in the system itself. The story is organized around three human characters—Samuel, Saul, and David—but God will clearly emerge as the ultimate guide of Israel's destiny.

Samuel's Dedication (1 Sam. 1:1—2:11)

The passage.—The story about the emergence of Israel's monarchy properly begins with Samuel. He profoundly influenced the entire period, serving as Israel's last judge, as one of her earliest prophets, and as a power behind the throne of her first two kings.

Samuel is clearly portrayed as a man chosen to perform his allotted tasks. He is born into a devout home, the son of a barren woman who fervently prayed for a son (v. 11) and who pledged to set him apart as a Nazirite (see Num. 6:1–8).

Special points.—Elkanah regularly took his family on an annual pilgrimage to the temple of the Lord at Shiloh (vv. 2,9). Such a practice was expensive and far beyond the means of ordinary working men. The "temple of the Lord" mentioned here and in 3:3 should not be confused with the place of worship constructed by Solomon.

When Samuel was about three-years old, Hannah brought him back to Shiloh where he began his religious training under Eli's leadership. Hannah's song on this occasion (2:1–10) praises Israel's God as the Lord of history. The Lord would surely judge the wicked and deliver the righteous (v. 9). This principle provides the theme for the ensuing chapters. Samuel's emergence as God's man of the hour will be paralleled by the precipitous decline of Eli's corrupt sons (2:12).

House of Eli Rejected (1 Sam. 2:12–36)

The passage.—As Israel's tribal structure was being strained to the breaking point, her central religious institutions were violently disrupted as well. Apparently the sanctuary at Shiloh and the core of Israel's priesthood were destroyed by the Philistines following their victory at Aphek (4:1–22). The biblical author foreshadows subsequent events as he explains why Eli's corrupt sons were to be rejected.

Eli's sons were guilty of both ritual and moral offenses. In the rites of sacrifice, they violated ancient customs regarding the priests' portion of the offering (vv. 13–17). Even more importantly, they were charged with immoral relations with the women who served at the entrance of the tent of meeting (v. 22). Because of their guilt, Eli's sons would be rejected as priests and God would find a man of his own choosing to follow them (vv. 34–36).

The context seems to imply that Samuel will be God's "faithful priest," but from what we can tell, he functioned only as a prophet and as a judge. More-

over, the corruption of his own sons prohibited them from becoming enduring leaders in Israel (7:15–17). The author apparently looked forward to an unnamed priestly line which would later emerge in the days of the monarchy.

Special points.—Although Eli's sons must bear the consequences for their actions, the author of these verses attributes ultimate responsibility for their downfall to God (v. 25). He stresses God's sovereignty so strongly that he sees everything that happens as the result of divine causation. Other biblical passages accord man a greater freedom in God's economy (Gen. 3:1–25; Rom. 1:18–25). Later prophetic demands for ethical conduct on the part of God's people also rest squarely on man's moral responsibility for his own conduct. Thus, within God's economy, men are free to determine their own destinies. They remain God's creatures, but they are free to accept or reject divine leadership (v. 30).

Samuel Begins His Ministry (1 Sam. 3: 1–21)

The passage.—The shift in religious leadership anticipated in the first two chapters, now comes into full view. God's actions will breathe a new vitality into the religious establishment at Shiloh which had become decadent through the years (vv. 1,21).

While sleeping in the temple as an attendant at the ark of the Lord, Samuel received a vision from God. The form of the story highlights the tragic novelty of the divine visitation. Samuel's youth would explain his interpretation of the nocturnal voice, but the entire passage implies that Eli should have been more experienced in such matters. Finally, after the third summons, Eli instructs Samuel to await God's revelation.

The burden of Samuel's vision lay in the proclamation of God's imminent judgment on the house of Eli. Even Eli himself was to be punished with his sons because he knew of their deeds and did not restrain them (v. 13). Samuel was reluctant to share the dread news with his aging tutor, but Eli demanded forthright answers from his young pupil. Eli courageously learned of his fate and submitted himself unto the Lord.

Even before God's judgment on Eli's house was carried out, Samuel's renown as a prophet of the Lord spread. Shiloh was no longer important solely as a ceremonial site. Now divine power was being evidenced in the personality of the new young leader who lived there.

Philistines Capture the Ark (1 Sam. 4: 1–22)

The passage.—Now that the major characters have been introduced, the author moves on to describe Israel's dire plight at the end of the period of the judges. In a series of engagements between Aphek and Ebenezer, Israel's army was completely routed, the ark of the Lord was lost in battle, the priests accompanying the ark were killed, and old Eli died upon learning of the disaster. Biblical records do not record it, but archaeological excavations indicate that Shiloh was also destroyed about this time. The heart of Israel's religious and political life was destroyed, and the Philistines were the *de facto* rulers of most of the country. The burden of leading Israel now fell to Samuel.

Special points.—The ark of the Lord appears to have been the focal point of Israel's national existence at this time. It represented God's presence among his people (v. 4) and called to mind his protection during Israel's wilderness wanderings (Num. 10:33) and the wars of conquest (Josh. 6). The loss of the ark in battle, therefore, was especially serious. It appeared that the Lord was unable to protect his people or even his own personal throne among men. The larger context, however, indicates that God was working in history to purge his corrupt priesthood and to bring his people under his leadership.

The Ark Plagues the Philistines (1 Sam. 5:1–11)

The passage.—The difference between ancient and modern perspectives is clearly demonstrated in the author's treatment of the events following Israel's defeat at Ebenezer. Modern readers look in vain for an analysis of the impact of the Philistine victory on Israel's struggling political institutions. Biblical materials are completely silent about conditions in Israel during this period.

The ancient reader's attention was focused, not on the political, but on the theological significance of Israel's defeat. Success in battle depended more on the power of a nation's god than on the prowess of its soldiers. From this perspective, it appeared that the Lord God had been defeated by Dagon at Ebenezer.

The Philistines celebrated their triumph by displaying the captured ark of the Lord in Dagon's temple at Ashdod. The victor and the vanquished were symbolically brought face to face. But then the unexpected happened! Dagon's image was first overthrown and then dismembered while a plague broke out among the people of the city. Sensing that Israel's God might be responsible for the disasters which had befallen them, the Philistines moved the ark on to Gath and then to Ekron. As death followed in its train, the Philistine leaders sought to return the ark to Israelite territory. God's power had been vindicated!

The Ark Returns to Israel (1 Sam. 6:1—7:2)

The passage.—As frantic preparations were made to return the troublesome ark to Israelite territory, Philistine priests devised one last test to determine the source of their affliction. First the people were to offer appropriate sacrifices (v. 4) to the Lord that he might lift the plagues which had afflicted them. Then the ark with the guilt offerings was to be placed on a specially prepared cart pulled by two cows. If the cows moved toward their calves which had been penned in Philistine territory, then all would know that the Lord had no part in the plagues which ravaged the land.

The cows, however, turned toward Bethshemesh, and the ark was restored to Israel. Amidst a joyous people, the cart and the cows became part of a sacrifice celebrating the Lord's return to his rightful home. Even Israelites were not exempt from death associated with the ark, however (v. 19). God does not play favorites according to biological or national heritage. All people must respect his holiness and live within his laws.

Special points.—The ark was soon moved from Beth-shemesh to Kiriath-jearim where it remained in obscurity for some twenty years (2 Sam. 6; but see 1 Sam. 14:18). Since a return to Shiloh was not even considered, it is assumed that Israel's former central sanctuary had been destroyed by the Philistines following their victory at Ebenezer.

Samuel Delivers Israel (1 Sam. 7:3–17)

The passage.—For some reason the Philistine advance stalled and little effort was made to follow up their victory at Ebenezer. Unfortunately, we are unable to reconstruct the practical factors which influenced Israel's political recovery. The recent plague among the Philistines, for example, must have restricted their hopes for territorial expansion. Beyond this, we are left with mere speculation. We are told nothing of the reorganization of Israel's army, the development of new leaders, or the reconstruction of her central government. Certainly some of these measures must have been attempted.

In keeping with the author's theological perspective (see 5:1–11), stress is laid on the religious foundations for Israel's improved fortunes. Called upon to purge themselves of the pagan elements which had crept into their worship, the people of Israel renewed their covenant with the Lord. Thus, the primary source for Israel's national unity was restored (see comments on 4:1–22).

A crucial test of Israel's strength under Samuel's leadership came in a Philistine attack on a national gathering at Mizpah. As in Joshua's days during the conquest (Josh. 1:5–7), the Lord intervened in the battle and routed the Philistines (v. 10). A monument named Ebenezer ("Stone of Help") was erected to commemorate the Lord's assistance (v. 13).

Special points.—The Lord's use of thunder in routing the Philistines may be symbolic. Hebrew poets, for example, frequently pictured God's participation in battle in terms of natural cataclysm (Ps. 18:7–15).

Samuel's Influence Fades (1 Sam. 8:1–22)

The passage.—Israel's political situation had stabilized for a time under Samuel's influence, but her underlying problem had not been solved. No system had been devised to provide a steady supply of capable, honest officials for public service. As Samuel grew old, the problem again became acute. He had installed his sons Joel and Abijah as judges in Beersheba, but they soon proved to be corrupt. Filled with despair, the elders of Israel asked for a king.

A change in Israel's form of government was no matter of little consequence. Every area of ancient life was affected. Under the judges, God had theoretically been Israel's absolute ruler. He had worked through the personalities of the elders who functioned roughly as a representative democracy. Their decisions were assumed to represent a disclosure of the divine will. Although a judge certainly influenced the decisions of the elders, he was by no means an independent agent. He operated within the framework of authority which they established. This system embodied the values which grew out of Israel's religious experience. The rights of the ordinary citizen were protected from arbitrary decisions resulting from the centralization of authority into one office.

Samuel rightfully recognized the inherent dangers in the proposed change in the form of Israel's government. Her entire political, civil, and religious philosophy could be sacrificed in the process. He, therefore, carefully outlined the impact that a typical Oriental monarch would have on the lives of ordinary men (vv. 10–18). Political stability would be achieved at the expense of personal liberty. The people would not be diverted, however and the Lord allowed them to have a king.

Special points.—The anti-monarchic attitude of this passage is abundantly clear (see also chap. 12). Other biblical passages, however, are much more favorably inclined toward the kingship (the major portions of chaps. 9–11 and Judg. 17:6; 18:1; 19:1; 21:25). In time God would make it clear that he would work with the new system just as he had with the old (12:14–15).

Samuel Meets Saul (1 Sam. 9:1–27)

The passage.—Once again the modern reader's interest in the mechanics of Israel's political reorganization is frustrated. Nothing is said of the fact that Judah and Simeon were no longer really considered a part of Israel's northern tribal organization (see Judg. 5). The record is likewise silent regarding the regional interests and parochial prejudices which had repeatedly undercut the effectiveness of Israel's weak central government. Certainly, each tribe must have advanced its own favorite son, or sons, as candidates for the throne.

The biblical author, however, again assumes his characteristic theological perspective. God selected Israel's king, first by revealing him to Samuel (chap. 8), and then by designating him before the national assembly at Mizpah (9:17–24). The divine hand is seen running through all of human history. God could use a search for lost donkeys for his own purposes or announce his selection of Saul as king before Samuel even met him (vv. 15–17).

In any case, the new king's selection appeared to be a wise political move. Saul came from a Benjaminite family which had already distinguished itself by its achievements. His tribe was centrally located and hence in a strategic position to unite the north and the south. Moreover, since the tribe was small, other groups would have little to fear or envy in Benjamin's growing influence. Perhaps equally important, Saul looked like a king. Standing head and shoulders above his fellows, he appeared to be a man who could capture the imagination of the people and lead Israel's armies to victory.

Special points.—The story of Saul's rise to power is divided into three shorter episodes: his selection by Samuel (9:3—10:16), his presentation to Israel

(10:17–27), and his winning of popular support (11:1–15).

Saul Designated King (1 Sam. 10:1–27)

The passage.—The reader can discern in the background of this passage some of the drama of the original experience. Saul's first meeting with Samuel left him stunned and uncertain. He had been royally welcomed (chap. 9), privately anointed, and confronted with the challenge of serving as Israel's first king (10:1). As evidence of Saul's divine selection, Samuel gave a detailed preview of his homeward journey. Nevertheless, Saul refused to tell his family about the kingship (v. 16).

The public phase of the selection of Israel's king came at a national assembly at Mizpah (vv. 17–27). God's will in the matter would be determined by using the sacred lot. In this procedure a two-sided object was thrown so that it indicated a positive or negative response. Questions were carefully phrased by the priests, and the results were considered indications of God's will. First by tribe, then by family, and then individually Saul was singled out. Still reticent about becoming king, Saul was found hiding in the baggage train!

The picture is ironic and real. Israel's new king was reluctant to accept the task, and, in spite of the decision of the sacred lot, the people were divided in their support of him (v. 27).

Saul Wins Public Support (1 Sam. 11:1–15)

The passage.—Israelite politics were in a confused state during this period. Saul had been anointed king by Samuel, and he had been chosen by lot in a national assembly. Nevertheless, he still was not king (11:15). Apparently partisan politics had so divided the people during the gathering at Mizpah that a final selection of a king could not be made at that time. Saul went home to Gibeah with a band of devoted followers and awaited an occasion to demonstrate his ability to unite the nation.

Such an opportunity came in the Ammonite attack on the Israelite town of Jabesh-gilead. The Ammonites were confident that Israel was too weak and fragmented to lend a trans-Jordan community assistance (v. 3). As a matter of fact, the attackers sought the complete humiliation of all Israel (v. 2).

Saul, however, resorted to strong measures to unite the nation. Infuriated by the Ammonites' audacity, he threatened to attack any Israelites who failed to come to the assistance of Jabesh-gilead (v. 7). This, apparently, was language his people could understand. Saul organized the enormous force which responded to his call and, attacking at dawn, completely routed the Ammonite army.

Finally convinced, the people of Israel formally installed Saul as their king in a special ceremony at Gilgal (v. 15).

Special points.—Israel's difficulty in selecting a king reflects the democratic nature of her government under the judges. Saul could not ascend the throne without the consent of his subjects.

Samuel Counsels Monarchy (1 Sam. 12: 1–25)

The passage.—With Saul's victory over the Ammonites, the lengthy struggle over Israel's form of government was finally resolved. Even those who had bitterly opposed the establishment of the monarchy gave in, and Saul was proclaimed king. With the monarchy now an accomplished fact, Samuel sought to unite the nation. In his speech he summarized the theological principles upon which God would deal with his people under the new system of government.

Samuel's own sentiments were never in doubt. He regarded the theocratic system under the old tribal league as Israel's legitimate political structure. After freeing his people from bondage in Egypt (vv. 6–8), God had repeatedly worked through the judges to deliver them from their enemies (v. 11). Samuel himself had most recently demonstrated that with an honest leader the system would work (vv. 1–5). Failures within the system were explained as the consequence of rebellion (vv. 9–10). Israel's call for a king during the Ammonite conflict, therefore, was seen as a sin against God's leadership (vv. 12,16–18).

Even under the monarchy, however, God would not abandon his people. His requirements of them would be essentially the same as they had been under the judges. He would bless Israel and her king as long as they were faithful unto him, but if they departed from the Lord's ways, they would be destroyed (vv. 22,24–25).

Samuel encouraged all of Israel's factions to work together. Only a united people under God's leadership would successfully resist the hostile powers who sought to overwhelm the nation.

Saul Rebels Against Philistines (1 Sam. 13:1–25)

The passage.—From the very beginning of Saul's reign, he faced two major conflicts: one against his Philistine overlords, and the other against Samuel, the man of God. The first would eventually cost Saul his life, the latter would contribute even sooner to the loss of his mental stability. The details of these two struggles are no longer precisely known, but their broad outlines can be discerned without difficulty.

Israel was in dire straits when Saul took office. The Philistines controlled most of the open country with local garrisons such as the one at Geba, and they appear to have been able to move freely throughout the land. Even more important was the Philistines' complete arms embargo on Israel. Iron was just coming into use in the eastern Mediterranean world, and the Philistines exploited their advantage over Israel by keeping the techniques of blacksmithing secret (13:19 f.). Saul, therefore, was forced to rely on small, poorly equipped forces who carried on a guerilla-type warfare (vv. 2,22).

In an effort to free Israel from foreign domination, Jonathan and a small band of followers attacked and defeated the garrison at Geba. As the Philistines raised an enormous army to quell the uprising, Jonathan dispersed his troops in the rugged terrain nearby (vv. 6–7).

In the meantime Saul was mustering another force at Gilgal. The morale of these troops was low, however, and desertions mounted steadily. Saul's situation was complicated by the fact that he was waiting for Samuel to come to perform the ritual ceremonies by which soldiers were consecrated for battle (Deut. 20:1–20; see 1 Sam. 21:4–5). After waiting for Samuel the prescribed seven days (10:8), Saul offered the preparatory sacrifices himself. When Samuel finally arrived in camp, he indicated that Saul would be rejected as king for his presumptuous action.

Special points.—Although other non-Levites are known to have offered sacrifice without incurring divine wrath (Judg. 6:25–26; 1 Kings 18:30 f.), apparently it was customary at this time for Samuel to bless the sacrifice (1 Sam. 9:13). In any case, another explanation of God's rejection of Saul is given elsewhere (15:1–35).

Jonathan Escapes Death (1 Sam. 14:1–52)

The passage.—This chapter contains an interesting story which clearly reveals the practical nature of Israelite theology. The story itself tells of an Israelite victory over the garrison at Michmash. The battle began with Jonathan's heroic attack on a small military outpost (vv. 1–20) and ended with the Philistines fleeing from the field of battle. Somehow, Saul's forces were unable to follow up their early successes as they should. Herein lay the theological problem.

Israel's triumph over the Philistines, surprising though it was, could be explained. Hebrew theologians had long pictured God going to battle for his people (Josh. 1:5; 6:1–27; etc.). If he had given the first victory, however, why didn't he continue sweeping the Philistines away? The standard answer and the most obvious one was that an Israelite had sinned and, thus, incurred the divine wrath (Josh. 7).

None of the principal characters was completely innocent. Saul had entered the battle at Michmash without awaiting divine counsel (v. 19). Also in the course of the fighting, he impetuously invoked a curse which deprived his men of the strength they needed to pursue the enemy (vv. 24–31). Likewise the people as a whole had incurred a ritual guilt by improperly disposing of the blood of animals they had killed for food (vv. 32–34); see Lev. 1:5; 17:10–15). Last and least, there was Jonathan who had inadvertently broken "his father's" oath by eating a bit of honey (v. 27).

Now the problem. What was to be done when the sacred lot settled on the one whose offense appeared the most innocuous, indeed who up to this point had been God's hero of the hour? Saul was prepared to execute Jonathan out of an awareness of divine obligation. The people, however, recognized that this solution would not adequately reflect the justice which is inherent in God's nature. Unconsciously, they relied more on their own innate spiritual perception than on any external means of understanding the divine will. They refused to allow any harm to come to Jonathan and decided that he should be ransomed instead. Thus, the judgment of the sacred lot was not openly defied, and yet the cause of justice was served.

Saul Rejected as King (1 Sam. 15:1–35)

The passage.—This chapter contains a second version of the reason for Saul's rejection as king (13:1–14). Again he is condemned for failing to carry out the Lord's commandments. In this instance, he failed to annihilate the Amalekites as he had been instructed to do (vv. 2–3).

The commandment to destroy the Amalekites and all their possessions was in keeping with a common Near Eastern custom called the *herem*. This practice was an outgrowth of the old holy wars in which all the spoils of battle were devoted to the national god. All living creatures were to be killed, all combustibles were to be burned, and all precious metals were to be placed in the god's treasury. Since all profit motives were removed, only the most dedicated soldiers would go to battle.

Saul's preservation of the Amalekite king and the best of their cattle was not the result of humanitarian nor religious motives (see v. 15). Rather, Saul was prepared to modify social custom or religious conviction to accommodate public opinion (vv. 21,24). A man of such character was hardly qualified to serve as Israel's king.

Saul Meets His Successor (1 Sam. 16:1–23)

The passage.—As Saul's reign wore on, his unstable character made it apparent that he could never provide a suitable foundation for Israel's monarchy. Samuel, however, either out of affection (10:24; 15:11,35; 16:1) or fear (v. 2), was reluctant to select a rival candidate for the throne. Finally, the matter could be put off no longer. Samuel was then led to Bethlehem where he was to find God's chosen leader. After seeing and rejecting all of Jesse's older sons, David was finally selected and anointed.

Again it must be understood that the divine appointment carried with it no office, title, or prerogatives. David's anointment at the hands of Samuel simply represented a future destiny to be worked out in human history.

David's first step toward the throne occurred when he became a member of Saul's court. In the first of two accounts of his introduction to Saul (16:14–23, see 17:1–58), David is portrayed as a musician and a warrior, recommended by a member of Saul's court to help soothe the king's murderous rages. Saul found comfort in his music and, with Jesse's permission, permanently attached David to his court as his armor bearer.

Special points.—The "evil spirit from the Lord" which came upon Saul (v. 14) represents the ancient Israelite view of God's sovereignty. All things, even evil (Isa. 45:7), were attributed to him. Today we would describe Saul's condition as a mental illness.

David Battles Goliath (1 Sam. 17:1–58)

The passage.—A second account of David's introduction to Saul is found in the story of David's victory over Goliath. In this account David was present

on the field of battle, not because he was Saul's armor bearer, but because he was bringing his brothers provisions from home. Until the time of his victory, he appears to have been unknown to Saul (v. 58); but through his newfound prominence, he became a close friend of Jonathan who immediately secured him a place in Saul's court (18:2).

The battle took place in the valley of Elah, one of the major passes from the Philistine plain up into the highlands of Judah. The two armies had retired to defensive positions on opposite sides of the valley, and neither commander was willing to surrender the advantage of height to carry the battle to the enemy. In the stalemate which followed, the Philistines were gaining a psychological advantage through their gigantic warrior who daily challenged the Israelites to individual combat.

Israel's champion was far from the untried boy envisioned by many modern readers. He may have lacked experience in the use of military weapons (vv. 38–39), but he was a strong and experienced fighter (vv. 34–36). Putting aside the normal battle garb, he selected ammunition for his sling from the bed of a stream: five stones, each about the size of a man's fist. With this formidable weapon, he felled the Philistine giant. Using Goliath's own sword, David beheaded his enemy, thus confirming the Israelite conviction that the Lord and not the force of arms determines the outcome of battle (v. 47). Unnerved by the unexpected defeat of their champion, the Philistines became easy prey for the jubilant Israelites.

Saul Seeks David's Life (1 Sam. 18:1–30)

The passage.—Following his victory over Goliath, David became a permanent member of Saul's court. There he

9. Bethlehem street scene (see 1 Sam. 17:12–15)

was befriended by Jonathan, Saul's son, and lionized by the people of Israel. As David's popularity rose, Saul's personality progressively deteriorated. Although David was taking no overt actions to become king, Saul sought to have his youthful adversary killed. First he attempted to do the job himself (vv. 10–11), and then he made an effort to get David killed by the Philistines (vv. 17–27). Clearly, God was protecting David from Saul's designs (v. 12).

Special points.—Saul's effort to kill David with a spear was attributed to "the evil spirit from God" (see comments on 16:14) which caused him to "prophesy" within his house (v. 10, KJV). At this time prophetic activity was closely associated with highly emotional or ecstatic behavior (see 19:18–24). Since in this context Saul tried to kill David, it is probably best to translate the phrase "and he *raved* within his house" (v. 10, RSV).

Saul's efforts to get David killed by the Philistines must be seen against the background of ancient Israelite marriage customs. The groom was expected to present the bride's family with a worthy gift as her purchase price. David felt

173

that his family was too poor to offer a gift worthy of a princess (v. 18). Saul sent messengers who assured David that the marriage price would be considered well paid with the evidence that David had killed 100 of the uncircumcised Philistines. Again Saul's plan to kill his rival collapsed. David was able to discharge his obligation twice over.

David Escapes Saul's Assassins (1 Sam. 19:1–24)

The passage.—When Saul's first attempts to kill David failed, he turned to other devices. His first efforts to get his servants to assassinate his young rival were thwarted when Jonathan temporarily convinced his father that David meant him no harm (vv. 4–5). David's popularity continued to rise, however, and Saul made another attempt on his life. Dodging Saul's spear, David fled to his own home followed closely by Saul's hired killers. Only a clever ruse devised by his wife Michal, Saul's daughter, allowed David to escape undetected. Michal's devotion to her husband reflects honor upon her and adds weight to the indictment of Saul's unjust attacks upon David.

Rather than moving toward Bethlehem as Saul might have expected, David fled to Ramah to seek counsel from Samuel. When Saul learned where he was hiding, troops were dispatched with orders to bring him back. Saul's plans were frustrated, however, when the soldiers fell under "the spirit of God" and began "prophesying" among Samuel's band. Saul decided to capture David personally, but he too was incapacitated by a "prophetic seizure."

Special points.—During this period, ecstatic or irrational behavior was apparently an important element in prophetic activity. At a later time greater stress was put on the moral and spiritual qualities of the prophet's ministry.

David and Jonathan Part (1 Sam. 20:1–42)

The passage.—In light of the many attempts on David's life, one wonders that there was any question as to Saul's intentions. Jonathan, however, had only recently arranged a truce between his father and his friend (19:1–7), and Saul's subsequent actions were subject to varying interpretations. His latest attack on David with a spear was associated with the evil spirit which afflicted him only periodically, and for which he could not be held accountable (19:8–10). Although David was convinced that Saul was trying to kill him in the incidents at his home and at Ramah, no overt attacks had been made. A test case was devised, therefore, by which God could reveal, especially to Jonathan, Saul's true attitudes toward David.

David decided to offer a false alibi for missing the king's ritual feasts associated with the arrival of the new moon (vv. 5–6). If the king accepted his explanation, David would know that he had misjudged Saul's intentions. A violent reaction to his absence from the ceremonies, however, would be taken as a final indication that David would never be safe in Saul's court.

Saul reacted, not only against David for his absence from court, but also against Jonathan for his lack of family solidarity. Saul could see that as long as David lived, Jonathan would never become king (v. 31). For Jonathan, however, the sacrifice of a friendship was too great a price to pay for the opportunity to reign. Now that his father's intentions were clear, he warned David to leave the king's court permanently. After a lengthy and emotional farewell, the two friends parted to pursue their divergent, even conflicting, destinies.

David, the Solitary Fugitive (1 Sam. 21: 1–15)

The passage.—David's break with Saul was finally complete. There follows an extended passage (through 28:2) dealing with David's fortunes as a fugitive. The story is told in such a way that God's guidance and protecting hand is seen underlying the entire narrative.

This chapter preserves two incidents which depict David's dire straits as a solitary fugitive from Saul's court. In the first of these he appeared before the priests of Nob asking for food and arms. In an effort to allay the suspicions of the fearful leader of the priestly band, David invented a secret mission supposedly undertaken at the king's command. Finally convinced by David's fanciful tale, the priest provided bread for him and his imaginary soldiers.

The second incident depicting David's helplessness during this period takes place in the Philistine town of Gath. Since Israel offered him no safe hiding places, David sought refuge among her enemies. Apparently he hoped to live inconspicuously among the Philistines, but suspicious soldiers seized him and brought him before Achish. When it appeared that his identity had been guessed, but before it could be proven, David feigned madness and escaped detection.

David Begins His Comeback (1 Sam. 22: 1–23)

The passage.—David knew that he could not successfully elude Saul within Israelite territory, nor could he withstand his forces single-handedly. After failing in his attempt to escape quietly into Gath, he moved back to Adullam on the frontier between Israel and Philistia. There in a region of steep ravines and numerous caves, David began gathering an army. In time he drew about 400 men from his own family and various malcontents from all Israel.

When Saul was informed that David was gathering troops and moving back into Israelite territory, his worst fears appeared confirmed. Seeking to make an example of anyone who offered David aid, Saul directed his wrath against the priests of Nob. Their leader Ahimelech admitted helping David, but he had been unaware of David's defection and had considered himself merely assisting an emissary of the king.

Saul's fury, however, could not be contained. Unable to get any native Israelites to take action against the priests, Saul finally persuaded Doeg the Edomite to carry out his orders. Ultimately the entire city was destroyed.

Special points.—By his actions at Nob, Saul alienated the entire religious community. Conversely, David gained the friendship of many who continued to uphold religious institutions associated with the period of the judges.

David Narrowly Escapes Capture (1 Sam. 23:1–29)

The passage.—Although David was immensely popular in many sections, he by no means commanded the loyalty of the whole country. This chapter gives but two of many instances in which Israelites would have been willing to turn him and his men over to Saul's forces.

The first incident occurred at Keilah, a small walled town just south of Adullam. The people there had reason to feel indebted to David since he had used his fledgling army to relieve a Philistine siege of the city. Nevertheless, the people admitted such fear of Saul that they would surrender David and his men to the king if they were called on to do so. Recognizing that the safety of his small band lay in the employment of different tactics, David abandoned the false security of the city walls and fled to the Wilderness of Ziph. There he could hide his men and use the guerrilla tactics which suited them best.

David's sojourn in Ziph brought him an unexpected dividend as Jonathan came forward to renew their covenant of friendship. Actually the two seem to have agreed to form a coalition government in which David would be the chief and Jonathan would be his second in command (v. 17). In any case, David was not without friends in high places.

In other areas, however, David had an ample supply of enemies. The Ziphites betrayed his position to Saul, and, except for divine providence, he would have been captured. Later generations pointed to a particular rocky hillside where Saul abandoned his search on one side while David was hiding on the other (v. 28).

Saul Delivered to David (1 Sam. 24: 1–22)

The passage.—In the struggle between Saul and David, the people of Israel were confronted with an agonizing dilemma. Their new government which had been established to help unify the nation was torn asunder by the bitter power struggle. The resultant division reopened the way for domination by foreign powers. Clearly the nation had to be united, but behind whom? Was Saul truly a demented autocrat senselessly pursuing an innocent man, or was David a political opportunist seeking to usurp power from the king?

The biblical author seeks to resolve this question in his account of the meeting between Saul and David in the cave at Engedi. With 3,000 crack troops at his command and with local citizens helping to locate his rival, the king seemingly had the upper hand. Once again, however, the Lord intervened—this time to deliver Saul into David's hands.

David now had the power, seemingly a God-given opportunity, to remove the one last obstacle blocking his and Jonathan's plan to restore stability to Israel's government (23:15–18).

David, however, was not anxious to assume personal control of matters under divine jurisdiction. He, therefore, restrained his men and cut off only the border of Saul's robe. If Saul was to be deposed as king of Israel, God would have to provide his own means for removing him from office. David would not lift up his hand against the Lord's anointed.

Saul was forced to admit that his suspicions had been ungrounded and that David would indeed one day rule over Israel.

David Marries Abigail (1 Sam. 25:1–44)

The passage.—To many modern readers, David's means of supporting his troops appears to be a form of illegal extortion. Life in the ancient wilderness, however, was vastly different from our own. While some property owners obviously objected to David's demands, his expectations do not appear to have been excessive by the standards of his own day. Apparently Nabal's servants and even his own wife felt that David was due some compensation for the protection he afforded Nabal's shepherds in the wilderness.

Although it is nowhere explicit, our author seems to imply that Nabal's re-

buff to David was politically motivated.
Nabal, like the Ziphites (23:19) and the
inhabitants of Keilah (23:12), remained
loyal to Saul. Abigail, on the other
hand, took provisions to David, not just
because he was a powerful warlord, but
because the Lord had appointed him
prince over Israel (25:30). The struggle
for Israel's throne had become a bitterly
contested issue which even divided many
families.

David's understanding of his role as
Israel's future ruler also seems to have
matured during this period. He had decided in the cave at Engedi that he
would not raise up his hand against the
lawful king. Now in Carmel he is led
to see that he should not use his power
to ride roughshod over his opponents
among the common people either
(25:26,33).

David, therefore, decided to forego
his brutal retaliation for Nabal's insult
(v. 22). Instead he left his judgment in
God's hands. Within a week Nabal was
dead, and his winsome spouse was soon
to become David's wife.

Ziphites Repeat Treachery (1 Sam. 26: 1–25)

The passage.—There are a number of
remarkable similarities between this incident and that in 23:19—24:22. On both
occasions David's position was betrayed
by the Ziphites. Saul employed 3,000
troops, and God delivered him into
David's hands. Likewise, on both occasions Saul said, "Is this your voice, my
son David?" and eventually ended by
confessing his injustices toward David.

The present context, however, portrays David in an even more daring role.
Taking only one companion, he stole
into the very heart of the enemy camp
and stood beside his sleeping king. He
took Saul's spear and canteen as evi-

dence of his opportunity to kill the king.
Confronted with this proof of David's
innocence, Saul reluctantly confessed
that he had misjudged his rival.

Special points.—In this passage (vv.
19–20), David recognized that he was
being driven from Israel. In a plea addressed both to God and to Saul, David
begged for some opportunity not to
have to leave his own people.

David used an interesting description
of Saul's pursuit: "like one who hunts a
partridge in the mountains" (v. 20,
RSV). This bird would not fly from danger unless abruptly startled, but it would
run along the ground. Hunters would
keep the bird moving until it was exhausted, and then it could be captured
with ease. This was exactly Saul's
strategy.

David Becomes a Vassal (1 Sam. 27: 1–12)

The passage.—David eventually realized that he and his soldiers could not
survive Saul's relentless pursuit in Israel.
He decided, therefore, to hire his men
out as mercenary soldiers to Achish,
king of Gath. This course of action was
fraught with a different kind of danger.
David's association with the Philistines
must have appeared treasonable at the
time, and there was the possibility that
his true motives would never be known.

Nevertheless, in spite of the obvious
dangers, David decided to live a double
life. Achish soon installed him and his
men in Ziklag, a small town on the
Israelite-Philistine border. David was expected to raid Judean towns seeking
spoil to be shared with his overlord
Achish.

Through cunning ruses, David was
able to convince Achish of his loyalty
without raising his hand against his own
people. He took spoil from Israel's

enemies and killed all the people to keep word of his duplicity from filtering back to the Philistines.

Special points.—The viciousness of David's actions against foreigners is easily recognized in the light of modern ethical standards. In David's day God was working to help his people understand how to treat their own king (24:1–7) or their fellow citizens (25:33–34) morally. Insights into the proper treatment of one's enemies would come as men were better prepared to comprehend God's message.

Saul Consults a Medium (1 Sam. 28:1–25)

The passage.—Israel's early efforts at establishing a monarchy appeared doomed as the Philistines made preparation for war. Israel's king was showing signs of increasing mental incompetence, and her most promising leader was a vassal of a Philistine king.

Badly alarmed by news of the Philistine mobilization, Saul earnestly sought instruction from the Lord, but he was denied guidance through the normal means of divine revelation. Cut off from legitimate prophetic (15:35) and priestly (22:11–23) counsel, Saul turned to the necromancers and wizards who were prohibited in his reign.

The biblical account does not seem to regard the consultation of the dead as an impossibility or even as a hoax perpetrated by the "witch" of Endor. Instead, such practices were regarded as contamination from the religious customs of Israel's neighbors (Deut. 18:9–14). The picture of a rejected king is thus completed as Saul laid aside his royal robes for a humble disguise and sought one last desperate means to receive a favorable word from the Lord.

The ghost of Samuel offered Saul little encouragement, however. In combat the next day, Israel's armies would be defeated and Saul and his sons would join Samuel in Sheol. Shattered by the emotional impact of Samuel's dire pronouncements and weakened by a daylong fast, Saul sank to the floor in a faint. Drawing strength from a meal prepared by the woman of Endor, Saul went out as a condemned man to meet his fate.

David Excluded from War (1 Sam. 29:1–11)

The passage.—During his 16 months as a vassal of Achish, David had been able to avoid any hostile acts against his own people. As the Philistines prepared for war against Israel, however, he was instructed to accompany Achish into battle. As the Philistine troops were passing in review, the leaders noted with alarm the presence of the Hebrews at the end of the column. Achish defended his decision to bring David and his men on the grounds that they had adequately discharged their duties since David had first deserted to him. The lords of the Philistines, however, perhaps remembering the defection of Hebrew mercenaries in the battle at Geba (14:21), insisted on sending David back to Ziklag.

Explaining that he himself had full confidence in David's loyalty, Achish reluctantly ordered his vassal to return to his home base. Although he was probably relieved, David's role as a loyal Philistine vassal required him to protest the decision to send him to the rear. Nevertheless, he and his troops were prepared to leave for home at first light the next day.

Amalekites Attack Ziklag (1 Sam. 30:1–31)

The passage.—After being suspended from the Philistine forces at Aphek, David and his men began a forced march back to Ziklag, which for some reason had been left without defenders. The weary soldiers covered nearly sixty miles in slightly more than two days, only to find their homes abandoned and in ruins.

Amalekite raiders had taken advantage of Israelite and Philistine preparations for war against each other by robbing and looting undefended towns in the southern portions of both countries. After taking captives to be sold in Egyptian slave markets, they melted back into the desert from which they had come.

David rallied his grieving men and sought divine guidance for his rescue attempts. Reinforced with a divine oracle assuring them of success, David's men began another forced march, this one to save their lost families. Their campaign was immeasurably aided by the discovery of an Egyptian slave who guided them to the Amalekite camp. Striking quickly before the Amalekites had an opportunity to harm their hostages, the Israelites routed the desert raiders.

David's men recovered their own goods and the spoil from many other cities as well. After distributing equal portions among his own troops, David shared the remaining booty with some of the more important communities in Judean territory. He wanted them to remember that while the Philistines were fighting Saul's army in the north, he was busy defeating one of Israel's inveterate enemies in the south.

Israel Defeated at Gilboa (1 Sam. 31: 1–13)

The passage.—The dread battle for which Saul had been preparing finally came to pass in the plain of Jezreel at the foot of Mount Gilboa. True to the predictions of the shade of Samuel (28:19), the day was a complete disaster. The Philistines scattered Saul's army, killed his three sons, and gravely wounded the troubled king himself. Finally, fearing that the Philistines would find him alive and make sport of him, Saul begged his armor bearer to take his life. When the young man refused, Saul fell upon his own sword. Israel was once again without a leader or a viable government to unite and protect them.

When the bodies of Saul and his sons were recovered the next day, they were exploited to the fullest by the Philistines. His armor was displayed in various Philistine temples nearby, and his decapitated body was exposed along with the corpses of his sons on the walls of Beth-shan. A measure of the respect that some Israelites retained for their fallen king is seen in the daring rescue of these bodies by the men of Jabesh-gilead. Remembering Saul's rescue of their city at the beginning of his reign, they risked their lives to give the bodies of the king's house a proper burial.

2 SAMUEL

Scott L. Tatum

INTRODUCTION

See the introduction to 1 Samuel.

David's Reaction to the Death of Saul (2 Sam. 1:1–27)

The passage.—The Amalekite claims to have killed Saul. It seems obvious that he was lying.

David's reaction was one of shock. The news of the death of the king of his nation and of his best friend Jonathan so overwhelmed him that he lost all desire for food.

The tribute of David to Saul and Jonathan reflects the high degree of loyalty in citizenship and in friendship.

Special points.—Some may raise the question about the justice of a man having to die for carrying out the judgment God had already pronounced on Saul for his sins. Keep in mind that God is capable of bringing about his will, and human beings are never wise to elect themselves as agents of God's judgment.

David Begins His Reign (2 Sam. 2:1–32)

The passage.—David had been anointed king of Israel much earlier by Samuel. He won the hearts of the people after his victory over Goliath and the Philistines. His popularity vexed the jealousy of Saul, and David became a fugitive. Saul sought to kill him. David had opportunities to kill Saul, but always spared him.

David sought for God's leadership. He asked if he should establish his throne. He inquired about the most appropriate place to begin. God led him to Hebron. He and his men with their families went where God had directed. They were accepted by the men of Judah, and David was anointed as king over them.

His right to be king did not go unchallenged. Abner, a cousin of Saul, and a commander of his army, made Ishbosheth king over Gilead. This set the stage for a civil war. The house of Saul and the house of David struggled for power.

Neither of the opponents seemed anxious for war. Abner suggested a "game of war" in an attempt at some kind of compromise settlement. The "game" turned into a bloody battle and the war was on. Asahel, David's nephew, and younger brother of Joab, chased after Abner. When he could not get him to turn away, Abner killed him.

Truth for today.—How may a person know the will of God for his life? David inquired of the Lord. God told him what to do and where to begin. There must first be a willingness to do God's will. God does not reveal his purpose for our lives simply to satisfy our curiosity. He does so in order that we may be obedient. Jesus said, "If any man's will is to do his will, he shall know whether the teaching is from God or whether I am speaking on my own authority" (John 7:17, RSV).

Abner's Revolt to David and His Murder (2 Sam. 3:1–39)

The passage.—The principal character of this passage is Abner. While David was growing stronger in his claim to

180

leadership of Israel, the house of Saul was growing weaker. It was not Ishbosheth who had the power, but rather Abner. Abner's taking one of Saul's concubines for himself was almost as if he were claiming royal rights for himself.

Abner sent messengers to David. He sought to make a covenant with him. David's condition was that Ishbosheth return Michal, Saul's daughter, who had been given to David as a wife. She seems to have hated David and was living with Paltiel. Abner arranged for the return. He came with some of his leaders to David and promised to unite Israel under his reign. David made a feast for him and sent him away in peace.

Joab, David's military leader, returning from a battle, heard about Abner's feast with David. He was very angry. He accused David of folly and Abner of deception. Joab secretly called for Abner's return and he murdered him.

Special points.—Joab and Abner were strong personal enemies. It may be that David arranged for Joab to be away while he was dealing with Abner. Joab took advantage of David's dependence on him to get his revenge against Abner.

Michal's return to David was probably against her will. Her husband, Paltiel, protested, but only briefly. David did not seek her return in love, but rather as a political move. This shows the low estate of womanhood prior to the coming of Christ.

The Murder of Ishbosheth (2 Sam. 4: 1–12)

The passage.—Ishbosheth was without a doubt a weakling. Abner had been the strength of his kingdom. When he was murdered, Ishbosheth's courage failed. His subjects were dismayed. Two captains of Ishbosheth's raiding bands, Baanah and Rechab, took advantage of the confusion and chaos. Realizing that

David would ultimately win the right to reign over all of Israel, they decided to get a part of the credit for themselves. They murdered Ishbosheth while he was sleeping in his bedchamber. They cut his head off and took it to David in Hebron.

When David saw what they had done he was enraged. They had claimed that they had done the work of God in redeeming David from his enemy. David disagreed. He reminded them that he had slain the Amalekite who had claimed he killed Saul. He said what they had done was worse. He ordered them killed.

Truth for today.—Jesus set forth the teaching that whosoever lives by the sword will die by the sword. The murderers of Ishbosheth did not gain positions of honor with David, but rather they met their deaths. Nations of the world would do well to learn this lesson.

David Established as King of All Israel (2 Sam. 5:1–25)

The passage.—After the death of Ishbosheth all of the tribes of Israel sent their leaders to David in Hebron. They made a covenant with him. In a spiritual ceremony they anointed him king over all of Israel. Thus David had been anointed three times—first by Samuel as God directed him, second by the tribe of Judah, and now by all of the nation.

One of the first acts of David as king of Israel was the capture of Jerusalem. Up to this time there had been no real center of national life. For Israel it became the most important city in the world. The Jebusites considered their stronghold so great that it could be defended by the "blind and the lame." They thus ridiculed David. Nevertheless David captured this stronghold of Zion.

Special points.—It appears strange that just at the time God was blessing David so much he seemed so utterly selfish. He built his own house before thinking of building a house for God. He took more concubines and wives for himself. We need to remember that David lived in a day when standards were not at all the standards of Jesus Christ. Women were not regarded as they are by Christians now. Women should thank God daily for the difference Jesus Christ made for them in life.

Truth for today.—With all of David's weaknesses and in spite of his apparent selfishness, his recognition of the hand of God in his life is admirable. In our day there is a great need for the people of God to be grateful that God has called them to salvation and to his service. David's practice of seeking God's will before undertaking anything is a good pattern for us today.

Bringing the Ark to Jerusalem (2 Sam. 6:1–23)

The passage.—David did many things to establish Jerusalem as the capital of his united kingdom. One of the most important of these acts was the making of Jerusalem the religious center of the nation. The ark of the Lord was the symbol of his presence among his people.

David made the occasion one of national celebration. He took thirty thousand men with him to accompany the ark from Baale of Judah, where it had been since its return from having been captured by the Philistines in battle during the days of Saul. David and all of his company made music and danced for joy as the ark was placed on a new cart for its trip to Jerusalem.

When they came to a rough spot in the road, the oxen pulling the cart stumbled and the ark shook. Uzzah reached out and touched the ark. He fell dead. David and his men regarded his death as an act of God. They be-

lieved the ark was too sacred to be touched except as prescribed as a part of worship. They halted the procession and took the ark aside into the house of Obed-edom. It stayed there three months. God blessed the house for the presence of the ark.

After three months David brought the ark of God into Jerusalem. He did so with ceremonies of worship. He sacrificed an ox and a fatling. He danced for joy before the Lord as the ark came into the city. It was placed in a specially prepared tent.

When Michal, Saul's daughter who had been given to David as a wife, looked out of her window and saw David leaping and dancing for joy, she despised him. After the great public ceremony when he returned to his home, Michal ridiculed David for his undignified abandon in worship. She accused him of vulgarity in public. David's reply to her indicates that he would no longer be a husband to her. She would remain in his house as a lonely, childless woman.

Special points.—Why was Uzzah struck dead for touching the ark? The people in the days of David interpreted everything that happened as an act of God.

In Numbers 4 instructions are given to the sons of Kohath who were to carry the ark. They were warned to carry it by the staves, but they were not to touch it lest they die.

God's Covenant to Establish David's Throne (2 Sam. 7:1–29)

The passage.—This is one of the outstanding messianic passages in the Bible. It contains God's covenant with David that he would establish his throne forever. David's response reveals the depth of his spiritual insight and the loyalty of his heart to God's will.

The occasion of the covenant was David's expression of his desire to build a temple for the Lord. It was his plan to provide a proper dwelling place for the ark of God. Nathan, the prophet, at first thought the idea was a good one. He encouraged David to proceed. That night, however, God revealed his will. David would not build the temple, but his son would instead.

God's message to David through Nathan contains some marvelous promises. God declared the values of his moving about with his people to bless them as they were pilgrims on their way to the Promised Land. He reviewed the history of his dealings with David. He had taken him as a poor shepherd lad and had made him king over all of Israel. He promised to make his name great. He declared he would appoint a place for his people Israel.

Instead of David building a house for God, rather God promised to build a house for David. He would establish his kingdom forever and make his name great. He said, "I will not take my steadfast love from him, as I took it from Saul, whom I put away from before you" (7:15).

David's idea of the special role of Israel in God's plan is important. Later Israel would forget God and take credit to themselves for their blessings. David did not make that mistake. He recognized that it was God who had driven out the enemy. As God had promised to magnify David's name, he in response made a covenant to magnify the name of the Lord forever.

A Summary of David's Victories (2 Sam. 8:1–18)

The passage.—For a long time the Philistines had been one of the major problems of Israel. Both Saul and David had spent much time in fighting them.

They were a constant threat to the security of the kingdom. David subdued them.

The Moabites were defeated and made servants to the Israelites. David put many of them to death, and the remainder of them were forced to pay tribute as a subjected people.

David extended his territories by defeating the Syrians. They were described as being in two groups. He conquered Zobah first and then the Syrians of Damascus. He slew twenty-two thousand men in the battles. The remainder of the Syrians were forced into the position of bringing tribute regularly to David. Much wealth of gold shields and bronze was brought back as spoil to Jerusalem.

David's Kindness to Mephibosheth (2 Sam. 9:1–13)

The passage.—David never forgot his love for Jonathan. It was a friendship as deep as life itself. He wondered if there were descendants of Saul to whom he might show mercy for Jonathan's sake. He was delighted to learn through Ziba that Jonathan had a son still alive. He learned the story of Mephibosheth. (Read the passage on Mephibosheth in 2 Samuel 4:4.) David sent for him.

Mephibosheth had every reason to be afraid of David. It was the custom in those days for any new king to destroy all of the descendants of rival dynasties. He fell on his face before David, but David assured him he had nothing but kindness for him. He promised to restore to him all of the lands that had formerly belonged to Saul. He would receive the income from the lands as long as he lived. Mephibosheth would always be a guest at David's table.

Special points.—It is difficult to understand the strange mixture of cruelty and kindness in David and those of his day. He could order the execution of thousands of men, women, and children. At the same time he never forgot the love he had for the friend of his youth, Jonathan. In every person there is both the capacity for severity and gentleness.

Truth for today.—The capacity for making lasting relationships is a quality of spiritual health. True love continues in spite of all circumstances. Not even death could make David forget Jonathan. His gratitude could not be expressed directly, but he sought some way to honor the house of Saul. He never got away from that awesome respect he had for "God's anointed." In our day there could well be a return to a higher respect for those who are specially singled out to serve the Lord.

The War with the Ammonites (2 Sam. 10:1–19)

The passage.—The king of the Ammonites died. David sent his servants to console the new king who had begun to reign in the stead of his father. He affirmed his loyalty to the Ammonites because of the friendship he had had with the deceased king.

The Ammonites insulted the Israelites who had come to them by shaving off half of the beard of each one. They also cut off their garments at their hips and sent them away in ridicule and disgrace.

David let his servants stay at Jericho until their beards had grown out. In the meantime he prepared to punish the Ammonites.

The Syrians were hired by the Ammonites to join in fighting Israel. Joab, David's general, realized that he was faced with a battle on two fronts. He divided his forces and prepared for battle. He chose to lead the battle against the Syrians and put Abishai in charge of the battle against the Ammonites. First the Syrians were defeated and then the Ammonites fled.

After this battle, the Syrians regrouped and came against Israel again. David led in a decisive victory over them. The Syrians decided it was not a good idea to help the Ammonites against Israel any more.

Truth for today.—One of the most inspiring texts of the Bible is found in verses 11 and 12. Joab said to Abishai, his brother, "If the Syrians are too strong for me, then you shall help me; but if the Ammonites are too strong for you, then I will come and help you. Be of good courage, and let us play the man for our people, and for the cities of our God; and may the Lord do what seems good to him."

David's Sin with Bathsheba (2 Sam. 11: 1–27)

The passage.—David's immorality began with the temptation of the eye. From the roof of the king's palace he saw Bathsheba bathing. She was very beautiful. It is not likely that his sin resulted from only one temptation. He probably entertained lustful thoughts from time to time. He may have gone to his roof on several occasions with the hope of satisfying his lustful curiosity. It could also be assumed that Bathsheba may have been aware of David's interest in her before he called for her to come over to the palace. The narrative in the Bible is necessarily brief. Much lengthy fiction has been written about this story.

David sent messengers to Bathsheba and invited her to come to his palace. Again it is not likely that she visited him only once. The adultery of David and Bathsheba resulted in her pregnancy. She sent word of her condition to David and he began to try to hide their sin.

His first attempt was to get Uriah, Bathsheba's husband, to return home and to appear to be the father of the baby. He sent for him from the battlefield. He inquired about the war with the Ammonites. He told him to go home to his wife. Uriah, either suspecting the problem, or trying to be fair with his men on the battlefield, would not go home. David then invited him to a feast and got him drunk. Still he would not go home to Bathsheba.

David then became a murderer. He sent a letter to Joab by Uriah himself, calling for his death to be arranged in battle. Uriah was to be placed in the hardest part of the fighting, and then the other men were to be withdrawn, leaving him to die. The deed was done. Word was sent to David of the death of Uriah. After a period of mourning, Bathsheba came to live with David in the palace. God was much displeased.

Truth for today.—We live in times of gross immorality. The stability of the institution of marriage is threatened on every hand. The sanctity of the unique relationship between husbands and wives is disregarded all too often.

Jesus spoke of the danger of the lust of the eyes. In Matthew 5:27–30 he called for purity of thought. Adultery, like other sin, begins with the entertainment of the idea in the mind. Jesus warned against the lustful look by saying, ". . . every one who looks at a woman lustfully has already committed adultery with her in his heart."

Sin almost never consists of one deed alone. One sin begets another. In an attempt to cover one sin, David committed almost all of the other sins. He set himself up as his own god. A woman became his idol. In the name of Jehovah he did the will of Satan. He dishonored motherhood and fatherhood. He murdered. He stole his neighbor's wife. He became a liar of the worst sort. His coveting was of the basest kind. In of-fending in one point he had broken all of God's law.

The Exposure of David's Sin (2 Sam. 12: 1–31)

The passage.—The Lord sent Nathan, his prophet, to David to expose him as a sinner. He began with a parable. There were two men in a certain city. One was rich and the other poor. The poor man had only one little ewe lamb that had been like a member of his family. When the rich man had a guest to entertain, instead of killing one of his many sheep, he stole his poor neighbor's lamb and killed it for his feast. As David heard the story he became angry. "The man who had done this deserves to die," he said. Nathan replied, "You are the man."

Nathan reviewed God's blessings upon David and exposed his sin fully. He prophesied the consequences that would follow the sins. The sword would never depart from David's house. His own family would be openly immoral. The child conceived in sin would die.

One of the most moving passages in the Bible follows. David acknowledged his sin. He asked God to pardon him. Read Psalms 32 and 51 for an understanding of the repentance of this man after God's own heart who had so grievously sinned.

Bathsheba's baby became very sick, and although Nathan had told him the baby would die, David prayed for it to get well. He would not eat, but mourned and prayed continually. After a week the baby died. David's servants feared to tell him, but David could tell by their actions that death had come. He washed himself and went to the house of God to worship.

He explained his actions by saying, "While the child was still alive, I fasted and wept; for I said, 'Who knows whether the Lord will be gracious to

me, 'that the child may live?' But now
he is dead; why should I fast? . . . I
shall go to him, but he will not return
to me" (vv. 22–23).

The birth of Solomon is recorded in
verse 24. The history of Israel concerns
itself with the struggle for the succession
to the throne. The tracing of the various claims makes an interesting study.

The conquest of the city of Rabbah
and the capture of the Ammonites is
recorded in verses 26–31. David took
the crown from the head of their king
and put it upon his own head, thus symbolizing his rule over them. He made the
Ammonites labor in the brick kilns and
perform other difficult tasks as his
slaves.

Special points.—It would seem that
Bathsheba would have been punished
for her part in the sins of David. While
it does not appear that she was punished with the same severity as he was,
it must be kept in mind that we do not
have all of the record. The Bible is seeking primarily to show God's dealing
with Israel leading up to the coming of
Jesus as the Savior of the world. Many of
our questions must go with only partial
answers. We may be sure that Bathsheba's grief over the death of their
baby was comparable to that of David.

Truth for today.—The overcoming
grace of God in spite of the sin of man
is seen in that God chose to use Solomon. Jesus was born of the line that
came from David and Bathsheba. No
one should ever feel that his background
disqualifies him for useful service for
God.

Sin does have severe consequences beyond the persons who are guilty. The
social implications of sin should be
taken into account. The death of Uriah
and many others in the battle at Rabbah, the death of the infant, the immorality of the children of David, and the

bloodshed for many years speak so
loudly, "Be sure your sin will find you
out." What David did in secret has become the most widely known act of immorality in the history of the world.

Amnon's Sin against Tamar (2 Sam. 13: 1–39)

The passage.—Amnon was the oldest
of the sons of David. The record of his
character may be given to show why he
was not chosen as successor to David.
The unfolding history also reveals the
weaknesses of Absalom and Adonijah.
It was Solomon who was clearly God's
choice.

Absalom and Tamar were children of
David by his wife Maacah. Polygamy
was an accepted social arrangement in
those days, but its evil consequences revealed it not to be the will of God for his
people. Children of the same father were
not supposed to marry (Lev. 18:9). This
and other of God's laws were often
broken, always with serious consequences.

Amnon made himself sick by his overwhelming sexual desire toward his half-
sister Tamar. He shared the knowledge
of his lust with his cousin Jonadab. He
gave Amnon the scheme he used to bring
about the rape of his half-sister.

Amnon pretended illness and when
David inquired about him, he asked for
Tamar to wait upon him. David granted
the request. Tamar prepared food for
him and at his request was feeding him
out of her own hands as he lay on the
bed. He seized her and raped her. Verse
15 declares that he then hated her with
a passion greater than the lust with
which he had sought to rape her. He
had her forcefully ejected from his
house. She went away crying aloud.

Absalom took Tamar to his home and
waited for an opportunity for revenge.
David heard of the ugly situation and

was very angry. He could not have escaped remembering the similarity of this sin to his own.

Two years later Absalom made a feast and invited all the king's sons. He also invited David. David did not go, but Absalom pressed him to insist that Amnon go. While Amnon was drinking at the feast Absalom commanded his servants to kill him. At first the news came to David that Absalom had killed all of his sons, but later he heard it was only Amnon who had been murdered. Absalom fled into exile.

Truth for today.—In these days of sexual permissiveness, stories like those of David and Bathsheba and Amnon and Tamar are being reenacted with alarming regularity. The circumstances may vary, but the results are always the same—guilt, shame, hatred, and death.

Absalom's Return from Exile (2 Sam. 14:1–33)

The passage.—Joab, realizing David's longing for Absalom, and at the same time his kingly pride, conceived of a plan to bring David face to face with his own conscience. He got a woman from Tekoa to pretend to be a mourner and to carry out the act that would bring David to admit the need for Absalom's return to Jerusalem.

The woman said she was a widow and had had two sons. They had quarreled with each other and one of them was killed. She said the family had risen up to claim the life of the remaining son because he had killed his brother. She said this would leave her in destitution and her late husband without any heir.

David gave orders that the remaining son should be granted immunity from the death penalty because the circumstances justified his pardon for his mother's sake and to carry on the name

of his father.

The woman then made the analogy. She said David was keeping the heir to the throne of Israel away from his people. She admitted that Joab had enlisted her to assist in bringing Absalom home. She said Joab had the wisdom of God upon him.

Joab brought Absalom back to Jerusalem, but David did not allow him to come to the palace. He lived in his own house apart.

Special points.—The ambitious selfishness of Absalom begins to show in this chapter and will unfold in the succeeding chapters. Bit by bit he set the stage to overthrow his father's throne and take it for himself. This was a part of the struggle for succession in the house of David. Ultimately, of course, Solomon came to the throne.

Why was Joab so interested in Absalom's return to Jerusalem? Perhaps there were three reasons. He knew David's love for his son was deeper than his pride would allow him to admit. He wanted to do what was best for the nation. He wanted to make sure a qualified heir was ready in case of David's death. He also probably thought Absalom showed the greatest promise and admired him for his ability and appearance.

Absalom's Conspiracy (2 Sam. 15:1–37)

The passage.—Absalom secured a personal bodyguard for protection and for appearance. He set about to undermine his father's throne. He sought popularity by claiming to have personal interest in those who found difficulty in getting to see David. He told every man that his claim was right and that if he were king he would hear him and grant his wish. When a man would bow before him he would kiss him and make him feel important. Absalom stole the hearts of the men of Israel.

Claiming he wanted to go to Hebron to worship, Absalom secured permission to leave Jerusalem. Secretly he had arranged for those who wanted to make him king to meet him at Hebron. The conspiracy was strong, and the numbers with Absalom increased.

David fled Jerusalem. He did not want the city to be destroyed in battle. He left only a few of his servants to care for the household. His faithful servants went with him.

The loyalty of Ittai the Gittite is best described in his own words in verse 21: "As the Lord lives, and as my lord the king lives, wherever my lord the king shall be, whether for life or for death, there also will your servant be."

David insisted that the ark of God remain in the city of Jerusalem. He trusted God to bring him back if it was his will. One of the saddest passages in the Bible is the description of David's leaving Jerusalem, weeping as he went. He was barefoot and had his head covered.

As David was leaving Jerusalem, Hushai agreed to return to Jerusalem to keep David informed of things he might hear there concerning Absalom's strategy.

David Flees; Absalom Enters Jerusalem (2 Sam. 16:1–23)

The passage.—As David was leaving Jerusalem he crossed the brook Kidron and went across the Mount of Olives. A little past the summit he met Ziba, the servant of Mephibosheth. He had two asses saddled and some provisions. He claimed to want to help David by providing these things for his journey. He also claimed that Mephibosheth had remained in Jerusalem and hoped to take advantage of the confusion to make himself king and thus reestablish the throne of Saul. David rewarded Ziba by giving him all of the property that belonged to Mephibosheth.

Ziba's story appears to be false. Read 2 Samuel 19:25–27 for Mephibosheth's version of what happened. He gave an understandable explanation and accused Ziba of lying. After David had heard both stories, not knowing which to believe, he divided the property in dispute equally between the two men.

Shimei, a relative of Saul, followed David along as he fled from Jerusalem and cursed him continually. He threw stones and dirt at him. David's servant, Abishai, wanted to cut off his head for these insults, but David would not consent. He left vengeance to the Lord.

As Absalom entered Jerusalem he found Hushai there. He could not know whether to trust him or not. He asked where his loyalty lay. Hushai claimed he would be loyal to Absalom, the new king, but we know he was a spy for David.

Ahithophel was Absalom's advisor. He had gone with him to Hebron and returned with him to Jerusalem. He suggested that Absalom take possession of his father's concubines. This would be an open sign that Absalom despised his father and that no one should hesitate to follow him and fear he would compromise with David. The break between father and son was complete. The tent of the concubines was pitched on the roof of the palace and Israel's moral shame was public. David's sin bore still more bitter consequences.

Special points.—Absalom followed the advice of Ahithophel in taking possession of David's concubines. Ahithophel was the grandfather of Bathsheba. Could he have been seeking revenge for what David did to her? Absalom was committing the same kind of immorality as that for which he had killed his half brother Amnon. Was it from the same rooftop where David's sin began? It may well have been.

David Is Saved by His Underground (2 Sam. 17:1–29)

The passage.—Ahithophel, Absalom's advisor, pointed out that it was David, and David alone who was the problem in Israel. He suggested gathering twelve thousand men to set out to kill David. He said all of Israel would return to Jerusalem like a bride for Absalom. At first Absalom thought the idea was a good one.

Absalom checked with Hushai. He said Ahithophel's advice was not good. He spoke of David's wisdom. He said he was angry and dangerous, like a bear robbed of her cubs. He was too wise to be caught with his soldiers, but would be well hidden. Hushai advised Absalom to wait until all Israel was behind him and then for him to go into the battle personally as the leader. Absalom accepted the advice of Hushai.

Verse 14 explains that God was watching over David. "For the Lord had ordained to defeat the good counsel of Ahithophel, so that the Lord might bring evil upon Absalom."

How the underground worked to keep David informed is shown in verses 15–20. Hushai worked through Zadok and Abiathar, the priests. They sent messages by a maidservant to David. On one occasion they were almost caught, but were saved when a woman hid them in a well and covered it and spread grain over it to disguise their whereabouts.

The Defeat and Death of Absalom (2 Sam. 18:1–33)

The passage.—David told his men to deal gently with Absalom. He knew he must defeat his son, but his love for him was strong.

Absalom, riding on his mule, became entangled in a tree. His head was caught and his mule ran from beneath him. He was left helpless, but alive. One of the men told Joab. He explained that he had seen Absalom but had not wanted to kill him because he remembered the words of David to deal gently with Absalom. Joab killed Absalom and ten others joined in the deed. Joab sounded the trumpet of victory. They buried Absalom beneath a great heap of stones.

Ahimaaz wanted to carry the news of Absalom's death to David. Joab forbade him to do so. He enlisted a Cushite, probably a slave to go. Ahimaaz insisted that he be permitted to go, and finally Joab consented. He outran the Cushite and came first to David. His courage must have failed him, because he was unable to give David the news. The Cushite arrived and told the story.

David was overcome with grief. He went to his chamber over the gate and wept. His lament is one of the saddest in the Bible. He said, "O my son Absalom! my son, my son Absalom! would God I had died for thee, O Absalom, my son, my son!" (v. 33).

Special points.—David put his military men in an impossible dilemma. How could they win the victory for David and at the same time deal gently with Absalom? Perhaps David had hoped Absalom could be taken alive and that reconciliation could be made. Perhaps he had actually considered allowing Absalom to have the throne. Likely he himself did not know his own mind in the matter. Possibly only the father of a rebellious son could know his mixed emotions. The key to the question lies in the lament of David in verse 33.

Joab's disregard for the command of David to deal gently with Absalom shows the power he had. His rebuke of David in the next chapter reveals his hard-hearted character. Nevertheless David was so dependent upon him and owed so much to him he was in an awkward position. Before David died he asked Solomon to make sure Joab was punished for the deaths of Abner and Amasa. He did not mention his disobedience to his order about Absalom, but this could not have escaped his memory.

David Returns to His Throne (2 Sam. 19:1–40)

The passage.—The mourning of David for his son continued for quite some time. What might have been the occasion of rejoicing for victory was turned into sadness for the nation because of the death of Absalom. Joab was angry. He thought David was acting foolishly. He had doubtlessly expected to be glorified for his part in the victory. He spoke harshly to his king. He said if he did not go out and speak words of encouragement to his people that they would turn against him. He said the conditions would then be worse than ever. King David complied.

Verses 9 and 10 tell of the strife and division that existed among the various tribes of Israel. David first appealed to the men of Judah to come back to his side. They responded to his claims of love and kinship and invited him to return to them and be their king. They met him at the River Jordan to bring him back home. Only about half of the men of Israel responded.

Shimei, who had cursed David as he left Jerusalem, met him at the River Jordan. He begged forgiveness for his crime against the king. David appeared to forgive him at the time, but in giving his final instructions to Solomon in 1 Kings 2:8–9, he told him to put Shimei out of the way.

Mephibosheth, Saul's lame son, also went out to welcome David home. David asked why he had not been loyal to him when he was leaving Jerusalem. Mephibosheth declared that Ziba had betrayed him and had lied about him to David. He claimed he had asked Ziba to saddle an ass for him so he could go with David. When Ziba failed him he could not go, because he was lame. Mephibosheth reminded David of his kindness in allowing him to live and eat at his table. He begged for mercy. David, not knowing whether to believe Mephibosheth or Ziba, settled the matter by dividing the property of Saul between them. Mephibosheth said he would be willing to give up everything for the joy of David's return home.

Barzillai the Gileadite was a very old man. He came to welcome David home. He was a wealthy man and had helped David in his time of trouble. David wanted to reward him by making him an honored guest in his palace. Barzillai said he had helped David with no hope of reward. He had done so because he loved his king. He wanted nothing in return. He recognized that he was too old to enjoy the pleasures of the king's palace. He wanted to return to his home.

Special points.—Notice especially the reaction of four men to the victory of David and the death of Absalom. Joab was impatient with David and expected special recognition. Shimei was the opportunist who had made a poor decision and tried to get back on the winning side. Mephibosheth, if he was truthful, was a poor man who had been wronged and desired to set the record straight. Barzillai stands out as a man of unselfish generosity. This passage is an interesting study in character.

The Revolt of Sheba (2 Sam. 19:41— 20:26)

The passage.—Jealously between the northern tribes of Israel and the tribe of

Judah flared into a war. The men of Israel felt that the men of Judah were claiming David as their king. The men of Judah pointed out that David was near kin to them. The men of Israel responded that they had ten shares in the king. They claimed to be the first to speak of bringing him back.

Sheba, a man of Benjamin, blew his trumpet and called Israel to revolt. He said, "We have no portion in David, and we have no inheritance in the son of Jesse; every man to his tents, O Israel!" (2 Sam. 20:1). The men of Israel followed him. The men of Judah followed David to Jerusalem.

David did not want Sheba's revolt to become a greater threat. He called on Amasa to return with the Judean soldiers. When he did not respond promptly, he sent Abishai after Sheba. Joab went also with many other men.

Amasa finally arrived to pursue Sheba. Joab murdered him. He tricked him by letting one sword fall from his belt. He appeared to greet Amasa as a brother. When he was close to him he drew out a hidden sword and thrust it into his abdomen. Thus Joab was in firm control again.

Joab pressed forward in pursuit of Sheba. The rebel took refuge in a fortress in Abel of Beth-maacah. Joab came and beseiged him. They were about to batter down the walls. A wise woman of the city agreed to exchange the head of Sheba for the safety of her city. It was agreed. In due time Sheba's head was thrown over the wall. Once again the threat of the throne of David was put down.

Special points.—Why did Amasa not respond quickly to the call of David to pursue after Sheba? It may be that the Judeans did not want to follow a fellow who had been on the side of Absalom, even if David had been willing to trust him. It could be that David was trying to curb the power of Joab. The men of Judah must have known Amasa was not the best one to lead them.

The Gibeonites Execute Saul's Sons (2 Sam. 21:1–14)

The passage.—There was a famine in Israel that lasted for three years. David asked God the reason for it. God replied it was because of the guilt of the house of Saul for putting some of the Gibeonites to death when Israel had sworn to spare them. David sought to make restitution to the Gibeonites. They demanded seven of the sons of Saul that they might hang them.

David spared Mephibosheth, but delivered seven other of Saul's sons. The Gibeonites hanged them as in public demonstration.

Rizpah, the mother of two of them, watched over their bodies for six months to protect them from the vultures and the beasts.

When David heard of her faithfulness and her mother love, he took their bones and those of Saul and Jonathan and gave them decent burial.

Special points.—The seemingly unjust punishment of sons for the crimes of their father reminds us of the privilege we have of living in days when the influence of Jesus Christ has brought a larger degree of justice to the world.

Truth for today.—The mother love of Rizpah is a pattern of loyalty and love to us. Though she was but a concubine to an evil king, she had the quality of love which has come down through the centuries in history as a memorial to her.

Another War with the Philistines (2 Sam. 21:15–22)

The passage.—The Philistines continued to plague the Israelites. This is but another brief account of the continuing conflict. On one occasion David was about to be killed, but Abishai came to his rescue. David's men urged him not to continue to place himself in such danger. A number of giants of the Philistines were killed in those battles.

David's Song of Thanksgiving (2 Sam. 22:1—23:7)

The passage.—This song reflects God's blessings on David throughout his life. Notice how much of it is contained in Psalm 18. David gave God the glory for all of his victories. He told of many times when he had called on God in times of distress. God always heard his prayers. He called God his rock, fortress, deliverer, shield, high tower, refuge, and savior.

The first seven verses of the twenty-third chapter are called David's last words. He declared that God had spoken to him. God had given him wisdom and judgment. God had made an everlasting covenant with him. By way of contrast the wicked are cast away from God. We are reminded of Psalm 1.

The Loyalty of David's Mighty Men (2 Sam. 23:8–39)

The passage.—This section is something of a review of the exploits of some of those who were so dedicated to David. They loved him, protected him, and were willing to lay down their lives for him.

On one occasion the Philistines were encamped in the valley of Rephaim near Jerusalem and occupied David's home town of Bethlehem. David expressed a wish for a drink of water from the well at Bethlehem. Three of his loyal friends broke through the enemy lines and at the risk of their lives brought him some water from the well. Because

they had risked so much because of their loyalty, David regarded the water as too sacred to drink selfishly. He poured it out before God as an act of worship.

Truth for today.—The world needs more Christians whose loyalty to Jesus Christ is like the loyalty of David's men. God's leaders should be respected as David's followers respected and loved him.

Almost anything can be used as an act of divine worship. Even a drink of water reminded David of God's gift. He was grateful to God for his friends and the risk of their lives for him. Though he had only a cup of water, it was his most precious possession. He gave his best to God. It was too sacred to waste on himself.

The Census and the Plague (2 Sam. 24: 1–25)

The passage.—For some reason, not fully disclosed, God was angry with Israel. This chapter tells us God moved David to number Israel. First Chronicles 21 states that Satan provoked David to number Israel. Sometimes humans have a desire to do something which Satan leads them to do and God allows them to do what they want to in order to reveal to them that they are wrong. The best interpretation here seems to be that the census was wrong. David's desire was so strong, God told him to go ahead.

Even Joab advised David against the census. The people did not want to be enlisted for further military duty.

After David realized he had sinned in taking the census, he repented. God gave David three choices: seven years of famine, three months fleeing from his enemies, or three days of pestilence. David threw himself on the mercy of God and chose the plague.

Thousands of people were dying.

God's mercy moved him to stop the plague. David begged God to let him alone bear the punishment.

Gad, the prophet of God, instructed David to build an altar to God on the site of the threshing floor of Araunah, the Jebusite. David sought to buy it from its owner. Araunah offered to give it to David along with animals for the sacrifice. David replied, "I will not offer burnt offerings to the Lord my God which cost me nothing." He insisted on purchasing the site at a proper price.

Truth for today.—One of the truly fine stewardship illustrations of the Bible is found in this passage. All too many people want to give as little as they can to God. They are willing for others to pay for the cost of the house of the Lord and the program of God's kingdom. A true Christian will not allow others to pay for his share of the support of the work of the Lord. He finds joy in sacrifice.

1 KINGS

Scott L. Tatum

INTRODUCTION

See the introduction to 1 Samuel. The books of Kings continue the books of Samuel.

David Chooses Solomon over Adonijah (1 Kings 1:1–53)

The passage.—David had two remaining sons who might have succeeded him, Adonijah and Solomon. Adonijah was the older, and Solomon, son of Bathsheba was the younger. This chapter tells of David's increasing infirmity, Adonijah's attempt to seize the throne, and David's choice of Solomon.

The aged King David was so weak that they attempted to revive him by giving him a beautiful young nurse as a companion. She could not stir his interest.

Adonijah made himself the king. He did something like Absalom had done (2 Sam. 15). He, like Absalom, had not been properly disciplined. He was handsome. He enlisted the aid of Joab, the military power in Israel, and Abiathar, the priest. He made a great feast to proclaim the beginning of his reign. Obviously Solomon was not invited. Nathan was not invited either.

Nathan and Bathsheba made plans to make Solomon the king. Bathsheba reminded David he had promised to let Solomon succeed him. Nathan came in to confirm the idea. They asked David to settle the matter since Adonijah had already laid his claim. David admitted his promise and pronounced that Solomon would succeed him.

Upon David's instructions Zadok the priest, Nathan the prophet, and other leaders of Israel placed Solomon on the king's mule and brought him to Gihon. There they anointed him king.

When Adonijah heard of it he was afraid of Solomon and went to hold on to the horns of the altar as a symbol of safety. Solomon promised not to kill him as the custom of kings was to slay their rivals. His promise was conditioned on his unquestioned loyalty.

Special points.—Up to this time there had been no particular plan established for the orderly succession to the throne of Israel. Both Absalom and Adonijah had sought unsuccessfully for it themselves. This whole section of history deals with the struggle for succession. For a brief while David and Solomon were co-regents. After the death of David the power was consolidated under Solomon, and Israel had her most glorious era of peace and prosperity.

The Death of David (1 Kings 2:1–12)

The passage.—When David realized he could not live much longer, he called Solomon to make his last wishes known. He challenged the new king to be true to God, to be strong, and to be courageous. He promised that God would keep his covenant and that there would always be a king on the throne of Israel.

He asked Solomon to punish Joab for the murders of Abner and Amasa. He urged him to be gracious to those who had been loyal to David his father. He requested that Shimei be punished for his disloyalty.

David died and was buried in the City of David. Solomon's kingdom was firmly established. He set about to deal with his enemies and rivals.

The Elimination of Solomon's Enemies (1 Kings 2:13–46)

The passage.—Adonijah, denied the throne he thought he deserved, had the audacity to ask for Abishag the Shunammite to be his wife. She had been David's nurse. Perhaps Adonijah still had some notion of setting up a rival throne. Perhaps he only wanted a beautiful woman for his wife. At any rate his request seems foolish. It cost him his life. Adonijah made his request to Bathsheba. She told Solomon. Solomon interpreted it as an insult and a threat. He sent one of his servants to kill Adonijah. He counted it wickedness that Adonijah should want one of his father's concubines.

Solomon banished Abiathar the priest. He sent him to Anathoth. He said he deserved to die, but he spared him because he had carried the ark of God and had shared the afflictions of David his father.

When Joab heard Adonijah had been killed, he was afraid for his life and ran to the tent of the Lord and caught hold of the horns of the altar to beg for mercy and safety from death. Solomon sent for him to come out. He would not. Solomon ordered him killed on the spot.

Shimei had been ordered by Solomon not to leave Jerusalem. He said he would die the day he left. After two years he left Jerusalem to recover some runaway slaves. Solomon had him killed for his disobedience.

Truth for today.—Jesus said, "All who take the sword will perish by the sword" (Matt. 26:52). The cruel lessons taught by the history of these passages

bear out this truth. Joab had been loyal to David, but he had been power-hungry and ruthless. His own ugly death was reminiscent of the many killings he himself had carried out.

The Wisdom of Solomon (1 Kings 3:1— 4:34)

The passage.—Solomon is well known for his wisdom. Unfortunately that wisdom was not used altogether. Solomon was foolish in marrying foreign wives, giving way to lust, and in his materialism.

God appeared to Solomon at Gibeon and offered to bless Solomon according to his request. Solomon praised God for his blessings to David. His one request of God was for wisdom. He wanted an understanding mind to be able to govern well. God granted his request and also promised him riches and honor as well as long life.

Solomon's wisdom is well illustrated in his dealing with the two harlots. Each claimed to be the mother of a baby and said the child of the other had died. Solomon told them to cut the baby in half so each mother could have a share. The true mother asked that the baby be allowed to live and be given to the other woman. Solomon granted the baby to its real mother. All of Israel recognized his profound wisdom. His wisdom is also shown in the very efficient organization of his government as described in chapter 4.

Israel prospered under Solomon. Its borders were greatly enlarged. There was peace. The people and Israel's neighbors also were happy with his reign and their welfare.

Special points.—Solomon's marriage to so many foreign wives was a matter of political expediency. The problem, in addition to the immorality of the situation, lay in the religious practices of his foreign wives. Solomon erected heathen shrines for them.

Truth for today.—The Bible warns against the marriage of Christians to non-Christians. "Be ye not unequally yoked together with unbelievers" (2 Cor. 6:14) or "Do not be mismated with unbelievers."

When we seek God's will first, he always adds other blessings to us. Solomon's primary desire for wisdom enabled God to bless him in many other ways, even in spite of his errors. "But seek first his kingdom and his righteousness, and all these things shall be yours as well" (Matt. 6:33).

King Solomon's Temple (1 Kings 5:1— 7:51)

The passage.—Hiram, king of Tyre, had built David's palace in Jerusalem. He established friendship with Solomon. Solomon told him of his purpose to build a house for the Lord. He asked Hiram for cedar and for laborers. The two kings made an agreement. Solomon also conscripted stonemasons and other workmen for the project. One of the greatest building projects in history was underway.

The dimensions of the Temple were 90 feet long, 30 wide, and 45 high. The vestibule was the same height and width as the main Temple, but was only 15 feet in depth. The inner sanctuary, later called the holy of holies, was a perfect cube of 30-foot dimensions overlaid with pure gold. The elaborate furnishings, carvings, overlays, and paneling are described in minute detail. The greatness of the building lay not in its size, but in its beauty and religious significance.

God made a covenant concerning the Temple. He promised Solomon he would bless him and Israel. He would dwell with them and never forsake them. They were in turn to obey his ordinances and keep his commandments (6:11–13).

Not only does this passage tell of the building of the Temple, it describes the entire complex of five buildings (7:1–8). All of these composed an impressive royal building program. The details of the metalwork, the symbolism of the pillars, the furnishings and fixtures of the various buildings and the significance of each could be the subject of a study requiring more space than is possible in a brief commentary. Many of our libraries have entire books devoted to a description of the Temple itself.

Special points.—It is interesting to notice that chapter 6 ends with the statement that Solomon was seven years building the Temple. Chapter 7 opens with the statement that Solomon spent thirteen years building his own palace. This is a commentary on Solomon's changing character. Worldly power and a desire for comfort and luxury gradually overcame his primary zeal to do the will of God.

Truth for today.—The elaborate and expensive furnishings of the Temple certainly justify our providing our best for the house of the Lord. Our dedication to God is often reflected in our devotion to his institutions. No institution should be wasteful, but if its existence is justified at all it should merit a quality in keeping with its relationship to our God.

The Dedication of Solomon's Temple (1 Kings 8:1—9:9)

The passage.—The dedication ceremonies for King Solomon's Temple began with the assembling of the elders and heads of the various tribes. It was to be a national sanctuary and the center of worship for all of the tribes. They brought the ark of God from its temporary resting place to its permanent quarters. They sacrificed so many animals that they could not be numbered.

When the priests came out of the holy of holies where they had placed the ark, a cloud filled the Temple. It symbolized the glory of God which filled the house.

Solomon made a long speech of dedication. He praised God and he blessed the people. He recalled David's desire to build the Temple. God had fulfilled the promise he had made to David. He declared the Temple as the dwelling place of the eternal God.

God's covenant to David and Solomon that the throne of David would be preserved is the subject of much of the dedicatory speech. Following his dedicatory speech there was a dedicatory prayer.

The Temple was to be a place of prayer. Solomon listed the objects of prayer which God would hear. Forgiveness for sin against God is a constant need. Offence against one's neighbor is another daily problem. In time of war God's people need to pray for deliverance. Drought was a frequent problem and the people of Israel would need to pray for rain. Various plagues and diseases would call the people to prayer. In verse 38 the term "whatever prayer" seems to cover all other kinds of need. Included in the listing were the prayers of foreigners and prayers from men far away in battle or in exile.

Solomon's prayer of dedication had been made on his knees with his hands outstretched toward heaven. He rose to bless the people again. They offered many more sacrifices to God.

God appeared to Solomon again. He promised to hear the prayers offered at the Temple. He renewed the promise to establish the throne of Israel forever. He warned that Israel would be cut off if they were to forsake God.

Special points.—The Temple was not just a private place of worship for Solomon and the royal family. It was for all the people. The passage in 8:41–43 gives special attention to the foreigner and his missionary significance.

The ark of the covenant was so called because it contained the tablets of stone on which the Ten Commandments were written. This was God's covenant with his people and the standard of their obedience and conduct.

Truth for today.—Sometimes it is good for us to remember that not all of our good plans will be brought to reality in our own lifetime. In 8:18 Solomon recalled that God said it was good for David to have the building of a Temple in his heart. Our dreams should exceed our grasp. Often others will get the joy of doing what we would like to have done for God.

Institutional religion is too frequently scorned in our day. Throughout the Bible there is the teaching that a strong base of operation for world missions is wise. The person who does not worship in a special place seldom worships anywhere else either.

The Glory of Solomon (1 Kings 9:10— 10:29)

The passage.—After Solomon's major building program was complete, he gave Hiram, king of Tyre, twenty cities in Galilee as payment for the gold, cedar, and cypress timber which he had supplied. Hiram was not well pleased with the bargain. We are not told how Hiram was eventually made satisfied.

The glory of Solomon's building was accomplished by forced labor. The people were compelled to spend a certain amount of time in the labor of building. The burden of this fell principally on the ten Northern tribes, and was a part of the difficulty that later arose between the two parts of Israel.

Solomon had regular times for offering sacrifices to God. The three times a year mentioned in verse 25 perhaps corresponded to the main feasts of the Hebrews throughout their history.

The visit of the Queen of Sheba to Solomon is indicative of his reputation all over the world. His glory was the talk of the royal palaces everywhere. The queen came bringing spices, gold, and jewelry as gifts to the famous king. She asked him very difficult questions, and he had the answers for her. There was nothing she asked about that he couldn't explain. After she had seen his glory and experienced his wisdom she uttered the famous lines, "The half has never been told."

The amount of gold mentioned in 10:14 would amount to more than sixteen million dollars. While this may not seem to be so much in these days of astronomical figures, it was tremendous in those days. This was typical of the other riches Solomon accumulated. His throne must have been one of the wonders of the world in his day. It was solid ivory overlaid with finest gold. It sat on an exalted platform surrounded by statues of lions. His drinking cups were of gold.

From all over the world people came to see Solomon's wealth and to hear his wisdom. As they came they brought additional wealth. The commerce of the world and the wealth of the world seemed to center in Jerusalem. It was said that silver became as common as stone.

Truth for today.—It is unfortunate that the Queen of Sheba was impressed only by the splendor and wisdom of Solomon. She went back to her land without knowing the God of Israel who had so blessed Solomon.

The Idolatry, Decline, and Death of Solomon (1 Kings 11:1–43)

The passage.—Solomon forgot that his blessings came from God. He forgot the high spiritual privileges that had come to him as God appeared personally to him. His power and glory detracted from his vision of the glory of God. His foreign wives led him away from God. He compromised by participating in worship with them and in providing for the building of altars to strange gods.

Solomon did what was evil in the sight of God. He did not follow in the ways of David's worship. God was angry because of his sins. God promised to take the kingdom away from him, with the exception of one of the tribes. For the sake of David God delayed the execution of the sentence until after Solomon's death.

Adversaries began to rise up against Solomon. First Hadad the Edomite organized resistance to Solomon. He had been an exile in Egypt, but returned after Solomon became king of Israel. Rezon of Syria became a troublemaker about the same time. It was said of both of these that God raised them up as adversaries.

The greatest threat came in the person of Jeroboam. He was a very able man. Solomon had made him one of the leaders in his forced labor system. The prophet Ahijah predicted that Jeroboam would take the Northern tribes away from Solomon's hand. His dramatic illustration was the tearing of his robe into twelve parts. He gave Jeroboam ten pieces along with his prophecy.

Ahijah's prophecy was much like the judgment that God had pronounced to Solomon. In it God gave the reasons for Solomon's loss of the kingdom. He promised to bless Jeroboam if he would serve God. Solomon learned of Jeroboam's opposition and sought to kill him. Jeroboam fled to Egypt.

Solomon died. The statement, "He

FON H. SCOFIELD, JR.

10. Shechem, ruins in the east gate area
(see 1 Kings 12:25)

slept with his fathers," came to be a common way of announcing the death of a king. Solomon was buried in the city of David—Jerusalem. Rehoboam, his son, reigned in his stead.

Special points.—When Solomon was old his wives turned his heart away from the true God. For a while Solomon was true to God and was blessed. For some additional years he lived a compromising life while maintaining a certain loyalty to God. After years of compromise his selfish glory and worldly riches were too much for his weakened religious loyalties. His wives' devotion to their worship was stronger than his.

Does God raise up adversaries? Certainly God used those enemies of Solomon to punish him for his disobedi-

ence. History is filled with examples of nations who turned away from God and were destroyed by their enemies. Isaiah 7:20 calls the foreign nations used to punish Israel "hired razors."

Truth for today.—What happened to Solomon can happen to anyone who puts pleasure, riches, and power above God. Not only are nations punished for the sins of their leaders, families can be made to suffer because of the sins of individuals. It is true that no one ever sins alone, and no one is ever punished without affecting others.

Jeroboam's Revolt Against Rehoboam (1 Kings 12:1–33)

The passage.—David had managed to hold Israel together, though they

199

maintained their tribal identity. Solomon reigned over them with a strong hand, but he became king not by their choice but by decree from David. When Rehoboam followed Solomon the kingdom became divided, and there follows a confused history of many kings in both parts of the divided nation. From this point on, there is a greater emphasis on the prophets and less and less emphasis on the kings except as they relate to the ministry of the prophets.

Rehoboam was foolish to listen to young advisors rather than the wisdom of well-trained older men. When Israel gathered at Shechem to make him king, Jeroboam and the assembly asked for tax relief and a more compassionate government. The older men advised him to lighten the load. The young men advised him to increase the load. They had been reared in prosperity and ease with the young prince and did not know the mind of the nation. Rehoboam told Israel that his little finger would be thicker than his father's thigh. Thereupon the ten Northern tribes of Israel went away from Rehoboam. The kingdom was divided. Jeroboam was made king of the Northern tribes.

Jeroboam knew that many of his people would want to go back to Jerusalem to worship God in the Temple. He therefore established a new religion for them and made two golden calves for them to worship. He placed one at Bethel and the other at Dan. He established his palace at Shechem.

Special points.—Though Solomon had many wives and concubines, we do not have record of any other sons that might have been eligible to succeed him but Rehoboam.

Truth for today.—Rehoboam was the son of the wisest man that ever lived, but wisdom is not inherited. Each generation must develop wisdom. It can profit from the experience of the past or suffer the consequences. Someone has said that neither wisdom nor grace runs in the blood.

Resentment usually boils over into strife. The ten Northern tribes were loyal to David and Solomon, but their resentment was building up all the time. When they got no relief under Rehoboam they finally rebelled. This should be a lesson for governments of the world today.

The Testing of the Prophet of God (1 Kings 13:1–34)

The passage.—An unnamed prophet of God came to Bethel from Judah. He saw Jeroboam in his heathen worship and cried out against the idolatry. When Jeroboam reached out to say, "Lay hold of him," his hand miraculously withered away. He asked the man of God to pray for him. He was healed. When he invited the prophet to go home with him he declined, because God had warned him not to do so. He was told to deliver his message and return home immediately.

An old prophet who lived at Bethel went to find the prophet from Judah. He insisted that God had told him to bring him back to Israel. He was lying, but the man of God made the mistake of believing him. He returned with him. While they were eating, the old prophet of Bethel received word from God that the younger would die for his disobedience. As he was returning home, a lion killed him. The older prophet realized that he had indeed been a man of God and brought his body back for decent burial. Read 2 Kings 23:15–20 for a reference to this story.

Special points.—Why would God place so severe a test on one of his servants? God had made clear his word.

There was no question about the directions. The young prophet should have listened to his own conscience. His mistake was not an innocent one. He knew better.

Truth for today.—In 1 John 4:1 we are warned, "Beloved, believe not every spirit, but try the spirits whether they are of God: because many false prophets are gone out into the world." The prophet from Judah should have known of the possibility of false prophets and should not have been so gullible. In our day there are those who would mislead us into going contrary to the will of God. We must obey God rather than men.

The Deaths of Jeroboam and Rehoboam (1 Kings 14:1–31)

The passage.—Jeroboam's wickedness went from bad to worse. His son became very ill. He sent his wife to Ahijah, the prophet of God. She disguised herself so he would not recognize her. Though the prophet was blind, God revealed the identity of Jeroboam's wife to him. He foretold the doom of Jeroboam. When Jeroboam's wife returned home her child died. In due time Jeroboam also died.

Meanwhile Rehoboam was king in Judah. He was almost as evil as Jeroboam. He led his nation away from God. They also built shrines to idols. Shishak, king of Egypt, came up to Jerusalem and stole the treasures out of the Temple of God. Rehoboam substituted shields of brass for the shields of gold that had been stolen. After the decline of his power, Rehoboam died.

Special points.—The heathen worship in Judah included both male and female prostitutes. The male prostitutes are called sodomites here, after the name of the ancient city God destroyed for its wickedness.

Truth for today.—When Jeroboam and his wife looked to Ahijah, the prophet of God, for prayer and counsel in the sickness of their son, they remind us of those who turn their backs on God and his church. In time of trouble they expect God and his people to minister to their desires.

Rehoboam's shields of brass substituted for the shields of gold are symbols of a religious glory that passes away from those who compromise their principles. The form of religion may remain, but its content is like brass compared to gold.

The Struggle Between Israel and Judah (1 Kings 15:1—16:34)

The passage.—Family quarrels are always especially bitter. Abijam, son of Rehoboam of Judah, and Jeroboam fought as long as Jeroboam lived. His death was recorded in the preceding chapter and this chapter summarizes and relates the reign of Abijam to the last part of the reign of Jeroboam. Only for the sake of David did God tolerate Abijam in spite of his sins.

Asa became king of Judah upon the death of Abijam, and he was a refreshing change for the better. He made partial religious reforms. Asa made an alliance with Benhadad of Syria and gave him many of the treasures of the Temple.

In Israel, Nadab ruled briefly and was succeeded by Baasha who overthrew him, destroying the descendants of Jeroboam. Baasha of Israel and Asa of Judah continued the civil war. Baasha's son, Elah, ruled briefly. Zimri overthrew him and destroyed all of his kin. He did not reign long, however, because Omri, his commander of the army, seized power. Zimri was killed in a fire that destroyed his palace. Omri began a new dynasty. He is most famous for his wicked son

Ahab.

Ahab did more wickedness than all of the kings before him. Jezebel, his wife, was a notorious Baal worshiper. Their wickedness was an abomination to God. His anger was great against their sins.

Elijah's Earlier Miracles (1 Kings 17: 1–24)

The passage.—This is a chapter filled with miracles. If we believe in God, we must recognize his limitless power. How these things were done, we do not know. If we could understand them and explain them in terms of the ordinary, they would not be miracles. God was proving his power in the worst of times. For a nation with a bad king God sent a good prophet—Elijah.

Elijah stood boldly before Ahab and predicted that it would not rain for three years except by his word. God told him to hide by the brook Cherith. He commanded the ravens to bring him food. When the brook dried up God sent him to Zeraphath where a widow fed him. Her meal and oil were miraculously replenished as she shared with God's prophet. When the woman's son became ill and there was no breath in him, Elijah took him up to his room on the roof and prayed that God would restore him to life. God raised him from the dead!

Special points.—Some have asked if the ravens were really merchants or Arabians. We are face to face with a series of miracles and an attempt to explain one of them away would still leave us a number of others even more amazing. It is better to accept them by faith in an all-powerful God.

The upper chamber was built on the roof of the flat-top house and could be reached by an outside stairway. Elijah may have attempted artificial respiration on the lad. It is consistent with prayer to carry out all we know to do ourselves and trust God to use our efforts or go beyond them.

Truth for today.—The book of James in the New Testament is a good commentary on the prayer life of Elijah. It tells us he was a man of like passions with us. He prayed earnestly that it not rain. According to his prayers the heavens were shut up. He prayed again and it rained according to his request. When we pray within God's will there is no limit to the power of prayer.

Truth for today.—One of the main teachings of this section of the Bible is that God punishes sin, though he loves sinners, and that he takes care of those who trust in him. The brook provided water until it dried up because there was no rain. God had a poor widow ready to help. Someone has said that Elijah became a foreign missionary. Zerephath was in Sidon. What a blessing he was to her and her family. Centuries later Jesus came to those same coasts and blessed another poor woman by healing her daughter.

Elijah on Mount Carmel (1 Kings 18: 1–46)

The passage.—After three years God told Elijah to go before Ahab again. Ahab had been looking everywhere for water for his horses. Obediah, a servant of Ahab who had remained true to God, was also looking for water for the king's horses when he met Elijah. Elijah told him to inform Ahab of his whereabouts. He feared at first, but trusted Elijah and did his bidding. When Ahab saw him he said, "Is it you, you troubler of Israel?" (v. 17). Elijah told Ahab that he and his family were the real troublemakers in Israel because of their sins.

Elijah challenged the prophets of Baal to a contest on Mount Carmel. He called all the people of Israel to witness

11. Samaria, palace of Omri and Ahab
(see 1 Kings 16:28–29)

it. He said to them, "How long will you go limping with two different opinions? If the Lord is God, follow him; but if Baal, then follow him" (v. 21).

Elijah directed that two bulls be brought. The Baal prophets chose one and he chose the other. It was agreed that the God who answered by fire from heaven would prove to be the true God.

The Baal worshipers called on him all day long, but there was no answer. As they raved on Elijah mocked them and told them to cry louder. He was not only taunting them, he was preaching to the people.

At the time of the evening sacrifice,

Elijah called all of the people together. He repaired the altar of the true God. He made a huge trench around it. He put the wood and the sacrifice in place. Three times he asked that all of it be drenched in water. It was all soaked and the trench was filled with water.

The prayer of Elijah in verses 36 and 37 is one of the most moving in all the Bible. He prayed for the miracle in order that the people might know Jehovah as the true God. The fire fell from heaven and consumed the offering, the wood, and the altar itself. Elijah ordered the prophets of Baal seized and killed.

Elijah then predicted rain and prayed for it. Just as God had answered with fire, he answered with rain. Elijah's servant was asked to look for a sign. At first he saw nothing in the sky. He went back to look seven times. Then he saw a small cloud the size of a man's hand. In a little while the sky was black with clouds, wind, and rain!

Special points.—Could the fire from heaven have been a bolt of lightning? If so, it came from a cloudless sky. If it was it would not in any sense disprove the miracle.

The destruction of the prophets of Baal seems severe. Throughout this section of the Bible there are similar accounts where capital punishment is inflicted on a wholesale scale. Compare this to Samuel's hacking Agag to pieces before the Lord in Gilgal. God himself, having all of the facts, is alone in a position to order the removal from the earth of persons or nations that are out of harmony with his purposes. We must be sure we know the mind of God. Our judgments must be made in the light of the truth we have after twenty centuries of Christian history. We cannot properly go back to the standards of conduct that prevailed before Christ came.

Truth for today.—Notice the calmness in prayer with which Elijah carried out his preparations on Mount Carmel. Contrast this with the frenzy of the prophets of Baal. It is not the loudness of prayer, nor the number of words, but faith in the true God that really counts. Read Matthew 6:7–8.

Christian people need to take a definite stand. Elijah asked why the people in Israel were "halting between two opinions." The Revised Standard Version uses the term "limping with two different opinions." The idea is of the person who hops from one position to the other. Read Matthew 12:25.

Elijah's Vision at Horeb (1 Kings 19: 1–21)

The passage.—When Ahab told Jezebel what Elijah had done on Mount Carmel, she swore to kill him. He fled to Beersheba and hid. He was so discouraged he wanted to die. God sent an angel to give him food to strengthen him. He went on to a cave in Mount Horeb.

God asked him why he was there. He replied that he was the only one left who was true to God. There was a great storm that tore through the mountain, but God was not in the wind. After the wind there was an earthquake, but God was not in it. After the earthquake there was a fire. God was not in it either. Then God spoke in a "still small voice."

God told Elijah to anoint Hazael to be king over Syria, Jehu to be king over Israel, and to anoint Elisha to succeed him as God's prophet. God revealed to him that there were seven thousand others in Israel who had not bowed down to Baal. Soon Elijah found Elisha and carried out God's directions as he anointed him as a prophet. He cast his prophet's cloak on him symbolizing the transfer of the prophetic ministry.

Special points.—Why was Elisha allowed to go back to his home for a farewell with his family when Jesus seemed to denounce this sort of thing in Luke 9:61–62? The circumstances were different. Elisha had already accepted the will of God for his life. He was not postponing a decision. What Jesus was urging was immediate decision. Excuses to delay doing the will of God are never acceptable. The feast of Elisha was a celebration of his dedication of himself to God. His parents shared his joy in finding God's purpose for his life.

Truth for today.—Elijah's discouragement after the victory on Mount

Carmel is so much like our moods sometimes are. No one is immune from despair. God is always ready to strengthen us, encourage us, and give us a fresh vision of himself. It may not be spectacular. Listen for the still small voice. Be ready to accept new challenges. Help prepare others to carry on.

Ahab and Benhadad (1 Kings 20:1–43)

The passage.—The Syrians and their kings, led by king Benhadad, beseiged Samaria. They demanded that Ahab surrender the silver and gold and the choicest of the women and children. Ahab was so weak militarily that he agreed. When he told the leaders of Israel what he had done they advised resistance. Benhadad was so overconfident that he was drinking himself drunk in his tent. Acting on the advice of a prophet of God, Israel attacked Benhadad's armies. The Israelites slaughtered the Syrians, but Benhadad escaped.

Benhadad regrouped his forces and came against Israel again. Israel defeated them again, and Benhadad fled. Realizing his peril, he appealed to Ahab for mercy. He promised to restore the territory Syria had taken from Israel. He agreed to give Ahab favorable trade advantage in Damascus. On those terms Ahab let him go.

God sent a prophet to Ahab to show him the folly of letting Benhadad go. The prophet had made a fellow strike him and wound him in the face so he would appear to have been in battle. With bandages and wounds as his disguise, he went before Ahab. He said that in battle he had been entrusted with a prisoner, but that he had let him escape. The penalty for letting a prisoner escape was death. By his very admission he pronounced the death penalty on himself. Ahab pointed out this truth. Then the prophet removed the bandages and revealed his identity. He told Ahab he had let Benhadad go when he should have destroyed him as the enemy of God's people. Ahab was angry over this revelation and went to his home nursing his resentment.

Special points.—The military weakness of Israel was apparently not as bad as Ahab thought. He seemed all too willing to surrender to Benhadad's demands. In his moral depravity he was willing to make peace at any price.

Verse 30 tells of the destruction of twenty-seven thousand men. Some have suggested that in the battle involving the storming of the city that large numbers of men were killed. Most interpreters regard it as a miracle.

Truth for today.—We can be too busy for the main business. Verse 40 is an indictment on many a person who needs to put first things first. "And as thy servant was busy here and there, he was gone." When Ahab let Benhadad go, he sinned against God's commandment. Ahab had been too concerned about getting back his lost territories. He wanted a place of special advantage to trade in the city of Damascus. We need a renewal of a sense of priorities. The will of God demands first place. Read Matthew 6:33.

Activism is sometimes used as an excuse for not doing the will of God. Dr. W. T. Conner used to say, "Activity around the church house is not necessarily religion." We can multiply our programs and our activities without deepening the spiritual lives of our people. We can join in every worthwhile endeavor in the community and "be busy here and there" and still not do the will of God.

Naboth's Vineyard (1 Kings 21:1–29)

The passage.—Near Ahab's summer palace at Jezreel, Naboth had a vineyard. Ahab wanted it very much and offered to buy it. Naboth could not sell it because according to the Israelite law a man's inheritance was his father's property and belonged in turn to his sons. Ahab knew this principle of justice, but still he had a passionate covetousness for the vineyard. He made himself sick over the matter.

Jezebel, his wife, determined to get it for him and so promised it to him. She arranged a great feast to honor Naboth. She had two base fellows to be there and to accuse him of blaspheming God and cursing the king. He was falsely charged and was stoned to death. According to 2 Kings 9:26 Naboth's sons were killed also. Ahab went down to Jezreel to take possession of the prize.

God sent Elijah to rebuke Ahab for his gross injustice and murders. He asked Ahab, "Have you killed, and also taken possession?" (v. 19). "In the place where dogs licked up the blood of Naboth shall dogs lick your own blood."

Ahab said, "Have you found me, O my enemy?" Elijah answered, "I have found you because you have sold yourself to do what is evil in the sight of the Lord." Not only did Elijah pronounce doom on Ahab, but on Jezebel as well. He predicted that dogs would eat her body in Jezreel.

Rather surprisingly Ahab humbled himself before God. We cannot know the depth of his repentance, but because he did humble himself before God, his judgment was delayed. Ultimately, however, the punishment came and the prophecy was fulfilled. Read 1 Kings 22:38 and 2 Kings 9:30–37.

Special points.—The phrase "sold yourself" used by Elijah to describe what Ahab had done in obtaining Naboth's vineyard means that he had become a slave of his own sin. Greed had become his god and would destroy him.

John 8:34 gives us the words of Jesus on this matter. Read also Matthew 16:26.

Truth for today.—There are some things that ought not to be for sale. Naboth recognized that. Someone has said that every person ought to have at least one thing that he would not sell for any price. This is true of a man's soul, his character, his reputation, his family, his church.

The Death of Ahab (1 Kings 22:1–40)

The passage.—After three years of peace in Israel, Jehoshaphat, the king of Judah, came to visit Ahab. They discussed the captivity of Ramoth-gilead by the Syrians. They made an alliance to go together to capture it. Jehoshaphat said, "I am as you are, my people as your people, my horses as your horses."

They asked their prophets if they should go up to battle. Four hundred who claimed to be prophets of God encouraged them to go to war. This is what they wanted to hear.

When the prophet Micaiah heard of the prophecy he was encouraged to agree. He replied that he must speak only as God directed. His first answer, however, did agree with the other prophets. We later learn that he wanted Ahab to go to his death. Ahab suspected this and insisted on the truth. Micaiah then prophecied truthfully that Israel would be scattered like sheep. He said God had caused the four hundred prophets to lie to entice Ahab into battle where he would die. Micaiah was put in prison for his prophecy.

Ahab went into battle disguised as a commoner. Jehoshaphat rode in the royal chariot. The Syrians were looking for Ahab to kill him and almost killed Jehoshaphat by mistake. When they recognized that he was not Ahab, they let him go. Ahab, however, was wounded by an arrow released at random. He died from the wound and his blood covered the bottom of his chariot. As they were washing it, the dogs licked up his blood as Elijah had prophecied. The death of Jehoshaphat is also related in verses 45–50. His reign is more fully covered in 2 Chronicles 17–20.

Special points.—The author of the books of First and Second Kings seemed to be more interested in recording the history of Israel, while the author of the Chronicles gave emphasis to the record of the prophets and kings of Judah. This explains the great amount of space devoted to Ahab and the little to Jehoshaphat.

The horns of iron used by Zedekiah in verse 11 were symbolic of the power he was claiming for Ahab and Jehoshaphat in battle.

Truth for today.—God can use even the false prophet to accomplish his purpose. Just as God can use heathen nations to punish those who have sinned; so when false prophets lead false men astray, the will of God can be brought to pass by them.

Be sure your sins will find you out. Every item of the prophecy of Elijah concerning the death of Ahab for the murder of Naboth was carried out in detail.

2 KINGS

Scott L. Tatum

INTRODUCTION

See the introduction to 1 Samuel. The books of Kings are a continuation of the books of Samuel.

Elijah Predicts Ahaziah's Death (2 Kings 1:1–18)

The passage.—Ahaziah, son of Ahab, succeeded his father on the throne of Israel. It was during his reign that Moab rebelled against Israel.

Ahaziah was injured in an accident in which he fell through some lattice from an upper floor of his palace. He sent his servants to inquire of Baalzebub whether he would recover.

Elijah met the servants of the king and warned them that they should seek guidance from God, not Baalzebub. He sent word to Ahaziah that he would die from his injuries.

When Ahaziah got the word he demanded that Elijah be brought to him. He sent fifty men to bring Elijah to him. Elijah called down fire from heaven and destroyed them. When the king sent fifty more, Elijah called down fire on them, and they were destroyed, too.

A third band of fifty men came and pled with Elijah to spare their lives. An angel told Elijah to go back with them to the king. He did so. He repeated his prediction that he would die of his injuries. He did die, and Jehoram, his brother became king.

Special points.—"The angel of the Lord" has been the subject of interest by some. This may have been an angel in the usual sense. Some have suggested it was a special manifestation of Jehovah or the pre-incarnate Christ.

Truth for today.—Ahaziah is a good example of the curse that comes to the children of evil parents. What could be expected of a man who had Ahab and Jezebel as father and mother? Notice 1 Kings 22:52. "He did what was evil in the sight of the Lord, and walked in the way of his father, and in the way of his mother."

Elisha Succeeds Elijah (2 Kings 2:1–25)

The passage.—Elijah knew that his work was complete. He asked Elisha to come with him to Gilgal. Elisha insisted on going on with him to Bethel and Jericho, even when Elijah and other of his friends urged him to stay behind.

Elijah caused the waters of Jordan to part so he and Elisha could go over on dry land. Elisha prayed to receive a double portion of the power of Elijah. Elijah told him that if he saw him when he was taken up into heaven, his prayer would be granted. Then he saw a chariot of fire and a whirlwind carry Elijah to heaven. He took up Elijah's mantle and became his successor.

Miracle-working power was Elisha's from the beginning of his ministry. With Elijah's mantle he struck the waters of Jordan and they parted for him as they had done for Elijah.

The sons of the prophets recognized the spirit of Elijah upon Elisha. They insisted that they go looking for the de-

AL J. STUART

12. Jericho, excavation of old city (see 2 Kings 2:4–5), traditional mountain of Jesus' temptation in background

parted Elijah. Elisha told them not to go. After their unsuccessful search of three days Elisha reminded them of his advice to them not to go.

The water in a spring near Jericho was bad. Elisha took a bowl of salt and cast it into the spring. He pronounced it pure. To this day the spring is used for its wholesome water.

When some small boys made fun of Elisha for being bald-headed, he pronounced a curse on them. Two she-bears came out of the woods and attacked them.

Special points.—Elijah's mantle was likely a leather cloak or outer wrap. It was a symbol of his authority from God. Even today reference is made to the mantle of one man falling to another. This means that the responsibilities and authority are passed from one to another.

Truth for today.—Elijah asked Elisha what he would rather have than anything else. He replied that he would like to have the spirit of Elijah. One prayer is always in order. Christians should pray for more of the power of the Holy Spirit. They must also be willing to pay the price.

The children in verses 23–25 were punished for their lack of respect for the man of God. Baldness was symbolic of weakness. Their irreverence is all too typical of the attitudes of many in our day. There needs to be a return to the

209

recognition of honor due to God's anointed.

Jehoram's War Against Moab (2 Kings 3:1–27)

The passage.—Jehoram, another son of Ahab, succeeded his brother Ahaziah to the throne of Israel. He was a wicked king, but not so bad as Ahab or Ahaziah.

When the Moabites rebelled and refused to pay taxes to Israel, Jehoram asked Jehoshaphat, king of Judah, to help him fight Moab. They made an alliance and started out to battle. They were also joined by the king of Edom.

There was a terrible drought and the armies of Israel and Judah were in danger of death from lack of water. Elisha was called for. He prayed for a miracle and God caused water to spring up for them in the ditches.

The water that came down from Edom by the miracle must have been muddy. The Moabites from a distance thought it was blood. They concluded that the three kings had fought each other and that the field was bloody.

When the Moabites came against the Israelites they were turned back and slaughtered. They had thought they would have an easy victory. They encountered a stinging defeat. So desperate was the king of Moab that he offered his eldest son as a sacrifice to his heathen god. Then the battle ceased.

Special points.—In verse 15 the music produced by the minstrel seemed to be just the encouragement Elisha needed. As the minstrel played, the power of the Lord came upon the prophet and he was capable of proclaiming the revelation of God. There is some indication that it was rather customary for there to be music played when the prophets of God were seeking God's will. Throughout history music has been a vital part of worship.

Verse 16 in the King James Version needs clarification of the words, "Make this valley full of ditches." In the Revised Standard Version it is clearer— "Thus says the Lord, 'I will make this dry stream-bed full of pools.' " This then was not a commandment to them to dig ditches, but a promise that God would fill the ditches that were already there with water.

God's Miracles Through Elisha (2 Kings 4:1–44)

The passage.—This chapter contains a number of stories of God's miracles through Elisha. Each one of them proves the power of Elisha as a prophet of God.

There was a widow of one of the prophets who was threatened by her husband's creditor with the enslavement of her two sons to satisfy the debt. Elisha told her to borrow all of the vessels she could find and to fill them with the oil she had. As rapidly as she poured, the oil kept multiplying until all the vessels were filled. She sold the oil and paid the debt. She had enough left to live on.

A Shunammite woman and her husband provided a room for Elisha in their home. He asked what they would like God to do for them. They had been childless and expressed the desire for a son. Elisha predicted they would have a son within a year, and they did.

When the child was old enough to work in the field he became ill and was taken to his mother. He died on her lap. The Shunammite woman went to see Elisha and begged for his help. Elisha went with her and raised the young man from the dead. The method he used suggests the possibility of mouth-to mouth resuscitation.

Another miracle took place when the young men in the school of the prophets had prepared and eaten poison food. By mistake they had cooked poison fruit. Elisha put meal in the pot and it became wholesome food.

Still another miracle was the feeding of a hundred men with a very small amount of food. Of course, we are reminded of the feeding of the five thousand by Jesus himself.

Special points.—In verse 24 the request of the Shunammite woman was to keep on whipping the beast so it would get her to Elisha as soon as possible.

Gehazi was unable to raise the young man from the dead by the use of the staff of Elisha. He laid it upon his body, but it did no good. Only Elisha's personal efforts were effective. It was as if he put his own warmth and his own breath into the child.

Naaman the Leper Is Healed (2 Kings 5:1–27)

The passage.—Naaman was the commander-in-chief of the Syrian army. He was wealthy, highly honored and respected, but he was a leper. In his household there was a little girl from Israel, who had been captured in a raid and was a slave. She suggested that Naaman seek help from Elisha, the prophet of God.

Naaman went to the king of Israel with a letter of introduction from the king of Syria and great riches to purchase a cure. The king of Israel was amazed and feared Syria was seeking a quarrel. Elisha heard about it and called for Naaman to come to him.

When Naaman came to Elisha's house, Elisha sent word for him to go wash in the river Jordan seven times. Naaman was angry. He thought Elisha

would go through some elaborate ceremony to cure him. He was sure the rivers of Damascus were better than all of the waters of Israel. He went away in a rage.

His servants pled with him to be calm and follow the simple prescription. He dipped himself seven times in the river Jordan and was completely healed. He returned to Elisha and tried to pay him, but Elisha would not take anything.

Gehazi, Elisha's servant, however, ran after Naaman and requested that Naaman give him money for the cure. He received the loot and returned to Elisha. Elisha knew of his sin and told him he would be smitten with leprosy. For his greed he was punished with the disease.

Special points.—Naaman asked for two loads of dirt from Israel to carry back to Syria. He probably had the idea that the God of Israel was identified with the land itself. Since he had found faith in the true God, he wanted to carry back home some of the land of that God. This primitive idea needed patient understanding.

Naaman also asked pardon from God for those occasions when he knew he would be asked to accompany his king into the heathen place of worship. He knew there would be the danger of compromise as he returned to a heathen environment and tried to be true to Jehovah. This problem is very real to people in all generations who try to live for God in a world that does not recognize him.

Truth for today.—No matter how humble a person's station in life may be, there are opportunities for witness for God. The little slave girl in Naaman's house is a good example. She had a strong, simple faith in God. She had a compassionate love for others. She knew the man of God would want to help. She did not allow resentment for her slavery to keep her from being kind. God rewarded her with an eternal place in history.

Elisha's Miraculous Power (2 Kings 6: 1–23)

The passage.—The sons of the prophets needed a larger house. Elisha went with them to the river Jordan to help them build a new one. One of the young men dropped a borrowed ax head into the water. Elisha miraculously made it float by throwing a stick into the water.

When Syria was fighting Israel, Elisha was able to warn the king of Israel as to the whereabouts of the Syrians. The king of Syria felt sure he had a spy in his camp, but his servants knew it was the God-given power which Elisha had.

The king of Syria sent to Dothan great armies and chariots and horses to surround the city where Elisha was. Elisha's servant looked out one morning and saw what he thought was a hopeless situation.

Elisha prayed for his servant's eyes to be opened. Then he saw that Elisha was protected by horses and chariots of fire around him. Elisha prayed that the Syrians be struck blind. He then led them to the king of Israel in Samaria. Rather than kill them, they fed them and sent them back to Syria.

Special points.—Spiritual insight is a rare blessing. Elisha could see God's powerful protection. His servant could see nothing but trouble. The horses and chariots of fire symbolized God's superior power. Elisha could say, "Fear not, for those who are with us are more than those who are with them" (v. 16).

The unusual mercy and kindness of Elisha to the armies of Syria is a refreshing change from the brutality of many of the other stories. He asked the king of Israel not to destroy them, but to feed them and send them home. In this act we see a foreshadow of the spirit of Jesus.

The Siege of Samaria (2 Kings 6:24— 7:20)

The passage.—Benhadad and his entire army besieged the city of Samaria. There ensued a terrible famine in the city. Food was so expensive and so scarce, people were eating refuse. Two women had bargained to eat the child of one of them and then the child of the other. After boiling the first child and eating it, the two mothers were arguing because the second mother had hid her child.

The king of Israel blamed the tragedies on Elisha and promised to behead him. He sent his servant to get Elisha. When he came to his door, Elisha predicted that the next day there would be plenty of food in Samaria and at cheap prices. The servant protested that it was impossible. Elisha told him it would happen, but the doubting servant would not live to see it.

There were four lepers who were at the gate of the city. They decided to surrender to the Syrians rather than starve to death. They knew the worst the Syrians could do would be to kill them, and they were destined to die if they did nothing. They ventured! They found the Syrian camp deserted. God had caused them to flee because they had heard the noise of a great army. The four lepers looted the tents. Remembering their starving city, and fearing punishment if they were caught, they went back to Samaria with the good news that food was plentiful and the enemy had fled. Elisha's prophecy of prosperity was fulfilled. The doubting messenger of the king, who had questioned Elisha's prophecy was trodden under by the people rushing out to get food.

Truth for today.—The four lepers spoke an evangelistic truth in verse 9: "We are not doing right. This is a day of good news; if we are silent and wait until the morning light, punishment will overtake us; now therefore come, let us go and tell the king's household."

Elisha's Wide Influence (2 Kings 8:1–15)

The passage.—In this section are two stories showing the broad influence of the prophet Elisha. Not only in Israel, but also in the neighboring nations he was well known and respected as God's man.

The Shunammite woman whose son Elisha had raised from the dead, had been in the land of the Philistines for seven years to avoid a famine in Israel. She had returned home and was appealing to the king to help her retain her lands. The fact that Elisha had raised her son from the dead and that he was living proof, caused the king to grant her petition.

The prophecy of Elijah that Elisha would anoint Hazael as king over Syria is recorded in 1 Kings 19:15–18. It is fulfilled in 2 Kings 8:7–15. Elisha had come to Damascus. Benhadad the king was sick. He sent Hazael, his servant, to inquire of Elisha if he would recover. Elisha replied, "Go tell him he will recover." He told Hazael that after his recovery from the illness, Benhadad would die. The reference was no doubt to his assassination by Hazael. Elisha wept because he said he foresaw the cruelty of Hazael to God's people Israel. Hazael carried the good news to Benhadad that his illness was not fatal. He did not tell him the rest of the prophecy, but he took it upon himself to carry it out by assassinating Benhadad the next day.

He took his throne for himself.

Special points.—In verse 11 "he settled his countenance steadfastly" means he stared at him or fixed his gaze upon him as if he were in a trance. Then he burst into tears. He foresaw the cruelty of Hazael to Israel.

Meanwhile in Judah (2 Kings 8:16–29)

The passage.—The scene shifts back to Judah in this passage. Jehoram, son of Jehoshaphat, was king there. He was wicked because he was married to the daughter of Ahab and Jezebel. The only reason God did not destroy Judah was for the sake of David, to whom the promise had been given that he would always have a successor.

In those days Edom revolted against Judah. The nations of Israel and Judah were declining in power and influence. Spiritually they were almost hopeless. After the death of Jehoram, Ahaziah, his son, reigned in Judah in his stead.

Jehu Becomes King (2 Kings 9:1–37)

The passage.—At the instruction of Elisha, one of the young prophets went to Ramoth-gilead and anointed Jehu king over Israel,. He did it secretly and commanded him to destroy the dynasty of Ahab. When Jehu's fellow officers heard the news they were ready to join in the revolt. They sounded the trumpet and proclaimed Jehu king. Joram, the king of Ahab's dynasty, had to be dealt with. He was in Jezreel recovering from battle wounds. Jehu set out furiously to go to Jezreel.

Joram's watchman saw the oncoming company and alerted his master. Joram sent a messenger to inquire if it was a peaceful band. The messenger inquired, but Jehu told him to fall in line behind him against Joram. A second messenger did the same thing. The watchman gave the reports and said he thought the driver in the lead chariot was Jehu "for he drives furiously" (v. 20). (This phrase has become an amusing proverb in our time referring to reckless drivers of automobiles.)

Ahaziah, king of Judah, was visiting Joram. Both of them set out separately in their own chariots to go to meet Jehu. They met at the site of Naboth's vineyard. At their first encounter, Joram realized Jehu did not come in peace. He turned and fled, but Jehu shot him with an arrow to the heart and he died. They cast his body to the ground in Naboth's vineyard, and God's prophecy was fulfilled.

Ahaziah fled also, and Jehu shot him in his chariot. He died at Megiddo. His servants took his body back to Jerusalem for burial.

When Jehu went to Jezreel, Jezebel looked out of her upstairs window. Jehu asked if there were any up there on his side. Two or three eunuchs looked out. He told them to throw her down. They did so and her blood was spattered on the wall. The horses trampled on her. When they went to get her body they discovered that dogs had eaten all except her skull and the palms of her hands. Once again the words of Elijah had been fulfilled.

Truth for today.—Dr. Robert G. Lee, noted Southern Baptist preacher, has a famous sermon entitled, "Pay Day Someday." In it he traces the story of Ahab and Jezebel from the time they coveted Naboth's vineyard until they both died according to Elijah's prophecy. His main point is that sin will find you out. "The wages of sin is death." God's retribution is sure for the unrepentant. Justice will ultimately come to pass. Years may go by, details of the sin may be almost forgotten by the persons guilty, but God remembers. The possession of Naboth's vineyard never

brought joy to Ahab and Jezebel. It brought guilt and death. "Thou shalt not covet."

Jehu's Massacres (2 Kings 10:1–36)

The passage.—Jehu set out to destroy all of the heirs of Ahab. At his word his servants cut off the heads of the descendants of Ahab and put them in baskets and sent them to Jehu at Jezreel. He continued the slaughter until none remained of the house of Ahab. While he was doing this, he also slew many of the kinsmen of Ahaziah, king of Judah.

Jehu set out to destroy the worshipers of Baal. He called for all of the priests of Baal to come to him. He said, "Ahab served Baal a little; but Jehu will serve him much" (v. 18). When he had gathered all of the priests and worshipers on the pretence of serving Baal himself, he had them slaughtered.

Special points.—Who was Jehonadab? He was a leader of the Rechabites. They were devout worshipers of the true God. Their lives were characterized by clean habits and morality. Verse 15 is a classic. Jehu asked, "Is your heart right, as my heart is right?" Jehonadab answered, "It is." Jehu said, "If it is, give me your hand." He gave him his hand and they rode together in the chariot. This passage is often used as the basis for a call to loyalty and godly friendship.

The Reformation in Judah (2 Kings 11:1—12:21)

The passage.—Athaliah was the daughter of Ahab of Israel. She seized the throne of Judah after the death of her son Ahaziah. She was the only woman to reign in either Israel or Judah. She sought to destroy all claimants to the throne, but Joash, son of Ahaziah, was hid from her and was spared. Jehoiada, the priest, led in having Joash crowned king. Athaliah was executed as a usurper. Joash is sometimes called Jehoash.

Jehoiada, the priest, led in a renewal of the covenant between Judah and Jehovah. They tore down the altars of Baal and pledged to be true to God. The reformation was not complete, however. The Temple was repaired. The people gave their offerings for the project.

It is unfortunate that the story of Joash does not end well. He had a good beginning. He used the Temple treasures to pay off Hazael, king of Syria, to keep him from taking Jerusalem. Joash was assassinated by his servants who conspired against him. Amaziah, his son, reigned in his place.

Truth for today.—Joash was blessed as long as God's servants directed him. He never seemed to develop his own loyalty to God. Too many people have only a secondhand religion. Each person must have a personal experience with God.

The Decline of Israel and the Death of Elisha (2 Kings 13:1–25)

The passage.—The spirit of gloom was heavy over the people of Israel during this period. Syria dominated them and reduced them to helplessness. Jehoahaz was king at Samaria, but was not capable of any outstanding work. After his death his son, Jehoash, succeeded him. He should not be confused with Jehoash (Joash) of Judah. He was a wicked king. He was followed by Jeroboam.

The death of Elisha is inserted at this point. It is almost as if God were saying there remained little hope for Israel. Although there were three victories for Israel recorded in verse 25, the general trend was defeat for Israel.

After Elisha's death and burial, a band of Moabites startled a funeral procession. They hastily placed the corpse in the grave of Elisha. When the body touched the bones of Elisha it revived.

War Between Judah and Israel (2 Kings 14:1–29)

The passage.—With this chapter it becomes very clear that both Judah and Israel are going down to defeat because of their rebellion against God. These two nations were never really one in spirit. Hostility was common between them. Only David and Solomon were able to keep them together briefly. Now for decades they would help to destroy one another.

Amaziah was at least partly loyal to Jehovah. His reformation left untouched most of the local heathen shrines. He was successful in his war against the Edomites. Encouraged by his victory, he challenged Jehoash of Israel to battle. In the war that followed, Amaziah lost heavily. He was captured. The walls of Jerusalem were torn down and the Temple treasures and the palace treasures were taken away. Later Amaziah was murdered by conspirators.

In Israel Jeroboam II succeeded Jehoash and had a long and prosperous reign. He was an evil man. Only by God's grace was Israel allowed to continue further into history. Zechariah, his son, followed him on the throne.

Truth for today.—In verses 26 and 27 the mercy of the Lord is revealed even to those who have turned against him. God did not forget his covenant with David and Israel. He kept trying to extend his love and mercy to his people. How tragic that they would not respond with their faithfulness.

A Succession of Kings (2 Kings 15:1—16:20)

The passage.—In these two chapters brief sketches of a number of kings are given. Azariah is usually better known as Uzziah. That is the name used in Chronicles and Isaiah and is more familiar. He reigned for fifty-two years in Jerusalem. He did right in the sight of God, although many of the people still worshiped heathen gods. His reign was marred by the fact that he became a leper. In 2 Chronicles 26:16–20 we are told it was for his spirit of pride and arrogance that he was smitten.

The passage from 2 Kings 15:8 to 15:31 is the record of the rapid succession of one king after another to the throne of Israel. In order Zechariah, Shallum, Menahem, Pekahiah, and Pekah reigned. Generally they were weak and cruel men. In the days of Pekah, Tiglath-pileser, king of Assyria, captured much of the land and carried away many of the people as slaves. Pekah was murdered by Hosea who seized the throne to be the last king over Israel.

In Judah, Jotham was king at this time. Little is said here of his reign. Read 2 Chronicles 27 for details. He built the higher gate of the Temple, but the morals of the people declined.

Ahaz followed Jotham. During his reign Rezin, king of Syria, and Pekah, of Israel, came up to besiege Jerusalem, but did not conquer it. Against the advice of Isaiah as recorded in Isaiah 7, Ahaz appealed to Tiglath-pileser of Assyria for help. He stripped the Temple of its treasures to finance the venture. Ahaz had an Assyrian altar built to replace the traditional altar at the Temple. This signified his allegiance to Assyria.

The Final Fall of Israel (2 Kings 17: 1–40)

The passage.—Hosea, king of Israel, had become a vassal of Shalmaneser, king of Assyria. When he sought to rebel, the Assyrian armies marched in and besieged Samaria. After three years it fell.

Verses 7–23 give a theological interpretation of the fall of Israel. Israel had not been true to God. The people had sinned both secretly and openly. They had worshiped idols rather than the true God.

The king of Assyria replaced the people of Israel with foreigners. This was probably the origin of the Samaritan people. They had a mongrel religion. "They feared the Lord, and served their own gods."

Truth for today.—The new inhabitants of Israel thought that each land had its own god. They asked the Assyrians for a man to teach them about the God of Israel. A priest was sent and the people set up a counterfeit religion. "They feared the Lord, and served their own gods." Today there are many who have a kind of allegiance to God, but they worship other gods in their daily lives.

Renewal in Judah Under Hezekiah (2 Kings 18:1—20:21)

The passage.—Hezekiah was a great reformer. He trusted in God and sought to destroy heathenism. Verses 5–7 tell us that he was the most righteous of all the kings. In order to preserve his kingdom, Hezekiah paid tribute to Sennacherib of Assyria. He even took treasures from the Temple to do so. At the same time he maintained a confidence in the Lord to deliver him from the enemy. The long and taunting challenge of the messengers from Sennacherib is recorded in 18:19–37. Hezekiah sought advice from Isaiah, who prophesied deliverance from God (19:6–7). Sennacherib would hear a rumor that would cause him to return to his own land. There he would be killed.

In connection with the threat from the Assyrians, Hezekiah received a letter

13. Gaza (see 2 Kings 18:8)

FON H. SCOFIELD, JR.

telling him there was no hope in his trusting his God. He took the letter to the house of God and spread it before the Lord. His prayer in 19:15–19 is one of the most beautiful and moving in all literature. Isaiah gave him God's reply of reassurance. God would save him. That very night the angel of the Lord killed a hundred and eighty-five thousand of the Assyrians. Sennacherib returned to Assyria. There he was assassinated.

Chapter 20 is the story of Hezekiah's remarkable recovery in answer to prayer. Isaiah had told him to make preparations to die. He prayed earnestly and wept before God.

Isaiah turned back to tell him God had seen his tears and heard his prayer. Fifteen years would be added to his life. God gave a sign. At Hezekiah's request the shadow of the sun went backward ten steps. The miraculous recovery of health came to Hezekiah as God had said.

A short time after he got well, Hezekiah received visitors from Babylon. He entertained them royally and showed them all of his treasures. After they had left, Isaiah warned Hezekiah that his people would be carried away captive to Babylon. Hezekiah took comfort that

217

there would be peace and security during his lifetime.

Special points.—The Scripture does not say that the sun went backward or that the earth reversed its rotation on its axis. The miracle had to do with a moving backward of a shadow. God can do all things, of course, but this passage does not say that God placed the machinery of the universe in reverse. The Bible does say that the shadow was moved back. Some interpreters say God's glory illuminated the area, moving the shadow in reverse. Obviously God is not bound by what we have chosen to call the laws of nature. God is free to operate his creation as he wills. As he can retract a shadow, so he can retract a pronouncement of doom for one who will repent.

Truth for today.—"What have they seen in thy house?" This question of Isaiah to Hezekiah may be a good question for us to ask ourselves. Do others see only the affluent riches of Christians today, or do they see Christ as Lord in our lives?

Manasseh and Amon (2 Kings 21:1–26)

The passage.—A period of great apostasy took place during the reigns of Manasseh and his son Amon. Manasseh rebuilt the heathen shrines which Hezekiah, his father, had destroyed. He built new altars to Baal. He burned his son as an offering. He practiced witchcraft. He desecrated the Temple of the Lord.

For the sins of Manasseh, God warned through his prophets that Judah would be destroyed. Jerusalem would see such evil that the ears of every listener would tingle. God said he would wipe Jerusalem as one wipes a dish.

The reign of Amon was but two years. He did evil as his father had done before him. He was so wicked that his own servants killed him. The citizens rose up and destroyed the murderers and placed the king's son, Josiah on the throne.

Truth for today.—From time to time there is a renewal of interest in fortune-telling. Some of it borders on witchcraft. The abuse of drugs is sometimes an attempt to have unnatural experiences and to "see visions." The downfall of a nation because of the sins of Manasseh in witchcraft should be a warning to any who might be tempted to think lightly of the serious problems of the abnormal in our day. The alcohol traffic is a part of the moral decay of our day.

The Spiritual Revival Under Josiah (2 Kings 22:1—23:30)

The passage.—Most of what is said in the Bible about Josiah relates to the reformation that came about during his reign. We learn from the general background of the passage that there must have been many in Judah who were trying to bring the nation back to God. The project of repairing the Temple was already being planned.

The book of the law of God was found in the course of the repair of the Temple. Probably it was portions of the book of Deuteronomy. When Josiah heard it read he realized how wicked his nation was. He led his people to repent. The public reading of the Word of God was a vital part of the spiritual revival. Josiah directed that the heathen shrines be destroyed and the idolatrous priests be removed. Cult prostitutes were driven out. Heathen altars were desecrated to render them unusable. Josiah carried his reforms throughout Judah and even into the territory formerly held by Israel.

The public celebration of the Passover in Jerusalem was instituted. Prior to this it had been a home ceremony.

Truth for today.—Spiritual revival in our day waits for a renewal of interest in seeking the will of God above all else. The Word of God is powerful still. Public reading of it by our leaders in the spirit of repentance would enable God to speak to the people. The secret of the revival under Josiah consisted of prayer, Bible reading, repentance, and forceful action against sin.

The Fall of Judah and the Destruction of Jerusalem (2 Kings 23:31—25:30)

The passage.—One of the purposes of the book of 2 Kings is to show how the sin of a nation can lead to its downfall. After Jehoahaz reigned but briefly, he was taken off the throne by the Egyptians. They replaced him with Eliakim and changed his name to Jehoiakim. Jeremiah was active as God's prophet in the last days of Judah. The Babylonians had defeated the Assyrians and had become the dominant power in the world. Nebuchadnezzar, king of Babylon, defeated the Egyptians and swept down upon Judah. For a while Jerusalem was spared, but when Jehoiakim tried to rebel, Judah was overrun.

Jehoiachin succeeded Jehoiakim. Like so many of the others, in spite of the need for God's help, he did evil in the sight of God. He was carried to Babylon along with the leaders of the nation, leaving the poorest people behind.

Zedekiah was the last king of Judah. He made the mistake of resisting Nebuchadnezzar. Jerusalem was besieged. The people were beginning to starve. Zedekiah tried to escape, but he was captured. The Babylonians killed his sons before his very eyes and then put his eyes out. They carried him away to Babylon. Jerusalem was burned. The walls were torn down. The people were carried into exile. God's justice had been accomplished. The need for redemption was never more apparent. The only hope lay in divine intervention. Salvation history moved on toward the coming of a Savior.

Special points.—For about ten years Jeremiah and Jehoiakim were opposing each other during the decline of Judah. They were about as different as any two men could be. Jehoiakim was wicked, selfish, and without scruples. Jeremiah was a man of truth and purity. He relied wholly upon God. He loved his nation, but he loved God more.

Jeremiah felt that it was absolutely God's will for him to prophesy the defeat of Judah. He predicted that Jerusalem would be destroyed by the Babylonians. He, of course, was accused of high treason. He was placed in a dungeon (Jer. 38:6). His life was miserable in the mire into which he sank. Later he was carried away to Egypt.

Truth for today.—The sins of our nation are as serious in the sight of God as the sins of Israel and Judah were. Why has God not destroyed America? Surely he has a high purpose for the people of our day. He has placed miraculous means of communication at our disposal. It is his will that we be a part of his program of redemption. We can be a part of salvation history. If we are not willing to become a missionary nation to bless the whole world, God will have to let America decay. No nation is indispensable.

1 CHRONICLES

Billy E. Simmons

INTRODUCTION

The first book of Chronicles is a record of a history of the Hebrew people from Adam through the reign of David. In a very general sense it may be said that 1 Chronicles parallels the Old Testament books of Genesis through 2 Samuel. Of course the material recorded in 1 Chronicles concerning the early history of the Hebrew people is not nearly so detailed as the material it parallels. In fact the first nine chapters of 1 Chronicles, which are in the form of a national genealogical table, parallels Genesis through Judges.

The reason for this approach to the writing of this material can best be explained when we understand that this material was written after the Exile. When the time came for the Jews to return to Judah after the exile, they were confronted with several problems. One of these was the correct distribution of the land by families. Another was the maintenance of religious rituals. To do this properly, they must have access to the Levitical genealogies. The various Levitical offices such as porters, singers, and priests were held by families. Therefore there was a need for proper records which must have been carefully preserved during the exile.

One of the primary reasons for the writing of this material seems to have been to show the importance of Judah in God's plan. The kingdom of Judah and particularly the Davidic dynasty is presented as the true Israel rather than the apostate, godless Northern Kingdom. The legitimate heirs of God's promises to David and his descendants are the people of the postexilic religious community.

Traditionally the authorship of the Chronicles material has been ascribed to Ezra. Though this has been challenged by some, there is no good reason to deny the possibility that Ezra did indeed author this material. However, it should be stressed that the book itself makes no claim to anyone as its author.

The date of composition for this material was approximately 400 B.C. Though some would place it a little later, this can be considered a fairly accurate date.

National Genealogical Table (1 Chron. 1:1—9:44)

The passage.—As was noted in the introductory statement, the first nine chapters are devoted to the early history of the Hebrew people. This history begins with Adam in chapter 1 and to some degree parallels the development of some of the earlier historical books of the Old Testament.

Chapter 1 deals primarily with the genealogical records of the patriarchs. Though there are brief historical statements included about some, this is primarily a genealogical record. The key verses which begin the genealogies of the various patriarchs are 1,8,17,28–29, 32,34–35, and 43.

Chapter 2 begins with the sons of Jacob, who is called Israel. (See Gen. 32:38.) The writer soon settles on Judah because of the importance of the Davidic line in the history of God's providential plan.

Chapter 3 continues the Davidic line giving the record of the sons born to David in Hebron (vv. 1–4) and in Jerusalem (vv. 5–9). The remainder of chapter 3 is devoted to the Davidic dynasty.

From 4:1—8:40 the genealogical information for the rest of the descendants of Jacob is given. The most notice was given to the tribe of Levi. The reason for this of course was the importance of the priestly tribe to the religious life of Judah.

Chapter 9 tells of the preservation of this genealogical material and of the duties of certain of the priests and Levites.

Special points.—To the average American reader of the Bible today, the least interesting sections are the genealogical tables. We care little about such details. However, to the Jew, these were of utmost importance.

It is quite remarkable that these genealogical tables were preserved through the years of captivity. However, this fact again points up the importance of this material to the pious Jew.

In using this material, the author is showing the returning exiles their historical connection with preexilic Judah. It was important that these returned captives realize that the exile had merely interrupted their religious institutions and national life. The use of this historical material gave them an important link with the past. It helped to create a needed continuity between preexilic and postexilic Judah.

The Death of Saul (1 Chron. 10:1–14)

The passage.—It appears that the writer has introduced Saul into the narrative simply to set the stage for the Davidic kingdom. (For the reader who is interested in a more detailed treatment of Saul's reign, see 1 Sam. 9 and

following.) None of the details of his relationship with Samuel and David are given by this writer. This is because these details were not germane to his purpose. He was primarily interested in the rule of David. Saul's death was simply a prelude or an introduction to this account.

Special points.—The author indicates in verses 13–14 that the death of Saul was the result of Saul's "transgression which he committed against the Lord." The question may arise in the reader's mind as to the exact nature of Saul's sin. The author evidently had two incidents in mind because of the nature of his explanatory note: (1) "against the word of the Lord which he kept not," and (2) "asking counsel of one that had a familiar spirit."

In the fifteenth chapter of 1 Samuel Saul was sent to destroy the Amalekites along with their king. Saul disobeyed the word of the Lord through Samuel. He kept the best of the animals and did not kill Amalek the king. Because of this, God rejected Saul as king. Though his reign continued for some years after this, God did not direct his reign as before.

The second transgression of Saul is a reference to an incident found in 1 Samuel 28:7–25. He had inquired of God, but God had not answered. He then sought out a spiritualist medium (called a witch in KJV), and asked her to bring up Samuel's spirit. In doing this, Saul broke an ancient command of God found in Deuteronomy 18:11.

It was because of these two specific sins that the author of 1 Chronicles declares that Saul lost his life.

The Beginning of David's Kingdom (1 Chron. 11:1–47)

The passage.—The Chronicles omits the brief reign of Ishbosheth, the son of Saul, over the Northern Kingdom and moves directly into the rule of David. The passage begins with David's being made king in Hebron and moves directly to the capture of the city of Jerusalem.

The securing of the fortress of Jerusalem as his capital city was David's first major project. This gave him a secure position from the physical standpoint. It was also a neutral site between Judah and Israel. For this city had belonged to the Jebusites and not to Israel or Judah before David captured it. (See Josh. 15:8,63; and Judg. 1:21.) This was a smart political move on the part of David in his consolidation of Israel and Judah behind him.

The passage concludes with a listing of David's heroes. Chief among these in the story of David's reign are Joab and Abishai, both the sons of Zeruiah. Benaiah the son of Jehoiada was also important in the later years of David's rule and the early part of Solomon's reign.

Special points.—Why would David refuse to drink the water from Bethlehem for which these three brave heroes had risked their lives? Perhaps David had forgotten about the Philistine garrison at Bethlehem when he made the wish. Probably he had not intended for these three men to risk their lives in this manner. Whatever the reason, David was touched by the dedication and bravery of these men. In fact, he was so moved by their heroics that he felt it would be sacrilege to drink that which represented their life's blood.

The Armies That Came to David at Ziklag and Hebron (1 Chron. 12:1–40)

The passage.—Ziklag was the city given to David by Achish, king of Gath, while David was hiding from Saul in Philistia. (See 1 Sam. 27:6.) David was exiled in Philistia for sixteen months (1 Sam. 27:7). During this time he was joined by men who became the nucleus

for his army as king of Judah and Israel.

After the death of Saul, David moved to Hebron at the instruction of the Lord (2 Sam. 2:1). The writer of Chronicles omits the intermittent civil war that occurred between Israel and Judah before the consolidation. (See 2 Sam. 2–4.) Evidently he did not consider this material of great importance to his purpose, for he moves directly into David's rule of the united kingdom.

Special points.—The question may arise as to why half of the tribe of Manasseh is mentioned in verse 31 and half in verse 37. You will remember that Moses allowed the tribes of Reuben and Gad along with one half of the tribe of Manasseh to settle on the east side of the Jordan River. (See Num. 32:33.) This allocation was made with the understanding that these tribes would assist the rest of Israel in the conquest of the Promised Land.

David Brings the Ark to the House of Obed-edom (1 Chron. 13:1–14)

The passage.—The ark had been lost in the disastrous battle of Ebenezer some eighty years prior to this time. The news of its loss precipitated the death of Samuel. (See 1 Sam. 4:11–18.) Because of the plagues of mice and tumors associated with the presence of the ark, the Philistines sent it back to Israel. It came to rest in Beth-shemesh, where it remained only briefly. Soon it was taken to Kiriath-jearim where it remained until David's time. (See 1 Sam. 6.)

David's sincere piety and his desire to serve God motivated him to bring the ark to Jerusalem. Since it had been in disuse for so long, much had been forgotten concerning God's commands concerning it.

In the process of bringing it to Jerusalem, one man lost his life. This caused

David to become angry and then fearful. Therefore, David allowed the ark to rest temporarily at the house of Obed-edom.

Special points.—As to why the ark had been left so long at Kiriath-jearim, there can be no dogmatic answer. Probably Samuel's death and the death of his sons was one of the main reasons. There probably was no one else in Israel who knew much about the ark and the rituals surrounding it. At any rate, during the reign of Saul, there had been no use of the ark (v. 3).

Why did God break forth and smite Uzza? (vv. 9–10). At least two reasons may be set forth in answer to this question. When God gave Moses commandments concerning the furniture of the holy place in Numbers 4:15, he said two things. (1) The furniture was not to be touched "lest they die" (v. 15). (2) Certain people were to carry the furniture in prescribed ways. When the ark was placed on a cart, this was a breach of this command. This problem was corrected later when David brought the ark to Jerusalem.

Three Episodes in the Life of David (1 Chron. 14:1–17)

The passage.—Verses 1 and 2 simply notify the reader that other kings were beginning to recognize David's rule. David accepted this as a sign that God had established his rule.

Verses 3–7 provide information concerning some of David's children.

The primary burden of this passage begins in verse 9 with the Philistine invasion. The domination of Israel by Philistia was the main international problem with which David wrestled early in his rule. You will remember that in his flight from Saul, David had become a vassal of Achish, king of Gath. (See 1 Sam. 27.)

Probably when David became king at Hebron, the Philistines still regarded him as a vassal-king. However, when he became king over Israel and Judah, he presented a definite threat to Philistine supremacy. This is the reason for their immediate invasion.

This passage records two battles. David and his forces won the first, but it was not decisive. In the second, however, God intervened to give the forces of Israel a decisive victory over the forces of the Philistines. These enemies were expelled from the territory of Israel. David thus achieved independence from the Philistines for Israel.

Truth for today.—David's obedience to God and his reliance upon God are in sharp contrast to the disobedience of King Saul. Because he relied on divine help, David was able to become a great king and give independence to his people. The lesson in 1 Chronicles 14:15 is one of eternal significance and validity for the Christian. "God is gone forth before thee."

When the Christian is willing to rely upon God for help and leadership in all of life's situations, God will go before him. Every follower of Christ should claim this truth personally as his very own.

David Brings the Ark to Jerusalem (1 Chron. 15:1–29)

The passage.—When David saw that the house of Obed-edom was prospering while the ark was there, he began to make elaborate preparations to bring it to Jerusalem. He determined that the ark would be brought in the manner prescribed by God. Earlier in the history of the nation God had given Moses instructions concerning the movement of the ark. (See Num. 4:15 and Ex. 25:14.) Only the sons of Kohath were to carry it, and it was to be borne by staves placed through rings attached to it.

David ordered the Levites to sanctify themselves so that they might be prepared for the task. When this was accomplished, David led the public procession in a joyous manner into the city of Jerusalem.

Some think that David composed Psalm 24 for this very occasion. Whether or not he did is impossible to ascertain. However, verses 7–8 of this psalm would fit such a procession beautifully. "Lift up your heads, O ye gates; and be ye lift up, ye everlasting doors; and the King of glory shall come in. Who *is* this King of glory? The Lord strong and mighty, the Lord mighty in battle."

Special points.—Verses 12–13 alert us to the fact that David had been made aware of the reason for God's displeasure with his earlier attempt to bring the ark to Jerusalem.

The Levites sanctified themselves according to the prescribed rituals of washings and refraining from ceremonial defilement. This was the general procedure in sanctifying oneself to come before God. (See Ex. 10:14–15.)

The word "sanctify" could also be translated consecrate. It basically means to set apart. In contexts such as this it means to prepare (set apart) oneself for service to God.

The Levites had been divinely appointed for the task of bearing the furniture used in worship. However, there was a need for further cleansing before they could appear before God for this specific task. This is why the ritual cleansing was required.

The reference to Michal in verse 29 is significant. She was Saul's youngest daughter and David's first wife. David had to leave her when he fled from Saul. When this happened, Saul gave her to another man. However, when David be-

came king, he demanded that she come back to him. (See 2 Samuel 3:12–16.) Though the Chronicler does not include it in his account, David expelled Michal from his presence after this. (See 2 Sam. 6:20–23.)

David had demanded that Michal be returned to him earlier for political reasons. He undoubtedly felt that his marriage to Saul's daughter would help him consolidate his kingdom. However, the cause for her hatred of David at this point is not readily apparent. It may be that she was jealous of David because of his popularity with the people.

David's Festival Sacrifice (1 Chron. 16: 1–43)

The passage.—When David and the people brought the ark of the Lord to Jerusalem, it was a joyful occasion. Burnt sacrifices and peace offerings were made before God. David blessed the people and gave them food for a feast.

At the conclusion of the feast, David left Asaph in charge of the service before the ark. At this time sacrifices were also reinstated in an orderly manner as prescribed by the Levitical law. The men who were left to do these things along with their specific tasks are enumerated in verses 37–42.

At the conclusion of the festivities, the people departed to their homes and David returned to bless his house.

Special points.—In verse 3 "a flagon of wine" should read "a cake of raisins" (ASV).

In verse 7 we read that David delivered a psalm into the hand of Asaph. This psalm continues through verse 36. With slight modifications it is also found in the Psalter as Psalm 105:1–15, Psalm 96, Psalm 106:1,47,48. All three of these Psalms are anonymous in the Psalter. However, David's use of them here is an indication that he was the author.

In verse 22 the phrase "touch not mine anointed" is used as a reference to the king. In the Old Testament, people were set apart to three offices by anointing. The offices of priest, prophet, and king were entered into by this method. (See Ex. 9:7 and 1 Kings 19:15–16.) This anointing was literally a smearing of oil on the person's head. This ceremonial act, when done by the proper individual, set apart by the person for service to God in one of these offices. One who had been set apart in this manner was not to be lightly regarded by his associates, for God's hand of approval was upon him.

God's Promises to David (1 Chron. 17: 1–27)

The passage.—Because of David's devotion to God, he desired to build a permanent home for the ark. Nathan the prophet's first response to David was in the affirmative. However, this was before God had revealed his plans to him.

God revealed to David through Nathan the prophet that he would not be allowed to build the Temple. However, God would continue to prosper David materially. Also, David's son would be permitted to build the house of God after David's death.

God also spoke to David of the more distant future when David's seed (Jesus Christ) would establish a spiritual and eternal kingdom.

David was so awed by Nathan's prophecy concerning his future in the plans of God that he went before the Lord to worship. In so doing, he made himself available to God for whatever the Lord had in store for him.

Special points.—The question may be raised as to why Nathan would have told David to build a Temple before inquiring of the Lord. No one can say with

any certainty. However, this seemed to be such a good idea that Nathan probably never thought that God would refuse the request.

We are told later (1 Chron. 22:8) that because David had "shed blood abundantly, and . . . made great wars" that he was disqualified from building the Temple.

The reference in verse 14 of David's house being established forever is a prophetic reference to the spiritual kingdom which Christ established.

Truth for today.—Though David may not have understood the full truth of God's promise to him, he was moved to praise God for his incredible goodness. Today Christians can look back on this promise with a more sure understanding of it than David had. Should it not fill us with awe as we wonder at the goodness of God? Should it not move us to praise God for his infinite and abounding grace?

David Subdues the Philistines and Moabites (1 Chron. 18:1–17)

The passage.—This chapter chronicles in summary fashion some of the military exploits of David. Generally speaking, this section parallels the eighth chapter of 2 Samuel. The intention of the Chronicler is to show that the Lord was with David and that he prospered him in whatever he did.

Israel's perennial enemy to the west was Philistia. For many years these people had dominated Israel and had garrisoned troops within the borders of Israel. (See 1 Sam. 10:5.) Under the leadership of David, the Israelites were able for the first time to effectively subdue them.

David consolidated his forces and also secured his borders to the east by defeating Moab, to the north by crushing Syria, and to the south by defeating

Edom.

The concluding paragraph of the chapter (vv. 14–17) gives a summary statement concerning David's administrative ability. There is also a list of David's chief administrative officers.

Special points.—In verse 17 the Cherethites and Pelethites are mentioned. These groups made up David's personal bodyguard. The Cherethites were probably Cretans by race. The Pelethites were Philistines. They were probably professional soldiers from the ranks of the decimated Philistine army. At any rate, they were mercenaries, and their loyalty to David was unquestioned.

More Conquests of David (1 Chron. 19:1—20:8)

The passage.—The material in this passage roughly parallels the information found in 2 Samuel 10–12. The Ammonites inhabited an area across the Jordan River immediately to the east of Israel.

In verses 1–5 the Chronicler outlines the cause for Israel's conflict with the Ammonites. They humiliated the messengers which David had dispatched on a mission of goodwill.

The Ammonites then hired Syrian mercenaries to fight with them against Israel. However, David's armies under the command of Joab and Abishai were able to soundly defeat them.

A year later David sent his army on the offensive against Ammon and completely subdued the country. In fact, the Ammonites became subservient to Israel.

Verses 4–8 of chapter 20 contain the final statement concerning the Philistine war. These events were later than the first Philistine wars recorded in 14:8–17. They may have been a part of the action described in summary fashion in 18:1. At any rate, they occurred before the rest which God gave David from his enemies. (See 2 Samuel 7:1.)

Special points.—In 19:4 we are told that Hanun shaved David's servants. Second Samuel 10:4 specifies that one half of their beards was shaved off. This was considered a terrible insult in the Orient. The men had to remain in isolation until their beards grew out. They would have been humiliated to appear this way publicly.

For a clearer understanding of 20:3 the reader should turn to the parallel passage in 2 Samuel 12:31. In that account it is said that David put the people under saws and harrows. That is, he made them work with these instruments. Instead of the reading in the King James Version in 1 Chronicles 20:3, the Revised Standard Version has "Set them to labor with saws." Though David could be ruthless with his enemies, we have no reason to believe that he would practice such sadistic cruelty. The reading in the RSV requires the changing of two letters in a Hebrew word. However, it better reconciles the record of 1 Chronicles with that of 2 Samuel. It is also more in keeping with what is known of the character of David.

The Numbering of Israel (1 Chron. 21:1–30)

The passage.—David was moved by Satan to take a census of the people of Israel. Soon after the census the prophet of Gad came to David with a message from God. The people of Israel were to be punished because of God's displeasure with David's actions. Gad had been sent to David with instructions for David to choose one of three possible punishments.

At the height of the judgment of God on the nation, Gad came once again to David with a message from God. David was to set up an altar at the threshing floor of Ornan.

When this was accomplished, God's

wrath was immediately stayed. David's commitment to God was once again affirmed.

Special points.—A question may arise in the reader's mind concerning why God would be displeased with David for taking a census. There doesn't seem to have been anything inherently wrong with the taking of a census. In the book of Numbers 1:1–2, God commanded Moses to take a census of the people. The problem with David's census was probably that David was placing his faith in the size and strength of his armies rather than in the promises of God.

The fact that Joab refused to number Benjamin and Levi (v. 6) among the tribes is puzzling. The Chronicler seems to indicate that these tribes were omitted because Joab was unhappy with David's decree.

David's use of the threshing floor of Ornan as a place of sacrifice has special significance. This was God's way of designating the place for the high altar of sacrifice within the Temple which was soon to be built.

Truth for today.—In verse 24, David made a significant statement. Ornan had sought to give David the threshing floor as well as the animals and materials for the sacrifice. David refused to take these things as gifts and said that he would not "offer burnt offerings without cost."

This statement contains a profound spiritual truth. It is not fitting that we should offer to God that which costs us nothing. God calls for the total commitment. This is costly, and it involves real sacrifice.

David's Charge to Solomon (1 Chron. 22:1—23:1)

The passage.—The threshing floor of Oran was recognized by David as the place where the Temple was to be built. Therefore David gathered a work force

of resident aliens to the nation of Israel. With this work force he began to gather material and make elaborate plans for the Temple.

David then called Solomon his son and gave him instructions concerning the building of the Temple. He recounted to Solomon his great desire to build the Temple. He also told Solomon why God had refused to allow him the privilege of building it. (See v. 8.) In effect, David told Solomon that he had gotten everything ready for construction. Now it was up to Solomon to actually complete the job.

David also called all of the princes of Israel together and charged them to support Solomon in this endeavor. He also admonished them to set their minds on spiritual matters now that God had given the land rest.

Special points.—David stated in verse 5 that Solomon was "young and tender." Probably Solomon was around twenty years old at this time. However, he was inexperienced in the affairs of state. David knew that Solomon would need his encouragement in this matter. Therefore he made elaborate plans for the building of the Temple.

In verse 8 David mentioned the fact that the word of the Lord came to him forbidding him to build the Temple. This is a reference to the instructions given him by Nathan in 17:4.

The Chronicler only mentions in summary fashion Solomon's accession to the throne. He omits all of the details given in 1 Kings concerning Adonijah's plot to become king. He says nothing of Bathsheba's and Nathan's intervention with David on behalf of Solomon. Neither does he mention Solomon's consolidation of power. However, these incidents were not in keeping with the purpose of the Chronicler. His primary intention was to trace some of the details concerning the plans for the building of the Temple.

It also should be noted at this point that though David had made Solomon king, he had not relinquished all power to him. Solomon did not become king in his own right until after David's death.

The Numbering of the Levites (1 Chron. 23:2–32)

The passage.—The chief burden of this passage is to show how David organized the Levites into functional groups. This was done according to their family groups.

A brief outline of the various ritualistic duties of the Levites is given from verse 24 through the end of the chapter.

Special points.—One of the most important contributions of David to the later religious life of Israel is found in this chapter. The division of the Levites into these groups for service in the Temple was utilized by all succeeding generations until New Testament times.

There were 38,000 Levites who were numbered in David's census. Twenty-four thousand of them were to do the physical work around the Temple. Four thousand were singers. Another four thousand were porters or doorkeepers. Six thousand of them were "officers and judges" (v. 4) who were charged with some of the more important functions.

In verse 29 the reading "meal offering" (ASV) is to be preferred to "meat offering."

The Divisions of the Sons of Aaron (1 Chron. 24:1–31)

The passage.—In this passage we find a continuation of assigning the various duties connected with the Temple. Aaron's descendants were to carry out the priestly duties. Thus they were divided by lot in courses. There were twenty-four courses in all. Sixteen were from the descendants of Eleazar and

eight from the descendants of Ithamar, the two surviving sons of Aaron.

Special points.—In verse two we are reminded of the death of Nadab and Abihu. In Leviticus 10:1–12 we find the record of their death. They were killed because they offered strange fire before the Lord.

The twenty-four courses mentioned in verse 4 continued down to New Testament times as the basis for rotating the various priestly duties. Though they did not continue consecutively until New Testament times, this grouping was the basis for the division of priestly duties.

In verses 20–31 the "rest of the sons of Levi" are delineated. These were the various Temple assistants that corresponded to the priestly courses outlined in the preceding verses. In verse 31 we are told that the pairing of the Levites and priests was done by the casting of lots in the presence of David.

The Consecration and Numbering of the Temple Musicians (1 Chron. 25:1–31)

The passage.—Many of the Temple services and rituals were accompanied by music. Therefore, David appointed certain musicians for these tasks. Their various duties are described in verses 1–7. In verses 8–31 they are divided into courses by lot. There were twenty-four courses to correspond to the number of the Levites and priests.

Special points.—Asaph, Heman, and Jeduthun had been appointed as musicians by David when the ark was brought to Jerusalem. (See 1 Chron. 16:5,41.)

In verse 1 prophesying with musical instruments is mentioned. Many of the Old Testament prophecies are preserved in poetic form. By the same token, some of the poetry (Psalms) is prophetic in nature. Music played an important part in the Hebrews' worship of God. This can be seen by the different instruments which were used in worship.

The Temple Porters (1 Chron. 26:1–32)

The passage.—This chapter has to do with the appointment of the porters and the division of their duties within the Temple. The primary function of the porters was to serve as gatekeepers. However, they also served as guards over the Temple properties and furnishings.

Up to this point, the various Temple officers have been divided into twenty-four courses which determined periods of service. However, the porters were divided by place of service. The number of the gates into the Temple determined the number of their courses.

Special points.—In verse 20 Ahijah of the Levites is mentioned. Though he was a Levite, he was also among the porters. This sacred trust assigned to the porters included guarding the various treasures stored in the Temple.

The Civil Organization (1 Chron. 27: 1–34)

The passage.—The basic organization of the Israelite nation under David is outlined in this passage. Verses 1–15 survey David's military organization. There were twelve army divisions, each having a complement of 24,000 men. Each of these army units was on active duty for one month out of the year.

In verses 16–24 there is a list of the regional or tribal organization. Each tribe had its own administrative officer or prince who was answerable to the king.

David's central administrative officials or counselors are listed in verses 25–34. These were the most important and influential officials in David's kingdom.

Special points.—In verses 23–24 mention is made of a promise to Abraham

and of an unfinished census. In Genesis 22:17 God had promised Abraham that he would increase his seed like the stars of heaven. The Chronicler seems to imply that the census was not finished because to have done so would have cast some doubt on God's promise. Reference is also made in these verses to David's military census which was displeasing to God. (See the commentary on 21:1–8.)

David Encourages Solomon (1 Chron. 28:1–21)

The passage.—David assembled all of the leaders of Israel so that he could encourage Solomon before them. He had carefully laid the plans for the building of the Temple. Also he had organized the priests and Levites for service in the Temple. In this passage he publicly committed the nation to the building of the Temple. He was also publicly giving the Levitical organization a permanent place in national life.

David rehearsed before the assembly his intentions to build the Temple and how God had refused to allow him. He then confirmed that Solomon was God's choice as his successor. From this point on, he encouraged Solomon to build the Temple in manner prescribed in the plans which he had made. He reminded Solomon that God would be with him in this endeavor. He also told him that all of the Levites and princes would support him in building the Temple.

Special points.—In verse 12 David appears to be saying that the plans for the Temple had been divinely inspired. Just as God had directed in the plans and erection of the tabernacle, so he guided in the plans for the Temple.

David's Final Words (1 Chron. 29:1–30)

The passage.—Chapter 29 is actually a continuation of the convocation assembled in the preceding chapter.

David challenged the leaders of Israel to share with him in a freewill offering for the Temple. This they did willingly and cheerfully.

After this David offered a marvelous prayer of thanksgiving and petition. He gave God thanks for the bountiful offering that had been freely given for the Temple. He also asked God to bless Solomon his son and to keep him in the way of righteousness.

Finally David called on the people to worship God and to recognize Solomon as their king. This they did gladly as they observed a feast which had been proclaimed for the occasion.

The final days and the death of David are then recorded in a concluding statement. The Chronicler reminds the reader that he had used certain ancient sources in the compilation of this account.

Special points.—In verse 4 David's personal contribution to the Temple is proclaimed. In today's currency it would be reckoned at well over one billion dollars.

In verse 9 the statement is made that the people responded willingly to the offering. This is reminiscent of the freewill offering taken for the tabernacle by Moses. At this time the people responded so freely that they had to be restrained. (See Ex. 36:5–6.)

In verse 29 two sources are mentioned besides Samuel. These are the works of Nathan the prophet and Gad the Seer. Undoubtedly the information concerning David recorded in 1 Chronicles which is not found in 2 Samuel was recorded in these books.

2 CHRONICLES

Billy E. Simmons

INTRODUCTION

In the Hebrew Old Testament, 1 Chronicles and 2 Chronicles are one volume. The title given to it in Hebrew is "the words of the days" or "events of past times." When the Hebrew Old Testament was translated into Greek, the material was divided into two parts. The title in the Septuagint (Greek Old Testament) is "things omitted." This title was a reference to those things which were added to the narrative of the books of Samuel and Kings. The title "Chronicles" comes from the Latin Vulgate version of Old Testament.

Second Chronicles traces the history of the Southern Kingdom of Judah from the reign of Solomon until the return of the exiles during the reign of Cyrus. The events relating to the Northern Kingdom are noted only as they have bearing on the history of Judah. The Chronicler seems to have been primarily interested in making the exiles aware of their historical and spiritual heritage.

For information pertaining to date and authorship of 2 Chronicles, the reader should see the commentary on 1 Chronicles.

God Appears to Solomon (2 Chron. 1: 1–17)

The passage.—Though David had established Solomon as king before his death, Solomon's formal inauguration did not occur until after David's death. Solomon led a solemn procession to the high place at Gibeon to appear before the Lord and offer sacrifices to him.

During the night, God appeared to Solomon asking him what he desired as king. Solomon's request was for wisdom to know how he ought to govern the people of Israel. Because his request was a prudent one, God added to him riches, honor, long life, and peace.

The final verses of this passage validate God's promise to Solomon. The prosperity of his kingdom is outlined in verses 13–17.

Special points.—In verse 3 the "high place that was at Gibeon" is mentioned. Gibeon was approximately seven miles northwest of Jerusalem. Here was kept the tabernacle of God. The high place was exactly what the name implies. It was a plot of ground higher than the surrounding terrain where sacrifices were made. Most of the "high places" in Israel had been contaminated for Jehovah worship by their use as places for heathen sacrifices. In fact, in Solomon's time the only legitimate places for divine sacrifices were Gibeon and Jerusalem. These were the two primary religious shrines before the construction of the Temple in Jerusalem.

Why Solomon chose to sacrifice at Gibeon where the tabernacle and brazen altar were rather than at Jerusalem where the ark was is not readily apparent.

Solomon Begins to Build the Temple (2 Chron. 2:1–18)

The passage.—Though David had laid careful plans for the building of the Temple, it remained for Solomon to

231

implement them. He began first by organizing a gigantic work force for the task. Then he contracted with Hiram, king of Tyre, for timbers from Lebanon and craftsmen to supervise the construction. His final act before construction began was to organize the aliens in Israel for the more menial tasks dealing with the construction.

Special points.—In verse 3 and throughout this section, the name of the king of Tyre is spelled "Huram" in the King James Version. The spelling should be Hiram. (See ASV footnote.)

In verse 7 Solomon asked Hiram to send him a man who was skilled in the craft of metal work. Archaeological remains attest to the fact that the Phoenicians were more highly skilled in the crafts than were the Israelites of this era.

Purple mentioned in verses 7 and 14 was the deep-red dye which came from a species of shell fish. It was called royal purple because it was very rare and costly.

The Construction of the Temple
(2 Chron. 3:1–17)

The passage.—Contained in chapter 3 is a record of the measurements of the Temple. Also the Chronicler has described many of the details of construction as well as the material which was used. The characterization is one of rare beauty and must have been especially impressive to the returned exiles who were the first readers of this material. The magnificence of Solomon's Temple provided a structural ideal for the Temple of the restored community.

Special points.—In 3:1 mention is made of Mount Moriah as the place where the Temple was constructed. The reader will remember this as the peak on which Abraham displayed his willingness to sacrifice his only son Isaac.

(See Gen. 22:2.)

The threshing floor of Ornan is also mentioned in this same verse. This is where David sacrificed to God to bring an end to pestilence. (See 1 Chron. 21:18—22:1.)

The second month is referred to in the second verse. This would correspond roughly to our April–May period. That is, their twenty-eight-day month would overlap the last part of our April and the first part of May. The fourth year of Solomon's reign would be 966 B.C.

In verse 3 and following, the cubit is mentioned as the standard measurement. A regular cubit was from the tip of the elbow to the tip of the middle finger. The generally accepted length for a cubit is eighteen inches. However, the earlier or "first measure" cubit was about three inches longer than the ordinary cubit.

The cherubim (vv. 7,10,11–14) were angelic creatures. They were winged figures usually with human form. They were symbolic of God's presence among men.

The "most holy house" of verse 10 is a reference to the inner sanctuary of the Temple. This compartment was to be separated from the rest of the Temple by the veil (v. 14). (See Ex. 26:31–33.)

The chapiter of verse 15 was the ornamented capital affixed to the top of each pillar.

The Furnishings for the Temple
(2 Chron. 4:1–22)

The passage.—This chapter actually could be considered as a part of the same context as the preceding chapter.

The Chronicler has gone into some detail in describing the various furnishings of the Temple. He also distinguishes between the artifacts constructed by Haram's workmen and Solomon's work force.

Special points.—The molten sea mentioned in verse 2 was placed here to show the need for purity of the person who approached God in worship. (See Ex. 30:21.) The molten sea consisted of a large bronze bowl approximately 15 feet in diameter. It was supported on the backs of bronze oxen. It was probably located near the entrance of the Temple before the altar. As was stated earlier, its purpose was to remind the people of the need for purity in approaching God.

Candlesticks in verses 7 and 20 should read lampstands, for candles were not used until much later in history.

Verse 17 "between Succoth and Zeredathah" or Zarthan according to 1 Kings 7:46. This location was to the east of Jordan and about midway between Galilee and the Dead Sea.

The Dedication of the Temple (2 Chron. 5:1–14)

The passage.—Upon the completion of the Temple, Solomon assembled all of the leaders of Israel along with the men of Israel for the purpose of dedicating it. After bringing the ark of the covenant from Jerusalem to the Temple, Solomon offered sacrifices to the Lord. Then the priests put the ark of the covenant in its place in the Temple. As they worshiped the Lord on this occasion, his glory filled the house.

Special points.—In verse 2 it is evident that Solomon has chosen his Temple to be a successor to the previous places of worship used by Israel. He so designated the Temple as a successor to the tabernacle when he had the ark of the covenant installed.

The seventh month (v. 3) would have fallen within our months of September–October.

In verse 4 we read that the Levites carried the ark. Solomon was careful

not to make the mistake that David made earlier (1 Chron. 13:10).

The "oracle of the house" in verse 7 is a technical term for the most holy place within the Temple.

It is interesting to note in verse 11 that all of the priests participated in the dedication. This was a very important event in the religious life of the nation. Therefore all twenty-four courses of priests participated.

The cloud which filled the house (vv. 13–14) is reminiscent of Israel's encounters with God during the Exodus. (See Ex. 13:21.) This cloud is called the *Shekinah*. It represented the presence of God with his people.

Solomon's Dedicatory Speech and Prayer (2 Chron. 6:1–42)

The passage.—In verses 6–11 Solomon gives a very brief oration. The main theme of this speech is the faithfulness of God. He also reminds the people that David had wanted to build the Temple, but God had not allowed it.

Verses 12–42 record Solomon's prayer of dedication. The main burden of this prayer can be seen in the recurring petition. Solomon prays that God will ever be attentive to the supplications of his people. He also asks that God will intervene on behalf of the people in times of crisis.

Special points.—Solomon's recognition of God's omnipresence in verse 18 shows the depth of his wisdom. Though he was building the Temple as a national shrine, he was aware that it could not contain God. Though God's presence pervaded the Temple, it was certainly not limited to the Temple.

Solomon's desire to see the Temple become a place of prayer for all nations (v. 32) is striking. Note the marked contrast in his attitude and that of the

Pharisees in the New Testament.

The recognition of the universal nature of sin in verse 36 is consistent with the biblical teaching of human depravity.

God's Response to the Dedication (2 Chron. 7:1–11)

The passage.—God responded to the worship of Solomon and the people with a marvelous manifestation of his power. He sent fire from heaven to consume the sacrifices. Also, his glory so filled the house that the priests could not enter.

At the conclusion of the festivities, Solomon sent the people away rejoicing.

Verse 11 is a summary statement indicating that God continually blessed Solomon.

Special points.—This great feast of dedication was planned to coincide with the Feast of Tabernacles. There was a special seven-day feast for the dedication followed by the Day of Atonement and the regular observance of the Feast of Tabernacles.

God Appears to Solomon a Second Time (2 Chron. 7:12–22)

The passage.—Some time later after Solomon had finished his palace, God appeared to him again. This time God reaffirmed his promises made earlier. However, he revealed to Solomon that the promises were conditional. They were contingent on Israel's faithfulness. He also said that, if Israel proved faithless, they would be exiled and the Temple destroyed.

Special points.—Verse 14 is probably the best known and most often quoted verse in all of 2 Chronicles. In this verse God outlines the conditions which Israel must fulfil if they are to know his blessings.

Truth for today.—One of the most marvelous truths to be found in all of the Old Testament is contained in verse 14. As we read this and apply it to Israel, we ought to realize that God still desires these traits in his people today. Those who wish to know fully the blessings of God must humbly turn from their sins. They must willingly yield themselves to God as they seek his face. When this is done, God's blessings will be received. This is true of nations as well as individuals.

Solomon's Reign Characterized (2 Chron. 8:1–18)

The passage.—Although Solomon's reign was not marked by war and bloodshed, he was able to expand his kingdom. This he did with the help of Hiram, king of Tyre. Those peoples who had not been destroyed by the early Israelites still had descendants in the land. However, Solomon exacted from them tribute and service to support his rule.

This passage also apprises us that Solomon made a political alliance with the Pharaoh of Egypt. This was consummated by a political marriage. Rather than have his Egyptian wife live in Jerusalem, he built her a house outside the city.

The remainder of the chapter is designed to show the grandeur of Solomon's reign. He was careful to offer the prescribed sacrifices and to establish the various courses of priests and Levites as David had decreed. He also was engaged in commerce with the surrounding countries.

Special points.—The only mention of any hostilities during Solomon's reign is in verse 3 of this chapter. "Solomon went to Hamath-zobah and prevailed against it." Nothing is said by the

Chronicler to provide us with a clue as to why Solomon engaged in this battle. Probably it was little more than a local revolt or uprising.

Though the Chronicler does not go into any details concerning Solomon's foreign alliances and marriages, we can learn of them from 1 Kings. The idolatry practiced by his Egyptian wife led to eventual apostasy in Israel. (See 1 Kings 11:1–8.)

The Wealth and Wisdom of Solomon (2 Chron. 9:1–31)

The passage.—The first section of this passage deals with the queen of Sheba's visit to Solomon. Though she had not believed reports that came to her, she was convinced when she saw the wealth and wisdom of Solomon.

The remainder of the chapter is devoted to describing the tremendous wealth of the kingdom of Solomon. The chapter concludes with a brief summary of the entire reign of Solomon.

Special points.—The queen of Sheba was from an area lying at the southern tip of the Arabian Peninsula. This land was especially noted for its spices and gold. She probably came to Solomon for trading purposes, but she tested his wisdom also.

In verse 14 the word "chapmen" is used. These were traders, and they traveled in caravans.

In verse 26 the extent of Solomon's territorial rule is described. This description corresponds to the promise of God to Abraham in Genesis 15:18. Thus he occupied the limits of the territory promised by God to Abraham.

Rehoboam's Bad Beginning (2 Chron. 10:1–19)

The passage.—Rehoboam, the son of Solomon, went to Shechem to be crowned king by Israel. However, before they were willing to acknowledge him as their king, they demanded lower taxes. Solomon's counselors (the old men) advised him to accept their terms. However, the young men prevailed, and Rehoboam refused the demand. Led by Jeroboam, the son of Nebat, the ten northern tribes then rebelled against Rehoboam.

Special points.—In verse 2 Jeroboam the son of Nebat is mentioned. He had been anointed king over the ten tribes north by Ahijah the Shilonite. (See 1 Kings 11:26–40.) He had fled to Egypt where he found refuge from Solomon. When he heard of Solomon's death, he immediately returned to Israel.

Only Two Tribes Left (2 Chron. 11:1–23)

The passage.—At first Rehoboam thought to lead the armies of Judah against the Northern Kingdom. However, God intervened and told Rehoboam that this division was from him. Therefore Rehoboam dispersed his army and occupied himself with matters pertaining to Judah.

He built several cities and strengthened his borders. The Levites and priests that had been dispersed throughout Israel migrated to Judah and Jerusalem. This migration strengthened the hand of Rehoboam.

The remainder of the chapter deals primarily with Rehoboam's domestic life. Evidently Rehoboam was content to govern the people God had given him. His was in no sense an expansionist reign.

Special points.—The devils mentioned in verse 15 appear, from the Hebrew word used, to have been goat idols. These were used in conjunction with the worship of the golden calves which Jeroboam had made.

The calves which Jeroboam made were undoubtedly patterned after the idols of the Egyptians. Jeroboam recognized that the national shrine that held together the United Kingdom was in Jerusalem. He also knew that unless he provided a shrine for the Northern Kingdom, the people would return to Jerusalem to worship. Then Rehoboam could eventually reclaim their political loyalty. (See 1 Kings 12:26–29.)

Rehoboam's Reign Summarized (2 Chron. 12:1–16)

The passage.—This chapter is a brief summary of the rule of Rehoboam the son of Solomon. Because of his departure from the law and teachings of God, the nation was punished. They were humiliated by Shishak, king of Egypt.

However, they turned back to God in humility. Because of this, God granted them "some deliverance" (v. 7). That is, he did not allow them to be totally destroyed.

The conclusion of the chapter (vv. 13–16) form a very brief summary of Rehoboam's seventeen-year reign. The Chronicler concluded that he was a king who "did evil, because he prepared not his heart to seek the Lord" (v. 14).

Special points.—In verses 9–10 we read that Shishak carried away the shields of gold. Rehoboam, therefore, made shields of brass in their place. His faithlessness reduced his treasures to imitations of the former glory that was Solomon's.

The Rule of Abijah (2 Chron. 13:1–22)

The passage.—The reign of Abijah the son of Rehoboam was brief. It was also almost completely occupied by war with Jeroboam and the Northern Kingdom.

This passage relates for us in somewhat more detail the nature of the conflict and the bravery of Abijah than does the parallel passage (1 Kings 15:1–8). Here his dependence on the Lord is more in evidence.

The Chronicler has told us that it was because of his trust in God that he was delivered from Israel. The odds seemed to be against Judah and Abijah. However, God prevailed against Israel and for Judah in the battle.

Special points.—In verse 2 we are told that Abijah ruled Judah for three years. His dates of rule were 913–910 B.C.

The covenant of salt in verse 5 is a reference to the permanence of God's promise to David. Salt was noted for its preservative powers. Meat that had been treated with salt would not spoil quickly. Thus the idea of permanence was attached to anything treated with salt.

In verse 20 the Chronicler states that God struck Jeroboam so that he died. The details of Jeroboam's death are not elsewhere recorded. However, Jeroboam's ruin and death were prophesied by Ahijah the Shilonite. This is recorded in 1 Kings 14:1–16.

Good King Asa Begins to Reign (2 Chron. 14:1–15)

The passage.—Chapter 14 records the beginning years of the rule of Asa. He was one of the most righteous kings to arise in Judah.

His first ten years were marked by peace. He took advantage of these quiet years by reinforcing his borders. He also built several cities and strengthened them.

After the ten years of peace, Judah was attacked by the Ethiopians led by Zerah. Through his dependence on God, Asa was able to rout the forces of the Ethiopians. So great was the victory, that the Ethiopians were not able to recover from their defeat.

Special points.—The targets spoken of in verse 8 were large shields which covered the entire body.

Zerah the Ethiopian (v. 9) has been identified by some as Osorkon I, the successor to Shishak in the twenty-second dynasty of Egypt. If this is correct, he was probably trying to duplicate Shishak's invasion of Judah.

Truth for today.—Asa's prayer recorded in verse 11 has a tremendous spiritual truth in it. God is able to bring victory out of much or little, many or few. God can use us for good if we will but dedicate ourselves to him. We may not think we have much to offer. However, God can take what we have and transform it into a mighty force for good.

Azariah's Prophecy and Asa's Reaction (2 Chron. 15:1–19)

The passage.—Azariah the son of Obed came to King Asa with a word from God. In effect God had said: "As long as Asa serves me I'll be with him."

When Asa heard this message from God, he was overjoyed. In fact so happy was he, that he began a new national program of reform immediately. He destroyed every vestige of idol worship that he could find. He led his nation in a great revival and renewal of trust in God. In fact, so widespread was his reform, that he removed his mother from her place as queen. This was done because she had been engaged in idol worship.

As hard as Asa tried, however, he was not able to completely eradicate idol worship from the land. But Asa himself was not defiled by any taint of idol worship.

Special points.—Except for this reference, Azariah and Obed are unknown. However, they are not the only obscure spokesmen for God in the Old Testament. God used an unnamed prophet to warn Jeroboam concerning his heathen altar. (See 1 Kings 13:1–10.)

In verse 3 the two words *"hath been"* which are in italics were supplied by the translators. This is called an emendation. Probably the emendation of the American Standard Version should prevail. It records: "Israel *was* without the true God."

Verses 9–15 record the making of a covenant to worship God. This occurred in the fifteenth year of Asa's reign or 895 b.c. The third month would have overlapped to our May–June period. Noncomformity to this covenant was punishable by death. This may appear to us to be a rather stringent step to take. However, idolatry had been so widespread that drastic measures had to be taken.

What happened to Maacah is not readily apparent. However, she was Asa's grandmother and not his mother. (See 11:22 and 13:2.) So, she was really the queen-grandmother. As to her fate, her age and influence in the kingdom probably saved her from death. She was more than likely removed from the court of the king. Perhaps she was confined to her home. Of course this is mere speculation, for nothing is said other than that she was removed from being queen.

The Last Days of Asa (2 Chron. 16: 1–14)

The passage.—Asa had trusted completely in the Lord for help earlier in his life. However, when Baasha, the king of Israel, besieged Ramah, he sought aid from Syria. His pact with Syria was honored, and the siege was lifted. However, the matter displeased God because Asa had not trusted him.

God sent the prophet Hanani to Asa

with a message of judgment. This so enraged Asa that he had the prophet imprisoned.

Verses 11–14 form a summary of the last few years of Asa's reign. He died of a disease that began in his feet. At the conclusion of a 41-year reign he died.

Special points.—Hanani the seer was the father of Jehu who was the prophet to Jehoshaphat, Asa's son.

In verse 10 Asa placed Hanani in prison. This is the first recorded persecution of a prophet. However, later in Judah's history this was commonplace.

The statement in verse 12 concerning physicians may raise a question in the mind of some. The Chronicler seems to be saying that Asa depended on the skill of men rather than on the goodness of God. Certainly medicine and physicians are God's gifts. However, God stands behind the cures effected by medicines and physicians. Just as Asa had relied on Syria rather than God, now he was relying on physicians rather than God.

Truth for today.—Asa turned from God in his later years to depend upon men. He had become established as king and for many years had reaped the benefits of God's blessings. He had come to take these things for granted. So, in his later years, when he fell into difficulty, he forgot to rely on God.

It is easy for us as Christians to fall into this same snare. As our years in the faith of Christ increase, we may have a tendency to rely more on our own strength and ingenuity than on God. Let us learn from Asa's bitter experience to ever rely on God for our sustenance.

Jehoshaphat's Good Beginning (2 Chron. 17:1–19)

The passage.—Jehoshaphat took up where his father left off in the matter of religious reforms. He began his reign by strengthening his boundaries against a possible invasion by Israel.

In the third year of his reign, he sent representatives throughout the cities of Judah. They were vested with the responsibility of teaching the law of God.

The nations round about Judah saw that God was with Jehoshaphat. Because of this they made no war against Judah. The Philistines and Arabians even sent presents to Jehoshaphat. His fame increased, and he became very great. The Chronicler illustrates his greatness by giving the names of his various army commanders, as well as the numerical strength of each.

Special points.—Jehoshaphat felt it necessary to strengthen himself against Israel. This was because wicked King Ahab was then in power.

"In the third year of his reign" (v. 7) probably was the first year of his sole rule. A comparison of 2 Kings 3:1 and 8:16 shows that his full reign of 25 years began three years before his father's death. This coregency was probably brought about by Asa's illness. (See 2 Chron. 16:12.)

Micaiah's Prophecy (2 Chron. 18:1–34)

The passage.—Jehoshaphat had come to terms with godless Ahab. He went to Samaria to visit Ahab. While he was there, Ahab talked him into going to battle with him. They called for Ahab's court prophets to bring them a word from God. However, these professional prophets were more interested in saying what Ahab wanted to hear than in bringing a word from God.

Jehoshaphat was somewhat suspicious of these court prophets. He insisted that they seek out a prophet who was not dependent on Ahab for sustenance. Ahab was not pleased with the suggestion. However, he gave in to the wishes of his guest and sent for Micaiah the son of Imla.

After a moment of jesting, Micaiah prophesied the defeat of Israel and the death of Ahab. To this Ahab responded by having Micaiah put in prison until he should return victorious.

Micaiah's prophecy proved to be from the Lord. Ahab was killed and Israel scattered. In the fray, Jehoshaphat narrowly escaped injury or death.

Special points.—The phrase "joined affinity with Ahab" in verse 1 has far-reaching implications for Judah. As far as future rulers are concerned, this is perhaps the greatest mistake Jehoshaphat made. For this included a political marriage between Jehoshaphat's son Jehoram and Athaliah the daughter of Ahab and Jezebel. This alliance brought all of the evils of heathenism into the ruling house of Judah.

Ahab sought to escape the judgment of God by disguising himself as a common soldier (v. 29). However, as we find in verse 33, God used the random shot of an enemy archer to strike the death-blow on Ahab.

Truth for today.—Jehoshaphat's unholy alliance with Ahab proved to be a disastrous step for him personally as well as for Judah. God's people today can learn from this that alliances with evil cannot produce the works of God. No matter how noble the cause may seem, if we must engage in an alliance with the world, we would be better off to forbear.

Jehoshaphat Is Reproved (2 Chron. 19: 1–11)

The passage.—When Jehoshaphat returned home to Jerusalem, Jehu the prophet of God was there to meet him. He had a word from God for the king. God reproved him for his questionable relationship to Ahab.

Evidently Jehoshaphat accepted the reproval as entirely justified. He satisfied himself for the time being with local and national reforms. He placed judges throughout the land of Judah. In Jerusalem he appointed the certain Levites and priests along with chief elders as judges in the central court.

Special points.—In verse 2, the prophet Jehu is not indicating that God's people should have no concern for the lost. He is merely indicating that God's people must never compromise their convictions in their dealings with the ungodly.

In verse 7 Jehoshaphat admonishes the judges to be impartial. Whoever does God's work must heed this admonition.

Jehoshaphat's Prayer and Jahaziel's Prophecy (2 Chron. 20:1–19)

The passage.—A conspiracy of several nations against Judah becomes evident. In this time of crisis Jehoshaphat humbled himself and proclaimed a fast throughout all Judah. Then, before the assembled congregation of Judah, Jehoshaphat called upon the Lord in prayer.

God was quick to answer the prayer of Jehoshaphat. He spoke his message through a Levite named Jahaziel. He assured the congregation of Judah that victory would be theirs. In fact, they would not even have to fight, for God would fight for them.

Special points.—In verse 3 we are told that Jehoshaphat proclaimed a fast. Fasting was not only a sign of grief; it also was used to dramatize the sincerity of one's prayer.

Truth for today.—The last phrase of verse 15 is a truth that should be claimed as a personal promise by every believer. "The battle is not yours, but God's." The Christian cannot live the victorious life in his own strength. Only as he yields himself to God through the direction of the Holy Spirit can he be victorious in life. Truly the battle is not ours. It belongs to the Lord.

The Last Days of Jehoshaphat (2 Chron. 20:20–37)

The passage.—God's promise through Jahaziel came rapidly to pass. Even before they went out to battle, God was at work. God brought about an ambush against the invaders. Evidently in the confusion of battle, all of the invaders were destroyed. Thus it was left for Judah to fall upon the spoils of war. They tasted a victory which they had not won by their own strength.

The remainder of Jehoshaphat's rule was quiet and uneventful. God was with him because he sought to do what was right. However, the Chronicler advises that not all of Jehoshaphat's decisions were good ones. But generally speaking, he was a godly king.

Special points.—The "ambushments," spoken of in verse 22, were probably bands of marauders from the region of Mount Seir. At any rate, God provided an unexpected adversary for the would-be invaders.

"The place was called the Valley of Berachah" (verse 26). The word "Berachah" means blessing. So the place was named valley of blessing because of the victory wrought by the Lord.

Why Jehoshaphat made another alliance with Israel (v. 35) is not readily apparent. Ahaziah was the son of Ahab. His rule was wicked and brief.

The Rule of Jehoram (2 Chron. 21:1–20)

The passage.—The rule of Jehoram was one of the darker chapters in the history of Judah. He had as his wife the daughter of the most infamous woman in all of Israel's history, Jezebel. Evidently Jezebel's daughter wielded a great influence on Jehoram. When Jehoram became king, he immediately put to death all of his brothers. This secured for him an undisputed claim to the throne.

Though he was very wicked, the Lord would not destroy the house of David. However, God warned Jehoram through a letter from the prophet Elijah. The message from God was one of judgment upon Jehoram and his family. It also contained a note of judgment for the nation of Judah because of their faithlessness.

The rule of Jehoram was marked by several invasions from surrounding nations. All of his wives and sons were taken captive, except for one son. Soon after this, Jehoram died from a disease of the bowels as Elijah had prophesied.

Special points.—Though his people are faithless, God is faithful. He had ample reason to turn his back on Judah and her king. They had become completely degenerate. However, God remembered his covenant with David and spared the nation.

Elijah was God's prophet to the Northern Kingdom. However, he never felt himself restricted by national boundaries. God had a message for Jehoram, and he used Elijah to bring it to him.

The disease with which Jehoram was stricken was a very painful and violent form of dysentery.

Even in death (v. 20) Jehoram had no honor. He was not given a proper state funeral. His burial place was not in the sepulchers of the kings.

Ahaziah and Athaliah (2 Chron. 22:1–12)

The passage.—This passage covers a span of only a few months. The influence of wicked Athaliah is seen from the very beginning of the passage.

Because of an alliance with Israel Ahaziah was in Samaria with Jehoram, king of Israel. They had done battle against Hazael, king of Syria, and were in the city of Jezreel to recover from the battle.

God used Jehu as his executioner against both these wicked men. When Athaliah saw that her son was dead, she usurped the throne and sought to kill every claimant to the throne. However, one of the king's sons was taken by the daughter of the king and hidden from her.

Special points.—The fact that the people of Jerusalem had a hand in making Ahaziah king (v. 1) suggests a possible dispute concerning who was to be king.

The statement in verse 2 that Ahaziah was "forty and two years old" when he began to reign may be an error of a copyist. Second Kings 8:26 states that Ahaziah was twenty-two when he began to reign.

For an expanded account of the death of Ahaziah see 2 Kings 9:1-29.

In verse 6 the spelling "Azariah" should be corrected to read "Ahaziah."

Truth for today.—The influence of a mother for good or evil can be seen from this passage. Had Athaliah been a godly mother, think what an influence for good she could have been in the kingdom. Every mother should take very seriously her role in shaping the young lives in her care. Truly as one somewhere has said: "The hand that rocks the cradle rules the world."

Joash Made King by Jehoiada (2 Chron. 23:1-21)

The passage.—Chapter 23 records a conspiracy of the priests and Levites under the leadership of Jehoiada. The true male heir to the throne had been kept in hiding during the reign of Athaliah. Now after six years Jehoiada decided it was time to overthrow Athalia and her wicked rule.

Jehoiada organized the priests and Levites for the coup. He gave them their instructions for guarding the king. Then he distributed weapons from the house of God for all of them.

When all was in readiness, Jehoiada and his sons anointed Joash king. The news came as a complete surprise to the wicked queen Athaliah. However, there was nothing she could do to resist because the revolt was so well organized. Also, it appears that the people in general had little sympathy for her. Therefore she was summarily put to death.

Jehoiada proceeded to make a three-way covenant between himself, the people, and the king. This covenant stated that they all belonged to the Lord.

From this point on, religious and political reforms were instituted. Baal worship was crushed and the worship of the Lord through sacrifices was reinstituted. Thus Jehoiada established Joash in the kingdom.

Special points.—It is made clear in 2 Kings 11:4 that these captains assembled by Jehoiada in 2 Chronicles 23:1 were elements of the royal guard. They were shown the king's son and sworn to his support. So in reality there were more than just priests and Levites engaged in this revolt.

In verses 4-8 the instructions were given to the Levites. Two companies of them should have been going off duty at this time. However, they were not dismissed. Instead, they kept a vigil around the king.

It is not certain what is meant by giving the king "the testimony" in verse 11. However, it may have referred to his duties as king similar to the document prepared by Samuel for Saul. (See 1 Sam. 10:25.) It also may have reference to the books of the law.

The Rule of Joash (2 Chron. 24:1–27)

The passage.—When Joash began to reign, he was only seven years old. Thus Jehoiada the priest probably had most of the responsibility for the affairs of state. As long as Jehoiada lived, he wielded an influence for good on Joash.

A tax was assessed on all the people of Judah for the repair of the Temple. Though the Levites were slow to implement this tax, the work finally proceeded. After some time, a chest was placed at the gate of the Temple for the purpose of collecting an offering. The proceeds from this were also used for repairing the Temple.

Jehoiada lived to the ripe old age of 130 years. During his life he was an influence for good on Joash. In fact, so great was his influence that he was buried among the kings. However, after his death, Joash forgot the good that Jehoiada had taught him. Soon after the death of Jehoiada, the people were again worshiping idols. Their leaders in all of this were Joash and the princes of Judah.

The son of Jehoiada, who was a prophet, stood before Joash and reproved him for his actions. This enraged Joash. Forgetting the kindness Jehoiada had shown him, he slew Zechariah the son of Jehoiada.

Because of his infidelity and rash actions, God's judgment came upon Joash and the nation of Judah. This judgment came in the form of an invasion from Syria. Though the Syrians came with only a small number of soldiers, they were able to completely despoil Judah.

After this invasion, some of the servants of Joash conspired against him. They murdered him in his bed. Though Joash was buried in Jerusalem, he was not given a state burial. His resting place was not in the sepulchers of the kings.

Special points.—Why the Levites did not hasten the work of gathering money to repair the house of God (v. 5) is not specifically stated. Perhaps it was because the priests were used to the present condition of things. They had come to accept the disrepair of the Temple as the normal condition of things. Perhaps a statement in 2 Kings 12:7 gives at least a partial answer. The king told the Levites to "receive no *more* money of your acquaintance." That is, they were to stop taking money from the worshipers for their own personal support.

The "collection" that Moses had laid upon the people in verse 9 was really a tax. The reference is to the situation recorded in Exodus 30:14–15. Every male Israelite twenty years old and above was assessed a sanctuary tax of one-half shekel. When Joash reinstituted this tax, there was an abundance of money for repairing the Temple.

Amaziah's Reign (2 Chron. 25:1–28)

The passage.—The first four verses of this chapter form an introduction to the rule of Amaziah. Verses 25–28 make up the concluding section. The rest of the record of Amaziah's reign centers around the two battles fought by Amaziah. The Chronicler has gone into some detail to show the moral lessons taught by these two events in the life of Amaziah. The parallel to this chapter is found in 2 Kings 14:1–20.

Amaziah's administration got off to a good start. The Chronicler observes that "he did that which was right in the sight of the Lord." He took vengeance on those who had slain Joash his father. However, he was careful not to harm their families. In so doing, he was following the Mosaic admonition that every person should suffer for his own sin.

In the early years of his rule, Amaziah went to war with Edom. He had hired mercenaries from the Northern Kingdom to augment his own forces. However, this was displeasing to God. He sent word to Amaziah by an unnamed prophet to send the Israelites home or face defeat. Amaziah was quick to follow the advice of the man of God. Because of this victory was his.

In the afterglow of victory, Amaziah forgot God. He took the idols which came with the spoil of the Edomites and began to worship them. Once again God sent an unnamed prophet to reprove Amaziah. However, he was not as anxious to listen to God's message this time. He had become enamored with his own greatness.

Amaziah had become so drunk on the wine of success that he challenged the Northern Kingdom to do battle with him. However, because he had forgotten God, he was decisively defeated.

The final days of Amaziah were neither happy nor peaceful. A conspiracy was formed against him. Because of this, he had to flee for his life. He was caught and killed in Lachish. However, he was given a proper burial in Judah.

Special points.—The meaning of the phrase "not with a perfect heart" in verse 2 is made clear by 2 Kings 14:4. Amaziah did not remove the high places. Also the people continued to sacrifice at these places.

The Mosaic ordinance referred to in verse 4 is found in Deuteronomy 24:16. Amaziah was at least true to the letter of the command in this case.

The statement in verse 17, "see one another in the face," is a challenge to do battle. Note verse 21 as a sequel to this statement.

Truth for today.—As we view the folly of Amaziah in worshiping the false gods (v. 14), we can see his error. How foolish, we say, to think that these gods which had no power could help him. However, there are many today who are bowing down before things that do not satisfy. Though our idols are more sophisticated, they are just as powerless as those Edomite idols.

Judah Under Uzziah (2 Chron. 26:1–23)

The passage.—Uzziah began to rule when he was only sixteen years old. His reign was long and eventful. However, the latter years of his reign were blighted by rash and foolish acts. In this sense he was much like his father.

As long as Uzziah followed the ways of the Lord, he had a prosperous and successful reign. However, when he became strong, he acted foolishly. He sought to usurp the prerogatives of the priesthood. He was reproved by the priests and became angry. However, God smote him with leprosy because of this rash act. His last days were spent out of touch with God's house and the people he had once ruled.

Special points.—Uzziah is called Azariah in the genealogical table found in 1 Chronicles 3:12. He is also known by this name in 2 Kings 14:21. His reign began in 790 B.C. and lasted for 52 years. His rule is reckoned until his death and not his illness with leprosy.

The prophet Zechariah mentioned in verse 5 was apparently well-known to the Chronicler. However, there is no other record of a prophet named Zechariah who lived during Uzziah's reign. Therefore, it is impossible to identify him further.

The word "harbergeons" of verse 14 is translated as "coats of mail" by the

American Standard Version. These of course had to do with the personal equipment of Uzziah's soldiers.

When Uzziah burned incense (v. 16), he was taking over a function that belonged exclusively to the priesthood. (See Ex. 30:7–8.) Only those who had been specially chosen of God and consecrated for this office could approach the altar of incense. (See Lev. 8:1–36.)

Verse 21 states that Uzziah dwelt in a "several house" after he was leprous. That is, he lived in a house set apart from others. He did not become an outcast as a commoner would have who contracted this disease. However, he was kept in quarantine. He had no more close contact with others.

At the time that Uzziah contracted leprosy, his son Jotham assumed the leadership of the king's house. That is, a coregency was instituted at this time.

Truth for today.—A most pathetic statement is made by the Chronicler in his estimate of Uzziah. "But when he was strong, his heart was lifted up to his destruction." How tragic that his strength which came from God was misused to his own downfall. This truth ought to be assimilated by every child of God. When one becomes strong, *i.e.,* wealthy or independent, the tendency too often is to forget God.

The Rule of Jotham (2 Chron. 27:1–9)

The passage.—The reign of Jotham was generally one of righteousness. He relied on God for his strength and was victorious over the Ammonites in battle. Little detail is given of the relatively brief reign of this godly king. Except for his battle with the Ammonites, the only other characterization of his reign mentions that he was a builder of cities, castles, and towers. However, the material in this chapter is somewhat more elaborate than the parallel passage in

2 Kings 15:32–38.

Special points.—Though Jotham was a godly king, he did not have a strong religious influence on the people. In verse 2 the Chronicler notes that "the people did yet corruptly." That is, they continued to sacrifice to the idols on the high places. (See 2 Kings 15:35.)

The Wicked Reign of Ahaz (2 Chron. 28: 1–27)

The passage.—The rule of Ahaz was marked by wickedness, shame, and defeat for Judah. Though his reign was no longer than that of his father Jotham, it was much more eventful.

The Chronicler first treats the spiritual apostasy of Ahaz. There was nothing good that could be said for him as a spiritual leader. Rather than following the ways of David he lived like the kings of the apostate Northern Kingdom. He worshiped almost all of the foreign deities with which Judah had any contact whatever.

After this the Chronicler recounts the pitiful political plight of Judah under Ahaz. During his administration, Judah was invaded from almost every side. Syria, Israel, Edom, and Philistia all in turn invaded Judah. Even Assyria, with whom Ahaz made an alliance, had no pity of Judah.

All of this was not enough to bring Ahaz to a realization of his sin. Rather, he worshiped the gods of Syria because he thought they would strengthen him. However, as the Chronicler puts it: "They were the ruin of him."

When Ahaz died, he was buried in Jerusalem. However, he was not deemed worthy of a place among the sepulchers of the kings.

Special points.—"The valley of the son of Hinnom" mentioned in verse 3 was of the southern boundary of the city of Jerusalem. It became the scene of many heathenistic rites in the later history of Judah. So atrocious were the acts committed there that it was made into a city dumping ground. This occurred during Josiah's reforms. The valley was held in contempt during New Testament times. And the perpetual fire that burned there was used by Jesus as an apt illustration of hell. The place is called Gehenna in the New Testament.

The phrase "burnt his children in the fire" in verse 3 is probably a reference to the worship of the Ammonite deity Moloch or Molech. This deity is also called Milcon in 1 Kings 11:5. Children were sacrificed to this idol by burning. This practice is condemned in Leviticus 20:1–5. In fact, the death penalty was to be assessed to the person worshiping Molech.

The prophet Obed mentioned in verse 9 is known only in this passage. Further identification of him is not possible.

The Beginning of Hezekiah's Administration (2 Chron. 29:1–36)

The passage.—Hezekiah was just the opposite of his wicked father in every way. He began his reign by opening the doors to the house of God. The sight which greeted him was not a pleasant one. For the house of God had been polluted with all of the trappings of sensual idol worship.

He immediately called together all of the Levites. He ordered them to sanctify themselves so they could clean up the house of God. As he charged them to sanctify the house of God, he reminded them that the pitiful plight of Judah was caused by unfaithfulness to God.

The Levites were quick to respond to the will of the king in this matter. They cleansed the house of God. Then they sanctified themselves from their ceremonial uncleanness. After this, they proceeded to ceremonially sanctify the Temple.

When they reported to the king that they had finished, he called the rulers of the city to the house of God. At this time, he reinstituted the sacrifices and all of the rituals that went with them. Then he invited the whole congregation to bring their sacrifices to the house of God. So great was the response that there were not enough priests to take care of the animals. Therefore the Levites had to help them.

Special points.—In verse 12 the representatives of three clans or family groups of the Levites are mentioned. These groups are the Kohathites, sons of Merari, and the Gershonites.

The uncleanness found in the Temple of the Lord in verse 16 was more than dirt and filth that had accumulated. The Chronicler has reference primarily to the idols and the materials used in their worship.

They threw these things into the brook Kidron. This was where Asa had burned the idol of Maachah. (See 2 Chron. 15:16.)

In verse 23 the priests placed their hands upon the goats that had been brought for the sin offering. This action symbolized the transferring of their sins to the goats. In this way they were designated as substitutes for their own lives.

A Solemn Passover Proclaimed (2 Chron. 30:1–27)

The passage.—So intense was Hezekiah's devotion to God that he proclaimed a passover. He established a decree to send a proclamation from one end of Israel to the other. The inhabitants of the Northern Kingdom who were under siege by Assyria were

invited to attend. A great number of
the inhabitants of Israel made light of
the intended passover. They had gone
so far in idolatry that worship of the
true God seemed like a joke. However,
some of their number did respond to
the invitation. These came to Jerusalem
for the passover.

The people of Judah came to the
feast in great numbers. When they
came to the feast, they first moved all
of the heathen altars out of the city.
These were thrown into the brook
Kidron.

As they began the feast, many of the
participants were ceremonially unclean.
For these Hezekiah interceded before
God. God heard the prayer and allowed this unusual situation to exist
without interveniton.

So great was the response and so
joyous the occasion that it was extended
for an additional seven days. For this
glad occasion, King Hezekiah furnished
the sacrifices necessary for the entire
assembly.

Special points.—Hezekiah's actions
in sending a proclamation to the Northern Kingdom may seem strange. However, at this time (724 B.C.) Israel had
been under siege by Assyria for some
time. Though the Northern Kingdom
did not disintegrate until 722 B.C., they
could not stop this action. As for the
Assyrians they probably would have
encouraged this seeming defection from
King Hoshea of Israel.

The proper time for keeping the passover was the fourteenth of the first
month (Nisan) on the Jewish calendar.
However, because the priests had not
properly sanctified themselves (v. 3),
this was impossible. Moses had made
provision for those who were unclean
during the regular time of passover to
keep it exactly one month later. (See
Num. 9:10–11.) Therefore, Hezekiah

had a good precedent for his actions
here. Since this passover was one
month late, it would have been held
in late April or early May, 754 B.C.

The Priests and Levites Reorganized (2 Chron. 31:1–20)

The passage.—With the conclusion
of the Feast of the Passover, there
came a resurgence of zeal for the true
God. The men went out into the cities
of Judah and destroyed all of the places
of idol worship. Before they returned
to their homes, they even went into
the areas of Ephraim and Manasseh.

Hezekiah then reorganized the priests
and Levites according to their courses.
He reinstituted Temple worship for all
of the prescribed sacrifices. Nothing
was overlooked in his zeal to repair
the spiritual life of the nation.

The king also set aside part of his
own substance for the various sacrifices. Then he commanded the people
of Jerusalem to support the priests and
Levites with the part of the offerings
that was rightly theirs. The response
of the people to his command was overwhelming. They began to bring an
abundance of things to the house of
God. In fact, they brought so much
that some was left over even after the
sacrifices and offerings were utilized.
These things they placed in a place of
safekeeping until they could be distributed to the priests.

All that Hezekiah did was in a right
spirit. He was sincere in heart and motive in seeking to reform the religious
life of the people.

Special points.—Verse 2 says that
"Hezekiah appointed the courses of the
priests and Levites." In other words,
he reinstituted orderly Temple worship
as it had been designed under David.
He reorganized the priests and Levites
according to their original courses.

This was necessary because, for some years, they had not been used in worship at all.

"The portion of the priests and the Levites" in verse 4 is a reference to what these groups received for their service in the Temple. Their portion consisted primarily of the tithes and firstfruits from the other eleven tribes. God had made provision for them, so they could give themselves to the work of the Temple. (See Num. 18:21–24 for a reference to this matter.) When the worshiper came to the Temple to make an offering to God, a tenth was to be given to the Levites.

The service of the priests began as early as three years of age according to verse 16. And even at this age, they would receive their portions directly from the Temple.

Assyria Invades Judah (2 Chron. 32:1–23)

The passage.—Sennacherib, king of Assyria, brought his forces against Hezekiah's kingdom. He was very sure he would be able to conquer so small a nation as Judah. However, Hezekiah relied on God for victory, and God caused the Assyrian forces to withdraw.

Hezekiah's first step was to shut off the water supply for Assyria. Then he called upon the people to trust in the Lord for deliverance from Assyria.

Sennacherib sent some of his generals to besiege Jerusalem while he laid siege against Lachish. These Assyrians taunted the people of Judah by saying that God would not be able to help them against Sennacherib. However, Hezekiah and Isaiah the prophet prayed, and God intervened.

Special points.—The brook that was stopped in verse 4 was probably the Gihon. This was done to deprive the Assyrians of a ready water supply.

The parallel account of this incident in the life of Hezekiah is found in 2 Kings 18:13—19:37. That account is somewhat more detailed than the one in 2 Chronicles. Some of the details evidently were not germane to the purpose of the Chronicler, for he omits them. For instance, before God delivered Hezekiah from Assyria, he payed large indemnities to Sennacherib.

A more detailed account of the prayers of Isaiah and Hezekiah mentioned in verse 20 can be found in 2 Kings 19:1–7 and 14–34.

The Last Days of Hezekiah (2 Chron. 32: 24–33)

The passage.—The Chronicler gives several of the events of the last fifteen years of the life of Hezekiah in a very brief summary.

Fifteen years before his death, Hezekiah became very ill, but God in his mercy spared him. The sparing of his life was in response to Hezekiah's prayer of petition for his life.

Though Hezekiah's life was marked by faithfulness to God, there were a few occasions when he did not seek God's counsel. When the ambassadors came from Babylon to visit him in his sickness was one of those times. This act of rash misjudgment proved costly for future generations.

However, Hezekiah can be remembered as one of the greatest and most godly kings of Judah.

Special points.—The Chronicler has not included many of the details of the last days of Hezekiah in this passage.

For a more detailed account of Hezekiah's sickness and the sign which God gave him (v. 24), see 2 Kings 20:1–11 and Isaiah 38:1–9.

In verse 31 the visit of the ambassadors from Babylon and the consequences of Hezekiah's actions are not given in detail. For a full treatment of this episode in the life of Hezekiah, see 2 Kings 20:12–19 and Isaiah 39: 1–8.

The Administrations of Manasseh and Amnon (2 Chron. 33:1–25)

The passage.—The rule of Manasseh was long and mostly very wicked. Though his father was one of the godliest of the kings of Judah, he was one of the most wicked. The greater part of his rule was spent leading Judah into heathenism. This led to political servitude to Assyria.

When Manasseh realized what his wicked actions had produced in his own life and that of the nation, he repented. He removed the strange gods from the house of God and repaired the altar of the Lord. He even reinstituted sacrifices to the true God. However, his repentance had little effect on the spiritual life of the nation. So great and so long had been his influence for evil that he could scarcely change their direction at this point.

The administration of Amnon is affixed to that of Manasseh almost as an afterthought by the Chronicler. Amnon seems to have been the product of his father's wicked life. Manasseh had little influence even on his son in his last days.

Amnon's reign was short and tragic. He was every bit as evil as his father had been in his youth. His own servants formed a conspiracy against Amnon and killed him.

Special points.—The list of heathen practices ascribed to Manasseh in verse 6 is formidable. He observed times or practiced augury. This was a type of divination based on chance events such as casting lots or sometimes even the flight of birds. He used enchantments or engaged in soothsaying. He even dealt with a familiar spirit. This was spiritualism or the attempt to make contact with the dead through spiritualist mediums.

The statement in verse 11 that Manasseh was taken "among the thorns" should read "in chains" (ASV).

Truth for today.—The tragedy of Manasseh's life is best mirrored in the life of his son Amnon. When Amnon was young enough to be influenced by his father, his father was a very wicked man. When Manasseh repented of his godless life, Amnon was already confirmed in his wickedness. How many times has this been the tragic story of parental influence in our own times. A man lives a life of wickedness before his children while they are young and impressionable. When the man is in middle age he is converted, and he can scarcely have any influence for good on his children. What a great trust the parent of a child has! Every parent should realize the extent of his influence in the lives of his children.

Josiah's Early Reign and Reforms (2 Chron. 34:1–33)

The passage.—Amnon had been killed before Josiah was old enough to be greatly influenced by his evil ways. Undoubtedly during his impressionable years, Josiah was under the influence of godly people. When he was sixteen years old, he began his reforms. So thorough were his reforms that he even exhumed the bones of the dead apostate priests and burned them.

After his purge of the land, he instituted an extensive program of repair to the Temple. It was during this time of repairing the Temple that Hilkiah found the lost book of the law. When the newly-found book was read to Josiah, he tore his clothes. He ordered

Hilkiah and others to inquire of God concerning the message of the book.

These men approached the prophetess Huldah to inquire of the Lord. She assured them that every curse written in the book would be brought upon Judah. However, because Josiah had been humble before God, Judah would be spared the wrath of God during his reign.

After this Josiah read the book of the law before all of the leaders of Judah. He made a covenant to keep the laws of God and commanded those present to do the same.

Special points.—The book of the law which Hilkiah found (v. 14) was probably Deuteronomy. The book contained many curses on those who did not keep the law. This sounds a great deal like Deuteronomy 28:15–47.

The word "college" in verse 22 should be "second quarter" (ASV).

The Last Years of Josiah's Administration (2 Chron. 35:1–27)

The passage.—In keeping with the reforms which he had instituted, Josiah kept a passover. Careful plans were laid in advance, for he was able to keep it at the prescribed time. This was the fourteenth day of the first month.

The Levites were organized in their courses and sanctified for the occasion. Then they prepared their brethren to take the passover in the proper manner. So well organized were the priests and Levites for this occasion that everything was carried out as prescribed by Moses. All of this was done in the eighteenth year of Josiah's reign.

Pharaoh Necho of Egypt wanted to pass through Palestine on his way to fight Nebuchadnezzar at Carchemish. Josiah went out to resist him. However, Necho was not interested in fight-

ing with Judah. He merely wanted to pass through the land. But Josiah was adamant in not allowing the Egyptian army to pass. He went out to do battle with them, but he disguised himself. In the course of the battle he was wounded and died soon after.

Special points.—A comparison of the passover in Hezekiah's reign (chap. 30) and that of Josiah leads to the conclusion that Josiah's reforms were more thorough. Though the passover of Hezekiah was equally important and impressive, it was one month late. Also, some of those who took it were not sanctified, and Hezekiah had to intervene for them. None of this confusion was present during Josiah's passover.

Verse 18 states that no passover like Josiah's had been kept since the days of Samuel. In other words, no other passover since the days of Samuel had met all the biblical standards as did Josiah's.

The encounter with Necho in verses 20–24 was really occasioned by the disintegration of the Assyrian empire. Egypt was competing with Babylon for supremacy of the ancient world.

Josiah disguised himself (v. 22) when he went to battle probably because of Necho's statement that God was behind his quest. Josiah was trying to escape his fate predicted by Necho.

"Jeremiah lamented for Josiah" in verse 25. Josiah and Jeremiah were closely allied in the far-flung religious reforms in Judah. Jeremiah outlived Josiah by several years, but throughout Josiah's rule, they were closely associated.

The Last Years of the Southern Kingdom (2 Chron. 36:1–22)

The passage.—This chapter records the last two decades of Judah's history before the Exile. Josiah's decision to go against Necho in battle brought Judah into servitude to Egypt. When Jehoahaz, the son of Josiah, had ruled for just three months Necho deported him to Egypt. This incident brought to an end the independent government of Judah.

Another son of Josiah replaced Jehoahaz. His name was Eliakim, but Necho changed it to Jehoiakim. His puppet kingdom lasted for eleven years. At this time Judah was invaded by Babylon and Jehoiakim was deported to Babylon.

For a brief period of just more than three months Jehoiachin was king. However, after this length of time he was also deported to Babylon.

Nebuchadnezzar then installed Zedekiah as ruler of Judah. Though he was a mere figurehead, his rule was marked by many evil practices which hastened the complete destruction of Judah. In his folly, he rebelled against Babylon. Nebuchadnezzar swiftly retaliated with a terrible vengeance. At this time the wall of Jerusalem was broken down and the Temple burned.

The Chronicler closes his account by rehearsing for the reader the decree of Cyrus. It was this decree that brought the remnant back to the land of Judah.

Special points.—In verse 9 Jehoiachin is said to have been eight years old. Second Kings 24:8 states that he was eighteen at this time. The reading in 2 Kings is to be preferred because of the characterization of his reign by the Chronicler. Also the fact that he was taken captive to Babylon would tend to support the older age.

The statement is made in verse 21 that the Exile lasted "until the land had enjoyed her sabbaths." Evidently this is a reference to the seventy-year period of the Exile. During this time the land was desolate. That is to say, no crops were cultivated. According to the law of Moses, the land was to be uncultivated every seventh year (Lev. 25:1–7). Evidently this custom had been neglected for many years. So, probably, the Chronicler was saying that this seventy-year rest was to make up for all the years the law had been neglected. There would be seventy sabbatical years in a 500-year period.

EZRA

Billy E. Simmons

INTRODUCTION

In the Hebrew Old Testament Ezra and Nehemiah are one book. Also in the Greek version of the Old Testament they are united and are called 2 Esdras. This was to distinguish this material from the Apocryphal book called 1 Esdras, which contains parts of these documents with some variations and additions. The fact that Ezra 2 is repeated in Nehemiah 7 seems to indicate that originally these were two distinct works.

The book of Ezra is named after its leading character. Ezra exercised a profound influence upon this era of Jewish history. He was a very strong personality who was totally dedicated to the doing of God's will as he understood it.

The history recorded by the book of Ezra covers a period of approximately eighty years. However, the book of Ezra treats only two comparatively short periods during this span of history.

Chapters 1–6 generally relate to the period from the decree of Cyrus in 536 B.C. to the completion and dedication of the second Temple in 515 B.C. Chapters 7–10 deal primarily with the period of history beginning in 458 B.C. when Ezra was given permission to conduct a second expedition to Jerusalem.

The book deals with decrees given by three Persian monarchs. These are Cyrus, Darius, and Artaxerxes. It was with the help of these three monarchs that the second Temple was built.

While the book does not claim Ezra as its author, the last four chapters were written largely in the first person. Traditionally the book has been ascribed to Ezra. There is no good reason why he could not have also compiled the first six chapters. He could have made use of royal decrees, certain letters, and genealogies as source material.

The Proclamation of Cyrus (Ezra 1:1–11)

The passage.—When Cyrus and the Persians overthrew the Babylonians, he immediately encouraged the Jews to return to Palestine. He made a decree that all Jews who did not wish to return to their homeland should help those who did. They were to contribute freely to the needs of the pilgrims as they returned from the seventy-year captivity.

Cyrus also decreed that the Temple should be rebuilt at Jerusalem. He brought out the vessels which Nebuchadnezzar had brought from Jerusalem. These he allowed to be brought back to Jerusalem. He also encouraged the Jews who did not return from exile to contribute to the offering for the house of God.

Special points.—In verse 1 the author states that the decree of Cyrus was in fulfilment of a prophecy by Jeremiah. Jeremiah made this prophecy in about 605 B.C. It is recorded in Jeremiah 25:12.

The decree of Cyrus recorded here pertains only to the Jews. However, he allowed all of the nations captured and exiled by Babylon to return to their homelands.

Verse 4 tells that all of the Jews did not return to Jerusalem. In fact, history records that the great majority of them remained in exile. They were treated well and most of them had never seen Judah. Seventy years is the normal life-span. So many of them had known nothing of their homeland. Only those who had a great religious zeal desired to make the long and dangerous journey to Palestine. Those who remained were later referred to as the Jews of the dispersion. Even though they did not return to Palestine, they retained their ethnic identity as well as strong ties with Palestinian Judaism.

Those Who Returned with Zerubbabel (Ezra 2:1–70)

The passage.—This passage consists primarily of a listing of those who returned to Palestine. The author has divided this list into eight groups.

The first group consists of the leaders, with Zerubbabel listed first (vv. 1–2). Also contained in this group are several other leaders.

The other groupings are as follows: (2) The list of Jewish families by heads of families (vv. 3–19). (3) The list of persons from various Palestinian towns (vv. 20–35). (4) In verses 36–39 the priests are listed by family groups. (5) The Levites are given in verses 40–42 with a breakdown by family groups as well as official Temple function. (6) The Nethinims are listed by family groups in verses 43–54. (7) In verses 55–58 there is a list of Solomon's servants by family groups. (8) The last grouping consists of those who could not show their genealogies to be definitely among Israel. This group is found in verses 59–63.

In verses 64–67 there is a statement which gives the totals of those who went on the first return to Palestine. The number of their beasts of burden are also enumerated here.

Verses 68–70 form a concluding statement to this section. The arrival in Jerusalem is recorded along with the various offerings made for the house of God.

Special points.—In verse 2, Zerubbabel is listed as the leader of this group. He was of the tribe of Judah and a descendant of David. He is also listed in the genealogy of Jesus Christ in Matthew 1:12–13. Though in the King James Version the spelling is Zorobabel in Matthew, the reference is to be Zerubbabel mentioned in Ezra.

The Nehemiah listed with Zerubbabel as one of the leaders of the returned exiles is not the Nehemiah for whom the Bible book was named. The Nehemiah who was governor of Judah and for whom the Bible book was named lived almost a century later than this.

In verses 36–43 it will be noted that over 4,000 priests returned to Palestine and less than 400 Levites joined the group. There is certainly no way to know why so few Levites chose to return.

The Nethinims (vv. 43–54) were probably descendants of the Gibeonites who tricked Joshua into not destroying them. (See Josh. 9.) This is assumed from the name Nethinim, for this title was given to those who did the menial tasks around the Temple.

It is uncertain what privileges the people of verses 59–62 who could not prove their Jewish lineage were given. They were allowed to accompany the others on this journey. However, they probably would have been excluded from any official function.

When the total number in each

group is tabulated, there is a discrepancy in the total figure given. The total given in verse 64 is 42,360. However, the total of the groups comes to 29,818. Perhaps this can be explained through errors of copying these numbers repeatedly by copyists through the years.

Work Begun on the Temple (Ezra 3:1–13)

The passage.—Soon after the Jews returned to Palestine they held a convocation in Jerusalem. They reinstituted the prescribed sacrifices and kept the Feast of Tabernacles.

They also made arrangements with Tyre and Sidon to send timbers of cedar from Lebanon for the house of God.

Two years after their arrival in Palestine from the captivity they were able to erect the foundation for the Temple. When this was completed, there was great rejoicing on the part of the younger generation. However, the older men who had seen the first Temple wept.

Special points.—In verse three it is said that "fear *was* upon them because of the people of those countries." Because of this they were acutely aware of the need for God's protection. It may be seen in the following chapters of Ezra that their fears were completely justified.

In verse 8 it is said that the Levites from twenty years old were used in rebuilding the Temple. It is significant to note that there were 24,000 Levites to see after the work of Solomon's Temple. (See 1 Chron. 23:4.) However, as was noted earlier, only 341 Levites returned from exile. This was a very small group to do the work demanded of them.

These older men who had seen the first Temple wept when they saw the foundation of the second one. (See v. 12.) Though the captivity was dated from the first carrying away in 605 B.C., the Temple was not actually destroyed until 586 B.C. Thus there had been no Temple for approximately 50 years. However, some were here now who remembered the grandeur of the first. Evidently this second Temple in no way compared to the first structure in plan or style of architecture. For this reason, these old men wept. However, there were those who had not seen the first Temple. For them this was a noteworthy and joyous occasion.

The Work Is Hindered (Ezra 4:1–24)

The passage.—Soon after the foundations of the Temple were laid an offer of help came to the Jews. However, it came from the people who had remained in Palestine from the time of the destruction of the Northern Kingdom. The Jews promptly refused to accept this offer of help.

The people of the land then did everything in their power to weaken the efforts of the Jews in their attempt to build. Their opposition continued through the rule of Cyrus until that of Artaxerxes.

These adversaries wrote to Artaxerxes reminding him that throughout history the Jews had been a rebellious people. The king read the letter and searched the annals of his kingdom for information concerning Israel and Jerusalem. He became convinced that it would be to his best interest to have the work stopped. Thus construction on the house of God ceased for some years.

Special points.—Judah and Benjamin are mentioned in verse 1 because the remnant consisted primarily of the descendants of these two tribes.

In verse 2 those who came to offer

their help mentioned that they had worshiped God since the days of Esarhaddon. This Assyrian king had been responsible for transplanting foreign people in the land of Samaria. These transplanted people intermarried with the Israelites who were left when Israel was overthrown. Through the years (about 150 now) these people had carried out a corrupt form of Jehovah worship. Now they have come to offer their help to these returned exiles. Had their offer been accepted, the true form of revealed worship probably would have been corrupted.

In verse 5 the statement "all the days of Cyrus . . . until the reign of Darius" covers approximately fifteen years. This was from 535–520 B.C.

Verse 6 begins a parenthetical statement of events which transpired some years later.

The races of people referred to in verse 9 are very difficult to identify. However, it is thought by some that these people originally came from Babylon, Media, and Persia.

The "great and noble Asnapper" (v. 10) is a reference to the Assyrian king Ashurbanipal. It was he who transplanted the peoples mentioned in verse 9 in Samaria.

The statement in verse 24 refers back to the statement in verse 5. The parenthesis of verses 6–23 is chronologically after verse 24. If this ,is not the case, the kings mentioned in verses 6–23 have been misplaced by the author. Verse 24 gives the additional information that it was in the second year of Darius (520 B.C.) that work on the Temple resumed.

Work Is Resumed (Ezra 5:1–17)

The passage.—After a work stoppage of approximately 15 years, Haggai and Zechariah began to prophesy. They encouraged the people to begin work on

the Temple again. Under the leadership of Zerubbabel and Joshua, work was once more begun.

When work was begun, the governor of the province named Tatnai came to investigate the activity. He questioned the Jews carefully concerning their permission to build the Temple. They told him that their permission to build had come from a decree made by Cyrus. Tatnai then wrote to Darius concerning the matter. He suggested that the king would do well to search through the royal decrees to see if Cyrus had really made such a decree.

Special points.—"Tatnai, governor of this side of the river" is a reference to the Persian province or satrapy west of the Euphrates River.

The letter to Darius beginning in verse 6 was concerned only with the Temple. There is no mention of the building of the city as in 4:12–16.

The Temple Is Completed (Ezra 6:1–22)

The passage.—When Darius the king received the letter from Tatnai accusing the Jews, he commanded that search be made among the archives. This was done and the decree of Cyrus was found. Then Darius made his own decree concerning the construction of the Temple. He even ordered that expenses be provided from his own coffers for the completion of this project. He also commanded that whatever animals were needed for sacrifices should be provided.

When Tatnai and his companions received the king's decree, they made haste to comply with it. The house of God was completed in the sixth year of the reign of Darius.

After the completion of the Temple, the returned exiles held a feast of dedication. At this feast they sacrificed a great number of animals.

Then they reorganized the priests and

Levites in their proper courses for Temple service. At the proper time, then, they were able to observe the solemn Feast of the Passover. This was possible because all of the priests and Levites had purified themselves in anticipation of this occasion.

Special points.—In verre 2 "Achmetha" is Ecbatana which was the capital of the Old Midian empire. Keil notes in his commentary that the records of the Persian empire were kept in an alaborate network of archives. The administration of these libraries centered in Babylon. However, there were branch libraries as far distant as Ecbatana.

The name "Artaxerxes" is added to those of Cyrus and Darius in verse 14. No doubt Ezra was careful to add the name of his own king because of the help he had been in maintaining the Temple.

The month of Adar in verse 15 corresponds roughly to our month of March. So it was in the early spring that the house of God was completed.

The sixth year of the reign of Darius was 515 B.C. So, when the work on the Temple really began in earnest, it took four and one-half years to complete it.

Verse 17 records a happy occasion in the life of the new nation. However, it is interesting to note how many more animals Solomon offered at the dedication of the first Temple. (See 2 Chron. 7:5.)

The Passover recorded in verse 19 occurred only a few weeks after the dedication of the Temple.

The Decree of Artaxerxes Concerning Ezra (Ezra 7:1–28)

The passage.—The chapter begins by giving the genealogy of Ezra. Then it makes mention of the fact that he went to Jerusalem and was a "ready scribe in the law of Moses."

The remainder of the chapter (vv. 11–28) is a record of the decree of Artaxerxes. He decreed that any priests and Levites who desired to go with Ezra to Jerusalem were free to go.

Ezra was commissioned as an official emissary of Artaxerxes to inquire concerning the affairs of Judah and Jerusalem for him. As such, he gave Ezra the permission to take a freewill offering from his kingdom to the Temple in Jerusalem.

Artaxerxes also decreed that his treasurer for the province west of the Euphrates give Ezra all the help he needed. Though he placed certain limits on certain materials, he was still very liberal. These things were to be used in the maintenance of the Temple.

His decree also stated that no tax could be levied on any of the official Temple workers. This included the priests and the Levites as well as the more menial officials.

The decree gave Ezra the command to serve as a teacher of the law for those who were ignorant of its teachings.

Special points.—Chapter 7 begins with these words: "Now after these things." Fifty-eight years passed between the events of chapter 6 and those of chapter 7. During this time the events in the book of Esther happened.

Ezra's genealogy is given in verses 1–5. It is interesting to note that he could trace his ancestry back to Aaron. He was also a descendant of Zadok who was one of David's priests and the leading priest during Solomon's administration. Thus Ezra's genealogy would have been very impressive to the community of Jews in Palestine.

The earlier scribes were merely secretaries or recorders of the law. However, even before the exile the scribes had become teachers of the law. This surely is the meaning of "scribe" as it is used of Ezra in verse 6.

Ezra Journeys to Jerusalem (Ezra 8:1–36)

The passage.—Ezra first gave a list of all of those who were to go with him from Babylon to Jerusalem. Before they began their journey, they camped for three days while Ezra made an inventory of those who were going with him.

When he had checked thoroughly, he found that there were no Levites among them. Therefore he sent to Casiphia and got a group of Levites and Nethinims to go with him.

Ezra then proclaimed a fast beseeching God's protection for the group as they traveled. By his own testimony, he was ashamed to ask the king for a company of soldiers to guard them. He had told the king how God would protect those who sought him. Now he felt he must invoke the blessing of God on his group as they journeyed.

At this point Ezra entrusted the Temple treasures to the priests and Levites who were among the group. Then they began their journey to Jerusalem. God was with them on the journey, and they arrived safely in Jerusalem.

Once they arrived in Jerusalem, they delivered the treasures they had brought to the house of God. Then they offered sacrifices to God for all Israel. After this they delivered the decree of Artaxerxes to the governor.

Special points.—The trip from Ahava to Jerusalem took four months. This is found in Ezra 7:9. They left Ahava in April and arrived in Jerusalem in July. The total distance covered was just short of 1,000 miles.

Twelve he-goats for a sin offering were mentioned in verse 35. This undoubtedly represented a sin offering for each of the twelve tribes of Israel. Even though the ten tribes North had long been dissolved, they were not forgotten in this offering to God. The feeling of family solidarity was still strong even among these returned exiles.

The lieutenants and governors mentioned in verse 36 were the Persian officials for all of the districts surrounding Judah.

Ezra's Prayer of Confession and Intercession (Ezra 9:1–15)

The passage.—After the official business had been taken care of, Ezra had an audience with the princes of the returned exiles. They told Ezra that the priests and Levites had not kept themselves pure from the abominations of the heathen. In fact, they had intermarried with the heathen thus bringing these abominable practices into the Jewish remnant community.

When Ezra heard this, he was overcome with grief. So moved was he that he was speechless for several hours.

At the time of the evening sacrifice, he offered his prayer to God. His prayer was one of confession for the sins of the people and intercession for them. In his prayer he rehearsed the commands God had given to the Israelites under Moses before they possessed the Promised Land. He also remembered that the Exile was brought about because of the disobedience to God's commands. He also recognized that the remnant community had no right to expect the blessings of God.

Special points.—In verse 3 it is recorded that Ezra tore his clothes and pulled out hair from his head and beard. To tear one's clothes was a sign of grief. However, to pluck out one's hair was a sign of violent indignation. Ezra was grief-stricken over the moral and spiritual life of the remnant nation. But more than this, he was filled with indignation

I. Hittite lions (Turkey)

II. Egyptian mummy case

III. Spring where Gideon selected his small band

IV. Gleaners near Nazareth

FON H. SCOFIELD, JR.

V. Gate house in Persepolis, ancient capital of Persia

VI. View of Bethlehem

FON H. SCOFIELD, JR.

VII. Traditional site of Jesus' baptism

VIII. Caesarea Philippi (Banyas)

FON H. SCOFIELD, JR.

IX. Synagogue in Capernaum (following time of Christ)

X. Colonnade in Capernaum

XI. Carved Ark of the Covenant, Capernaum

FON H. SCOFIELD, JR.

XII. View of Bethany

XIII. Beautiful (Golden) Gate, Jerusalem

XIV. Roman aqueduct, Caesarea

V. LAVELL SEATS

XV. Dome of the Rock (Temple site), Jerusalem

XVI. Detail, sarcophagus from Antioch (Turkey)

over their condition. He felt that they had been derelict in their responsibilities to God.

From the indications in the following chapter, Ezra's prayer was public. It led to repentance and confession among the people.

It is also noteworthy that this great prayer of Ezra contained no plea for pardon. It is primarily one of confession, though there is a note of intercession in it.

Ezra Institutes Reforms (Ezra 10:1–44)

The passage.—After Ezra completed his prayer many people gathered to him weeping because of their sin. They encouraged Ezra to issue a proclamation that all foreign wives must be divorced and that their children must be sent away with them.

This gathering resulted in a proclamation that all Jews should report to Jerusalem within three days. The purpose for the assembly was to determine who was guilty in this matter. Then by judicial decree they would be forced to put away their foreign wives. However, the problem was a very complex one. Also, the weather was inclement. For these reasons there was a delay in the proceedings concerning this matter.

In the final analysis, the guilty parties were brought to court. Then they were forced to send away their foreign wives.

The concluding part of the passage is a list of those with foreign wives. Among this list were seventeen priests, ten Levites, and eighty-six men of the congregation of the remnant. Each had to put away his foreign wife and offer a ram as a trespass offering.

Special points.—In verse 8 the phrase "all his substance should be forfeited" is used. The word "forfeited" is literally "devoted." Probably the goods of those who refused to comply with Ezra's proclamation were to be appropriated for the maintenance of the Temple.

In verse 15 the phrase "were employed about this" probably should read "stood up against this." This is the reading in the American Standard Version. In other words, only the two men mentioned in verse 15 stood up in the assembly to oppose this plan.

It may be difficult for us today to understand how the purpose of God could have been served by dividing these homes. This, however, was a crucial time in the history of the messianic community. Ezra was doing what he could to see to it that the true form of worship was preserved. As he viewed it, this could not be done as long as heathenism infiltrated the family and religious life of the nation.

NEHEMIAH

Billy E. Simmons

INTRODUCTION

As was noted in the introduction to Ezra, these two books were treated as one in the Hebrew and Greek Old Testaments. The book of Nehemiah should quite logically be regarded as a sequel to Ezra. However, Nehemiah is not so much a recitation of the history of the period as it is the record of some important events.

The book of Nehemiah covers a period of approximately twenty years beginning in 445 B.C. and lasting until his return to Jerusalem from Babylon. The purpose of his coming was to correct some problems which had arisen during his absence.

It is evident from Nehemiah 8:1–9 that the careers of Ezra and Nehemiah overlapped.

Concerning the authorship of this document, it may be said that the book claims to be "the words of Nehemiah." On occasion Nehemiah is mentioned in the third person. However, the bulk of the material was written in the first person. There seems to be no good reason to deny that this document was compiled by Nehemiah.

Nehemiah Prays for the Remnant (Neh. 1:1–11)

The passage.—Nehemiah recounts an incident that happened to him in Shushan. A certain Hanani came from Judah to the palace where Nehemiah was. Nehemiah asked him concerning the Jews who had left the captivity. The report which Hanani gave was a very disturbing one.

So disturbed was Nehemiah by the report from Judah that he wept for several days. Then he fasted and prayed to God.

The prayer of Nehemiah was one of intercession for the remnant of Judah. He did not ask for more of the Jews in exile to return to Judah. He asked for the divine protection of those who were already there.

Special points.—The month of Chisleu (v. 1) corresponded roughly to our month of December. "The twentieth year" would have been the twentieth year of the reign of Artaxerxes. This was 445 B.C.

Whether or not Hanani was actually Nehemiah's blood brother cannot be definitely ascertained. However, in 7:2 Nehemiah again refers to him as his brother. This would lead to the speculation that Hanani was in reality Nehemiah's blood brother.

The destruction of Jerusalem mentioned in verse 2 probably does not refer to that of 586 B.C. as some think. It would be difficult to explain Nehemiah's shock if this were the case. However, what destruction was referred to by Hanani is impossible to say.

Nehemiah Arrives in Jerusalem (Neh. 2:1–20)

The passage.—As Nehemiah fulfilled his official duties before Artaxerxes, the king noticed that he was sad of countenance. Therefore he inquired concerning the reason for Nehemiah's sadness.

When Nehemiah related his reason to the king, he asked Nehemiah to make his request. Nehemiah asked for the privilege of going to Jerusalem and rebuilding the city. The king granted this request along with his request for material to build the gates of the city, a palace, and a castle.

When Nehemiah arrived in Jerusalem with his armed escort, he made a secret inspection of the situation by night. He found the walls to be in a very bad state of repair. Then he challenged the Jews to rebuild the walls. His enemies, Sanballat, Tobiah, and Geshem, made fun of his efforts to have the walls rebuilt. However, Nehemiah was able to answer them satisfactorily.

Special points.—It was noted in 1:11 that Nehemiah was the king's cupbearer. As such it was his responsibility to taste the wine before the king drank it. This was to make sure it was not poisoned. Among the Persian rulers, this was a very important position. Therefore, Nehemiah's presence at the king's court was the normal thing.

The fact that the king was willing to grant Nehemiah's request is evidence that Nehemiah was in a favored position in the court. It also is evidence of the providential hand of God at work among his people. These Persian rulers were instruments of God, though they were not of the messianic race.

Those Who Repaired the Wall Listed (Neh. 3:1–32)

The passage.—In this chapter Nehemiah lists the names of those who worked on various gates and sections of the wall. In all, eight different gates are listed along with the sections of the wall adjoining them.

Special points.—The first gate listed is the sheep gate. It was in the northeast corner of the city. From there Nehemiah moved in a counterclockwise direction describing the gates and sections of the wall along with the workmen.

Opposition to the Project Arises (Neh. 4:1–23)

The passage.—When Nehemiah's enemies saw that the building program was making progress, they began systematically to intimidate the Jews.

These enemies decided to actively fight against the rebuilding of the wall of Jerusalem. Many of the Jews became disheartened and feared for their homes and families. However, Nehemiah encouraged them to continue in the work and to be willing to defend themselves against their enemies. He set up a continual guard around the city so that the work could go forward without needless interruption.

Special points.—In verse 12 the phrase "from all places whence ye shall return to us" is used. The reference is to the Jews who were working on the walls and living in towns outside Jerusalem. The people of these towns wanted the Jews working on the walls to stop and return home to defend their families against these enemies.

"Habergeons" in verse 16 refers to a coat of mail. Probably in Nehemiah's day a leather coat covered with thin sheets of metal were used.

Nehemiah Institutes Reforms (Neh. 5: 1–19)

The passage.—This chapter seems to be a sort of parenthesis to the story of rebuilding the wall. Nehemiah learned that many of the people with money were charging usury. In this way many of the poorer people were losing all they had, for they had not been able to cultivate their lands.

Nehemiah called the nobles together and persuaded them to stop the practice of usury and to restore the property which they held in pledge. This they did willingly.

Nehemiah also recounts that he had not exacted from the people that which was usually taken from them by governors.

Special points.—In the first five verses three classes of people are listed who were complaining of hardship. (1) There were families who had no property, and the building was working a hardship on them. (2) Some families who had property were having to mortgage it to meet expenses. (3) There were others who were having to borrow money to pay taxes. They had pledged their crops and when there were none their children were taken as slaves in payment.

In verse 7 Nehemiah accuses the rich Jews of charging interest on loans made to other Jews. The Old Testament does not condemn the loaning of money with interest except to another Jew. (See Ex. 22:25.)

The Walls Are Completed (Neh. 6:1—7:4)

The passage.—So enraged was Sanballat at the progress being made on the walls, that he tried to lure Nehemiah out of the city. He sent letters repeatedly to Nehemiah saying he wanted to confer with him. However, Nehemiah suspected a trap and refused to go.

When this plan failed, Sanballat tried to intimidate Nehemiah by sending an open letter to the Jews accusing Nehemiah of sedition. Then he hired false prophets to predict an attempt on Nehemiah's life. They encouraged him to hide in the Temple. However, Nehemiah suspected the plot and refused to be drawn into a trap.

Finally, to the dismay of the enemies of the Jews, the walls were finished. Then Nehemiah set special guards around the city to keep watch over the city by night.

Special points.—"One of the villages in the plain of Ono" (v. 2) would have been approximately twenty miles to the north of Jerusalem.

The month of Elul mentioned in verse 15 corresponds roughly to our month of August. The length of time taken in building the wall mentioned also in verse 15 was fifty-two days. This sounds like a comparatively short time for such a monumental task. However, it should be remembered that the wall had not been destroyed completely. They were repairing only the breaks in the wall.

A List of Those Who Returned with Zerubbabel (Neh. 7:5–73)

The passage.—The wall had been completed, and Nehemiah now set himself to the task of populating the city of Jerusalem. It was his desire to populate the city with Jews who could find their genealogies listed in the register of those who had returned with Zerubbabel.

Except for verses 70–72 the list given here is exactly like the one found in Ezra 2:1–70.

Special points.—The Tirshatha mentioned in verses 65 and 70 was the Persian title for the governor of Judah. The reference in this section is probably to Zerubbabel.

The Reading of the Law (Neh. 8:1–18)

The passage.—On the first day of the seventh month, Ezra the priest read publicly the law of God. It was read before the men and women, and it took from early morning until noon. When the people heard the words of the law, they began to weep. However, Nehemiah, Ezra, and the Levites reminded the people that they should rejoice rather than weep.

The next day the people gathered together again so the law could be explained to them. It was discovered that during the seventh month there was supposed to be a feast. The Jews were to take branches and build booths to dwell in for seven days.

Therefore the people went out and got branches and built booths to dwell in during the feast. This feast had not been observed properly since the time of Joshua. During the observance, there was much gladness, and the law was read every day.

Special points.—Why Ezra has not been mentioned in the book of Nehemiah up to this point is not easily explained. Quite possible he had been away in Babylon during the repairing of the wall. At any rate, as a priest, he was the appropriate one to read the law and instruct the people in it. Nehemiah, you will remember, was neither a priest nor a Levite.

The feast observed at the beginning of the month was the Feast of Trumphets. This was the festival of the new moon. The seventh new moon of the year was the most sacred of all during the year. During this month the Feast of Trumphets would be followed by the Day of Atonement. This then would be followed almost immediately by the Feast of Tabernacles. This feast commemorated the forty years of wilderness wanderings when the Israelites dwelt in tents.

Possibly the point being made in verse 17 that since the days of Joshua the feast had not been properly observed is that the Jews had not dwelt in booths.

A Public Confession (Neh. 9:1–38)

The passage.—Just two days after the glad Feast of Tabernacles the people came together in a solemn assembly. This was a solemn public confession of

their sin, and it was to be directed by certain of the Levites. When they came together, the book of the Law was again read aloud. Then they confessed their sins.

The Levites led in this public confession. This included a lengthy recounting of the history of Israel from the time of Abraham to the present. The main theme which runs throughout the confession is the faithfulness of God and the faithlessness of his people.

The confession concludes with a lament that they are in servitude to foreign kings in the land which God had given to their forefathers. Then a solemn covenant was written. This was a renewal on the nation's part to keep the covenant made at Sinai.

Special points.—In verse 2 it is said that "the seed of Israel separated themselves from all strangers." That is to say there would be no intermarriage with the heathen that surrounded them.

One-fourth part of a day in verse 3 represents three hours. The Jews divided the twenty-four-hour day into two twelve-hour segments. These were from 6 P.M. to 6 A.M. and from 6 A.M. to 6. P.M.

The Covenant Is Sealed (Neh. 10:1–39)

The passage.—The passage begins with a list of those whose names were affixed to the covenant. Nehemiah the governor heads the list. Following him is the list of priests.

The covenant is then given with an emphasis on three main points. (1) There was to be no intermarriage with the heathen people of the land. (2) There was to be no buying or selling or any business transactions on the sabbath or any other of their holy days. (3) They were also pledged to recognize and practice the year of release which occurred every seventh year.

The rest of the chapter has to do with

the support of the Temple. The people agreed to tax themselves one third of a shekel for its support. They also pledged their firstfruits for God's use. And, they agreed that the priests were to share with the Levites in the tithe.

Special points.—The observance of the seventh year mentioned in verse 31 is a reference to the Mosaic ordinance found in Deuteronomy 15:1–2. The third part of a shekel which was to be exacted for Temple support was a concession. The Mosaic ordinance found in Exodus 30:13 called for each male over twenty to pay one-half shekel for support of the tabernacle. Perhaps this concession was made at this time because of the poverty of the remnant community.

The Inhabitants of the Land Listed (Neh. 11:1—12:26)

The passage.—Nehemiah's plan to populate Jerusalem with Jews whose genealogies could be proven is now unfolded. It was alluded to in 7:4–5 but was interrupted by the special seventh-month feast and the covenant. At this time lots were cast to bring one tenth of the people into Jerusalem to dwell. The rest were to dwell in other cities.

The remainder of chapter 11 consists of a list of those who dwelt in Jerusalem along with the other cities where Jews lived. In verses 3–24 the inhabitants of Jerusalem are listed. The other towns where Jews lived are found in 11:25–36. Chapter 12:1–9 contains a list of the priests and Levites who returned with Zerubbabel. The rest of the passage (12:10–26) is a genealogy of Levites and priests as well as high priests who lived after the exile.

Special points.—Probably Jerusalem had few permanent inhabitants at this time. There was great danger in living in a city whose walls were broken down.

There were bands of marauders roaming that part of the world in search of unprotected cities to pillage.

The Jaddua mentioned in verse 22 as living during the reign of Darius the Persian has been the center of a controversy. Some have assumed that he is the Jaddua who lived during the time of Alexander the Great. In this case the Darius mentioned would be Darius III (335–331 B.C.). Josephus mentions such a person in his *Antiquities.* Though the controversy cannot be resolved dogmatically, there are several possibilities. Josephus is not always correct in his chronology. It may be possible that he is not correct in this case. There is also the possibility that there were two high priests named Jaddua. There is a third but remote possibility that this Jaddua lived to be approximately one hundred years old. This would place him in both periods.

The Walls Dedicated and Temple Service Organized (Neh. 12:27–47)

The passage.—This passage records the dedication of the walls of Jerusalem and the formal organization of Temple services. For this gala occasion the Levitical singers were brought in from surrounding towns. The people were purified before the actual ceremonies began. Then Nehemiah led one group and Ezra another in a procession around the city. When they came to the Temple, they offered sacrifices with gladness. Then the services of the Temple were set in order.

Nehemiah Institutes Reforms (Neh. 13:1–31)

The passage.—At the time of this dedication the book of the Law was read publicly to the people. Then Nehemiah instituted these final reforms.

Tobiah was made to move out of the

Temple where Eliashib had prepared him a private lodging. Nehemiah notes here that while all of this had been going on he was not at Jerusalem. He had gone to Babylon for a time.

The Levites also had been deprived of their rightful offerings and had to leave the Temple and work their lands for substance. Nehemiah then set to work to correct this problem.

The next problem he confronted was the breaking of the sabbath. Many were working, and commerce was carried on contrary to the law. Nehemiah had to threaten the use of force to correct this.

Some of the Jews had also intermarried with the heathen during his absence. This enraged Nehemiah, for he found that their children could not even speak Hebrew. He made them swear that they would not allow this practice to continue.

Special points.—Though nothing is said of Nehemiah's return to Babylon before verse 6, he had evidently been gone for some time. Just when he left and when he returned is impossible to determine with certainty. Undoubtedly he left Jerusalem in 432 B.C. after serving twelve years as governor. Probably he was gone for several years. However, it is impossible to say exactly when he returned in relation to the events in chapter 13.

ESTHER

Russell H. Dilday, Jr.

INTRODUCTION

Purim, one of the most joyful of all Jewish holidays, is observed in the spring of the year, usually during the month of March. This happy day celebrates the downfall of the villain Haman as recounted in the book of Esther.

In temples and synagogues throughout the world today Purim is marked by family services during which the "megillah" or the story of Purim is read. Great merriment and noise accompanies the reading of the story, and Purim is the only time behavior of this kind is allowed in the sanctuary. Whenever the name of the villain Haman is mentioned, the children hiss, boo, and wave special Purim noisemakers called "greggers."

As part of the Purim festivities children usually dress in costume. And naturally the most popular outfits are those of Queen Esther and King Ahasuerus, which allow the children to wear regal crowns and robes.

A traditional Purim pastry called "hamantaschen" is served. These are three-cornered pastries filled with prune or poppy seeds and are supposed to resemble Haman's hat. Hamantaschen are often available in the bakeries during the Purim week and are usually served at temple following a Purim service.

All these present-day observances date back to the events described in the book of Esther. In fact, the purpose of the book is to explain the origin of this Jewish feast and to suggest motives for its observance.

King Ahasuerus in the book is traditionally identified as Xerxes, the Persian king who ruled from 485–464 B.C. The book of Esther was written after that, possibly as early as 450 B.C.

How Esther Came to Be Queen of Persia (Esther 1:1—2:23)

The passage.—In the third year of his reign, King Ahasuerus of Persia gave a banquet in honor of the great leaders of his kingdom. On the seventh day of the feast the king, "when his heart was merry with wine" (1:10), commanded his queen, Vashti, to appear and show her beauty to his guests. She refused and Ahasuerus divorced her and made a public example of her banishment.

Upon the advice of his servants, Ahasuerus had fair young maidens brought to Shushan from all parts of the kingdom from among whom he would choose a new queen (2:4). Among the fair maidens was a Jewish girl named Esther. She lived with her cousin Mordecai who had been carried into captivity from Jerusalem. Her beauty was so natural that without having to go through the year of beauty treatments required by the other maidens she captured the king's affection (2:12–16). She was crowned Queen of Persia by the king himself.

Meanwhile, Mordecai overheard two enemies of King Ahasuerus plotting to assassinate him. Mordecai told Esther, who in turn warned the king, who in turn had the matter investigated. The plot was indeed genuine, and the two traitors were executed. King Ahasuerus recorded Mordecai's name in his chronicles as the one who had acted to save his life.

Special points.—The identify of King Ahasuerus has been most often linked with King Xerxes of Persia who reigned from 485 B.C. to 464 B.C. History records enough of the deeds of Xerxes to vouch for his likeness to Ahasuerus.

The banquet in 1:4 didn't last 180 days, or half the year, as it might appear. Instead, a display of the glories of the kingdom was carried on in all parts of the land for 180 days followed by a banquet lasting only seven days.

The phrase "none did compel" in 1:8 means that the guests were allowed to drink all they wanted to drink, which usually happened at Persian banquets. There is nothing in the phrase to indicate moderation.

Queen Vashti refused to risk her dignity and reputation as a queen and a wife before the drunken guests (1:12). This explains the reason for her banishment.

"Esther" was a Persian name meaning star (2:8). Her Hebrew name was Hadassah, which means "myrtle."

Esther did not reveal her Jewish nationality (2:10) because Mordecai had no doubt instructed her to remain silent. Being a descendant of a captive people and a foreigner in the land, she would not have received the favorable treatment in the palace had it been known she was Jewish.

Truth for today.—This story is an illustration of how seemingly unrelated events like a feast, a divorce, a beauty contest, an alert ear overhearing a devious plot can all be seen as a part of God's plan. Minor events and apparently insignificant happenings may be used by the Creator to carry out his purpose. It is an encouragement to us to trust God day by day since we cannot see the future.

How the Jews Were Condemned to Death (Esther 3:1—4:17)

The passage.—It so happened that King Ahasuerus decided to honor one of his princes, Haman, by promoting him above all the princes and commanded all his subjects to bow down before Haman in reverence. Mordecai, the Jew, refused to worship Haman, probably because it was against his religious belief. This angered Haman, and he devised a plan not only to kill Mordecai but also all the Jews throughout the kingdom.

By accusing them before the king as lawbreakers (3:7–11) Haman persuaded Ahasuerus to issue a decree in every province that called for the destruction of all Jews and the confiscation of their possessions for the king's treasury. By the casting of lots (3:7) the thirteenth day of the month Adar (February–March) was chosen as the day of execution.

Mordecai, in mourning, sent a copy of the fatal decree to Esther and called upon her to intercede with the king on behalf of her people (4:8). Esther explained that to go before the king without being summoned was a crime punishable by death. But she agreed to risk her life and speak to the king (4:16).

Special points.—In 3:4 Mordecai apparently had to explain his refusal to bow down to Haman by admitting he was a Jew, and as a Jew he believed worship belonged only to God and not to man.

In 3:12 the question is raised, why was the decree issued on the first month of the year and the extermination of the Jews delayed until the thirteenth day of the twelfth month, nearly a year later. The idea may have been to encourage the Jews to escape quickly and leave their property and possessions behind. In this way Haman would have accomplished his purpose without the need of a massacre. However, it must be remembered that the date for the killing of the Jews was set by casting lots. This time interval gave the Jews opportunity to take action and avoid the tragedy. Now this appears to have been just by chance, but it is an evidence of the providential watch-care of God overruling the plans of men for his purpose.

Truth for today.—In this passage we see revealed an interesting study of character traits of the main personalities in the story. Mordecai's courageous nonconformity needs to be repeated by men today. Romans 12:2 commands, "Be not conformed to this world." Mordecai was one of those who had courage to resist the popular patterns of action and stand by his convictions.

The arrogant vindictiveness of the politician, Haman, is another study in character, warning us against the folly of egotism. King Ahasuerus represents the despotic and careless ruler who fails to think through his decisions and unknowingly injures others by his acts. The quiet and humble bravery of Esther is the highlight of the story. Mordecai suggested to her in 4:14, "Who knoweth whether thou art come to the kingdom for such a time as this?" In other words, "You have attained your royal position as queen for a time like this to use your position and power and prestige to save your people." How often God may bless a person with opportunity for one reason —so he may use that opportunity for God.

How Haman's Plot Was Reversed (Esther 5:1—7:10)

The passage.—Risking the possibility that the king would not receive her and instead put her to death, Esther went before Ahasuerus uninvited. He did receive her graciously and promised to grant her any request she might make. She replied by requesting the king and wicked Haman to come to a banquet she had prepared (5:4). They did and Esther still did not make her desire known to the king but instead asked them both to return to a banquet the next day (5:8).

On his way home Haman, happy at being so royally entertained by the queen, passed Mordecai in the king's gate. When Mordecai refused to bow before him he was enraged, and upon the advice of his wife and his friends he resolved to put Mordecai to death the next day. A gallows 50 cubits high (about 83 feet) was built, and Haman planned to ask the king the next day for permission to hang Mordecai (5:14).

That night the king was unable to sleep, and instead of counting sheep he had a servant read to him from the book of records. It so happened that he read the account of how Mordecai saved the king's life by warning him of an assassination plot (2:23). Since no reward had been given to Mordecai, King Ahasuerus called in Haman, who happened to be outside his chambers, to ask his advice as to the best way to honor someone whom the king favored. Haman, selfishly assumed that the king planned to honor him and suggested the gaudy processional in 6:7–9.

Much to his surprise, the king then commanded Haman to extend the honor he had suggested to Mordecai, the Jew. Haman, perplexed and afraid, honored the man he had secretly planned to kill.

Now he was not so anxious to attend the queen's second banquet. At the dinner Esther exposed the entire plot against the Jews to the king. And in anger King Ahasuerus sentenced Haman to be hanged on the gallows he had built for Mordecai.

Special points.—Esther seems to have been reluctant to present her petition to the king (5:4,8). This was either because of fear or because of a desire to find just the right time for a favorable response to her request.

The gallows (5:14) may have been a type of stake on which the victim was impaled and lifted up in a crude form of crucifixion rather than hanging by a rope.

In 6:10 the question is raised, how did the king know Mordecai was a Jew. The answer is probably because the book of records included that fact in its account. King Ahasuerus evidently forgot that he had issued a decree to kill all Jews when he decided to honor Mordecai.

Truth for today.—There is a lesson in this section illustrating the truth that "pride goeth before a fall." Haman's childish and intemperate boasting reveals how impressed he was with himself. It has been said that God knew what he was doing in putting man's arms in front to make it difficult for him to pat himself on the back. But in spite of the difficulty, man seems at times quite able to do it. In a thousand ways he knows how to parade his virtues before others in his conversations as though he were leading them through a tour of his trophy room. Perhaps we need to learn the lesson of Haman. His sudden and dramatic and humiliating downfall illustrates the truth, "The first shall be last and the last first."

How the Jews Were Saved from Death (Esther 8:1—10:3)

The passage.—Mordecai was advanced to Haman's position by the king, and Esther pled with the king to reverse the edict calling for the annihilation of the Jews. The request was granted and a counter-edict was published giving the Jews permission to defend themselves and destroy their enemies who were planning to kill them and take their property (8:11).

Supported by the royal officials (9:3) the Jews inflicted a great defeat on their enemies especially in the city of Shushan where the Jews were given an extra day to carry out their revenge. A feast was then instituted under the name of Purim to celebrate their victory (9:21–23). Chapter 10 briefly relates the power and greatness of Mordecai who now was the hero of his people.

Special points.—Perhaps the major problem coming to our attention in this passage and in the entire book for that matter is the bloody vengeance of the Jews upon their enemies. Mordecai and Esther were certainly justified in doing what they could to save the Jews in Persia from the danger of an irrational and bloodthirsty foe. The motivation of self-defense is always acceptable. But it seems they went further than was necessary in the authorizing of the slaying of "little ones and women" (8:15–17). Some historians have estimated that as many as 75,000 people were killed by the Jews in Persia; in Shushan especially. Haman and his ten sons were all hanged publicly (9:13), and an additional day was granted for the slaying of their enemies there.

The account shows us something of the recklessness of human life and the lack of concern for personality that prevailed among the sovereigns of the most celebrated nations of the Eastern world. It must be remembered that the Jews of that day were prone to live under the rule of "an eye for an eye, and a tooth for a tooth." Even though they had also been taught "vengeance is mine saith the Lord," it was not until the coming of Christ and the teachings of the New Testament that this truth was effectively brought home to men.

One thing is clear—the Bible never covers up the weaknesses and sins of its heroes. Even though Esther was a person whom God used as an agent for a great purpose, she was not perfect and this passage reveals it plainly.

One other problem must be mentioned and that is the fact that the name of God in every form is entirely absent from the book. This may be because the writer having lived so long in Persia found his religious feelings and national patriotism dulled. On the other hand, he may have thought it safer to keep his feelings and opinions in the background as he wrote. A better answer is found in the fact that the observance of the Feast of Purim was one of noisy merrymaking. The author may have feared that the name of God in the passage when read at the feast might lead to irreverence. Whatever the reason for omitting his name, the tone and spirit of the book certainly give evidence of faith in the God of Abraham, Isaac, and Jacob.

JOB

Russell H. Dilday, Jr.

INTRODUCTION

The book of Job is a real-life drama written mostly in poetic form. It has been evaluated as one of the greatest books in literary history. Martin Luther called it "magnificent and sublime as no other book of Scripture." Alfred, Lord Tennyson spoke of it as the "greatest poem of ancient and modern times." Carlyle called it "the world's great book." The writer of the book of Job has been designated as "the Shakespeare of the Old Testament."

The author of the book is not named in the ancient manuscripts, and no clue as to his identity has been given by tradition. Whoever he was he takes a well-known historical character named Job, who lived probably in the patriarchal age and uses his experiences as the basis for his book. Job was a highly regarded personality in Jewish history. Ezekiel names him in chapter 14 of his prophecy, along with Noah and Daniel, as an example of a godly man. James refers to Job in chapter 5, verse 11. This is the only New Testament reference to him. There appear to be other references to a man named Job in certain nonbiblical traditions, but the only other information we have about him is found in this book that bears his name.

The first scene in the drama pictures Job in the land of Uz as a wealthy landowner with thousands of sheep, camels, oxen, and donkeys. He has a large family and has led them to worship Jehovah. Job is described as "blameless and upright, one who feared God" (1:1).

The next scene takes place in heaven where the servants of God come to report their work. One of the officials called "the satan" suggests that Job is good only because God has rewarded him with wealth. And so permission is granted to test Job by a series of disasters which take away his possessions and his family. Job continues to be faithful and blameless. "The satan" then suggests that Job's sufferings have not gone deep enough; that Job himself must be attacked. And so a painful and loathsome sickness falls on Job and he becomes an outcast but still refuses to blame Jehovah.

The scene changes next to an ash heap where three friends of Job: Eliphaz, Bildad, and Zophar, find him and come to "comfort him." There follows then a series of dialogues between Job and his friends which make up the bulk of the book. Following the dialogues, Jehovah appears and speaks, and Job submits to him in repentance. Finally Job is vindicated and his losses are restored twofold.

The purpose of the book of Job is to discuss the problem of suffering. Why do the righteous suffer? The traditional Jewish explanation was that all suffering was due to and proportionate to sin. The book of Job challenges that concept by describing the intellectual struggles and the spiritual agonies of a man who suffered miserably and who tried to harmonize his experiences with his belief in an all-powerful, all-wise, all-loving God.

Two of the important answers the book of Job gives to the problem of suffering are: (1) Suffering may come to good men as a trial or test to demonstrate, strengthen, and establish their faith. (2) The ultimate answer to suffering is hidden in the wisdom of an all-powerful God. To know this God in a personal way is enough. Job cried for an audience with God to argue his case. But when God appeared and Job saw his majesty and glory he ceased to be bothered by the problem of suffering. In the presence of God his complaints all vanished away and only God was left. There were no more doubts as to God's reality and power and goodness. It is as though Job, who was looking for an answer, now in the presence of God is satisfied just to know there is an answer. This appears to be the ultimate message of the book of Job in regard to the problem of suffering.

Satan's Effort to Make Job Curse God (Job 1:1—2:13)

The passage.—The prose introduction describes Job's life as perfect and ideal. He was wealthy, having seven thousand sheep, three thousand camels, five hundred teams of oxen, five hundred she-asses, and very many servants. He had seven sons and three daughters (perfect numbers) who loved each other and for whom Job prayed continually (1:5). He was a godly man, blameless, upright, fearing God and turning away from evil (v. 1).

In heaven one of God's special messengers questions the sincerity of Job's faith and piety. He suggests that Job serves God only because God blesses him and that if he lost everything he would curse God. And so God permits Satan to try Job's faith within certain limitations (v. 12).

A terrible series of catastrophes begins to fall upon Job, all in one day, and all in the day he was praying and sanctifying his children. First, a messenger appears to tell how an Arab tribe called the Sabeans attacked Job's herdsmen. They killed his servants and took away his oxen and she-asses. "While he was yet speaking" another servant comes to tell how lightning had annihilated his flock of sheep and their keepers. In sequence, a third servant appears with the news that the Chaldeans had stolen his camels. And fourth and most severe was the news of the death of all his children in a windstorm. In spite of these breathtaking calamities, Job "did not sin or charge God with wrong" (v. 22).

Job's second great trial came about when Satan suggested that the test had not been severe enough and Job's life itself must be threatened. Again permission was granted within limitations (2:6), and a loathsome disease (probably a form of leprosy) afflicted Job from head to foot. In spite of this and in spite of his wife's suggestion that he "curse God and die" Job did not sin with his lips (v. 10).

We are next introduced to three of Job's friends who come to see him to "mourn with him and comfort him." First is Eliphaz, the Temanite. He is the oldest of the three, kindly, pious, relying on mystical revelations as his source of truth. Next is Bildad, the Shuhite. He is less sympathetic, depends on ancient authority as his source of truth. Next is Zophar, the Naamathite. He is the youngest and relies on neither revelation or ancient tradition. He, himself, knows all he needs to know and can state the truth with absolute dogmatism. They sit down with Job and begin the long dialogue that makes up the majority of the book.

Special points.—Job's wealth is described by implication (1:3). The seven thousand sheep would imply the ownership of large tracks of pasture land. The camels were used for trade and suggest that Job was a merchant. The oxen were used to till the soil, suggesting that some of Job's lands were cultivated and that he was an agriculturalist. The she-asses were useful because of their milk. Job was a dairyman too. All of these combined support the scriptural claim that Job was the greatest man in all the East.

How could Job offer sacrifices to atone for his children's sin (v. 5)? According to the patriarchal customs in Job's day, the father served as the priest for the family. Job's sacrifice was a burnt offering given as an atonement for the sins of his family. This sacrificial practice within the Jewish family was the background for the complicated sacrificial system to be developed in the Jewish nation later.

The "sons of God" who presented themselves before the Lord (v. 6) were probably angelic beings. These were special messengers created by God to form the council of heaven and carry out his bidding in specific assignments.

The word "satan" in this passage is always used with the article, "the satan," indicating that the word was not being used as a proper name. The word means "the adversary." The satan here is described as one of God's messengers whose duty it was to discover whether good men were really good and to bring the guilty ones before Jehovah for judgment. He is not described as the leader of the forces of evil but rather as a divine "attorney general" who prosecutes men before God in judgment. His power was limited only to those actions God gave him permission to take.

Truth for today.—This passage teaches that often suffering comes as a test or a trial. The test is not to prove to God that a man's faith is genuine. He knows that because of his omniscience. But suffering may be the occasion to demonstrate genuine faith in a convincing manner to other people. When an individual faces suffering with courage and optimism and faith as Job did, his experience will prove the genuineness of his faith. Job's refusal to curse God or "sin with his lips" proves that man with the help of God is capable of real and unselfish goodness and can love God just for God's sake alone, without the bribery of rewards.

Job's Cry for Death (Job 3:1–26)

The passage.—Those who think of Job as an example of great patience have apparently overlooked this chapter. For here Job loses his composure and his self-control and breaks out into a passionate cry for death. His lament, which begins the poetry section of the book, is neatly divided into three parts:

(1) I wish I had never been born (3:1–10).

(2) I wish I had died at birth (3:11–19).

(3) I wish I could die now (3:20–26).

"I wish I had never been born" (3:1–10). With his wailing lament Job curses the night he was conceived (3:3,6–10). He wishes that the night he was conceived would continue forever without ever breaking into the dawn of a new day. He also curses the day he was born (vv. 3–5). He wishes that the day might be swallowed up in darkness and that his birthdate might be erased from the calendar (v. 6). He despises the very idea of a birthday celebration (v. 7).

"I wish I had died at birth" (vv. 11–19). With this cry Job turns to the next possibility. "If I had to be born, then

why couldn't I have died immediately?"
In this way he would have escaped all
of his sorrow and would have been at
peace (v. 13). As his mind dwells on the
fascinating idea of the calmness of
death, he names over the variety of
people who have found rest there: kings
and princes, slaves and prisoners, great
and small (vv. 14–19).

"I wish I could die now" (vv. 20–26).
Now Job's anguish and impatience intensify. He complains that it is unfair
for God to give life to anyone who is
bitter and who wants to die (vv. 20–21).
Then more specifically he asks, "Why
does God give life to one single individual whose life is hidden and hedged
in by suffering?" (v. 23). This of course
is a reference to himself.

Job's three friends have sat quietly
with him in mourning for seven days.
Now suddenly Job has broken the silence with this speech of bitter and
violent complaint against God. Job who
had "sinned not with his lips" now un-
leashes a torrid and impatient tirade
against God. His friends are shocked
at his tone of mind and the debate
about Job's attitude begins.

Special points.—The blackness Job
wishes would obscure the day of his
birth (v. 4) probably refers to sun
eclipses or sandstorms. In other words
he wishes that his birthday each year
might be obscured by frightening omens
and dark forebodings.

In verse 8 "the mourning" should be
"the leviathan." This is noted in the
margin of the King James Version. The
leviathan was the snake-monster of
ancient mythology who could swallow
up the sun and cause an eclipse. The
verse seems to be saying then, "Let
those who can, curse the day and release some monster to blot out the sun."

In verse 12 the translation should
read, "Why did the knees receive me?"
and refers either to the mother's knees
or the knees of the father on whose lap
the newborn baby would be placed.

Truth for today.—Job's speech seems
to blame God for all that has happened
to him, when in fact the first chapters
have explained that satan was the one
who touched Job with suffering. God
only permitted satan with certain limitations to bring the tragedies.

Today when a terrible tragedy occurs, it is often said, "This is God's
will," as though God were to blame for
the experience. Job's suffering is a reminder to us not to blame God for
everything that happens to us. It might
be that the automobile accident was
caused by a drunken driver who violated the will of God. It might be that
the heart attack came because of a
driving greed and ambition for material
wealth which was not God's will at all.
It might be that the employee was fired
because he failed to carry out his duties
which had nothing to do with the
providence of God. In each of these
cases to blame God or to say, "This is
God's will," would be to make the same
mistake Job made in chapter 3.

Eliphaz's First Speech (Job 4:1—5:27)

The passage.—This beautifully constructed speech by Eliphaz is made up
of three suggestions to Job:

(1) Why don't you practice what you
preach (4:1–11)?

(2) How can anyone be right who
complains to God like you do
(4:12—5:7)?

(3) Why don't you rejoice since God
through suffering is only trying
to help you (5:8–27)?

Eliphaz wonders why Job could forget all the good things he has said to
comfort others in their trouble (4:3–5).
He wonders how Job can be so impatient and despondent when he has

been so skilful in explaining suffering to his friends. "After all everyone knows that only sinful men suffer and God always blesses good men" (vv. 7–8). The traditional Jewish explanation for suffering comes out here; that is, that all suffering is result of sin; and that if Job is a righteous man, then his suffering will not bother him. This offers little help to Job in his misery.

In the second part of his speech Eliphaz warns Job against the danger of complaining to God. In a dream Eliphaz has heard of a voice saying, "Can mortal man be more just than God?" (v. 17). "What right do you have, being a man, to complain to God," is the essence of his comment. There is very little comfort for Job in this part of the speech either.

The last part of the speech of Eliphaz is a suggestion. "If I were you, Job, I would stop complaining and trust God in humility for his help" (5:8). This is a reminder to Job that if he is a righteous man, then he should rejoice in his suffering because it opens the way to richer blessings from the Creator (vv. 17–27).

Special points.—The destruction of the wicked is likened in chapter 5, verses 10 and 11, to the breaking up and destruction of a den of lions. It is interesting to notice that there are five different Hebrew words for "lion" used in these two verses: lion, roaring lion (fierce lion), young lion, strong lion (old lion), and lioness. The parallel of this picture of destruction is in the breaking up of the home of the wicked described in 5:2–5.

In 4:19, "houses of clay" refers to the earthly bodies of men made of dust and standing upon dust. The phrase "crushed before moth" means that man's earthly life is as fragile and as easily destroyed as a moth when it is crushed.

In 5:5, the word "saint" literally means "holy ones" and probably refers to angels.

The numbers "six" and "seven" in 5:19, are round numbers symbolizing completeness. The idea is that God shall deliver in "many troubles" or in "all troubles." Notice that God's care of the righteous here is promised in three dimensions:

(1) He shall bless his own person (5:18–23).
(2) He shall bless his possessions (5:24).
(3) He shall bless his posterity (5:25–26).

Job's Reply (Job 6:1—7:21)

The passage.—Eliphaz has indirectly implied that Job is to blame for being impatient and complaining. He has used against Job such words as "confounded," "impatient," "passion," "fool," "godless man." All of these critical implications have wounded Job deeply. His reply is that of an innocent man who cannot believe what his friend is inferring about him. Job in this speech is defending the harshness of his complaint and despair as being justified.

First, he compares his complaints over against his calamities, and he claims that his troubles are far heavier than his cries of impatience (6:1–4). In other words, his complaints are not out of proportion to his sufferings. Next he argues that as friends they should have taken the position that his complaints proved he must really be suffering unjustly. For every effect there must be a cause. Job reminds them that this is what they would have decided if they had heard a dumb animal crying out (vv. 5–7). Job's defensive attitude of impatience quickly drives him to cry out again for death (vv. 8–13).

Job had freely expressed to his friends in chapter 3 his miserable state expecting them to sympathize and reinforce him. Instead he is disappointed that they came to him with accusations and rebukes (vv. 14–21). He says, "If I had come to you asking for a hand-out or a loan or asking you to risk your lives for me, then I could understand your being afraid. But I only came asking for sympathy" (vv. 22–23).

Finally, his speech throws down a challenge to the three friends. If they are accusing him of sin, if they believe he is not justified in his complaints, if they believe he has no right to speak because he is a sinner, then let them name his sins. What has he done to deserve this suffering? (vv. 24–30).

Chapter 7 is a repetition of his complaint about life in general. This is Job's terrible indictment of God's dealing with man. Life, he says, is too short and too evil to have come from a God who is all-wise and just (7:1–10). Even the God-given ability to feel misery is itself an added misery of life (vv. 11–21).

Special points.—In verse 29 the phrase "return, I pray you," appears to mean, "adopt another course," that is, "Proceed on to some other argument than that of my guiltiness and try to find another explanation of my calamities."

In 7:2, the shadow which the servant earnestly desires probably refers to the shade of a tree. A slave in the heat of the day under difficult labor yearns for the shadow of the evening or the shade of a beautiful tree. In verse 9, "the grave" refers not so much to the place of burial as it does to the general abode of the dead. It is even possible to substitute the word death for grave and retain the same meaning here. In verse 12, Job is speaking with irony as he says, "Is a man like me a sea monster or a part of the ocean that he must be watched and subdued with plagues lest he prove dangerous to the universe?"

In verse 19, the phrase "till I swallow down my spittle" was a proverbial phrase used in the early days, like our phrase "the twinkling of an eye." It signified just the passing of a moment. What he is asking here is that he would be let alone for just a brief time.

Bildad's First Speech (Job 8:1–22)

The passage.—Bildad has listened to Job's answer to Eliphaz and is particularly offended by Job's complaint against God. He believes that Job has been in error questioning the wisdom and the goodness of God. Therefore, Bildad begins his speech with a defense of the goodness of God (vv. 1–7). God's goodness is reflected in two unalterable precepts: "those who suffer must have sinned" (v. 4) and "those who are rewarded must have been righteous" (v. 6).

Then he turns to another point in Job's defense that he considers improper. That is Job's assertion that all men are oppressed under an unfair burden of suffering. In answer to this Bildad refers to the great wisdom of ancient men which refutes Job's claim (vv. 8–19). Bildad uses the picturesque language of the ancient philosophers to show that righteous men never suffer and that the wicked are always punished (vv. 11–13).

He ends his speech with the prediction that if Job is righteous, God will eventually restore him and reward him for his goodness (vv. 20–22).

Special points.—In verse 4, Bildad says "if thy children have sinned." He obviously believes that they have, and the verse really means "*since* thy children have sinned, God has cast them away for their transgressions."

The "rush" in verse 11 is probably the papyrus plant of Egypt which often grows to twice the height of a man. The "flag" is the "Nile-reed." The ancient wisdom referred to in this verse therefore must have come from Egyptian philosophers.

In verse 22, Bildad is defending himself and his friends as Job's helpers. They are not his enemies as he seems to assume. They have come to comfort him.

Job's Reply to Bildad (Job 9:1—10:22)

The passage.—Job's reply is not a carefully organized speech. It is rather a passionate, hurried outburst filled with indignation and despair. Instead of comforting him, Bildad has only aroused his desire to intensify his complaint.

First, Job argues, "How can man defend his innocence before God when God's might and majesty prevent man from approaching God?" Job believes that God's unapproachable might is like an earthquake that moves mountains (9:5–6). It is like an eclipse that blots out the sun (v. 7). His power created the stars and keeps them in the heavens (vv. 7–9). His ways are beyond man's understanding (v. 10). He destroys the innocent and the guilty alike (vv. 21–23). In the light of all of this Job sees no hope in being able to come before God and declare his defense.

Job regains his composure again, and in chapter 9, verse 25 and following, he proceeds more calmly to speak of his own condition as an example of the mistreatment that all men everywhere receive. Life is brief (vv. 25–26). Life is vain (vv. 27–31). Next Job repeats the complaint that God is not a man and therefore no man can approach him and plead his case (vv. 32–35).

In chapter 10, Job tries to discover some secret in God's mind that would explain why he has afflicted such terrible suffering upon him. Several guesses are proposed as to why this may have happened.

(1) Does God enjoy punishing the innocent and smiling upon the wicked? (v. 3).

(2) Is God blind, or does he have difficulty seeing correctly so that he mistakes the guilty for the innocent? (v. 4).

(3) Is God so limited in time that he is afraid his victim will escape before there is an opportunity to finish his punishment? (vv. 5–6).

(4) Could it be that God created Job just so he could punish him? (vv. 8–17). Job is overcome by the contradictions in such an argument. Why would God who created him by his own hands now use his hands to suddenly crush him into dust again? Why would God so graciously guide and protect him in past years and now suddenly turn against him?

Job's speech ends with another pathetic cry for death and a dreary description of the land of darkness that must be waiting for him beyond the grave (vv. 18–22).

Special points.—The names in 9:9, are constellations of stars probably denoting the "Big Dipper," "Orion," and the "Seven Stars."

The phrase in verse 13, "the proud helpers do stoop," should be translated "the helpers of Rahab did stoop." Rahab was a name given to the sea monster of ancient mythology.

Job is saying, "Even the powerful sea monster and his helpers could not stand up against God. How then can I being a mere man hope to approach him?"

The "post" in verse 25 is a messenger or a courier speeding to deliver his message. Life goes by with the same speed.

The "swift ships" in 9:26 refers to

the two-man skiffs made of bulrushes or reeds. They were lightweight and therefore very swift.

In verse 30 the "daysman" was an arbiter, a mediator, or an umpire.

In 10:5–6 Job wonders if God's life is limited in time like a man's life is so that he has to hurry up his efforts at punishing Job lest he run out of time.

Truth for today.—Job expresses the universal need of man for a mediator between himself and God (9:32–33). He knows he is separated from God by a great gulf. God is perfect; man is imperfect. God is unlimited; man is limited. God is all-powerful; man is weak. Man cannot approach God. He needs someone who will intercede for him. He needs an umpire or a mediator who can "lay his hands on us both" (v. 33) bringing man and God together.

This is exactly the reason God sent his Son. Jesus is described as "the one mediator between man and God" (1 Tim. 2:5). Jesus has entered "heaven itself to appear in the presence of God for us" (Heb. 9:24). John says, "If any man sin, we have an advocate with the father, Jesus Christ the righteous, and he is the propitiation for our sins" (1 John 2:1–2). How Job would have rejoiced to hear these words in his day.

His pathetic description of death in 10:21–22, as "the land of darkness without any order where even the light is darkness" cries out for the eternal life promised through faith in Jesus Christ. How Job would have rejoiced to know that God sent his only begotten Son that whosoever believeth on him shall not perish but have everlasting life.

Zophar's First Speech (Job 11:1–20)

The passage.—In his first reply Job has not emphasized his innocence. He has merely claimed that his suffering is out of proportion to his sin. But in his reply to Bildad, Job has vehemently denied any guilt and Zophar turns to that denial as the basis for his argument. Job may be unaware of any sin he has committed, but God knows he has sinned and will remind Job about his failures. Zophar points out to Job that if God did speak to him as he seems to wish him to do, he would declare Job's sins (vv. 5–6). Zophar declares that God's infinite wisdom detects man's hidden sins and he sends sudden calamities like those Job is suffering as a punishment (vv. 7–12).

He ends his speech by calling upon Job to repent, put away his evil, and then prosperity and happiness will come to him again (vv. 13–20).

Special points.—In verse 3, "lies" refers to Job's boasting claims of innocence. Zophar is saying, "How can I keep quiet in the presence of such exaggeration?"

Job has claimed his suffering is not proportionate to his sin. However, in verse 6 Zophar claims the opposite. God has sent less suffering than Job deserves.

Verse 12 may be translated "a vain man can just as easily become a wise man as a wild ass's colt can become a man."

The phrase "many shall make suit unto thee" (v. 19) means literally "many shall stroke thy face"; that is, "many will flatter or praise thee."

Truth for today.—While the speech is insensitive and cruel, and application of it is painful to Job, Zophar's condemnation of man's pride (vv. 7–12) is justified and needs to be repeated today. Those who declare today that God is dead or who create self-made ideas of God to suit their own fancies need to understand that the human mind is too limited to grasp the fulness of God. God is "higher than the heavens, deeper than hell, longer than the earth, and broader than the sea" (vv. 7–9). A black preacher summed up this warning against human pride by saying, "Man's arm is too short to box with God."

Job's Reply to Zophar (Job 12:1—14:22)

The passage.—Job is angry at his friends now and for the first time he turns on them in earnest. His reply is full of sarcasm as he denies their claim to be superior to him. "You really think you are something, don't you?" (12:2). "You think all wisdom will die when you die" (v. 2). "Do you think you are the only ones who know these things?" (v. 3). "Even the beasts of the field and the fowls of the air and the fish of the sea and even the ground could teach you a thing or two" (vv. 7–9). "You are physicians of no value" (13:4). "Your best demonstration of wisdom would be to hold your tongues" (v. 5). Job reminds them that they, too, stand under the same severe judgment as he does and that they should beware lest it fall upon them. This speech of Job's is divided into three major sections.

(1) Job claims to know far more about the wisdom and power of God in the world than they do (chap. 12).

(2) God's wisdom and power do not explain his sufferings. Job still desires to meet God and declare to him in person his innocence. He wants to hear God himself explain why the suffering has come (chap. 13).

(3) The mystery of his suffering overwhelms him and again Job sinks back into a sorrowful description of the wretchedness of man and his inevitable death. The despair of Job is interrupted at one bright point as he wonders about the possibility of life after death (chap. 14).

Special points.—Verse 14 in chapter 12 is better understood if the word "city" is inserted after "breaketh down."

In 13:7–8 Job accuses his friends of taking God's side just because he is God, without any regard to the circumstances or without even trying to understand Job's side.

Verses 14–15 are difficult to understand. Verse 14 probably means "why should I make such a strenuous effort to preserve my life when God intends to destroy it after all?" Verse 15 is translated by Moffat to read, "He may kill me—what else can I expect? But I will maintain my innocence to his face." These verses have generally been interpreted to support the idea of Job's patience. However, it appears that Job's patience has come to an end and he once more is flinging his case into the presence of God.

Job likens God's dealings with him as an imprisonment (vv. 27–28). "Thou settest a print upon the heels of my feet" means "Thou drawest a line around the soles of my feet." In other words, God rigidly controls his movements, even marking out the steps he can take.

"As the waters fail from the sea" (14:11) probably refers to evaporation. "The flood" refers to a stream of water.

Job believes that when man dies his death is forever. He will never be raised out of his sleep (v. 12). He will continue to be held in the shadowy, dreamy half-world of the dead which the Hebrews called Sheol. The word "Sheol" is generally translated "grave" in the book of Job.

In verse 17 Job sees God as carefully treasuring up man's sins in a bag so that none of them will be lost when he brings judgment against them.

Truth for today.—In this passage Job hints at the idea of life after death (v. 14). It is only a hint, for the idea of immortality was not very strong among early Old Testament writers. There is no concept in the Old Testament of man's possessing immortality as a natural part of his human nature. The idea of natural immortality comes from Greek philosophy and not Scripture. The Bible instead teaches that if man is to live after death, it will be only because God chooses to keep him alive and gives him eternal life as a gift of his grace. Man cannot claim immortality as an innate part of his make-up. He can only trust God for life beyond the grave.

Job, in this passage, catches just a glimpse of the glorious truth that comes to full light in the New Testament. It is Paul who later is able to declare with positive assurance, "The gift of God is eternal life through Jesus Christ our Lord" (Rom. 6:23).

Job's yearning question, "If a man die, shall he continue to live?" is his way of saying that if there were life after death, it would help him to understand and to explain his sufferings. Job could stand the torment in this life if he knew there would be a better life to come. This is the same thing that encouraged Paul to say, "For I reckon that the sufferings of this present time are not worthy to be compared with the glory which shall be revealed in us" (Rom. 8:18). "For we know that if our earthly house of this tabernacle were dissolved we have a building of God, an house not made with hands, eternal in the heavens" (2 Cor. 5:1).

Eliphaz's Second Speech and Job's Reply (Job 15:1—17:16)

The passage.—The second cycle of speeches between Job and his friends begins in chapter 15. The debate in the first three speeches centered around God and his wisdom and justice. But now the theme shifts. Job's three friends are shocked at his irreverence toward

God and his unkind sarcasm against them. They are more and more convinced as they hear him speak that Job must indeed be very wicked. They suspect that he has been cleverly concealing his sins through the years and that now God is finally punishing him. And so the speeches in this second cycle turn to the theme of the fate of the wicked under the providence of God. Eliphaz is the first to speak again.

Eliphaz, who is the oldest of the three, begins his speech by rebuking Job's unkind treatment of his friends. He rejects Job's claim to be wiser than they are. And he rebukes Job's irreverence before God. Job proves he is not wise when he argues with such loud and empty words (vv. 2–3). Eliphaz believes that such arguments can come only from a very wicked man (v. 46). Eliphaz then begins to return the sarcasm Job has leveled at them by asking, "Do you think you were the first man ever born?" "Do you have a private line of communication with the Almighty?" (vv. 7–9). "After all, some of us are old enough to be your father; who are you to try to teach us?" (v. 10). Then Eliphaz instructs Job in the doctrine that all evil men who disregard God will inevitably be punished (vv. 17–35).

Job's reply is given in chapters 16 and 17. He is disappointed that his friends have taken his complaints as a proof of his guilt instead of his innocence. Now Job who has been hurt by the feeling that God has turned against him feels the added pain of knowing his friends have turned against him too. There is nothing left for Job but his own sense of his innocence. And he clings to that tenaciously in his reply to Eliphaz. The reply has four sections:

(1) Job rejects the speeches of his friends as monotonous and empty (16:1–5).

(2) He reviews his loneliness as both God and man have deserted him (16:6–17).

(3) He expects to die under this false accusation and be numbered as a transgressor. But his innocent blood will cry out for vindication. He still believes somehow that the justice of God will prevail and prove his innocence even after his death (16:18—17:9).

(4) Even though his friends have predicted that if he repent, God will heal and restore him, Job renews his belief that he will die and that his only hope is in the grave (17:10–16).

Special points.—Verse 4 in chapter 15 means "you are doing away with reverence before God and you are hindering worship and prayer."

In verse 12, chapter 15, Eliphaz is asking, "Why do you get so excited and why do your eyes blink and flash in anger?"

Verse 26 in chapter 15 describes the wicked man's assault upon God. "He runs upon God with a stiff neck, with the thick bosses of his shield." The "bosses" were the thick, curved side of the shield carried by the warriors. It was the convex side of the shield always turned toward the enemy.

Compare 15:27, with Psalm 73:7. "Fatness" in the Old Testament is often used as a symbol of undisciplined pride, which makes a man insensitive to the Spirit of God.

Moffat translates the last clause of chapter 15, verse 30, "His fruit is whirled off by the wind." This is a desolate picture of the destruction of the wicked.

In 16:12–13, Job sees himself as the target for God's archers. He has become the "bull's-eye" for every sharp arrow of suffering. The arrows strike the vital parts of his body and pour out his life upon the ground ("reins" is the

word for kidney).

In verse 16 of chapter 16 the word "foul" means "inflamed" or "red." It pictures a man's face which has become swollen and red from excessive weeping.

Chapter 17, verse 3, Job refers to a custom in his day of guaranteeing an arrangement or promise by "striking hands." This same custom is referred to in Proverbs 6:1, 11:15, 17:18. Job is calling for God to give his pledge or his promise by "striking hands" with him as a guarantee that he will be vindicated.

Truth for today.—One of the high points in the book of Job is reached in Job's statement, "The righteous shall hold on, and he that hath clean hands shall become stronger and stronger" (17:9). This is a courageous insight into the problem of innocent suffering. The righteous man will not be misled by the mysteries he sees in the world around him which he cannot understand. He will cling to his righteous life in spite of the mysteries. He will not be good just because it pays to be good. (This was Satan's accusation against Job.) In fact, Job says that the wrongs and the injustices which he sees in the world around him will make the inner joy and peace of the righteous man deeper and more valuable. Therefore, instead of faltering he becomes stronger and stronger. There is a high moral grandeur in the resolution of the righteous man to hold on to the right in spite of the cost.

Bildad's Second Speech and Job's Reply (Job 18:1—19:29)

The passage.—Bildad like Eliphaz points his second speech to the theme of the destruction of the wicked. His speech differs from Eliphaz in that he sees this destruction coming from outside man. It comes from nature itself which rises up against the sinner. Eliphaz on the other hand sees the sinner's punishment coming from within him, through his own conscience. Bildad like Eliphaz rebukes Job for his harsh criticism of his friends. He has called them annoying comforters (16:2), scorners (v. 20), mockers (17:2), and blind, ignorant advisers (vv. 4–10). It appears to Bildad that Job thinks of his friends as unclean beasts (18:2–3).

He also is angry at Job for his irreverent accusation of God, saying that God has torn him in his anger (16:9). Bildad tells Job it is not God who tears him in his anger but rather in his uncontrolled fury against God, Job is tearing himself (18:4).

Bildad then uses a variety of graphic figures of speech to describe the downfall of the wicked. While he is talking about sinners in general, it is obvious that he has Job in mind and is suggesting that Job's sufferings are those of a sinful man who is being punished by God. (1) The sinner's light will go out (vv. 5–7). (2) He will be trapped by his own errors (vv. 8–11). (3) Destruction will devour him like a wild animal (vv. 12–14). (4) His race and name will become extinct (vv. 15–17). (5) Bystanders will be astounded by his fate (vv. 18–21).

In answer to Bildad, Job recognizes that his description of the wicked is a direct reference to Job himself. The disease that "devours his skin" (v. 13) obviously points to Job's own painful disease. The "fire that burns up the sinner's home" (v. 15) must refer to Job's houses which were burned up by lightning. Job takes Bildad's speech personally. He hears Bildad saying that his suffering must be a sign that he is a sinner.

In this second reply to Bildad, Job adds nothing new to the argument. He repeats the dark description of desertion, alienation, and hopelessness which he feels (19:1–22). He turns his eyes to the future and hopes that somehow God will vindicate him before generations yet to come (18:23–27). In these verses the message of Job reaches another high point in courageous faith in a God who will justify righteous men. Job then ends his speech with a guarded threat that the judgment of God may also fall like a sword upon his friends (vv. 28–29).

Special points.—"Mark" in chapter 18, verse 2 means "act with wisdom" or "listen and understand."

"The grin" (18:9) is a word for a hunter's trap that bares its teeth like a "grinning fiend" ready to snap around the victim's heel when he sets it off.

In chapter 18, verse 13, the figure is used "firstborn of death." The firstborn in a family was always honored as the leader, the strongest, the most important member of the family. Bildad uses it here to mean "the strongest child of death" or "the very deadliest death." The "king of terrors" in 18:14, is another name for death.

The "ten times" in 19:3 is a figure of speech meaning "as much as possible."

In verse 20 "the skin of my teeth" refers to the gums around the teeth. Job is saying that the only part of his body not affected by his disease is this skin around his teeth. In other words he has barely escaped total destruction by disease.

Job wants his case written down permanently so that others in years to come might read it and sympathize with him. He knows however that regular methods of writing are temporary and perishable, and so he desires that his words be indelibly carved into rock with a chisel and that the chiseled-out letters be filled with lead to make them permanent (19:23–24).

The "redeemer" in chapter 19, verse 25, is a word (*goel*) meaning a close relative who takes care of a man's property and his good name after his death. The redeemer or goel would avenge a man's blood if he were unjustly slain. Job says, "God is my redeemer" (goel).

"Yet in my flesh shall I see God" (v. 26). The word "in" also means "from" or "out of" as the margin of the King James translation points out. The passage then can also be translated "*without my flesh I shall see God.*"

Truth for today.—The great climax of the book of Job comes in this passage as Job asserts his faith in God who will vindicate him even after death. Men may desert him. His family may fail him. But God never will. The faith of Job seems even stronger when it is noted there was very little hope of life after death among the Hebrews at this time.

Job doesn't understand how it can be, but he is certain that if his body is buried and the worms destroy it, he will still remain alive; he will see God and be vindicated. Job knows that since God is just, there must be a reward beyond the grave. The nature of that reward is not thoroughly described until the New Testament. But it was enough for Job just to know it would come and that he would be there in person to receive it. While Job still cannot understand the injustices he experiences in this life, he clings nevertheless to this faith in a God who has the last word even after death.

Zophar's Second Speech and Job's Reply (Job 20:1—21:34)

The passage.—Zophar is angry. Job treated his first speech with sarcasm. He has threatened him and his friends with the sword of judgment (19:29) and now in his reply to Bildad, Job has condemned God for deserting him and at the same time praised God for being his redeemer after death. Zophar cannot remain silent any longer in the presence of such bitterness and inconsistency. He seems to interrupt Job's reply with his passionate second speech.

Zophar says that the prosperity of the wicked is only temporary and the sweetness of sin soon turns sour (20:1–14). Man's hunger for sin will quickly be satisfied and he will become sick of it all (vv. 15–29). The picture Zophar paints here is that of a rich man of power who is suddenly brought down to poverty and weakness. Zophar is very blunt. He is saying to Job in this speech, "Thou art the man."

In response Job denies Zophar's philosophy. It is sometimes true that the wicked are destroyed by their sin but not always. Job's experience has caused him to doubt the popular Jewish answer that "all sinners suffer and all righteous men prosper." Job has seen wicked men prosper, have children, and die in peace (21:6–16). At other times he has seen the wicked destroyed (vv. 17–21). The facts of life therefore prove that there is no set pattern that can allow Zophar to make such a generalization. Wicked men do not always suffer. And good men do not always prosper.

Job reminds Zophar that he and his friends must not impose their petty principles upon God or quote their cheap philosophies so easily. Do they think they are wiser than God? (vv. 22–34).

Special points.—The "organ" referred to in 21:12 is a musical instrument called the "pipe" which is played like a flute.

In verse 4 Job calls himself "impatient" (RSV). This contradicts the usual idea of Job as the symbol of patience. James 5:11 speaks of the "patience" of Job. But there patience means "endurance." Job can hardly be described as a patient man when he throws his complaints so forcefully against man and God. But he did endure and he never gave up until he found God's purpose in it all. Job can more accurately be described as the symbol of endurance rather than the symbol of patience.

In verse 32 Job describes the honorable burial of the wicked. These verses may be translated, "And he is carried to the grave and they keep watch over his tomb. The clods of the valley are sweet unto him and all men draw after him as there are innumerable before him." Job is saying that the wicked man often has a beautiful funeral. Innumerable memorials are placed before his grave and other men imitate him as a high example after his death. This is another illustration proving Zophar's argument is wrong.

Eliphaz's Third Speech and Job's Reply (Job 22:1—24:25)

The passage.—The theme of the first cycle of speeches was "the nature of God." The theme of the second cycle of speeches was "the fate of wicked men." This last cycle of speeches turns from these broad subjects to speak specifically about "the sinfulness of Job." What his friends had only hinted at before is now expressed openly. They begin to charge Job directly with sin.

Eliphaz is the first to speak. He suggests that the cause of Job's sufferings should not be sought in God or his treatment to men. After all it is no loss to God if a man sins, and it is no profit to God if he is righteous. The reason behind man's suffering must be sought in man himself. It is inconceivable that God would punish a man be-

cause he is good, and so therefore a man's suffering must be directly related to his own sin (22:1–4).

With pointed, direct accusation Eliphaz begins to name the sins Job must be guilty of committing: inhumanity, avarice, abuse of power, oppression of the poor, injustice (vv. 6–10). Did Job think he could hide these sins from God? Did he think God was so far away in heaven that he didn't see? (vv. 12–20). Eliphaz's speech concludes with an exhortation to Job to reconcile himself to God. If he will, then God will bless Job again (vv. 21–30).

Job seems to be too overwhelmed by the mystery of God's providence to defend himself against Eliphaz's charges. The injustices and the cruel wrongs that go unpunished in the world, the misery of the innocent, the happy lives of the wicked—all these seem to indicate that God no longer is in control of the world (24:1,12). A part of the injustice Job sees is his own personal suffering. Job longs again for the opportunity to find God and argue his case before the judgment seat (23:1–12). Another part of the injustice he sees is in the lives of humanity in general. Job lists at length the sins of the wicked which he believes cry out for punishment. But God seems to overlook them (24:3–12). In fact, it appears to Job that at times the wicked are even helped by God, protected by God, and brought at last by God to a peaceful death "like all others" (vv. 13–25).

Special points.—The "arms of the fatherless" in chapter 22, verse 9, are the rights and the means of support which sustain the orphans. Job is accused here of taking away what little support the orphans may have.

In chapter 24, verse 3, Job mentions "the ass" and "the ox" of the orphan and the widow. The implication is that these are the only animals they have by which to work their small fields and provide food for their families. Without these they are completely impoverished. Job has seen wicked men who were guilty of such oppression that seemingly were never punished.

The robbers in chapter 24, verse 16, "dig through houses." The houses in Job's day were made of an adobe-like clay or soft brick. In order to break in a thief would literally dig himself an entrance in a wall of the house.

Truth for today.—Eliphaz makes the mistake of assuming that there could be no such thing as a personal relationship between God and man. "Can a man be profitable unto God? Is it any pleasure to the Almighty that thou art righteous? Or is it gain to him that thou makest thy ways perfect? Will he enter with thee into judgment?" (22:2–4). Eliphaz here is declaring God's holiness, his "otherness," but he makes no mention of God's immanence, his closeness. He cannot imagine God coming down to man in condescending love. Neither can he imagine man being able to approach God with a feeling that he will be personally accepted.

It was to correct this misconception that God became man in Jesus Christ. The God whom all the world had thought of as a distant, unapproachable Creator, through Christ became "bone of our bone and flesh of our flesh." It is through the incarnation of Christ that God became known as "Immanuel—God with us." He revealed himself as a God who will enter with us into judgment and take pleasure in our righteousness.

Job cries out, "Oh, that I knew where I might find him, that I might come even to his seat. I would order my cause before him." He has searched forward and backward, right and left for God, but he cannot find him (23:3–9). The promise given to man in later years is "Ye shall seek me and find me when ye shall search for me with all your heart" (Jer. 29:13). Job needed to know this promise and would have rejoiced to hear Jesus say, "When ye have seen me, ye have seen the Father. I and the Father are one."

Bildad's Third Speech and Job's Reply (Job 25:1—26:14)

The passage.—In a very brief speech Bildad tries to subdue Job's arrogant assumption that he would be found guiltless if he stood before the judgment seat of God (23:3–7). How could man who is like a worm ever consider himself pure before the omnipotent maker of the universe (25:1–6). This is another repetition of what has already been said in the earlier speeches and it seems to indicate that the friends of Job have about exhausted their argument.

In his reply, which is also brief, Job mocks Bildad's speech as an empty and helpless contribution to his problem (26:2–4). To prove that he has added nothing that Job did not already know he proceeds to give a far better picture of the greatness of God than Bildad has given. He still fails to see, however, how the knowledge of God's greatness solves the mystery of his sufferings (vv. 5–14).

Special points.—The "armies" in 25:3 refer to the stars in the sky at night. God controls the numberless stars like a mighty army. "His light" in verse 4 refers to his control over the sun by day. Bildad uses these descriptions to picture the majesty and universal power of God.

Job describes the majesty of God in broader dimensions than Bildad. He sees God's power manifest not only on the earth and in the heavens but in hell too (that is Sheol, the abode of the dead).

The statement in chapter 26, verse 7, "He hangeth the earth upon nothing," is a remarkable example of accuracy in light of the modern scientific concepts of space and gravity. All of the other ancient cosmologies of that day were proposing a wide variety of superstitious theories. Some believed that the earth rested on the back of a giant turtle. Others proposed that it stood on the back of a huge man named Atlas. In contrast to these, this passage describes the earth as suspended in space and attached to nothing; in perfect consistency with man's later discoveries.

Verse 14, in chapter 26, means "Lo, these are just the outskirts of his ways, and how small a whisper is that which we hear of him. Who could understand if the full thunder of his power were unfolded?"

Job's Concluding Address (Job 27:1— 31:40)

The passage.—The dialogues between Job and his friends have now ended. Their arguments have all been exhausted. In fact, the third speaker, Zophar, does not speak at all in this last cycle, and after a pause, Job sums up his defense. The line of thought is difficult to trace in this concluding discourse. Some of the ideas seem to contradict what Job has said earlier. As a result some interpreters believe that portions of this passage are the words of Zophar, whose speech is missing from the third cycle. Others find certain misplaced sections which they attribute to the two other friends. However, the inconsistency in Job's speech could also be a result of the trauma of his suffer-

ing. He is not thinking clearly. His words often come in torrents. Inconsistencies are to be expected from one who is struggling with the heavy mysteries of life.

In chapter 27, Job renews his claim of innocence before God (vv. 1–6). He follows this with another dreary description of the destruction of wicked men and declares with an oath that he is not one of the wicked. Until he dies he will not admit his guilt. His conscience sustains his innocence (vv. 7– 23).

In chapter 28 the theme is "wisdom cannot be attained by man." Job uses poetic pictures to illustrate this truth. (1) Man digs for valuable treasures and precious stones and he finds them. But there is no mine from which wisdom can be uncovered and brought out (vv. 1–14). (2) Man can purchase merchandise in the marketplace, but wisdom is not for sale at any price (vv. 15–22). God created wisdom and keeps it secretly hidden from man. Man's only wisdom is to fear God (vv. 23–28).

In chapter 29, Job paints a pathetic word picture of his former prosperity and respect. He reviews with sadness the happiness he enjoyed with his family, his prosperity, his feeling of acceptance by God, and the respect and reverence shown him by his friends (vv. 2–10). He remembers that he earned their respect by benevolent and humane treatment of others (vv. 11– 17). He had looked forward to the future with calm assurance (vv. 18–20). In contrast to the rejection of his three friends, he remembers his pleasant relationships with his fellowman in the past (vv. 21–25).

Chapter 30, Job reviews his present state in sharp contrast to the happy picture drawn in chapter 29.

14. Grinding grain
(see Job 31:10)

In chapter 31 the long discourse ends with a series of protests from Job by which he clears himself of all offenses. The last verse says, "The words of Job are ended."

Special points.—The "dust" and the "clay" in 27:16 stand for great abundance. The wicked man is described as having silver as abundant as dust and as possessing as much clothing as there is clay in the ground. Costly clothing was one of the symbols of wealth in ancient days.

"He openeth his eyes and he is not" (27:19) points out the suddenness of the sinner's destruction. It is similar to 2 Kings 19:35: "When they arose early in the morning behold they were all dead corpses."

Verses 6–11 in chapter 28 describe the mining of gold. The miner keeps the location of his claim secret so that not even the birds and animals know about it (vv. 7–8). He digs beneath the mountain and hollows out "rivers" or "tunnels" in the rock (vv. 9–10). Then he suddenly discovers the vein of gold and brings it out into the light (v. 11).

The "crystal" in verse 17 refers to "glass" which was very rare and valuable in ancient days.

In 29:2, the "candle of God" should be "the lamp of God." God's lamp represents his shining favor reflecting on Job to prosper him.

Job says in verse 6 that his steps were "bathed in butter." This is another figure of speech describing his wealth. He was literally engulfed in those things that represented prosperity.

In 30:18, Job tells how his disease has caused him to lose weight. His emaciated condition makes it possible to bind up his loose-fitting outer garment as tightly around his waist as the collar around his neck. He has in a sense taken up all the "notches on his belt."

In 31:33, Job may be referring to Adam's hiding from God in the Garden of Eden. On the other hand since the word "Adam" means "man" Job could be saying "if I covered my transgression like other men."

Chapter 31, verse 35, literally says "Behold my *tau*—let the Almighty answer me." *Tau* is the last letter of the Hebrew alphabet and was used in ancient days as a personal mark instead of a signature. This verse may be saying, "Here is my signature. Let God answer it."

Elihu the Bystander (Job 32:1—37:24)

The passage.—Elihu the Buzite has been listening to the debate as a bystander. Being younger than Job and his three friends, he has politely refrained from speaking. But now when the debate is over and there is a pause in the conversation, he speaks. He is incensed at Job for his complaints against God and he is angry at the three friends for failing to convince Job of his improper attitude. He corrects Job in his speech at several points.

(1) Job is wrong in saying that God is hostile toward him and refuses to hear him or to speak to him. Elihu quotes a number of passages from Job's speeches which make that claim, and then sets out to refute them (33:8–13). To correct Job's misconceptions Elihu reminds him that God does speak to man in many ways. For example, he

speaks in dreams and visions (vv. 14–18), and he speaks through angelic messengers sent to those who suffer (vv. 19–28). If Job will only listen to what God is already saying and take his words to heart he will be restored.

(2) In chapter 34, Elihu refutes another of Job's untruths. Job has accused God of injustice in his dealings. He claims that God has afflicted him without reason. Elihu answers by pointing out the absurdity of such a claim. Injustice in God who is the ruler of all is inconceivable. "Shall not the judge of all the earth do right?" (Gen. 18:25). The words of Job have incited Elihu's indignation. He believes there has never been anyone as irreverent or impious as Job (34:7–8). Elihu draws the conclusion that Job has added to his other sins the grave sin of defiant and mocking impiety. He deserves to be punished in the furnace of severe affliction (vv. 34–37).

(3) In chapter 35, Elihu attacks the statement of Job that a man does not profit by doing right. His answer is that neither godliness nor unrighteousness affects God. He is too exalted to be touched by anything human. Therefore, the advantages and profits of righteousness must come upon man since they do not affect God (vv. 5–8). If there are those rare cases where man's righteousness doesn't seem to pay it is because he has approached God in the wrong way (vv. 9–16).

In concluding his speech, Elihu explains to Job that the afflictions which come to man are examples of God's great wisdom whereby he encourages man to listen to him (36:5–15). Job, therefore, should not complain because he is suffering. He should rather rejoice that God is using suffering to lead him into a happier and wiser life (vv. 16–25). If Job would simply look and listen he could see the evidence of God's greatness and holiness in the clouds, in the wind, and in the rain (vv. 26–33).

The same theme is carried over into chapter 37. Job should be impressed by God's majesty revealed in nature. He should humble himself before the unapproachable greatness of God (vv. 14–24).

Special points.—Elihu is the only one of the speakers to call Job by name (33:1). This may be because of his desire to be respectful since he is young, or it may be his way of emphasizing the importance of what he is about to say.

Verse 6 in chapter 32 should read, "Behold before God I am even as thou." Elihu is not claiming here to speak as the representative of God. He is rather claiming to understand Job's situation since he too is a man like Job.

The "ransom" in 33:24 which God looks for in order to forgive man could be man's repentance or his afflictions which are sufficient to pay the price of his sins.

In chapter 34, verses 16–19 express the idea that injustice in God is impossible. Abraham had the same idea in Genesis 18:25. Years later the apostle Paul said, "Is God unrighteous? God forbid, for then how shall God judge the world?" (Rom. 3:5).

In chapter 35, verses 14–15, Elihu is suggesting that the reason God has not answered Job is that he is merciful. If he should come to speak to Job while he is rebellious and complaining, he could only come in anger and in judgment. His silence is a sign of his mercy.

The word "hypocrite" in 36:13 is more accurately translated "godless."

In 37:16 the "balancing" of the clouds describes the marvelous way in which these heavy rain-laden clouds seem to be suspended in the air.

Truth for today.—Elihu's speech has a great deal of truth in it. Apparently Job realizes this because he has no answer for him. Elihu is right when he points out the error of blaming God for suffering. He is right in uplifting the justice and righteousness of God. He correctly notes that if justice were not at the heart of things, the entire universe would collapse. There is great assurance still today in realizing that "behind the dim unknown standeth God within the shadows, keeping watch over all his own."

Elihu is correct in showing the various ways in which God speaks to man. He has spoken by direct revelation, in dreams and visions (33:15–16). He has at his disposal thousands of angelic messengers which he at times sends to speak to man (vv. 23–24). He can communicate his power through nature (chaps. 36–37). God also speaks in the same way today. But far superior to these is his revelation of himself through his Son. "God who at sundry times and divers manners spake in times past unto the fathers by the prophets hath in these last days spoken unto us by his Son whom he hath appointed heir to all things, by whom also he made the world" (Heb. 1:1–2). When we remember that for centuries struggling men groped in darkness for a clear message from God, we should rejoice that through Christ he has revealed himself to us so clearly. Paul was impressed with this and says, "Wherefore, I am made a minister according to the dispensation of God which is given to me for you, to fulfil the word of God even the mystery which hath been hid from ages and generations but now is made manifest to his saints, to whom God would make

known what is the riches of the glory
of the mystery among the Gentiles,
which is Christ in you, the hope of
glory" (Col. 1:25–27).

The Lord Speaks to Job (Job 38:1—39: 30)

The passage.—The last act in the
drama of Job begins. Satan has accused
Job of serving God because God prospers him. He has predicted that if Job
suffers, he will reject God. God permits
the trial and now Job has endured that
trial successfully. Although Job has
sinned during his testing, it has not
been the kind of sin Satan predicted.
He has not rejected God, but has continued to cleave to him. He has even
expressed profound depths of faith far
deeper than he had known in his happier days (chap. 19). During his suffering Job's insights into the ways of
righteousness have been sharpened and
focused (17:9). And so now the Lord
who permitted the trial and had been
watching from a distance interposes to
bring it to an end and to bestow upon
Job the fruit of his suffering.

Rather than explaining to Job intellectually that his afflictions were not due
to his sin, God simply reveals himself
in majesty and mercy and filling Job's
mind with an awareness of himself that
he has never had before. In the presence of God, Job's heart is filled with
joy, and at the same time with an
embarrassed regret for his past thoughts
and words. He repents in dust and
ashes.

The Lord's first answer to Job is in
chapters 38–39. He asks Job, "Shall
mortal man contend with God?" In essence his message to Job is, "You have
been asking for a chance to argue your
case before me. Now you have your
chance. Here I am. What do you want
to say?" (38:1–3). He then paints a

panoramic picture of the acts of creation: in the earth (vv. 4–11), in the
sea (vv. 8–10), in the dawning of the
sun (vv. 12–15), in light and darkness
(vv. 19–21), in the snow and hail (vv.
22–23), in the stormy wind, the rain
and the lightning (vv. 24–27), in the
dew, the frost and the ice (vv. 28–30),
in the movement of the stars (vv. 31–
38), among the animals (chap. 39). God
then asks, "Were you there when these
mighty acts took place? Do you still
want to share your wisdom with the
God who made the world?"

Special points.—The "whirlwind" in
38:1 is often used in the Old Testament as the manner in which God veils
himself to speak to man. He hides his
glory behind a storm cloud when he
descends to the earth.

The "sons of God" in verse 7 is
another name for the stars which sang
together.

The "dayspring" is the word for the
"dawn" (v. 12).

The word "death" in verse 17 is the
word "Sheol." It means the place of
the dead. Job is told that God's presence and power reach even deeper than
the depth of the sea. They extend to
the very place of the dead itself.

In 39:1 wild goats are mountain
goats, a species of Chamois. The "hind"
is the deer. The "unicorn" in verse 8
is probably the wild oxen. The one-
horned animal called the unicorn was
an imaginary animal of mythology. In
the Bible this word seems to refer to
the wild oxen.

In verse 13 "peacock" should be
"ostrich." These verses all describe the
ostrich which is noted for its cruelty
and stupidity (Lam. 4:3). This is the
way God made it (39:17). But while
God did not give the ostrich wisdom,
he did give it speed. When it "lifts itself
on high, it scorneth horse and rider"

(v. 13). This means that when the ostrich runs at full speed it can outrun
a race horse. The speed of the ostrich
has been measured at nearly 30 miles
per hour, and its stride from 22 to 28
feet at a single bound.

Verse 20 should read, "Can you
make him leap like the grasshopper?
The glory of his snorting is terrible."

Verse 25 should read, "As often as
the trumpet sounds he says, Ha, Ha!"
The war horse only laughs at the dangerous sounds from battle.

Truth for today.—The more man discovers about nature, the more he should
wonder at the greatness of God. When
men stood on the moon for the first
time and looked back at the earth
"hanging on nothing" (26:7) their first
words were, "In the beginning God
created the heavens and the earth." Scientific discoveries do not contradict
faith. They simply expose more reasons
to declare the glory of God.

The Lord Speaks Again (Job 40:1—41: 34)

The passage.—Job is silenced by the
glory of God presented before his very
eyes. He covers his mouth in shame
and refuses to say another word (40:
1–5). The Lord speaks again. This time
his question to Job is, "Shall man
charge God with injustice in his rule
of the world?"

Job has accused God of mismanagement and injustice in his control over
the world. With cutting irony God invites him to try to rule the world if
he can. "If you think you can do it
better than I, come ahead and try"
(vv. 8–14). God uses two simple illustrations of his creative power to suggest
to Job, "Here are two creatures I have
made. See if you can do the same"
(40:15—41:34). The two creatures are
the "behemoth," probably the hippo-

potamus, and the "leviathan," probably
the crocodile.

Special points.—The behemoth in
40:15, is the name the Hebrews gave
to the "water ox" or the hippopotamus.
The margin of the King James Version
suggests elephant, but the description
in this passage fits the hippopotamus
better.

The leviathan in 41:1 is the crocodile. In verse 18 he is described as
breathing smoke and flames. "Neesings"
means "sneezing" and refers to the way
the crocodile exhales in shallow water.
When the stream from his nostrils is
reflected in the sunlight, it appears to
be smoke rising from the water.

The Epilogue (Job 42:1–17)

The passage.—Job responds briefly
to what God has said. He admits that
he has spoken unwisely. He has made
assumptions on the basis of hearsay.
But now he has seen the glory of God
for himself. The effect of this deeper
knowledge of God is to cause him to
repent in dust and ashes (42:1–6).

The last verses of the book of Job
are written in prose rather than poetry
(vv. 7–17). They tell how Job is commanded to intercede for his three
friends who have displeased God by
their treatment of him. He does so
and then Job is restored to a level of
prosperity double that which he formerly enjoyed. He is again blessed with
children and dies old and full of days
(vv. 10–17).

Special points.—The fact that Elihu
is not mentioned in the eiplogue with
the other friends has led some to assume that his speech was not a part
of the original book but was added by
a later editor.

Job's daughters (42:14) are given
beautiful names. Jemima means "dove."
Kezia means "perfume." Keren-hap-

puch means a cosmetic-like "mascara."

Truth for today.—In summary, the book of Job gives several important insights into the problem of suffering.

(1) It denies the age-old philosophy that suffering is due to past sin. This is often true but not invariably so.

(2) Job's idea that man suffers because of God's indifference or his arbitrary injustice is also refuted. God is pictured as concerned, interested, and in control of mankind.

(3) Elihu adds the truth that sometimes suffering is used to educate man or to lead him to maturity. Through suffering man learns things he would not otherwise learn. Job, for example, gained new insights into life after death and God's greatness.

(4) The last speeches from the Lord show suffering should not produce rebellion but an increased faith. Just as man cannot understand all of the intricate workings of nature and must trust God to operate the universe, so he must trust God in his personal life, even though he cannot understand every experience.

PSALMS

Russell H. Dilday, Jr. (1–41) and
J. Hardee Kennedy (42–150)

INTRODUCTION

Through the years, several different names have been given to the book of Psalms. In Hebrew its title means "praises." In the Greek version of the Old Testament the book goes by the name "melodies." In one ancient manuscript the book was called the "psalter," indicating that the Psalms were to be sung to the accompaniment of stringed instruments. It may have at one time been considered as a book of prayer (Ps. 72:20). Most readers have understood the book to be a collection of hymns used in private and public worship by the Jewish people.

The Psalms have had a powerful appeal to believers throughout the centuries. In no other book in the Bible can one find recorded such a variety of religious experiences. It is impossible to read very far in this book without immediately identifying a particular facet of one's life with a similar experience in the life of the author. The book of Psalms has a timelessness which makes it equally applicable to every age.

The literary form of the Psalms is poetry, but the poetry is unique in that it has no rhyme and very little rhythm to it. Hebrew writers used such things as accent and parallelism to distinguish their poetry from prose. By accenting certain words in a line of poetry the writer was able to create a pleasing but unpolished kind of rhythm. Parallelism is the method by which the writer would state an idea and then reinforce it by repeating it, varying it, or contrasting it in a second line. There are three major kinds of parallelism found in the Psalms: (1) Synonymous—in this form of parallelism the second line repeats the first line in slightly different words (Ps. 1:2).

(2) Antithetic—in this form of parallelism the second line repeats an opposite idea to that in the first line (Ps. 1:6).

(3) Synthetic—in this form of parallelism the second line adds other thoughts to the first line to reinforce the original idea (Ps. 7:1).

The book of Psalms is itself divided into five sections called "books," each section closing with a doxology of praise. The five divisions correspond to the ancient five books of the law.

Book One, Psalms 1–41
Book Two, Psalms 42–72
Book Three, Psalms 73–89
Book Four, Psalms 90–106
Book Five, Psalms 107–150

The first book (Pss. 1–41) consists of Psalms which in their titles name David as the writer (with four exceptions: Pss. 1,2,10, and 33). This first division of the book of Psalms is unique also in that the most frequently used name of God is "Lord" (Yahweh), whereas in the other sections the name "God" (Elohim) is used more frequently. Since each Psalm differs in theme from the others, there is no practical way to outline the thought of the book. Efforts have been made, however, to classify the Psalms according to subject. There are Nature Psalms, Character Psalms, Penitential Psalms, Worship Psalms, Assurance Psalms, and Psalms dealing with subjects such as the Word of God, Suffering, and the Messiah.

The Two Life-Styles (Psalm 1)

The passage.—This familiar psalm presents the radical differences between the godly man's life-style and the way of life of the wicked man. With three verses the poet portrays the blessedness or happiness of the godly man who rejects the example of sinners (v. 1) and whose chief interest is to fulfil the law of God (v. 2). His life will be like a tree, cultivated and cared for under the best circumstances so that it never fails to produce fruit (v. 3).

The closing verses describe the opposite pattern of life in the experience of the ungodly. His life is unrooted and unstable (v. 4). He cannot endure the judgment of God, nor can he be included with God's people (v. 5). The inevitable destiny of the unrighteous man for whom God has no regard is destruction (v. 6).

Special points.—"Blessed is the man" can be translated, "Oh, the happiness of the man" (v. 1).

There is a progressive intensification of wickedness described in the verbs of verse 1: "walk," "stand," "sit." These verbs describe a process whereby the man who only walks with the wicked at first, soon begins to "stand" with the wicked, and eventually feels at home enough to "sit" with those that scorn God. The nouns in the verse also show this progressive seriousness of sin: "ungodly" describes a man who occasionally is out of step with right conduct. "Sinner" is a man whose wicked misconduct has become habitual. "Scorners" means the hardened, arrogant man who mocks

God.

"Rivers of water" (v. 3) refers to manmade irrigation ditches. "Planted" means "transplanted." The picture then is of a tree carefully transplanted by an irrigation ditch where it is tended and cared for by a careful gardener so that it bears fruit.

"Knows" (v. 6) means "cares for or regards."

Truth for today.—Anyone who considers himself strong enough to control sin should heed the warning of this passage. There is a subtle, almost invisible, quality about sin that draws its victims into a deeper and deeper involvement. The verbs "walk," "stand," and "sit" and the nouns "ungodly," "sinners," and "scorners" all hint at this subversive build-up of influence in immorality. Once a person allows sin to get a start in his life, it begins to drag him along in its undertow. Eventually he "sits in the seat of the scoffers" hardened and at ease in his sin. To resist this subtle intensification of sin the godly man must be morally stabilized (v. 1), spiritually oriented (v. 2), creatively productive (v. 3), and eternally secure (v. 6).

The Victory of God's Kingdom (Psalm 2)

The passage.—Like Psalm 1, this passage contrasts the two ways of life among men, this time among nations instead of individuals. The first scene in the poetic picture takes place in the courts of the earthly kings who rebel against God (2:1–3). The second scene takes place in heaven where God laughs at their rebellion and promises judgment when his Anointed One (Messiah) shall come (vv. 4–6). The next scene pictures the kingdom of God's "anointed." The psalmist describes this ideal king's relationship to God (v. 7), his worldwide authority (v. 8), and his power (v. 9). In the last scene the poet urges men to be wise (v. 10), to serve God (v. 11), and to give homage to his anointed (v. 12).

Special points.—"Bands" (v. 3) refers to the harness of a work animal. The rebellious nations considered God's control as a kind of slavery from which to be freed.

"The anointed" (v. 2), "the king" (v. 6), and "the son" (v. 7) are all terms most often interpreted as pointing to the Messiah.

"Thou art my son, this day have I begotten thee" (v. 7) was a phrase used in the legal adoption of a child according to the ancient laws written in the code of Hammurabi. This verse seems to be the basis for the "voice out of heaven" at the baptism of Jesus (Mark 1:11).

A Prayer for Help (Psalm 3)

The passage.—According to the superscription, this psalm was written by David when he was running away from Absalom his rebellious son. The danger he experienced during those days led him to write this prayer for help.

First, he describes the perils he faces because of his numerous enemies (v. 1). So dangerous is his condition that many around him believe that he is beyond help (v. 2).

He next describes the protection of God which gives him confidence (vv. 3–6). The reason he can face his trouble with courage is his belief that God is his shield and his sustainer.

Last he voices the prayer in his heart. He calls upon God to deliver him from his enemies and bless his life (vv. 7–8).

Special points.—The term "selah" in verses 2, 4, and 8 was probably a musical term giving instruction to the singers or the instrumentalists who sang and accompanied the psalm. It probably meant "sing louder here" or "play louder here." In this way it was similar to the modern musical term "forte." However, the term could also have marked a musical pause intended to give emphasis to a thought. "Selah" could be translated "stop and think about that for a while."

In verses 3–4 the writer lists the reasons why he is confident God will help him. He is confident because God has been his shield, his glory (or honor), and his "lifter-up" (in victory over his enemies).

A Prayer of Confidence (Psalm 4)

The passage.—This psalm carries a firm note of optimistic trust from the first verse to the last, with no word of complaint as found in Psalm 3. The psalmist appeals to God who has often delivered him from trouble in the past (v. 1). He then challenges his enemies to stop terrorizing him and turn instead to God in repentance and worship (vv. 2–5). The psalm concludes with an expression of the joy of trusting in God for help (vv. 6–8).

Special points.—The word "Neginoth" in the title of this psalm means "stringed instruments." Psalm 4 was apparently intended to be accompanied by stringed instruments.

The phrase, "Thou hast enlarged me," in verse 1 means, "Thou hast given me room." It describes one who is under pressure and hedged in by difficulty. He appeals to God and God opens up a way through which he may escape.

"Leasings" in verse 2 means "lies."

Truth for today.—David uses an easily understood illustration of the joy one finds in trusting God. He has more gladness in his heart than other men have when their grain and wine abound (v. 7). Those who are looking for happiness in material possessions should understand this. A personal relationship with God through Christ is the only thing that can create real joy within man's heart.

If his happiness is based on wealth, profits, or income, then his happiness comes and goes depending on the amount of material possessions. Should the grain and wine not abound, then there is no happiness. But if happiness is founded on the unchanging God, it is always lasting and rich. The writer of Ecclesiastes after searching for happiness in knowledge, pleasure, and wealth came to the conclusion: "Let us hear the end of the whole matter. Fear God and keep his commandments, for this is the whole duty of man" (Eccl. 12:13).

A Prayer of Worship (Psalm 5)

The passage.—In this psalm, David is not fleeing for his life as in Psalm 3. But he is in Jerusalem and is preparing to go into the Temple for the morning sacrifice (5:3). However, even here in the safety of the city at the time of the morning worship service there are those who are devising some plot against him (v. 10). These enemies are described as arrogant, foolish, boastful, deceitful, lying, blood-thirsty flatterers (vv. 5–6,9). The only way he can hope to escape their treachery is for God to intervene and show him the way (v. 8). He is certain that anyone who puts his trust in God shall be rescued and blessed (vv. 11–12).

Special points.—The word "Nehiloth" in the title of this psalm means "wind instruments" and probably suggests that the psalm was to be accompanied by woodwinds.

"I worship toward thy holy temple" literally means "I fall down in the direction of thy holy temple." This describes the custom of praying with the body bowed toward the direction of Jerusalem as Daniel did in Babylon.

David's prayer at the end of this psalm has three requests:

(1) That God will reveal his will plainly to him (v. 8).

(2) That God will destroy his enemies (v. 10).

(3) That all those who trust God may sing for joy (vv. 11–12).

The Prayer of a Sick Man (Psalm 6)

The passage.—David's trouble in this psalm is not enemy threats as in the preceding chapters but rather a personal sickness that has weakened his body and soul (6:2–3). So serious is his illness that he is afraid he might die (v. 5). He sees his sickness as God's punishment upon him and he petitions God to release him. After describing his condition in detail, he then declares his certainty that God will answer his prayer and will turn back the trouble that threatens him.

Special points.—The word "Sheminith" in the title of this psalm means "eighth." It may refer to the lower range of music indicating that the psalm was to be sung by male voices such as tenors and basses.

The word "vexed" in verse 2 literally means dried up. Not only are his bones rotting away, but his soul also is losing its health.

In verse 5 the word "grave" is the Hebrew word "Sheol" and refers not so much to a burial place as it does to the general abode of the dead.

Truth for today.—This psalm seems to reflect the traditional viewpoint that suffering, especially sickness, is due to sin. As David cried to the Lord from his illness, he asks, "Oh, Lord, how long?" (6:3) as though he believes that his sickness is God's punishment upon him. This false viewpoint expressed also in the book of Job was still widely accepted during Jesus' day. The disciples asked Jesus if it were the blind man's sins or his parents' sins that led to his blindness.

The New Testament corrects this misconception. Sickness is not always God's punishment for sin. Today when misfortune is encountered there are those who say, "This tragedy is God's will." But to blame God for all the misfortune that comes our way is wrong. Many of our problems come as results of our own foolishness and sin. While sickness may be used by God as judgment and punishment for sin, it may not always be used that way. Many righteous people suffer illness and physical distress. Many scholars believe Paul's "thorn in the flesh" was probably the disease of malaria. He prayed for healing and deliverance, but God instead gave him grace to endure it. David is confident that God will hear his prayer and give him the strength he needs (6: 9).

A Prayer for Help in Persecution (Psalm 7)

The passage.—This psalm is a lament in which David cries out to God for justice in the midst of bitter persecution. The superscription at the beginning of the psalm indicates that David is writing about his persecution under Saul, as described in 1 Samuel 24–26. "The words of Cush the Benjamite" probably refers to some slanderous rumor spoken by one of the many servants of Saul to arouse his anger against David (2 Sam. 21). David says the bitter persecution he is facing from this enemy has all the fury of a wild beast of prey (7:1–2). In verses 3–5, David proclaims his innocence from the charges leveled against him by his enemy. He has not been guilty of fraud and dishonesty. He has not wronged his friends.

In verses 6–8, David appeals to God to arise in justice and vindicate him in his claim of innocence. He has complete faith in the fair outcome of such a trial since God is a righteous God (vv. 9–11).

Apparently, even as David lays his case before God, his enemy comes to attack him again. But David is confident that his evil schemes will "backfire" and he will destroy himself (vv. 15–16). The psalm closes with a doxology of thanksgiving for God's help (v. 17).

Special points.—"Mine honor" in verse 5 is another word for "my soul." David is willing to lay his soul in the grave, to submit death, in case he has ever acted dishonorably.

A Psalm to the Glory of God (Psalm 8)

The passage.—This hymn of praise is one of the best known of the Psalms. Its imaginative thought and artistic form have caused readers in all ages to respond to it (Matt. 21:16, 1 Cor. 15:25, Heb. 2:6–7).

The psalm opens and closes with the same refrain, "Oh, Lord, our Lord, how excellent is thy name in all the earth!" Following the opening refrain there is a beautiful description of God's glory revealed in nature (vv. 1–3). His glory is seen in the earth, in the heavens, in the moon and the stars. So great is his glory that when men try to express it, their words are like the babbling of babes and infants (v. 2). God's majesty is beyond the power of human tongue to express.

In the light of God's glory the significance of man seems very small (v. 4). And yet in spite of his insignificance, man is no accident. He was created by God for a high purpose—to have dominion over creation (vv. 5–8).

The doxology with which the psalm begins is used to call man back once more to the majesty of God (v. 9).

Special points.—The word "gittith" in the superscription does not refer to a musical instrument but rather to a tempo to which this psalm was to be accompanied. Most scholars believe that it refers to a marching tempo popular in the land of Gath.

The moon and stars are the work of God's "fingers" (v. 3). In other places the Scriptures speak of the work of God's "hands." Here David may be suggesting the careful deftness and artistry of God's creative work in the heavens.

"Established" in verse 3 is another way of saying "created."

The "son of man" in verse 4 is another word for man. This is an example of poetic parallelism in which an idea is emphasized by repeating it again using other words.

The word "visitest" in verse 4 should be translated "care for."

In verse 5 the phrase, "a little lower than the angels," is David's reverent way of saying, "a little lower than God." Man is thus described as being created in the image of God.

Truth for today.—Human injustice and racial prejudices arise when men forget about the dignity of man as God created him. This psalm reminds us that God made man "a little lower than divine." It reminds us of Genesis 1:26, "Let us make man in our image, after our likeness, and let them have dominion . . ."

When one remembers that each person in the world, without regard to his racial background or social status, has been created in God's image, crowned with glory and honor, and given dominion over the works of God, it is unforgivable to degrade or dishonor that person.

Two Psalms of Praise and Supplication (Psalms 9–10)

The passage.—Some students of the Old Testament believe that Psalms 9 and 10 should be considered as one

psalm because the two are printed as one in some of the ancient manuscripts. Another reason for considering them as a unit is that the verses of these psalms form an alphabetical acrostic. The first word in each verse begins with a different letter of the Hebrew alphabet, so that verse 1 begins with "a," verse 2 with "b," and so on throughout the two psalms. Some of the verses are out of order, but the acrostic carries through Psalms 9 and 10. Whether or not they were originally one psalm, the two do fit together for discussion.

In Psalm 9:1–8, David sings thanksgiving to God for turning back his enemies, for maintaining his just cause, for rebuking the nations, for destroying the wicked, and for judging the people with equity.

In verses 9–12, he praises God for his care of the afflicted. He is a dependable defender and helper in time of trouble. Therefore, David appeals to God for his mercy in deliverance (vv. 13–14).

Psalm 9 concludes with a description of the judgment of God upon the nations. David prays that the proud nations may be reminded that they are only men (v. 20).

Psalm 10 begins with a plea for God's intervention in the affairs of men to turn back the tyranny of oppressors (vv. 1–2). His help is needed because of the uncontrolled wickedness of the enemy (vv. 3–11). The psalm closes with a prayer to God to rise and defend the afflicted (vv. 12–18).

Special points.—The word "muthlabben" in a superscription of Psalm 9 is difficult to interpret. It literally means "death is white," and is probably the name of a popular melody in ancient times to which this psalm was to be sung.

Psalm 10 has no superscription, which gives added evidence to the belief that these two were at one time printed as one psalm.

Faith Finds a Refuge (Psalm 11)

The passage.—David, in this psalm, is fearful for his life and is being advised to flee to the mountains for safety. The historical situation that occasioned the psalm is probably the rebellion of Absalom.

In the first verses David's faith is expressed. He is advised by his friends to find a hiding place in the mountain regions outside the city. But David sees this suggestion as an invitation to compromise, to take the easy way out, to choose the path of cowardly expediency. He rejects this advice and instead expresses his faith in God who will be his hiding place (vv. 1–2).

The last verses tell where David's faith is founded. His faith is founded upon the Lord who is in his temple but at the same time seated on his heavenly throne. Being both eminent and transcendent, close at hand and far removed in the heights of heaven, he can see the threats of the enemy. David believes he will destroy the wicked who threaten him, for he is a righteous God (vv. 4–7).

Special points.—Verse 2 should read, "They have fitted their arrows to the string to shoot in the dark at the upright in heart." The picture here is of a band of robbers waiting in the darkness to ambush their unsuspecting victim.

The "horrible tempest" in verse 6 is the "scorching wind" of a volcanic eruption. It brings with it the fire and brimstone from heaven. This points back to the destruction of Sodom in Genesis 19:24.

The Loneliness of the Righteous (Psalm 12)

The passage.—How often have the people of God felt outnumbered and alone in the midst of universal moral corruption. This seems to be the mood of Psalm 12. Everywhere he looks the author sees wickedness. This leads him to believe that there are no faithful, godly people anymore (v. 1). Honesty and humility have disappeared (v. 2). Lying, flattery, hypocrisy, insincerity, and boasting are the order of the day (vv. 3–4).

God responds to the godly who are surrounded by an immoral society. He promises to protect the moral man from the influence of the wicked (v. 5).

The closing verses of the psalm praise the words of God which stand in contrast to the empty, flattering words of the proud generation (vv. 6–8).

Special points.—"Flattering lips" in verses 1 and 2 means literally "smooth lips" and refers to the smooth talk of a boisterous, loud-mouthed flatterer.

"Double heart" in verse 1 denotes a hypocritical man who speaks one way and lives another.

Truth for today.—A contemporary theologian described life in the twentieth century for the believer as the life of "moral man in an immoral society." The believer has often been called upon to live out his faith in an unsympathetic world. In fact, Jesus predicted bluntly that his disciples would encounter this kind of uncooperative environment. Under these circumstances, believers are tempted to withdraw to the safety of some kind of insulated monastic life. The Bible, however, declares that the Christian's role is to be in the world but not of the world; to permeate and invade the diseased society about him with the healing salt of the gospel. This psalm should encourage the modern-day believer as it points to the Word of God as the source of strength and guidance. It reminds him that God is able to save by many or by a few and that while the believer may be outnumbered, he has unlimited power available to him through Christ.

A Brief Prayer for Deliverance (Psalm 13)

The passage.—This abbreviated cry from David has been used to express the deep feelings of troubled people in every generation since it was written. In 1539, for example, John Calvin selected it to be included in a hymnbook of worship.

The psalm begins with a stormy complaint (vv. 1–2). The stormy lament begins to decrease in intensity as the writer appeals to God for help (vv. 3–4). Then it ends with the quiet, calm certainty of faith (vv. 5–6).

Special points.—Verse 2 should read, "How long must I bear pain in my soul and have sorrow in my heart all the day? How long shall my enemy be exalted over me?"

The Fate of Godless Men (Psalm 14)

The passage.—This psalm is identical, almost word for word, with Psalm 53. The book of Psalms is itself divided into five books (see Introduction). This particular passage happened to be included in both book one and book two. David's concern here is for the widespread occurrence of practical atheism among his people. He describes in verses 1–3 the depravity and the foolishness of the man who says, "There is no God."

However, he sees a day of retribution coming in which the judgment of God will fall upon the ungodly (vv. 4–6). At the same time God will deliver the righteous and restore their fortunes (v. 7).

Special points.—The atheist's plea "there is no God" (v. 1) is better understood as "God is not here." The kind of atheism David is talking about here is not so much philosophical as it is prac-

tical. People were apparently not denying the existence of God intellectually. They were simply living as though he did not exist. In verse 3 the phrase "every one of them is gone back" means "every one of them has fallen away." That is, they have backslidden and broken their relationship to God.

Truth for today.—In this passage David links atheism very closely with such things as foolishness, wickedness, corruption, abominable iniquity, and depravity. It is still true today that when men either deny the existence of God philosophically or begin to live as though he did not exist, then the quality of life will suffer. When a society forgets God then its life-style becomes depraved, corrupt, and sinful. History will support the accusation of this psalm that such practical atheism is foolishness.

How Man Can Approach God (Psalm 15)

The passage.—In contrast to the foolish atheist described in chapter 14, David here talks about the virtues of the godly man. These virtues are actually conditions which must be met if a man is to approach God.

In order to have access to God a man must:

(1) Live up to the standards of righteousness (v. 2).

(2) Speak honestly (v. 3).

(3) Never slander or gossip (v. 3).

(4) Be thoughtful of his friends (v. 3).

(5) Refuse to insult his neighbor (v. 3).

(6) Never tolerate someone else who insults his neighbor (v. 3).

(7) Reject the reprobate and accept the godly (v. 4).

(8) Keep his word (v. 4).

(9) Never take advantage of others (v. 5).

(10) Refuse bribes (v. 5).

Finally, in verse 5c the reward is promised to those who keep these 10 requirements. They shall become as stable as a rock, able to withstand any crisis.

Special points.—The psalm was apparently designed to be used in the temple or in the home as a catechism of instruction. It could be sung as a response or used in a question-and-answer teaching exercise. First the question is asked (v. 1). Then the answer is given (vv. 2–5b).

The word "backbiteth" in verse 3 can also be translated "slander" or "gossip." A very literal translation of the word would be "he does not go footing-about with his tongue."

The latter part of verse 4 means that in business affairs his word is his bond, even if he has made a deal in which he is the loser. If he "swears to his own hurt, he will not change."

In verse 5 the injunctions of the Jewish law forbade a merchant to take interest on the loans he made to his fellow countrymen (see Ex. 22:25, Deut. 23:19, Lev. 25:36). Interest rates in the ancient world were extremely high, often from 20 to 50 percent.

The Blessings of Fellowship with God (Psalm 16)

The passage.—David is in danger of death as he writes this psalm (vv. 1,10). But there is no expression of bitter complaint or gloomy fear. The psalm instead speaks with a bright hope, a settled calm, and an inward joy based on the confidence that God will supply every need.

David prays that he may always live in the shelter of God's providential care (vv. 1–4). He knows there is nothing good in life apart from God. In contrast, those who worship other gods

have multiplied sorrows.

He then testifies how richly God has supplied his needs (vv. 5–8). These blessings of God give him an eternal security not only in this life where there is fulness and joy, but in the life to come where there are pleasures forevermore (vv. 9–11).

Special points.—In verse 4 David speaks of the "drink offerings of blood" which were offered by the heathen in their worship services. In the worship of Jehovah only libations of wine were offered to the Lord (Num. 28:7–8). David abhors the detestable practices of the pagan.

In verse 6 "the lines are fallen unto me in pleasant places" refers to the division of land by measuring property lines. In other words, David is saying, "As God has marked out my share or allotment in life, he has always given me fertile and pleasant fields."

In verse 7 "my reins" literally means "my kidneys." Ancient writers believed that the seat of man's emotions and will was not to be found in his heart but in the other organs deep inside his body.

A Prayer for Vindication (Psalm 17)

The passage.—The Scriptures carry numerous warnings about the dangerous power of the tongue to destroy. False accusations and vicious gossip can be a brutal form of persecution. It is this particular persecution that David is facing as he looks to the Lord in Psalm 17. We are not told what the false accusations are, but apparently he has been charged with dishonesty (vv. 4–5).

First he prays for justice (vv. 1–5). God is his last court of appeal. His cause is just; and he is honest. But apparently no one believes him and no one can vindicate him but God (v. 2).

Next he prays for mercy (vv. 6–12). He is confident that right would prevail if he were judged by God, but he wants more than justice. He pleads for "the lovingkindness" or "mercy" of the Lord. Because of his past experiences with God he knows God will deal with him in love. This love is in sharp contrast with the merciless arrogance of his deadly enemies (vv. 9–12).

Last, he prays for deliverance (vv. 13–15). It is a fierce cry for vengeance against those who persecute him. David sarcastically prays: "May their belly be filled with what thou hast stored up for them." It sounds like a blessing, but he actually is praying that God's wrath would fill the life of his enemies to their discomfort (v. 14).

Special points.—The word "sentence" in verse 2 means "vindication." David is saying, "If I am to be vindicated, it must come from thee."

The beautiful phrase in verse 8, "apple of the eye" refers to the round pupil of the eye. David wants God to protect him as carefully as a man would protect his valuable eyesight. The Hebrew for this phrase is literally "the little man of the eye."

The "shadow of thy wings" (v. 8) suggests a mother bird protecting her young.

In verse 11 David expresses his hope in life after death.

Thanksgiving for Victory (Psalm 18)

The passage.—David's prayer in Psalm 17 has now been answered. He has been delivered from the hand of his enemy Saul (see the superscription). And now David pauses to thank the Lord for his help. His dramatic experience of deliverance has given David an enlarged concept of God which he wants to share. He has come to know God as a rock, a fortress, a buckler,

a horn, a tower (v. 2).

He has also come to know God as one who answers prayer (vv. 3–16). David called for God's help at the most dangerous time of the battle, and in answer to his prayer there came a powerful and miraculous intervention by God to save him. An earthquake, volcanic rock, fire and smoke, foreboding darkness, hailstones, thunder and lightning all accompanied this impressive demonstration of God's power. David was rescued from overwhelming enemy forces which outnumbered him (vv. 17–19).

As David thought back over the experience he had come to believe that God's deliverance was dependent upon David's faithfulness and obedience to the Lord's commandments (vv. 20–27). He concludes, "With the merciful thou wilt shew thyself merciful" (v. 25).

It is with confidence then that David faces the future. He knows now what God can and will do for his own when they call upon him from a faithful and obedient heart. The list is quite impressive:

(1) He will give him insight and wisdom (v. 28).

(2) He will lead him through opposition and over obstacles (v. 29).

(3) He will reinforce his strength (v. 32).

(4) He will give him enthusiasm and energy (v. 33).

(5) He will give skill and strength to his hands (v. 34).

(6) He will keep him from falling (v. 36).

(7) He will give him victory over his enemies (vv. 37–42).

(8) He will trust him with authority and responsibility (vv. 43–45).

The psalm concludes as it began with a hymn of praise to the God who delivers (vv. 49–50).

Special points.—Psalm 18 is the longest of the psalms in the first book. It was quoted by the writer of 2 Samuel and can be found almost word for word there in chapter 22.

"The horn" in verse 1 refers to the horn of a wild animal like the wild ox in Deuteronomy 33:17. The horn symbolized authority. David is saying, "God is the champion of my salvation."

The "temple" referred to in verse 6 is the "heavenly temple," the place in heaven where God dwells.

"My candle" in verse 28 probably refers to the light of wisdom and insight that God instils into man's mind. It may also mean that God ignites that specific individual ability which each person has but without God may remain darkened and hidden.

"Thy gentleness hath made me great." This phrase in verse 35 should be translated, "Thy help hath made me great." However, the mistranslation found in the King James Version does carry a wonderful truth. The gracious gentleness of God does indeed make man great.

The mention of David's own name in verse 50 does not, as some believe, rule out his being the author of the psalm.

Truth for today.—This psalm obviously is based on an experience of David's that was deeply meaningful to him. As he communicates what he has learned about God in that experience it reminds us that we too have the same responsibility to communicate. The most convincing evidence an unbelieving world can hear today is the evidence of personal experience. When the Christian declares what he has learned about God from the experiences of answered prayer, deliverance from trouble, supernatural strength in a crisis, or the simple consciousness of the presence of God, he has declared the most powerful witness he could share.

God's Glory in Heaven and in His Word (Psalm 19)

The passage.—Psalm 19 is at the same time one of the most familiar Psalms and one of the noblest examples of Hebrew poetry. It proclaims the greatness of God in two spheres.

First, in verses 1–6 it tells of the glory of God in creation. The writer does not call upon people to sing praises to God. Instead he reminds them that a song of praise has already been raised in the heavens. By day and by night the beauty of the sky speaks of God's greatness. The sun has a leading role in this heavenly drama and sings its solo part for all the world to hear (vv. 4–6).

Second, the theme of the psalm shifts from nature to God's law in the Scripture. Creation declares God's power and glory but the Scriptures declare his wisdom and will (vv. 7–11). A variety of synonyms are used for God's Word here: the law, testimony, precept, commandment, fear, ordinances. Six statements of truth about the law are followed by six effects the law has upon man. For example, the first of the six states, "The law is perfect (statement). It revives the soul (effect)."

The psalm closes with a prayer for an obedient and faithful life (vv. 12–14).

Special points.—The "firmament" (v. 1) is another word for "heaven." This is an example of parallelism in which the same idea is repeated with different words.

In verse 4 the phrase "their line" means "their sound."

There is little difference in the

meaning of the various words for law used in verses 7–11. However, what the writer states about the law of God is significant. It is perfect, that is, without flaw—(v. 7). It is sure (dependable) —(v. 7). It is right (correct)—(v. 8). It is pure (shining)—(v. 8). It is clean (free from pagan contamination)—(v. 9). It is true (trustworthy)—(v. 9).

An Intercession for a King (Psalm 20)

The passage.—The scene is a worship service at which the king brings his sacrifices and the people join him in prayer for God's help. The first part of the psalm (vv. 1–5) is addressed to the king. The people express their hope that God will accept his sacrifice and answer his prayer.

The last half of the psalm (vv. 6–9) seems to follow a pause. Perhaps the people wait as the king offers his sacrifice and makes his prayer. Then in some way God demonstrates his approval and it is obvious that his sacrifice has been acceptable. The writer then assures the king that God has heard him and will help him.

Special points.—Verse 9 should read, "Give victory to the king, O Lord. Answer us when we call."

Thanksgiving for the King (Psalm 21)

The passage.—"May God grant you your heart's desire and fulfil all your plans" cried the people in Psalm 20:4. Now because of God's blessings upon their king, they are able to say, "Thou hast given him his heart's desire" (v. 2). This is another of the so-called royal psalms in which the people come before the Lord on behalf of their king. David is probably the king referred to in both Psalms 20 and 21.

The first part of the psalm is addressed to the Lord (vv. 1–7). So numerous and splendid has been the help God has given him that the king can rejoice in it (v. 1).

The second part of the psalm is addressed to the king as the people predict future victories and success for him (vv. 8–12). Verse 13 is a prayer for God to hasten the day of victory, so they can praise him for it.

Special points.—The crown of fine gold in verse 3 may be a reference to the incident in 2 Samuel 12:30 when David, after conquering the city of Rabbah, set the Ammonite crown on his own head. It was noted for the weight of its gold and its ornamentation of precious stones.

"Find out" in verse 8 means "to seize."

A Cry of Loneliness (Psalm 22)

The passage.—The moving lament of this psalm coming from one who has been forsaken, humiliated, and afflicted puts it in sharp contrast to the joyful tones of Psalm 21. It probably comes from the time of David's persecution at the hands of King Saul. Jesus knew this psalm well and his own sufferings were so similar to those David described. From the cross Jesus used the first verse to express his own painful agony and dereliction, "My God, my God, why hast thou forsaken me?"

The psalm is messianic in that David by inspiration saw his own sufferings as prophesies of the sufferings of the Messiah. The Gospel writers pointed out these similarities in their accounts of the crucifixion (Mark 15:29 = verse 7; Matt. 27:43 = verse 8; Matt. 27:35 = verse 18).

The first division of the psalm is the cry of painful agony to God from one who was being scorned, despised, and mocked (vv. 1–11). His enemies have surrounded him like wild animals. He is wounded and they stand about and gloat as they wait for him to die (vv. 12–18). He cries to God to come to his aid and save him (vv. 19–21).

Suddenly the tone of the psalm shifts as in the second half the writer lifts a prayer of thanksgiving to God (vv. 22–31). He is confident that God will bring him through the crisis and all the ends of the earth shall see it and turn to the Lord (v. 27).

Special points.—The superscription literally means "to the choirmaster according to the deer of the morning's dawn." Some have seen this as a reference to Jesus as the animal sacrifice in the early morning. But the phrase is probably the name of a familiar tune to which the psalm was to be sung.

My "darling" in verse 20 means my "life." It is dear to him because it is his only life.

The unicorn in verse 21 was the wild ox of Syria which was known for its fierceness. It is now extinct.

Truth for today.—The fact that Jesus made a verse of this psalm one of his seven last words gives it a special sacredness. We approach it reverently as through it we are allowed to know a part of what was in the mind of the Lord as he died for the sins of the world. It shows us that Jesus suffered separation from God for us.

Since the psalm ends with a positive note of victory, it may be that Jesus in addition to his cry of dereliction was expressing his confidence in a God who brings conquest out of defeat.

A Testimony of Trust (Psalm 23)

The passage.—This psalm, like the Lord's prayer, is one of the best known passages in the Bible. Even those who have no commitment to the kingdom of God have recited and found strength in it. It is simple, brief, and unimpressive from the standpoint of literary art. But its realistic appeal to human need and its clear assertion of God's care have won for it the highest place in the world's admiration.

David as a shepherd himself thinks of how he cares for his sheep. The conviction floods his mind that God cares for his people exactly the same way. And so from personal experience David paints a word picture of God as a God who cares.

Verses 1–4 picture God as a Shepherd. Man is described here as on a journey throughout which the Shepherd God leads him step by step. He provides every need (v. 1). He brings his people to oases of refreshment and strength (v. 2). He renews life with spiritual energy (v. 3). His will for man always leads him to the right pathways (v. 3). He gives courage in times of danger (v. 4).

Then David changes the image and pictures God as a generous host (vv. 5–6). These verses picture man at the journey's end in his Father's house. Here God gives him safety from the enemy and prepares for him a table of perfect provision. The enemy can be seen outside but in the Father's presence there is safety (v. 5). The anointed head and the overflowing cup symbolize the abundance of God's care (v. 5). The great climax of the psalm reminds the reader that God as a Shepherd and a Host will give his people victory over death (v. 6).

Special points.—The rod and staff in verse 4 represent God's defense and guidance. The rod or club was used to drive off wild animals and enemies. The staff was used to give guidance to the flock and to lift them back on the pathway when they fell. The rod and staff in the hands of God comfort or give assurance to the psalmist.

A Processional Hymn (Psalm 24)

The passage.—This psalm was composed at a time when the ark of the covenant was taken with the army into battle. After the battle is over the ark is returned to Mt. Zion. The psalm celebrates the entrance of the ark into the city. The ark of the covenant represented to the Jewish people the very presence of God, himself. And so this psalm hails the triumphant entry of God. It also specifies who is qualified to enter the city with God (vv. 3–6).

The first six verses are very similar to Psalm 15 (see exposition of Psalm 15). The last verses described the joyous procession arriving in Jerusalem at the gates of the Temple (vv. 7–10). This psalm was probably sung responsively as the ark was put back in its sacred place.

A Poetic Prayer for Help (Psalm 25)

The passage.—This is one of nine alphabetical psalms. Each verse begins with a successive letter of the Hebrew alphabet in the form of an acrostic. (In the present form, however, one letter is missing and two letters are used twice.) In verses 1–7 the psalmist is praying in faith for vindication (v. 2), for guidance (v. 4), for instruction (v. 5), for mercy (v. 6), and for forgiveness (v. 7).

In verses 8–15 the psalmist describes the uprightness of God. His steadfastness and love encourage him to continue his prayer. And so in verses 16–21 the prayer continues as the psalmist asks for deliverance and protection.

A Testimony of Faithfulness (Psalm 26)

The passage.—In 2 Samuel 15:6 there is an account of Absalom's rebellion in which he uses bribery to steal the allegiance of the men of Israel against David. This may be the incident behind this psalm. For here David contrasts his own faithfulness with the hypocritical, bloodthirsty men who use bribes (v. 10).

First the poet prays for vindication on the basis of his integrity before God (vv. 1–3), on the basis of his conduct with his fellowman (vv. 4–5), and on the basis of his love for God's house (vv. 6–8). He then prays that God will not count him with sinful men (vv. 9–11). The psalm ends with confident rejoicing that God will answer his prayer (v. 12).

Special points.—The word "dissemblers" in verse 4 means literally "not-real men." It refers to hypocrisy.

The washing of the hands in verse 6 was an act symbolizing innocence (Deut. 21:6–8; Matt. 27:24).

"Gather not my soul with sinners" (v. 9) means "sweep me not away with sinners."

A Hymn of Confidence (Psalm 27)

The passage.—This psalm has two divisions which differ so drastically in theme and mood that some have believed they are two separate psalms brought together as one.

The first division (vv. 1–6) is a joyful hymn of bold confidence in God. God is a source of light in the darkness of despair or trouble or conflict (v. 1). David longs to dwell in the presence of such a gracious God (v. 4).

The second division is a frantic plea for help (vv. 7–14). The poet here is threatened by his enemies and looks to God for deliverance. In the last two verses he allows his faith in God to encourage his soul (vv. 13–14).

Special points.—The word "pavilion" in verse 5 means "tabernacle" and refers to the tent-like gathering place of ancient Israel.

Verse 13 means, "How could I have doubted that I would see the goodness of the Lord in the land of the living?"

An Answered Prayer (Psalm 28)

The passage.—Like Psalms 26 and 27, this psalm expresses both a longing for the sanctuary of God and a prayer for the Lord's help. The circumstances are like those David faced during the persecution by Absalom. He prays for divine assistance, and he believes that God has heard and will answer his prayer (v. 6). In the last two verses David uses his experience of answered prayer to encourage the nation (vv. 8–9).

Special points.—"The pit" in verse 1 is another word for "the grave." It means death.

"Oracle" in verse 2 means "sanctuary."

The Psalm of the Seven Thunders (Psalm 29)

The passage.—David has witnessed a fierce rainstorm. As the thunder peals in rapid succession he seems to hear seven successive messages of the glory of God.

There is first a call to worship (vv. 1–2) as David invites the angels (literally the sons of God) to praise the Lord. Then he hears the sevenfold thunders of "the voice of the Lord" (vv. 3–5,7–9). The response at the end of the dramatic display of power pictures God as in complete control (vv. 10–11).

Special points.—"The waters" in verse 3 refers to a lake or a sea. This is probably the Mediterranean over which the storm approached.

"Sirion" in verse 6 is another name for snowcapped Mt. Hermon. The word means literally "to glitter." This verse

seems to picture the earth trembling during the height of the storm.

The "flames of fire" in verse 7 refers to lightning.

Truth for today.—Nature preaches powerful sermons. In Psalm 19 David says, "The heavens declare the glory of God." Psalm 29 is an illustration of that verse as the storm declares its sermon. Meteorologists have described the powerful energy of a single thunderstorm. The towering cumulonimbus clouds rise to fifty thousand feet and higher. The updrafts and downdrafts inside the cloud can rip an airplane to pieces. There is hail and ice and lightning in addition to the torrents of water. The wind accompanying such a storm can reach destructive velocity. All of this powerful energy is a minute reflection of the power and the glory of God.

Just as a thunderstorm subsides after its power has been spent, so David pictures the calm after the storm in verses 10–11. The psalm ends with the word "peace" like a rainbow after the rain.

Thanksgiving for Healing (Psalm 30)

The passage.—David has recovered from a serious illness which he believes God sent as a punishment (v. 5). He prayed earnestly for healing, and the words of his prayer are quoted in verses 9–10. God answered the prayer and healed the sickness (v. 2). David therefore rejoices; his mourning is changed to dancing (v. 11), and he sings glory to the Lord (v. 12).

Trusting Life in God's Hands (Psalm 31)

The passage.—The words of surrender in verse 5 were the dying words used by Martin Luther, John Knox, John Huss, Polycarp, Bernard, Henry V, Jerome, and Melancthon. However, they are best known as the last words of Jesus on the cross. The psalmist's cry for help in this passage has appealed to people everywhere who are in distress. It is a prayer asking for deliverance from trouble (vv. 1–8), from sickness (vv. 9–12), and from slandering enemies (vv. 13–18). Like so many other psalms it closes with thanksgiving for God's answer (vv. 19–24).

Special points.—Parts of this psalm are very similar to other Scripture passages. See Psalm 71:1–3, Jeremiah 20:10–12, Lamentations 1:20, 3:54.

The "net" in verse 4 was used by hunters to trap wild animals and birds.

Truth for today.—Jesus added only one word to verse 5 when he spoke from the cross. But what an important word it was—"Father." On the lips of our Lord this phrase of commitment was not a sigh of defeat but a proclamation of faith. When David used it he was hoping God would deliver him from death. But when Jesus used it he was expressing his confidence that through death his Father's will would be accomplished in victory. Because of Jesus' death and resurrection believers can commit their lives into the hands of the Father with the conviction that he is able to keep that which they have committed unto him against that day.

The Way of Forgiveness (Psalm 32)

The passage.—This is one of seven psalms dealing with repentance and forgiveness (Pss. 6,32,38,51,102,130,143). The first two verses set the theme. "Happy is the man who finds forgiveness" (vv. 1–2).

David next shares his personal experience. He has been seriously ill. He believes that the illness is the result of his refusal to repent and confess his sins (v. 3). Under conviction, he acknowl-

edges his sin before God, and he is forgiven (v. 5). The blessings and joy of healing and forgiveness lead him to praise God (vv. 6–7).

He then calls upon others to learn from his experience. They should not stubbornly refuse to repent but trust God who is merciful (vv. 8–11).

Special points.—The psalmist uses three words for sin in verses 1 and 2. "Transgression" means breaking loose or tearing away from God. "Sin" means that which is not pleasing to God or misses the mark of his will. "Iniquity" means perversion or distortion. He then uses three words for forgiveness. "Forgiven" means lifted-away. "Covered" means hidden or invisible. "Not imputed" means erased or not recorded.

Truth for today.—The same steps to forgiveness must be followed today. Sometimes it takes a crisis such as illness to awaken the guilty to the fact that he has sinned. He must then not keep silence (v. 3) but acknowledge his sin before God (v. 5). The Old Testament psalmist has pointed in this passage to the same promise found in the New Testament: "If we say we have no sin, we deceive ourselves, and the truth is not in us. If we confess our sins, he is faithful and just to forgive us our sins and to cleanse us from all unrighteousness" (1 John 1:8–9).

A Call to Worship (Psalm 33)

The passage.—Obviously, this psalm was written to be sung by the congregation. It was to be accompanied by the lyre and the harp played skillfully and loudly (vv. 2–3).

The first section praises the power of God's word in creation and history (vv. 4–9). The second section praises the power of his wisdom (counsel) in dealing with the nations (vv. 10–14). The third section praises God's all-seeing eye as he watches over his world (vv. 13–19). The last section praises God as a shield (vv. 20–22).

Special points.—In verse 15 the meaning is not that God makes all men similar or equal. The idea is simply that he makes all men. The verse is better understood if it is translated, "He fashions the heart of them all."

God's Goodness (Psalm 34)

The passage.—The occasion for this psalm is described in the superscription. David planned to escape from the Philistines by pretending to be insane (1 Sam. 21:10–15). The plan worked and David composed this psalm to thank God for his deliverance (vv. 4–6). David then invites the people to "taste and see" for themselves that the Lord is good (v. 8).

Special points.—This is another alphabetical psalm in which the verses begin with consecutive letters of the Hebrew alphabet.

Verse 6 means "those that look unto God will be lightened and their faces shall not be ashamed."

A Prayer for God's Defense (Psalm 35)

The passage.—David had enemies of all kinds. In this psalm he pictures them as false witnesses who accuse him (vv. 11,21), as opponents in a battle (vv. 1–4), as hunters trying to trap him like an animal (vv. 7–8), as mockers (vv. 15–16), as wild beasts (v. 17). David sees God as his last court of appeals. He prays that God will come to his defense (vv. 1–10). He prays that God will proclaim his innocence before the public (vv. 11–25). He prays that God will vindicate him by punishing his enemies and rewarding his friends (vv. 26–28).

The Two Ways of Life (Psalm 36)

The passage.—The life-style of the godly and the life-style of the godless are contrasted here as they were in Psalm 1. The wicked man is described as hearing a sinful voice deep inside his heart that tempts him (v. 1). In his wickedness he speaks lies, plans evil while in his bed, walks in a sinful pathway, and embraces evil (vv. 3–4).

In sharp contrast the second section speaks of the steadfast love of God that surrounds the life of the righteous (vv. 5–9). A good man is protected by God (v. 7), is provided for richly in God's house (v. 8), and receives life and light like a fountain (v. 9).

The psalm ends with a prayer that God's favor will always surround the writer to protect him (vv. 10–12).

Special points.—In verse 11 the phrase "come against me" should be translated "trample me."

Verse 12 should be translated "may evildoers be appalled, may they lie prostrate and be unable to rise."

Why Do the Wicked Prosper? (Psalm 37)

The passage.—The often debated question of why evil men prosper and good men suffer is the theme of this psalm. The basic thought running through the psalm is: do not be angry about the prosperity of the ungodly. Wait on the Lord. The happiness of the wicked will suddenly come to an end as will the suffering of the righteous. In the end good will triumph and evil will be punished.

First the poet gives wise advice to his readers about how to handle the inconsistencies in life (vv. 1–11). Even though they see the wicked enjoying blessing and the righteous afflicted, they must not lose faith in God's justice.

He described the fate of the wicked

(vv. 12–20), reminding his readers that "his day is coming" (v. 13).

Then the poet points to the certainty of reward for the righteous (vv. 21–31). The conclusion of the psalm (vv. 32–40) contrasts the final fate of the righteous (v. 37) and the wicked (v. 38).

Special points.—This psalm is written in the form of a double acrostic. The letters of the Hebrew alphabet are used twice to begin each of the verses.

The word "fret" in verse 1 means "to grow hot." This verse is repeated in Proverbs 24:19.

Truth for today.—The concept of life after death is very dim in the Old Testament. For that reason, writers like David longed for the wicked to be punished and the righteous be rewarded in this life. The New Testament clearly proclaims that after death man will face the judgment of God. No matter how inconsistent this life may seem, the New Testament promises that in the judgment right will triumph and evil will be punished. The idea of eternal life adds a helpful dimension to the answer of the problem this psalm deals with.

A Prayer for God's Help (Psalm 38)

The passage.—This is another of the penitential psalms (see Ps. 32). David prays at a time when he is deathly sick, in mental anguish, lonely and deserted by his loved ones, and guilt-ridden because of his sins. It may be he is describing his feelings after his sin of adultery (2 Sam. 11–12). The superscription indicates the psalm was used by worshipers when they brought a memorial sacrifice.

First David writes about the sufferings of sickness and sin which he is facing (vv. 1–8). The description of his disease is very similar to the symptoms Job suffered.

In verses 9–14 he laments the desertion of his friends and loved ones. This also sounds like Job, whose friends and family failed to sympathize with him.

In conclusion, David expresses his hope of release from suffering, and he prays for God's help (vv. 15–22).

Special points.—"I go mourning" in verse 6 literally means "I go black." It refers to the Jewish practice of wearing sackcloth and ashes to express sadness.

The closing cry for help is worded to show that David has not lost faith. He still believes God is a God of salvation (v. 22).

A Humble Prayer for Understanding (Psalm 39)

The passage.—Like so many of the preceding psalms, David writes this prayer in a time of suffering. At first he resolved to bear his affliction silently. But resentment over the injustice he has received builds up within him until he breaks the silence and speaks (vv. 1–3).

He calls on God to tell him how short and transient his life will be. This will encourage him because, if life is short, it means that his suffering will be short too (vv. 4–6).

David then asks, "What am I hoping for?" He answers his own question, "My hope is in thee" (vv. 7–13). Although there is no clear idea of life after death expressed in this psalm, there is a firm faith in the God who lives forever (vv. 12–13).

Special points.—The word "bridle" in verse 1 should be "muzzle."

In verse 3 the thoughts and emotions rubbed together and the frictions between them produced a blazing fire. Unable to contain the pain, the psalmist had to speak.

The "handbreath" in verse 5 was a

small measurement. Nine of them make a yard.

Praise and a Plea for Help (Psalm 40)

The passage.—This psalm has two divisions which may at first have been written as two separate psalms. The last half (vv. 13–17) is repeated independently as Psalm 70.

The first section (vv. 1–12) is a hymn of praise for God's deliverance. The word picture of God's lifting the poet out of miry clay and setting his feet upon a rock has been a favorite of readers through the years (v. 2.) With a joyful new song in his heart, the poet proclaims God's goodness to the congregation (vv. 9–10).

The second section (vv. 13–17) is an appeal for God's help (see exposition of Ps. 70). Since David has not withheld his praise and witness to God's goodness he prays that God will not withhold his tender mercies.

Special points.—Verses 7–9 are quoted in Hebrews 10:5–10 and is the message of the Messiah when he comes into the world. Just as David moves to his throne through suffering, so the Messiah moves to his throne after giving himself as the sacrifice for sin.

In verse 16 the words "aha, aha!" are an exclamation of sarcastic delight which rejoices in another's misfortune (compare Ps. 35:25).

God Delivers the Righteous (Psalm 41)

The passage.—After an introduction which states the general truth that God will strengthen and preserve the righteous (vv. 1–3), David gives his own testimony. The testimony is in the form of a drama.

The scene in verses 4–6 is a sickroom where David is alone and bitterly complaining. Into the sickroom comes his enemies who gloat over his misfortune saying, "When will he die and his name perish?" (v. 5).

In verses 7–9 the scene shifts to some gathering place of his enemies where they continue to rejoice in his trouble. David knows there is at least one trusted friend who has treacherously joined his enemies (v. 9). The faithless friend David was thinking about here could be Ahithophel (2 Sam. 16:23).

The scene then shifts back to the sickroom (vv. 10–12) as David prays in solitude that God will uphold him in his integrity. Verse 13 is a benediction which closes not only the psalm but the first book of 41 chapters. The same kind of benediction is added after Psalm 72, Psalm 89, and Psalm 106.

Special points.—Verse 3 should read, "The Lord sustains him in his sickbed. In his illness thou healest all his infirmities."

Verse 10 is quoted by Jesus in John 13:18 to show that the treachery of Judas Iscariot was a fulfilment of Scripture. The treachery of a friend like Ahithophel was typical and predictive of the treachery of Jesus' friend, Judas.

Verses 11–12 indicate that David's prayer for help was answered.

Truth for today.—This psalm proclaims the happiness of the man who is compassionate, who considers the poor or the weak (v. 1). It teaches that the one who takes a compassionate attitude toward life will tend to receive compassionate understanding from life. "Whatsoever a man soweth, that shall he also reap." A life of loving concern will produce happiness and fulfilment.

In 1 Corinthians 13 Paul says love is not puffed up, thinketh no evil, rejoiceth not in iniquity. By contrast, in this psalm the enemies gloat over the sickness of the writer and rejoice in his suffering.

David says this negative way of life will always end in defeat (v. 11). On the other hand the one who sympathizes with the weak in loving compassion will be preserved (vv. 1–3).

Longing for the Sanctuary of God (Psalms 42—43)

The passage.—Psalm 42 and Psalm 43 form one poem. In several Hebrew manuscripts they are joined together. The theme of the two psalms is the same, the psalmist's fervent desire to worship God at the Temple in Jerusalem. Three stanzas comprise the total poem, 42:1–5; 42:6–11; and 43:1–5. Each stanza ends in a refrain of virtually identical words.

Special points.—The psalmist was prevented from sharing in a pilgrimage to the Temple in Jerusalem. His reaction was one of painful regret. In deep emotion he expressed his yearning for the house of the Lord.

References to "Jordan, Hermonites" (Hermon, RSV), and "Mizar" (42:6) indicate that the psalmist was at the headwaters of the Jordan River in the region of Mount Hermon. They suggest his remoteness from Jerusalem. The great distance that separated him from the sanctuary seemed to alienate his spirit from God.

Memories intensified the psalmist's disappointment. He recalled his former participation in such pilgrimages and festivals, a joyous privilege. He remembered "the house of God," "the voice of joy and praise," and "a multitude that kept holyday" (42:4).

Complaints against enemies and oppressors (42:9–10; 43:1–2) describe aggravated distress. These enemies construed the psalmist's plight, illness or exile or other calamity, as evidence of the indifference or powerlessness of his God. Their sneers were like a sword in his bones. This was their taunting question: "Where is thy God?" (42:10).

The basic source of the psalmist's grief was not absence from the Temple but a desolating sense of separation from God. His longing for personal fellowship with "the living God" (42:2) was like the searing thirst of a panting deer hotly pursued or overcome by thirst in a time of drought.

Changing moods are reflected vividly. The refrain at the end of each stanza is a self-exhortation to faith in the face of distress. The thunderous waterfalls fed by Hermon's snow and the swirl of Jordan's flooded tributaries seemed to illustrate the restlessness of the psalmist's thoughts and feelings. But God's lovingkindness in the past was a quieting certainty for the future.

The final stanza displays a rising tide of confidence and joy. The circumstances of regret and perplexity were unchanged. But faith rebuked those circumstances. God's light and truth would lead the psalmist once again to the "holy hill . . . unto the altar of God" (43:3–4). They would lead to inspiring worship at the Temple and to renewal of personal communion with God. This experience of the presence of God (the face of God, 42:2, RSV) would be the psalmist's "exceeding joy" (43:4).

Bewilderment of God's People (Psalm 44)

The passage.—Israel had suffered defeat. God's face seemed to be turned from his people. The reasons were not clear.

The psalmist recalled God's great mercies to Israel in the past (vv. 1–3). He made those mercies the ground of confidence for the present and the future (vv. 4–8). But he described the present defeat (vv. 9–16) and asserted such faithfulness of the people as made their

humiliation inexplainable (vv. 17–22).
Finally, he appealed to God for speedy
deliverance (vv. 23–26).

Special points.—The specific setting
of the psalm is not indicated. Situations
such as those in the days of Jehoshaphat (2 Chron. 20:1–30), Hezekiah (2
Kings 18:13—19:37), and Josiah (2
Kings 23:26–30) suggest themselves.

The psalmist fixed attention on the
people's entrance into Canaan. That historic victory was not due to military
prowess but to God. God's past performance was a basis of hope in the
current calamity.

At points exhortations addressed to
God were almost violent (vv. 11–13,
23–24). The distraught psalmist did not
recognize clearly that the innocent
sometimes suffer. He did not understand
that even God's people may be covered
with "the shadow of death" (v. 19; deep
darkness, RSV).

Perhaps the psalmist's perception of
God's ways was deepened through
suffering. The basis of the final appeal
was not the self-respect of Israel but
the character of God. Let God deliver
his people for his "mercies' sake" (v. 26;
steadfast love, RSV).

Celebration of the King's Marriage (Psalm 45)

The passage.—The poem celebrated
the marriage of an Israelitish king to a
foreign princess. The particular king
cannot be identified. Solomon, Ahab,
Joram, and Jeroboam the son of Joash
have been suggested.

Following an introductory word on
the inspiration of his theme (v. 1), the
poet addressed the king (vv. 2–9). He
paid tribute to the ruler's noble appearance, secure throne, and royal attendants. Afterward, he turned his attention to the queen (vv. 10–17). He
urged her full devotion to the king, de-

scribed her magnificent bridal attire,
and prophesied her continuing fame.

Special points.—Psalm 45 is one of
the Royal Psalms. Other psalms related
especially to the king are 2, 18, 20, 21,
72, 89, 101, 110, and 144.

The psalm apparently was composed
to celebrate an actual occasion. That it
was written as an idealistic prophecy, an
allegory, describing the Messiah as
bridegroom and his church as bride is
most improbable.

Moral earnestness and national ideals
filled the poet's thought. The king was
urged to use his skill and valor to maintain "truth and meekness and righteousness" (v. 4), not merely to subdue
enemies.

The psalmist had an exalted conception of the kingship. In the debated
phrase "O God" (v. 6), the king probably was not addressed as God. Rather,
the king's throne was declared to be
God's throne, or to be like God's throne
(Your divine throne, RSV), standing
"for ever and ever."

God in the Midst of His People (Psalm 46)

The passage.—This is a hymn of triumphant trust in God. Jerusalem and
Judah had been under the threat of
calamity. God had intervened. Perhaps
the occasion was the deliverance of
Jerusalem from Moab and Ammon in
the days of Jehoshaphat (2 Chron.
20:1–30), or Sennacherib's abandonment
of the siege of Jerusalem in the time of
Hezekiah (2 Kings 18:13—19:37).

The hymn consists of three stanzas,
verses 1–3, 4–7, and 8–11. God was
declared to be the present helper amidst
hazards, the sure source of inward security, and the victor over men's militant
violence.

Special points.—The destructive physical powers described in verses 2–3

(volcano, earthquake, storm) probably were symbols. They represented feared military powers that threatened Judah.

The river flowing out of the heights of Jerusalem, where no river actually is found, symbolized spiritual resources. In the most terrifying circumstances, God is readily available (a very present help, v. 1).

The Lord demonstrated that he is sovereign God. His sovereignty is destined to reach all nations (the heathen . . . the earth, v. 10). Therefore, let violent oppressors leave off!

Truth for today.—This psalm inspired Martin Luther to write the hymn, "A Mighty Fortress Is Our God." Both psalm and hymn are perennial sources of comfort and strength.

Faith often finds increased reality in times of trouble. Adversity did not destroy the psalmist's faith. It was the occasion for enriched experience with God, the stimulus for eloquent witness to what God had done.

Praise to God the King (Psalm 47)

The passage.—God's deliverance of Israel from extreme peril filled the psalmist with triumphant joy. He called on all peoples (people . . . earth, vv. 1–2) to acclaim the Lord as king, vv. 1–4). He exhorted them to acknowledge the enthronement of the Lord as king over all rulers (princes . . . shields, v. 9) and nations (vv. 5–9).

Special points.—This hymn of kingship is related in theme and spirit to Psalms 93,95–100. Its immediate connection is with Psalms 46 and 48. The three psalms apparently arose out of extraordinary expressions of divine mercy in times of grave danger.

Ceremonies for crowning a king at Jerusalem suggested the description of the Lord's enthronement over all the earth (2 Kings 11:12). The processional march toward the Temple probably was the backdrop for the exclamation, "God is gone up with a shout" (v. 5).

There is a paradox in the emphasis on the Lord's conquering the nations (v. 3) and exalting Israel (v. 4). Obviously, Israel could rejoice. But how could subdued nations welcome the Lord's supremacy? The implication is that the Lord rules with mercy and justice. Moreover, his choice of Israel is a means of ministry to all humanity (earth, v. 7). All may become spiritually "the people of the God of Abraham" (v. 9).

Praise to the Protector of Zion (Psalm 48)

The passage.—The psalm expresses praise to the Lord as protector of his people. Jerusalem had been spared. The Lord had protected "Zion" (v. 2), the visible symbol of the invisible God.

Three stanzas are recognizable. "Beautiful for situation" in the mountains of Judah, Zion was the setting for praise to the Lord (vv. 1–3). Enemies had fallen back in defeat, evoking praise to the Lord who granted deliverance (vv. 4–8). The covenant love (lovingkindness, v. 9) of God in preserving his own people inspired increasing gratitude (vv. 9–14).

Special points.—In theme and spirit this poem is a counterpart to Psalm 46, a sequel to Psalm 47. The first poem celebrates the deliverance of the nation from peril. The second praises the majesty of the Lord as deliverer. The third describes the glory of the city which was delivered.

Jerusalem was related peculiarly to the Lord. Perhaps the obscure expression "the sides [districts] of the north" (v. 2), much like that used by other ancient peoples to designate the abode of their gods, had this sense (Isa. 14:13).

The city's high elevation and physical grandeur were exhilarating. Of far greater meaning was the fact that there the Lord specially manifested himself to his people.

Hope for the Future (Psalm 49)

The passage.—The author was a teacher of wisdom. His instruction (parable, v. 4; proverb, RSV) concerned the problem (dark saying, v. 4; riddle, RSV) of suffering inflicted by foolish men who prospered. The appeal to all implied the importance of the problem for all (v. 1–4).

Prosperous, arrogant men inflicted suffering on the psalmist. But death was coming, and their wealth could not buy an escape (vv. 5–12). These persecutors were herded toward the gloom of Sheol, but God would rescue and receive the psalmist (vv. 13–20).

Special points.—The refrain (vv. 12,20) placed emphasis on the fact that death comes to all. The man of affluence does not continue to live indefinitely in his "pomp" (RSV).

The emphasis was enforced by means of two key ideas. First, material wealth can not buy off death (vv. 7–9). One can not "ransom himself" (RSV; redeem his brother) so that he may "live for ever." Second, one's earthly advantages cease at his death, "his glory shall not descend after him" (vv. 17–19).

All men experience death (vv. 10–11). But when the psalmist should come to that experience God would receive him (v. 15). This was confident expectation of continuing life with God.

The True Religion That God Requires (Psalm 50)

The passage.—The psalm falls into four parts. In the introduction God is represented as revealing himself in a solemn call for judgment on Israel (vv.

1–6). There follows a prophetic message concerning the true sacrifice that God requires (vv. 7–15). Then superficial religion is denounced (vv. 16–21). The conclusion combines warning to faithless men and promise to those whose manner of life (conversation, v. 23) demonstrated loyalty to God.

Special points.—In Moses' times God revealed himself at Sinai to establish covenant with Israel and to declare his requirements. Now he revealed himself at Zion to judge the faithless and to renew loyalty in the covenant people (my saints, v. 5).

The Judge was described by titles which attested his jurisdiction. He acted as both God of awesome power (mighty God) and covenant grace (Lord, v. 1).

The emphasis on dynamic faith in contrast to ceremonial religion is similar to that of Isaiah 1:10–17; Jeremiah 7:21–26; Hosea 6:6; Amos 5:21–27; Micah 6:6–8. Israel offered sacrifices with strict observance (vv. 8–13). What God desired was not meaningless ceremonies, but spiritual worship in humility and thanksgiving.

A Cry for God's Forgiveness (Psalm 51)

The passage.—This is a psalm of personal religion, of repentance and renewal. It is the expression of a heart overwhelmed by shame, broken by guilt, and delivered from despair to joy.

The superscription connects the psalm with David's repentance for his sin with Bathsheba (2 Sam. 12:1–14). The connection is appropriate. But verses 18–19 apparently were added much later, perhaps during the Exile or just prior to Nehemiah's mission.

Verses 1–2 record a heart cry for God's forgiveness. In verses 3–5 a personal confession makes genuine repentance the basis for appeal. An urgent petition for cleansing and renewal follows in verses 6–12. Assuming God's merciful answer, commitment to praise and testimony is made in verses 13–17.

Special points.—The so-called Penitential Psalms include 6, 25, 32, 38, 39, 40, 51, 102, and 130. Psalm 51 is the most famous of all. It expresses supreme concern for the inward, moral nature of sin and forgiveness.

Three words describe the psalmist's sin: "transgressions" (v. 1), meaning rebellion; "iniquity" (v. 2), denoting perversion; and "sin" (v. 2), signifying variance from right. Three words characterize forgiveness. The penitent prayed that God would blot out (v. 1) rebellion, "wash" (v. 2; knead or tread) out perversion, and "cleanse" (v. 2; pronounce clean) from sin.

Verse 5 records the psalmist's conviction that he was entangled in the reality of sin by membership in the human race and in human society. He did not mean that sin is transmitted biologically, or that physical conception and birth themselves are evil.

For the psalmist forgiveness was a creative experience (vv. 6,10–12), deeply inward, radically transforming. It was the work of God's Spirit, creating and sustaining in him a moral reconciliation, a joyous fellowship, and a radiant witness.

Truth for today.—Sin seals the lips of testimony. Only when one is filled with the joy of God's salvation does he have a radiant, winsome word.

Victory over sin is never possible until a new creation is a reality of experience. The broken, willing spirit is the sinner's preparation. The Spirit of holiness works out the divine purpose.

The Fall of a Tyrant (Psalm 52)

The passage.—The psalm is concerned with a cruel tyrant. The superscription connects it with David's indig-

nation at Doeg, a betrayer of him and Abimelech (1 Sam. 22:9–23).

The poem comprises three divisions: verses 1–4,5–7, and 8–9. The oppressor is described as an unscrupulous schemer. Divine judgment is pronounced on the materialistic monster. The security of the psalmist and the downfall of the traitor are contrasted.

Special points.—The phrase "the goodness of God" (v. 1) probably means "against the godly" (RSV). As a godly man, the psalmist was subjected to the mischief of a braggart.

Fear and laughter (v. 6) did not represent contradictory emotions. God's acts of judgment would produce awe in the "righteous." The same acts would remove the oppressor and bring gladness.

The tyrant trusted in material riches, the psalmist in the covenant love of God (mercy, v. 8). In judgment the tyrant would be uprooted like a fallen tree. The psalmist would have security like that of "a green olive tree" (v. 8) inside the Temple courts.

Man's Folly—Past and Present (Psalm 53)

The passage.—This is a second version of Psalm 14. Both psalms describe the universal moral perversity of mankind.

In Psalm 53, three parts appear: universal corruption and its root cause (vv. 1–3), oppression of the people of God and God's intervention (vv. 4–5), and prayer for the full restoration of Israel (v. 6).

Special points.—Like Psalm 14, this psalm traces the problem of mankind's corruptness to its source—the refusal of men to seek God. It is concerned with the resultant evil, men's cruel oppression of fellow men.

Unlike Psalm 14, here the consistent

designation of deity is "God," a general term, rather than "Lord," the name of the covenant God of Israel. The substitution is appropriate. The moral state of mankind, not of Israel only, concerned the psalmist.

"The fool" (v. 1) represented a class of men, the "depraved" (RSV; filthy, v. 3). This moral state was not the result of a speculative conclusion that God is nonexistent. It was the consequence of rejection of God and his moral principles.

Variations appear in verse 5 as compared with Psalm 14:5–6. Perhaps the original psalm was adapted and applied to a current or recent attack upon Israel by ungodly oppressors.

The expression "bringeth back the captivity" (v. 6) means "restores the fortunes" (RSV). Compare Job 42:10. The psalmist prayed for a radical renewal of the moral and national life of Israel.

Prayer Concerning Arrogant Foes (Psalm 54)

The passage.—The psalm consists of three parts: verses 1–3, 4–5, and 6–7. At the beginning the psalmist prayed for deliverance from ruthless enemies. He then professed confidence in the Lord, his chief upholder. In conclusion he promised a sacrifice of thankfulness when prayer had been answered and rescue experienced.

Special points.—The superscription links the psalm to David's reaction to plans of the Ziphites of Judah to betray him into the hands of Saul (1 Sam. 23–26). In the psalm itself the term "strangers" (v. 3) probably classified the enemies as insolent men (the proud, Psalm 86:14), not as foreigners or non-Judahites.

Threatened by those who would take his life, the psalmist appealed for deliverance by the Lord's "name," and vindication by the Lord's "strength" (v. 1; might, RSV). The name of the Lord was no mere title. It represented the God who acts in behalf of his oppressed people and vindicates their uprightness and loyalty.

The psalmist did not think abstractly, distinguishing between sinners and their sin. He desired that God would "reward evil" to the enemies, even "cut them off" (v. 5). He was convinced that God's moral "faithfulness" (RSV; truth, v. 5) demanded punitive judgment.

Man's Treachery *Versus* God's Trustworthiness (Psalm 55)

The passage.—A prayer in anguish opens the psalm (vv. 1–8). So fierce was the hostility directed against the psalmist that he longed continually for escape, protection, and rest.

An outcry of anger follows (vv. 9–15). The psalmist's mood turned to indignation. The bitter fact was that his own friend was now his adversary. But calmer words mark the conclusion (vv. 16–23). God would deal justly with the enemies and with him.

Special points.—Perhaps the psalm refers to David's experience in the time of Absalom's rebellion and reflects the treachery of Ahithophel (2 Sam. 15–17). Or possibly it reflects the trials of Jeremiah and the treacherous actions of his friend Pashhur (Jer. 20). The specific episode can not be identified.

Extreme pressures induced the psalmist's longing of heart, his fantasy, described in verses 6–8. Strife was on the city walls (vv. 9–11). Treachery was in the words and actions of his friend (vv. 12–14).

Betrayal by a respected friend (equal . . . acquaintance, v. 13), not hateful assault by others, inflicted the deepest hurt. This deceiver had shared as a "companion" (RSV; guide, v. 13) in the services or worship.

Prayer that God destroy the plotting and confuse (divide, v. 9) the tongues of violent men is understandable from a moral viewpoint. The plea that "death seize upon them" (v. 15) and that God "bring them down into the pit of destruction" (v. 23; the lowest pit, RSV) is far less so.

Faith in a Time of Fear (Psalm 56)

The passage.—The psalm portrays strong tension between fear and faith. The psalmist cried out of fearful persecution. But his loyalty was unswerving; he affirmed his confidence in God. According to the superscription, David's experience as a captive of the Philistines is reflected here (1 Sam. 21–22).

The psalm has two parts: verses 1–4 and 5–11, with verses 12–13 as the conclusion of both. In the first part, the psalmist cried out for God's mercy. He was trampled (RSV; swallow me up, v. 2) by enemies, an army in fierceness and number. In the second part, he appealed for a judgment of retribution on these enemies. Their plots were cruel, their actions criminal.

Special points.—Verses 4 and 10–11 are almost identical, suggesting a refrain. The two pairs of key terms are "God" and "trust," "fear" (afraid, v. 11) and "flesh" (man, v. 11). These pairs were set in contrast. With faith in God, the psalmist would not be overwhelmed by fear of the worst that earthy powers could do.

One certainty was the principal source of confidence: "God is for me" (v. 9; Rom. 8:31). The persecuted psalmist was sustained by the conviction that God was concerned. Even his bitter tears would be treasured up and noted in the heavenly record (v. 8; Mal. 3:16).

Deliverance from enemies was fore-seen as if already present. It was viewed as a rescue from "death" and "falling" to a joyous "walk . . . in the light of the living" (v. 13). The psalmist must respond in thanksgiving and pay a vow made in the hour of crisis.

Protection in a Time of Peril (Psalm 57)

The passage.—This is a companion piece to Psalm 56. The two psalms are much alike in style and theme. Both are concerned with vicious enemies, persevering faith, and divine deliverance of the persecuted. Each has a superscription pointing to David's harrowing experiences when a fugitive from Saul (1 Sam. 22–24).

An outcry for God's protection, voiced in confidence, is expressed in verses 1–5. A complaint of the enmity and plotting of enemies, overbalanced by faith, completes the poem in verses 6–11. The repeated refrain, verses 5 and 11, is an appeal to God to demonstrate his power.

Special points.—A young bird seeking protection under its mother's wings (v. 1) was favorite imagery for psalmists (17:8; 36:7; 91:1,4). If the image suggested divine protection, it first pictured the movement of an imperiled one toward God.

Persecutors were described as ravenous "lions" (v. 4). Apparently they were searching near the hidden place where the intended victim was sleeping. They were represented also as hunters. Crafty and determined, they set a trap for the intended prey (net . . . pit, v. 6).

Confidence in the covenant love and the faithfulness (mercy . . . truth, v. 3) of God was no temporary emotion. Steadfastness sustained this hounded man: "My heart is fixed" (v. 7). He would "awake the dawn" (RSV; will awake early, v. 8) with praise to his protector.

God the Righteous Judge (Psalm 58)

The passage.—Corruption masquerading as justice was the psalmist's concern. First, there is an indictment of pretentious judges who pervert justice (vv. 1–5). Afterward, there is a petition to God for removal of these corrupt officials (vv. 6–9). Finally, there is an expression of joyous vindication: the evil system falls, for there is a "God that judgeth" (vv. 10–11).

Special points.—The most nearly satisfactory rendering of "O congregation" in verse 1 is "you mighty ones" (or, *you gods,* RSV). Those addressed were judges. They were men of authority, officials bloated with self-esteem.

Likewise, the judges probably were not called "sons of men." Rather, they were asked concerning the rightness with which they judged the sons of men (RSV).

The words of corrupt judges were as dangerous as snake's venom. The biased, unprincipled officials were as deaf to appeal as the deadly snake that ignores the shrill piping of expert "charmers" (v. 5).

The prayer in verses 6–9 invoked punishment on officials who dispensed violence rather than justice. Expressed in graphic symbols, it is sevenfold: broken teeth, fangless jaws, vanishing water, withered grass, dissolving snail, untimely birth, and burned thorns. Righteous men would rejoice, for right will prevail (v. 11).

The God of Refuge (Psalm 59)

The passage.—The prayer consists of an appeal for divine help (vv. 1–5), a description of extreme danger (vv. 6–10), a plea for judgment on enemies (vv. 11–13), and a testimony of joyous confidence (vv. 14–17). The concern was twofold: deliverance of the psalmist from bloodthirsty men (v. 2), and

demonstration of God's care over "Jacob" (v. 13), his people.

Special points.—If this was a prayer of David (superscription; 1 Sam. 19), he was like a besieged outpost awaiting a relieving force. But while the prayer was personal (vv. 1–4), the praying man represented Israel (my people, Jacob, vv. 11,13). Perhaps the enemies were called "the heathen" (vv. 5,8) because they were aliens to God. But the term was the usual designation for non-Israelitic nations.

Enemies planned to take the psalmist's "life" (RSV; soul, v. 3). Their hostility was unprovoked (without my fault, v. 4). Yet they prowled nightly, like scavenger dogs in the streets (vv. 6–7, 14–15).

The persecuted man was sustained by a conviction: "My God in his steadfast love will meet me" (v. 10, RSV). Such is the force of the words, "The God of my mercy shall prevent me." Just so, the concluding word was a testimony of assurance. "God is my defence" (vv. 9, 16–17; fortress, RSV).

Lamentation Changed to Confidence (Psalm 60)

The passage.—A national lament, this poem reports Israel's defeat in battle. The failure was viewed as proof of divine displeasure toward Israel. Yet only God could reverse the circumstances. This he would do.

There was first a lamentation, asking divine help (vv. 1–5). A message followed—the answer from God (vv. 6–8). Lamentation was changed to confidence (vv. 9–12).

Special points.—Israel's flight before the foe was an unforeseen defeat and a national humiliation. The superscription points to battles fought by David and Joab (2 Sam. 8:3–8,13–14; 1 Chron. 19:6–9). In the lament itself the specific military defeat and the historical period are not identified.

Verse 4 probably is irony. The Israelites believed themselves to be God's people, but present reverses mocked that claim. The God-given "banner" (Ex. 17:15, margin) in this instance had led to flight, not to victory. This, then, is the probable sense: that they might flee from the bow (not "that it may be displayed because of the truth").

God's answer to shaken, staggering Israel (vv. 6–8) was a ground of confidence. All nations are his. He deals with them in sovereign wisdom. As Judah was his "scepter" (RSV; my lawgiver, v. 7), so Moab would be his washbasin and Edom his property (I cast out my shoe, v. 8; Ruth 4:7).

A Prayer to God from Afar (Psalm 61)

The passage.—This is the prayer of a king for himself, or of a subject for himself and his king. It consists of two parts: a far-away cry for God's help (vv. 1–5), and a fervent prayer for the king's welfare (vv. 6–8).

An assault by enemies was the occasion. But a sense of far-offness from God—and great distance from the sanctuary—was the problem. Spiritual security was the paramount concern, the urgent need.

Special points.—What the psalmist most desired for himself was unattainable through his own strength. He described it as "the rock that is higher than I" (v. 2). He longed for closeness to God, spiritual security.

What he asked for the king was a stable reign. Steadfast love and faithfulness (mercy and truth, v. 7) would be like guardian angels. Such was the appeal.

While yet troubled, the psalmist expressed confidence. God had heard and answered his request (or, "hast given

me the heritage," v. 5). Deeply inspired, he vowed to live a life of daily thanksgiving.

Trust in God Alone (Psalm 62)

The passage.—Poised and patient trust in God alone is the theme of this psalm. The psalmist expressed quiet confidence, yet acknowledged that he was assailed by foes (vv. 1–4). Repeating the profession of faith, he exhorted others to trust in God rather than human resources (vv. 5–10). Finally, he told of a message from God, assuring the triumph of justice (vv. 11–12).

Special points.—The psalmist professed utter faith in God's help. The term "only," occurring in verses 1 (RSV), 2, 5, and 6, declared singular reliance on God. All human schemes and possessions were described as a delusion (vanity, lie, v. 9).

The psalmist waited on God "in silence" (v. 1, RSV). This is the better rendering of the statement, "Truly my soul waiteth upon God." He was so assaulted as to be like a leaning wall and a rickety fence (terms applied to the psalmist, not to the assailants). Yet he experienced inward calm and strength even while sorely mistreated.

The style of verses 11–12 (once, twice) is like that of Proverbs 6:16; 30:15; and other such passages. As a teacher of wisdom, the psalmist declared a message of assurance. God's "power" and steadfast love (mercy) guaranteed justice for all.

The God Who Satisfies (Psalm 63)

The passage.—This is a prayer for fellowship and communion with God in the sanctuary. Longing, confidence, and praise are blended in verses 1–4. Deep satisfaction—spiritual assurance and security—is expressed in verses 5–8. Public shame of defeated enemies is predicted in 9–11.

Special points.—The superscription relates the psalm to David's flight from Absalom (2 Sam. 15–17). The expression *dry and thirsty land* (v. 1) readily suggests the wilderness of Judah through which David passed. Reference to "the king" (v. 11) is of interest in the same connection.

As in Psalms 42–43, the psalmist longed for the sanctuary and lamented his distant relation to God. His sense of separation was intensified by the threat of enemies.

Yet the psalm is marked by spiritual growth and deepening insight. Thirst (v. 1), hunger (v. 5), and yearning to look upon God (v. 2) expressed intense desire for fellowship with God, not mere longing for a holy place and sacred ceremonies. Fulfilment came in joyous consciousness of divine care, spiritual security, and sure defeat of criminal adversaries.

Communion with God inspired a poetic description of the twofold nature of faith. The believer "clings" (RSV; followeth hard) to God, and God sustains (upholdeth, v. 8) the believer.

The Ultimate Triumph of Right Over Wrong (Psalm 64)

The passage.—This is another psalm of distress and prayer because of bitter foes. But it is much more. It is a profession of confidence in the ultimate triumph of right and defeat of evil. In tone and content it resembles Psalms 56–59.

Almost overwhelmed by enemies who schemed in snug secrecy, the psalmist prayed for divine protection (vv. 1–6). He expressed conviction that God would frustrate the evil plotters and make their defeat a lesson to others (vv. 7–9). He concluded with an exhortation to gladness because of the righteous judgment of God (v. 10).

Special points.—Here, as in many other such psalms, enmity was expressed through malicious, defaming words. Slander was like a "sword" and "arrows" (v. 3) in its destructiveness. Evil accusations were concocted in the depths of perverse hearts (v. 6).

Because God is righteous, the psalmist was sure that the principle of retributive justice operates. Shooting an arrow was the figure employed both for the assault of the evil men and for their overthrow (vv. 4,7). As the enemies had set a trap for the feet of another, so they themselves would stumble (vv. 5,8).

Verse 10 is probably an exhortation (RSV) rather than a forecast. In view of God's goodness and justice, let his people rejoice.

Thanksgiving for Harvest (Psalm 65)

The passage.—This is a song of national thanksgiving. Perhaps the specific occasion was the end of a drought, when the people were saved from famine. Since rain apparently had come while grain was still in the field (vv. 11–13), the probable season was the beginning of barley harvest (Lev. 23:10–14).

In verses 1–4 the psalmist sang of an assembly gathered for offering praise and performing vows at the sanctuary. In verses 5–8 he declared God to be the true hope of Israel and all peoples. In verses 9–13 he celebrated the provident gifts of rain and abundant harvest.

Special points.—Three considerations made offering of praise and performing of vows at the sanctuary to be especially appropriate. God had answered prayer, forgiven the rebellious, and made his house a blessing.

The singer caught a glimpse of true worship becoming universal (all flesh, v. 2). God's acts in behalf of Israel were both awesome and righteous (terrible things in righteousness, v. 5). They would be witnessed by peoples far and wide as tokens of God's control of all nature and all nations (vv. 5,8). They would motivate these peoples to reverence God and rejoice (are afraid . . . rejoice, v. 8).

The productive season was the climax of the year. Expressed in poetic symbols, when the joyous earth was arrayed in fruitfulness and plenty, then God placed a crown of splendor on the year (vv. 11–13).

Thanksgiving for Deliverance (Psalm 66)

The passage.—This hymn celebrated God's deliverance of his people. Verses 1–12 treat thanksgiving and praise in the people's public worship. Verses 13–20 report thanksgiving and payment of vows by an individual.

Special points.—Allusions were made to the dryshod crossing of the Red Sea and the Jordan (sea . . . flood, v. 6), but a recent deliverance was the occasion for the hymn (vv. 8–12). So extraordinary was the recent deliverance that it had significance for "lands" and "nations" (vv. 1,7). The destruction of Sennacherib's army in Hezekiah's time was an event of such international impact (2 Kings 18:13—19:37).

The "we" part of the hymn (vv. 1–12) reviewed God's mighty acts in the history of Israel. Perhaps the review was an introduction to the "I" part (vv. 13–20), which is a personal testimony to answered prayer.

The individual whose prayer had been answered and who now fulfilled his vow was the king or some other prominent person. He first addressed God in thanks and commitment (vv. 13–15). He then entreated the people to hear his testimony to answered prayer (vv. 16–19).

The psalmist sounded a universal note. This was his central theme: God's wondrous works in Israel should lead all people to worship him.

A Prayer That All Peoples Worship God (Psalm 67)

The passage.—This festive song is a prayer that God's blessings to Israel would bring God's blessings to all peoples. Perhaps a bountiful harvest was the immediate occasion (v. 6), but the abundant crop was only an example of God's goodness to Israel. The mission of Israel to the nations, the bestowal of blessings through a people specially blessed, was the wider concern.

Special points.—Petition was linked inseparably with purpose in the prayer. Each stanza, verses 1–3, 4–5, and 6–7, consists of these two elements. Petition is clear in verses 1 and 4: "God be merciful. . . . O let the nations be glad." Actually verse 6 has the same force: May God bless (God . . . shall bless).

Purpose was first made explicit: that God's way and salvation be made known to all nations (v. 2). Then it was expressed as a refrain concluding the first and second stanzas (vv. 3,5). Possibly the refrain was present also at the end of the last stanza (v. 7) in early usage, giving completeness to the song.

The character of God was declared the moral stimulant for nations to worship him. The verbs "judge" and "govern" (v. 4) signify rule and guide. God governs and guides men with consistent uprightness.

Song of a Triumphal Procession (Psalm 68)

The passage.—A triumphal procession, both the event and its meaning, is described in dramatic poetry. Perhaps the original occasion was the transference of the ark of the Lord from the house of Obed-edom to the new tabernacle on Mount Zion (2 Sam. 6:2–19). If so, the poem was used also in subsequent celebrations of victory.

A prelude of praise to the God of greatness and goodness (vv. 1–6) is followed by a review of some of God's triumphs in the past (vv. 7–18). The Lord is praised as the present deliverer of his people (vv. 19–23). He is pictured as the victor honored by a triumphal procession of reunited Israel (vv. 24–27) and by the tribute of non-Israelite kings (vv. 28–31). The conclusion is a doxology (vv. 32–35).

Special points.—The God of might (vv. 1–2) was recognized also as the God of mercy (vv. 5–6). He puts hateful enemies to flight; he is the "father of the fatherless."

Several historical allusions were adapted from the Song of Deborah in Judges 5. Especially noteworthy are verses 7–9, 12–13 as compared with Judges 5:4–5, 16. Similarly, certain expressions have parallels in the Blessing of Moses in Deuteronomy 33.

The concluding doxology included all the earth in praise to the Lord. The mission of Israel to the nations was implied, the sure and decisive victory of the Lord anticipated.

Suffering for Conviction (Psalm 69)

The passage.—Undeserved suffering —suffering due in large part to devotion to God—is the theme. Essentially the same theme appears in Psalms 22, 35, 44, and 109.

The psalmist's plight is indicated in a distressful outcry in verses 1–5. The cause of the plight, unswerving loyalty to God, is expressed in a testimony in verses 6–12. The psalmist's prayer for God's help is recorded in verses 13–18. An extension of the prayer to include condemnation of persecutors follows in verses 19–28. The psalmist's praise for the sure help of God forms a fitting

conclusion (vv. 29–36).

Special points.—The superscription relates the psalm to David, but it is not linked readily to any known episode in his life. Indeed, verses 33–36 seem to refer to the Babylonian exile and to longing for restoration to the land of Israel.

The psalmist's calamity was rooted in the antagonism of many. Unprincipled men hated him (vv. 4,12). Friends and kindred misunderstood him (v. 8). He was like a person swept away by flood waters, near to drowning and despairing of help (vv. 1–3,14–15).

This was the chief agony: the psalmist suffered because of uprightness (not sinlessness, v. 5) and loyalty to God (vv. 7–11). His situation could turn others from uprightness and loyalty (v. 6).

Yet God would act (vv. 32–33). He is just, and he answers prayer. This ultimately was the source of hope and confidence.

An Urgent Prayer for Deliverance (Psalm 70)

The passage.—This psalm is a repetition of Psalm 40:13–17, with a few variations. It begins and ends with an urgent plea (make haste, vv. 1,5) for personal deliverance. It includes a fervent prayer for the frustration of enemies (vv. 2–3) and for the joy of the Lord's people (v. 4).

Special points.—This fragment of Psalm 40 appears at this point probably because of similarity to Psalm 69. Both begin with a note of urgency. Both invoke divine judgment on enemies. Both appeal for personal deliverance from desperate circumstances.

Further, these five verses form an appropriate postscript to Psalm 69 because that psalm has much in common with Psalm 40. Especially noteworthy are the references to mire, urgent rescue, and seekers of the Lord.

Perhaps the most interesting variation from Psalm 40 is the substitution of divine names. "Lord" is changed to "God," except in the second part of verse 1. On the other hand, "God" is changed to Lord in the latter part of verse 5.

The Prayer and Praise of an Old Man (Psalm 71)

The passage.—The psalm is composed of petition (vv. 1–11) and praise (vv. 12–24). More strictly analyzed, the two elements are commingled in a prayer.

Even while assaulted by enemies and perhaps afflicted otherwise, an aged man (vv. 9,18) expressed mature faith. This he did through personal confidence and by testimony to other people.

Special points.—The psalmist made strong appeals for both deliverance and protection. He symbolized the God-given security that he desired as a "rock of refuge" (RSV; v. 3). The symbol was a favorite with psalmists.

Confidence in God was induced by a lifetime of experience. From his youth to the present the psalmist had known a relationship of personal trust and divine instruction (vv. 5,17).

The aged sufferer was "a wonder unto many" (v. 7). Perhaps this was because his lifelong devotion to God had not excused him from persecution. Or, perhaps it was because of his astonishing deliverance in previous crises.

Petition for rescue was linked with a noble purpose. The psalmist would be spared in order to teach the new generation the message of his God (v. 18).

A Prayer for the King and His People (Psalm 72)

The passage.—This is a prayer for the king and his people. It seems especially designed for the ruler's coronation. It magnified his relationship to God and his responsibility for maintaining justice.

The prayer comprises five appeals for divine blessings on the king and his subjects. These are just administration (vv. 1–4), continuing dynasty (vv. 5–7), worldwide dominion (vv. 8–11), increasing righteousness (vv. 12–14), and prosperity and fame (vv. 15–17).

Special points.—The superscription relates the psalm to King Solomon. Perhaps the relationship was suggested by references to the royal son, expansive kingdom, and tribute wealth (vv. 1,8,10, 15). Possibly the prayer was written for Solomon, not by him. The viewpoint of a loyal subject, especially concerned for the poor, is reflected (vv. 2,4,12–13).

Many expressions may be rendered either with future (prophetic) force or with wishful (prayerful) sense. For example, "He shall judge" probably should be interpreted as "May he judge" (v. 2). This pattern of rendering through most of the psalm, as in RSV, makes forceful the prayerful yearning of the psalmist.

Verses 18–19 do not belong to the psalm itself. They are a doxology. They close the second of the Psalter's five books, Psalm 42–72.

Verse 20 appears to be an editorial note. It may indicate that after the formation of an early collection of Davidic psalms other groups of psalms were added.

A Serious Challenge to Faith (Psalm 73)

The passage.—If God is just, why do some evil persons prosper while some righteous persons suffer? Because of this problem the psalmist had passed through inner conflict. He described his experience and the conclusion to which it led. Now he would teach this truth: "Truly God is good. . . ."

The psalm begins with an assertion of reestablished faith (vv. 1–3). The wicked are viewed as specially advantaged by wealth and security (vv. 4–14). Then their state is reassessed: the long-range benefits belong to the godly (vv. 15–26). The conclusion is a personal testimony to the goodness of God's presence—a contrast to the fate of the wicked (vv. 27–28).

Special points.—An experience of worship in "the sanctuary of God" (v. 17) was the turning point. The troubled psalmist gained a changed outlook, a long-range view. He had thought his feet were slipping. Now he recognized that those who prospered at the expense of right were "in slippery places" (vv. 2,18).

The psalmist recoiled at the thought of the wicked awaking to their sad delusion, "their end" (vv. 17–20). But he could contemplate no termination to his own joyous communion with God (vv. 23–26).

Truth for today.—Inadequate religious understanding results in confused values and shaken faith. The rewards of righteousness and the consequences of sin may not be evident fully in present circumstances. Wealth and power are not tests of the worthwhileness of faith in God.

Distress of God's People (Psalm 74)

The passage.—Like Psalms 44 and 79, this is an outcry of dismay and sorrow. Calamity had fallen on the land. The Temple had been destroyed. Seemingly the Lord had abandoned his people.

The introduction is an appeal to God to turn from wrath and to consider the plight of Jerusalem (vv. 1–3). There follows a description of the devastation wrought by the enemy (vv. 4–8). The appeal to God is resumed (vv. 9–11). The mood abruptly changes. God's past acts of mercy and power are recalled (vv. 12–17). With rising hope the appeal

to God is renewed (vv. 18–23).

Special points.—The probable historical background was the fall of Jerusalem to Nebuchadnezzar's army in 586 B.C. (2 Kings 24:10—25:12). The description of the havoc wrought by the enemy fits that event.

Destruction of the Temple (sanctuary, v. 7) and other "meeting places" (RSV; synagogues, v. 8) brought distress. But the supposition that calamity was proof that the Lord had cast off the people of his covenant (v. 2) brought consternation.

The appeals of the psalmist implied hope. The divine character had been demonstrated from "of old" (v. 12). God's power (vv. 12–17) had subdued the powers of Egypt (dragons . . . *leviathan*) and preserved Israel.

Divine faithfulness (vv. 18–23) to the covenant had ensured God's identification with his beloved (turtledove, v. 19). Thus, the enemy's contempt for God's people was contempt for God also.

God Alone Is Judge (Psalm 75)

The passage.—This psalm celebrates God's mighty act of judgment. The poem is developed in four parts: verses 1, 2–5, 6–8, and 9–10. The people, represented by the psalmist, express joyous thanks. A word from God assures his righteous control over the moral order. Just so, the psalmist declares that God alone is judge and rejoices that righteousness will triumph over evil.

Special points.—The psalmist's thought was focused on a calamity, a judgment, giving deliverance to his people (vv. 1,8). Whether this deliverance was past or future is not clear.

Verse 2 is difficult to render. The emphasis probably is on the appointed time for God's judgment, as in RSV

Even if the human situation is chaotic and justice seems delayed, God's action accords with the moment for a righteous reckoning.

Verses 2–5 are much like prophetic messages delivered by Amos and Isaiah. This was the word of assurance: the God who is both sovereign and just maintains the moral order. He makes the "pillars" steady.

From the divine message the psalmist drew crucial implications. From no direction (vv. 6–7) comes final authority in life and history except from God. The ultimate experience of men in relation to God's moral reign is either exaltation or debasement, joy or dismay (vv. 7,10).

Praise to God Triumphant (Psalm 76)

The passage.—This song of deliverance has four stanzas. God has manifested his safeguarding presence in Jerusalem and Judah. Because of his intervention, enemy warriors lie still in death. Through his irresistible judgment the oppressed have been restored. Let tribute be given to the all-victorious God. Such were the psalmist's thoughts in verses 1–3, 4–6, 7–9, and 10–12.

Special points.—Poetic pictures of men in the deep sleep of death and of horses and chariots lying still on the battlefield suggest the destruction of Sennacherib (2 Kings 18:13—19:37). Perhaps that mysterious overthrow of the enemy was the common background of this psalm and Psalm 75.

The basic theme is the same as that of Psalms 46 and 48, divine deliverance of Judah and Jerusalem. In verse 1 "Israel" is synonymous with "Judah." Israel as the Northern Kingdom had been overthrown. Similarly, in verse 2 "Salem" is identical with "Zion." In Jerusalem the Lord was worshiped, and in the sanctuary his dwelling among his

people specially was made known.

The exact sense of verse 10 is uncertain. The probable meaning is that in the divine purpose even violent acts will be overruled for ultimate good. That is, the resultant judgment will lead the wicked to recognize God and inspire the righteous to praise him. This is the response anticipated in verses 11–12.

Hope in Spite of Gloom (Psalm 77)

The passage.—Apparently the cry to God represented the nation's plight, not individual distress only. It arose out of deepest gloom, though no specific crisis was indicated. Of supreme concern was the absence of any sign of God's compassion and power.

The present gloom was contrasted with past blessing (vv. 1–10). Remembrance of God's acts in history (vv. 11–15) revived courage. It inspired praise of God as the deliverer of his people (vv. 16–20).

Special points.—Verses 1–3 are unclear because of the uncertain time viewpoint (tenses) involved. The rendering in ASV may be helpful. Apparently the psalmist resolved to pray and hope in spite of past disappointment.

The empty present was a despondent contrast to the acts of God in "the days of old" (v. 5). Yet remembrance of what God had done kindled boldness to hope for what he could do—and would do.

The psalmist's agonizing questions (vv. 7–9) as to whether the God of covenant had forgotten his people had one dominant concern. Had God changed? The word rendered "years" (v. 10) probably means "has changed" (RSV).

The supposition that God was not what he once was—this was the psalmist's "infirmity" (grief, RSV). When that supposition was forsaken he found God's historic deeds a source of hope and praise (vv. 16–20).

Lessons from History (Psalm 78)

The passage.—Like the author of Psalm 49, this psalmist was a teacher. His purpose was to instruct the present and future generations through lessons drawn from the past (vv. 1–8).

Israel's history was a record of rebellion against God (vv. 9–16). Faithlessness in the face of divine faithfulness demanded chastisement (vv. 17–31). Repentance was superficial (vv. 32–39). Defiance and ingratitude were the more grievous because of God's wondrous acts (vv. 40–55). Continued rebellion brought severe judgment (vv. 56–66). Finally, God abandoned Ephraim and chose Judah, Jerusalem, and David (vv. 67–72).

Special points.—Several psalmists recited history in order to apply spiritual lessons. Note especially Psalms 105, 106, and 136. In the present instance emphasis was on a stark contrast: God's faithfulness and Israel's faithlessness.

The recital was adapted to the teacher's purpose to illustrate truths. For example, the plagues in Egypt were mentioned, but perhaps only seven of the ten (vv. 42–51). Again, major episodes were recounted, but not in strict time order. The plagues were mentioned "after" the wilderness wanderings (vv. 9–20,42–51), the giving of water "before" the manna and quails (vv. 23–29).

Truth for today.—Religious instruction is indispensable. Each oncoming generation must be taught to recognize God's hand in life and history. Each youth must be led to distinguish between a changing society and moral values that do not change.

Continual resistance to God destroys opportunity, cuts off the future. The abandonment of Shiloh and Ephraim is an ancient illustration. A strife-ridden church, devoid of spiritual power and purpose, may be a modern illustration.

Lament over Jerusalem (Psalm 79)

The passage.—The psalmist voiced the people's lament over the destruction and sorrow of Jerusalem (vv. 1–4). A plea for divine help (vv. 5–7) was accompanied by confession of sin and concern for the honor of God's name (vv. 8–10). An answer would ensure thanksgiving by the people (vv. 11–13).

Special points.—The background was similar to that of Psalm 74. Perhaps both psalms reflect the fall of Jerusalem and the burning of the Temple in 586 B.C. (2 Kings 25:1–17). Verses 1–3 describe invasion, desecration of the Temple, destruction of the city, and unburied corpses.

Urgent argument for God's intervention was based on the honor of his name. God had chosen Israel and Jerusalem. Now the continuance of his covenant, the trustworthiness of his promises, was at issue (vv. 1,5). The reputation of his name, the reality of his power, was in question by pagan nations (vv. 4,9–10).

Worship was anticipated as a natural response to God's intervention (vv. 11–13). Let God demonstrate his faithfulness and power! His people would offer their praise and thanksgiving.

A Song of Sorrow (Psalm 80)

The passage.—This song of sorrow has three main parts, each ending in a similar refrain. The beginning is a plea for God's help (vv. 1–3). There follows a description of divine wrath, the occasion for Israel's affliction (vv. 4–7). The conclusion is a prayer for God's favor, resulting in praise (vv. 17–19). The inset (vv. 8–16) is an allegory comparing Israel to a vine.

Special points.—"Shepherd" is a tender, appealing title. It suggested God's leadership and care for Israel, and Israel's dependence on God. It is promi-

nent in psalms connected by superscription to Asaph (74:1; 77:20; 78:52–
53, 70–72; 79:13). Perhaps it recalled
Jacob's relation to God (Gen. 48:15). It
applied to Moses and David as leaders
of Israel.

The refrain (vv. 3,7,19) is a modified
form of Aaron's blessing (Num. 6:24–
26). For the psalmist it was a plea that
God restore the fortunes of Israel.

Ephraim, Manasseh, and Benjamin
loomed large in the psalmist's concern.
The misfortunes of Joseph—tribes of
the center and north—were his grief
(vv. 1–2). Possibly the fall of the
Northern Kingdom to Assyria in 721
B.C. was the occasion (2 Kings 17:5–6;
18:9–11).

Israel was compared to a vine in three
stages. There was the transplanting from
Egypt (v. 8), the spreading growth from
the Mediterranean to the Euphrates
(sea . . . River, v. 11), and the destruction by ferocious enemies (boar
. . . beast, v. 13).

A Hymn and a Prophecy (Psalm 81)

The passage.—A hymn (vv. 1–5*b*) and
a prophecy (vv. 5*c*–16) are combined in
this psalm. The former is a summons to
the people to celebrate a religious festival. The latter is a message from God to
be announced to the people. The message contrasts God's faithfulness (vv.
6–10) with Israel's waywardness (vv.
11–16).

Special points.—References to the
trumpet (literally, ram's horn), "new
moon," "time appointed" (full moon,
RSV), and "feast day" (v. 3) suggest the
Feast of Tabernacles, or possibly Passover. The hymn summoned a national
remembrance of God's redemption of
Israel from Egypt (v. 5).

A possible rendering of the difficult
third part of verse 5 is as follows: "I
hear a voice I had not known" (RSV).
Possibly ancient Israel responded to

God's act of deliverance as a new revelation. In that act the people heard a
voice speaking mercy and redemption
(v. 5*a-b*).

Another interpretation is more probable. A prophet at the sanctuary referred to his experience in receiving the
message that he was to proclaim. The
divine word, recorded in verses 6–16,
had come through a strange voice.

Verses 11–16 compose a passage of
pathos. They tell of what might have
been. Israel could have had the "finest
of the wheat . . . honey out of the
rock" (v. 16). Instead, they were victims
of their enemies because they had become enemies of their God (v. 15). But
the way of repentance and obedience
was still open.

Judgment on Unjust Judges (Psalm 82)

The passage.—This is a psalmist's
vision of divine judgment on corrupt
human judges. The God of supreme
authority takes position as judge (v. 1).
Corrupt judges are arraigned (vv. 2–4).
Their ignorance is described (v. 5), and
their downfall is proclaimed (vv. 6–7).
In conclusion, God is urged to take
possession of all nations in righteous
judgment (v. 8).

Special points.—In verse 1 "the
mighty" and "the gods" apparently were
human judges, not superhuman beings.
They were so designated because in office and authority they were to represent
God (Deut. 1:16–17; Psalm 58:1; John
10:34–35).

Corrupt judges were charged on two
counts: partiality to the powerful rich
and unconcern for the defenseless poor.
Observe the near parallel in Isaiah 3:
13–15.

Misrule emerged out of ignorance.
Such blindness was dangerous. It threatened "the foundations" of an orderly
and ethical society (v. 5).

Divine judgment set forth a contrast.

Now in high position, these perverters of justice would die like common men. They would fall like other officials who failed their trust.

Truth for today.—The principle of government, whatever the particular form and expression, is ordained of God (Matt. 22:21; Rom. 13:1–7). Responsible citizenship is an obligation. Officials are accountable ultimately to God for their public trust, for their opportunity to promote the betterment of people.

A Cry for Judgment on a Confederacy of Enemies (Psalm 83)

The passage.—Whereas Psalm 82 is a cry for judgment on corrupt judges, Psalm 83 is a cry for judgment on corrupt nations. A plea was made that God assert himself against the confederated enemies of Israel (vv. 1–8). He was urged to act in judgment as desolating as historic judgments in the past (vv. 9–18).

Special points.—Like other psalms associated with the name Asaph, Psalm 83 is strongly national. The psalmist reacted to the political power and economic greed of surrounding peoples. These enemies coveted Israel's land and plotted the nation's destruction.

The sweeping survey of hostile tribes and nations moved clockwise. Attention moved from southeast, south (Edom . . . Ishmaelites) to west (Philistines . . . Tyre) to northeast, east (Assur [Assyria] . . . Lot [Ammon and Moab]). A specific historical period when all of these powers were allied against Israel is not known.

The psalmist prayed that the nations might suffer the fate of those overthrown by Deborah and Barak (Judg. 4–5) and by Gideon (Judg. 7:1—8:12). They hated God and plotted the destruction of his prized and protected people (thy hidden ones, v. 3).

Yet the prayer for punishment was positive. It voiced hope that those humiliated would seek God (vv. 16,18)—that judgment would lead to redemption.

Joy in the House of the Lord (Psalm 84)

The passage.—This is a song concerning God's house and joyous worship there. In verses 1–4 attention is on the loveliness of the Temple and the happiness of those who dwell there. Verses 5–7 describe the joy of those who overcome hindrances in order to appear before God in his house. The final stanza, verses 8–12, records the pilgrim's prayer and confidence in going to the Temple.

Special points.—In devotion to the Temple and joyous worship there, this psalm is a companion to Psalms 42–43. Several expressions are essentially the same. Perhaps the three poems had the same author.

Note references to the journey to Jerusalem. They suggest kinship to the Pilgrim Psalms, 120–134.

Happy indeed were those having access to the Lord's house! The psalmist almost envied birds that nested within the Temple precincts. He considered the priests supremely privileged in their continuous service there.

God's highways were in the heart of the devout pilgrim (v. 5). He joined a procession that gained spiritual exhilaration as it journeyed toward the Temple. Because of expectancy even a dry valley seemed well watered.

The psalmist considered the humblest place in God's house better than any other privilege. Yet he did not love the Temple and its ceremonies for themselves. Rather, he loved the God who withholds nothing good "from them that walk uprightly" (v. 11).

God in the Past, Present, and Future (Psalm 85)

The passage.—This psalm reflects three dominant concerns of the discouraged community of Israel. Serious attention was focused on divine mercies in the past, urgent needs in the present, and prophetic assurance for the future. The respective thoughts are in verses 1–3, 4–7, and 8–13.

Special points.—Possibly the psalm represents the small community at Jerusalem after the Exile. The days of Nehemiah and Ezra were marked by opposition without and within. Hardships stifled the early enthusiasm of the returning exiles.

The expression "brought back the captivity" (v. 1) probably had a broader reference than the Babylonian Exile. Emphasis was on God's mercy in past years. In Israel's crises God had restored "the fortunes" (RSV) of his people.

The basis of the prayer was God's mighty, merciful acts in the past. Once again the whole life of the nation needed renewal. Deliverance from present troubles depended on a fresh demonstration of God's covenant relation (steadfast love . . . salvation, v. 7, RSV).

God's past performance inspired confidence for the future. Renewal of both spiritual and material well-being would come. Heaven and earth would meet, creating meaning and harmony in the relationship of God and men (vv. 10–13).

Truth for today.—In our time and situation, too, prayer for revival must be a broad and deep concern. As for the individual, the whole person needs renewal. God's claims are upon the total life. As respects the community, morality and compassion in human relations and public institutions are sure evidences of God's work in individuals.

Prayer of a Servant to His Sovereign (Psalm 86)

The passage.—This is the prayer of a person of deeply felt need. He was devout, utterly humble and sincerely trustful. At the beginning (vv. 1–7) and at the conclusion (vv. 14–17) he petitioned God for help. He linked these pleas with fervent praise (vv. 8–13).

Special points.—The exact nature of the psalmist's crisis is not told. But he considered the circumstances extremely serious. The "day of trouble" involved those who hated him (v. 17) and affliction which brought him to the brink of death (lowest hell, v. 13; depths of Sheol, RSV).

This humble, teachable man of prayer had a deep consciousness of belonging to God. Seven times he used the term "Lord" (vv. 3,4,5,8,9,12,15) when addressing God. The title emphasized God's sovereignty and authority over his life. In contrast, he referred to himself as God's "servant" and "the son of thine handmaid" (vv. 4,16).

All nations had their gods, but the psalmist praised him who is "God alone" (v. 10). In a coming day all peoples would acknowledge the singleness of the true God. His greatness and goodness are beyond compare.

More than renewed help and protection were asked. The psalmist entreated God to answer his prayer in such a conspicuous way as to impress the godless.

A Vision of the Coming Zion (Psalm 87)

The passage.—This brief psalm is a prophetic vision. The true God reigns supremely. Believers out of the nations, not Israelites only, worship him.

Analysis is difficult, but three parts seem clear. The Zion of God's creation is glorious (vv. 1–3). It is the spiritual birthplace of various national groups (vv. 4–6). It is the source of abundant joy (v. 7).

Special points.—Of all the dwelling-places of Israelites, Jerusalem (the gates of Zion, v. 2) was most celebrated. The city was the religious and political capital. The Temple, the center of worship and the symbol of the Lord's presence, was located there.

In God's announcement (v. 4) Jerusalem apparently represented the spiritual Zion to come. What was envisioned was not merely a return of scattered Jews to the land. The dominant thought was that of joyous, universal acceptance of God as Lord and King.

The Lord was described as registering his people (v. 6). Enemies of Israel—Egypt (Rahab), Babylon, and Philistia—were seen joining Israel in a common allegiance (v. 4). The Lord was envisioned as recording them also as his people.

Non-Israelites would share in the heritage of Israel because of allegiance to the God of Israel. Relationship would not depend on physical birth at Jerusalem, but on spiritual birth into Zion.

Truth for today.—The vision of Psalm 87 finds fulfilment in Jesus Christ. Under his lordship national and racial friction is replaced by love and reconciliation. Only in practicing and preaching the gospel is there hope that the alienated will find acceptance.

Praying in Darkness (Psalm 88)

The passage.—This is a psalm of gloom, the saddest in the Psalter. It consists of the agonizing complaints of a sufferer (vv. 1–9a, 13–18) and his searching questions as he despairs of life (vv. 9b–12). The movement from complaints to questions in verse 9 is clarified in RSV.

Special points.—The psalmist had suffered long and grievously. He was approaching death. Instead of friends he had only "darkness" (v. 18). His aloneness suggests the possibility that he was a lifelong victim of leprosy.

That suffering was due to divine judgment was confidently assumed. "Thy wrath lieth hard upon me . . ." (v. 7). Yet no sin was mentioned, no repentance evidenced, no confession made. The assumption represented a popular religious belief. But the psalmist apparently knew no sin in his life that resulted in this terrible affliction.

With strength failing, the sufferer fixed his eyes on death. For him this meant Sheol (or destruction, v. 11; Abaddon, RSV), the shadowy and dreaded realm of the departed. Would God allow him soon to go into "the land of forgetfulness" (v. 12)? No! Let God help now!

Even in the darkness the suffering man addressed his outcry and questions to God. At the brink of despair he claimed a personal relationship—"God of my salvation" (v. 1). There is this single gleam of light.

God's Promise and Israel's Plight: A Dilemma (Psalm 89)

The passage.—The Lord's covenant with David (vv. 1–4) is the theme that unifies this psalm. The Lord is praised for his supreme power and faithfulness (vv. 5–18) and reminded of his special promises to David (vv. 19–37).

The plight of the present-day Davidic ruler and his people is described (vv. 38–45). The Lord is implored to honor his covenant and restore the Davidic rule (vv. 46–51).

Special points.—A devout man faced a dilemma. He had concluded that the Lord's "mercy" (*steadfast love,* RSV) and "faithfulness" in covenant were everlastingly dependable (v. 2). Now that conclusion seemed contradicted. The promises to David appeared to be "made void" (v. 39).

A Davidic king was defeated in battle. His crown was in the dust. The circumstances suggest the downfall of Judah and Jerusalem to the Babylonians. Per-

haps they reflect the time of Jehoiachin
(2 Kings 24:8–17).

The hymn of praise (vv. 5–18) magnified the Lord's power, faithfulness, righteousness, and justice. These attributes
were a fourfold guarantee of the covenant promises.

The recital of the covenant did not
overlook the provision for divine chastisement (vv. 30–32; 2 Sam. 7:14). But
the present calamity was severe. Did it
nullify God's promises and cast off his
anointed line? If the psalmist was to be
reassured in his brief lifetime, God must
act soon (v. 47).

Verse 52 is a doxology closing the
third of the Psalter's five books, Psalms
73–89.

**The Unchanging Refuge for Changing
Man (Psalm 90)**

The passage.—Two main sections
comprise the psalm. In verses 1–12 the
enduring life of God is contrasted with
the brief life of man. In verses 13–17 a
prayer is made for the renewal of God's
favor. Reflection on the God-man contrast was preparation for prayer that the
Sovereign, Eternal God would bless
troubled Israel.

Special points.—This psalm is like
stately music. A beautiful adaptation is
found in Isaac Watts' hymn, "O God,
Our Help in Ages Past."

The superscription refers to Moses.
Hence, the psalm is possibly the oldest
in the Psalter. So understood, it
expressed the prayer of the Israelites
who wandered in the wilderness and
died without seeing the Promised Land
(Num. 14:20–23).

The occasion was an affliction of the
Israelites (v. 15). The nature of the
calamity was not indicated, only its long
duration.

The psalmist set forth one key religious idea. The "Lord" (a title indicating

sovereignty) is the true "dwelling place"
(home, refuge) of each succeeding generation. Whereas man's life is brief and
changing, God abides.

Brief days are troubled by sin. Few
recognize the need for repentance (v.
11). But for himself and his people, this
was the psalmist's prayer: "Return, O
Lord . . . let it repent thee . . ." (v.
13). Merciful forgiveness could make
days of gladness equal to days of grief.

Faith That Casts Out Fear (Psalm 91)

The passage.—The theme of this
psalm is deep confidence and trust (v.
1), faith stronger than fear. Verses 2
and 9 are the psalmist's personal affirmations: the Lord is "my refuge." In
each instance the verses that follow,
3–8 and 10–13, declare providential care
over one who has made God his refuge.
In conclusion, a message from God
(vv. 14–16) confirms the security of one
who trusts in him.

Special points.—"Most High" and
"Almighty" are significant titles for
God. They were intended to describe
God's worldwide dominion and sover-
eign power. The same titles appear in
Genesis 14:17–24 and 17:1–8.

The personal affirmation of faith in
verse 2 is clear, but that in verse 9*a* is
somewhat obscure. A clearer rendering
of the latter verse is as follows: "Because
thou, Lord, art my refuge . . ." (RSV,
margin).

The psalmist described faith in terms
of both security and happiness. The believer has a "secret place" (v. 1), protection and care, known peculiarly to God.
God's "shadow" is like that of
the mother bird hovering her young, or
the giant rock protecting a weary traveler. Security is a reality even when dangers are hidden (snare of the fowler, v.
3), and whether they threaten "by night"
or "by day" (v. 5).

15. Date palm
of Palestine
(see Psalm
92:12)

Also, the believer experiences deeply satisfying spiritual fellowship. The answer to prayer is assured, and the proofs of God's love are seen (vv. 14–16).

Rejoicing in God's Mighty Acts (Psalm 92)

The passage.—Joyous gratitude prompted this psalm. The contents fall into three parts. To praise the Lord for his mighty acts is good (vv. 1–4). These mighty acts are seen in the punishment of the wicked and the deliverance of the righteous (vv. 5–11). Praise is especially inspired by the lifelong blessing of the Lord upon the righteous (vv. 12–15).

Special points.—The psalm expressed the praise of the community of Israel, not that of the psalmist alone. Surely an extraordinary act of God was in the immediate past. Perhaps the Babylonian exile had ended.

Steadfast love and constant dependability (lovingkindness . . . faithfulness, v. 2) characterized the Lord who had made and maintained the covenant. How appropriate to offer praise to him "in the morning" and "every night!" (v. 2; Ex. 29:38–42). How natural "to sing" and to play the "harp!" (vv. 1,3).

Verse 8 announced the supreme certainty: "Lord . . . most high for evermore." Therefore, evil men with temporary wealth would "perish" (v. 9). The righteous, with resources unchanging, would be like the evergreen "palm" and "cedar" (v. 12).

Truth for today.—God's hand is current in history, in today's events. Moral distinctions matter in personal and national affairs. Now, as long ago, only the person who is dull and silly (brutish man . . . fool, v. 6) refuses to recognize this reality.

The Lord Is King (Psalm 93)

The passage.—This brief, magnificent hymn acclaims the enthronement of the Lord. He reigns as majestic, eternal King (vv. 1–2). His kingdom is supreme and secure above opposing powers (vv. 3–4). His reign is marked by spiritual revelation and worship (v. 5).

Special points.—The spirit and theme of this hymn recall Psalm 47. Moreover, the psalm is a prelude to Psalms 95–100, a collection of Royal Psalms.

Perhaps the restoration of Israel from Babylonian exile was the occasion. From the first the Lord was Israel's king (Ex. 15:18; 1 Sam. 8:7). But defeat and captivity seemed to offer proof of an abandoned throne. Now his everlasting kingship was proclaimed anew.

The floods, increasing their fury to thunderous billows (vv. 3–4), symbolized threatening human powers. But the opposition of evil and chaotic powers to the Sovereign Lord was futile.

The will (testimonies) of the King as revealed to his people was dependable (sure, v. 5). His holy presence would mark the appointed place for their worship.

Prayer for Divine Judgment (Psalm 94)

The passage.—An age-old problem concerned the psalmist. How are arrogance and cruelty in the world to be reconciled with the fact of God's goodness and power?

The community's lament in verses 1–15 is combined with the individual's testimony in verses 16–23. God is urged to intervene against the wicked (vv. 1–7), the wicked are admonished (vv. 8–11), and a blessing is assured for the righteous (vv. 12–15). The reflection on personal struggles is followed by triumphant thanksgiving (vv. 16–23).

Special points.—Echoes of Psalm 73 and Job are here. Similarities in theme and major ideas are striking.

Those who crushed the Lord's people (heritage, v. 5) apparently were fellow Israelites, not foreigners (v. 8). Dull and foolish (brutish . . . fools), they ignored moral responsibility. Further, they assumed that the "God of Jacob" (v. 7) was only one of the many gods.

The God of "vengeance" and the "judge of the earth" were parallel expressions (vv. 1–2). The psalmist prayed for the triumph of moral order and its just consequences, not the visitation of spite and hate. Yet total justification of the psalmist's attitudes and emotions may not be assumed.

Through adversity God's people would learn the way of faith, awaiting vindication and justice (vv. 12–15). When the psalmist's foot had slipped— faith had staggered—the Lord's steadfast love (mercy, v. 18) held him. The lesson of his personal experience applied to the perplexed community of Israel.

The Great King (Psalm 95)

The passage.—Here an invitation to worship (vv. 1–7b) is followed by a warning against disobedience (vv. 7c–11). The former is a hymn of praise. The latter is a prophetic message to the worshiping congregation.

Special points.—This psalm shares a common theme with Psalms 96–100. All express joyous worship of the Lord as the supreme ruler.

Apparently the worshipers, in procession, first were invited to approach the Temple (come, or proceed, v. 1). Afterward, they were invited to enter the sanctuary (come, or enter, v. 6).

The first invitation called for praise that was fervent and loud—song and shout. The second emphasized reverence and humility.

Associated with the first invitation was the conception of the Lord as the "great God" and "great King" (v. 3). In sovereign power he created the world. Associated with the second invitation was thought of the Lord as "our maker" (v. 6). In great compassion he became the Shepherd of Israel.

The psalmist asserted the Lord's supremacy "above all gods" (v. 3). The extent of his creation and sovereignty left no place for other gods.

Perhaps a prophet or priest announced God's message to the congregation. Emphasis was upon the current situation, the present generation (To day, v. 7). Let these people avoid the rebellion and suffering of their fathers. Let there be no repetition of Meribah and Massah (provocation . . . temptation, v. 8; Ex. 17:1–7).

The Universal King Is Judge (Psalm 96)

The passage.—This is a joyous song of victory. The Lord reigns as judge of all! The first stanza (vv. 1–6) is a general exhortation to praise the Lord for his wondrous deeds. The second stanza (vv. 7–9) is a summons to the nations to acknowledge him in praise and offerings. The final stanza (vv. 10–13) is a call for the world, nations and nature, to acclaim him sovereign and judge.

Special points.—Perhaps this psalm was associated with Israel's return from Babylonian exile. The wondrous new expression of divine mercy called for "a new song" (v. 1) of praise. "Honour and majesty" (v. 6) described the Lord who was to be praised, while "strength and beauty" (v. 6) marked his new sanctuary in the restored community.

The psalm, in some form, may be older. It appears in 1 Chronicles 16: 23–24, with other psalm portions and with certain changes. The occasion was David's bringing the ark to Jerusalem.

Expectation of the Lord's universal reign prevails in references to the "nations," "earth," and "world." Likewise, heathen "gods" were declared "idols," weak and worthless in contrast to the Lord. Both ideas are prominent in Isaiah 40–66.

The psalmist anticipated the revelation of the Lord in holy splendor ("beauty of holiness," v. 9). He expected worldwide establishment of the Lord's kingship and judgment. The result would be salvation and abounding joy.

The Universal King Is Supreme (Psalm 97)

The passage.—The supreme greatness of the Lord is portrayed in three stanzas. First, the Lord is described in an awesome manifestation of himself (vv. 1–6). Then his victory over false gods is acclaimed (vv. 7–9). In conclusion, his care for his people is declared to be the inspiration for their joyous worship (vv. 10–12).

Special points.—Again, presumably the return of Israel from exile was the background. That deliverance reestablished the certainty of the Lord's kingship.

The manifestation of the Lord was a reminder of that to Moses at Sinai. References to "clouds," "lightnings," and earthquake (earth . . . trembled, v. 4) indicated the wonder of it.

Once more, the Lord's superiority to pagan gods was emphasized by contrast. His exalted supremacy over "graven images," "idols," and "all gods" (vv. 7,9) was demonstrated by his deliverance of his people.

Perhaps verse 10a should be read as follows: "The Lord loves those who hate evil" (RSV). If so, the three verbs of the verse depicted the Lord's active relationship to his people. He loves, preserves, and delivers his own.

The reason for joyous worship was described as a daybreak of well-being for the righteous. The light of day comes (Light is sown, v. 11; Light dawns, RSV). The Lord rules!

The Universal King Is Victorious (Psalm 98)

The passage.—In this instance also a hymn concerning the Lord's kingship is developed in three stanzas. The first stanza celebrated the Lord's mighty act on behalf of Israel (vv. 1–3). The second called for the whole earth to hail him as king (vv. 4–6). The third urged the material creation to rejoice in his coming as righteous judge (vv. 7–9).

Special points.—The great event of divine deliverance (marvellous things, v. 1) was doubtless the return of Israel from captivity. It was wholly God's act, accomplished by his power (*his right hand . . . arm*, v. 1). It was God's saving act, demonstrating his love and faithfulness (his mercy and his truth, v. 3) in covenant.

The nations saw far more than an exhibition of power. They witnessed a revelation of moral character. In full view were the proofs of love and fidelity to promise. On this basis the whole earth was urged to salute the victorious Lord.

The Lord's coming for the full establishment of his reign was anticipated with triumphant joy. The psalmist appealed for the jubilation of men and nature. The universal sway of righteousness and equity (v. 9) would bring radical correction to human relationships and even to the physical environment.

The Universal King Is Holy (Psalm 99)

The passage.—Like Psalms 96, 97, and 98, this psalm proclaims the victorious kingship of the Lord. The hymn of praise is composed of two parts, verses 1–5 and 6–9. First, the nations were summoned to praise the Lord, the God exalted in Zion and known for righteousness. Afterward, the Lord's dealings with Israel were recalled, acts of both mercy and chastisement.

Special points.—The two parts of the hymn end in refrains that are virtually identical. "Exalt ye the Lord our God . . . for he is holy" (v. 5). "Exalt the Lord our God . . . for the Lord our God is holy" (v. 9). The common emphasis is God's holiness.

Attention was drawn to the Lord's exaltation in Zion, that is, Jerusalem and the Temple. There the "cherubims" (v. 1), figures above the ark in the most holy place, symbolized his presence.

Likewise, attention was focused on crucial events in Israel's history. The ministries of Moses, Aaron, and Samuel were recalled. In those affairs the Lord had revealed his compassion and forgiveness in combination with chastisement.

In spite of attention to Jerusalem (or Temple, his footstool, v. 5) and to the history of Israel, the universal note was sounded again. The Lord was acclaimed absolutely supreme and unutterably sublime. Let all peoples, Israel and the nations, worship the God of holiness—the God of "great and terrible name!" (v. 3).

Worship Because of Who God Is (Psalm 100)

The passage.—Although extremely brief, this is a vigorous and eloquent hymn. The psalmist urged worship with joy and gave the reason (vv. 1–3). In parallel, he appealed for thanksgiving in the Lord's house and gave the reason (vv. 4–5).

Special points.—Joy (vv. 1–2) and thanksgiving (v. 4) in worship were considered appropriate because of the Lord's character and acts. The Lord redeemed his people and chose them to be his own (made us . . . sheep of his pasture, v. 4). Joy was the spontaneous result.

The Lord is "good." In "steadfast love" (RSV; mercy, v. 5) he proved his "faithfulness" (RSV; truth, v. 5) to succeeding generations. Grateful praise was the natural response.

The exhortation to joyous worship of the Lord was directed to all peoples. The term "lands" in verse 1 is a singular noun meaning earth. Such worship was not limited by nationality or geography.

Truth for today.—True worship begins with a humble awareness of who God is. It involves recognition of his sovereign greatness, redeeming love, and complete worthiness of our trust.

Joyfulness and gratitude arise spontaneously in genuine recognition of the true God. But they are also necessary ingredients in the worship that he requires.

True worship of the true God is the basis of unity for divided humanity. Let the church take seriously its stately hymn "Old Hundred."

Resolutions of a Ruler (Psalm 101)

The passage.—The high resolves of a ruler, probably a king, are set forth in this psalm. His ideals for personal life are the subject in verses 1–4. His standards for public action are treated in verses 5–8.

Special points.—The superscription connects the psalm with David. Perhaps it was an expression of his lofty purposes when the ark of the covenant was brought from the house of Obed-edom to Jerusalem (2 Sam. 6:6–19).

Actually the psalm is a statement of principles appropriate for any responsible ruler. It probably was recited by several Israelite kings in their coronation ceremonies.

Private life came first, and properly so. The ruler would esteem the character (mercy and judgment, v. 1) of the Lord. He resolved to conduct himself with integrity, yearning to have the Lord as guest in his home. Baseness and disloyalty (wicked thing . . . them that turn aside, v. 3), as well as perverseness (froward heart, v. 4), would be allowed no acceptance or approval (I will not know, v. 4).

As head of government, the ruler determined to appoint to office men committed to the same personal standards. His favor would be on "the faithful of the land" (v. 6). He would dismiss any who practiced deceit and falsehood. Righteousness throughout the capital city was his noble, if impracticable, ideal.

Hope for the Afflicted (Psalm 102)

The passage.—Dismal complaints and strong assurances form this psalm. The prayer for the Lord's speedy help (vv. 1–2) is an introduction. Three main divisions follow: an outcry of suffering and despair (vv. 3–11), a vision of glorious restoration (vv. 12–22), and a testimony to the ground of hope (vv. 23–28). The last division is a climax as well as a conclusion.

Special points.—The psalm originated near the close of the Babylonian exile.

Allusions to prisoners, Zion's dust, and restoration make this dating virtually certain.

The intense suffering was the experience of an individual. But the individual represented the captive, sorrowing Israelite community. Loneliness (v. 7), abuse by enemies (v. 8), and consciousness of God's wrath (v. 10) were experiences common to all.

A glorious restoration, God's achievement, was envisioned for the future. It would have two major results. First, the afflicted people would be returned and Jerusalem rebuilt. Second, the nations would see this act of God's goodness and reverence him (v. 15).

The hope of the suffering psalmist was solidly grounded. The material world and the human order are transitory. But God the Creator is forever "the same" (v. 27). His love and his purpose do not fail.

Praise for the Lord's Goodness (Psalm 103)

The passage.—The psalmist's theme was the enduring goodness of the Lord. The theme was developed in four main parts: (1) Self-exhortation to praise the Lord for blessings personally received (vv. 1–5); (2) Gratitude for the Lord's fatherly goodness to the Israelites (vv. 6–14); (3) Reflection on the Lord's enduring faithfulness in contrast to man's passing life (vv. 15–18); (4) Exhortation to the heavenly hosts and the created world to praise the Lord of universal sovereignty (vv. 19–22).

Special points.—This poem is one of the special treasures of the Psalter. Beautiful phrases, profound thought, and broad scope are distinguishing features.

The psalmist called on his total personality (my soul, v. 1) to praise the Lord. The mercies received were abundant, material and spiritual. They were also deeply satisfying, renewing life itself.

Both the revelation to Moses and the whole history of Israel were an exhibition of the Lord's power and grace. Divine forgiveness loomed large in a review of this heritage.

The *"holy name"* (v. 1) that the psalmist magnified represented God's character. Verse 8 reflected the historic description of character in Exodus 34:6.

The closing note returned to that of the beginning (vv. 1, 22). The psalmist would share with all creation in praise. In contrast to mortal affairs (man, v. 15), God's goodness is a reality in every generation.

Praise for the Lord's Manifold Works (Psalm 104)

The passage.—Creation is the subject of this majestic poem. Yet not creation itself, but creation's reflection of the Creator is the preeminent concern.

A description of the creation (vv. 1–23) is followed by meditation on its wonders and meaning (vv. 24–30). In conclusion, the Creator himself is praised (vv. 31–35).

Special points.—In a general way the psalmist gave a poetic version of Genesis 1. But he was not concerned primarily with the initial creation. His thoughts were those of a worshiper presently looking at God's marvelous works.

This psalm, like Psalm 103, begins and ends with "Bless the Lord, O my soul." The spirit of thanksgiving prevails in both. Possibly they were composed by the same author.

The psalmist conceived of the Creator as "clothed with honour and majesty" (v. 1). He described the Creator's work as comprehensive and total—animate and inanimate, large and small.

Meditation on the Creator's "works" and "riches" (v. 24; creatures, RSV) was an experience of worship. In what God had wrought were variety and wisdom, power and purpose.

The Creator was identified as the God of righteousness. God's order must not be marred by sin (v. 35*a*).

A single word is placed at the end of the poem: Hallelujah! The word is translated "Praise ye the Lord" (v. 35*c*).

Praise for the Lord's Faithfulness to Covenant (Psalm 105)

The passage.—One truth filled the consciousness of the psalmist. The Lord "remembered his holy promise" (v. 42).

The Israelites were exhorted to praise the Lord for his wondrous works (vv. 1–6). They were to recall his covenant with the patriarchs and his care over their early descendants (vv. 7–15). They were to review his provisions for the chosen people when they were in Egypt, at the Red Sea, and in the wilderness (vv. 16–42). The Lord's faithfulness constrained the present generation, heirs of the covenant, to be loyal and obedient (vv. 43–45).

Special points.—Interpretation of this psalm depends on two key expressions. First, "Remember . . ." (v. 5). Again, "He hath remembered . . ." (v. 8). From the beginning the Lord had been faithful to the people whom he chose and redeemed. Let the present generation take note and respond with loyalty.

The present generation was probably the community newly returned from Babylonian exile. These people needed the lessons of history. Struggling against great odds, the restored community could draw reassurance from proofs of the Lord's care for his continuing people.

Verses 1–15 appear in a hymn associated with David's bringing the ark to Jerusalem (1 Chron. 16:8–22). Portions of the psalm, therefore, may have had an early origin. Another possibility is that the psalmic verses were borrowed and incorporated into the hymn used in later commemorations of Israel's history:

Praise for the Lord's Mercy to Sinners (Psalm 106)

The passage.—This psalm celebrates the Lord's persevering love in spite of Israel's rebellion. The introduction (vv. 1–5) consists of exhortation to thanksgiving for the Lord's goodness, prayer for another expression of divine goodness to Israel, and confession of the nation's sin.

The body of the psalm surveys Israel's history of rebellion (vv. 6–39) and summarizes the results in divine wrath and mercy (vv. 40–46). The conclusion (v. 47) returns to prayer for the Lord's goodness once more.

Special points.—A companion piece to Psalm 105, this psalm probably came from the same poet. The preceding psalm reviewed Israel's history in order to show proofs of the Lord's faithfulness. This psalm reviewed that history in order to cite examples of Israel's faithlessness.

Many specific acts and attitudes of revolt were cited (vv. 7–39). Summary statements were considered sufficient reference to episodes reported more fully in Exodus and Numbers.

The psalmist's confession reflected a deep sense of guilt. It reflected also a perception of the unity of his generation with the "fathers" (v. 6) in their rebellion against God.

Yet the Lord's goodness inspired joy (vv. 1,47). It encouraged prayer for mercy anew and hope for Israel's complete restoration.

Verse 48 is a doxology closing the fourth division of the Psalter, Psalms 90–106.

A Song of the Redeemed (Psalm 107)

The passage.—Two broad divisions comprise the psalm, vv. 1–32 and 33–43. The redeemed people first were exhorted to offer thanks to the Lord for his wondrous acts of deliverance. Then they were challenged to respond in praise to his providence of love.

Special points.—The exhortation was addressed to the "redeemed" (v. 2). At an earlier time the Israelites were delivered from the bondage of Egypt. More recently they were released from exile in Babylon. Indeed, the reference to all points of the compass implied a gathering from wide dispersion (v. 3).

Here, as in other psalms, the term "mercy" (v. 1) or "lovingkindness" (v. 43) is the key thought. The term represented the Lord's love in covenant with his people. It described that love as strong and enduring (steadfast love, RSV).

The acts of the Lord's steadfast love were summarized in four pictures. Wanderers were delivered, or redeemed, from the wilderness (vv. 4–9), captives from prison (vv. 10–16), the sick from death (vv. 17–22), and the seafarers from shipwreck (vv. 23–32).

Note the double refrains. "Then they cried." . . . "He delivered." . . . "Let them thank the Lord" (vv. 6 and 8, 13 and 15, 19 and 21, 28 and 31, RSV). Such words are like a poetic rendering of the stories in Judges.

The challenge, likewise, was directed to the redeemed. Acts of God brought blessing or penalty. Let the redeemed "give heed" (RSV; observe, v. 43). Let them perceive the expressions of the Lord's steadfast love in such providences.

A Hymn of Victorious Prayer (Psalm 108)

The passage.—Here Psalm 57:7–11 and Psalm 60:5–12 are combined. Verse 6 connects the two parts in the new arrangement. The result of the union is a hymn of victorious prayer.

Special points.—Reasons for combining the two psalmic fragments are not known. Perhaps the new composition was designed for use by the worshiping community of Israel after the Exile.

Both of the older psalms expressed lament over stressful situations. But portions selected for this new arrangement expressed the bold faith of Israel "among the nations" (v. 3).

Petition and assurance were commingled in the prayer. Appeal was made to God to deliver the Israelites (thy beloved, v. 6) from "trouble" and "enemies" (vv. 12–13). Yet that victorious accomplishment was sure. God's shout of triumph had been heard already (vv. 7a, 9c).

A Plea for Just Rewards (Psalm 109)

The passage.—The psalm consists of appeals to God for help against malicious enemies. Four successive appeals appear in verses 1–5, 6–19, 20–25, and 26–29. The conclusion, verses 30–31, is a resolution to praise God for the answer confidently expected.

Special points.—The enemies were described as false accusers who assaulted with "words of hatred" (v. 3). They attacked without cause, returning "evil for good" (v. 5).

Unlike other parts of the psalm, verses 6–19 describe an enemy rather than enemies. One persecutor was especially vicious and merciless.

The denunciation of this chief persecutor is the most extensive and passionate in the Psalter. Of course, prayers for severe judgment on the wicked occur in Psalms 35,69, and others.

The distraught psalmist, devoutly religious, was concerned greatly about moral "reward" (v. 20). The fact of God's justice required retribution. Curses must fall on a pitiless persecutor who poured his curses on others (v. 17). Desperation must overtake a godless tyrant who drove others to death (v. 16).

An increased meaning for love has come through Jesus Christ. Yet in some ways the psalmist's pleas anticipated the fuller revelation. Specifically, he prayed for the reward of blessing on himself as a loyal believer. But his confident expectation of the answer magnified the Lord's goodness, not his own worthiness (vv. 21,31).

The Priest-King (Psalm 110)

The passage.—The purpose of the poem was to acclaim the ruler as both priest and king. The declaration was made in two parts, verses 1–3 and 4–7. Kingship was emphasized in the former, priesthood in the latter.

Special points.—This is the most famous of the Royal Psalms. In the New Testament it is quoted more frequently than any other psalm. It found special fulfilment in Jesus our Lord.

The ideal ruler was envisioned as possessing both kingly and priestly functions. A combination of these offices was actually the case in the early days of Israel's history. It was the case also in the much later period of the Maccabees. This psalm, therefore, probably applied originally to a Davidic ruler in pre-Exilic times.

An explicit word from the Lord introduced a description of the ruler (my Lord, v. 1) as king. Another such word introduced a description of the ruler as priest (v. 4). Perhaps in ceremonial use of the psalm a prophet or priest pronounced these divine messages.

The ruler would have three characteristics as king. He would enjoy great power, continuing youth, and enthusiastic cooperation of his subjects.

Likewise, he would have three characteristics as priest-king. He would function by divine appointment and not by hereditary position, thus like Melchizedek of ancient Salem (or Jerusalem; Gen. 14:18–20). He would serve continually and not by temporary assignment. He would press for a victory of righteousness and not simply hold office.

Private and Public Praise (Psalm 111)

The passage.—Praise of the Lord was the concern of the writer, his own and that of others. He began with a promise of praise (v. 1). He continued with an explanation of reasons for praise (vv. 2–9). He concluded by pinpointing the meaning of praise (v. 10).

Special points.—This psalm and Psalm 112 probably came from the same author. In addition to similar contents, they have the same arrangement. Each is an acrostic or alphabetic poem. Each has twenty-two lines (RSV), the number of letters in the Hebrew alphabet. The successive lines begin with the successive letters.

Together these psalms seem to function as an introduction to Psalms 113–118. This larger group, known as the Hallel, or Hymn of Praise, was used in the Jewish festivals of Passover, Pentecost, and Tabernacles. The expression "Praise ye the Lord" marks the group.

The writer yearned for wholehearted praise in private devotion and in congregational worship. The term "assembly," meaning an intimate group, described the former. The term "congregation" (v. 1) designated the latter.

The Lord's works were ample reason for praise. What he had done in behalf of his people expressed his greatness (vv. 2–3) and his goodness (vv. 4–9). The covenant-keeping God had delivered the people from Egypt and settled them in the Promised Land.

Praise was considered natural for those who practice heavenly wisdom. It arises out of reverent recognition of the greatness and goodness of God.

The Blessedness of a God-Fearing Man (Psalm 112)

The passage.—The God-fearing man is the subject of the psalm. His divine blessings (vv. 1–3), manner of life (vv. 4–6), and spiritual outlook (vv. 7–10) are celebrated.

Special points.—In effect, this psalm is an expansion of Psalm 111:10. There it was declared that reverence for the Lord is the beginning of wisdom. The present psalm describes the well-being of the person for whom profound reverence for God is a way of life.

The blessedness of the God-fearing man was represented as abundant (vv. 1–3). Also, it was described as both spiritual and material, and as affecting oncoming generations.

Moral qualities attributed to God in Psalm 111 were applied here to the God-fearing person. Note the terms "gracious," "compassion," and "righteous" in verse 4. The implication is that a life of reverence takes on likeness to God.

The life of reverence was portrayed as free of fear and possessed of enduring righteousness. Faith in God puts fear to flight. Righteousness is real only in a relationship to the God of enduring righteousness.

Praise the Lord! (Psalm 113)

The passage.—This is a hymn of praise to the Lord. It begins with a fervent call for praise (v. 1). It concludes with a shout of praise (v. 9c). Two emphases link these exclamations. The Lord is worthy of universal praise (vv. 2–4). He is the exalted God who cares supremely for needy men (vv. 5–9b).

Special points.—This is the first in a group of five psalms of praise. The use of the group in traditional Jewish worship has been noted already in comments on Psalm 111.

Attention was focused on praise to "the name of the Lord" (vv. 1–3). The Lord's name represented his character. Further, it stood for what he made known concerning himself to his people.

Possibly the psalm reflected joy because of Israel's return from Babylonian exile. Restoration of the nation was God's accomplishment. It revealed his power and fulfilled his promise. Just so, it glorified his name.

The Lord was declared to be beyond compare. Whereas he "dwelleth on high" (v. 5), yet he "humbleth himself" (v. 6). He is the exalted God. Yet he concerns himself with lowly human beings. His compassion reaches a woman grief-stricken by childlessness, and a man whose wretched lot is a "dunghill" (v. 7; ash heap, RSV).

Truth for today.—The psalmist anticipated the gospel of Jesus Christ. God is awesome in greatness. He is infinitely above us and beyond us. Yet in Jesus he has come to us. In his Spirit he now lives in us.

God's Deliverance of Israel from Egypt (Psalm 114)

The passage.—The familiar subject of this little poem is the deliverance of Israel from Egypt. In four brief stanzas, each consisting of two verses, four dominant thoughts appear. The people of Jacob were delivered from Egypt (vv. 1–2). The physical creation cooperated in the deliverance (vv. 3–4). Why was it so (vv. 5–6)? God's presence was the adequate explanation (vv. 7–8).

Special points.—No other historical event was so revered in Israel as the deliverance from Egypt. That event expressed the Lord's purpose and power, election and redemption, in Israel. That event broke the hold of oppressors whose hostility made them a "people of strange language" (v. 1). It laid divine claims on the whole life of the whole "house of Jacob," both "Judah" and "Israel" (v. 2).

Possibly, though not certainly, the return from captivity in Babylon was the backdrop. Even that deliverance was not so extraordinary as the coming out of Egypt. Yet, like the deliverance from Egypt, it demonstrated the power and faithfulness of the Lord.

Apparently the crossing of the Red Sea (sea) and the crossing of the "Jordan" (v. 3) were fused into one thought. Both events were dramatic responses of the physical creation to the act of God.

God's presence alone explained the behavior of waters and mountains in the events of the past. In the present, too, his wonder-working presence would bring a blessing to the people.

The Lord in Contrast to Idols (Psalm 115)

The passage.—The psalmist magnified the superiority of the Lord. His words were an answer to ridicule by the idol-worshiping heathen.

The Lord was implored to vindicate his name by acting in behalf of his people (vv. 1–2). Idols were scorned as senseless and powerless (vv. 3–8). Israelites were exhorted to trust the Lord and wait patiently (vv. 9–11). Assurance was linked with petition to God (vv. 12–15). Praise was offered to the Lord (vv. 16–18).

Special points.—The psalm was de-

signed for responsive singing. Compare Ezra 3:11. The first and final portions (vv. 1–8, 16–18) apparently were sung or chanted by the chorus or the congregation. The central portion (vv. 9–15) was rendered partly by the leader and partly by the congregation. In verses 9–11 the latter half of each verse was a response.

Idol-worshipers had challenged the effectiveness of Israel's God. Their gods could be handled and seen. The Lord could be seen only in his work. Hence, the psalmist prayed for the Lord to act.

In contrast to the sovereign God "in the heavens" (v. 3), the idols were "the work of men's hands" (v. 4). They possessed neither life nor power.

The exhortation to faith was addressed to "Israel," the "house of Aaron," and those who "fear the Lord" (vv. 9–11). Apparently Israel was the worshiping congregation; Aaron was the priest; and the God-fearers were both together.

The psalmist was confident of the divine blessing even while he prayed for it. On the condition of faith the blessing was sure for "small and great" (v. 13), without human distinction.

Deliverance from Threatened Death (Psalm 116)

The passage.—In an especially personal manner the psalmist expressed gratefulness and made a thank-offering to the Lord. He had been at death's door. The Lord had restored him.

The psalmist's thanksgiving (vv. 1–2) was followed by an indication of the serious illnesses from which he had recovered (vv. 3–4). The Lord was praised as merciful helper (vv. 5–11). Offerings and vows were made in worship (vv. 12–19).

Special points.—The psalmist declared, "I love the Lord" (v. 1). He knew the Lord to be personal and concerned for a human being's welfare.

Dreaded enemies, "death" and Sheol (RSV; hell, v. 3), were visualized as hunters. They set traps and waited to take their victim. The picture-like phrase "sorrows of death" means literally traps of death (RSV).

In verse 6, as in Psalm 19:7, the expression "the simple" has a good sense. The term applied to the psalmist. When he declared that the Lord "preserveth the simple" he gave his personal testimony.

The exact meaning of verses 10–11 is somewhat uncertain. The rendering by RSV is helpful. "I kept my faith, even when I said, "I am greatly afflicted; I said in my consternation, Men are all a vain hope.""

The psalmist had made vows which he would fulfil if permitted to get well. Now recovered, he acknowledged publicly his obligation and fulfilled his commitment.

Praise the Lord, All Nations! (Psalm 117)

The passage.—Briefest of all the psalms, this is a hymn calling for all nations to praise the Lord.

Special points.—In some manuscripts this psalm is made the conclusion of Psalm 116, in others the beginning of Psalm 118. But it is not appropriate in either position. Its brevity alone probably accounts for these arrangements.

The basis or occasion of praise was the Lord's "steadfast love" and unswerving "faithfulness" (RSV; merciful kindness . . . truth) to Israel in the covenant. This emphasis was a frequent one in the words of psalmists and prophets.

But the exhortation to "all ye nations" and "all ye people" (peoples, RSV) expressed a concern for human beings far beyond the borders of Israel. Indeed, it implied clear recognition that the ulti-

mate objective of Israel's calling was the salvation of men everywhere.

A Glad Song of Victory (Psalm 118)

The passage.—Deliverance from danger and death was celebrated at the Temple. A call to praise the Lord (vv. 1–4) was followed by an individual song of thanksgiving (vv. 5–20). A congregational hymn magnified the same theme (vv. 21–25). Pronouncement of benediction and chanting of thanks concluded the ceremony (vv. 26–29).

Special points.—The psalm was used in a celebration of victory. Deliverance from an enemy in warfare is described in verses 10–14. The specific occasion can not be determined.

Victory was credited to the help of the Lord. Two divine attributes were especially demonstrated by the Lord's acts: goodness and steadfast love (good . . . mercy, vv. 1,29).

Apparently the call to praise was sung or chanted by several groups. Perhaps verse 1 represented the full chorus or congregation. Then parts were specifically designated for the congregation (Israel, v. 2), the priests (Aaron, v. 3), and both (God-fearers, v. 4).

In verses 5–20 the pronouns "I," "me," and "my" indicate individual thanksgiving. Possibly the individual was the king. If so, he represented the people. The enemies were the nation's enemies. The victory was a deliverance for the people.

In verses 21–25 a gradual transition is made to the pronouns "we," "us," and "our." The congregation sang of the "Lord's doing" (v. 23). He had snatched victory out of seeming defeat. A rejected stone was made the cornerstone (v. 22).

Responsive chants by the priests inside the Temple were a feature of the worship. Observe their answer in verse 20 and their benediction in 26. Perhaps the congregation sang in a processional approach to the Temple. Note the joyous entrance in verses 26–27.

Delight in the Law of the Lord (Psalm 119)

The passage.—This is a psalm of joyous meditations on the law of the Lord. There are twenty-two sections, each relatively complete within itself. Stated another way, the sections are successive meditations and not parts of a logically developed theme or argument.

Special points.—Like Psalms 111, 112, and others, this is an alphabetical poem, or an acrostic. The twenty-two sections are headed by successive letters of the Hebrew alphabet. Each section contains eight lines. Each of these lines begins with the letter that stands at the beginning of that particular section.

To the psalmist the law of the Lord had the broad meaning of divine revelation. It consisted of what God had taught his people, not merely Mosaic legislation. Observe the variety of descriptive terms: "law" (v. 1), "testimonies" (v. 2), "ways" (v. 3), "precepts" (v. 4), "statutes" (v. 5), "commandments" (v. 6), "judgments" (v. 7), and "word" (two terms, vv. 9,41).

To this psalmist the law was the opposite of "a yoke upon the neck" (Acts 15:10). The law was from God, and it expressed his wise and gracious will. It was a means for living in fellowship with the God who gave it. This was the essence of his attitude: "O how love I thy law! it is my meditation all the day" (v. 97).

Brief statements of wisdom and moral guidance resemble portions of Proverbs. Compare verses 9–16 with Proverbs 3:13–18.

The complex structure of this longest psalm may seem to indicate artificial literary effort. Actually, however, the poem is characterized by deep feeling and earnestness. The writer was a sufferer (vv. 81–88,153–160), and in great suffering he found the law a source of comfort and correction (vv. 67,71).

The Cry of One Assailed by Enemies (Psalm 120)

The passage.—Assailed by foes, the psalmist voiced deep distress and sorrow. He confidently appealed to the Lord for help (vv. 1–2). He then addressed his enemies with a forecast of judgment on them (vv. 3–4). Finally, he expressed a dismal lament for his situation, surrounded by those who hated peace (vv. 5–7).

Special points.—This is the first in a group of fifteen psalms (120–134) described in each instance as "A Song of degrees." The superscription means literally A Song of Goings-up (Ascents, RSV). The note possibly alludes to the return from Babylonian exile. But it more probably refers to the pilgrimage of worshipers to the Temple feasts in Jerusalem.

"Mesech" and "Kedar" were not exact geographical areas. The former apparently referred to a region to the north of Israel near the Black Sea (Gen. 10:2; Ezek. 32:26). The latter probably specified Arabian tribes to the east, beyond Ammon and Moab (Gen. 25:13).

Possibly the psalmist was an exile. If so, he shared the fear of returning exiles for these tribes along the way. The more probable assumption is that he was in the land of Israel. He described fellow Israelites, his persecutors, by these names that represented bitter hostility.

What kind of judgment would overtake the enemies? The psalmist answered his own question (vv. 3–4). They would receive what they had given. Piercing words of "lying lips" (v. 2) would return as actual "arrows" (v. 4). Fires of slander from "a deceitful tongue" (v. 2) would return as condemnation burning like the intense, prolonged heat of a broom tree fire (juniper, v. 4).

The Lord Is Keeper (Psalm 121)

The passage.—Four pairs of verses comprise the psalm, each pair affirming sure reliance on the Lord. The Lord is helper (vv. 1–2), keeper (vv. 3–4), protector (vv. 5–6), and guard (vv. 7–8). The psalm as a whole reflects spiritual quietness and peace.

Special points.—The latter part of verse 1 is actually a question, not the completion of a statement. Observe the rendering of RSV: "From whence does my help come?" Verse 2 is the answer.

Possibly the psalmist was a pilgrim journeying to Jerusalem for one of the annual feasts. If so, perhaps the pilgrim's exciting first view of "the hills" (v. 1) around the city or the Temple inspired his words.

The question and answer of verse 1 possibly represented the psalmist's communion with himself. Presumably verses 3–8 were assurance given by others as he made the pilgrimage. Or, possibly they were a priest's benediction pronounced on him as he started back home. But only the superscription (degree, or goings-up) suggests connection with a pilgrimage.

A situation of uncertainty and danger was implied. But the psalmist faced such circumstances in peaceful, unshakable reliance on God. In contrast to certain other psalmists, he displayed no anguish or tension.

Truth for today.—In the psalmist's experience great faith corresponded to a great God. He trusted in the God of power and goodness. Just so, his God's protection was as real "by night" as "by day" (vv. 5–6). His God was as certainly a keeper for a life-time as for a

day, for one's "coming in" as for one's "going out" (v. 8). These divine certainties are still the counterbalance for human uncertainties.

Joyous Arrival at the House of the Lord (Psalm 122)

The passage.—This is a song of Zion. It expresses the joy of the pilgrim who had just arrived in Jerusalem (vv. 1–2). It reflects the memories called up as he viewed the city (vv. 3–5). It recalls his exhortation that others join him in prayer for the beloved city (vv. 6–9).

Special points.—Verses 1–2 express joyous fulfilment. The pilgrim had reached his longed-for destination! Some had said, "Let us go . . ." (v. 1). Together they came. Now their feet actually rested on the pavement inside the city gates!

What an overpowering sight! The pilgrim saw the city "compact together" (v. 3). It was literally so from the viewpoint of a man from the open country. It was religiously and politically so from the standpoint of one familiar with the history of Israel.

Jerusalem was the spiritual center. There "the tribes" (v. 4) went up to worship the Lord. It was also the political capital, the seat of "the house of David" (v. 5), where justice was administered to the nation.

Memories of the past turned to hopes for the future. As the pilgrim had exhorted others, so he himself prayed for the future welfare of Jerusalem. He appealed for peace and prosperity. He offered his prayer for the sake of his fellow Israelites (my brethren, v. 8) and for the sake of the Temple (the house of the Lord, v. 9).

Eyes That Look to the Lord (Psalm 123)

The passage.—The psalm is a prayer for God's mercy in the face of scorn and contempt. First, in verses 1–2, the eyes were turned toward the heavens in vigilant expectation of divine mercy. Afterward, in verses 3–4, the lips expressed anguish of soul in prayer for divine mercy that seemed too long delayed.

Special points.—The entire Israelitish community was the object of scorn and mockery. Who were those who held the people in "contempt" (vv. 3,4)? Perhaps they were their own public officials, cruel and corrupt at the time. Or, possibly they were pagan nations and rulers.

The specific time and occasion reflected in the psalm are not indicated. However, the trials of Nehemiah's period come readily to mind (Neh. 2:17–20; 4:1–5).

The psalmist alone addressed God in verse 1. He and others spoke in verses 2–4. In the former case he spoke in behalf of the community. In the latter, he joined others of the community in fervent prayer.

The psalmist likened himself to an Oriental servant whose eyes were always on his master. The comparison was appropriate. His eyes were turned to the Master who "dwellest in the heavens" (v. 1). Even while trials continued, he waited in hope of mercy.

Yet the limit of endurance seemed near. With hearts "exceedingly filled" (v. 4) with anguish, these abused people voiced a cry of urgency to the God of mercy.

Thanksgiving for Rescue from Enemies (Psalm 124)

The passage.—An unforgettable rescue of Israel from dangerous enemies occasioned the psalm. Credit was given to the Lord for taking the nation's side (vv. 1–5). Praise was offered to the Lord for past help and future hope (vv. 6–8).

Special points.—In the superscription the psalm is connected with David. However, in some of the early translations this reference is omitted.

Perhaps an older psalm was adapted to celebrate a great deliverance at a later time. The particular occasion may have been the return from exile in Babylon, or victory over the opposition of Sanballat and Tobiah in Nehemiah's day.

Observe the pronouns "we," "our," and "us." The psalm represented the nation's experience. It was an appropriate expression of gratitude and praise by the community in worship.

Vivid language was used in verses 3–7 to describe dangers, or enemies, that had threatened the nation. Note these expressions: "swallowed," "overwhelmed" (swept away, RSV), "stream" (torrent, RSV), "proud waters" (raging waters, RSV), "prey," and "snare of the fowlers."

The worshiping people recognized only one source of adequate help. They acclaimed the "Lord, who made heaven and earth" (v. 8). Apart from him they would have been overcome completely.

The Abiding Security of God's People (Psalm 125)

The passage.—Spiritual security is the theme of this psalm. The psalm itself falls into two parts: an expression of confidence in God (vv. 1–3) and a prayer and warning (vv. 4–5).

Special points.—The confidence of those trusting in the Lord was compared to "mount Zion, which cannot be removed" (v. 1). The comparison was meaningful to Israelites. Mountains were a symbol of all that was immovable and enduring.

The Lord's care for his people was likened to the wall of mountains "round about Jerusalem" (v. 2). The city was

high. The surrounding mountains were
higher, especially the Mount of Olives
on the east, the Hill of Evil Counsel on
the southeast, Mount Scopus on the
north, and the rising plateau on the
west. The God of eternal faithfulness
had chosen both the people and the city.

Because of the Lord's faithfulness, the
domination of pagan oppressors ("rod
of the wicked," v. 3; scepter of wickedness, RSV) would be broken off. Oppression would not be permitted to
drive the people of faith to despair and
rebellion.

The psalmist prayed for justice. Let
God show special goodness to those who
remained "upright in their hearts" (v.
4) during trials. But let those who "turn
aside" (v. 5) beware of serious consequences.

Perhaps the restless, troubled times
were those of Nehemiah. In the struggling community resettled at Jerusalem
some proved the Lord's faithfulness.
Others sold out to the enemy.

Abounding Joy, Yet Tears (Psalm 126)

The passage.—A joyous testimony
(vv. 1–3) and a confident prayer (vv.
4–6) comprise the psalm. What the Lord
had done for Israel was so good and
great as to be unbelievable. Yet, present
needs were serious and urgent.

Special points.—The phrase "turned
again the captivity" in verse 1 may mean
"restored the fortunes" (RSV; Job
42:10). Here, however, reference apparently was made to the return from
the Babylonian exile. The Lord's act of
deliverance was so marvelous as to be
like a dream.

When the reality of liberation and
return dawned upon the Israelites, they
were captured by joyous enthusiasm, by
"laughter" and "singing" (v. 2). Even
other nations (the heathen, v. 2) acknowledged the Lord's mighty act in

behalf of Israel.

But early enthusiasm had waned.
Now there were pressing needs, if not
disappointment. Perhaps the difficult
times of Nehemiah were reflected, or
possibly those of Haggai (Hag. 1:1–11;
2:15–19).

"Turn again our captivity" (v. 4). Was
this an appeal that yet other exiles be
returned? Or, was it a plea that the
fortunes of the poor community be restored? Probably the latter. As winter
rains turned dry watercourses of the
Negeb, south of Judah, into flowing
streams, so let divine mercies turn
Israel's poverty into plenty.

This was a prayer of confidence. God
is sovereign over the seasons, both
physical and spiritual. Tears in planting
time would be followed by rejoicing in
harvest.

Dependence on the Lord (Psalm 127)

The passage.—Utter dependence on
the Lord is the unifying theme of this
song. In work (vv. 1–2) and in family
life (vv. 3–5) there is indispensable need
of divine favor.

Special points.—Superficially observed, work and family appear to be
separate themes. Are two poems, vv.
1–2 and 3–5, artificially put together?
No. Actually, there are two emphases in
a larger unifying theme: dependence on
the Lord. In work and in family relationships the divine blessing is
necessary.

The two parts of the psalm appear to
be meditations—connected meditations
—of a wise man. Each verse is a wise
saying. The similarity of such sayings to
those of the book of Proverbs is
obvious.

The last clause of verse 2 is obscure.
Not "so he giveth his beloved sleep,"
but "for he gives to his beloved in sleep"
(RSV), is the probable sense. This was

no encouragement to laziness. Rather, it was a warning against the assumption that endless, frantic toil for material things is the whole of life.

For the psalmist religion was practical. Like a rugged pioneer, he was concerned for elemental needs and common tasks. Two convictions had emerged. No human enterprise could succeed without God's help (v. 1). A flourishing family, with resultant benefits, could not be viewed as human achievement but rather as a gift (heritage, v. 3) from the Lord.

The Blessedness of the God-Fearer (Psalm 128)

The passage.—The subject of the poem is the God-fearing man. In verses 1–4 a tribute is paid to the God-fearer, with emphasis on productive work and happy family. In verses 5–6 a benediction is pronounced on the God-fearer, with concern for the well-being of both family and nation.

Special points.—Fear of the Lord meant devout reverence or worshipful regard for the Lord. Stark fright and cringing terror were not the thought of the psalmist.

Fear of the Lord affects human conduct, so the psalmist was convinced. The "one that feareth the Lord" is the one "that walketh in his ways" (v. 1).

Work was an emphasis continued from Psalm 127. There the success of every human enterprise was dependent on the Lord. Here honest and productive work marked the ethical life of a worshiper of the Lord.

Likewise, happy and prosperous family life was a continued emphasis. In Psalm 127 such happiness was the gift of the Lord. Here it was the result of reverent recognition of the Lord.

The wife privileged to have many children was described as a "fruitful vine." Healthy, vigorous children were likened to "olive plants" (v. 3; shoots, RSV). Such figures were forcefully descriptive of a society which cherished large families and considered childlessness a shame.

Truth for today.—In the benediction, verses 5–6, family and nation were considered interdependent. The insight is sound. A flourishing national life is dependent ultimately on happy and prosperous families.

The Pledge of Israel's Survival (Psalm 129)

The passage.—This is a psalm of the community. The dominant concern was survival in anxious, threatening times. Deliverances of Israel in the past (vv. 1–4) encouraged hope for the nation's future (vv. 5–8).

Special points.—Israel's past was reviewed from the time of Egyptian bondage onward (youth, v. 1; Hos. 11:1). The history of the people was a record of multiplied afflictions. But it was a record of amazing deliverances also.

The expressions "plowed upon my back" and "made long their furrows" (v. 3) refer to oppression. A nation thrown on her face and an enemy plowing furrows on her back—these are pictures of cruelty. Perhaps the strips of whip lashes suggested the description. Similarly, the term "cords" (v. 4) denotes bondage.

But Israel had survived every crisis. There was a single, all-sufficient explanation. "The Lord is righteous" (v. 4).

Verses 5–8 are partially prayer and partially prediction. The present enemies of Israel were like self-sown "grass," voluntary growth, in crevices on "housetops" (v. 6). Like such grass, let these cruel powers pass away quickly.

Enemies of the people in covenant with the Lord deserved no blessing from the Lord. Let no benediction, no word of encouragement, be pronounced on them.

The specific enemies threatening the people were not identified. Perhaps the hard circumstances of Nehemiah's period account for the psalm.

The God of Mercy and Pardon (Psalm 130)

The passage.—This is a penitential plea for divine forgiveness. The devout psalmist first turned to the Lord in repentant prayer (vv. 1–6). Then he turned to the assembled worshipers with a word of expectant faith (vv. 7–8).

Special points.—From deep waters of affliction (the depths, v. 1) the penitent worshiper cried out to God. He had a deep and clear sense of sin. Yet he did not give a graphic portrayal of guilt and suffering. Rather, he magnified divine forgiveness.

The basis of the repentant man's confidence was the Lord's mercy. Indeed, he was sure that should the Lord "mark iniquities" (v. 3), no one would have hope. Mercy, in contrast to strict account, was the basis of pardon.

The psalmist turned to the Lord with both patience and impatience. There was concentration on the "word" of promise, a quiet confidence (I wait, v. 5). Yet there was expectancy, an eagerness greater than that of the watchman awaiting the dawn ("they that watch for the morning," v. 6).

In verses 7–8 the personal pronoun "I" is replaced by references to "Israel." Possibly the personal prayer (vv. 1–6), the original poem, was enlarged so as to apply to the whole nation.

By the Lord's mercy the penitent worshiper was lifted from depths of distress to heights of hope. The triumphant experience of an individual was possible for a nation. "Let Israel

hope. . . ." Let a penitent community depend on divine "mercy" for "plenteous redemption" (v. 7).

Schooled in Calm Confidence and Humility (Psalm 131)

The passage.—The psalmist's personal confession (vv. 1–2) and his exhortation to Israel (v. 3) comprise the poem. He had learned the way of quiet trust and childlike humility. Let Israel learn the same patient confidence in the Lord.

Special points.—Comparison of the psalm with Psalm 130 is instructive. This psalm is a confession of humility. Psalm 130 is a prayer of repentance. Both are intensely personal except at the end. Each concludes with an appeal to the whole community.

The figure of the "weaned" child (v. 2) held a twofold suggestion: giving up and finding contentment. The child gave up the mother's breast and learned contentment and security without it. Similarly, in his maturing process the psalmist turned from his own ambitions and learned to wait on God.

The disciplined life was not a natural endowment. The psalmist had known the inclination to haughty looks and ambitious schemes. But humility and patience had replaced selfish struggle.

Let Israel learn this same lesson. Perhaps this was the problem-plagued community after the Exile. Not in restless struggle, but in calm confidence the people should wait on God.

David's name appears in the superscription. Possibly this is true because the psalm seemed to illustrate the spirit of David's life (2 Sam. 7:18–29).

Sure Blessings for David's Sake (Psalm 132)

The passage.—Prayer (vv. 1–10) and promise (vv. 11–18) are the two parts of the psalm. Both relate to deep concern for God's blessings on David's royal house and on the sanctuary in Jerusalem.

Special points.—The psalm probably was designed for public ceremony. Apparently the congregation spoke the prayer. A prophet or a priest recited the divine promise in response.

The Lord was implored to remember the royal house and the Temple for David's sake. Perhaps the better rendering for verse 1 is "Remember, O Lord, in David's favor" (RSV). Such is the emphasis in verse 10: "For thy servant David's sake."

David's primary concern was to find a "place" for the ark of the covenant, symbol of divine presence. Building the house of the Lord was a matter of conscience and resolute purpose. It cost him "hardships" (RSV: afflictions, v. 1). Yet it won the eager response of his people.

The prayer echoed famous stories concerning the ark. "Ephratah" was another name for the Bethlehem district. The expression "fields of the wood" (v. 6) described Kiriath-jearim. Narratives in 1 and 2 Samuel recount the background episodes.

In substance, verses 11–18 were a poetic version of 2 Samuel 7:5–16. The Lord chose Zion, promising to "dwell" there (v. 14), bless her spiritual ministers (priests), and give joy to her devoted ones (saints, vv. 9,16). Likewise, he promised continuing vigor and prosperity for the Davidic dynasty (horn of David to bud . . . a lamp, v. 17).

The Blessings of Brotherly Fellowship (Psalm 133)

The passage.—The psalm is a beautiful tribute to brotherly togetherness. In verse 1 the blessings of such relationship are exclaimed. In verses 2–3 the blessings of such relationship are illustrated.

Special points.—By "brethren" (v. 1) the psalmist referred to members of the covenant community. The harmonious togetherness of Israel, not that of a single family, was the thought.

Brotherly relationship in covenant had outward expression in religious festivals. Perhaps the psalm was used in such ceremonies in Jerusalem.

The psalmist's emphasis was in the phrase "dwell together" (v. 1). Israel's togetherness was expressed in postexilic times by the settling of returned exiles at Jerusalem. The specific occasion may be reflected in Nehemiah 11:1–2.

Brotherly togetherness was compared to perfumed oil (precious ointment, v. 2) used in anointing Aaron as high priest (Ex. 30:22–33). Its growing influence would be like the spreading oil running down from the head to the beard and to the collar (literally, mouth; skirts, v. 2) of the robes.

Also, brotherly fellowship was likened to the abundant dew of Mount Hermon. Its spiritual effect on the community would be like the physical effect of this rain-like dew should it fall on the dry hills of Jerusalem.

Jerusalem was connected especially with the Lord's choice and promise. To the nation whose center was "there" (v. 3), the Lord promised renewed and continuing life.

A Benediction (Psalm 134)

The passage.—Bless and be blessed—these are the essential ideas of the psalm. Observe the exhortation (vv. 1–2): "Behold (come, RSV), bless ye the Lord." Observe the response (v. 3): "The Lord . . . bless thee. . . ."

Special points.—This is the last of the so-called pilgrim psalms (120–134). It was apparently a farewell to the Temple. With the festival concluded, the procession of worshipers departed for home.

Verses 1–2 represent the departing worshipers' exhortation to the priests. Let these "servants" at the Temple "bless the Lord." The lifting of their hands was the appropriate posture of blessing.

The reference to the "night" seems to imply nighttime services at the sanctuary (1 Chron. 9:33). Presumably the Feast of Tabernacles was the occasion.

Verse 3 represents the priests' response, that is, a priestly blessing (Num. 6:24). The blessing was based on the conviction that the Lord who "made heaven and earth" and dwelled in "Zion" had the power to bless.

Praise to the Lord for His Power and Mercy (Psalm 135)

The passage.—This hymn of praise magnified the Lord's power and mercy. The priests, and then the worshiping assembly, were summoned to praise the Lord (vv. 1–4). A recital of the Lord's wondrous acts included phenomena of the physical world and events in history (vv. 5–12). An affirmation of the Lord's power and faithfulness set powerless idols in contrast (vv. 13–18). A new summons to praise was addressed to all Israel (vv. 19–21).

Special points.—In a sense, this psalm was an extension of Psalm 134. As there, so here, the Temple was the setting. In both psalms the groups exhorted were priests (ye that stand in the house) and general worshipers (in the courts, v. 2).

The Lord's great acts were manifest in marvelous features of the creation (heaven . . . earth . . . seas, v. 6). Similarly, his great acts were manifest in Israel's exodus from Egypt, wilderness wanderings, and conquest of Canaan.

In the past the Lord's supremacy

over "all gods" (v. 5) of the nations had been demonstrated by his choice, deliverance, and protection of Israel. His name, representing his person and purpose, had not lost its power. In the future he would "vindicate" (RSV; judge) Israel and "have compassion" (RSV; will repent himself, v. 14) on his people. What a contrast to powerless, ineffective idols!

Finally, all Israelites were called to worshipful praise. From "Zion"—the Temple—should ring out their witness to the Lord.

Thanksgiving for the Lord's Steadfast Love (Psalm 136)

The passage.—With thanksgiving throughout, the psalm sustains consistent emphasis on the Lord's steadfast love. At the beginning is an invitation to worship (vv. 1–3). Then attention is focused successively on the Lord's acts in creation (vv. 4–9), deliverance of Israel (vv. 10–22), and mercy for Israel and sustenance for all (vv. 23–25). The conclusion is a word of praise (v. 26).

Special points.—The psalm was designed for responsive chanting or singing in one of the religious festivals. All verses end in an identical refrain: "for his mercy endureth for ever." This refrain probably was sung by the congregation in response to the sentences sung by the priestly choir, or by the choir in answer to a leader.

As in Psalm 135, the Lord's acts in creation and in deliverance of early Israel are major themes. The leading ideas concerning creation (vv. 4–9) are similar to those of Genesis 1. The exodus, the wilderness wanderings, and the settlement (vv. 10–22) correspond to the stories of Exodus, Numbers, and Joshua.

All of the Lord's acts demonstrated his "steadfast love" (RSV; mercy). He had "made the heavens" (v. 5), "brought out Israel" (v. 11), and given a "land for an heritage" (v. 21). More recently he had lifted the nation from "low estate" (v. 23), perhaps the Babylonian exile.

To the God who "remembered" (v. 23) his covenant and "rescued" (RSV; redeemed, v. 24) his people, let all give thanks!

Emotional Memories of the Exile (Psalm 137)

The passage.—This psalm recalls the exile in Babylon. Verses 1–3 describe experience so bitter that the people had no heart to sing the songs of Zion. Verses 4–6 declare the psalmist's undying devotion to Jerusalem. Verses 7–9 record prayer for a divine curse on enemies.

Special points.—The "rivers" and the "willows" (vv. 1–2) were unforgettable features of the land of exile. The species of poplar flourished along the Euphrates and its irrigation canals.

Exiles who "sat" and "wept" (v. 1) in mourning could not sing the "songs of Zion" (v. 3). A song concerning the Lord seemed utterly inappropriate beyond the borders of Israel (in a strange land, v. 4). Besides, the songs of Zion were not ditties of "mirth" (v. 3).

In passionate loyalty to Jerusalem, the psalmist almost threatened himself with a curse. The city must be above his "chief joy" (v. 6). Rather than dishonor Jerusalem, he would lose his skill as harpist and his voice for singing.

Retribution was invoked on both Babylon and Edom. Nebuchadnezzar's army had destroyed Jerusalem and had taken the people captive in 586 B.C. When the city fell, the descendants of Esau took cruel advantage of the plight of Judah (Obad. 10–14).

Truth for today.—When the Lord's people are silenced by sorrow they become victims rather than victors. More-

over, every new set of circumstances, however foreign, is a fresh opportunity to demonstrate faith.

The temper of the psalmist's words was this: Blessed is one who deals with you as you have dealt with us. But the moral constraint on the Christian's motives and actions is this: "Blessed are the merciful . . ." (Matt. 5:7).

Gratitude for Fulfilment of God's Word (Psalm 138)

The passage.—A notable fulfilment of God's word was the occasion of thanksgiving. The psalmist resolved to give wholehearted praise to the Lord (vv. 1–3). He then predicted that all rulers would offer homage to the Lord (vv. 4–6). Finally, he professed his trust in the Lord's continuing care (vv. 7–8).

Special points.—The particular fulfilment of divine promise apparently was Israel's return from exile. Although David's name appears with the psalm, certain manuscripts of early translation add the names Haggai and Zechariah. Perhaps the older Davidic poem was given this revised form after the Exile.

As in Psalm 82:1, the term "gods" (v. 1) probably applied to earthly rulers. In the midst of the mighty the psalmist would praise the Lord.

The Lord's faithful performance would have great effect on these "kings of the earth" (v. 4). Their response apparently would result from such testimony as that expressed by the psalmist.

The fulfilment of divine promise was considered greater than all previous acts revealing the divine character (name, v. 2). Observe this rendering: "thou hast exalted thy word above all thy name" (RSV, v. 2 note).

The psalmist's worship was inspired by the Lord's great "glory" (v. 5). It was encouraged by the Lord's "respect unto the lowly" (v. 6).

Verses 7–8 are a reminder of Psalm

23. The future could be trusted to God. Because of love in covenant (mercy; steadfast love, RSV), God would complete (perfect) his purpose in his own people.

A Tribute to the Greatness of God (Psalm 139)

The passage.—This psalm is a personal meditation addressed to God. It consists of four stanzas: verses 1–6, 7–12, 13–18, and 19–24. Each stanza magnifies an awesome characteristic of God. The respective characteristics are perfect knowledge, universal presence, sovereign control, and moral constraint.

Special points.—The psalmist declared that God knew all about him. Furthermore, God cared for him with precious and numberless thoughts.

Verse 4 has this sense: "Even before a word is on my tongue . . . thou knowest it" (RSV). Absolute knowledge was—and is—"too wonderful" (v. 6) for human comprehension.

The terms "spirit" and "presence" in verse 7 apparently had the same meaning. Emphasis was on the reality of God's presence everywhere. That reality is unhindered by factors of place or time or circumstance.

The psalmist credited his life to the creative work of God. "For thou didst form my inward parts, thou didst knit me together . . ." (v. 13, RSV). The expression "the lowest parts of the earth" (v. 15) was possibly a poetic description of the womb. The expression "substance . . . unperfect" (v. 16) was a reference to the embryo. And quite likely the days of life, not bodily parts, were considered "written" (v. 16) by the foreknowledge of God.

Of God the psalmist inquired, "Do not I hate them . . . that hate thee?" (v. 21). Evil could have no permanent place in God's world. Applying this

truth to himself, he prayed for genuine uprightness and for divine leading into life and peace (way everlasting, v. 24).

Prayer for Deliverance from Schemers (Psalm 140)

The passage.—Protection from scheming enemies was the psalmist's concern. He prayed to be delivered from their malicious plots (vv. 1–3) and shrewd traps (vv. 4–5). He asserted confidence in the Lord's protection (vv. 6–8) and appealed that the mischief-makers suffer their own mischief (vv. 9–11). In conclusion, he expressed assurance that the Lord would make justice to prevail (vv. 12–13).

Special points.—Pointed, poisonous tongues were the weapons of the enemies. Vicious slander, secretly plotted, was intended to inflict deadly wounds.

The fourfold reference to the hunter's traps (snare, cords, net, gins, v. 5) probably indicated deeds, not words only. If so, traps suggested acts of subtlety and cruelty.

The psalmist's confidence in the Lord's help was a spiritual experience, not a religious sentiment. It was based on a personal bond with the Lord: "Thou art my God . . ." (v. 6).

Prayer for the recoil of mischief on those who plotted it (v. 9) was an expression of strict justice. Indeed, such justice—God's justice—would "maintain the cause of the afflicted" (v. 12). But the plea that the enemies suffer the fate of Sodom (burning coals . . . fire, v. 10) was apparently charged with fierce emotion. No reference was made to the larger conception of the saving mercy of God.

Prayer for Deliverance from Sin and Sinners (Psalm 141)

The passage.—Like Psalm 140, this is a prayer for deliverance. The psalmist first appealed that his prayer be acceptable to the Lord (vv. 1–2). Then he prayed that he be preserved from the evil that surrounded him (vv. 3–4). Preferring the rebuke of the righteous to the hospitality of the wicked, he declared the sure punishment of evildoers (vv. 5–7). Finally, he voiced a plea for personal deliverance from enemies (vv. 8–10).

Special points.—The psalmist urged the Lord speedily (make haste, v. 1) to receive and accept his prayer. He would have his prayer ascend as the smoke of incense. He would have the lifting of his hands to represent a true dedication, "as the evening sacrifice" (v. 2).

Verbal supplication apparently was substituted for the sacrificial rite at the Temple. Perhaps this was a spiritual advance over exclusive dependence on the sanctuary. Or possibly the time was the early postexilic period when there was no Temple.

The prayer was twofold. First, the psalmist prayed that he be preserved from evil in a corrupt society. He was tempted with respect to speech, thought, and actions (lips, heart, works, vv. 3–4).

Second, the psalmist prayed that he be protected from personal foes. As in Psalm 140, the hunter's traps (snares, gins, nets, vv. 9–10) may suggest treacherous acts, not slanderous words only.

Leaders of wickedness would be punished and "their bones" (RSV; not our bones, v. 7) scattered at the grave. Then their followers would remember the psalmist's words (hear my words, v. 6).

Prayer for Deliverance from Distress (Psalm 142)

The passage.—Distressed and lonely, the psalmist sought help from the Lord. His appeal (vv. 1–3*a*) was followed by references to enemies and loneliness (vv. 3*b*–4). The appeal was renewed, with anticipation of deliverance and thanksgiving (vv. 5–7).

Special points.—Psalms 140, 141, and 142 are strikingly similar. All are personal prayers for deliverance from enemies. They have common features of language (for example, hunter's trap), and all have David's name attached. Presumably all had the same author and came from the same Davidic collection. Nevertheless, in their present form they may represent the unsettled conditions after the Babylonian exile.

In Psalm 142 the psalmist prayed aloud (with my voice, v. 1). His distress was almost overwhelming.

The psalmist's chief distress was not plotting enemies but utter aloneness. The *right hand* (v. 4) was the position of the protector. But he saw no one there to care and to help.

In his extremity the psalmist cried unto God. This was his confidence: "Thou art my refuge . . ." (v. 5).

The psalmist was possibly imprisoned literally. But his "prison" (v. 7) was more likely his deep distress. Even as he prayed he anticipated release. He foresaw the encircling companionship (compass me about, v. 7) of "the righteous" who would share his joy.

Truth for today.—Prayer is the prime source of comfort and courage in times of persecution. But for the Christian it is an occasion for solemn reminder that vengeance belongs to God, not to man. And it is an experience of maximum meaning only when it inspires forgiveness.

Penitential Appeal (Psalm 143)

The passage.—This is a penitential prayer in six parts. The psalmist's appeal for divine mercy (vv. 1–2) led to a description of cruel enemies (vv. 3–4).

Encouraged by the Lord's past goodness (vv. 5–6), he prayed for speedy help in the present (vv. 7–8). He pleaded for divine deliverance and guidance (vv. 9–10), then for deliverance in contrast to the fate of his enemies (vv. 11–12).

Special points.—The psalmist thought of his extreme affliction in terms of "darkness" and death (dead, v. 3; pit, v. 7). Only two circumstances were specified: persecution by enemies and personal guilt.

Recalling the Lord's goodness in the past, the psalmist was encouraged. The Lord had intervened in behalf of his people. His "works" (v. 5) had demonstrated his faithfulness and vindicated his people.

The basis of confidence was the character of God. Particular emphasis was placed on divine "righteousness" in association with "faithfulness" and "steadfast love" (RSV; lovingkindness). Divine character was especially magnified in verses 1, 8, 11, and 12.

Acutely aware of personal sin, the psalmist recognized that by strict righteousness he could not receive acquittal (be justified, v. 2). He prayed repentantly, therefore, with reliance on God's merciful goodness.

The penitent desired of God more than pardon. He asked for counsel (teach me, v. 10) in fulfilling the divine purpose. Likewise, he desired more than rescue from troubles. He asked that enemies be "cut off" (v. 12) as a vindication of his servantship to God.

Divine Blessings on the King and the Nation (Psalm 144)

The passage.—This is one of the Royal Psalms. Verses 1–11 report the king's praise and prayer. Verses 12–15 describe the nation's future prosperity and peace.

Special points.—There are numerous similarities, even parallels, in thought and language between this psalm and other psalms. Especially impressive are comparisons with Psalms 8 and 18.

The king acknowledged the gifts and goodness of the Lord. To divine help he owed his success in war and in national leadership. Indeed, he viewed man's frailty in stark contrast to the Lord's greatness.

The particular king was not named. The title "David his servant" (v. 10) was probably a designation of the typical ruler of the Lord's people, not a historical reference to King David. Yet this title, together with literary parallels to Psalms 8 and 18, likely account for David's name in the superscription.

The king prayed for a manifestation of divine power like that of the past. Volcano (smoke, v. 5) and storm (lightning, v. 6), mysterious physical forces, were symbols of God's awesome might.

The king was threatened by overwhelming danger (great waters, v. 7). The foreign power was called "strange children," literally, sons of a strange land (vv. 7,11). Evidently a treaty had been violated. The "right hand," uplifted for an oath, was a hand of "falsehood" (vv. 8,11).

The plea for national prosperity and peace (vv. 12–15) has the appearance of a separate poem. Yet divine blessings on the king would benefit the entire nation. This evidently was the point of essential unity.

Truth for today.—Two unchanging fundamentals were expressed in the concluding prayer. First, a nation's continuance depends on the vigor and beauty of its younger generation. Note references to "our sons" as sturdy saplings; to "our daughters" as beautiful, ornamented corner pillars. Second, a nation's ultimate well-being depends on its relationship to the Lord. Note the classic exclamation: "Happy the people whose God is the Lord!" (RSV).

Praise to God the King (Psalm 145)

The passage.—Here the psalmist spoke in behalf of Israel. His subject was God the King. He offered praise for divine majesty, goodness, providence, and love.

Beginning with exuberant praise (vv. 1–3), the psalmist recalled God's wondrous acts in history (vv. 4–7). He acclaimed God's perfect goodness as displayed toward men (vv. 8–9). He then turned toward the whole creation, expecting universal praise of the Lord (vv. 10–13b) and describing universal mercy from the Lord (vv. 13c–20). He concluded with another ascription of praise (v. 21).

Special points.—This is an alphabetic poem, an acrostic. Each two-line couplet begins with a letter of the Hebrew alphabet in regular order.

One couplet (one alphabetic letter) missing from most Hebrew manuscripts is omitted at verse 13 in KJV but supplied as verse 13c, d in RSV. The two lines complete the acrostic. They are drawn from one Hebrew manuscript and several ancient translations. See the note in RSV.

Even perpetual praise to the Lord was declared inadequate, for "his greatness is unsearchable" (v. 3). In history he is the God of "mighty acts" (v. 4). In relation to men he is the God of "compassion" (v. 8; Ex. 34:6).

Time limits and national boundaries were considered no barrier. God's kingdom is "everlasting" (v. 13). His providing hand is open to "every living thing" (v. 16). He saves all who "fear" and "love" him (vv. 19–20). Therefore, let "all flesh" (v. 21) praise him!

Praise to God the True Helper (Psalm 146)

The passage.—The Lord's unfailing help is the theme of the psalmist's song.

Indeed, the singer promised lifelong praise (vv. 1–2). He described man's transitoriness and unreliability (vv. 3–4) in contrast to God's unfailing help in time of need (vv. 5–9). In conclusion, he acclaimed the God of help as everlasting king (v. 10).

Special points.—This is the first of the five Hallelujah Psalms with which the Psalter closes. The word "Hallelujah" at the beginning and ending of each psalm means "Praise ye the Lord."

Observe the strong note of trust in the Lord. The psalmist's whole-life commitment to praise (v. 2) had its stimulus in the Lord's unswerving, enduring trustworthiness.

The psalmist evidently had suffered a betrayal of confidence. His disappointment related to a ruler (princes, v. 3) whose purposes (thoughts, v. 4) had perished with him.

But trust in the Lord would not be frustrated. The foundation of confidence was threefold. God is mighty, merciful, and abiding.

As respects sovereign power, the Lord "made heaven, and earth" (v. 6). As regards compassion, he "executeth judgment [or justice] . . . giveth food to the hungry" (v. 7). As for continuance, past experience inspired future hope. The "God of Jacob" (v. 5) most certainly "shall reign for ever" (v. 10).

Praise to the God of Purpose and Providence (Psalm 147)

The passage.—This is another hymn of praise. It falls naturally into three parts, each beginning with an exhortation to praise the Lord. Praise the Lord for restoring Jerusalem and gathering the outcast people (vv. 1–6). Praise him for sustaining the provident physical order (vv. 7–11). Praise him for giving prosperity and peace to his people (vv. 12–20).

Special points.—The mood of joy probably reflects a specific occasion. Attention was on the restoration of Jerusalem. Possibly a religious festival in Nehemiah's time was the setting.

The Lord's work was pictured as in process. The verbs "doth build . . . gathereth together" (v. 2) have this force: is building . . . gathers. The God who determines the "number" and "names" of the stars was capable of this accomplishment.

The Lord who expressed goodness to Israel exercised providential mercy toward all creation. Falling "rain" and growing "grass" (v. 8) were evidences, as were food for "beast" and attention to "ravens" (v. 9).

Yet reverent response in a trusting heart (fear him . . . hope in his mercy, v. 11) was God's primary concern. Images of physical strength and human pride (strength of the horse . . . legs of a man, v. 10) were set in contrast.

Mercies were general. But restoration of Jerusalem was special—like winter turned to spring! God's dealings with this people were unique (vv. 19–20).

Supreme Praise to the Supreme God (Psalm 148)

The passage.—Heaven and earth are summoned to highest praise of the Lord. In verses 1–6 the summons is directed to heavenly beings and bodies. In verses 7–14 it is addressed to earthly persons and things.

Special points.—Following the call for heaven's praise, a reason for praise was given (vv. 5–6). Creatures (angels, hosts, v. 2), bodies (sun, moon, stars, v. 3), and orderly movements (decree, v. 6) are God's creation.

Likewise, after the call for earth's praise, a reason for praise was given (vv. 13–14). God alone is supremely glorious above all creation, "earth and heaven" (v. 13). Also, his goodness to his people was peculiar cause for worship.

The conception of creation was that of Genesis 1. God "commanded" with authoritative, effective word. Resultantly, "they were created" (v. 5). Further, sun and moon were to reflect praise to God their maker.

The Lord exalted "the horn of his people" by restoring the well-being of the nation after the Exile. They were "near unto him" because he had chosen them and they had committed themselves to him (his saints, v. 14).

The God of Israel is also God of "all people" (v. 11; peoples, RSV). Irrespective of position or sex or age (vv. 11–12), all should acclaim his praise.

Praise to the God of Victory (Psalm 149)

The passage.—A song in the mouth (vv. 1–5) and a sword in the hand (vv. 6–9) were two expressions of victory. The first was marked by joy, the second by heroic action. Together they offered praise to the God who gives victory.

Special points.—Faithful Israelites, gathered in worship (congregation of saints, v. 1), were exhorted to praise the Lord. A recent monumental experience called for "a new song" (v. 1). Perhaps that experience was restoration from the virtual ruin of the Babylonian exile.

The reason for praise was twofold. The Lord was "Maker" and "King" (v. 2, RSV). This nation was his workmanship. Jerusalem was the place chosen for his name. Also, the Lord was restorer. He changed humiliation into "victory" (v. 4, RSV). Such is the force of the phrase "will beautify the meek with salvation."

Praise was to be private as well as public. In the security of the home at night "upon their beds" (v. 5; couches,

RSV), let royal men worship.

The faithful were exhorted also to praise the Lord by use of the "sword" (v. 6). Use of the sword was literal in Nehemiah's day (Neh. 4:16–18). Perhaps in the psalmist's thought it was partially symbolical. If so, it was moral earnestness opposed to evil men, those with "judgment written" (v. 9) against them in God's books (Job 13:26; Isa. 65:6).

To those devoted to God (saints) belongs "honour" (v. 9). They express his honor.

Hallelujah! (Psalm 150)

The passage.—The thought of this final psalm is totally of praise to the Lord. The five Hallelujah Psalms (146–150) and the Psalter as a whole reach a resounding climax.

Special points.—Like the four psalms preceding, this psalm begins and ends with the word "Hallelujah." The word means "Praise ye the Lord."

In verses 1–5 is a tenfold "praise him." The only phrase not preceded by this expression is the last (v. 6), and it is the most comprehensive of all.

The terms "in his sanctuary" and "firmament of his power" (v. 1) possibly were parallel designations of the heavenly source of praise. Or, they contrasted the earthly and the heavenly sources.

The stimulus of praise was God's "mighty acts" and "excellent greatness" (v. 2). Perhaps both acts and character were meant.

Every instrument was to be used to praise God. The blasting ram's horn (trumpet, v. 3) and the jingling tambourine (timbrel, v. 4) had their functions.

The psalmist's thought and feeling were overmastering. He exhorted "everything that breathes" (v. 6, RSV) to praise the Lord!

Truth for today.—Essentials of meaningful worship remain the same. True worship begins with reverent recognition of God. It continues in wonder and humility before his infinite greatness and goodness. It finds expression in joyous trust, obedient action, and adoring praise.

PROVERBS

Conrad R. Willard

INTRODUCTION

In the book of Proverbs, God made his divine will and truth more easily understood. Wisdom is the theme of the book and is often equated with righteousness.

"The Proverbs," as the King James has it, is actually a title derived from the first two words of the collection of sayings. Expanded it would read, "The Proverbs of Solomon the son of David, the King of Israel" (1:1). As indicated within the book, others contributed additional proverbs and wise sayings (25:1, 30:1, 31:1).

Many proverbs are comparisons. They compare a universal truth, in rhythmic phrases, to something simple; some familiar object, person, or action. The comparison may be either to something similar or, it may find its emphasis by showing contrast. They reveal truth, needed for right living.

The book of Proverbs represents an attempt to distil great truths into a few words. They draw from the experiences of daily life in Palestine, hundreds of years before the birth of Christ. Since memorization was, at the time Proverbs was being written, probably one of the most effective methods of teaching and learning, brevity was helpful. Thus a well-turned phrase became easier to remember than a complex law or theological doctrine. Because of the universal nature of the truth they contain, and, of course, because they are likewise divinely inspired, Proverbs is often referred to by New Testament writers. The book was well known to informed Jews in the times of Jesus. Jesus frequently used a phrase or comparison to illustrate a divine truth. Some of these can be found in his Sermon on the Mount (Matt. 5,6,7).

Most scholars agree to Solomon as the author of Proverbs. Some think revision or addition was done, as indicated in chapters 25, 30, and 31. Regardless of questions concerning its authorship, its divine inspiration as the word from God is apparent to all who read it.

Importance of Being Wise (Prov. 1:1–33)

The passage.—The suggestion here (it continues throughout the book) infers that we will not do well with life, unless we understand our relationship to God. We are asked to learn the meaning of justice, judgment, and fairness. The earlier in life we acquire this wisdom, the more competent we will become in living.

Getting knowledge and wisdom is more than getting facts. We should have respect and reverence for the Lord. Without this, knowledge about almost anything has limited significance. Reverence for our creator connects all knowledge to God's plan for the ages. Without an eternal God, all our plans are ultimately doomed.

Special points.—The term, "fear of the Lord" (v. 7), means we are to respect his power to create, control, discipline, and destroy.

Ancient teachers often spoke to their pupils as father to son. Thus there frequently occurs at the beginning of a proverb, "My son." Though Solomon may have indeed instructed his own sons.

Even a bird is frightened away from a trap being set in its presence. But those who murder to get wealth apparently do not see that they are setting a trap for themselves (vv. 10–19). With every choice, God gives us a right way to follow (vv. 20–23). Disregard for God's way leads to destruction. Obedience brings security and freedom from fear (vv. 24–31).

The "dark sayings" in verse 6 probably refers to proverbs and sayings in general. Condensing into a few words an important truth about life, may, at first, make it harder to understand. But since it has a deeper meaning than it appears to have, it wears well and does not grow stale or meaningless with time or repetition.

Truth for today.—This first chapter of Proverbs sets the tone for the entire book. The wise and prudent person will benefit from the experiences of others, found in these guidelines for life. God-inspired truths about life are first learned, then understood, then applied at the time of our own temptations and opportunities.

The world doesn't need a new set of rules. We haven't lived up to the old, simple, and obvious ones yet. These are words from God. They represent the combined wisdom of generations of human trial and error. They are true, helpful, needed, and inspired of God. Our ever-present inclination to do wrong makes them relevant. No one is too wise. Indeed, but for Jesus, no one is wise enough.

Profit in Wisdom (Prov. 2:1–22)

The passage.—There is almost a tone of desperation as Solomon stresses his plea to seek understanding and wisdom. The phrases, "incline thine ear unto wisdom and apply thine heart to understanding" (v. 2), "criest after knowledge and liftest up thy voice for understanding" (v. 3), "seekest her as silver and searchest for her" (v. 4), show the urgency in finding God's way for our life. This wisdom does not come automatically or naturally. We will find it if we search earnestly (v. 5). Its rewards are priceless. It will shield and guard and preserve. More than that, even the process of getting it will be a pleasant experience.

God-given understanding will deliver us from the ways and aims of evil people who are headed for destruction (v. 22).

Special points.—This chapter refers to the security we find when we listen to God's voice and obey his instructions. One specific and tragic evil to be avoided is adultery. Sexual relationship outside of marriage is doomed from the start. The controlling of one of life's strongest drives requires divine help. It is readily available to all who seek it. This may account for the repeated reference to adultery in Proverbs.

The "strange woman" and "the stranger" (adventuress) referred to in verse 16, may mean any woman other than a man's own wife and to an unbelieving woman, (one from an alien, heathen nation).

Truth for today.—Some of the greatest problems confronting Solomon and his sons are still with us. Israel fought for stable existence as a nation. She struggled even more desperately to preserve her righteousness. The two were linked together in a subtle way. Young, potential leaders were being seduced by wanton, alien women, to whom, evidently, marriage vows meant little.

Adultery results in moral confusion. It lowers self-respect and weakens the structure of the family as an agency for teaching righteousness, and, as a refuge of strength for the individual. Adultery is a house slanted toward the death of the spirit. Divine wisdom is essential for deliverance from its temptation and torment.

Getting the Right Directions (Prov. 3:1–35)

The passage.—The theme of wisdom, understanding, and knowledge continues through verses 1–27. If we acknowledge God in every area of life, he will lead us to make wise and right decisions. If we use good judgment, we will not rebel and become bitter when we suffer for our sins. His chastisement is but the sign of his love.

Happiness will come to those who are wise enough to obey both the natural and the spiritual laws of God. Suffering we do willingly for a righteous cause, can bring a deep, inner peace. Most of the world's suffering is mental and spiritual and not physical. Trust in God and the acceptance of his wisdom makes the soul rejoice, even though we do not understand at the moment the reason for our suffering.

The last part of the chapter contains three brief warnings: Don't withhold good from the deserving; don't fight with someone who has not harmed you; and don't envy anyone who lords it over you. The conclusion is a statement similar to the Beatitudes; to the lowly he gives grace; to the wise, glory.

Special points.—Throughout the book, ideas are often repeated. This was probably done for emphasis and to assist in learning the central truth. However, none of them are *exact* repetitions. There is something to be learned from each of them. Verse 13 says, "Happy is the man that findeth wisdom." Verse 18*b* says, "Happy is every one that retaineth her" [wisdom]. One refers to finding wisdom, the other to retaining it.

Truth for today.—Social and ethical problems, such as the unequal distribution of wealth and the prosperity of the wicked, have been the blight of almost every age of man. While the aim of wise and Christlike living is not material gain, righteous living will improve most circumstances.

The Springs of Life (Prov. 4:1–27)

The passage.—Written as a father instructing his children, the entire chapter may be read as though God was speaking to all men everywhere. Its message is universal. It is good doctrine and therefore helpful. It was the same message the writer received from his father and had stood the test of time and experience. Obedience to God's law removed the stumbling blocks that are scattered throughout life's pathway (v. 12). It is equated to life itself (vv. 13,22).

The abundant life, which God placed within man's reach, lies untouched by many. For the righteous, life is like the dawn of a day that is to end in the eternal brightness of God's glory. Wickedness blinds and leads into an ever-darkening pathway (vv. 18,19). Keeping the heart pure and keeping life free from sin should be an obsession. From the heart, spring ideas and actions that make the difference between man as an animal and man as an abundant, expectant, and joyous spiritual life as the child of God.

Special points.—Verse 2 sets forth in bold language that the Bible is true and good and *for* our good. *We* may choose the wrong way, but *God* never leads us that way. There is no point in blaming God for the evil we do.

Of all things that are to be guarded, the heart is the most vital. Love, compassion, repentance, forgiveness, and life eternal begin in the heart. "With all diligence" (v. 23), means vigilance, alertness, and constantly keeping and guarding.

Truth for today.—Though the Bible is the word of God, it always has been under attack. It is challenged, ridiculed, accused of being outdated, and falsely charged with being filled with errors, contradictions, and myths. But even its bitterest critics do not claim it is not *good.* When its divine laws are forsaken, the beauty in life fades and turns sour.

The Sanctity of Marriage (Prov. 5:1–23)

The passage.—The heart of chapter 5 is found in verses 15–19 where the marriage relationship is exalted. The sexual urge is also a gift from God. Fulfilment of it is reserved for marriage. Practiced outside of marriage it is an act of disobedience. The same admonition applies to both husband and wife. Let your emotions for love be stirred by the steadfast love of your partner in marriage.

Verses 3–14 and 20–23 clearly describe both the bitter-sweet introduction of immorality and its tragic, sad end. Whether a prostitute, or the wife of another man, is referred to here, her suggestion sounds reasonable and her offering seems desirable. It leads to remorse and death.

Special points.—The phrase, "How have I hated instruction" (v. 12), deserves special attention. It was the cry of one who had rejected the instructions that would have forestalled the loss of honor (v. 9); the ruin of the rest of life (v. 9); the loss of possessions (v. 10), and finally, total destruction.

Lest women feel some discrimination in this passage, verses 22–23 place the blame where it belongs. The sinfulness of the woman is assumed. The sinfulness of the man is spelled out, "His own iniquities shall take the wicked himself," and, "He shall die without instruction" (vv. 22–23).

Truth for today.—Few sins are as tempting as infidelity to marriage vows. It degrades all persons related to it. Contrary to popular and worldly views, it does not bring happiness.

Children, wives, husbands, parents, and friends are all shamed and hurt. It's never a case of, "It's my own life and I'll do as I please," or "It's not my fault." All attempts to justify immorality finally come "before the eyes of the Lord" (v. 21). Today, the church stands as the silent, yet sad and compassionate witness against the adulterer. Its testimony is true and vital.

Danger in Deception and Delay (Prov. 6:1–35)

The passage.—If we inadvertently have guaranteed the honesty of someone we do not know, by guaranteeing the integrity of a friend, then we should ask to be released from such a pledge immediately (vv. 1–5).

Poverty will rob as an armed bandit if we are lazy. Even the ant knows it must work for what it eats. It doesn't need a boss or superintendent to remind it of that (vv. 6–11)!

The Lord hates arrogance, lying, murder, evil ideas, evil desire, perjury, and anyone who creates a division in his church (vv. 16–19).

Close companionship with the word of God will help overcome lust. The lustful person is defying God as well as the husband of the one with whom the sin is consummated. A hungry thief may be forgiven by his victim, but the adulterer is not forgiven by a jealous husband (vv. 20–35).

Special points.—"Stricken thy hand" (v. 1), could be compared to co-signing a note, by today's commercial practices.

The man who "winketh with his
eyes," "speaketh with his feet," and
"teacheth with his fingers" (v. 13), is
cunningly implying something that is
not true.

Truth for today.—The Lord hates
the man who "soweth discord among
brethren" (v. 19). There are many ways
to create trouble and division in a
church. But one of the most common
is to falsely accuse a brother in Christ
of not being true to the Lord and to the
Bible. This is often done by setting up
a "straw man." The discord sower then
flails away at the nonexistent person
who is guilty of the sin he is describing.
However, all along, he is cunningly referring to someone casually known to
his hearers. Thus, in his heroic attack
upon evil, he receives the plaudits of
all who do not personally know of the
true faith of the one being attacked. It
is a form of public gossip.

Probably the best summary of the
section on adultery in chapter 6 is that
the adulterer "destroyeth his own soul"
(v. 32).

The Way of an Adulteress (Prov. 7:1–27)

The passage.—This chapter describes
the way of an adulteress. It is in contrast to chapter 8 which sets forth the
way of wisdom. In chapter 7 there is
an eyewitness account of the seduction
of a young man by a prostitute. The
illustration is realistic and needs only
brief interpretation.

The prostitute (vv. 10,26) (though she
is married) introduces herself by referring to her faithfulness to her religion
(v. 14). The deceptiveness goes all the
way back to the serpent in Eden.

Special points.—"Bind them upon thy
fingers" (v. 3), is an admonition to keep
God's word and wisdom where it is
always near—as a ring is to the hand.
The young man mentioned in chapter 7

did not keep wisdom near enough. Failure here cost him his life (v. 23).

Whatever resistance he had, melted
away with the woman's pleasant, pro-
vocative, and persuasive conversation.
"All at once" (v. 22, RSV) he forgets
the rest of his life. At that instant, from
his heart, came an issue of death and
not life. The "all at once," reveals once
again that sin is conceived in the heart.
The intent was evident. He had rejected
wisdom. He was *willing* and had willed
to sin. Having rejected wisdom, he does
not now understand he is about to be
destroyed.

Truth for today.—The use the adulteress makes of a celebration that
should be religious and holy, should
make us take another look at the way
Sunday and Christmas are used. Sunday,
as a day away from work, may turn
into a day away from God. Office
Christmas parties may become an invitation to dissipation and sin.

The Way of Wisdom (Prov. 8:1–36)

The passage.—Wisdom calls. She
stands at the gate, where all who enter
may see and hear. She calls to all men.
Her message is noble and right. She is
the opposite of the harlot mentioned in
chapter 7. Though she also speaks to
fools and those with little understanding,
her speech is not deceptive. Her products wear better. By her (wisdom)
kings reign, princes rule and decree
justice. She offers lasting riches and
honor.

Wisdom loves with a true love. She
offers something better than silver and
gold. She promises an inheritance. She
has her origin in God. Portions of verses
23–31 are referred to in John 1:1–5 and
in Ephesians 3:9–11. Chapter 7, verse
27, says that the way of the harlot leads
to death. But in chapter 8, verse 35, it
says that whoever finds divine wisdom

finds life.

Special points.—"Doth not wisdom cry?" (v. 1). God makes every effort short of force to make the way of righteousness clear and appealing. He places wisdom at the crossroads where no man can avoid seeing. Wisdom stands on a high hill so we can see her when we are in the valley. She cries out so that we can hear her above the noise and turmoil of the world. She does not speak like the adulteress. The adulteress, in chapter 7, made her deceitful and flattering speech at a lonely street corner in the dark of night.

This matchless wisdom of God is now available to all who will partake of it. Our sinful nature leads us astray from the obvious and right choice. All we can learn about these two behavior patterns would dictate our choosing the right way—the way of the wisdom of God.

Truth for today.—In a world that seems to try so hard to find peace and happiness, it is good to know it is always near. All we need for happiness ("Blessed" means happy) is wisdom (v. 34). It is as near as our next decision.

Wisdom's Invitation (Prov. 9:1–18)

The passage.—A summary of chapter 8 may be seen in verses 1–6, as well as a summary of chapter 7 in verses 13–18. Verses 7–12 contrast a scorner to a man of wisdom.

In the first section of this chapter a type of the Christ that was to come may be discerned, in that Jesus did what these verses said wisdom would do. Jesus prepared a spiritual feast for men; simple men; *all* men. A vivid contrast may be seen between this and the foolish woman, who is much like the wanton, shameless world of Satan. We have a choice and Christ offers life. The only other choice is death.

Special points.—Verses 7, 8, and 9

show why the invitation of wisdom is to the simple and not to the scorner. The ordinary man will listen and perhaps accept, while the scorner is already wise in his own eyes.

"Stolen waters are sweet" (v. 17). The world lures us away from the way of life in Christ, by tempting us with the things that are hardest to resist.

Truth for today.—Though their final destinations lie in opposite directions, the road of righteousness and the road of sinfulness often seem to run side by side. At times we have difficulty knowing which road we are traveling, so tempting is sin and so urgent is the voice of the Lord. But we can always know which road we are on if we follow the wisdom of God, the Bible. It will point us to Christ who saves us from our sins.

Contrast Between Good and Evil (Prov. 10:1–32)

The passage.—Verses 18, 22, and 26 are double-barreled statements, aimed at a single truth. With the possible exception of verse 10, the remaining verses of this chapter contrast good and evil. Verse 7 offers a good example of this contrast.

Verse 10 contrasts two evil practices. "Winketh with the eye," reveals craftiness, malice, and complicity with other wicked comrades. It is a form of sly deception. With it a person may convey evil thoughts without saying a word. A fool brings punishment upon himself by speaking when he should keep silent (v. 13).

Wealth buys privileges and material security the poor never know (v. 15). Having little or nothing is often the undoing of the poor. This may refer to the way God blesses the industrious and punishes the lazy person. But for the poor whose poverty is the result of something beyond his control, the words

of Jesus take added meaning: "Blessed
be ye poor: for yours is the kingdom of
God" (Luke 6:20).

Special points.—The hunger of the
soul is mentioned in verse 3. The world
is filled with people dying for lack of
spiritual food. Jesus said that God
would provide for man's physical and
natural needs, just as he does for birds
and flowers. It is up to us to seek the
kingdom of God *first.* The material
things will come in their natural order
as we need them.

In a country where chimneys were
unknown, smoke from the household
fire could bring pain to the eyes. The
lazy and unfaithful messenger brought
pain and disgust to those who sent him.
In like manner, his feeble efforts were
as unsavory as the bitter taste of
vinegar.

Truth for today.—Integrity, honest
work, purity, and common sense all lead
to a life with which both God and we,
ourselves, will be pleased. Foolishness,
laziness, unfaithfulness, and all sin only
leads to a disappointing and sorrow-
filled life.

The Upright and the Wicked (Prov. 11: 1–31)

The passage.—Deceit, dishonesty,
and pride are steps that lead to self-
destruction and are an abomination to
the Lord. One of the saddest notes
sounded in the Bible is found in verse
7, "When the wicked dies, his hope
perishes" (RSV). He may have survived
by his craftiness during his lifetime, but
death ends his hope of being redeemed
from his evil ways.

Verses 9–14 show the contrast between righteousness and evil as it affects
a neighbor, the community, or the
nation. An evil gossiper and talebearer
can destroy a neighbor or throw an entire city into turmoil. Therefore, the

combined counsel of wise leaders is
needed (v. 14).

The "hand join in hand," in verse 21
may imply a group banded together in
an evil pursuit. Though they agree to
support one another, they will be
punished anyway. The fact that many
are involved in an evil business will in no
way justify it.

The blessings of a generous heart are
contrasted to a selfish and miserly one.
The one who gives freely, shall receive
freely from God. Those who withhold
blessings they could grant, shall finally
lose them anyway.

Special points.—Both verses 4 and 28
warn that material possessions will not
support us where we need help most.
The pursuit of wealth has been the goal
of both poor and rich. It is a false god.
It cannot save the soul. The wealth of
the universe is exactly where it was the
day God finished his creation.

The family was the earliest refuge
known. To cause trouble within the
family is to sow seeds that bring a bleak
harvest. There is no inheritance of value
to one who by rebellion and rejection
has shamed those who have been nearest
to him.

Truth for today.—The belief that
crime doesn't pay may arise from the
frequency of the arrest and conviction
of criminals. We are apt to take more
lightly a statement that *evil* doesn't pay,
because so much evil apparently goes
by undetected. But verse 21 says that
the wicked shall not go unpunished.
Every sinful act must be accounted for.

Jesus' cross is stark evidence that evil
is unprofitable. It is costly beyond our
imagination.

The Good Life (Prov. 12:1–28)

The passage.—Only a stupid or
brutish person will refuse to learn the
lessons about life that bring peace and

happiness. Life has no permanence if filled with sin. But it will find purpose and stability if it is righteous.

Good can come to us in this life if we will follow these wise and helpful instructions. A good wife (one who is virtuous and righteous) makes of man a king. Her holy and regal qualities are the crown that brings to them both, a private, yet substantial, kingdom (v. 4).

Special points.—"Despised, and hath a servant" (v. 9)—means it is better to be our own humble self than to boast about things we do not have. A man who can afford luxury, yet quietly goes about his business, is better than one who boasts that he is rich, while in reality he can't even buy his food!

"Recompence of a man's hands" (v. 14) refers to the good that comes back to bless the one who has either spoken wisely or done a good deed.

The statement that "there shall no evil happen to the just" (v. 21) is a way of saying that trials and troubles may come to the righteous, but God will watch over them and give them final and complete victory. Of course, righteous living will help us avoid many of life's trials.

Truth for today.—Of all the proverbs in this chapter, few have the potential to bring the healing and happiness as the one mentioned in verse 18. Angry words can pierce the heart. Yet, speaking to someone who is lonely or discouraged, may bring healing to their broken spirit. There may be someone waiting to hear the words that only *we* can speak to them.

Righteousness and Riches (Prov. 13:1–25)

The passage.—Guarding the lips is like guarding the soul. Silence may have the strength of a mighty speech. Evil thoughts, displayed in words, may be the undoing of a soul (v. 3).

Many references are made to both poverty and wealth and how they are to be considered. Some are poor but pretend to have riches. The rich may pretend poverty to avoid carrying their share of the load (v. 7).

A man's great wealth may be the source of his trials, since others will make demands upon him that only his money will satisfy. The poor are ignored and avoided by those who would be their enemies if they were rich (v. 8).

Special points.—Verse 23 means that even the poor man, who may have a small farm, may yet reap a rich harvest. On the other hand, there are fields, (meaning the fields of the rich), that will produce little, because of bad judgment, or evil and selfish actions.

Lack of discipline (v. 24) is a sign of a lack of love.

Truth for today.—Our character is known or greatly determined by our companions. Each of us has his responsibility to be faithful. We are in the world, but we are not to have the world in us. Since it is our privilege to be witnesses for Christ, we should watch closely, lest we fail in our effort to successfully bear the good news of salvation to this lost world.

Patience and Prudence (Prov. 14:1–35)

The passage.—Like wisdom is to life, a wise woman is to her family. By faithfulness and industry, she makes the home a place of refuge and strength (v. 1).

Good judgment and a sound mind are gifts of God and should be used at all times. A fool is known by his refusal to use the common sense God has given to him. "The simple," in verse 15 does not refer to those who are mentally retarded, but to those whose foolishness is seen in their deliberate rejection of

God's will.

Perpetuating the poverty of a people, by whatever action, or inaction, is an insult to God, who created us all (v. 31). Kindness and mercy, shown to the poor of this world, honor God.

Special points.—"The heart knoweth . . ." (v. 10). The heart is a private world, where we, only, know the depth of our depression and despair. Others may sympathize, but they cannot feel our burden. In the same way, God gives to each of us a supply of secret, happy thoughts, of which, no one else is ever aware.

Laughter can come even if our soul is burdened by sin. We may even try to cover our spiritual fears by seeking entertainments that will make us laugh. But the outcome of such behavior is only to sink back into the reality of the real circumstances that made us sad. True joy comes from within. It springs spontaneously from a heart and mind that knows all is well. Happiness like this doesn't end when the laughter stops.

In verse 19 we are reminded that the immoral, the thief, the greedy, as well as most sinners, are seeking happiness in some form, however perverted it may be. It may be that, in their own perverse way, they are humiliating themselves before good and righteous people, vainly attempting to share in the joy the righteous person has.

Truth for today.—We can convince ourselves that what we are doing is right and justifiable, though it actually may be wrong and sinful. This sad, but true fact shows the deception we practice on ourselves. Half-hearted surrender of life to Christ and Sunday rituals are not enough.

God Sees Everything (Prov. 15:1–33)

The passage.—God both sees our sins and knows our sorrow. A fact that

brings comfort to the godly and fear to the sinner (vv. 3,11).

Many of the disappointments in life could be avoided if we would take time to consider the results of our rash speech (vv. 1–3,7,18,22,26,28). If we reject the instruction to be found in God's Word, evil is sure to disrupt our life.

Special points.—Sacrifices brought, or made, to God by those who have an unholy and selfish motive, are not acceptable to God. A sacrifice is not holy in itself. Even heathen people sacrifice to idols. Sacrifices are to be made for good and righteous purposes.

"The afflicted" (v. 15), probably refers to those who continually complain, rather than to those who suffer some mental or physical handicap. The verse implies that those who do not trust in the ultimate goodness and love of God, will continually suffer from the results of their fears.

"Establish the border of the widow" (v. 25), means that God will watch over those who are unable to defend themselves.

Truth for today.—Since God sees all that we do and is aware of our needs, it is best to accept our humble station in life and trust in him for the rest. It is better to eat hamburgers in a home where people love each other, than to eat steak where bitterness exists.

The Conduct of Life (Prov. 16:1–33)

The passage.—Man has the free will to set his goals for life and then to try and attain them. But it is God who is the doer: the Creator of the mouth that speaks, the hand that lifts, and the feet that walk. Man can plan and propose, but all plans are subject to the working laws of the universe, which God has made.

Verses 10–15 set forth the responsibility of governments to act with righteous judgment, since they hold their authority by the grace of God. If they are divinely ordained, we are obliged to obey their rules for the common good of all.

The power of persuasive speech is described in verses 21–30. The sweetness of words that bring learning and the "burning fire" in the speech of the ungodly are pictured.

Special points.—That God made the wicked for the day of evil (v. 4) might seem unjust upon first reading it. But God does not force them to do their evil and sinful deeds. Each has his opportunity to obey. His rebellion is his own act. But God turns even the wickedness of men to his glory. Not *because* of their sin (for he desires none to be lost), but *regardless* of their sin.

Long life ("hoary head," v. 31) is a crown of glory only if it represents righteous living. Men may gamble with life, but the final word about the matter will come from God.

Truth for today.—Iniquity is taken away by the mercy and truth of God. Jesus was that mercy and truth. By his atoning death, we are made ready for the final court of all men for all time. This proverb may also apply in our relationships to others. When a sincere confession of the truth is made and forgiveness is called for, mercy should be shown and the offense removed from the relationship. Don't pour fuel on your anger (v. 32). Be the conquering ruler of a great city—the city of your own soul.

About Proper Conduct (Prov. 17:1–28)

The passage.—The crucible and the furnace are used to remove impurities and to improve the quality of silver and gold. So the Lord tests and improves his own. But only the Lord tests the hearts of men. They are not to put one another to the test (v. 3). An appropriate rebuke from the Lord "goes deeper" (v. 10, RSV) into one who earnestly tries to find and do his will. The disobedient may have a hundred painfilled experiences to warn him of impending disaster ahead, but he will say they are only there by chance. He will never see the restraining hand of God in them (v. 10).

If we are wise, we will, at the earliest opportunity, stop an argument that might lead to a greater trouble. Letting a fight begin is like letting the first trickle of water flow through a crack in a dam. If it is not soon stopped, it may never be.

Special points.—Verse 8 says that buying the favor of a person with a gift or a bribe, makes one think that money is the key to everything. The greatest deception is worded upon the one receiving the bribe. Inflamed by a desire to get more money in the same manner, he works feverishly at the same evil to get another "gift."

Covering (v. 9) or forgiving a transgression or an offense is a way of showing love. God is the avenger for sins committed. Telling someone they have been sinned against, when there is no useful purpose to be served, will only cause senseless trouble to arise between people, even between friends.

Truth for today.—A Christian should always seek to be a peacemaker. It is not always a pleasant task. Striving within the church lessens its influence on the world. We will reach a greater spiritual maturity, if we cultivate an attitude of patience, openness and love.

The Power of the Tongue (Prov. 18:1–24)

The passage.—Some have interpreted verse 1 to mean that a man deliberately separates himself from the counsel of others, so he can set forth his own views. Others (and I agree with this latter interpretation) see in this proverb, one who goes away from the bustle of life, to more thoroughly seek the facets of God's wisdom.

Our words have far reaching significance. Much beyond what we ever expect them to have (v. 4). Deep satisfaction is to be gained if we say the right thing at the right time. "A man's belly," in verse 20, may be equated with his conscience. Death and life may be determined by what we say. We may use the tongue to successfully plead for our life, or the lives of others. With the tongue we may utter sinful words that will lead others away from the love of God and bring condemnation upon our own souls.

Special points.—It is best not to believe everything you hear about someone (vv. 8,13,17). Do not pass judgment too soon, since only in eternity will the matter be settled in full. One who pronounces judgment even before he hears both sides of the story is a fool (v. 13).

Truth for today.—"He who is slack in his work is a brother to him who destroys" (v. 9, RSV). Few church members would tolerate anyone who maliciously began to tear down the church building or the fellowship itself. Anyone who would be such an obvious waster in God's house would be condemned by all. But what of the Christian who by indifference, nonattendance and nonsupport brings about the same results? The Bible says the two are as brothers from the same family.

Keeping the Soul (Prov. 19:1–29)

The passage.—No one should be in such a hurry that he does not have time to get the understanding necessary for the well-being of his soul. To miss the way, simply because we claim not to have the time, would be great foolishness. Our waywardness often causes us grief, for which we sometimes blame the Lord (vv. 2–3).

We are to give to the poor according to their need and our ability (v. 17). (See also James 2:15–16.) Giving to those who are in need is like lending money to the Lord. He will consider it so and will repay in full, with interest.

We may have many plans for our life, but God has only one.

Special points.—Verses 4, 6, 7 give the favorable position enjoyed by the prosperous. By way of contrast, it would almost seem that to be poor is to be neglected by the Lord. But God is friend to the poor.

"A poor man is better than a liar" (v. 22). This phrase, taken alone, would seem to rank poverty slightly higher than deceit. But such is not the case at all. Taken as a whole, the entire verse means that the poor can promise little or nothing as a material gift. His lack of funds does not diminish his desire to be kind. He does not deceive anyone about his desire to be kind, as those do who are able to give, but do not.

Truth for today.—If we keep God's commandments, he will keep us from all that is really harmful. Obedience to the Word of God is the sum of divine wisdom.

Observations About Conduct (Prov. 20: 1–30)

The passage.—Beverage alcohol mocks a man, in that it at first dulls his senses and seems to give him a sense of well-being. But later it makes him appear foolish to others. Ultimately he appears a fool to himself (v. 1). Leaving tasks undone that need to be done results in a loss at the time others are receiving good wages for their labor (v. 4).

There is a commonly accepted hypocrisy that incites us to devalue an item we bargain for. Later, we inflate its value beyond its worth, to make it appear that we were wise and shrewd. Both actions are deceptive (v. 14). The soul of man is a light given by the Lord. It is also to be used *for* the Lord. We reveal what we are by our use of the conscience and what we do for and to the soul.

Special points.—Though they may not appreciate it at first, children who are raised in a home where honesty and the righteousness of God are upheld receive a rich inheritance (v. 7).

I have never heard anyone say that he was sinless. Cleansing our own soul from sin is impossible (v. 9). We are dependent upon the grace of God through Christ, for the cleansing of our soul from sin.

It is wise to require collateral from those who guarantee the credit of someone who is a stranger to the laws of the land (v. 16).

War is a court of last resort. Counsel and negotiation should be sought and used. Caution is the better part courage (v. 18).

Severe punishment may bring reform in an evil life. It may not only improve behavior, but cause remorse and genuine repentance, which can bring salvation to the soul (v. 30).

Truth for today.—Most people will talk about the good deeds they have done. Some even allude to goodness they intend to do, or think they may have done. How much better it would be if all this goodness, all these good deeds, were a reality. If all the good that is boasted of were actually ac-

complished, what a better world we would live in.

Various Observations (Prov. 21:1–31)

The passage.—God is the God of nations and their leaders, just as he is the God of individuals within the nations. He is their Lord, whether they recognize him as such or not. The reign of the mighty is always uncertain (v. 1). Righteous deeds and decisions are more acceptable to the Lord than religious rituals.

In verses 9 and 19 we have a comment on some things that are "better . . . than." The entire family may be included, when the corner of the housetop is recommended as a better living place, than a house with a contentious, brawling, angry woman. When necessary and appropriate, the Bible calls attention to our failures. This includes men or women, parent or child, rich or poor, king or slave.

"Hardeneth his face" (v. 29) means restraint in showing emotion. The sinner tries to hide his true feelings and actions by keeping a straight face. This is a form of hypocrisy. Outwardly, there is no revelation of the evil that is going on. Hardened criminals eventually develop a severe expression. The long discipline of controlling their expression finally betrays what it meant to hide.

Special points.—The instruction of a wise man (v. 11) in the ways of the Lord, is usually a matter between the man himself and the Lord. The man learns, changes his ways, and pleases the Lord. On the other hand, the person who has publicly ridiculed instruction from the Lord, will be punished openly. His punishment will make the foolish, who themselves might make the same mistake, become wise about the matter.

Secret gifts for evil purposes are

bribes, and are thus a sin. But appropriate gifts, given quietly and without publicity, to God, to the needy, the deserving, or to rectify unintentional injury or insult, may stop a trouble at its outset (v. 14).

Verse 18 may refer to the heathen King Cyrus, who was thought to be the deliverer of the Jews from the captivity of Babylon. It also may refer to the way the Egyptians suffered, when the death angel passed over God's people before they fled.

A nation may be armed to the teeth, but ultimate security is found only in the Lord.

Truth for today.—Now and then there arises a movement that extols the glory of man to the exclusion of God. They preach a doctrine of man's glory to the point that they make God unnecessary. Then they say, "There is no God," or, "God is dead." Such folly comes and goes with the ages.

There is no way man can contend with or be wiser than God. No one has ever defeated God. No one can tell God what to do. We *can pray* to him and *trust* him and *accept his only begotten son, Jesus, as our Savior.*

Study God's Word (Prov. 22:1–29)

The passage.—Both the rich and the poor are made in the image of God. Both are subject to his laws. Both have available his free grace. Both will stand before him in judgment. The greatest and the humblest are together made in his image (v. 2).

The lazy will claim there is a lion in the streets to keep from going to work. They will use any excuse, no matter how unlikely or unbelievable, to keep from carrying their share of the load (v. 13).

Verses 17–21 is a direct appeal to the reader to hear and apply the word of the Lord as found in the Bible. Excel-

lent things have been written so that the reader may come to trust in the Lord. If we know his word, we can give a truthful answer to those who ask about our God.

Special points.—Riches are far easier to come by than a good name. Only a lifetime of good conduct deserves a good name. A good name is the long-planned and much-studied product, of deliberately choosing the way of God, rather than the way of the world. Others may confer a title of honor upon us, but only God can add the crown of glory to life.

The "bountiful eye" in verse 9 refers to the gentle countenance of a generous person. He *looks* like he is going to help the needy person, and he *does*. In return, his compassion is rewarded by the blessing of God.

"Remove not the ancient landmark" (v. 28; see also 23:10) is the biblical source of the name for Landmark Baptists (a group who separated from Southern Baptists). They were so called, when one of their leaders used this term to hold on to existing policies.

Truth for today.—The program of religious education in most churches has many subtitles, such as Sunday School, Church Training, and Vacation Bible School. It undergoes spasmodic renovation and rejuvenation, but it still is the church's way of teaching the Bible. There are thousands of children in our church schools today who learn about Jesus because their Sunday School teachers are teaching the Bible. There is no substitute for Bible teaching, especially to children.

Evils to Be Avoided (Prov. 23:1–35)

The passage.—Verses 1–8 call for wise and temperate manners, in the court of a king or in the presence of an envious, selfish man. Do not gorge on the delicacies set before you. They may be there to test your character or to get something from you which you did not intend to lose. The implication here is that the man was not in a position to merit such an invitation, therefore, he should beware.

The stern discipline suggested in verses 13–14 is not to be interpreted to be violent beating, with an instrument that would maim or injure. It is rather the offering of a gentler way, to prevent the child from suffering a much worse fate. Learn the lessons of life while young and avoid trouble later on. The passage is followed by a stated desire that both parent and child enjoy happiness, each one because the other is wise and happy.

With the world nursing millions of alcoholics, verses 29–35 needs little interpretation. The woe, sorrow, strife, delirium tremors, and beds made of sidewalk and gutter, are enough to see that the sting of alcohol, if not more deadly, is far more frequent, than that of a serpent.

Special points.—"Buy the truth," (v. 23) does not mean that it may be purchased with money, though a good education, which costs money, may be part of the way we can possess truth.

However, truth includes a knowledge and fear of the Lord. This wisdom and truth of God must be bought, whatever the price. Without it, life will miss its mark.

The last verses of this chapter (vv. 32–35) report the tragic condition of one who is the victim of drunkenness. He can neither think nor see intelligently. He reels as a ship wallows in a rough sea. Finally, in the last verse, he makes his own sad little speech, "I was so drunk I didn't even feel it when they beat me up. When I wake up, I will want another drink."

Truth for today.—The Bible gives good and wise advice to all the sons of the world. Many lives would be saved from tragedy and early death if this advice were used. As stated earlier, many of the proverbs were written as a father speaking to his son. With conditions as they are, both parents and children could use these admonitions. But it is only the young who still have a chance to redirect life.

Strength, Justice, and Industry (Prov. 24:1–34)

The passage.—Wisdom is as a house that is filled with pleasant and precious riches (v. 4). These are diamonds of grace, rubies of mercy, pearls of forgiveness, and a multitude of gems that bring peace, love, and happiness. They are the riches of the soul that all the money in the world cannot buy.

As honey, dripping from the honeycomb, is golden, pure, and sweet, so wisdom tastes delicious to the soul. It nourishes and gives the promise of more and better things yet to come.

God-fearing people should never rejoice at the punishment of their enemies. The Lord will be displeased with an attitude of pride and triumph. "I told you so," is *never* appropriate.

Verse 29 is a reverse twist of what we know as the Golden Rule. Do not say, "I will do unto others as they have done unto me." In this proverb it was used as advice for those who would give damaging testimony against a neighbor and friend.

The last section (vv. 30–34), is a warning about a little laziness leading to a lot of poverty.

Special points.—"Falleth seven times," (v. 16), may refer to the sinning of a just man, who by repentance and because of his love for God, is able to rise again. The phrase may also mean that an evil person is wasting his time in trying to destroy a just or righteous man, since he will be struck down only to rise again. "Seven times" means merely often.

Kissing the lips of one who has acted with sound judgment is merely a way of saying he has gained respect and is genuinely appreciated. In Oriental lands, kissing was as much a show of respect as it was of intimate affection.

Truth for today.—I think verses 11 and 12 apply to the church today. If we fail to bring the saving gospel of Jesus Christ to those who are about to be forever lost, and if we excuse ourselves by saying that we did not know they were dying, or that we did not know God in Christ would save them, then the keeper of our souls shall surely call us to account.

Appropriate and Inappropriate (Prov. 25: 1–28)

The passage.—The first seven verses have to do with kings and those who appear before them. Removing the dross, so that silver may be refined, has a useful application. It illustrates the usefulness life may have when we have removed the evil and the unnecessary.

Too much of even a good thing can become offensive (vv. 16,17,27). It may be a good idea to be friendly and visit with a neighbor. But even a friend can become sated with our companionship, if we come too often or stay too long. In so doing, the friend is not only lost, his friendship may turn to disgust or hate. In much the same way, describing one's goodness can be sickening.

If we are hungry and try to eat, while having a tooth that is broken or infected, we are annoyed. But if we are in mortal danger and our only way to escape is to run, to have a broken or dislocated foot is indeed a disaster. The broken tooth may be an inconvenience, while the broken foot could be the difference between life and death. Trusting an unfaithful person is like trusting a broken foot in an emergency.

Special points.—"A soft tongue" (v. 15), reminds us that the mind and the spirit of man is reasonable. Sometimes, gentle and kind reasoning may bring about an effect that violent punishment could not do. Jesus used a similar illustration in his parable of the importunate widow (Luke 18:1–8).

"Vinegar upon nitre" (v. 20). Vinegar is an acid. "Nitre," as it was then known, was a carbonate of soda, mixed with a few other elements. This nitre was used in washing and sometimes in cooking. To pour vinegar upon nitre was to neutralize it. It became a form of useless salt that would have been discarded. Singing light and happy songs to someone in sorrow would dilute the therapy that comes with weeping. Being neither happy nor sad is like feeling nothing.

Truth for today.—We may express sympathy to those who grieve. We may tell others we rejoice in their moment of success. We may attempt to comfort when it is not needed. We may express our feelings to others in a thousand ways, sometimes appropriately and sometimes inappropriately. But saying the right thing at the right time is an act that lasts, like a beautiful painting, for a long, long time.

The Foolish and Deceitful (Prov. 26:1–23)

The passage.—Honor and respect for the foolish and disobedient is not becoming to them (v. 1). There are times when it is best not to try to answer someone who asks a foolish question. There are also times when silence is the best answer to one who sets a trap by his question. At times, the best answer is *no* answer. On the other hand, do not let silence to a foolish question be your condemnation. Occasions arise when an answer to an evil person will properly reveal his false ideas.

Special points.—Those who honor people who don't deserve it will actually cause them trouble. The pity in it is that the one about to suffer, is like an innocent bystander (v. 8).

"Taketh a dog by the ears" (v. 17) implies a lack of understanding of the danger involved in reaching the hands to the head of a snarling dog. So is the person endangered who interferes in a quarrel that is none of his business. Christians are to act as peacemakers when their intercession or mediation is helpful. They ask for trouble when they take sides in an issue that really has nothing to do with them.

Truth for today.—"I have something that I just can't wait to tell you." "Did you know that . . . ," and there follows a tale of gossip that is sure to hurt someone. At first, when the message was announced, there was hope that it would be good news. But too many times that is not the case. Lips that burn to spread information that can bring sorrow are like a junky piece of pottery. It is glazed to look valuable, but it is worthless (vv. 18–28).

Moral Lessons (Prov. 27:1–27)

The passage.—Frank criticism, if it is constructive, is much better for us than someone who secretly appreciates and loves us, though most of us prefer the latter (vv. 5,6).

Verses 9 and 10 lack their fullest meaning, unless we remember that the practice of polygamy in ancient Israel (evil though it was), was not conducive to brothers being neighbors. (The nomadic life patterns of modern American families produces a somewhat similar result.) Therefore, it was, and still is, good advice to cultivate friends who live nearby. Many times they are able to offer a helping hand in a day of trouble, when it would be almost impossible to call on a brother.

"Face answereth to face" (v. 19) is a reminder that the heart mirrors the man. A man reveals his true character by the things he thinks about.

Verses 23–27 simply advise us to be busy with our own affairs. To do so is to insure the provision of our needs.

Special points.—Anger can be cruel, to both the one who is angry, and the one at which the anger is directed. Sudden anger is akin to temporary insanity. "Wrath" (v. 4), may be another and more violent expression of displeasure. But neither of them brings the drawn-out suffering as does envy and jealousy. Envy is a smoldering fire that is not easily vented and burned out. An outburst of anger may clear the air, and through reconciliation and forgiveness, heal its own wounds. Not so with envy. Jealousy and envy plot and scheme all sorts of evils to be done. All the time, they are burning away the strength of the one holding them.

"Iron sharpeneth iron" (v. 17). The file sharpens the sickle. The hammer beats out the plowshare. Yes-men are useless to an organization. They sharpen no one's wits; not even their own.

Truth for today.—From the first verse of this chapter, we learn a wonderful lesson about living. We are to prepare for tomorrow, but not presume upon it. We may dream of the tomorrows, but we are not to demand them of God, as if our plans for them were better than his. It is best to speculate about tomorrow only if we ask for God's will to be done. The future is not to be feared. It is in the hands of a loving God.

Destinies of the Evil and the Good (Prov. 28:1–28)

The passage.—When a man who knows the problems of poverty oppresses the poor, it is a sin upon a sin. While those who have plenty may never be able to understand the pain of hunger, the poor *do* understand. If, knowing this, a poor man is placed in authority and becomes oppressive, he further destroys the hope for relief from hunger (v. 3).

Sinners praise others who are guilty of sin. Having forsaken the laws of God, they promote sin as something to be desired. Only the innocent may condemn. Only those who have turned from the ways of sin are set to stem the tide of sin that sweeps the world. Evil men do not understand, or do not want to understand, the judgment of God. Those who have known the joy of being cleansed by forgiveness, know how efficiently the laws of God work (vv. 4–5).

Those who flatter and give praise where it is not earned, may, at first, please whom they have flattered. Constructive criticism, or a rebuke aimed at helping a person lead a better life, will not at first be liked. Later, the critic will be better liked, because he told the truth—and it helped!

Special points.—The guilty are always running from justice. Fear haunts them day and night. They live in fear of being discovered in their sin. They often betray themselves by being too cautious. Because they know of their guilt, they make excuses for actions which no one challenges or questions. But the righteous are freed from such fears. They can be bold and forthright, because they have kept the laws of God. They have confessed their sins and have been forgiven (v. 1).

Wealth that is unjustly gained will ultimately find its way into the hands of one who is compassionate. God is merciful, but he is also just (v. 8).

Truth for today.—Those who keep sinning in secret, though they may outwardly prosper, are not building a bank account with the Lord. They *think* they are making it successfully, but there is no foundation for their eternal home. Indeed, if discovered, they may lose it all, here and now. Only a full confession of sin and turning away from it, merits the mercy of God (v. 13).

Repent or Suffer (Prov. 29:1–27)

The passage.—Verses 2 and 4 commend the leaders of governments who are God-fearing and righteous. But corruption can infest that which starts out to be a peaceful administration. When bribes and other evils enter, the common citizens suffer. Many a government has fallen, because those who are second or third in command were greedy and evil.

A foolish person will speak rashly when angered, saying things that ought never to be said. A wise man will hold back his replies until he has had time to think about the results of such an outburst. "Count ten, before you speak," we say. It's a good idea. The idea behind such a statement is the Word of God (v. 11).

Those who assist a thief are as guilty as the thief himself. They know the penalty for the evil action. They hear the plans for robbery being laid, but tell no one. Therefore, one can only surmise that whoever knowingly involves himself this way, really hates himself.

Special points.—Godly people find time to work to help the poor. They take up the cause, even in court if necessary. "Considereth" doesn't mean just to "think about it!" The wicked do not care what happens to poor people. They are principally concerned about what happens to themselves. A classic example of this is the way big-time criminals drain nickles and dimes from the pockets of simple-minded people. These poor people are to be pitied, as well as condemned, for their unwise investments. They are lured on in the hope of sudden wealth, which rarely comes to any of them in their lifetime.

"Where there is no vision" (v. 18) refers to the absence of an open revelation of the word and will of God. It does not necessarily mean that if there are no plans being made, the people will perish. Rather, it calls for prayer, preaching, and consecration, so that God's plan for life may be known.

Truth for today.—One of the great lessons on the judgment of God is to be found in the first verse of this chapter. Those who have had fair and frequent warning about the result of sin and, who have continued, although they fully understood the final outcome, shall "suddenly be broken beyond healing" (RSV). If there is never any repentance, never any belief in Christ, never the acceptance of God's forgiveness, then that life will not be saved.

God's Word Is Wisdom (Prov. 30:1–33)

The passage.—This chapter by Agur is added to the proverbs by Solomon and is in every way as inspired. Agur begins by stating his own inadequacy in understanding the wisdom of so great a God. Every word of God is pure and to which no other word is to be added.

Agur then makes a plea (vv. 7–9). He asks to be made acceptable to God. As he looks about, he sees men who are guilty of not heeding the lessons given from God to Solomon (vv. 11–14). The remainder of the chapter is a series of illustrations, using animals, people, and objects, which picture sin, wisdom, and

strength. All of these word pictures prove the truth to be found in Proverbs. Although the word of God needs no defender, there is no greater proof of its accuracy, than the reality in its references to nature and human nature.

Special points.—Verses 18–20 describe the way an adulteress tries to cover her sin, so that no one will find it out. An eagle in the air, a snake on a rock, a ship in the sea, and love itself leave no visible trail.

"Conies" (v. 26) are small animals, about the size and color of a rabbit, though of a different animal family.

Truth for today.—There is danger, of course, in the world of today of being guilty of the sins described in verses 11–14. It is an age that rebels against parental judgment and discipline. It attempts to reject the principles and laws of the Bible, as well as the God who inspired it. It is an age that casts off both mother and father, to let them die alone. At least some of this generation is corrupted by unforgiven sin, yet they justify to themselves their immorality.

If such accusations are groundless, the righteous will toss them aside as meaningless. But if this word from God is fitting for the world of today, the righteous will know it and pray for the salvation that is in Christ Jesus the Savior.

A Virtuous Woman (Prov. 31:1–31)

The passage.—These proverbs are still another addition to the proverbs of Solomon. They were written by King Lemuel. His name means, "unto God." There is no other information about him in the Bible.

The opening part of this chapter is an admonition to beware of foreign women (a thing that troubled Israel without end), and some advice concerning the use of strong drink. Alcohol may be used as a medicine. Overindulgence dilutes the judgment. The remaining verses offer a description of a virtuous woman (vv. 10–31).

"Virtuous woman" as used here, means far more than being chaste and morally pure. In the days when women were degraded and considered only as the property of men, it was with great insight and inspiration that this prophecy exalted her to her deserved position of honor. She is faithful, industrious, wise, farsighted, compassionate, concerned, bold, respected, artistic, talented, kind, loved, and praised by her husband and children. She is an ideal woman. She is so lovable and good that no valued thing in this world can equal her.

Special points.—The use of wine in biblical times (v. 6), was both for intoxication and for medicinal purposes. Drinking wine and other strong drink to become intoxicated, or drunken, was condemned. But in a day when there were only a few effective medications, wine was used as a sedative to ease the suffering of the dying. It was also recommended for those who were mentally depressed. Of course, it must not have been effective all of the time, as medicine today. Addiction to alcoholic wine must have been rather common, since the Bible contains repeated warnings against its use.

Truth for today.—The struggle to gain equal rights for women continues to this day. This inspired description of womanhood gives to her the respect she has earned, by her intelligence, self-sufficiency, generosity, optimism, and loveliness.

In the book of Proverbs, the good and the evil of both men and women are described, without restraint.

ECCLESIASTES

Conrad R. Willard

INTRODUCTION

The title for this book is taken from its opening sentence. "Ecclesiastes" means "the Preacher." The content and tone of Proverbs, Ecclesiastes, and the Song of Solomon are similar. Solomon was reputed to be a wise king. His wisdom was the gift of God. Yet his carnal nature led him astray. His many wives, some of them foreign, led him into excesses that ultimately caused his downfall. Thus Proverbs reflects wisdom gained from mistakes he had made. God has used his sensuous, poetic song, the Song of Solomon, to mean far more than its authors could foresee. But it is in Ecclesiastes that we find the thwarted spirit and the broken heart of Solomon.

His "all is vanity" (1:2) reveals the folly, so frequent in his life. That he, Solomon, the king, could be so exalted by the world, yet so wrong in his relationship to God, is probably the key to it all. Solomon saw that crime *did* pay —at least in the eyes of the world. It made him heartsick to know this. He began to look to a judgment beyond this life. In the closing verses of the book, he finds something that is for everyone and is *not* vain. "Let us hear the conclusion of the whole matter: Fear God, and keep his commandments: for this is the whole duty of man" (12:13).

Ecclesiastes is like a page torn from the book of life. It catches us when we are depressed; when we can find no answer to our call for help. But it serves its purpose by instructing us through many lessons. We cannot read this book without thanking God for the light that is in Jesus Christ. Solomon saw the weakness of man and the foolishness of this world. However his faith may have faltered, he held the lamp through his night, until the day was to dawn in Jesus.

Words of the Preacher (Eccl. 1:1–18)

The passage.—The title of the book is found in its first phrase. The word "Preacher" is the English equivalent of Ecclesiastes. It refers to a speaker, or one who calls students or disciples together to teach them. Although Solomon's name appears nowhere in the book, it is generally understood to be his work. Solomon was the only son of David who was king in Jerusalem.

From verse 2, we get the idea that the author has a pessimistic outlook on life. An attitude that may have been caused by Solomon's spiritual degeneration, after he had risen to power.

The section including verses 4–11 seems to explain further verse 2. The author sees the world as a meaningless daily grind. He seems to be saying, "What's the use in anything. In a little while, no one will know or care anyway!" Lest anyone think the author had completely lost his faith, or that his tirade against life was inexcusable, the last verses of the book set the entire work in its proper perspective. "Fear God, and keep his commandments: for this is the whole duty of man" (12:13).

Special points.—"No new thing" (v. 9) reminds us that only God can

377

create out of nothing. We may re-arrange matter to suit our particular and immediate need, but all is subject to the laws of God. Only in the person and work of Jesus did God give man something new and different and redemptive.

Verse 11 concludes the first pessimistic speech, saying that nothing will be remembered. Although God remembers it all, historians record extremely little of what goes on in the world. Only a few names and incidents survive.

Verses 17 and 18 characterize the limitations of man, if not indeed his depravity. Without God, a man is lost. No one can understand divine wisdom or man's tendency to err, without divine help. The more we really know about ourselves and the world we live in, the more we come to depend upon God. The Savior, Jesus, was needed. He was in the beginning with God. His entrance upon the world's stage was a part of God's plan for the ages.

Truth for today.—Solomon was no hermit, soured on the world. Ecclesiastes is not a book that says there is no God. But Solomon, writing out of the depth of his God-given wisdom, saw that, man, left to himself, was hopeless. "What difference does it make?" some people say, implying that they might as well do as they please, or what their evil nature urges them to do. But this vanity of vanities is an opinion voiced without the faith, hope, and love that is in Jesus.

Vanity of Seeking Pleasure (Eccl. 2:1–26)

The passage.—The author tries everything he knows about to find satisfaction for his soul; pleasure, entertainment, accomplishment, and wealth. He tried to forget his troubles by drinking. He got busy building great buildings, gardens, and orchards. He acquired servants and entertainers. His wealth was greater than any who had gone before him in Jerusalem. By all standards of the world, he had achieved success. But still he was not satisfied.

Solomon saw that wisdom excelled folly and that righteousness excelled sinfulness, as far as light excelled darkness (v. 13). Lacking peace for his soul however, he "hated life" (v. 17). He saw clearly that all God had made was good and that a man should enjoy the results of his labor. He saw that disobedience and sin led to pain and trials, just as joy comes to the prudent. A life that was lived in defiance of God was a vain and useless life (v. 26).

Special points.—Verse 11 states that the author found "no profit" in all that he had accomplished. His material wealth, when balanced against his trust in God, did seem worthless. Since he had built his buildings and gardens, sought gratification of his senses, and tried to please himself only, he began to understand the delusion of the world. He could take nothing with him when he died. All of it had to be left to someone else, perhaps one who would not appreciate it anyway (v. 18).

Truth for today.—Solomon's testing and tasting of the world's gifts was a trial and error method, which many today are pursuing. They will try anything, in the maddening race to find satisfaction.

"What shall a man give in exchange for his soul?" said Jesus (Matt. 16:26). Yet there are many who foolishly bargain away their one eternal soul, for the perishable baubles of the world. We can join Solomon in his vexation and wonderment that men could be so foolish.

God's Providence (Eccl. 3:1–22)

The passage.—Change is a sign of life. In this life the change is from one extreme to another. Some changes are not under man's control and some are. The alternating seasons of life, such as weeping and laughing, scattering and gathering, and getting and losing, are the mark of this world. Only God is changeless. We keep discovering and unlocking the mysterious, beautiful world God has made. Although we have been examining it for thousands of years, there is yet much about the world and the universe it is in, that we do not know. No one can find out why God made so many things. No one knows all that went on before they reached their present state. No one knows what will come of it all (v. 11).

The last seven verses of the chapter remind us that we are absolutely dependent upon God. We cannot unravel the mystery of life, unless we trust in him.

Special points.—The statement in verse 19 that "man hath no preeminence above a beast" is in reference to the first half of the verse. There, it states that both man and beast alike, die. Their bodies return to the dust of the earth in the same manner. Insofar as the body is concerned, man has little or no advantage over the beasts of the field. A dog has a keener sense of smell, a leopard can run faster, a turtle lives longer, and an eagle has better eyesight. It is in the realm of the mind and the spirit that man has superiority. Only man is made in the image of God.

Verse 20, "all go unto one place," refers to the body at the time of physical death.

Truth for today.—It is a great shock, or at least it should be, to find wickedness in the place of righteousness and justice. Our mind says, "If you can't depend on the people at church and at the courthouse, then who can you depend on?" It is no easy matter to answer. Solomon resolved it by saying that both the people in the place of righteousness and the people in the place of justice would someday stand before the same God, just like everyone else.

Life's Hopelessness (Eccl. 4:1–16)

The passage.—A penetrating look into the affairs of men reveals an abundance of high-handed injustices. Some are the victims of greedy men who have money as their God. Others fall victim to self-centered individuals, who seek their own personal success or well-being, even if it means misery and suffering for others. Such victims weep with no one to comfort them. This observation prompted the author to conclude that under these conditions, those who had never been born were better off (vv. 1–3).

The outlook was also dark for those who had apparently succeeded in some areas of life. Their success and diligence would be met by envy and jealousy from their neighbor (vv. 4–6).

Verses 7–12 describe the plight of the lonely. The last verses of the chapter probably refer to Solomon's backward look at his own days of success and power. If reformation in his own life was coming too late to be of any significance, he could also see that even a young man, assuming the mantle of kingship, would also be passed by. Time and changing whims of the people would erase the memory of his goodness from their minds.

Special points.—Verses 2 and 3 state that the dead are better off than the living and that those who are not yet born, who have not seen the evil of this world, are better off than either the living or the dead. It is an interpretation of life without hope and without God.

Verse 8 refers to one who is so self-centered that he ignores the neighbor or the family God has given to him. It may refer to one who really does live alone, but who strives as hard to accumulate wealth, as one who had posterity to whom he could leave it all. It is as though he had spent his life of painful labor to accumulate riches which no one could ever use or enjoy.

Truth for today.—The simple, clear statement, "Two are better than one" (v. 9) is a true foundation upon which much of life is built. God made man *and* woman. He told them to multiply. It is divine wisdom that teaches us to relate properly to other people. Each of us needs the presence, strength, and comfort of having people close to us. This principle is true in the world of the spirit and in the church. We are links in a long chain of witnesses to the power of God in Christ.

Rash Vows, Riches, and Labor (Eccl. 5: 1–20)

The passage.—Good conduct is to be the rule when we come to the house of God or go about his business (v. 1). God's house is not to be a place of worldliness, but it is to be a place where the world may come for help. Prayer, the reading of the inspired Word of God, and public worship can solace troubled hearts.

Silence before God is a good policy. It is better for God to speak to us than for us to speak to God (v. 2). It is better not to make a promise to God, than to promise and not do it. Yet vows and promises should be made and accomplished as soon as practical (vv. 4–5).

Worldly riches are a grave peril. Yet it is not so perilous to have them as it is to be obsessed with *wanting* riches. Of this, both the poor and the rich can be guilty (vv. 10–11). The poor man who labors for what it takes to live on sleeps as well or better than the man who is troubled about retaining his excessive wealth. But, to some, God gives the

stewardship of great and expensive possessions. If such has come by righteous means, then, like the laborer, the rich man is to enjoy the gift, sharing with others, as God has with him (vv. 18–19).

Special points.—"A dream cometh," in verse 3, refers to the disturbed sleep that follows troubled and anxiety-ridden activity. It is unprofitable to put faith in dreams resulting from disturbed sleep. This triggering of the subconscious mind is compared to the babbling of meaningless vows. Neither are to be trusted. They are unreal.

In the discussion on wealth and labor, in verses 9–20, there are two summaries. One is found in verses 15–16, which says that we leave this world with no more than we brought into it. The second is found in verses 18–20; God will bless both the rich and the poor who do his will with something far better than their memory of the joys of this life.

Truth for today.—If all the vows made to God were actually done, what a better world this would be. Making a promise of faithfulness to God, if he will but deliver us from some impending trouble, is all too common. Failure to fulfil our commitment means we were foolish enough to attempt a trick on God, or, we make ourselves liars by not doing what we have said we would do.

Christians take a vow to live a life surrendered to God's will. This dedication of life brings to us the eternal riches of God's glory. We have no excuse for failure. We can only accept God's mercy and love in Christ, in the places and times where we fail.

Unwise Use of Wealth (Eccl. 6:1–12)

The passage.—Improperly used wealth is vain and is a common error (vv. 1–2). Though a man be rich, blessed with a large family, and live a long life, if he has not turned his soul to God, he has missed the mark completely. Riches, honor among men, long life; things that are usually the sign of God's blessings, may be misused. The standards of man do not reach high enough to bring happiness to the soul (v. 11).

Special points.—"Though he live a thousand years twice told" (v. 6) describes the improbability of a man achieving satisfaction, if he makes his heart too small for God. Though God give him more than any other man seems to have, if he does not use his capacity to enjoy it, he fails in life.

Wealth in itself does not bring happiness. The *stewardship* of life's gifts, not simply the fact that we possess them, is the important thing.

Truth for today.—"The power to enjoy" (v. 2, RSV) the God-given blessings of life is missing in much of the church today. For example: America is one of the richest nations on earth, yet we take millions of mood elevators and tranquilizers. Our suicide rate is high. Millions of souls in this land are so unhappy that they have blotted out the rest of us, by drinking themselves into insensibility. Wealth does not assure the happiness of a nation.

The power to enjoy is what we want. This is what we are lacking. Only Christ, living in the heart, guiding the mind and hand and eye, can bring the power to enjoy gifts from God.

Happiness and Wisdom (Eccl. 7:1–29)

The passage.—The statement in verse 1, that the day of death is better than the day of birth, is true if we have obeyed God. If we have lived so as to earn a good name, have done his will, then heaven will, of course, be better than anything we have known in this life.

The assertion that it is better to go to the house of the mourning than to go to the house of the feasting is another way to be reminded of the brevity of

life. Throwing away life's golden moments only to bring life to an untimely end may be the meaning of "the house of feasting" (v. 2). We need this reminder. Verse 20 says that all men are guilty of sin (compare Rom. 3:23).

Special points.—"Be not righteous over much" (v. 16) is a caution that at first might seem to contradict other important teachings of the Bible. But it is not a contradiction. It is a warning against being so good in our own eyes, that we become self-righteous. It can refer also to those who would try to impress others with their outward display of righteousness.

In verse 15, Solomon sees that the best that is in this world is evil when compared to the eternal glory of God. The righteous may die an untimely death, while the evil may live long and be prosperous, but final victory belongs to those who are on the Lord's side (v. 18).

Truth for today.—Solomon's unholy relationship with many women (1 Kings 11:1) led to a life that ended with bitter experiences. The more he looked back at life, the worse it looked to him. His conclusion that he could find "one man among a thousand," may refer to Adam, the forerunner of all men. That only Adam, made in the image of God, was at one time free from evil. But Adam sinned, and thus became the father of sinful men. How significant then, that Jesus the sinless man comes to earth (1 Cor. 15:47). Man has no other God-given example to follow, no other Savior.

Final Failure of the Wicked (Eccl. 8:1–17)

The passage.—A general admonition to obey those in authority. It is not wise to strike out at the God-sanctioned leaders of the people. To rashly reject their commands will bring punishment. Evil rulers are reminded that man does not control his final end. He does not know what will happen. Evil man keeps on with his bickering and war, but this does not settle the matter. No man has power over the spirit. Only God, who is just, can even all accounts as they should be (vv. 1–8).

Verses 11–14 reveal that God knows about the success of the evil and the suffering of the righteous. God does not always settle accounts with evil men on the day they commit their sins.

The recognition of God as the infinitely wise Creator and man as the limited creature is set forth in the final verses. Man simply cannot know all that God has done and is doing in this world. It is a tribute to the majesty and authority of God.

Special points.—Whatever evils we may try to avoid, verse 8 lists four that are impossible: to stop the turn of events that is God's call to end life; to avoid the time of death; to evade the struggle of life; and to be delivered into heaven by sinful living.

The subject of one man's authority over another is further explored in verse 9. Evil rulers, whatever their rank, will finally be overthrown by their own evil actions and judgments. People who govern themselves by electing their own leaders may bring destruction upon themselves by sinful actions.

Truth for today.—True wisdom cannot be found without God's help. Whatever we discover about ourselves, or the world we live in, must be related to God if it is to have significance. That God is working in this world, in and through man, helps us to see a plan that is more majestic and grand than the little purposes we have for the moment. God reveals himself and all of his plan that we need to see, through the Bible, Jesus, the Holy Spirit, and his marvelous

creation about us. We are not thwarted by lack of understanding. We are, rather, honored and exalted to be included in a scheme so vast. By God's grace, we share in it all, as his children.

On Death and Wisdom (Eccl. 9:1–18)

The passage.—The imperfections of this world are easily seen by all who observe. That which appears outwardly to be true, may indeed, not be true at all. There are many experiences that are common to both good men and bad (vv. 1–3). Death, which is one of these common experiences, puts an end to the activities of life. Therefore, men should enjoy the good that God has given to them, while they can (vv. 7–10). The white garments referred to in verse 8 were, as they are now, symbols of purity and happiness, as contrasted to dark or black apparel.

Evil circumstances, or even death itself may come unannounced. The outward success a person may enjoy at the moment cannot stay the hand of death. A wise man may prove useful, but still go without recognition and suffer the fate of the foolish. This truth is illustrated by the beautiful story of a "little city" (v. 14) that was saved by the wisdom of a poor man.

Special points.—"Live joyfully" (v. 9) is a command from the Word of God that is too often ignored. We are to live so that those about us can see the good that God has built into this world. We can enjoy this life more if we learn to share its burdens with others. In the same way, happiness will come to any who will help those who are nearest. Though there is much in this world that cannot be understood, there is still room for the joy of living. It is the gift of God.

Verses 11 and 12 remind us that there is a certain unpredictability about life. Races are not always won by the swiftest runners; riches are not always the mark of the smartest men; the strongest do not always win the fight; and, some men of great talents are not always honored. Therefore, this world and its illusions are not to be trusted. It can be deceptive.

Truth for today.—God has set many signposts along the road of life. The Bible is one of these clearly-defined instruction points. It warns of the lure and attractiveness of pleasure and pride. It repeats again and again, in many different life stories, that unrighteousness can only lead to destruction. It warns that the things of this world cannot be depended upon. Only the Lord is steadfast and eternal. Solomon had tasted the good that is in the gifts from God. He also experienced the sorrow and bitterness that accompanies disobedience.

Avoiding Life's Pitfalls (Eccl. 10:1–20)

The passage.—A sin committed, though it may seem of little significance at the time it is done, may, at a later time, become the ruin of an entire life. As a whole body of water may become polluted and unusable by one careless incident, so a sin can pollute the soul (v. 1). If a person sets a trap to ensnare another (v. 8), he will fall into the pit himself. The act of deception practiced against another person is the pit of sin and its punishment into which he has already fallen.

Laziness and indifference permit natural processes of decay to set in, whether it be a life or a house. The call to be wise and industrious is seen in verses 10 and 18. Neither should we be careless with our speech. Judging or condemning another is not to be practiced. Even whispered condemnation has a way of finding the ears of the one condemned.

Special points.—"Princes walking as servants" (v. 7) is another reminder of

our out-of-joint world. It is quite true that some of the world's finest are people of humble circumstances. Many never receive public recognition, wealth, or even expressions of gratitude. Yet, they are quietly faithful to the Lord and in the performance of their assigned tasks. Jesus said, "Blessed are the meek" (Matt. 5:5).

"Money answereth all things" (v. 19). Money cannot be eaten. It cannot be worn. It cannot be used as shelter. It cannot buy peace of mind, forgiveness for sin, or the needs of the soul. But money is the answer to the things the sinful seek. It provides the food, drink, power, and luxuries that satisfy the senses. In the context of the entire verse (v. 19), money answers the two goals of the sinner.

Truth for today.—The Bible is a deep well from which may be drawn refreshing and life-giving water for the soul.

Drink this: If the ax is dull, and we don't sharpen it, then we must strike a harder blow (v. 10). If the methods we are using in the church to bring the lost to Christ are dull and ineffective, then we must put more effort into it. Either improve the old way, or try harder with what we have. For many, it is easier to limp along with a dull ax and a weak effort.

Attempt (Eccl. 11:1–10)

The passage.—Approaching the end of his sermon, Solomon gives some sound advice. He speaks with full knowledge that man's life is fraught with sin, broken promises, and unattained dreams. Nevertheless, he advises charity and generosity. Such action will find its reward at a later time. Gifts are to be given with no thought of reward to the donor. This explains why the bread is given as though it were bread thrown into a river, with no hope of seeing it again. In the providence of God, it has a way of returning to feed the giver.

Caution' is a good quality, but at times, hesitation may cause an opportunity to pass that will never return (vv. 4–6). If God opens a door, we are to enter. If he provides food, we are to eat. As with life itself, which no man can explain, so is the wisdom and work of God. Verses 9–10 call for the young to use God-given talents and abilities, and to be faithful, for a final judgment lies ahead.

Special points.—In verse 5, lack of knowledge about the way of the spirit is compared to lack of knowledge about the facts of human birth. While it is true that we may know more about pro-creation, genetics, heredity, and cell structure than did Solomon, the fact of life itself is still an enigma to mankind. He may even discover acids or elements that generate movement or life. Yet a single cell and the whole universe are shrouded in a mystery known only to God.

Truth for today.—People who give are happier than people who receive. The stewardship of life is the greatest challenge we will ever have. To be able to give is a blessing. Yet there are many, who by thinking of themselves too much, do not see the needs of others about them to which they could give. At whatever age, it is never too early, or too late, to learn the happiness and the blessing of giving.

Life's Problem Solved (Eccl. 12:1–14)

The passage.—One of the most beautiful chapters in the Bible. An exhortation to the young to consider the ways of the Lord while there is still time (vv. 1–7). Each verse refers to the progres-sive maturing of life. Until the "silver chord" is loosed (v. 6), or, until death comes.

In the final verses, the book commends itself as being filled with that which is right and true. "The conclusion of the whole matter" (v. 13) is that to fear God and keep his commandments is the whole duty of man. It will prepare him for the final judgment that is to come.

Special points.—"The voice of the bird" (v. 4) is a difficult phrase and has been interpreted various ways. The most likely of which is that it refers to the thin, high-pitched voice of an aged man. When the doors are closed, the mill is stilled and the music is low, death may be not too far away.

"The silver cord" (v. 6) is a mystical reference to the thing that binds the eternal soul to an earthly body. When this cord is loosed, the soul is freed. The breaking of the golden bowl probably refers to the death of the body that held the precious water of life.

Truth for today.—The Word of God is enough. Most of what is wrong in this world could be set right if the words of this book were obeyed. Few statements in the history of man speak with the force and clarity of verse 13. The duty and obligation of all men everywhere is to fear God and keep his commandments.

Further progress will, of course, be impossible until we have met these conditions. His kingdom is as near as our surrender to his blessed will. To think—all these years we have flourished in our sin and sorrow. All we have needed to do was to fear God and obey his commandments. Accepting Jesus as our Savior fulfils them both.

SONG OF SOLOMON

Conrad R. Willard

INTRODUCTION

"The Song of Songs, which is Solomon's," is unique among all the books of the Bible. It does not contain the name of God. It does not directly preach moral or ethical values or doctrines. It is never quoted in the New Testament. Yet it has been confirmed as divinely inspired by both Jews and Christians.

Many books have been written to explain its meaning. Some have supposed it to contain a hidden message from God and have filled many pages with their speculations. It evidently grew out of some, now obscure, historical situation, concerning the physical attractiveness of man to woman and woman to man. That it was written to mean *only* this, seems improbable. By its inclusion with other divinely inspired Scripture, it sanctions the relationship between man and woman, established in the Garden of Eden.

There are three principal ideas that have been used throughout the centuries (since before the time of Christ), to explain its meaning. The *first* is: It is an allegory. The characters referred to in the book represent something or somebody else. Usually, under this method, Solomon is taken to be God and the maiden is taken to be Israel. (Or, Solomon represents Christ and the maiden represents the church.) The *second* is: The lovers and their situation are *typical* of the love of Christ for the church. The book may be a relatively accurate account of Solomon with one of his wives.

But the reason it has been declared inspired, lies in its similarity to the deep and complete love God has for his people and Christ has for his church. The *third* is: It is the account of ideal human love and affection. They hold that the love herein described is innocent. Therefore, the subject matter stands upon its own merit.

I believe the second to be most accurate. The Bible would not be complete without it.

Introduction of the Maiden (Song 1:1–17)

The passage.—The book takes its title from the first verse. It is a song (or poetic drama), that excels all other songs. The content reveals the following characters: King Solomon, a maiden, women in the palace and probably a shepherd who loves the maiden. (One speech may be by the maiden's brothers.) The book does not say that the song was composed by Solomon. It was undoubtedly written about him.

Following the title verse is a series of monologues and dialogues. One or more of the women refer to the attractiveness of the king (vv. 2–4). The maiden says she is dark-skinned because she has worked in the sun too long. Yet she knows she is beautiful. She longs for a shepherd she loves (vv. 5–7). Someone answers that she should go look for him (v. 8). She is likened to an exquisitely beautiful and adorned mare from the finest stables (vv. 9–10). The women offer to adorn her (v. 11). Then the maiden praises the king, though at times, she seems to speak longingly for her true love—the shepherd (vv. 12–17).

Special points.—"I am black, but comely" (v. 5), may be a reference to some of the experiences of Solomon. As was the custom of Oriental kings of his day, he had many wives. Some of them came from distant places. The inclusion of an explanation of her color implies she was not from Jerusalem.

The reference in verse 9 to a "company of horses in Pharaoh's chariots" was intended as a compliment to the maiden, though it may sound awkward by today's standards.

Truth for today.—A poem about the true love of a young girl who rejects the proposal of a king to marry the one she loves is beautiful sentiment. But this poem may be the revelation of something far more grand than the love two people might have for each other. Almost since the time it was written, Bible scholars have seen the characters of this little drama representing something highly significant. They picture Solomon, or the shepherd, as representing God or Christ. They see the maiden as being Israel or the church.

Except for the love of God, the noblest and tenderest emotion known, is the love of another person. God planned it to be that way from the beginning. Thus, in its highest form, human love may be used as a type of divine affection that Christ has for his church, or that God has for his people.

The Bride's Memories (Song 2:1–17)

The passage.—Since the characters in this drama or poem are not named, the speaker and the one spoken to can be determined only by what is said. Therefore, it would seem as though the maiden speaks all that is in chapter 2, with the possible exception of verses

2 and 15. Verse 7 is a refrain that recurs other places in the poem. Verses 3–6, 8–14, and 16–17 seem to be addressed to her shepherd lover—her true love.

Special points.—"The little foxes" (v. 15) is a reference to the small foxes that infested Palestine and were destructive to the vineyards. The beauty and productiveness of a vineyard would be reduced by the invasion of these pests. In like manner, small irritations and problems may eat away at a happy love relationship.

Truth for today.—Until further revelation, this divinely inspired song of love yields its sweetest notes as an allegory. The love of a husband and wife is sacred, reassuring, and intimate. It has similarities to the love of Christ for his church. Little sins, like little foxes in a vineyard, may eat away the fruit of the spirit.

The Maiden's Dream (Song 3:1–11)

The passage.—The speech of the maiden continues. Though she may have been taken to the king's palace to become his bride, she longs for her true love. Her speech here seems to be a dream, or the fantasy of her imagination (v. 1). She dreams of searching throughout the city for the shepherd. She finds him and takes him to her home (vv. 2–4).

Except for verse 5, which is the repeated refrain of the song, the rest of the chapter is a eulogy of the king. It is probably the speech of the other women of the king's court.

Solomon is praised for being wise and thoughtful. He made for himself a chariot large enough to sleep in. It was made of cedar, silver-trimmed, gold-lined, and upholstered with rich purple fabric. It was paved with love.

Special points.—"I charge you, O ye daughters of Jerusalem" (v. 5)—a phrase that appears in 8:4, as it does in 2:7. This short and repeated saying lends strength to the interpretation of the work as a song or poem. This repeated call to the "daughters of Jerusalem" to let love be as God made it to be, not forced or unnatural, may have a deeper meaning than first appears. It could be a reminder that God, the creator, has a plan whereby his love will, at the right time, be made known. But even in its simpler application, to husband and wife, true love is not forced.

Truth for today.—The longing desire this maiden has for Solomon (or the shepherd, depending upon which interpretation is used) becomes a beautiful expression of love. It is the way we see people when we love them. We overlook their faults and see only their good points. Therefore, if a deeper and hidden meaning is intended here, it is easy to see how great and majestic God was to Israel. How great is our salvation in Jesus Christ, the redeemer of our souls.

Love's Beauty (Song 4:1–16)

The passage.—All the verses are in praise of the maiden, except verse 16. In this verse the maiden speaks. Since the first seven verses deal mainly with the physical beauty of the maiden, some interpreters think Solomon, in his worldliness, is the speaker. These also hold that verses 8–15 are the speech of the shepherd, which is her true love, since it does not dwell upon her physical attributes, but upon the purity of love itself. However, the entire section seems to be of the same intent. It is a play upon words of love between a man and the woman he loves. It brings to intensity the response of the maiden.

Special points.—The entire chapter is the inspired description of love between man and woman. It strengthens the bonds of marriage. This divinely inspired book alone gives ample proof that God's simple and basic life relationships are his gifts.

The language of almost any translation is quickly understood. Only when it is forced into meaning something for which it was not intended, do difficulties arise. There is a temptation to make the "garden" of verse 12–15 represent the church; to see in this "garden" unlimited beauty and healing. But to yield at this point would lead to absurdities at other places in the chapter.

Truth for today.—One of the greatest gifts of God to man is his capacity to love and to be loved. There are obvious and specific differences between physical love, the love of friends, and the divine love of God. From these three divisions, which have been used for centuries, we have assumed that there is no relationship between these emotions. The Song of Solomon brings them closer together. Excluding blind and insane lust, our ability to feel for others and to love them is very closely linked to our tendency to love God and have compassion that identifies us as a Christian. Thus, this chapter heightens our understanding of one of our most basic responses to the God who created us, and all that is about us.

Love's Dream of Beauty (Song 5:1–16)

The passage.—Verse 1 is a speech made by the lover, about his satisfaction with the maiden. He encourages his friends to join the celebration of his great joy. Except for verse 9, which is probably by the other women of the palace, the remainder of the chapter is the eulogy of the lover by the maiden.

The words, "I sleep, but my heart waketh" (v. 2), may indicate that the entire speech is actually the report or account of a dream. This explanation fits with the interpretation that the maiden is still longing for her shepherd lover, but is still in the palace of the king. A simpler interpretation is that she is simply praising the one she loves, which, if so interpreted from the beginning, is Solomon.

Special points.—Punishment suffered by the maiden (v. 7) is to show the love she has, and to show her determination to find the one she loves. Her desire to find him was born of pure and chaste intent. Her tormentors punished her as though she were a woman with sinful intent. In 1:5, the maiden says she is black. In 5:10 she pictures her lover as being white. The contrast may be either used to describe the situation between Solomon and one of his wives, or, it may be used simply to contrast her humility with the excellence she saw in the one she loved.

Truth for today.—Everything God has made is good. Godly men and women see the beauty which God has created in the one they love. The simple beauty and longing to be loved is surely understood by almost anyone who would read these lines. But the Bible has truth interwoven into every sentence it contains. Divinely inspired, it keeps teaching us lessons we need to learn. It keeps revealing the glory and purpose of God. It glows on every page, with the light of man's redemption and the glory of God. If we listen for the still small voice of the Holy Spirit, we may hear more than the beautiful song of love from a maiden from the court of Solomon.

Overwhelming Beauty (Song 6:1–13)

The passage.—Others ask of the maiden some questions about the one she loves (v. 1). Verse 2 is her answer. He has gone to work and to eat in his garden (vv. 2–3). Verses 4–13 could be the speech of Solomon or the shepherd. It is at least an extended poem praising the maiden. Some Bible scholars think

that verse 10 may be the speech of the women of the palace. Some think verse 12 is the voice of the maiden. But its continuity permits it to remain as a single speech.

One of the strongest arguments supporting the idea that this young woman was in the palace of the king are phrases found in verse 13. "Return, return, O Shulamite" (v. 13), indicates that she was leaving.

Special points.—"Tirzah"—A city located in the mountains and noted for its beauty. The name signifies sweetness. Like Jerusalem, it was used to describe the surpassing beauty of the maiden.

"Terrible as an army with banners" (v. 4)—probably refers to the attention she attracted when she passed. It is as if her beauty held the gaze of others, as an army marching by in full dress.

"Shulamite," as used in verse 13, is the nearest thing to a name ever given to any of the characters appearing in the drama except King Solomon. It means she was a woman from the territory of the tribe of Issachar, south-east of Nazareth. In 1 Kings 1:3, the same region is referred to as Shunem. It was, then, in the time of Solomon, the source of beautiful women.

Truth for today.—Whether or not the original intent of this song of songs included an application beyond the characters mentioned, it lends itself well to the intimate relationship God has with his people. If each description is applied to some part of both human love and divine love, the analogy does not fit. But if we can see that God loves his own with tenderness and intensity; if we can also see that one brings glory to the other, then a truth of God has been plainly demonstrated.

The King and His Love (Song 7:1–13)

The passage.—The desire and appreciation man has for woman is seen clearly in this chapter. For those who think that the song contains a description of the love for both Solomon and a native shepherd, this portion is assigned to Solomon. It is thus held to be evidence of decadency and lust on the part of the aging king. To those who hold that the entire song is a dialogue between King Solomon and his bride, this passage is looked upon as part of a tender love song. It is probably the most difficult portion of the book for those who interpret Solomon and the maiden to mean Christ and the church.

Special points.—"Held in the galleries" (v. 5) means that Solomon was entranced by the beauty of her hair.

"Mandrakes" (v. 13)—an aromatic plant that grows in the middle-east. Like roses, both its flower (like a small apple) and its fragrance were symbols of love and affection.

Truth for today.—No other book in the Bible describes in such detail the thoughts and actions of strongly attracted man to woman and woman to man. This attraction and affection is the gift of God. Marriage is a part of God's plan for man upon earth. Infidelity and the breaking of this marriage bond is treated with utmost seriousness. Adultery is a sin. It threatens the tender relationship between man and woman as husband and wife. It also defies the law of God.

The powerful emotional relationship of man to woman may be the symbol of a stronger and longer lasting relationship between God and his people. To apply the symbolism in each detail may miss the larger truth.

The Marriage Vow (Song 8:1–14)

The passage.—Verses 1–4 continue as the speech of the maiden. In them she further describes her love. Verse 5 is a brief speech by other persons. The maiden vows her undying love and pledges herself for life (vv. 6–7).

Verses 8–14 are either a speech by the brothers of the maiden and then a short statement by her, or it is a longer speech by the maiden as she recalls things that had happened earlier. Perhaps she remembers what her brothers had said about her when she was but a young girl.

Special points.—The references to brothers of the maiden, found in verse 1 and in verses 8,9 imply she has returned to her native home in Shulam (Shunem). She desires to be so closely related to the one she loves that she longs to have him in her home (vv. 1–3).

"Set me as a seal upon thine heart" (v. 6)—the supreme vow of faithfulness and love. "Be thou like to a roe . . ." (v. 14), completes the symmetry of the entire song. As she refers to the one she loves in chapter 2, verse 9, she now desires him, alone.

Truth for today.—In 1 Corinthians 13:1–13, the apostle Paul describes the attributes and work of love. As God reveals himself in his Holy Word, he reveals his love for us. The Bible teaches us to love one another. It describes the nature and purpose of the love of husband and wife. It tells us that God is love and that he loved the world, and sent his only begotten son to die for our sins.

Love is one of our most commonly used emotions. It affects us from the cradle to the grave. It is the symbol of the divine relationship between God and man.

Therefore, the Song of Solomon, in its simple beauty, may extol for us the one quality and act in life that is greater than either faith or hope. Human, physical love is not, of course, the highest point of our journey. But it may point us on, to a love that is divine—from God—for eternity.

ISAIAH

James E. Carter (1–39) and
Peter McLeod (40–66)

INTRODUCTION

The book of Isaiah is a high-water mark in Old Testament prophecy. With majestic expression, deep insight, and spiritual sensitivity the message is presented. Long a favorite Old Testament book of Christians, it is also quoted extensively in the New Testament.

The prophet.—Little is known about Isaiah himself. We know that he was the son of Amoz and that he lived and ministered in Jerusalem. He was married and had at least two sons. Since he had access to the rulers of the nation, he may have come from a noble family.

Beginning at the death of King Uzziah, *c.* 742 B.C., his prophetic ministry extended nearly half a century through the reigns of four kings of Judah. He had a group of followers; they may have been responsible for the collection of Isaiah's materials. As a prophet he was more concerned with forth-telling than fore-telling.

Conditions.—Uzziah reigned at the end of Judah's days of glory. At the time of his death the nation enjoyed material prosperity; but it suffered from a weakened spirituality.

The international situation had its effect on both the kingdom and Isaiah's ministry. At least three political crises are reflected in the book. In these times of crisis God's messenger spoke.

Contents.—Various literary forms are found in Isaiah 1–39. Some historical information along with oracles concerning Judah and foreign nations as well as "woes" are included.

Significance.—God is revealed as the "Holy One of Israel." There are messianic promises that find their fulfilment in Jesus Christ. The covenant relationship with God, the standards of righteousness, the consequences of rebellious sin and the faithful remnant of believers are emphasized. These themes still need understanding.

See also the introduction to Isaiah 40—66 preceding the discussion of chapter 40.

A Day in Court (Isa. 1:1–31)

The passage.—A brief introduction identifies Isaiah as the prophet responsible for these passages.

The first chapter establishes the character of the prophet's message. Presented as a trial at law the charges of God against his people are expressed. The heavens and the earth are called as a jury. God is both the plaintiff and judge. The people of Judah are the defendants. The prophet is the witness.

The charge is that the people have been unresponsive to God. Even the animals know their master, but these people have not recognized their dependence on God. Devastation is the result of sin. They may plead by their religious exercises, but they have lacked heart. Pardon is possible, but they must seek forgiveness. Judgment will be the inevitable result of their rebellious course.

Special points.—Vision (v. 1) has been used as a technical term for prophecy. It was God's revelation.

The city or the nation is often personified. The "daughter of Zion" (v. 8) is a reference to the city of Jerusalem.

Because of the complete devastation (vv. 5–9) some would date this passage as late as 701 B.C. Whatever the period, the message remains: Judah has sinned and the result is punishment.

Worship was actively practiced but it had not become a part of life. God is the "Holy One of Israel" and their lives are to reflect his character. They have a covenant with him.

Due to the context some have interpreted verse 18 as an expression of irony. Traditionally it has been understood as the possibility of pardon.

The "oak" and "garden" (v. 29) refer to pagan worship practices. They are futile.

Truth for today.—Our response to God grows out of our relationship to him.

Worship must result in character. Empty forms and unaffected lives are not pleasing to God. The experience of forgiveness will show in the quality of life.

Peace and Punishment (Isa. 2:1–22)

The passage.—An ideal Jerusalem is presented in verses 2–5. At some future time the house of God will be exalted. People from all over the world will be attracted to learn the teachings of God. God's sovereign rule will be acknowledged. The result will be universal peace. Instruments of war will be turned to implements of agriculture. War will be neither learned nor practiced.

That is the ideal Jerusalem. The real Jerusalem was different. Punishment was in store for them because of their rebellious and deceitful actions.

The Day of the Lord would bring the vindication of God. The people had become haughty, made foreign alliances, become proud of their attainments, and turned to idols. But God would have the last word.

Idolatry was doomed. The proud people would be humbled. They would grovel in the caves and among the rocks for protection.

Special points.—Isaiah 2:2—12:6 is generally considered to be a section of prophecies concerning Judah and Jerusalem.

The "last days" is usually associated with the messianic reign. In verse 1 it could also mean some future date.

Mount Zion, the center of Jerusalem, is exalted above all else. It is understood as the center of God's activity.

The "day of the Lord" was thought to be a time of God's victorious action over his enemies. Isaiah shows that the people of Judah are the enemies of God because of their sin. In the caves and the clefts of the rocks, ancient places of refuge, they would try to hide from God. The things that stood tall, hills and trees, would be flattened.

Truth for today.—The quest for peace must end with God. When God is acknowledged as God and human accomplishments are seen in proper perspective, peace will be on its way. The ways of God result in peace. The ways of rebellious sin result in destruction.

Crisis in Society (Isa. 3:1—4:1)

The passage.—Cutting through the religious observance and the civic pride, Isaiah pointed to the problem in Jerusalem as it really was: a crisis in leadership.

He pictured God removing everything that had given stability to society. Five groups of leaders are removed from their places of responsibility. So critical had leadership become that the person who had a coat on his back was chosen to lead.

The reason for the rottenness was the corruption of the leaders. They had refused to practice social justice; they had abdicated their trust.

The luxury-loving women were responsible too. They would feel the pinch of judgment. Conditions would be so bad that seven women would ask one man for marriage simply for the protection and standing it would afford.

Special points.—The "stay and the staff" are society's stabilizing features.

A Purified People (Isa. 4:2–6)

The passage.—Isaiah's third vision of Jerusalem is a prophetic vision. He sees it as a purified city.

The real reason for God's judgment is not punishment but salvation. The prophet has hope, a hope grounded in faith in God. The people can be cleansed of the sin and filth of their lives and given a place of standing with God. These are the remnant that remain with their Redeemer.

In the messianic age that follows the day of the Lord there will be material plenty, moral purity, and the protection of God.

Special points.—In some prophetic incidences "branch" has a messianic reference; in verse 1 it is more a reference to the fruitfulness of the land.

Verses 5 and 6 remind the reader of the Pentateuch and the references to the "glory" of the Lord. These are the manifestations of the presence of God that both hide and reveal God.

A Parable with Purpose (Isa. 5:1–30)

The passage.—On the occasion of a festival the prophet publicly sang a song, as would a minstrel. The song concerned a vineyard owned by a friend. The friend had given the utmost care to the vineyard. It had been cleared, fenced,

planted with choice vines, and even equipped with a permanent watchtower. Everything indicated that this was to be a permanent installation. But at the time of harvest it yielded bad fruit.

What should be done with such a vineyard? It was left to itself, abandoned to its own fate.

The identification is made clear in verse 7: the vineyard was Israel, God was the friend. The nation had not produced.

He then followed with a series of six woes or laments. The woes pronounced against greed (vv. 8–10), drunkenness (vv. 11–12), skepticism (vv. 18–19), moral blindness (v. 20), self-sufficiency (v. 21), and perversion of justice (vv. 22–23) tell Israel's story. The cause is the rottenness at the root in forsaking the law of God.

A tragic result will follow. In fact, the prophet spoke of it as already having happened, so certain would judgment be. An unnamed foreign foe would be the instrument of God's judgment.

Special points.—The parable is used as an attention-gaining device. Not often in the Old Testament is a parable used. But in each case, it drove home the intended lesson.

It is somewhat unusual for Isaiah to use such a familiar term as "well-beloved" for God. He did not identify God as the friend of whom he spoke until he applied the parable to the listeners.

In the original there is a play on the words "justice . . . bloodshed" and "righteousness . . . cry" in verse 7 (RSV). They are words that sound very similar but have vastly different meanings.

A woe is a lament, almost a sound of anguish. Each of the woes is for a reason: a breakdown of relationships.

Truth for today.—The parable sounds so contemporary as to be almost shock-

16. A watchtower in the hill country of Palestine
(see Isa. 5:2)

ing. Surely God has lavished abundant care and blessings upon us. But what has been the return? We have not acted in ways consistent with his nature nor have we developed character that conforms to his will. We cannot ignore God with impunity. What is sowed must also be reaped. This is a law of nature that has a distinctly spiritual application.

Judgment may come by simply abandoning us to our own devices and desires. Or judgment may come in unexpected and unacknowledged ways. God has his own way.

And what of the woes? If there were things that caused God's displeasure in Isaiah's day, we can be sure they are displeasing to him now. God's character has not changed. Oppression, rapacity,

injustice, arrogance, and self-sufficiency bring their own results. They carry with them the seeds of destruction. Perhaps God would again like to penetrate our preoccupation with a lesson for us to hear.

A Commissioning Call (Isa. 6:1–13)

The passage.—At some event in the Temple, either in a public worship service or in private prayer, in the year of King Uzziah's death (742 B.C.), Isaiah had a life-changing vision of God. Likely the death of Uzziah was a traumatic experience in the life of the young Isaiah. While in the Temple the physical surroundings faded into the background and Isaiah had an encounter with God.

He had a new consciousness of God.

393

He saw God as sovereign over all the world. His majesty filled the place as though royal robes had filled the Temple. Created creatures were present to serve him. In reverence, humility, and service the seraphim stood in his presence. In antiphonal singing they expressed the holiness of God.

Struck by his own sinfulness Isaiah confessed his sin before the holy God. From the altar one of the seraphim took a coal to touch it to his lips signifying his forgiveness.

Having been forgiven of sin, Isaiah made a commitment of his life to God. Upon hearing the question, "Whom shall I send, and who will go for us?" he quickly answered, "Here am I; send me" (v. 8).

With Isaiah's commitment came a commission from God. He commanded him to go and he gave the prophet a message. The message is presented from the standpoint of its inevitable result. It was not the purpose of the message to make the people unrepentant; because of the people's sinfulness it was known that this would be the result.

How long was he to minister? To the very end. Even until a time of devastation and destruction he was to be faithful in announcing God's word.

But it would not all be fruitless. A remnant (v. 13) would remain. From the stump of the fallen nation would come the seeds of new life. There was always hope when God was at work.

Special points.—While some interpreters consider the reference to King Uzziah's death (v. 1) simply a method of dating the experience, most understand it to indicate a shattering experience for Isaiah. In his grief he went to the Temple and there saw God.

Why should Isaiah be so conscious that his lips were unclean (v. 5)? Perhaps it is because of his responsibility as a spokesman for God. Perhaps, too, it is because promises are broken and covenants are renounced with the mouth.

Only in this passage are seraphim mentioned in the Bible. They are pictured as living creatures who were attendants of God. Their real significance may be in what they conveyed by the use of their three pairs of wings: reverence, humility, and service.

The remnant (v. 13) became a prominent part of Isaiah's message. Some who were faithful to God would remain to serve and worship him.

Truth for today.—When do we encounter God? For many people their most realistic experience with God has been in a time of deep personal need when they threw themselves completely on God. It is not just at the crisis times that God approaches us, but at those times we are often most receptive to him.

At any time that we become conscious of God in his holiness and glory we become aware of our own unworthiness. The purity of God convicts us of our uncleanness.

With every confession of sin and plea for forgiveness God gives purification. Sin is drastic and must be dealt with drastically. But God answers in forgiving grace.

Concern for others is a result of encountering God and experiencing forgiveness. We must share what we have felt.

Others may not always be receptive to our message. Faithfulness is our responsibility. The results are God's business.

An Encounter with the King (Isa. 7:1–25)

The passage.—At a time of national crisis Isaiah confronted King Ahaz while he was inspecting the defenses. The kings of Syria and Israel had formed an alliance against the king of Assyria.

Ahaz had refused to join the alliance and they were preparing to attack him. He was frightened and about to panic.

With Isaiah was his son, Shear-jashub, whose name meant "a remnant shall return." The presence of the child was a living prophecy.

Isaiah counseled Ahaz to be calm, to stand firm, and to have faith in God. His salvation would come from God, not from military alliances formed in panic.

Isaiah went on to state that the objects of his fear were already burned out. In but a few years they would no longer be threats.

Then, either in a continuation of that encounter or at a later date, he challenged the king to ask a sign from God to prove his truthfulness. Feigning a piosity which he did not possess Ahaz refused to put the Lord to the test.

So Isaiah gave him a sign. A young woman known to both of them would conceive and bear a son whose name would be Immanuel, which means "God with us." He would be a symbol of the presence of God and the truthfulness of the prophecy. Before he reached young manhood the feared kings would be destroyed.

Christians recognize that this sign finds its ultimate fulfilment in Jesus Christ.

Then Isaiah followed this with four threats introduced by the words "in that day." They tell of invasion and ruin.

Special points.—Since his son was able to accompany him, Isaiah had earlier named the boy Shear-jashub. His presence would be both a threat and a promise.

The word translated "virgin" in the KJV and "young woman" in the RSV in verse 14 means "a young woman of marriageable age." Since the sign was given to Ahaz, apparently Isaiah ex-

pected it to occur during their lifetime. Otherwise it would have little meaning to the king.

Christians have been convinced that this prophecy was fulfilled in Jesus Christ. While there may have been an immediate fulfilment, its ultimate fulfilment was in the birth of the Savior. Matthew 1:23 quoted the Greek version of the Old Testament to substantiate the virgin birth of Jesus.

The Davidic kingdom of which Ahaz was the king was unfaithful to God. But a new Davidic kingdom would at sometime be established, a kingdom of faith.

Truth for today.—Faith, not fear, is to be the response of the Christian. In the face of overwhelming problems deliverance does not come through panicked actions, but through faith in God.

The promise of Immanuel, "God with us," strengthens the believer. God is with us in Jesus even to the "end of the age."

Further Signs and Symbols (Isa. 8:1–22)

The passage.—Before two witnesses the prophet wrote the words "Belonging to Maher-shalal-hashbaz" on a large piece of wood in letters that all could read. Later at the birth of his second son the child was given the same name which means "spoil speeds, prey hastens." The sign and the boy's name were signs of God's message: Syria and Israel would be destroyed. It would be done even before the child could talk.

The symbol of water was used to convey a similar thought. Judah had rejected the quiet waters of Shiloah that flowed into a pool in Jerusalem. Assyria would be as a river in flood that swept them before it.

God was the only source of strength. They should have feared him; instead they refused his counsel.

Isaiah retired for awhile from public life (vv. 16–18). He was to wait patiently on God while the names of him and his children would be signs of God's presence in Jerusalem.

The awful results of people turning from faith in God to superstition are shown. After the Assyrian invasion the people would know keep distress.

Special points.—This chapter refers to the same political crisis as chapter 7. Ahaz did not heed Isaiah's counsel. Instead he formed a coalition with the king of Assyria.

In verses 1–8 the previous theme of the doom of Syria and Israel was repeated. The difference is that he named the invading conqueror: Assyria.

Possibly in the time of withdrawal mentioned in verses 16–18, Isaiah began to write these autobiographical sections.

Truth for today.—Faith in God may be the dividing factor between people. Those who trust in God separate themselves into a community of belief. This differs from the superstitions that attract the attention of so many. Waiting on God becomes the test of obedience.

A Promise of a Delivering King (Isa. 9: 1–7)

The passage.—An abrupt shift takes place between the gloom of 8:22 and the light of 9:1. A promise is given of the return of lands that had been humiliated by capture by the Assyrians. Verse 1 is the prose introduction to the well-loved prophetic poem of verses 2–7.

Great joy is described (vv. 2–3). People who had known oppression and occupation have been transformed into people who know joy as the joy of a successful and fruitful harvest.

The reason for the joy is found in verses 4–6. Each of the verses begin with the word "for." The transformation has come about because the yoke of the oppressor was broken, because the military garments were destroyed,

but mainly because of the birth of a child.

The child is the deliverer. Cast as a king in whom God has placed his strength and power this one shall inaugurate a reign of peace and plenty.

Four descriptive names are given to the promised king. The first two, Wonderful Counselor (RSV) and Mighty God, deal with the character of the king. The second two, Everlasting Father and Prince of Peace, refer to the character of his reign. Wisdom, power, concerned care, and peace will mark this promised deliverer.

He is promised a permanent reign of justice and righteousness. It is possible through the zealous activity of the Lord.

Who is this king? In the end it can only be Jesus Christ. He alone fulfils these expectations. This could well be an expansion of the suggestion first made in 7:14. Possibly it was originally used at the coronation of a new king. But Christians see its ultimate fulfilment in Christ, the king.

Special points.—Some interpreters consider verse 1 to be related to 8:21–22. It is considered here to be a prose introduction to the poem.

The "day of Midian" (v. 4) refers to the victory of Gideon in the Midianite invasion (Judg. 7). Again a victory for God would be enjoyed with even the garments of war destroyed.

The people of Judah rested in the promise that a descendant of David would sit on their throne forever. This hope was directed to the messianic hope, that God would send the Messiah to rule. This passage is an affirmation of the ideal Davidic king, the Messiah.

Truth for today.—In the coming of Jesus Christ we have been given the one who fully meets the characteristics of God's deliverer. His wisdom, power, concern, and peace have been demonstrated to all.

His kingdom is not a kingdom of the world but a kingdom of the heart entered by faith in him. It is a kingdom without end.

However originally used, these words bring joy and light to the lives of Christians. God has fulfilled his promise in the birth of a child.

Words of Warning (Isa. 9:8—10:4)

The passage.—Three passages of doom and warning against the Northern Kingdom are given. These are followed by a similar warning to Judah to heed the experience of their northern counterparts. Each ends with the same refrain (9:12,17,21; 10:4).

The people had not profited from the chastening given because of their sins. The destructive power of evil that devours as a fire and turns brother against brother is mentioned (vv. 18–21).

Surely this would serve as a warning to Judah. In 10:3 the prophet addressed three questions to those who had been oppressive. But he did not wait for an answer. There would be no place to hide from God.

Special points.—The "word" (9:8) is the prophetic word. It is a word of judgment upon Israel.

"My people" in 10:2 indicates that the prophet has turned to Judah in his thinking.

An Instrument of God (Isa. 10:5–34)

The passage.—Isaiah described Assyria as the rod of God's anger. He could hardly imagine a kingdom becoming so powerful or lasting so long without the decree of God. Assyria was understood as the instrument used by God for judgment upon his people.

But the king of Assyria did not understand it in that light. He considered his success due to his own cunning power. He had no intention of being an agent of God.

However, an agent of God he was. In verse 12 and verses 15–19 it is clear that he was used only as God allowed him. The ax is not greater than the man who wields it; the king of Assyria was not greater than God.

A remnant of people faithful to God would return. They did not trust their military might but placed their faith in God.

The Assyrian army is shown advancing toward Jerusalem. The cities are named in order of their distance from Jerusalem until they overlook the city itself. That is far enough. As a forester clears the forest, God would remove the Assyrian.

Special points.—"The rod of my anger" (v. 5) refers to Assyria as the instrument of God's judgment. While God is described as showing human emotion, it is not to be considered capricious. These are ways of describing God's displeasure against rebellious sin. He acts within his redemptive purpose.

Truth for today.—The prophetic view of history is presented in this passage. People can be used for the purposes of God even when they are unaware of it. That the unrighteous one was being used by God did not make him righteous. God's judgment was being expressed.

It all is under the control of God. History has a purpose. And God is in sovereign control of that purpose. Our hope lies in finding God's purpose.

God's Messiah and His Work (Isa. 11: 1–16)

The passage.—From the stump that represented the Davidic line of kingship would come a new shoot, a new growth. This new king would be empowered with God's spirit. His reign would be just and peaceful.

Three pairs of characteristics would mark him. They denote his intellectual, practical, and religious strength. He would operate with a reverential awe, a fear, of the Lord. His judgments would be fair and righteous. Hearsay and appearances would not alter his decision.

All of creation would benefit from his peaceful reign. Even the natural enemies of the animal world would be at peace. A child could safely play among the most dangerous snakes. So safe would they be that a small child could serve as a shepherd to them.

The reason for this peaceful transformation is that the knowledge of God would cover the earth as waters would blanket a sea.

Like a flag flying high above the crowd the promised one of God would rally the people around him. His appeal would not simply be to the Israelites, but all the people of the world would come to him.

The exiled from Israel would return. From all over the known world they would return by way of a highway constructed for them. In peace they would dwell together. Through his Messiah God's rule would be known throughout the earth.

When would this come about? Obviously it would be realized only during the reign of God's promised deliverer, the Messiah. This passage should likely be linked with 7:14 and 9:6–7. The full realization of it can only be in Jesus Christ, our Lord. Only as Christ rules in the hearts of men can God's perfect kingdom be known. Possibly, however, the passage was first composed when a new king came to the throne. With each new king came new hope. But these hopes were constantly crushed. Only in Christ are these hopes realized.

Special points.—The "stump of Jesse" (RSV) and the "root of Jesse" refer to the Davidic line of kings. Jesse was David's father. The messianic hope centered in a descendant of David.

In the Old Testament "the Spirit of the Lord" (v. 3) is spasmodic and special. It is understood as the power of God given to a person for a specific task. Often it was understood as only for a limited time. It is the empowering of the promised king by God's spirit that enabled him to have the necessary characteristics for the reign of peace.

The "fear of the Lord" (v. 3) is not a craven fear of God. It is the reverential awe that one has in the presence of God. Both the "fear of the Lord" and the "knowledge of the Lord" (v. 9) have to do with piety or religion. It is the knowledge of God derived from experience with him.

The "ensign" (vv. 10 and 12) is a standard or a flag raised for all to see. It is the Messiah.

Truth for today.—How we long for peace in our day. But the efforts for peace all seem to be directed in the wrong directions.

Real peace comes only as the Prince of Peace comes to dwell in the lives of people. Only as the reign of God through Jesus Christ is realized in human lives will the desire for peace be realized in human experience.

The perfectness and the extent of this peace seem to be fanciful expressions. Dreams and visions are not limited by the confines of our experience. As all of God's creation has been touched by the wickedness of man, destroying not only human relationships but also God's good earth, so the peace of God can reach to all of God's creation. When all are at peace with God and with one another there is no limit to its healing effects.

Rallying around the flag of God's grace as known in Jesus Christ we can have peace through him whom God has sent.

A Song of Salvation (Isa. 12:1–6)

The passage.—Following the thrilling description of the Messiah and his work is a song of salvation. Faith in God has always provided joy for the believer.

After the Exodus the people of Israel sang a song of deliverance (Ex. 15: 1–18). A new exodus, a new deliverance, is expressed at the hands of God's great deliverer. This, too, brings forth a song of praise.

The song centers in the activity of God. It is God who has delivered; he has provided salvation.

From the deliverance of God comes great joy. This is a joy that cannot be silenced. It is expressed in praise to God.

The praise to God becomes a witness of God to all the nations. God is great in his activity on behalf of his people; and all must know it.

Special points.—This chapter ends a major section of the book of Isaiah. It is significant that the section closes with a song of praise. Throughout the section the prophet has expressed faith in the ultimate victory of God. Judgment may be necessary; but in the end God will be victorious.

"In that day" (v. 1) is a reference to the day of God's activity, the time that God would act to bring about his will.

The "Holy One of Israel" is one of Isaiah's favorite designations of God. It emphasizes the holy character of God. Since God is holy those who believe on him and serve him are to be holy too.

The metaphor of the "wells of salvation" in verse 3 is very interesting. In a land where people were dependent on wells for water the wells were important. God makes provision for our salvation.

Truth for today.—A recovery of joy is imperative. Right standing with God produces the greatest joy. God has richly provided salvation and sustenance for us. Our praise should express our joy in him.

Babylon's Doom (Isa. 13:1–22)

The passage.—The prophet was not only concerned with Judah but with the surrounding nations as well. In chapter 13 he pronounced a terrible doom on Babylon.

God is pictured as personally leading the forces in battle against the Babylonians. He gathered the armies together. He prepared them for battle.

The day of the Lord would dawn as a day of judgment against the enemies of God's will. The destruction would be complete and terrible. All of creation is seen as suffering from these decisive acts.

The Medes are identified (v. 17) as the instruments of God's judgment against Babylon. So complete would be the devastation that Babylon would remain uninhabited.

Special points.—Chapters 13 through 23 deal with prophecies concerned with foreign nations. Many of them begin with the designation "The burden of . . ." (KJV) or "The oracle concerning . . ." (RSV). Such an "oracle" or "burden" announced doom to a people.

Because of its content many interpreters consider this section to be very late in its composition.

The "day of the Lord" (v. 9) was the day of God's decisive activity. The people of Israel considered it to be a time of the vindication of God and the victory of God over his enemies. Their enemies were considered God's enemies.

Truth for today.—Can these passages of doom for ancient enemies have any meaning for us today? Yes, indeed.

They show us that God is not narrowly concerned with one nation. His interest and his active intervention reach to all the nations of the world. God is the sovereign ruler of all the world.

All history is in the hand of God. It has a destination; God is at work in it.

Warnings of God's Judgment (Isa. 14:1–32)

The passage.—God's choice of Israel once again is expressed in 14:1–4. A great reversal would take place. Those who had been the slaves would become the captors.

Following this is a taunt, a mocking, ironic statement, against the king of Babylon. Not only would Babylon fall, as was asserted in chapter 13, but the king would suffer an ignominious downfall himself. From the pinnacle of power to the depth of degradation with burial in a common grave on a battlefield would he fall. People would wonder how they had once feared this one who then lay crushed by the power of God.

Not only Babylon, but also Assyria would fall. God's purpose would not find its fulfilment in Assyria (vv. 24–27). His purpose for them was destruction.

Philistia is also warned (vv. 28–32). They may have found temporary relief from oppression, but it would only be temporary. From the north still would come destruction. Relief is found only in the place of the Lord.

Special points.—A prose introduction (vv. 1–4) and conclusion (vv. 22–23) are features of the poem that deals with the downfall of the Babylonian king.

"Sheol" (v. 9, RSV) is a reference to the abode of the dead. It is a common

expression in the Old Testament and actually carries no connotation of either blessedness or punishment. The "pit" (v. 19) is a common grave on a battlefield.

The reference to the death of King Ahaz (v. 28) is for dating. The Philistine cities on the Mediterranean seacoast did revolt briefly against the power of Assyria but were ultimately crushed.

Truth for today.—Pride always falls before the presence of God. The once mighty conqueror of a portion of the world could be brought to humility by death. We live by God's grace.

The Doom of Moab (Isa. 15:1–9)

The passage.—The area of Moab was located just to the east of the Dead Sea. For some time it had independent existence. At other times it was a vassal state to Israel or to other stronger nations.

This passage is a lament over the destruction of Moab. It is not known what caused the destruction. But the destruction seemed to be both swift and comprehensive. The people have suffered. They clog the roads as refugees. Even the land was made desolate. It is a picture of despair.

Practically all the known settlements of Moab are mentioned and even some of these locations are uncertain. In general the locations are listed from south to north which may, or may not, indicate that the destructive force came from the south.

Special points.—The date and the cause for this passage are very uncertain. Moab is seen to be in deep distress.

The Appeal of Moab (Isa. 16:1–14)

The passage.—The first five verses voice an appeal of the people of Moab for refuge in Judah. They offer a gift of lambs as a part of their appeal. They even assert that if mercy is shown to them the perfect Davidic kingship would be more completely established.

But the appeal is rejected. Moab had once stood in arrogant pride. Now the nation would know sorrowful despair.

A picture of the complete destruction of vineyards (vv. 6–11) indicates that the "pride of Moab" may have been in its wine. Continual prayers offered to their god (v. 12) will avail nothing.

Just as at some former date Moab's prayer for deliverance was not answered so would it not be answered in that time of difficulty (vv. 13–14).

Special points.—"Sela" is in Edom. From there the refugees appeal to Judah.

The "battle shout" (RSV) of verse 9 is contrasted with the usual vintage shout during harvest.

The Doom of an Alliance and Idolaters (Isa. 17:1–14)

The passage.—The alliance between Syria and Israel that occurred late in the eighth century B.C. was doomed. They could not hope to stand against the strength of Assyria. It is explicit (vv. 1–6): the destruction will be as thorough as a harvest. Only the gleanings would be left of these people.

For that matter Assyria would also feel the rebuking power of God. While not named (v. 12–14) it is assumed that Assyria is the enemy in view. They roared; but they would be quieted.

Interspersed (vv. 7–11) is a statement against idolaters. The altars constructed by their own hands and the plants used in some pagan worship rites would bring no peace. Deliverance is from God alone.

Special points.—The "pleasant plants" (v. 10) refer to a fertility diety. Contrast the "Rock of your refuge" (RSV).

A Message to Ethiopia (Isa. 18:1–14)

The passage.—A group of envoys from Ethiopia approached the king of Judah (probably Hezekiah) seeking an alliance. Likely they were attempting to enlist allies to revolt against Assyria.

To these tall people with smooth, glossy skins Isaiah replied that God was watching the situation. When he was ready for the power of Assyria to be broken he would move as in a harvest. With a pruning hook of judgment he would lop off those offending people and they would be left to destruction. God was watching and waiting.

Then (v. 7) these same people would come to give tribute to God. To Mount Zion where God was honored they would come to honor the deliverer.

Special points.—The "whirring wings" is probably a reference to the swarming insects of the Nile Valley.

"Tall and smooth" is their physical appearance.

The Doom of Egypt (Isa. 19:1–25)

The Passage.—Since an Ethiopian dynasty ruled Egypt in the late eighth century, Isaiah turned from the reception of the Ethiopian ambassadors to Egypt. In both poetic (vv. 1–15) and prose (vv. 16–25) statements he foresaw the doom of Egypt.

Egypt suffered from both natural calamities and civil disorders. They would turn to magic and sorcery, but this would avail nothing. In the end a fierce dictator (v. 4) would rule. Their vaunted wise men would fail.

All of this is seen as coming from the hand of God. God could use military power, natural calamities, and civil disorders as his instruments.

The pronouncement of doom is followed by a statement of international understanding and goodwill. Both Egypt

and Assyria are shown as converting to
God. With spiritual unity there would
come peace. Israel was seen as fulfilling
its purpose of ministry in the world.

Special points.—God's active concern
with the affairs of nations is described
with the words "the Lord is riding on a
swift cloud" (v. 1). To Egypt God would
come in judgment.

Notice (v. 22) that the smiting of
Egypt has the purpose of the healing of
Egypt. God's judgment is not solely for
destruction; it is basically for salvation.

Israel was described as "a blessing in
the midst of the earth" (v. 25). Originally God had called these people to
serve as a blessing in the world (cf. Gen.
12:1–3), but too often they had failed.
When God's people perform their ministry, God's blessings are known in the
world.

Truth for today.—International peace
and understanding seem to be elusive
dreams. They have a spiritual basis.
When God is acknowledged and worshiped, people can have a unity of faith.
God's people have to be the instruments
of God's peace.

An Enacted Parable (Isa. 20:1–6)

The passage.—The alliance promoted
by the Ethiopian dynasty of Egypt revolted against Assyria in 714–711 B.C.
The center of the revolt was the Philistine city of Ashdod on the Mediterranean coast.

To show the futility of dependence on
Egypt Isaiah removed his shoes and
outer garments and walked around barefoot and in a slave's loincloth for three
years. Every time he was seen he was
giving eloquent testimony that the revolt was doomed and that Egypt was
undependable. These people would be
led away as naked slaves.

Apparently Judah did not join the
alliance. Isaiah's influence may have had

something to do with their refusal. Isaiah's enacted parable was not wasted on
the others, however.

Special points.—The "Tartan" (v. 1)
was the Assyrian commander-in-chief.
It was a title rather than a name.

The "isle" (KJV) was a "coastland"
(RSV).

The Fall of Babylon (Isa. 21:1–17)

The passage.—The prophet had a
"stern vision" of the fall of Babylon. He
set himself as a watchman but the only
result he saw was that of a defeated
people.

He was appalled at the destruction.
It seems that they had been busy eating
and drinking and the conquering force
had come upon them unaware.

His vision then shifted toward the
Arabian peninsula. Likely the same ones
who had struck against Babylon had also
struck against the trade routes that
crossed Arabia.

Edom was a neighboring nation south
of the Dead Sea. Even though Dumah
was the name of an Ishmaelite tribe, the
word of doom seems to be directed to
Edom. Morning followed night, then
night again. There was no relief from
their night of doom.

And it was no better for the people
of Arabia. They would know the terror
of oppression.

Premature Rejoicing (Isa. 22:1–25)

The passage.—The occasion for the
great rejoicing in Jerusalem is not definitely known. Likely it was the deliverance of Jerusalem from the hand of
Sennacherib in 701 B.C. or possibly the
escape of Jerusalem from any retribution in the crushing of Ashdod in 711
B.C.

At any rate Isaiah was upset by the
reaction of the people. They had done
nothing of which to be proud. Rather

than depending on God they had strengthened their defenses and checked the water supply. Feasting and merriment were not what they needed. Humility and repentance should have been their stance.

Shebna, the steward (vv. 15–25), had displayed unbecoming ambition. He was to be deposed and replaced by Eliakim. Eliakim would serve well. But he seems to have been removed from office too (v. 25).

Special points.—The "valley of vision" is not identifiable. It seems to have been a place where Isaiah had a vision.

The Doom of Tyre (Isa. 23:1–18)

The passage.—Tyre was the capital city of the Phoenicians. Their ships plied the Mediterranean, trading in many ports.

The glory of Tyre and Sidon would not last. They would return to discover that they had no home port to which to go. This judgment, too, would come from the hand of God. No nation was outside the active interest of the Holy One of Israel.

For a period of seventy years the importance and trade of Tyre would diminish. After that time she would be back to her old trade again. Like an old harlot seeking admirers, the Phoenicians would seek trading rights again. As before, they would prostitute everything for commercial gain.

But there is a difference. Tyre would have come to know God. Their profits would go to his glory.

Special points.—The seventy years is a period of exile and punishment.

The Desolation of the Earth (Isa. 24:1–23)

The passage.—The judgment of God upon the world is presented in vivid

terms. Judgment has come because of sin; man's sin has polluted the whole world.

No one will be able to escape this judgment. Regardless of position and rank all people will feel its effects. Cities will be reduced to rubbish. Festivities will cease; there is no cause for joy.

Yet there is hope. A remnant of those faithful to God will remain (v. 13). Lest those who are God's faithful remnant rejoice too quickly (vv. 14–16), the prophet reminds them that woe still follows.

A scene of God's great judgment day (vv. 21–23) closes the chapter. God will reign in his city and will judge all the world.

Special points.—Chapters 24—27 form a collection of prophecies dealing with the last days. The themes of judgment and God's reign run through them.

It is very difficult to date these passages. Most interpreters consider them to be a collection of prophecies on a common theme given over a period of time.

The "city of chaos" (v. 10, RSV) is not identified. It could be every city. As a result of God's complete judgment there would be chaos in every city.

Verse 13 suggests the remnant. In "that day" or the "day of the Lord" when God acts decisively there is a twofold aspect: judgment and salvation. God does not move in judgment without at the same time giving opportunity for salvation.

Verses 21–23 points to the new age. The golden age of God's complete reign figures in these passages.

Truth for today.—Judgment is a legitimate aspect of God's character. Since God is holy and righteous, he has certain demands that must be met.

Sin pollutes people as well as the earth. Sin cannot go on unchecked.

Yet the judgment of God is not simply negative; his desire is to save.

A Hymn of Thanksgiving (Isa. 25:1–12)

The passage.—Apparently at the overthrow of an enemy city (v. 2) a hymn of praise and thanksgiving is offered to God.

It is God who has done mighty things and has given refuge to his people.

Looking toward the messianic golden age God will spread a feast for his people. It will apply to all people, all the redeemed of the world. The things that frighten men, death and sorrow, will be abolished. God bestows the good things of his grace.

Moab is singled out as one of the enemies of God's people that will be destroyed. In the figure of a man struggling for his life in a pit of dung, Moab's destruction is asserted.

Special points.—It is not definitely known which city is mentioned in verse 2. It could be any enemy city.

Verses 6–8 reflect the Jewish belief in a great messianic feast in the times of God's reign. The universality of God's grace is affirmed, for "all peoples" will be a part of the feast.

The abolition of death (v. 8) is a striking feature. In the Old Testament the idea of a future life developed late. With the resurrection of Jesus Christ this becomes a sure hope for the Christian.

Notice that verse 9 posits salvation in God alone. God's people are delivered by God's action.

The "mountain" (vv. 6,10) carries us back to the place of God's ultimate reign: Mount Zion in Jerusalem (see 25:21–23).

Truth for today.—In these times when men are extremely well impressed with their progress and abilities, we must remember the source of salvation. Salvation comes from God.

The deliverance that God gives to us through Jesus Christ removes the haunting fears from our lives and bestows upon us God's grace and strength. We surely enjoy the richness of God's blessings when he rules in our lives.

A Psalm of Praise (Isa. 26:1–21)

The passage.—That salvation has come from God is expressed in the song composed to be sung by all of Judah. Perfect peace can come only to the mind guarded by God.

God gives guidance to those who follow him. They can even have the assurance of life at the hand of God, whose grace is like the dew that covers the dust.

Special points.—The definition of faith as trust, reliance on God, commitment to God is expressed in verses 3–4.

One of the clearest expressions of belief in the resurrection of the body in the Old Testament is found in verse 19. This is the first occurrence in the Old Testament of a belief in resurrection.

Truth for today.—Peace of mind is found in trust in God. A search for wholeness in life ends with commitment to the Lord of life. God keeps guard over the one who trusts in him.

A Song of a Vineyard (Isa. 27:1–13)

The passage.—God will be victorious over all the forces of evil as symbolized by the monster.

Israel has indeed known the care of God. Like a carefully kept vineyard, God's people have experienced his care.

Then why have they suffered so much? The suffering is for the removal of their sins. Those who have mistreated the people of God, even though they were used in this manner as God's instruments, will ultimately know desolation.

As a great homecoming the people of

God will be gathered to him to share his reign. From all over the world they will come to worship God.

Special points.—The reference to Leviathan (v. 1) is symbolic of all the forces of evil. It originally meant a many-headed sea monster.

The parable of the vineyard is also mentioned in 5:1–7. Here it is reversed. God has shown great care for it.

An Inadequate Alliance (Isa. 28:1–29)

The passage.—Beginning with an older message that had originally been delivered to Israel before the fall of Samaria, the prophet warns against foolish actions.

Samaria, a city on a hill, was compared to the garlands around the head of a reveler. But the flowers faded and fell at the hand of God's judgment. Like an early ripened fig that was eaten whole, the city was consumed.

A reference to the remnant (vv. 5–6) connects the older prophetic utterance against Israel to its present application for Judah. God will have a remnant. But look at his remnant at that time!

The leaders, both political and religious, reel drunkenly. Their celebrating has left no room for the celebration of worship. Mockingly they ask the prophet if he would teach them lessons as a child would be taught. They would be taught all right. If they could not learn them in Hebrew, they would learn them in a foreign tongue. The word of the Lord would be heard.

They had made an alliance. It was not really a covenant for life as they thought but rather a covenant with death. It was as insufficient for deliverance as sleeping on a short bed with narrow covers would be insufficient for rest. Faith in God would be their only refuge.

A parable of a farmer tells them how they should react at that time. The farmer acts purposively. So does God. They should use the same discernment.

Special points.—Chapters 28 through 33 contain a series of "woes." They are usually dated *c.* 705–701 B.C. A crisis had arisen following the death of the king of Assyria. Hezekiah, the king of Judah, joined in resistance against Assyria. Eventually an alliance was made with Egypt. Hezekiah had refused to do this in a previous crisis. And Isaiah counseled against it in that crisis. Throughout this section is Isaiah's repeated word: only faith in God would save.

In verses 1–6 notice the contrast between the crown of faded flowers that was Samaria and the crown of glory that was God.

The "covenant with death" (v. 15) may have had reference to the name of a Cananaite diety of infertility; it could also imply the result of the covenant with other nations: death.

Verse 16 indicates that the relationship between God and his people should be one of trust.

A parable is found in verses 23–29. Appropriate actions need to be taken at appropriate times both by the farmer and the faithful.

Truth for today.—From whence comes security? We have run around from place to place and fad to fad in an attempt to find security for life. All the time it is found in faith in God. When it comes down to the end, all the external grasps at security are insufficient, like short beds and narrow covers.

When God Delivers (Isa. 29:1–24)

The passage.—Before he captured the Jebusite city that became Jerusalem, David laid siege to it. Looking back to this experience, it is indicated that siege would once more be experienced by Jerusalem. But then God would deliver.

Her enemies would be like dust; they would be blown away like the chaff.

The people had deluded themselves (vv. 9–14). They would not understand the prophetic word that had been given to them. Practicing a formal religion they had not given themselves to God. But nothing that is done, even the forming of alliances, can be hid from God (vv. 15–16).

In his own time God would act to deliver his people. Their handicaps would be removed. They would praise God.

Special points.—"Ariel" was a pre-Israelite name for Jerusalem. It is probably used as a play on the word for "altar stone."

The people were in such a spiritual stupor that the word of the Lord through the prophet was as a "book that is sealed."

Verse 17 shows a tremendous change. Lebanon, known for its forests, would be turned into a garden; the garden would be turned into a forest.

Truth for today.—Faith in God is a matter of heartfelt commitment to him. Some may be able to repeat the right words and appear at the right places but have no real, heart knowledge of God. There is a distinction between an intellectual knowledge and a knowledge growing out of an experience with God.

It is only when God is known with the heart as well as the mind, when his word is a part of the life as well as the lips, that the ways of God can be known.

Spiritual insecurity is the result of spiritual stupor. Which way is God moving? We do not always know beforehand. When God begins to act we will be better able to discern it and to move with him if our hearts are aligned with him.

The Futility of Misplaced Faith (Isa. 30: 1–33)

The passage.—The embassy from Judah made its way into Egypt seeking an alliance. Isaiah made it clear that their plan was not God's plan. What they were doing was both bad politics and bad religion. Egypt would be no more help than a shadow. She was as helpless as a monster sitting still. Only God had strength.

Isaiah was led by God to write his teachings. The rebellious people had not heeded them; they wanted more pleasing words. But their wall was about to tumble on them.

God does not just deal in judgment. Again (vv. 18–28) it is expressed that God is gracious. He waits on them to turn to him. He has the way; they need to walk in it.

The chapter closes with the assurance of the destruction of the Assyrians.

Special points.—"Rahab" (v. 7) is the monster earlier called Leviathan. Here it is a powerless force.

They were interested in horses (vv. 16–17). With a note of irony Isaiah told them they would need fast horses to carry them in retreat.

"Tophet" (KJV) or "the burning place" (RSV) of verse 33 is a reference to the practice of sacrificing children by fire. The Assyrian army is the victim.

Truth for today.—How often we have misplaced our trust. In panic we have turned to the nearest apparent source of strength. All the time God waits for us to turn to him. At any time that we turn to him in faith he receives us and treats us graciously.

Constantly we have to be reminded of the truth of the Holy One's message: "In returning and rest shall ye be saved; in quietness and confidence shall be your strength" (v. 15). And too often our report is the same: "And ye would not."

God has a way in which we should walk. It is the way of quiet confidence in God. Faith in him is not futile.

Whom Do You Trust? (Isa. 31:1–9)

The passage.—In another reference to the Egyptian alliance Isaiah pronounced shame upon those who went to Egypt for help. They were looking for help from the apparent sources: horses and chariots. Their real help would come from the spirit of God. He is wise, wiser than they, and when he acts things happen.

And act God will. Isaiah is assured that God will act to save Judah and Jerusalem. Using the metaphors of both a lion who will not be frightened away and a mother bird who protects her nest he showed that God would protect them.

In the day of God's activity they will discard their idols. It will then be apparent to them that they did not deliver. The Assyrian foe would fall, some from the sword and some from the sheer power of the spirit of God.

Special points.—Verse 2 has a rather ironic reference to the wisdom of God. They thought the Egyptians were wise and that they were wise in consulting them. But God is wise, too; he will bring judgment on their plans.

The summation of the source of power is so vivid in verse 3 that it has become one of the most familiar verses in Isaiah. The Egyptians could do only the things that men can do; God could do all that God can do.

The metaphors are mixed in verses 4 and 5, but the intent is plain: God would watch over and protect Jerusalem. Some interpreters see that God is fighting against Jerusalem in verse 4 and fighting for it in verse 5. It could be that both express God's protection.

Truth for today.—Whom do you trust? That becomes one of our most significant questions. We can trust human ability and military might. This may deliver from a present crisis but it will not give ultimate deliverance.

The contrast between the power of God and the strength of men is apparent. The Lord does not stumble: he will uphold all.

The Results of Righteousness (Isa. 32:1–20)

The passage.—The prophet looked forward to the day of righteous rulers. He was convinced that if the leadership was righteous the effects would filter down to society. They could serve as God's protection to people in trouble. They would begin to think well and to plan nobly.

A warning was given to the women who frivolously danced at the harvest festival. In only a year there would be no cause for complacency. The crops would have failed and wild animals would graze in the fields.

But judgment is not the last word. The spirit of God would ultimately be poured out on the people. Then a great transformation would be known. Then the effects of righteousness could be enjoyed in the lives of the people.

Special points.—There are differences of interpretation of verses 1–8. This could be taken as a messianic passage. Then the king would be God's promised deliverer. It is more likely, though, that this passage is hypothetical rather than predictive. Here he is referring to what would happen in the life of the nation when a righteous ruler ascended the throne.

Verse 2 has four figures that express the protection of God.

The reference to the complacent women in verses 9–14 reminds one of the earlier reference to the court women of Jerusalem in 3:16—4:1. In this passage, the women are the celebrating women unmindful of the calamities at hand.

Notice (v. 15) the results in the life of a nation when the spirit of God is accepted.

Truth for today.—What can one man do? If it is true that righteousness filters down, it is also true that righteousness floats up. One man who practices righteousness can have a great effect on those around him. The noble person would think noble thoughts and devise noble deeds. With this example others would follow, good would result.

Deliverance from Distress (Isa. 33:1–24)

The passage.—At some unknown time an unspecified assailant, probably Assyria, moved against Jerusalem. They had acted treacherously. The indication is (vv. 7–9) that they had broken treaties and had devastated the land.

A prayer pleading for the graciousness of God in their time of distress is offered (vv. 2–4).

As an answer to the prayer there is an assertion of God's exaltation. He is the one who would deliver Jerusalem in its distress.

Truly it is God who delivers. "Now I will arise . . ." (v. 10, RSV), affirmed God. And when he moved all would know the power of the consuming fire of his judgment. Not only would the heathen feel it, but also the unrighteous in Judah.

Moving from this to the future Isaiah saw the ideal reign of God. There would be peace and forgiveness of sin. The streams would supply life-giving water,

not bring warships.

Special points.—The call to both the "far" and the "near" in verse 13 indicates that both the heathen and the unrighteous Jews would feel the fire of God's judgment.

Verses 14–16 are considered by many to be a liturgical dialogue. When the sinners in Judah fear, who could stand before God? The only ones who could stand before God would be those whose lives were pure.

Verse 23 is probably a continued reference to the unfriendly ship of verse 21. It is interrupted by a statement that God saves.

Observe in verse 24 the relationship between physical illness and the forgiveness of sin. Sin creates many problems.

Truth for today.—Who, indeed, "can dwell with the devouring fire?" (v. 14, RSV). The characteristics of the righteous man are sorely needed. God has never changed his standards of righteousness. Faith stands in the fire.

A Day of God's Judgment (Isa. 34:1–17)

The passage.—A call is issued to all the nations of the world to hear their sentence of judgment pronounced. Their sin had finally become all that God could stand and he is pictured striding forth as a vengeful warrior. As sacrificial animals are slain for the sacrifice, God would lay low those who had opposed him and his will. A bloody picture of slaughter is painted.

One nation, Edom, was chosen as representative of all the nations. Edom lay southeast of Judah and was an ancient enemy. At times they had dealt very treacherously with their Judean neighbors.

Following the statement of the outpouring of God's wrath is a scene of utter desolation (vv. 9–17). Here the land is utterly ruined. The cities are uninhabited. Where once people lived then the strangest collection of animals would be at home. This is destined in God's book; it is God's judgment.

Special points.—Chapters 34 and 35 go together. They express the related concepts of God's judgment and salvation. Either picture alone is incomplete.

Because of their style many interpreters date them later than the period under discussion. They feel that these chapters are more closely related to the material found in the latter part of Isaiah. However, much of this same sentiment had been expressed already.

In verse 1 the nations are summoned to the pronouncement of judgment. God's active interest is not confined to Judah alone. All the world exists under his rule.

The key to this activity is the "day of vengeance" mentioned in verse 8. This is the Day of the Lord. At this time God's actions and interests will be vindicated.

The completeness of God's judgment is seen in verse 12 when the site of a once powerful nation would be called "No Kingdom There" (RSV).

The main significance of the birds, animals, and demonic creatures in verses 14–15 is the expression of desolation. The demonic creatures were thought to inhabit uninhabited, ruined places.

That the destruction is the result of the decree of the Lord is apparent from verses 16–17. God had measured it out himself.

Truth for today.—The concept of the judgment of God has fallen into disrepute among many people. But God's judgment and salvation are related truths.

Never is the judgment of God presented as capricious and unprovoked. God always acts in ways consistent with his mercy and his grace. There are always repeated opportunities for repentance and return.

Rebellion and sin cannot go on unanswered. God is moral. And God is just. Something has to be done about the continued drift in sin. God would be less than himself if there were no judgment, no punishment for sin. Salvation is always present; it is God's desire. But some people will not accept it.

A Highway of Holiness (Isa. 35:1–10)

The passage.—From the dark picture of judgment the prophet turned to the light of God's salvation.

The salvation of God would be so complete that the very land would be transformed. Nature itself would take up the joyful refrain to God.

The people who had been weak and feeble would be strengthened. Those who had known physical disabilities would no longer be troubled by them. Even in desolate places God's transforming presence would be known.

A highway of holiness would be built. Upon this pilgrim's way those who have known God and have been cleansed by a relationship with him would move to God's new and perfect Jerusalem. It would be a safe journey. Free from the marauding animals God's redeemed would go to him.

Joy and gladness would be the result. Those who know God in redemption will have joy as the mark of their lives.

Special points.—The Day of the Lord is also a day of salvation. The prophet carried them to that day of God's perfect redemption and rule.

Lebanon, Carmel, and Sharon were places of luxuriant growth. The whole land would be that fertile.

In verse 4 "vengeance" refers to salvation. At this time the vindication of God is the salvation of God. He will come to save.

Notice that the highway of God is a holy way. Character counts.

Truth for today.—What a salvation it is that God offers! The redemption of God is so complete that it absolutely transforms. Men are made new when they know God in salvation.

The transforming experience with God makes all previous limitations seem insignificant. God acts in strength and power to those who come to him.

The redeemed are the people of God. They are to share in his character. Holiness marks God; those who walk with him are to be holy.

A Demand for Surrender (Isa. 36:1–22)

The passage.—In a historical narration the story of the attack on Jerusalem by Sennacherib, king of Assyria, is presented. The date was *c.* 701 B.C. The place of initial confrontation was the water conduit where Isaiah had confronted the king years before (see 7:3).

An Assyrian official, the Rabshakeh, met with Judean officials. The Assyrians demanded the surrender of Jerusalem. Tauntingly, he gave five arguments for surrender, all asked as rhetorical questions. The questions were: Do you think words are a substitute for military power? Do you think you can rely on Egypt, a broken reed? Do you rely on the Lord, all but one of whose altars for worship had been removed by the king? Can you repulse a single Assyrian company? What if the Lord had sent the Assyrians?

So telling were these questions that they asked him not to speak in Hebrew so that the people could not understand him. Instead he shouted the taunts in Hebrew, adding that no other nations had been delivered from them.

With torn clothes, the sign of mourn-

ing, the Hebrew officials reported the demand to King Hezekiah.

Special points.—Chapters 36 through 39 are historical. They relate the crisis presented by the invasion of the Assyrian king, Sennacherib. Similar material is found in 2 Kings 18–20. The date is generally considered to be *c.* 701 B.C.

Some interpreters think that this material contains references to two invasions by the Assyrians at different dates. Traditionally, it had been considered one invasion.

"Rabshakeh" is a title rather than a name. Apparently he was a civilian official who accompanied the army.

The three Hebrew officials were Eliakim, the prime minister, Shebna, rather a secretary of state, and Joah, a recorder or press secretary.

Psychological warfare is not new. So unnerving were the taunts of the Rabshakeh that he was asked to speak in "Syrian" (KJV) or "Aramaic" (RSV) which had become the language of diplomacy.

Apparently, too, he knew of the activities of both the king and Isaiah. He made references to the removal of all altars except the one in Jerusalem (v. 7) and to the possibility that the Assyrians might be acting as God's agents (v. 11).

Truth for today.—In more than one crisis has the taunting question of the reality of religious faith been asked.

If the Judeans had to determine whether they would trust in the frail support of Egypt or their faith in God, so have we many times had to decide where true faith would be placed. They could see the Egyptian horses and chariots; they could not see God.

How often have we talked like Christians and acted like materialistic worldlings? The proof of our faith is in our practice when we face the crisis.

An Amazing Deliverance (Isa. 37:1–38)

The passage.—Upon hearing the Assyrian demand for surrender, King Hezekiah assumed the stance of mourning and went to the Temple to pray. He also sent word to Isaiah asking him to pray for the people.

Isaiah's reply was that the king had no cause to fear Sennacherib. He would hear a rumor about an uprising and depart. He would die violently in his own land.

When it was learned that the Egyptians under their Ethiopian king were about to fight the Assyrians a letter was sent to Hezekiah. Again he was reminded that their gods had not delivered other nations and was advised to surrender.

This time Hezekiah took the letter to the Temple and laying it out before the Lord prayed for deliverance.

His answer came in a prophecy from Isaiah. The girls of Jerusalem were shown taunting the Assyrian king. He had mocked God. And he would exist no longer than God allowed. God would break him.

Further, the king was assured that by the third year life would be normal again. The king of Assyria would not shoot as much as one arrow into the city.

There was an amazing deliverance. The Assyrians were killed in some mysterious way in great numbers. The army left. Some time later Sennacherib was killed by his own son in his own land.

Special points.—It is interesting to observe the king who had earlier rejected Isaiah's words turn to him for help in their time of crisis. But he could not depend only on other's prayers; he prayed too.

The death of the Assyrian soldiers was attributed to "the angel of the Lord." How it happened is not indicated.

Truth for today.—The proper stance for the believer is repentance and prayer when faced by problems. We cannot expect a miraculous deliverance in every case. We can expect to find a strength, a comfort, and a guidance from God. This results in witness to God.

The Recovery of the King (Isa. 38:1–22)

The passage.—Hezekiah, the king, had become seriously ill. It was the duty of Isaiah to tell him that his sickness would be fatal.

This message distressed the king. With deep feeling he turned to the wall and prayed for recovery.

Then Isaiah had the happy honor of telling the king that he would recover from his illness. As a sign the shadow on the sundial would recede ten steps. He would have fifteen years more life. The last two verses of the chapter describe the medical treatment Isaiah gave him.

Hezekiah expressed his gratitude to God for his delivery by a psalm. The first part of the psalm described his plight in suffering. At the height of his life it looked as though he would be removed from life.

Then in the latter part of the psalm he gave praise for deliverance.

Special points.—There is some problem with the dating of this illness. Isaiah's account placed it during the crisis with Sennacherib. Some think that it should be placed at an earlier date in order to include all the years of Hezekiah's reign. It is difficult to date it with certainty.

The "dial" mentioned in verse 8 may not have been a traditional sundial. It may have been an architectural feature of the palace whereby the shadows caused by the sun were seen on steps.

Many interpreters consider the psalm (vv. 10–20) to be a liturgical psalm used in worship upon recovery from illness.

Truth for today.—We can easily identify with Hezekiah when faced with his own death. At times of severe illness we, too, call upon God in sincere prayer even when we do not normally spend much time in prayer.

Even though we do not usually receive the definite promise of further life we have a hope that he did not have—Jesus Christ. Christ has transformed death.

An Unwise Revelation (Isa. 39:1–8)

The passage.—At some time after Hezekiah's recovery from illness he received messengers from the king of Babylon, Merodach-baladan. Ostensibly, the embassy was to congratulate him upon his recovery. Actually, they had come to attempt to enlist Hezekiah in military action against the Assyrians. Proudly Hezekiah showed his visitors all his treasures.

Suspecting something amiss Isaiah approached the king. When he discovered that the visitors were from Babylon and that the king had shown them all of his resources he was dismayed.

The prophetic word was that this unwise revelation would be regretted. The day would come when all this treasure as well as the people of the land would be carried to Babylon. They would defeat them.

With resignation the king accepted this. At least he would have peace the remainder of his reign.

Special points.—The material in this story is very similar to an account in 2 Kings 20.

It is known that Merodach-Baladan was a king of Babylon and that he encouraged revolt against the Assyrian power. At one time Hezekiah had led the nations in the general area in activities against the Assyrians. Isaiah was always opposed to this.

The king had forgotten the vow that he made to God to serve him humbly. When the opportunity came to show off before other leaders, he foolishly showed them all that he had.

The words of Isaiah (vv. 5–7) anticipate what actually happened. Babylon became the dominant world power after Assyria. It was Babylon that defeated Judah and carried them into captivity.

When the king said that the word of the Lord was "good," he meant that it was acceptable. They would continue in peace and security throughout his life.

Truth for today.—What has one done with the life that has been given to him? This is an essential question that we all must answer.

All of us have not been given the assurance of a specified length of time that we have to live. But all of us have now the gift of life. How we use that life is extremely important.

We can take a long view or a short view. The short view of life looks only at the pleasure, the profit, or the comfort of the moment. It does not look beyond the immediate to determine the ultimate results of actions and attitudes.

The long view looks beyond the moment to what can result from decisions. Decisions made one at a time determine our lives.

The God whom we serve, the Holy One of Israel proclaimed by Isaiah and revealed through Jesus Christ, calls on us to take the long look. To live well life must be lived in faith in God. God's promises are known. Jesus Christ has come. Through him God saves.

INTRODUCTION TO ISAIAH 40—66

In Isaiah 40—66 Hebrew prophecy reaches its highest point of victorious, joyous expression. The prophet shares with the people the exciting news that the days of judgment have passed. Israel's iniquity has been pardoned; and God, like the good shepherd, has come to feed and guide his flock.

Between Isaiah 39 and Isaiah 40 we are confronted with a time span of almost two centuries. Assyria has long since passed from the scene, and Babylon has been ruling the world for over half a century. But even Babylon is tottering on the precipice of destruction. On the horizon Persia led by Cyrus is emerging as the new world power to be reckoned with.

In 539 Cyrus defeated the Babylonian army under the crown prince Belshazzar (Dan. 7). His victory signaled a significant change not only for Babylon but also for the captive Israelites. For among his first acts as the new sovereign were a series of decrees permitting subject peoples who had been taken captive by the Babylonians to return to their homeland.

As the prophet surveys the rapidly changing world scene he discerns the hand of God directing the affairs of men. He is also confident that God's work with Israel in the past has been a preparation period for the great mission which is to be hers in the new age that is about to dawn.

In our day, a day of mass disorientation and disillusionment, the message of Isaiah 40—66 brings new hope and new meaning to both personal and national problems. For this prophet proclaims lucidly the stirring truth that man's sin cannot defeat the ultimate purposes of God, that regardless of how hopeless the situation may appear we must never forget that God is still in control of the affairs and destiny of mankind.

The Call and Commission of God's Prophet (Isa. 40:1–31)

In this chapter we have the call of the prophet and his commission to share the message of God's new and dramatic intervention in the affairs of men. The joy and triumph of this passage sets the stage for the following chapters where the prophet will interpret the meaning of history and proclaim the "new things" that God has planned for his people.

The call of the prophet (40:1–11).— "Comfort" is the keynote of the prophet's message (v. 1). He is to remind the discouraged Israelites that God's judgment is past (v. 2). Their sins have been forgiven and God himself has come to empower and lead his people. He strikingly contrasts the weakness of man's passing power with the strength and permanence of God's promise (vv. 6–8).

The commission of the prophet (40:12–31).—Beginning with verse 12 the prophet's message changes from the joyful proclamation of his call to a sharp penetrating argument of God's sovereignty and power. With biting sarcasm he pours scorn on man-made idols, and underlines the fact that Jehovah and Jehovah alone is worthy of mankind's respect and devotion.

In the concluding verses, he reminds the people of Israel once again that God has not forgotten their plight (v. 27). Rather God has noted their need and has provided the spiritual power to meet both present and future challenges (vv. 28–31).

Truth for today.—The late Soviet cosmonaut Titov reportedly stated that during his flight in space he saw "no sign of God." That statement graphically pinpoints the basic spiritual problem of modern man. For in a world filled with exploding crisis situations contemporary man sees "no sign of God" and many are convinced that God is either dead or he is uninterested and uninvolved in the human struggle. Isaiah's message is as relevant today as it was to the discouraged Israelites. "Behold your God." God is interested! He is involved and he can be known and experienced by those who have the faith that helps them to mount up with wings like eagles, run and not be weary, walk on and not faint (v. 31).

God's Call to the Nations (Isa. 41:1–29)

The nations who in chapter 40 were so greatly feared by Israel are in chapter 41 called into court by God in order to hear his judgment upon them. The entire chapter provides us with one of the most incisive discussions of comparative religion to be found anywhere in the Bible.

It is also in this chapter that the term "servant" which is original with Isaiah and central in his thought, first appears.

God's call and the issue to be discussed (41:1–7).—The prophecy begins with God summoning the nations together in order to decide who it is that controls and directs human history. He makes two stinging points. First, he asks who it is that empowers the rising conqueror from the East (v. 2). Second, he pours scorn once again on the total inability of man-made idols to influence human events. His triumphant conclusion is "I the Lord, the first, and the last; I am he" (v. 4b).

God's servant (41:8–20).—God now turns to Israel as she stands among the assembled nations and reminds her that she is his chosen "servant." He assures her of her unique role in the world as God's witness and encourages her as in chapter 40 with the promise of his presence and power (vv. 10,13,20).

The challenge and proof of God's sovereignty (41:21–29).—God again challenges man-made idols to prove their power by interpreting past events and predicting the future. Their futility is summed up in verse 26b: "Not one declared, not one foretold, Not one heard a sound from you" (NEB). In the concluding passage (vv. 25–29a), God affirms his control of human affairs by his direction of the new rising conquerors.

Truth for today.—An old German-Jewish philosopher who had had to flee from the Nazi persecution in Germany was sitting on a park bench in New York's central park. As he sat thinking about some of life's ultimate questions —Who am I? Why am I? What is the purpose of existence?—his entire appearance reflected his difficult circumstance. His pocket was threadbare and his shirt collar ragged. Suddenly a policeman nudged the old man with his night stick and inquired, "Old man, what are you doing here?" The philosopher, lost in reflection, did not respond. The policeman nudged him again. "Old man, what are you doing here?" With searching in his eyes and pathos in his voice the old man responded "I wish to God I knew!"

Jesus Christ, unlike other great world religious leaders, did not say that he was seeking truth. Rather in John 14:6 he stated "I am the way, the truth and the life." Jesus was truth and in a personal experience of faith one can know the ultimate truth about God and life through Jesus Christ. Beside this claim and its reality other religious claims pale into insignificance.

The Servant of God (Isa. 42:1–25)

This is the first of what many interpreters call the "servant" poems in Isaiah. In this passage God not only reveals the role and responsibility of his servant, he also reveals his goal for history. Not that Israel will conquer for the sake of conquest but rather to establish God's justice among nations.

God introduces his servant (42:1–4). —In these verses God's special relationship with the servant and the servant's special relationship to the world are beautifully and touchingly described. The servant is God's "chosen one" in whom he delights and upon whom he has bestowed his spirit (v. 1). The servant's relation to the world is one of peace and nonviolence (vv. 2–4).

The mission and ministry of the servant will result in his being a light to the nations (v. 6), opening the eyes of the blind and setting captives free (v. 7).

The new song (vv. 10–13). Following his announcement of new things (v. 9), the prophet sings a "New Song." He calls the whole world to recognize and praise God for his power not only to promise victory but like a conquering warrior to be *victor*.

God's self-restraint (vv. 14–17). — In stark contrast with his warrior metaphor in verse 13, God now confirms his self-restraint. He has in the past held himself in check (v. 1), but like a woman in childbirth his purpose can be held back no longer.

The deaf and blind servant (vv. 18–25). —The prophet here laments that Israel appears to have learned so little from her past history. God's judgment in the past was intended to have been redemptive but Israel his servant was so blind that she could not see what was happening and was so spiritually insensitive that she could not understand.

Truth for today. —In every crisis situation God has his "servant" picked, pruned, and prepared for the occasion. The Bible is replete with illustrations of this truth, e.g., when the people of Israel cried for deliverance from the slavery of Egypt God responded by calling and empowering Moses. Later when the infant nation needed strong national leadership God led in the choice of David as king. During the period of exile and restoration the prophets served as God's spokesman for justice and righteousness. But it is in the incarnation that this truth is epitomized: "In the fulness of time," Paul tells us in Colossians 4:4, when everything was prepared and ready, God sent his own Son to meet man in his greatest crisis.

Today, as the "servants" of God, Christians are called upon to proclaim the good news of the gospel and minister to the need of man. Like Israel, our call is both a privilege and a responsibility.

God's Amazing Grace (Isa. 43:1–28)

This passage begins with the words "But now," thereby relating it to the preceding statement. This connection is important as the prophet now turns from the past to the future and proclaims more in detail the theme he began in 41:8–10.

In verses 1–5, God through his prophet again encourages the people: "Have no fear." He reminds them of their special relationship to him: "I have paid your ransom, I have called you by name and you are my own" (v. 1*b*), and of their future rich with promise (vv. 5–7).

The Lord alone is God and Israel is his witness (*vv. 8–13*).—The scene here is similar to that in chapter 41, where God has summoned the nation but there is a new element in that Israel is summoned as God's witness (v. 10). The message that the witness is commissioned to carry to the world is the truth of God's sovereignty. The concluding verse of the passage climaxes God's message through Israel. "I am God; from this very day I am He. What my hand holds, none can snatch away; what I do, none can undo" (v. 13,NEB).

Cease to dwell on days gone by (*vv. 14–21*).—As if to underscore the reality of the message in verse 13, the prophet turns now to the theme of Israel's coming salvation. God is planning a new exodus for his people for this Babylonian captivity. This new exodus will be a "new thing" (v. 19), superseding even the first exodus in glory and power.

God's indictment of Israel (*vv. 22–28*).—The final passage begins with a sea of negativism. The prophet turns from the present to the past and reminds the people of their failure to call for God (v. 22*a*), and their failure to serve him (v. 22*b*). But true to his message of comfort (40:1), he also reminds them that God's judgment is past and their sins have been forgiven (v. 25).

Truth for today.—Pastor Robinson of the pilgrim fathers was seeking to encourage and strengthen his congregation for the long move from Holland to an utterly new world. As he stood on the wharf preparing for this voyage he said, "God has yet more light to break forth from his word."

The prophet expresses this same thought beautifully in 43:18. This is a startling imperative because it runs counter to the Old Testament emphasis upon remembering. For what kept Israel going was its remembrance of a God who delivered them from Egypt, brought them from the wilderness and established them in the Promised Land. But Isaiah was attempting here to restore a sense of balance for, in essence, what he was saying was that the past was meant to be a guide post and not a hitching post.

As believers we need to be aware of our rich historical past yet at the same time be sensitive to the areas in the contemporary world, where the spirit of God is breaking through and doing "new things."

Fear Not (Isa. 44:1–28)

In this chapter there is a repetition of the themes introduced in the earlier chapters: Israel as God's witness, her message to the world, and a rebuke of idols and idol worshipers.

Outpouring of God's Spirit upon Israel (*vv. 1–5*).—With characteristic abruptness the prophet turns with a "but now" to declare God's grace to the undeserving people. With the encouragement again to "have no fear" (v. 2), God promises to pour his spirit out upon Israel and her offspring. The experience of the early church in Acts 2 is an example of the literal fulfilment of God's promise to his people.

The Redeemer of Israel, the Only true God (*vv. 6–23*).—The message to which Israel is to be a witness in the world is once again described. The people are encouraged not to be afraid but to look to God as their "rock."

The stupidity of idolatry is described again with contempt and sarcasm in verses 9–20. Isaiah, like other great Hebrew prophets, had a passionate devotion to Jehovah, the invisible God who required of man that he act justly, love mercy, and walk humbly before

God (Mic. 6:8).

God's sovereignty revealed in Cyrus (vv. 24–28).—God, in this passage, identifies himself as the creator of the world and the controller of historical events. He illustrates this sovereignty by promising the rebuilding of Jerusalem and the Temple with the assistance of Cyrus, the Persian conqueror. The term "shepherd," used to describe the role of Cyrus in God's plan, refers to an important officer or administrator.

Truth for today.—In Mark 4:35–41 we have the significant account of Christ subduing the forces of nature and transforming what appeared to be imminent tragedy into a triumph of faith. The turning point in the entire incident came when the disciples ceased to regard Christ as a passenger and called upon him to be the pilot when he ceased to be cargo and became the captain of the vessel. The prophet in this chapter encourages the people to "fear not" because God had become the "captain" of their ship of state and he was redemptively directing their affairs. The same encouragement needs to be given to believers today. Our fear of the present and the future can be dispersed when by faith we turn the helm of our life over to Christ and allow him to be the pilot and not simply a passenger in our life.

God's Sovereignty (Isa. 45:1–25)

The prophet, having introduced the name of Cyrus in 44:28, now proceeds to explain and enlarge upon the Persian King whom God had annointed.

Cyrus (vv. 1–8).—In verses 2–6, God addresses Cyrus directly and he reveals that the power and achievements of Cyrus are the result of his role in God's plan for his servant people, Israel (v. 4). It is God and God alone who has called Cyrus even though Cyrus does not know it.

The Creator is beyond criticism (vv. 9–13).—These verses seem to indicate that there were those among the exiles who questioned the prophet's conviction that Cyrus was the instrument of God's purpose. The prophet's response is sobering. The creator is beyond criticism of his creatures. It is an interesting historical footnote that Cyrus, regarded as the greatest of Persian monarchs, is also acclaimed as one of history's most enlightened imperialists. This underlines the fact that in God's providence "all things work together for good."

Conversion of the Gentiles (vv. 14–25).—The end result of God's working through Cyrus will be the acknowledgement by Gentile nations that God is both sovereign and Savior.

The worldwide scope of God's invitation is verse 22. "Look unto me and be saved you peoples from all corners of the earth; for I am God, there is no other" (NEB) represents one of the prophetic peaks in the Old Testament. Here the missionary role of Israel and God's desire that the whole world shall be his kingdom is more lucidly and powerfully set forth than in any other part of the Old Testament.

Truth for today.—In every age God through his spokesman has struggled to achieve the reality of an unhindered gospel. Both the prophets in the Old Testament and the apostles in the New Testament sought constantly to communicate the universal dimension of God's message. The gospel of God's grace is for all men regardless of culture or color.

During World War II some American soldiers carried a dead comrade to a French graveyard and asked the priest's permission to bury this friend in the church cemetery. The priest graciously but firmly stated that the rules of his church would not allow him to comply with this request. Saddened, the soldiers took their dead friend and buried him just beyond the fence of the graveyard. In the morning when they returned to pay their last respects they looked and looked but failed to find the newly dug grave. While they were looking the priest came out and informed them that during the night he had been unable to sleep as he wrestled with his conscience, so he had decided the issue by personally moving the cemetery fence so that it included the grave of the dead American. Rules raised the barriers but love moved them.

The God Who Carries and the God Who Must Be Carried (Isa. 46:1–13)

The prophet calls the attention of Israel to the lesson that they should learn from the fall of Babylon. The theme of the entire chapter is a favorite with the writer: the contrast between the powerless idols and the power of God, the difference between the God who carries his people and the God that people carry.

Bel and Nebo (v. 6), were the greatest gods in the Babylonian religion, yet they were helpless to save their country and people in their time of need. The result was that they went with the people into captivity. The prophet used this tongue in cheek example to remind Israel once again of the power and patience of the living God who had carried them as his burden since the beginning of time and would continue to do so until the end of history.

Isaiah returns to this recurring theme in an attempt to stir up faith, trust, and hope in the dispirited and discouraged Israelites.

Truth for today.—If one could use a sanctified imagination he could almost hear the prophet singing to his people. "Be not dismayed whate'er betide, God will take care of you."

The apostle Paul in Philippians 4:19 states: "My God shall supply all your need according to his riches in glory by Christ Jesus." For Paul, like Isaiah, this truth was not simply a pious platitude. Rather it was a triumphant witness to their personal experience. Thank God that his faithfulness does not depend upon our worthiness but upon his love and grace.

The Judgment of Babylon (Isa. 47:1–15)

From beginning to end this chapter is one long oracle of doom upon Babylon. She is pictured as a young woman who must descend from her throne and sit in the dust. She must exchange dainty ease for coarse drudgery.

Like other great world powers Babylon had assumed that she would reign forever (v. 5). She had been God's instrument in disciplining his unfaithful people (v. 6). But she had been guilty of arrogant self-assurance and brutality (v. 6). In her infatuation with power she had assumed that there was no one to whom she would ever give an account (v. 7). She has sown to the wind and she is about to reap the whirlwind of God's judgment.

In verses 12–13, the prophet explains for the benefit of God's people the futility of astrology and magic. With biting sarcasm he points up the utter uselessness of such tragic substitutes for a personal faith in a living God.

Truth for today.—Robert G. Ingersoll was one of the most flamboyant agnostics in American history. For years he travelled throughout the nation giving dramatic lectures in which he proclaimed his doubts about God, future life, judgment, and hell. One night when he was addressing an audience in a small town in New York he had convincingly presented his case against a future judgment. When he was finished an obviously drunk man stood up in the rear of the hall and said, "I sure hope you're right brother Bob, for I'm counting on that."

Modern man does not like to think of God in terms of judgment, justice, or wrath. We are much more agreeable with a God fashioned after the permissive philosophy of our day. The only problem with this idea is that it is neither biblically nor practically true. The principle of reaping what we sow, of harvesting what we plant, is woven into the warp and woof of life. The prophet Ezekiel proclaimed the sad news of the destruction of Jerusalem as the inevitable fruit of the people's faithlessness to God.

Isaiah opens his prophecy with the lament that his people had fallen under the judgment of God because they called evil good, and good evil. This same thought is evident in the preaching of the apostles in Acts 17:31. These biblical writers were not hell-fire and brimstone, morose iconoclasts looking at the world with a jaundiced eye.

Rather, they were sensitive, perceptive human beings who knew that for men and nations there was a pay day someday, and that what we sow we ultimately reap.

Now I Show You New Things (Isa. 48: 1–22)

It has been suggested that this chapter may have been a sermon delivered by the prophet to a congregation of the exiles in one of their synogogues on a day of penitence. Regardless of the truth or fiction of the suggestion, like all good sermons, this chapter has three clear-cut divisions.

"New things" (*vv. 1–11*).—The main thrust of this passage is a stern reminder that God had predicted the disaster that had overtaken Israel. He reminds them of this so that they have no excuse for attributing it to any other power human or divine. Similarly on the eve of their liberation from captivity, he predicts new things so that when they occur they will know that God alone is the Lord of human events.

God first and last (*vv. 12–16*).— Turning from his call to repentance, the prophet's sermon now turns from the sin of Israel to the greatness of God. He reminds his listeners that without their help he created the world (v. 13), and called Cyrus (vv. 14–15). It is as though God were saying "I can expect nothing from my people. I, the first and the last, will do it all."

Redemption by God's grace (*vv. 17–22*).—In these concluding verses, the prophet reminds the people of their past history and the fact that if they had listened to God's commands they would not be in their present situation. Nevertheless, true to his message of comfort and hope, this prophet reminds Israel of this coming redemption, and their release from captivity.

Truth for today.—The greatest experience in life is to comprehend the truth that we are loved by God. Not because of what we have done or what we can do, but rather because of what God in Christ has done for all men.

A modern playwright traveled around the world looking for evidence of man's spiritual realities. His conclusion at the end of the trip was that the world is hopelessly fragmented and that there are no "centers" around which and upon which men can build their lives. The people in Isaiah's day had come to the same conclusion. The prophet's message needs to be our message, that even in the midst of a changing world scene the unchanging truth of God's grace and love are "centers" around which and upon which we can build our lives for time and eternity.

The Servant of the Lord Called and Commissioned (Isa. 49:1–26)

The first six verses of this chapter constitute "the second servant song" of Isaiah, the first being chapter 42:1–4. The servant, Israel, who was introduced in the first song speaks in this second to the nations of the world telling them of his call (v. 3) and commission (v. 5) by God. Verse 6 represents another of those prophetic peaks. Here again, the prophet pinpoints not only Israel's privilege but also her responsibility as the servant of God to be a light to the nations. The commissioning of the servant is discussed in verses 8–13. The promises made in 42:6 are repeated, but with a new sense of urgency. God through the prophet is again encouraging the dispirited people to have faith in the purpose of God.

The tenor of the chapter suddenly changes in verse 14 from one of encouragement to one of discouragement. The long years of exile had taken their toll spiritually. Israel had a sense of being forsaken and forgotten by God. In verse 15, the prophet's portrayal of God's affection for his people is powerfully poignant. Again God reiterates his concern and care for his people, declaring in verse 26 "that it is I, the Lord, who saves you, I your ransomer, the Mighty One of Jacob" (NEB).

Truth for today.—There are periods in the life of every believer when the challenges and demands of daily living

sap our reserves of spiritual vitality and reality. For this reason we need to constantly care for and replenish the "wells" of spiritual meaning and power in our lives. The prophet reminds us in this chapter that one of these wells is the awareness of God's presence and power. Many are attempting to teach and preach from dry wells. We need to realize that the greater the output, the greater is the need for input.

Israel's Banishment Is Not Permanent (Isa. 50:1–11)

The metaphor in verses 1–3 in this passage liken God's covenant relationship with Israel to a marriage. The people supposed their present plight was due to one or other of two causes: (1) God had finally divorced them, or (2) he had sold them to a creditor. God is pictured as asking where the bill of divorce is and to which creditor the children had been sold. Their plight, Israel is told, is the result of their own sin. But God reminds them that the banishment is not permanent for his hand is not shortened that it cannot save (v. 2).

In an autobiographical passage (vv. 4–11) the prophet, speaking for the true Israel, declares that it was God who taught him and that he was not rebellious at the teaching. To those who spat on him and insulted him (v. 7), he made no response. Instead, he placed his faith and trust in God, believing that he would ultimately be vindicated (v. 9).

Truth for today.—In Exodus 13:17–18 we read that God led the children of Israel not by the shortest route but by the way of the wilderness. God had some lessons that the Israelites needed to learn and the wilderness was to be their schoolroom. Today the Jewish people celebrate the Feast of Sukkos which is a remembrance of their wilderness wanderings. They have never forgotten that it was in the wilderness they became a nation. It was there that they were transformed from a slave people to the servants of God.

Every believer, like the children of Israel, has his "wilderness experiences" where it appears that God is distant, even divorced from his struggles. God's message through his prophet is assuring that the wilderness is not permanent. It is simply a cleansing and refining experience.

The Encouragement of Zion and the Coming Salvation (Isa. 51:1–23)

The tenor of this chapter is one of urgency and expectancy. The prophet uses such vigorous verbs as "Harken" (v. 7), "Listen" (v. 4), "Awake" (v. 9), "Raise yourself" (v. 17). His hope is that he can arouse Israel to action so that she will respond to God's mighty acts with faith and joy. He reminds them of the rock from which they have been hewn (v. 1), and that as God blessed Abraham so he promises to bless them (note v. 8). As he proved to be their conqueror in the past so he will continue to give them victory in the future. Therefore, they should not fear man (v. 12), but continue to place their faith and trust in the power of God (v. 16).

Jerusalem is portrayed as reeling like an intoxicated man after having drunk to the last dreg the bowl of God's wrath. But the good news is that God's judgment has passed from their hands to the hands of their tormentors, and the promise to Jerusalem is that "you shall never again drink from the bowl of my wrath."

Truth for today.—A pastor received a letter from one of his members who was serving in the armed forces. The young man wrote that the stabilizing factor in his life during the difficult years in service had been the quiet advice of his mother. "Son," the mother had said, "wherever you go and whatever you do, don't ever forget who you are."

That priceless piece of advice has been a redemptive factor in many lives. For example, it was when the prodigal son "came to himself," when he realized who he was and to whom he belonged, that he moved out of the hog pen and went back to his father's house.

May we never forget the rock from which we have been hewn!

Your God Reigns (Isa. 52:1–12)

The opening verses of this chapter are inextricably wed to the concluding verses (vv. 17–23) of chapter 51. Jerusalem was there pictured as staggering with intoxication because she drained the bowl of God's wrath (v. 17). But with God's judgment in the past Jerusalem is now encouraged to put on her beautiful garments for she is about to be set free from her captivity to foreign powers.

Verses 7–12 are a hymn expressing joy that the exile is past and God is going before his people into Jerusalem.

The Man of Sorrows (Isa. 52:13—53:12)

We now come to the most familiar passage in Isaiah. This is the fourth and last of the servant songs and is well known as the song of the suffering servant. The theme of this great passage is the atoning work of the servant in the world through his vicarious sacrifice. The New Testament writers believed that Jesus in his life and death fulfilled the prophecy inherent in this servant song. Modern biblical scholarship, however, has generally followed the Jewish interpretation of the passage, believing that the servant here as in earlier passages refers to a redeemed Israel. Yet, whether one thinks of the servant depicted in this passage as national or individual, most will agree that the picture painted here finds its actualization only in Jesus Christ, the suffering Savior.

The passage can be outlined as follows:

52:13–15—The introduction of the servant.
53:1–3—The sorrow of the servant.
53:4–6—The suffering of the servant.
53:7–9—The death of the servant.
53:10–12—The satisfaction of the servant.

Truth for today.—In a recent survey taken to pinpoint the factors that determined why people joined particular churches, it was determined that the churches were chosen on the basis of:

(1) the personality of the pastor
(2) the education program of the church
(3) the music program
(4) the location
(5) the denominational tie

All of these factors have one thing in common. They revolve around the contribution that the church can make to the life of an individual or his family, rather than the contribution they can make to the life of the church. This fact points up the urgent need for the people of God to rediscover the servant role of the believer.

In John 13 when Jesus washed his disciples' feet he was giving a concrete example of how his followers should relate to the world. God's ,call is not a call to privilege but to service—towel service where and when it is necessary.

The old song states "Must Jesus bear the cross alone and all the world go free? No, there's a cross for everyone and there's a cross for me." I am not sure that there is a cross for everyone but I do know that there is a towel.

The Consolation of Israel (Isa. 54:1–17)

This chapter represents an abrupt change in tenor and theme from the previous passage. For here the prophet recaptitulates the emphasis of 44:1–5, 49:14–21, and 51:1–3. He expresses again the joys of redemption and fellowship with God. It appears as though Isaiah used this passage as a parenthesis between the double climax of 52:13—53:12 and chapter 55.

The prophet again encourages Israel to fear not (v. 4). The metaphorical language likening God's relationship with his covenant people to the relationship between a husband and his wife is commonly used both in the Old Testament and in the New Testament. God, like a good husband and father, promises his protection and love.

Truth for today.—Periodically every believer needs to refurbish and reinforce the memory of high spiritual moments in his life. The memory of high spiritual hours can often serve as an effective antidote against our "valley" experiences.

This is what Paul did in 2 Corinthians 12:1–10. Paul in this passage describes the many difficulties he found in his ministry. Suddenly into the midst of his sobering recounting, he interjects an account of a high spiritual moment—"I knew a man."

Isaiah, Paul, and many other great spiritual giants have known and expressed the value of remembering those moments when spiritually they were at their best. They understood that the mountaintop and not the valley moments in life help us to see ourselves and the world as God sees us.

The Banquet of the Lord (Isa. 55:1–13)

Nowhere in the Old Testament is the spirit and substance of the New Testament message more clearly anticipated than in chapter 55. It is the Old Testament counterpart of the parable of the great supper (Luke 14:15–24).

The entire passage pulsates with a passionate appeal for all men to open their eyes to the riches of God's love and grace and to accept by faith and repentance his free gift of salvation.

In verses 1–5 God is portrayed as standing in the marketplace encouraging men to "listen to me and you will have good food to eat and you will enjoy the fat of the land. Come to me and listen to my words, hear me, and you shall have life" (NEB). The invitation to the banquet is accompanied by an invitation to repentance (vv. 6–13). The urgent invitation of verse 6 is sobering for it suggests that delay might be fatal. Let the wicked forsake his ways and return to the Lord now.

Truth for today.—It is significant that it never had to be proved to man that God was a God of wrath, judgment, or power. Man accepted these aspects of the personality of God without question. The result was that God had to prove decisively to man that he was first and foremost—love. In the life, death, and resurrection of Jesus we have God's dramatic and historic intervention into the life of the world in order to prove to man once and for all that he was love. Yet the message of the cross is double-edged. It reveals not only the love of God but also how seriously he judges sin.

God's loving invitation to all men is to come, for all things are now ready. But the tenor of the invitation is one of urgency. Love redeems but sin destroys.

Encouragement for Ethical Conduct (Isa. 56:1–12)

The mood and materials in this chapter represent a distinct change in emphasis from that encountered in chap-

ters 40–55. The form is not that of prophecy but of exhortation concerning the spirit and structure of worship in the Temple.

The welcome of all to worship (vv. 1–8).—The passage begins with the command to maintain justice and do right (v. 1). In the interim period, waiting for God's full salvation, high standards of ethical and community life were to be maintained.

In verses 3–8, we have one of the most significant passages in the Old Testament regarding the welcome and treatment of foreigners. When the foreigner was converted, he was to be welcomed to the worship of God in the Temple. Oftentimes the Bible has been used, and wrongly so, to further the idea of separation and segregation. But in this passage the prophet once and for all lays to rest any biblical basis for segregation among believers.

Condemnation of corrupt leaders (vv. 9–12).—Two leadership groups were identified and criticized. Israel's watchmen (prophets and religious leaders) and shepherds (community leaders and government officials) are accused of blindness, cowardice, idolence (v. 10), and greed (v. 11).

Truth for today.—There is no such thing as a "social" and a "spiritual" gospel. In the New Testament sense the gospel is either social and spiritual or it is not the gospel at all. Our relationship with God is inextricably wed to our relationship with our fellowman. It is an oft forgotten fact that great evangelical leaders of the past such as Luther, Wesley, Booth, Moody, and Spurgeon were also significant social reformers. They realized that the task of the church was not that of simply "saving souls" in the abstract, but the redemption of man's total being.

The great Scottish poet Robert Burns

once wrote that "man's inhumanity to man makes countless thousands mourn." No one stated that truth with more savagery and poignancy than the prophets of Israel. Name any of the prophets —Jeremiah, Amos, Micah, Isaiah—all of them were rebels against the abuses of the social and religious institutions of their day. Their message had a disturbing relevance because they exposed the hypocrisy of a religion that was patently pious but totally insensitive to the hurts of humanity.

Condemnation of Corrupt Leaders (Isa. 57:1–21)

Maintaining the demand for high ethical conduct the prophet in this chapter condemns in the strongest possible terms those within the community who practice injustice and idolatry.

The condemnation (vv. 1–10).— Spiritual vitality is dying and no one seems to care. Idolatry and injustice are rampant but no one seems concerned. It is obvious that the people have forgotten, if they ever learned, the lesson of their past history.

The reason for Israel's apostasy (vv. 11–13).—Disappointed and distressed, God asks the reason for Israel's apostasy. As in the past, he warns the people that when they need help most their idols will be helpless.

God's persistent grace (vv. 14–21).— The message in these verses is the promise of forgiveness, restoration, and peace to the godly.

The final verses (vv. 20–21) describe vividly the end result of the wickedness described in the above verses. "The wicked are like a troubled sea, that cannot rest, whose troubled waters cast up mud and filth. There is no peace for the wicked, says the Lord" (NEB).

Truth for today.—It is no secret that many today are turned off by religious institutions and religious leaders. As never before in this century the church is the center of much controversy. The result is that there is presently little ease for those in Zion.

Part of the contemporary disenchantment stems from our persistent use of "stained-glass language," the using of words that have little meaning to the contemporary Christian and no meaning at all to the world outside the church. The prophets, especially Isaiah, did not have this problem. His language is lucid, his condemnation of sin precise. Those who heard his message had no difficulty understanding its meaning. Paul said in 1 Corinthians 14:19: "I had rather speak five words with my understanding, that by my voice I might teach others also, than ten thousand words in an unknown tongue." In a day when it is difficult to catch the ear much less the heart of the unredeemed world, we must make sure that when we have their ear they hear and are able to understand.

The Purpose and Meaning of Fasting (Isa. 58:1–14)

The prophet in this chapter condemns the shallowness of performing religious functions such as worship and fasting without an accompanying ethical concern for your fellowman. Like Amos and Micah, Isaiah insists that God's supreme concern is for justice, mercy, and humility rather than perfunctory religious acts.

The passage begins with God's summoning the prophet to make a proclamation to the house of Jacob concerning their sins. But the people are hard to convince for they say they delight in approaching God (v. 2).

This leads the prophet to a discussion of the contrast between a true and false fast. Verses 6–8 provide a profound interpretation of a true fast.

In the concluding verses 13–14, God reminds his people that his promise of his presence and power is conditional upon the practice of high ethical conduct in their personal and community life.

Truth for today.—Repeatedly in the New Testament, Jesus took great pains to differentiate between a religion of the spirit and a religion of rule and regulations. In his parable of the new patch on an old garment in Luke 5:36, he was clearly disassociating himself and his followers from the legalistic and joyless religion of the Pharisees. Far too often the gospel has been presented in terms of what we are required to do rather than what we are released to become. The result is that God has become a cosmic policeman, checking our faults and tabulating our failures. In his discussion of the meaning of true fasting Isaiah like Christ is telling us that real religion is a religion of the spirit, that evidences itself not only in our relationship with God but also in our relationship with our fellowmen.

Sin and Confession (Isa. 59:1–21)

Gloomy over national conditions the people again began to feel that God had deserted them and they begin to charge him with indifference. But the prophet, bringing God's message, states that their condition is not due to God's inability to save or hear; rather their sins have separated them from God.

In verses 3–8 the prophet exposes in detail the sins of the people. The end result of their wilful disobedience is that they "look for light but all is darkness, for the light of dawn, but we walk in deep gloom" (v. 9b, NEB).

While verses 9–11 are in the form of an explanatory declaration to Israel about her sin, verses 12–15a are in the form of a confession. First, the prophet confesses the sins of apostasy, transgressing, denying, and turning away from God, then hollow speaking, oppression, and uttering words of falsehood. In the final section of the chapter God is pictured as a warrior coming to judge and redeem. The word picture of God as a warrior is a particularly significant one for it shows the seriousness with which God regards the struggle against sin.

Truth for today.—In a national survey American doctors stated that 75 percent of the patients who come through their offices have no basic physical problem. Their problem is a spiritual one that evidences itself in physical symptoms. In the great majority of cases the spiritual problem is one of guilt. People today are literally hagridden with a debilitating sense of guilt.

The Bible gives the only permanent antidote for guilt in 1 John 1:9: "If we confess our sins, he is faithful and just to forgive us our sins, and cleanse us from all unrighteousness." Confession and cleansing can mean the beginning of a new life physically and spiritually for both individual and nation.

Promise of the New Jerusalem (Isa. 60: 1–22)

The vigor and exultation of this passage stands in stark contrast to the gloom of chapter 59. The dominant theme of chapters 56–59 was judgment, but beginning with this chapter the hope and aspiration of chapters 40–55 is again present.

The prophet draws impressive word pictures with the words "light" and "darkness." These words are spiritual symbols, light representing fellowship with God and darkness is life apart from God. Although darkness covers the earth, Israel will be covered with the light of God's glory; and nations will stream out of their darkness into the light of God at Jerusalem. Using a sanctified imagination the prophet urges the people to "lift up your eyes and look around, they flock together, all of them, and come to you."

The prophet strikes the apocalyptic note obviously to encourage the people to look beyond their immediate lack and discouragement and see the day when God will create a "new" Jerusalem. The final verses paint a beautiful picture of a land at peace, a picture which is repeated in Revelation 21:22–26.

Truth for today.—Sir Walter Scott tells how as a young boy in Scotland he would stand on the porch of his home and watch the old gas lamplighter switch on the lights throughout the town. As he moved from place to place Scott followed his path by the small pools of light that he left behind. As he got closer to home the young Scott would run in and call to his mother, "Mother, Mother, come and see a man who is punching holes in the darkness." This is an excellent definition of the mission of God's people in every age: to punch holes in the moral, spiritual, social, and political darkness of the world and allow the light of the gospel to bring direction and healing. The "new Jerusalem" can be located wherever the people of God are allowing their "light" to shine.

The Spirit of the Lord Is Upon Me (Isa. 61:1–11)

The opening verses of this chapter have special significance for believing Christians, for Jesus used this passage in Luke 4:16–19 to interpret his mission and ministry in the world. How they applied in this particular context is not entirely clear. The speaker does not refer to himself as the servant but the task that rests before himself is

similar to that of the servant in 42:1, 48:16, and 50:4.

In verse 6, the people of Israel are called priests of the Lord. The prophet here returns to the truth of Israel's universal mission and her responsibility as the bridge to help bring God to man and man to God.

The blessing promised in return for Israel's faithfulness is described in verses 7–9.

With characteristic joy the prophet concludes this passage with a hymn of thanksgiving for the grace and greatness of God.

Truth for today.—"But ye shall be named the priests of the Lord" (v. 6). No truth in God's Word has had more revolutionary or rewarding results than the doctrine of the priesthood of every believer. Once thought to be the private preserve of Protestantism, the priesthood of the believer is now widely discussed and preached in the Roman Catholic Church.

The term "priesthood" weds beautifully both the privilege and responsibility of the people of God. It emphasizes our vertical relationship with God and our horizontal relationship to mankind.

The New Jerusalem (Isa. 62:1–12)

In this chapter we find a repetition of a theme already introduced in chapters 40–55 and 60 and 61. The subject is the "new" Jerusalem that will become the religious capital of the world. No longer will it be called forsaken and desolate. Rather it shall be named Hephzibah (my delight is in her) and Beulah (wedded). In verse 1, the prophet promises persistent intercessory prayer on behalf of the "new" Jerusalem and in verses 6–7 he encourages the people to join him in this prayer pact until God makes their dreams a reality. Here we meet the prophet as intercessor more vividly than anywhere else in the Old Testament. It is significant that the intercessory prayer for the coming of God to redeem and rebuild Jerusalem is mingled with the confident assertion that God is coming to save.

In the concluding verses the inhabitants are encouraged to put feet to their prayers and go out and prepare a highway for the people—a holy people, the ransomed of the Lord—who will come to a city not "forsaken" but "sought out" (v. 12). The prophet here, as on other occasions, is urging the people to look beyond the poverty of their present situation and see with eyes of faith the life and glory of their future with God.

Truth for today.—The apostle Paul stated in 1 Corinthians 15:19: "If in this life only we have life in Christ, we are of all men most miserable." Paul, like the New Testament writers Peter and John, recharged the batteries of their souls with the "blessed hope" that one day God would wrap up time, set the wheels of eternity rolling, and establish a new heaven and a new earth. The promise of Christ's return and the future glory of believers is a truth that has played a primary role in the lifestyle of almost every great spiritual giant in the church. It inspired hope, bred consistency, and encouraged urgency. Many of the problems we face in the church today, such as apathy, inconsistency, and indifference would be erased if Christians gave greater attention to the promise and warning that sooner than we expect Christ will fulfil his promise to "come again and receive us to himself" (John 14).

God's Judgment of the Nation (Isa. 63: 1–6)

The setting for this vivid and sobering passage is the country of Edom and one of its chief cities, Bozrah. In 597 and 587 when Nebuchadnezzar's armies destroyed Judah and Jerusalem the Edomites took advantage of the weakened conditions of Judah and took over the southern part of Judea.

Repeatedly in Jewish apocalyptic thought God is pictured as judging the Edomites for their treachery. In this passage the prophet uses this figure to announce God's judgment, not only of Edom but all nations. The prophet's God has a sensitive conscience. He cannot stand aloof from the struggle against evil. Rather he takes to the field of battle on behalf of his people. This passage foreshadows the incarnation in the New Testament where God uniquely and decisively identified himself with man and his struggle against evil.

Truth for today.—God is no Saturday afternoon grandstand quarterback divorced from the struggle of his people in the game of life. Rather he is on our team, in the game, running interference for us so that we can make the winning plays and know victory over the forces of evil. If the incarnation means anything, it means that God takes sin and its power so seriously that he concretely identified himself with man in the human struggle for victory over the power of sin.

The Prophet's Intercessory Prayer (Isa. 63:7—64:12)

It is significant that immediately following the terrible picture of God's coming judgment we have inserted this beautiful intercessory prayer.

The prayer begins with the prophet's recounting "the Lord's acts of unfailing love" (63:7, NEB). In doing so he grasps for superlatives to express God's graciousness.

In verses 10–14 the prophet remembers and interprets Israel's past history and God's involvement with them. Like other nations in time of crisis and danger Israel remembered God's empowering of Moses and the exodus from Egypt. The tenor of the prophet's prayer turns in verses 15–19 from remembrance to a plea for a sense of God's fellowship. "Stand not aloof; for thou art our father, though Abraham does not know us nor Israel acknowledge us. Thou, Lord, art our father" (v. 16, NEB).

In 64:1–5a the prophet makes a strong appeal for God to dramatically display his power on behalf of his people.

In the final passage (vv. 5b–12) the prophet came to the heart of his prayer. Speaking for all the people he acknowledges "We have sinned" (v. 2b).

We all become like a man who is unclean; "We have all withered" (v. 6). "We are the clay" (v. 8). His appeal is to the mercy and love of God for he recognizes that they have no way of meriting God's grace.

With eyes tearfilled and a heart broken by repentance the prayer concludes "After this, O Lord, wilt thou hold back, wilt thou keep silence and punish us beyond measure?" (v. 12, NEB).

Truth for today.—In this passage Isaiah reveals the true "prophet heart." In this regard he stands with Moses who prayed that his name would be removed from the book of life rather than for God to punish the disobedient Israelites; with Paul who prayed in Romans 9:3: "For I could wish that I myself were accursed and cut off from Christ for the sake of my brethren, my kinsmen by race"; and with Christ who said, "O Jerusalem, Jerusalem," (Luke 13:34a). The true prophet always proclaims God's message with paradoxical emotions. On the one hand he scathingly condemns sin but on the other hand he is profoundly burdened for the sinner.

God's Response (Isa. 65:1–25)

Here we have God's response to the preceding intercessory prayer. His answer in verses 1–7 is that he was ready to hear all that sought him but Israel did not turn to him. Instead they turned their back on his open invitation and pursued rebellious and idolatrous practices.

God then announces in verses 8–10 what he is going to do about the situation. This represents the heart of God's response to the prayer in chapter 64. Though all have sinned a remnant will be spared.

In verses 11–16, those Israelites who trusted fate and fortune rather than God are warned of their coming judgment. But for the loyal remnant God again promises blessing.

The concluding verses ring with the joyous affirmation, "Behold I create . . ." (v. 17a). The present world is to be entirely rennovated and transformed as the setting for the new redeemed community in the final passage presents a beautiful and touching picture of the life-style of the redeemed community. It will be one of fulfilment and peace.

Truth for today.—For almost two thousand years the words of Jesus have challenged us to think big, act bold, and claim the audacious promise of prayer power, but somehow we have been intimidated by the simplicity and profundity of it all. His promise in John 15:7 and then again in Luke 11:9, appears too good to be true. Yet every believer who has ever claimed the promise of God in prayer has found like Isaiah that "it shall come to pass" (v. 24). The truth is that God is much more willing to hear and answer our prayer than we are to ask.

Final Promise of Salvation and Judgment (Isa. 66:1–24)

This final chapter gives unity to the entire book. Throughout the book there has been the repeated plea for a deeper sensitivity to human need and less concern for formal religious strictness. In this concluding passage the prophet reiterates this demand. For Isaiah's viewpoint the people were overly absorbed in the reconstruction of the Temple (vv. 1–3), and at the same time overly involved in pagan practices.

His call is for obedience to God's Word (v. 5) in the light of coming judgment (v. 6).

Using the example of childbirth the writer portrays God's promise to bring forth a new people (v. 7–9).

The concluding verses are a mixture of promised salvation and judgment. In fact, the chapter ends with one of the most sobering statements in the entire book. The prophet's obvious disgust with the people leads him to conclude that they seemingly have learned little from their past and the effect of God's judgment is pictured in "the dead bodies of those who have rebelled against me; their worm shall not die nor their fire be quenched, and they shall be abhorred by all mankind" (v. 24, NEB).

Truth for today.—The late President Kennedy once stated that "the nation that fails to learn from her mistakes is doomed to repeat them." Throughout the Old Testament the history of Israel is a recurring cycle of apostasy, judgment, and repentance. They simply failed to heed the warning that "righteousness exalts a nation, but sin is a reproach to any people" (RSV).

The shores of history are littered with the bones and debris of dead states and fallen empires that likewise failed to learn from their past.

It is sobering reading to note how the Greek glory in the age of Pericles was soon replaced by the drunken riots of Alcibiades or how the enlightened Roman Caesars degenerated into neurotic Neros and the once noble praetorian guard became a gang of assassins willing to sell the throne to the highest bidder.

When Alaric's Goths finally poured over the walls of Rome, it was not because the walls were low but because Rome itself was low.

Nearly a thousand years lapsed between the fall of western Rome and the rise of the Renaissance. Those thousand years are well known as the Dark Ages, for they represent a time of regression in which nearly all western European social institutions were inferior to those that had gone before.

Today one wonders if the future of our civilization will be a regression or a renaissance.

JEREMIAH

J. Leo Green

INTRODUCTION

The word "Jeremiah" probably means "The Lord shoots or hurls." It is used in two ways in this study. First, it refers to a prophet who labored for the Lord in Judah for forty years (627–587 B.C.). Second, it serves as the title of a book containing materials from, about, or in some way related to that prophet.

The prophet.—We know more about Jeremiah than we know about any other prophet. He was born about 650, toward the close of the long reign of the wicked Manasseh. He was reared in Anathoth, a tiny town three or four miles northeast of Jerusalem, in the territory of Benjamin. Anathoth was located in a hilly, rocky, arid area, and was the habitation of the country priests, descendants of Abiathar (1 Kings 2:26–27).

Several influences helped to prepare Jeremiah for his life work. Among these were a godly Hebrew home, the preaching of the prophets (especially Hosea), life in a rural village, and proximity to the capital, only an hour's walk away. But the thing that really set him forward on his course as a prophet was his experience of call (Jer. 1:4–19).

Jeremiah exercised his ministry during the darkest, most difficult, and most dangerous period in the history of Judah. It was a day of recurring crisis and rapid change, resulting in ultimate catastrophe. Jeremiah was the prophet of the decline and fall of the Southern Kingdom.

Five kings occupied the throne of Judah during his prophetic career: Josiah (640–609), Jehoahaz (609), Jehoaikim (609–598), Jehoaichin (597), and Zedekiah (597–587). Babylon was the rising world power. She would eventually destroy both Jerusalem and Judah and deport the Judeans into exile. To get the historical background, one should read 2 Kings 21—25 and John Bright, *A History of Israel* (Philadelphia: Westminster, 1959), pp. 288–319.

During his long, stormy, and eventful ministry, Jeremiah remained faithful to God. A sensitive, reserved, poetic, impatient, intensely human individual, he was often torn between natural inclination and divine vocation. He had inner doubts and difficulties and spoke freely and frankly about them to God. As far as we know, he never succeeded at anything he ever did. He was not privileged to marry. He had few intimate friends. He was criticized and conspired against. According to tradition, he was eventually killed by the people he loved so much and served so long. Yet he became "an iron pillar" and "a bronze wall," one of the spiritual giants of the ages.

The prophecy.—The book Jeremiah is the inspired record of the utterances and experiences of the prophet. It may be divided into three parts, with an historical appendix. Part I is sometimes called "The Words of Jeremiah" (chaps. 1–25). It contains prophecies of various types, with some biographical and autobiographical materials interspersed. Part II is often referred to as "The Biography of Jeremiah" (chaps. 26–45).

This is chiefly a record of the experiences of the prophet from 609 to 587, with particular stress on the suffering which he encountered in the service of God. Part III is a collection of prophecies concerning foreign peoples (chaps. 46–51). The appendix, an excerpt from 2 Kings 24:18—25:30 (with some modification), deals with the destruction of Jerusalem, the disposal of the rebel leaders and the Temple furnishings, the deportation of the Judeans, and the deliverance of Jehoaichin, the Davidic ruler imprisoned for 37 years in Babylon (chap. 52).

Jeremiah is one of the longest and most important books in the Bible. It is also one of the most difficult. It is not arranged according to any consistent logical, chronological, or topical principle or pattern (though there are evidences of topical and chronological arrangement in places). To derive the most from the study of Jeremiah, therefore, one should seek a reconstruction of the process of the composition of the book, starting with chapter 36. This is not easy, but it can be rewarding. He should then endeavor, as far as possible, to set the messages and experiences of the prophet in chronological order and historical context.

Further, he should recognize that there is an unusual abundance and wealth of literary forms and stylistic devices in Jeremiah. He should also realize that the book is a blend of prose and poetry. The poetry is some of the best in the Old Testament. The prose is that which was characteristic of the period.

Scholars are not agreed as to the date and authorship of the book. We are told that in 605–604 Jeremiah dictated his prophecies to Baruch (36). The probability is that Baruch was responsible not only for that recording of his prophecies but also for "the biography of Jeremiah" and for the basic structure of the book itself. There may have been later additions and adaptations by inspired men.

The important thing is that we have the book. It was given by inspiration of God. It has in it the divine Word, not only for Jeremiah's day, but also for our day, if we will permit the Spirit to communicate it to us.

Jeremiah's Call and Commission (Jer. 1: 1–19)

The passage.—Verses 1–3 serve as a sort of preface for both the first chapter and the chapters that follow. The preface provides important information concerning the prophet: his name, the name of his hometown, his priestly family background, and the place and date of his ministry.

The account of the call-experience begins with verse 4. It consists of three parts: the divine call through ecstatic vision (vv. 4–10), the divine communication through symbolic perception (vv. 11–16), and the divine charge through admonition and assurance (vv. 17–19).

The call proper starts with the revelation of the divine purpose (vv. 4–5). Since before birth, God has set Jeremiah apart to be "a prophet to the nations." Next comes the human response to this staggering revelation (v. 6). Jeremiah pleads inadequacy and youthful inexperience. God's reply follows (vv. 7–10). It deals with the preparation of the prophet (vv. 7–9) and the portrayal of the nature and scope of the prophet's task (v. 10). God always equips those whom he calls. There are three elements in Jeremiah's equipment: a conviction of divine authority (v. 7), a consciousness of the divine presence (v. 8), and a communication of the divine word (v. 9).

The prophet's task is to be extensive

in range (v. 10*a*). He is to be God's representative with authority to declare his word. That word determines the destinies of the nations. Moreover, his work is to be destructive in its immediate objective but constructive in its end result (v. 10*b*). He is to be a prophet of both judgment and salvation. The judgment aspect will predominate.

In verses 11–16 God, through symbolic perception, communicates two profound insights. The first is that he is awake and watching over his word to perform it. The second is that he is presiding over the movements of the nations and will use them for the carrying out of his word.

The call-experience closes with a divine charge (vv. 17–19). Jeremiah is to get ready for strenuous action. He is not to play the coward lest he be surrendered to the consequences of his cowardice. His message will cut across the character and conduct of his countrymen. His ministry will be opposed by governmental personnel, priests, and people. They will not prevail over him, for God will be with him and will make him "a defensed city, an iron pillar, and brazen walls"—that is, a person nobody and nothing can defeat or down.

Special points.—Jeremiah's call came in a time of impending world crisis (627). The north was "boiling" with possibilities. Against the background of the rapid decline of Assyria, a struggle for world supremacy was already in its early stages. It was just the sort of situation that called for a true spokesman for God.

The prophet's call likely came as the consummation of a growing religious experience. One day it all crystallized in the conviction, in confrontation with God, that everything in his background and life had worked together under the

hand of God to get him ready for the task to which he was now being summoned. Jeremiah believed in predestination, but it was predestination to service.

The call came in the form of a conversation between God and Jeremiah. When compared with that of Isaiah or Ezekiel, it is distinguished by simplicity. This has serious implications for our understanding of the prophet's ministry and message. Both in personal experience and in public proclamation he would emphasize that true religion is direct, dynamic personal fellowship with God, expressing itself in godly living.

The call was accompanied by two needed insights. Both came through ordinary sights: a blossoming almond branch and a boiling pot. The "waketree" bursting into bloom was a token of the coming of spring. It suggested that God is "continually awake" in the realm of history as well as nature, watching over his ethical purpose to carry it out. The wide-mouthed pot, present around most Hebrew households, was tilted away from the north, ready to empty its seething contents southward. This meant that "the North held the forces for the fulfilling of the Word" and that God would use those forces in the accomplishment of his purpose.

The call was concluded with a charge in which Jeremiah was not promised sympathy or success but struggle and strength—and victory.

The truth for today.—God is alive and active in his world. He is at work in nature (v. 11), in history (vv. 10,11,13–16), and in the human heart (vv. 4 ff.). This faith in the living God who is in control and is carrying out his purpose in life is something we greatly need in this day of crisis and change.

God works through his word. That word is still a powerful thing. It is effective in toppling structures of evil and in building assurance in the midst of defeatism and despair.

God has work for us to do in his world. He expects us to be up and about it. If he singles us out for a hard task and we shrink from it, as did Jeremiah, we should set over against our awareness of our inadequacy the assurance of his presence with us to perform his purpose (word).

The Sin of the People (Jer. 2:1–37)

The passage.—Chapter 2 belongs to a collection of prophecies (2–6) which come primarily from the early period of the prophet's activity (627–622). One of the great chapters of the book, it exhibits a remarkable unity. It centers around a single subject: the sin of Israel, God's people. Four aspects of that sin are stressed: the essence of it (vv. 1–13), the suffering caused by it (vv. 14–19), the seriousness of it (vv. 20–29), and the stubbornness of the people in it (vv. 30–37).

In the opening section (vv. 1–13) the prophet lays bare the essence of the people's sin. It is unfaithfulness to God. Their unfaithfulness has manifested itself in apostasy and idolatry. To Jeremiah, this turning away from the true God to false gods is utter folly.

The second section (vv. 14–19) emphasizes the suffering which the people have experienced because of their infidelity. It starts with three short, sharp questions (v. 14). The answer to the first two is: "No! He is a son!" Then what is the explanation of the hardship which Israel, the son, has endured at the hands of the Assyrians (v. 15) and the Egyptians (v. 16)? The explanation is given in verse 17 in the form of another question. Israel has become a "prey" to pagan powers because of rank apostasy.

The next section (vv. 20–27) dwells on the seriousness of the people's sin. Their sin is deep-seated and of long standing. The prophet employs some raw facts and forceful figures from everyday life in a rural community to portray the passionate plunge of the people into paganism. To be sure, the people have not renounced their bond to their covenant God. They acknowledge him in a formal way on special days and occasions. But, to get their fields blessed and their flocks multiplied, they have turned their backs on the true God and their faces to the Baals: they have one God for sacred days and other gods for ordinary days. When they get into trouble, they cry out to the covenant God, even try to press legal claim upon him, when, in fact, they have rebelled against him.

The final section (vv. 30–37) shows the stubbornness with which the people persist in their sin, despite God's goodness to them and his efforts to correct them through chastisement. They claim to be guiltless and continue to engage in idolatrous practices and in faithless diplomacy in foreign courts. But neither their protestations of innocence nor their political plotting and planning can avert the penalty of their apostasy.

Special points.—The overall pattern used by the prophet is the covenant lawsuit. God is plaintiff, prosecutor, and judge. The people are the defendants. The heavens are the jury. The charge is unfaithfulness to God. The prophet is the divine messenger who delivers the indictment and the sentence.

There is a sharp contrast between Israel's early devotion (vv. 1–3) and her later defection (vv. 4–13). Verses 2–3 contain a poem of great pathos and power, in which we feel the pain of a brokenhearted God whose wife (Israel) loved him and was loyal to him during "the honeymoon days," before she came into contact with the fertility cult of the Canaanites.

In verses 4–13 we get another glimpse of the suffering love of God. The accusation continues, first by indirection in verses 4–8 (as in verses 2–3), then by open indictment in verse 9. The climax comes in verse 13, one of the outstanding verses in the Old Testament. The "two evils" are apostasy and idolatry (the pagans were guilty of one, idolatry). The amazing fact, which has brought pain to the heart of God (vv. 2–3) and horror to the heavens (vv. 10–12), and which has resulted in national deterioration (vv. 4–8), is that God's people have forsaken him, the fountain of the waters of life, to cut out of the rock for themselves cisterns, cracked cisterns that can hold no water.

Verse 18 indicates that the people were placing their trust in man-made alliances rather than in reliance on God. They were drinking of "the waters of Sihor" (the Nile—Egypt) and "the waters of the river" (the Euphrates—Assyria) in preference to "the fountain of living waters" (God).

Note the seven strong figures in verses 20–26. They stress the depth and gravity of the apostasy of the people.

In verse 32 the prophet uses a touch from village life to emphasize the imcomprehensibility of Israel's conduct.

The truth for today.—Sin is no triviality. It is something deep and dark and terrible. It is a betrayal of God's love. It is spiritual adultery.

There is a dynamic connection between sin and judgment. They are two sides of the same coin, two parts of a single process. Rebellion against the sovereign will of God will result in inevitable retribution.

Idolatry is absurdity. It is leaving the true God of grace and glory for "gods" which have no real existence and can give no assistance. It is forsaking the fountain of fresh, ever-flowing, life-giving water to hew out, at great expenditure of energy and effort, cracked cisterns which can hold no water. It leads to a tragic fragmentation and disintegration of life.

While men, in their folly, are seeking substitutes for the God they have left, as they must and do—whether pleasure, possessions, position, power, education, scientism, formalism in religion, or something else—God is like a lovely fountain at the head of a valley, amid flowers, shrubs, and trees. The way to the fountain is open. There is no charge of admission. The water is sufficient, and it satisfies. The invitation is extended: "Ho, every one who thirsts, come to the waters!" (cf. Isa. 55:1; Rev. 22:17).

The Need and Nature of Repentance (Jer. 3:1—4:4)

The passage.—The theme is repentance. The key word is "turn" or "return." The theological logic is obvious. The people are guilty of terrible sin (2:1–37). Sin leads to judgment (2:35). The judgment can be averted and a right relationship with God restored only through real repentance. Hence the prophetic calls for a radical turnabout in character and conduct.

There are four principal parts to the passage: a condemnation of the people (3:1–5), a comparison of Judah and Israel (3:6–18), a contrast in conduct (3:19–20), and the people's cry and God's call (3:21—4:4).

In the first part (3:1–5) the prophet brings an incisive indictment of the prevailing attitude of the covenant people. By engaging in pagan or semipagan worship, they have played the harlot. As a consequence, they have an inadequate conception of the character and claims of God. Therefore, they have no real sense of the need for a radical inner change.

In the second division of the passage (3:6–18) Israel and Judah are compared to the disadvantage of the latter. Both are referred to as adulterous (apostate) sisters. But Judah is said to be the more guilty of the two. The stated reason for this conclusion is that Judah has had the warning example of Israel and has given no heed to it. There follows an earnest summons to return to God. The reason for the call is that God is a God of grace who will not keep his anger forever. The section ends with a plea and a promise: a plea for repentance and a promise of restoration and redemption.

Next we have a brief but beautiful poem in which God speaks (3:19–20). There is a sharp contrast between the way God has treated his people and the way they have treated him. In love, he gave them a pleasant land and a position of privilege among the peoples of the world, yet they have betrayed his love.

The final portion of the passage (3:21—4:4) brings the pleading begun in chapter 3 to a climax. The prophet hears the cry of a confused, frustrated, yearning, apostate people, who are disappointed with their worship and way of living (v. 21). This is followed by the command of God to turn back to him that he may forgive and heal (v. 22a). The people respond with their confession, which is more an expression of regret or remorse than of true repentance (vv. 22b-25). The passage concludes with God's clarion call for a repentance that is radical (4:1–4).

Special points.—Jeremiah employs both of Hosea's favorite figures—the husband-wife relationship and the father-son relationship (3:1–5,19–20; cf. 2:2–3)—to emphasize God's loyal love and Israel's flagrant faithlessness.

The historical reference in 3:6–11 is to the destruction of the Northern Kingdom in 721 because of its sin, the reformation under Hezekiah in Judah a little later, the temporary and superficial character of the "return," and the unprecedented pagan reaction under Manasseh. Judah did not profit from Israel's experience. She did not return to God with her whole heart.

In 3:14–18 Jeremiah looks forward to the day when God will rule over a redeemed, regenerated, reunited community, made up of Israelites, Judahites, and Gentiles, who will have such a mature conception of God and such a vital relation to him that they will depend upon a firsthand knowledge of him rather than upon any external forms and supports of religion. Even the ark of the covenant, the most sacred symbol of God's presence in ancient Israel, will no longer be remembered or missed!

Chapter 3:21—4:4 is in the form of an imitation of a liturgy. It builds to a strong climax in 4:1–4. Here God tells Israel that a superficial return is not enough. She must come all the way back to him (v. 1a). This return will involve a repudiation of idolatry in all its forms (v. 1b), a recognition of the lordship of God (v. 2a), and a radical revision and rearrangement of life (vv. 3–4). This is a painful process, like the plowing up of fallow ground or the circumcising of the heart. But it is necessary. Only in this way can God's promise to Israel be fulfilled, and her high destiny be realized (v. 2b; cf. Gen. 12:3; etc.). The alternative is ruin (v. 4b). God's "fury" is the retribution which follows one's refusal to respond properly to his loving purpose and pleas.

The truth for today.—The living God will not tolerate a partial allegiance. He requires complete commitment.

Sin, which is spiritual adultery, breaks

our relationship with God. Reconciliation can come only through radical repentance.

Real repentance is not mere regret or remorse. It is much more than elaborate ritualism in religion. It is a sincere return to God, which involves inner transformation, issuing in outer action.

This is the supreme need of the present hour. The need is acute, desperate. Through the practice of our pet idolatries (including empty formalism in religion) and the application of the philosophy of self-assertion, we have been pushed to the brink of unprecedented disaster. Only repentance and God can save us. It is, as Jeremiah said, "Repent or perish!"

The Ruin That Threatens (Jer. 4:5–31)

The passage.—Jeremiah has spoken of the sin of the people and of the need and nature of repentance. The next logical step is to stress the certainty and necessity of judgment, if the people do not turn back to God in true penitence, trust, and obedience. This he does in 4:5—6:30.

One of the most arresting features in 4:5—6:30 is a series of eight powerful poems portraying the coming of a foe from the north against Judah. As vivid and brilliant as these poems are, the primary emphasis in them is not on the description or identity of the enemy but upon the moral indictment of the people and the imminence of the judgment.

Five of the eight poems appear in 4:5–31. They are artistically arranged, are quite lyrical in character, and depict the successive stages in the invasion of the land, from the initial sounding of the alarm to the final death-shriek of the city as she sinks before the slaughterer. The first poem (vv. 4–10) centers about the warning of the watchman on the wall. The second (vv. 11–18) pictures the advance of the adversary. The third (vv. 19–22) is concerned with the anguish of the prophet as he contemplates that approach. The fourth (vv. 23–28) contains a vision of the cosmos reverting to chaos. The final poem (vv. 29–31) presents a brief but graphic portrayal of the assault of the enemy and the death-agony of the Holy City.

Special points.—There has been much difference of opinion about the identity of the foe from the north in these poems. It should be remembered that Jeremiah began his ministry with the conviction that calamity was coming upon Judah in the form of an invasion from the north and that this calamity was the judgment of God upon a rebellious, unrepentant people (1:13–16). This conviction was central to the message of the prophet throughout his ministry. At the outset, he did not identify the particular agent to be used by God (cf. 1:13–16; 4:5—6:30). He may have had the Babylonians in mind. However, it is perhaps better to assume that he had no specific people in mind at first. In any case, his primary concern was the moral condition of his countrymen and a sense of impending crisis. He must call the people to repentance. Later, following the fall of Nineveh (612) and the battle of Carchemish (605), he spoke specifically and openly of Babylon as the enemy from the north and of Nebuchadnezzar as God's "servant."

In verses 19–22 we have the first direct indication of Jeremiah's identification with the people in their sin and their suffering. The anguish expressed here would be experienced again and again in the years to follow. It stemmed from his love for his people.

The poem in verses 23–28 is a masterpiece. It speaks of a world catastrophe. Cosmos has reverted to chaos. Light is gone! The mountains and the hills, symbols of strength and stability, are no longer stable and secure, but are shaking and swaying and sinking! There is no man about, and the birds have fled! The cultivated land is a desert, and fortified cities are in ruins! And Jeremiah is looking on—as man faces the ultimate outcome of his choosing to live as a rebel against God! What a picture!

The clue to the understanding of this vision is to recognize that the prophet views the destruction of the universe. This, in turn, becomes symbolic for him of the destruction of Judah.

The truth for today.—This poem of unusual power (vv. 23–28) speaks to our contemporary situation. It pictures "the shaking of the foundations." We, too, are living in a day of grave crisis. Chaos threatens to invade and destroy cosmos. An atomic explosion of gigantic proportions! the end! no exit!

But we should remember that if sin leads to destruction, repentance leads to salvation. The same Bible which contains the picture of chaos also contains the promise of a new heaven and a new earth (cf. Isa. 65:17–25; Rev. 21–22).

The Reason for the Ruin (Jer. 5:1–31)

The passage.—This is a unique chapter. It tells about "a private prophetic project," by means of which the moral necessity for judgment was indelibly impressed upon Jeremiah. God put him out where the people were. He sent him through the streets of Jerusalem in search of "a man" of genuine piety and real integrity. The prophet went first to the "poor," the uneducated masses—peddlers, shopkeepers, donkey drivers, ordinary laborers. His search was in vain. Then he made his way to the "great," the jet set of Jerusalem. The result was the same.

As a consequence of this experience and his reflection upon it, Jeremiah brought one of the most penetrating and devastating indictments of a decadent society to be found anywhere, in the Bible or outside it. There are four major elements in the indictment or critique, four evidences of the deterioration that comes when there is no vital, personal, life-changing relationship with God. They are: corruptness of conduct (vv. 1–9), self-complacency (vv. 10–19), sheer callousness (vv. 20–29), and a conspiracy of evil from the center to the circumference of community life (vv. 30–31). The prophet drove home the truth that the loss of the ultimate loyalty, the lack of a right relationship with God, leads to moral and spiritual degeneration and to eventual disaster.

Special points.—Wanted: a man! What kind of man? One marked by "judgment" and "truth." "Judgment," in this context, is true religion on its practical side as a divine ordering of life. It is God's revealed way of life for his people. "Truth" is a firmness in one's relationship with God which shows itself in a stability or integrity or fidelity in one's relationships with others in the community. It is both trust and trustworthiness.

As Jeremiah went through the streets, the squares, and the shops of the capital city, peering into faces and observing attitudes and actions among both small and great, he discovered that the people were guilty of perjury (v. 2), of apostasy (vv. 5b, 6b, 7a), and of adultery (vv. 7b-8). Prosperity had not brought gratitude and godliness but depravity (v. 7b). The people were defiant. They would not repent (v. 3b). Such corruption must end in retribution (v. 9).

The particular manifestation of unfaithfulness to God pinpointed in verses

10–19 is that of apathy (vv. 12–13). Lacking in true piety and moral integrity, the people were also guilty of indifference. The primary reason for their apathy was their perversion of the doctrine of election (v. 12). In this, they were supported by the popular prophets, peddlers of a superficial and baseless optimism (v. 13). They had settled down into a comfortable sense of false security: "It can't happen here!" When true prophets, like Jeremiah, sought to shake them out of their self-complacency, they rejected their efforts by calling them windbags whose word of judgment was not the word of God (v. 13). But they would find that they were mistaken. Sin would lead to judgment (vv. 14–19; vv. 15–19 constitute the sixth poem about the foe from the north).

The aspect of the people's sin emphasized in verses 20–29 is callousness (cf. v. 21*b*). They had no sense of reverential awe in the presence of the great God of majesty and might (v. 22), no gratitude for his goodness to them (v. 24), and no regard for his covenant laws (vv. 26–28). Neither God's power nor his grace nor his law could get to them. They were hardened, encrusted, calloused. God must deal with them in divine visitation (v. 29).

The chapter comes to a crashing and climactic close with an appalling picture of a conspiracy of evil throughout community life (vv. 30–31). Hence, the question: "What will ye do in the end thereof?" A very good question for the beginning!

The truth for today.—The relevance of this chapter is almost terrifying. It presents a vivid picture of present-day society in America—corrupt, complacent, calloused, with a conspiracy of evil from its center to its circumference. Such a society tends to perpetuate itself. It is made up of corrupt individuals. Corrupt individuals produce corrupt structures and institutions. These breed more corrupt individuals. When the corrupt individuals and institutions become complacent and calloused, the problem is compounded. A difficult thing to deal with, the sin of the settled!

What can be done to change such a society? The only hope lies in the change of the human heart through the grace of God (cf. 4:4*a*,14; 17:9–10; 29:13; 31:33–34; 32:39; John 3:3; 2 Cor. 5:17).

Wanted: men and women of true piety and ethical integrity! Wake up, America! Let God into the situation that he may create his great society!

Rebellion, Ritualism, and Retribution (Jer. 6:1–30)

The passage.—This chapter closes the section which began with 4:5. It is more miscellaneous in character than 4:5–31 and 5:1–31.

There are five parts to the passage: the siege of the city (vv. 1–8), the sinfulness of the city's citizens (vv. 9–15), a system of sacrifice and ceremony no substitute for surrender to God (vv. 16–21), a sound like the roaring of the sea (vv. 22–26), and an assayer of the attitudes and actions of the people (27–30).

The remaining two poems about the foe from the north appear in verses 1–8 and 22–26. They are not outstandingly different in content from the other six. Verses 1–8 are quite dramatic in character. Verses 22–26 stress the cruelty of the invader and the agony his presence creates.

The prophet emphasizes the sinfulness of the people in verses 9–15 and the inadequacy of empty ritualism to meet God's requirements in verses 16–21.

In verses 27–30 Jeremiah is given a

confirmation of his call and a new conception of his work. He is to be not only a proclaimer and an exhorter but also a tester of the attitudes and actions of the people. He presents his current analysis of the situation.

Special points.—Several outstanding scholars render verse 2: "Daughter-Zion, I have likened you to a meadow delightful." Verse 3 picks up the figure, as the invaders are compared to shepherds (the commanders) bringing their flocks (the soldiers) to graze in that meadow.

Verse 11a indicates that Jeremiah is about to explode. He is so intimately involved with God and his word that he shares the pathos (emotion) of God.

There are three elements in Jeremiah's early indictment of the popular prophets and priests (and their people): greed for material gain (v. 13a), a spirit of superficial optimism (v. 14), and the lack of a sense of shame in the presence of sins committed (v. 15a). Nothing shocks or shakes them up any more—they have even lost their ability to blush.

"Incense" (from Sheba) and "sweet cane" (from India) were used in worship. Note the emphasis in verses 16 and 20: no amount of ceremonialism can suffice as a substitute for self-commitment.

There is a powerful wordplay in verse 30: a people who persistently reject God will eventually be rejected by God and men.

The truth for today.—Verse 16 is one of the outstanding verses in Jeremiah. Several things stand out in it. The first is a challenge to serious thought: "Stand at the parting of the ways and gaze at the guideposts. See where you are headed, lest you wind up in a wilderness or over a precipice. Ponder your paths! Think upon your way!" This challenge to serious thought needs to be issued to many in our day: those who follow the crowd, those who go in for novelty for novelty's sake, those who choose pleasure or money or position as the highest good in life, those who worship at the shrine of science or scholarship or institutional religion.

Second, there is a command to careful inquiry into "the old paths," with a view to ascertaining "the good way." This is no brief for an unprogressive, unthinking conservatism. Jeremiah was a "rebel prophet." He dared to cut across many hallowed customs and conventions of the day. At the same time, he was soundly grounded in the faith of the fathers.

"The old paths" were paths of real faith, spiritual worship, ethical conduct, and glad obedience. Among these would be found the good way, God's way—good because it had been ordained from eternity and set in the structure of reality, good because it had been tested and found to be true. It was not necessarily the easiest or shortest or most popular way. But it would be the good way—good in its commencement, its continuation, and in its consummation.

Third, there is a call to action: "And walk in it." It is not enough to think and inquire. There must be a positive response. The eternal paths of God alone can lead to salvation and security.

Fourth, there is an accompanying promise: "And ye shall. . . ." "Soul" is the total life of the person. "Rest" is settling down after restlessly wandering around. It is the relaxation of the whole life in a situation that makes this possible. It involves sharing the "rest" of God. The only way to it is that of commitment to the God of covenant grace, who has manifested himself supremely in the Incarnation, crucifixion, and resurrection of Jesus Christ, our Savior and Lord. In belief in the atonement of Christ on the cross is found rest

for the accusing conscience; in faith in
a loving Father is discovered rest for the
anxious mind; in fellowship with the
Holy Spirit comes rest for the troubled
heart; in complete commitment to and
cooperation with the will of the Lord
God—Father, Son, and Holy Spirit—is
found rest for a distracted will.

Finally, there is the people's choice:
"We will not. . . ." There are two ways
we can take in life, according to Jeremiah. One leads to "rest"; the other, to
ruin. Each person, each nation must
choose which path he or it will follow.
Israel chose the road to ruin. Will we?

Religious Rites and Right Relationships (Jer. 7:1—8:3)

The passage.—The contents of this
unit may be divided into four parts: a
sermon on the source of security (7:1–
15), a prohibition of prayer for a
profligate people (vv. 16–20), cultic conformity or complete commitment (vv.
21–28), and the valley of sacrifice—"the
valley of slaughter" (7:29—8:3).

For some years Jeremiah had been
watching the growth of "the Temple
superstition," that is, trust in the
Temple and that which transpired in it.
Then one day, with a holy fire in his
heart, he appeared in the Temple area
on the occasion of a religious
observance, probably the fall festival of
609 (cf. 26:1). Taking his life in his
hands, he denounced the cherished
Temple worship, indicated that an
ethical and spiritual religion alone is acceptable to God, and declared that God
was going to destroy the whole business,
Temple and all, if the people did not
return to a right relationship with him
(vv. 1–15).

Jeremiah has been called "the supreme intercessor" among the prophets.
Yet, because the people were so corrupt
that repentance was seemingly im-

possible and judgment inevitable, further
intercession for them was forbidden by
God (vv. 16–20; cf. 11:14; 14:11).

The clue to the interpretation of
verses 21–28 appears to be the preservation of a balance between verses 22
and 23. Jeremiah did not mean that
there was no sacrifice in the days of
Moses. There was. Nor did he repudiate
the cult lock, stock, and barrel. He was
not objecting to the cult as such, but to
a cult emptied of its original content and
real purpose. He was stressing the truth
that God's first and fundamental requirement is *not* cultic conformity *but* complete commitment, expressing itself in
obedience.

The people are rebuked again for
their apostasy and are told that in the
valley where they have slaughtered their
children in worship they will be
slaughtered. The slaughter will be so
great that, with the burial grounds full,
Tophet, the valley of slaughter (human
sacrifice), will be used (vv. 29–34).

In the time of divine retribution, the
bodies of the dead will be brought forth
from the graves to be exposed to the
heavenly bodies which they worshiped.
This—the very deepest shame—would
mean restless wandering in the underworld (8:1–3).

Special points.—As we move from
chapter 6 to chapter 7, we become
aware of a significant shift in time and
in language and style. Timewise, we
have moved from the period prior to
622 down to 609 (cf. 26:1; 2 Kings
22–23). Also, we find ourselves reading the first of Jeremiah's prose sermons.

The "Temple Sermon" (vv. 1–15) is
one of the greatest sermons of biblical
times and of all time. It appears to be
in the form of a legal brief. There are
four parts to it: a vigorous denunciation
of the whole priestly program (vv. 1–4
—the statement of the case); a pointed

declaration of God's demands (vv. 5–7 —a resumé of what God expects and has promised); an indignant indictment of worship divorced from life (vv. 8–11 —the direct accusation); and a graphic description of the impending destruction (vv. 12–15—the sentence).

This sermon on the basic issue of security nearly cost the prophet his life (26:7–24). It is no wonder, for in it he blasted some of the hallowed beliefs and practices of the people of his day and openly broke with the Josianic reformation.

The truth for today.—God does not desire a perfunctory and pretentious ritualism in religion. He wants real repentance, regeneration, and reformation. Wickedness and worship he cannot take!

Like the people of Jeremiah's day, so the people of our day are frantically searching for security. The prophet would tell us, as he told his countrymen, that security is not to be found in mere reverence for a holy book, however important this may be. It is not to be had through external reformation of life, as significant as this may be. It does not come through an elaborate ritualism in religion, as necessary as ritual is, in its proper place. The only security there is lies in a right relationship with God, expressing itself in right relationships with our fellowmen, all kinds and colors. This can never come through an act of Congress or through feverish activity at the church house. It can come only through complete commitment to the will of God. No foxhole religion—only an ethical fellowship with the living God! Security cannot be found in anything short of this! Then or now!

A Sinning People and a Suffering Prophet (Jer. 8:4—9:1)

The passage.—This section is related to the one preceding it in that it deals with the same basic theme and dates, in all probability, from the same general period. It may be divided as follows: the prophet's painful perplexity over the people's apostasy (8:4–7), wisdom and the word of God (vv. 8–13), the collapse of the spirit of the people in the face of a catastrophe (vv. 14–17), and the compassion of the prophet for his countrymen (8:18—9:1).

Jeremiah is staggered by the mystery of evil. The persistence of the people in their apostasy is so unnatural and incomprehensible. Migratory birds know and obey the God-given law of their being and well-being. Not God's people! Their irrational, headlong plunge toward destruction both perplexes and pains the prophet (vv. 4–7; cf. 2:13,21,32; 5:22–23; 6:16).

Stung by the remark in verse 7, perhaps the people reply: "We have wisdom. We know how God rules. We have it in a book!" Jeremiah expresses further amazement. How can a people who have rejected the word of the Lord claim wisdom, for there is no wisdom apart from that word (God's revelation of his will and a proper response to that revelation). Because they have rejected his word, God has rejected them. They will experience retribution (vv. 8–13).

In verses 14–17 we have a lament of the people. They are in utter despair. The reason? They are under the judgment of God because of their sin. Things haven't turned out as they expected (cf. v. 15 with 7:9). It is a time of terror, not triumph. And the worst is yet to come.

The lament of the people is followed by a lament of the prophet (8:18—9:1). Here are some of the most poignant and powerful lines in the book. Jeremiah scales the peak of pain as he expresses his sorrow over the suffering of his people.

Special points.—There has been much difference of opinion concerning the reference to the making of the law into a lie by the false pen of the scribes (8:8). This much seems clear. The law was being manipulated in the interests of ecclesiasticism. The external and ceremonial elements were being emphasized to the exclusion of the ethical and the spiritual. It is also highly probable that this activity was related to the Josianic reformation and the prophet's assessment of it (cf. 11:1–8,15–16; 7:1–15; 26).

The situation shortly after the death of Josiah in 609 provides a suitable setting for the double lament in 8:14— 9:1 (8:23, in Hebrew Bible).

Snake-charming was an art practiced in the Near East, including Israel. But no one skilled in this art would be able to charm the serpents coming against God's people (8:17). Some crises had been averted by various devices, such as faithless intriguing in foreign courts. Not this one!

To get the force of the statement in 8:20, we must recognize that the harvest and the summer were two different seasons. If the spring grain harvest failed, the late summer fruit harvest was unusually a success (or vice versa). If both failed, stark tragedy stared the people in the face. The proverb speaks of the tragedy of wasted opportunity. There comes a time when it is too late!

The answer to the first two questions in verse 22 is: "Yes. Gilead is famous for its medicinal herbs and physicians." The answer to the third question is: "There is a remedy available. It has not been applied."

A gross misrepresentation, one of the ironies of biblical interpretation, is based largely on 9:1. Though he loved deeply and suffered greatly, Jeremiah was not "the weeping prophet," but one of the great minds and spirits of the ages, who never wasted time weeping when there was work to be done for God.

"O That . . . I Might Leave My People!" (Jer. 9:2–26)

The passage.—The material in this section is miscellaneous in character and appears to emanate from the reign of Jehoaikim. It may be divided as follows: the prophet's despair over the depravity of the people (vv. 2–9), impending ruin and the reason for it (vv. 10–16), raise a dirge because of the ruin! (vv. 17–22), the true basis of boasting (vv. 23–24), and "circumcised—yet uncircumcised" (vv. 25–26).

Jeremiah is the most human of the prophets. He runs the gamut of emotions and frankly and honestly expresses what he feels. The lament in verses 2–9 is quite different from that in 8:18—9:1. There he identifies himself with his people in their suffering and sin. Here he wishes to separate himself from them and be done with them. Why? They are all just a bunch of rascals! The prophet pinpoints certain aspects of their sin: adultery, duplicity, dishonesty, cruelty. All are traced to their source in a lack of true piety (vv. 3*b*, 6*b*).

Verses 10–16 begin with a brief lament, followed by a fairly lengthy prophecy, which continues the description of imminent destruction suggested in verses 7–9, and, in a rather unique way, designates the cause of it.

In verses 17–22, Jeremiah is at his poetic best, as he describes, in the form of a dirge, the work of Death, the grim Reaper, as he goes through the land, leaving in his wake such an abundance of bodies that no one can bury them.

A blistering broadside is launched against a false pride which boasts in wisdom, power, and/or wealth, rather than in a right relationship with the sovereign God of grace, justice, and righteousness (vv. 23–24).

All who do not have the kind of relationship spoken of in verses 23–24 are uncircumcised spiritually (though they may be circumcised physically) and—whether pagan or Israelite—will experience divine judgment (vv. 25–26).

Special points.—In verse 2, Jeremiah expresses a very human desire, the desire to run away. The inn in the desert was usually sparsely furnished, for people only spent the night there. Sometimes there was an innkeeper. He had no responsibility for the guests. He could talk and trade stories with them. Then in the morning they would be gone. Perhaps Jeremiah longs to be such an innkeeper, to have human intercourse without responsibility, to be a looker-on at life. Yet he knows that the inn is not there, that there is no escape from reality and responsibility.

"Lovingkindness" (grace, loyal love), "judgment" (right decision), and "righteousness" (the practice of the principles of right action, or conformity to the code of conduct proper for God, or one in right relationship with him) are covenant words and have a very rich content and connotation (v. 24).

"Covenant" referred to a vital relationship between God and his people. It was rooted in his "grace" and expressed itself in "loyal love" of the people for God and each other. The relationship was sustained by the practice of "judgment" (justice) and "righteousness"—i.e., the code of conduct befitting one in that relationship. The maintenance of the relationship resulted in a state of "peace" (completeness, totality, harmony). From this "totality" —this state of harmonious relationships with self, God, and others—flowed "blessing"—i.e., inner vitality or lifeforce, and that to which it led for the

individual and the community: joy, fertility, prosperity, victory. In this one should "glory" (boast).

The truth for today.—A wrong relationship with God results in wrong relationships with one's fellowmen. Conversely, a right relationship with God (the knowledge of God) will lead to right relationships with others.

You can't run away. Many people, even the best people, have wanted to down through the ages. Some have tried it—as did Jonah. But you simply can't run away—from self, sin, suffering, or the sovereignty of God. The inn just isn't there. The great souls are those who stick, when they really want to run—as did Jeremiah, one of the spiritual giants of the ages.

Every generation has its set of values, its system of priorities. As in Jeremiah's day, so in our day some place wisdom (culture, scientism, education) at the head of the list. Others give first place to power (personal or collective). This means everything. It gets their ultimate allegiance. Still others put wealth—the accumulation of things—at the top of the ladder of value. But there is no true basis for boasting in these.

The only authentic basis for boasting (rejoicing, glorying) is to be found in God. A right relationship with him is the thing that matters supremely. We are to put him first in our lives and let him fill us with those qualities which he has and which he only can bestow. This is what abides—God, the knowledge of God, grace, justice, righteousness—and in this we should "boast" (glory, rejoice).

Idolatry and Calamity (Jer. 10:1–25)

The passage.—This chapter falls into three parts: God and the gods (vv. 1–16), the coming calamity (vv. 17–22), and a cry for compassion in chastisement (vv. 23–25).

Verses 1–16 form a separate and striking section which focuses on the folly of idolatry. The prophet presents a sharp contrast between the power of the God of Israel and the powerlessness of the gods of the pagans. There are three major emphases in the passage: first, a warning to God's people not to adopt the superstitious practices of the pagan peoples around them; second, an exposure of the absurdity of trying to materialize deity; third, a strong stress on the reality, sovereignty, and power of the God of Israel.

Verses 17–22 contain a short oracle (vv. 17–18), a touching lament (vv. 19–21), and a brief ejaculation (v. 22). The subject is the coming calamity.

In verses 23–25 the prophet utters a prayer. He prays first that God will not chastise his people with mathematical exactness, but that in wrath he will remember mercy. The prayer closes with a request for retribution to be poured out upon those who have ravaged God's people and their land.

Special points.—With superb sarcasm, the prophet reveals the irrationality of idolatry (cf. vv. 3–5,8–9,14–15). With sublime skill, he sets in clear relief the uniqueness of the God of Israel—his sovereignty, his wisdom, his grace, and his power (cf. vv. 6–7,10,12–13,16). Why leave him for a mere nothing, a chunk of wood, a scarecrow deity?

In a profound sense, man belongs to Another. Apart from the recognition of the priority of his relationship to God, he cannot find freedom and fulfilment, but experiences increasing self-deception and frustration (v. 23). There is here a remarkable expression of the paradox of the human situation, recognized by Augustine, Dostoevski, Kierkegaard, Holderlin, Rilke, and modern depth psychologists.

The truth for today.—The temptation to idolatry is ever present. Men today, as in the prophet's day, have a flair for idolatry. Their idolatry takes many forms (not necessarily metal—maybe mental; less tangible, but nonetheless real); sensual pleasure, lust for power, love of money, a hunger for fame, formal religion—anything short of God that represents the totality of reality for those involved.

The folly of idolatry is that men fashion their gods with care, fasten them securely in place, fall down before them, and find that those gods are nothingnesses and that they cannot give their worshipers any help, but, instead, cause them to become like them. Wooden deities! Wooden devotees! Hollow scarecrow gods! Hollow men!

Jeremiah and the Covenant (Jer. 11:1—12:17)

The passage.—This unit may be divided into four parts: crusader for the covenant (11:1–14), empty cultus and inescapable catastrophe (vv. 15–17), the prophet's first confession (11:18—12:6), and God's people and the pagans (vv. 7–17).

In verses 1–8 Jeremiah is enjoined to herald "the words (terms) of this covenant" to the people in the city and in the country, with particular stress on the curse (retribution) that comes from not giving heed to them (cf. Deut. 11:28; 27:26; 28:15–68; 29:20–21). He is to remind them that he is speaking of the covenant God made with them at the time of the deliverance from Egypt and that their well-being in the land God gave them has been and is dependent upon their obedience to his will (Deut. 2:30; 4:20; 6:3; 7:8; 8:18; 26:15). The prophet accepts the commission.

Verses 9–14 suggest that there was

resistance to the preaching of the prophet.

Verses 15–17 indicate that, in their present state, the people have no business in God's house. A mechanical rigmarole of ritual cannot remove their guilt. Hence there is no basis for exultation. Instead, there is going to be divine visitation.

In 11:18—12:6 we have the first of the prophet's "confessions." There are five of them, priceless passages which give us intimate glimpses into the inner life of God's servant. There is nothing like them elsewhere in the Bible. The other four are: 15:10–21; 17:9–10,14–18; 18:18–23; 20:7–18.

There are three parts to the first: the conspiracy (vv. 18–23), the complaint (12:1–4), and the challenge (vv. 5–6). The conspiracy takes place in Jeremiah's hometown, has as its objective the killing of the prophet, and involves his family members and neighbors. It provokes a complaint on his part against the rectitude of divine providence. God responds with a stern challenge.

Verses 7–17 have a common theme: the relationship of the covenant people to pagan peoples. Verses 7–13 contain God's dirge over the devastation of his heritage (see 2 Kings 24:1–2 for the probable historical background). His complaint corresponds to that of Jeremiah in verses 1–4. Just as the prophet has experienced great pain because of rejection by his people, so God experiences great pain because of his people's rejection of him and the retribution which this inevitably entails.

Verses 14–17 are concerned with God's dealings with the devastators. Though unaware of it, the people who have invaded Israel have served God's purpose. It is also a part of God's purpose that they, along with the Judeans, be carried into captivity by the Babylonians (cf. 25:8–9; 27:4–11; etc.). But, in time, they also will experience restoration to their own area.

Special points.—The crucial question in 11:1 ff. is: what covenant? Consider the historical situation (2 Kings 22—23) and of the content of the passage itself. It thus is a reasonable conjecture that "this covenant" refers to the Mosaic covenant of Sinai as renewed in 622 B.C. under the leadership of Josiah and the guidance of Deuteronomy. (According to most scholars, Deuteronomy was the book of the law found in the Temple.)

If this conclusion has validity, considerable light is shed on a very thorny problem, that of discovering Jeremiah's relation to the Josianic reformation. It would appear that the prophet was sympathetic with it and gave it his support for a season (vv. 1–8). Later, as he saw it deteriorating into an empty formalism, he became critical of it (vv. 15–17; cf. 8:8), and eventually broke openly with it (cf. chaps. 7, 26).

It is also likely that Jeremiah's advocacy of the reform movement had something to do with the plot in Anathoth (11:18–23; 12:6). It meant the closing of the local sanctuary. This put the prophet's priest relatives and friends out of a job. Clergymen do not like to be defrocked. So, they set about to deal with their meddling kinsman and fellow townsman!

The conspiracy called forth the complaint in 12:1–4. In the complaint, Jeremiah revealed several things: he was confused by the inequities of life (v. 1); he was concerned about God's reputation (v. 2); he was conscious of his own integrity (v. 3); he came to God with his case and committed it to him (vv. 1–4; note the presence of the lawsuit motif).

The prophet was in deep water. He was wrestling with the problem of the justice of God in his dealings with men.

He received an answer to his plea. It was not the kind he wanted but the kind he needed. He was in need of a challenge, not soothing comfort. And God provided it: "If a few footrunners have worn you down in your race for me, what will you do when you come up against thoroughbred horses? And if you fall flat on your face on level ground in a pleasant meadowland in your move for me, what will you do in the tangled, lion-infested jungles of the Jordan? Cheer up, Jeremiah, the worst is yet to come!" This was a call to courage, a challenge to heroic endurance (v. 5).

The challenge had implications for Jeremiah. There was a recognition of past service. There was also a revelation of future suffering. God had confidence in his servant. His servant must place his confidence in him. Together they would make the higher hurdles ahead.

The imprecations in 11:20 (?); 12:3; and elsewhere (cf. 15:15; 17:18; 18:21–23; 20:12[?]) pose a problem. From the Christian standpoint, there is no justification for the attitude expressed, but there is an explanation. At least three things should be kept in mind. First, Jeremiah never really succeeded at anything he ever did. He was constantly frustrated and fouled up, ridiculed and reproached, criticized and conspired against by the people whom he loved, served, and sought to save.

Second, like other Old Testament believers, he did not distinguish between sin and the sinner. His enemies were God's enemies. In praying for their destruction, he was giving expression primarily to his devotion to God and his desire for the vindication of his cause.

Third, he nowhere refers to a belief in a life after death. He thought in terms of earthly retribution. It was now

or never—all of which shows the difference that Christ and the empty tomb have made.

The truth for today.—We live in a day of much religious activity. Perhaps, when we go to church, we need occasionally to ask, "Why am I really here?"

As Christians, we are to hate sin but love the sinner. Also, we are to learn to pray: "Father, forgive them, for they know not what they do."

Sooner or later, we have to learn that the problem of reconciling a good God and a bad world must be solved on a personal basis and that we must be able to live without having all of the answers to the enigmas of life.

God's method, when his servants are down, frequently involves a call to courage, a challenge to endurance—not "You *are* really having a hard time!" but "Go on to the tougher still!" This is psychologically sound. If one responds properly to such a call, he becomes the better for it.

Life is full of testing times. The trials of the human pilgrimage tend, in the providence of God, to be graduated—the footmen before the horses, the land of peace before the jungle of the Jordan. The lesser trials are intended to prepare us for the greater. Victory in the lesser is a pledge and a promise of triumph in the greater, for the same God who helps us with the footmen will also aid us with the horses. Nothing is too hard for him!

Two Parables, a Plea, and Some Pessimistic Predictions (Jer. 13:1–27)

The passage.—This new section (cf. v. 1) contains five prophecies of various types coming mainly from the reign of Jehoaikim.

The first is the parable of the linen lioncloth (vv. 1–11). It consists of two parts: the story of the symbolic act (vv.

1–7) and the significance of the act (vv. 8–11).

In this bit of acted out symbolism, the Euphrates stands for the Mesopotamian area. Jeremiah represents God. The lioncloth—something highly prized by the Oriental male and worn close to his person—symbolizes Israel. Israel was God's treasured possession, his covenant people. At one time there had been a beautiful relationship between him and them. But pagan influences from the land between the rivers had separated God's people from him and made them "good for nothing," as far as his purpose was concerned.

The parable of the wine jars (vv. 12–14) contains words of warning. Using a popular proverb or a portion of a drinking song for his purpose, Jeremiah drives home the truth that, when the day of reckoning dawns, the people will not have the spiritual insight or moral energy to deal with it. Reeling against each other, they will perish together.

There follows a plea to give up pride and grant glory to God (the worship of true obedience) before it is too late (vv. 15–17).

Verses 18–19 present a picture of degradation and deportation for the king (Jehoaichin) and the queen mother (Nehushta). The captivity is a reality (597). No help will come from Egypt to the south.

The section closes with a prediction of the punishment of a reprobate people (vv. 20–27).

Special points.—The symbolic act was used in law, medicine, and worship. Since it was familiar to the people, the prophets employed it for communication purposes. It was an intensified form of prophetic proclamation. It was both illustrative and effective. It not only pictured that which was to take place but also propelled it toward actualization (cf. Jer. 13,16,19,27,28,32,43,51).

There is much question about the two round trips to the Euphrates—a total of at least 1,400 miles. The record reads like a simple, matter-of-fact narrative. Could not Jeremiah have made the trips as proof positive of his deep earnestness in the exercise of his ministry and as evidence of his complete readiness to do whatever God wanted him to do in order to get the precise message across?

The truth for today.—To the extent that God's people permit anything— pride, paganism, or whatever—to rob them of a right relationship with God they become ineffective for the carrying out of his kingdom purposes.

A sinful way of life tends to stultify the moral and spiritual faculties so that when the day of crisis comes we lack the insight and strength to meet it.

Verse 23 presents a penetrating portrayal of the power of habit, especially evil habit. The impossibility which it suggests becomes a glorious possibility through the grace of God in Jesus Christ (2 Cor. 5:17).

Drought and Other Disasters (Jer. 14:1—15:4)

The passage.—We have here a carefully integrated composition in dialogue form and prepared most probably in imitation of a liturgy. The emphasis on the certainty of captivity points to the reign of Jehoaikim as the historical setting for the passage.

This very dramatic and dynamic passage may be divided as follows: the plight of the people (14:1–6), the people's plea (vv. 7–9), God's reply through the prophet (v. 10), the punishment of the people for their perversity and of the prophets for their false promises (vv. 11–16), the prophet's pain for the people (vv. 17–18), the people's second petition (vv. 19–22), and God's response to their prayer (15:1–4).

The section starts with a powerful piece of pure poetry which portrays a natural calamity that has created a great emergency and caused much grief (vv. 2–6). The calamity suggests an even greater national catastrophe: captivity. In the verses that follow, there is a superb literary production (a blend of poetry and prose), in which the prophet skilfully interweaves the two disasters —drought and destruction—with an increasing stress on the latter. The people are past the point of no return. Their doom is writ.

Special points.—This prophecy resembles a penitential liturgy and may have been uttered by the prophet at the Temple in a time of penitence and prayer during the crisis caused by the drought.

The attitude of the people is arresting. They do not ask, "How are we letting God down?" but "Why is God letting us down?" They have a perverted conception of election. They present a perfunctory confession of their sin and press upon God his obligation to protect his "name" (honor, or character), his "glorious throne" (power), and his "covenant" (contract; here is the perversion referred to)—they have a threefold grip on him (cf. vv. 7–9,20–22).

Here is a group of people who have gone so far in sin and ceremonial worship that they are ignorant of the character of God and of the claims of true religion. Their attitude is: "All we have to do to get forgiveness and deliverance is to chase up to the 'church,' give God a brief salute, go through a few prescribed rites, and then leave, free once again to do as we please."

How can people be such fools? We share the prophet's perplexity and pain. All over this land and in many parts of the world there are multitudes acting in the same way. They forget that the great Savior-God is also a God of righteousness and that biblical faith, which begins with redemption through grace, also involves an ethical exaction.

God's attitude in this prophecy is also arresting. It is one of great severity. His patience has run out. Intercession is no longer of any avail (14:11; 15:1; cf. 7:16; 11:14).

The truth for today.—Foxhole religion was not born during the World War. It has been around for quite a spell. Men may give their loyalty to the gods of their choosing when the sun is shining, but when the storm strikes they strike out for the Temple and the God of grace and glory.

There is suggested here the basic difference between biblical faith and pagan religion, whatever its name or sign. Pagan religion attempts to put God (or the gods) at man's disposal. Biblical faith seeks to place man at God's disposal.

God is God, and he will not permit his people indefinitely to practice rebellion against his will and a religion that seeks to tether him to their wishes. Sooner or later he steps in to set things straight.

Judah's Winnowing and Jeremiah's Woes (Jer. 15:5–21)

The passage.—This unit contains some of the most poignant and important material in the book. It may be divided into two sections: the punishment of an apostate people (vv. 5–9) and the price of being a prophet (vv. 10–21).

In a personal lament, Jeremiah pictures the pathetic plight of Jerusalem (vv. 5–9). Because the people have left the Lord and keep walking away from him, instead of turning back to him in true repentance, he is not going to alter his course of action (repent) any more, but will take them to the gates of the cities (or the border of the country) with his winnowing fork, pitch them into the air, and let the wind carry them into captivity.

In verses 10–21, we have the prophet's second confession. There are three parts to it: the prophet's perplexity and pain (vv. 10–12), his prayer (vv. 15–18), and God's reply to the prayer (vv. 19–21).

The prophet is painfully perplexed by two things: the failure of his people and the frustration of his preaching (vv. 10–12). He bemoans his birth because he is at odds with everybody, is forever citing his countrymen to the bar of divine judgment. All are hurling curses at him—and this despite the fact that, through prayer and preaching, he has been seeking to save them from a tragic fate. He is not made of iron. Can he be expected to stand up against an unlimited amount of opposition?

The prayer, one of the most unconventional ever recorded, follows (vv. 15–18). First, Jeremiah pleads that God will remember him and visit him—this he needs, by this he lives—and that he will wreak vengeance on his foes (v. 15). Next, he proclaims his joy in belonging to God and in being the medium of revelation (v. 16). Third, he protests the loneliness which is his lot as a spiritual leader who must constantly proclaim judgment (v. 17). Finally, he plumbs the depths of pain as he gazes into the face of God and asks, "Are you like . . . ?" (v. 18).

God answers the prayer, but it is not an easy answer (vv. 19–21; cf. 12:5). Jeremiah must do two things. First, he must repent. His attitude of resentment and rebellion has impaired his relationship with God. He must practice what he has preached: repentance. Second, he must rid himself and his message of all that is unworthy. Not all in the tester (cf. 6:27) is pure metal. The dross must go. If he will do these two things, he will be restored as God's true and trusted messenger, will cause the crowd to turn ultimately to him for the word of the Lord instead of his going over to the crowd, will become a fortified wall of bronze (cf. 1:18), and will be defended and delivered from evildoers.

Special points.—Verses 13–14 appear in 17:3–4 and are more in context there.

The figure in verse 18 is very daring. There are wadis (brooks) aplenty in Palestine. During the rainy season they are full to overflowing, but during the hot summer months they are bone dry. Woe to any one who goes to one of them seeking water for personal or agricultural purposes in a time of need. In the depths of agony, Jeremiah, who once had spoken of God as "the fountain of living waters" (2:13), now asks whether he is like "waters that fail," i.e., a God who is quite promising in good times but does not perform in times of real need.

Jeremiah was having "soul-trouble." What was the difficulty? Two things, it would seem—aside from the fact that he was human and was undergoing terrific inner and outer distress. First, he was the victim of self-concern. Encircle the pronouns "I," "me," and "my." They occur 18 times in four verses (vv. 15–18). Self had moved to the center of the stage. Second, the prophet was temporarily interpreting his commission more in terms of comfort than in terms of character and kingdom service. God had told him that he would have a hard time but that he would be with him (1:17–19).

The truth for today.—Does God fail his people, let them down in the clutch? No! Inadequate or inaccurate conceptions of him will. The wrong brand of religion will. God, never!

Real prayer is not the presenting of pretty, polished speeches to God. It is the pouring out of the soul before God —dregs and all. It is a practice in honesty.

The greatest battle that any one fights is the battle with self.

When a servant of God is in the throes of doubt and distress, the real question becomes: Will he run away, or will he stick and struggle through? The only real way out is through a deeper surrender to God and a more sincere service of God. A greater commitment leads to a greater certainty.

The Great Renunciation (Jer. 16:1–21)

The passage.—Autobiographical in character, this passage appears to have originated during the reign of Jehoaikim. However, it gives expression to a conviction which must have come to Jeremiah much earlier, for marriage was a state much to be desired among the Israelites and they ordinarily married at a rather early age.

The chapter may be divided as follows: Jeremiah forbidden to marry (vv. 1–4), the prophet not permitted to take part in mourning or merrymaking (vv. 5–9), Judah to be punished for her sin (vv. 10–13), a second exodus greater than the first (vv. 14–15), no escape from God (vv. 16–18), and the God of all the earth—the light of all men (vv. 19–21).

Special points.—The prophet was denied the delights of family life and the joys of participation in normal social life. He was not even to weep with those who wept.

This tremendous denial was a part of God's plan for him. His giving up of a life made bright by the presence of wife and children and by ordinary human intercourse was to be a sign that ca-

tastrophe was coming upon the country and that parents and children would die horrible deaths from sword, starvation, and disease.

There was nothing wrong with marriage as far as the prophets were concerned (cf. Hos. 1–3; Isa. 8:1–4,18; Ezek. 24:15–27). But Jeremiah was gripped by the conviction that giving up marriage and family was God's will for him and a part of his witness to his people. There is a parallel between him and Paul at this point, and there is something in 1 Corinthians 7:26 which is reminiscent of Jeremiah 16.

The point is that each person should commit himself to God's will for his life. This may mean one thing for one, another for another. But only in the doing of his will do we find peace and power.

Miscellaneous Materials (Jer. 17:1–27)

The passage.—One has called this chapter a "miscellaneous file." On the surface, it seems to lack organic unity. A careful study, however, will disclose a dynamic, though elusive, relation of the chapter to its context and of the different parts of the chapter to each other. The reign of Jehoaikim provides the most likely setting for the contents of the chapter.

The chapter consists of seven sections: Judah's sin and the certainty of her punishment (vv. 1–4), a psalm contrasting true and false character (vv. 5–8), the prophet's penetration of the human predicament (vv. 9–10), a proverb about a partridge (v. 11), a passage about the true place of sanctuary (vv. 12–13), a prayer for healing and help (vv. 14–18), and a proclamation about the sanctity of the sabbath (vv. 19–27).

The sin of Judah is deepseated (cf. 2:22 f.). It is indelibly inscribed upon her heart (the center of her being) and upon the horns of her altars (the cult she is observing), and it cannot be removed by an empty, elaborate ritualism (vv. 1–2). Its price must be paid. The penalty is captivity (vv. 3–4: cf. 15: 13–14).

The psalm in verses 5–8 presents a picture of two trees which represent two types of persons. One turns from God and trusts in man, making the "flesh" his strength (arm). This secularization of life lands him in a desert of dryness and death. The other puts his faith in the Lord. The basic orientation of his life toward the spiritual and eternal rather than the material and temporal leads to life, beauty, joy, stability, strength, and fruitfulness.

In a remarkable wisdom-like passage in poetic form, the prophet lays bare in a single sentence the secret of the world's predicament: a deceitful, diseased heart, defiant of God's control (v. 9). Only God can know the inner being of man (v. 10).

There follows a proverb about a partridge (v. 11). Just as a mother partridge that takes over another bird's nest and hatches the eggs discovers that later the young abandon her because they are "an alien brood," so the man who acquires wealth in the wrong way will find that it will leave him one day and fly away.

Salvation and security are to be found in the sovereign God whose spiritual presence fills the universe and who is personally present among his people (vv. 12–13).

Verses 14–18 contain the prophet's prayer for healing and help. His stern sermons about judgment have provoked antagonism and angry audience reactions. He wonders whether he may have crossed the line between dedication to the glory of God and the good of the

people, and a desire for personal vindication. He longs to be purged of all selfishness and sin, that he may be a true witness for God. Verses 14–18 (plus verses 9–10) constitute the prophet's third confession.

Verses 19–27 concern the sanctity of the sabbath. The fathers broke the covenant, as indicated by their desecration of the sabbath. The people are enjoined to learn from their example and to keep the sabbath holy. If they don't, they will suffer.

Special points.—There is a remarkable anticipation in verses 9–10 of the "discovery" of modern depth psychologists and of the emphasis of certain contemporary writers and theologians. The human heart seeks to cover up its real problems and motivations, suffers from a fatal malignancy, and, in living in revolt against God, becomes the center of conflict, which, if not resolved, means disaster.

Jeremiah reiterates, in various ways, that anything and everything outside a right covenant relationship with God will end in frustration and failure. In verses 12–13, he turns the coin over and says that the true place of sanctuary is a throne of glory set on high from the beginning. The phrase "a glorious high throne" (a throne of glory set on high) is very suggestive. It suggests the real presence of God on earth, in the sanctuary, and among his people. It also goes beyond this to refer to the transcendent Being whose majestic spiritual presence fills the world.

The sabbath has been called the grandest institution in the religion of Israel. Some regard it as the sign of the Mosaic covenant. It was an outer token of Israel's relationship to God and tantamount to dedication to and worship of him. Its proper observance symbolized her loyalty to her covenant God. Originally (and until quite late) the sabbath was a delight, a day of rest, rejoicing, and renewal (cf. Isa. 58:13–14).

The truth for today.—There are two ways through life. Man may take either. He may choose the way of faith or the way of "unfaith," the way of submission to God or the way of rebellion against God. There is no other alternative. He then must decide, and his choice will have consequences. One way will lead to dryness and death. The other will lead to delight and life.

If the primary cause of man's problems is a corrupt heart, the only cure for those problems is a changed heart (v. 9; cf. 31:33–34; 32:39). This comes through the grace of God in Christ (2 Cor. 5:17).

God's throne of glory, symbol of his personal presence and universal sovereignty, is "the place of our sanctuary," our "hope," the center and source of salvation and security in any and every situation. The same God who reigns also redeems. He who is afar off comes very near. He who was really present among his people in a particular way in the sanctuary in Old Testament days is *really* present among us in Jesus Christ, our Savior, "the Lord of glory," who became flesh and dwelt among us and whose glory we beheld.

Proper sabbath observance is not synonymous with puritanical legalism, and there is much to be said for corporate worship and personal renewal—physical and spiritual—on a set day, and also for an open public witness to the reality of inner dedication of life to God.

Perplexity, Parable, and Plot (Jer. 18:1–23)

The passage.—Chapters 18–20 constitute an editorial unit. The unit contains materials of diverse character,

coming most likely from the reign of Jehoaikim.

Chapter 18 may be divided into three parts: the parable of the potter and the clay (vv. 1–12), a poetic portrayal of the unnaturalness of the people's apostasy (vv. 13–17), and a plot and a protest (vv. 18–23).

In verses 1–12 we have one of Jeremiah's prose sermons (cf. 7:1 ff.; etc.). It begins with a personal experience (vv. 1–4), which becomes a parable and is expanded into a prophecy (vv. 5–12). God can do as the potter does: he can adjust to a changed situation. If his people cooperate with him, he can make them the kind of people he wants them to be, a true covenant community. If they refuse to cooperate, he must deal drastically with them in loving discipline, in order that, if possible, they may be made over into a people he can use effectively for the achievement of his purpose.

Verses 13–19 stress the unnaturalness and incomprehensibility of Israel's sin (cf. 2:10–13; 5:20–25; 8:7; etc.). Her apostasy is contrary to the practice of pagans and to the established patterns in nature. Because of her conduct, so unnatural and incomprehensible, she must experience the judgment of a holy God.

Verses 18–23 are regarded as Jeremiah's fourth "confession." Verse 18 tells of a plot against the prophet by the religious leaders of the day, and verses 19–23 record the prophet's passionate protest. He pleads his innocence (vv. 19–20) and prays for the destruction of those who are opposing him (vv. 21–23).

Special points.—The visit to the pottery is one of the most interesting and important episodes in the Bible. For one thing, it sheds much light on the matter of inspiration and revelation. It gives us a brief glimpse into the revela-

17. A potter
at work (see
Jer. 18:1–4)

tory process. It shows how God caused a new truth to be born in the prophet's brain and how, under inspiration, he communicated the revelation to the people in words which they could understand and which would suit their situation.

In the second place, the experience here recorded is significant because the parable of the potter and the clay has become "the classical illustration" of the divine sovereignty in relation to human freedom. God is sovereign, but he works with free men. Man is free, but only to choose the response he will make to God.

The experience at the pottery is important, too, because it shows not only the sovereignty and freedom of God but also his love and patience. In his marvelous grace, God gives men a new opportunity to rise to his purpose.

A fourth reason for the tremendous significance of the visit to the potter's house is that it marks a turning point in the prophet's career. He was now convinced that the nation was doomed. But what did this mean? Was God defeated? Was he casting Israel off forever? Jeremiah was plunged into a Gethsemane of perplexity and agony. In a most unlikely place, he was given light

453

on this painful problem. He learned
that the captivity did not mean doom
but discipline. Beyond the judgment that
must come upon Judah there lay a future of hope. In short, the experience at
the pottery meant the entry of a new
element into Jeremiah's message and
marked the beginning of a new epoch
in his ministry. From this time forward
began he "to build and to plant." In the
years that would follow, the blacker the
circumstances around him would become, the brighter his forecasts of the
future of God's people would be.

The truth for today.—God is the
divine potter. As potter, he is sovereign
over life. The clay is under his control.
But he is not amusing himself with it.
He is about something and knows what
he is about. He has a purpose for all of
life and for every life. Man is not the
product and plaything of blind fate.
God's purpose includes both nations and
individuals. We cannot always fully understand his purpose, but we can rest in
the assurance that it is beneficent because it is divine. The highest wisdom of
man is to seek to find and fit into the
divine purpose.

Though God is a potter with a purpose, there is always the possibility of
perverting his purpose. We can resist
the touch of the potter's hand, and the
vessel can be marred. God can and does
fail at times. He fails because he has
granted man the power of choice. We
can say yes or no to him. This means
that there is ever the possibility that we
will frustrate his purpose and turn his
beautiful dream for us into a frightful
nightmare.

Also, God's wonderful patience and
perseverance appear in the process of
the remoulding of the vessel. God does
not let go of man easily, but stands ever
ready to give him the second chance—
and the ten thousandth. This is the gos-

pel of his infinite grace.

As to ancient Israel, so to us, God
offers a fresh start, a new beginning. To
refuse his offer is to rob ourselves. To
accept it is to find forgiveness and the
fulness of life in Christ.

A Parable and a Proclamation (Jer. 19: 1–15)

The passage.—The material in this
chapter is concerned with events which
probably transpired in the early part of
Jehoaikim's reign. They are included
here because of the symbolic act and
the allusion to a potter's vessel (cf.
chaps. 18, 20).

There are two parts to the chapter:
the parable of the potter's pitcher (vv.
1–13) and the proclamation in the Temple (vv. 14–15). In verses 1–13 Jeremiah
is directed by God to purchase a potter's vessel, to take it—along with some
of the leaders of the people—to the
southern section of the city, and to
smash the vessel in the presence of the
people, accompanying this symbolic act
with a prophetic pronouncement. He
does what he is told to do.

Verses 14–15 record the story of
the prophet's trip from Tophet to the
Temple, where he delivers the same sermon—briefly but pointedly. The point
was that the people's persistent rebellion against God was going to result
in terrible retribution.

Special points.—In chapter 19 we
encounter a new literary type for the
first time: biographical narration. Someone else is telling a story about Jeremiah
(probably Baruch).

The "potter's earthen vessel" was the
most delicate, artistic, and costly member of the pitcher family. It had a slen-
der, narrow neck. Once broken, it was
almost impossible to mend it. It was an
apt symbol for Jerusalem in Jeremiah's
illustrated sermon.

"The valley of the son of Hinnom" was south-southwest of the city. There the audience could see Tophet, the place where human sacrifice was offered to Baal (in 32:35, Molech).

There is a blending of a sermon in speech and a sermon in symbolic act in verses 3–13, including both accusation and announcement of judgment.

The truth for today.—There comes a time when God's patience runs out. When it does, religious opportunity passes, and God's grace gives way to his wrath. Has America passed the point of no return, or will we turn back to God before it is too late?

Agony and Victory (Jer. 20:1–18)

The passage.—This chapter, one of the most significant in the book, contains one of the earliest references to open, outright persecution of the prophet because of his preaching. Also, it preserves the last and greatest of Jeremiah's confessions.

The confession is made up of two parts: verses 7–13 and 14–18. A tenable conjecture is that verses 14–18 were spoken before verses 7–13. If this be the case, the contents of the chapter may be analyzed as follows: the situation (vv. 1–6), the struggle (vv. 14–18, 7–10), and the assurance (vv. 11–13).

The situation is that of intense suffering. Angered by the sermon in the Temple, Pashhur, the chief of the Temple police, beats Jeremiah and puts him in the stocks. There, for perhaps 24 hours, he undergoes indignity, physical torture, and terrific mental anguish. When Pashhur decides to release him the next day, the prophet drenches him with denunciation and gives him a name which makes him a double sign of the essence of the sermon he preached in the Temple (vv. 1–6).

At some point during the agonizing experience, Jeremiah breaks forth in a bitter outcry (vv. 14–18). He curses the day of his birth and the man who brought the news to his father from the women's quarters concerning his new son. He asks why, once born, he was permitted to live and spend his days in shame and sorrow. He has reached a dead end—and this for doing the will of God. Black despair grips him.

Having given vent to his feelings about his coming into the world, he gets down to the matter of his work in the world. Having reached a dead end, he goes back to his call. In his intense struggle with the realities in the situation and with God's relation to them, he addresses God directly in verses 7–10. He accuses him of seducing him, of overpowering him, and getting him into the ministry without revealing the extent of the responsibility and the suffering involved. His faithful communication of the divine word has made him a day-long joke to the people. He would like to go back to the life of an ordinary layman, but, when he thinks this way, something catches fire in his bones, and he cannot put it out or hold it in. He is painfully conscious of the cruel taunts of the crowd, including some of his familiar friends.

Now comes the assurance: agony followed by victory (vv. 11–13). Confidence in God's saving presence and sovereign power causes the prophet to move upward out of the depths. His foes are on the losing side, not he! God is going to win, and his servant will be vindicated. A dead end becomes a doorway to victory!

Special points.—One of Jeremiah's favorite expressions was *magor-missabib,* "terror-all-around." He did a daring and clever thing in giving this name to Pashhur, thereby making him "a walking sermon," a living confirmation of the truth of his preaching (vv. 3–6). Later, the milling crowd turned it on him: "There's old Terror-all-around! He's denounced us aplenty. Let's denounce him!" (v. 10).

In verses 7 ff. we have one of the most impressive and illuminating passages in the prophetical literature of the Old Testament. As no other passage, it takes us "into the depths of the prophet's soul" and "into the secrets of the prophetic consciousness." Talk about prophetic constraint and compulsion, this is it (vv. 7–10; cf. 1 Cor. 9:16). A major mark of a true prophet was a sense of call. His supreme mission was a faithful communication of the divine word.

In this final confession, Jeremiah emerges from his dark night of the soul into the sunshine again, God's iron man, whom nothing and nobody can down, a prophet of courage and hope, committed to the will of God whatever the cost. The promise of his call has been fulfilled (1:18). He can now minister to his people effectively amid the gathering shadows and in their darkest hour.

The truth for today.—Jeremiah would tell us that prayer is conversation with God. As such, it is a two-way affair, not a monologue but a dialogue. It is not a chore but a joy, as is any conversation with a good friend. It is vital and varied, not stale and stagnant—not saying the same old things over and over. It is not complicated and sophisticated but simple and childlike.

Jeremiah made prayer a practice in honesty. At times, the prophet seemed to border on blasphemy. Actually, he was simply disclosing the intimacy and honesty which characterized his communion with God and which made prayer so meaningful in his ministry. Such prayer can change our lives.

The way to greater certainty and more effective service is the way of deeper commitment to God.

Jeremiah as Statesman-Prophet (Jer. 21: 1–14)

The passage.—This chapter reveals Jeremiah in a new role, that of statesman-prophet. Also, no longer is he hounded by "the higher-ups." He is a national figure and is sought out by the king in a national crisis.

There are two parts to the chapter: Zedekiah's request and Jeremiah's reply (vv. 1–10), and the responsibility and delinquency of the royal house (vv. 11–14).

Weak-willed, well-meaning Zedekiah became king of Judah in 597. He was under the influence of the nationalistic party, and favored revolt against the Babylonian overlord, in reliance on Egypt. He came close to rebellion in 594–593, but apparently held off, possibly because of the dynamic and dramatic preaching of Jeremiah (see chaps. 27—28). With the accession of Pharoah Hophra in Egypt in 589, the fireworks started. Zedekiah was deeply involved. Nebuchadnezzar marched westward in late summer or early autumn, blockaded Jerusalem, and began subjugating the surrounding towns and cities. A few months later he laid siege to the Holy City. The incident recorded in 21:1–10 took place during the blockade.

Quite distraught, Zedekiah sent to Jeremiah a delegation of two men to ask the prophet to inquire of the Lord for a word concerning the situation which the city and country were facing. Evidently he expected an assurance of divine deliverance such as Isaiah gave Hezekiah in the crisis of 701 (cf. Isa. 37:36 f.). In his response, Jeremiah stated that the people would not be able to repel the enemy, but would retreat within the city, for God himself would fight against them. Many would perish, and those who survived would be turned over to Nebuchadnezzar. Moreover, he counseled surrender to the enemy as the wise course and forecast that the city would be captured and consumed by fire (vv. 1–10).

Verses 11–14 contain a prophecy addressed to the royal house of Judah. In verses 11–12 there is the proclamation of a principle: the Davidic dynasty was responsible, under God, for the establishment of justice in society in keeping with covenant law (Ex. 22:20–23). Stability and continuity were dependent upon a faithful discharge of this responsibility. Since there had been delinquency in this area, the royal house was under the judgment of God. Retribution would come upon both court and city (vv. 13–14).

Special points.—The unusual expression "his life . . . for a prey" (v. 9) probably originated in the army. When an army came home in triumph, it brought booty. But when it came in defeat, there was none. The returning soldiers were likely asked, "What booty or prey do you have?" After an unsuccessful campaign, the answer may have been a shrug of the shoulders and something like this: "Booty? Prey? My life is my booty. I managed to get back alive. That is my prey, my prize of war."

The attitude of Jeremiah in verses 8–10 raises two questions: Was he a patriot or a traitor? Did he love his country? The answer to the second is that he loved his country so much that he was willing to sacrifice everything he held near and dear if, by chance, the soul of the nation might be saved. The answer to the first is: it depends on what one means by patriotism. If he means "My country, right or wrong," Jere-

miah was no patriot. If he means "I want above all else that my country be in line with the will of God," then Jeremiah was an example of the enlightened type of patriotism so greatly needed today.

In verses 11–12 Jeremiah reveals that good government is absolutely indispensable to the well-being of a nation. When it goes, life begins to fall apart. Judgment is inevitable.

Jeremiah and the Rulers of Judah (Jer. 22:1—23:8)

The passage.—This section contains a collection of prophecies concerning the Davidic kings. It may be analyzed as follows: Jeremiah's first encounter with Jehoaikim (22:1–9), his lament over Jehoahaz (vv. 10–12), his judgment-speech again Jehoaikim (vv. 13–19), a dirge over Jerusalem's disaster (vv. 20–23), oracles against Jehoaichin (vv. 24–30), and false rulers and a true Ruler (23:1–8).

The maintenance of justice was a major duty attached to sacral kingship in the Near East. In Judah, the obligation was intrinsic to both the Mosaic and the Davidic covenants. A proper discharge of this responsibility was essential to the preservation of the stability and continuity of the covenant community (cf. 21:12).

In his first recorded appearance at court as God's messenger, Jeremiah reiterated this basic principle of kingship, probably in the presence of Jehoaikim soon after his accession (22:1–9). Josiah, father and predecessor of Jehoaikim, faithfully executed the covenant stipulations in his dealings with his subjects (vv. 15b–16). But not the son! He was a selfish, heartless tyrant who practiced injustice and unrighteousness (vv. 13 ff.). Neither Jehoahaz nor Jehoaichin

ruled long enough to reveal the direction
his administration would take. Zedekiah
and his colleagues fell far short of the
ideal (23:1–4). But one day there would
appear a righteous Branch, the Messiah,
who would succeed in his service to
God and man, would make possible salvation and security, and would completely carry out all covenant stipulations
in his relationship with God's people as
king (vv. 5–6).

Special points.—Jeremiah's clash with
Jehoaikim catapulted him onto the stage
of history as a statesman-prophet. This
marked a turning point in his career. He
did not leave the role as long as the
state stood.

As the prophet parades before the
reader the men who were kings of Judah
during his ministry, he ranges from commendation (Josiah, 22:15b–16) to lamentation (Jehoahaz, Jehoaichin, 22:10–
12, 24 ff.) to condemnation (Jehoaikim
and, by indirection, Zedekiah, 22:13–19;
23:1–4) to anticipation (the ideal king
of the future, 23:5–6).

The complex on the kings moves forward toward a climax, beginning with
the proclamation of the basic principle
of kingship in 22:1–9 and ending with
the promise of the Messiah and the
prediction of a unique new Exodus in
23:5–8.

One is impressed with Jeremiah's
raw courage, his capacity for righteous
indignation in the presence of entrenched evil, and the clarity of his view
of the realities of the present and the
glories of the future, read in the light of
the divine purpose.

The Polemic Against the Prophets (Jer. 23:9–40)

The passage.—This remarkable section concerning the prophets may be
divided into four major parts: deep distress (vv. 9–12), a sharp distinction (vv.

13–15), an incisive indictment (vv. 16–
32), and a prophetic discourse (vv.
33–40).

Jeremiah begins with a graphic expression of inner pain. He is in agony because of his realization of the awfulness
of sin and the revelation of God's antagonism to it—the divine words of
denunciation and doom which he must
utter. More specifically, he is undergoing
terrible inner distress because of the
general corruption that is so widespread
and because of the tragic consequences
to which it will inevitably lead. The bitterest part of it all is that the priests
and prophets share and support that
corruption. They are lacking in that
"aloofness of character" which enables
God's servants to touch the life of a nation with healing power. For such men
judgment is certain (vv. 9–12).

In verses 13–15 the prophets of Israel and those of Judah are compared,
to the disadvantage of the latter, who
are considered to be more guilty than
the former. Lacking in moral character,
the prophets of Judah are also lacking in the capacity for moral leadership.
Instead of leading the people into a
deeper fellowship with God and a more
ethical relationship with their fellowmen, they are strengthening the hands of
evildoers and are poisoning the life of
the land. Retribution is inescapable.

Lacking in moral character and in
the capacity for moral leadership, the
popular prophets are also lacking in an
authentic message. Their message is devoid of all moral content and challenge. Hence it is the word of man and
not the word of God. It originates in
the human cranium and not in the council of the Lord. The Lord is against such
prophets and will bring them to book
(vv. 16–32).

The discourse in verses 33–40 revolves
around a wordplay. The word for "bur-

den" literally means "a lifting up, a thing lifted off." Thus it can refer either to the lifting of a load (burden) or to the lifting up of the voice (oracle, usually doom-oracle). Since Jeremiah's preaching, with its emphasis on sin and judgment, was a bit burdensome and boring for some of the "brethren," they would ask him, "What is the burden of the Lord today? We know that it has to be a heavy doom-oracle. So what is it this time?" One day the prophet turned the question on the questioners: *"You are the burden of the Lord! And he is tired of carrying you and is going to cast you off!"* Because of the sarcastic spirit shown, they were forbidden to use the expression in the future and were told that they were going into exile.

Special points.—One of Jeremiah's greatest trials and tasks was the necessity of combating the influence of the priests and the prophets of his day—especially the prophets. He was convinced that they were largely responsible for the superficial optimism, the insensitivity to social and ethical issues, and the moral and spiritual corruption so widely prevalent among his countrymen. They were the supporters of the established order and the chief obstacles to his preaching.

The ecclesiastical conflict began early in his career and continued to the end. It resulted in an open clash in 594–593 (cf. chaps. 27–28). That clash provides the point of greatest illumination for the polemic in 23:9–40.

We have in this polemic the most penetrating analysis of true and false prophecy to be found in the Bible. The problem of distinguishing between a true prophet and a false prophet was and is both acute and elusive. A careful study of 23:9 ff., in the context of the content of chapters 27–28 and of other references to the prophets in Jeremiah, can enable one to form a list of criteria that can be helpful. When it is all sifted down, the solution for the problem lies partly in the conduct of the man and the content of his message, but primarily in the sense of divine constraint, the deep consciousness of having true insight into the will of God for the present situation, and the faithful communication of the "word" for that situation. The "word" itself has a self-authenticating power which is difficult to resist by one who gives it a fair hearing. The problem becomes less difficult when both prophet and people are in a right relationship with God and have the Spirit of God within them.

The truth for today.—Prophetic preaching can play a very important role in the life of a people. On the one hand, a poisoned prophetic spirit can and will gradually poison the life of a nation. On the other hand, true prophecy can have a transforming power (vv. 14–15,22).

The God of biblical faith is not a little local god, whose presence, purpose, and power are limited to a particular place and people. Nor is he a "next-door-neighbor" sort of deity, with whom one can be quite "chummy" and from whom he can easily escape. He is a majestic sovereign God, whose spiritual presence pervades the entire universe. He is a God at hand—yes, but also a God afar off. He is both transcendent and immanent, and there is no way to avoid encounter with him (vv. 23–24). How big is your God?

The word of man is straw (chaff): it has no real substance and provides no sustenance. The word of God is like wheat, which gives life; like a fire, which consumes anything and everything contrary to God's character and will; and like a hammer, that breaks in bits all opposition and smashes any and all illusions and falsehoods in which men place their confidence. The word of the living God is a dynamic, creative, powerful thing (vv. 28–29)!

The presence of sincere, God-called, committed, courageous prophets among God's people to proclaim his word is a token of his love for them. Sad is the day when the sun goes down on the prophets in any land—including our own—and when there is "no vision" (no true prophetic perception)! For where there is no vision, the people perish.

A Vision of Two Baskets of Figs (Jer. 24:1–10)

The passage.—Possibly it was the summer of 597. Earlier that year Nebuchadnezzar had carried the upper crust of Judean society into captivity (v. 1). Among the exiles was the young king, Jeconiah (Jehoaichin). It was a time of tragedy.

People were bringing their figs to market in the city. Jeremiah saw two baskets of them. They became a medium of revelation.

Verses 1–3 tell of the prophet's experience. As he thought about the historical situation and about the sight of the figs, he fell into a trance. He noted that one basket had delicious, edible figs in it (first-ripe figs were a delicacy), and that the other basket contained overripe, rotting (naughty) figs, unfit for human consumption. He also observed that these baskets were "set before the Temple of the Lord."

Verses 4–10 give the explanation of the prophet's experience. The good figs represent the exiles in Babylon (vv. 4–7). God looks on them with favor. They are the hope of true religion in the future.

Stripped of illusions and false securities, they will respond properly to their

suffering. They will "return" to God "with their whole heart." As an act of grace, God "will give them a heart to know" him. In short, through genuine repentance they will come into a vital, personal, life-changing relationship with God. They will be the true covenant community of the future. Through them God will carry forward his purpose of salvation. This will involve restoration to their native land.

The bad figs represent the Judeans left in Judah and those living in Egypt (vv. 8–10). The former, in particular, are characterized by a spirit of self-righteous superiority. They look upon themselves as the remnant who survived the judgment. They scorn the captives. Terrible sinners, they—good riddance!

The Judeans in Egypt are likely members of the pro-Egyptian party who sought refuge in that land in 609, or 601, or 597.

Because of their arrogant self-righteousness, their reliance upon false conceptions of religion, and, in some cases, their rank paganism (cf. Ezek. 8:5 ff.), God cannot use the group symbolized by the basket of rotting figs.

Special points.—One should note the emphasis on repentance, God's grace, and the words "pull down," "pluck up," "build," and "plant," so prominent in 1:10 and elsewhere in the book. He should also observe the position of the baskets of figs: "set before the Temple of the Lord." This indicates that the primary emphasis is religious. It may also suggest that mere reliance on the presence of the Temple will not save those who survived the captivity of 597.

But there are three things that stand out sharply. First, God can be known anywhere—in Babylon or in Jerusalem —if sought with the whole heart. This was a tremendous revelation in Jeremiah's day (cf. 29:13), when so much trust was placed in the external supports of religion.

Second, in the midst of terrible tragedy, the prophet had hope. Though it was dark about him, he saw a light ahead. God was still at work, and his work was going on.

Third, Jeremiah's hope for the future of religion centered from this time forward in the exiles (cf. 29—33). This insight was vindicated in signal fashion in historical experience.

The Cup of God's Wrath (Jer. 25:1–38)

The passage.—The date is 605, not long after the battle of Carchemish. The passage consists of two parts: a summation and a proclamation (vv. 1–14), and the presentation of the cup to the nations (vv. 15–38).

The summation is in the form of a reproach (vv. 3–7). Speaking from a heart filled with loving compassion and righteous indignation, Jeremiah reminds the people that for 23 years he has faithfully preached God's word to them. Like other God-called prophets through the ages, he has urged upon them the absolute necessity of that fundamental "turning" so essential to a secure "abiding" in their God-given land. The only response has been constant disobedience and continual idolatry.

There follows a proclamation of disaster (vv. 8–14), so integral to the preaching of Jeremiah through the years. There is a peculiar poignancy in the declaration that the coming calamity will mean the cessation of the sights and sounds of a happy everyday existence (v. 10; cf. 7:34; 16:9; 33:11).

Verses 15–38 relate a personal experience of the prophet. In vision, Jeremiah is commanded to present a cup of the wine of the wrath of God to particular nations that they may drink it and stagger like crazy men. This he does.

The cup of wine represents God's basic antagonism to the sinfulness of the nations (cf. chaps. 46–51). Their reeling signifies the retribution that is coming upon them because of their sin. The righteous Ruler of the universe will bring not only Judah but also other nations to book.

Special points.—The victory of the Babylonians at Carchemish (605) constituted a strong confirmation of Jeremiah's preaching for many years concerning judgment in the form of a coming of a foe from the north. It is not surprising that a new urgency entered his preaching in 605. The crisis was at hand. It was now or never. The rebels must repent!

In verse 9 Nebuchadnezzar is spoken of by God as "my servant." In the light of recent study, we now know that this does not mean that Nebuchadnezzar was a devout worshiper of the true God but that he was his "vassal," subject to his sovereign will and obligated to provide his army for the carrying out of his sovereign's purpose. This is another expression of the prophet's theology of history.

The mention of "this book" (v. 13), when set in the context of Jeremiah's dictation of his prophecies in 605 (cf. 25:1; 36:1), suggests that the present passage may have been the conclusion to that "book" (36:4,32).

It is possible that Jeremiah originated the powerful, awesome figure of the cup of divine wrath. The grim figure and the reality it represented must have caused horror and anguish in his sensitive soul.

The truth for today.—True repentance is the only way to escape from retribution and experience redemption. "Repent or perish!" is a cry that needs to be sounded loud and clear in our day.

The cup of divine wrath is a cup from which we all have to drink. Life places it to our lips, this cup of the consequences of our wrong choices. Its contents can be very bitter, whether the recipient be a nation or a person.

Jesus himself cried out in agony in Gethsemane: "Abba, Father, all things are possible to thee; remove this cup from me; yet not what I will, but what thou wilt" (Mark 14:36, RSV). In his case, the cup was not for his sin but for ours. On that same night, he presented a cup to his followers and said: "This is the blood of the new covenant, which is poured out for many" (Mark 14:24, ASV). He transformed Jeremiah's image into a figure for the price of our salvation, his pouring out of his blood on the cross. If through "turning" from our sin in true penitence and trust we come into a saving knowledge of the grace of God, the cup of God's eternal wrath *can* pass from us!

The Story of the Temple Sermon (Jer. 26:1–24)

The passage.—Chapter 26 may be divided into three sections: the setting of the sermon (vv. 1–3), the substance of the sermon (vv. 4–6), and the sequel of the sermon (vv. 7–24).

The occasion was a religious observance in the accession year of Jehoaikim. It was likely the fall festival in 609. Crowds of people had come to the Holy City to worship. Jeremiah was commanded to deliver God's word to them —without deletion or dilution. The purpose was to try to get them to return to a right relationship to the covenant Lord.

Only the essence of the sermon is given (vv. 4–6; for a fuller record of it, see 7:1–15). Simply stated, it is this: If the people do not change their way of life and commit themselves to the sovereign will of God, God will destroy the Temple, as Shiloh was destroyed earlier (*ca.* 1050 B.C.), and he will make Jerusalem "a curse" to all the countries of

the earth (i.e., when they wish to pronounce a curse, they will say, "May you become as Jerusalem!").

The central emphasis in the chapter is on the response the sermon got and the reaction it provoked. It caused quite an uproar. This is no surprise, for it struck at some of the most cherished and hallowed beliefs and practices of the day (such as the inviolability of Jerusalem and the indestructibility of the elect).

As the story unfolds, we note the determination of the priests and the prophets to dispense with Jeremiah (vv. 7–11), the prophet's self-defense (vv. 12–15), and his deliverance (vv. 16–24). Jeremiah was charged with being a false prophet (cf. Deut. 18:20). When put on trial, he met the charge head on. Through the intervention of the laity and in the providence of God his life was preserved. The story of Urijah is inserted to indicate the danger in which Jeremiah was (vv. 20–23).

Special points.—This is the first chapter in what is often called "The Biography of Jeremiah." That "biography" (chaps. 26–45) is a very unusual, exciting, and significant work. In it, Baruch tells how Jeremiah walked the way of a cross because of his commitment to the divine purpose. Theologically speaking, the implication is that suffering and the service of God are somehow interwoven. There are foreshadowings of the concept of the Suffering Servant and of the cross of Calvary.

Some may be puzzled by the use of the word "repent" in verse 3. This particular term is employed mainly in connection with God in the Old Testament. It signifies a change of mind or an alteration of decision or course of action with regard to a person or situation. There is an element of emotion involved (often, grief). God longs to forgive and save, if only the people will truly "turn" to him in penitence, trust, and obedience.

There is a noticeable difference between the attitude of the laity and the clergy in this crucial situation. The laity are more open to the truth. They do not have entrenched interests to defend. Hence they more readily recognize the ring of reality in the prophet's words.

Jeremiah's defense is most inspiring. He retracts nothing, but reaffirms that God has *really* sent him to speak all the words he has spoken. What transparent sincerity! What fearless courage! What utter devotion to God whatever the cost!

The truth for today.—Three things stand out. First, empty, elaborate ritualism in religion is not enough. God desires and requires real repentance and right relationships. Second, commitment to God costs. Third, there is need today, as in Jeremiah's day, for the individual who will stand against the crowd and for his convictions regardless of the cost.

A Sermon in Symbol and Speech (Jer. 27:1–22)

The passage.—It was 594 or 593. Diplomats from surrounding countries had come to Jerusalem for a caucus. Their purpose was to plan a revolt against Nebuchadnezzar. Nationalistic prophets were fanning the flames of rebellion. Jeremiah demonstrated his superb statesmanship by delivering a penetrating and timely sermon. Because the situation was so crucial, he resorted to the intensified form of prophetic proclamation used on earlier occasions (cf. 13:1 ff.; 16:1 ff.; 19:1 ff.; 35:1 ff.). He directed the sermon first to the rulers of the nations (vv. 1–11), then to King Zedekiah of Judah (vv. 12–15), and finally to the priests and the people (vv. 16–22).

Although he adapted the message to the audience addressed, the message itself was essentially the same. The will of God, the Lord of history, was that the nations, including Judah, submit to the yoke of Babylonian overlordship. The only alternative was disaster.

Special points.—There is an involved textual problem in 27:1 and 28:1. The interested reader is referred to the more technical commentaries for a discussion of it. It is obvious that the two chapters deal with the same general situation. Critical textual study brings 27:1 and 28:1 into harmony, so that both passages refer to the fourth year of the reign of Zedekiah.

The allusion in the term "yokes" (v. 2) is to wooden yoke-bars which were bound with leather thongs. Apparently only one yoke was made. It symbolized submission to Babylon.

One can imagine the dramatic situation. The delegates from the various nations were meeting in the statehouse. In walked the preacher with a plowman's ox-yoke around his neck. All had seen such a yoke, but not on a man!

To the startled group Jeremiah said, in effect: "I want you to take a message back to your respective rulers. The great Creator and Controller of this world has a purpose which he is working out in history. His purpose now is that you submit to the yoke of Babylonian supremacy. That supremacy will last until Babylon's time of reckoning arrives. But for you to resist now is to resist God, and there is no future in that kind of enterprise. Don't listen to these prophets who are filling you with false hopes and lies. Submit and survive!"

As a demonstrator, a one-man protest movement, Jeremiah must have created quite a sensation! With some variations and adaptations, he addressed the same sermon to Zedekiah and to the priests and people in Jerusalem.

The reference to Nebuchadnezzar as God's "servant" (v. 6) does not mean that the king was a worshiper of the true God but that he was subject to him as sovereign and, as a vassal, was obligated to serve him with his army.

We are impressed not only with Jeremiah's ingenuity in getting his sermon across but also with his consistency in interpreting events in terms of a theology of history.

Jeremiah and Hananiah (Jer. 28:1–17)

The passage.—The conflict between Jeremiah and the prophets was becoming more acute. Finally, it broke into open clash. Chapter 28 records the incident.

There are four parts to the chapter: Hananiah's prophecy of release and restoration (vv. 1–4), Jeremiah's reception of the prophecy and his response to it (vv. 5–9), Hananiah's symbolic action and verbal proclamation (vv. 10–11), and Jeremiah's final declaration and vindication (vv. 12–17).

Hananiah, evidently a leader among the prophets, met Jeremiah in the Temple precincts. The latter was still wearing the yoke. In the presence of the priests and the people in the area, Hananiah announced that he had received a revelation from the Lord. It was that in two years God would break the yoke of Babylon and bring home Jehoaichin, the captives, and the Temple furnishings.

Jeremiah responded with a hearty "Amen," but, upon reflection, reminded Hananiah that, in the past, the burden of proof had rested on the purveyors of a bright and breezy optimism and not on the proclaimers of the stern word of ethical judgment.

In a fit of fury, possibly, Hananiah broke the yoke from Jeremiah's neck and reiterated his prophecy of an early release from Babylon. By this symbolic act he hoped to cancel out Jeremiah's utterance and set his own in motion toward fulfilment.

Since inspiration was lacking at the moment, Jeremiah went his way to pray about the matter and wrestle it through. He had to reply to Hananiah, and reply he did, as soon as the word of the Lord came to him.

That word was twofold: a message for Judah (vv. 13–14) and a message for Hananiah (vv. 15–16). The message for the nation was that, instead of a yoke of wood that might be broken, God had forged a yoke of iron which none could break. The policy of revolt implied in Hananiah's prophecy would result in total subjection to Nebuchadnezzar.

The message for Hananiah was that, since he had not been "sent" by God, had "taught rebellion against the Lord" (in advocating a policy contrary to the will of God), and had caused the "people to trust in a lie," he must die (cf. Deut. 13:6; 18:20). And he did—two months later (v. 17).

Special points.—It is obvious that in chapter 28 the phrase "the prophet" is constantly used in connection with the names of Jeremiah and Hananiah. This is intentional, not accidental. The prophets are being set over against each other.

They engage in open clash. Both speak in the name of the Lord. Both speak with conviction and apparent sincerity. Both employ the proper formula. Both engage in symbolic acts. Yet both cannot be right.

We call Jeremiah a "true" prophet and Hananiah a "false" prophet. But how do we know? How did the people know? Study this chapter carefully and then examine 23:9–40 in the context of the experience here portrayed. The difference lay primarily in the strong sense of call, the intimate communion with God, the character of the man, and the ethical content of the message. One who is Spirit-led can usually distinguish between the two.

The Prophet's Communication with the Captives (Jer. 29:1–32)

The passage.—The first major Babylonian captivity came in early 597. Jeremiah was deeply concerned about the well-being of the exiles. Because of his concern he communicated with them. The correspondence took place between 597 and 594.

The first letter (vv. 1–23) was carried to the captives by an important delegation of the king. In it the prophet gives some counsel for the present and a forecast of the future.

He urges the exiles to face up to the facts. They are to be there a long time. They should settle down, engage in normal activities, and seek the well-being of the area assigned to them. They must not pay attention to the prophets, for they are preaching a lie (two are mentioned by name and their tragic fate predicted—cf. vv. 21–23).

Although they are not coming back in the near future, as some of the prophets are saying, they are coming back, after 70 years. God has plans for them, a future of hope. Meanwhile, they are not necessarily separated from him, for they can find him in intimate personal relationship in Babylon as in Jerusalem—without Temple, land, priests, sacrifice—if they seek him with all the energy of intellect and will. Then, in God's own time, he will bring them back to the place from which he sent them into exile.

It is not surprising that the letter had repercussions, making a second letter necessary (vv. 24–32). A certain Shemaiah, a prophet in Babylon, wrote letters to Jerusalem about Jeremiah's letter. One of these went to Zephaniah, chief of the Temple police, urging him to deal with this dangerous fanatic. Zephaniah showed the letter to Jeremiah, and did nothing about it.

Jeremiah wrote another letter to the exiles warning them of the falsehood and folly of Shemaiah's viewpoint and predicting that because this man had no mandate from God and no true message from God, no member of his family would participate in the restoration "the good that I will do. . . ."

Special points.—Chapter 29 is a very important chapter. It sheds much light upon Jeremiah and upon his conception of God and religion. First, it indicates that he was now an impressive and influential person among his people.

Second, it reveals his raw courage. He dared to shatter the illusions and false hopes of the exiles and to stand up against the prophets who were encouraging the exiles in them.

Third, the correspondence discloses that Jeremiah was a man of indomitable faith. Because of his realism, he was pessimistic about the immediate future. Yet he was optimistic for the long pull. He was sure that God had plans for his people and that he would carry them out.

Fourth, his communication with the captives reveals that Jeremiah was a man of penetrating insight. He saw that true faith is not dependent upon geographical locality or cultic conformity. One can know God anywhere, if he meets the conditions.

Finally, we note that Jeremiah enjoined prayer for the enemy. This is the only place in the Old Testament where this is done.

Jeremiah both personalized and universalized the religion of his people.

The Good That I Will Do (Jer. 30:1-24)

The passage.—The chapter may be analyzed as follows: a preface (vv. 1-3), a people saved by the Lord (vv. 4-9), a people saved from afar (vv. 10-11), a people saved from within (vv. 12-17), a people saved unto God (vv. 18-22), and a people struck by the storm of the Lord (vv. 23-24).

The preface states the theme of chapters 30-33: the glorious future of the people of God.

Following the general introduction, the prophet paints a vivid picture of the day of the Lord. It will be a day of distress (vv. 5-7a) and a day of deliverance (vv. 7b-9).

God tenderly assures his people that, though he must chasten (correct) them in just measure, he will not leave them in captivity, but will save them "from afar" (cf. 31:2). Therefore they are not to fear (vv. 10-11).

In sharp contrast to a picture of an incurable condition of sin and guilt (vv. 12-15) is set a promise of healing and health (vv. 16-17). God will save his people from within.

There follows a remarkable portrayal of an ideal theocracy (vv. 18-22). The prophet describes the rebuilding of the city and community, the joy of the citizens thereof, and the reign of God among them through a chosen prince. The covenant ideal will be realized.

At the close of the chapter, there is a reference to the storm of divine judgment to be encountered by the people who oppose God (vv. 23-24; cf. 23: 19-20). The alternative? The salvation of the Lord, or the storm of the Lord!

Special points.—Chapters 30-33 contain a collection of prophecies of hope

known as "the book of consolation." They have a distinctive introduction (30: 1-3) and a common theme. Each chapter also has its separate heading (30:4; 31:1; 32:1; 33:1).

The day of the Lord is the day of his activity when he intervenes in human affairs to set things right. It involves judgment and salvation. The primary allusion in verses 5-7a is to the captivity of 587. The reference to "David their king" is messianic (v. 9; cf. 23:5-6; 30:21; 33:15).

"Jacob" was the ancestor of all the Israelites (vv. 7,10,18; cf. 31:1).

The phrase "all thy lovers" (v. 14) designates the political allies of Judah who deserted her in the day of divine visitation (588-587 B.C.).

There is something very striking in verse 21. The prince (king) referred to is God's representative among the people. The unique feature is the manner of his approach to God. It is through "standing bail or surety" by offering his life in pledge. In this way he keeps access to God open. Are there foreshadowings here of something profound and far-reaching?

The Optimism of Grace (Jer. 31:1-40)

The passage.—There are several parts to this tremendous chapter: love and hope (vv. 1-6), faces aglow over the goodness of God (vv. 7-14), Rachel's grief and God's gracious promise (vv. 15-22), the renewal and repopulation of Judah and Israel (vv. 23-30), God's new thing (vv. 31-34), and God's double seal (vv. 35-40).

The wonderful love of God is the basis for Jeremiah's glowing hope of a glorious homecoming (vv. 1-6).

God, who is father to his people, will redeem and restore them. Like a good shepherd, he will guide and guard them. With songs on their lips, they will return from exile with faces aglow over the goodness of the Lord. In their new life, they will have joy and plenty and tranquility (vv. 7–14).

Mother Rachel, long dead, is pictured as weeping and wailing because her children have been carried into captivity (v. 15). God assures her that her labor in giving birth to them and in caring for them has not been in vain. It will be rewarded. They will be brought back from captivity (vv. 16–17).

While the mother is weeping, the children are also weeping. They confess that they deserve the discipline they have received and pray a prayer of penitence (vv. 18–19). God responds to the penitent prodigal with an assurance, an injunction, and a prediction (vv. 20–22).

There is to be a great reversal which will involve both parts of the people of God (vv. 23–28). The renewal which the reversal will entail will be on the basis of individual response to God's call to repentance and participation in his redemption (vv. 29–30).

The prophet is speaking of a new order in human affairs, a wonderful new thing which God will create (cf. v. 22). That new thing is the subject of the noblest of Jeremiah's prophecies, that of the new covenant (vv. 33–34). That covenant will be marked by pardon and grace, by firsthand fellowship of the individual with God, and by direct illumination concerning the will of God.

At the close of the forecast of the new covenant he will make and the new man he will make, God sets a double seal. The first is placed directly by the hand of God (vv. 35–37). It involves his faithfulness, as seen in the fixed order of nature. This order is a guarantee of the permanence of the new Israel. The second part of the seal is the promise of the new Jerusalem (vv. 38–40). This involves the action of man.

Special points.—Note verses 2–3. God appears from afar (Jerusalem) to his people suffering in the "wilderness" (a figure for the captivity, a period of discipline and deprivation). In response to their seeking "rest" (cf. 6:16), he assures them that he loves them with "an everlasting love" (the word for a love that springs spontaneously from within and seeks out the beloved—i.e., election love; cf. 2:3) and that with grace ("lovingkindness"—the word for love which stresses loyalty, even to those unworthy of it—i.e., covenant love, here grace; cf. 2:3) he is drawing them (seeking to bring them into a right relationship with him).

In poetic quality, verses 1–6 and 15–22 are scarcely surpassed in Jeremiah. Note especially the pictures in verses 4–6 and 15 and the dramatic quality of verses 15–22.

Verses 18–19 depict the kind of repentance necessary to participation in God's redemption of his people. Verses 29–30 emphasize the necessity for a sense of ethical responsibility on the part of the individual.

The greatest prophecy in Jeremiah is the new covenant passage (vv. 31–34). It deals with God's new thing spoken of in verse 22. Several observations need to be made. First, the unique structure of the passage stresses that God's new thing is to be radically different and that what is here said about it *is* revelation.

Moreover, the revelation comes in a particular life situation as the solution of a problem. The collapse of the old covenant (with the destruction of the nation) created the question: How can a holy God maintain a relationship with a sinful people? The answer comes in the form of the new covenant concept.

Further, the revelation involves both continuity and discontinuity. There will be continuity. Like the old, the new covenant will be rooted in and rest on the divine initiative—God will act in sovereign grace. Also, it will have as its intent the realization of a dynamic relationship between God and man. Again, it will include at its center the law—not a new law—as the expression of God's will for his people. Moreover, it will be a covenant made with the whole people of God. It will transcend the national entity but not community and group solidarity.

If there is to be continuity between the new and the old, there is also discontinuity. For one thing, the new covenant is incorporated in the promise. Formerly, covenants were made, not promised. The taking up of the covenant into the promise marks the end of the history of God's previous dealings with his people. Again, the new covenant includes an eschatological dimension.

Further, it involves the creation of a new man through a new divine deed. God will put his will straight into the heart of man so that the necessity of communication through external methods will be circumvented. This is Jeremiah's way of speaking of the work of the Holy Spirit in the making of a new man, who not only has illumination as to what God's will is, but also has the power to respond in obedience to that will. This new man knows God firsthand. And it all roots in redemption, the forgiveness of sins.

This picture of a new man, forgiven and in fellowship with God in a new community, with the ability to discern and do God's will, has no parallel in the Old Testament.

The truth for today.—God's love underlies the trying experiences of life. It is a perpetual love, a powerful love, and a personal love.

God's wonderful new thing is available today. Jeremiah's picture of the faith of the future finds fulfilment in the New Testament faith. It includes the forgiveness of sins through Christ (the grace of our Lord Jesus Christ), the fellowship with the Father in love, "from the least . . . to the greatest . . ." (the love of God the Father), and the fulness of the Spirit (the communion of the Holy Spirit). God alone, in his marvelous grace, can deal effectively with our sin and make us new creatures in Christ.

A true repentance and a personal sense of ethical responsibility are essential to participation in God's great salvation.

God's faithfulness guarantees the permanence and future glory of his people.

And I Bought the Field (Jer. 32:1–44)

The passage.—This interesting and illuminating chapter consists of the preface to a prophecy in symbolic act (vv. 1–8), the account of the purchase of a piece of real estate (vv. 9–15), the prayer of the prophet (vv. 16–25), and the response of God (vv. 26–44).

In the preface, two things are emphasized: the prophet's imprisonment (vv. 1–5) and his presentiment (vv. 6–8).

Verses 9–15 tell of Jeremiah's purchase of a piece of property at Anathoth as a tangible token of his faith in the future of God's purpose and people.

There follows, in verses 16–25, a beautiful but agonizing prayer. In one of those afterthought situations, in which the prophet realized the contradiction between his action and the actual situation around him, he sought clarity through prayer.

God's response dwells on two things: because the guilt of Jerusalem is so great, her destruction is sure: because her God is a God of grace, her restoration is certain (vv. 26–44).

Special points.—The court of the guard (prison) was a portion of the palace where prisoners with dangerous views were kept under the direct supervision of the king. Confinement was semipublic (cf. 37:21; 38:1 ff.; the date was likely 587).

Jeremiah had a presentiment concerning the coming of his cousin which he identified as the word of the Lord (vv. 6–7). This was confirmed in experience: "Then I *knew* that this was the word of the Lord" (v. 8). An interesting insight into the matter of inspiration and revelation!

The incident recorded in verses 9–15 is most instructive and inspiring. It is a very illuminating illustration of the process involved in an ancient business transaction. But it is much more. It is a concrete revelation of the fact that in Judah's darkest hour Jeremiah, the so-called "weeping prophet," was her supreme optimist! No trafficker in tears and tragedy this man, but a true prophet of gallant courage and gigantic faith!

Verses 37–41 are very important and should be compared with 31:31–34.

The truth for today.—No matter how dark it may become about us, there is always a light ahead. God holds the future and has a future for his people.

Clarity and certainty in the midst of confusion and inner conflict will often come through earnest, intimate, honest communion with God.

Happy Days Ahead (Jer. 33:1–26)

The passage.—The overall emphasis in chapters 30–32 continues in chapter 33. The outlook is bright. The subject is the happy future of God's people. The divisions of the chapter are obvious: the rebuilding of the Holy City (vv. 1–9), the restoration of joy (vv. 10–11), the return of good farming conditions (vv. 12–13), and the rule of the Davidic king (vv. 14–26).

Verses 1–9 give us a glimpse into the heart of the great preacher during the final days of the siege of Jerusalem. He is convinced that all of the suffering and the severity of the judgment has been caused by the persistent sin of the people. Moreover, he is certain that though God's face is hidden now he will ultimately show it and save his people.

When restoration comes, there will be a rebirth of joy (vv. 10–11). Also, in the new age, there will be pastoral peace in the land (vv. 12–13).

The closing section stresses God's abiding faithfulness to his people, as seen especially in his restoration of them and in his raising up of a righteous Branch of the line of David to rule over them in justice (judgment) and righteousness (vv. 14–26).

Special points.—Note the emphasis on the grace of God and on the joy of salvation.

Not only is there joy when God's people are in right relation with him, but also there is a sense of security (freedom from fear).

Compare the portrayal of the rule of the messianic king here with that in 23:5–6.

The stability of the natural order is referred to again as an indication of the enduring quality of God's new spiritual order (cf. 31:35–37).

Experiences of the Prophet During the Siege of the City (Jer. 34:1–22)

The passage.—The two incidents recorded in this chapter took place during the siege of Jerusalem. The first occurred most likely in the spring of 588, some time after the experience described in 21:1–11. The second came later, shortly before and after the Babylonians raised the siege of the city in order to deal with the Egyptians who were advancing from the south to aid the Judeans (v. 22; cf. 37:1 ff.).

In verses 1–7 we are told that Jeremiah felt divinely constrained to give King Zedekiah some counsel during the crisis. The counsel was that it was useless to resist the enemy. The city was doomed to destruction. The only wise course was to surrender to Nebuchadnezzar in compliance with the will of God. Should this be done, the king might receive leniency of treatment, an honorable funeral, and lamentation befitting a ruler.

Verses 8–22 are concerned with a covenant violation and the accompanying oracle of condemnation. As the siege wore on and the picture became blacker, the king took an unusual step. He led the people in the making of a solemn covenant to free all Hebrew slaves. Then, when the siege was lifted and it seemed that deliverance had come, the people reversed the earlier action and reenslaved those who had been released. This was an act of treachery and blasphemy. It fired the spirit of Jeremiah. He delivered a scorching oracle of condemnation in which he declared that a people so corrupt deserved the fate which was surely coming upon them.

Special points.—We are struck by the prophet's consistency. For years he had known that the Babylonians were the appointed agents of God's judgment on Judah. He stuck by that conviction. He would not compromise in his preaching.

Hebrew law provided for the release of slaves after six years (Ex. 21:2–6; Deut. 15:1–18). But this law had suffered neglect. Now, in extremity, the people needed God. Accordingly, they got busy complying with his covenantal commands. They even went beyond the law and let all slaves go, whether their time was up or not. There would be fewer mouths to feed; they could use more fighting men; most of all, they wanted God's favor.

The royal decree to free the slaves was issued in covenantal form, and the covenant was sealed in a most solemn fashion (vv. 18–20; cf. Gen. 15:7–17; Ex. 24:6–8). Then it happened. The Babylonians left. God had stepped in and saved! The people could use their slaves now. There was work to be done. Accordingly, they slapped them back into servitude. And Jeremiah "lowered the boom" on them for this blatant breach of a solemn covenant made before God.

Foxhole religion stands condemned in divine presence. God accepts those whose faith, though rooted in redeeming grace, expresses itself in ethical conduct.

The Parable of the Rechabites (Jer. 35:1–19)

The passage.—There are three parts to chapter 35. The first part relates the story of a symbolic act (vv. 1–11). The second part recounts the significance of that act (vv. 12–19).

Acting under divine command, Jeremiah went to the "house" (community) of the Rechabites and asked them to go with him to the Temple. There, in a particular "chamber" (council room), he set before them pitchers of wine. He urged them to drink. They refused. They gave as their reason faithfulness to a vow taught by their founder and taken by them. The vow prohibited drinking wine and living in houses. They made it clear that they had obeyed the teaching of their founder in all particulars. Their presence in Jerusalem (a city of houses) was no violation of that teaching. They were simply seeking temporary security in a time of crisis.

The significance of the symbolic act

recorded in verses 1–11 is set forth by the prophet in verses 12–19. Addressing the covenant community as the messenger of God, he showed how the simple act in the Temple pointed up the sharp contrast between the fidelity of the Rechabites and the infidelity of the Judahites. The former had obeyed to the letter the teachings of a human founder. The latter had constantly disobeyed the teachings of the eternal God. God had shown his love for them by sending prophets to call them to repentance and by dealing out fatherly discipline. They had not only rejected correction and refused to repent, they had paid God no attention at all.

This course of action could lead to but one end: the destruction of the nation. On the other hand, because of their fidelity, the Rechabites would experience stability and continuity.

Special points.—Who were the Rechabites? They were a protest group. They were distantly related to the Israelites (1 Chron. 2:55; Judg. 1:16). They were also devoted servants of Israel's God (2 Kings 10:15–17). For centuries they had lived in Southern Palestine (Judg. 4:17; 5:24; 1 Sam. 15:6).

The thing which set these people apart was their way of life. They lived in tents, as the Israelites had done during the wilderness sojourn. They did not plant vineyards or drink wine.

What was the reason for this unusual behavior? The Rechabites were repudiating the pagan elements which had entered the religion and life of the Israelites from the culture and cult of the Canaanites, and they were reverting to the simplicity and purity of religion and life in "the good old days."

About 601, Jehoaikim rebelled against Nebuchadnezzar, his overlord. The Babylonian ruler sent soldiers from neighboring vassal states to put down the revolt (2 Kings 24:1 ff.). Finally, Nebuchadnezzar had to come himself in 598.

During this stormy period, most likely, the Rechabites moved into Jerusalem for safety (vv. 1,11). The presence of these "teetotalers" in the capital must have been quite a curiosity. Jeremiah was divinely directed to use them as an object lesson (on symbolic acts, see 13:1 ff.).

The truth for today.—The primary application for us in this chapter is a powerful lesson in loyalty. Jeremiah was not advocating the practices of the Rechabites but the principle behind those practices. That principle was loyalty. The prophet was convinced that the supreme concern of every person and nation should be to enter into a right relationship with God and to be faithful to the requirements of that relationship.

In a day marked by moral relativism and religious compromise, we desperately need the prophet's emphasis on the moral quality of loyalty. There should be loyalty to our best selves, loyalty to family, loyalty to country (in an enlightened sense), loyalty to church, and, above all, loyalty to God in Christ.

The Indestructible Word (Jer. 36:1–32)

The passage.—This important chapter falls into three parts: the word recorded (vv. 1–8), the word read and rent (vv. 9–26), and the word rewritten (vv. 27–32).

Verse 1 sets the stage for the story that follows. It was a crucial hour (605). Nebuchadnezzar had just defeated the Egyptians at Carchemish and was pressing southward into Palestine.

God commanded Jeremiah to secure a book-scroll. On it he was to write the prophecies he had delivered from the time of his call (627) up to the current crisis (605). The purpose was to seek to persuade the people to repent and receive forgiveness (vv. 2–3).

Verses 4–8 record Jeremiah's obedience to the divine directives. He dictated his prophecies to Baruch. Baruch was instructed to read them to the people on the occasion of a fast. During the months of waiting the son of Neriah was having his problems (cf. vv. 1,9; 45:1–5).

Finally a fast was proclaimed in December, 604. The probable reason was the danger posed by the presence of the army of Nebuchadnezzar in Philistia.

There were three readings of "the book." First, it was read in the presence of the people (vv. 9–10). The place was "the chamber (council room) of Gemariah," in the upper court of the Temple, near the New Gate (cf. 26:7 ff.).

The second reading was in the presence of "the princes" (vv. 11–19). The ministers of state were in session in the statehouse, just down from the Temple. When they heard what had happened, they were alarmed. They sent for Baruch and "the book." Upon hearing the contents of the scroll, they were concerned about its origin and about the safety of Jeremiah and his scribe. They *knew* the king, and to the king they must report.

The third reading of the book-scroll was in the presence of the king (vv. 20–26). Jehoaikim was sitting before a fire in the portion of the palace exposed to the winter sun. As he listened to three or four columns, he would slash them off and cast them into the fire. In this way he was showing his contempt for the words read. He was also seeking to cancel out their effectiveness.

What now? When Jeremiah heard about the destruction of the record of

his prophecies, he dictated a second time and "added . . . many like words" (vv. 27–32). This time his purpose was not to persuade the people to repent but to preserve the revelation for future generations.

Special points.—Chapter 36 is unusually significant. First, the story which it relates is told with great skill. The artistry of the inspired writer is seen in the way he allows the reader to feel the situation building toward a climax. This is quite evident in the three readings of the scroll. The first is described very briefly, the second more at length, and the third in greater detail. The center of interest throughout is the fate of the scroll.

Second, the chapter is unique in that it contains the only detailed account of the production of a prophetical book in the Old Testament. It sheds much light on the way in which at least some of the prophetical literature came into being. It also is the starting point for the composition of the prophecy of Jeremiah and for the study of the process of its composition.

Third, the chapter records a pivotal experience of the prophet: his first dictation of his prophecies. He was "shut up"—i.e., "surrounded," then "held back, restrained." Since he was free to move about the city, Jeremiah was not in prison. He was simply debarred from the Temple area, probably because of his "Temple sermon" (cf. 26:1 ff.; 7:1–15). He felt constrained to make a last-minute appeal to the people. Hence he dictated his prophecies of 23 years to Baruch that they might be read in a public assembly at the Temple. This was something new in the ministry of Jeremiah, and the public reading of prophecy was something new in the history of prophecy.

Pervading the story is the conviction

that God's word is indestructible. Once uttered, it will not return void. It will endure and be effective. It must be passed on. Even when fulfilled, it will continue to have perennial meaning, relevance, and power.

The truth for today.—From this story come insights of abiding value. First, God speaks to man. He desires to communicate and have communion with him.

Second, he speaks in various ways. He spoke to Jehoaikim through a godly father, Josiah. Most of us have at least one "Josiah" in our lives. Also, he spoke to Jehoaikim through trouble. He also addresses us through trial. Further, he spoke to Jehoaikim through the written word. He speaks to us through the written word, the spoken word, and the "living" Word.

Third, God's word may be accepted or rejected. God does not override the human will. Man can say yes or no to God. Jehoaikim said no.

Fourth, though God's word can be rejected—even rent—it cannot be abrogated. It is going on. It is indestructible (Isa. 40:8).

The Prophet in Prison (Jer. 37:1–21)

The passage.—We learn from the chapter itself that the events it records took place during the siege of Jerusalem. The contents of the chapter center around a request for prayer by the king and the response of the prophet (vv. 1–10), the accusation and arrest of the prophet (vv. 11–15), and the prophet's conference with the king (vv. 16–21).

During the temporary lifting of the siege of the city (cf. 34:8–22), Zedekiah sent a second delegation to Jeremiah with an earnest entreaty that he pray for the people (vv. 1–5; cf. 21:1–2). The request provides another eloquent testimony to the position Jeremiah occupied as intercessor supreme.

The prophet's response was that time had run out. The Babylonians would be back. If they had only wounded men left, they would destroy the city (vv. 6–10).

Jeremiah decided to go out to Anathoth to transact some business. He was arrested by the officer in charge at the Benjamin Gate on the north side of the city and was accused of treason. Though he stoutly denied the charge, he was turned over to the government officials, was beaten, and was placed in a maximum security prison. There, if left long enough, he would die (vv. 11–15).

After he had been in prison for many days under the house of the secretary of state, the king sent for him. His stated purpose was to discover whether the prophet had a word of the Lord for him (vv. 16–21).

Special points.—By this time the prophet was suffering greatly. Yet he was still faithfully and fearlessly proclaiming the word of God in a difficult and dangerous situation.

There is a textual problem in verse 12. The nature of Jeremiah's mission is not certain. The probability is that the allusion is to the redemption of some family property.

The situation in verses 16–21 is quite dramatic. In reality, the king was much more bound than the prisoner before him. Several things stand out in the secret conference. First, Jeremiah retracted nothing. He stood by his conviction as to what God's will was. He was now "an iron pillar." Second, he asserted his innocence and argued for the integrity of his preaching as over against the falsity of that of the "king's preachers." Third, he urgently asked for clemency. He had no martyr complex.

He had a healthy desire to live and would do anything honorable to insure the realization of that desire. Fourth, there was one thing he would never do: compromise his conscience.

Final Experiences Before the Fall of the City (Jer. 38:1–28)

The passage.—The events in this chapter took place after those referred to in 37:1–21 and shortly before the capitulation and destruction of the city. As ever, Baruch's central concern is the suffering of God's servant.

There are three parts to the passage: a dauntless prophet and a determined opposition (vv. 1–6), a daring deliverance (vv. 7–13), and a desperate individual (vv. 14–28).

There is only one way to silence a man like Jeremiah, and that is to kill him. This the officials determined to do. However, they were foiled by one of the unsung heroes of the Bible, Ebedmelech, an Ethiopian eunuch and a palace official of some importance.

Zedekiah was in deep distress. The siege, one of the most horrible in history, had lasted a long time. Provisions were low. People were dying of disease and starvation. Some were deserting. The king was desperate. He sent for Jeremiah. This was the last interview the prophet had with the ruler before the final debacle.

Special points.—In the court of the guard, a part of the palace where "problem" characters were kept under the surveillance of the king, Jeremiah had considerable freedom, and he used it. He kept uttering the same sort of seditious words he had spoken before. On the problem posed by the prophet's counsel in verses 2–3, see remarks on 21:8–10.

The weakness and vascillation of Zedekiah are seen throughout this chap-

ter. His response to the demands of the princes in verse 5 reminds one of the words of Pilate centuries later in a similar situation (Matt. 27:23–24).

Jeremiah knew Zedekiah. In the conference described in verses 14–28 he was much more cautious than before. His reservation was born of bitter experience. Only after assurance that the king would not kill him or turn him over to those who would, did the prophet speak. His message was the same as before (vv. 17–18).

There is a touching tenderness, an unusual solemnity, and a poetic artistry in the prophet's final appeal to the monarch (vv. 20–23). The humanity of Jeremiah is seen in his compliance with Zedekiah's last request (vv. 24–27).

The Fate of Jerusalem and Jeremiah (Jer. 39:1—40:6)

The passage.—The tremendous tragedy in the summer of 587 had been foreshadowed in Jeremiah's call-experience (1:13–16), and its possibility had been a vital part of his preaching for forty years. It is only proper that Baruch's story of his ministry should include an account of the great catastrophe, and that he should interweave with the fate of Jerusalem the fate of Jeremiah, who loved the city so much and had served it so faithfully and suffered so deeply in his efforts to save it (cf. 52:4–16; 2 Kings 25:1–12).

Verses 1–10 deal with the capitulation and destruction of the city and the dispensation made of the king and the citizenry. Verses 11–14 give a brief account of the release of Jeremiah from the court of the guard into the custody of Gedaliah, son of Ahikam (cf. 26:24) and soon to be the governor of the Judean province of the Babylonian Empire. Verses 15–18 contain an oracle of promise to Ebed-melech. Chapter 40:1–6 tells of Jeremiah's choice at Ramah.

Special points.—Verses 1 and 2 (39) are introductory. They indicate that the siege of the city lasted from January 588, to July 587.

Following the surrender of the city, some of the chief Babylonian officers set up a center of military government "in the middle gate" (v. 3—probably the principal eastern gate of the Temple, now known as the Golden Gate) to administer the affairs of the conquered country. The city itself was demolished about a month later (cf. 39:1; 52:4,12). Most of the citizens were carried into captivity. A few of the poor were left in the land to care for the fields and vineyards.

There is some confusion in the stories concerning the fate of Jeremiah (cf. 39:11–14 and 40:1–6). The probability is that, when the city was put to the torch, Jeremiah was released by order of Nebuchadnezzar through Nebuzaradan. The order was likely carried out by a subordinate. Later, when the captives were being collected, by some mishap the prophet was bound, along with the rest of the prisoners, probably by someone not aware of his special status. They were herded off to Ramah, the headquarters for getting the captives ready for the long trek to Babylon. Then Nebuzaradan discovered the error, set Jeremiah free, and gave him the choice referred to in 40:4–5.

The promise to Ebed-melech is out of order, chronologically, but is probably put where it is because of the sharp contrast between the tragic fate of Zedekiah because of his unfaithfulness to God and the brighter future of Ebed-melech because of his faithfulness to God (on "your life as a prize of war," see 21:9).

Verse 6 (40) is one of the most eloquent sentences in the book. Because of a deep devotion to God, a love for people, and a sensitivity to human need, Jeremiah chose to stay with the unpromising group left in Judah rather than to enjoy a life of ease and honor in Babylon.

The Failure of the Fresh Start (Jer. 40: 7—41:18)

The passage.—The section requires little exposition. Gedaliah, the new governor, persuaded the guerrilla groups scattered about the country to join the Judean community and promised their commanders that he would stand between them and "the Chaldeans" (vv. 7–10). Hearing about the promising new start back home, Judeans who had fled to Moab, Ammon, and Edom returned to Gedaliah at Mizpah, and they gathered the late summer fruit harvest in great abundance (vv. 11–12).

Things were looking bright. How long the period of peace and prosperity lasted we do not know. The biblical record suggests that the time was short. This much we do know: it came to an end. Despite a warning by Johanan, Gedaliah was assassinated by Ishmael, a nationalist of the seed royal and a Chaldeanhater, and thus the willing instrument of Baalis, king of Ammon, for extending his power in Palestine (40:13—41:3).

As the story unfolds, we have a dastardly piece of treachery and sadism (41:4–9), the capture of the people of Mizpah (v. 10), Johanan's pursuit of Ishmael and the rescue of the Judean captives (vv. 11–14), and the escape of Ishmael to Ammon and the movement of the Judeans southward to a lodging place near Bethlehem because of fear of reprisals from Nebuchadnezzar (vv. 15–18).

Special points.—One of the most unusual features of the record of Gedaliah's administration and assassination is the total absence of any reference to Jeremiah. We know nothing about his activity during the period.

Despite this remarkable silence, this may have been the easiest, happiest time of his ministry. For a brief season he was free from the burden of proclaiming judgment and was at liberty to set forth the glowing prospect and glorious promises regarding the future of God's people. In all likelihood, from this period come some of the grandest products of Jeremiah's genius as a poet-prophet, i.e., portions of "the book of consolation," notably chapters 30–31. This would include the greatest prophecy of all, that of the new covenant (31:31–34).

The Flight to Egypt (Jer. 42:1—43:7)

The passage.—Light had suddenly turned to darkness. The fresh start had resulted in failure. What now? Enter Jeremiah!

To go or not to go—that was the question. Should the fugitives face the music in the homeland, or should they flee to a foreign land? It was not an easy choice.

The passage tells of the people's request of Jeremiah that he discover God's will for them (42:1–6), the prophet's reply after ten days of prayer (vv. 7–22), and the response of the people to his reply (43:1–7).

Special points.—Much is said or implied about Jeremiah and prayer in 42:7 ff. For one thing, it is made clear that Jeremiah was known as a man of prayer. Also, it is apparent that the king and the people turned to him in times of trouble with earnest requests that he pray for them. But that which is most illuminating is that prayer was preparation for the receiving of revelation (this does not exclude reflection), and that Jeremiah persisted in it *until* the reve-

lation was clear (observe the threefold repetition of "Thus saith the Lord," vv. 9,15,18). When the word came and he was inwardly certain, he told it as it was.

But, though the people had solemnly pledged that they would abide by God's word when made known (42:5–6), when the word came they rejected it (43:1–3). Public opinion and mass emotion are fickle things.

The people not only refused Jeremiah's counsel but also accused him of palming off on them words of Baruch as the word of God (43:3). This is an unusual twist and an unexpected tribute to the influence of Baruch who kept himself in the background at all times in his writing (but cf. 45:1 ff.).

Having sensed their reaction and decision before he finished speaking (42:9–22), Jeremiah vigorously denounced the people for their flagrant violation of their pledge made in solemn oath before God. Such action could have but one result: a widening of the chasm between them and him. This, in turn, would bring down upon them the very calamities they were seeking to avoid.

The truth for today.—Prayer can and should play an important role in our discovery of God's will for us in a given situation.

When we have promised to do God's will when disclosed, it is the part of wisdom to keep that pledge. Failure to do so can lead only to trouble. Ulterior considerations and motivations must not be permitted to enter the picture.

When in a crisis situation, we should act in faith, not in fear, for that which we fear tends to come upon us.

The Finale (Jer. 43:8—44:30)

The passage.—The story of Israel has come full circle. It started in Egypt, when a group of slaves experienced deliverance by God's grace and power, and ventured forth in faith toward the Promised Land. Jeremiah had spoken about this from the earliest days of his ministry (cf. 2:2–3, etc.). Now a crowd of fugitives returned to Egypt in fear. This was not the kind of covenant community God had intended to create.

The story of Jeremiah comes to a close. We are granted two glimpses of him in Egypt. In both cases he is doing what he has done for forty years. He is puncturing illusions and preaching reality.

The first illusion was that, since the people were in Egypt, they were safe. They were beyond the reach of Babylon. By means of a symbolic act at night, the prophet shattered that illusion (43:8–13). The Babylonians would invade and ravage Egypt.

The second illusion which Jeremiah exploded was that the people could worship other gods alongside their covenant God and get away with it. They could not. In seeking to do so, they were in grave danger of losing God altogether (44:1–30).

Special points.—In the prophet's preaching in Egypt we recognize the boom of the same old artillery. Will the fire never go out in this man's bones and being—now in his sixties?

The audience reaction in 44:15–19 is very interesting. Jeremiah had said that idolatry was the major reason for the catastrophe that had befallen the city and country (vv. 1–14). The people stated, that, as they saw it, it was the other way round. Things had gone well with them during the period (under Manasseh?) when they were worshiping other gods, especially the queen of heaven (a prominent Assyrian goddess, whose worship was quite popular among women). It was when they gave all this

up and had the big cleanup campaign under Josiah (2 Kings 23) that things started to go wrong. This was a real switch! From blaming the supreme tragedy of 587 on the apostasy and idolatry of the people to blaming it on the purification and centralization of worship of the true God in the great "revival" of 622!

Jeremiah ended on a stern note, a verbal blast (44:20 ff.). This must be set in the context of his long ministry of service, suffering, and sacrifice, motivated by loyal love for God and people. It must also be set in the context of the people's long history of persistent apostasy and rebellion.

With an appeal to history to prove who was right, he or the people (vv. 28–30), the greatest prophet of ancient Israel dropped from sight. Tradition claims that his countrymen killed him. Later, they "canonized" him. Next to Jesus, he was the most successful failure of biblical days.

Baruch and Jeremiah (Jer. 45:1–5)

The passage.—This is a short but significant chapter. In recording the story of the suffering of God's servant, Baruch consistently remains in the background. Only here does he step out of the shadows and show something of himself as a human being. For this reason, the passage is sometimes called "The Confession of Baruch."

There are three parts to the chapter and the experience it records: the occasion (v. 1), the complaint (vv. 2–3), and the challenge (vv. 4–5). The occasion was Jeremiah's dictation of his prophecies to Baruch in 605, following the victory of the Babylonians in the battle of Carchemish (36:1 ff.). Chapter 45 fits into the time slot between verse 8 and verse 9 of chapter 36.

The complaint is a very frank expression of despondency. Although specific reasons for the complaint are not given, it is probable that there were at least three. First, Baruch was staggered by the words dictated to him concerning the seriousness of the people's sin and the shattering consequences of that sin. Second, he had probably suffered some already because of his association with the prophet of doom. In his imagination, he likely envisioned greater suffering ahead when he read the prophecies in public. Third, he saw an end to any dreams he had of personal popularity and prestige. And so, he poured out his lament.

The challenge follows. It comes from God through Jeremiah. Since Jeremiah had had times of despondency, God could use him to help his friend.

First, God made it plain to Baruch that what he was suffering was relatively insignificant when set alongside what *he* was suffering (v. 4). *He* was having to pull up what he had planted and pull down what he had built (cf. 1:10). And there was terrible pain in the pulling up and pulling down!

Second, God called Baruch's attention to the fact that he must serve him on his terms. He charged him to stop putting self at the center, to give God priority, and to be prepared to take the consequences (v. 5).

Special points.—Some scholars reject this chapter, largely because of its position in the book and the character of its contents. The conclusion is unwarranted. The date is reliable. The position in the book is likely due to Baruch's desire to make the chapter a sort of personal signature and seal to his account of the prophet's "passion," and to provide some theological insight into the reason for the preservation of the stories about the prophet's martyrdom.

The calamity which was coming was not an accident. It was coming through the action of God. And it was causing God great pain. There is here a most unusual revelation of the cross in the heart of God because of the sin of man.

But God does not suffer alone. Sometimes his servants must suffer. They are not to indulge in self-pity or cherish personal ambition (vv. 3,5). They are to rise to the challenge to true greatness. God promises his presence and protection (on "thy life . . . for a prey," see 2:9).

In a difficult day which tests the souls of the best of men, God's word to Baruch may have a peculiar personal relevance for many. The world's supreme need now is life that is completely committed to the will of God whatever the cost.

Prophecies Concerning Egypt (Jer. 46: 1–28)

The passage.—Chapters 46–51 constitute a separate "book" with its own heading (46:1). This "book" contains a collection of prophecies against foreign nations. It is the least read part of Jeremiah. This is unfortunate, for it contains some of the best poetry in the prophecy and it is essential to a full understanding of the ministry and message of the prophet.

At the beginning of the "book" of foreign prophecies there are two prophecies concerning Egypt. The first deals primarily with the defeat of the Egyptians (46:2–12); the second describes the consequences of that defeat (46:13–28). Each has its own preface (vv. 2,13). Verse 2 suggests that the background of the first prophecy was the victory of the Babylonians over the Egyptians in the famous battle of Carchemish in 605 B.C. Verse 13 appears to place the second prophecy a little later than the first—either during Nebuchadnezzar's push southward after his triumph in 605, or during his activity in the Philistine plain in 604.

Special points.—When Jeremiah heard the news of the outcome of the battle at Carchemish, he was deeply moved. He composed a prophecy (vv. 3–12), which for sheer poetic power is scarcely surpassed by anything in the book. As the Egyptians prepare for the struggle, the reader hears the officers barking out their orders (vv. 3–4). He observes the collapse of the courage of the Egyptians as they confront the enemy, and he notes their ensuing panic (v. 5). He sees their attempt at flight and their fall to the ground (v. 6). He listens to the prophet as he taunts Pharoah Neco for his pride and pompous aspirations, which rise like the Nile at floodstage (vv. 7–8a). He is fascinated as the resurgence of Egypt under a new dynasty is pictured (vv. 8b-9), only to be brought to a stop by a decisive setback on another river, the Euphrates (v. 10). This is a tragedy for which there is no remedy (vv. 11–12). Outstanding poetry, this!

In the second prophecy (vv. 14–28) Jeremiah pictures the invasion and devastation of Egypt by the Babylonians. The sacred bull Apis, highly revered as the incarnation of a god, has left the land because God has driven him out (v. 15). This means that the country will collapse. The pharoah will not be able to protect it and will be nicknamed "Big Noise who missed his chance" (v. 17).

In sharp contrast to the fate of Egypt is the future of Israel (cf. vv. 18–26 and 27–28). Instead of destruction, there will be deliverance. Egyptians will be carried into exile; Israelites will be brought back from exile.

In verse 10 the phrase "the day of the Lord" occurs. The day of the Lord is the day of his activity. It is the day when he steps in to set things straight.

In these two prophecies concerning Egypt, Jeremiah expresses his conviction that God reigns and that he is active in history, directing and overruling the movements of men to his own glory and the ultimate vindication of his moral government of his universe.

A Prophecy Concerning Philistia (Jer. 47:1–7)

The passage.—The second in the series of foreign prophecies is directed against the Philistines, Judah's immediate neighbors. Its date is uncertain (possibly 609, 605, 604, or 601). Like the oracles on Egypt, it is marked by unusual literary power. Its theme is the disaster that is coming upon the Philistines from the north.

It begins by portraying the predicted invasion as a great flood which will overflow the entire country and all the cities in it, so that the citizens will cry out in consternation and lamentation (v. 2). Mingled with the weeping and wailing will be the noise of stamping stallions, rushing chariots, and rumbling wheels. In fear fathers will forsake their children and flee (v. 3). The treaty with the Phoenicians will be of no help (v. 4a).

Why all of this commotion, lamentation, and frustration? The Lord is going to bring destruction upon the Philistines (vv. 4–7).

Special points. The shaving of the head and self-mutilation were signs of grief and distress (v. 5).

The prophecy comes to a dramatic and powerful close in verses 6 and 7 with an address to the sword of the Lord, a question from the people as to when the sword will cease its activity, and the answer of the prophet in the form of another question: "How can it be quiet (at rest), when the Lord has given it a charge . . . ?"

"The sword of the Lord" is one of the prophet's most forceful and fearful figures. The sword represents God's righteous judgment. That judgment is not only coming upon Judah but also upon other countries. The Philistines, too, must drink of the cup of divine wrath (25:17–20).

A Prophecy Concerning Moab (Jer. 48: 1–47)

The passage.—This lengthy prophecy is a collection of utterances concerning Moab. In the prophecy there is a graphic portrayal of the destruction of Moab and of the reaction of the prophet and the people to that destruction. There is also a brief concluding promise of a restoration of the fortunes of Moab.

It is not easy to outline the passage because of the miscellaneous character of its contents. The following analysis is suggested: the downfall of Moab (vv. 1–10), disaster and disillusionment (vv. 11–17), devastation and derision (vv. 18–28), a dirge over a land now desolate (vv. 29–39), and destruction and restoration (vv. 40–47).

The land, along with its major cities, will be laid waste by an invasion from the north. The people will discover that the objects of their confidence—including their army and their deity (Chemosh)—will let them down in the time of crisis. The nation's power (horn) will be broken, and the country will become the object of ridicule, a laughingstock among the nations. Along with the prediction of retribution, however, there is a promise of restoration.

Special points.—Because of a lack of internal evidence and the inadequacy of our knowledge of Moabite history, it is difficult to determine the exact occasion of the prophecy. The probability

is that it dates from the period shortly after the battle of Carchemish (605) and deals with Moab in the light of the significance of Nebuchadnezzar's victory for her.

There is an unusually large number of place names in the passage. For the study of these, one should have available *The Westminster Historical Atlas of the Bible* (1956) by Ernest Wright and Floyd Filson.

Much of the material in chapter 48 is borrowed material. The chief passages involved are: verses 29–39 (cf. parts of Isaiah 15–16), verses 43–44 (cf. Isa. 24:17–18), and verses 45–46 (cf. Num. 21:28–29). It is possible that Jeremiah was using material from other men— mainly Isaiah—or that both Jeremiah and others were employing anonymous sayings treasured and transmitted by the fellowship of the faithful.

Verse 10 has been called "a bloodthirsty verse." It is the sort of scriptural statement that must be used with care by the Christian. The work of the Lord is not to be done with indolence, but it must be the work of the Lord.

The reasons for Moab's downfall are three: trust in material things rather than in the true and living God (v. 7), self-complacency (v. 11), and pride (vv. 26,29,42).

Verse 11 describes Moab as "settled on his lees." This is a figure for stagnation and self-satisfaction. The Moabites have not been poured from vessel to vessel (have not known trouble) and, therefore, have not learned through discipline. Instead, they have rested back on themselves, as wine left too long on its lees (sediment). The result is self-complacency.

The truth for today.—The sin of the settled is a common sin among the prosperous and the proud. It is subtle and deadly. Someone has said that good causes are not defeated so much by open opposition as by being sat on by nameless nobodies. Complacency does clog the wheels of life and leads eventually to catastrophe. For God does not permit it to continue indefinitely. There comes a tilting, a pouring out, a shaking up, a shattering. Man is compelled to reckon with reality (v. 12).

The nation that magnifies itself against God is headed for disaster. God is the supreme factor in life. Man's relationship with him determines his future and ultimate fate. This was true of ancient Moab. It is true of modern America. If the widespread tendency to usurp the position and prerogatives of God is not reversed by a return to a right relationship with God, we are doomed.

Prophecies Concerning Various Peoples (Jer. 49:1–39)

The passage.—Chapter 49 contains prophecies against the Ammonites (vv. 1–6), the Edomites (vv. 7–22), the Syrians (vv. 23–27), the Arabian tribes to the East (vv. 28–33), and the Elamites (vv. 34–39).

Only one of the prophecies is dated. It is assigned to the accession year of Zedekiah (597). The others likely come out of the period between 604 and 593. They are prophecies of judgment. In two cases there is a promise of restoration (vv. 6,39; cf. 46:26; 48:47).

Special points.—The Gadites (v. 1) lived in Gilead, just north of Ammon. After Tiglath-pileser's invasion of Galilee and Gilead in 734–733, the Ammonites had taken over the territory of the Gadites. This explains the way in which the prophecy against the Ammonites begins (v. 1).

The reason for the judgment upon the capital (v. 2) and the other cities of Ammon (v. 3) is arrogant self-sufficiency and secularism (v. 4; cf. 48:11,26,28).

There is a close relationship between the prophecy against Edom and the prophecy of Obadiah (cf. vv. 9–10a with Obad. 4–5; vv. 14–16 with Obad. 1–4). Also, much of the material in the prophecy appears elsewhere in Jeremiah.

The Edomites and the Israelites provide the classic case of fratricidal hatred and strife in Old Testament times. Like their ancestor Esau, the Edomites were "profane" (Heb. 12:16), that is, they were secularists. There is only one mention of Edomite gods in the Old Testament (2 Chron. 25:20). They had a religion, but apparently they gave it little place in their lives. They were interested in that which went on in front of the Temple (*profanum*).

Despite their earthiness and evil, the Israelites, descendants of Jacob, were "fane." They could never escape from their hunger for the things of God. At the center of their life was a temple (*fanum*). They had their priests, their prophets, and their psalmists. They gave us our Bible and our Christ. The Edomites left nothing of abiding value. One who visits ancient Edom today finds eloquent testimony to the fulfilment of the prophecy of its utter destruction (vv. 8–10).

Kedar was the name of a nomadic tribe in the desert to the east of Palestine. Hazor appears to be a collective name for the seminomadic Arabs or the villages in which they lived. Elam was a strong state to the east of Babylonia in the area now known as Iran. The Elamites were outstanding archers. "The bow of Elam" (v. 35) represents their military strength.

The truth for today.—Edom came to symbolize evil incarnate, secularism in essence. The struggle between the Edomites and the Israelites was more than a personal feud. In some sense and measure, it represents the fundamental antagonism between sin and righteousness, between faith and "unfaith," between God and "the flesh." In this struggle that rages through the ages, God is going to win. Every entrenched evil will one day come down.

The place from which Hitler planned to rule the world at Berchtesgaden, Germany (with its "eagle's nest"), is now a place for religious retreats. Here is another concrete evidence that God reigns and that it is a part of the structure of reality that what is "fane" will last and what is "profane" will not!

A Prophecy Concerning Babylon (Jer. 50:1—51:64)

The passage.—This is a long prophecy, or collection of prophecies, against Babylon, the world power from 605 to 539. It is a difficult passage and has been the source of much debate.

Because of its length and looseness of connection, it is impossible to outline it with any degree of satisfaction. One's approach to the study of it may be made in one of two ways. First, he may group the various parts around major motifs (cf. H. Cunliffe-Jones, *Jeremiah*, pp. 270–80). Or, second, he may come at the material by observing the alternation throughout between the emphasis on the doom of Babylon and the emphasis on the deliverance of Israel: two sides of the same coin, God's action in setting the situation straight (Howard Kuist, *Jeremiah and Lamentations*, pp. 135–7).

Special points.—The symbolic act recorded in 51:59–64 is dated in 594–593. It is a very dramatic and significant incident. Through the intensified form of prophetic proclamation Jeremiah was indicating that the word of destruction had been set in motion toward fulfilment (cf. 13:1 ff.; 19:1 ff.; 27:1 ff; 32:1 ff.; 43:9).

Certain key ideas stand out in the section on Babylon. First, kingdoms built on force and fear and fraud will one day fall (cf. 50:2–3,13–16,39–40, 44–46; 51:5,7–8,13,24,26,33,39–40,54–58). "The mills of God grind slowly, but they grind exceeding small."

Second, the way to the restoration of a right relationship with God is repentance (cf. the picture of the people in penitence in 50:4–5). Nothing is said about the possibility of repentance on the part of the Babylonians. Time had run out for them. They were past the point of repentance and redemption. This happens. It is a part of reality.

Third, the true God of this world is infinitely great, the majestic Creator and Controller of the universe (51:15–16). He is the portion of his people (51:19).

Fourth, anything short of God, any man-made deity, any idol, will prove to be "a work of delusion" and will perish —and, along with it, the one who gives it his allegiance (51:17–18).

Fifth, God is Redeemer (50:33–34; cf. Job 19:25; Isa. 43:14; 44:6; 47:4; 48:17; 49:7; 54:5). The full revelation of this aspect of God's character and activity comes in Christ, "in whom we have our redemption, the forgiveness of our sins" (Col. 1:14).

The Appendix (Jer. 52:1–34)

The passage.—The concluding chapter of Jeremiah deals with five things primarily. They are: the destruction of Jerusalem (vv. 1–16), the despoiling of the Temple (vv. 17–23), the death of many of the instigators and supporters of the revolt (vv. 24–27), the three deportations of the Judeans (vv. 28–30), and the deliverance of Jehoiachin (vv. 31–34).

Special points.—Chapter 52 is an excerpt from 2 Kings 24:18—25:30, with minor variations. There is one major omission (2 Kings 25:22–26), and there is one important addition (vv. 28–30). The addition is significant because it contains material not found elsewhere in the Bible.

Rather strangely, Jeremiah is nowhere mentioned in the concluding chapter. Why, then, was it added at the end of the book that bears his name? Perhaps there are two reasons. First, it emphasizes the fact that Jeremiah's prophecies concerning the fate of Jerusalem came true. Second, it tells of the release of Jehoaichin, a Davidic ruler, after 37 years of imprisonment in Babylon. This was probably regarded as a symbol of promise, a foregleam of the fulfilment of the beautiful forecasts of the glorious future of God's people given by Jeremiah.

The final chapter appears to say, therefore, that God's word through his prophet had been fulfilled and would be fulfilled.

LAMENTATIONS

J. Leo Green

INTRODUCTION

The book which we call "Lamentations" has no distinctive title in the Hebrew Bible. It carries as its caption the first word in it: 'Eykah, "O how!" The book appears in the third division of that Bible, known as the Writings, and is classed as one of the five festal Rolls (the other four being Song of Songs, Ruth, Ecclesiastes, and Esther). The Septuagint and the Vulgate place the book after Jeremiah and give it the heading "Dirges" or "Lamentations." The English versions have expanded this to read "The Lamentations of Jeremiah."

The book of Lamentations consists of five poems which are bound together by a common theme and a common use. These poems deal with the conflict between fact and faith caused by the terrible calamities which came upon Judah and Jerusalem between 609 and 587 B.C. (cf. 2 Kings 23–25). The poems were employed—possibly prepared—for liturgical purposes, primarily a catharsis of grief and guilt, on the anniversary of the destruction of the Holy City by the Babylonians in 587. Since A.D. 70, orthodox Jews have read Lamentations in the synagogues to commemorate the fall of Jerusalem to the Romans. Various Christian groups have used and still use selections from the book in worship during Holy Week.

The poems in Lamentations are striking in their structure. The first four are acrostics. This means that there are 22 stanzas in each poem and that each stanza begins with the appropriate letter in the Hebrew alphabet. In chapters 1–3 the stanzas normally have three lines each. In chapter 4 each stanza is made up of two lines. Chapter 3 is a triple acrostic, each of the three lines in each stanza beginning with the proper Hebrew letter. The fifth poem (chap. 5) has 22 stanzas (the number of letters in the Hebrew alphabet), but it is not an acrostic.

The reason for the use of the alphabetical arrangement in the poems is not known. Possibly it was intended as an aid to memory or as an indication of continuity and completeness. Despite the rather rigid character of the structure, the poems in Lamentations pulsate with passion and power. They are marked by an unusual variety and vitality of emotion: vigorous expressions of grief, contrite confessions of guilt, earnest petitions for mercy, strong affirmations of hope.

In the main, the poems are not only acrostics, but also adaptations of the personal lament, with the dirge rhythm predominating (except in chap. 5). It would appear that the account of the national catastrophe was couched in the form of the individual lament in order to convey its deeply personal character and significance. The result is a classic case of literary beauty rising out of deep agony.

There is disagreement as to the date and authorship of the book. The traditional view is that Jeremiah composed the poems after the fall of Jerusalem. This position is based upon a reference in 2 Chronicles 35:25, a statement at the beginning of 1:1 in the LXX, and similarities between the prophecy of Jeremiah and the book of Lamentations.

If there are similarities between Jeremiah and Lamentations, there are also marked differences. Because of these differences, primarily, most modern scholars ascribe a part of the book to Jeremiah (e.g., chaps. 2,3,4) and the rest to some other writer(s), or they deny the Jeremianic authorship altogether and assign the poems to various unknown writers living during the Exilic and post-Exilic periods.

The Desolation and Distress of Jerusalem (1:1–22)

The passage.—The first poem is usually divided into two parts. The first part (vv. 1–11) starts with a sigh of sorrow: "How . . . !" There follows a vivid portrayal of the present misery of Jerusalem as compared with her former prosperity. Once full of people, she is now empty and lonely, for her inhabitants are gone. Once great and highly regarded, she has descended to the depths. Once powerful, she is now weak. Once the mistress of others, she is now a vassal. Her former glory is gone; her appointed feasts have ceased; foreigners have invaded and desecrated her sanctuary. All of this has come upon her because of her sin.

In the second part of the poem (vv. 12–22) the city speaks (cf. vv. 9,11). Her pent-up passion pours forth in torrential flood as she describes her desolate condition. Yet there is no resentment. Freely she confesses that she has rebelled against the divine will and that the Lord is in the right. She appeals to him, her only hope. She prays that those

who have taunted and tormented her may also receive a just recompence from God.

Special points.—This chapter contains a poem of unusual pathos and power. In language of solemn beauty it takes the reader back into the situation of suffering and sorrow that produced it.

Whether referred to as "the city," "Judah," "Zion," "the daughter of Zion," or "Jerusalem," the covenant community is personified as a widow throughout the poem. In keeping with this, the pagan nations are personified as "fickle, fair-weather lovers" (cf. vv. 2,19).

Observe the sharp contrast that is drawn between a glorious past and a ghastly present. Also, note how frankly and frequently the suffering of the present is spoken of as the consequence of terrible sin (vv. 5,8,12,14,18,20,22).

The "pleasant things" (vv. 7,10) are likely the Temple treasures.

The plaintive cry in verse 12 appears in Stainer's "Crucifixion" as a plea addressed by the crucified Christ to every professing Christian.

The truth for today.—It is a basic law of life that we reap what we sow. All suffering is not caused by sin, but all sin will ultimately lead to suffering (cf. vv. 13–15 especially).

So often, in our preoccupation with our own problems and pain, we forget the hurt and heartache of others. We do not identify with the community as did the inspired poet of long ago. We need an acute awareness of the needs of humanity and a willingness to do what we can to alleviate those needs.

There comes to mind a painting in which Christ is bound to an altar (not a cross) in a public place. His body is bent under the weight of great suffering. On his head rests a crown of thorns. Close by is the inscription: "To the Unknown God." People from all walks of life are passing by: rich and poor, lettered and unlettered, old and young, religious and irreligious. Only one, a woman, glances at the suffering Savior—a brief look of shock. "Is it nothing to you, all ye that pass by?" Our neglect of Christ is often the source of our neglect of others.

The Lord's Doing (2:1–22)

The passage.—This poem may be analyzed as follows: a graphic picture of destruction as divine visitation (vv. 1–10), a detailed portrayal of distress and despair among the people (vv. 11–17), and an earnest plea for deliverance enjoined and uttered (vv. 18–22).

In his anger, God becomes as an enemy to his people (v. 5). He places them under a cloud of disgrace (v. 1). He scorns his altar and disowns his sanctuary (v. 7). He marks off the city ("the beauty of Israel") for destruction (v. 8). He demolishes the Temple ("his footstool") with ease (v. 6). The exultant cries of triumphant soldiers are heard, as the place of worship is ravaged (v. 7). Altar and sanctuary, palace and stronghold, ramparts and walls, gates and bars, the Holy City and the habitations of Jacob—all are torn down (vv. 2,5,7,8). King and country are dishonored. Priest and prophet are silenced (v. 9). The community engages in mourning over its desolate, God-forsaken state (v. 10).

As the lament continues, the poet becomes more specific in his portrayal of the suffering of the people during the siege and sack of the city (vv. 11–17). He is overwhelmed by what he sees and hears (vv. 11,13): the fainting of infants because of famine (vv. 11,12), the failure of the prophets (v. 14), the contempt of onlookers (v. 15), and the rejoicing of the foes (v. 16). The magni-

tude of the calamity is beyond measure (v. 13).

In the closing part of the poem (vv. 18–22) the people are urged to pour out their hearts in God's presence in a plea for help (vv. 18–19). They respond with the prayer recorded in verses 20–22.

Special points.—This poem differs from the first in several ways. Like the first, it is an acrostic, but, for reasons not known, the order of the sixteenth and seventeenth letters is reversed (cf. chaps. 3,4). Moreover, the poem stands higher on the ladder of literary excellence.

Also, the tone is such as to place it nearer to the time of the tragedy of 587 B.C. In fact, it appears to be an eyewitness account of that tragedy.

Further, the poet places greater stress on the cause of the catastrophe and on God's activity in connection with it. The Lord is made the subject of approximately half of the statements in the poem.

Finally, the poem closes with a prayer but without the element of imprecation in it.

For clarity and for the arrangement of the text as poetry, the RSV (or some other modern version) should be used. The RSV rendering is to be preferred in verses 6, 11, and 18 especially.

The truth for today.—The wrath of God is a reality (cf. vv. 1,2). If we break out of the circle of God's will, we find ourselves in the larger circle of his wrath (judgment). However, through repentance we can move from this circle into the wider circle of his forgiving mercy and redeeming grace. In the light of the Christian relevation, therefore, the answer to the burning question in verse 13, "Who can heal thee?" is obvious: the Great Physician.

God has a purpose which he is working out in history. His faithfulness in the achievement of that purpose sometimes requires that he appear more like an enemy or an archer with bow bent than like a father or a shepherd (vv. 4,5,17).

Religious leaders bear a heavy responsibility (v. 14). If they fail, the people fall.

Hope in the Midst of Despair (3:1–66)

The passage.—This lengthy chapter is difficult to outline. The analysis which one makes may be determined either by the change of speaker or by the character of content. The latter is used as the guide here.

According to subject matter, there are four parts to the poem. First, there is an expression of despair in the midst of great suffering (vv. 1–18). By means of a vigorous vocabulary and a variety of imagery, the speaker depicts the extent of his misery and the depth of his despondency. So acute is his suffering and so complete is his sense of isolation from God and men that his state seems hopeless.

There follows a psalm of hope (vv. 19–39). The speaker turns from a description of his misery to a contemplation of God's mercy. As he thinks about the faithfulness, the goodness, and the steadfast love of God, he finds hope. With such a God in control of the world, why should he, a man, complain about the suffering caused by sin?

Next, we have a plea for penitence (vv. 40–47). Instead of questioning God's ways, the people are urged to examine their ways. To him against whom they have sinned they must make confession.

The poem ends with a petition for vindication (vv. 48–66). Overwhelmed by affliction and moved by deep emotion, the speaker calls upon God to judge his cause. The divine response brings assurance of the redemption of his life and of retribution upon his enemies.

Special points.—Chapter 3 is somewhat different from the other chapters in the book. For one thing, it is longer. Also, it has a more elaborate structure. It is a triple acrostic. Moreover, the atmosphere in it is less gloomy and more hopeful. Further, it is more personal and profound.

The last point raises a question: Is the poem to be given an individual or a collective interpretation? Who is "the man" in verse 1—some particular person (e.g., Jeremiah), or the personification of the community? It is difficult to be certain on this subject. Since the people speak in verses 40–47, perhaps it is best to regard "the man" as an individual sufferer whose intensely personal experiences are intended to represent the suffering and sentiment of the community.

There are many parallels between this poem and parts of Jeremiah, Job, and the Psalms (cf. the more detailed commentaries for specifics). It is not difficult to see why many identify "the man" as Jeremiah and consider him to be a typical sufferer who is representative of the people of God.

The emphasis upon the universality of God's rule (vv. 35,38) and upon the individuality of religion (vv. 24 ff.) poses a problem: If a good God is in control of the universe, how can one explain the suffering of the righteous? The solution presented here is that, since the God who sent the affliction will also show compassion in his own time, the sufferer is to seek him, submit to him, and wait for his salvation (vv. 25–33).

Observe that, though the name of God appears only once in the portrayal of the man's affliction (vv. 1–18; cf. v. 18), it occurs often in the psalm and prayer which follow (vv. 19 ff.). In this way, it is emphatically indicated that the speaker's hope centers in God and in him alone.

The climax of Lamentations is reached in verses 19–39. These verses should be studied with much care and prayer.

The truth for today.—In the world in which we live, suffering is as certain as death and taxes. It is a raw, rugged reality. We cannot evade it. We cannot fully explain it. There is ever an element of mystery about it. But we can know God in such a way as to be released from it and rise above it—and recognize its disciplinary value.

The antidote to despair is hope. The basis for hope is the strong, steadfast covenant love of God, who is faithfully working out his purpose in the world and who is going to win in the end.

At times God's face seems to be hidden in an impenetrable cloud, and his ways appear to be completely beyond human comprehension. If we earnestly seek him and eagerly, expectantly wait on him, however, he will answer our anguished pleas, saying, "Fear not" (v. 27). Then we can face the future with faith.

"It is good for man that he bear the yoke in his youth" (v. 27; cf. Heb. 12:7–11). "The yoke" is the yoke of discipline, the discipline of God's will and way. If accepted in one's early years, it will likely remain with him through life and will result in good. This points up the imperative importance of proper parental instruction by word and deed.

Past Glory and Present Misery (4:1–22)

The passage.—In the first part of this poem (vv. 1–11) the author describes the distress of the people during the siege of Jerusalem. The city and its citizens are helpless and worthless (vv. 1–2). Under the stress of suffering due to famine, mothers become cruel to their children. Leaders are lost, and those accustomed to living in luxury lie on the refuse heaps (city dumps; vv. 3–5). The chastisement of God's people is greater than that of the sinners of Sodom (v. 6). The Nazarites (probably nobles here) are terribly emaciated because of hunger and hardship (vv. 7–8). More fortunate are those who died by the sword (v. 9). Compassionate women, accustomed to doing deeds of kindness, cook their own children for food (v. 10). The horrors experienced are the judgment of God upon the people (v. 11).

In verses 12–16 the poet designates the delinquency of the prophets and priests as the primary cause of the unbelievable catastrophe. Guilty, confused, unclean men, victims of moral and spiritual leprosy, they are under the curse of Cain, doomed to wander and find no rest.

Verses 17–20 depict the despondency and despair of the people as the end draws near. The hope of help from Egypt fades (v. 17). The enemy breaks into the city and begins chasing and catching the people in the streets (v. 18). King Zedekiah and others seek to escape but are caught (cf. 2 Kings 25:4–7; Jer. 39:1 ff.; 52:6 ff.).

The final portion of the poem dwells on the doom of Edom (vv. 21–22). The Edomites may gloat now, but their time is coming. They, too, must drink from the cup of God's wrath (cf. Jer. 25:14 ff.; 49:7–22).

Special points.—This chapter resembles chapter 2. It sets us down in the midst of the situation in Jerusalem in 587 B.C. In fact, so concrete and accurate are the details given that one can scarcely resist the impression that the poet lived through the horrors of the siege.

The contrast between what was and what is is very sharply drawn. This is especially the case in verses 1–11.

The poet stresses the suffering of different groups, but he gives special attention to the actions and reactions of women and children. Jackals (not sea monsters) are kind to their young, but ostriches are noted for their neglect of their offspring (v. 3).

Much of the blame for the national catastrophe is placed upon the religious leaders who have betrayed their calling (vv. 12–16; cf. 2:9,14; also, Jer. 2:8; 5:13; 6:13–14; 8:10–12; 14:13–15; 18:18–23; 23:9–22; 26; 27—29).

The phrases "the breath of our nostrils" and "the anointed of the Lord" refer to the king, Zedekiah.

The Edomites, though related to the Israelites, were their most persistent and pestilential foes (see Isa. 34:1 ff.; 63:1–6; Ezek. 35:1–15; Obad. 1–21; etc.).

"The cup" of God's wrath is a fearful and forceful figure for God's basic antagonism to sin and the inevitable retribution which comes as a consequence of sin (cf. Jer. 25:14 ff.; 49:12; 51:7).

Remember, O Lord! (5:1–22)

The passage.—The final poem begins with an earnest appeal to God (v. 1). This is followed by a vivid portrayal of the pathetic plight of the people (vv. 2–18). Then comes a concluding prayer for restoration and renewal (vv. 19–22).

The Lord is called upon to consider the disgrace which has come upon his covenant people (v. 1). The sadness of their condition and the severity of their affliction are set forth in graphic fashion. Their land has been turned over to foreigners (v. 2). Their fathers have been killed or carried off into captivity, leaving them orphans and their mothers widows (v. 3). Ironically, they have to buy water and wood in a country rightfully theirs (v. 4). They suffer under the yoke of servitude (v. 5). They have had to pay homage to aliens to get bread, and are ruled over by slaves (servants) because of the sins of their forebears (vv. 6–8). They are raided by Bedouin bands from the desert, and have become victims of raging fever brought on by hunger (vv. 9–10). Women and virgins, princes and elders, young men and boys are subjected to appalling indignity and distress (vv. 11–14). A deep sense of shame and despondency has settled upon them, as Zion lies desolate, with jackals prowling among her ruins (vv. 15–18). But God is King everlasting (v. 19). Let him not continue to reject them, but, instead, let him renew and restore them (vv. 20–22).

Special points.—Unlike its predecessors, this poem is not an acrostic, though it has 22 stanzas. Also, it is a prayer, not a dirge. However, in literary excellence it stands alongside the other four poems.

The situation in Palestine sometime after the fall of Jerusalem seems to provide the historical setting of the poem. There is no direct allusion to the Exile and no mention of the siege of the city or the slaughter of its citizens. Those left in the land are experiencing tyranny from within at the hands of a pagan conqueror and violence from without at the hands of raiders from the desert (cf. the unusual phrase "the sword of the wilderness"). Jerusalem is in ruins. All of this points to a time somewhat removed from the tragedy of 587 B.C.

Egypt and Assyria are used to indicate geographical areas to which some of the people have had to go for survival (v. 6).

Verse 7 reflects an attitude which created a problem after the fall of Jerusalem (cf. Jer. 21:29; Ezek. 18:1–32). The present generation felt that it was suffering for the sins of the preceding generation (but cf. v. 16).

The officials are spoken of as "servants" either because they were subject to Babylonian overlordship or because they were former slaves who had secured their positions by appointment or by their own prowess (v. 8).

"The crown" refers to the former status of Judah as an independent kingdom, now lost (v. 16).

The word rendered "remainest" in verse 19 means "sit" (here, as king) and is best translated "dost reign."

Verse 22 poses a problem, The literal translation runs thus: "For if thou didst reject us completely, thou wouldst be angry unto much (i.e., too angry) with us." Because of the somber (and in some versions, hopeless) note sounded, the Jews, when they read the passage in the synagogues, repeat verse 21 after verse 22, so that its words may be the last to fall upon the ear.

The truth for today.—The habit of evasion is one to which all of us are addicted in varying degrees. We try to pass the buck, to put the blame on someone else (v. 7). But this cannot be done. To be sure, we suffer the consequences of the sins of others in some measure, and corporate responsibility is a reality. Primarily, however, we are responsible to God for our own deeds (cf. v. 16).

We live in a world that is torn by strife and tormented by sin and suffering. Can we feel the anguish experienced and expressed in Lamentations and the agony of our age without praying with the suffering saints of long ago: "Restore us to thyself, O Lord, that we may be restored! Renew our days as of old!" (v. 21)? Must we not recommit ourselves to God?

Hope can dwell in the midst of any situation, however difficult and demanding, if it is grounded in the sovereignty of the living Lord (v. 20), who has re-vealed himself supremely in Jesus Christ.

George Frederick Handel's biographer tells of the time when the health and wealth of the famous composer were at their lowest ebb. His money was gone. Jealous rivals had ruined him. He was partially paralyzed. His creditors were threatening to imprison him. Bankrupt and broken in body at the age of sixty years, he became terribly depressed. He hobbled through the streets of London in despair. Life was almost too much for him. He was tempted to give up.

Then he rebounded, upon receiving a letter and a package from Charles Jennens, and began to compose the music for *Messiah.* Day after day he wrote, walked about the room, wept, and continued to write, crying, "Hallelujah," with tears freely flowing down his cheeks. Finally he went to bed exhausted and slept for seventeen hours, but on his desk was the score for *Messiah.*

When *Messiah* was first given in London in 1743, the audience was so deeply moved by it that, when the "Hallelujah Chorus" was reached, the king and the people stood to their feet, starting a custom that has continued ever since. "The Lord God omnipotent reigneth, and shall reign, King of kings and Lord of lords, forever and ever. Hallelujah!"

After his composition of *Messiah* Handel carried heavy burdens and, in fact, actually became blind. But he never surrendered to despair. He was held by the conviction that God reigns.

It was this same conviction which gave help and hope to the suffering people of God who speak in Lamentations (cf. 5:19). It is also the basis of hope for us today.

EZEKIEL

Fred M. Wood

INTRODUCTION

Ezekiel was carried captive to Babylon in 597 B.C. He began preaching four years later and we have a record of his ministry until 571 B.C.

The book has two logical divisions. Chapters 1–24 contain messages delivered before the destruction of Jerusalem in 586 B.C. The theme is twofold. First, those in Babylon must realize they will not return to their homeland soon. Second, those in Judah will soon be coming to Babylon. Sinful Jerusalem is ripe for judgment. Chapters 25–48 were delivered after the city fell. Their message is different. God is with his people. He will destroy their enemies and restore them to their homeland.

The second half has three major divisions. Chapters 25–32 consist of prophecies directed against the foreign nations. Chapters 33–39 deal with God's assurance Israel will be delivered from captivity and once more be a glorious nation. Chapters 40–48 contain Ezekiel's description of the restored Temple and future city of God.

The book is simple and clear in arrangement. Most of the sections have dates attached to them and the material is almost entirely chronological.

Ezekiel was a priest who became a prophet. He was an unusual man—thoughtful, sensitive and a man of visions. He was lonely, yet intelligent, and a man of keen discernment coupled with deep faith.

Although in some ways legalistic, he recognized form and ritual were vain without the spiritual vitality of a transformed life. He was a dedicated man caught in the crosscurrents of history. Strongly conscious of God's demands upon the people and yet sensitive because of the crisis, he identified with his people but never compromised his loyalty to God.

Most scholars agree this book is as free from critical problems as any in the Old Testament. This does not mean there are no radical students who cast doubts upon its integrity, but the general field of scholarship accepts the book as a thoroughly reliable literary vehicle of the message of the prophet. One of the most respected scholars says there has scarcely any doubt been cast even by the extremist critics upon the unity and authenticity of the book. We can be assured in studying the content that we are dealing with the message that Ezekiel spoke from God to the people of his day.

Ezekiel's Vision of God (Ezek. 1:4–28)

The passage.—The complex and minute details of this vision defy description. All attempts to reproduce it on the artist's canvass have been futile. It is not necessary to understand every detail in order to grasp the meaning. This experience had two great purposes. First, it enabled the prophet to realize that his God was ever present, thoroughly resourceful with all power at his disposal. Second, it thrust him into service with assurance.

This revelation of God meant the

491

Divine Presence is neither static nor stationary. God is able to move about freely. He sees everywhere and acts in history. Ezekiel was conscious that what he saw was but an imperfect semblance of the essential nature of God.

The exiles needed confidence. In a foreign land without their Temple, they were tempted to despair. This vision reinforced the truth that God is present in every situation and is uniquely able to meet any emergency in history.

Special points.—The first three verses contain the date and superscription. Verse 1 is in the first person while verses 2–3 are in the third person. In all probability the last two were added by one who collected Ezekiel's works in order to clarify the time of the prophet's ministry and give additional information about it. Nothing of the Bible's authority is lost if we concede the addition of these two verses by an editor in order to give a fuller picture.

It seems best to conclude "thirtieth year" means the age of Ezekiel at his call. This was the time a priest entered his work. Also, it was the age John the Baptist and Jesus began their active ministry.

Did Ezekiel actually see four living creatures? He says that he saw "the likeness" of them. Words were inadequate. The emphasis is not on the literalness of the objects but rather on the spirit which was the Divine Principle and acted as guide. The unity of God and the vital energy by which he acts upon the creatures is the dominant theme.

Truth for today.—We cannot retreat to any location in order to escape God nor be sent to a place where his divine providence is absent. His spirituality does not do away with his personhood nor diminish his power. He has aligned himself with his people to work out his

purpose and to meet their need. He still lives and reigns although national boundaries fall and his institutions are abused by those who despise his name. The self-revealing God can make himself known in all circumstances.

The Commission to Present God to a Rebellious People (Ezek. 2:1–7)

The prophet, fallen prostrate before God's glory, was told to arise. He had been energized by the Spirit, set on his feet, given his commission and a warning concerning it.

The task would not be easy. The nation had been historically rebellious. The present generation was equally obnoxious and stubborn, but the prophet must deliver the message. He was not responsible for his success but only for his faithfulness in declaring the word of God among them. He must not be overcome with fear but must keep constantly before him the fact that even if his message is seemingly rejected it will still have a profound influence upon them—more than the prophet can possibly realize.

Special points.—Only one other time in the Old Testament is "son of man" used to address a person (Dan. 7:13). Jesus' use of it is not parallel with Ezekiel's. He identified himself with the messianic figure of Daniel as the truly representative man.

Some feel the phrase emphasizes the great distance between God and man while others feel it was used to magnify the dignity of man and his potential worth. The truth may be somewhere between these two extremes. God wanted to identify Ezekiel as a member of the human race. He was far inferior to God but not in the sense that he should feel crushed or void of all goodness. He is contrasted with God but not abased. Even though a fallen creature, he is still the climax of God's creation. He must be humbled before the majesty of God but he need not forever cringe in awe. God wants man to stand erect before him and realize his dignity as a transformed child of God.

Although there is no fully developed doctrine of the Holy Spirit in the Old Testament, we certainly see the truth in embryo. The "Spirit" means the vital life-giving principle that comes from God. This divine impulse is spoken of in connection with many of the prophet's actions. The New Testament gives us the ultimate teaching.

Truth for today.—If we are to serve God, we must recognize that we are to become dead to the world with both its prizes and threats. Although we must, of course, have a "decent respect for the opinion of mankind," at the same time we are answerable to God and him only. There never has been a period in the history of the world when it was popular to speak the plain unpleasant truth of God's demands. We must be as winsome as we can in our personality but our first loyalty must always be to speak the word of truth without fear.

God's Symbolic Communication with the Prophet (Ezek. 2:8—3:3)

One who begins as a spokesman for God is always conscious of an inward hindrance. With Ezekiel it was the sinister dread that perhaps there was present in him the same rebellious spirit that characterized the people to whom he would minister. This command was a test of his obedience.

The scroll, written on both the front and the back, indicates an intensification of the message. There is no place for the prophet to add his own words. He must deliver a "thus saith the Lord."

As Ezekiel faced his ministry it seemed bitter and unpalatable. Life always appears hard and discouraging from without and the destiny in store for us seems forbidding. When we enter the conflict, however, our heart is sustained by the inward joy of God's presence.

Special points.—Even the most insistent literalist must agree this passage is symbolic. This does not mean, however, that it is without spiritual value. Here is one of the highest concepts of the prophetic gift. We must avoid a crude and mechanical understanding of inspiration. This does not mean that he was to reproduce in instalments the facts that were delivered to him. He was rather given the faculty of distinguishing God's truth from any other thoughts that would invade his mind and threaten his judgment. The eating of the book symbolized self-surrender. He was to be conscious of a new power at work within him. It would act as a spiritual impulse. He could then declare, without compromise, the truth that would be revealed to him as the need for understanding arose.

Truth for today.—Making God's will our own is still a major problem. We shall grow in comprehension and insight as we assimilate unwanted elements into our soul's experience. Faith means, among other things, the willingness to receive our task from God and remain perfectly willing to let him show us from day to day how we can serve him and his purpose most effectively. We shall find unanticipated joys as the bitter becomes sweet in God's service.

Further Explanations and a Temporary Command to Keep Silent (Ezek. 3:4–27)

The called prophet needed orientation. He was reminded again of the people's unwillingness to hear but promised he would be made strong in order to bear this refusal. In order that he might understand their problems and sympathetically identify with them, he "sat where they sat" for seven days.

He was then given stern words concerning his responsibility. This was followed by a statement that his tongue would be made unusable so he could not preach to the people. He was reminded at the close once more he would speak to rebellious people.

Special points.—What were the "cords" placed upon the prophet? The binding was probably in a spiritual sense. The sinfulness and unresponsiveness of the people would limit his freedom in preaching. One's spirit can be crushed when people refuse to give a sympathetic hearing.

What about his dumbness? To say he was literally speechless until the Fall of Jerusalem (24:27) is to dispute clear statements that he spoke during this period. Some have suggested he was "role playing" in order to underscore his message. The more probable truth, however, is he was "dumb" in that he could not make contact with the people. They "tuned him out" when he became sharp and definite concerning their sins.

Truth for today.—True strength is not found in hard, ruthless individuals whose actions are ungodly. The man who sets his conscience in opposition to the wicked standards which prevail is the person of real courage. The weak man is the one who compromises for the sake of expediency.

Bitter and unsympathetic attitudes toward others are often mellowed when we enter into their experiences. That which is seen in the vision must be expressed in practical service. No one can stay on the mountain of inspiration. He must come down to the valley of practical living.

God deals with men as they permit him. When they will not hear him, he often withdraws. This does not mean they are entirely ignored, but often God must wait before he can make full revelation unto them.

Symbolic Warnings of Jerusalem's Destruction Followed by Prophet's Explanation (Ezek. 4:1—5:17)

The passage.—These four "dramatic parables" are actually one prophecy depicting the certainty and thoroughness of the coming punishment upon Jerusalem. God's decision was not a sudden or arbitrary one. He had observed the progressive moral deterioration.

The object lesson concerning food gave a twofold message. Living conditions during the siege would be horrible and the exile would continue their lack of the normal conveniences of life. The barber's razor emphasized that only a nucleus would be spared when the devastation came. A thorough purging would make the remaining seed usable for God's redemptive purpose.

The prophet concludes with an explanation. The nation has plunged into wickedness and God must come in judgment in order that both Israel and her neighbors shall see and know God will not allow his people to escape deserved judgment.

Special points.—Did Ezekiel actually perform these deeds? Although preaching of this type may seem strange to moderns, the Oriental would consider it a normal means of communication. To them, words and actions were so closely related that if one did something similar to what he was predicting, he was helping it occur.

The 390 days and 40 days are probably to be understood as concurrent. The possibility of performing such a deed is easily explainable. The text nowhere says the prophet stayed on his side twenty-four hours a day. He probably did it at certain periods each day.

Truth for today.—When God chooses a people for special privilege, a greater responsibility is also thrust upon them. Punishment will always be in proportion to opportunity. Every generation needs to learn afresh the moral laws of the universe. What God has done, he will do again when men turn away from him. The harvest for sin may be delayed, but it will not be suspended. Judgment will come because God's character demands it. Man cannot sin with impunity. Wickedness carries with it the seed of its own destruction.

Prophecy Against the Mountains and People with Promise of a Remnant Surviving (Ezek. 6:1–14)

The passage.—Ezekiel addressed the mountains of Israel because it was there the "high places" of idolatrous worship were found. The ravines and valleys were also included in the pronouncement of judgment. When the Jews first entered Canaan and took over the worship sites their religious ceremonies were, no doubt, pure. Canaanitish customs, however, became incorporated into Jehovah worship. The pagan religion appealed to the baser part of man's nature. Israel's moral life began to decay. Stern measures had been taken to eliminate it. Ezekiel adds to his predecessors in his fierce condemnation of this nature worship.

There is some hope for the people. A few will be left alive and will remember their God. The wickedness of their sin will become loathsome even to their own eyes. God's work shall not have been in vain. They shall return to him.

A tremendous punishment, however, must come to Israel. The pestilence, sword, and famine shall take their toll. The dead bodies and the desolate land will convince the people God will not tolerate sin in the lives of his people.

Special points.—How do we explain God's harsh attitude? Some have pointed out we are still in the pre-Christian period of revelation and should not expect New Testament ethics in Old Testament days. As conscience became more enlightened, God would reveal himself in more humane ways.

This is not, however, the entire story. The type of religion practiced at the "high places" was immoral to the core. It was a cancer upon the spiritual life of Israel and must be dealt with in a drastic way. There are times in a nation's history that severe measures must be taken to preserve any semblance of purity in religious life. The wrath of God is just as much an essential part of his nature as his love.

Truth for today.—There runs throughout the Bible a teaching that the land itself is under a curse because of the people's sin. The best ecology known to man is clean living. Purity of deeds will result in purity of land. Polluted lives means a polluted environment. We need to get the individual right first! The other will then be forthcoming!

Lamentation Concerning the Doomed and Desolate Land (Ezek. 7:1–27)

This section concludes the "first cycle of threats" against Israel (chaps. 4—7). It is more a restatement of principles and denunciations previously stated than a new prophecy. The prophet spoke under great emotion because he was convinced the end was near. There are many short sentences—often without conjunctions. They express the urgency the prophet felt as he saw the inevitability of the coming judgment.

Chapters 4—7 fit beautifully into the overall literary structure of the book but could be isolated and considered as a unit within itself. This seventh chapter forms an excellent conclusion to the section. It brings to a climatic and comprehensive conclusion all the prophet has said concerning Israel's sin and the imminent judgment.

Special points.—The word "land" can be translated "earth." If so, the coming catastrophe is viewed as worldwide. Quite often the prophet spoke of local punishment for sin against the background of a universal judgment. Either translation is acceptable.

Truth for today.—People are more than atoms vibrating under unconscious forces. They are subject to a righteous God who has revealed himself in moral purity. Because of his essential nature, God must manifest himself in judgment when men ignore his spiritual laws and rebel against his commandments.

If Israel, chosen for a particular purpose, could not escape judgment for sin what about us moderns? The same course of evil that brought trembling and shame to Israel will bring overwhelming horror to our nation or any nation in any generation.

Great economic systems cannot prevent the destruction of an ungodly nation. A morally bankrupt nation will soon be a financially unstable one. The living God is the moral absolute. Obedience or disobedience to his standard colors all the areas of both national and personal life.

Series of Visions Showing Jerusalem's Sin and Coming Destruction (Ezek. 8:1—11:25)

These four chapters are a distinct unit. The prophet, up to this time, has declared the coming judgment through symbolic messages. In this section he is carried in spirit to Jerusalem where he witnesses some of the actual wickedness that is taking place.

Abominable Practices in the Temple (Ezek. 8:1–18)

The passage.—Ezekiel was shown, in vision, the perversions of worship practiced in the Temple. There was an "image of jealousy" north of the altar gate thoroughly displeasing to God and dishonoring to his glory. It was likewise present in the Temple.

The prophet dug in the wall, found a door, and witnessed many vile abominations. The people were convinced God had forsaken the land. The prophet was warned he would see even greater abominations. The iniquities grew more intense as he moved from one abomination to another. The "women weeping for Tammuz" was followed by twenty-five men facing toward the east in worship of the sun. Their backs to the Temple suggested their rejection of God. The ceremony in which the men "put the branch to the nose" was probably some type of obscene rite.

Special points.—Ezekiel nowhere makes the claim he was carried literally to Jerusalem. There is nothing to indicate Ezekiel was psychotic as some have claimed. He was certainly in great spiritual ecstasy but this does not mean he had the emotional problems of the mentally ill person. The fact that he may have been familiar with a type of religious practices the people were engaging in at Jerusalem does not minimize the voice of God speaking to him. He was carried in spirit to the city. This was God's work and we cannot understand completely the methodology involved.

Some scholars believe the "image of

jealousy" related to the Adonis-Festival which was a sex-oriented religion. The "women weeping for Tammuz" was also related to the fertility rites. Tammuz was probably the Syriac name for Adonis. According to the myth, the god died each year and was resurrected. His death was commemorated with weeping and his return was hailed with joy. The women, in their various activities, would yield themselves to prostitution.

Truth for today.—We become like that which we constantly admire and worship. If our God has no character, there is no constraint to personal morality. God's command to his people was that they should be holy because he was holy.

Immorality and injustice go hand in hand. People who are depraved and licentious in their personal living standards do not really desire justice for all people. They may pretend to do so in order to "present a good front," but their claims are only pretense. When people reject the God of righteousness, unbridled indulgencies of all kinds usually follow closely.

Decree to Destroy All Except Those Who Are Grieved Because of Sin (Ezek. 9:1–11)

The passage.—God's patience had been exhausted. He could not tolerate such abominations as Ezekiel had seen in the Temple. His character demanded that he come in judgment.

Surely there were a few who were concerned for righteousness! These could be spared. The prophet, however, doubted any were sufficiently grieved at the wickedness of the land to warrant sparing their lives. He felt such punishment would be so nearly universal the nation would be destroyed.

Special points.—Was this command actually carried out? According to verse 11, the man reported he had obeyed orders completely. We should remember this was a vision. Although the abominations Ezekiel saw were actually being practiced, it is not necessary to believe there was a wholesale killing at that time.

There were three invasions of the city. In 605 B.C. and 597 B.C. there must have been a number killed in the fighting. This vision of Ezekiel came after these two invasions but it also came before the final destruction in 586 B.C. when there was a mass slaughter.

Truth for today.—God is always looking for those who will not yield to the pressures and temptations of the world. He will keep them from the judgment that comes to the wicked. Sometimes it seems good people suffer but God will eventually honor those who honor him.

A great spiritual truth is suggested by God's word, "Begin at my sanctuary." Judgment must always begin with God's people. There is a distinct difference between the sin of God's redeemed child and one who is lost. The unregenerate are subject to the general law of sin and retribution but God's born-again family feel the special chastisement of God's discipline.

Lifted out of context, the words of the man clothed in linen provide a great spiritual challenge for us. His report was, "I have done as thou dids't command me" (1:11, RSV) Would to God we could be so obedient in all of our responsibilities!

Destruction of City by Fire and a Fresh Revelation of God's Glory (Ezek. 10:1–22)

The people were destroyed in chapter 9. Now the city is to be burned. This is symbolized by the scattering of coals which were taken from under the throne.

In the previous chapter God's glory was on the threshold of the house (9:3). Here it is sitting upon the throne above the cherubim. In verse 4, however, it returns to the threshold of the house and filled all the area with brightness. It is very difficult to trace the schedule and activities of God's glory. Perhaps this is the prophet's symbolic way of saying that no place can "corner" God or his majestic nature.

As one studies verses 9–18 he should review the vision in chapter 1. The differences are small and probably without any significance. The same truths are emphasized about God. He is active in the affairs of history and aware of the needs of his people. Nothing escapes his all-seeing eye. He possesses infinite resources to work out his redemptive purpose in the world.

Special points.—Ezekiel makes it very clear that these were likenesses of things rather than the thing itself. The phrase "in form resembling a throne" (10:1) makes it clear we are dealing with symbolism. There is no particular merit in trying to reproduce the vision in picture form. The prophet himself was vague about the content. We are dealing with symbolism and should be quite content to accept the in-depth message of God's glory without trying to create our own "graven images" to act as a crutch for spiritual worship. All scholars point out that Ezekiel went to great efforts to refrain from "anthropomorphic" descriptions of God. Deity cannot be explained in human terms apart from the incarnation when God became man in Jesus Christ.

Truth for today.—When mortal sin comes into conflict with God's glory the fires of judgment must fall. It will either purify and make one ready for

service as in Isaiah's inaugural vision or it will be a consuming fire to destroy.

As God's glory was mobile, so we must be flexible in our spiritual lives. Many changes are taking place today. We must be able to cope with these quick transitions and carry godly lives into the midst of any situation.

Judgment upon Leaders and Promise of Nation's Restoration (Ezek. 11:1–25)

The passage.—Leaders in iniquity must be punished. These men were deceiving the people by lulling them into a false security. This caused the nation to plunge more deeply into sin.

When Ezekiel witnessed the death of Pelatiah, he became desperate. He felt this indicated Israel would be left without even a remnant. God assured him his eye was upon the people and that he determined to work out his redemptive purpose through them. They would be restored to their land and given a moral transformation. This would give them the inner power to obey God. Those who insisted upon being unusable, however, would be dealt with appropriately by God's avenging hand.

Special points.—The contention by some scholars that 11:1–13 should be placed after 8:15 is not valid. They point out the city had already been purged (chap. 9) and devastated by fire (chap. 10) and there would be no people left. We should remember we are dealing in visions. Ezekiel nowhere claims the executioner's work had been literally accomplished nor the city literally burned. He is declaring coming judgment and giving pictures of activities in the city that demanded this judgment. We make a great mistake when we try to press the visions as literal happenings and insist each must follow the other in a chronological continuity. Also, the twenty-five men in 11:1 are not the same as in 8:16. The first group are the sun worshipers while the second are outstanding political leaders.

Again, Jaazaniah in 11:1 is not the same man mentioned in 8:11. They have different fathers. Azzur could be the grandfather of both men since family relations are sometimes designated this way but it is more likely they are two separate men.

Verse 3 poses a slight problem for it seems to indicate the opposite of what it means. The wicked politicians did not believe judgment was near. The best interpretation is they were urging the people not to build houses but rather prepare for war with Babylon. Ezekiel would consider this an evil act for he had warned the city was doomed. Jeremiah had also been telling the people to surrender to Babylon for this was God's will.

Truth for today.—No nation ever rises above its leadership. Wicked men will contend to the very end their position is right and God's way is not practical. Such men will ruin a nation rather than repent of their evil ways. The writer of Proverbs wisely said, "When the wicked beareth rule, the people mourn" (29:2).

Messages Showing the Moral Necessity for Jerusalem's Destruction (Ezek. 12: 1—19:14)

This section is not quite as cohesively unified as the immediately preceding one. There is, however, a relatedness of subject matter which binds these chapters together. They seem to possess generally the same date as 8:1—11:25 since no new date is added until we reach 20:1.

There seems to be a more spiritual view of Israel's guilt in this section. There are three general concepts which,

although not entirely new, are presented with a little more depth of insight. First, individual responsibility means one cannot be held responsible for the sins of others. Second, those who escape judgment will be witnesses to others concerning the resourcefulness of God and his ability to deliver from sin. Third, the final answer in spiritual matters is for the people to receive a new heart.

Flight from the Doomed City (Ezek. 12: 1–20)

The passage.—The city is doomed! The people must not take it lightly! The prophet gives the coming captivity a historical dramatization. The exiles' baggage should convince even the rebellious house of Israel there is "death in the city." The digging through the wall is an added sign.

The eating and drinking with quaking, trembling, and fearfulness symbolizes the terror that shall seize the people. They cannot ignore the judgment by making fun of previous prophecies. The proverbs the people have concocted will not avert or even delay the coming judgment. God has decreed the city's doom and it will come to pass shortly.

Special points.—There is no reason to doubt these events occurred literally. By this time, the people were probably coming to Ezekiel's house to hear his messages. The leaders may have begun to take him seriously even though many of the captives were still rebellious. There are no physical impossibilities connected with the actions attributed to him.

The "prince" referred to the king. Ezekiel spoke of his coming to Babylon and yet not seeing it. According to 2 Kings 25:7 and Jeremiah 39:6–7, the words of Ezekiel were literally fulfilled. This must be accepted as predictive prophecy. There is no alternative.

Truth for today.—It is sometimes necessary for God to expose the shallowness of our illusions. If ungodly leaders are giving us false hope, it is an act of mercy for God to reveal the vanity of such unrealistic optimism. The coming of God's word to man has always been an important event. It may be attractive, tender, and consoling. It can unfold our responsibility and urge us to the performance of duty. Sometimes, however, when moral conditions deteriorate sufficiently, God's word produces a certainty of coming terror because of entrenched evil in the land.

God's decrees are immutable. Blind and rebellious unbelief cannot break down his words. Those who set themselves against divine truth will find their words are only bubbles—baseless and hollow.

Condemnation of False Prophets and Prophetesses (Ezek. 13:1–23)

The passage.—Why did the Israelites entertain such delusive hopes regarding their future welfare? To a large extent, it was because the prophets of the day held out such hopes to them. The term "false prophet" is not found in the Old Testament but this is the term scholars have chosen to identify those spokesmen who misguided the people by giving them a false concept of God and his dealings with the nation.

The first sixteen verses refer to the prophets while the last seven are against the prophetesses. A fox finds his natural place among conditions of decay. They undermine anything which is still standing. A fox will enter through a breach in a ruined building and flee from one to another. All of these speak of a false prophet's characteristics. They add to the decay of a nation by failing to take a stand but rather exploiting the people for personal gain. They thus intensify the national danger.

There are several women mentioned in the Old Testament as prophetesses (Miriam, Deborah, Huldah, the wife of Isaiah). The Lord has endowed many women with fine gifts to speak for him. The women of Ezekiel's day, however, did not represent the true prophetic movement. They were associated with sorcery and witchcraft. Following their own imagination, they led the people astray. They pretended they could foretell future events. They exploited the people through their "magical arts." One prominent scholar says, "Prophetesses is too good a name for them; witches or sorceresses would suit the description better."

Special points.—The "pillars to all armholes" is more properly "magic bands upon all wrists." Recent scholarship believes these bands were put upon the ones who consulted the prophetesses conveying the idea they were bound or fastened to the magic influences upon them and perhaps symbolizing the power which the sorceresses had to bind and loose.

"The handfulls of barley . . . and pieces of bread" may refer to items used in the process of divination rather than the traditionally accepted interpretation that they represent the fees given to the prophetess. The bread would be crumbled or the barley scattered. The observer would watch it closely and then listen to a pronouncement from the sorceress. This was morally revolting to God, among other reasons because it was perverting certain types of offerings and rituals which had been commanded by God in the Old Testament.

Truth for today.—Everyone who speaks for God must constantly reexamine his message. Only by keeping strict discipline upon our motives can we avoid self-deception. Every nation that ever fell was influenced to a large extent by misguiding teachers. Spokesmen for God can never relax their supreme regard for truth and must never yield to the popular cry to relax one's discipline and blend in with the worldliness of the day.

Condemnation of Insincere Inquires and Time Serving Prophets (Ezek. 14:1–11)

Although this section was delivered to the elders of Israel, it was intended for a larger audience—those in Babylon and perhaps Jerusalem. There was a group who came to the prophet for advice and yet did not really want it. They had already decided their course of action. They had committed themselves to idolatry and did not intend to take seriously any command from the Lord or his prophet. These people should not even be dignified by the prophet with an answer. If he is deceived by their hypocrisy, the Lord will deceive the prophet and destroy him. This act of God is redemptive in purpose. It is in order that the people shall cease from their sin and turn to God.

The latter part of the chapter reveals the seriousness of the situation. If three of the most righteous men who ever lived were present in the land, they would not be able to avert the coming judgment. They alone would be spared but could not effect the deliverance of any save themselves. The prophet does admit, however, the possibility of a remnant surviving. They will be a consolation for the people in Babylon when they come to join them. Their presence will be a testimony to the resourcefulness of God and his ability to show mercy even in the midst of judgment.

Special points.—Scholars have found a great hero named Daniel (spelled slightly different) in the Ras-Shamra text who dates from the fifteenth century

before Christ. This man was righteous and judged equitably the cause of widows and orphans. There is just as great a problem, however, if not greater, in including a non-Old Testament character with Noah and Job as including a contemporary. Ezekiel's reference to him only enhances the greatness of the man who was so faithful to God during the time of the exile.

The prophet is not inconsistent when he speaks so strongly of the impossibility of one escaping and then refers to a remnant. There was always implicit within every prophetic oracle the fact that a remnant would survive. Isaiah enunciated this principle many years before and every prophet faithfully observed it.

Truth for today.—Those who serve God in leadership positions need to possess keen powers of discernment. It sometimes takes years of experience to recognize the "phonies" but more than that we must be genuine ourselves and without pretense in our religious life.

There are times in the history of a nation when a few righteous people can avert judgment on the land. Total destruction of a people has been delayed a generation because a Hezekiah or Josiah in the political realm or a Wesley or Whitfield in the religious realm have called the country back to at least a partial repentance. There does, however, come a point of no return. Where do we stand in our nation?

Worthless Vine, Inhabitants of Jerusalem, to Be Consumed (Ezek. 15:1–8)

The prophet perhaps anticipates the arguments of the wicked people in Jerusalem. Has God not chosen them and blessed them in an unusual way? Surely he cannot cast them as "rubbish to the void."

Ezekiel, however, says he can—and

will. He goes so far as to compare them to a vine. Even when complete, it was virtually worthless for any constructive building. When damaged by fire, it was absolutely worthless.

The teaching is clear. Even at its best, Jerusalem was not much. Now that she has become infected by sin, Jerusalem is utterly without value. God must act in accordance with his true character. The guilty must be punished.

Special points.—The figure of comparing God's people to a vine was a favorite one in the Old Testament (Isa. 5; Hos. 10; Jer. 2:21). The comparison is not between the wood of the vine and that of other trees. The particular tree Ezekiel mentioned is not fruit but a wild vine that grows in the forest. It is inferior because it is nonfruitbearing and produces no wood which can be used as timber.

Truth for today.—Man is very much like a vine. He is capable of producing fruit. He may become like the God in whose image he is made. If he fails, however, he is completely worthless. When one possesses a moral nature and fails to develop it or perverts it, he becomes inferior to the animals who do not have a moral nature at all.

Man is completely dependent upon God. When he neglects the help that can be supplied through fellowship with his creator he fails to realize his possibility. A collective number of men cannot be independent of God any more than a single individual without suffering dire consequences.

Israel's Infidelity Allegorized (Ezek. 16: 1–63)

The passage.—Few nations have possessed the proud national consciousness of Israel. Patriotic feeling burned brightly. Israel's past made it impossible for her to be indifferent to the elements

of greatness in her history. Ezekiel, however, did not share her pride. He traced her history through three stages—"foundling child," "unfaithful spouse" and "abandoned prostitute."

The language is offensive to modern taste. His purpose was seemingly to present the people's wickedness in a most repulsive way in order to shock them into utter disgust concerning their moral condition.

The sin of Judah was so terrible it made Samaria, and even Sodom, look good. Nevertheless, the section closes with a promise of restoration not only for her two sisters but for Judah as well. God will forgive her and once more establish his covenant with her. Although Ezekiel does not specifically say it, one truth is always present in his messages. God will forgive and restore Israel in order that he might work out his long-range redemptive purposes through her.

Special points.—Ezekiel does not consider Israel's beginning at Sinai, in Egypt, or even with Abraham who left Ur, at God's command, to begin a new people. Israel's moral deterioration caused him rather to identify her with the Canaanites. Ezekiel's point is that Israel has likewise been pagan all along. Infidelity was in her lifeblood. She has always been abominable and disgusting even as the Amorites and Hittites who were the most famous and corrupt of all the Canaanitish people.

Truth for today.—This is more than a narrative concerning a nation. It is the story of a human soul. We enter society uncared for until God the Redeemer comes. He loves us, saves us, trains us, and far too many times we reward him with infidelities and shameless idolatries.

Yet God continues to woo us for he is the ever-loving Father and Husband. He has made us for himself and has redeemed us in order that we might be fit instruments for the working out of his purpose.

Ingratitude is the greatest of sins. We need to remember constantly our lost condition before salvation and that we are what we are by grace and grace alone.

Allegory Concerning Zedekiah's Rebellion and the Future Messianic Kingdom (Ezek. 17:1–24)

The passage.—Ezekiel had a high concept of the monarchy's dignity. He represented it as a cedar in Lebanon. On the other hand, he regarded Zedekiah's administration as infinitesimal. The eagle replaced the cedar with a vine which grew along the ground.

The great rivalry between Babylonia and Egypt is evident in this allegory. There had existed a strong pro-Egyptian party in Judah for many centuries. Isaiah reckoned with it. It probably extended back to the days of the Exodus. Israel could never quite believe Assyria and later Babylon were really stronger than the once great Egyptian monarchy.

The disheartened nation is encouraged, however, by the prophet's description of the future. Israel, although politically impotent, will make its contribution in another area. God has designed for her a spiritual mission. The young twig will bear fruit and become a noble cedar. Perhaps Jesus had in mind this passage in his parable of the mustard seed (Mark 4:30–32).

Special points.—The fruit bearing of the cedar signified more than the return from Babylon under Zerubbabel. It was definitely a prediction of the coming messianic kingdom. The Jews have interpreted this more in terms of political prosperity and security but Christians see this spiritually fulfilled in the coming of Christianity and the extension of

God's spiritual rule in the hearts of people.

Truth for today.—Whatever fantasies we may possess of our own importance, God always has the last word. He cannot use a nation or an individual that ignores his pronouncements concerning moral and spiritual issues. On the other hand, God never casts his people away entirely. If there is any trace of usableness, God's grace will offer every opportunity to be of service. No child of God has ever gone so far in rebellion but that he can return, find forgiveness, and dedicate himself afresh to God's plan for his life.

Individual Freedom and Responsibility (Ezek. 18:1–32)

The passage.—This chapter has one great theme. Man is responsible for his own actions. He cannot blame his father for his own sin. Neither can he benefit from his father's good deeds. He must make his own choices and his destiny is based upon these decisions.

Ezekiel begins with a categorical denial of the popular proverb in Israel. He lays down a general principle and then illustrates this principle rather tediously through three generations.

Anticipating the objection of some, he points out the possibility of a wicked man repenting and even a righteous man sliding backward in devotion. He reconciles these with the fairness of God and closes with a heartfelt call to repentance. Twice he makes it clear that God is compassionate and finds no joy in punishing the wicked (vv. 23–32). The seeds of the New Testament doctrine of the new birth are found in the concluding part of the chapter.

Special points.—The critics have contended Ezekiel oversimplified the matter of morality to an "atomistic basis." They insist punishment does not follow quite so automatically. If this were the only word we had from Ezekiel, we might accept the charge as valid. We must realize, however, this is but one chapter from a thoroughly comprehensive analysis of Israel's moral and spiritual life. Of course, our father's actions do affect us and our actions affect our children, but we are not hopelessly enslaved by our family background.

The concluding verses open up the doorway of opportunity. We need not become bewildered or cynical at life and its demands. We are not left to our own abilities. Each of us is responsible for his own moral actions but we can always change because God is more than just— he is merciful.

Truth for today.—Some behavioral schools have overemphasized the effect of childhood influences. Massive organizations and computer programing have dwarfed personal initative. We need a reevaluation and restatement on the individual's worth and responsibility.

The strongest team is no more effective than the individual performance of the weakest member. Rugged individualism which leads to unconcerned isolationism is bad but so is any system of thought which buries the individual's responsibility beneath a maze of corporate machinery. One of Christianity's greatest contributions is recognizing the competency of the individual and the corresponding obligation.

God is concerned with the future of every man. He will give a new spirit and motivation to all who turn to him in repentance and faith. In God's highest revelation, Jesus Christ, there is always a "land of beginning again."

A Lamentation over Three Weak and Wicked Kings (Ezek. 19:1–14)

Shadows crept into the royal house of the last four kings of Judah but two exercised an unusually profound feeling of pity among their countrymen because of their melancholy fate. It may be that Jehozhaz (vv. 1–4) and Jehoiachin (vv. 5–9) were in captivity (Egypt and Babylon) simultaneously while Ezekiel spoke these words.

This oracle is in the Qinah metrical scheme (that of a dirge). It is a graphic description of the spiritual bankruptcy of the country because of its continual rebellion against the Lord. The third part of the chapter (vv. 10–14) dealing with Zedekiah makes it clear the tragedy that has come on the land is due to Judah's "stem" not to Babylon. Ungodly kings, ruling with the permission of ungodly people, have brought Judah to a weakened condition which makes her vulnerable to a foreign invader. The prophet gives lyrical expression to the nationwide feeling of sadness. The spiritual insensitivity of the two young kings plus the headstrong and yet vacillating Zedekiah have paved the way for national destruction.

Special points.—The "mother" of verse 2 refers to the nation Judah rather than to the physical mother of these kings. She is compared to a lioness probably because the nation of Judah is symbolized as a lion (Gen. 49:9).

Jewish scholars interpret the "whelp" of verse 5 as referring to Jehoiakim rather than Jehoiachin. The former, however, was not taken with hooks and put in a cage and taken to Babylon. He died, probably during the turbulence during the invasion in 597 B.C. There is every reason to believe Jeremiah's prediction of his burial was literally fulfilled (Jer. 22:19). The context supports our accepting the "whelp" as Jehoiachin. We have a parallel—all three of the men mentioned in this chapter were taken captive.

Truth for today.—Most wicked men suffer grievously before death overtakes them. Few descend in peace to the grave. Sin carries with it its own destruction. Judah's fire went out from its own stem and consumed its branches and fruit. We are punished by them. The moral structure of the universe guarantees that in the long run sin pays off the sinner—usually in the same area in which he has violated the moral law.

Israel's History Summarized and Her Future Described (Ezek. 20:1–49)

The passage.—This final group of oracles (chaps. 20–24) were all delivered within three years of Jerusalem's fall. There is actually no new teaching in this section but rather a restatement and deeper intensification of the prophet's basic message. The end was drawing near but Ezekiel kept his composure in spite of his obvious excitement.

When some of the elders came to the prophet asking for a message he summarized Israel's history and drew appropriate lessons from it. He recalled the nation's sins while in Egypt, the travels in the wilderness and their continued transgressions after reaching the Holy Land. Every action of God was for "the sake of his name" by which he meant that the Lord would not be despised and minimized in the sight of other nations. The people's sinfulness renders them unworthy to carry on dialogue with him as an equal.

The deserved judgment, however, will be followed by a mighty act of deliverance because of God's mercy. The nations must know he is God. They must see him punish sin but they must also realize that he has the power to preserve his own people and use them to accomplish his redemptive purposes.

Special points.—The visits of the elders indicates Ezekiel had come to be a respected person. Probably they came periodically to ascertain his evaluation of the political situation. It also indicates Babylon allowed Israel some type of self-government. God was jealous for his name. The entire personality and essence of one's being is wrapped up in one's name. To profane God's name was to profane his moral character. To recognize his attributes and assign him the position of Lord in life is to sanctify and reverence his name.

The picture of passing under the rod and going in by numbers is from the custom of the shepherd in counting his flock. Every tenth animal was dedicated to the Lord and any cull was separated from the flock. This insured purity. Jesus spoke of separating the sheep from the goats.

Truth for today.—When we ask for God's leadership there must be evidence of our sincere desire to follow his revealed will. A mere occasional coming to him is not sufficient. It is comforting, however, to know that God never leaves his children in the wilderness of suffering and frustration. There is always a future for failures. God is always seeking how he can use us not how he can punish us. It is not his will that any should perish. He wishes all men to come to repentance and be of service in bringing his purposes to pass in this world.

God's Judgment Sword Drawn for Israel's Punishment (Ezek. 21:1–32)

This literary vehicle is a striking one. Judgment, when it comes, will cut off both the righteous and the wicked. The prophet is commanded to give evidence before the people of his breaking heart and bitter grief. In verses 8–18 irregular and unorganized words come forth as the prophet pictures the sword flashing back and forth in judgment.

A secondary literary vehicle is employed in verses 18–23. The prophet is commanded to draw a symbolic sketch for the sword of Babylon's king. A signpost will mark two different ways for the king to take. One alternative is to

Ammon and the other to Jerusalem. The king is pictured as using various means of divination as he seeks to determine which path to take. The lot falls upon Jerusalem. The city's doom is sealed. The time of Israel's final punishment is near. Ruin is decreed for the land. A final section reminds the Ammonites they will not escape punishment.

Special points.—There is no way to determine whether or not the events in verses 21–22 occurred literally and, if they did, were seen by Ezekiel. We can be sure it is descriptive of the custom of the Babylonian kings. Actually, these were religious men. They believed in following indications given by higher powers but their methods were crude and their knowledge of God was both limited and perverted.

Truth for today.—The things which we trust the most can be swept away in a moment. When our religious institutions become meaningless and unrelated to life God must act to remove them and bring us back to reality in worship. God's judgments are threatened long before they are executed. His sword remained in the sheath for many years during the wanderings and rebellions of the Jews. Likewise, he is patient toward us and is slow to anger. Surely, the goodness of God should lead us to repentance.

Evil people rejoice when judgment comes upon good people but their joy is shortlived. Judgment must begin at the house of God but it extends to all unrighteous people. God chastises "his own people" to correct them. "Others" reap, in time, the law of sin and retribution.

Jerusalem's Sins Graphically Described and Fate Decreed (Ezek. 22:1–31)

This indictment against Jerusalem resumes the thought of 20:1–44. The emphasis here, however, is on the present sins rather than the past history of Israel. This chapter is, in a sense, an apologetic. The Lord is defending himself for the action he must take. The abominable deeds that have made the city a reproach to the nations are enumerated. The city has become bloody. He mentions the word seven times which indicates the violence in the land. Israel has become dross. She must be melted by the judgment of God. All classes of people are guilty of unworthy acts. The Lord needs an intercessor but he cannot find one. His wrath must be poured out and the people consumed because of their iniquity.

Special points.—The expression "strike my hands together" (v. 13, RSV) indicates a strong feeling of emotion. It may indicate either displeasure or rejoicing. In this context, of course, it expresses the Lord's displeasure at the conduct of his people. In 26:6 Ammon performed the same act when she rejoiced over Judah's suffering.

Truth for today.—Moral corruption and social injustice go together. We never find great humanitarians among those who violate the laws of chastity and purity. Unbridled indulgence in the realm of the flesh produces selfish exploitation in the ethical realm.

When moral absolutes are ignored there is no depth to which a city will not sink. Right worship and right living are inseparable. When religious leaders lower the standards the people lose all sense of control and discipline. They plunge headlong into vices of the lewdest kind.

God must consume filthiness with the fires of judgment. His purpose is never merely punitive, although at the time it may appear to be. He rather desires to melt the dross in order to obtain pure metal from a worthless mixture. Even when the clouds seem darkest God is seeking to find a way to work out his purposes. He is always seeking for a man, a spiritual leader, to act as his representative and hold back the tide of inevitable judgment even if only for a short time.

Israel and Judah's Sin Allegorized by Two Sisters (Ezek. 23:1–49)

The frank and intimate language of this allegory reminds us of chapter 16. In the earlier chapter, however, the emphasis is on Israel's idolatry and corrupted religion. The theme of this chapter is the political alliances of Israel and Judah with foreign nations.

Ezekiel pictures these alliances as disloyalty to Jehovah and uses the figure of adultery. As Israel and Judah allied with the foreign nations in treaty they adopted their religion which was sensual and based upon immoral sexual conduct. Part of the worship ritual was actually engaging in sexual practices with the priestesses who were dedicated to these false gods.

Israel (Samaria) and Judah (Jerusalem) are compared. Judah has the greater guilt because she had Israel's example before her but failed to learn the obvious lesson that sin brings death to a nation.

A closing word gives a stern warning to all women concerning immorality in their personal lives. The frank language of the prophet conveys the point with clarity. No one who heard Ezekiel speak or who reads his prophecy can fail to understand the message that lewd living produces a deteriorating society.

Special points.—This is one of the chapters in the Bible that does not lend itself to public reading. Many consider such descriptions vulgar and offensive. This, however, is God's word and his message to the people. The prophet is seeking to make sin appear as monstrous as possible.

There is no actual trace of idolatry during the Egyptian bondage but there are indications the Israelites adopted many Egyptian customs. Ezekiel speaks of both kingdoms as existing as far back as the days of Egyptian bondage. The germ of the two kingdoms does appear from the very beginning of Israel's history. Judah and Ephraim stood apart as strong tribes. This attitude, no doubt, paved the way for the later division.

Truth for today.—The secular forces are constantly seeking to undermine Christian convictions. When one breaks relationship with God and turns to those whose ideals are not compatible with the ethical righteousness of God's character, moral deterioration soon takes place. Because woman is made for the highest, when she corrupts herself she can sink lower than any man.

God's people need to be aware constantly of the need for witnessing. It is not necessary, however, to enter into alliances of any kind with non-Christians in order to influence them. The wise Christian will "keep his distance" from moral impurity but, at the same time, he will seek to "build bridges" to the individual in an effort to lead him to the forgiveness that is in Christ.

Final Prophecy of Jerusalem's Fall (Ezek. 24:1–27)

Judah's midnight hour finally came. The first two verses of this chapter give the historical facts concerning the beginning of the siege. All the prophet had been predicting was about to occur. The people would recognize all that he said was indeed the Word of the Lord.

Verses 3–14 contain an allegory delivered to the people. The siege and capture were pictured as a rusted caldron set on a fire. It represented the city while the pieces of flesh inside the caldron represented the people of Jerusalem. The fire represents the siege and the rust represents the filthy lewdness of the people. Also, the rust was suggestive of the blood which had been spilled by the violence and the casual attitude of the people toward murder.

Even the death of Ezekiel's wife was used by God as an object lesson. He is told not to mourn for her even though she is "the delight of your eyes" (v. 15, RSV). The sanctuary at Jerusalem was also the pride of the people. It would be taken from them. They may pine away to each other but not make a great display of mourning.

Special points.—How could Ezekiel have known the exact day? It has been suggested that he was in touch with Babylonian leaders. It has also been suggested that he obtained the date by calculating backward after he received news of the city's fall. It has been suggested that he possessed an unusual gift which was intensified and directed when he "passed into a trance." Even such a scholar as G. A. Cook, author of International Critical Commentary, speaks of "Ezekiel's peculiar faculty for seeing remote events happening before his eyes." We can express it in the simpler language of faith. God revealed this to him.

The declaration of God that the fugitive will report the fall "on that day" raises a problem of distance. The best translation is probably "time" or "period" since the word for "day" in Hebrew is ambiguous.

The promise of God "your mouth will be opened" and "you shall . . . be no longer dumb" have to do with the declaration of God in 3:26 (see comments on this section). Ezekiel had indeed spoken but the people did not listen. For all intent and purpose, he may as well have been dumb. Now, however, it will

be different. They will listen gladly to him in his subsequent messages.

Truth for today.—God may delay his judgments but they always come. The time of grace runs out and sin must be dealt with drastically. One does not escape God's judgments by ignoring his messenger.

Nothing in this world is permanent. The things and people dearest to us will some day be taken away. If we are to come through our times of grief with faith, we must have spiritual resources before the tragedy comes.

Sometimes the fountain of tears that we feel like shedding must be sealed up within us. Often we can witness best by doing our mourning in private and showing little grief publicly. This does not mean that we do not bear heavy sorrow but rather that we find our comfort in our personal communion with God.

Prophecies Against Foreign Nations (Ezek. 25:1—32:32)

These chapters constitute the first division of the second half of Ezekiel's prophecies. They are, in a sense, a part of the prophecies of restoration because Israel's enemies must be destroyed before she can become once more secure in her own land.

Many of the prophetic books have messages directed against the foreign nations. What is their purpose? First, it is to underscore the fact that God's moral sovereignty extends to all people. Again, Israel was prone to despair when Jerusalem fell and the people were carried into captivity. These prophecies would encourage them as they faced the dense darkness of the people in whose land they lived.

There are prophecies against seven nations. Many scholars see this as a symbolic number signifying completeness. God is against *all* the enemies of his people. They are accountable to him for their moral shortcomings.

Prophecies Against Nearby Neighbors (Ezek. 25:1–17)

The passage.—These four nations were geographically closer and historically more intimately connected with direct and open hostility to Israel. The prophecies should probably be dated after the destruction of Jerusalem. These nations were a constant threat to Israel's restoration. We can visualize the prophet as he stands imaginatively in the ruins of the city and makes a semicircle in his thrust of prophetic messages. Beginning with Ammon, he moves in a clockwise motion and finishes with the message against Philistia.

Special points.—The Ammonites and Moabites were the descendants of the two sons of Lot by the incestuous relationship with his daughters (Gen. 19:30–38). Fellowship between them and Israel was strained for centuries. There were frequent conflicts and wars. They settled their land early and resented the fact they were pushed out by the Israelites.

The Ammonites' *Aha* was the same sin for which Obadiah condemned Edom except Ezekiel is a bit more definite in specifying the actual occurrence. It was the destruction of the Temple when Jerusalem was sacked in 586 B.C.

Edom was actually more closely kin to Israel than Moab or Ammon. The inhabitants were descendants of Esau, brother of Jacob. Their strategic location was of great commercial importance. It controlled a major caravan route. This judgment pronounced upon them was literally fulfilled. In the second century B.C. John Hyracanus defeated them and compelled them to adopt the Jewish faith. Their prestige, however,

had been taken away by Arabian tribes much earlier. Herod the Great of New Testament days was an Edomite.

Most scholars believe the Philistines came from Crete about 1500 B.C. They were non-Semitic and became the perpetual enemies of Israel. Their country was about fifty miles long on the western coast of Palestine. They lived mainly in five fortified cities (Gaza, Gath, Ashkelon, Ashdod, and Ekron) and were a constant menace to the Israelites for several centuries.

The prophet is not quite as definite concerning their fate as that of the others. He does, however, make it clear they will be extinguished. This was fulfilled in the several centuries preceding the birth of Christ as Jewish culture absorbed this area.

Truth for today.—The verdict of history is that no group of people can oppose God and his purpose without suffering dire consequences. There is a moral law within the universe which guarantees evil will be destroyed. Sin contains within it the germ of its own self-destruction.

Many times those who are closest to us resent most strongly God's blessings upon us. We must, nevertheless, remain true to the revelation which God has given to us regardless of the enmity aroused by others when we are faithful and receive God's blessings. God must be vindicated. Evil must be destroyed. The world must come to know and recognize God's presence and his eventual triumph over all entrenched evil.

Prophecies Against Tyre and a Brief Fragment Against Sidon (Ezek. 26:1—28:26)

The passage.—There are five main divisions in the material. First, Ezekiel predicts the destruction of the great city (26:1–14). Tyre had rejoiced at

Jerusalem's destruction because it meant profit to her. Many nations will come and destroy her completely. The walls will be broken down and the soil scraped from her. The land will be completely exploited. Tyre will become a bare rock never to be built again.

Next, the prophet enumerates and enlarges upon the consequences of Tyre's fall (26:15–21). Her partners in commerce will be shocked for they had considered her impregnable. Her geographical isolation suggested a military security.

God's decree is that Tyre will descend into the Pit to be remembered no more. The once proud prince of commerce will come to a terrible end. People will search in vain for her. Her greatness will vanish forever.

In chapter 27 Tyre is symbolized as a great ship. It is constructed from the best material, furnished with choice equipment and manned by the most skilful personnel. Verses 5–11 describe in great detail the furnishings. Verses 12–15 tell of the merchandise with which she was involved in trading. This added great wealth and made her one of the richest cities in the world. The great ship Tyre is steered into dangerous waters where it is caught in a storm. Both men and merchandise are destroyed.

The latter part of the chapter describes the utter consternation of the people who knew Tyre. They weep bitterly and are horribly afraid when they witness the dreadful end of the once great city that has been brought to utter destruction in the midst of the sea.

Chapter 28 turns from the city to the ruler who is called "the prince of Tyre." He personifies the spirit of the proud metropolis. A severe indictment is brought against him as the prophet specifies the particular sin which was the foundation for all the other iniquities. By equating himself with God, the prince committed blasphemy. He attributed all his prosperity to his own wisdom and ruled out any dependence upon God. A terrible fate awaits him.

Verses 11–19 contain the final prophecy which is a lamentation over the king. The prince of Tyre is symbolically placed in the Garden of Eden where there is perfection. Because of his great desire for splendor, his pride led him to corruption. Those who sought his punishment were appalled because of his dreadful end.

A brief oracle against Sidon, Tyre's nearby neighbor (vv. 20–23) with a word of assurance and comfort to Israel (vv. 24–26) completes this larger section.

Special points.—Many scholars believe the prophecies against Tyre are, in reality, veiled references to Babylon. It is significant that Ezekiel has no word against Babylon as most of the other prophets.

There is some plausibility in this suggestion. Babylon and Tyre were both great commercial powers. The rejoicing of Tyre in 26:2 sounds more like Babylon. Also, it would have certainly been unsafe for Ezekiel to have spoken so strongly against Babylon while a captive in the land.

On the other hand, certain portions, especially chapter 27, do not fit Babylon at all. Then, too, in chapter 26 Ezekiel represents Babylon as attacking Tyre. This seems a bit out of place if Tyre symbolically represents Babylon. Furthermore, the fragment against Sidon would be a bit out of place following a prophecy against Babylon. It fits more naturally if Tyre is actually Tyre. The theory is not really proved in any sense of the word.

In 26:1 the date presents a problem

since Jerusalem fell in the fifth month of the eleventh year. Also, from 33:21 we see Ezekiel did not receive news of it until months later.

Various suggestions have been made for textual correction but the best explanation is that Ezekiel received a vision revealing to him that the same moral and spiritual principles governing Jerusalem likewise prevailed concerning Tyre.

Truth for today.—There is no security apart from a personal relationship with God. The spiritual factor in history is not as outwardly evident as the economic and political factors, but it works silently and surely. In the long run to have "much wealth but little soul" will cause any civilization to crumble.

There is always the temptation for a strong state to arrogate to itself absolute authority. This leads to usurping the place of God by declining to recognize an authority higher than its own. This is one of the greatest dangers of our day.

It is in God we find the power both to win and maintain inward serenity even in the face of seeming insecurity. God vindicates the individual who remains faithful to him regardless of the pressures brought by the ungodly forces of pride and greed.

Prophecies Against Egypt (Ezek. 29:1— 32:32)

There are seven oracles against Egypt. With one exception (30:1–19), they are assigned a date in the text. Chronological order prevails among the first six with the exception of the second message (29:17–21). The final of the seven messages describes the entrance of Egypt into the lower world where she joins other nations that have preceded her. This dirge is a fitting conclusion not only for the messages against Egypt but for the entire book of foreign prophecies. It is entirely unrelated to the dating scheme of the prophecies concerning Egypt.

Ezekiel has a different attitude toward Egypt from that of Tyre. He makes no mention of her political greatness nor of the years the Israelites spent in bondage nor of the Exodus. He mentions only slightly her vacillating policy. He does spend some time in figurative description, however, concerning her status and her shocking fall.

Little is said concerning the current events of Egypt's political life. Actually, the few years which preceded his prophecies had been a time of activity. Pharaoh Necho had suffered a severe setback in the struggle for international power between Babylon and Assyria at the Battle of Carchemish in 605 B.C. Hophra had become king in 588 B.C. He defeated Tyre and Sidon and for a short while was the supreme power in Lebanon. While Nebuchadnezzar was besieging Jerusalem for eighteen months Egypt was strong enough to threaten Babylon but not strong enough to break the siege.

The significant thing about Egypt is that she does not disappear from history like Assyria and Babylon. She merely grows weaker under the succeeding international powers. We do not have enough records of Egyptian history to be dogmatic concerning a literal fulfilment of all the small details Ezekiel prophesied. The main thought is that Egypt was to be reduced to helpless impotence. This was certainly fulfilled.

General Announcement of Coming Judgment upon Egypt (Ezek. 29:1–16)

This proclamation of God's purpose to punish Egypt by reducing her in size and prestige is appropriately placed at the beginning of the seven messages. Egypt is represented as a great dragon lying in the midst of his waters and proudly proclaiming the Nile belongs to him. The prophet warns she will be exposed to those who will exploit her to satisfy their ravenous appetite. Egypt has been guilty of great pride and failed to be a source of help to Israel in her need. The sword will come upon the land and she shall become a desolation and waste. The people shall be scattered and the cities shall lie waste for many years. God will regather the people, restore their fortunes, and bring them back to their land, but Egypt shall remain an insignificant power among the nations. Never again will Israel rely upon her for help.

Nebuchadnezzar to Receive Egypt as Reward for Besieging Tyre (Ezek. 29:17–21)

Nebuchadnezzar labored thirteen years to capture Tyre but failed to secure any reward for the toil. God will, therefore, give him Egypt for plunder. Her wealth shall furnish wages for Nebuchadnezzar's army.

In the future God will bless Israel and vindicate her in the sight of the Egyptians. The "horn" of which Ezekiel speaks is probably a symbol of power rather than an individual leader. Israel was delivered from captivity after the fall of the Babylonian Empire in 536 B.C.

Egypt's Complete Destruction Graphically Described (Ezek. 30:1–19)

Because Egypt was an international power, her fate affected the entire world. Thus God's activity concerning her constitutes a great intervention in history. Ezekiel calls it a "day of the Lord."

Not only will Egypt be destroyed, those who support her will likewise fall. The wealth of the land will be dried up (symbolized by the Nile). Several cities are specifically mentioned and judgment decreed against them. The conclusion is as in other prophecies of this type—this is done in order that all men may recognize the true character of God.

The Breaking and Scattering of Egypt Among the Nations (Ezek. 30:20–26)

The background of this short oracle is a recent defeat of Pharaoh by some army. It was probably Egypt's attempt to break the siege of Jerusalem in the last days before it fell to Babylon.

Since Pharaoh's arm has been broken and not bound up, it is incapable of wielding a sword. God will break both of Egypt's arms and make strong the king of Babylon against him.

Babylon is God's agent of destruction. It is his will that Egypt be scattered among all nations. When it occurs God will be vindicated and people will come to a knowledge of both his holiness and power.

Pharaoh, the Great Cedar, to Be Cut Down (Ezek. 31:1–18)

In chapter 29 Egypt was a dragon. Here, her pride is pictured as a lofty cedar tree. The first nine verses describe her in beautiful poetry. She surpasses all other trees and is envied by all.

Verses 10–14 describe in prose the punishment. The tree will be cut down by foreigners and left lying on the ground. Birds will settle on its ruins.

The last four verses tell of the consternation among the nations at this catastrophe. Those in the grave will mourn. The nations will quake at the sound of the fall. Those who have sought its aid will perish with it. The last verse of this section makes it clear by stating emphatically the prophecy refers to "Pharaoh and all his multitude." There is no misunderstanding the personification.

Lamentation over Pharaoh (Ezek. 32:1–16)

This section and the one following it could be considered as one prophecy with two different divisions. The first is a lamentation while the second is a funeral dirge.

Ezekiel once more pictures Pharaoh as a dragon whose feet trouble the waters and make the rivers foul. He will be dug out and thrown on the ground. His blood will drench the land and there will be a cataclysmic shock upon nature. Babylon is again specified as the instrument of punishment and spoken of as the most terrible among the nations.

Thoughts expressed in previous prophecies are reiterated and some new details are added. Both the poetical and prose sections make it clear Egypt will be stripped of her pride. When the land is completely purified the people will recognize the Lord. Ezekiel instructs the daughters of the nations to sing this lamentation concerning Egypt and her inhabitants.

Egypt's Descent into the Lower World (Ezek. 32:17–31)

This dirge concludes the foreign prophecies. It is a weird funeral march and contains only the cold comfort that all the other nations are sharing the common fate of Egypt. Those who live by physical force and are motivated by greed are, at last, victims of the sword.

The prophet, first, consigns Egypt and her inhabitants to the netherworld. She joins the others who have preceded her in death. A number of kingdoms are present. The list is representative of the world with which Israel has been associated for nearly two centuries.

Some scholars attempt to make the number come to a total of seven in order to coincide with the seven nations against whom Ezekiel prophesies (Ammon, Moab, Edom, Philistia, Tyre, Sidon, and Egypt) and also to signify fulness or completion. This is not, however, a satisfactory approach but satisfies those who love to think in this vein. The greater truths, however, are moral and spiritual.

Special points.—Does 29:18–20 imply Ezekiel made a mistake in 26:7 ff.? Not necessarily! There is a great debate among scholars as to whether Babylon actually conquered Tyre. Some historical records tell of Tyre's fall to Nebuchadnezzar. Many scholars believe the people of Tyre, when they saw the inevitability of the city's fall, loaded all the wealth of the city in ships and fled leaving Nebuchadnezzar with no booty.

In some of his prophecies Ezekiel used current conceptions of the grave as a framework through which he sought to convey spiritual truths. We should remember that the Christian today cannot use these as a basis for doctrinal beliefs concerning the future life or the state of man after death. The zenith of revelation was reached in Christ. This does not mean that Old Testament teachings are false but rather every statement must be viewed in light of historical context and the stage of progressive revelation reached by the writer and his audience.

Truth for today.—National greatness does not guarantee permanence. When a nation is so filled with vaunting pride and prevailing vice that she ignores the moral principles which are written into the structure of the universe, national decay has begun. If we allow pride to overleap our sound judgment, the end is not far away.

All the military genius in the world plus superior economic planning cannot be substituted for humble trust in God. Those who are full with this world's goods can soon be emptied. Both nations and individuals who are wise will seek the wealth that does not pass away. Purity of life and integrity of character serve as a basis for stability and give true meaning to life. Those who leave God out will, in the end, all be alike—unmourned by their equally ungodly friends and separated from God in eternity as they were in the days of their flesh.

Prophecies of Hope (Ezek. 33:1—39:29)

The fall of Jerusalem brought a new phase to Ezekiel's ministry. He had been prophesying doom to the overoptimistic people. Now, he becomes a prophet of comfort for the discouraged people. It is a mark of prophetic genius to know when the people need condemnation and when they need encouragement. There is a time for each emphasis.

Although the foreign prophecies (chaps. 25–32) are in a limited sense prophecies of restoration since they speak of the destruction of Israel's enemies, the true prophecies of hope begin with this section. The people were stunned at Jerusalem's fall but the prophet dared to speak of a new Israel. Some of Ezekiel's deepest insights are found in this section.

A Message Concerning Personal Responsibility (Ezek. 33:1–20)

When Ezekiel began his ministry God outlined the specific duties of a watchman (3:16–21). As he begins the second phase of his ministry, God reminds him once more of these tremendous truths. This second phase was not accompanied by the unusual phenomenon of the first. As one matures, God can speak to him in more mature ways. The visions and ecstatic experiences have a place in one's development but they are not the ultimate in God's dealings with men.

The first nine verses outline the parallel between the prophet and a watchman. They pinpoint the prophet's unique responsibilities. Verses 10–20 deal with the matter of one's individual's responsibility for his sin. God has no displeasure in the death of the wicked but he must judge in accordance with his character. To allow wickedness to go unpunished would be injustice.

Truth for today.—A modern pastor has many responsibilities but major priority must be given to caring for the spiritual life of those whom he serves. His message will not always be received but he must warn people whatever the cost in personal popularity.

Result of Jerusalem's Fall upon the Prophet's Ministry (Ezek. 33:21–33)

The Message.—The final fall of the city brought Ezekiel great freedom. He had been limited in effectiveness as a prophet until God vindicated his words concerning Jerusalem's approaching doom. He had to battle constantly the stubbornness of the people who insisted the land belonged to them and would not be taken away. The prophet insisted their wickedness demanded God's punitive action.

The last section is a strange one. It pictures neurotic people who adore the preacher, are fascinated by his message but are entirely unaware of God's moral claim upon their life. The tragedy is this type of person exists today. Some greedy and preoccupied people still admire preachers for oratory but never seem to feel the moral constraint of the message.

Special points.—When 33:21 is compared with 2 Kings 25:1–10 there is a serious problem. There have been a number of fantastic proposals by technical scholars to resolve it. The best solution seems to be there were many premature rumors of the city's fall. The people were slow to accept Ezekiel's messages concerning the city's capture. They believed Jerusalem would be spared at the last moment as in the days of Hezekiah. It was not until one who had seen the city fall gave an eyewitness account that the people finally accepted the truth. He may have hired out as a camel driver or some similar job. He could have come with the captives and made his escape. We do not know all the details but it is quite possible it would have taken him eighteen months. This would be the first absolutely authenticated word.

Truth for Today.—Blind unbelief causes people to sink deeper into the pit of frustration. It intensifies the practice of wickedness and leads to eventual ruin piled on top of ruin. People caught in the whirling law of sin and retribution mock the most earnest pleadings of God's spokesmen. They may be fascinated by the oratory and charmed by the sincerity but they are too far steeped in infamy and too rebellious in nature to give heed to the message. Depraved people can resist so many appeals their hearts become hard. It is a dangerous moment when one neglects hearing so long that the mind and heart leave the warm and hopeful zone to enter the Arctic Circle of spiritual freeze. For this type of person there is virtually no hope. Oh that men may "come before winter" while the day of opportunity is still present!

Selfish Rulers Rebuked and God's Future Blessings Assured (Ezek. 34:1–31)

The passage.—The prophet goes directly to the root of Israel's problem in a strongly worded denunciation of the political rulers. The people have been subjected to exploitation and misgovernment. Rather than healing the people, the leaders had enriched themselves at the expense of their subjects.

There is, however, a better future for God's people. He will not allow the strong to continue their abuse of the weak. The selfish tyranny of the corrupt political administrations will fall under the judgment of a righteous God. All civic relations will come under the regulation of his righteous will. The human abuses by powerful leaders will give way to the compassionate Shepherd who will rescue his sheep from the wilderness of adversity and exploitation.

Special points.—There is no doubt Ezekiel's promise of the "one shepherd, my servant David" has messianic implications. He is certainly not suggesting reincarnation. A succession of sovereigns hardly suffices to fulfil the promise of Ezekiel. It requires a unique individual.

The ultimate fulfilment of this passage is, of course, found in Jesus of Nazareth. In a spiritual sense, Jesus is sitting on the throne of David today. Every born-again believer is a citizen of God's spiritual kingdom of which Christ is the head.

Whether or not the promises of material prosperity will be fulfilled literally in a millenial kingdom is a question upon which scholars are divided. Some contend vigorously the promises of unprecedented fertility and material progress which did not come to pass after the Babylonian exile must be realized in a future literal reign of righteousness on earth with Jesus Christ as both the religious and political leader. Others insist a spiritual fulfilment of this prosperity in terms of the peace that comes to the hearts of believers is a more meaningful fulfilment than insisting upon a materialistic one. Christendom will, no doubt, never be united in this area of interpretation.

Truth for today.—God loves his people. He is concerned with their problems and acts in history to meet their needs. Both political and religious institutions have a tendency to become corrupt as time passes. Human beings have a way of becoming power-hungry.

It is necessary for God to be both merciful and severe. There is a time when his compassionate heart reaches out in tenderness toward all men. There are also occasions when he must be stern. Both the love and the righteous wrath of God are essential parts of his character. To emphasize one to the exclusion of the other, is to present only half the picture.

God is forever acting in history to bring his purposes to pass. He does not always act in the immediate present to relieve the sufferings of his people. He is, however, working all things to the good of his people. If suffering comes, it is in order that character may be developed. When vindication comes, whether soon or late, God's people will praise him and know that God's way was best.

Edom's Doom and Israel's Glorious Future (Ezek. 35:1—36:38)

The passage.—The prophet follows his promise of the good shepherd ruling in righteousness with a word concerning the land. Edom, Israel's perpetual enemy, had insisted on her right to the land. God's verdict is against her.

The oracle seems superficial and obvious when first read but deepens with further study. Mount Seir, which stands for Edom, is a symbol of all those who despise their birthright as Esau and live for the lust of the moment. The picture of God's glorious future for his people

and their land must be preceded by a word concerning the coming judgment on all of those who, like Edom, have chosen to live for themselves and despise the people of God.

The abused and exploited land of Israel is still precious in God's sight. Although it has been made desolate and crushed from all sides by God's enemies, God will both judge those who have mistreated it and will bless the land with material prosperity.

This was the native land of Ezekiel. Shining through the inspiration of God's Holy Spirit we see the prophet's impassioned love for his native soil. He loves its traditions, takes pride in its history, and delights to describe the various features of the landscape with which he was familiar. He cannot believe the now barren earth will lie untilled nor that the cities will remain uninhabited.

God's blessings upon Israel are not, however, all material. The individual will be changed. The people will be ashamed of their sins and turn from them. This passage anticipates the New Testament doctrine of the new birth.

Modern-day ecologists would do well to note the close relationship between purity in one's personal moral life and freedom from environmental pollution. Ezekiel's constantly recurring theme is the basis for God's actions. He wants the world to know of his holiness as well as his love.

Special points.—The similarity between Ezekiel's portrayal of Israel's transformation and Jeremiah's promise of the work of God in the New Covenant (31:31–34) is obvious. The same Holy Spirit was, of course, the inspirer of both prophets. It is, nevertheless, possible that Ezekiel was familiar with the ministry of Jeremiah and his profound picture of the work of God's Spirit in the future. This does not detract from

God's inspiration but rather reveals there was harmony and fellowship between these two great prophets.

In this day when overpopulation is a problem it is interesting to see God promising this handful of captives an increase of inhabitants for the cities. The last two verses of chapter 36 are not anticlimactic. Neither are they a fragment added by a later editor as some radical scholars have suggested. The scarcity of Israelites was a real issue. The population had been terribly reduced by disastrous wars since the days of Hezekiah. God's promise of future inhabitants in the cities brought great encouragement to the lonely and miserable remnant who were discouraged as they thought of the tremendous task of building once more a strong and prosperous nation.

Truth for today.—God's enemies will eventually be destroyed. Their own hatred will contribute to the process. Those who rejoice over the disasters of righteous people are sowing seed for their own oblivion. To oppose God's plan in history is utterly futile and leads only to confusion, devastation, and eventual ruin.

God's greatest blessings are not the material ones. Transformation of life through the giving of a new spirit is always his ultimate bestowal upon those whom he loves. God's purposes in history do not come as quickly as man wishes. We want our blessings now. God is more interested in developing character than in providing freedom from present inconveniences. We are not to judge God's work until we see the culmination of it. The discipline of our present suffering is needed in order that we shall be developed to our fullest potential. The final evidence will vindicate his work. A surgical operation sometimes seems cruel and unnecessary especially if one should walk in on the middle of it. God interprets his own work.

Israel's Future Symbolized as a Resurrection of Dry Bones (Ezek. 37:1–28)

Israel had been completely disintegrated as a nation and this posed a serious theological problem. Could the Lord still be alive if his Temple had been destroyed, his land polluted, and his people dispersed? The feeble and demoralized remnant in Babylon was at the depth of discouragement.

The valley of dry bones, representing the death of the nation, took on life when the prophet spoke to them. First, there was flesh only but then God breathed into it and it lived. Like in the Garden of Eden, it was when the Spirit came into the flesh that true life was imparted.

An even greater feature of the restoration is set forth. Judah and Israel will be reunited under one sceptre. This cleavage between the two groups was much older than the monarchy. There is evidence it dated all the way back to days of Egyptian bondage. It would be more than political unity. Ezekiel believed the completeness of the union required divine force to make it a reality. Ezekiel, like Jeremiah, always considered the ten Northern tribes as part of any concept of Israel which might exist. The future Israel would not march under two banners but under one.

Special points.—There is not sufficient evidence to be certain concerning the fate of the ten tribes captured by Assyria in 722 B.C. In 605 B.C. Babylon defeated Assyria at Carchemish. There is good reason for believing the Jewish captives were taken to Babylon. Representatives of all twelve tribes returned, following the decree of Cyrus. In New Testament days the people considered themselves as twelve tribes rather than two. Paul, before Agrippa, spoke of "our twelve tribes, instantly serving God day and night" (Acts 26:26).

Truth for today.—Although this passage does not teach the resurrection of the body, the implications are certainly present. The God who raised up a dead nation and reestablished it in its homeland is certainly capable of raising up a dead body.

Regardless of how deep into rebellion and wickedness an individual has gone, God can restore him and make him a new person in Christ Jesus. The same God who breathed into man the breath of life in Eden can transform a sinful life and make it anew in Christ Jesus.

By whatever standard Scripture is measured, this chapter is one of the most profound in the Old Testament. Although the destructive effects of sin have exposed one to the sad ravages of death, he is not hopeless. In Jesus, God's power is unlimited to raise a sinner from spiritual death and make him truly born again of the Spirit. What God does for the individual he can do for a nation in our day. Although it seems to be the "eleventh hour" in our nation's existence, a great turning to God in repentance and faith can bring deliverance and spare us the judgment which seems inevitable because of the moral crisis in our land.

Invasion and Defeat of Israel's Great Enemy, Gog (Ezek. 38:1—39:29)

The passage.—This highly controversial oracle of Ezekiel is considered by many today as directly predictive of events taking place in the Mid-East. Some go so far as to identify Gog as Russia, insisting the Hebrew word translated *prince* should be *Russia* by translating the consonants in the Hebrew word.

These chapters describe an event that takes place after Israel has been resettled in her land. The implication is she has been there for a long time. Gog believes his campaign against God's people is of his own planning, but, in reality, it is a part of God's plan to reveal his holiness and his power in the eyes of many nations. The devastation upon Gog's forces is cataclysmic. Gog will be utterly defeated. It will require a lengthy time to burn the weapons of the enemy and bury the dead.

God will then declare his glory among the nations and Israel will realize his greatness and serve him faithfully. God's holiness will be vindicated and his spirit poured out upon his people. This message closes the section dealing with the restoration of Israel to her land. Although it is not definitely stated, it implies no other enemy will ever threaten the security of the land or the people.

Special points.—Is Gog Russia? One would be unwise to limit the power of God and his ability to predict future events through his spokesman. On the other hand, one weakens his case by resorting to false exegesis to prove a point. The Hebrew word transliterated *rosh* means chief, head, or leader. It is a proper modifier of a word meaning prince and the two words seem properly translated by most versions as "chief prince." The proper noun "Mesech" is similar to Moscow but it is a strained and forced interpretation to say this is a direct prediction of the present-day Russian capital.

In what sense may Gog be associated with Russia? In Ezekiel's prophecy Gog was the enemy of Israel located in her homeland. Israel has been reestablished in her homeland today and Russia seems to be aligned against Israel politically. From this standpoint Russia is rosh—not because rosh is to be interpreted linguistically as Russia but because she seems to be an enemy of Israel today.

There have been other suggestions concerning Gog. The passage has been interpreted apocalyptically. Great events convey spiritual truths in such writings. They are symbolic of times when God delivers his people in time of great need and crisis. The vagueness of this oracle argues for its apocalyptic nature.

Again, Gog has been interpreted as the "barbarian within the soul." In this sense, he represents the powerful forces of brutality that would destroy everything which has been built in the name of reason and humanity at any period in history. This passage shows that such forces as these cannot be ultimately victorious. Forces are at work to destroy society but God is stronger than these evil powers.

The New Testament's teaching of "spiritual Israel" should not be overlooked. If Christianity has inherited the promises made to Abraham (Gal. 3:29), Gog would not be an enemy of national Israel but rather of spiritual Israel. In this case, these two chapters, if predictive of events yet to come, would refer to a great movement against Christianity in the latter days rather than a great movement against Israel.

Each student of the Scripture must study and decide for himself. This is no passage for a novice to interpret with dogmatism.

Truth for today.—God is present in history even when it seems the forces of evil seems to be in control. When it fits into God's redemptive purpose, he moves in to claim the victory for himself and his people.

Often the wicked man becomes puffed up with his own importance. If he has temporary success, it is because God is allowing it. We may suffer without suc-

ceeding but it is in order that later we may succeed and see God's glory. It may be, however, that we are suffering in order that someone else can succeed after us.

It is not possible for us to know whether history, as we know it, will be consummated in our generation. These are truths that are known only to God. Our duty and privilege is to be in God's will so that whatever comes to pass in our world we will have a relationship with him that enables us to find peace within our own heart regardless of external circumstances.

Ezekiel's Picture of the Restored Temple and the Ideal City of the Future (Ezek. 40:1—48:35)

Ezekiel combined the creativity of the idealist with the legalism of the pragmatist in outlining the future Temple. These chapters are highly controversial as to fulfilment. Many scholars see no actual value in them for today's world while others believe this Temple will be rebuilt literally.

There are three main divisions in this larger section. In 40:1—43:27 the prophet gives a picture of the New Temple. He follows it with an outline of the worship ritual in 44:1—46:24. The two concluding chapters (47:1—48:35) tell of the Healing Waters and the Division of the Land.

Picture of the New Temple (Ezek. 40:1—43:27)

The passage.—Ezekiel was placed on a high mountain and told to observe in order that he might declare to Israel all that he would see. Around the Temple area there was a wall about nine feet thick and nine feet high. The wall, which covered the perimeter of the Temple area, was approximately 750 feet on each side.

There were three (no Western gate) gates into the Temple area. A building behind the Temple came against the wall on the Western side. Outside the entrance, there were seven steps leading up to each of the gates. There was a threshold in front of each gate and then a corridor about 42 feet in length. There were guard rooms on each side of the corridor. When one came to the end of the corridor there was another threshold which widened into a porch. There was then another gate which opened into the outer court. Each of the three gateways were designed identically.

Ezekiel was carried into the outer court. One hundred cubits across the outer court from each of the three gates one found himself facing eight steps leading to another gate. Ezekiel went up the eight steps of the South gate and entered a similar arrangement of gateways, threshold, long corridor with rooms on either side, and then another threshold followed by a gate leading into the inner court. He was now on a second level of the city.

This inner court was 150 feet square. On the West side of it was the vestibule leading to the Temple. There was an altar in the inner court in front of the Temple. There were ten steps leading up to the Temple. This made the Temple on the third level above the city.

Throughout both the outer court and the inner court were a number of chambers for the use of the priests. There were tables at the North gate of the outer court as one entered the vestibule going toward the inner court. These tables were for the slaughtering of the sacrifices.

The prophet was then shown the Temple which had two main divisions—the nave and the Most Holy Place. There were buildings around the Temple and chambers for the priests who ministered in and near the Temple. There were smaller buildings where the priests were to deposit the garments which they used in ministering.

When all of the measurements were completed Ezekiel was brought to the Eastern gate and shown the glory of the Lord coming from the East and entering into the Temple by this gate. God would dwell with his people and Israel was to defile the Temple no more.

This section is concluded with a description of the altar and instructions concerning sacrifices. The priests of Zadok's family were to be in charge of the rituals. An eight-day ceremony of atonement was to be held. The great emphasis was on the cleansing of the altar which was to serve as a basis for cleansing the whole Temple.

Special points.—The wall around the Temple area was important. Likewise, the gates, corridors, and guardrooms were significant. The Temple was to be protected. In time of war the enemy always sought to capture the worship area of a nation and destroy its gods. A battle between two nations was essentially a battle between the gods of these nations. Israel's Temple and other holy places must be preserved. There was great military strategy in the planning of these gateways.

It is true that Ezekiel is very tedious in describing these various parts of the Temple area. Sometimes it seems he is unnecessarily meticulous. At other times it seems he is vague. Some scholars wish to explain the ambiguities on a "corrupted text" but it is not necessary to resort to this escape. If one will read the text carefully and make notes as he goes along, this material can be mastered. Ezekiel is logical—unusually technical but logical. The priestly side of his character shows up strongly in this section.

There is no need to reflect at length on the method of inspiration God used to convey this message to the prophet. Ezekiel was certainly in ectasy. His experience has been called a "trance-vision," and this is a satisfactory designation if one speaks of it in a reverent manner. Whether it seems as relevant as other Scripture or not, we have no right to ignore or minimize it. We should rather study it carefully and seek to hear the message God was speaking to the exiles and the application for us.

Truth for today.—God is with his people always. He brings fresh encouragement every morning. Ezekiel foresaw a time when God's purposes would be worked out in history. He believed the institutional life was essential to the religious progress of a nation.

This is a day when many minimize the institutional church. The non-church related organizations and "cell groups" are receiving much attention and praise. There is, of course, always the danger that organized religion will become static if not actually corrupt. Christianity, however, needs the local, congregationally controlled organizations known as churches. When these churches lose vitality the pendulum swings and public reaction turns against them, but institutional religion is necessary to both the propagation of the Christian faith and the conserving of its values. *We need our churches and we need to support them.*

Duties of Priests and the Prince and Other Ordinances Concerning Worship (Ezek. 44:1—46:24)

The passage.—Although these chapters are devoted to instructions which border on legalism, the prophet begins with a dynamic approach. God has entered the Eastern gate and no one else may come through it. Every time the prophet is confronted with the glory of God he is overcome with awe and reverence.

At first glance, the command to exclude foreigners seems bigoted. A closer examination, however, reveals God's disapproval of them was not an arbitrary prejudice. It was because they were lacking in moral transformation. They were uncircumcised in *heart* as well as flesh. Ezekiel was more than a legalist. He was a person of true spiritual discernment.

The prophet is very practical. The Levites who were unfaithful to God must take menial places of service while the sons of Zadok who have refrained from apostasy are assigned the more spiritual aspects of Temple service and ministry. Other indications of the practical approach include the choice of clothing. One cannot perform his work in the best manner when he is physically uncomfortable. Priests shall avoid extremism in either direction concerning their hair and shall remain "tee-totalers" while performing sacred duties. A religious leader's choice of a companion is likewise considered important. Anything which compromises the ability of a priest to serve unfettered, must be eliminated from his life. Even his personal possessions influence his ministry. He must be carefully regulated concerning them.

Any temporal ruler must also be a man of spiritual discernment. He must cooperate with the spiritual leaders of the land and must recognize his limitation in authority over the religious institutions. He has responsibilities to perform but these do not give him the right to dominate either the religious life or the spiritual leaders.

Special points.—Nothing in these chapters should be interpreted as to support the acceptance of governmental aid for churches or church-related institutions. The community of Israel was quite different from the pluralistic society of modern America. The nation Israel was God's chosen people in a unique sense. As a corporate personality, Israel was a redeemed people. This is simply not a parallel situation to our contemporary problem.

The problem of understanding the reason for the people's entering by one gate for worship and leaving by the other has been solved in a twofold manner. Some have spiritualized by saying that when a man comes from worship he should be a "changed man" as a result of his encounter with God. He thus "takes a new route." More practical minded people, however, see this as a problem in traffic control without any spiritual significance. Some pastors would probably like to see members get out of the rut of sitting in the same seat and going out the same door every service. If members would "circulate" a little more they might meet new people and add to the fellowship and spirit of the church.

Truth for today.—One of the greatest cleavages in modern Christendom is between those who look at religion legalistically and those who view it creatively. There is a type of legalism which repels. Yet, there is a type of freedom which is not liberty at all but rather anarchy. There is a proper place for firm, hard guidelines in religious life. Without them, religion could degenerate into a subjectivism in which each man would mount his own horse and ride out in various directions.

God has revealed certain standards as right and has set forth certain actions as wrong. Sometimes it is necessary for the man of God to "spell these out" in no uncertain terms. He must do so with love but he must do so uncompromisingly. Moral standards will not be brought to bear upon society with vague generalities about God's requirements. Religion is the true basis of equity and God's norms must be clearly and unmistakably set forth.

Streams of Healing Water and Division of the Land (Ezek. 47:1—48:35)

The passage.—The prophet, like the people, could not go out the East door. He was led around to the North gate and brought on the outside of the wall to the Eastern entrance. The healing water began at the threshold of the Temple. Ezekiel emphasized the importance of the religious institution! As the stream moved forward it became deeper. Land that was once barren became fertile as the streams flowed through it. Even the Dead Sea became alive with freshness!

The last section of Ezekiel's book is a mixture of legal enactments and spiritual symbolisms. Sometimes it is difficult to know which way a passage should be interpreted. Here, however, there is no doubt. We see a beautifully symbolic picture of God's transforming grace. The two essentials for living are provided by the waters—healing and food.

The section dealing with the allotment of land seems anti-climactic after the picture of God's grace, but it has a meaningful message. Although Ezekiel was in many senses a mystic, he had a practical approach to the realities of life. He foresaw an ideal city. Yet he recognized the necessity for organization. He furthermore saw the essential need for fulfilment of life in any geographical situation—the presence of the Lord.

Special points.—Will this be fulfilled literally? There are those who maintain with dogged determination that it must be or God's Word fails. If one belongs to this category, he looks forward to it being done in the last days before the grand and glorious appearing of Jesus Christ.

There are serious problems connected with looking forward to a restoration of the land according to the Ezekial pattern. Of course, one must never limit God and say it cannot be done. The question to ask, however, is whether there are not greater truths to be seen when we recognize that Ezekiel spoke to people of his day in terms they could understand. This does not mean he spoke anything falsely. It means rather that he was preparing the people for the coming of the Christian gospel. The zenith of God's revelation is Jesus Christ—not a restoration of the Jewish monarchy. Whatever God wishes to do with the Jewish people is his work and we, as Christians, will accept it gladly. We should be careful, however, about building a dogmatic case from Old Testament prophecies, the fulfilment of which are controversial among the best of scholars.

Ezekiel is pointing, as all of the prophets, to the coming of a messianic age. Jesus Christ was the fulfilment of the messianic passages. The body of believers constitutes the new Israel. We need to interpret the Old Testament always in light of this fact.

Truth for today.—Salvation is all of grace. As the barren land was transformed by the flowing stream, so a sinful life is forgiven on the basis of God's mercy. As one then develops in his Christian life, he finds the rivers of God's grace flow deeper and deeper.

Everyone is important in God's sight. No one was overlooked in the division of the land. God's "eye is on the sparrow" and even the very hairs of our head are numbered.

Although Ezekiel emphasizes Israel's redemption more than her mission to the nations, there is, nevertheless, a missionary message implicit within his words concerning the stream. All the barren and unclean places are to be purified. What a foundation upon which to build a great missionary message!

DANIEL

Fred M. Wood

INTRODUCTION

Although several of the stories in it are among the best known in the Bible, Daniel has been called "one of the least understood books" among all Scripture. In fact, some of the material is highly controversial and it has become the "battleground" of the scholars. This is especially true of chapters 2 and 7–12.

Daniel is the major character. In fact, practically all that is known of Daniel is contained in this book which bears his name. His friends, Hannaniah, Mishael, and Azariah, however, share some of the spotlight. All four Hebrew lads were brought to Babylon in 605 B.C. by Nebuchadnezzar in the first of three deportations (605, 597, 586 B.C.) of the Jews.

Two definite divisions are evident. Chapters 1–6 contain dramatic stories of Daniel and his three friends which occurred in the reigns of Nebuchadnezzar (chaps. 1–4), Belshazzar (chap. 5) and Darius the Mede (chap. 6). Many of us learned these in our childhood and thrill afresh when we read them again. The last six chapters, which almost seem like a separate book, contain four visions (7:1–28; 8:1–27; 9:1–27; 10:1—12:13) of Daniel. The interpretation of this material has been a major problem. Chapters 2 and 7 provide the principal link that connects the two parts of the book.

The theme of the first is the certain victory of individuals who are faithful to God and his moral demands. The theme of the writer is clear and unmis-takable. He believed the intense agonies of persecution could not last long and no all-out attempt to annihilate true religion could possibly succeed if God's people would be faithful to his commands. Chapter 2, however, deals more with the triumph of the kingdom of God in the world than with individuals.

The problem of chapters 7–12 centers around the many technical predictions. The writer speaks of minute happenings in the second century B.C. This complete division has as its background the Maccabean period of Jewish history when the Greeks dominated the Jews and sought to force Hellenistic customs upon them. Many interpreters hold that Daniel foresaw this period through God's inspiration. Others, however, assign the writing to the later period and believe that someone wrote under the name of Daniel to inspire the people of that day to rise up and contend vigorously for the Hebrew faith. These scholars hold that the intent was not to deceive people but rather to impress upon them that Jehovah their God would protect them if they remained loyal to his law.

It is not the purpose of this commentary to investigate the claims of both sides with respect to authorship and interpretation of the book. There is spiritual truth in these chapters regardless of the human author. The permanent message is that God will not be thwarted nor his purposes in history defeated. Individuals who hold firm in crisis will be vindicated. Likewise, the nation that refuses to yield to the on-slaught of ungodly forces will share in God's redemptive purpose for the world.

A Noble Example of Faithfulness to God's Requirements (Dan. 1:1–21)

The passage.—This chapter shows it is not necessary for a young man to "sow his wild oats." Daniel and his three friends were far away from home. They changed Daniel's name but they could not change his nature. Although he was a slave, he was as free in Baby-lon as he had been at Jerusalem for the Lord lived within his heart.

Daniel's opposition to the "establish-ment" was justified. He believed the rich food which was offered him would be detrimental rather than beneficial in realizing a high goal for his life. He was willing to put his convictions on the testing block and let the evidence speak for itself. His sincerity and personal charm produced a winsomeness that completely won over the ones in charge of his training.

His three friends were not so out-spoken as Daniel but shared his deep convictions. They likewise participated in the victory. By remaining faithful to God's purpose for him, Daniel won per-sonal vindication. The last verse tells of Daniel's longevity—he outlasted the Babylonian Empire.

Special points.—At one time the his-toricity of Daniel 1:1 was doubted. It was claimed there was no supporting evidence for the 605 B.C. invasion of Jerusalem. This notion, like other ones doubting the integrity of biblical state-ments, has been discarded by many competent scholars.

The problem of what kind of food the Chaldeans offered Daniel has not been solved. It was, no doubt, an abun-dance of rich delicacies. Daniel's strict training influenced his decision. There were, no doubt, other rituals connected with idol worship that were just as re-pulsive to him as the type of food placed on the menu. It was not so much asceticism of the body, as such, which Daniel advocated and insisted upon but rather a discipline of life that included moral purity as well as proper diet.

Truth for today.—God's followers must serve in the wider world but there are limits to their participation in the customs of that world. It is often diffi-cult to maintain one's religious convic-tions but often one must decide where his loyalty lies.

One should never be afraid to put God to the test. It was concerning stewardship rather than personal mor-als, but the basic principle is the same. God said, "put me to the test" (Mal. 3:10, RSV).

Too often we are not so much op-posed to religious convictions as we are unaware of their relevance to life. Our belief in God should make a noticeable difference in our way of life. It should convince others of their need for a simi-lar relationship to God.

Nebuchadnezzar's Dream and Daniel's Interpretation (Dan. 2:1–49)

The passage.—It was generally be-lieved that dreams were a way the gods made known their will. People were, therefore, reluctant to disregard them. Kings employed astrologers and divin-ers to keep their minds at rest. An old tradition said, "A dream not interpreted is like a letter not read." This chapter represents more than merely an encour-agement to keep alive the Jewish hope for a coming messianic kingdom. It ac-tually belongs to all people in all gen-erations. There is contained here the seed of a philosophy of history which has stood the test of time. In every generation people have turned to this vision for proof of the truth that God "is the governor among the nations" (Ps. 22:28). The nucleus of the entire chapter is found in verses 31–45. The preceding and succeeding verses are the framework which provides a historical and literary setting for the description of the world empires.

The new kingdom is, of course, the most important aspect of the vision. It is necessary, however, for the old kingdoms to be destroyed before the new one can become universal. The new kingdom will not be just another kingdom but will be a consummation of the historical processes. It will challenge every injustice and inequity and will destroy all things not in harmony with God's purposes for the world. The kingdom will be a confrontation to every greedy ambition of power-hungry tyrants. It will fill the earth and never be destroyed. In God's "plan of the ages" all people must come to live according to his purposes for them.

Special points.—Scholars differ as to the identification of the three nations following Babylon. There is, however, substantial agreement that the stone which smites the image is connected with the messianic age which is connected inseparably with the Messiah. Some scholars are reluctant to see the prediction of a personal Messiah in Daniel's interpretation but see it rather as only a messianic age.

Some scholars identify the second, third, and fourth kingdoms as Media, Persia, and Greece while other scholars see the three as Medo-Persia, Greece, and Rome. The difference is their feeling concerning the basic message of the book.

The futuristic school of thought, with a strong emphasis on the millenium, believed the fourth kingdom represents the Roman Empire and the whole

period of the times of the Gentiles. During the church age the Gentile period has been temporarily postponed for the parenthetical church age period. It will recommence at the rapture of the church and will continue through the tribulation period until the grand and glorious appearance of Christ. To this school, the great stone represents the second coming of Christ in glory.

It is not possible to offer evidence for these schools of thought. There are many fine commentaries that discuss these positions in depth. One should familiarize himself with all of the evidence before reaching a conclusion.

Truth for today.—God will never transfer his sovereignty to those who are temporarily in charge of activities in the secular world. Neither will he abdicate his authority until the agnostics make up their minds whether or not they believe in him. The God who revealed himself in history is the one who is in control of history. Whether we are to look for it in an apocalyptic moment or in progressive realization, the time will come when the kingdoms of this world will become the kingdom of our Lord.

Although things may look dark when we evaluate the world situation in terms of human strength, there is an eternal sunlight visible on the horizon when we remember that the future belongs to God. The ages of time are to him as a day. We can have strength for living now because we not only have hope for the future but we are a part of the future in God's redemptive purpose.

Refusal of Three Youths to Worship the Idol of God (Dan. 3:1–30)

The passage.—The Babylonian Empire did not last many years but it produced some unusually ambitious and aggressive kings. They, like all monarchs of that day, were vain men. They often erected images of themselves and required the people to give homage to them. This story fits in well with all we know concerning the historical situation of that day.

The three young men give us an unforgetable lesson in faithfulness. There are times when God's servant can do nothing in opposition to the entrenched forces of evil but be willing to die for the sake of his conviction. The blood of the martyrs has indeed been the seed of the church. Far too often, religion seems to be considered a way of escape for men and women in danger. It is, however, much more! These three young men realized life could have true meaning only if they opposed the degrading idolatry which was thrust upon them. They dared to resist even though it meant personal confrontation with the king.

The fury of the king was in harmony with the temperamental outbursts of spoiled monarchs. The heating of the furnace to seven times its usual strength reflected a tantrum unworthy of a ruler and more characteristic of a small child. It is to Nebuchadnezzar's credit, however, that when he saw God's mighty act he was willing to make amends for his error. The three young men were given places of honor in the kingdom.

Special points.—Scholarship has not been able to attach any specific values to the titles given the various officials in verse 8. In all probability, they are merely a catalog of Assyrian, Babylonian, and Persian titles. They represent the various administrative functions of the day—civil, military, and legal.

The musical instruments are also varied. Three, the harp, psaltery, and bagpipe, are Greek. The horn and sackbut come from either Aryan or Semitic backgrounds. The pipe is definitely Semitic. The writer adds, "all kinds of music" which parallels "all the rulers of the provinces" in verse 2. This, of course, indicates the bigness of the occasion.

Who was this fourth person the king saw? A literal translation is "son of deity." This certainly implies a divine person—a supernatural being of some type. The Jewish position is he was an angel. Christian expositors, through the centuries, have taken the position this was a preincarnate appearance of the second person of the Trinity.

Truth for today.—Conditions in our country have not yet reached the critical stage that calls for God's people to suffer physical abuse. There are many social pressures put upon Christians who hold firm to their convictions. Even the economic squeeze is sometimes invoked. Quite often Christians lose in the business world because they will not "go along" or because they "do not fit" in certain circles. There are certain indications on the horizon that "it could happen—even here." God's people must always be ready to stand firm in their witness regardless of the cost.

Whatever happens to God's people, he will be with them. It is this consciousness that gives strength for the meeting of crises. When wicked people see Christians holding firm and posessing inner strength they will honor God and God's servant. It is not easy to maintain one's integrity in the face of opposition but this is the very essence of the Christian faith.

Nebuchadnezzar's Madness, Punishment, and Exaltation (Dan. 4:1–37)

The passage.—Pride causes one to put himself in the place of God. This leads to a loss of perspective and is a distortion of true values. In his madness, such a man considers himself to be beyond any human limitation. When the crisis comes sudden panic arises. The man of pride always overextends himself.

A man can learn lessons about God without becoming a completely spiritual person. Nebuchadnezzar seems to have learned some great lessons from his experience even though there is no evidence that he became what we would call a "regenerated man."

Most scholars concede this story has a historical basis. It was probably given by Nebuchadnezzar to explain a lapse in his administrative function and probably his sanity. There is every reason to believe it reflects a complete nervous breakdown probably caused by the exhaustion of a power-hungry tyrant. When his emotional security returned he gave a graphic testimony concerning the restoration of his inner peace. The entire chapter is actually a doxology of praise to the God of Israel for his mercy. Although Daniel's name is not mentioned, his presence seems to hover in the background of every sentence.

Special points.—Why is the language of the king's decree scriptural in nature when it is, in reality, a document of the state? It has been suggested the Old Testament writer was putting words in the mouth of the king. Others have suggested that Nebuchadnezzar's association with Daniel had caused him to become familiar with the Hebrew Scriptures. The most likely suggestion, however, is that since the Babylonian and Jewish religions were both Semitic there were many parallel thoughts. Nebuchadnezzar could have been quoting from Babylonian sources which paralleled the Hebrew accounts. Also, he could have absorbed Hebrew thinking into his religious life because of its affinity to his own philosophy.

While it is true that the monuments and inscriptions are entirely silent as to historical evidence for a period of degrading madness during Nebuchadnezzar's reign, scholars have nevertheless been slow to deny its possibility. Nebuchadnezzar was a strange man and many unusual things happened during his reign. This "lightning stroke of terrible calamity" is an event which seems entirely within character for him. His haughty boast as he viewed the grandeur of his kingdom represents a normal reaction. His particular type of mental illness is not unknown. Even his sudden recovery is not without precedent. Quite often when calm comes to one's troubled soul, with an upward glance his reason is restored. The whole story has the smack of reality and there is no reason to cut it to pieces with rationalistic scissors.

Truth for today.—A lack of internal resources to match our outward responsibilities still produces exhaustion and breakdown. The self-centered, self-pleasing disposition that has been called an "egocentric predicament" is the original sin of mankind. We cannot, of ourselves, cope with the problems of this competitive world.

Human nature can be changed but every little reform movement in our life is not divine transformation. A fundamental change in character comes only by a deep experience with the One who is "our refuge and strength" and a "very present help in trouble." Outward props are perilous substitutes for a life committed to inner spiritual values.

Man's extremity is always God's opportunity. When we come to the place that we can throw our all in complete dependence upon him we can become linked to his great creative processes.

This is the only hope of a man in crisis. Jesus said it another way, "Ye must be born again."

Belshazzar's Feast, Handwriting on the Wall, and Babylon's Fall (Dan. 5:1–30)

The passage.—Oriental revelry, with extravagance and luxurious passion, dominates this story. The reader's imagination is stirred as he enters into the night with its growing madness, mysterious horror, and final tragedy for the Babylonian monarch.

The story begins with a crashing overture. Belshazzar seems to be celebrating some great victory or festival. The graphic description is similar to the one which opens the book of Esther. At the height of intoxication, Belshazzar made a daring decision. He ordered his servants to bring the vessels of gold and silver which had been taken from the Temple in Jerusalem. They were used as wine goblets while Belshazzar in his orgy praised his own gods. The orgy was probably a religious festival in praise of the Babylonian gods accompanied by an open defiance of the God of Israel whose moral requirements were known over all the world.

The vigor of Belshazzar's youth and the flush of the wine faded from his cheeks when the handwriting appeared. His cry of panic brought the astrologers and soothsayers but they stood impotent before the divine pronouncement. The words of Daniel, at first reading, seem discourteous and almost rude. It was difficult for him to be other than firm in the face of such dissipation and indulgence.

The immediate fulfilment of Daniel's words do not necessarily indicate he was aware of the exact military situation. He was basing his warning on moral criteria and knew the deterioration of national character meant inevitable tragedy.

Special points.—This chapter has felt the dissecting knives of the historical critics. One, at first, is overwhelmed at their claims, but sober reflection gives reassurance that the negative evidence is not as convincing as one might initially surmise.

There is ample room for accepting the historicity of Belshazzar and Darius the Mede unless one has made up his mind to dispute the historical integrity of the biblical record. There is good reason to believe Belshazzar was a co-regent at the time which explains his promise that the successful interpreter would be the "third ruler" in the kingdom.

The "Eupharsin" of verse 25 and "Peres" of verse 28 are not in contradiction. One is the active and the other the passive form.

Truth for today.—Those who want the Bible to be relevant should major on this chapter! Each verse shouts aloud the short-lived nature of ungodly living. The licentiousness and immorality of Babylon finds its parallel in today's "sexual wilderness." The king's guilty conscience because of aggravated rebellion reflects the stupidity of the depraved human heart. The profaning of holy things finds its parallel in our modern world's attempt to destroy all distinctions between the sacred and the secular.

The destiny of nations is still in the hands of a sovereign God. Sin shortens the existence of both governments and individuals. Unless we heed the lessons of history a calamity can come upon us as suddenly and even more devastatingly than came to the God-defying Belshazzar and his drunken associates who were weighed in the balances and found wanting.

Daniel's Deliverance from the Den of Lions (Dan. 6:1–28)

The passage.—This is the first record of hardship for Daniel. He has been successful in every previous venture but God placed a severe testing for him in order that he might take his place among the preeminent. Daniel's friends were tempted to commit an act which was wrong. Daniel was called upon to discontinue an activity that was right. It is difficult for us to evaluate the severity of Daniel's punishment in contrast with that of his three friends. The fiery furnace seems more severe but Daniel spent the "entire night" in the lions' den. The command of Darius, however, exceeds that of Nebuchadnezzar in the thoroughness and comprehensiveness with which he acknowledges the supremacy of Israel's God.

This command of the king for universal recognition of Jehovah and complete vindication for Daniel is a logical conclusion to the first half of the book. Many scholars believe these chapters existed separately and circulated independently before being combined with the other six chapters to form the book as we now know it. This is a very probable conclusion and does not militate against a high view of inspiration. Several of the Old Testament books give internal evidence that certain sections stood by themselves before being incorporated into the larger collection of material.

Special points.—There is no great problem with accepting the historicity of Darius the Mede nor understanding his friendliness toward Daniel. Darius had, no doubt, heard of Daniel's interpretation and prediction. He would not wish to lose the services of such a distinguished man whose experience was immense, whose honor was impeccable, and who even seemed to be biased in favor of the new administration.

The extensive administrative organization is in keeping with modern findings concerning the extent of the Persian Empire. It was necessary to keep a strong hand upon governmental affairs. The early Persian kings were inclined to be benevolent and tolerant, but the insecurity of their position made them subject to sudden emotional changes. Disobedience of a command was taken personally as posing a threat to the ruler's authority. This explains somewhat the seeming vacillation of Darius with reference to Daniel.

Truth for today.—Men of strong conviction attract the attention of their superiors but also arouse the jealousy of their peers. There is a natural antagonism between good and evil comparable to the eternal struggle between light and darkness.

The believer is always safe in God's hands. The path of duty is also the path of safety. A man who is in the will of God is immortal until his work is completed. The contrast between the misery of the king in his palace and the peace of Daniel while in the lions' den represents the difference between one who has no internal resources and one whose mind is fixed on God.

The vindication of Daniel brings encouragement to us who find ourselves under pressure because of our attempt to hold high standards in contemporary life. Although we realize God does not work miracles lavishly, we still can be confident that he knows of our situation and will intervene at the proper time for our deliverance and honor us as we have sought to honor him. God may not come as quickly to our rescue as we feel he should, but faith continually whispers in times of discouragement that help is near and God will not tarry long.

The Vision of Four Beasts and the Heavenly Court (Dan. 7:1–28)

The passage.—It is not fair to call the last six chapters of this book "unquestionably inferior to the first part." Some important concepts are presented which inspired hope for the persecuted Jews. The writer believed God was in control of history and his purposes could not be thwarted. The two main sections of the book are tied together by the striking similarity of chapters 2 and 7. Both of these tell of four oppressive empires that will be terminated by God's sovereign activity in history. The drama will then end with the triumph of God's kingdom on earth.

Although the first three kings are represented as terrible, it is the fourth who comes with monstrous cruelty and surpasses his predecessors in destruction. The terror which this beast spreads comes from one specific individual who heads up the intense terror.

When the tyranny seems unbearable the Almighty appears surrounded by his attendants. The judgment of the heavenly court is that the wicked kingdom must be destroyed. Although Daniel was greatly alarmed and visibly affected, he pondered carefully the vision as he reflected on God's presence with his people in both their present and future crises.

Special points.—Scholars are divided on the identification of the four beasts. The same basic approach should be taken here as in chapter 2. Those who put great emphasis on the predictive nature of prophecy believe the fourth kingdom is Rome. Those who emphasize the contemporary nature of prophecy believe it is Greece. They feel these words were given to comfort the people in the time of Antiochus Epiphanes rather than a blueprint for events at the second coming of Christ.

Truth for today.—Brute force cannot permanently conquer. Every political dictator will be replaced by another —usually a more cruel and ferocious one. God's people, however, will outlast all their enemies. God made the world for righteous people and in his time they will inherit it. Since God is on the side of his people, they cannot afford to become impatient.

Vision of the Ram, He-goat and Little Horn (Dan. 8:1–27)

The passage.—The interpretation of this vision is less controversial because the writer explains the countries represented by symbols. Also, a shorter period of time is covered. These seems no doubt the vision deals directly with Antiochus Epiphanes, his presumptuous and overbearing conduct and his fall. We know the Greek Empire fragmented into four kingdoms at Alexander's death. We also know from history that Antiochus Epiphanes met a sudden death, although we do not know the cause, and faded from the scene as though by a divine stroke.

The crisis concerning the Greeks desecration of the Jewish sacrificial system in the Temple was one of the greatest in the history of Israel. The people needed a prophet to assure them of God's presence and Judaism's certain triumph. The thrilling story of Jewish resistance, led by the Macabees, is one of the greatest traditions among the Jews of today. The critical period lasted about three and one-half years. The "broken without hand" is translated elsewhere "by no human hand" and indicates God's direct intervention in behalf of his people against the mad

Greek ruler.

Special points.—Those who insist Rome is the fourth kingdom in chapters 2 and 7 appeal to this chapter for proof of their position. Daniel here connects Media and Persia as one kingdom. If this pattern is followed in the other two chapters, Greece becomes the third kingdom and Rome the fourth. The other school of thought, however, insists that this is not a valid conclusion.

The latter part of this chapter seems to indicate the writing of it was many years before the events took place. This argues for the early date of Daniel, but those on the other side insist the writer was on the contemporary scene but wrote in a way as to make it appear Daniel had actually written the book several hundred years earlier. A thorough study should be given before reaching a dogmatic conclusion.

Truth for today.—All of us have that within our nature which desires to know something of the future. This sometimes has caused unwise speculation and even wild schemes. God has wisely concealed from us details concerning that which is yet to come, but he has given us certain assurances. He is in control of the future. We do not know what the future holds but we know who holds our future. We can serve him with assurance that the victory will be ours at the end. An army does not have to win every battle to win the war. There will, at last, be an end to those who oppose God and his way of life. Those who rebel against God and set themselves against the divine will are doomed. Judgment has already been pronounced against them. The righteous will survive and be vindicated. If we could see into the future and witness the doom of the wicked, we too would be astonished and sick.

Daniel's Prayer, Gabriel's Answer, and the Seventy Weeks (Dan. 9:1–27)

The passage.—Although Daniel's prayer occupies the major thrust of this chapter, far more interpretive emphasis has been given to the vision of seventy weeks. This is, of course, because of the natural curiosity of people concerning anything that holds itself to be predictive in nature. Few passages in all the Bible are more controversial as to meaning than the last seven verses of this chapter.

The prayer is aflame with the purifier of sincere repentance. It is similar in nature to those of Ezra (9:6–15) and Nehemiah (see chaps. 1 and 9). It includes a confession of national sin and an admission of deserved punishment and concludes with a heartfelt plea for mercy and restoration. Few prayers show such fervor and spiritual concern. Daniel was deeply disturbed concerning the future of God's people.

The vision which follows the prayer is somewhat grotesque but it seems to have met Daniel's need, although he surely did not understand every detail of its fulfilment. The six brief clauses in verse 24 summarize God's spiritual intentions for the future.

Special points.—The problem in interpreting verses 24–27 is the point of beginning. The date usually given for the command to restore and build Jerusalem is 536 B.C. There have been basically two schools of thought with reference to the "weeks" of years.

One school has insisted these seventy weeks should begin from the destruction of the Temple in 586 and is an enlargement or some say a "correction" of Jeremiah's seventy years of exile. This would bring the fulfilment down to the days of Antiochus Epiphanes.

Others, however, associate the beginning with the general period of Ezra-Nehemiah and bring the seventy weeks to the time of the birth of Jesus or his triumphant entry into Jerusalem.

Millenarians believe the sixty-nine weeks of years were fulfilled at the death of Jesus and we now live in a parenthesis period. They contend the seventieth week will be the seven year tribulation between the rapture and the grand and glorious appearing of Jesus. This will be the time of "Jacob's trouble." There are, however, some divisions of thought within the school of pre-millenialism concerning this seventieth week of Daniel.

The subject is much too complex to be settled in such a short commentary. If one is interested in further study, there are many fine exegetical commentaries dealing with all of these various schools of thought.

Truth for today.—The Christian should realize his indebtedness to Judaism but should also be aware that we live in the fulness of God's revelation. Jesus Christ has come, and *he* is the hope of the world.

Christians are heirs of the promises to Abraham. Scholars speak of Christianity as "spiritual Israel" and this is an accurate designation. The question, of course, arises, "What about national Israel?"

It is difficult to be dogmatic. There are many competent Christian scholars, sincere and dedicated, on both sides of the question concerning the future of national Israel. We have witnessed a great phenomenon in the last twenty years. It cannot be ignored. The Jews are once again in their homeland.

On the other hand, we must remember that our commission from the risen Lord is to be witnesses of the living Christ. The personal visible return of Christ is taught in the Scriptures but the mystery of the end is locked up in the heart of God. Our task is to be faithful in leading people *now* to repentance and faith. This is God's redemptive purpose and we have the privilege of sharing in it.

Daniel's Final Vision with Prologue and Epilogue (Dan. 10:1—12:13)

The passage.—The previous visions of Daniel indicated a dark future for Israel. He was anxious for a further word from the Lord. The Old Testament abounds with the truth that God reveals himself only when men are willing to pay the price in spiritual discipline. Daniel's mourning and fasting was related to his intense desire to know more concerning the historical situation and Israel's relation to it.

Daniel, like Ezekiel, groveled in the dust when he was overpowered by God's presence. In the Old Testament ecstatic experience is almost always followed by complete immobility. God is not willing, however, for his servants to remain in this position. He respects their dignity and wishes them to rise and stand erect.

This epilogue (10:1–18) clearly teaches that nations, like individuals, have patron angels assigned as guardians of their destinies. This entire subject is dealt with in a limited fashion in this passage but we are certainly led to believe that God sits above the waterfloods of history and retains his sovereignty through his divine messages.

Scholars are fairly well agreed that 11:1–35 gives a "selective account" of history from Persia down to some place in the latter part of the reign of Antiochus Epiphanes. Many details are given concerning war and the family life of the Greek period especially during the reigns of Antiochus the Great (222–187 B.C.) and Antiochus Epiphanes (175–164 B.C.).

Although Antiochus the Great afflicted the Jews, it was Epiphanes who was the "mad monster" and defiled everything the Jews held sacred. The first twenty verses of chapter 11 form a preamble to the madman's reign. The intricate details concerning the family life of both the Seleucid rulers of the North and the Ptolmies who reigned in Egypt have convinced many scholars this section was written by a man on the scene rather than predicted by Daniel during the Babylonian exile.

Verses 20–35 are universally accepted as outlining the wild career of Epiphanes. A certain vagueness is present, however, beginning with verse 36. Scholarship divides at this point. Those who believe this book was written during the Maccabean period as contemporary history contend the author knew Epiphanes would come to an end but was not exactly certain as to the nature of it. It is a historical fact that Epiphanes died very suddenly and under strange conditions—perhaps mental illness being a part of the cause.

Those of the futuristic school contend verses 36–45 leap over the centuries and give us a picture of the final battle in connection with the second coming of Christ. This is basically the same group who interpret chapters 2 and 7 as giving in the fourth kingdom a picture of the restored Roman Empire in Europe at the consummation of history. They, of course, interpret the first few verses of chapter 12 as the period of tribulation immediately preceding the grand and glorious appearing of Christ.

The epilogue (12:5–13) concerns the length of time until the end of the events which were to come. Daniel was not satisfied with the "time, two times, and half a time" and inquired further. He is told the struggle between good and evil will continue and is informed of the number of days involved in the "time table." One group of scholars identifies these days with the period of Antiochus Epiphanes and the desecrating of the Temple while others associate them with the tribulation period between the "rapture of the church" and "the grand and glorious appearing" of Christ. Daniel is not given any interpretation to satisfy his curiosity. He must wait for the mystery to be revealed.

Special points.—What can the ordinary Christian do when two groups of scholars disagree? Everyone cannot be a technical student but must depend upon those who have the time and ability to delve deeper into the historical background of the Scriptures and methods of interpretation. History has taught us to exercise caution with reference to mathematics in dealing with the second coming of Christ. On the other hand, we must never allow ourselves to lose sight of his glorious promise to return.

Messages of the Old Testament prophets and other writers were usually identified closely with the contemporary situation. This is a strong argument in favor of applying this section, in its entirety, to the time of Antiochus Epiphanes. On the other hand, to rule the predictive nature of prophecy out completely is to ignore some clear-cut teachings of Scripture. There are many examples in the Old Testament where a statement has a dual application—one to the local situation and the other to the birth of Jesus in Bethlehem. We must be careful not to limit God in his ability to speak through his messenger concerning the second coming of Christ. On the other hand, we must also be cautious lest we make the Scriptures say more than God meant for them to reveal.

Truth for today.—During crisis periods people become unusually interested in predictions of the future. This is based on both man's natural curiosity and also his desire for security and assurance. We live in such a period now. This passage as well as several in Ezekiel hold a fascination for some modern writers.

Whatever interpretation should be accepted as valid, God's eternal truth concerning his people is valid in all generations. He will not allow his cause nor his people to be stamped out. It may be necessary that Christians be disciplined and even severely chastised but it is all for a purpose. The dross must be burned out in order for God's image to be reflected in the gold of Christlike character.

The victory will be the Lord's and his people. Some who suffer for the cause of righteousness will be vindicated while still living. Others may be forced to wait until the world to come. We divide time but to God even the present is a part of eternity.

The most important thing to learn from this section is not the mystery of date, authorship, or historical sequence. There is a deeper truth. God has a redemptive purpose in history. Daniel was a part of it. The Maccabean family made their contribution. We, in our day, are also members of God's family and share in his eternal purpose. Whatever comes and whoever rules on earthly thrones, the Christian knows that ultimate authority belongs to God. Therefore, our first loyalty must be to him

HOSEA

Donald F. Ackland

INTRODUCTION

To understand Hosea we must know something of the historic background. In 922 B.C., the kingdom built by David and Solomon was divided. Ten tribes formed the Northern Kingdom (Israel) under Jeroboam I. The two hundred years of its existence were marred by:

Religious apostasy.—After the division of the kingdom, Jeroboam set up a new priesthood, made two calves of gold, and established shrines at Dan and Bethel (1 Kings 12:25–33). Although Jeroboam probably intended to continue the worship of Jehovah, the door was opened to idolatry. Ahab, seventh king of Israel, married Jezebel, daughter of the Sidonian priest of Astarte. A temple of Baal was built in Ahab's capital, Samaria (1 Kings 16:29–33). Ruthless reform was attempted by Jehu (842–815 B.C.), but of succeeding kings it is monotonously recorded, "He did that which was evil in the sight of the Lord" (2 Kings 15:9,18,24, etc.).

Political intrigue.—The Northern Kingdom had nineteen kings, many of whom died violently. Hosea probably began his ministry toward the end of the reign of Jeroboam II (786–746 B.C.) and continued till the fall of Samaria (722 B.C.). In this period, political violence increased. Jeroboam's son, Zachariah, reigned six months and was assassinated by Shallum. He reigned one month and was killed by Menahem who, after a ten-year reign of terror, died a natural death. Pekahiah, his son, reigned two years and was slain by

Pekah who met his death at the hands of Hoshea, vassal king whose end is unknown (2 Kings 14:23—17:6).

Foreign alliances.—The turmoil of the times caused Israel's kings to seek help in foreign alliances. They turned to Syria and Egypt, but neither availed against the conquering Assyrians. In 722 B.C. Samaria fell and Israel went into captivity.

Hosea was apparently a native of Israel who ministered to his own people. Through his personal experience he obtained deep insights into the character of God, particularly in his stedfast love toward Israel.

The Prophet's Story (Hos. 1:1—2:1; 3:1–5)

The passages.—Hosea married a woman named Gomer. To them were born three children who were named at the instruction of God. While some believe 3:1–5 to describe a second marriage, it is more acceptable to relate these verses to Hosea's experience with Gomer. She was unfaithful to her husband and sank so low in sin that she sold herself into slavery. Her husband sought her and redeemed her with half the price of a slave (Ex. 21:32) plus a balance paid in grain. He took her home and (by implication) restored her as his wife after a period of probation.

Special points.—Does "a wife of whoredoms" (harlotry, RSV) mean that God told his prophet to marry a woman already committed to an immoral life (1:2)? Not only is this contrary to the

536

character of God but it violates the purpose of the record, namely, to present Gomer as an illustration of the nation Israel. The statement must relate Gomer's subsequent condition.

The names of Hosea's children had prophetic significance. *Jezreel* (1:4) figured in Israel's history as a place of judgment. Read 2 Kings 9 for Jehu's acts of vengeance against the house of Ahab at Jezreel. In the same locality, God would again bring judgment on Israel (1:5).

"Lo-ruhamah" (unpitied, or, not obtaining mercy) is thought by some to reflect Hosea's suspicion that this was not his child. God's purpose in the name, however, is clearly stated in 1:6. He would withdraw his mercy from Israel. Note marginal alternative in KJV for the conclusion of this verse. See also RSV.

The name of the third child, "Lo-ammi," "not my people," expresses the final step in the breach of relationship between God and Israel (1:9). He would disown them. Did Hosea mean to deny that he fathered this child?

The triumph of divine love is seen in 1:10—2:1. A day of restoration would come for Jezreel, the unpitied would obtain mercy, and the disowned would be reinstated. These promises were fulfilled in Christ (Rom. 9:22–26; 1 Pet. 2:10). The same glorious prospect is found in 3:4–5. Although Israel would be sent into exile without government and the comforts of religion, she would find salvation in repentance. "David their king" may be messianic and point to him who came of David's line (Luke 2:4,11).

Truth for today.—God speaks to men in varied ways, sometimes through life experiences. Sorrow and joy can either deepen our knowledge of divine love or steel our hearts against it. Those who learn the lessons of life may in turn be teachers of others.

God's Message Summarized (Hos. 2:2–23)

The passage.—These verses may be seen as a summary of God's message to Israel through Hosea. The nation's sin is described in terms of adultery, with God as the aggrieved husband (Isa. 54:5; Jer. 3:14; 31:32). Instead of worshiping the true God, the people had turned to Baal to whom they attributed nature's bounty (v. 5).

This indictment is followed by a pronouncement of coming judgment (vv. 6–13). Israel would find no true satisfaction in idolatry (v. 7). She would eventually lose everything: her material resources (vv. 9,12) and her religious observances (v. 11). Note the incredible reason: "she . . . forgat me" (v. 13).

But God's love would triumph (vv. 14–23). He would give Israel a new wilderness experience. As he had brought her out of Egypt, so he would bring her out of this bondage. Judgment would be a thing of the past ("Achor," see Judg. 7) and replaced with hope and a song (v. 15). Some of the conditions of that day would be: idols forsaken (vv. 16–17), security enjoyed (v. 18), relationship restored (vv. 19–20), nature harmonious and productive (vv. 21–22), and judgment stayed (v. 23).

Special points.—Baalism was a fertility cult. Nature's productivity, attributed to the god, was believed to be stimulated by human sexual activity. Hence, Baalism fostered immorality in the name of religion. These evil notions furnish undertones throughout this passage.

There is deep irony in verse 8. The precious metals used to overlay heathen idols came from God!

Both *Ishi* and *Baali* are equivalent

terms meaning "my lord" or "my husband." The point made (v. 17) is that all association with idolatry will cease. Even words reminiscent of past unfaithfulness will be no longer used.

The chapter closes with plays on the names of Hosea's children (v. 23). "Jezreel" (God sows) will no longer refer to judgment but to blessing. The other two names are given positive instead of negative meanings. A lost relationship is reestablished, expressed in the affirmation, "Thou art my God."

Truth for today.—A nation's greatest sin is to forget God. Idolatry is the substitution of things for God and those thus guilty must suffer the penalty. But God, though offended by sin, continues to seek a way of salvation for sinners.

The Nation Indicted (Hos. 4:1–19)

The passage.—God had complaints against Israel other than idolatry. It is amazing that it should be said of this favored people, "There is no faithfulness or kindness, and no knowledge of God in the land" (v. 1, RSV). Priests and prophets alike are guilty. Together they are destroying the nation, their "mother" (v. 5).

Ignorance of the ways of God is attributed to the faithlessness of the priests (vv. 6–11). God rejected them because of abuse of their office. They encouraged others in sin to satisfy their own appetites. But they would never find satisfaction (v. 10). Through sexual indulgence and insobriety, practiced in the name of religion, they had lost the power to think straight (v. 11).

God's prophets held idolatry in scorn. In verses 12–14 Hosea exposed heathenism's folly and vice. God's people were seeking counsel from blocks of wood, a commentary on verse 11. Their immoralities were leading their wives and daughters into sin. The Mosaic law had severe penalties for unfaithful women, but these were abrogated because of the shocking example of the men: "for the men themselves go aside with harlots" (v. 14, RSV).

The concluding verses (15–19) contain several obscurities. They begin with an apparent appeal to Judah to avoid the sins of the Northern Kingdom whose commitment to evil is described, with its consequent penalty (v. 19). Read the passage in the RSV.

Special points.—"Controversy" (v. 1) belongs to the language of litigation; God had a case against his people. The final phrases of verse 2 are clarified by the RSV: "they break all bounds and murder follows murder." Among several suggested renderings of verse 4, the RSV is as acceptable as any, "Yet let no one contend, and let none accuse, for with you is my contention, O priest." Because of bad example, the people are becoming like the priests (v. 9).

Gilgal (v. 15) was a center for idol worship (12:11). *Beth-aven* (house of evil) is probably a caustic alternative to Bethel (house of God). By making the second part of verse 16 a question, the RSV aids understanding. For *Ephraim* (v. 17) read Israel, here and subsequently in Hosea. *Wind* is used (v. 19) to typify overwhelming disaster that will sweep the offenders away and persuade them of the futility of their idol worship.

Truth for today.—Heavy responsibilities accrue to leaders, whether political or religious (James 3:1). The New Testament describes all believers as priests (1 Pet. 2:9), implying that every Christian has a responsibility to fulfil for others.

The Lord's Withdrawal (Hos. 5:1—6:3)

The passage.—In this chapter, as elsewhere in the Minor Prophets, many textual problems are resolved by the RSV.

The entire nation—priests, people, and king—is summoned to listen to God's words (5:1). The nation is committed to evil (v. 4). A generation has been raised who are strangers to the ways of God (v. 7). Though some go through the motions of worship, their insincerity is such that God withdraws himself so that he cannot be found (vv. 7,15).

The character of the impending judgment begins to be revealed at 5:8. Trumpets of war are heard in cities of Judah (*Gibeah, Ramah*) and Israel (*Beth-aven*, or Bethel). The description of events seems to cover an extensive period of campaigns and alliances. Syria joined with Israel in attempting to compel Judah to unite against Assyria (2 Kings 16:5).

Judah was apparently not without blame. Her leaders are condemned as "those who remove the landmark" (5:10, RSV), that is, those who take illegal possession of property. God's judgments are impartial against Israel and Judah alike (vv. 12,14). Although both kingdoms might appeal to Assyria for protection, nothing could avail against the judgments of God (v. 13).

The words of 6:1-3 are often put into the mouths of the people and interpreted as a shallow response to God's plea (5:15). In light of 6:4, this is a reasonable position. However, they may be heard as words of Hosea exhorting the people to "return unto the Lord." The One who has chastised them is the One who will heal. Therefore the prophet pleads, "Let us know, let us press on to know the Lord" (6:3, RSV).

Special points.—Mizpah and *Tabor* (5:1) (the RSV adds Shittim, 5:2) were idolatrous shrines that ensnared God's people. At such shrines, Israel had committed spiritual adultery, forsaking Jehovah, to whom she was espoused, for false gods (vv. 3-4). There is probably reference to the occasions and characteristics of Baal worship in verse 7: "Now the new moon shall devour them with their fields" (RSV). Each new moon was kept as a religious festival at which fertility rites, intended to bring rich harvests to their fields, were observed. Before another new moon appeared, those fields would be destroyed.

The expression, "After two days . . . in the third day" (6:2) means, "After a short while." No reference to Christ's resurrection should be read into it. The promise of rain (v. 3) is not only a reminder of the dependence of Palestine on adequate rainfall but also declares the Lord (not Baal) to be the controller of nature. For adequate harvests the early winter (*former*) and spring (*latter*) rains were essential. God would send both on a repentant people.

Truth for today.—God's judgments are impartial: Judah, as well as Israel, must bear the consequences of sin. No nation may consider itself immune from the judgments of God. Correspondingly, no people that sincerely repents will be rejected by a God who waits to bless.

The Divine Dilemma (Hos. 6:4—7:16)

The passage.—God is now the speaker. However we interpret 6:1-3, we are faced with God's evaluation of Israel's *goodness* ("love," RSV) as short-lived. There is almost despair in the heart of God as he considers the deliberate waywardness of his people. Both Israel and Judah defeat his purposes of grace. Though he has sent his prophets with warnings and judgments (6:5), they persist in their evil ways. Among these are: insincerity in religious practice (6:6), contempt for divine justice (7:2), unawareness of decadence resulting from evil relationships (7:9), and disregard of God himself (7:10,13).

Textual difficulties in this passage account for a variety of interpretations. Perhaps we should see 7:3–7 as a description of intrigue within the nation evidenced by the murder of many of Israel's kings (see Introduction). The picture seems to be of people who, while aflame with passion as an oven, control their emotions so as to deceive their kings and princes. While posing as their friends (7:3,5) they are plotting their deaths (v. 7).

Israel's foreign alliances next come under divine rebuke (7:8–13). Threatened by enemies, they turned to other nations for help, and not to God. "Like a silly dove" (v. 11) they flit from place to place looking for allies. God will deal with them as silly birds, catching them in his net and punishing them (v. 12).

The concluding verses of chapter 7 return to the subject of Israel's desertion to Baal. The phrase "for grain and wine they gash themselves" (v. 14, RSV) refers to the frenzied worship of idolators (cf Elijah and the prophets of Baal at Carmel, 1 Kings 18:26–28). In times of adversity, instead of turning to the God who redeemed them (v. 13), they plunged deeper and deeper into the enormities of Baalism. Suffering at God's hand and the contempt of other nations awaited them (v. 16).

Special points.—The particular offence for which *Gilead* is condemned (6:8) is not known. The circumstances in which priests were accused of murder (v. 9) are also unknown. The RSV's "they murder on the way to Shechem" suggests attacks on religious pilgrims, Shechem being a famous shrine. Whatever the crime, its seriousness is underlined by the statement "they commit villainy" (RSV).

There is wide agreement for making

the last phrase of 6:11 ("when I returned the captivity of my people") the opening phrase of chapter 7. Thus the chapter begins by stating that whenever God attempted to change the lot of Israel he was confronted by new transgressions.

The description of *Ephraim* (Israel) as "a cake not turned" (7:8) suggests the unpalatable and useless. By cultivating associations that caused her to turn her back on God, Israel denied herself the one relationship that would have given her a worthwhile role in the world.

Truth for today.—Hosea impressively presents the predicament of God on account of man's sin. As a God of holiness he abhors sin. As a God of love he seeks the welfare of the sinner. Justice and mercy met at the cross where God provided a remedy for sin. But judgment still awaits those who reject the remedy.

The Wind and the Whirlwind (Hos. 8:1— 9:17)

The passage.—Hosea saw the disasters confronting Israel as the result of their sin. They had "sown the wind" by living in reckless defiance of God's laws; they would "reap the whirlwind" of defeat and exile (8:7). In the role of watchman, the prophet sounded yet another note of warning (v. 1). The enemy was already hovering as an eagle over the land; "house of God" must be so understood. Last-minute appeals to God (v. 2) would be useless. Israel had "spurned the good" (v. 3, RSV) and must bear her punishment.

The people could never accuse God of concealing the reasons for his judgments. Again in these chapters Israel's offences are repetitiously recited. God had been banished from their politics (8:4a) and their religion (v. 4b). They had sought safety in alliances with pagan nations (vv. 9–10). Though favored with God's law they had turned from it (v. 12). Their sacrifices were made occasions for personal indulgence (v. 13). Palaces and fortified cities (v. 14, RSV) had become symbols of a materialistic culture that had no place for God. The warnings of the prophets had been received with scorn amounting to hatred (9:7–8).

Because of these iniquities, sentence is passed on Israel. "They shall return to Egypt" (8:13; 9:3) should be interpreted figuratively. They had been delivered from bondage in Egypt but would experience a new captivity like that from which God had saved them. In exile they would be compelled to eat unclean (ritually forbidden) food. The Lord recalls his initial dealings with Israel whom he found as "grapes in the wilderness" (9:10). But his hopes were not fulfilled in them for they "consecrated themselves to Baal" (RSV).

At 9:14 we probably hear the voice of the prophet in agonized pleading. His request of God may mean that it would be better for Israel to cease having children than to bring them into a situation of national apostasy and disaster. History attests the fulfilment of verse 17.

Special points.—The RSV will help the student understand some of the obscurities of this passage.

References to "the calf" (8:5–6) relate to the golden calves made by Jeroboam (1 Kings 12:28). Though at first intended for the worship of Jehovah, they inclined the people to idolatry. Verse 11 probably means that altars raised for the atonement of sin became occasions to sin. Hence God's words of rejection, "I have spurned your calf, O Samaria" (v. 5, RSV). Compare the earlier statement, "Israel has spurned the good" (v. 3, RSV).

"The prophet is a fool, the spiritual man is mad" (9:7) should perhaps be read as the railing of the people against

God's messenger. Though sent as a watchman, traps were set for him and hatred expressed even in the house of God. "Gibeah" (v. 9) had been a place of infamy in Israel's history (Judg. 19:16–30) and now history was repeating itself. "Gilgal" (v. 15) was a center of Baal worship (4:15). This section that begins, "Israel has spurned the good" (8:3, RSV) concludes, "My God will cast them off" (9:17, RSV).

Truth for today.—The law of cause and effect operates in the spiritual realm. "Whatsoever a man soweth, that shall he also reap" (Gal. 6:7). The history of man is a cycle of ingratitude. He is in jeopardy; God saves him; he forgets to honor God; he returns to the misery from which God delivered him. For Israel this meant from captivity (Egypt) to captivity (Assyria).

Outworkings of Judgment (Hos. 10:1–15)

The passage.—The concept of Israel as a *vine* was introduced at 9:10. This figure also appears in Psalm 80:8, Isaiah 5:1–7, Jeremiah 2:21. Here the RSV reads, "Israel is a luxuriant vine" (v. 1). The more the nation prospered, the more it abandoned itself to sin.

The results of this infamy will be severe. Verse 3 probably refers to the nation's overthrow. Because of their rebellion against God they have lost their *king.* But they ask themselves, "A king, what could he do for us?" (RSV). Their experiences have made them cynical. Neither God nor man can help them. Verse 4 would then express their lack of confidence in rulers.

Another consequence will be disillusionment with idols (vv. 5–8). They become anxious for the safety of their gods, the golden *calves.* Well they might for they will be carried away to Assyria and the *high places* (sites of pagan worship) will be destroyed. Deserted by their gods and threatened by their enemies, the people will call on *the mountains* to cover them.

Loss of freedom will follow (v. 11). Israel is compared to an ox once employed to thresh corn. It was an easy and rewarding task, for the ox could eat as it worked. But a new and hard task would result from exile. The ox would be yoked to a plow and made to serve a demanding master.

The overthrow of the nation and its monarchy is declared in verses 13–15. The things in which Israel trusted— *mighty men* and *fortresses*—will fail her. Her idolatry will be her downfall.

There is a break in the pronouncement of doom at verse 12. Is this the voice of Hosea pleading, even at the eleventh hour, for a change of heart? If so, his plea fell on deaf ears (v. 13).

Special points.—See comment on 4:15 for *Beth-aven.* In verse 8, the word is abbreviated to *Aven.* For *Gibeah* see comment on 9:9. The statement *as Shalman spoiled Beth-arbel* (v. 14) has no explanation from recorded history.

Truth for today.—Man's sin contains the seeds of his own destruction. The things he substitutes for God become a source of disillusionment. The blasé attitude of many today reflects the emptiness of life without God.

The Compassion of God (Hos. 11:1— 13:16)

The passage.—Hosea 11 is one of the greatest chapters of the Bible. It begins in a mood of divine reminiscence. God recalls his tender relationship with Israel whom he called out of Egypt (v. 1). Two metaphors are used: the love of a father (v. 3) and the care of a master (v. 4). God's goodness is contrasted with Israel's ingratitude.

Verse 8 presents the amazing picture of God in a dilemma. What can he do in face of his people's rebellion? His love will not permit him to abandon them. Verses 10–11 anticipate release from exile. As Hosea purchased his wife out of slavery so God would bring Israel out of foreign bondage.

But the way of divine love was beset with problems. Israel's conduct was treacherous (11:12—12:1). Like their ancestor, *Jacob* (12:3–6), they needed a transforming encounter with God (Gen. 28:10–22; 32:24–32). A second reference to Jacob (12:12) is hard to explain. The verse may have been displaced.

In 12:7–8 Israel is condemned for materialism and commercial dishonesty. For this God would make them homeless, as when they lived in *tabernacles* (tents) in the wilderness (v. 9). Their sin was inexcusable. God had sent them his *prophets* (v. 10) and *by a prophet* (Moses) had given them deliverance from *Egypt* (v. 13).

Chapter 13 continues the theme of a privileged people that has sinned beyond recovery. It begins, "When Ephraim spoke, men trembled; he was exalted in Israel" (v. 1, RSV). But idolatry had brought the nation to ruin. The God of the Exodus (v. 4) had been forgotten, for which cause he had become their destroyer (vv. 7–8).

The meaning of the remaining verses depends largely on punctuation which is absent from the Hebrew and must be supplied by the translator. The RSV is probably right in rendering the declarative statements of the KJV as questions. Hence we have, not promises of help, but expressions of despair and judgment. For example, "Shall I redeem them from death?" (v. 14). Israel is so committed to evil that the God of all mercy has to say, "Compassion is hid from my eyes" (v. 14, RSV).

Special points.—*Admah* and *Zeboim* (11:8) were cities of the plain (Gen.

14:2) that shared the fate of Sodom and Gomorrah.

God likens himself in 11:10 to a *lion* whose roar is responded to by its cubs; so Israel will be recalled from captivity. But in 13:7 the lion is used as a beast of prey to typify God's judgments.

The *oil* with which Israel tried to buy Egyptian aid (12:1) was made from olives. For *Gilead* (v. 11) see 6:8, and *Gilgal* see 4:15.

Contempt for the idolators is brought out in "Men kiss calves!" (13:2, RSV). Kissing an idol was an act of submission. The fact that Paul had verse 14 in mind when he wrote 1 Corinthians 15:55 declares the victory of divine compassion in Christ.

Truth for today.—Few spectacles are more pathetic than a great nation in decline. There are examples in recent history. Those who transgress the commandments of God expose themselves to this eventuality. Yet it is not God's will to consign nations or individuals to destruction. He appeals for love and loyalty today in the name of him who conquered death.

Salvation in Prospect (Hos. 14:1-9)

The passage.—The ultimate message of the prophets is not doom but hope. Some regard this chapter as inconsistent with the rest of Hosea. But though God may judge men for their sins he never abandons them. Hosea 14 expresses that everlasting mercy that came to full fruition in the gospel of Christ.

The chapter contains a call to repentance (v. 1), prayer of penitence (vv. 2-3), divine response (vv. 4-8), and a postscript (v. 9). If it had no fulfilment in Israel's history, it graphically presents what might have been. God replies to his repentant people with promises of restoration and prosperity. The RSV makes verse 8 read, "O Ephraim, what have I to do with idols? It is I who answer and look after you. I am like an evergreen cypress, from me comes your fruit."

The concluding verse calls on the reader to understand and apply the teaching of the book. "The ways of the Lord are right" (straight, just, constant) and men stand or fall as they relate to them.

Special points.—"Take with you words" (v. 2) implies words of sincere confession, repentance, and faith. These would be more acceptable than *calves* (young bulls) offered in meaningless sacrifice.

Asshur (v. 3) was the god of the Assyrians; *horses* were emblems of military might.

Truth for today.—Hosea's presentation of God's persistent love finds its fullest meaning in the gospel of our Lord Jesus Christ. Grace has triumphed where law failed. In Christ it has become true of the church: "Once you were no people but now you are God's people; once you had not received mercy but now you have received mercy" (1 Pet. 2:10; cf. Hos. 2:23).

JOEL

Donald F. Ackland

INTRODUCTION

The immediate occasion for Joel's prophecy was a plague of locusts of unprecedented severity. The poetic imagery with which the catastrophe is described does not exaggerate the facts. Many accounts, both ancient and modern, of devastation from this cause justify Joel's figures of speech.

The prophet saw in this tragedy a warning of the coming *day of the Lord* (1:15; 2:1,11,31), that is, a time when God would openly assert his authority over men in redemption and judgment. Other prophets saw this as a future event only. Joel declared that ultimate divine intervention was prefigured in contemporary happenings. So a locust plague became a warning of greater judgment to come.

We know little more of Joel than is told in 1:1. References such as 2:1,15,23,32 indicate that his ministry was to Jerusalem and Judah. Opinions differ as to the period in which he served. His name means "Jehovah is God."

A Contemporary Calamity (Joel 1:1–20)

The passage.—Addressing himself to *old men* with long memories (v. 2), the prophet asked their confirmation of the exceptional nature of the locust attack. The consequent suffering is related to four groups: *drunkards* (v. 5) had no wine to satisfy their craving; *priests* (vv. 9,13) could not function for lack of cereal and drink offerings; *husbandmen* and *vinedressers* (v. 11) had no harvests

to gather; and *beasts of the field* (v. 20) were without water or pasture.

In the midst of his description of natural desolation, Joel calls for repentance (vv. 13–14). The priests, dressed in *sackcloth,* an expression of grief, should spend the night prostrate before God. They should also summon a public *fast* by which the people as a whole might confess their sin. At other times, Israel viewed *the day of the Lord* (v. 15) as a time of judgment on their enemies (Ezek. 30:3). They needed to recognize God's judgment against themselves.

Special points.—The words translated *palmerworm, locust, cankerworm,* and *caterpiller* (v. 4) described four stages in the development of locusts and not four different species. Perhaps Joel's purpose was to indicate the continuing nature of the plague, amounting to years (2:25).

The locusts are described as a nation (v. 6) because of their number and organization. They have saw-like *teeth* capable of destruction far out of proportion to their size.

Verse 8 is addressed to the nation which is compared to a young woman mourning the death of her espoused husband. For *meat offering* (v. 9) read "cereal offering" (RSV). *Fire* and *flame* (v. 19) and the reference to *rivers* being *dried up* (v. 20) suggest that drought was added to existing terrors.

Truth for today.—We may no longer regard natural disasters as punishment for particular sins. But we must recognize the inseparable connection between cosmic disorder and human sin (Gen. 3:17–19; Rom. 8:20–22). Suffering is the consequence of rebellion against God and is the shared experience of fallen humanity.

Greater Disasters Threatened (Joel 2:1–27)

Some authorities regard 2:1–11 as an elaboration of the calamity already described. Others believe that the prophet now uses a natural disaster as a figure and warning of impending invasion. It would be appropriate to speak of Judah's enemies as *the northern army* (v. 20)— "the northerner," RSV—whereas locusts usually came from the south.

Joel provides a vivid picture of a relentless and ruthless adversary against whom no defence can be mounted. Yet the destroyer is under the command of God (v. 11) and fulfilling his purposes.

The same God, through his prophet, calls his people to repent and return (vv. 12–14). Superficial emotionalism will not suffice; but God will surely respond to those who truly seek him. He will restore their harvests making it possible for them to bring again "a meat offering and a drink offering."

In answer to the divine overtures, a new call goes out for a *fast* and *a solemn assembly* (v. 15). Old and young are summoned. The prayer of the priests (v. 17) is difficult to relate to locusts. It seems to refer to deliverance from oppressing nations and the humiliation of defeat.

Repentance brings its promised reward (vv. 18–27). God rehearses those blessings with which he will endow his returning people. Inserted in the passage is a song of joy (vv. 21–23).

Special points.—The comparison of locusts to *horses* (v. 4) may refer to the similarity of a locust's head to that of a horse. Verse 6 reads in the RSV, "Before them people are in anquish, all faces grow pale." Following verses are also clarified by this version. It would not be unusual for *the sun* and *the moon* (v. 10) to be obscured by flying locusts.

Orientals express sorrow by tearing their *garments* (v. 13). God asked for an inward, sincere act of repentance. For *fats* (v. 24) read "vats."

Truth for today.—Going through the motions of religious profession and performance, without sincere intent, is an ever-present danger. It is possible to perform the accepted routines—walking the aisle, submitting to baptism, tithing one's income—without the commitment of life that alone makes these things valid.

The Day of the Lord (Joel 2:28—3:21)

The passage.—After promises of material restoration and prosperity, consequent upon the nation's repentance, Joel anticipates a future outpouring of spiritual power (2:28–32). On the day of Pentecost, Peter applied these words to the descent of the Holy Spirit (Acts 2:16–21). Prior to Pentecost, the Spirit had come upon certain people at certain times to equip them for specific tasks. The promise given through Joel was that God would send his Spirit on all his people. Peter's inclusion of Joel's statement about *the sun* and *the moon* (v. 31) would imply that this part of the prophecy had also been fulfilled, possibly in the events recorded in Luke 23:44–45.

Interpretation of chapter 3 will depend on whether we regard it as historically fulfilled in the experience of national Israel or prophetic of God's dealings with the church and his final judgment of the nations. If we take the former approach, uncertainty concerning the date of Joel's ministry makes the identification of the events difficult.

The basic message of the chapter is

clear. God has purposes of mercy toward his people and judgment against those who oppress them. He accuses the offending nations of brutality toward Israel whom they have "scattered among the nations" (v. 2) and sold into slavery (*cast lots,* v. 3; also v. 6). The parceling of Israel's captured territory was regarded as an offence against God himself (parted my land, v. 2) as also was their spoiling of the Temple (v. 5).

For his afflicted people God had assurances of restoration but to their enemies (and his) he said, "I will requite your deed upon your own head" (v. 7, RSV). Verses 9–17 describe "the day of the Lord" in terms of judgment. A call to war (v. 9) brings the armies of wickedness to *the valley of decision* (v. 14), where God sits on a throne of judgment (v. 12). Note that the decision is God's, not man's, whose wickedness has come to full *harvest* (v. 13) and the *sickle* of divine judgment is applied.

In vivid contrast to his opening description of the destruction of the land by locusts, Joel concludes with a picture of nature abounding in peace and plenty (v. 18). Israel's traditional enemies, *Egypt* and *Edom* (v. 19), representative, perhaps, of all her enemies, have been punished and *Judah* and *Jerusalem* (v. 20) are for ever secure "for the Lord dwelleth in Zion" (v. 21).

Special points.—Whatever interpretation we give to this passage, it is important to note that Peter (Acts 2:21) and Paul (Rom. 10:13) related 2:32 to the gospel of our Lord. It is likely, therefore, that chapter 3 has significance far beyond the historic context in which it was given.

The valley of Jehoshaphat (v. 2) is not mentioned elsewhere in the Bible. Probably no recognizable location is intended. The significance of the name is in the meaning of Jehoshaphat, "Jehovah judges." The same thought is found in the later phrase, *valley of decision* (v. 14). *Tyre* and *Zion* (v. 4) were cities of Phoenicia, and "all the coasts of Palestine" becomes "regions of Philistia" in the RSV. These were long-time enemies of Israel.

The call to war (v. 10) reverses the gracious promise of Isaiah 2:4 as it bids the nations acquire every possible weapon and enlist every available man, "Let the weak say, 'I am a warrior'" (RSV). The accumulated military might of a sinful world is about to be judged. God has vast spiritual forces at his command—"thy mighty ones" (v. 11).

Familiar Bible concepts are met in the harvests of field and vineyard (v. 13) and references to *sun, moon, stars* (v. 15) and earthquake (v. 16) as providing nature's accompaniment to God's acts of judgment.

The closing verse is otherwise rendered, "I will avenge their blood, and I will not clear the guilty" (v. 21, RSV). It should be associated with verse 19. The concluding phrase, "for the Lord dwelleth in Zion," then climaxes verse 20.

Truth for today.—God's people find their greatest assurance of deliverance and security in the promise of God's presence in their midst. For the church, and all who comprise the church, that presence is made real in the gift of the Holy Spirit (1 Cor. 3:16).

AMOS

Donald F. Ackland

INTRODUCTION

The turbulent history of Israel, the Northern Kingdom, has been reviewed in the Introduction to the prophecy of Hosea. The long reign of Jeroboam II, which lasted forty-one years (2 Kings 14:23–29), introduced a time of comparative peace and prosperity between two prolonged periods of internal strife and foreign aggression. Jeroboam's contemporary was Uzziah, king of Judah, whose reign was of equally long duration.

As a shepherd, Amos may have found a good market for his wool in northern cities. But he realized that economic prosperity can bring evils that destroy a nation. Although a native of Judah, he heard God calling him to be his messenger to Israel (7:15).

Using language of surprising refinement, rich in analogies from nature, Amos thundered against self-indulgence, injustice, dishonesty, immorality, and corrupt religion. He warned individuals and nations of impending judgment, so much so that some have seen his prophecy as one of unrelieved gloom.

This, however, is not the case. In spite of major emphases on condemnation and punishment, Amos' prophecy is shot through with tender concern for Israel (7:2,5). His concept of a sovereign God, active in judgment against evildoers, is tempered by the divine plea, "Seek ye me, and ye shall live" (5:4).

All that we know of Amos is found in the book that bears his name. These items of personal history will be discussed as they arise in the text.

The Judgment of the Nations (Amos 1: 1—2:16)

The passage.—After a brief personal reference (1:1), the prophet proceeds immediately to his message. God has spoken from *Jerusalem.* The *roar* of his voice brings disaster to "the pastures of the shepherds" (RSV) and the tree-lined Carmel range (v. 2).

Following this slight reference to the territory of Israel, Amos proceeds to deliver God's judgments against neighboring nations (1:3—2:5).

The charge against Syria, whose capital was *Damascus,* is inhuman conduct for which defeat and captivity would be the consequences (1:3–5). Philistia, represented by the city of *Gaza,* is accused of wholesale enslavement for which she would suffer extermination (1:6–8). Offences similar to Philistia's are attributed to Phoenicia (*Tyre*), with destruction as punishment. *Edom,* composed of descendants of Esau, was accused of insatiable hatred leading to unpitying violence, for which God would send an ordeal of fire (1:11–12). *Amon* had been guilty of what we today call genocide, the attempted extermination of a people. Exile would be their lot (1:13–15). Finally, *Moab*'s aggressions had involved even the desecration of the dead, for which suitable retribution would follow (2:1–3).

We may imagine the prophet's audi-

547

ence listening with demonstrated approval to these verdicts. But Amos now turns to *Judah,* sister state to Israel. A new criterion of judgment is introduced as Judah is charged with breaking God's laws and embracing lies (idols). For these offences against revealed truth, penalties similar to those pronounced on heathen nations would follow (2:4–5).

Israel itself became the next subject of Amos' pronouncements (2:6–16). The long list of indictments includes: corruption of justice (v. 6); oppression of the poor (v. 7a); degradation of religion (vv. 7b-8); ingratitude for divine blessings (vv. 9–11); and opposition to God's witnesses (v. 12). For such conduct the consequence would be ignominious military defeat.

Special points.—The word "herdman" (1:1) is rendered "sheepmaster" in 2 Kings 3:4, where it refers to a king. Amos was apparently a sheep owner. *Tekoa* was in Judah, about twelve miles south of Jerusalem, in rugged wilderness country. We are not able to date the earthquake which is also mentioned in Zechariah 14:5.

The expression, "For three transgressions . . . , and for four" (1:3) suggests repeated offences. *Hazael* and *Benhadad* were Syrian kings (v. 4). The "bar of Damascus" (v. 5) probably means the fortified gate of the city.

By "the law of the Lord" (2:4) we should understand the total revelation of God. The following reference to his *commandments* relates specifically to the Mosaic legal code.

In verse 6, "sold the righteous for silver, and the poor for a pair of shoes," may describe abuses of the process of law. The first phrase refers to bribery of a judge, the second to the practice of giving a shoe as token of a completed legal transaction (Ruth 4:7).

Further oppression of the poor is indicated in verse 7—"they that trample the head of the poor into the dust of the earth" (RSV). The second half of the same verse has reference to religious prostitution. Father and son commit immorality on *clothes* taken in pledge while they drink *wine* obtained by extortion (see RSV).

Nazarites (2:11), or "Nazirites" (RSV), were persons dedicated to the austere life as a protest against indulgent times (Num. 6).

Verse 13 reads in the RSV, "I will press you down . . ." Israel is pictured as loaded down with its sins.

Truth for today.—There is a moral law to which all men are answerable. God sits in judgment on every nation and holds them responsible for their actions. Though aggression may seem to bring glittering prizes, in the outworkings of history God will assert his sovereignty and justice will prevail. Those who, possessing the knowledge of God's nature and will, sin against the light, will not escape.

The Abuse of Privilege (Amos 3:1–15)

God's complaints against Israel are elaborated in 3:1—6:14. It is possible to identify three separate messages, each beginning with the summons, "Hear this word" (3:1; 4:1; 5:1).

The passage.—The prophet's first sermon begins with a statement of the base ingratitude of Israel. God had brought them out of Egypt and had entered into covenant relationship with them. This is the significance of "You only have I known" (v. 2), "known" describing the most intimate of relationships, based on mutual consent.

Did these statements by Amos provoke violent reaction among his listeners? He apparently found it necessary to justify what he had said, which he did in a series of illustrations of cause and effect (vv. 3–8). Four of these were taken from his own rural background, two from urban life. They are climaxed by verse 8 which states that behind the prophet's ministry was the action of God to which he could do no other than respond.

Then, using a dramatic method frequently employed by the prophets, Amos called on other nations to witness the charges against Israel (vv. 9–15). He pictured a nation committed to evil, whose prosperity could not hide her turmoil and whose wealth had been gotten by oppression (vv. 9b-10).

Sentence of doom was pronounced (vv. 11–15). An invader would ravage the land, destroying its luxurious palaces together with its idol shrines, a reference to Assyrian conquest.

Special points.—Insight into Amos' background is given in verse 3—"Do two walk together, unless they have made an appointment?" (RSV). For two persons to meet in the wilderness around Tekoa would indicate some prearrangement. The meaning of "gin" (v. 5) is "bait" or "trap." In each illustration the point is cause and effect.

"Ashdod" (Philistia) and "Egypt" (v. 9) were traditional enemies of Israel. Verse 12 provides a picture of complete destruction. The reference to "two legs, or the piece of an ear" echoes Exodus 22:13 where such remains were evidence of death. Only pieces of costly beds and remnants of rich material (Damascus may mean "damask") would remain to attest the luxury of an overthrown culture.

Heartless Indulgence Reproved (Amos 4:1–13)

The passage.—Amos held wealthy women, compared to an aggressive breed of cattle (*kine of Bashan,* v. 1),

responsible for oppressing the poor. They demanded of their husbands more and more of life's good things. Their end would be ignominious. Their enemies would drag them "away with hooks" (v. 2) through gaps ("breaches," v. 3) in the city's walls. Ancient monuments depict just such treatment of prisoners. The fact that "into the palace" ("into Harmon," RSV) has no satisfactory translation adds to the grimness of the picture.

The Bible contains no more bitter denunciation of meaningless religious ritual than in verses 4–5. "Come to worship and sin," is the prophet's cry. The people worshiped God in ways that appealed to themselves ("this liketh you," or, KJV marg., "so ye love"), not in ways that God approved. Their religion was centered in self.

These people refused to learn life's lessons. God had chastised them in the past, but they had not profited from the experience (vv. 6–11). Five misfortunes and calamities are listed: famine (v. 6), drought (vv. 7–8), crop failure (v. 9), war (v. 10), earthquake and fire (v. 11). Five times the disappointed cry is heard, "yet have ye not returned unto me, saith the Lord."

"Therefore, . . . prepare to meet thy God, O Israel" (v. 12). This is a warning of coming, final judgment. The seriousness of the words is emphasized by the majesty of the speaker (v. 13).

Special points.—*Bethel* and *Gilgal* (v. 4) were religious shrines, ostensibly dedicated to Jehovah, but tending to idolatry. The RSV makes "after three years" read "every three days," apparently referring to a schedule of activity followed by pilgrims. The use of leaven (v. 4) was forbidden by Mosaic law. The ironic command to "proclaim and publish the free offerings" suggests giving for the sake of personal notice.

Truth for today.—Even Christians need to be warned against the perils of formality in religious practices. That which is intended for the praise of God can be made to cater to human pride and perversity. Motivation is the all-important factor in determining the acceptability of worship.

Aggravated Sin and Inevitable Punishment (Amos 5:1—6:14)

The passage.—Prophets used various methods to attract attention to their message. We may think of Amos standing in a public place intoning the words of 5:1–2. They are in the form of a lament, in which, anticipating events, he depicted Israel as a young woman come to an untimely end. The same poetic form is found in verses 16–17, but there God is the speaker.

Israel's catastrophe was the result of ignoring the pleadings of God, "Seek ye me, and ye shall live" (5:4). The routines of religion as observed at Bethel, Gilgal, and elsewhere would not suffice; these places, in fact, would be destroyed. A rebellious nation must seek the true God whose greatness is described in exalted language perhaps reproducing an ancient Hebrew hymn (vv. 8–9).

Charges of injustice against fellowmen follow (5:10–17). The processes of law were being used in favor of the rich and against the poor. For these oppressive acts God would send appropriate punishment (v. 11).

Verse 13 presents a problem of interpretation. It is probably an ironic comment on the failure of good men to speak out against prevailing ills. The only remedy was to abandon wickedness, redress wrong, "and love the good" (vv. 14–15). Otherwise God himself would take up the lament against his people (vv. 16–17).

Unfortunately, Israel cherished false hopes based on pride (5:18–20). They talked about "the day of the Lord" as though it would bring them advantage. Amos wanted them to know that it would be to their undoing for God's judgments would be unleashed against his rebellious people. There would be no escape; it would be like fleeing from a lion only to be attacked by a bear, or taking refuge in a house and being bitten by a serpent.

In 5:21–27 the prophet brings earlier themes into relationship. The people were guilty of superficial practices of worship (vv. 21–23) and the veneration of false gods (v. 26). They were also guilty of social injustices (v. 24). For these reasons, their orthodox rituals were no more acceptable to God than their idolatries. Verse 24 may be considered the key verse of the prophecy. For *judgment* read "justice." God has no use for religion divorced from social justice.

Addressing himself to the nation's leadership (6:1–6), Amos deplores their complacency (at ease) in a time of national peril. Their trust was in material things, "the mountains of Samaria" (v. 1), the defenses of the city or the resources of government. Their complacency was evident in their self-indulgence and unparalleled luxury.

To alert them to their danger and bring about repentance, Amos describes the horrors that would accompany the siege of Samaria (vv. 8–11). There would be wholesale death from enemy action or plague, together with indiscriminate destruction of property. Two absurd suggestions about horses and oxen (v. 12a) are used to emphasize the utter unreasonableness of Israel. They despise justice and honor and boast about military achievements (vv. 12b–13). But divine retribution is near in the

Assyrian aggressor (v. 14).

Special points.—Once again the concept of Israel as a woman is introduced (5:1), this time tragic in death. The phrase "house of Joseph" (v. 6) also refers to Israel. In verse 7, turning "judgment to wormwood" means perverting justice so that it becomes a bitter thing instead of a refuge for the poor. God is described (v. 8) as creator of "the seven stars" (Pleiades, RSV) and "Orion," well-known constellations of the heavens.

Justice, normally administered in "the gate" (5:10,12,15) was being perverted as rich landowners took "exactions of wheat" (v. 11, RSV) from their tenants. Innocent people (the just) were being punished by judges who accepted bribes (v. 12).

We should probably understand 5:25 as meaning that God did not expect *only* sacrifices and offerings in the wilderness. These were then brought as evidence of acknowledged sin and repentance, elements that were absent from the type of worship Amos criticized.

Moloch and Chiun (5:26), which become "Sakkuth" and "Kaiwan" in the RSV, were Assyrian deities. The tense here should be future as Amos describes the people going into captivity carrying these false gods.

Why attention was called to Calneh, Hamath, and Gath (6:2) is uncertain. The prophet may have been inviting comparison between the greatness of Samaria and these lesser cities. The word "viol" (v. 5) is rendered "harps" by the RSV. The cumulative picture of these verses is of luxurious living in disregard of others' need and impending judgment (v. 6).

Pride (excellency, v. 8) and selfish indulgence would be the nation's ruin. Even though as many as ten men in one house (v. 9) might survive one disaster,

they would all ultimately die in the horrors of siege. When the dead are brought out of devastated homes, and one survivor is found, people will be so demoralized with fear that they will shrink from speaking even the name of God (v. 10). Total devastation is described in verse 11—"The great house shall be smitten into fragments, and the little house into bits" (RSV).

The latter part of 6:12 repeats the idea of 5:7 (see comment). Verse 13 reads in the RSV, "you who rejoice in Lo-debar, who say, 'Have we not by our strength taken Karnaim for ourselves?' " This is usually taken as a reference to two minor victories by Israel which gave her false confidence. "Hamath unto the river" (v. 14) denotes the farthest boundaries of Israel as established by Jeroboam II.

Truth for today.—Warnings against the selfish, God-forgetful enjoyment of prosperity are as relevant today as when Amos lived. Affluence too often leads to moral decline, social irresponsibility, and formal religion. God's dealings with Israel should be a present warning against the abuse of wealth and a call to renewed dedication to him as sovereign Lord of the universe.

Preparatory Visions (Amos 7:1–9)

The character of the book of Amos changes after chapter 6. Spoken messages give place to mainly biographical content.

The passage.—God gave Amos three visions to prepare him for his work: locusts (vv. 1–3), fire (vv. 4–6), and plumbline (vv. 7–9).

Amos saw locusts devastating the land and pleaded with God to forgive Jacob (Israel) . . . "for he is so small" (v. 12). The word "repented" (v. 3), as applied to God, has no parallel with human repentance. Literally, God "was sorry" and withheld his judgment.

Then Amos saw a vision of fire (drought) and again interceded with God (v. 5). His prayer was heard.

His third vision was of a plumbline held against a wall (Israel) to reveal its crookedness (vv. 7–8). The nation has miserably failed to meet God's standards of righteousness, and punishment is accordingly pronounced. The answer of Amos to this vision is his ministry. "The Lord hath spoken, who can but prophesy?" (3:8).

Special points.—By *the king's mowings* (v. 1) we should understand the early crop that was claimed by the king. The second crop, on which the people depended for their own use, was destroyed. A plumbline (v. 7) is a weight on the end of a string used to test the straightness of a wall. By saying, "I will not again pass by them" (v. 8) God meant that he would not again withhold judgment.

A Biographical Interlude (Amos 7:10–17)

The passage.—The faithful prophet carried his message to Bethel where there was a shrine patronized by the king himself. Amaziah, priest of Bethel, reported the words of Amos to the king adding his own interpretation that they were treasonous. This led to a personal confrontation between priest and prophet. Amaziah ordered Amos to return to Judah. The latter replied by affirming his divine call and restating his message of warning, with personal application to Amaziah.

Special points.—By using the word "seer" (v. 12), Amaziah expressed his scorn. It meant "visionary." In his reply, Amos disclaimed any professional standing ("a prophet's son," v. 14), and described his beginnings as "a herdman, and a gatherer of sycomore fruit." Au-

thorities disagree on the precise meaning of "gatherer" (lit., "pincher").

Concluding Visions (Amos 8:1—9:15)

Two more visions were granted to Amos, the first of a basket of summer fruit (8:1–14) and the second of God himself at work in judgment and redemption (9:1–15).

The passage.—The Hebrew has a play on words in 8:1–2 that is not brought out in the English. The words for "summer fruit" (v. 1) and for "end" (v. 2) have a similar sound. The harvested fruit and the similarity of sound combine to convey the idea of a nation that has run its course.

Former charges against Israel are repeated in 8:4–10 with significant additions. We see greedy merchants begrudging the time taken for worship (vv. 5–6). Even while engaged in worship they are plotting against the poor. To previous judgments was added spiritual famine (vv. 11–14). Because God's people had despised his messengers there would be a time when they would crave "the words of the Lord" and not be satisfied. In that day the people would realize the vanity of their false faiths.

Finally there was granted to Amos a vision of the Lord himself (9:1–15). An act of judgment takes place at a shrine that may have been Bethel (vv. 1–4). Crowds are assembled for worship when disaster comes in likeness to an earthquake—a reference, perhaps, to 1:1. This is a portent of final judgment, destruction by war.

In verses 5–10 we see the judge himself. He is Lord of all nature (vv. 5–6) and nations (vv. 7–10). All history is under his control. His sovereignty is particularly displayed in his judgments against Israel (vv. 8–10), "the sinful kingdom."

But the mood changes before the prophecy closes. In 9:11–15 we see God at work in restoration and redemption. While the promises are in terms of material recovery, a messianic note is to be recognized in "the tabernacle of David" (v. 11). Gospel writers saw such prophecies fulfilled in the coming of Christ (Luke 1:32).

Special points.—The *new moon* and *the sabbath* (8:5) marked religious festivals. An *ephah* was a measure and a *shekel* a weight. Deceit in trading is indicated. For 8:6 see comment on 2:6.

The word "hell" (9:2), rendered "Sheol" in the RSV, means the place of the dead. A blow is delivered to racial pride in verse 7 where God claims that he is at work in all history, controlling the movements of Gentile nations as well as directing the destiny of Israel.

Truth for today.—The history of Israel witnesses to the inexorable outworkings of divine justice. "Now these things happened to them as a warning, but they were written down for our instruction" (1 Cor. 10:11, RSV). The greater the privileges we enjoy, the greater our responsibility before God.

OBADIAH

Donald F. Ackland

INTRODUCTION

This is the shortest book in the Old Testament. It tells of the doom of Edom as God's judgment for offenses against Judah, with concluding promises of restoration for Judah and Israel.

Edomites were descendants of Esau. Their territory (Edom, or Ser) lay south of the Dead Sea. Among its principal cities were Sela (Petra) and Teman.

The spirit of contention shown at the birth of Jacob and Esau (Gen. 25:22–23, 26) continued through many centuries. The Edomites refused Moses permission to enter their territory (Num. 20:14–21). There were clashes between Edom and Israel during Saul's reign, but David subdued them (2 Sam. 8:14).

In later years, the Edomites repeatedly rebelled. In the reign of Jehoram they formed an alliance and invaded Judah (2 Chron. 21:8–10,16–17). Some scholars think that this event is described in Obadiah 10–14. Others feel that the reference is to the destruction of Jerusalem by Nebuchadnezzar. Since nothing is known about Obadiah as a person, these conflicting opinions influence scholars in dating the book.

After the fall of Jerusalem, the Edomites were expelled by enemies and settled in southern Judah (Idumea). The Maccabees (Jewish patriots, 166–66 B.C.) conquered this territory and incorporated it under Jewish rule. Eventually, the Romans wiped the Edomites from the pages of history.

Overthrow of Edom (Obad. 1–9)

The passage.—Since there are close parallels between Obadiah's words and Jeremiah 49:7–22, Obadiah may be an echo of Jeremiah's prophecy or both prophets may reproduce an earlier common source. In either case, the message is *from the Lord* (v. 1). The nations are summoned against Edom which God will make small and bring to humiliation (v. 2).

Though the Edomites pride themselves on their impregnability (vv. 3–4), God will bring them down. Their destruction will be complete (v. 5) and will be brought about by their own allies, "men of thy confederacy" (v. 7).

Special points.—The description, "thou that dwellest in the clefts of the rock" (v. 3), is appropriate for the mountain strongholds of the Edomites, still to be recognized in the existing ruins of Petra. Edomites were renowned for their wisdom (v. 8). *Teman* (v. 9), a chief city, stands for Edom as a whole.

Charges Against Edom (Obad. 10–14)

The passage.—Disregarding ties of kinship (thy brother Jacob, v. 10), the Edomites had taken sides with Judah's enemies. They had found scornful pleasure in Judah's defeat (v. 12). Furthermore, they had actually joined in pillaging the distressed people (v. 13) and had turned attempted escapees over to their foes (v. 14).

Judgment of the Nations (Obad. 15–16)

The passage.—Obadiah, as other prophets, refers to coming judgment as "the day of the Lord" (v. 15). Edom and other nations that have celebrated their victories in Jerusalem (my holy mountain, v. 16) will be made to drink deeply of God's wrath until completely destroyed.

Restoration of Israel (Obad. 17–21)

The passage.—Jacob (Israel) and Joseph (Judah) shall as a reunited people burn up their enemies, including Edom, as stubble (v. 18). In expanding their borders they would overcome the Edomites, settled in Idumea (*the south,* v. 19), a prophecy fulfilled under the Maccabees.

Special points.—Jerusalem's freedom from occupation by unbelievers is indicated by *there shall be holiness* (v. 17). Some of the place names of verses 19–20 are problematic, but the picture of extended borders is clear. For *saviours* read "deliverers" (v. 21). This concluding verse may have messianic implications as suggested by the final phrase.

Truth for today.—Because God reigns (the kingdom shall be the Lord's, v. 21) eventual justice is inevitable: "as thou hast done it shall be done unto thee" (v. 15).

JONAH

Donald F. Ackland

INTRODUCTION

Few books of the Bible have been more misused than the book of Jonah. Interest has been focused on the whale (actually, "great fish") while the intended message has been largely overlooked.

Jonah's identity as an historic individual is not in question. He is mentioned in 2 Kings 14:23–27 as a patriotic preacher who encouraged Jeroboam II, king of Israel, in his recovery of lost territory.

Jeroboam's success was in part due to the temporary decline of Assyria, a power that, according to secular history, had threatened Israel on at least two occasions. The Assyrians achieved a reputation for incredible brutality and their decline gave satisfaction to countries, like Israel, that they had attacked.

We can imagine Jonah's amazement when God called him to be his messenger to Nineveh, capital of Assyria (1:2). He had no inclination to be a missionary to these hated people. So he ran away from his assignment and (as he hoped) from God.

As a result of his experiences at sea and inside the great fish, Jonah obeyed God and preached to the Ninevites. But when, as a consequence of their repentance, God withheld his judgments, Jonah was angry. He is still angry when the story ends with God's question, "Should not I spare Nineveh?" (4:11).

The book of Jonah was written to teach readers of all times that the universal God is impartial in his dealings, patient with the worst offenders, and ready to grant forgiveness to all who repent. It provides an Old Testament foundation for Christian missions.

We have no reason to suppose that Jonah wrote the book that bears his name. Who wrote it and when we cannot tell. The story bears all the marks of true biography and was so accepted by our Lord (Matt. 12:38–42; 16:4; Luke 11:29–32).

The Prophet's Flight (Jonah 1:1–17)

The passage.—Jonah was called of God to be a messenger of judgment against Nineveh as the reference to "their wickedness" (v. 2) indicates. But, as he later acknowledged (4:2), he knew from the first that God would forgive the Ninevites if they repented. It was this prospect that caused him to run away. He did not want to be the vehicle of divine grace to an enemy nation.

The seamen on the ship by which he traveled were heathen. When a fierce storm arose, they prayed to their gods and took measures to make the vessel more seaworthy. Then they cast lots (v. 7) to determine who was responsible for the anger of the gods, to which they attributed the storm.

When Jonah was indicated as the offender, he asked the crew to throw him overboard. They were at first unwilling, but when the storm persisted they asked forgiveness of Jonah's God and then threw him into the sea. The man who would show no mercy to Nineveh became the object of God's mercy. He was swallowed by a "great fish" in which he remained for "three days and three nights" (v. 17).

Special points.—Jonah's destination, Tarshish (v. 3), is considered to have been a port in Spain. The significance may be that it was the furthermost point westward to which a traveler of those days could go. It is specifically stated that he fled "from the presence of the Lord." In his spirit of racial prejudice he wanted to get away from the demands of an all-merciful God.

The willingness of Jonah to be sacrificed to save the lives of the pagan crew suggests a change of heart. In a common danger he had been able to identify with these non-Hebrews whose concern for him (v. 13) was in sharp contrast to his lack of compassion for the Ninevites.

The Prophet's Prayer (Jonah 2:1–10)

The passage.—Many commentators believe that the original story of Jonah did not include this prayer (vv. 2–9) which they regard as a later addition. However, most of the statements are appropriate to Jonah's experience. Many echoes from the psalms create the possibility that Jonah found comfort and assurance in recalling the words of others. He concluded by acknowledging his indebtedness to God as his deliverer.

Special points.—By "the belly of hell" (v. 2) Jonah meant the place of the dead (Sheol). Anticipating escape from his living tomb, he spoke as though this had already happened: "yet hast thou brought up my life from corruption" (v. 6). His deliverance would be like life from the grave. Our Lord saw in Jonah's experience comparisons with his own (Matt. 12:40).

Verse 8 is rendered: "Those who pay regard to vain idols" (RSV) and reflects the conduct of the heathen seamen (1:5). Such can never know God's mercy. But Jonah makes his vows to the Lord (v. 9) who answers by delivering him (v. 10).

The Prophet's Preaching (Jonah 3:1–10)

The passage.—Rescued from sea and fish, Jonah was again called to be God's messenger to Nineveh. This time he obeyed and under his preaching the people repented. When the Lord saw this, he repented (v. 10), that is, he withheld his judgments.

Special points.—A "city of three days' journey" (v. 3) would be some seventy-five miles across. Since no known cities approach this size, it may be that Jonah's ministry was to a larger area of which Nineveh was the center.

The Prophet's Complaint (Jonah 4:1–11)

The passage.—When God responded to the repentance of Nineveh by withholding his judgments, Jonah was angry and took an I-told-you-so attitude. This, he told God, was why he did not want to accept the mission in the first place. He knew God would embarrass him by failing to support his preaching. He was ready to die!

Then God taught him a lesson with a gourd and a worm (vv. 6–7). The plant afforded needful shelter for Jonah, but was killed by the worm. The prophet's anger blazed again, this time because the plant had died. He had more pity for a plant than for the people of Nineveh.

There the story abruptly ends, leaving the reader to make the application.

Special points.—Jonah's booth (v. 5), that is, shelter of leaves and branches, must have been inadequate. God provided additional shade for the prophet in a gourd (v. 6), thought to be a castor-oil plant which has large leaves. The 120,000 "persons that cannot discern between their right hand and their left" (v. 11) were children.

Truths for today.—Israel's narrow nationalism caused her to despise other nations and fail as the messenger of God's redemptive love for all mankind. For many centuries, Christians were similarly neglectful of their responsibil- ity. Even today, missionary activity is hampered by lack of support.

The story of Jonah teaches many lessons, among them the power of prayer and the effectiveness of preaching. But supremely it reveals the character of God whose love is universal and whose forgiveness is available to all.

MICAH

Donald F. Ackland

INTRODUCTION

To Micah, the events of history were the outworkings of the purposes of God. He witnessed much evil, both in Judah and Israel. He spoke as the representative of God who was no idle spectator of man's wrongdoing but the righteous judge.

But Micah also recognized purposes of redemption in the activity of God. His prophecy is rich in messianic promises that reach their high point in the naming of Bethlehem as the birthplace of the coming Redeemer-King.

The book begins by mentioning three reigns during which Micah prophesied (1:1). The full period would cover the years 742–687 B.C. It is likely that his active ministry covered only part of this time. His home was Moresheth-gath (1:1,14), situated in the foothills between the coastal plain and the highlands of Judah. There is a reference to Micah in Jeremiah 26:18–19.

Messenger of Judgment (Mic. 1:1–16)

The passage.—Using the familiar setting of a court of justice, the prophet begins by calling on all nations to listen to God's case against Israel and Judah. The great Accuser is depicted as descending from his heavenly temple (vv. 2–3). The majesty of his presence causes mountains to melt (v. 4).

Micah describes the coming fate of Samaria (vv. 6–7) and Jerusalem (v. 9), capital cities of Israel and Judah respectively. We see the prophet delivering his dramatic message stripped to his loincloth (naked, v. 8) and wailing like a mourner.

Specific warnings are addressed to a number of towns, some identifiable, others not (vv. 10–15). This difficult passage is made more intelligible by the RSV. The prophet tells parents to shave their heads ("Make thee bald," v. 16) as a sign of mourning because of the captivity that awaits their children.

Special points.—The RSV has "of Moresheth" for "the Morasthite" (v. 1). The phrase "high places" (v. 5), pagan shrines, identifies Jerusalem's sin as idolatry. The same charge is made against Samaria (v. 7) whose shrines had been built with *hires,* payments made to religious prostitutes.

For *dragons* and *owls* (v. 8) read "jackals" and "ostriches" (RSV). "Declare ye it not in Gath" (v. 10) echoes David's lament over Saul (2 Sam. 1:10). Gath was a Philistine city. As a sample of several puns on place names, *Aphrah* means "house of dust."

Sins of Violence (Mic. 2:1–13)

The passage.—Micah addresses himself to oppressors of others (vv. 1–5). Because they violently rob others of their land, God will bring evil on them "from which ye shall not remove your necks" (v. 3). Like oxen, they will be forced to do the will of their conquerors. In this changed situation they would say, "how hath he removed it from me" (v. 4), "How could God do this to me?" When the land was redivided (after invasion) there would be nobody to stake

559

a claim (cast a cord by lot, v. 5) for them.

It was inevitable that Micah should meet with opposition. In verse 6 we hear interruptions from his audience, "Prophecy ye not" ("Stop this preaching"). In reply, Micah adds to former accusations. Inoffensive travelers are being attacked and robbed (v. 8). Women and children are being driven from their homes (v. 9).

Still addressing his interrupters, Micah tells them that the kind of preacher they want is one who will preach "of wine and of strong drink" (v. 11), that is, either approving intemperance or accepting intoxicating beverages as the reward of smooth talk.

The chapter concludes with promises of restoration in which God appears first as a shepherd gathering his sheep together (v. 12) and then as a king leading his people out of captivity (v. 13).

Sins of Leadership (Mic. 3:1–12)

The passage.—Now Micah exposes the sins of political leaders who might be expected "to know judgment" (v. 1). Here, as often in the Old Testament, "justice" is the better translation. They are described as ravenous beasts, tearing and consuming their victims. The offence is compounded by the fact that they assume the role of religious people. But God will not hear the prayers of such (v. 4).

Next, false *prophets* are accused: men who are friendly enough when they are well treated but become antagonistic to those who do not reward them (v. 5). God would publicly discredit them. When the time came that they needed a message, it would not be granted (vv. 6–7).

By way of contrast, Micah claimed, "I am full of power by the spirit of the Lord" (v. 8). He was conscious of di-

vine enduement. The evidence of this was the faithfulness of his message. Unlike the false prophets, he would "tell it like it is."

In verses 9–11, rulers, priests, and prophets are all indicted for abusing their offices. Hardened in conscience and hypocritical in spirit, they strike a religious pose, and say, "Is not the Lord among us? none evil can come upon us." But they are wrong. Justice will overtake them (v. 12).

Truth for today.—As prophet of the common people, Micah expresses God's concern for all who are oppressed or deceived, either by corruption in government or insincerity in religious leadership. Unfortunately, these evils went hand in hand because of collusion between church and state. Only as spokesmen for God are free from obligation to the state can they faithfully fulfil their mission. There is always need for men of Micah's stamp who will speak for righteousness and justice, regardless of consequences.

The Coming Kingdom (Mic. 4:1–13)

The passage.—The eyes of Micah are shifted from the immediate scene to a glorious future, "in the last days" (v. 1). In words that largely duplicate Isaiah 2:2–4, he describes a new Jerusalem, elevated above its surroundings, and drawing to itself people of "many nations" (v. 2). Their purpose will be to learn of God's ways. God will reign from this city, put an end to war (v. 3), and give the blessings of prosperity and peace (v. 4).

Verse 5 recognizes that these conditions belong to the future as the prophet acknowledges the existence of many religions. Israel has first to undergo severe trials, variously described in verses 6, 9–10. Nevertheless, her final victory is assured. She will trample her enemies, who "know not the thoughts of the

Lord" (v. 12), as a fearsome animal with horn and hoofs (v. 13) of metal.

The Coming King (Mic. 5:1–15)

The passage.—Having anticipated the coming kingdom, Micah proceeds to describe a leader "that is to be ruler in Israel" (v. 2). Exalted language is used about this one who will be a shepherd ("feed his flock," v. 4, RSV) and a bringer of peace (vv. 5–6).

The remainder of the chapter contains statements about "the remnant of Jacob" (v. 7), that is, Israel surviving in captivity. They would serve both a beneficent purpose and one of judgment (vv. 8–9). Finally, the prophet lists things in which Israel had falsely trusted and from which God will purge them (vv. 10–15).

Special points.—While references to Assyria (vv. 5–6) lend support to the opinion that the promise of a "ruler in Israel" (v. 2) had early fulfilment in an earthly leader (some suggest Hezekiah), the language used describes more than a man. Christian faith, supported by Matthew 2:5–6 and the historic circumstances of Christ's birth, sees this as an inspired prophecy of our Lord's birthplace, person, and mission.

The Lord's Controversy (Mic. 6:1–16)

The passage.—Returning to the setting of a court of justice, Micah calls on "the mountains" to witness God's complaints against his people (vv. 1–2). An opportunity is given Israel to state their grievances (v. 3). Since they have none to offer, they are reminded of God's historic dealings with them (vv. 4–5).

Speaking for and to the people, Micah asks rhetorically what kind of sacrifice they should bring to this gracious God (vv. 6–7). The answer of verse 8 states in brief "the whole duty of man"— justice and kindness to their fellows and a humble walk with God.

Charges of dishonest trading follow (vv. 9–16). Because wealth had been accumulated by deceitful means, God would visit the people with judgment. They had followed in the ways of evil kings, Omri and Ahab (v. 16).

Repentance and Recovery (Mic. 7:1–20)

The passage.—Taking a final look at the nation, Micah reaches the conclusion that "there is none upright among men" (v. 2). The moral collapse is such that confidence can be placed in nobody (vv. 5–6).

"Therefore," he says, "I will look unto the Lord" (v. 7). In doing this he finds hope. In the "darkness" of exile, God will be a "light" to his people (v. 8). They must bear their punishment but after that God will "execute judgment" for them (v. 9). Enemies that have mocked them will be "trodden down" (v. 10). Jerusalem will be rebuilt and her "boundary will be far extended" (v. 11, RSV), while desolation will afflict others (v. 12).

After a prayer to God to be a shepherd to his scattered people (vv. 14–15) and a description of the effect of Israel's restoration on the nations (vv. 16–17), the prophecy ends with a hymn of praise to God, the redeemer of his people. Micah's name means "Who is like Jehovah?" so verse 18 contains a play on his name.

Truth for today.—Micah's prophecy concludes with a reminder that sin is the obstacle to fellowship between God and man and that this fellowship can only be restored as God provides a way to deal with sin. Thus the ancient prophet points to the need of a Savior, to whose coming he bears witness, although the greatness of his salvation was not known until he was proclaimed as "the Lamb of God, which taketh away the sin of the world" (John 1:29).

NAHUM

Donald F. Ackland

INTRODUCTION

Unlike other prophets, Nahum's preaching was not concerned with the sins of Judah and/or Israel, but with the coming doom of Assyria. Nineveh's repentance under the preaching of Jonah (Jonah 3:5) was apparently short-lived. Nahum saw the capital of the Assyrian empire as "a bloody city . . . full of lies and robbery" (3:1).

Some recoil from this prophecy as vengeful and alien to the spirit of Christ. But this is to misunderstand its setting and purpose. Micah did not engage in personal vindictiveness. He was the messenger of divine justice against a nation whose incredible atrocities are recorded in secular history.

Nahum means "comfort" or "comforter." Although the note of comfort is not prominent in his prophecy, it is repeatedly expressed (1:3,7,12–13,15). Those who suffered under ruthless aggression were assured that God reigns in history and will bring even the worst of tyrants to an accounting.

Nahum's prophecy must be dated between the fall of the Egyptian city of No-amon, or Thebes, in 663 B.C. (see 3:8–10) and the destruction of Nineveh by the Medes and Babylonians in 612 B.C. His home, Elkosh (1:1), has never been positively identified. Majority opinion favors a site about twenty miles southwest of Jerusalem.

God of Vengeance (Nah. 1:1–15)

The passage.—Micah's prophecy is introduced as "the burden of Nineveh" (v. 1), "burden" literally meaning "that which is lifted up," as the hands of a prophet when making a pronouncement of doom. In a context of judgment against "his adversaries" and "his enemies," God is described as "jealous," "avenging," and "wrathful" (v. 2, RSV).

God's might in judgment is first seen in disasters and convulsions of nature (vv. 3a-6). "Who can stand before his indignation?" asks Micah (v. 6) as he proceeds to describe God's dealings with his enemies (vv. 7–15).

These verses contain many problems for the student. It is not easy to distinguish God's words of assurance to his people and those of judgment against their enemies. An unnamed leader, "a wicked counsellor" (v. 11), is picked out for particular reproof. His name will not be perpetuated through offspring, his idols will be destroyed, and God will bury him (v. 14). On the other hand, Judah is given the "good tidings" that her religious festivals will be preserved (v. 15).

Special points.—Bashan, Carmel, and Lebanon (v. 4) may be mentioned as normally fruitful areas. Even they will languish in drought. God's judgmental actions will bring an utter end (vv. 8–9). There will be no "second time" for his enemies to repeat their aggressions (v. 9). History records that the Assyrians were engaged in drunken revelries when the city of Nineveh fell (v. 10).

The Fall of Nineveh (Nah. 2:1–13)

The passage.—Many times other cities had been alerted to the approach of

Assyrian armies. Now Nineveh itself is summoned to "man the ramparts" (v. 1, RSV). The enemy is described as "the shatterer" (RSV), that is, the coalition of Medes and Babylonians. Verse 2 is a parenthetical explanation of Nineveh's fate. "For the Lord is restoring the majesty of Jacob as the majesty of Israel, for plunderers have stripped them and ruined their branches" (RSV).

The picture of confusion in the besieged city (vv. 3–10) is a masterpiece of Hebrew poetry. Finally, the question is asked, "Where is the dwelling of the lions?" (v. 11). The lion was a favorite symbol in Assyria and here is appropriately used to describe the nation itself. To the Assyrian lion that once ravaged others (v. 12) the Lord says, "I am against thee" (v. 13). Divine retribution will overtake this tyrant race.

Special points.—Readers are again referred to the RSV for many improved translations in this chapter. For example, verse 5 is therein rendered, "The officers are summoned, they stumble as they go." Those who see verse 4 as a foreview of the modern automobile degrade the purpose of prophecy. The setting is Nineveh in the seventh century B.C.

Secular sources tell that the flooding of the Tigris added to the terrors of the siege (v. 6). Huzzab (v. 7) is thought to refer to the Assyrian queen. Verse 9 describes the spoiling of the city's treasures by her enemies. "Nineveh is like a pool whose waters run away. 'Halt! Halt!' they cry; but none turns back" (v. 8, RSV) graphically describes a people in flight who cannot be brought under control. In consequence of these fearful conditions the prophet exclaims, "Desolate! Desolation and ruin! Hearts faint and knees tremble" (v. 10, RSV).

Why Nineveh Fell (Nah. 3:1–19)

The passage.—The vivid word picture of Nineveh under siege continues into the opening verses of this chapter. The RSV captures the stark brutality of the language—"hosts of slain, heaps of corpses, dead bodies without end—they stumble over the bodies!" (v. 3).

Then the viewpoint changes. All this carnage is the result of Assyria's moral wickedness. She is described as a prostitute of "graceful and . . . deadly charms" who "betrays nations with her harlotries" (v. 4, RSV). The charge is the corruption of others by deceit. For this, Assyria will be treated as an immoral woman, exposed to public shame and derision (vv. 5–6).

Some time before, a great Egyptian city, No-amon (Thebes), has been overthrown in spite of protective waters (v. 8) and strong allies (v. 9). Nineveh will experience a like fate. In her death agony she will reel like a drunken man (v. 11). The city will fall as "firstripe figs" into the hands of the enemy (v. 12). In their helplessness, her defenders will be as "women"; her "gates" will be burned (v. 13).

In taunting words, the prophet tells the Assyrians to draw water and strengthen their defenses in preparation for the attack (v. 14). But this will be in vain. Let them multiply themselves as locusts (see RSV) and they will vanish away as do "grasshoppers . . . when the sun ariseth" (v. 17). No measures they may take to protect themselves will avail.

The final words of Nahum are addressed to the king of Assyria (vv. 18–19) whose "shepherds slumber," whose leaders are asleep. In consequence of their self-indulgent complacency, the nation is scattered beyond recovery. The wounds inflicted on Assyria are beyond cure, a fact that causes those who have suffered her cruelties to rejoice. "All who hear the news of you clap their hands over you. For upon whom has not come your unceasing evil?" (v. 19,

RSV).

Special points.—In the Old Testament, "whoredoms" ("harlotries," v. 7, RSV) usually refers to idolatry. Here it seems to apply to Assyria's commercial and military compacts with other nations who have been deceived into a relationship that is essentially immoral. Notice the charge, "Thou hast multiplied thy merchants" (v. 16). Besides engaging in military aggression, the nation had sought to enrich itself through the unscrupulous pursuit of trade.

Truth for today.—The theme of the wrath of God is avoided by many. Yet if there is to be a moral order God must act in judgment against sin. While the punishment of the individual offender lies beyond the grave, nations are called to account at the bar of history. "He that leadeth into captivity shall go into captivity; he that killeth with the sword must be killed with the sword" (Rev. 13:10).

No nation, however strong, can resist the outworkings of divine justice. The greatest aggressors of history have eventually come to a day of reckoning. Though retributive justice may seem slow in coming, yet it is certain and final.

But the mercy of God is to be seen even in his judgments. Israel of old and Christians of the first century were comforted in their afflictions by the knowledge that God's kingdom will prevail. This must be our confidence.

HABAKKUK

Donald F. Ackland

INTRODUCTION

Who has not been perplexed by events that challenged one's understanding of the character of God? And who has not wanted, in such circumstances, to take his questions direct to God? Habakkuk had his problems, asked his questions, and received God's answers. As a result of his dialogue with God, he exchanged his doubts and perplexities for a strong faith, expressed in chapter 3.

The reference to Chaldeans or Babylonians (1:6) helps us to date Habakkuk. In 605 B.C., Nebuchadnezzar of Babylon won a victory over the Egyptians at Carchemish that opened the Palestinian area to his conquests. Habakkuk 1 appropriately describes conditions either immediately before or after this event.

This places Habakkuk in the reigns of Jehoiakim and preceding kings (2 Kings 23:31—24:7). The social injustices mentioned in Habakkuk 1:2–4 also fit this period of Judah's history. Habakkuk and Jeremiah were contemporaries (Jer. 25–26).

Of Habakkuk the man nothing is known beyond this short book. Some see his name as that of a plant; others think it means "to embrace."

Questions and Answers (Hab. 1:1—2:4)

The passage.—Twice Habakkuk addresses God (1:2–4,12–17) and twice he receives answers (1:5–11; 2:1–4). His first questions are concerned with social injustices in his own land, matters that have long been the subject of his prayers (1:2). In conditions of widespread vio-lence the processes of justice have broken down: "the law is slacked, and judgment doth never do forth" (v. 4).

God's answer (1:5–11) adds to Habakkuk's perplexity. God is about to use "that bitter and hasty nation," the Chaldeans (v. 6), as the instrument of correction. Their ruthless conquests are described: they carry everything before them as they occupy the territory of others (v. 6); in the violence of their aggressions they follow their own standards of justice (v. 7); their mounted troops advance like ravening beasts (v. 8); they strike terror as they take multitudes captive (v. 9); none can resist them (v. 10); they make might their god (v. 11).

In reply, Habakkuk expresses his astonishment (1:12–17) that a holy God would use such an instrument to accomplish his purposes. Why would he permit a brutal invader to wage war that involves the innocent with the guilty, causing him to destroy "the man that is more righteous than he" (v. 13)? Habakkuk portrays the Chaldeans as treating "men as the fishes of the sea" (v. 14), heartlessly gathering them into the net of conquest as though they were worthless. Moreover, they make the implements of conquest the objects of worship (v. 16).

At this point Habakkuk takes his problem to a place of quiet retreat (2:1). His purpose is twofold: to listen attentively to God and to escape from the clamor of argument. We are led to suppose that his perplexities are widely shared and that he is beset by people who think he, as a prophet, should be able to answer them.

This time God instructs the prophet to "write the vision" (revelation) so plainly that it may be read by a man while running (2:2). Fulfilment, however, will not come immediately; it will be gradual, but certain (v. 3). This is particularly appropriate of the contents of verse 4, the full meaning of which awaited the coming of the gospel (Rom. 1:17). A better rendering of this important verse is: "Behold, he whose soul is not upright in him shall fail, but the righteous shall live by his faith" (RSV).

Special points.—Again prophecy is described as "the burden" (1:1), see comment on Nahum 1:1. The word came to refer to prophetic utterance. Habakkuk is also said to *see* his message since it came to him, as to other prophets, in visions (cf. 2:2). Verse 7 should be understood as saying that the Chaldeans have their own standards of justice. The phrase, "their faces shall sup up as the east wind" (v. 9), is a KJV attempt to handle an obscure passage. The RSV reads, "terror of them goes before them," but this is one among several suggestions. Verse 11 has similar problems for the translator.

An ancient Hebrew rendering of "we shall not die" (v. 12) reads "thou shalt not die," addressed to God. This conforms to the sense of the verse. The KJV word "drag" (v. 15) is rendered "seine" by RSV, that is, a net that is dragged.

The outstanding verse of Habakkuk is 2:4 which literally describes the man who is "puffed up," arrogant, self-sufficient. This aptly describes all offenders. There is good authority for "my soul is not well pleased with him." God takes no pleasure in self-centered sinners; "but the righteous shall live by his faith" (RSV).

The Five Woes (Hab. 2:5–20)

The passage.—Still referring to the "proud man" (v. 5), the prophet speaks in behalf of all nations and all people who are victims of his aggressions.

Woe to the plunderer of others for he himself shall be plundered (vv. 6b-8).

Woe to him who seeks wealth and security at the expense of others. Retribution will overtake him (vv. 9–11). This may have been spoken against Jehoiakim.

Woe to those who build cities by violence. People will not forever submit to working for nothing. And God's kingdom will prevail (vv. 12–14).

Woe to those who lead others into indulgence and immorality. They will drink from "the cup of the Lord's right hand," that is, his judgment. *Lebanon* is specifically mentioned as a scene of such gross behavior (vv. 15–17).

Woe to the maker of "dumb idols." His self-made gods have "no breath [spirit] at all," no teaching to give. But God reigns and all must give heed to him (vv. 18–20).

Special points.—The words "thick clay" (v. 6) are rendered "pledges" (RSV), that is, possessions of others obtained by oppression. For *"booties"* (v. 7) read "booty" (RSV), or "spoil." Verse 11 is a poetic way of saying that the house that is unethically obtained will become a snare to its owner. Verse 14, which echoes Isaiah 11:9, is a pearl of divine promise in an unlikely setting.

A Song of Faith (Hab. 3:1–19)

The passage.—This concluding psalm has given rise to the speculation that Habakkuk may have been a Levite, skilled in leading worship.

It opens with the prophet's prayer for God's intervention (v. 2) and proceeds to describe God coming forth to save his people (v. 13). There are many obscurities, but even with these the majestic movement of the psalm can be appreciated, specially in the RSV. The writer sees God on the march for the deliverance of his people. Hence, he concludes with a great statement of prevailing faith (vv. 17–19). Come what may, this man "will rejoice in the Lord" (v. 18).

Special points.—"Shigionoth" (v. 1) appears also in the title of Psalm 7. It may be a musical notation though some translate it "for adversity." The recurring word "Selah" (vv. 3,9,13), frequently found in the Psalms, is variously understood. It could be a musical instruction or a paragraph mark. The concluding words are rendered by the RSV—"To the choirmaster: with stringed instruments" (v. 19).

Truth for today.—Questions and doubts are inevitable for the thoughtful and concerned person. They should not be suppressed but brought into the light of divine revelation. God gives understanding to those who sincerely seek answers from him.

God's ways are not our ways. By sometimes inscrutable means he works out his purposes. He may even include unbelievers in his plans; but this does not mean that they will escape the penalty of their evil deeds. The "puffed up" person or nation must bear the consequences of his pride. The only way of salvation is the way of righteousness and faith.

ZEPHANIAH

Donald F. Ackland

INTRODUCTION

The theme of Zephaniah is readily recognizable by the frequency of the phrase, "the day of the Lord." To Zephaniah, "the day of the Lord" would be a time of universal judgment. Although efforts are made to relate his prophecies to events in or near his times, the probability is that the goal of his teaching was the consummation of all things. He saw the final triumph of good over evil and the ushering in of that kingdom which God himself would rule in righteousness (3:15).

Zephaniah's lineage is given to the fourth generation (1:1), making him the great-great-grandson of a man named Hizkiah (Hezekiah). If Judah's king of that name is indicated, which would seem to be the reason for the genealogy, Zephaniah was of royal blood. His name means "hidden of Jehovah."

The statement that God's commission came to him "in the days of Josiah" (1:1) raises the question as to whether he was active before or after the reforms of that king (2 Kings 22:1— 23:28). Since the evils denounced by Zephaniah correspond to those that occasioned Josiah's reforms, it is usually assumed that his ministry preceded them, around 625 B.C.

Judgment on Judah (Zeph. 1:1 to 2:3)

The passage.—There is a finality about the opening words of the prophecy (1:2–3) that suggests an ultimate and universal "day of the Lord" with justice triumphant and evil vanquished. But beginning with "Judah, and . . . all the inhabitants of Jerusalem" (v. 4), Zephaniah warns of approaching individual judgment on rebellious nations.

The warning is given at a time when the worship of Baal and other pagan practices are prevalent in Judah (1:4– 6). For those who engage in such idolatry "the day of the Lord" (v. 7) will come as "the day of the Lord's sacrifice" (v. 8) to which "he hath bid his guests" (v. 7). It was customary to summon people to a sacrifice (1 Sam. 16:2–5). This time, however, they are gathered to learn their fate.

As judgment approaches, cries are heard from various parts of Jerusalem (v. 10). None will escape of those who take the complacent, contemptuous attitude, "The Lord will not do good, neither will he do evil" (v. 12), that is, God is indifferent and will do nothing. Dreadful events will soon prove that God is active against evildoers.

But there is a way of escape from these judgments. The "shameless nation" (2:1, RSV) is called on to assemble in repentance "before you are driven away like the drifting chaff" (v. 2, RSV). The fate of the proud is sealed; but those who "seek righteousness, seek meekness" (humility) have hope of escape "in the day of the Lord's anger" (v. 3).

Special points.—For "the stumbling-blocks with the wicked" the RSV has, "I will overthrow the wicked" (1:3). "Chemarims" (v. 4) were priests of Baal. Practices condemned are: worshiping sun, moon, and stars on housetops

(Jer. 19:13) and combining the worship of God with that of idols (syncretism), "Malcham" being either Molech or Milcom, both pagan deities (v. 5); wearing foreign "apparel" (v. 8), probably in relation to worship; leaping over "the threshold," maybe explained by 1 Samuel 5:4–5, and "violence and deceit," or fraud (v. 9).

In 1:10–11, several sections of Jerusalem are mentioned: "the fish gate," "the Second Quarter" (RSV), "the hills," and the hollows (Maktesh). For "candles" (v. 12) read "lamps." The phrase "on their lees" refers to the thickening of wine when it is left unstirred. It is applied to those who have become settled in complacency and unconcern.

Judgment on the Nations (Zeph. 2:4–15)

The passage.—Zephaniah broadens his message now to include Philistia (vv. 4–7), Moab and Ammon (vv. 8–11), Ethiopia (v. 12), and Assyria (vv. 13–15). If we take "Ethiopians" (v. 12) to mean Egyptians, all these people had at some time or another been oppressors of Israel.

Of Philistia it is said that she shall be destroyed and left with no inhabitant (v. 5). The people of Judah will occupy her coastal plain (v. 7). Moab and Ammon will be overthrown as completely as Sodom, and . . . as Gomorrah (v. 9). At this point the prophet anticipates the time when God will prove his superiority over idols "and men shall worship him, every one from his place" (v. 11).

The fate of the Ethiopians (Egyptians? v. 12) is briefly stated. Assyria, represented by its capital, Nineveh (vv. 13–15), indulgent, complacent, and boastful ("I am and there is none beside me"), meets its nemesis as "a desolation, a place for beasts to lie down in!" And so it is.

Special points.—Gaza, Ashkelon, Ashdod, and Ekron (v. 4) were all Philistine cities. Cherethites (v. 5) is an alternative for Philistines. "O Canaan" may be a mistranslation; some versions so treat it.

In the description of the coming desolation of Assyria, the RSV has many interesting variations: "Herds shall lie down in the midst of her, all the beasts of the field; the vulture and the hedgehog shall lodge in her capitals; the owl shall hoot in the window, the raven croak on the threshold; for her cedar work will be laid bare" (v. 14). What a fate for "the rejoicing city that dwelt carelessly" (v. 15)!

Appeal to Jerusalem (Zeph. 3:1–8)

The passage.—Although Jerusalem is not named as "the oppressing city" (v. 1) references to "her God" (v. 2) and "the law" (v. 4) leave us in no doubt. Four classes are specifically condemned: princes (officers, RSV), judges, prophets, and priests (vv. 3–4). In each case, their conduct is a betrayal of their trust. In contrast, God is described as "righteous" (RSV); "he will not do iniquity" (v. 5).

The fate of other nations should have been an example to Jerusalem (v. 6). So the Lord hoped (v. 7a). But the city persisted in its sin: "they rose early, and corrupted all their doings" (v. 7). Verse 8 is probably an appeal to any in Jerusalem who will respond to the prophet's warnings by turning to God whose judgments are certain.

The Lord's Remnant (Zeph. 3:9–20)

The passage.—Although verses 12–13 probably refer to the remnant of Judah that would return from exile, the passage as a whole anticipates the gathering together of the redeemed and the establishment of God's spiritual kingdom. God will call out for himself a cleansed people who will come from far places to worship him (v. 10). The shame of past sin will be put away and pride will give place to a humble spirit (v. 11).

In the new Jerusalem there will be freedom from fear because "The Lord thy God in the midst of thee is mighty" (v. 17). He will defend his people over whom he will reign as king (v. 15). "He will renew you in his love; he will exult over you with loud singing" (v. 17, RSV). Because of this gracious relationship, God's redeemed remnant will "get them praise and fame in every land where they have been put to shame" (v. 19). The vindication of the saints is the theme of Zephaniah as of John in Revelation.

Special points.—"Pure language" (v. 9) is literally "pure lips." This is Zephaniah's parallel to Isaiah 6:5–7. Some authorities revise verse 10 to mean that God's worshipers (suppliants) will come from the south (rivers of Ethiopia) to furthest north, a universal gathering. The phrase "for the solemn assembly" (v. 18) may be the conclusion to verse 17, as in the RSV, which continues: "I will remove disaster from you, so that you will not bear reproach for it."

Truth for today.—The recent "God is dead" philosophy was anticipated in Zephaniah's day by those who said, "The Lord will not do good, neither will he do evil" (1:12). To such expressions of unbelief the activity of God in history provides the answer. He visits the consequences of transgression on all, Hebrew and Gentile alike.

There is a glorious goal, however, even to God's works of judgment. His chastisements are intended to purge and transform. In place of the evil kingdoms of this world he will set up his own spiritual kingdom in which the redeemed remnant will be forever secure.

HAGGAI

Donald F. Ackland

INTRODUCTION

After destroying Jerusalem in 587 B.C., Nebuchadnezzar sent its people into exile in Babylon. Fifty years later, Babylon itself was overthrown by Cyrus, king of Persia, who gave permission for the Jews to return home (Ezra 1–2). One of the first acts of the repatriates was to rebuild the Temple altar (3:2) and lay the foundations for a new sanctuary (3:10). But the schemes of their adversaries resulted in a ban on further work (Ezra 4). Although this ban was lifted by Darius (6:7), the people were disinclined to resume building until God sent two prophets, Haggai and Zechariah (5:1), to stimulate them for the task.

Our knowledge of Haggai is confined to the statements of Ezra and the opening verse of Haggai's prophecy. His name means "festive," suggesting that he might have been born during a religious festival. Some interpret 2:3 to indicate that Haggai himself had seen Solomon's Temple, which would make him an old man. But this is conjecture. His book consists of four messages (1:1–15; 2:1–9,10–19,20–23) all delivered within a four-month period in the year 520 B.C., "the second year of Darius" (1:1).

Reproach for Delay (Hag. 1:1–15)

The passage.—Speaking as the mouthpiece of God, Haggai addresses first the leadership and then the people themselves. Though they are offering excuses for carrying forward the building of God's house, they have provided homes for themselves (vv. 2,4). Perhaps part of their excuse is their impoverished condition (v. 6); but this, says the prophet, is God's visitation expressing his displeasure (v. 9). He calls on them to bestir themselves, gather needed materials, and return to work (v. 8).

Haggai's exhortations are heeded. Twenty-four days after hearing the prophet's words the people return to their task, encouraged by the assurance, "I am with you, saith the Lord" (v. 13). The will to work is quickly followed by the promise of divine help.

Special points.—Zerubbabel was grandson of Jehoiachin, king of Judah at the time of the Babylonian conquest. Joshua was grandson of the high priest of the same period (v. 1). Both men, presumably, were born in Babylon.

For "ceiled houses" (v. 4) it is usual to understand homes with wood paneling, a luxury for those days. However, the prevailing state of poverty casts doubt on this interpretation. The word can mean "roofed." The people's homes were complete whereas God's house was unfinished. The phrase, "a bag with holes" (v. 6), is readily understood by those who have experienced inflation. Money no sooner comes than it goes!

Exhortation to Build (Hag. 2:1–9)

The passage.—About a month after work is resumed, Haggai brings another message from the Lord. He begins by recognizing the physical inferiority of the new Temple compared with that of

Solomon (v. 3). See Ezra 3:12. Then he encourages his listeners with promises. Repeated assurance of divine help is given (vv. 4–5). God will work mightily in his universe in their behalf to provide "the treasures of all nations" (v. 7, RSV) for the embellishment of his house. It will be greater in glory than Solomon's Temple (v. 9).

Special points.—The returned exiles are referred to as "the residue of the people" (cf. "remnant of the people," 1:14). Not all Jews returned from Babylon to Palestine. The cosmic upheavals (v. 6) associated with the statement, "I will shake all nations" (v. 7) could describe the conditions of widespread disorder prevailing around the year 520 B.C. Many countries were in revolt against Persia and Greek influence was increasing. The point is that God will so control history that honor will be brought to his house.

Although "the desire of all nations" (v. 7) has often been referred to the Messiah, the translation is faulty and should read "the treasures of all nations" (RSV). We may more confidently see messianic promises in verse 9.

Promise of Blessing (Hag. 2:10–19)

The passage.—After an interval of two months, the Lord speaks again through his prophet. Questions are addressed to the priests. Does the possession of "holy flesh," meat consecrated to God, mean that everything touched by it will be rendered holy? The answer is no. But, on the other hand, that which is ritually unclean, does it not defile everything in contact with it? The fact that this is so makes the point that evil spreads its influence more readily than good. The neglect of God's house is an evil that has infected the life of the nation.

The consequences are seen in the fail-

ure of crops (vv. 16–17). But now that the people have changed their ways better days are before them. Behind the questions of verse 19 are promises of coming blessing. There will be seed in their barns and their trees will again produce.

Encouragement for a Leader (Hag. 2:20–23)

The passage.—This was a second message in one day (v. 20). Once again mention is made of cataclysmic events. Their immediate significance is for Zerubbabel. Under the direction of God, these happenings will bring advancement to him. God will make him "as a signet" (v. 23), a ring indicative of assigned authority. Of his grandfather, Jehoiachin (here called *Coniah*), God had said if he were "the signet upon my right hand, yet would I pluck thee thence" (Jer. 22:24–25). But for the man who has led the restoration of the Temple God has honors in store.

Special points.—Many see the violent events of 22–23 as those that introduce the messianic age. The promise to Zerubbabel is also interpreted in terms of messianic purpose. He would continue the Davidic line of kings and foreshadow in himself the coming great Deliverer. Zerubbabel has a place in Luke's genealogy of our Lord where he is called Zorobabel (Luke 3:27).

Truth for today.—The function of God's messengers is defined in the ministry of Haggai. He spoke only as the Lord directed him and faded into the background as he faithfully discharged his mission.

The book of Haggai is a commentary on the truth, "Them that honour me I will honour, and they that despise me shall be lightly esteemed" (1 Sam. 2:30). The ingratitude of the human heart is illustrated in a failure to fulfil a clear duty to the Lord who had brought his people back from exile. Our readiness to find excuses for default in spiritual obligations is exposed in their conduct. How soon initial enthusiasm in doing God's will can be lost!

But the long-suffering patience of God is evidenced in his willingness to forgive and bless. While his chosen people continued to display characteristic instability, he was working out his purposes toward the day when he would "give peace" (Hag. 2:9) through his Messiah-King.

ZECHARIAH

Donald F. Ackland

INTRODUCTION

Of the three books that bear the names of prophets of the restoration, Zechariah's is by far the longest and the most difficult to understand. Haggai dealt with practical matters in a plain, direct style. Malachi's message is carefully organized. Zechariah, however, though concerned with Haggai about the building of the Temple (1:16; 4:9; 6:12–15), used a complicated and varied style and dealt not only with immediate issues but also with future, end-of-the-age events.

The book of Zechariah falls into two sections. In chapters 1–8 the setting is mainly historic as the prophet addresses himself to the need for completing the Temple. In chapters 9–14 his eyes are on the future, chiefly in the context of messianic expectation and the coming "day of the Lord" (14:1).

Zechariah is described as "the son of Berechiah, the son of Iddo the prophet" (1:1) and as "the son of Iddo" in Ezra 5:1. The probability is that, in the Ezra passage, "son" is used in the sense of "descendant." In Nehemiah 12:16 Zechariah's name appears in a list of priests. There are reasons for considering him a young man, born during the Babylonian exile. His name means "Jehovah has remembered."

A Call to Repentance (Neh. 1:1–6)

The passage.—Two months after "the word of the Lord" first came to Haggai (Hag. 1:1), God called Zechariah into service (1:1). Hence, we can date this prophecy as beginning in 520 B.C. during the ministry of Haggai. The reference to "the fourth year of king Darius" in 7:1 indicates that Zechariah prophesied for at least two years. We do not know whether he lived to see the dedication of the restored Temple in the sixth year of Darius (515 B.C.).

Under instruction from the Lord, Zechariah calls the people to repentance. He reminds them, doubtless with reference to the Exile, of God's displeasure with their fathers (v. 2). Prophets had been sent among them, "but they did not hear, nor hearken" (v. 4). The fathers and their prophets have died, but the message is still valid (v. 6). In this verse, some authorities read "you" instead of "your fathers." If this reading is accepted, the latter part of verse 6 becomes the response of Zechariah's audience. They acknowledge the justice of God's ways and repent of their sins.

Truth for today.—The primary purpose of God's communication to men is to call them from sin to repentance and forgiveness.

The Heavenly Horsemen (Zech. 1:1–17)

Exactly two months after the foundation stone of the Temple was laid (Hag. 2:18), "upon the four and twentieth day of the eleventh month" (1:7), Zechariah begins to rehearse a series of eight visions followed by a coronation scene (1:7—6:8). His purpose is to encourage the people to proceed with the building and bring it to completion.

The passage.—In a night vision, the prophet sees horsemen riding mounts of different colors, with a rider upon *a red horse* in the foreground (v. 8). He sees also an *angel* (v. 9) of whom he asks, "O my lord, what are these?" The rider on the red horse explains that the horsemen are God's "patrols" (RSV) engaged in a mission of inspection. Thereupon, Zechariah hears their report: "all the earth sitteth still, and is at rest" (v. 11).

The rider on the red horse, now described as "the angel of the Lord," intercedes with God in behalf of "Jerusalem and . . . the cities of Judah" (v. 12). The Lord's answer becomes the prophet's message. The prevailing peace does not mean that God is indifferent or inactive. He is "jealous for Jerusalem" (v. 14) and angry with "the nations" (RSV) "that are at ease" for their harsh treatment of his people (v. 15). The Temple and city of Jerusalem will be rebuilt (v. 16), and all the cities of Judah will "overflow with prosperity" (RSV) with Jerusalem again favored of God (v. 17).

Special points.—We must resist the temptation to speculate on all the details of the vision. The *myrtle trees* (v. 8) were a common feature of the Jerusalem landscape; *the bottom* describes a valley or "glen" (RSV). The full period of Babylonian exile was *three score and ten years* (v. 12; see Jer. 25:11).

Truth for today.—God is at all times fully informed on earthly events and has a master plan for establishing justice and introducing eternal felicity and peace.

The Four Horns and Carpenters (Zech. 1:18–21)

The passage.—The second vision relates to God's statement in verse 15. Zechariah sees *four horns* (v. 18), frequently used in the Bible as symbols of

power (Mic. 4:13). They represent nations that *have scattered Judah, Israel, and Jerusalem* (v. 19). Then God shows the prophet *four carpenters,* or "smiths" (RSV). Their task is to *fray* (or, "make afraid") the horns (v. 21). The RSV has "terrify them." These destructive nations are themselves reduced to fear as they are *cast out,* destroyed.

Special points.—Perhaps the number four is chosen to represent all enemies of Israel from North, South, East, and West. Their offence is stated in verse 15. God had appointed them instruments of his justice, but they had been excessive in cruelty.

Truth for today.—Ruthless aggressors are destined to be destroyed as God provides his own instruments of judgment.

The Man with the Measuring Line (Zech. 2:1–13)

The passage.—If the Jews contemplated rebuilding Jerusalem as a walled city, this third vision may have had the purpose of dissuading them. However, the contents of this chapter have meanings reaching beyond the circumstances of Zechariah and his times.

The prophet sees *a man with a measuring line in his hand* (v. 1), evidently in preparation for building walls. One angel sends another to tell the *young man* that Jerusalem will not need walls (v. 4). Its condition will be like that of unwalled villages whose inhabitants, men and animals alike, will live in unrestricted freedom. God himself will be the city's defence and *the glory in the midst of her* (v. 5).

In view of this prospect, the prophet sounds a call to Jews still in exile to join their repatriated brethren (vv. 6–9). God is about to act in judgment against offending nations. His sensitivity for his afflicted people is conveyed in the statement: "He that toucheth you toucheth the apple [pupil] of his eye" (v. 8).

Then Zechariah breaks forth into a song of joy (vv. 10–13) which seems, in part, to describe conditions in the gospel age. God's presence among his people, who include *many nations* (v. 11), indicates that the church is in view. The closing verses show God as ready to descend from *his holy habitation* (heaven) to invest the new earthly sanctuary with his presence (vv. 12–13).

Special points.—Babylon was to the east of Palestine. The description, *the land of the north* (v. 6), may be accounted for by the fact that the highway to Babylon took a northward course before veering east. The phrase, *After the glory* (v. 8) is obscure and is variously explained. But the context is clear: God will vindicate his people by turning the tables on their enemies. The oppressed will become the oppressors (v. 9).

Truth for today.—We need to be sure that our measuring lines are adequate for God's plans. Those who trust in him can afford high hopes and wide horizons.

The Cleansing of the High Priest (Zech. 3:1–10)

The passage.— Zechariah now sees "Joshua the high priest" (Hag. 1:1) being accused by Satan of unworthiness for his office. The Lord immediately rebukes Satan and describes Jerusalem (represented in Joshua) as "a brand plucked out of the fire" (v. 2), that is, brought back from exile by God's action and for his purposes. Orders are given to remove Joshua's *filthy garments* and give him a complete change of raiment (vv. 4–5).

The high priest is now charged by God to "walk in my ways" (guard his personal life) and "keep my charge" (fulfil the responsibilities of his office). If he will do these he will judge (rule)

God's house and "have right of access" (RSV) to the court of heaven itself (v. 7).

There follow several messianic promises to Joshua and his companions who are described as "men of good omen" (v. 8, RSV). The terms "servant," "branch," and "stone" are all familiar Old Testament designations of the Messiah (Isa. 52:13; Jer. 23:5; Isa. 28:16).

The description of the stone as having *seven eyes* (v. 9) should probably be understood in the light of 4:10. God's eyes will be on the stone to give it protection and purpose. The inscription on the stone appears to be related to the statement: "I will remove the iniquity of that land in one day." This was basically an assurance of divine cleansing for Jerusalem, its priest and people (see 5:5–11). But the words are most significant applied to the atoning work of Christ.

Truth for today.—God needs cleansed instruments for his work (2 Tim. 2:21). Though the best of men sometimes succumb to sin, there is cleansing provided in Christ (1 John 1:7,9).

The Golden Candlesticks and Two Olive Trees (Zech. 4:1–14)

The passage.—Following the promise of pardon comes a promise of power addressed to Zerubbabel (vv. 6–10), governor of the returned exiles (Hag. 1:1). Zechariah sees a golden lampstand with seven lamps supplied with oil from a bowl on the top of the lampstand. On either side of the lampstand are olive trees.

The interest of the prophet centers in the olive trees of which he asks, "What are these, my lord?" The attending angel does not answer but speaks a word from God to Zerubbabel. His monumental task of rebuilding the Temple will be successfully concluded. This will be done "Not by might, nor by power, but by my spirit." The headstone will be laid to accompanying cheers ("Grace, grace unto it," v. 7).

Again Zechariah asks, "What are these two olive trees . . . ?" The "two anointed ones" of the answer (v. 14) are probably Zerubbabel and Joshua, the political and spiritual leaders respectively.

Special points.—In a number of ways, this is the most difficult vision of the eight. This is recognized in Zechariah's own questions. Although some of the details of the lampstand and its oil supply are ambiguous, the intended message comes through clearly. Assurance is given of a task carried through to completion by the supply of God's Spirit.

Verse 10 is clarified in the RSV which reads: "For whoever has despised the day of small things shall rejoice, and shall see the plummet in the hands of Zerubbabel. These seven are the eyes of the Lord. . . ." Here human endeavor and divine oversight and protection are brought into relationship. As Zerubbabbel works the Lord watches over his activity to prosper it.

Truth for today.—No matter how difficult the task, those who do the Lord's work may trust in his enduement of adequate enabling. His servants today have the resource of the indwelling Holy Spirit.

The Flying Book (Zech. 5:1–4)

The passage.—In the sixth vision, the prophet sees a flying scroll of unusual proportions (30 by 15 feet). Its message is one of judgment addressed particularly to those who steal and swear falsely by God's name. Presumably theft and profane oaths were common sins that were hindering the operation of God's will for his people.

The Woman and the Measure (Zech. 5: 5–11)

The passage.—This time the prophet sees an *ephah,* that is, a measuring vessel. Like the scroll of the previous vision, it is of abnormal size. Inside is a woman to whom the interpreting angel gives the name *wickedness* (v. 8). When she tries to get out of the vessel, the angel shuts her in with "a talent of lead" ("leaden cover," v. 7, RSV). Then two other women with wings like a stork pick up the ephah and carry it to "the land of Shinar" (v. 11), or Babylonia.

However strange this vision may seem to us, it graphically suggests the ridding of the land of Judah of sin and wickedness. It anticipates the new Jerusalem of which it is said, "There shall in no wise enter into it anything that defileth" (Rev. 21:27).

The Four Chariots (Zech. 6:1–8)

The passage.—The last of the visions is of *four chariots* proceeding from between *mountains of brass* (v. 1). Attention is focused on two of the chariots that go *into the north country* (v. 6), that is, toward Babylon (see comment on 2:6). The final words of the vision are, "Behold, these that go toward the north country have quieted my spirit in the north country" (v. 8). The work of judgment against Babylon being complete, the wrath of God is appeased.

A Messianic Incident (Zech. 6:9–15)

The passage.—The visions being concluded, Zechariah is instructed to take certain prominent repatriates to "the house of Josiah" (v. 10; to gather *silver and gold* for the purpose of making *crowns* to put on the head of "Joshua . . . the high priest" (v. 11).

In doing this, Zechariah is to speak prophetic words concerning "the man whose name is The BRANCH" (see comment on 3:8), who shall be "a priest upon his throne" (vv. 12–13). The reference to Christ, who is both priest and king, is unmistakable (Heb. 8:1). The Temple that he builds is his church into whose service not only Jews but also "they that are far off" are called (v. 15; Eph. 2:13).

To mark the importance of the occasion, instruction is given to place the crowns in the Temple as a memorial (v. 14).

Special points.—Some scholars believe that the name of *Joshua* the priest has been substituted here for Zerubbabel, governor of Jerusalem. But the messianic purpose of this coronation is best served by the character of Joshua who in name ("Hoshua" is the Hebrew form of "Jesus") and office (priest-king) typifies the person of our Lord.

Truth for today.—The Lord provides men for his work and, in the outworkings of history, has raised up a supreme Builder who takes men and women and uses them as stones for his spiritual temple (1 Cor. 3:16; 1 Pet. 2:5).

Obedience Better than Fasting (Zech. 7: 1–7)

The passage.—Now (7:1—8:23) comes a historic interlude for which the actual date is given (7:1). Two years have passed since Zechariah's call (1:1). Some men come from Bethel ("the house of God," v. 2) with a question concerning fasts instituted during the Exile (v. 3). Should these be continued now that the Temple is being rebuilt?

Zechariah's reply falls into four parts each of them introduced by the same phrase, "The word of the Lord came."

In answering (vv. 4–7), the prophet goes to the heart of all religious practice. What is the motive of this fasting? He mentions two fasts in particular: that of the fifth month which commem-

orated the burning of Jerusalem (Jer. 52:12–13) and that of the seventh month which recalled the murder of Gedaliah, governor of Jerusalem (Jer. 41:1–2).

These fasts, Zechariah charges, are self-centered: "did not ye eat for yourselves, and drink for yourselves?" (v. 6). As with so much religious activity, God is left out. The people need to return to the teaching of former prophets from which they could learn the things that please God (v. 7).

The Message of the Prophets (Zech. 7: 8–14)

The passage.—Renewed in his awareness that he is speaking for God, Zechariah spells out the message of the prophets which, if responded to, would have prevented the disaster of exile. In the spirit of Isaiah and Amos, he declares God's demand for social justice with the plain implication that the things condemned were the things practiced "when Jerusalem was inhabited and in prosperity" (v. 7). The spirit in which the former generations of Israel spurned the prophets' pleas is shown in the statement: They refused to hearken, and pulled away the shoulder, and stopped their ears" (v. 11).

This answer to the inquirers from Bethel, therefore, becomes a lesson from history. Instead of fussing about the observance of fast days, these people need to profit from the past and do these things that are really acceptable to God. For failure to do so, their fathers went into captivity (v. 14). Note the tragic words of verse 13—"as he cried, and they would not hear; so they cried, and I would not hear."

Truth for today.—The tendency to make religion an end in itself persists. There is continuing need to heed the teaching of psalmists, prophets, and apostles—and of Jesus himself—that the acceptable worshiper is he who fulfils his duty toward both God and man.

Prospects of Restoration (8:1–17)

The passage.—Historic sequence is maintained as Zechariah proceeds from the scattering of the people (7:14) to their restoration. This is the work of the Lord who is "jealous for Zion with great jealousy" (v. 2). Glorious prospects are offered for the future of Jerusalem: the old will dwell in healthful security and children will play unthreatened and carefree (vv. 4–5). That which is too marvellous to believe will come to pass (v. 6). Further repatriations of exiled Jews are promised (vv. 7–8). These verses may be read as an anticipation of gospel ingatherings the world around.

In light of these things, the people are encouraged to new effort (vv. 9–15). Great changes have taken place since they responded to the challenge of prophets, such as Haggai, to proceed with the building of the Temple. God's attitude toward them has changed (v. 11) in consequence of which harvests will be plentiful (v. 12). Therefore, "fear not, but let your hands be strong" (v. 13).

The promises of God should not be received with presumption but in earnest desire to measure up to his requirements. Hence the prophet's exhortations to high standards of social morality (vv. 16–17).

When Fasts Become Feasts (Zech. 8:18–23)

The passage.—The answers to the question of 7:3 conclude with a promise that, conditional upon a right response to the Lord's moral requirements (7:9–10; 8:16–17), the fasts of the Exile will become cheerful feasts (v. 19). To the two fasts previously mentioned

(7:5) are added two more: in the fourth month for Nebuchadnezzar's capture of Jerusalem (Jer. 52:6) and in the tenth month for the siege of the city (Jer. 52:4).

The felicity of God's people will result in Jerusalem becoming a place of international worship as "many people and strong nations shall come to seek the Lord of hosts in Jerusalem, and to pray before the Lord" (v. 22). In verse 23, "ten men" means "a considerable number." This whole paragraph is appropriate to the Pentecostal events of Acts 2 and subsequent Gentile ingatherings into the church as the result of the preaching of the gospel by Jewish believers.

Truth for today.—A more obvious element of joy in our Christian living would be a magnetic appeal to others, who would say, "We will go with you" (v. 23).

Israel Preserved and Blessed (Zech. 9:1—10:12)

The passage.—At this point we enter the second half of the prophecy, attributed by many to the later years of Zechariah. These concluding chapters contain much that is obscure. At the same time, they have a rich messianic content, second only to the writings of Isaiah.

For "burden" (9:1) see comments on Nahum 1:1 and Habakkuk 1:1. Problems of interpretation begin with 9:1 which is considerably changed by the RSV: "The word of the Lord is against the land of Hadrach and will rest upon Damascus. For to the Lord belong the cities of Aram, even as all the tribes of Israel." Zechariah foretells the judgment of God against Israel's enemies: the Syrians (vv. 1–2a); the Phoenicians (vv. 2b–4); and the Philistines (vv. 5–6). The last mentioned are to be converted to Judaism and will become "a remnant for our God" (v. 7, RSV) and assimilated into the nation "as a Jebusite" (Josh. 15:63).

Before proceeding to other descriptions of divine action against his people's foes, Zechariah introduces the coming Redeemer-King (9:9–10). In Matthew 21:5 and John 12:15 his words are applied to Christ's entry into Jerusalem. This royal visitor of humble mien will give peace to his people and to the nations and will reign "even to the ends of the earth."

In a sudden return to his previous theme, the prophet now offers the prospect of release for "prisoners out of the pit" (9:11) as God makes Judah his bow and Ephraim (Israel) his arrow (see RSV). The reference to Greece (v. 13) anticipates the campaigns of Alexander, 200 years later. Victory is assured because "The Lord of hosts shall defend them" (v. 15). Verse 17, and possibly 10:1, describe the restored productivity of the land.

Further assurances of success against their enemies are found in 10:3–5. In addition, Zechariah sees a time of restoration for the Northern Kingdom of Israel (the house of Joseph, v. 6; Ephraim, v. 7). Though widely scattered, God says "they shall remember me in far countries" (v. 9) and be brought back from Egypt and Assyria (v. 10). In the second century B.C. there were considerable colonies of Jews in both places. They were to return in such numbers that "place shall not be found for them" (v. 10). In fact, Zechariah compares their repatriation to a second Exodus (v. 11a).

God's Shepherd Rejected (Zech. 11:1–17)

The passage.—The sudden transition from promises of blessing to new calamities (11:1) should remind us that there were probably intervals between Zechariah's utterances. Here (vv. 1–3) he

describes the ravages of an enemy advancing from North to South through Lebanon and Bashan to "the jungle of the Jordan" (v. 3, RSV).

A call comes to the prophet to "Feed the flock of the slaughter" ("the flock doomed to slaughter," v. 4, RSV), who are oppressed by their owners (possessors) and leaders (shepherds, v. 5). In responding, Zechariah chooses two staffs which he calls "Beauty" (grace) and "Bands" (union). They typify the principles of God's government of his people, namely, to bless and unite them. Also he removes "three shepherds" (leaders) apparently in the interest of the flock (v. 8a).

But for all his care, the people behave so badly that the prophet "loathed them" (v. 8) and he accordingly breaks the staff Beauty in token that he quits his job. Having asked for his wages, he is given thirty pieces of silver (v. 12), which the Lord describes ironically as a "lordly price" and tells the prophet to cast the money into "the treasury in the house of the Lord" (v. 13, RSV). Having done this, the prophet breaks his other staff, symbolizing the future scattering of Israel. Under God's instruction, Zechariah next impersonates a foolish (worthless, RSV) shepherd to dramatize the punishment that will befall a disobedient, ungrateful people (vv. 15–17).

Special points.—In Zechariah's first impersonation (vv. 4–14) Christians see a portrayal of the Good Shepherd whose God-assigned mission of redemption was rejected by the Jews of his day. The thirty pieces of silver, the price of a slave (Ex. 21:32), was the amount paid to Judas for betraying Jesus (Matt. 26:15). Matthew recognizes this as fulfilment of prophecy which, however, he attributes to Jeremiah, not Zechariah (Matt. 27:9). Among several proffered explanations is that Jeremiah is placed first among the prophets in the Hebrew canon and the whole section of the Old Testament may have been named accordingly.

God's Purposes for Judah (Zech. 12:1–14)

The passage.—The final message of Zechariah begins at 12:1, introduced as before (9:1) as "The burden of the word of the Lord." The repetition in this last section of the book of the phrase "in that day" (12:3,4,6, etc.) may be taken to mean that the prophet is looking beyond contemporary history to events in the undefined future.

Chapter 12 begins with a statement of the creative power of God (v. 1) who promises, through his prophet, to "defend the inhabitants of Jerusalem" (v. 8). Zechariah uses a number of analogies—"cup of trembling" (v. 2), "burdensome stone" (v. 3), "hearth of fire," and "torch of fire" (v. 6)—to describe the triumph of the city over its adversaries. The people living in the surrounding country (the tents of Judah) will be saved first and those within the city will not have cause to boast (v. 7). God himself will be the deliverer and will make the feeble strong "as David" and the royal house "as God," or, "as a god" (v. 8).

The greatest blessing from God will be a "spirit of grace and of supplications" (v. 10). In repentance for their sin, "they shall look upon me whom they have pierced," a statement referred in John 19:37 to the Lord Jesus. Zechariah describes the intensity of the people's mourning (vv. 11–14). Men and women of all families will join in "a great mourning in Jerusalem."

The Purifying of the People (13:1–9)

The passage.—Repentance leads to cleansing. So the prophet speaks of a coming day when there shall be "a fountain opened . . . for sin and for uncleanness" (v. 1). For ultimate fulfilment we must look to the cross. Repentance will also produce reform: idols will be put away (v. 2) and false prophets will be eliminated (vv. 3–6). So thoroughly will this be done that parents of a false prophet will put him to death and the guilty will try to hide their identity. Verse 6 may relate to a man who is seeking to explain scars that others conclude to have been obtained in the observance of pagan rituals.

The Lord himself is now heard saying, "Awake, O sword, against my shepherd" (v. 7). This shepherd stands in unique relationship to God, being described as "my fellow" ("the man who stands next to me," RSV). Our Lord referred this verse to himself in Matthew 26:31. After the shepherd is smitten, the sheep are scattered, although there is reason to believe that "I will turn my hand upon the little ones" (v. 7) is a pledge of protection for some. Those who have come under God's displeasure, presumably for their treatment of the shepherd, are purged by chastisement. The purpose is one of grace for a remnant return to God and are received and acknowledged by him (v. 9).

"The Day of the Lord" (Zech. 14:1–21)

The passage.—Once again Zechariah sees Jerusalem as a ravaged city (vv. 1–2), suffering the worst consequences of siege and enemy occupation. Some regard this as a prophecy of the fall of Jerusalem to the Romans (70 A.D.). Since it is impossible to fit the rest of the chapter into such a scheme of historical interpretation, it seems better to recognize the chapter as a symbolic description of the conflict between good and evil and the final victory of the Lord.

When the enemy has done his worst against the Holy City and its inhabitants,

"Then shall the Lord go forth, and fight
against those nations" (v. 3). The reference to the mount of Olives (v. 4) recalls the promise of Acts 1:10–12 that
this will be the site of Christ's return.
As the feet of the descending Lord touch
the mountain, a great cleft is made that
provides a way of escape for the beleaguered survivors in Jerusalem (vv. 4–5).
Natural convulsions (vv. 7–8,10–11)
frame the proclamation that "the Lord
shall be king over all the earth" (v. 9).

Descriptions of judgment on those nations that fought against Jerusalem follow (vv. 12–15). Those who escape turn
to the worship of God and "keep the
feast of tabernacles" in Jerusalem (v.
16). The disaster of drought is pronounced on "whoso will not come" (v.
17).

Finally, the prophet sees "in that day"
a new Jerusalem wholly consecrated to
God (vv. 20–21). The "bells of the
horses," representing secular life, will
bear the same inscription as the head-
dress of the high priest (Ex. 28:36).
Domestic cooking vessels will be used
for the ritual of the Temple. In short,
the distinction between secular and sacred will be abolished, for all will be
yielded to the service of God.

Special points.—Azal cannot be positively identified as a place name. See

alternative rendering in RSV. For "the
earthquake" (v. 5) see comment on
Amos 1:1. "Geba to Rimmon" (v. 10)
describes the boundaries of Judah. The
reference to Egypt (v. 18) is probably
an acknowledgement that since that
country depended on the Nile for irrigation, some other punishment would be
devised for it (see v. 18, RSV). An alternative rendering of "the Canaanite"
(v. 21) is "a trader" (RSV); see John
2:14. But the meaning may be that the
new Jerusalem will be free from those
who would pollute it, Canaanites being
idolators (Rev. 21:27).

Truth for today.—Through the many
obscurities of ancient prophecy shine
glimpses of a coming Redeemer-King.
Though the portrait was blurred and incomplete, many among the Jews cherished the hope of Messiah's coming and
lived in daily expectation of his appearing.

To us is given the inestimable blessing of living after his coming and in the
realized benefits of his life and death.
An obligation to witness to Jesus as Savior and Lord is the consequence of our
privilege. Moreover, there are other
promises yet to be fulfilled that should
keep us alert for his return to set up his
eternal kingdom.

MALACHI

Donald F. Ackland

INTRODUCTION

The historical situation of the third of the prophets of the restoration was very different from that of Haggai or Zechariah. The Temple had been restored and its services resumed. Indeed, sufficient time had elapsed for the priesthood to become degenerate and the worshipers in the Lord's house careless concerning sacrifices and offerings. Intermarriage with foreigners and divorce were common, and a spirit of cynicism possessed the people.

Similar conditions prevailed during Nehemiah's period as governor and were the occasion of his reforms (Neh. 10: 28–39; 12:44–47; 13:10–13,23–31). It is thought, therefore, that Malachi prophesied during Nehemiah's governorship, possibly during his visit to Babylon (Neh. 13:6). This would date him some 80 or 90 years after Haggai and Zechariah.

Malachi means "my messenger," which could be a personal name. Another possibility is that "My Messenger" is the title of the book, based on 3:1. The division into four chapters disregards the design of the prophecy, which consists of seven groups of affirmation, objection, and elaboration.

God's Love Declared (Mal. 1:1–5)

The passage.—Verse 2 sets the pattern for the entire message: affirmation, "I have loved you"; objection, "Wherein hast thou loved us?"; elaboration, "Was not Esau Jacob's brother?" to end of verse 5.

Through the prophet, God declares his love for his people. To this is given an impertinent reply that could be rendered, "If God is a God of love, why this, that, and the other?" Disappointment, complaint, and cynicism are reflected in the words. Malachi elaborates on the initial affirmation by an appeal to history (vv. 3–5).

Special points.—The brothers Jacob and Esau were ancestors respectively of Israel and Edom (for Edom, see Introduction to Obadiah). God's love for Israel is shown in contrast to his attitude toward Edom, a tribe that perpetuated the materialistic unbelief of its founder.

Priestly Sins Condemned (Mal. 1:6—2:9)

The passage.—A father has a right to expect honor from his son, and a master from his servant; but God complains concerning the priests that they "despise my name" (1:6). In quick succession come the indignant rebuttals: "Wherein have we despised thy name?" (v. 6) and "Wherein have we polluted thee?" (v. 7).

In the development of the original accusation, the priests are described as offering maimed animals in sacrifice (vv. 8–11), displaying professional boredom toward their sacred tasks (v. 13), and showing partiality in the application of the law (2:8–9).

Special points.—The RSV aids understanding of this passage. The pointed question is asked: Would anyone give an earthly ruler the worthless animals now

583

being offered in sacrifice to God? (v. 9). Better to close the Temple doors than so to abuse its altar (v. 10).

Favored Israel is twice rebuked with the example of the Gentiles (1:11,14). The repeated phrase, "shall be" (v. 11), should be "is." God is receiving more reverential worship from other nations than from his own people. The words contain a promise of coming worldwide worship of Jehovah.

Truth for today.—Do we show greater deference to people than to God? His resistance to religious formalism is such that no worship at all may be better than empty ritual.

Compromise and Unfaithfulness in Marriage (Mal. 2:10–16)

The passage.—This third charge begins with a statement that needs to be kept in its context: "Have we not all one father?" God is both father and creator to Israel, a fact that should unite the nation in resistance to corruptive influences such as intermarriage with idolators (v. 11).

Associated with this sin is that of divorce. Some are apparently repudiating existing marriages to form alliances with heathen women. Yet, faced with the charge of "profaning the covenant" (v. 10), these people ask, "Wherefore?" (v. 14).

Verses 14–16 contain one of the strongest statements on the marriage bond to be found in Scripture. God is declared to be the witness to such contracts (v. 14). Verse 15 is problematical but a possible meaning is that "godly offspring" (RSV) is God's purpose for marriage, a purpose that is frustrated when unbelievers are taken as partners. The words of verse 16, "he hateth putting away," are God's verdict against the practice of divorce.

Special points.—Whose are the "tears,

. . . weeping, and . . . crying out" (v. 13)? They could be from cast-off wives or from worshipers dismayed that God does not accept them. In either case, the teaching is that by our treatment of others we determine our acceptability with God.

Certainty of Judgment (Mal. 2:17—3:6)

The passage.—The fourth affirmation is, "Ye have wearied the Lord with your words" (2:17). The people's retort is, "Wherein have we wearied him?" The cause of God's weariness is the cynical suggestion that he has abdicated as judge of men's moral conduct and is actually biased in favor of the wrongdoer. This is the old problem of the prosperity of the wicked, used, in this case, to repudiate God's moral authority in the world. Men can do as they please, for God is indifferent to their behavior; so men reason.

As a corrective to such cynical unbelief, God himself announces the sending of "my messenger" to prepare the way for "the messenger of the covenant," who is none other than the Lord himself (3:1). This second messenger will purify the priesthood (v. 3) and bring all offenders to judgment (v. 5). Yet, because God is unchangeable, in wrath he will remember mercy and the sons of Jacob will not be consumed (v. 6).

Special points.—Whatever application 3:1 may have had to Malachi's times, Matthew 11:10 identifies John the Baptist as "my messenger," and, by inference, the Lord Jesus as the divine "messenger of the covenant." In him, mercy and judgment meet.

Reconciliation Rejected (Mal. 3:7)

The passage.—This one tragic verse contains God's indictment of sin, his offer of reconciliation, and man's denial of any need to repent.

When Men Rob God (Mal. 3:8–12)

The passage.—The sixth of God's statements is "ye have robbed me" (v. 8). Back comes the question, "Wherein have we robbed thee?" The answer is: "In tithes and offerings." Because God's rightful dues have been withheld, the land is "cursed with a curse" (v. 9; see also v. 11). But all this can be changed if the people will make amends and "bring the tithes into the storehouse," the Temple (v. 10).

Truth for today.—Those who withhold from God impoverish themselves. Those who fulfil their stewardship obligations cannot escape blessing. Yet our motive must not be gain but gratitude.

The Profitableness of Obedience (Mal. 3:13—4:6)

The passage.—Over the people's protest, "What have we spoken so much against thee?" (v. 13) God reproves their skepticism. "It does not pay to serve God," they say. Proof to the contrary is given in the experiences of those "that feared the Lord" (v. 16). Their names will be entered in a book of remembrance and God will make them his "jewels" (special possession, RSV). Thus will be revealed the difference "between him that serveth God and him that serveth him not" (v. 18). A day of judgment is coming for all that do wickedly (4:1); but for those that "fear my name" a better day will dawn, ushered in by the rising of the Sun of righteousness in whose rays are powers of healing (v. 2).

The prophecy ends, and the Old Testament closes, with a call to "remember . . . the law" (4:4) and the naming of Elijah as the forerunner of "the great and dreadful day of the Lord" (v. 5). Jesus identified John the Baptist as this promised Elijah (Matt. 11:14).

MATTHEW

Wayne E. Ward

INTRODUCTION

Matthew's Gospel is the fullest record we have of the teaching of Jesus. For Bible teachers this means that it is the incomparable record of the Greatest Teacher who ever walked upon this earth. It is a treasure beyond value.

In the very earliest manuscripts of the Greek New Testament, from the third and fourth centuries A.D., Matthew stands first in the New Testament order of books. One of the main reasons is the fact that Matthew was one of the original twelve apostles, while Mark and Luke were not; and the Fourth Gospel, also attributed to one of the twelve, John, was not written until some years later.

Another important reason for the position of Matthew is the fact that it begins with the genealogy of Jesus, the important beginning place for Hebrew Christians, and takes the form of five distinct "books" or collections of the teaching of Jesus. This five-book structure parallels the five books of the Pentateuch which begin the Old Testament and made Matthew a logical choice to begin the New Testament.

One of the early Christian writers, Papias, in the second century, said that Matthew collected the teachings of the Lord in five books in the Hebrew tongue. This would mean that the original parts of Matthew's Gospel were in Hebrew (or the dialect of Hebrew, called Aramaic), in which language Jesus almost certainly spoke them originally. This would help to account for the fact that Matthew is such a Jewish Gospel, appealing often to the Old Testament quotations, and presenting Jesus as the Messiah of the Hebrew people.

Matthew gives a little signal to mark the end of each of his five books: "and when Jesus had finished all these words," or words very similar to this, mark the end of each of the five blocks of teaching which Matthew has collected under five major topics.

After the first two chapters on the birth of Jesus, book one begins with chapter 3 and goes through the Sermon on the Mount, to the end of chapter 7. In 7:28, Matthew gives his little signal, "And it came to pass, when Jesus had ended these sayings," marking the end of the teaching of Jesus on the subject of "discipleship." Chapters 3 and 4 are narrative, telling about the baptism of Jesus, his temptation, the beginning of his public ministry and the call of the disciples. Then chapters 5, 6, and 7 bring together the teachings of Jesus about what it means to be a disciple, a follower, of him. Each of the five books begins with a chapter or two of narrative, describing events in the ministry of Jesus, and then concludes with a summary of Jesus' teaching on the particular subject which is stressed at that point in his ministry.

After book one on "discipleship," the second book takes up the theme of "mission" as the apostles are sent forth to preach and heal. The word "apostle" means "missionary," or "one sent" with the message of the gospel. Book two ends at 11:1. Book three is concerned

with the "kingdom of heaven" and records the wonderful miracles of the
kingdom power and the parables of the
kingdom in Matthew 13, ending at 13:
53.

Book four ends at 19:1, and it deals
with the subject of the rejection of the
kingdom and Jesus' plan to build "the
church," the fellowship of his committed
disciples who will have the "keys of the
kingdom." So this portion of Matthew's
Gospel may be called "the kingdom
and the church." Then book five is concerned with "the coming judgment," embracing both the warnings of Jesus about
the impending destruction of the city of
Jerusalem and the coming of the Son of
man upon the clouds of glory at the
end of the age. This book ends at 26:1,
and the final chapters on the passion
and resurrection of Jesus complete the
Gospel of Matthew.

This simple outline made this Gospel
a very convenient book for use in teaching early Christian converts about Jesus,
and there is clear evidence that Matthew was used as the primary textbook
for the indoctrination of young Christians from the earliest centuries.

We do not have full information
about when the Gospels were written or
their relationship to each other. Many
scholars believe that the earliest part of
Matthew's Gospel was the collection of
the teachings of Jesus, probably by Matthew in the Hebrew language, in Antioch, about A.D. 40–50. Then they believe
that this material was combined with
the material in Mark's Gospel and
another special source called M (for
Matthew's special source) about A.D 85
to give us the completed Gospel as it
stands today.

The Genealogy and Birth of Jesus (Matt. 1:1–25)

The passage.—Usually a genealogy
makes very dull reading, but this genealogy of Jesus was dramatic evidence
of the messiahship of this Son of David,
to a devout Jew.

By beginning with the designation of
Jesus Christ as the "son of David" and
the "son of Abraham," Matthew is showing that Jesus is the fulfilment of the
promise to Abraham that his seed would
bring a blessing to the nations (Gen. 12:
1) and also the fulfilment of the prophecies that the Messiah would be the son
of David, reigning upon the throne of
the ideal kingdom (Isa. 9:7).

Then Matthew stresses this Davidic sonship of Jesus by a remarkable device. He
divides the genealogy into three parts:
from Abraham to David, from David to
the Exile of the Davidic royal line (the
kingdom of Judah, not the kingdom of
Israel), and finally from the Exile to Jesus. In order that the reader cannot
miss it, Matthew carefully points out
that there are fourteen generations in
each of these three groups. Not only is
fourteen a double seven, the most sacred number of the Hebrews, but it is
the numerical equivalent of the Hebrew
name, David. The Hebrews used letters
to count, somewhat like Roman numer-
als are used, and the three Hebrew consonants of the name David add up to
14. Even the passing of the generations
in the long centuries of expectant
waiting for the Messiah was shouting
the promise of David's greater Son!

It is also quiet significant that Matthew includes the names of some of the
women, as well as the men, in tracing
the lineage of Jesus. The ones he chose
to mention are surprising: Ruth, that
daughter of the hated Moabites; and
Tamar and Rahab, whose sinful background is chronicled in the Old Testament with the words "the harlot." It
seems that Matthew is trying to remind us that God works his purpose
through frail and sinful human beings
and that God was able, in spite of hu-

man weaknesses, to accomplish his purpose in bringing the Savior into the world in the "fulness of time."

The genealogy is traced to Joseph "the husband of Mary, of whom was born Jesus," even though Matthew has made it clear that Joseph was not actually the father of Jesus. This is because the legal genealogy in Jewish law is traced through the man, as head of the family, even if he is a step-father or foster father. Also, it is clear that Mary is of the line of David herself, and even in his physical descent through Mary Jesus is of the "house and lineage of David."

In the remainder of the chapter, verses 18–25, Matthew spells out explicitly the virgin birth of Jesus. In the most modest and simple words he explains that before Joseph and Mary came together as husband and wife, Mary was found to be with child by the Holy Ghost. Like any normal person, Joseph would have found this difficult to believe if the angel of the Lord had not appeared to him in a dream to confirm the fact that this baby was conceived by the Holy Ghost. His name JESUS was also revealed by the angel of the Lord because this name means "Savior," and he was to save his people from their sins.

With a pattern which echoes throughout the Gospel, Matthew then cites the Old Testament passage (Isa. 7:14) which is fulfilled by the virgin birth of Christ: "Behold, a virgin shall be with child, and shall bring forth a son. . . ." Throughout his gospel, Matthew stresses the fulfilment of the Old Testament words and events in the life of Jesus. The word he uses for "fulfilment" could be literally translated "confirm" or "support," as it is often used throughout the Septuagint, the Greek translation of the Old Testament. Matthew means that

God is confirming the words and deeds of the Old Covenant in the words and deeds of Jesus, the Promised Messiah. Some of the newer translations of the Old Testament use the words "young woman," rather than "virgin," in Isaiah 7:14, to translate the Hebrew word *almah*. Matthew, however, is following the text of the Septuagint which has the clear and unambiguous word *parthenos,* virgin. But it is important to remember that the great doctrine of the virgin birth of Christ does not depend upon a dispute about the translation of a Hebrew word, but upon the plain and unmistakable statements of Matthew and Luke that before Mary and Joseph came together, "she was found to be with child by the Holy Ghost."

Chapter 1 ends with the final confirmation of the fact that Mary and Joseph did not come together as man and wife until after the birth of Jesus. The idea of the "perpetual virginity" of Mary is a fiction created in the later church; Matthew plainly implies that Mary and Joseph lived a normal husband-wife relationship after the birth of Jesus and even names their children in Matthew 13:55.

Special points—Two important points stand out in this first chapter of Matthew. First, God's purpose worked out through all the centuries of Israel's history, through the line of David, to bring his Son into the world to be the Savior of men. Second, God brought his Son into the world through the miracle of the virgin birth. It is not the virgin birth which made Jesus Christ divine. He was already the divine Son of God from all eternity. Rather, because he was already the divine Son, God chose this appropriate means of bringing him into the world to be the Savior of all who follow him. God might have chosen any means to bring his Son into human flesh, but the clear teaching of Matthew's Gospel is that God chose the means of conception in the womb of the virgin Mary by the Holy Spirit.

Truth for today.—In all the long years since the coming of Christ into the world, some men have mocked the Christian promise of the second coming of Christ and the resurrection from the dead. Matthew's account of the long centuries of waiting for the promised Messiah simply reminds us that eventually, in God's good time, Jesus came. It should encourage every Christian to believe more firmly that God keeps his promises—no matter how long the time of waiting may be. Though the centuries roll by, the purpose of God will never fail!

The miracle of Christ's birth underlines the fact that God has not left his world to run automatically. All the births in all the centuries would never have produced the Son of God. Only by the divine act of intervention into the human process, by the miraculous conception of Jesus through the Holy Spirit, did the Son of God become a man—bone of our bone, and flesh of our flesh—to live, suffer, be tempted, and die for all men. This divine act of incarnation, God becoming man, is the center of our Christian faith.

Events at the Birth of Jesus (Matt. 2:1–23)

The passage.—The visit of the Wise Men, the flight of Mary, Joseph, and the Babe into Egypt, and Herod's slaughter of the infants make up the entire account of Matthew in chapter 2.

These Wise Men (or Magi) were from the East, probably Persia, and belonged to that ancient group of scholars who studied the movements of the heavenly bodies and applied these signs in the skies to the interpretation of events upon earth. Astronomers have speculated about what they saw—whether a conjunction of planets to make an enormous star in the evening sky, or a comet with a tail which seemed to point down toward Judea, and eventually to Bethlehem itself. Some have even tried to date the birth of Jesus from the astronomical records of a brilliant conjunction of three planets in 5 B.C. One thing is certain from Matthew's account: they saw an unusual star in the sky, and they believed that it was the sign of the coming of the promised King of the Jews because it stood over the land of Judea.

Tradition has always assumed that there were three Wise Men, but the Scriptures do not say. Apparently, because three gifts are named (gold, frankincense, and myrrh), three Magi are posited. Being royalty themselves, they quite naturally came to Herod's palace, expecting the new "King of the Jews" to be born in the royal family. It is interesting that Herod called for the keepers of the Scripture, and that he listened anxiously to the words of Micah 5:2 prophesying the birth of the Messiah in Bethlehem, even though he did not like what he heard!

Many interpreters have pointed out the significance of the three gifts of the Wise Men: gold, appropriate for a king; frankincense, usually offered on the altar to a deity; and myrrh, a strange gift to a baby, because it was used in anointing for burial. No doubt early Christians saw great significance in the future meaning of such gifts in the life of Jesus.

The flight into Egypt to escape the sword of Herod and the return to Nazareth are seen by Matthew as an amazing recapitulation of the experiences of Israel in the life of the true Son of Promise. Hosea 11:1, "Out of

Egypt have I called my son," originally spoken to Israel, is applied to Jesus who is truly God's Son. In a strange and miraculous way God's promised Messiah is living through some of the tragic experiences of his people, Israel.

Special points.—Verse 11 says the Wise Men came "into the house" and found Mary and the child. Some readers have wondered how they could be in a house if the birth took place in a stable as Luke says. Of course, the word for "house" might include such a place as the stable room on the back of the inn of Bethlehem; but it is more likely that some time had passed and they were temporarily in some other dwelling in Bethlehem. Traditionally, the visit of the Wise Men (or Three Kings) has been celebrated in Latin countries twelve days after Christmas, January 6th. The giving of gifts is reserved for this day, and the interval is the famous "twelve days of Christmas" in poem and carol.

The reference to Rachel "weeping for her children" (v. 18) is especially appropriate because she died in childbirth there, and her tomb stands at the northern entrance to Bethlehem until this day.

Truth for today.—Some people are repelled by the accounts of heavenly signs, angels appearing in dreams, and other miracles which attended the birth of Jesus. In this scientific age they just assume that such things could not have happened, and they miss the whole point of the biblical teaching. It is a strangely unscientific assumption that we know everything and can explain everything that happens in terms of natural law—now and always. This is simply not true, and the best modern scientists know it.

What is important is this: the true believer in God knows that there are many things in God's working which are

beyond our understanding, whether scientist or ordinary layman. Matthew is pointing out what every man of faith must know: God is at work in human life and history, and he will bring his purpose to completion in his own time, no matter how many Herods may try to stop him, and no matter how many unbelievers may reject him. God is the God of miracle. This world is a miracle of his creative love, and the miracle of the coming of his Son into the world is the only hope for our salvation.

The Baptism of Jesus (Matt. 3:1–17)

The passage.—This short chapter has one purpose: to show how Jesus was inaugurated for his mission as Messiah through his baptism by John the Baptist.

John prepared the way for the ministry of Jesus by his preaching in the Jordan Valley of Judea, and he even gave the keynote by calling men to repent and prepare for the kingdom of heaven. His dress and manner recalled the prophet Elijah, and his preaching fulfilled the promise of Isaiah 40:3.

The most important part of John's preaching was the promise of the Mightier One who was coming after him, who would baptize with the Holy Spirit and fire. The real importance of John's ministry is found in his preparation for Christ.

The baptism of Jesus was a dramatic sign of his identification with John's message of the inbreaking kingdom of heaven, and the coming of the Holy Spirit upon him was his anointing as the Messiah (Messiah means "Anointed One," that is, anointed with the Spirit).

Special points.—John's message from Isaiah and his food of locusts and wild honey are identical with references in the Dead Sea Scrolls, which were found in 1947 in caves not far from where

John was preaching. This has led many scholars to believe that John had some connection with this community of Qumran, which copied and preserved the scrolls.

John naturally felt unworthy to baptize Jesus, but Jesus insisted that it be done to "fulfil all righteousness." This means, to carry out God's plan of salvation. By this act the Savior was being inaugurated for his public ministry, and by the coming of the Holy Spirit upon him, God was giving his seal of approval to his beloved Son.

Truth for today.—John's example of humility in drawing attention, not to himself, but to Jesus, is exemplary for us today. The heavenly confirmation which came to Jesus was both for his own inner assurance and for a witness to others. This is the same reason for a public act of surrender and commitment to Christ on the part of Christians today. We need the inner confirmation of the divine blessing upon us, and the world needs the testimony of the life which is openly committed to Christ.

The Temptation of Jesus and the Calling of the First Disciples (Matt. 4:1–25)

The passage.—Chapter 4 brings us to the keynote theme of what we have called book one of Matthew's gospel—the book of discipleship. Jesus goes through the ordeal of temptation in the wilderness and then begins his public ministry by preaching the kingdom of heaven and calling his first disciples, Peter and Andrew, James and John, to follow him.

The forty days and nights in the wilderness are an echo of the forty years that Israel was in the wilderness, and the hunger of Jesus is a reminder of the hunger of Israel when God sent the manna. The three temptations of Jesus touch the very heart of the human problem of sin; and they reverse, in the most pointed way, the failure of Adam and Eve in the garden. Stones into bread—the temptation to center everything on man's material and physical needs. Jumping from the pinnacle of the Temple—the temptation to exploit and manipulate man's religious instincts. Gaining the kingdoms of the world by worshiping Satan—the temptation to grasp political power as the ultimate means to obtain selfish ends.

Like John, Jesus preached the reign of God, the inbreaking power of God in the hearts and lives of men, calling them under his lordship, and showing forth his power in miracles of love and healing. Then the very beginning of that reign was dramatically demonstrated by the calling of his first disciples to be "learners" in his kingdom. The healing of all kinds of diseases, and the casting out of demons, were not just miracles to excite awe. They were powerful signs that the kingdom of God was really breaking into the lives of men, and their purpose was to demonstrate the truth of Jesus' words. The miracles were the visible signs of the kingdom words which Jesus proclaimed.

Special points.—An interesting construction in the Greek language occurs in the words of Satan in the first two temptations: "If thou be the Son of God . . ." (vv. 3,6). This is a conditional sentence (called first class by the grammarians) which assumes the truth of the condition stated. A more accurate translation would be, "Since you are the Son of God. . . ." Satan knew that Jesus was; that was never in dispute. Satan's purpose was to try to get him to use his divine power in the wrong way, defeating God's ultimate plan of salvation.

Many people assume that since Jesus was the Son of God he could not have been really tempted. Others suppose that if Jesus had done what Satan suggested, he would have ceased to be the divine Son. Both of these ideas seem to miss the point entirely. If Jesus was not really tempted, if he could not have yielded to the temptations, then the whole account is a farce. It would make the gospel a deception. He really was tempted, and he could have taken the path Satan suggested.

If Christ had followed Satan's way, he would not have lost his deity, but we would have lost our Savior! Christ is the divine Son of God, and nothing Satan or man can ever do can change that fact. But, if God in Christ had not been willing to turn down all the easy alternatives, and go to the cross of Calvary for our sins, we would be utterly without hope in this sinful world. Let us bow the knee in trembling gratitude as we see Jesus struggling in the wilderness. There was won the victory of divine love over the power of the Evil One. What was at stake in that awesome struggle was not his deity but our salvation! Thanks be unto God that Christ won the victory there.

Truth for today.—After the excitement and thrill of the baptism in Jordan, and the coming of the Holy Spirit upon him, Jesus was led by that same Spirit into the agony of the wilderness. It is always so. A Christian is never more vulnerable than he is in the afterglow of a thrilling spiritual experience. Both the mountain peaks of Christian joy and the valleys of temptation are part of the experience of the disciple of Jesus. If it happened to our Lord, it will certainly happen to us.

The example of Jesus shows us exactly how the kingdom of God is coming into this world: he called men to follow him, and he taught them by word and deed what it means to be a disciple in his kingdom. The next three chapters

in Matthew's Gospel are concerned with the meaning of discipleship in the kingdom of heaven. This is still our task today—to call men to follow Jesus, and to show them by word and deed what it means to follow him.

Characteristics of Kingdom Disciples (Matt. 5:1–48)

The passage.—Chapter 4 ends on the note that great multitudes followed Jesus. Chapter 5 begins, "And seeing the multitudes, he went up into a mountain. . . ." This has caused many readers to assume that Jesus gave the sermon which follows to the multitudes. But that misses the point that "when he was set, his disciples came unto him. . . ." Jesus was actually getting away from the throngs, and he was addressing these words to those who were seriously trying to be his disciples. The phrases "when he was set" and "he opened his mouth" are formal expressions describing the most important utterances of a rabbi to his students.

Matthew gives first the Beatitudes, the joyous shouts of exclamation over the attitudes and the activities of disciples in the kingdom: the "poor in spirit" recognize their helplessness and have no one to trust but God; "they that mourn" are keenly conscious of their sin and deeply sensitive to the needs of others; "the meek" are the teachable, those who are always willing to learn new truth and new ways; those who "hunger and thirst after righteousness" have an insatiable longing for a deeper relationship with God.

These first four Beatitudes have summarized the basic attitudes of the true disciple. The next three describe their characteristic activity: they "show mercy," bending down in the spirit of Christ to bind up the wounds and lift the spirits of the broken lives; they are "pure in heart," which means singleness of purpose—they are absolutely committed to one overriding mission in life —to live as a disciple of the kingdom; they are "the peacemakers," actively involved in making peace and reconciling the hostile and estranged. Jesus concludes these seven Beatitudes with the weaning that such a life will bring persecution. Yet, every one of these Beatitudes is prefaced with the word "Blessed," which is really a shout of joy: "Oh, the happiness!" Such a life is the secret of true happiness, no matter how difficult the way may be.

Then Jesus uses two simple, but powerful, figures of speech to describe the true disciples: They are *salt,* which savors, purifies, and preserves, as they are to do in society. They are *light,* which cannot be hidden.

The remainder of the chapter shows the relationship of Jesus to the law: he came not to destory, but to fulfil. In five antitheses, or contrasts, he sets his own teaching over against the popular interpretation of the law by the scribes and Pharisees. Jesus is not rejecting the law but giving it the true spiritual meaning which God intended. The perverted legalism of the scribes has overridden and all but destroyed the true meaning of the law. In all of these contrasts Jesus appeals to the deepest motives of the human heart, going behind the overt act which violates the law to the sinful attitudes which prompt wrong actions:

(1) "Thou shalt not kill"—but Jesus condemns the anger, which leads to the sound "Raca" (the clearing of the throat to spit on someone), and finally to an ugly name of utter contempt (translated "thou fool"). The end of this evil motivation is destruction of the hated one.

(2) "Thou shalt not commit adultery" —but Jesus goes further and condemns the feeding of the lust which culminates in adultery.

(3) "Thou shalt not forswear thyself" —that is, do not break your solemn oath. But Jesus says we should keep our word even without being bound with an oath.

(4) "An eye for an eye"—not equal revenge but turning the other cheek is Jesus' teaching.

(5) "Love thy neighbor"—but Jesus says, "Love your enemies," doing good to them that curse you.

Jesus concludes this section with the most staggering demand of all: "Be ye therefore perfect, even as your Father which is in heaven is perfect." This means that his disciples have an absolutely perfect standard at which to aim, and they cannot be satisfied with aiming at anything less!

Special points.—The saying about divorce in 5:32 has caused much agony and sharp disagreement. Jesus is stating an absolute ideal of faithful marriage, and anything which breaks it is a failure of the ideal. This does not mean that it cannot be forgiven; even as Christ can forgive the word of anger, or the striking back, or the hatred of enemies, he can forgive this failure to reach the ideal in marriage. But the problem of a broken marriage cannot be legalized away—it must be faced, acknowledged, and redeemed by God's grace.

The entire Sermon on the Mount is the statement of an absolute ethic. Any attempt to work out little legalistic loopholes so that we may "keep" the Sermon on the Mount is a perversion of its purpose. Jesus gave it to us to stand there as a constant challenge and rebuke. It sets before us a goal which we will never reach until we have come into the presence of the heavenly Father. It brings us to our knees in repentance, and to our feet for a new effort to follow him more perfectly every day.

Truth for today.—Nothing is needed more today than the challenge of this Sermon. People are confused by changing moral standards, shocking conduct on the part of young and old, and the relativism of all values. Here Jesus gives us an absolute standard of life and moral conduct. No matter how far we miss the mark, we know where the goal is. It is the certain assurance that the Christian disciple needs in this troubled world.

Activities of Kingdom Disciples (Matt. 6:1–34)

The passage.—Jesus goes even deeper into the requirements of discipleship by describing two types of activity: the specifically religious acts of almsgiving, prayer (including forgiveness of others), and fasting; and the kind of life the disciple must live in the hard and competitive struggle of the work-a-day world which concentrates on gaining worldly treasures.

Almsgiving must not be paraded before men; the disciple must not give in order to be praised or rewarded. Prayer is intimate communion with God, not a display to impress men. It should be simple and direct, like a child speaking to a father. One cannot even seek forgiveness from the Father unless he is willing to forgive those who have wronged him.

Fasting, like prayer and giving, is an intimate act of devotion to God and must not be advertised to the world by parading the signs of fasting.

In blunt language Jesus rejects the worldly drive to gain material treasures. The disciple must not be concerned with earthly treasures, but heavenly ones, that will never fade away.

Even the accommodation of trying to do both (serve two masters) is rejected by Jesus. One must make his choice: he must reject material treasures and seek heavenly ones, or he cannot be a kingdom disciple.

The final section of this chapter clinches the point of the disciple's activity in this material world. Jesus gives an extreme and challenging statement: Do not worry about tomorrow—do not be anxious about material needs! Concentrate on one thing: the kingdom of God; that is, the doing of God's will "on earth, as it is in heaven." Jesus does not deny material needs, even saying that "all these things shall be added unto you." It is a matter of priority. The kingdom of God comes first, and these other things have to take a secondary place.

Special points.—In older versions (such as the King James) some strange and contradictory words have been added by a later editor, centuries after the time of Christ: "and thy Father which seeth in secret shall reward thee *openly*" (6:4,6). Some editor could not stand the thought of Jesus that only the Father would know of his prayer and almsgiving, so he added the word "openly" in both verses. He wanted public credit for his piety—like the Pharisees. These words were added to later Greek manuscripts, flatly contradicting the teaching of Jesus—and proving his point! Men want the praise of men for their piety, even if they have to change the words of Jesus in order to justify it.

In the Lord's Prayer, 6:9–14, the words "forgive us our debts" stand in the body of the prayer; and the word "trespasses" appears only in Jesus' explanation at the close of the prayer in 6:14–15. The form of the prayer which uses "trespasses" comes from the English Book of Common Prayer and is used mainly by those churches which have their background in the Anglican

Church.

Truth for today.—The mad struggle for material possessions which so characterizes our world today makes these words of Jesus all the more relevant. The disciple of Jesus cannot let this materialism dominate him. He must major on "seeking the kingdom of God and his righteousness." The attitude of worry and fretting about what may happen tomorrow must not characterize the Christian disciple.

The other emphasis of this chapter is upon the right motivation in religious activities. More important than what we do is the attitude with which we do it. Perfunctory attendance upon religious services, because it is the expected thing, will never fulfil the meaning of true discipleship. Religious devotion is an intimate and deeply sincere relationship with the heavenly Father—never a public display. We should not pray, or give, or worship in order to "keep up appearances" before men, but in order to express our love and obedience to the heavenly Father.

Facing the Alternatives of Discipleship (Matt. 7:1–29)

The passage.—The Sermon on the Mount is concluded with this crisp and challenging chapter on the alternatives which the Christian must face—the decisions which he must make. Instead of passing judgment on others, the disciple of Jesus must first pass judgment on himself. Rejecting the passive attitude of simply waiting, the disciple must ask, and seek, and knock. He must actively do unto others what he would have others do to him. He must choose the narrow way and reject the broad way which the crowd follows to destruction. He must discriminate between true and false prophets, between good and evil fruit. The true disciple must *do* the will

of the Father, not simply talk about it. He must build his house upon the rock, to withstand the wind and flood, and not upon the sand, where it will be destroyed. The point of this whole chapter is crystal clear: the disciple of Jesus Christ cannot be blandly adjustable to all the prevailing patterns of society. He must make his choice for the "strait and narrow way," in the firm assurance that when the final record is in, no matter how it may look to the world, that choice will be vindicated.

Special points.—"Give not that which is holy unto the dogs" appears to be a harsh discrimination in the midst of a passage which warns against passing judgment. But it is a reminder that even though we are not the final judge of men, whether ourselves or others, we must constantly make some distinctions in our ministry of holy things, according to the response that is given. Even as the Christian disciple must choose between alternatives, and cannot have it both ways, the one who hears the gospel must respond positively, or it can never become effective in his life. It is like the warning of Jesus about "shaking the dust off of the feet." Instead of trying to batter down the door of rejection, press on to the open doors of response—which was always the way of Jesus.

"Judging" means "to pass condemnation upon." Although it is always necessary to make some judgments and distinctions, Jesus is warning us against "playing God." He makes the final judgment; we are all under his ultimate decision.

The final words of the chapter stress the authority of Jesus in his teaching, and the authority of Jesus will be the keynote of the miracles which fill the next two chapters.

Truth for today.—Although spoken almost 2,000 years ago, these words have never been more relevant than they are today. In a pluralistic society where one religion is supposed to be as good as another, and one way of life as good as another, Jesus still stands on the great divide and says, "Choose!" Every man will walk the broad way with the crowd unless he deliberately chooses to leave it, by a strong and decisive act of faith, and follow Jesus up the narrow way. Every man's house will be swept away on the surging sands, unless he carefully chooses to build it upon the difficult and demanding rock.

With an eloquence which is undimmed by myriad translations and rolling centuries of time, Jesus has set the alternatives once and for all—follow me into the life that will never fade away, or go with the world into everlasting destruction.

Great Miracles of Jesus in Galilee (Matt. 8:1—9:38)

The passage.—These chapters open book two of Matthew, the book of mission. They cover a major portion of the great Galilean ministry of Jesus, and they show in concrete action how the reign of God was coming into the world through the words and deeds of Jesus. First, Jesus goes into the sinful, suffering society of first century Galilee and actively helps the broken and sinful. Then, he sends his disciples out, two by two, to carry on this same mission beyond his own outreach. These are the examples and the marching orders for his disciples for all time.

The first three miracles which Matthew records in chapter 8 emphasize the great authority or power of Jesus over diseases: with a word he takes away the leprosy which was the horrible scourge of that day; like the centurion who understood about authority, Jesus simply gave a command, and his will

was carried out in the healing of the centurion's servant (and the centurion was a hated Roman!); when Peter's mother-in-law was sick with a fever, Jesus simply "touched her hand" and she was well again. The total impact is clear: the mighty power of God is at work in the quiet words and deeds of this Man!

Along the way, Matthew records a few words of the teaching of Jesus, but they are always in the context of interpreting some action or situation which has arisen in his public ministry. Chapters 8 and 9 are simply filled with action. Chapter 10 will summarize the teaching of Jesus about the mission of his disciples in the world.

The next three miracles of Jesus stress the mighty power of Jesus over different areas of life: concluding chapter 8 he stills the tempest (power over nature) and casts the demons out of two demoniacs (power over evil spirits). The third one, in chapter 9, is the most awesome of all: he dares to forgive sins as he heals the "sick of the palsy." *Power over sins* belongs to God alone, but Jesus has dared to forgive sins and demonstrate it by the visible sign of freeing the man from his paralysis! The gauntlet has been thrown down to the scribes and Pharisees: Jesus is presuming to do the work of God, and backing it up with awesome miracles which they cannot deny.

After the brief interlude of the call of Matthew, and the dinner in his house which provoked the self-righteous Pharisees and even the fasting disciples of John, chapter 9 is concluded with the final cycle of miracles—emphasizing unusual faith on the part of the recipients.

First is the raising of the daughter of the ruler, who believed that if Jesus would just lay his hand on her, she would live. Telescoped within this miracle, while Jesus is on the way to raise the little girl, is another dramatic demonstration of faith: a woman just touches his garment and is healed! Confronting the two blind men who call upon him for help, Jesus asks simply: "Do you believe I am able to do this?" In childlike faith they answer, "Yes, Lord." Then comes the key word: "According to your faith be it upon you." Without their faith, not even Jesus could have healed them. Faith is the key.

Finally, the dumb man is freed from the demonic power that bound him, and the crowds are awe-struck: "It was never so seen in Israel." The concluding words of the chapter bring into focus again the theme of mission: there is a great harvest to be gathered, but where are the laborers? In the next chapter, Jesus will send his disciples forth into the Galilean mission, setting the pattern for the mission of his church until the end of time.

Special points.—The cycles of three miracles in each group suggest that Matthew has selected and arranged them under particular subjects, to aid memory and understanding as they were taught to young Christians. Like John, he could not record all the miracles that Jesus did, so he made a selection.

Some people have criticized Jesus for letting the evil spirits go into the swine and send them to their death in the sea, destroying valuable property! Certainly Jesus did not have to destroy the herd of swine in order to heal the demoniacs. He cast out demons many times without sending them anywhere. It may be that he gave the demoniacs a powerful visual sign of their deliverance—their tormentors were sent into the depths of the sea. Some interpreters have thought that a devout Jew would consider this an appropriate fate for the loathsome swine or evil spirits. It may be that Jesus is rebuking our concern with property values, when the lives of two men have been gloriously redeemed. In any case, this much is clear: the powers of evil which destroy men have met their match in Jesus! He can utterly banish them, to the depths of the sea. In the power of Jesus is our hope!

Truth for today.—Although the heart of Matthew's Gospel is the teaching of Jesus, these chapters remind us that actions often teach louder than words. The narrative of Jesus' action in the midst of the throngs of Galilee carries the powerful message that he really cares for people; and he is not afraid to get involved in helping them, whatever the risk.

The mission of the disciples—then and now—is to do what Jesus did: to go into the midst of human sickness, conflict, and fear, and do everything possible to help. The same Holy Spirit who empowered Jesus will empower those who go in his name.

Rising above the whole mission of the disciples is the assurance that the power of Jesus triumphs over disease, sin, and death—over the forces of nature and the sinister evils of the spiritual realm. In his power the mission cannot fail!

The Mission of the Twelve (Matt. 10:1–42)

The passage.—The opening verses of this chapter give us the names of the twelve disciples, or *apostles,* as Matthew designates them here. "Disciple" is a general word for any learner, or follower, of a great teacher. "Apostle" means "one who is sent," which is exactly what Jesus did here. He sent the twelve forth into Galilee.

With the warning that he was sending them out as sheep in the midst of wolves, Jesus gave them a fourfold commission: (1) preach the kingdom of heaven;

(2) heal the sick and leprous; (3) raise the dead; and (4) cast out devils. This embraces both the physical and spiritual needs of men, and it concerns both this world and the world to come.

Jesus also gives the most specific instruction he ever gave on how to face persecution, when they are dragged before kings and councils, or betrayed by their closest friends and relatives. In fact, there is guidance here for much more than the preaching mission in Galilee. There is the command of the Lord which will guide the mission of his church through all the ages and in all the nations—until he comes again.

The whole purpose of this chapter is to summarize the teaching of Jesus concerning the mission of his followers in the world. Those who receive his disciples are receiving Jesus; and even a "cup of cold water," given in the name of a disciple, shall have its reward.

Special points.—The order and names of the twelve apostles vary somewhat in the four lists given in the New Testament (Matt. 10:2–4; Mark 3:16–19; Luke 6:14–16; Acts 1:13). There have been many ways of harmonizing these lists (with Levi equated with Matthew, etc.), but one remarkable thing is found in all four lists. The twelve names are always grouped in the same three groups of four names each. More surprising still is the fact that the first name in each of these three groups is always the same: Peter, Philip, and James the son of Alphaeus. The possibility of that happening accidentally is beyond imagination. It almost certainly indicates some type of organization of the disciples into groups, with specific leaders and responsibilities.

The command to go to the house of Israel, and not to the Gentiles or Samaritans, raises a problem. Jesus himself went to Gentiles and Samaritans.

Why would he forbid his disciples to do this?

Apparently Jesus is telling them where to start in their mission. They must begin at home, and with their own people. Christ is the Messiah of the Jews, and the long years of preparation for his coming involved the covenant people. Therefore, the mission must begin with them.

Verse 23, "Ye shall not have gone over the cities of Israel, till the Son of man be come," is one of the most discussed verses in the Bible. Albert Schweitzer thought this meant that Jesus expected a divine figure, like the Son of man in Daniel, to bring in the kingdom before the disciples finished the Galilean preaching mission. Schweitzer thought that when this did not happen, Jesus turned in an act of desperate commitment to try to force the kingdom to come by his death on the cross.

Some have tried to explain that Jesus simply meant to overtake the disciples before they finished the Galilean mission. Others have just decided that Jesus was mistaken because the kingdom did not come and the Son of man did not appear from heaven on the clouds of glory.

A much more obvious explanation stands in the chapter itself. In verse 18 Jesus tells them that they will be dragged before governors and kings, for a testimony against them and the Gentiles. Obviously, they are to begin their mission to Israel, but they cannot wait until all Israel has been evangelized before they go on to others. In verse 23 Jesus is saying that he, the Son of man, will come at the end of the age; but the disciples will not even have reached all the cities of Israel before the end comes. It is a message of utmost urgency. It means that the mission of the disciples of Jesus is limited in its time of opportunity. They must make the most of the opportunity they have now. Almost 2,000 years have passed since Jesus gave this warning, but it is all the more urgent because of that very fact. The task will never be finished before Jesus comes, but the urgency of the mission should challenge us to the supreme effort in every moment of opportunity that remains.

Truth for today.—Some people ridicule organization and administration in our churches today. The fact that Jesus himself organized his disciples into certain groups, and apparently appointed leaders with specific responsibilities, ought to say something. If the Son of God himself employed simple administrative means to increase the effectiveness of his disciples, how much more should we!

The debate about the relative importance of evangelism and social action could be settled in a moment, if people would only listen to the command that Jesus gave his disciples. He stressed *both* the preaching of the kingdom and the meeting of physical needs. Also, the ridiculous argument that Christians should be concerned with this world only and forget about "pie in the sky bye and bye" would be utterly rejected by this commission which Jesus gave. He stressed the resurrection of the dead, the liberation of men from the powers of evil, and preparation for the coming kingdom. This means concern for the world here and now, but with ultimate concern for the life which goes beyond this world.

Sometimes the "giving of a cup of cold water" is construed as an act of meeting human need which is a substitute for Christian discipleship. Some even argue that one does not need to confess Christ, or join his church, if only he will help to meet the needs of his fellowmen. Jesus certainly commands his followers to serve the needs of men, but he says this must be done "in the name of a disciple." This means that the motive must be to carry out the command of Christ to serve him as a disciple and to bring others to be his disciples. In some communist nations and in some social programs, the motive for social action is to make people more subservient and more enslaved to the system. It is possible to "help" people for the wrong motive, and Jesus makes clear that the motive for social action is of paramount importance.

The Signs of the Kingdom (Matt. 11:1—12:50)

The passage.—Matthew begins his book three with the first verse of chapter 11: "And it came to pass, when Jesus had made an end. . . ." After book one on the requirements of "discipleship" and book two on the "mission" of his apostles, Jesus is concerned with the inbreaking power of the kingdom of heaven. In chapters 11 and 12, Matthew records the questions and the conflicts which arise in response to Jesus' ministry. His preaching and his marvelous miracles have heralded the power of the kingdom. Something is happening in the life and ministry of Jesus which is more wonderful than anything the world has ever seen. But the response to this amazing Teacher is strange indeed!

First, even John the Baptist is having some doubts about him. Of course, while he lies there in prison, John is probably wondering why Jesus does not do anything to help him, if he is indeed the Messiah. John sends two of his disciples to ask Jesus if he really is the "Coming One." The answer Jesus sends is a hard and challenging one. It is the clue to his whole understanding of the kingdom of heaven: Go tell John what you see and hear in my ministry! Then the decision was left squarely up to John. It is only by faith that one can see the power of God working in the words and deeds of Jesus. Not even Jesus can make the decision for John and quietly give him reassurance. John, and every man, must make that "leap of faith" for himself.

The words of praise for John the Baptist are the most laudatory that Jesus ever spoke. John was the forerunner of Messiah and the first proclaimer of the kingdom. Without the preparation of John, Jesus could not even have begun his ministry. John was the transition point—from the law and the prophets (the Old Testament) to the fulfilment in the Messiah. His importance was beyond all measure.

Then Matthew records the severe words with which Jesus rebuked that generation. They rejected John the Baptist because he was too ascetic, and they rejected Jesus because he was just the opposite—too sociable! They were just negative to the message of the kingdom, no matter how it came.

Chorazin and Bethsaida, cities of Galilee which had seen the miracles of Jesus and the disciples on their preaching mission, are worse than Sodom and Gomorrah, Tyre and Sidon. Those wicked cities would have repented if they had seen the deeds and heard the preaching which Galilee had received.

The closing part of chapter 11 is one of the most amazing prayers of Jesus. It sounds like the Gospel of John. Jesus thanks his Father that he has revealed "these things" (the signs and preaching of the kingdom of heaven) to the "babes" (the simple and unsophisticated), rather than to the high and mighty. It is ever so: the lowly and humble are willing to respond to the message of God, when the brilliant and the powerful are often too proud to accept it. Jesus

calls the lowly ones "who labor and are heavy laden" to come to him; and they are the ones who respond.

Chapter 12 is concerned entirely with the response of one other group to the signs of the kingdom in the ministry of Jesus: the scribes and Pharisees. From beginning to end, this chapter records the bitter and vindictive reaction of these entrenched leaders of the religious establishment of Israel. They feel threatened by the loving freedom and spiritual power of this amazing teacher from Galilee. Because they are not able to control him and make him fit into their system, they are determined to kill him.

When Jesus and his disciples eat some grain while passing through the fields on the sabbath, they jump quickly to accuse him. His answer infuriates them more: he, the Son of Man, is Lord even of the sabbath. They hardly expected such an answer as that. He was even claiming a lordship which belonged to God alone. To them it was blasphemy!

So blind were these religious leaders that they could not even thank God for the miraculous healing of a man with a withered hand. Because Jesus had done this on the sabbath, they plotted to kill him. Then, before the crowds, they accuse Jesus of doing these mighty works in the power of the evil one, Beelzebub. This horrible blasphemy against the Holy Spirit who was working these miracles in the ministry of Jesus brought forth from the Master the strongest indictment he ever pronounced: this sin of blasphemy against the Holy Spirit will not be forgiven in this world, or the world to come!

It seems shocking that some of the scribes and Pharisees could come forward then and demand a sign. What more could they want? Dozens of signs and miracles had been wrought in their midst, but they were unwilling to accept them. Jesus does promise one sign that is the most important of all: the sign of Jonah. He means that just as Jonah was three days and nights in the belly of the whale, so he will be in the "heart of the earth." It is a veiled reference to his coming death and resurrection, the greatest sign of all. The whole destiny of mankind will turn on whether that sign is accepted or rejected!

The last verses of chapter 12 bring us to one of the most poignant moments in the entire ministry of Jesus. Doubted even by John the Baptist, despised and ignored by the cities of Galilee, hated by the Pharisees, it now seems that even his family is worried by his outlandish words and deeds. Apparently they have come to call him away from the crowds, and, perhaps, to take him home. In words that ring with pathos and heartache, Jesus points to the only "family" he really has—his disciples, those who "do the will of my Father in heaven." None of his own family (except perhaps his mother), became a Christian disciple, until after his death and resurrection.

Special points.—Many people are shocked that John the Baptist could have doubted Jesus when he had proclaimed his coming, prepared the way, and even baptized him for his messianic mission. But this only shows that doubt can come to anyone, especially when things are not going well. The basic problem for John was that Jesus was not doing what he expected. It is always hard to accept God's way of doing things, when it does not conform to what we want or expect. We are not told how John responded to the message which Jesus sent back, and that is probably not accidental. Matthew wants to leave us with exactly the question which John faced: you see the deeds and hear the words of Jesus; now, do *you* believe that he is the Messiah?

The unpardonable sin of blasphemy against the Holy Spirit is the point of most serious disagreement in this passage. The words which describe it are clear enough: when the Pharisees observe the miracles of the Holy Spirit's power and attribute them to the prince of devils (Satan), Jesus says this blasphemy against the Holy Spirit will never be forgiven, in this world or the coming one.

What does this mean? Jesus could even ask the Father to forgive those who crucified him. Why could he not ask the Father to forgive this? Or, is the unpardonable sin a sin which could only be committed during the ministry of Jesus when people attributed his miracles, performed in the power of the Spirit, to the devil? Some interpreters believe that the sin which has no forgiveness could only be committed then.

Oh, that this were only true! Matthew records this not just because of historical interest. It is a warning to all of us. The only way anyone can ever respond to Jesus and the Father is through the work of the Holy Spirit. If men blaspheme him and reject him, they are literally closing the only door they have to forgiveness and salvation. Men might hear Jesus, and even turn away from him, only to have his words brought powerfully into the heart by the Holy Spirit. There is the ultimate point of decision. Only the Spirit can convince and convict, even if one is standing right there looking at the deeds and listening to the words of Jesus. If the Spirit is rejected, the only line of communication is broken. There is no other hope!

The really tragic fact is that the Pharisees knew perfectly well that God was working in this man. The Holy Spirit had convicted them of that. But they hated Jesus so much that they were going to call the work of the Spirit the work of the devil anyway! This is deliberate spiritual blindness which has no cure. The only cure would be the power of the Spirit, and that is precisely the cure that is being rejected.

Truth for today.—The primary message of these two chapters on the response of different people to Jesus can be found in this twofold truth: there is an awesome responsibility upon men as they react to the kingdom message of Jesus and his disciples; and there is an awesome responsibility upon the followers of Jesus to be faithful to this message, no matter how violent the response.

When doubts come, or when opposition comes, the ultimate question is still the same: under the impact of the ministry of Jesus and the witness of the Holy Spirit, will each individual accept for himself the inbreaking reign of God in the hearts of men? It is the only door, and it can be opened only from the inside, by the believing one himself.

Parables of the Kingdom (Matt. 13:1–58)

The passage.—In this chapter, at the climax of book three, Matthew has collected the main parables of Jesus about the kingdom of heaven. His purpose is to show that the kingdom is working in the midst of men, even though the responses are varied.

With the famous parable of the sower, Jesus is really stressing the different kinds of response to the message. The seed is the same (the Word) and the sower is the same (Jesus), but the soils are different in the way they receive the seed.

The parable of the tares is a reminder that the weeds and the good grain often grow side by side now. The "enemy" who came and sowed the tares is certainly Satan, who tries to undermine the work of the kingdom. But judgment belongs to God. In his own good time, God will bring the harvest and make the separation between weeds and grain.

The parable of the mustard seed stresses the great results that can come from small beginnings. Though the kingdom may now appear to be as small as a mustard seed, one of the tiniest of seeds, it can become mighty like the mustard plant which shelters the birds on its branches.

The parable of the leaven is similar in meaning. Though the leaven is very small in relation to the three measures of meal, it will eventually leaven the whole lump by working from within. So the kingdom of heaven may be hidden in the world, but it works quietly from within, permeating the whole of society.

The intervening interpretation of the parable of the tares (vv. 36–43) is intended to make clear that the children of the kingdom and the children of the wicked one live side by side in the world. They are not separated now. But, at the end of the age, there will be a separation and judgment.

The parable of the hidden treasure and the similar one about the pearl of great price teach the same thing: a man should be willing to give up everything else to gain the Kingdom. It is the highest value of all.

The final parable of the net with good and bad fish is like the parable of the tares. Both good and bad may be attracted to the Kingdom; but at the end of the age, the wicked will be separated from the just and cast "into the furnace of fire."

Matthew gives the signal for the end of book three with his regular transition in 13:53, "And it came to pass, that when Jesus had finished these parables. . . ." The sad words about the rejection of Jesus in his own country (Nazareth) give us a clue to the next book in Matthew's collection. Having been rejected by everybody from the religious rulers in Jerusalem to the neighbors in his own hometown, Jesus will now turn to a series of withdrawals into regions outside Galilee. There he will prepare his disciples for the work they must carry on after his death and resurrection.

Special points.—The parable of the sower has a special warning for those who confess Christ and then do not grow as Christians and bear fruit. The seed that fell on stony ground sprang up quickly, but soon withered away. A temporary response to Jesus, which does not go on to maturity and bear fruit, is not a saving faith.

In 13:55 Matthew gives the names of four brothers of Jesus and mentions "sisters" in the plural, indicating at least two. This helps us to understand more about the large family in which Jesus grew up. Most interpreters believe that Joseph had died some years earlier, and Jesus probably carried the responsibility for running the carpenter shop and supporting the family until the boys were old enough to help. It may account for the "silent years" during his "teens" and twenties, and the delay of his public ministry until he was thirty.

Truth for today.—The fact that Jesus was rejected by the religious authorities of his day should be a warning to religious leaders today. There is always a danger that established religion will reject the prophetic voice of Jesus. But these parables tell us that the kingdom of God goes right on working, no matter what the religious leaders do. Some people will respond, though they be lowly and insignificant to the world. God's power does not have to work through official channels.

These parables of the kingdom also give us another important teaching: the time of judgment is coming. The attitude of indifference which is so characteristic of men today would be shattered by this truth, if only it could get through to their minds and hearts. It is a tremendous responsibility to live in this world. The gift of life brings the responsibility to use it wisely in this world and set the right direction for the world to come. Some men may think that it does not matter how they live, if they can just "get away with it" now. Jesus says the time is coming when a final separation will take place. That judgment will be decided by whether a man is growing and bearing fruit in the Kingdom now!

The Withdrawals of Jesus from Galilee (Matt. 14:1—15:39)

The passage.—With the beginning of book four, in Matthew's outline, there is a complete shift in the ministry of Jesus. Having been rejected by the religious leaders, the cities of Galilee, and his own hometown, Jesus now turns to a period of withdrawals into regions outside of Galilee. He is trying to get his disciples alone and prepare them for the crisis that is coming.

At first the crowds still try to follow him. The report of the beheading of John the Baptist was the occasion for the first withdrawal of Jesus. He knew that this meant the time was fast approaching when his ministry would be interrupted, so he was anxious to concentrate on getting his disciples ready.

Because he went by ship across the sea to a "desert place," it is likely that the location of this first withdrawal is Perea, on the east side of Galilee and the Jordan. But the crowds followed him around the lake, and their hunger was so great that Jesus was moved with compassion. Five thousand men plus women and children were fed with the five loaves and two fish. We know from John's Gospel that they wanted to make him king, and Jesus had to send the crowd away and literally force his disciples to get into a boat and leave. Jesus spent the night in prayer. He may have been fighting the old temptation to "turn the stones into bread" and be the popular Messiah the people wanted.

In the closing part of chapter 14, Jesus comes to the disciples, walking on the water. In this intimate encounter with the small band of disciples, Jesus revealed himself and his heavenly power in a way that he had never disclosed himself to the multitude. It is small wonder that "they that were in the ship came and worshiped him."

Even as the news about the death of John the Baptist precipitated the first withdrawal, a clash with the scribes and Pharisees led to the second. They made a contentious attack upon Jesus because his disciples did not practice all the ceremonial washings which the Pharisees required. This withdrawal took Jesus and his disciples up along the Mediterranean coast toward Tyre and Sidon.

The healing of the daughter of the Canaanite woman is one of the most important examples of the ministry of Jesus outside of Israel. Her faith was so great that it overcame all the cultural barriers, and Jesus answered the prayer of this distraught mother.

Returning from this northwestern region along the sea, Jesus came to a mountain "nigh unto the sea of Galilee." This may have been along the lower slopes of Mount Hermon, north of the sea of Galilee. There the crowds found him again and stayed with him three days. As before, because there was no food in this desert place, Jesus fed the multitude from a few loaves and fishes.

This time the number was about 4,000 men, beside women and children.

Special points.—Although Jesus worked many miracles, he would not intervene with his miraculous power to save John the Baptist. In a similar way, he would not call on his heavenly power to save himself when he faced the cross. He used his miracles to demonstrate the inbreaking kingdom of God in the lives of men, but he would not invoke them to remove the cross of suffering from himself or his disciples. He plainly told them that they must take up their cross and follow him. Eventually all of his faithful disciples sealed their witness by their suffering and death.

The withdrawal of Jesus into regions beyond Galilee was not accidental. It was an object lesson for the disciples. They would also be rejected by their own people, but they would follow the example of Jesus and go outside their homeland—even to the ends of the earth.

Truth for today.—There is much criticism today of the church which "retreats behind its walls." Ridicule is even heaped upon the idea of worship as a form of service to God. Some recognize only social action outside the walls of the church as valid Christian service.

Jesus stressed action in the marketplace and in the midst of teeming society. But he also stressed withdrawal for prayer and spiritual renewal. Matthew has just given us two whole chapters which balance withdrawal and involvement—social action and spiritual retreat. If Jesus needed this, it would be almost blasphemous for his followers to say that they do not!

The ministry of Jesus beyond Galilee, and to people as hated and despised as the Canaanites, shows us that the gospel has no boundaries. It must be proclaimed at home, but it must not stop there. It must be carried to the ends of the earth. No one is excluded from the love of God. No one should be left out in the sharing of the gospel.

Peter's Great Confession and the Foundation of the Church (Matt. 16:1–28)

The passage.—In this chapter we have the turning point of the Gospel of Matthew and the ministry of Jesus. All of the work of Jesus had been building up to this point: the time when one or more of his disciples would freely accept him and confess him as the Son of God. Not until that time could he really build his church, because his church was to be composed of confessing believers. Not even Jesus could force that confession. It had to come voluntarily, inspired by the Father above.

Again it was the harrassment of the Pharisees which led Jesus and his disciples to withdraw to the other side of the sea. The Pharisees demanded from Jesus a "sign from heaven," ignoring all the signs of his ministry. Jesus rejected this contemptuous demand and warned his disciples against the "leaven" of the Pharisees. This time, the permeating power of leaven is used as a symbol of the sinister workings of these wicked religious leaders, rather than the power of the kingdom of heaven. Both good and evil work inwardly, expanding and permeating society.

Near Caesarea Philippi, probably somewhere up the slopes of beautiful Mount Hermon, Jesus decided to confront his disciples with the most important question of all: what did they believe about him? Simon Peter led the way in confessing Jesus as "the Christ, the Son of the living God."

It was this act of confession by Simon which gave Jesus the opportunity to proclaim the foundation of his church. The keys of the kingdom, the power of

binding and loosing men from their sins, are given here to Peter (or perhaps the disciples), and later (Matt. 18:18) to all who confess him as Lord. The keys signify the power to proclaim the gospel which liberates men from sin. The rejection of this gospel also leaves men bound in sin, without hope in the world.

Directly after this marvelous confession of Christ, Jesus warns the disciples of the coming crisis and his death in Jerusalem. When Peter remonstrates with him over such a somber prediction, Jesus rebukes him with stern words: "Get thee behind me, Satan!" The old temptation from Satan, which Jesus had conquered long ago, is coming again through the mouth of the first disciple to confess Jesus as Messiah!

Chapter 16 closes on the note of promise that the Son of man will come in his kingdom. If a man should gain the whole world and miss this, he has lost all that really matters.

Special points.—The important passage on the founding of the church has been a battleground in Christian history. Roman Catholics have insisted that the church was founded upon Peter and that he alone was given the "keys"—the power to accept or excommunicate members of the church.

A careful reading of the original passage (vv. 18–19) shows the impossibility of such an interpretation. Jesus says "You are Peter [*Petros*]," that is, "a stone." Then Jesus adds, "And upon this rock [*petra*]," that is, a "ledge of rock," he would build his church. He does not call Peter the rock foundation on which the church is built. In fact, as Peter himself says in his first epistle (1 Pet. 2:48), Christ is the foundation, on which the living stones of the apostles and believers are built into a spiritual house. Peter certainly knew that he was not the foundation of the church. The

Christ whom Peter confessed was and is that foundation.

The power of "binding and loosing" has been interpreted by some to mean that when Peter, or the church, accepted or excluded members, condemned or absolved their sins, that even heaven was bound by that decision. The passage actually says just the opposite. The verb used is in the past perfect tense: "What you bind on earth *has been bound* in heaven." The church can only do on earth what God has decreed in heaven. Heaven controls the work of the church on earth; the church does not control heaven!

Truth for today.—With all of the disagreement today about the church, it is wonderful to have such a clear scriptural teaching on what the church really is, and what her purpose is in the world. Those who truly confess Christ as Son of God and Savior, who build their lives upon him, and carry the keys of living and proclaiming his kingdom, are the ones who make up his church. All the creeds and ecclesiastics in the world cannot make a church. Only the voluntary confession of Christ, and obedience to his commission, is the essence of the church.

This should be a warning to all Christians today that real church membership is not guaranteed by belonging to a particular denomination, having been baptized, or having been born of Christian parents. Only a deliberate and responsible decision to confess Christ and obey him can make one a true member of his church.

Christ's Special Teaching to the Church Which He Is Building (Matt. 17:1—18:35)

The passage.—In these two chapters which complete book four on "the kingdom and the church," Jesus gives some special revelation and teaching to those who have confessed him as Lord —that is, to his church. He reveals himself to them in a more intimate way than he ever has before, and he gives them specific instructions on relationships within the church and to the world outside.

Chapter 17 opens with the beautiful account of the transfiguration. Before the confession of Christ as Son of God, he could not have revealed himself to his disciples in this way. It would have overwhelmed them and destroyed the voluntary response of faith by which they confessed him. The fact that Jesus took only Peter, James, and John with him to the mount of transfiguration may suggest that only they had reached the point of spiritual maturity where they could be shown the heavenly glory of Jesus. The other disciples may not yet have been ready for this powerful revelation of the deity of Jesus. Jesus must have given this marvelous disclosure of his glory to those who had freely confessed him as Lord—as a confirmation of their confession and a spiritual strengthening for the ordeal which lay ahead.

Coming down from this glorious experience on the mount, Jesus had to face immediately the helplessness and unbelief of his disciples. Their inadequacy in the face of a suffering boy and his pleading father only dramatized the wide gulf between the power of Jesus and the spiritual immaturity of the disciples. They still had to grow a great deal, and Jesus knew that time was running out for his training of them.

After this experience of failure on the part of the disciples, Jesus makes a second prediction of his death and resurrection. Like an ominous drumbeat, these warnings are now coming as a reminder that the time is short. Their master will soon be taken away from them, and they must be ready to pick up the task which he passes on to them.

Chapter 17 closes with the unusual account of Jesus' payment of the tribute for himself and Peter, with the coin from a fish's mouth. It means that Jesus affirms the obligation of himself and his church to obey the just laws of society.

Chapter 18 is composed entirely of teaching which Jesus gave to his church on their relationships within the fellowship, and to the world outside.

The dispute about "the greatest in the kingdom of heaven" brings an exhortation to humility, like a little child. The warning against offences is a stern reminder of the danger of causing another to stumble. The Christian must be responsible for the way his deeds and words may hurt another.

The one lost sheep outside the fold requires more concern than the ninety-nine inside. This certainly shows the priority Jesus placed on reaching outside to those who are lost, rather than being preoccupied, as too many churches are, with their own membership.

The most practical guidance for dealing with personal conflicts is given by Jesus in this chapter. Go to your brother, whom you believe has wronged you, and seek to make it right! If no understanding is reached, take two or three others, as mediators and witnesses. If this fails, tell it to the church. If the offender will not hear the church, consider that person as one *outside*—a heathen and a publican. This does not mean to consign the person to hades, but to view him as a person to be reached and won by the redeeming love of Christ.

The exhortation to limitless forgiveness is followed by the humbling story of the ungrateful servant who had been forgiven so much—but would not forgive even the least of his debtors! Jesus closes his exhortation to the church on this note: you must forgive because you have been forgiven so much.

Special points.—Some interpreters see the transfiguration as a fulfilment of the promise that "some standing here" shall see the "Son of man coming in his kingdom" (Matt. 16:28). But Jesus still prophesied the coming of the Son of man upon the clouds of glory *after* the transfiguration. Obviously, he believed it was still in the future. The entire book five of Matthew's Gospel is on this theme of his coming.

Moses and Elijah signify the Law and the Prophets, the two divisions of the Old Testament canon of Scripture at the time of Jesus. Their conversation with Jesus means that they are testifying to him and his mission as the Messiah. The warning which Jesus gave to the three disciples, not to tell of the vision until after his resurrection, was to prevent someone from believing in him just because of this overwhelming experience. All men have to come to him by faith, and the disclosure of his heavenly glory is reserved for those who have already committed themselves to him by this simple act of trust.

Perhaps the most overlooked point in all this instruction to the church is the matter of initiative when someone has been hurt by a brother in the fellowship. Usually, when a person feels that he has been wronged, he will swell up with outraged pride and wait for the offender to come and try to make it right. Jesus exactly reverses this order: instead, the one who feels that he has been offended must take the first step! He must go to his brother and seek an understanding. The wisdom of this is obvious on a moment's thought. Some people have gone for years nursing grudges against people who did not even know they were being accused, much less what they were accused of doing. Only the one who has been hurt is in a position to take the initiative. Also, the problem of carrying a bitter feeling of resentment will quickly become the greatest evil of all. That means that the person most in need of immediate action is the one who feels that he has been wronged.

Truth for today.—These two chapters of instruction for the church give practical guidance for today. The transfiguration experience reminds us that the church needs the mountaintop experiences when the heavenly glory of her Lord shines through. It is the only way the church can be fortified to meet the challenge in the valley below.

The payment of the hated tribute money (or Temple tax) shows that Jesus, by word and example, counseled obedience even to irritating laws, when a principle was not at stake. He was not looking for an occasion to make trouble. He was exhorting his church to live peaceably, if at all possible.

Perhaps the words of Jesus about dealing with conflicts between brethren are the most urgent of all today. Bitterness and hurt feelings are more the rule than the exception in many churches. A careful, step-by-step following of the instruction of Jesus could overcome any misunderstanding. Clearly, the ideal is for brother to be reconciled to brother, without spreading the problem or hurting anyone else. Taking "two or three others" is a next step to widen the base of understanding and consideration, without involving the whole church.

The final exhortation to bring it to the church, if other steps fail, is a warning that conflict between brethren is a problem that concerns the whole church. It can undermine the fellowship and destroy the witness of the church in the community. How important it is to put into practice what Jesus says here!

Teaching on the Way to Jerusalem (Matt. 19:1—20:34)

The passage.—With Chapter 19:1 begins the last book of Matthew's Gospel, book five on "the coming judgment." Everything in this book, which runs from 19:1 to 26:1, is concerned with the coming judgment, in two senses: the judgment that Jerusalem is facing when her Messiah comes through the gates, and the judgment that all the nations will face when the Son of man comes upon his throne. This is consistent with all the teaching about judgment in the Gospels. There is a judgment which is taking place now, as men and nations are confronted by the gospel of Jesus Christ. And there is a judgment to come at the end of the age, when all nations shall be gathered before the Son of man on his throne.

On the way up to Jerusalem, to meet the last crisis, Jesus comes into the outlying borders of Judea, beyond the Jordan River. There he teaches again, as he had done in the Sermon on the Mount, that marriage is intended in the purpose of God to be an indissoluble union. Divorce, even though granted by Moses, is a failure of God's intended purpose.

Jesus receives and blesses the little children along the road. He calls upon the rich young man to give all his wealth to the poor and follow him. Jesus points out the difficulty of leaving possessions to follow him and blesses his disciples for doing exactly that.

In chapter 20, Jesus gives the parable of the laborers in the vineyard, indicating that even the Gentiles who come in later will have the same share in the kingdom.

The mother of James and John asks

that her sons be given the first places in the kingdom, drawing from Jesus the reminder that the greatest in the kingdom must be servants. Coming out of Jericho, on the last leg of the journey up the mountains to Jerusalem, Jesus heals two blind men who call him "Son of David!" The promised Son of David is about to come to Jerusalem for the last time, with their last opportunity.

Special points.—The saying of Jesus about divorce (19:9) adds something to his earlier teaching in the Sermon on the Mount. The warning that remarriage constitutes adultery is modified by the exception, "except it be for fornication." In 5:32, this exception is related directly to the divorce, rather than the remarriage. This seems to give more freedom to the innocent party in a marriage which has been destroyed by adultery.

In both cases, Jesus is firmly stating the ideal—so strongly, in fact, that the disciples decide it is best not to marry! Marriage is an awesome responsibility, and divorce is a serious failure to attain the ideal purpose of marriage. Only forgiveness and the grace of God can heal the broken hearts and lives in a broken home.

The cry "Son of David," from the blind men of Jericho, is a reminder that the promised Messiah is coming to his city. Even the blind men can "see" who he is. Matthew is almost asking the question, "Why can't you religious leaders see who he is, when even the blind men can see?"

Truth for today.—This whole passage moves with relentless step to the moment of decision. The primary thing it is telling us today is this: We cannot avoid the decision about following Jesus. Neither wealth, nor position, nor family problems, nor favored religious status can relieve us of the necessity of making our response to him. This is the most important issue of life, and the implications of it reach to all eternity.

Jesus' Triumphal Entry into Jerusalem (Matt. 21:1–46)

The passage.—Chapter 21 has one theme: the entry of the promised Son of David into Jerusalem. The Holy City is given her last opportunity to receive her Messiah.

The shouts of the children and the lowly explicitly fulfil the promise of the psalmist that these are the ones who will recognize him (Ps. 8:2). The cleansing of the Temple fulfils the prophecy of Malachi that the "Lord shall suddenly come to his temple" (3:1). The gauntlet is thrown down to the Temple authorities. Jesus paints their picture more plainly than they can stand in the parable of the wicked husbandmen who kill even the son that is sent to them! The chief priests and the Pharisees are determined to do exactly that—kill the Son.

Special points.—The fig tree which bore no fruit and withered away is a picture of Israel. It is a graphic object lesson to the disciples. Because the nation has not fulfilled its covenant promise, it will wither away.

The following promise about "prayer which removes mountains" should be understood in this context. Jesus is not suggesting that the disciples should pray for mountains to be removed into the sea, but illustrating the limitless power of prayer. Absolutely impossible things can happen "if they ask in prayer, believing."

Truth for today.—The main warning in this chapter is addressed to religious leaders of all time. Exactly at the point where Jesus should have been most welcome—the religious center of the Temple—he was most hated and rejected. The priests had a very lucrative business going in the buying and selling in the Temple. This money motive had blinded them to the terrible perversion of the religious institution. This is always the danger of institutionalized religion. All too often, in the history of the church, this blindness has been repeated. This passage stands there in the Gospel as a warning to us all!

The Last Conflicts with the Leaders in Jerusalem (Matt. 22:1:—23:39)

The passage.—Like a great crescendo in a symphony the crisis is building up to the climax of the rejection and crucifixion of Jesus by the leaders in Jerusalem. In these two chapters Matthew shows how each religious and political party threw down their last challenge to Jesus—trying to ensnare him and give a basis for his arrest and conviction. The Herodians, the Sadducees, and the Pharisees all threw their sharpest lawyers and their most controversial questions at Jesus to trap him. But he quietly answered them, devastating their arguments, and exposing the hypocrisy of them all.

Chapter 22 opens with the parable of the great wedding feast, a blunt warning to the Jewish leaders that when they reject the invitation to the messianic banquet, the Gentiles and the outcasts will be brought in. Then the Herodians and Pharisees tried to trip him up on the question of tribute to Caesar. It brought from Jesus the sweeping principle that Caesar has his due, but God's claim is supreme. They were stunned and speechless at his answer.

The Sadducees fared no better. Bringing out their "old saw" with which they worked on all their enemies, they asked a question about the resurrection. Because they did not believe in a resurrection, they liked to ridicule the idea by asking a silly question: If a woman married in succession seven brothers, to whom would she be married in the resurrection? Jesus demolished their question by exposing their naive assumption. They assumed that there would be marriage in the resurrection just as in this world, when, as Jesus said, the Scriptures and the power of God deny it.

The Pharisees had saved their attack and awesome public influence for the last round. They intended to put the finishing touches on this upstart Teacher from Galilee: "Which is the great commandment in the law?" This was the question which they agonized over constantly. They could never solve it, and they were intending to break Jesus with it. "Love God" and "Love your neighbor" came the answer! And in this simple and all-embracing double commandment of love they recognized the essence of all the commandments. In awe and amazement they still redoubled their plotting to kill him.

Chapter 23 is an unbroken pronunciation of woe upon the scribes and Pharisees. It is the most powerful and sustained denunciation that Jesus ever gave of anyone; and it ends with Jesus weeping over this great city that he loved so much—but could not gather to himself!

Special points.—The poor man who was thrown out of the wedding feast for not having a wedding garment (22:11–14) has always excited some sympathy. Brought in unexpectedly from the highways, how could he possibly have a wedding garment? Of course, all the others had been brought in the same way. They had wedding garments only because they had been provided. Obviously, this guest had refused his. Jesus is saying that even those who are brought into the kingdom after the Jews and their leaders have refused the invitation must also meet some conditions—like the wedding garment. Otherwise, they, too, will be rejected. It is a warning to the Gentiles not to be too smug about their acceptance in the kingdom, taking everything for granted. As the Jews stumbled and fell, so can they!

The harsh words with which Jesus indicted the religious leaders are so severe that some interpreters cannot accept the fact that Jesus spoke them. But what they miss is the heartbreak that runs through every word, and the tears of Jesus as he reaches out his arms over Jerusalem. Jesus had to make clear the nature of their sin in the plainest words, as a warning to them and to all of us who would follow. And still he reaches out his arms inviting them and us to come to repentance.

Truth for today.—One important truth runs through this passage: The greatest danger of religious leaders and institutions is hypocrisy. They appear white on the outside, like tombs, but inside are rotting bones. They discuss great questions like the resurrection and the supreme commandment, not to learn truth, but to use as a club over someone's head.

Matthew did not preserve this harsh indictment of the Pharisees by Jesus, just to place some blame on them. He knew that these words were also addressed to us, and that religious leaders must face their judgment for all time.

The Signs of Judgment and the Second Coming of Christ (Matt. 24:1—25:46)

The passage.—With these two chapters on the teaching of Jesus concerning the coming judgment, Matthew ends book five. After this last book of teaching, he places the narrative of the cross and resurrection at the conclusion of his gospel.

Matthew 24 weaves together the teaching of Jesus on two aspects of judgment: the coming destruction of Jerusalem, and the coming of Jesus at the end of the world. Every sign, whether famine or earthquake or war, is a reminder that turmoil and tragedy will mark history until Jesus comes. The impending destruction of Jerusalem, like the time of tribulation and judgment in every age, is simply a preview of the final great tribulation and judgment at the end of the age.

Chapter 25 is composed of three powerful parables of the coming judgment: First, the parable of the five wise and the five foolish virgins is a warning to be always ready, with "oil in the lamps." The bridegroom will come when he is least expected, even though he may have tarried long.

Second, the parable of the talents, teaching the responsibility of every servant to be a good steward of what he has been given, be it great or small. The time of reckoning is coming, when the King will require all to give an account of their stewardship.

Third, the much-loved and much-misinterpreted parable of the last judgment, when the sheep and the goats are divided by the Son of Man upon his throne of glory. The basis of judgment is the way they have treated the Son of Man through the way they have treated his brethren.

Special points.—The "abomination of desolation" standing in the holy place of the Temple (24:15) is some desecration of that sacred altar. It had happened when Antiochus Epiphanes slaughtered swine on the altar back in the second century B.C., and it happened again when Titus desecrated the Temple and destroyed the city with a Roman army in A.D. 70.

Every sign Jesus gives of his coming and the end of the world has been fulfilled. The meaning of the signs is this: In times like these, just like the ones in which we live, the Lord will come. It can happen at any moment.

The lightning shining from East to West means that the coming of Christ will be visible in the whole earth. It will not be necessary to be at a certain spot in order to see him.

Those who are "taken away" from the field and from the mill (24:40–41) are not raptured, as some interpreters have said. They are taken away to destruction, as in the flood of Noah (v. 39).

The three great parables of chapter 25 all point to the final judgment. The parable of the virgins emphasizes eternal vigilance; the parable of the talents responsible stewardship; and the Son of man on the throne emphasizes the basis of final judgment: the way men have treated his "brethren" and, therefore, the king himself.

Many interpreters have lifted this completely out of context and argued that the final basis of judgment for all men will be how they have treated the hungry, sick, and imprisoned. Certainly one does not have to depend upon this passage but can go to a score of places to demonstrate the concern of Jesus for suffering humanity. A man who does not actively follow the example of Jesus in serving the needs of broken and suffering men cannot be his disciple.

But this parable has a different thrust. It is a warning to all men that the way they treat the followers of Christ is the way they are treating him. Who are "the least of these my brethren"? Over and over again in this Gospel, Jesus tells us who his brethren are. It is a theme of the Gospel of Matthew, but some careless interpreters ignore that completely and give their own meaning to "the brethren." His disciples are his brethren and family (Matt. 12:48–49). Those

who do the will of his Father are his brethren (v. 50). Jesus means that if men ignore or reject his church, his followers, they are rejecting him; and they will be cast into everlasting punishment.

Truth for today.—It is surely one of the most perverse distortions of Scripture that men could use this very passage today to heap contempt upon the church, and urge "social action" as a substitute for Christian discipleship. For a true Christian, discipleship involves "social action" to meet the needs of men. But the man who ignores or rejects Christ and his brethren is facing certain condemnation, no matter how much he may protest that he did not realize that he was actually ignoring the King!

Notice also the exactly opposite attitude of those who cast their lot with the lowly and suffering brethren of the Son of man. In compassion they met the needs of the brethren of the rejected and crucified Son of Man, not seeking any reward. What a surprise was in store when this despised and rejected One was seen upon his throne!

The Last Supper, Betrayal, and Trial of Jesus (Matt. 26:1–75)

The passage.—Matthew has completed his collection of the teachings of Jesus. Now, in a powerful and moving narrative, he tells the story of the passion of Jesus.

After the plotting of the chief priests and rulers, and the symbolic anointing of Jesus in the house of Simon the leper, there follows the beautiful account of the Last Supper. Then Matthew records in great detail the agony in Gethsemane, Judas' betrayal of his master with a kiss, the shameful trial before Caiaphas, and the denial of Jesus by his most outspoken disciple—Peter! The chapter ends on the tragic but hopeful note that Peter went out "and wept bitterly."

18. Traditional site of the Last Supper (see Matt. 26:18)

Special points.—Jesus and the gospel writers saw great significance in his anointing by the woman in Bethany. It was a premonition of his coming death and a beautiful act of adoration at a time when almost all were rejecting him.

The struggle in Gethsemane was real. If Jesus had not been able to win the victory and pray "Thy will be done," the world would still be without a Savior. Jesus had to go through that agony alone; but the Last Supper with his disciples, and the exhortation to do this in remembrance of him, gives a continuing invitation to his followers to share as deeply as they can in his sacri-

fice and suffering.

Truth for today.—The celebration of the Lord's Supper, an almost universal observance in Christendom, is the visual embodiment of the truth of this passage. Jesus was betrayed and denied by his own disciples. The Supper calls us to a soul-searching self-examination. We, too, are capable of denying and betraying him.

The Supper calls us also to a deeper spiritual union with Christ in his suffering and death for us. Visible signs speak more eloquently than words. The simple elements of bread and the fruit of the vine (the word "wine" is never used in

613

connection with the Lord's Supper anywhere in the Bible!) are a reminder of
our dependence upon God for physical
sustenance, and upon the sacrifice of
Christ's body and blood for spiritual
rebirth.

The Crucifixion of Jesus (Matt. 27:1–66)

The passage.—The most heartbreak-
ing story in the history of the world is
told in this one chapter. Jesus was taken
after daybreak from the high priest's
house to Pontius Pilate. When Judas saw
that happen, he knew what was coming
and could not face it. Slinging the betrayal money down in the Temple, he
.went out and hanged himself.

Pilate is portrayed as willing, or even
anxious, to release Jesus. The crowd
would not have it, even choosing the
infamous criminal, Barabbas, rather
than Jesus. Pilate had Jesus scourged,
and then delivered him over to be
crucified.

The quiet agony on the cross is told
with amazing detail and great dignity.
The soldiers gambling for his robe, the
thieves on either side, the mocking
scribes and priests—they are all there.
And when the horrible deed is finished,
a relative stranger, Joseph of Arimathea,
and the faithful women are there to take
him down for burial. This chapter ends
on the pathetic attempt of the priests
and Pharisees to seal the tomb and keep
him there!

Special points.—Only Matthew tells
us that some of the saints arose and
came out of their graves *after* the resurrection of Jesus. Some interpreters dis-
count this completely because only
Matthew mentions it, and they do not
trust his historical sources.

It is important to notice what is said.
These are not called resurrections, such
as Jesus experienced. They simply "appeared" to many who knew them in

Jerusalem and, apparently, disappeared
again. There is no suggestion that they
continued to live on in a genuine resurrection from the dead.

These appearances must have been reported among the disciples in Jerusalem,
and it is almost certain what they meant.
The disciples believed that Jesus went
into the abode of the dead with the
glorious news of his victory on the cross
(1 Pet. 3:18–22; 4:6). This brought
ecstatic rejoicing to those who had long
awaited his coming. Jesus knocked the
lock off the door of Hades, and some of
them got out for a little while, in a kind
of preview of that day when all his
disciples will follow him through the
open doorway of the tomb into resurrected glory! This is surely the spiritual
meaning of these appearances, whatever
form they took and however they were
reported.

Truth for today.—The overwhelming
truth for us today is that we cannot
blame the death of Jesus on someone
else. We are guilty of doing the self-
same things today.

We deny him, forsake him, or even
betray him to his enemies. Like the
disciples we can be more concerned with
our sleep than with the agony of Jesus
for a lost world. We can even join the
crowd that mocks him on his cross, or
the soldiers that gamble for his robe
while he dies for them. Matthew holds
up a mirror in this chapter. If we look
carefully, we may see ourselves!

The Resurrection of Jesus and His Com-mission to His Disciples (Matt. 28:1–20)

The passage.—Most biographies end
at the grave, but for this life the grave
is just the beginning. Matthew ends his
Gospel on the triumphant note of the
resurrection of Jesus and his commission
to his disciples to go to the ends of the
earth making disciples.

The faithful women, especially the two Marys, are singled out by Matthew as the last to leave the body of Jesus at his burial and the first to the tomb on Easter morning. To them the angel gave the first news of the resurrection: "He is not here: for he is risen, as he said" (v. 6). Hurrying to tell his disciples, they meet Jesus on the way. Falling at his feet, they worship him!

Even the enemies of Jesus are shaken by this momentous event. The frantic guards run from the tomb to the chief priests and are "paid off" to tell the fictitious story that his disciples stole his body away. This saying is still being reported among the Jews at the time of the writing of this Gospel, some fifty years later.

Upon a mountain in Galilee, Jesus appeared to the eleven disciples and gave them the commission which has guided his followers until this day—and will be their guide until the end of the world. All authority in heaven and earth was claimed by Jesus. Upon the basis of that supreme authority, he commanded his disciples to carry out three particular activities in their mission to the world:

(1) Make disciples in all nations;
(2) Baptize them in the name of the Father, Son, and Holy Spirit;
(3) Teach them to observe all his commandments.

To this Great Commission is added the promise which has sustained his followers in the face of suffering, pain, and death: "Lo, I am with you always, even unto the end of the world." Every disciple who has gone out in the strength of this promise can testify that it has always proven true. From highest mountain to deepest valley, in joy and in sorrow, in life and in death, not one of his disciples has he ever forsaken!

Special points.—The account of the angel of the Lord descending and rolling back the stone is taken by some to mean that the stone was rolled away to let Jesus out of the tomb. This misses the whole point. Jesus had already risen! The stone (or closed doors and walls) presented no barrier to him.

The stone was rolled away to let his followers in—to let men see "the place where the Lord lay." This is another element in the remarkable testimony to the resurrection of Jesus. The tomb was empty. His body had undergone a marvelous transformation. He could both limit himself to the conditions of this physical existence (by walking with them, or preparing a meal and eating with them) and transcend the limits of this natural order (by appearing and disappearing, passing through closed doors, ascending beyond the clouds). This is the best clue we have to the nature of the resurrection body in the life to come: if we are to be like him, as he says, we will have a transformed body which can both experience the kind of reality we know now, and go beyond it.

It is interesting that in the Great Commission the first command in the English versions is to "Go!" In the original Greek, the word for "go" is a participle, meaning "as you go." The first imperative, or command, is "Make disciples!" This states the priority in the mission of the church. The next command, to baptize, is the visible sign and public declaration of that discipleship. The final command, to teach them the commandments of Jesus, is the content and the continuing task of the church in the world.

Truth for today.—The overwhelming significance of the resurrection today lies in this one fact: Jesus Christ is alive and reigning in the midst of his disciples. The resurrection is not just an ancient record in history. True, it is an actual historical event; and the evidence for it is of absolute importance. But, a person could believe that Jesus arose from the dead and still be utterly lost and without hope in the world.

One must meet the risen Christ himself: The evidence of the Christian writings, all of the New Testament, and the witness of Christians through the centuries make their contribution to belief in the resurrection of Christ. But the final and decisive step comes when the individual man truly meets the risen Christ in his own inner experience and cries out like the disciple of old, "My Lord, and my God!"

All of the wonderful Gospel of Matthew is intended to bring the reader to this point. The Son of David who moved down the dusty roads of Galilee must be met and accepted in our own hearts as the Son of God who gave his life for us all.

MARK

Landrum P. Leavell

INTRODUCTION

The opening words of this book stake out the claim of priority. If it is the earliest written record of the life of Jesus, it is the most important writing in the Bible. The books of the Old Testament preserve the historical record of God's relationship to the Jewish people. He promised them the Messiah. Those centuries were but prelude, being consummated in Jesus Christ.

It is believed that Mark's Gospel was written primarily for Roman readers. This could explain why Mark did not trace the genealogy of Jesus and seek to prove the fulfilment of prophecy. Had this Gospel been intended for a Jewish audience, surely some attempt would have been made to prove the identity of Jesus Christ.

Romans were noted for their common sense and practicality. With Rome ruling the world, they understood power and authority. Mark gives emphasis to the power and authority of our Lord, with the miracles prominently described.

Even a superficial reading of Mark will show the rapidity with which the narrative moves. It is filled with verbs of action. The word "straightway" appears forty times in this Gospel, and is only found forty times in the remainder of the New Testament. This word appears ten times in the first chapter.

The weight of scholarship holds that Mark was an associate of Peter. In 1 Peter 5:13, Peter refers to "Mark, my son" who was his companion in Babylon. This could imply that Peter was instrumental in winning Mark to Christ.

Vivid detail is found throughout the Gospel. This suggests the account of an eye witness. If Mark was with Peter, and had possession of notes from Peter's preaching, this accounts for the minute details found in many places. A number of writers from early centuries refer to Mark as an "interpreter of Peter."

Three languages were used prominantly by early Christians. These were Hebrew, Greek, and Aramaic. Many scholars believe that Peter spoke in Aramaic, which could explain the presence of a number of Aramaic expressions found in Mark. The number of peculiarly Latin terms is understandable if these discourses were originally delivered in Rome.

This Gospel, like Matthew, Luke, and John, does not contain the name of the author. Early Christian tradition and modern scholarship hold the author to be John Mark, referred to in Acts 12:12 and Acts 13:13. As was frequently done in that day, John had both a Jewish name and a Roman name. John is Jewish, and Mark or Marcus is Roman.

Surely part of Mark's purpose in writing his Gospel was to provide a written record of the earthly ministry of Jesus Christ. This undoubtedly came through the prompting of the Spirit.

John Mark was associated with both Paul and Barnabas as well as Simon Peter. Paul and Barnabas took him with them when they went out on one of their missionary journeys. During the travels, Mark left them at Perga in Pamphylia. This led to a misunderstanding between Mark and Paul which was later resolved. Acts 15:39 reveals that Barnabas took Mark and moved out in the proclamation of the gospel. Colossians 4:10 reveals that there was a kinship between Barnabas and Mark.

The date of this Gospel has been placed from approximately A.D. 50 to A.D. 70. If Mark is the first written Gospel, it had to exist before Matthew and Luke. There are strong reasons to date it within 25 to 30 years following the crucifixion of Christ.

I. THE GENESIS OF THE GOSPEL (MARK 1:1–20)

The passage.—Although Mark probably wrote primarily for Gentile readers, he begins by linking his account to the Old Testament. The obvious difference in these opening verses as compared to Matthew and Luke can probably best be explained by the different audiences to whom these Gospels were addressed. A Roman audience would not be nearly so interested in Hebrew genealogy as would a Jewish audience.

The message of John the Baptist was a clarion call for repentance. The baptism of John was a repentance kind of baptism, or one that gave proof of repentance.

The popularity of John's ministry is shown in verse 5. Undoubtedly the crowd was composed in part by curiosity seekers. Yet there were many who genuinely repented, as proven by their willingness to follow Jesus when he began his public ministry.

Special points—Much has been said about John's asceticism. Some have suggested he was an Essene. John did not withdraw from the world in disgust; he attacked in the power of God.

There is a movement abroad today away from the institutional church. Some feel the church moves too slowly, while others feel the church is moving too rapidly, especially in social ministries. There is a need for men like John. He stood his ground, condemned hypocrisy, and called for repentance and godly living.

Beginning in verse 9 Mark shows how Jesus was approved. He received the approval of John, known far and wide as God's prophet. To this was added the approval of John's baptism. Then came the certification of God himself, at the time of the baptism. On the basis of this authentication, Jesus embarked on his earthly ministry.

In verse 15 we find the assertion of God's unique sovereignty. The age of the eschaton had finally dawned. The coming of Jesus Christ marks the embarkation of man upon the last days.

II. GREAT GALILEAN MINISTRY (MARK 1:21—6:13)

Authority (Mark 1:21–45)

The passage.—The concentration of the early ministry of Jesus in this province was doubtless by design. It was the rural, agrarian area of Palestine as compared to the more urban Judea. The people who lived there were removed from the strong influence of the religious leaders in Jerusalem. Through this area ran the arterial highway connecting Egypt, Syria, and Arabia.

Mark moves quickly to establish Jesus' authority. It was not the conferred authority marked by a robe, crown, and scepter. It was the inherent authority of a Spirit-controlled personality. It was obvious to those who listened that Jesus was not like the scribes.

Mark records four illustrations showing Christ's authority over illness. The first showed how an unclean spirit yielded to the authority of the Son of God (1:23–28). Jesus came into the world as the Redeemer, but ministered to human need in such a way as to teach and to save.

The fever of Peter's mother-in-law (1:29–30) is an entirely different kind of sickness from that of the unclean spirit. Jesus had authority over this fever, and the proof of the cure is in her ministry to them.

There seems to be a distinction in Mark between demons (1:32–34) and unclean spirits (1:23–28). Whatever the malady caused by these, Jesus Christ had authority over both.

Perhaps the most tragic illness of that day was leprosy (1:40–45). It did not immediately kill, but left one maimed and crippled. Jesus touched this leper, in defiance of the ritual law. This serves to substantiate the priority Jesus gave to persons over the petty legal restrictions of the Jewish law.

Special points.—We must allow latitude in our approach to the subject of demons. It is not possible for us to positively identify these with modern day mental illness or psychoses. Whether or not these exist today in the same form cannot be stated.

It is certain that the people of the first century believed in demons. It is apparent that Jesus shared this belief, at least to the point of getting to the source and effecting a cure. We are on safe grounds when we interpret every illness, of whatever nature, as an opportunity for Christian ministry.

Criticism (Mark 2:1—3:6)

The passage.—In chapter 2 through 3:6 we see the criticism of Jesus growing among the scribes and Pharisees. They were critical because he forgave sin. It was their belief that no one could forgive sin save God only. Since they did not acknowledge Jesus as God, they judged his actions to be blasphemy. In Old Testament times those guilty of blasphemy were sentenced to die by stoning.

There was widespread belief in those days that physical maladies were a result of sin. The friends of Job thought him to be guilty of gross sin because he suffered so. It naturally followed in their thinking that restoration depended upon forgiveness. Perhaps it was for this reason that Jesus first forgave the sin of a victim of palsy (2:1–12). The Pharisees had no way of knowing whether or not the man's sins were actually forgiven. The man knew, but Jesus provided the proof in commanding him to take his bed and carry it out.

In 2:13–17 we find the call of Matthew. It has been pointed out that he left everything except his quill. His sacrifice was greater initially than that of the fishermen apostles, for he could not return to this political position of tax-collector.

The Pharisees were horrified when Jesus went into the home of a despised publican to eat a meal. Jesus made no effort to defend these people and their sin, but stated their need. Publicans had plenty of money. Their problems were not economic. Adequate financial resources, however, cannot solve the problems of personal sin. These were spiritually sick and needed the Great Physician.

In 2:18–22, Jesus is criticized for refusing to fast. The only fast prescribed in the Torah was on the Day of Atonement. The oral tradition had developed so far beyond the Torah that every Monday and Thursday were designated as fast days. Jesus did not approve fasting for fasting's sake. It is not necessarily a mark of piety because the calendar indicates it is time to fast. This practice becomes meaningful when transcendent values are given priority, causing mundane, lesser things to fade into insignificance.

It is likely that 2:19–20 reveal the shadow of the cross falling upon Jesus. He referred to himself as the bridegroom, and pointed to a time when he would not be with them.

In 2:21–22 Jesus showed the incompatibility between the Jewish system and Christianity. The Jewish system, like an old garment, had served over a long period of time. The Christian faith is not an appendage to be sewn on an old garment. Ritual forms, ritual sacrifices, and special days are outward expressions only. The Christian faith, like new wine, cannot be contained in the vehicle of the old system.

In 2:23 through 3:6 we find two criticisms centering in sabbath regulations. Jewish leaders had reduced their sabbath laws to a total of thirty-four. Under each of these thirty-four laws there were six divisions!

The feeling of some Jews toward the Sabbath was so strong that they would not defend themselves on the sabbath. Military enemies, knowing this about the Jews, sometimes attacked on the sabbath, knowing the Jews would not resist.

The Pharisees' concept of faith centered in the word "ritual." As long as they did the right thing at the right time, they felt themselves to be orthodox and acceptable to God. Jesus taught that man's highest expression of faith was not in ritual but in service. The sabbath as an institution should not receive top priority. The sabbath was made for man, not vice versa.

The conflict in 3:1–6 stems from the same source. Their beliefs were so distorted that they held institutions to be of greater worth than persons. In verse

4 Jesus asked a question, which if they had answered honestly, would have condemned them. Jesus called the man into the center of the crowd, and in the presence of all healed his withered hand.

In 3:6 we find the strange coalition of Pharisees and Herodians. Here and in Mark 12:13 are the only two references to this party. These politically oriented people were supporters of Herod the Great. Though he was half-Jew, he had an appointment from the Romans that gave him authority in that part of the Roman Empire. The Herodians wanted one of Herod's descendents in that position once more, that they might reap the benefits of a good working relationship with Rome.

Special points.—The word which Jesus spoke in 2:2 was the gospel. It included his own identity and the fulfilment of the messianic promise.

Fasting has validity today when associated with supreme values. When preoccupied over the illness of a loved one, fasting comes easily. When we are wrapped up in spiritual concerns, the thought of food is secondary. Fasting today should be Christ honoring, not for promotion of self.

Truth for today.—In the emphasis on forgiveness in 2:1–12, we must keep in mind the obligation both to forgive and receive forgiveness. These are equally difficult.

The incident in 2:15 f. points up an aspect of Christian responsibility. We are responsible to those considered to be outcasts from society. They are sometimes well-to-do, like these publicans, as well as the economically disadvantaged.

In 2:21–22 Jesus sounded a relevant warning. We can be so wrapped up in the system that we lose sight of our purpose. We must remember that there is never any finality in the system or the methods. There is finality in our message, but the new wine will not long be contained in old wineskins. The wineskins of method are easily antiquated. We must remain willing to let the system go, but preserve the new wine at all costs.

Popularity (Mark 3:7-35)

The passage.—In 3:7-35 we see the ever growing popularity of Jesus. This interesting section reveals certain responses to the ministry of Jesus. Because of the tremendous throng of people, it was necessary to get into the boat and push out a little way into the Sea of Galilee. Though the Pharisees had established their opposition to him, it is obvious in verses 7-11 that the common people loved him and followed him.

In 3:13-19 is found a response from those called to be apostles. This significant moment in the earthly ministry of Jesus required withdrawal from the multitudes. Luke's Gospel adds the interesting sidelight that Jesus spent a night in prayer before selecting the twelve.

In 3:14 it is said that Jesus "ordained" these men. The word is better rendered "made." It does not involve ordination in the modern sense, with a special service to which all church members are invited. It would appear obvious that Jesus related some of the costs involved and the sacrifice they would be called upon to make.

There is a good possibility that the number "twelve" is significant. The number could symbolically refer to the twelve tribes of Old Testament times.

Much has been said regarding the difficulty in correlating the names of these men by the lists that appear in different places. These men are named in four separate New Testament passages, with one name appearing differently three times. Some suggest there must have been more than twelve men, others insist the lists are not accurate, but it is both reasonable and possible for one man to have been known by three separate names.

In 3:20-27 we find the response of religious leaders and the comment Jesus made. His ministry was identified with the work of Beelzebub, "the prince of devils." Jesus pointed out that Satan would not destroy his own house, yet Satan's house was being destroyed.

In 3:28-30 Jesus speaks of blasphemy against the Holy Spirit, which is sometimes called the unpardonable sin. This is refusal to accept obvious truth. It is apparent that a Christian cannot commit this sin.

In 3:31-35 we discover the response of Jesus' family to his ministry. These were his mother and his half-brothers, and he used their coming to point out a basic spiritual truth. Kingdom citizenship does not depend upon flesh and blood, but rather upon spirit. This is the kindred spirit we possess in seeking to accomplish God's purpose through faith in Christ.

Teaching by Parable (Mark 4:1-35)

The passage.—In 4:1-35 Jesus taught by parable. This was a favorite method of his.

Some say there is no connection between these four parables. A close relationship can be seen when they are read and studied from the standpoint of the witnessing obligation of every Christian.

In 4:1-20 we have the parable of the sower and the soils. Interpreters generally emphasize one or the other, but not both. Neither should rule out the other. The sower has an obligation to sow faithfully, while the hearer is obliged to hear and respond. The Christian witness knows that all hearers will not respond affirmatively. The sower knew that all soil would not be productive. This did not deter him from faithfully scattering the seed. He broadcasts the same good seed regardless of the reception it might gain.

In 4:21–25 the parable of the candle points up the Christian's responsibility for action. Someone may have questioned the value of bearing witness or sowing seed if the response was to be as limited as the preceding parable suggested. Jesus pointed out that a Christian has no choice. The purpose of a saved life is to dispel darkness. In 4:24–25 we are taught that faithfulness in shining will determine reward.

In 4:26–29 we discover the mystery of growth. The point appears to be that we are not equipped to know the results of either our sowing or shining. The results may come many years later, but they come. The Zealots had their own methods of getting results, but Jesus said the kingdom would not come about according to their methods.

The parable of the mustard seed is recorded in 4:30–34. Its connection with the three preceding parables can be seen in encouragement to those who are reaping meager results. It is not up to us to measure the response, but to sow the seed. A well known saying reminds us that "great oaks from little acorns grow." This is another way to express this parable.

Teaching by Miracle (Mark 4:35—5:43)

The passage.—Turning from teaching by parable, Jesus began to teach by miracle. In 4:35–41 Jesus established himself as Lord over nature. In withdrawing from the multitude, he and the disciples put out onto the Sea of Galilee. This ordinarily placid body of water was subject to violent storms. The minute details in 4:38 and following undoubtedly came from an eyewitness.

Jesus commanded the storm to "be muzzled," using a verb form that implied immediate action, proclaiming the miraculous element of his word. This was not a gradual diminution of the wind and waves, but immediate calm. The disciples were originally frightened by the storm, but 4:41 points out their fear in the presence of One who has power over the storm.

In 5:1–20 Jesus showed himself to be Lord over demons. In this incident it is apparent that demon possession is marked by attempted suicide, insanity, and self-destruction. The text pictures Jesus as a believer in the presence and power of demons. To hold otherwise is to question the integrity of the Gospel writer and place the entire Gospel account in question.

Whatever one may choose to believe about demons, the text is quite clear that Jesus had authority over them. Whoever or whatever they might be, this was a malady that kept men from being whole and Jesus could restore possessed men to wholeness. Among the problems this miracle raises is that of the destruction of property. This may well be an underscoring of the supreme value of human personality. Humans are more important than institutions like the sabbath and they are of vastly greater worth than material possessions.

In 5:21–24, 35–43 Jesus proved his power over death. Mark weaves this experience with another showing Jesus' lordship over disease in 5:25–34. This serves as substantiation for the authenticity of Mark's account, for it is perfectly natural to find an interruption in the activity of Jesus.

Jairus, who held a position of authority and respect in the synagogue, came to beseech Jesus to intercede in behalf of his little girl. As they walked away together, out of the crowd came a woman who had a physical problem which had plagued her for twelve years. She had spent all her money for medical attention, but without relief. In addition to her physical illness, she was considered ceremonially unclean, as described in Leviticus 15:25.

When she touched Jesus, he knew that power had gone forth from him. It cost Jesus to heal. He was conscious of the flow of the power of God through him to another.

Moving on more quickly with only three of the apostles, they went to the home of Jairus. When the professional mourners had been cleared out, Jesus took the little girl by the hand and restored her alive.

Teaching at Home (6:1–28)

The passage.—In 6:1–13 we find some reactions to the ministry of Jesus in his native Galilee. Their astonishment at his apparent wisdom stemmed from the fact that they had known him in his youth. The omission of any reference to Joseph may imply that he was already dead, or could possibly allude to the fact of the virgin birth.

Jesus pointed out the difficulty of a hometown boy being accepted by his peers. John 6:5 can mean that the mighty works of Jesus were not the miracles of healing and restoration from physical infirmities. The greatest work he desired to accomplish was opening up and transforming minds, changing attitudes and direction. He could heal physical ills with or without personal faith, but the inner transformation can only come when one is willing to believe and accept.

Beginning in 6:7 Jesus sent out the twelve apostles. Their ministry was spiritual, and their physical needs would be supplied by those to whom they ministered. They were not to engage in debate or argument with those who rejected their message, but were to move on offering the gospel to those who would hear and heed.

Mark gives the details on the death of John the Baptist in 6:14–29. He made it perfectly clear that John was not an enemy of the state. He was not put to death because he endangered Roman interests. His message of repentance and righteousness conflicted with the personal life of Herod Antipas. Mark will also show that Jesus was not a seditionist, and made no attempt to overthrow Rome.

Special points.—In 4:41 fear came upon those who witnessed the miracle. In 5:15 those who saw the restored man were afraid. In 5:33 the woman made whole was fearful and trembling. In 5:42 those who witnessed the miracle were filled with great amazement. This seems to be the natural reaction to the miraculous ministry of our Lord, both then and now. This fear hardens some persons and makes them cynical and doubtful. It warms the hearts of others and makes them believe more strongly.

III. GETTING BEYOND GALILEE (MARK 6:30—10:52)

Some of the most important events in the ministry of Jesus are found in this section of Mark. There are four withdrawals, in which Jesus and the disciples sought to get away from the crowds for periods of rest and instruction. Due to the overwhelming popularity of his cause, people continue to flock to the side of Jesus Christ. Included in this section is the record of the journey toward Jerusalem. The shadow of the cross can be seen with growing clarity. This section covers approximately six months of the earthly ministry of Jesus.

Crowds and Miracles (Mark 6:30–56)

The passage.—Every human periodically needs rest and relaxation. Jesus called the twelve apart to refresh themselves or to rest up. In addition to the tension created by the crowds, perhaps they were distracted over the death of John the Baptist. Chapter 6, verse 32 states the Pharisees' purpose, but their plan was aborted.

In verses 33–44 the record of the feeding of five thousand appears. Clearly, Mark recorded this as a miracle. To hold otherwise brings the integrity of Mark and the divinity of Jesus into question.

Another miraculous event is found in verse 45–52. It was about three hours before sunrise, with a stiff wind blowing, that Jesus walked to the boat on the water. The amazement of the disciples led to the hardening of their hearts. This could be due to the attempted imposition of the role of an earthly ruler upon Jesus. Whatever the cause, they hardened their own hearts.

The final four verses of this chapter describe a return to Galilee. Word had reached these people concerning the healing of the woman with the issue of blood. They also desired to touch the tassel of his garment. They gladly followed Jesus as long as he fed and healed them. When he outlined the claims made by discipleship, the crowds melted away. The greater blessings, those of the spirit, were sublimated to physical concerns then and now.

Conflict and Withdrawal (Mark 7:1–37)

The passage.—In chapter 7 we find Mark's record of the continuing conflict between Jesus and Jewish tradition. In verses 3, 5, and 8 we find the word "tradition." This is the oral law, not God's revelation recorded in the Old Testament. They had come to look upon their man-made rules as sacred and binding.

Beginning in verse 10 we find an illustration of their hypocrisy. The word "Corban" in Hebrew means "gift." One of the Ten Commandments requires that honor be given parents. This includes provision for their physical needs. Some were known to evade this parental duty by giving their estate to the Temple rather than to parents. It was easy from that point to find a loophole and keep one's property, giving it neither to the Temple nor one's parents. The hypocrisy is in saying one has given his property to God, and neither doing this nor caring for aged parents.

In verses 14–23 Jesus clarifies and condemns the sin of the spirit, not just the sin of the flesh. The Jews judged a man by his outward conformity to law. The spirit, attitude, and motive of an individual more clearly reveals his true nature. Man tends to look on outward appearances, but God ever looks on the heart.

A second withdrawal is described in 7:24–30. This one takes Jesus into Gentile country. This is a difficult passage to interpret, but can be seen as a test of this Greek woman's faith. There is also the possibility that Jesus did this as a lesson for the twelve. Some have suggested it may reflect an inner struggle with Jesus.

Another withdrawal, this time away from Phoenicia, is recorded in verses 31–37. Returning to the area around the Sea of Galilee, a deaf and dumb man was brought to him for healing. He could speak, but with an impediment. The importance of this healing may be in light of the fact that the man was a Gentile who was healed by a Jew. In the presence of the twelve the wall of separation was beginning to be destroyed.

Ministry and Miracles (Mark 8:1—9:1)

The passage.—In 8:1–9 we have the miracle of feeding the four thousand. Some commentators hold that this is merely a repetition of the previous miracle when five thousand were fed. That view would question the integrity of both Mark and Matthew, for both record the two feedings. The feeding of the five thousand involved a Jewish crowd. This feeding, taking place in the Decapolis region, involved Gentiles primarily.

It is possible that this is another step in the breaking down of the wall of prejudice. Jesus showed no partiality because of race. His ministry was to all men, both Jew and Gentile.

In 8:10–21 there is another record of the Pharisees' attempt to trap Jesus. Though Dalmanutha cannot be positively identified, it is obviously on the southern shore of the Sea of Galilee, and out of strictly Gentile country.

Beginning in 8:13 through 9:29, we find the fourth withdrawal. During this time Jesus sought to give the twelve greater understanding regarding his purpose. In 8:21 he asked if they were not beginning to perceive. The miraculous feeding of two multitudes should have given them new insight.

The leaven of the Pharisees must have been spiritual blindness. This sin led to the rejection of Jesus Christ in favor of the maintenance of tradition. The twelve must interpret Jesus and his ministry in light of what he was doing, not in terms of their preconceived ideas of the Messiah.

Beginning in 8:22 we have the only recorded instance of a gradual healing. It was a miracle, but was brought about in a different manner. In order, this man looked up, looked through, and looked in. This could be descriptive of the gradual comprehension of the truth of the ministry and purpose of Jesus. The twelve did not suddenly grasp the intention of Jesus. Their understanding was slowly opened.

The supreme confession of Peter recorded in 8:27–30 comes when Jesus was finally alone with the apostles. Peter scored one hundred on this theological question. He was much slower to learn about emotions, for Jesus later had to ask the third time, "Lovest thou Me?"

In 8:31 through 9:1 Jesus issued his call to commitment. It is apparent that the twelve were not ready for Jesus to die, nor to die themselves.

The Kingdom had come already when Jesus spoke the words in 9:1. They had not yet seen it and were still looking for signs. They will understand the kingdom better in light of the cross and resurrection. The verb form here is best translated "having come" or "has come." The kingdom came with Jesus, but the disciples could not see it because they were looking for the wrong thing.

Transfiguration and Teaching (Mark 9:2–50)

The passage.—The transfiguration, recorded in 9:2–13 has deep and rich theological implications. This scene included Moses representing the law, Elijah representing the prophets, and Jesus Christ as the fulfilment of both. Both Moses and Elijah had triumphant departures. The exodus of Jesus would be a greater triumph than either of the others.

The earthly body of Jesus was not able to contain the divine effulgence. This may be comparable to the resurrection body which will be given the redeemed for eternity. It is a wonderful foretaste of glory, both for the apostles and modern-day Christians.

The experience of the twelve in 9:14–29 is as modern as today. They were powerless in their ministry, due to the fact that they were prayerless.

During a brief visit back to Galilee,

Jesus insisted on his role as suffering Servant. They still had not accepted the messianic role of Jesus, holding to their own image and ideas.

The paradox of Christian greatness is beautifully described in 9:33–50. These teachings were prompted by the fact that the twelve were still jockeying for position. Jesus did not denounce greatness, he merely taught that it came in a different way than men suppose. Greatness comes through service. It involves the same spirit that leads to kindness toward a child. Such kindness is rendered without thought of reward. A child can scarcely repay. We extend kindness and service to all, even those who cannot give in return. In 9:40 Jesus seems to be dealing with prejudice. Like the twelve, we must be slow to criticize those who use different methods from our own.

Responsibility and reward are outlined in 9:41–48. How important it is for the trumpet to sound a certain note. To do otherwise can cause a babe in Christ to stumble, and this has serious consequences. Chapter 9, verse 48 points up the horror of hell, where there is no death nor any cessation from punishment.

The concluding verses of chapter 9 suggest our influence may well be determined by our harmony with one another. This may refer back to the person described in verse 38.

Teachings on Discipleship (Mark 10:1–52)

The passage.—Beginning in chapter 10 Jesus sets his face toward Jerusalem.

Jesus' teaching on divorce is found in 10:1–12. The purpose in marriage is that two persons shall become one. Anything short of that is failure and a compromise of God's purpose. The New Testament gives one reason, which God

approves, for divorce. There is absolute silence regarding remarriage, even if the reason for divorce is biblical. It is always hazardous to try to speak where the Bible is silent.

The necessity of childlikeness is found in 10:13–16. This passage points up the kind of mind with which Jesus can work. It implies a willingness to receive and to follow. It also involves wonder and awe.

The grave danger of great riches is told in 10:17–31. This polite person referred to Jesus in a complimentary fashion. Jesus tried to find out if he actually believed he was God. In referring to the commandments, Jesus was not implying that salvation came in keeping them. This was rather the quickest way to unmask this egocentric individual. A man is not saved by giving away his possessions. He becomes a Christian when he is willing to renounce anything that stands between himself and Christ.

Once again in 10:32–34 there is the reiteration of the dire happenings in store for Jesus. Against that background, it seems all the more incongruous for the apostles to continue to be concerned about personal rank. It was necessary in 10:35–45 to reinforce the lesson on greatness. That which the apostles desire cannot be bestowed, it must be earned through humility and service.

It was near the city of Jericho that Jesus blessed blind Bartemaeus. Likely the crowds were gathered along the road to greet travelers on the way to the Passover in Jerusalem. Though Jesus told him to go his own way, Bartemaeus joined him and his followers.

Special points.—Three theological concepts are underscored in Mark 6:29 —10:52. Jesus is identified as the Christ in 8:29, and in 8:31 as the Son of man and suffering Servant. Jesus accepted the identification as Messiah, but rejected their concept of that One. God's Messiah was to be a Servant identified with all humanity. Stephen was the only other person in the New Testament to refer to Jesus as "Son of man."

IV. THE SHADOW OF THE CROSS (MARK 11:1—14:52)

On to Jerusalem (Mark 11:1–26)

The passage.—Jesus began the last phase of his public ministry from Bethany, about two miles from Jerusalem. The coming of the King (11:1–11) was marked by careful preparation. Though he was King Messiah, he was not the warrior type. He came in fulfilment of the prophecy in Zechariah 9:9. A conquering king would enter a defeated city *after* the battle. Jesus entered Jerusalem *before* the battle. A warrior king would ride upon a white horse, with the bound prisoners following him. Jesus came on a donkey, symbolic of peace, not to imprison but to liberate.

Like all Jews, past and present, Jesus loved Jerusalem. He afforded them one more opportunity to acknowledge him and to be saved. Also, his ministry had reached the point where he now was ready to face the leaders of Judaism on their own home grounds.

Returning to Jerusalem the next day, Jesus pronounced an awesome judgment upon barrenness (11:12–14). In all likelihood, the leafy tree without fruit was representative of the sham and emptiness of the religious practices in Jerusalem. Just so, the judgment of God was to come upon those practitioners of religion who were being weighed and found wanting.

The cleansing of the Temple (11:15–19) was a challenge both to the greed and irreverence of those people. The Temple was designed to be a place of worship and reverence. With the tur-

moil, noise, and confusion created by the presence of the money changers, the purpose of the Temple was prostituted. This act was an indictment against the religious leaders who allowed these practices. It was a direct confrontation with their authority and spirituality.

Returning to the city the next day, the disciples observed the withered fig tree (11:20–26). Jesus answered Peter's question with a call to definite spiritual exercise. His followers were to be men of unswerving faith and prayer.

Opposed by Leaders (Mark 11:27—12:44)

The passage.—In 11:27–33 Jesus both confounded the religious leaders and clarified his authority. As he frequently did, Jesus asked a question in response to a question. He wanted them to state their attitude toward the ministry of John the Baptist. This put them in an indefensible position. If they had stated John's ministry was of God, they would have stood condemned for not listening to and obeying John. Had they denied the divine authority of John, they would have incurred the wrath of the people who universally believed John to be a prophet sent from God. Jesus made no attempt to further identify his authority. Since they would not be honest in regard to John, he felt no need to pursue the matter with them.

The parable found in 12:1–12 appears in all three Synoptic Gospels. It is a direct attack upon the hypocrisy of the religious leaders. The parable applies to the entire nation Israel. God is pictured as the owner, and has provided everything necessary for the harvest. The treatment afforded the servants is comparable to the reaction of the Jews toward the prophets and others whom God sent. When the tenants, who were the Jews, killed the son of the owner, they rejected both the heir and the owner. In rejecting Jesus, they rejected God also. This dastardly deed was not done in ignorance, for 12:7 points out their recognition of the heir. According to verse 12 the point of the parable was not lost. They wanted to kill him then, but were more afraid of the crowd than they were of God.

After the Sadducees were soundly rebuked, other groups came to try their hand at intimidating Jesus. The Pharisees and Herodians came next in 12:13–17. After Herod the Great's death, in about 4 B.C., his rule over all Palestine was ended and the province divided. The Herodians wanted a descendent of Herod returned to authority.

The Pharisees, bitter enemies of Jesus, were opposed to all taxation by a foreign nation. They put the question, believing that any answer would condemn Jesus. If he said taxes should be paid, the Jews would despise him for taking the side of the Romans. If he said they should not pay taxes, this would make him guilty of sedition. The Romans would not tolerate that.

With divine insight Jesus answered the question in 12:17. He underscored a principal as operative today as it was then. Christians belong to two kingdoms, and owe allegiance to both.

The Sadducees returned for the next skirmish with Jesus. In this dialogue we find rich insights into the resurrection. They thought their hypothetical illustration of the man with seven brothers would stump him. The answer was that things pertaining to this life do not hold in the life beyond. We get beyond human family relations in heaven to become members of God's family. The clinching argument is found in 12:26 when Jesus stated that both God and these patriarchs are living. If the Sadducees had known the Pentateuch, which

was the only Scripture they accepted, they would have known that God is Lord of the living.

Out of the crowd came a fairminded scribe who knew that Jesus had answered every question honestly and with greatest insight. In his openness to the truth of God, Jesus said this man was not far from the Kingdom. This did not mean he was saved, but that his openness could lead to saving faith.

The opponents of Jesus realized they had been bested. In 12:34 we read there were no further questions. They did not give up, but were aware of the fact that they had been completely defeated.

After handling all their questions without a flaw, Jesus put a question to them. In 12:35–40 he attacked one of the popular misconceptions of that day. The Jews were looking for the restoration of the Davidic Kingdom and for a son of David to reign. Jesus rejected their idea, for he was not David's son, he was David's Lord. He did not come to restore David's earthly kingdom, for the one he established had little in common with David's. The rebuke of the scribes was doubtless based on their perpetuation of the erroneous ideas regarding the restoration of David's earthly kingdom.

There is a sudden change in the tone and attitude of Jesus in 12:41–44. Whereas he had been in combat in the ring with his opponents, he now views the devotion of a poor widow. Jesus knew both the precise amount of the gift and the spirit of the one making it. Though infinitesimal by comparison to the gifts of the wealthy, Jesus indicated this poor widow gave more than anyone. It was not the biggest gift in terms of total value. It was the best and highest gift measured in terms of love and sacrifice. The rich made no sacrifice in their contributions. This devoted lady probably went without supper that night in order to make her gift.

Coming Events (Mark 13:1–37)

The passage.—All 37 verses of Mark 13 compose what has been called "the little apocalypse." This great discourse is a difficult passage to understand for a number of reasons. One is that it is written in veiled language. Also, Jesus pointed here to the destruction of Jerusalem, the end of the world, and the second coming of Christ all in one passage! These words were written for comfort and hope. By observing carefully, this chapter may be separated in such a way as to understand that to which Jesus was pointing. In 13:1–4 the obvious reference is to the destruction of the Temple in Jerusalem. Between verses 2 and 3, it appears that Jesus and the disciples have left the main part of the city and walked over to the nearby Mount of Olives. Sitting there and looking across the valley at the Temple, they continued the same discussion.

In verse 4 the four apostles, Peter, James, John, and Andrew asked specifically when those events would take place and by what sign they would be accompanied. Rather than answering directly, Jesus dealt with some other matters of vital importance first (13:5–8). He warned them against any who might claim to have special insight, and then warned against false Christs.

The next section (13:9–13) describes the era leading up to A.D. 70 and the destruction of Jerusalem. The predictions in verse 9 actually came to pass in Acts. Tension within an individual home was also predicted. This would be especially true of a Jewish home divided over loyalty to Christ. The latter portion of verse 13 points out that the

genuinely saved are those who endure. Pseudo-believers may turn back and forsake what they once claimed. The true believer will be faithful to the end.

The matters discussed in 13:14–23 obviously do not fit the end of the world and the second coming. They do have reference to the destruction of Jerusalem. These verses underscore the necessity of haste. Those in the city are to flee to the country. Those watching the approaching army from the housetop should not reenter the house for possessions, but flee directly to safety. The plowman in the field is not to take so much time as to pick up his cloak. The expectant mothers and those with young children will face dire circumstances. Except for the Lord's elect, the Christians, it would have meant disaster for everyone. Yet because of his people, God made these days short in duration. Jesus also forewarned them that these events were not to be construed as his return.

The next section (13:24–37) refers to the ultimate end of the age and the coming of Christ. It is a dramatic portrayal of his coming.

In 13:28–30 Jesus reverted again to the destruction of Jerusalem. Some hold that Jesus made an error in verse 30, thinking he would return again in a short period of time. This does not get support if we read verse 32. The thing that did occur in that generation, which they lived to see, was the fall of Jerusalem within 40 years.

Again in 13:31–37, our Lord points to his return. Since there is no time schedule given, we are to spend our time taking heed, watching, and praying. The positive assurance of our Lord's return is based upon the total fulfilment of his prophecy concerning the destruction of Jerusalem. The first has already been done. The second remains to be done, yet we are to be busy in the meantime.

Preparing for the Cross (Mark 14:1–52)

The passage.—The first nine verses of chapter 14 relate the beautiful story of Mary's extravagance. This incident becomes the more meaningful when we realize that Jesus was in the last days of his ministry. The first two verses relate the plan of the scribes and chief priests to kill Jesus, but not to kill him during a feast time for fear of the people. Their plan ultimately had to be changed, for Jesus was killed during the time of a feast.

The parallel story to this in John 12 states that Lazarus, recently raised from the dead, was present at this meal with his sisters, Mary and Martha. It was a custom of the times to pour a few drops of perfume upon an arriving guest and rinse the dust from his feet. Mary emptied the entire box on the feet and head of her Master.

This box and its contents were valued at 300 denarii. The magnitude of this extravagance is revealed in the knowledge that a denarius was the average working man's wage for one day's work. This perfumed ointment from India was regarded as a gift fit for a king.

There was immediate criticism for this generous act. This is the natural reaction of a materialist to anyone who gives something away. The greedy, unregenerate person, like Judas, cannot understand an act of generosity.

In a brief but significant section, 14:10–11, we read of Judas' traitorous bargain. Sin was the ultimate cause of Judas' downfall. He was an ambitious, money-loving young businessman. He had an overriding ambition. He wanted to get to the top as quickly as possible. He had done nothing in violation of the law. He was not a sinister, evil sort of person. He was rather an unsaved man who had been in close association with Christians. He is like the unsaved church members of our day, who when the chips are down, reject Jesus and accept the world offers.

The conspirators changed their minds about killing Jesus at feast time. Judas' betrayal made it possible for them to proceed immediately with their plans.

Mark next records the last Passover and the first Lord's Supper (14:12–26). It was the last Passover for these men, for Judas killed himself, Jesus was crucified, and the other eleven apostles thereafter observed the Lord's Supper. This was the Christian fulfilment of the Passover Feast. The sacrificial system of the Old Testament, represented by the Feast of the Passover, is now fulfilled in the Lord's Supper of the New Testament. This is Christ's new covenant sealed with the blood of the sinlessly perfect Son of God.

The tragic denials of Peter are disclosed in 14:27–31. Comfort should have been derived from verse 28, but the truths of verse 27 caused them either not to hear or not to understand his resurrection.

Jesus' agonizing moments in Gethsemane's shadows are described in 14:32–42. This small enclosure, filled with olive trees, was a favorite place of repose for Jesus. He asked the same apostles who had seen his glory on the mount of transfiguration to come and witness his agony. The victory came through prayer (v. 41), and even at that triumphant moment he knew the presence of his enemies who had come to take him.

Mark's rapidly moving drama now records the betrayal kiss and arrest of Jesus (vv. 43–52). Among the shadows of the ancient olive trees, and in the dim light of the torches, it was hard to tell

19. The Garden of Gethsemane (see Mark 14:32)

one person from another. Judas had obviously agreed in advance to signal which one Jesus was. The signal would be the greeting of a traditional kiss, customary from a disciple to his master. The kiss on the forehead was all the soldiers needed.

John revealed that Peter took the sword and tried to kill a soldier. It could have been the bad light or poor aim, but he only got an ear! Luke reminds us that Jesus healed the ear.

There are a number of interesting possibilities regarding 14:51–52. This is the only Gospel which records this incident and it is entirely likely that this person was the author, Mark himself. Most New Testament scholars believe that the Passover meal was eaten in the home of Mark's mother (Acts 12:12). If this be the case, it is entirely possible that the young man, John Mark, was in bed when the soldiers came to his home. The curious lad may have wrapped a bed sheet about himself and gone out to see what would take place. When all the apostles started running (v. 50), Mark probably ran with them. In their attempt to capture this fleet young man, the soldiers came out with a sheet, or a linen cloth, and nothing more!

V. THE HEART OF THE GOSPEL (MARK 14:53—16:20)

The Trial of Jesus (Mark 14:53—15:20)

The passage.—The full details of the trial of Jesus must be pieced together from all four Gospels. There are two sections to the trial, before the Jews and before the Romans. Each of these two consists of three phases.

The Sanhedrin's illegal trial (14:53–65) was held in violation of their own rules. It was decreed that they could not meet at night nor during any of the great feasts. Their law also required that if a death verdict were given, a night must elapse before it was carried out in order to have time for reconsideration. Their animosity had reached the point that they were not interested in administering justice, they were interested in killing Jesus.

During the testimony, Jesus did not speak. Finally Caiaphas asked Jesus if he were the Messiah. This could be construed as insurrection against Rome and would be grounds for death. Jesus responded positively in language which incited the wrath of the Sadducees. Pandemonium broke loose, and their great hour arrived. They used the occasion to spit on Jesus, to strike him, and call upon him to show them his ability to prophecy.

The denials of Peter are fast moving and decisive (14:66–72). The redeeming feature of this is that Peter knew he was wrong and wept bitter tears of remorse. As inexcusable as his conduct was, we can be grateful it was not unforgiveable.

The trial of Jesus before Pilate is found in 15:1–20. He was the legal representative of the Roman Empire. He was despised by the Jewish people at large. Perhaps the question Pilate asked Jesus stemmed from unbelief. It would be hard to believe that this Galilean peasant, dressed in the garb of an ordinary working man, could be King of the Jews.

The offer to release a prisoner brought about the release of Barabbas. Having asked for their opinion regarding Barabbas, Pilate asked them what he should do with Jesus. Roman justice was trampled under foot as the people cried for the crucifixion of Christ. The Jews were not allowed to give the death penalty. Only the Romans could do this. Crucifixion was a common method of punishment under the Romans.

Scourging was the ordinary prelude to crucifixion. Since a man could easily be beaten to death, the number of lashes was limited.

Even the Roman soldiers caught the spirit of the crowd. When they led Jesus away, they made mockery of him by dressing him in purple, crushing a crown of thorns upon his brow, spitting in his face, striking his head with a reed, and bowing their knees in mock worship.

Crucifixion and Burial (Mark 15:21–47)

The passage.—The crucifixion represents the zenith of man's rejection of God and rebellion against his revelation (15:21–37).

With his entire back one open raw mass of bleeding, quivering flesh, the weight of the cross probably caused Jesus to stumble. The soldiers compelled Simon of Cyrene to carry the cross. This was a city on the coast of North Africa. Simon had likely come to Jerusalem for the Passover, and was identified as "the father of Alexander and Rufus." These could have been two outstanding Christians, and one may be referred to in Romans 16:13.

The procession finally reached the hill shaped like a skull. In present-day Israel, Gordon's Calvary more nearly fits the New Testament description than the traditional site inside the ancient city.

Jesus was offered wine mingled with myrrh as a form of sedation. When he tasted it, he would not drink it.

Having nailed him to the cross, the soldiers began gambling for his garments even before he died. Others in the mocking multitude joined their voices in reviling Jesus. Just as during his ministry, they continued to ask for a sign. They wanted proof that he was the Christ, which would be given in the form of his coming down from the cross. Even this they would not have believed.

In verse 37 we find again the voluntary nature of Calvary. Jesus' life was not taken from him, he gave it. In his dying breath Jesus permitted his spirit to leave. He was in control to the very end.

The completeness of redemption is described in 15:38–39. The rending of the veil in the Temple was significant. It was torn from the top, indicating an act of God and not man. This was the veil which secluded the holy of holies. Man now has direct access to God through Christ, and not through human priests.

It is likewise significant that the Gentile centurion recognized the acknowledged Jesus as the "Son of God."

Mark mentioned the names of some devout disciples in 15:40–41. Mary Magdalene was a woman Jesus healed, Salome was Jesus' aunt, the mother of James and John, Mary had already been taken away by John. These were Galilean women who loved Jesus and had ministered to him on many occasions. Their reasons for being present were both intimate and also less personal. Jesus afforded all womanhood a dignity never known previously.

The burial of Jesus is told in 15:42–47. Joseph of Arimathea, a well-known Jew and a member of the Sanhedrin, was a secret disciple of Jesus (19:38).

Perhaps Joseph was grieved for having failed to defend Jesus in the preceding trial. He asked Pilate for permission to give the body of Jesus a decent burial. Joseph purchased a supply of linen and Nicodemus provided the spices for burial (v. 39). When the body was prepared and placed in the tomb, a stone was rolled against the door.

The Risen Christ (Mark 16:1–20)

The passage.—The glorious finale to redemption's story is recorded in 16:1–8. The women waited until the sabbath was over, at sunset on Saturday evening, then began to assemble spices to anoint the body. Early Sunday morning they began to walk from Bethany to Jerusalem.

It is little wonder they were astounded upon reaching the tomb. Not only was the body gone, an angel of God was sitting there. In fear they did not follow instructions. They were told to tell the disciples and Peter, but they said nothing. These women were the first to know the most earthshaking fact ever revealed to man. Jesus Christ, the Son of God, ever liveth to make intercession for us!

From 16:9–20, we have a passage not found in the most reliable ancient Greek manuscripts. Some of these verses are found in other gospels that are not disputed. The truth of these verses is not in question. The textual question concerns the original ending of the Gospel of Mark.

Aside from the textual question, the emphasis in these final verses seems to be on the authority of Christ. In this sense, it gives a parallel to Matthew's concluding verses. Whatever one's approach to the authenticity of these verses, the point is clear that the power and authority of Jesus Christ is supreme.

The command of the angel to "go—tell . . ." is reiterated throughout the New Testament. This is still our task.

LUKE

Malcolm O. Tolbert

INTRODUCTION

The superscription "The Gospel according to Luke" is not a part of the original manuscript. The Gospel itself is anonymous. Tradition, however, has unanimously attributed the Third Gospel to Luke, the physician and missionary companion of Paul mentioned in Colossians 4:14, Philemon 24, and 2 Timothy 4:11. It was probably written around A.D. 80–85, although some interpreters hold that it may have been written as early as A.D. 60.

The layman may know that the same man wrote both Luke and Acts. He may not know that originally both were written as parts of the same work. It is necessary to read Luke and Acts together to get the whole story that Luke wished to tell. These two books constitute the largest block of material contributed to the New Testament by any single author.

Why did Luke write his Gospel? He must have felt that those already in existence did not meet the need completely (Luke 1:1–4). It is also possible that he wanted to correct erroneous ideas that his prospective readers held about the Gospel (see commentary on 1:1–4). Luke wanted to set the record straight for them.

Much of Luke's material is found in no other Gospel. We would be much the poorer had the Third Gospel never been written. The concept that most Christians have of Jesus is shaped to a great extent by Luke's special material, e.g., the story of the penitent sinner (7:36–

50) and the parable of the prodigal son (15:11–32). The reader will also find that Luke gives much attention to prayer, the Holy Spirit, social outcasts, women, and the use of wealth in his writings.

The Third Gospel begins with a preface (1:1–4), the only one of its kind in the four Gospels. In it the author speaks of his method of writing and his purpose. This is followed by the birth and childhood narratives (1:5—2:52). Luke's introduction to Jesus' public ministry (3:1—4:13) consists of the call and preaching of John the Baptist, followed by the baptism, genealogy, and temptation of Jesus.

The first part of Jesus' ministry is centered in Galilee (4:14—9:50). It begins with his rejection in Nazareth and reaches a climax in the great confession and transfiguration (9:28–36).

The turning point in Jesus' ministry is reached in 9:51, where we are told that he "set his face to go to Jerusalem." The section which follows (9:51—19:27) is usually designated "The Journey to Jerusalem." It is dominated by the rejection and death which await Jesus at its end. In this section we find much of the special material presented in Luke's Gospel.

The ministry in Jerusalem (19:28—22:53) is followed by an account of the trial and crucifixion (22:54—23:56a). The Gospel is brought to a close with the resurrection narratives (23:56b—24:53). In 24:46–49 the stage is set for the story which follows in the book of Acts.

The Preface (Luke 1:1–4)

The passage.—In this introduction to the Third Gospel we learn that it was not the first written account of Jesus' ministry. At least one of these earlier documents, the Gospel of Mark, appears in our New Testament and was used by Luke. He was not an eyewitness to Jesus' ministry. But the information available to him was based on the testimony of eyewitnesses.

Luke dedicated his work to Theophilus. He intended it, however, for a much wider audience. Perhaps he hoped that the dedication to Theophilus would secure a hearing for the gospel in certain important political and social circles.

Special points.—"Ministers of the word" (1:2) may have been the early teachers whose particular responsibility was to impart a knowledge of the gospel to new converts. The first of these teachers were people who had actually been with Jesus, witnessed his acts, and heard his teachings. The gospel account was first passed on orally in the relatively brief period of two or three decades before it was put into writing.

Luke must have felt that his work met a need that other accounts had not filled. He wanted to present the gospel materials "in order" (v. 3), that is, "to write an orderly account" (RSV). His contribution, therefore, was the bringing together of materials assembled from various sources both written and oral into one, orderly work.

Theophilus (v. 3) means "friend of God." He is not mentioned elsewhere except in Acts 1:1. It is generally thought that he was a Roman of noble rank with some influence in ruling circles. The title "most excellent" was appropriate for a person of such standing. Theophilus may have been a prospective Christian whom Luke hoped

to bring to open faith in Jesus. More likely, however, he was an official who had a distorted, erroneous notion of the Christian faith. This idea is seen in verse 4: "That you may know the *truth* concerning the things of which you have been informed" (RSV). One of Luke's purposes was to show that Christianity was not a political threat to Rome. Some of the ruling class, perhaps Theophilus among them, believed that it was.

Truth for today.—Modern Christians can have confidence in the essential reliability of the Third Gospel. Luke had access to information coming from eyewitnesses. He wanted to present a faithful account of Christian beginnings. This written record serves the function today that the original eyewitnesses discharged in the first generation. It tells of the incarnate experience of him who is the risen, living Lord of the church.

Christian Beginnings (Luke 1:5–80)

The passage.—Three major themes may be seen in the first two chapters of Luke. They are: (1) the nature of the relationship between John and Jesus, (2) the close relationship between Judaism and Christianity when the latter began, and (3) the gift of the Holy Spirit and the revival of prophecy as the sign of the dawning messianic age.

John the Baptist is a very important figure in gospel beginnings. The early Christians understood that he was the "forerunner" mentioned in Malachi 4:5–6. His appearance was a signal that God's Messiah was about to begin his work. Luke makes it clear that John's role in redemption history, while one of great significance, was not the central one. This emphasis, also noted in other gospels, was probably made necessary because some people believed that John was the Messiah.

Furthermore, Luke shows that Christianity began in the very heart of Judaism. The first scene is set in the Temple. The speeches by the angel, Zechariah, Mary, and Elizabeth are woven in large part from Old Testament texts. They teach that Jesus was Israel's promised Messiah. Luke's position is that Christianity, rightly interpreted, is the continuation of genuine Judaism.

Special points.—Herod (1:5) the Great was the ruler of Palestine at the pleasure of the Roman government from 37–4 B.C. At this time there was a multitude of Jewish priests, about 20,000 according to some estimates. They were divided into 24 courses or divisions, each of which served in the Temple for a week twice during the year. Because there were so many in each division, priests were chosen by lot to perform certain functions, such as the burning of incense (1:9). This ritual took place within the sanctuary proper of the Temple area, which only priests were allowed to enter. The "multitude of the people" (v. 10) refers to male Israelites assembled in the Court of Israel in front of the sanctuary.

Verses 16–17 are based on Malachi 4:5–6. They teach that John the Baptist was destined to fulfil the role of Elijah in the messianic age. His appearance is the signal of its beginning. Notice the relationship between the Holy Spirit and the prophetic gift in verses 15, 41, and 67. According to a current Jewish expectation the revival of prophecy through the gift of the Holy Spirit would be a sign of the messianic age. Luke seems to teach that this expectation is being fulfilled.

Surprisingly little is told about Mary in the New Testament in contrast to the emphasis placed on her in subsequent Christian history. "Highly favored" (1:28) simply means that she is the object of God's grace. The wonder is that

God chose a simple Galilean maid who did not anticipate such an honor to be the mother of Israel's Messiah. His name *Jesus* (v. 31), the Greek equivalent of the Hebrew Joshua, means "the Lord is salvation."

Luke teaches that the conception of Jesus was supernatural. However, "come upon" and "overshadow" (v. 35) do not denote sexual activity. They represent the activity of the Spirit in a way very similar to Genesis 1:2: "And the Spirit of the Lord moved upon the face of the waters." In Luke, God's Spirit is shown to be active in bringing into being a new creation or a new humanity.

Further discussion of the virgin birth may be found in the comments on Matthew 1:1–25.

The universal note, so prominent in Luke's writings, first comes to the surface in verse 79. Those that "sit in darkness" are the Gentiles.

Truth for today.—God acts in mighty and unexpected ways as he directs history toward its goal. He also uses human beings as the instruments of his grace and power. We rightly respect those men and women who have served God well. The emphasis, however, must be placed on what God does.

Christians do well to honor Mary as the mother of the Lord, but this should not exceed the bounds of propriety. The New Testament shows that early Christians did not worship Mary in any sense, nor does she have a central place in subsequent events. The major figure in the Gospel here and elsewhere is Jesus. There can be no rival to him for the love, admiration, and obedience of his followers.

Jesus' Birth and Childhood (Luke 2:1–52)

The passage.—Only Matthew and Luke tell anything about the birth and early childhood of Jesus. His public

**20. Old stable with inn above at Bethlehem
(see Luke 2:7)**

ministry climaxed by his death and resurrection was the focal point of interest among the earliest Christians.

Luke's reference to the census is his explanation for the presence of Joseph and Mary in Bethlehem at the time of Jesus' birth. The Lucan story emphasizes the humble surroundings of the birth. The first notice of the wonderful event is given to lowly shepherds. This is in keeping with Luke's teaching that the gospel is especially for the downtrodden and dispossessed.

The stories about Jesus' childhood tie him to Jewish piety and especially to the Temple. He is recognized as the fulfilment of Israel's hopes and expectations by the devout Simeon and Anna. He lingers behind in the Temple when his parents leave Jerusalem after observing passover. There he engages in questions and answers with the doctors or learned rabbis. Luke teaches that Jesus was reared as a genuine Jew. Judaism both cradled him and was fulfilled in him.

Special points.—Caesar Augustus ruled the empire from 27 B.C. to A.D. 14. "Taxed" (2:1) should be translated "enrolled." The verse describes a census conducted for the purpose of forming tax rolls. Mary is Joseph's "espoused wife" (v. 5) in the KJV, but "his betrothed" is the reading supported by the best Greek manuscripts. Since the area where guests slept was filled, Joseph and Mary had to find shelter in the stable.

637

Shepherds would not have been in the field in December. Sheep were tended in the open between April and November. We do not know, therefore, exactly when Jesus was born. December 25 was adopted as the date to celebrate his birth in the fourth century by Christians in the West.

The reading of the KJV for verse 14 is not supported by the best manuscripts. The better text is "on earth peace among men with whom he is pleased." The Gospel does not promise the cessation of war and strife upon the earth in this age. It does affirm that men who belong to God will experience a peace that is not dependent upon outward circumstances.

Luke seems to have fused two separate rites, purification and the redemption of the firstborn in verses 22–24. The mother of a newborn child was supposed to offer a lamb and a pigeon or a turtledove for her purification (see Lev. 12). The poor could substitute another pigeon or a dove for the lamb. Verse 24 indicates, therefore, that Mary was poor. According to Numbers 18:16 the price for the redemption of a male offspring was five shekels.

The "consolation of Israel" (v. 25) and the "redemption of Jerusalem" (v. 38) both refer to the messianic hope of the Jewish people. They looked for a king who would liberate his people and reestablish the Davidic dynasty in Jerusalem. Simeon and Anna point Jews who have such hope to the baby Jesus as its fulfilment.

"Passover" (v. 41) celebrated the deliverance of Israel from Egypt. It was one of the three pilgrim festivals that male Jews were supposed to observe in Jerusalem. Those who lived in Palestine attempted to celebrate at least one there. Jesus joined the elders for the annual trip when he was twelve (v. 42). At this age he assumed responsibility as a member of the covenant community and was under the same religious obligations as other males.

Jesus was surprised at the anxiety expressed by Mary over their failure to find him. He did not understand why they should have thought that he would be in any place other than the Temple. "About my Father's business" (v. 49) is better translated "in my Father's house." According to the Third Gospel, Jesus had a consciousness of a unique relation to God at this time.

Truth for today.—Jesus was born in a stable and not in a palace. How uniquely suitable was this place of his birth! So many people of the world are poor, ill-clad, diseased, despised. They would feel uncomfortable in the affluent surroundings of the rich. But nobody is out of place in a stable. The poor, humble, little people of the world can gather around the manger and feel that the baby born there really belongs to them.

The Ministry of John the Baptist (Luke 3:1–38)

The passage.—During the reign of Tiberius Caesar, events were transpiring in an obscure corner of his empire which passed unnoticed by the larger world at the time. John and Jesus, members of the subject Jewish nation, set something in motion that was to affect the world more profoundly than did the reign of the mighty Tiberius.

There are more questions than answers about John the Baptist. Exactly what were the factors that shaped his life? What was the substance of his message? What was the extent of his influence? We can only guess at the answers. John the Baptist was important to the gospel writers for one reason.

He was the herald of the Lord's coming, the sign that the day of the Messiah had dawned.

The brief account of John's proclamation indicates that he was a stern preacher of righteousness and judgment. For him the coming of the Messiah meant that the ax was "laid unto the root of the trees." He challenged the widespread assumptions that religion was a matter of race and ritual. He demanded a practice coherent with profession.

Jesus' baptism accompanied by the descent of the Spirit constituted his ordination for his public ministry. The genealogy emphasizes the universal significance of that ministry. Luke traces the ancestry of Jesus to Adam. This is his way of saying that Jesus belongs to the whole of mankind.

Special points.—*Tiberius* (v. 1) succeeded Augustus in A.D. 14. Therefore, John's ministry began in A.D. 28–29. Upon the death of Herod the Great in 4 B.C., Palestine had been divided among his three sons, Archelaus, Herod (Antipas), and Philip. In A.D. 6 Archelaus had been deposed, and Judea had become an imperial province under the administrator of a governor. *Pontius Pilate* was the fifth of these governors.

High priests were supposed to serve for life. But under the Romans they were removed often for political reasons. Annas (v. 2) had been high priest from A.D. 6 to 15. His son-in-law Caiaphas held the office from A.D. 18 to 36. Annas, however, may still have been the dominant figure.

Baptism of repentance (v. 3) means that John's baptism was not empty ritual. Repentance on the part of sinners was demanded as a prerequisite. *For remission of sins* does not mean that baptism itself was the means of forgiveness. Rather, the repentant persons expected God to respond by forgiving them of their sins.

Herod (Antipas) was married to the daughter of Aretas the Nabatean (Arabian) king. He divorced her in order to marry Herodias, his half-brother's wife (v. 19). John, worthy successor to the prophets, challenged this evil in high places. As a result, he was imprisoned and finally beheaded. According to Josephus the place of his imprisonment was Machaerus, a fortress east of the Dead Sea.

Truth for today.—Repentance is a decisive act, affecting all of life. It makes a difference in the way a person speaks, acts, thinks, earns his living, and relates to other people. No doubt John would call on many modern church members to "bring forth fruits worthy of repentance," were he among us today. There are far too many contradictions between what we say we believe and the way we live in the world.

The Beginning of Jesus' Ministry (Luke 4:1–44)

The passage.—In his baptism Jesus accepted his role as God's Messiah. In the temptation he had to decide what kind of messiah he would be. Great pressures were exerted on him during his ministry to force him to become a popular messiah, appealing to the baser, more hostile elements of his people. The temptations are presented in dramatic, vivid form. This must not obscure the fact that Jesus was tempted in the same way that we are (Heb. 4:15).

Luke makes the rejection in Nazareth the first major incident in Jesus' Galilean ministry (cf. Mark 6:1 ff.). The rejection of Jesus by his own hometown is the first step in the ultimate rejection of Jesus by his own people, the Jews.

Capernaum became the headquarters for Jesus' activities in Galilee. His ministry began there with a series of mighty works. These indicated that the power of God was breaking into history in the person of Jesus. His victory over the forces of evil and disease that held men captive demonstrated his messianic authority.

Special points.—The clash between Jesus and the devil (v. 3) was a power struggle between the two kingdoms, the kingdom of God and the kingdom of evil. Actually it was a clash between God's purpose and prevailing popular expectations and desires. Some people expected the Messiah to reproduce the miracle of Moses' day when manna was supplied in the desert. In the first temptation (vv. 2–4), Jesus refused to base either his faith in God or the demonstration of his messianic power on the ability to produce bread in the desert.

In the second temptation (vv. 5–8) Jesus was confronted with the possibility of establishing a world power by worshiping the devil. To worship the devil means to use the devil's methods to gain one's purposes. Many people advocated the liberation of Israel by force of arms. If Jesus had followed this path he would have been worshiping the devil. Jesus rejected sensational methods to capture public support in the third temptation (vv. 9–12).

In a synagogue service any visitor might be invited to read a Scripture passage or to bring a sermon (v. 16 ff.). The passages read by Jesus from Isaiah (vv. 18–19) set forth the mission of the Messiah in characteristic Lukan terms. The gospel is for the oppressed and afflicted. The anger of the congregation (v. 28) arose from the references to incidents which showed Gentiles receiving blessings denied to Israelites. In his writings Luke teaches that Israel excluded itself from the gospel. One of the main problems was its failure to understand that the gospel recognized no racial boundaries.

In the ancient world mental illness was explained in terms of demon possession (5:33). The gospel was a power that liberated men from the dark, hostile forces that oppressed them. One of the greatest demonstrations of Jesus' power was his ability to make emotionally disturbed people whole.

Truth for today.—The fact that a person has dedicated his life to God does not mean that he has won the battle over evil. A person may decide to follow God's call to be a preacher or a missionary. But he must always struggle with the question: What kind of preacher? What kind of missionary? The desire for popularity, for success, for acceptance are strong pressures that may operate against God's purposes for our lives. The decision to be true to God often means that the believer must face misunderstanding, contempt, and rejection. It was certainly true with Jesus.

The gospel is for everybody, especially the excluded, oppressed elements of society. This kind of gospel inflames prejudiced people. This was one of the reasons that Jesus was crucified. Church members who exclude people from their fellowship on the basis of race or class considerations are playing the role of Jesus' enemies.

The gospel still meets human need today. It is the power that liberates men from that which enslaves them in the twentieth century as it did in the first.

Popularity and Hostility (Luke 5:1—6:11)

The passage.—The first two stories of chapter 5 bring out the immense popularity of Jesus with the people at this stage of his ministry. Several points are made in the call of Simon and the other fishermen. They are as follows: The call of Jesus determines the role of the disciple in the Christian community. Jesus' disciples are to accept and be governed by his authority even when circumstances seem to doom their enterprise to failure. The power of Jesus determines the outcome of their efforts. Furthermore, the call to follow Jesus is a call to break with the old way of life. From fishing for fish, the disciples turn to fishing for men.

In 5:17 a series of controversy stories begins. In the first one Jesus' enemies are offended by his assumption of the authority to forgive sins. In succeeding incidents, they are aroused by his association with sinners, by the failure of his disciples to fast, and by the disregard for sabbath traditions. The climax is reached when Jesus' opponents come to the conviction that they cannot afford to allow him to continue his course unhindered: they must do something with him (6:11).

Special points.—The lake of Gennesaret is another name for the Sea of Galilee (5:1).

Jesus instructed the cured leper to follow the requirements set forth in Leviticus 13–14 (5:14). The accredited authorities had to pronounce him cured if he was to be restored to society. The incident may also show Jesus' respect for the Mosaic law.

The Pharisees, from whose ranks came some of Jesus' principle antagonists, were characterized by their scrupulous observance of the great body of oral traditions. These interpreted the meaning of the written law.

Palsy (5:18) is an archaic English word used to designate various kinds of paralysis. The cure of the paralyzed man was a response to the faith of those who brought him to Jesus. But faith was not essential to Jesus' healing power (see 17:11–19). *Son of man* (5:24) is a title found in the Gospels only on the lips of Jesus, who avoided the use of Messiah (Christ). Son of man is a figure of power and glory associated with the end-time in some Jewish writings. Jesus interpreted it in the light of the Suffering Servant of Isaiah. The Son of man must suffer and be rejected before he is exalted to a position of glory and power.

Levi (5:27) is identified as Matthew in the First Gospel (Matt. 10:3). He was a publican or tax collector. Tax collectors were generally despised by other Jews for two reasons. They were in the service of the hated Roman government. Moreover, they used their position to exploit their countrymen, often collecting more than was legitimate.

Sinners (5:30) refers to the large number of common people who did not observe the oral traditions as scrupulously as the Pharisees expected. Both tax collectors and sinners were outside the pale of respectability.

Fasting (5:33) was required by the law only on the Day of Atonement. Pharisees, however, fasted twice a week. Jesus did not believe that fasting should be a pious ritual. The "new garment" and the "new wine" (vv. 36–37) are the teachings of Jesus: the "old garment" and "old bottles" (wineskins) represent Judaism. These verses teach the basic irreconcilability between the teachings of Jesus and the traditions of the Pharisees.

The law enjoined Israelites to keep the sabbath holy, refraining from work on the day. Jewish scribes or experts in the law had devised a host of regulations that defined activities to be classified as work and, therefore, prohibited on the sabbath. By plucking grain and rubbing the husks off, the disciples violated these oral laws (6:1–5). The grain was wheat or barley and not what we call corn. Jesus also violated these regulations when he healed a man on the sabbath (vv. 6–11). It was against the oral law to do this unless a person's life was in danger.

Truth for today.—When Jesus looked at a man, he saw not only what he was but also what he could become. Simon was indeed a "sinful man," as the gospels tell us. But Jesus knew that he had the possibility of becoming Peter, which means a "rock." Christians have to be optimistic about people, since they believe that God can work a transforming miracle in any life.

There is no one outside the circle of Christian love. The Christian is not "too good" to associate with people whom others despise. In fact, the only way that he can be good is to be open and accepting to all kinds of men.

People are more important than anything, including sacred religious rules and practices. The worship and service of God can never conflict with love and service to man. Jesus' enemies were interested in protecting their institutions. Jesus was interested in people. In the light of his actions, we must constantly ask the question: "Are our religious institutions and rules keeping us from responding to human need?"

The Great Sermon (Luke 6:12–49)

The passage.—The notices about the choosing of the Twelve and mighty works performed by Jesus set the stage for his great sermon. The sermon is addressed specifically to disciples. It delineates the kind of attitude and life that Jesus expected of his followers.

Most of Luke's sermon has parallels to the Sermon on the Mount in Matthew 5–7. The sermon in Matthew is, of course, much larger. This is due

to the tendency of Matthew to gather related materials into one section. Both begin with a series of beatitudes and end with the parable of the two foundations. Much of the material in Matthew's sermon is paralleled elsewhere in Luke.

Special points.—Jesus chose twelve of his disciples for a special role. No doubt they represented the twelve tribes of Israel. By his choice of the twelve Jesus declared that the community created by him was the new Israel and that he was its King-Messiah. "Apostles" (v. 13) refers specifically to the twelve here. Elsewhere in the New Testament it often has the general sense of missionaries. The list begins with Simon, the most important. Peter, the name given to him, really should be translated "rock." Judas, the traitor, appears last in the list. Most of the twelve are hardly more than names to us.

Blessed (v. 20) means "how fortunate" or "how happy." In his description of the fortunate, happy people Jesus turns the concepts of the world upside down. They are the poor, the hungry, etc. These words describe persons who recognize their need, depend solely upon God, are burdened by the sin and evil of the world. On the other hand, the unfortunate are the rich, the full, etc. They are the people who receive their satisfaction from their wealth, the pleasures of the moment, etc.

How are the needy and persecuted to respond to those who exploit and oppress them? Jesus says: "Love your enemies" (v. 27). What does it mean to love one's enemies? The believer meets hostility with active goodwill, expressed in deeds that are totally unexpected.

The prohibition against judging (v. 37) is based on the fact that all men are sinners; all need forgiveness. God alone is capable of judging. When a person judges his fellowman, he is usurping a role which belongs to God. This does not mean that we are to be blind to the needs of our brother. Rather, we must see his sins in the right perspective. The beam, or log, is in our eye; the mote, or speck is in his (v. 42). My sins in comparison to my brother's must be seen in the ratio of log to speck, and not the other way around.

"Lord" is a title which emphasizes the authority of Jesus (v. 46). Jesus teaches that practice must not contradict profession. Mere words are not enough. The person whose life is shaped by Jesus' teachings is on a secure foundation. He will be able to stand in the flood, which represents the crisis of God's judgment.

Truth for today.—What does it mean to be a good Christian? It means that we take the teachings of Jesus seriously as the standard for our lives. A good Christian is a person who depends completely on God, aware of his own spiritual bankruptcy, hungry for God's presence and blessings. The good Christian loves people who do not like him. The good Christian is not judgmental, harsh, or critical in his attitude to others. In humility he seeks to help his brother with his needs, conscious always that he needs God's grace more than does his brother. By God's grace he seeks to develop a good, generous, loving character from which will flow genuinely good deeds. Compare these ideas taught by Jesus to the concepts that we generally have of qualities of good Christians.

Of course, when we allow the teachings of Jesus to speak to us, we are made conscious of our sins. They represent the demand of the gospel, bringing us under the judgment of God. We do not love as we ought; we do not forgive as we ought; we are harshly critical of others. What is the answer to this problem? God loves us more than we deserve to be loved. He forgives us. But his forgiveness and love do not release us from the demand of the gospel. Rather, they make us more responsible to be loving, forgiving, and good.

The Nature of Jesus' Mission (Luke 7:1–50)

The passage.—Jesus healed a centurion's slave at a distance by the power of his word. This miracle performed for a Gentile was no doubt used as a justification for the wider mission to the Gentiles about which Luke speaks in Acts. Also the faith of the centurion, superior even to that of the Jews (v. 9), foreshadows the time when many Gentiles will believe in a Savior rejected by his own people. In the second miracle Jesus restored a young man to life in Nain, the modern village of Nein. This was near Shunem where Elisha had raised a boy from the dead (2 Kings 4:21–37). The people's reaction is expressed in the words: "A great prophet [like Elisha] is risen up among us" (v. 16).

Deeds of this sort constitute the answer to John's question (v. 20). John sent messengers because he was in prison (cf. Matt. 11:2). Perhaps his doubts about Jesus were due to his expectation that the Messiah would execute God's judgment on evildoers. But the evil Antipas still ruled Galilee while John languished in his prison. Jesus challenged John not to allow his preconceived notions to blind him to what God was actually doing. In his subsequent evaluation of John, Jesus cautioned his hearers not to misjudge the wilderness prophet. His moment of doubt does not mean that he was a weakling.

Special points.—"Centurion" (v. 1)

was technically the commander of a hundred infantrymen in a Roman legion, but the size of his command varied with the size of the legion. The "elders of the Jews" (v. 3) is a designation for important people in the community. The centurion was one of the few men to grasp the extent and significance of Jesus' authority (v. 8). Disease was as subservient to the authority of Jesus as were the centurion's soldiers to his command.

"He that should come" (v. 19) translates a participle, "the coming one." This was probably a current title for the Messiah. Because Jesus did not fit the mold that people expected, many of them were offended (v. 23) and rejected him. Jesus warned John against such a course.

John may have had his momentary doubts, but he was not a "reed shaken with the wind" (v. 24). He was a courageous prophet. But more than that, he was the forerunner of the messianic age promised in Malachi 4:5–6 (v. 27).

The "least in the kingdom," however, is greater than John (v. 28). This cannot refer to John's inherent worth. Jesus had already affirmed that John had no superior as a prophet. "Greater" must be understood in terms of privilege. To share in the time of salvation inaugurated by Jesus is greater than to be the forerunner of this period.

"Justified God" (v. 29) means that the response of the people to John's message had proven the rightness of the way God had acted. The religious leaders, who prided themselves on their theological perception, had failed to see what God was doing.

The "children in the market place" (v. 32) illustrate the peevish and arbitrary attitude of the people who rejected both John and Jesus. They wanted the austere, ascetic John to play the happy game of wedding. They wanted the joyous, sociable Jesus to play the sad game of funeral.

The two debtors, one owing five hundred pence (denarii) and the other fifty (v. 41) represent the sinful woman and the Pharisee from his point of view. He was less of a sinner than she, he thought. The point is that neither could pay his debt. What difference did it make that one was smaller than the other?

Truth for today.—God does not always do things the way that men expect him to do them. Even the great John the Baptist had to learn this. If the Gospels teach us anything at all, they teach us that God acts in surprising, unexpected ways. One of the chief reasons why people rejected Jesus was that he did not fit their notions about what God's Messiah would be.

We need to throw away our preconceived notions about how, when, and where God is going to act. Only then may we be open and alert to what he is actually accomplishing in our midst. We may discover, for example, that he is doing much of his work outside organized religious channels. Also it may be that he is using some surprising people as his modern prophets.

An Itinerant Ministry (Luke 8:1–56)

The passage.—"Soon afterwards" (8:1) marks the transition to another phase of Jesus' activities. He now embarks on an itinerant preaching ministry that calls for rapid visits to various places. The chapter begins with some teachings of Jesus, followed by four miracles. The general theme of "hearing the word" may be the bond uniting verses 1–21. The last two miracles (vv. 40–56) are unusual in that one is set in the context of another, the only example of this in the Gospels.

Special points.—Luke alone explicitly says that the material needs of Jesus and his disciples were met, at least in part, by some women of means. "Seven demons" (v. 2) describes the severe emotional disorder from which Jesus had healed Mary Magdalene.

The parable of the sower (vv. 4–8) is based on the common experience of Palestine farmers. The various responses of hearers to the gospel are illustrated by the different kinds of soil into which seed might fall. "Rock" (v. 6) is shallow soil which covers underlying rock. The parable teaches that the indifference, lack of commitment, and even hostility with which men receive the Word must not lead believers to despair. The seed will fall on good soil and will bear fruit. God himself guarantees the result of the harvest.

Why did people not understand and respond to the teachings of Jesus? The answer is that the parables of Jesus are vehicles of revelation to those who are perceptive, the disciples, but their truth is hidden from the others (v. 10). Is God himself responsible? In a sense he is, for he has chosen to reveal himself in ways that man in his arrogance and rebellion will not accept. But the real problem is man's own spiritual blindness—his refusal to see what is right before his eyes.

The meaning of the three sayings in verses 16–18 is obscure. In this context they probably mean that the gospel is a light that was not intended to be hidden. It is to be given the widest possible proclamation. The failure to respond to the gospel upon hearing it may result in the loss of further opportunities (v. 18).

Why did the family of Jesus wish to see him (vv. 19–21)? Mark (3:31–55) implies that they wanted to interrupt his ministry because of the report that Jesus was crazy. But Jesus makes it clear that the narrow claims of family and race cannot disrupt his larger relationships with those who have responded to the gospel.

Jesus "rebuked the wind" (v. 24), as he had already rebuked demons and disease. The manifestation of Jesus' lordship over the forces of nature is one more sign of the breaking in of the kingdom of God.

"Gadarenes" (v. 26) probably should be Gerasenes. This is a place of uncertain location on the east side of Galilee. It is the only instance in Luke in which Jesus set foot on pagan soil. The demoniac was violently insane. Legion (v. 30) was a Roman division of about 6,000 men, but here it stands for a host of demons. The "abyss" is the nether region (hell), the prison for demons. Some people object to this story because they feel that the destruction of a herd of swine is not in keeping with Jesus' character. But swine, considered unclean by the Jews, was a more appropriate house for evil spirits than was a man.

Truth for today.—One of our major problems is the tendency to evaluate what we do statistically. And when the statistics do not show an increase in baptisms, money, and churches, a general cloud of pessimism descends upon us. When shall we ever learn one of the major truths of Scripture? The victory of God does not depend on numbers. Nor is it deterred by the character of human response.

We can preach the gospel with confidence in its power. Many will reject it or be indifferent to it. But occasionally the seed will fall on good soil. When it does, God guarantees that it will take root, grow, and produce a harvest. Our hope and optimism must not be based upon what we do, nor upon the results of what we do. Faith will stand the test only if it rests in God's power to guarantee his kingdom.

Revelations to Disciples (Luke 9:1–50)

The passage.—Chapter 9 begins with the mission of the twelve, which is really an extension of Jesus' own mission. It was a rapid tour of Jewish communities for the purpose of proclaiming the breaking in of the messianic age through preaching and miracles of healing.

This is followed by a series of incidents and teachings that revolve primarily around two of the principal themes of the Gospel: (1) who Jesus is, and (2) what it means to be a disciple. The great confession (vv. 18–27) and the transfiguration (vv. 28–36) are, of course, the crucial events that mark a real turning point in the ministry of Jesus. From this time he is less concerned with his public preaching and more concerned with teaching the inner circle of his followers about the meaning of his life and theirs in the light of his impending death.

Special points.—The twelve were commanded to "take nothing" (v. 3) when they set out on their preaching mission. They were to depend for food and shelter on the hospitality of the inhabitants of towns in which they preached. Some Jews returning to their homeland from Gentile country would shake the dust of the pagan lands from their feet. This act by the disciples (v. 5) symbolized that the city which rejected them was regarded as pagan.

Herod's question: "Who is this?" (v. 9) is really the primary question that the Gospels answer. An insight into the answer is given to the disciples by the feeding of the five thousand (vv. 10–17), the only miracle recorded in all Gospels. This miracle took place near Bethsaida, the capital of Philip's territory north of the Sea of Galilee. By feeding the people in the desert, Jesus showed that he was the prophet like Moses that God had promised to raise up (Deut. 18:15).

Peter recognized Jesus as God's Christ, or Messiah (9:20). But he did not understand that the Messiah was to suffer and die (v. 22). Nor did the disciples understand that they were also required to walk the way of the cross, if they were going to follow him (vv. 23–27). To be ashamed of Jesus (v. 26) meant to refuse to confess him for fear of persecution or hardship. Some early Christians did deny Jesus in times of testing, but others were faithful to death.

Verse 27 is difficult. To "see the kingdom" could refer to the end of the age, of course. But it may refer to some special manifestation of the kingdom's power and glory in this age, such as the transfiguration or Pentecost.

The transfiguration (vv. 28–36) followed closely on Jesus' prediction of his death. It gave to the three disciples a glimpse of his deity and of the glory that awaited him beyond the cross. Moses and Elijah were both closely related to the messianic age in Jewish thought. The Messiah was to be a prophet like Moses: Elijah was to be his forerunner.

The power struggle among the disciples (v. 46) is almost inconceivable in light of Jesus' teaching about the meaning of the cross. Jesus explained that greatness among his disciples was to be understood in terms of service to the little ones of the world (v. 48).

Truth for today.—The Greek word that we translate "disciple" means "learner." This is a good definition if you are thinking about a disciple of some Jewish rabbi or Greek philosopher. But it falls far short of defining what Jesus meant by disciple. Primarily a disciple is one who follows him along the way of the cross. The path to glory for the disciple also leads through suffering and humiliation.

We have substituted beliefs about Jesus for commitment to follow him. You can believe certain things about Jesus without its costing you money, position, or prestige. But if you dare to follow Jesus, that is something else altogether! You may have to give up your job; or move to another country. You will have to cut across the grain of accepted social values and prejudices. It is much safer to believe in Jesus with the top of the head than to make the dangerous decision to follow him.

The Meaning of Discipleship (Luke 9:51—10:42)

The passage.—Verse 51 marks a decisive point in the ministry of Jesus as presented in Luke. When the divinely determined time arrives, Jesus decides to go to Jerusalem, aware of the fateful consequences of such a decision. The rest of Jesus' public ministry unfolds under the shadow of the cross.

Most of the subsequent episodes in this passage illustrate what it means to follow this Jesus who goes to his death. The encounter with three prospective disciples, the mission of the seventy, the lawyer's question and the parable of the Good Samaritan, and finally the conflict between Martha and Mary—all these shed light on the meaning of discipleship.

Special points.—The Samaritans (9:52) occupied the territory between Judea and Galilee. They accepted the Pentateuch as their Scriptures. They had their own priesthood and built a rival temple on Mount Gerizim, which had been destroyed by the Jewish ruler John Hyrcanus. Bitter hostility existed between Jews and Samaritans.

"The Son of man has nowhere to lay his head" (9:58) does not mean that Jesus was without shelter. Homes of friends evidently were open to him. What Jesus meant was that there was no place in the world where he was safe. A disciple had to be prepared to share this experience.

One of the highest duties of a Jew was to care for his father and give him an honorable burial upon his death (v. 59). But Jesus taught that the claims of the kingdom must take precedence over all others, no matter how sacred. The spiritually "dead" (v. 60) who have not responded to the proclamation of the kingdom can care for duties of secondary importance.

The mission of the seventy, like that of the twelve, was a rapid preaching campaign. The disciples, therefore, are told to "salute no one on the road" (10:4, RSV). They did not have enough time to stop for the long, ceremonial greetings customary in the East.

"Son of peace" (10:6) describes a person receptive to the message of peace or salvation. "Sodom" (v. 12) represented the epitome of human wickedness as well as divine judgment. The greater opportunity extended to the people of Jesus' day implied a greater judgment on those who refused to repent.

The cure of the demon-possessed by the disciples represented a victory over the powers of evil and darkness. This was greeted by Jesus as an indication of God's ultimate, decisive triumph over Satan (v. 18). Verse 19 cannot be interpreted literally. The fact of the matter is that the disciples were indeed *hurt* by their enemies. Some of them suffered martyrdom. But they could suffer no ultimate, decisive harm. God guaranteed their future, no matter what happened to them in the world.

The "wise and prudent" (v. 21) were men who arrogantly depended on their own intellectual capacities. The "babes" were humble folk who were receptive to God's revelation of himself in Jesus.

The "lawyer" (v. 25) was a scribe, one of the Jewish religious experts. His answer to Jesus' question (v. 27) combines Deuteronomy 6:4 and Leviticus 19:18. Deuteronomy 6:4 is the Shema, the basic Jewish confession of faith.

The limits of a person's obligation to love would be determined by his definition of "neighbor" (v. 29). As generally interpreted, a neighbor was a fellow Jew. Pharisees might even exclude people like tax collectors and sinners. The parable of the good Samaritan (vv. 30–37) teaches that such limitations are wrong. The lawyer had asked the wrong question. He should have asked: To whom can I be a neighbor? Only with this attitude could he fulfil the commandment of love.

The parable also teaches that there can be no conflict between love for God and love for the neighbor. The priest and Levite both served God in the temple. They avoided the helpless man for fear of defiling themselves and becoming temporarily unfit for temple service. For all they knew, the naked man could have been a Gentile. Or, he could have been dead. Touching a corpse resulted in ritual impurity (see Num. 19, esp. vv. 11,13,17–19).

"One thing is needful" (v. 42) may be understood in two ways: (1) Only the spiritual part chosen by Mary was essential; or, (2) a simple meal of one dish would have sufficed.

Truth for today.—Jesus wants no superficial disciples, men so carried away by the enthusiasm of the moment that they are blind to the realities of the future. He always emphasized what it cost to follow him. Would he not chill the ardor of some of our evangelistic meetings just as he cut through the superficial enthusiasm displayed by one

of his prospects for discipleship? We have tended to emphasize one aspect of the gospel, rightly proclaiming that salvation is a free gift of God's grace. But have we at the same time emphasized that grace is also costly? Have we also stressed that love for God is not expressed adequately by worship in church alone? Jesus taught that service for God involves serving people who are deprived, hurt, and avoided by others.

Prayer and Spiritual Discernment (Luke 11:1–54)

The passage.—The materials in chapter 11 fall into two distinct categories. Verses 1–10 contain teachings of Jesus on prayer, beginning with the Lord's Prayer. Verses 11–54 depict the spiritual blindness of people who did not see what God was doing through Jesus right before their eyes.

Points for special emphasis.—"Abba" was the Aramaic word Jesus used for "Father" (v. 2). It was the intimate word used by the Jewish child to address his human father. By his use of the word Jesus was teaching that God is a loving Father to whom his children can go with complete confidence. The "kingdom" is the kingship or rule of God that his children long to see established completely and eternally.

"Keep on asking, keep on seeking, keep on knocking" would better translate the sense of the verbs in verse 9. The preceding parable illustrates this idea. God's children should never become discouraged when there seems to be no response. Of all the good gifts that God can give his children, the Holy Spirit (v. 13), the presence and power of God in their lives, is the greatest.

Jesus' enemies declared that he received power to do his mighty works from Satan (v. 15). Jesus showed them that their argument was illogical (vv.

17–18) and inconsistent (v. 19). The meaning of Jesus' mighty deeds was that a power greater than that of Satan was in the world, namely, the rule of God. The "finger of God" is the power of God (v. 20).

Jesus cured a dumb man (v. 14). But the cure itself, i.e., the explusion of the demon, was not enough (vv. 24–26). Man needs to be filled with the presence of God in order to be able to withstand future assaults from evil.

The "sign" (v. 29) desired by the people probably was some great celestial display, such as an eclipse of the moon or sun. The person of Jesus, "the Son of man," was the sign God had given to men (v. 30). People would be judged by their response to him.

Washing (v. 38) was practiced for religious purification and not for personal hygiene. The problem with Pharisaism was its concern with exterior or ceremonial purity. It did not come to grips with inner depravity (v. 39).

Since touching the dead was especially defiling, care was used to avoid contact with graves. "Graves that appear not" are unmarked graves (v. 44). The religious leaders are similar to such graves in that it does not appear from the outside what they are on the inside.

A vast body of oral traditions had developed by the first century. These prescribed what people had to do to keep the law. They are the "burdens grievous to be borne" laid on the people by the legal experts (v. 46). The Scriptures, rightly interpreted, are the "key of knowledge" (v. 52). By their wrong interpretations the legal experts had shut both themselves and the people they influenced out of the kingdom.

Truth for today.—The idea of Father is the key to Jesus' teaching about God. We can have implicit confidence in his love and care. Jesus' teaching on prayer is based on this concept of God. We can pray confidently if we believe in God as Father.

The secret of the serenity in Jesus' life was just this—his ability to trust God completely with the future. This is the way to freedom from anxiety in our own lives. How much better we would be if we could turn all our concerns about tomorrow over to God. This would liberate us to live creatively and confidently today, which is all that God ever gives to us. Life is given to us one day at the time, but God keeps tomorrow for himself.

Lack of faith is one of our problems. Spiritual blindness is another. God is ever active in his world, but often we do not see what he is doing. Spiritual blindness causes men to call the truth a lie, good evil, and God the devil. For example, some people have made God the great segregationist. The Bible teaches us, however, that God is at work to bring people together. When we attribute the divisions among men to God, we are really making him the devil.

Trusting God (Luke 12:1–34)

The passage.—Two different situations in the disciples' lives are presupposed in this passage. In both their faith in God will be tested. In the first instance, the test of faith is the hostility that the disciples will encounter when they dare to proclaim their loyalty to Christ (vv. 4–12). In the second, the need for faith in God is urged as the antidote to anxieties about material needs (vv. 13–34).

Special points.—Leaven (v. 1) usually stands for evil, in this case the hypocrisy of the Pharisees. All secret things, however, will be exposed by the light of God's judgment (v. 2).

Verse 3 says that disciples cannot keep their faith secret. Persecution, in which they may even be killed (v. 4), must not keep them from confessing Jesus openly (vv. 8–10).

Criticism of the "Son of man" is forgiveable (v. 10). Son of man can mean "a man." However, if it is the title Jesus often used for himself, the statement means that criticism of Jesus as a person is forgiveable. In Mark 3:28–29 (cf. Matt. 23:31–32) "blasphemy" against the Holy Spirit (12:10) is clearly the sin of attributing the mighty deeds of Jesus to the power of the devil instead of the power of God. In the Lukan context it is not so clear what is meant.

"My soul" (v. 19) is a Semitic way for a person to speak of himself. Translate the phrase "myself" in the English idiom. "Soul" (v. 20) is life. "Thy soul shall be required" means "you are going to die." The rich man could amass a quantity of goods, but he could not extend his life so as to enjoy them.

A cubit (v. 19) is the distance from the elbow to the tip of the middle finger, approximately 18 inches. The word translated "stature" can also be translated "span of life," which is preferable (see RSV).

Truth for today.—Traditionally we have thought that the injunction in verses 8–9 is fulfilled by what we call a "public profession of faith in Jesus." But this is not what Jesus had in mind at all. Generally, people who profess faith in Jesus before a church do so before a friendly, sympathetic audience. This is certainly not the supreme test of our loyalty.

But what about those times when under the stress of social or business pressures we have taken positions or said things that were not in keeping with our character as believers? What about those times when we have felt an urge to speak out for Christian principles and attitudes but were deterred by the prejudices of others in the group? These are more similar to the circumstances anticipated in the text.

There may be sins that are unforgiveable, but there are no persons who are unforgiveable, no matter what they have done. The problem is that God can only reach us if we respond to his efforts. If we say that the voice of God is the voice of the devil, then God cannot possibly get through to us. This is the sin against the Holy Spirit. It was the problem that Jesus confronted.

Teachings About the Future (Luke 12:35—13:9)

The passage.—Some of Jesus' sayings teach that the kingdom of God is already present in the world, manifesting itself in his person. This meant that his contemporaries were faced with the necessity of making a decision. When God confronts men as king, they must decide if they will submit to him or rebel against him.

In other sayings Jesus teaches that the Kingdom is yet to come. The fulness of God's rule will be manifested at the end of this age. Both aspects of Jesus' teaching are found in this passage.

In 12:35–48 the future appearance of the Kingdom at the end of this age is in view. Here Luke emphasizes that the end of the age and the coming of the Son of man cannot be predicted. Jesus' followers must be prepared for his return at all times. In 12:49–59 Jesus calls on his hearers to make a decision now in light of the fact that God's rule has broken into history. Jesus' mission, to be accomplished through his death (12:50), will result in divisions (vv. 51–53) as people make their decisions for and against him.

Special points.—The servant prepared to serve his master at a moment's notice will have his "loins girded about"

(v. 35), i.e., the long robe will be gathered up around his waist to permit freedom of movement. In 12:38 the night is divided into three watches according to Jewish custom. The second watch was from 10 P.M. to 2 A.M.; the third, from 2 A.M. to 6 A.M.

The idea in 12:47–48 is that greater knowledge, opportunity, and trust imply greater responsibility. Leaders have more responsibility than followers in God's kingdom.

"Fire" (v. 49) represents the divisions caused by the ministry of Jesus. His "baptism" is the suffering and death which lie ahead.

A "cloud out of the west" (v. 54) brought moist air from the Mediterranean Sea and so indicated the possibility of rain. The south wind (v. 55) blew off the hot, dry desert country. Jesus castigates the spiritual blindness of his people. They can interpret the signs of weather correctly. But they do not see what God is doing in their midst.

The Galileans (13:1) were slain while offering sacrifices in the Temple. There is no mention of this incident outside Luke. Josephus, the Jewish historian, tells of similar acts of cruelty committed by Pilate. The "tower in Siloam" (v. 4) was a fortification built to guard a spring and reservoir which provided water for Jerusalem. Some people evidently believed that the incidents recounted in the passage were a punishment brought about by sin. Jesus contradicted this kind of theology.

The "fig tree" (13:6) is a symbol for Israel (Hos. 9:10). The parable illustrates the patience of God with Israel. But this patience has its limits.

Truth for today.—Suffering and misfortune were popularly explained as a punishment for sin in Jesus' day. Jesus did not accept that theology. In fact, his own experience is a complete contra-

diction of it. He, the best of all men, knew the bitter, dark depths of human suffering. He taught that his followers would also know their share of suffering and misfortune. Jesus believed that it pays to serve God, but not necessarily in terms of economic prosperity or good health.

The idea that suffering is the direct result of sin can lead to either of two extremes. The sufferer may feel hopeless, cut off from God by his misfortune. The nonsufferer may become arrogantly self-righteous.

The truth is that all men are sinners; all need to repent; all need the grace of God; all can be confident that they will receive it.

The Nature of the Kingdom (Luke 13:10–35)

The passage.—The power of the kingdom is manifested once again in the cure of a crippled woman (vv. 10–17). The growth of the kingdom is illustrated by two parables (vv. 18–21). The difficulty of entering the Kingdom is emphasized by the parable of the closed door (vv. 23–30). In the last part of the passage we are reminded once again that Jesus is on his way to die. Threatened with the possibility of death by Herod (vv. 31–33), Jesus replies that he will die in Jerusalem and not in Galilee. The passage ends with the poignant lament over Jerusalem.

Special points.—For the problem of healing on the sabbath see comments on 6:1–11. Disease is seen as a frustration of God's purpose for man. So Jesus says that the crippled woman was bound by Satan (13:16).

The parable of the mustard seed (vv. 18–19) probably illustrated the contrast between the small beginnings and eventual greatness of God's kingdom. "Leaven" (v. 21) is often a symbol for evil, but here it stands for God's rule. The parable illustrates the mysterious and irresistible working of that rule. The parables of the kingdom in general teach that God's kingdom is guaranteed by his own power and purposes. It does not stand or fall with human activity.

The question in verse 23 is both irrelevant and impertinent. It is not my business to determine whom God is going to admit to the kingdom. I have the responsibility to make sure that I am not one of the persons on the outside of the closed door. Jesus consistently cautioned against getting the impression that it is easy to enter the kingdom (v. 24). Changed lives rather than words are the criterion (vv. 26–27). Verse 29 contains a prediction that Gentiles will occupy the places claimed by the religious leaders.

"Herod" (v. 31) is Herod Antipas, ruler of Galilee. Jesus was not swayed by threats. He had a God-given task to perform, which Herod could not thwart. At the appropriate time he will go to Jerusalem where he is destined to die. The result of Israel's rejection of Jesus will be the destruction of her "house" (v. 35). "House" probably represents Jerusalem. Verse 35b in the Matthean context (Matt. 23:37–39) is clearly a prediction of Jesus' return at the end of the age. Here it may refer to the triumphal entry into Jerusalem (see Luke 19:38).

Truth for today.—Too many people are like the man who wanted to know if only few will be saved. They are always trying to determine who is not going to be included in that number. You get the idea that they will be distinctly disappointed if God decides to save many people, especially the ones that they have decided are not going to make it.

What we need to understand is that it is God alone who judges and God alone

who saves. This is an area where no human being has the competence to operate. We cannot determine in any case who is saved and who is not. We cannot do this even with the Bible. The reason is that having the Bible does not make us God.

We need to be concerned above all about our own personal response to God. The gospel is not a standard by which we can judge others. It is a personal message addressed to each one of us. We should not seek to use it as a club against others but, rather, strive to hear what it is saying to each one of us.

The Demands of the Kingdom (Luke 14:1–35)

The passage.—The teachings of Jesus in chapter 14 are placed in the setting of a sabbath dinner at the home of a leading Pharisee. The passage begins with an account of a healing which once again violated Jewish sabbath traditions (vv. 1–6). This is followed by a series of comments on the right conduct of guests and host (vv. 7–14). Beginning with the parable of the great banquet (vv. 15–24), the last part of the chapter emphasizes the demands of the kingdom on disciples.

Special points.—For "chief rooms" (v. 7) we should read "chief places of honor" (RSV). These would be the ones nearest the host. The teachings of Jesus lead to the principle enunciated in verse 11. In the kingdom of God human values are turned upside down. It is the humble man, the person who defers to others, who is first in God's sight.

The pious platitude uttered by a self-assured guest (v. 15) serves to introduce Jesus' parable of the great banquet (vv. 16–24). The religious leaders were sure that they had reserved places in God's kingdom. But Jesus taught that it is not enough just to be invited. A person has to accept the invitation. Because they failed to accept God's invitation, arrogant religious people would discover that places they thought were reserved for them would be given instead to the people that they despised and ostracized (v. 21). The people from the "highways and hedges," from outside the city, would probably be Gentiles.

"Hate" (v. 26) means to love less. Jesus never taught that we should hate anybody. He did teach that the demands of the Kingdom must come first. We must be willing to deny claims of family, culture, job, and anything else if they interfere with our loyalty to God. This is essentially what is meant also by bearing one's cross (v. 27). The disciple is to walk the way of self-denial and commitment to God if it costs him his life to do so.

"Salt" (v. 34) is the element of self-sacrifice absolutely essential in the life of the disciple. Salt does not actually "lose its savor," but it could be mixed with other substances so as to lose its strength. Such salt was good neither for food nor fertilizer (v. 35).

Truth for today.—What do you think would happen to us if we actually took seriously our responsibility to follow Jesus in all areas of our lives? Suppose we started to accept and associate with people of all races, classes, and moral levels. Suppose we started to go to the kinds of places and do the kinds of things that he did. Suppose we suddenly became totally generous, completely dedicated to serving others, entirely oblivious to thoughts of self-interest and advancement. What kind of criticism, misunderstanding, and even hatred do you think would beat against us from a scandalized society? Do you think that we would begin to understand what it means to "bear a cross" after Jesus?

God's Joy over the Recovery of the Lost (Luke 15:1–32)

The passage.—Chapter 15 consists of three parables, the lost sheep, the lost coin, and the prodigal son. The last two are found only in Luke. Verses 1–2 should be considered the introduction to each one of the parables. They were told in response to the indignation of religious leaders who were scandalized by Jesus' association with tax collectors and sinners.

Special points.—The inclusion of Israel's rejected people in the kingdom of God was made concretely visible when Jesus received them in table fellowship. In so doing, he extended to them the grace of God. The joyous fellowship between Jesus and the tax collectors and sinners offended the scribes and Pharisees (15:2). They believed that close association with such people caused a religious person to become ritually impure.

The joy of the shepherd who finds his lost sheep (v. 5) is a picture of God's joy over sinners attracted to Jesus. So also is the joy of the woman (vv. 9–10) and the Father (vv. 22–24) when they found something precious to them. "In heaven" (v. 7) is a common phrase used by Jewish people to avoid mentioning God's name, for which they had great reverence.

The "silver coins" (v. 8) were drachmas, each one of which was worth about 30 cents. One drachma was a day's wage for a working man. The "lamp" (v. 8) was necessary because the small hut was poorly lighted. By sweeping the clay floor, the coin was eventually recovered.

The depth of misery into which the prodigal sank after leaving home is graphically described in verses 15–16. No Jew would have had anything to do with swine if he could possibly help it. They were considered unclean. But the prodigal was reduced to such desperate straits that he found it necessary to tend pigs. The husks were pods of the carob tree, used for animal fodder.

The son's restored status is symbolized by the robe, the ring, and the shoes (v. 22). Such a robe was given to honored guests who arrived after a long trip, dusty and travel-worn. The ring and shoes say that he was received as an heir and a son. Slaves went barefoot.

The parable of the prodigal son really should be called the parable of the elder brother. The resentment and cheerlessness of the older son at the joyous reception of the returning prodigal typified that of the religious leaders.

Truth for today.—A joyless, self-righteous approach to religion is often taken by people who claim to be following Jesus. Self-righteous legalism is expressed by contempt for the people who do not live up to a certain prescribed code of conduct. It is strange that people erect in Jesus' name the very kind of institution that he challenged.

The truth of the matter is that the kinds of people whom Jesus received would probably not be welcome in the average church today. Unless they cut their hair in a prescribed manner, dress in a certain way, and move in decent, respectable circles, religious people feel uncomfortable around others. Perhaps this is why more sinners are not being transformed in our society.

The Danger of Wealth (Luke 16:1–31)

The passage.—Chapter 16 begins with the parable of the dishonest steward and ends with the parable of the rich man and Lazarus. Neither is found in the other Gospels. They are a part of the special materials that indicate Luke's emphasis on the danger of wealth.

Special points.—The "steward" (v. 1) was an administrator in charge of his employer's property and business. The owner ordered him to give an account (v. 2), that is, to turn in the records of the transactions made during his term of employment. A hundred measures of oil (v. 6) was about 875 gallons; a hundred measures of wheat (v. 7), about a thousand bushels.

It is entirely possible that the parable of the dishonest steward describes an incident that had actually happened. We are not to suppose that Jesus condoned the trickery of the steward whom he pointedly describes as "dishonest" (v. 8). He saw a lesson in the story for his followers. The crafty steward took advantage of the possibilities available to him in the present to prepare for the crisis that lay in the future. Like the steward, all men face a crisis in the future when they must give an account to God of their stewardship. They should use their wealth in such a way as to provide for that crisis.

Money is called "unrighteous mammon" (v. 9, RSV) because it is often earned and used in evil ways. It should be used to help people. "When ye fail" (v. 9) should be "when it fails." Money fails when a man dies. However, when God receives the generous man in heaven he will find the "friends" whom he has made through the responsible use of wealth.

The "least" (v. 10) is material wealth, of little value when compared to the "true riches" of eternity (v. 11). Wealth does not belong to the person who uses it. All things belong to God (v. 12). Only that which the Christian receives in the next life will be his "own," his to enjoy forever.

"Justify yourselves before men" (v. 15) means "you try to prove to other people that you are religious by your pious acts." But God knows men's "hearts." He pierces through the religious cover to see the motives.

Keeping the law was the ultimate goal of Pharisaism. The "law and the prophets" constitute a phase of redemptive history that ended with John the Baptist (v. 16). A new era had dawned with the proclamation of the kingdom of God. "Every man is pressing into it" probably refers to the people who were responding eagerly to the gospel.

A "tittle" (v. 17) was an ornamental flourish added to a Hebrew letter. The phrase emphasizes the point that the law had not become void. It had been fulfilled. Verse 18 is an example of this fulfilment. There were provisions for divorce under the law. But the radical demands of the kingdom go beyond the law and emphasize God's original purpose for an indissoluble union in marriage.

The opulence of the rich man is contrasted with the extreme misery of the beggar (vv. 19–20). The cloth of the expensive outer garment is called purple because of the costly dye used in its manufacture. Linen is the inner garment. "Lazarus" means "one whom God helps." Upon his death he went to "Abraham's bosom," a symbol for heaven. The rich man in torment is pictured as being within sight and sound of heaven.

The parable teaches that a life dedicated to material values and lived in isolation from human need is also separated from God. It also teaches that men are not genuinely converted by sensational acts. The rich man had the witness of Scripture. *Moses* (the law) and the "prophets" teach man's responsibility for the poor, for which he must answer ultimately to God.

Lesson for today.—Often our approach to Christian giving is pragmatic. We urge people to give because of what can be done with money. Jesus was interested in what could be done for needy people with money. But he was also interested in the welfare of the rich. He understood that the gravest danger facing a person of means was idolatry. Wealth is a potential rival to God in a man's life. He can depend on it for security, happiness, and fulfilment, leaving God out of his life. We show that we have left God out of our lives when we have no compassion for God's unfortunate children.

There was a great gulf fixed between the rich man and Lazarus in eternity. It was but a continuation of the gulf between the two on this side of the grave. The only problem was that God was identified with the poor man on the other side of the gulf. This teaches us that we should be careful how we shut people (of other races, the poor) out of our lives. We may be closing God out also!

Forgiveness, Faith, Duty, Gratitude (Luke 17:1–19)

The passage.—The sayings and incidents in the passage are not held together by any unifying theme. They touch on the various aspects of the believer's life indicated in the heading.

Special points.—"Offences" (v. 1) translates a Greek word which originally referred to the bait stick of a trap. In the New Testament it often refers to those things which a person may do or say to cause another to fall into sin ("temptations to sin," RSV). "One of these little ones" (v. 2) are not only children but any of the more limited, humble, less enlightened members of the community.

Note that the Christian has a responsibility not to hurt his brother; he also has a responsibility if the brother offends him (vv. 3–4). He must seek reconciliation with his brother and practice forgiveness in his relationships with him.

The disciples may have asked for a greater faith (v. 5). The underlying Greek phrase also allows for the meaning: "Give us faith." A "grain of mustard seed" (v. 6) was proverbial for its smallness. Jesus teaches that the least amount of faith will open up miracle-working possibilities. Of course, we should not interpret verse 6 literally. God does not waste his power in performing senseless, sensational acts. The removal of the tree is but an illustration of the mighty deeds that men of faith can accomplish.

The parable of the unprofitable servant (vv. 7–10) simply teaches that our service for God should not make us feel that God owes us something. The point at issue is not how God thinks of his servant but how the servant thinks of his work for God. "I trow not" may be omitted. It is not a part of the original text. It is also a good example of the outmoded English often found in the KJV.

Verse 11 reminds us once again that Jesus is on his way to Jerusalem. "Through the midst of Samaria and Galilee" probably means "on the frontier between Samaria and Galilee." The miracle that occurred here has an unusual slant. Jesus did not actually heal the men on the spot. They were instructed to show themselves to the priests (see Lev. 13:1 ff.) in the confidence that they would be healed before they reached their destination. All the lepers must have believed Jesus, but verses 15–19 show that genuine faith involves more than believing in the miracle-working power of God. It also involves the recognition that God's mercies are undeserved. Gratitude, therefore, is an essential part of true faith. The point in the story is that a "Samaritan," a despised foreigner, was the one who had genuine faith.

Lesson for today.—When we compare our concepts of the Christian life to those of Jesus, we see how narrow, limited, and provincial we are. We set limits on our responsibility for others. If our brother offends us, we feel that this cancels our responsibility to relate to him. We respond to his desire for reconciliation with limited expressions of love and forgiveness.

Our ideas about the possibilities of faith are also very restricted. We do not really believe that God's power can and will remove the mountainous obstacles that we confront. By contrast Jesus sets before us breathtaking vistas of what we could do if we had the tiniest bit of faith.

If we do the least thing for God, we want everybody to notice it and praise us for it. We often act as if we feel that we are doing God and the church a favor if we teach a Sunday School class, for example. Jesus taught that it is impossible for us to do enough for God.

We build fences around forgiveness, faith, duty, and gratitude. In passages like this one Jesus exhorts us to tear those fences down in order to achieve the possibilities of the Christian life.

The Certainty of the Kingdom (Luke 17:20—18:8)

The passage.—One of Luke's primary aims apparently was to eliminate speculation about the end of the age. In this passage he says three things about the coming of the Son of man at the end of history: (1) He is sure to come. (2) No one can predict when he will come. (3) Christians should not be plunged into despair by delay in his coming.

Special points.—"With observation" (v. 20) is better understood if we read "with signs to be observed" (RSV). Discussions about signs that would help them to recognize the approach of the end-time evidently preoccupied Pharisaic circles. But Jesus taught that there is no basis for predicting the date of God's coming kingdom. Furthermore, the kingdom (rule) of God was not something out there—foreign and isolated from them. "Within you" (v. 21) is one of the most debated phrases in the New Testament. It can mean that the rule of God is inside the individual, that it is personal and spiritual. Or, more probably, it should be "among you" (see RSV). Jesus in their midst was the demonstration of the power of God's rule. People looked for the Kingdom out there, heralded by sensational wonders. They needed to look in their midst to see the revelation of the Kingdom in the person of Jesus.

Christians will face difficult times of persecution when they will long to see "one of the days of the Son of man" (v. 22). This probably refers to a mighty manifestation of God's power as, e.g., the transfiguration. Such a manifestation would give them courage. During difficult times, they could become easy victims of sensational preachers who proclaim that the end of the world is at hand (v. 23). Jesus cautioned his disciples not to be misled. No person or group of persons will have special, inside information denied to others. The coming of the Son of man is like "lightning" that flashes across the whole sky (v. 24). It will be recognized by all men at the same time.

The point is illustrated by Noah and Lot (vv. 27–30). Life was going on as usual when people were surprised by the great crises of those days. When the end comes, Jesus' followers are not to act like Lot's wife (vv. 31–33). They are not to try to hold on to the things of the old age.

Verse 36 is not found in the best Greek manuscripts and should be omitted. In verse 37 the saying of Jesus shows once again that questions of when and where with reference to the end of the world are useless. The "eagles" symbolize God's judgment that will take place at the appropriate place and time.

The parable of the importunate widow (18:1–8) urges Christians not to lose faith in God if he seems to delay in the execution of final judgment and salvation. "Though he bear long with them" (v. 7) means that God is patient with his children who continue to cry out to him. God can be trusted. But Jesus raises the question: Can the same be said about man? When the end comes will all men have lost heart (v. 8)?

Truth for today.—According to the biblical view, history does not go in circles. It is proceeding toward a goal. That goal is determined by the sovereign will of God. God is the God of the future. Jesus called on men to trust God with the future.

This liberates us to live in the present which God gives to us. This present moment is the only one that belongs to us. We should receive it gratefully and live it responsibly.

Too many people try to live in either the past or the future. Some are unable to enjoy the present or achieve its possibilities because they are crying over something that happened in the past. Others try to live in the future. They worry about what might happen—possible catastrophes, misfortunes, needs. They can't enjoy the meal they eat now because of worrying about whether they will have enough to eat in a tomorrow that may never come. By contrast, faith in God should lead us to live joyously and fully in the present.

Jesus' Approach to Jerusalem (Luke 19:1–46)

The passage.—The public ministry of Jesus draws rapidly to a close. At the beginning of the passage Jesus has reached Jericho, some 15 miles northeast of Jerusalem. There he exercises a transforming power in the life of Zacchaeus. This is the last of those recorded incidents that illustrate the openness of the religious outcasts to Jesus in contrast to the spiritual blindness of religious people. The rest of the passage sets forth the meaning of Jesus' fateful entrance into Jerusalem.

Special points.—As an important border town and commercial center, Jericho required the service of tax collectors like Zacchaeus (v. 2) who charged customs on goods traveling the Jerusalem highway. Although he was perhaps initially drawn to Jesus by curiosity, Zacchaeus was transformed by Jesus' unconditional acceptance of him. His repentance was expressed concretely as a new sensitivity to social justice in keeping with teachings like those of John the Baptist (cf. Luke 3:11–14). In spite of the fact that he was a Jew, a "son of Abraham" like other Jews, Zacchaeus was treated as an outcast or a "lost" person. But Jesus came seeking just such despised, lost Jews (v. 10).

The messianic expectations of the disciples were raised to fever pitch by their approach to Jerusalem. Evidently they believed that Jesus would establish his kingdom once he arrived in the Jewish capital (v. 11). The parable of the pounds is Jesus' answer to such false ideas (vv. 11–27). Like the king in the story, Jesus must also go away for an indefinite length of time. Like the king also, he will return at an unexpected moment.

It has been suggested that the parable of the pounds in Luke is based upon the well-known experiences of Archelaus. Although named in Herod's will as heir to Judea with the title of king, Archelaus was opposed by a Jewish embassy when he went to Rome (a far country— v. 12) to be confirmed as ruler of Judea. In the deeper meaning of the parable, the "citizens who hated him" (v. 14) may be the Jewish people who rejected Jesus. The nobleman gave "pounds" to his subjects to be used in his absence. Each had a value of twenty to twenty-five dollars. These represent the responsibilities and opportunities entrusted to believers during the absence of their Lord. The parable teaches that Christians are not to sit around waiting for their Lord to return. They are to be busy serving him in the present so that they can render a good account of their stewardship at his return.

Bethany (v. 29) was about one and one-half miles east of Jerusalem. The location of "Bethphage" is unknown. At this point Jesus secured a "colt" to make his entrance into Jerusalem. Evidently this was a conscious fulfilment of Zechariah 9:9. By fulfilling this prophecy, Jesus declared that he was Israel's King-Messiah. Both his humility and his mission of peace were symbolized by the animal on which he rode.

Jesus wept over Jerusalem (v. 41) because he saw so clearly the fate that awaited the city. When they rejected him, the Jewish people in effect chose a course of revolutionary nationalism. This led to the rebellion against Rome and the terrible destruction of Jerusalem in A.D. 70. This is depicted in verses 43–44.

Pilgrims who visited Jerusalem required animals for sacrifice. They also needed to exchange their foreign money for the half-shekel used to pay the Temple tax. In order to supply these needs a lucrative business had developed in the Temple. Jesus' first act in the Temple was to drive the people out who made a commerce of religion (vv. 45–46). Probably this act was also very symbolic. According to some Jewish thought, the Messiah would make his appearance in the Temple at the beginning of his reign. By cleansing the Temple, Jesus declared that he as Messiah had wrested control of it from the religious leaders.

Truth for today.—The story of Jesus' encounter with Zacchaeus illustrates his complete freedom to relate to people in need. Everybody criticized him when he went to Zacchaeus' house. But Jesus simply did not allow prejudice nor social customs to erect a barrier between him and any human being.

Jesus infuriated people so much because he refused to be controlled by their social codes. Then as now the rule was: Good people associate with good people; bad people associate with bad people. But here he was, a good man, who spent most of his time with bad people.

It is here that Jesus blazed a trail that so few of us dare to take. We simply do not care to pay the price that will be demanded if we associate with the kinds of people that Jesus would identify with, were he among us today. We do not wish to risk the ostracism and anger that would be the result. There is no greater barrier to genuine discipleship in modern society than our fear of public opinion.

So we move in our closed circles; worship him in our closed churches. And brag on him for being so loving and open to people! But he doesn't want us to brag on him. He wants us to follow him.

Controversies in Jerusalem (Luke 19:47—21:4)

The passage.—We are told in 19:47 that the Jewish religious leaders were determined to destroy Jesus. Their rage was due in part to his cleansing of the Temple. Jesus' popularity with the people, however, constituted a major deterrent to the plans of his enemies (v. 48). Insofar as they were instigated by the leaders, the series of controversies described in chapter 20 were designed to destroy Jesus' popularity. Jesus clearly emerged from those conflicts as the victor over his enemies.

Special points.—Representatives of the groups named in 20:1 constituted the Sanhedrin, the Jewish supreme court. Their question (v. 2) was provoked by Jesus' action in cleansing the Temple. If Jesus had authority for what he did, it clearly did not come from regularly constituted Jewish authority. Would he be so bold as to claim God's authority for his act?

The dishonesty of the questioners was revealed by Jesus' counter-question (v. 4). If they admitted that John's authority came from God, they would have to admit that Jesus who was baptized by John received his authority from the same source. Unwilling to do this and unwilling to anger the people, the religious leaders beat a cowardly retreat (v. 7).

The "vineyard" (v. 9) is a figure for Israel. The servants (vv. 10–12) are the prophets. The son who is killed is Jesus (vv. 13–15). Because Israel failed to recognize God's ownership, the vineyard will be given to "others" (v. 16), that is, Christians. The "stone rejected" by the Jewish people (Jesus) will become the cornerstone of a new edifice (v. 17). But the stone is also a stone of judgment. All attacks on it will be shattered. Furthermore, it will fall in judgment on those who reject it (v. 18).

Tribute (v. 22) was the direct personal tax levied on citizens of Palestine by the Roman government. Since it was a symbol of their subjection to Rome, the ardent nationalists violently hated and opposed the tax. Jesus' enemies hoped to elicit an answer that would either anger the people or make him betray the Roman government.

Jesus' answer (vv. 23–25) was based on accepted ancient custom. Money belonged to the ruler who minted it. It symbolized the ruler's sovereignty over the territory in which it circulated. By carrying Caesar's money in their purses, the Jewish people were admitting his right to rule over them. Since the money belonged to Caesar to begin with, they had no choice but to return it upon his demand. Then Jesus added an unexpected injunction: Render "unto God the things that are God's." Man bears God's image and so belongs to him. Man should pay taxes to Caesar, but his life and devotion belong to God alone.

The Sadducees (v. 27) accepted as their Scriptures only the first five books of the Old Testament. They claimed that a doctrine of the resurrection was not found there. They put a question to Jesus which they thought pointed up the absurdity of belief in the resurrection (vv. 28–33). It was based on the practice of levirate marriage (*levir* means brother). The brother of a deceased man had the obligation of marrying the widow to raise up heirs for him (see Deut. 25:5–10). Notice that Jesus did not argue with the Sadducees about their concept of Scripture. He simply used a passage from Exodus (3:6), a book that they accepted as Scripture, to show that their denial of the resurrection was erroneous (vv. 37–38).

Jesus seized the initiative in 20:41 when he questioned the accepted Jewish concept of the Messiah. The people expected a descendant of David to sit on his throne in Jerusalem. Jesus rejected the idea that the Messiah was to reestablish the Davidic dynasty. Psalm 110:1 implies that the Messiah was much more than David's son; he was also David's Lord (20:42–44).

Truth for today.—The statement of Jesus in 20:25 (and parallels) is the only one in the Gospels that deals with the relation of the disciples to Caesar. It has

been made to bear the weight of many arguments about the Christian and the state, some of which are very erroneous.

To begin with Jesus taught that all of life is under the control of God. We are responsible to God for every act, whether it be in the social, political economic, or religious sphere of life. The idea that the gospel should have nothing to say about political and social matters is a perversion of the teaching of Jesus.

Caesar has no authority which rivals God. In the last analysis, it is God and not Caesar who must determine what is right for the Christian. The follower of Jesus does not allow president or king to set the standards by which he judges his moral life. Only God can do that. Taxes may be Caesar's due, but to God must go life's supreme allegiance.

The Destruction of Jerusalem and the End of the Age (Luke 21:5–38)

The passage.—As we have noted elsewhere, one of the primary purposes of Luke was to warn against false notions about the end of the world. To some people such terrible events as the destruction of Jerusalem which took place in A.D. 70 indicated that the end was near. In times of great difficulty, predictions about the return of Jesus abound. Luke teaches that the end of the world is not connected with any of the crises of history.

Special points.—The Jewish historian Josephus informs us that the Temple in Jerusalem was constructed of huge blocks of white marble, which from a distance looked like a gleaming, snow-capped mountain peak. The "gifts" (v. 5) with which the Temple was adorned had come from various people, including King Herod and Caesar Augustus himself. The massive structure gave an appearance of stability and permanence, but Jesus predicted that it would be destroyed completely (v. 6).

Jesus did not give an answer to the disciples about the "time" and "signs" of this event (v. 7). Indeed, he steadfastly refused to answer this kind of question. Instead, he warned his followers not to be misled by predictions that the time of the end was near. The inclination is to see in such terrible events of history a sign that the end of the world is at hand.

Jesus taught that neither "wars" (vv. 9–10), nor natural disasters (v. 11), nor the persecution of his followers (v. 12) would indicate the approaching end of the age. Persecutions will come from Jewish as well as Gentile sources. The *synagogues* also functioned as local Jewish courts. "Kings" and "rulers" are Gentile authorities.

Persecution is to be viewed as a time of witnessing rather than as a sign of the end (see 21:13 in the RSV). But Christians are not to be preoccupied by what they will say in their witness before their persecutors (vv. 14–15). Their Lord will give them their message (cf. Luke 12:11).

Verse 18 cannot mean that Jesus' followers will not be harmed by their enemies. Some of them, we know, were beaten, imprisoned, and killed. But Jesus affirms that the ultimate security of his disciples is in God's hands. Persecutors can kill Christians, but God will give them life in the age to come. This is the promise in verse 19 which should read: "By your endurance you will gain your lives" (RSV).

The siege and destruction of Jerusalem are depicted vividly in verses 20–24. "Days of vengeance" ascribes the fate of Jerusalem to the judgment of God. It is the punishment resulting from the city's rejection of Jesus. Pregnant women and women with small children (v. 23) will have special problems when Jerusalem is besieged. They will not be able to flee fast enough. We know that Jewish Christians escaped the horrible fate of their countrymen by fleeing to Pella.

The "times of the Gentiles" (v. 24) is the period when Jerusalem will be dominated by pagans. This time has its appointed limits. The Romans will not rule forever.

Clearly the first part of our passage has to do primarily with the destruction of Jerusalem. But it is not so clear how one should understand verses 25–32. Is the subject the end of the world which is to take place at the coming of the Son of man? If "this generation" is given its usual meaning, we should assume that verses 27 and 31 refer to special expressions of God's power, such as the transfiguration and Pentecost, that the disciples experienced during their lifetime.

Truth for today.—There are two extremes to be avoided in our attitude toward the future. On the one hand, we can become engrossed in thinking about the future, in speculating about what is going to take place, and in figuring out the calendar that God is going to follow. Of course, it doesn't really matter in the long run what kinds of predictions anyone makes. God is going to order the future in his own way. Our predictions will not change his plans.

The real problem is that people who become overly concerned with the end of the age do not live responsibly in the here and now. Their speculations are really an escape from the world with its challenges and difficulties.

On the other hand some people live as if there were no tomorrow. They are only concerned about the present. They forget that they are more than a stomach to be filled or a body to be clothed. They are eternal spirits who have basic needs not met by food and drink. They also forget that they cannot always run from God to whom they are accountable for what they do in the present.

The Night Before the Crucifixion (Luke 22:1–70)

The passage.—Luke sets forth the events that occurred on the night of Jesus' arrest. The celebration of the Passover at which the Lord's Supper was instituted, the agony in Gethsemane, the arrest, and the denial by Peter are the salient experiences of those fateful hours.

Special points.—Technically the Passover occurred on the 14th of the Jewish month called Nisan. On this day the Passover lamb was slain. The Passover meal was eaten that night. Since the Jewish day ran from sundown to sundown, this was the beginning of Nisan 15. The "Feast of Unleavened Bread," a seven day festival, began on this date also. Because they were so closely associated, both could be called either "Passover" or the "Feast of Unleavened Bread" (as in v. 1).

The Jewish leaders had decided not to move against Jesus during the Passover for fear of inciting the people (see Mark 14:2). But when they were promised help by Judas (Luke 22:4), they changed their minds. Evidently Judas' part in the plot was to lead Jesus' enemies to a place where they could seize him without creating an incident.

During the Passover, many thousands of pilgrims flocked into Jerusalem. The residents were obliged to open their homes to these pilgrims, providing them with the facilities for celebrating the Passover. Jesus, no doubt, had made prior arrangements with someone for the use of his house. The disciples designated to purchase the lamb, sacrifice it, and prepare the Passover meal would be led to the house by a "man bearing a pitcher of water" (Luke 22:10). Since this was a task usually performed by women, he would be easily identifiable.

The breaking of the bread and the blessing of the cup (vv. 19–20) were an integral part of the Passover meal. Indeed, all the evidence indicates that the Lord's Supper continued to be observed in the early church in connection with a fellowship meal.

The sharing of the bread and the cup on that night took on a new significance, however, because of its relationship to the crucified and risen Lord. Perhaps the key phrase in the description of the Last Supper is "new testament in my blood" (Luke v. 20). The word "testament" is often replaced in other versions by the word "covenant." Neither of these accurately translates the underlying original. The Greek word in its biblical sense refers to an act of God whereby he seeks to redeem his people and to establish a relationship with them. The phrase "new covenant" reminds us of Jeremiah's prophecy (Jer. 31:31–34). In the Last Supper this prophecy was fulfilled by Jesus; the new covenant was established. Through the death of his Son God redeemed the believing remnant and constituted the new Israel.

In verses 35–38 Jesus emphasizes to his disciples that their situation is about to change drastically. On their earlier missions (Luke 9:1–6; 10:1–12), Jesus' followers could count on the hospitality and generosity of the people (Luke 22: 35). But that is no longer the case. They are going to be objects of hatred and hostility. In this changed situation the disciples will go hungry unless they have their own provisions (Luke 22:36).

Jesus' remark about the sword is puzzling (v. 36). In any case, it cannot be taken literally. This would contradict the total thrust of the teaching and acts of Jesus. Also, only "two swords" would be useless as weapons of defense (v. 38).

Jesus' statement, therefore, must be a way of emphasizing that the disciples are about to enter a time of great peril —a point that apparently was lost on them.

At daybreak, after several hours of abuse and heartbreak, Jesus was led before the "council." This was the Sanhedrin, the highest judicial authority among the Jewish people. Under the Romans the Sanhedrin still enjoyed extensive powers. This apparently did not include the power to execute capital sentences.

Truth for today.—The denial by Peter may have been the saddest experience of all for Jesus during that night before his death. The question may be asked: Why did Peter do it? He did not intend to. Obviously he didn't want to, for he was stricken immediately with overpowering remorse.

Having had the same kind of experiences, most of us can identify with Peter. Under the pressure of public opinion, because we want to fit in or get ahead, we sometimes say or do things that are unworthy of Christians. Even while we say and do them, we are aware that this does not represent our best self.

There are two aspects to Peter's experience that give us hope. One is the fact that God's grace is great enough to forgive men such unfaithfulness. The other is that people can become better than they now are. Tradition tells us that Peter was martyred for his Lord. Thus, we also can hope to become stronger in our faith.

The Trial and Crucifixion (Luke 23:1–56)

The passage.—In Luke the trial of Jesus is presented in such a way as to emphasize two points. First, the guilt of the Jewish leaders is underlined. They frame the charges of insurrection against Jesus (v. 2—not in parallel passages);

they insist that he be crucified (23:5, 18–24). Second, it is obvious that the responsible governmental officials find Jesus innocent of the charges against him. Three times Pilate affirms that Jesus is not guilty (vv. 4,14,22). Herod Antipas, tetrarch of Galilee, reaches the same conclusion (v. 15. The description of Jesus' appearance before Herod is found only in Luke). The centurion in charge of the crucifixion also declares that Jesus is innocent (v. 47). All this is in keeping with Luke's purpose to show that Christianity from its beginning was no threat to the Roman government.

Special points.—The Sanhedrin had condemned Jesus on the charge of blasphemy, punishable by death under Jewish law (22:70–71). But such a charge would have had no weight with the Roman governor. Consequently the religious leaders accused Jesus of treason on three counts—attempting to stir the Jewish nation to revolt, telling fellow Jews not to pay their taxes, and presenting himself as their king (23:2).

Ironically Barabbas seems to have been guilty of the very crime for which Jesus was accused. He had been involved in an uprising against the government in which men had been killed (v. 19). When the Jewish leaders chose Barabbas the insurrectionist, they showed where their real sympathies lay. This also revealed the hypocrisy of their charges against Jesus.

"Simon" from Cyrene in North Africa was probably in Jerusalem to observe the Passover (v. 26). Condemned men were forced to submit to the additional indignity of carrying the cross bar to which their hands would be affixed. Because of the beatings to which he had been subjected, Jesus lacked the strength to do this.

The women who wept over Jesus needed to save their tears for their own doomed city (vv. 27–31). In their rejection of God's redemption the people had set their course toward the confrontation with Rome that resulted in such terrible suffering and slaughter. The "green tree" (v. 31) represents the spring, the time of budding; the "dry" represents the fall and winter. The crucifixion of Jesus constitutes the planting of a seed that will bear a disastrous harvest. Just three people were crucified by the Romans on that day. In A.D. 70, after Jerusalem fell, we are told that the Romans crucified Jews in such numbers that there was no more room for crosses.

Crucifixion was accomplished by nailing or tying the arms and legs of the victim to the cross. The agony was sometimes prolonged over a period of days. Death resulted from exposure, shock, and eventual suffocation, when the body was so exhausted that breathing in that position was no longer possible. Comparatively speaking the death of Jesus occurred rapidly.

Joseph was a "counsellor" (v. 50), that is, he was a member of the council or Sanhedrin. Luke inserts the comment that he had not agreed with the decision of the council about Jesus (v. 51).

The day on which Jesus was crucified was the "preparation" (v. 54), a term by which Friday was known. The sabbath began at 6 P.M. This meant that the burial of Jesus had to be hurried in order not to violate the sabbath laws.

Truth for today.—God hangs on a cross! The ultimate in identification! This is what it means for the Word to become flesh. There are no safe places, no walls to get behind, no fortresses in which to hide. There are no holy retreats where a man can spend his life free from obscenity and evil. There are no nice clean places where he can escape from dirt and germs. This is, at least in part, what the cross means to those who dare to take seriously Jesus' command to follow him.

The Resurrection (Luke 24:1–53)

The passage.—According to Luke, the resurrection appearances occurred in or near the city of Jerusalem. The ascension apparently is placed at Bethany, just outside the city of Jerusalem. If we had the Gospel only from Luke's pen, we would surmise that he conceived of the ascension as occurring on the day of the resurrection. In Acts, however, we read that the appearances of the risen Lord took place during a 40 day period (1:3).

Special points.—The women had to wait until the sabbath had passed to visit the tomb. Otherwise they would have broken the sabbath traditions forbidding work. The "first day of the week" was already some twelve hours old before they arrived at the tomb at daybreak (v. 1).

The story told by the women about the empty tomb did not convince the despondent disciples that Jesus was alive (vv. 11–12). As the earliest Christians knew, an empty tomb does not prove anything. Nothing less than the appearance of the risen Lord to them could have convinced them of the reality of the resurrection.

The death and resurrection of Jesus are interpreted as the fulfilment of Moses (the Law), the prophets, and the Psalms (vv. 27,44). There are, of course, no Old Testament passages that describe in exact detail the experiences of Jesus. But early Christians could read the Old Testament in the light of God's revelation in Christ and see that he fulfilled such passages as Isaiah 53.

Verse 30 is reminiscent of the Last Supper and of Jesus' fellowship meals with his disciples, no doubt deliberately so. Jesus revealed himself to the two disciples in the breaking of bread. So it was on such occasions afterward in the life of the church. In their fellowship meals they recognized the presence of the Lord.

One chapter of redemptive history was fulfilled in the experiences of Jesus. There remained yet another to be fulfilled in the life of the church (v. 47). The proclamation of the gospel to the Gentiles fulfilled Old Testament passages like Isaiah 52:10 and 40:5.

The "promise of the Father" (v. 49) is evidently a reference to Joel 2:28–32 (see Acts 2:14 ff.). The presence and power of the Spirit of the risen Lord would equip the disciples for their mission to the nations.

Truth for today.—The witness of the early church was not based on the empty tomb but on the encounter of the disciples with the risen Lord (see 1 Cor. 15:3–8). This is always the basis of a genuine resurrection faith.

The witness of the apostles comes to us in the witness of Scripture. But we never really believe in Jesus solely because of arguments based on their experience. We are assured that he is risen only when we encounter him in our own lives on some personal Emmaus road. When this happens, we too are filled with great joy (v. 52) and are transformed into victorious proclaimers of the gospel.

JOHN

J. P. Allen

INTRODUCTION

An eyewitness account has a different ring to it. The one who sees it happen paints it in livelier colors. He recounts details others miss. You can almost feel he was there.

John's narrative is like that. He saw more than any other writer. He stood by the river and heard the signal of his teacher, John the Baptist, "Behold the lamb of God." From that first moment young John followed Jesus. Through the three and one-half years John was nearest. He alone of the disciples was witness to the crucifixion. He went all the way into the tomb after his Lord arose.

So it is no wonder John's key word is "witness." The term appears twenty seven times in the Fourth Gospel, but is not so used in Luke, for instance, at all. And there is a single purpose to witnessing—to compel belief. That is always John's theme. He tells precisely why he wrote, "But these are written, that ye might believe that Jesus is the Christ, the Son of God" (20:31).

John was especially impressed with the wondrous deeds he witnessed. He not only saw the miracles, he also perceived why his master did them. So John calls them "signs," and this becomes a central word in the Fourth Gospel. A sign is a mighty work, but its deeper design is to manifest the true nature of the Christ who worked it. So, it is a miracle—with special meaning.

Writing later than the other Gospel writers, John selects certain miracles and builds his book about them. Note again his reason for writing, "And many other signs truly did Jesus . . . which are not written in this book: But these are written. . . ." (20:30–31).

John has a good sense of drama. He sees the redemptive purpose of God unfold as if on a stage. Following his brief prologue, Act 1 continues through chapter 12. A series of characters appear at stage center, each one touched by Jesus' words or deeds. These bear witness that God has come to man, and whoever believes has the right to sonship to God.

At chapter 13 a change occurs. The action becomes more private. The curtain closes on an intimate group which sits with Jesus at his supper, and then witnesses his agony and death and resurrection.

This, then, is what happened to John. He believed, he followed, he changed. He entered into personal experience with the Word, now become flesh. He became a friend to him who was before the creation. It is the way it should happen to us all.

God Comes to Man (John 1:1–51)

The passage.—Matthew and Luke had already told of the birth events. John starts from further back. He wrote toward the end of the first century when some were skeptical that Jesus was God. Others doubted that he was truly man. John affirms both. He identifies Jesus as the eternal Son, the Word, agent of creation. He leaves no room for doubt.

Such is the nature of the famous prologue, verses 1–18, done in classic style. But his purpose was not speculation or debate. He established a base for the climax of verse 14, "And the Word became flesh and dwelt among us" (RSV).

The rest of the chapter is a firsthand account of how Jesus the man related to other men. It is the way God wishes to act with his sons.

Special points.—The first actor on the stage is John the Baptizer—always referred to as merely "John." It is noteworthy that the author of this Gospel, John the disciple, never refers to himself by name. He calls himself, "the disciple whom Jesus loved" (21:20), and "the other disciple" (20:4), and one of the "sons of Zebedee" (21:2). It is a good evidence of his authorship.

One can be sure of the preparation young John received from the Baptizer. John was *his* disciple, and an apt one, before he was Jesus'. The forerunner surely taught his small group all he knew about the promised Messiah. On a wonderful day John the Baptist baptized that Messiah. And then there was silence. We know that Jesus was six weeks in the wilderness of temptation, but they did not know that. They had to be perplexed by his absence.

Then one day, verse 29, the forerunner saw Jesus reappear. No doubt he eagerly told John, and Andrew of Bethsaida (v. 40), that he was back. It was time to change masters, John the Baptist must have said; follow him not me. He gave them a sign so they would recognize Jesus whom they had not seen.

It was the "next day" (v. 35) that John would never forget. Writing years later, he even remembered what time it was when he first heard Jesus' voice inviting him to "come and see" (v. 39).

Now the circle begins to expand. One finds another. Note that there was

available a number of spiritually-minded men. Often the Jews of Jesus' day are branded as shallow and traditional beyond hope. Their rulers tended to be, but the Mosaic law did produce some good soil for the gospel sowing. Jesus chose learners who were responsive and offered promise.

Truth for today.—There is an excellent contrast in the two sections of this chapter. It begins in the misty reaches of eternity. The glory and majesty of an eternally existing God give the reader a sense of insignificance. How remote is the God whom no man has ever seen (v. 18)!

Suddenly God acts to close the gulf between. He comes to men. And when he does, he likes them, talks to them, associates with them. He is now within reach. That is the basic note of the "good news" in Christ.

Regard also the invitation of Jesus. His first call was not to full belief in himself. It was to the adventure of following him: "Come and see." Those who kept company with him usually arrived at a vital personal faith. It is never faith in a doctrine, but in a person. Jesus' basic call is still the same, "Follow me."

The Beginning of Signs (John 2:1–25)

The passage.—John now proceeds to show how signs produce faith in some, rejection by others. The key in this chapter is the repetition of the idea concerning belief (vv. 11,22,23).

Two signs are described and others only stated. One of the miracles took place before the eyes of the disciples. The second was verbal, and its meaning was not clear to them until after the resurrection—the greatest miracle.

Special points.—You need to see it as John saw it. He had followed a new master, but he knew very little about

him. There were already five disciples:
John, Andrew, Peter, Phillip, Nathanael
(possibly James). Jesus understood their
need to have reasons for believing. An
opportunity came quite naturally at the
wedding festival to which they had been
invited.

Cana was near enough to Nazareth
for Mary to be there, and in some authority. When the wine failed she undertook to relieve the embarrassment. Jesus
and his friends were outside the banquet
hall, since they were near the water jars.
These had contained water used in the
Jewish rites of purification (v. 6). As
such they were strictly not permitted
near food or drink.

Mary probably meant for Jesus to
send for more wine. His response to her
was not disrespectful. It likely was his
way of reminding her that the new
status between them was never again to
be a simple mother-son relationship. He
was committed to another role, another
kingdom.

In a moment Jesus decided what he
would do. The six stone jars there suggested the sign to him. The number is
important—six. It was the worst number
to the Jews, falling just short of the perfect seven. And the water pots were identified with ceremonial law. So then,
what if he filled each container with
water to the brim? Would not this signify fulfilment, completion? And, what
if the water next drawn from the well
should suddenly become wine? Could
that not suggest that spirit (the lively
wine) was superior to formal law the
water)? Would not the entire episode declare to those who saw that he, himself,
had the right to bring the old ways to
fulfilment and originate the new?

This is what Jesus did, and a splendid
reason for doing it. He had no interest
in merely making wine. He was revealing himself. His mission was not to make
the wedding feast merry. It was to lead

men to believe in him as creator and
Lord of his new kingdom.

Did he accomplish his end? Verse 11
makes it plain, "And his disciples believed on him."

The word "sign " appears again in
verse 18. The Jewish leaders had rallied from their shock after Jesus drove
the animals from the Temple area.
They demanded some token of his authority. He really gave them a sign, it
was just that they did not recognize it.

You cannot but wonder if Jesus casually laid his hand on his own breast
when he said, "Destroy this temple, and
in three days I will raise it up" (v. 19).
Whether he did or not, it was his meaning. That supreme act of his divine nature, his resurrection was full proof of
his authority over God's Temple. He was
God; but they were then incapable of
accepting it. But at the right time, "his
disciples remembered" (v. 22), and that
was the important thing. When they
remembered, they believed.

Truth for today.—We who follow
Christ need the same prod to faith that
John did. In the prologue he declared,
"All things were made by him" (1:3).
Our discipleship is not of a mild-man-
nered teacher who pleads for loyalty.
We follow One whose power made the
worlds. He speaks and everything in na-
ture recognizes his authority. He has the
rights of Creator.

And we are his new creation. Freed
from legalisms and mere regulations, we
are sons of a spiritual realm. It is high
above every form of ritual religion. As
the water looked at its creator and
blushed into wine, so we are free from
dead works, and alive to his vital presence.

A New Kind of Birth (John 3:1–36)

The passage.—The last word in the
preceding chapter leads to the first sentence of this famous section of John—

"man." Jesus knew the nature of men. They were easily impressed by miraculous works, but likely to miss the deeper issues of faith. So, he did not lightly trust himself and the secrets of his kingdom to them, "for he knew what was in man" (2:25).

But, "There was a man" (v. 1)—and with this man Jesus did open the mysteries of the new birth. John now uses the interview with Nicodemus to show how a new kind of kingdom demands a new kind of birth.

Special points.—Since Nicodemus was a Pharisee the story assumes more importance. He sat on the highest court of the Jews, but he recognized God at work when he observed Jesus' signs. He was spiritually sensitive even though his training was largely legalistic.

Word had come to the Sanhedrin concerning certain miracles Jesus performed. Most called it trickery. Nicodemus felt these were impossible for any man "except God be with him" (v. 2). So, the signs accomplish their purpose. Nicodemus was moved to seek out the new teacher.

That he came "by night" has caused some to suggest cowardice. It is more likely that it was wise caution, since he was only in the seeking stage. He was not ready to openly accept the teachings of Jesus. That he did so gradually, and without fear, is indicated by further references in 7:50 and 19:39.

Jesus answered Nicodemus' unspoken question. He knew what the young lawyer wanted to know. In essence Jesus responded something like this. "Now listen to me (the "verily, verily" in verse 2 is John's usual expression of force). You sense that I am from God, and you are right. And I have not come to teach or renew the old Mosaic system. Instead, I will make possible a radical new relationship with the Father that does not depend on race or natural birth. It

will be such a realm as not to be recognized from outside. You will have to enter it by a personal experience so drastic that it can only be called being born again. Only then can you see it."

No wonder Nicodemus was puzzled. His deepest conviction was that men were in God's kingdom when they were from Abraham. The new idea startled him. He could only murmur, "How can these things be?" (v. 9).

Jesus tried to aid his faith by illustration (v. 6). Flesh and spirit are in obvious contrast. And the spirit is the higher order. Nicodemus knew that there were spiritual factors which could not be experienced by the fleshly body. So, then, there were also other realms that required spiritual perception, Jesus told him. So he would have to come alive to heavenly realities through faith (v. 12). It was what God had always wanted, as he could understand if he remembered the salvation of Israel in the wilderness (v. 14).

Most of all, the new relationship with God would be through a new sacrifice (v. 16–18). One wonders if Nicodemus did not see this clearly in the years following the death and resurrection of Jesus.

Truth for today.—It is plain that God desires a relationship, not mere obedience to commandments. Like a father, he wants a loving trust, not fear. When any person exercises that faith in Christ, the resulting life can only be described as having come from "being born all over again."

Perhaps the concluding part of this chapter should suggest a related truth. After birth, comes growth and maturity. That is as much a part of God's plan as is the first step of spiritual rebirth. John the Baptist reflected that maturity when he was able to conquer the jealousy others suggested to him in Jesus' popularity (v. 26). It takes a man, not an infant, to say, "He must increase, but I must decrease" (v. 30).

The Second Sign (John 4:1–54)

The passage.—This section contains two episodes both of which lead to belief. It is as though John illustrates the widening scope of believers. They come from all walks of life and all areas of the country.

Nicodemus was from Jerusalem. What a contrast when John next introduces us to a woman from Samaria. There follows then a nobleman from Galilee, attached to the service of the king. Like the ripples on a pond, the good news radiates outward from center. There is no shore where it does not touch.

Special points.—Many details of the humanity and character of Jesus are seen if the imagination is used. He sat on the well curb while his disciples went into town to buy food. Thus some of their travel habits are revealed.

He was tired, although young and strong from carpenter's labors. He had no rope to draw with (v. 11). There might very well have been a bucket made of animal skin there. But long ropes were valuable things not easily made. He looked up and saw the woman approaching, her drawing rope coiled about her waist. Almost certainly he remained quiet while she lowered the vessel, the splashing water increasing his thirst. As she poured the water into her carrying jar for the return trip, he spoke, "Give me a drink" (v. 7, RSV).

The conversation which followed begins on a clever, breezy note because the woman chose that direction. Either his clothes or his speech indicated he was a Jew. She could not resist making an issue of it, and that she was a woman (v. 9). Her voice had a sharp edge of sarcasm. No matter how often Jesus tried to direct the subject upward from cold water

to the water of life, she cleverly changed directions (vv. 11,15).

She was about to leave when Jesus touched the exposed nerve of her moral life. She still tried to divert him (vv. 19,25), but Jesus pressed his advantage. She was sensitive enough to her sin to respond to his apparent authority.

The woman returned to her village in such haste that she forgot the jar (v. 28). The record of her witness and the belief by so many is in harmony with John's purpose in writing. The proof of Jesus' word about the ripe harvest (v. 35) is seen in his happy visit to the Samaritan city (vv. 40–42).

Jesus went on to Galilee, into Cana, site of the first recorded sign. At the close of a day filled with teaching, he looked into the face of a heartbroken father. A man of authority in government, yet he had walked the 20 miles from Capernaum because his little son was gravely ill. His grief appealed to Jesus and moved him to speak life and health into the boy across that distance.

The joy of recognition that it was Jesus' word that had saved his son is felt in the climax in verse 53. Again the idea of belief is basic.

John adds a comment in verse 54 that confirms the nature of the miracle. It was a sign. It demonstrated the human compassion of Jesus, and yet declared more. It affirmed that he was not only Lord of created things (water, wine), he was also in authority over life. It revealed the character of the Messiah who created life, and who has the power to recreate it.

So John conforms to his central theme. Life is from God, and it comes through faith. He opened the book with that idea in the prologue (vv. 4,12) and he never leaves it.

Truth for today.—Another note is sounded by each of the two narratives in chapter 4. It is the importance of invitation. The Samaritans "asked him to stay with them; and he stayed there two days" (v. 40, RSV). The father "begged him to come down" (v. 47, RSV) to where his son was. In each case Jesus was able to do his work because he was accepted.

In contrast, remember how on another occasion men begged Jesus to leave their territory (Mark 5:17). He did. But after all, this was the condition stated in John 1:12. God's gifts are always "to all who received him" (RSV). They still are.

Jesus Declares Himself (John 5:1–47)

The passage.—John's reference to another "feast of the Jews" (v. 1) calls attention to a major contribution by this Gospel. Without his help we likely could not figure the length of Christ's ministry. He makes four references to feasts, and they all are probably passovers. He states that three of them are (2:13; 6:4; 12:1).

If this one is taken to be a Passover also, then the work of Jesus is seen to be about three and one-half years. It again offers insight into John's purpose. How swiftly he passed events by, wishing to spend most of his narrative on the last week! Three Passovers (two full years) are recorded in six chapters. Only seven episodes are told out of the labors of 24 months. Thus carefully John chooses material to help men believe.

In this section another sign of healing occurs. Out of it, Jesus for the first time makes a public declaration of who he is.

Special points.—Jesus returned to Jerusalem for the Feast of the Passover, as he usually did. The sense of worship was strong in him. But he was also moved by mercy.

Bethesda means "House of Mercy," and Jesus went to a popular place in the city by that name. A multitude of invalids had been drawn there by the legend that there was healing in the bubbling spring waters. It is important to note that verse 4 appears in none of the early manuscripts. It is omitted in all later versions. John does not assert that the waters were stirred by an angel. He only suggests that popular belief.

One man, a cripple, was healed. Jesus did no mass healing, so he left the others as they were. He avoided appearing to be simply a miracle worker. He wanted his true nature to be seen, not merely to produce excitement.

This sign had a different element from the previous ones—it was public. The others included by John had been observed only by small groups. Likewise, it had two immediate effects. It demonstrated Jesus' authority over chronic illness. Chiefly, in it he claimed to be Lord over the sabbath (v. 9).

Sooner or later this issue had to be faced, and now it was. Jesus could never agree with the harsh sabbath rules under which the people lived. But in order to manifest God's real purpose in man and the sabbath, Jesus had to declare who he was. He knew it would cause open conflict. He would have to break with the rulers of the Jews. It would ultimately lead to his death.

So the amazing claim was made, "My Father is working still, and I am working" (v. 17, RSV). And the Jews did not miss the significance of that. He "called God his Father, making himself equal with God" (v. 18, RSV).

Now that the sign had led to Jesus' bold claim, the rest of the chapter deals with John's great themes—"life" and "witness." In verses 21–29 Jesus told plainly how men have life only from the Father. There was testimony to the truth of that. There was the witness of John the Baptist in words (v. 32–35). Higher still was the witness of the Father through the signs of his Son (vv. 36–38, RSV).

Truth for today.—It was a significant question Jesus asked of the lame man by the pool. "Do you want to be healed?" Do not too easily reply, "Well, of course he did." He who had received alms and been carried on the backs of others for 38 years would have to go to work. Was he ready for that?

Whoever receives the gift of eternal life from Christ has to be prepared to accept the burdens of maturity. With growth comes responsibility, self-giving, perplexity, disappointment. It is no easy thing to come into his kingdom. His is not a cheap salvation. It is a costly crusade. John is fond of this idea.

The Bread of Life (John 6:1–71)

The passage.—A whole year has gone by since chapter 5. Jesus spent that time in Galilee where the open-minded people made it easier to teach than in Judea. Now he withdraws to the east side of the lake of Galilee. There is need to be away from the press of great multitudes. There he began a six-months period of special training for his disciples in nearby districts. It is now one year before his death.

But there was to be no escape. Great throngs were attracted to him because "they saw the signs which he did" (v. 2, RSV). The size of the crowd was increased by the journeys to Jerusalem on the way to the Passover (v. 4). His popularity was at its peak.

Special points.—The miracle of feeding the multitude is a deliberate sign which Jesus planned. He surveyed the mass of hungry people and, turning to Philip, brought up the subject of feeding them. It would not ordinarily have been done. Many were Passover pilgrims and had foodstuff in their camps. Others lived nearby.

But Jesus saw opportunity to make a declaration of a vital truth. He, himself, would feed them. He would give them bread and fish, enough to satisfy. Yet, for those who understood, he would be seen as the one who served living bread. He, in and of himself, was sufficient to nourish men's souls. All they had to do was receive him. They would have to take him so personally that it could only be described as eating his flesh (v. 48–56).

The narrative is filled with vivid details. The disciples asked the people to be seated by family groups, in ranks, aisles between the squares. Being springtime the grass was green, as Mark vividly pictures (Mark 6:39). Looking down the hill westward, the brilliant colors of their robes and turbans looked like cultivated garden plots. That is the word Mark used.

Jesus bent down to divide the lad's lunch and two heaps of bread and fish began to grow. The twelve probably had to be aroused from their amazement and sent to serve the multitude. The baskets they used were their travel luggage. And the fragments they gathered up were of the unused pieces, not scraps of discarded food. There was more than they could eat.

The instant reaction of the crowd (vv. 14–15) forced Jesus to withdraw. The popular excitement was calmed for a while, but revived the next day. They followed him across the lake to Capernaum (v. 24).

The lesson Jesus then taught was too hard for them. They had not seen the sign and its truth, they had only eaten their fill (v. 26). In a higher way than their forefathers had received bread from heaven (v. 32), God now had sent the eternal food of the soul. He said it plainly, "I am the bread of life" (v. 35).

The Jews whispered their doubts (v. 41) and then broke into bitter dispute (v. 52). Even some of his followers stumbled (v. 60) and finally turned away (v. 66). It became a crisis for the twelve (v. 67). But Jesus stood firm. He refused the role of popular hero or king. He had not come to make people more comfortable. His work was to give himself, his body, his blood. Only by this gift could men have eternal life (v. 54).

Truth for today.—There is no clearer picture of what man must do to be saved. He is saved by the person of Christ. He must accept him in a personal transaction as vital as eating is to physical life.

One may say of books in a library, "look at all that knowledge." But this is not knowledge. It becomes so only if the books are taken inwardly by personal acceptance. So also groceries become food only when consumed.

This is God's offer of life in his Son. Accept him!

Open Hostility with the Jews (John 7:1–53)

The passage.—Another evidence of John's use of time is seen in verse 1. In a single sentence he covers the events of six months. He refers to the end of Jesus' ministry of special training around Galilee.

It is now October and the Feast of Tabernacles, only six months before the crucifixion. The feast was celebrated for seven days with a holy convocation on the eighth. It was a joyous commemoration of Israel's dwelling in tents in the wilderness.

The Jewish leaders have made Jesus an open issue (vv. 11,12). So the question is, will he go up to Jerusalem and risk the hostility of the rulers?

Special points.—Jesus' brothers enter the picture here in a surprising way. Apparently they have unworthy motives. Their names appear in Matthew 13:55. They were actually his half brothers, all younger than he, and were for years under his care and support. They had been friendly when John wrote 2:13, but certainly they had not accepted his messianic claims. Verse 5 makes that clear. They either wished to involve him in difficulties, or gain from his popularity, or cause a showdown. In any case, they were acting beyond their rights.

It here appears how sensitive Jesus was to timing. He knew what was ahead, but he refused to let others force him to be a victim of circumstances. He would act, not merely react. He was in control; he would give his life, not just have it taken. So he spoke of his time, "My time is not yet come" (v. 6). The word means "season," the fitting and proper season for showing himself to the world (v. 4).

The time was really nearer than the brothers thought. Jesus would, indeed, go up to Jerusalem, but not on their terms. He went and found the city in a turmoil over him.

John portrays three groups in the bitter debates. "The Jews" (v. 11) refers to the hostile ruling class. The depth of their feelings is seen in the literal reading of verse 11, "Where is that fellow?" On the other hand, "the people" (v. 12) denotes the Galilean crowd. They were divided but were asking honest questions. The third attitude is seen in "the people of Jerusalem" (v. 25, RSV). They knew their leaders better than the visitors to the city. They knew that Jesus' charge that they wanted to kill him (vv. 19–20) was true.

Jesus would not remain in hiding. He boldly disputed with his accusers. And on the last great day of the feast he made another startling claim. One of the

features of the worship had been the
daily pouring out of the drink offering.
With that in his mind, Jesus cried out,
"If any man thirst, let him come unto
me, and drink" (v. 37). With courage
he declared that God would no more
honor the ceremonies of the ancient
wells of salvation. Henceforth there was
to be a new source of the Water of life.
It would be in him.

Truth for today.—There is a significant truth in verse 17. It is a supreme
test for knowing what is God's will. "If
any man's will is to do his will, he shall
know . . ." (RSV). In Jesus' usage, that
was to be their way of knowing whether
God had sent him. In ours, the same
principle applies. Whoever wants to
know God's will must *want to do* that
will before he can know it. It doesn't
say, "if any man's will is to *know* his
will." The question is on doing.

God never submits his will to us for
our approval! He shows himself to us if
we desire to act. Our acceptance is to
be in advance. Then one truly wants it.
God always reveals the next step to us
while we are on the way to doing what
we already know to do.

The Light of the World (John 8:1–59)

The passage.—John dwells on the disputes between Jesus and the Jews far
more than any other writer. He does it
because it is testimony about himself
from the mouth of Jesus. In dialogue
many facts about a man emerge. It is
good for Jesus' friends to hear him talk
about himself.

The scene is in the Temple area (v.
20). It is the same or following day
from chapter 7.

Special points.—The section from
7:53—8:11 presents a problem. It was
not a part of John's original text. No
manuscripts before the 12th century
show it. And after it appeared it varied

in location. Sometimes it was found at
the end of John, sometimes after 7:36,
and also after Luke 21. Thus it is
omitted in nearly all 20th-century
versions.

The narrative has every mark of
truthfulness. It is probably an apostolic
tradition. John clearly says that many
deeds of Jesus were not written (20:30;
21:25). Indeed all the stories of Jesus'
life were told orally before they were
ever put in writing. Most scholars accept it because it is so much like Jesus,
in attitude and action. One wonders if
it was put here because it illustrates
verse 15.

The real theme of the chapter appears
in verse 12. Recall how John gives fuller
treatment to each of the main topics of
his prologue. The subject in chapter 6
was "life." Now "light" comes up for
discussion (1:4,5,9).

Light is the means of seeing, and by
seeing we know. In the feast just passed,
candles had burned in the Temple
courts in memory of the pillar of fire
by night. Jesus now claimed to be the
one medium of divine knowledge.

The issue of light is not merely intellectual truth. Whoever has it "will not
work in darkness, but will have the light
of life" (v. 12, RSV). The result of the
light is conduct in life. The emphasis is
on *walk*.

In verse 19 Jesus makes another telling point against those who should be
teaching the Jews. He actually accused
them of not even knowing God. This
was their proudest boast that they knew
all truth about God. What strong judgment this was against those who were
wilfully blind. See the charge repeated
in verse 55 and in 5:37–38; 7:28; 16:3.

There appears more frequently now
the suggestion of Jesus' death. In verse
21 he spoke of going away. In verse 28
the prophetic phrase "lifted up" is the

first hint of crucifixion.

"Many believed" (v. 30), but the word probably implies only a kind of consent, not a true acceptance. This is obvious because immediately he began to test them. The proof of discipleship is simple, "If you continue in my word, you are truly my disciples" (v. 31, RSV).

Truth for today.—The word "continue" is a vital point in being a Christian. Jesus summoned no temporary followers. That is his word, "follow." The direction in the Scriptures is faithfulness "to the end." In the New Testament there is no room for any "inactive" membership in the body of Christ!

A Blind Man Sees (John 9:1–41)

The passage.—This chapter dramatizes Jesus' bold claim, "I am the light of the world" (8:12). Whoever asserts that he is light had better be prepared to prove it. So Jesus uses another sign. He heals a man, no question about that. But the fact of his blindness is important. Darkness fled before the sight Jesus gave him. That is the point not to miss.

The dialogue here has unusual charm. There is subtle humor and irony. See the ruffled dignity of the Jewish rulers in contrast to the majestic calm of the Master. This chapter is excellent for training in oral reading. The voice has to be used to mark the change of characters, the quotes, and the punctuation.

Special points.—The blind man was probably a well-known character. About him the disciples asked Jesus what was an honest question. "Who sinned?" (v. 2, RSV), they inquired. They assumed that sin always brought specific suffering. So they were puzzled about a man who had been born under such a curse.

Jesus denied that rigid rule. The parents were not declared sinless, only that one man's suffering was not punishment for one sin. Neither did Jesus imply that the man was born for the sole purpose of being miraculously restored. His short statement was that the sight of human suffering was a call not for speculation but for service. It was an opportunity for God to manifest his grace.

Jesus did not here explain the mystery of pain. What he did do was associate others with himself in responding to the darkness in which men live. He could give sight, and he would (v. 5).

The clay pack Jesus made from spittle was used probably for several reasons. The act encouraged the man's faith. It was something he could know was being done to him. Also there was then as always a sense of the curative powers of saliva. But chiefly it pointed up the significance of the water that washed away the clay. That water was from Siloam, "Sent" (v. 7).

It was from that same pool that the drink offering had been drawn (see the comment on 7:37). Jesus sent the man to wash. But he himself had been "sent" from the Father. He constantly declared this. So Jesus fulfilled all the blessings that Siloam typified. This even enlarged the "sign." As the waters of Siloam washed away the clay and the blindness, so he who was sent would illumine the darkness of the world.

Note now how the excitement builds. First the neighbors (v. 8) could scarcely believe. They asked the natural question, "How?" (v. 10). Much more serious issues arose when he confronted the Pharisees (v. 13). They summoned the man's parents who were frightened (v. 22). The man was called up the second time (v. 24), but this time he was too bold for them (v. 30). They cast him out of the synagogue (v. 34).

The issue of faith is made very clear when Jesus, with great kindness, sought the man (v. 35). He believed; and Jesus drew the profound contrast between those who accept light when it is sent and those who are wilfully blind (v. 39).

Truth for today.—A meaningful parallel is apparent in the chapter. There is progression in the man's confession of faith. It is a type of ours.

When he first referred to his benefactor he said, "The man called Jesus" (v. 11, RSV). That was all he knew. After he had time to know and consider more facts he stated, "He is a prophet" (v. 17). More than a man; a man from God, he affirmed. Truly the man once blind has begun to see. The climax is when he has his eyes fully opened. He believed and confessed that Jesus was "the Son of God" (v. 35).

The Good Shepherd (John 10:1–42)

The passage.—John never introduces a fresh topic with his double "verily, verily." It is rather a solemn prelude to repetition or emphasis. So in this section Jesus is continuing to reveal his true status, as opposed to the false leadership of the Pharisees.

In chapter 9 these rulers had assumed that they were the spiritual guides for the people. Jesus' point of view was that they were but hirelings, or worse. Their estimate of human values had been seen in their dealings with the man born blind. Jesus had already declared that they did not know God. They failed on both counts—God and man.

So Jesus presents an allegory which shows the clear contrast between true and false teachers. Note that the Pharisees were so spiritually dull that they did not even comprehend the meaning of the story (v. 6).

Special points.—The word picture of the sheep and the fold is not so clear today. It was to the first hearers. The fold was an open yard, surrounded by a low wall. Several flocks were given by their shepherds into the care of the porter (v. 3). In the morning the shepherd called for his own flock and led them out again.

One who climbed over the wall, then, could not be the true shepherd, but a thief. The real shepherd entered by the gate. When he spoke, his familiar voice was recognized and his sheep followed him to pasture.

The distinction is sharp between the benevolent shepherd and the plundering robber. Here are contrasted religious teachers who would serve themselves by means of the flock, and those who would serve the sheep. Without apology Jesus declared that he was "the door" (v. 7) and "the good shepherd" (v. 11). He was both—the way into the fold of safety, and the great provider.

Note the complete salvation the Lord described. "If any one enters by me, he will be saved" (v. 9, RSV). That is narrow, indeed, as the truth is narrow. But that is not all. Those who are his believers "will go in and out and find pasture" (v. 9, RSV). So a normal life, a daily routine is suggested. Under his guidance they follow and are fed. No provision is made for any flock not willing to be led in fellowship with him.

Perhaps the greatest affirmation in the passage appears in verse 10. In a sentence Jesus declared his purpose in coming. What does he want of us? He came for life, a full and abundant life! His self-sacrifice never stands in more vivid outline than here.

But he claimed to have "other sheep" (v. 16). The great love he showed was not alone for his disciples, or even Israel. There may be separate folds but his flocks are all his. The inclusion of men of all races and times is one of John's themes (11:52; 12:32; 17:20). See also Matthew 8:11.

Truth for today.—Our word "pastor"

is the Latin for "shepherd." It is a highly suggestive term. It places every minister who leads a church under the high obligation of loving and nourishing his flock. It summons every member to follow and feed and grow. And finally, the shepherd does not have the lambs; the sheep do. He leads, they reproduce. Together they produce "babes in Christ" and grow them to "men in Christ."

A Dead Man Lives (John 11:1–57)

The passage.—Did he not say that he came so that we might have life? (10:10). The most celebrated statement in this chapter strengthens that claim. "I am the resurrection, and the life," Jesus said (v. 25). Not "this is the way to," but "I am!"

So lofty a theme needs more than language. Did Jesus actually tell his friends that the power of resurrection was within his authority? He did; and his greatest promise required his greatest sign. The death of his close friend became the occasion of this vital lesson in who he was.

Special points.—The story of the Bethany family is one of the warm insights into the life of Jesus. John put it plainly in verse 5. With them, in Bethany two miles east of Jerusalem, he had his home so often. His relationships with people were very real. He had a genius for friendships. He then, as now, had his inner circle of friends. These were not arbitrarily chosen. They were those who responded to him.

But Jesus was away, about one day's journey. He was probably at the other Bethany, beyond Jordan, where he had gone in 10:40. The sisters sent a messenger with the news of Lazarus' illness. The response of Jesus (v. 4) is not that his friend would not die. Indeed, he was probably already dead. John discloses the time schedule. One day each way

for the journey, and a delay of two days (v. 6), account for the four days since death (v. 17).

The action of Jesus in tarrying has sometimes been a puzzle. Note that the sisters did not ask him to come. They would not presume so much, and they knew there was danger for him in Judea. He delayed probably to avoid any issue of trickery, the accusation that the man was not really dead. He knew it was the right time for a dramatic sign. His own death and resurrection was drawing near. So he was concerned for the disciples' sake (v. 15). He simply declared that for Lazarus it would not be a victory for death, but the occasion for the manifestation of the glory of God (v. 4).

He met Martha first, likely having sent for her (v. 20). She in turn called for Mary (v. 28). The narrative shows in vivid detail how Jesus responded to doubt and grief. He involved himself in the suffering of death because he intended to break forever the tyranny of death.

One of the drama-packed moments of the Bible comes as Jesus called loudly to a man in the opened tomb (v. 43). Imagine the shock and amazement when the shrouded figure emerged into the light! What were the immediate reactions of Mary and Martha? What kind of homecoming procession must it have been?

One thing is not questionable—the results. "Many of the Jews . . . believed" (v. 45). The wise among them saw the miracle for what it was—a sign (v. 47). That was Jesus' ultimate goal.

Truth for today.—Generations of Christians have faced death with a new faith since Jesus emptied a tomb. It is no surprise to us that his own stood empty. He not only talked like one who had power of life over death. He acted like it! And that is the sure ground of our faith in him.

The End of Signs (John 12:1–50)

The passage.—This chapter closes what was called, in the Introduction, Act 1 of John's drama of redemption. Until now the author has presented a selection of "signs." Each was chosen by John to offer testimony that Jesus was indeed the Christ. Each produced belief or unbelief in those who saw.

From this point on, however, Jesus discloses himself in private. The signs are concluded. Indeed, the word occurs twice in the chapter, but not again except in summary. The transition is clearly marked by two significant sentences. "He departed and hid himself from them" (v. 36, RSV). It was a symbolic statement. He had been available for light if anyone would see. The verdict is tragic. "Though he had done so many signs before them, yet they did not believe in him" (v. 37, RSV).

Special points.—Three incidents are featured here. All of them reveal the relation to Jesus which has been developed during his ministry. The anointing in Bethany (vv. 1–11) depicts the devotion of those who loved him. The triumphant entry into Jerusalem (vv. 12–19) shows him to be the popular idol of the multitudes. The inquiry of the Greeks (vv. 20–36) suggests the longing for truth by the hungry Gentile world.

As always, each episode results in belief or rejection. The discontent of Judas in the first scene, the anger of the rulers in the second, and the reply of Jesus in the third are typical. They prepare us for the coming tragedy of unbelief.

The banquet was for Jesus—and Lazarus (v. 2). That was fitting. Although Martha served, as usual, the supper was not in their home but in the house of Simon the Leper (Mark 14:3).

One may be certain that he also had been touched by the power of Jesus. The occasion drew a crowd. Both guests of honor were great curiosities (v. 9).

Mary's devotion was an offense to Judas. It tested his own coolness and deceit. Jesus' verdict left no doubt, "Let her alone" (v. 7); it was symbolic to him. See how conscious he was of the end.

John discloses something not found elsewhere. Amid the splendor of the triumphal march, John gives the reason for the crowd (vv. 17,18).

The writer of the Gospel also knows the visit of "certain Greeks" (v. 20) is significant. Not only was there popular excitement among the Jews, the word had spread beyond. These Greeks may have been converts to Judaism, but John wrote late enough to know that many Gentiles turned willingly to the gospel.

It was this barrier of distrust between Jew and Gentile that caused the agony of Jesus in verse 27. He understood that only an event of the magnitude of the death he was about to die would crumble the wall. This was why Jesus responded with such emotion to the simple request of Greeks to see him.

Thus the cross appeared in prospect (v. 32). By his sacrifice "all men," regardless of race or nation, could stand on common ground with him. Nothing else would avail.

Truth for today.—We are the ministers of this reconciliation. If human hatred, cruelty, and injustice could be healed by education or culture it would have been done long since. No, the problem is too deep in the human kind. A power outside ourselves must bring us together. A person, not a force, must change us.

We, through John, have seen the signs of Jesus. He was Lord of creation, provider of food, source of light, restorer of life. Fragmented mankind is hopeless without his personal touch. To this end we have been entrusted with his message, his good news: "And I, if I be lifted up from the earth, will draw all men unto me."

Into the Shadow (John 13:1–38)

The passage.—John's purpose is illuminated by the attention he gives to the death of Christ. He spends almost one half of the book on the last few days. He was there. He experienced all of it, and he alone did. He knew how vital to the gospel was this central fact of Jesus' sacrifice for sin.

Great attention to detail is given to the scenes in the upper room and the hours that follow—five chapters. No other event in the Gospels receives so much treatment. The intimate experiences of the last supper were not shared by the public. The curtain has closed, and only his willing followers receive the purifying and strengthening for the end.

Special points.—Contrary to what one might expect, the supper did not begin in a quiet mood of devotion. To understand the disciples' frame of mind is the only way to know what happened.

Jesus rose to wash their feet because they were angry with one another (v. 4). A bitter debate had arisen among them because of pride (Luke 22:24). Thus no one of them was ready to act in the servant's place. Jesus broke their sullen tension by arising from his couch to perform that humble role.

He announced plainly that he had done it as an example (v. 15). But there was a deeper purpose than to teach humility. Jesus simply had to deal with Judas, and he chose this avenue. Judas was very much in John's mind in this chapter. The writer had deep-scarred memories of the shock of that awful disclosure.

So Jesus included a double meaning. He said that the twelve did not need a complete bath. Only the feet needed cleansing. This was their custom and well known. But, he added, not *all of them* were clean (vv. 10–11). One of them was defiled. Again he brought up the subject, so that when the traitor struck they would know that Jesus knew who it was (vv. 18–19).

The question of who would betray him was much on their minds (v. 22). Out of their curiosity, one of the delightful eyewitness scenes of the book is sketched. John was reclining on Jesus' right side. Judas was likely at his left. Somewhere further to the right Peter was in the line of sight of John's gaze. It was he who caught John's eye and made a lip motion for him to find out who it was (v. 24). John decided that he would, and did.

Reclined on the dining couches as they were, as John leaned backward to whisper to Jesus his left shoulder touched the breast of his Lord. This alone could account for the comment of verse 23. It was the place for a friend and John never forgot that nearness. Years later he drew the picture in vivid detail.

Truth for today.—There was cleansing as a result of the supper. Judas, who did not love him, was removed from the circle. Peter, who did love him, was warned.

And, after the cleansing, what? There was the tenderness of love. Jesus called them, "Little children" (v. 33). He told them of his love (v. 34).

These remain as goals for our discipleship. It is one of the reasons our Lord commanded us to observe the supper. We need to be purified, and warned, and loved.

He Is with Us (John 14:1-31)

The passage.—This is one of the tenderest chapters in the Gospels. The distress over Judas' withdrawal and the rebuke given to Simon Peter had left the room full of tension. Jesus responded to that in the most intimate language. He talked of their heavenly home, of making a place for them. He promised that they will not be left like orphans (v. 18). He spoke of a fellowship more bold than any mere man could have dared (v. 20).

It is helpful to notice that this section concludes the events in the upper room. Verse 31 makes it clear that they departed. That fact will give better perspective to the conversations which followed.

Special points.—Remember how John chose to include in his narrative the things Jesus said and did which carried out his expressed purpose. John wanted to interpret his Lord so as to promote belief in him. So he always liked the statements which summarized who Jesus was. The classic one for brevity and fullness now appears. It is the theme of the book put into a single sentence (v. 6). Jesus was the way for men to come to God. He was the source of truth about God. He was the author of life in God. Indeed, this is all John had been concerned with from the first chapter.

The fact that Christ was the way did not depend on his physical presence. That would be a difficult lesson for the disciples to learn. They must walk with him in that way after they could no longer see him in the flesh. So he promised them "another Counselor" (v. 16, RSV). The word "counselor" means "helper," "advocate." He would come to them (v. 18) and be comforter and teacher. He would be to them as Holy Spirit (vv. 17,26) the same as he had been with them as Jesus of Nazareth. All references to the Holy Spirit in

this chapter are made in terms of "I" and "He," and never "It." He is not a ghost; he is a person. It might have been far better if Christians had formed the habit of omitting "the," and calling him just "Holy Spirit," even as they do "Lord Jesus."

These important words must have fallen on a room heavy with silence. Gone were the crosscurrents of jealousy. The mood of their great Teacher was different from what it ever had been before. They certainly sensed it. They were stirred from that quiet retreat with his word, "Arise, let us go hence" (v. 31).

Truth for today.—If Christ is "the way," then Christianity must be a "way." It is not, therefore, strange that this was the first title by which believers were called (Acts 9:2; 19:23). Christianity *is* a way—not a way of doing certain things, but a certain way of doing everything.

And, our Master does not instruct us from afar. He is with us. A question was once asked: "Why, when Jesus left his disciples, did he not tell them everything that they should do?" The apt answer was, "He did not leave them."

Living with Him (John 15:1-27)

The passage.—Unless one is careful he will suppose all the final discourses of Jesus took place in the upper room. He had already left there (14:31), but had not yet gone out of the city toward the garden (18:1). Obviously the little band had to be somewhere in Jerusalem during this interval.

Here is a possible explanation of what happened. Leaving the scene of chapter 14 late at night they walked toward the brook Kidron. Because it was the Passover the moon was in full cycle. They might well have passed the Temple in the bright light. As they lingered at this sacred place Jesus spoke to them of what they must do while they were separated for a while. Then he prayed (chap. 17).

This suggestion has been made because of Jesus' next words. The beautiful sculptured vine across the face of the Temple might have inspired the line, "I am the true vine, and my Father is the husbandman" (v. 1).

Special points.—There is another explanation for the use of the vine analogy here. The Memorial Supper, using the fruit of the vine, was still on their minds. The vineyard was common in Palestine, and the force of Jesus' picture of himself and his work would not be lost.

The powerful application is that of vital union. The branch bears no fruit of itself. It is the connection with the vine that makes its life possible (v. 4). Indeed, the fruitless branch is intolerable. The vinedresser will cut it away, as Judas has well illustrated (vv. 2,6). There is no place in Christ's vineyard for "inactive branches."

The fruit which issues from abiding in him will appear quickly. Immediately there is joy (v. 11). Love is another evidence (v. 12). A special product of obedience is reported by John, and it is unique to him in this sense. "Friend" is a warm and meaningful word. No one would dare to presume so much if Jesus had not stated it clearly, "You are my friends" (v. 14, RSV). This places his followers in a permanent state of new dignity which men never had before.

That high calling is not of man's doing. His disciples are appointees, men under commission, to go (v. 16), and to identify with him (v. 18), and to be his witnesses (v. 27). So, the fruit-bearing goes on.

Truth for today.—There really are no options as to the demands of discipleship. No one can follow Jesus on his own terms. Jesus himself defined the terms. The word "disciple" means

learner. When we bear that name, we do not declare ourselves to be saints. What we have said is that we go to school to him. We learn from him. We start as babes, we mature, we' grow toward manhood, we err, we stumble. But we are always instructed, always disciplined—if we "abide in him."

The Cost of Discipleship (John 16:1–33)

The passage.—While walking through deserted streets at that late hour Jesus continued his quiet instruction. When he was no longer to be seen in the flesh they would still have his friendship. But they must maintain contact, like a twig to its vine (chap. 15). And, there was a compelling reason.

He told them plainly that there would be hardships (vv. 1–4). They understood that language and became sorrowful (v. 6). So Jesus took them into his further confidence. He explained their benefit from his going away, and promised their ultimate victory. This was his last opportunity to teach them before his death. He would prepare them as best he could for their ordeal ahead.

Special points.—Under the stress of persecution they would need a defense. Obviously Jesus could not be physically present with all his believers at all times. How, then, could they have his counsel and his strength? If he went away, he said, it would be to their advantage (v. 7). This must have startled them. Yet when the Comforter came, he would be to them as a "Lawyer," an advocate for their defense.

A significant point is made in regard to the Holy Spirit. "I will send him unto you," Jesus said (v. 7). But note that though he would come to the believers, "He will convince the world of sin" (v. 8, RSV). The Christians, therefore, are the link between the Spirit's convicting work and the unbelievers. He must work through us with those who do not know him.

For us the Holy Spirit becomes "guide" (v. 13). The first disciples could not possibly understand the scope of the kingdom (v. 12). No era can foresee the nature of the gospel's application to the life of the age to come. Yet this is no barrier. The Master himself is present to interpret and apply. Thus no epoch is dependent on the methods of the past. No problem in the future is too much for Christ to guide his church to the attack.

An insight into the humanity of the eleven disciples is given in verses 17 and 18. "We do not know what he means" (RSV), they murmured to one another. It is a confession often spoken, one to be expected. They had stumbled at his "a little while." They did not realize what a very little time remained. The cross would appear in a few hours.

But their sorrow would in another brief time "turn into joy" (v. 20, RSV). He must also have had in mind even a fuller joy than the resurrection—that of Pentecost.

Truth for today.—The last word of the section is prophetic, "I have overcome the world" (v. 33). Jesus was always sensitive to fulfilment. He spoke in terms of expectancy. The victory is actually in prospect when the deciding force is applied. The issue is not seriously in doubt!

You can say that polio is conquered —since Dr. Salk. That is true, even though the vaccine needs to be applied. There are battles yet to be won; but Jesus already has accomplished the victory.

The Lord's Prayer (John 17:1–26)

The passage.—If any words of Jesus deserve to be called "his prayer," these would merit that title. "He lifted up his eyes to heaven" (v. 1). This is his prayer

for his people, his church—then and now.

It is noteworthy that on this last night, in three places, Jesus was in prayer: at the supper, here, and in Gethsemane. In the quiet and deserted street of the old city, by the light of the moon, Jesus and his disciples stood still and hushed. He addressed God as his Father. The burden of the prayer was that God should be glorified. To do that, the Son must be glorified (v. 1).

Special points.—"Glorify" is an important word. To us it means to make great. To Jesus it meant to reveal the true character of someone. In the New Testament the word always involved the manifesting the purpose of something in keeping with its nature. A peach, then, is the glory of a peach tree. The ultimate purpose of the seed and the bloom is to produce the fruit. There is no other way for a peach tree to be "glorified" except to produce peaches. Jesus came to fulfil God's design.

In the entire prayer, this was Christ's only personal petition. It related only to the purpose of the Father to redeem men by the cross. Jesus wanted his own "glory" to be in that purpose (v. 3). And as the time of death approached, the whole redemptive plan of God drew close to realization. All sacrifice was now to find its true meaning.

Jesus had a keen awareness of his mission (v. 4). He declared that he had "finished" his work. It is the same word he would utter on the cross. It reflected in him utter satisfaction. There was no failure or incompletion of his assigned mission. Jesus called it his "work."

In apparent anticipation of the events of the morrow, Jesus remembered his nearness to God in the beginning (v. 5). One's mind is immediately taken back to the first verse of John. How clearly the author saw the divinity of Jesus. So, it is obvious that the cross was not the end. It was a climax. For one who is God there would be a return to that status after his release from the imprisoning flesh.

One of Jesus' petitions was for the oneness of his disciples (v. 11). In the sentence he referred to God as "Holy Father." It is the only instance in the New Testament of this excellent address to God in prayer. The high ideal of "that they may be one" is modified by a condition: "as we are." The basis for unity of believers is obviously to be found in like natures with one another. This was the case in the identical natures of Jesus and God. A basic harmony is required. And the kinship must be with the Father, not of human agreement.

Truth for today.—The close of the prayer from verse 15 sets forth Christ's high expectancy of us. He asked that we not be taken out of the world. There is no escape for us from the perpetual task of changing sons of evil to sons of God. This clear statement is always a warning to Christians.

We are to be *in* and *with* the world, always touching it, always changing it. But we are not to be of its nature. Our spirit must prevail; not the world's. This is the call to apartness, not to aloofness. No glory comes to Christ by reason of our isolation. Jesus prayed for us to be *in* the world. It is our job to stay there!

The Arrest and Trial (John 18:1–40)

The passage.—John records more details of the crucial events of the trial and crucifixion than the other writers. He saw it all, and somehow seems to have it more vividly in his mind. His special closeness to Jesus would account for that. Young John suffered deeply through these trying hours.

This chapter portrays three scenes.

The action moves quickly from the garden to the Jewish court to the Roman tribunal. John watched as Judas gave the traitor's kiss. He witnessed Simon Peter's sword-play. He was jostled by the arresting mob as he accompanied Jesus to the house of the high priest. He heard Peter's profane denial and Annas' empty chatter. It must have been with apprehension that he saw his Master disappear into the residence of the Roman governor. How rapidly events were moving! What a long night for John!

Special points.—The garden had been quiet; too quiet for the weary, sleepy disciples. But the noisy approach of the soldier band interrupted the stillness of Gethsemane. John adds a note of interest. It was a place Jesus had often brought the disciples for prayer (v. 2). How little we know of the details of their life with the Lord. It is a sad commentary that it was his habit of prayer that gave Judas a chance to deliver him up.

The effect of Jesus on those who sought him offers a puzzle. Undoubtedly they expected the "fugitive" to hide or run. When he stepped forward boldly and declared, "I am he" (v. 6), it could have accounted for their falling to the ground. But John seems to be saying more. There must have been a quality of majesty or strength which took them back. After all, it is important that he give himself—not that his life be taken from him. Thus he had even the soldiers at a disadvantage had he wished to escape.

There can be little doubt as to why John tells that it was the "right" ear Peter cut off with his sword (v. 10). It depicts a hefty swing with the blade at a man's head. His swift movement to the left exposed the right ear to the sharp edge. No wonder Jesus rebuked Peter so sharply.

As Simon stood in the chilly, open courtyard by the fire (v. 18), you cannot but wonder where John was. He was present (v. 16), and likely had taken his place much nearer Jesus. He must have witnessed the drama of Peter's denial with great distress.

Dawn was approaching, and since they could not put Jesus to death (v. 31), his accusers dragged him off to face Pontius Pilate.

Truth for today.—We have still not learned to handle swords. They represent the use of force to assert right or correct wrongs. But violence breeds violence and enmity is deepened. Jesus shows how to handle evil. All the way back to the city, they laid aside or sheathed their weapons. Why not; they were not needed! His aggressive love disarmed angry men. It is a force even one's enemies cannot handle.

Condemnation and the Cross (John 19:1–42)

The passage.—The other gospel narratives had already told the story of the Lord's death. John goes more fully into the trial before Pilate since only the Roman tribunal could impose the death sentence.

John also provides some of the events of the cross which we would not otherwise know. He tells, for instance, that Jesus bore the cross on himself at the beginning (v. 17), before Simon of Cyrene. He gives a full account of the casting lots for Jesus' coat (vv. 23–24). He recites how the title above the cross was written (vv. 20–22). He mentions the conversation about Mary and himself (vv. 25–47). He tells of the cry, "It is finished" (v. 30), and of the spear thrust (v. 34). Obviously, John was there.

Special points.—The encounter of Pilate and Jesus produces some moving scenes. A man who wanted to do right, but didn't have character enough to decide right, always arouses interest—and pity.

Clearly this was the way the governor was at first (18:28–38). The Jews asked him for the death penalty with no further trial. He promptly refused that. Next they accused Jesus of a political crime. Jesus did him the courtesy of telling Pilate what kind of king he really was. The only possible conclusion was, "I find in him no fault at all" (18:38).

The brutal scourging (v. 1) prior to a verdict was unlike what might be expected of Pilate at this stage. It is probably best to assume that he did it to ease the rage of the rulers and perhaps arouse the pity of the people. There was still no guilt to be seen in Jesus (v. 4).

The accusations were not over. A religious charge was next to be made (v. 7). It led to one of the many trips the bewildered Roman made from outside where the Jews gathered to inside where Jesus waited in solemn dignity (see 18:29,33,38; 19:5,9,12,13).

Pilate wavered, but could not be moved until the accusers hit him at his weakest point. He turned coward when they threatened to report him to Caesar (v. 12). It was a real threat. At least three times Pilate had been roughly handled by the monarch in Rome because he lacked skill in dealing with the Jews. His insensitivity to their holy places, taxation, and cruelty had caused the leaders to appeal to Caesar. Pilate was afraid of yet another charge. Thus the fatal sentence, "Then he handed him over to them to be crucified" (v. 16, RSV).

The inscription over Jesus' head as he hung on the cross (v. 20) seemed to John to be prophetic. Hebrew was the language of the people, Latin of govern-

21. **Gordon's Calvary, regarded by some as the site of the crucifixion (see John 19:17)**

ment, and Greek the common tongue of the world. How the Jews must have winced under the irony of the title (v. 21–22). It was Pilate's last hope of revenge on them, and he would not change it.

When John added verse 35 to the account, it indicates the depth of his feeling when he knew his friend and Lord had died. He saw the gaping wound and flow of blood. There was no remote question in his mind—Jesus was dead! It was, up to then, the high watermark of his testimony.

Truth for today.—It is not enough to stand sorrowfully at the foot of the cross. To wag the head or cluck the tongue does not adequately respond to what happened. It was not a tragedy.

It was a deliberate act of sacrifice. You regret a tragedy. A sacrifice must be accepted.

From the first, John said Jesus was the "Lamb of God." When the Lamb was offered up as a sacrifice for sin, it was our sin. The only way to have the pardon is to accept the sacrifice as one's own.

Raised from the Dead (John 20:1–31)

The passage.—John tells the story of the resurrection as he had recorded so many earlier events. He returned to the "staging" method. Three sets of characters are shown on the stage. They came face to face with evidences that Jesus lived. You could guess that the result was *belief.*

685

Peter and John were the first pair, running to the tomb which was reported to be empty. Mary Magdalene next spoke with one whom she took to be the keeper of the garden. Thomas was the central character in the third scene. It had two parts, one with Thomas absent, the other present. The time was Sunday through the following Sunday.

Special points.—It appears as though Peter and John had spent the night together. They were awakened by the anxious cries of Mary Magdalene who had been very early at the tomb. Her news excited the two men to great haste, as they both ran toward the garden (v. 4).

Note some genuine conclusions which may be drawn. John, indeed, does not mention his own name, as he never does (vv. 2,3,4,8). The very number of indirect references to himself stresses the point. Also, the speed with which John outran Peter strongly suggests his youthfulness in contrast to Simon's age. Moreover, each acted in character when he arrived breathlessly at the tomb. John hesitated; Peter rushed in.

One of the most profound truths in the Gospel is disclosed in John's testimony. He stooped to peer into the darkened vault, but saw only vaguely. When Peter dashed into the tomb, John followed. Immediately he saw the graveclothes, lying undisturbed. Even the face napkin was folded, as if everything had been done in an orderly fashion (vv. 6,7). Instantly he knew the truth. No one had stolen the body. If so, the cloths which wound the body would have been gone.

Only one conclusion could be drawn. Jesus, by the power of his divine nature, could not be held by death. In majestic calm, he had simply left the shroud—bodily had flowed out of its folds, and walked out of the grave! "And he saw, and believed" (v. 8). It was the condition of the clothing that he observed. It told him all he needed to know. John was the first to believe Jesus had risen without seeing him.

Mary Magdalene, having notified the men, returned to the garden tomb. It was her name, spoken as only Jesus had done, that told her it was he. Her impulsive move toward him brought a strange response. The language makes it clear that what he said was "Do not hold me" (v. 17, RSV) rather than not to "touch" him. Mary must learn that the conditions had changed. The old forms of friendship and discipleship could no longer prevail. They would not have his physical nearness. So, she might as well know from the first how to relate to his presence in spirit, not flesh.

That Jesus responded to Thomas' doubt was like him (v. 27). John probably witnessed the lesson Thomas had to learn with a smile. It had not taken nearly so much proof for *him* to believe.

Truth for today.—It is reassuring to observe what Jesus did when he rose from the dead. He showed himself, not to those who had killed him, but to those who loved him. We might have done it differently. How it would have confounded Caiaphas and Pilate and the rest if he had stood before them!

But he sought the fellowship of his own. They needed to be certain that he lived. For to them, and to us, he gave his commission (v. 21). In the same manner as the Father sent the Son—to reveal God's salvation—so he sends us, also his sons. If we live with him, we will tell.

The Final Scene (John 21:1–25)

The passage.—Jesus associated with his disciples for some six weeks after his resurrection. He gave them time to become accustomed to the fact that he lived. There were ten appearances; coming to them only now and then. They must not learn to depend on his presence as before.

This chapter records an event by the lake, and appears only in John. Seven disciples are shown to be together. They were back in Galilee. It was their home, and besides, Jesus had said he would meet them there (Matt. 28:10,16). This is not that appointed time, they were waiting for that. Meanwhile they decided to go fishing.

Special points.—The picture of Jesus calling out, fisherman style from a hundred yards off, "Have you any fish?" (v. 6, RSV) is a realistic one. Their answer is age old. The miracle resulting from his instruction was so much like Jesus that John instantly recognized him. Again it was Peter who acted abruptly (v. 7).

The breakfast on the Galilean beach is the warm, intimate scene with which John brings the Fourth Gospel to a close. Eating appears to be a major activity during the vital period before ascension (Luke 24:30,41–43). It is almost as though Jesus is establishing a pattern for the future. He will be with his own in the normal places and activities of their lives. This idea is reinforced by Revelation 3:20.

There was a strained silence during the meal (v. 12), and naturally so. No one must have been quieter than Simon Peter. The memory of his swearing he didn't know Jesus was still vivid. What could he say in the presence of others?

It was a merciful relief when they finished and Jesus invited Peter to walk with him. John makes it clear that the dialogue did not take place around the breakfast fire (v. 20). Difficult as it was being alone with his Master, there was now the opportunity to remove the barrier of that awful denial. Jesus did not chide him. He only asked him if he loved him.

Two things must be noted. Jesus modified his question by the addition of "more than these" (v. 15). He probably motioned toward the other disciples when he spoke. After all, Peter had claimed that although the others might deny Jesus, he would not. The other thing is the play on words they used. This often happens when two people are healing a misunderstanding.

Two words for love were used, one stronger than the other. When Jesus asked if Peter loved him, he used the strong word. In his reply, Peter was afraid to use that so he responded with the weaker word. Both of them heard the difference. The second question and answer retained the identical terms they had first used. But on the third time, Jesus came back at Peter with his own weaker word for love. That is why Peter was "grieved" (v. 17) by the third question. It was not repetition that bothered Simon. It was as though Jesus had said: "Well, by your own definition, do you love me?" He could only answer the truth; yes, he did.

Truth for today.—One result of John should be your own intimate encounter with Jesus. In a private place, with issues known only to you, comes his question, "Do you love me?"

The answer is known only to you. If you do, he will cleanse you and he will assign you a task.

ACTS

Wayne Dehoney

INTRODUCTION

Acts narrates the expansion of the gospel throughout the heart of the Roman Empire. The events begin with the ascension of Jesus Christ and Pentecost (A.D. 29) and extend through Paul's imprisonment in Rome (A.D. 61).

Acts links the earthly ministry of Jesus Christ with the coming of the Holy Spirit in whose power the amazing events of Acts took place. The book shows how the gospel broke through religious, racial, and national barriers. In the early chapters Christianity is merely a sect of Judaism. Later the gospel spreads from Jewish converts, to Samaritans (half Jews), to proselytes (Gentiles who had become Jews), to God-fearing Greeks, and finally to pagans.

The tragedy and conflict throughout the book of Acts is the resistance of the Jews to the universality of the gospel. By the end of Acts, many Jewish Christians (Judaizers) have repudiated this universalism, the unbelieving Jews have repudiated Christianity, and both unite with Roman authorities to persecute Paul. But Acts ends in triumph. The unhindered gospel is finally preached to all people!

The book of Acts is an invaluable source to present-day Christians as it portrays the early church at work in faith, in fellowship, in evangelism, in stewardship, in living and dying for the Lord.

Acts was written about A.D. 62. The author is Luke, "the beloved physician" (Col. 4:14), who also wrote the Gospel

of Luke. He was Paul's companion in the latter part of his ministry.

The Promise of the Spirit (Acts 1:1–26)

The passage.—Luke connects Acts with his Gospel as a continuing account of what happened after the resurrection. Jesus promises to send the Holy Spirit to the waiting praying disciples. The baptism of the Holy Spirit will empower them to be witnesses to the ends of the earth. After witnessing the Lord's ascension they return to Jerusalem to wait for the Spirit.

While waiting for the gift of the Spirit, the early church (numbering about 120) engages in a "business" session. Peter describes the gruesome death of the traitor Judas and asks the group to fill the vacant apostleship. Two meet the qualifications and Matthias is chosen.

Special points.—Theophilus (literally "friend of God," v. 1). Luke addressed both his Gospel and Acts to this patron. Many believe he was a Gentile Roman official, converted to Christianity.

"Restore again the kingdom to Israel?" (v. 6). The crux of the conflict in early Christianity. At first the disciples saw Christianity as merely an extension of Judaism. Jesus answers (a) God's dates are not your business, (b) I will not bring in the kingdom—but you will establish this kingdom by your witness, (c) the Holy Spirit will empower you to carry this witness to the ends of the earth.

The brothers of Jesus (v. 14) named

in Mark 6:3 (James, Joses, Juda, and Simon) were half-brothers, the physical children born of Joseph and Mary. There is no scriptural basis for the doctrine of the perpetual virginity of Mary which attributes these half-brothers to Joseph by a previous marriage.

The death of Judas (v. 18). Matthew says Judas "hanged" himself. Apparently, he was later cut loose or fell and "burst open in the middle" (RSV).

Truth for today.—Mission frontiers are not always geographical. Frequently they are moral, spiritual, and social and lie at the doorstep of the church. Sometimes it seems easier to send missionaries to Africa than to reach across racial lines at home. In the early church, even the disciples felt the kingdom of God was to be the exclusive possession of a limited few.

The Coming of the Spirit (Acts 2:1–41)

The passage.—The disciples are together on the day of Pentecost when a rushing mighty wind fills the room. Firelike tongues appear and the disciples receive the ability to speak in other tongues. Gripped by the power of the Spirit, they go forth to witness to the pilgrims from many nations gathered in the city. Peter's sermon declares the fulfilment of Joel's prophecy that God would pour out his Spirit on all flesh. He declares that "Jesus of Nazareth, who was crucified, and whom God raised up, is the Chirst of God." Peter charges the convicted multitude to (a) repent, (b) accept Jesus Christ as Savior and Lord, (c) be baptized, and (d) receive the gift of the Spirit. Three thousand are converted and baptized.

The Christian community draws together in a common fellowship, teaching, praying, worshiping in the Temple and in homes, and sharing material resources.

Special points.—"Wind" (v. 2), "tongues of fire" (v. 3), "speak in other tongues" (v. 4)—authenticating the passing phenomenon of the Spirit. The disciples spoke in other or "foreign" tongues and were understood by the hearer each in his own language.

"Repent, and be baptized . . . for the remission of sins" (v. 38). Actually "repent, and let each of you be baptized in the name of Jesus Christ because of the forgiveness of your sins." The preposition "for" is "causal." For example, a man is executed "for murder"—that is, not "in order" to commit murder but "because" he has. Forgiveness follows repentance, not baptism (cf. Acts 3:19).

"Such as should be saved" (v. 47) does not imply certain persons were predestined to be saved. A better translation "and the Lord added . . . *those who were being saved*" (RSV).

Truth for today.—A belief in the presence of the Spirit is more than mere doctrine. To be vital, it must be an experience.

Teaching doctrine was an important activity of this new fellowship. Some argue it makes no difference "what" is believed, as long as a person believes "something"! But the world's most disastrous war was fought, not because some vicious people believed nothing, but because they strongly believed something so hideous that the rest of the world spent life and wealth to halt its spread!

Peter's Second Sermon (Acts 3:1–26)

The passage.—Peter, accompanied by John on the way to the Temple to pray, heals a lame man at the gate. The man follows them into the Temple area, leaping, praising God, and creating wonder and amazement among the multitude of worshipers.

Peter seizes the opportunity to preach

the gospel. He attributes the miracle to God, glorifying Jesus, a living power in their midst. But, they, the Jews are guilty of killing Jesus whom God sent. They have rejected the one promised in prophecy. The fact of the resurrection now calls for a new evaluation of Jesus. Then Peter gives an urgent invitation to "repent" and "turn" and receive "forgiveness." Peter's preaching results in many converts bringing the total number of believers in Jerusalem to 5,000 men (4:4).

Special points.—"The hour of prayer" (v. 1). Peter and John were the evident leaders of the Jerusalem church at this time. Yet they remained faithful Jews and were entering the Temple for the three o'clock prayer service. There is yet no apparent break between Judaism and Christianity. The thousands of converts are Jews. Christianity is still exclusively a Jewish religion.

The miracle of healing was more than a wonder. It was a sign (4:22). The miracle-working power of the Spirit was given to the apostles not to astound the crowd with magic but to demonstrate that Jesus has saving power over both the physical and the spiritual.

Truth for today.—Daily routines offer many wayside opportunities for witnessing. The apostles, hurrying to prayer meeting, saw a lame man. Because they were alert to such unexpected opportunities and sensitive to the man's need, not only was the man healed, but the door was opened for Peter to preach and 2,000 were saved A hundred wayside opportunities for witnessing open to the alert Christian every day!

"Such as I have give I thee" (v. 6). The beggar asked for money. What else would buy bread? What else can satisfy a gnawing appetite or clothe a naked body? Peter had no gold, but possessed something far greater, Jesus Christ! He shared what he had and the lame man received the greatest gift that life can offer.

The Church Strengthened in Persecution (Acts 4:1–37)

The passage.—The religious authorities, alarmed by the preaching of the resurrection of Jesus and the number of converts, imprison Peter and John.

On trial before the Sanhedrin, the apostles turned the table on the Jewish court. When the Sanhedrin cannot deny the fact of a miraculous happening, they demand "by what authority do *such as you* (uneducated, common men) preach in the temple and claim to do the works of God?" Peter boldly answers, "By the name of Jesus whom you crucified." In the presence of the beggar healed by the power of Jesus, the Sanhedrin is impotent. They release the apostles but charge them to be silent. Peter disregards the threat and continues preaching.

Meanwhile the church has been gathered in prayer during the imprisonment and trial. The freed apostles appear before them and challenge all to be bold in their witness. The church is shaken by a fresh infilling of the Spirit.

A new depth of fellowship emerges from this first test of persecution. Members voluntarily share their material resources.

Special points.—The Sadducees were an aristocratic wealthy religious minority. Collaborating with the Romans to preserve order among the Jews, they controlled the Temple.

The preaching of Peter and John disturbed the Sadducees because (a) they were unlearned men unauthorized to preach in the Temple. (b) The growing new movement could disturb the Roman authorities and threaten the peace. (c) Theologically, they did not believe in the resurrection. The Jew believed the resurrection would bring about the destruction of the existing "order," thus implying the destruction of Rome, a dangerously revolutionary doctrine. (d) The preaching of the "kingdom" was inflammatory propaganda. The Sadducees saw a threat to the peaceful status quo that protected their landed wealth and established position with Rome.

The Sanhedrin was a 70-man Jewish supreme court with authority over Jewish law and internal affairs.

Truth for today.—Peter, boldness in the face of opposition! Can this be the same Peter who, not many days before, in the same place, and before the same people, had denied his Lord? Now he defies the murderers of Jesus, ignores their threats, and generates a new boldness among all believers to "obey God and not man." The difference is the filling of the Spirit (v. 8) and how desperately we need this Spirit-empowered courage today!

Barnabas was a nickname meaning "son of encouragement." Later, he stood up in defense of the young man, John Mark. He persuaded the Jerusalem disciples to receive Paul (9:27). He was sent to receive the Gentiles at Antioch (11:19–24). "The ministry of encouragement" calls Christians today. Young people need a Barnabas to encourage them. New converts need a Barnabas to strengthen them. Preachers, teachers, and missionaries need a Barnabas to stand by them.

The Church Grows in Spite of Internal Problems and External Persecution (Acts 5:1–42)

The passage.—Ananias and Sapphira pretend to give all to the church. Their hypocrisy and deceit is punished by immediate death. Believers and non-believers are awestruck by the swift judgment of God.

The apostles and Christianity gain favor with the multitudes and the church grows. Sick are brought from near and far to be healed by the apostles.

The religious leaders, seeing the popularity of the movement, are filled with frenzied jealousy. The apostles are re-arrested. Gamaliel restrains the Sanhedrin from stoning the prisoners. He reasons, "If this movement is of man, it will fail. If of God, you cannot overthrow it."

The apostles are beaten, ordered to cease all activity in the name of Jesus, and released. They rejoice in suffering for Jesus. Undaunted by the threats of the religious authorities, they continue teaching and preaching.

Special points.—The sin of Ananias and Sapphira was hypocrisy. They "agreed together" to live a lie before God and the church. Such a sin carries severe consequences!

Miracles continue as a "sign" of God's Spirit in this new movement. Some are healed by the touch of the apostles' shadow! While some would question the plausibility of this, if we grant the possibility of *any* miracle, then *all miracles* are possible in any extreme!

Gamaliel (v. 34) was the most famous rabbi of his day. Grandson of Hillel, he represented the liberal wing of the Pharisee sect. Paul studied under Gamaliel. Perhaps Paul was present at this council meeting, for he appears to have been a member (26:10). When the council later stones Stephen, Saul is an observer (7:58).

Truth for today.—Cromwell instructed the artist to paint his portrait "warts and all." The inspired writers of the Scripture never ignore the human factor. We see hypocrisy, murmuring (chap. 6), dissension and sharp contention (chap. 15) in the early church. It is comforting assurance that even in sin and weakness, God's power can still be manifested and his work flourish. In spite of human frailty, God uses his church.

Christ was preached in the Temple and great numbers of *Jews* were converted. Later they will reject Christianity not because they cannot accept Jesus as the Messiah, but because they refuse to accept the uncircumcised Gentile as a Christian brother. Even today, the divisive issue in many churches is not "who is Jesus" but "who is my Christian brother."

To obey God rather than man (v. 29) has been the watchword of Christians in the face of persecution and death throughout the centuries. Martin Luther declared "Here stand I! God help me, I can do no other!" In World War II, Martin Niemoeller spent eight years in prison in Germany for obeying God rather than Hitler. A missionary refuses a huge salary to represent an oil company saying, "I have a previous commitment—to God!"

Lay Leadership in the Early Church (Acts 6:1–15)

The passage.—In the growing church distributing food and money to needy church members absorbs much of the apostles' time. Dissension and murmuring against the apostles for allegedly neglecting certain church members divides the fellowship.

At the request of the apostles, the church elects seven men to administer the relief funds. The apostles now can concentrate on their responsibilities of preaching and teaching. This action brings harmony to the fellowship and increases the effectiveness of the apostles. The number of disciples multiply greatly and even many priests are converted.

The lay witnessing and wonder working of Stephen, one of the seven, arouses bitter opposition. He is arrested and brought before the Sanhedrin, where false witnesses accuse him.

Special points.—Grecians and Hebrews (v. 1). The Greek-speaking Jews were from other countries residing in Jerusalem; the Hebrews were the native Palestinian Jews. The Grecians appeared to emerge as leaders as indicated by the Greek names of the seven. The cleavage was not unlike the present-day conflicts in a church between "old-timers" and "newcomers."

"Libertines" (v. 9). Literally freedmen, Jews taken as prisoners to Rome, and later freed. There were many synagogues in Jerusalem built by Jews of various countries (Cyrene, Alexandria, Cilicia, etc.). Stephen, a Greek-speaking Jew, was zealous in witnessing in these synagogues.

Blaspheming "this holy place, and the law" (v. 13). Greek-speaking Jews cleverly twist the words of Stephen to incite the conservative traditionalist, the Pharisees. They charge Stephen with disrespect for the Temple, Moses, and their traditions.

Truth for today.—The "seven" laymen were selected to tend "this business." Some erroneously interpret this to mean *"the* business" of the church. Of course, a congregation *may* assign to deacons responsibility for the financial, physical, and business affairs of the church. But in the Jerusalem church the seven were charged with (a) peacemaking, healing the breach in the fellowship, (b) strengthening the ministry of the apostles by shielding them from criticism and relieving them of menial secondary tasks, (c) functioning as undershepherds to the congregation. These seven were not a board of directors running the church. They were spiritually-minded servants of the congregation undergirding the preaching and teaching of the apostles.

Stephen's enemies accused him of changing the "customs" (v. 14) in regard to the "holy place and the law" (v. 13). The divisive issues in a church often do not relate to the will of God or the authority of the Bible but to the traditions and social practices that are challenged by change. Racial discrimination in the church is ultimately defended not by the authority of the Bible but by a sacredness of our traditional social practices!

Stephen's Defense and Martyrdom (Acts 7:1–60)

The passage.—Before the Sanhedrin Stephen reviews Hebrew history—in the light of Jesus Christ. Stephen declares: (a) God has never limited himself to one land. Abraham came from outside Palestine; God dealt with Jacob and Moses in Egypt; gave the Ten Commandments in Arabia. (b) The Jews have deified the Temple building, yet the tabernacle was not bound to any land. (c) Israel has been repeatedly stubborn and blind to the spirit of God and rejected his prophets. (d) Now, these very Jews who claim to defend the law are guilty of its destruction because they crucified Jesus.

With animal-like fury, the crowd seizes Stephen. While praying for his executioners, Stephen is stoned. A young rabbi, Saul of Tarsus, is a silent witness to the violence.

Special points.—Why the turn of events from broad popular support (even many priests believing, 6:7) to this wild massive opposition? The Pharisees now understand the full *universal implication* of the gospel. Layman Stephen, declaring the universality of God's reve-lation in Judaism, has preached Jesus as the *universal Savior* for all men everywhere. The "middle wall of partition" that the Jews have built to set themselves aside as God's chosen people has been challenged. The Pharisees cannot stand such heresy! Stephen has drawn the line that will mark the continuing controversy in the book of Acts.

The Sanhedrin could not impose a death sentence without approval of Roman authority. So Stephen's death was the result of lynch mob action rather than a formal legal execution.

Saul, a young Pharisee, had probably disputed with Stephen in the synagogue of the Cilicians (6:9). He watched the garments of the executioners at Stephen's stoning.

Truth for today.—The Jews had let their devotion to a *house* of worship take the place of loyalty to God. Throughout Christian history men have tended to deify buildings and sanctify places. Fellowship often is broken by a proposal to move the church *location* or to modify or replace the physical *facility.* "God is a spirit" and he dwells not in houses of wood but in the hearts of men and in the body of the believers which is the true church.

The first Christian martyr was a layman! Stephen's death did not destroy his witness. The centuries to follow would reveal that "the blood of martyrs is the seed of the church."

Philip the Evangelist (Acts 8:1–40)

The passage.—The stoning of Stephen unites Pharisees and Sadducees against the church. Saul is a leader, ravaging the church, beating, imprisoning, and killing Christians. Persecution scatters the church abroad.

One of the seven, Philip, preaches in Samaria. God authenticates his witness with many miracles and conversions.

The apostles in Jerusalem send Peter and John to investigate the Samaritan revival. When the Samaritan converts receive the Holy Spirit, Simon the magician asks to buy the power of the Spirit and is rebuked by Peter.

Philip's next encounter is with an Ethiopian eunuch. When he explains that Jesus is the Messiah, prophesied in Isaiah, the eunuch believes and is baptized. Philip continues his evangelistic preaching in all the cities along the coast.

Special points.—The events of this chapter seem very significant in Luke's judgment. Stephen proclaimed the universality of God's love for all men.

Then the gospel spreads, first, to the Samaritans who were half-Jews, a mongrel race outside the Covenant in the eyes of the Jews. Then immediately, the gospel is preached to a Gentile, an Ethiopian, a "God-fearer" but not a Jew!

Baptism, an act of obedience and an expression of faith (v. 36). Jesus commanded it (Matt. 28:19). Believers are baptized: 3,000 at Pentecost (2:38); Samaritans (8:12); Saul (9:18); Cornelius (10:47–48); Lydia (16:15); the Philippian jailer (16:33); the Corinthians (18:8); the Ephesians (19:5). Paul states the symbolism of immersion (Rom. 6:3–7) to be the death, burial, and resurrection of Christ and the believer's personal experience of death to sin and resurrection to new life in Christ.

Truth for today.—Every major advance of Christianity has been characterized by fervent lay witnessing. Persecution scattered the early church. As the "scattered ones went everywhere witnessing," the gospel marched in seven-league boots across the Roman Empire. The first missionary-evangelist was a layman, Philip. The first recorded revival outside Jerusalem was led by a layman in Samaria!

Today, after gathering in church on Sunday, modern transportation and communication scatter the members across the face of the earth. What a revival would sweep our world if today "the scattered ones went witnessing!" (v. 1).

Saul's Conversion (Acts 9:1–43)

The passage.—On the way to Damascus to persecute Christians, Saul encounters the resurrected Lord. Struck to the ground and blinded, he is converted. In Damascus, a disciple Ananias lays hands on Saul and his sight is restored. He is baptized and commissioned to preach.

Christians and Jews are amazed by the preaching of the one-time persecutor. When the Jews plot to kill him, Paul escapes by night in a basket over the wall. When Saul arrives in Jerusalem, Barnabas speaks up in Saul's behalf. Soon his bold preaching arouses the enmity of the Jerusalem Jews. Saul is brought to Caesarea and sent home to Tarsus.

Peace follows and the church prospers. Peter preaches in the coastal cities, healing a paralytic at Lydda and raising Dorcas, a believer, from the dead. Peter takes up residence in Joppa with Simon the tanner.

Special points.—Tarsus was surpassed only by Athens and Alexandria as a center of culture and learning. Here Saul was born of well-to-do orthodox Jews of the tribe of Benjamin, and a Roman citizen by birth. A Pharisee, equipped to practice the trade of tentmaking, he was sent to Jerusalem to be trained as a rabbi under the great Gamaliel. His conversion occurred in A.D. 34 (cf. chaps. 9,22,26). He spent three years at an oasis in the Arabian desert near Damascus in study and meditation ("many days," v. 23 and Gal. 1:17). After a brief visit in Damascus and Jerusalem, Paul returns to Tarsus. In the ensuing years he undoubtedly debated with the Jews in the synagogue and witnessed to Gentiles throughout Cilicia.

Eventually Paul will attract the attention of the church at Antioch and 13 years after his conversion they will send him on the first missionary journey (A.D. 47, Acts 11:25 ff.).

Truth for today.—To be "converted" is to be "turned around." A Christian is one who has been "turned around" by Christ and faces in an opposite direction. Paul, the persecutor, has become a preacher! The world is constantly amazed at the change Jesus Christ makes in a life.

"Brother Saul" (v. 17). While some were suspicious, Ananias showed the true Christian spirit of accepting the new convert Saul on the face value of his profession of faith in Christ. This remains the mark of a true New Testament fellowship—*the acceptance of a new believer as a brother* in Christ on profession of faith. Yet often we withhold acceptance of the prostitute, the drunkard, the person of another race or social level, saying, "Let them *prove* their sincerity, *first.*"

The Conversion of Cornelius (Acts 10:1–48)

The passage.—Cornelius, a God-fearing Roman centurion in Caesarea is instructed by an angel to send for Peter.

In Joppa, God speaks to Peter commanding him to eat of the ceremonially "unclean" food he sees in a thrice-repeated vision. Peter understands that God has directed him to put aside Jewish custom and accept the invitation of the Gentile Cornelius to come into his house.

In Caesarea, Cornelius gathers kinsmen and friends to hear Peter. The apostle declares that God (whom Cornelius already reverenced) had sent Jesus of Nazareth to be "judge of the living and the dead" (v. 42, RSV). When the hearers believe, the Holy Spirit comes upon them.

The Jewish Christians accompanying Peter are amazed at the immediate evidence of the Holy Spirit validating the salvation of these Gentiles. The new converts are baptized.

Special points.—Caesarea, 50 miles northwest of Jerusalem, was the Roman capital of Palestine, and residence of the governor. Here Paul was imprisoned (24:27) and Philip lived (8:40). Cornelius was captain of the Italian band, the elite palace guard. He was a devout "God-fearer," student of Judaism (but not circumcised), seeking a fuller revelation of the living God.

The Holy Spirit came upon the believers *before* they were baptized (v. 44). Conversion was already a reality when baptism was administered. Both circumcision and baptism are *symbolic* rites. In Acts, Luke is explicit to demonstrate that Jewish circumcision is not necessary to salvation and here he incidentally demonstrates the same thing about baptism.

Truth for today.—Who first brought the gospel to Rome? There were believers, even "in Caesar's household" (Phil. 4:22) almost from the beginning. Could this army officer, Cornelius, have been transferred shortly to Rome and established the band of believers in Caesar's household?

Certainly, Cornelius carried his Christian witness wherever he was assigned for military duty. Modern-day Christian "centurions" are a dynamic missionary force. Christian military personnel have established mission work and churches throughout the world while on overseas duty.

The Church at Antioch (Acts 11:1–30)

The passage.—In the Jerusalem church when Peter is criticized for eating with the Gentile Cornelius, he explains: It was God's doing. God told Cornelius to send for Peter. God told Peter to go to Cornelius. When Peter preached Jesus, the Gentiles were converted. God approved all by sending the Holy Spirit. But when they hear that Peter has baptized Gentiles without requiring circumcision, the "circumcision party" opposes Peter.

A report comes from the church at Antioch which was founded by Jerusalem refugees and men from Cyprus and Cyrene. There, also, Gentile converts in great numbers have been received without circumcision. Barnabas is sent to investigate.

Convinced that the converts are genuine, Barnabas brings Saul from Tarsus to Antioch to assist him in teaching. Here disciples are called "Christians" for the first time.

Later, the Antioch Christians send Barnabas and Saul with relief for the famine sufferers in Jerusalem.

Special points.—The "circumcision party," later called the "Judaizers," who will bitterly oppose Paul. There were two issues here: (a) Can Gentiles be saved without circumcision and (b) may a Jewish Christian eat with an uncircumcized Gentile Christian?

Antioch. Third in size in the Roman Empire, surpassed only by Rome and Alexandria. Located 80 miles southeast of Tarsus, and 300 miles north of Jerusalem. Later, Antioch becomes a strategic center of Christianity.

Truth for today.—We quickly condemn these Jewish Christians for refusing to accept with equality the Gentile believers. But the disapproval of Peter eating with Cornelius is painfully similar to the attitude of white Christians who "refuse to eat with Negroes."

We may recall sermons "proving" from the Bible that God intends for the races to be segregated even when the parties involved are all Christians. How often have we heard, "Let them go to *their* churches. Let us have *our own* church for our people."

The "circumcision party" is ever with us, drawing circles and excluding others of certain social or racial classes as being unfit, unworthy, or even incapable of experiencing God's grace.

In the years to follow, the Jerusalem church, filled with prejudice, declined in influence while the openhearted Antioch church increased. The refining judgment of history still operates to prosper the church that proclaims the "open" gospel.

Persecution Under Herod (Acts 12:1–25)

The passage.—Herod Agrippa executes the apostle James and imprisons Peter. God miraculously intervenes to deliver Peter. There is great rejoicing when Peter joins the disciples in a home.

Herod orders the execution of the guards who permitted Peter's escape and returns to Caesarea. To honor a Phoenician delegation, Herod dresses in royal regalia and delivers an eloquent oration to the people. As the people shout, "It is the voice of a god, and not of a man," the judgment of God falls quickly. Herod dies a horrible repulsive death!

With Herod's death, official persecution subsides. The word of God multiplies. Barnabas and Saul return from Jerusalem to Antioch bringing John Mark along.

Special points.—The Herods were a cruel and bloody line of kings. Under the Roman government, they took control of Judea sometime before Christ. Herod the Great (37 B.C.–A.D. 4) slew the children of Bethlehem. His son, Herod Antipas (A.D. 4–39) killed John the Baptist (Mark 6:14–29). This is Herod's grandson, Agrippa I, king of all Palestine (A.D. 41–44) who executes James. It is his son, Agrippa II before whom Paul is tried (Acts 25:13 ff.).

Agrippa I was half-Jew and Edomite. Reared in Rome, and anxious to curry popular support as the new king, he quickly identified with the Jewish majority in their opposition to the heretical Christian sect.

Not "Easter" (v. 4) but the Jewish Feast of the Passover. Herod intended to execute Peter immediately after the Passover celebration.

Truth for today.—Waiting on the Lord is often difficult for a Christian. But when that waiting is spent in prayer, it is never wasted. The Christians waited in prayer for the release of Peter from prison.

It is easy to be discouraged. The temporary triumphs of wickedness will not prevail. By waiting in prayer, the Christian may look with hope beyond the moment to see the continuing victory of God in the years and centuries and millenniums.

Peter, on the night before his scheduled execution, slept so soundly that the angel "prodded" to awaken him. What a change in a man who had been cowed into denying Christ by the accusations of a mere servant girl (John 18:17).

How Peter had grown in Christian courage. In the last verse of his last letter (2 Pet. 3:18) Peter challenges the Christians in Asia, to "go on growing." How well do we sleep in the face of trouble? It is a good measure of our Christian growth and maturity.

Paul's First Missionary Sermon (Acts 13: 1–52)

The passage.—Barnabas and Saul are sent as missionaries by the Antioch church. They pass through the island of Cyprus preaching in the synagogues. At Paphos the Roman governor is converted. God validates Paul's witness when a false prophet is temporarily blinded. Hereafter Saul is called Paul, his Roman name.

At Perga John Mark deserts the party. They travel northward by foot to Antioch in Pisidia. On the sabbath Paul preaches in the synagogue.

His first recorded sermon reviews Jewish history, declares Jesus the fulfilment of promise and offers forgiveness and salvation. Many Jews and God-fearing Gentiles believe.

On the next sabbath, when the whole city comes to hear Paul, unbelieving Jews drive Paul and Barnabas out of Antioch and they come to Iconium.

Special points.—The first missionary journey (A.D. 47–48). Cyprus was the island home of Barnabas. Disciples from Cyprus had come earlier to the church at Antioch (11:20). There had probably been a Christian witness in Cyprus from Pentecost on. Luke considered the conversion of the Roman governor the significant event of the Cyprus mission.

Luke does not mention, and Paul only hints at, the hardships suffered on the foot journey from Perga to Antioch. From the hot coastal region, the road twists northward through treacherous valleys and over rugged mountains to reach the 4,000-foot Galatian tableland. The journey was full of perils "of waters" and "of robbers" all the way (2 Cor. 11:26).

Some scholars believe that Paul contracted malaria as he passed through the infested coastal swamps of Perga and reoccurring attacks were his "thorn in the flesh." It is apparent he was ill when he arrived at Antioch, for Paul expresses gratitude to the Galatian highlanders for their care (Gal. 4:13 f.).

Truth for today.—In Antioch we see the first organized Christian mission.

The Spirit led some Christians to *send* missionaries. They were commissioned with the laying on of hands and "sent . . . away" (v. 3) or literally "released." The church "gave up" for missionary service two of its most gifted and outstanding leaders. Yet, how difficult it is for us to "give up" our most capable young people, our most talented pastors, our most dynamic leaders for the mission fields!

Unfortunately, there are many church members who really do not believe in evangelistic and missionary endeavors. Some believe only "superior" people are capable of receiving the gospel. Others do only lip service to spreading the gospel. The missionary church at Antioch is a worthy example for present-day churches!

Preaching in Galatia (Acts 14:1–28)

The passage.—Paul and Barnabas remain in Iconium, preaching, working miracles, and winning great multitudes. After first preaching in the synagogue they are driven out, and preach to the Gentile populace. Finally, threatened by mob violence Paul and Barnabas flee to Lystra.

In the pagan city of Lystra, when Paul heals a cripple, the crowd believes they are gods. The pagan priest prepares to offer them sacrifices but Paul explains they are mere men and preaches to them of the living God.

Later, unbelieving Jews who have followed Paul to Lystra, stone him and leave him for dead. But Paul is revived and taken back into the city.

They continue to Derbe where many pagans are converted. Then Paul and Barnabas retrace their steps revisiting the new converts in Galatia. The believers are strengthened to face persecu-tion. Church congregations are organized and pastors elected.

Returning to Antioch, they report to the church how God has opened the door of faith to the Gentiles.

Special points.—Gentile opposition in Iconium (v. 4). Christianity divided the Jews because of doctrine, the pagan Gentiles because of morality. Imagine the tension between a Christian wife and a pagan husband who worships idols and believes in infanticide! Thus the whole city, Jew and Gentile alike, became "pro" or "anti" Paul.

Zeus was the king of gods; Hermes, the god of speech or the messenger of gods (v. 12). Paul interrupted his sermon to heal the cripple. The crowd reverted to their native tongue and it was only later when the priest came with the sacrifices that Paul was horrified to learn that these people were worshiping them as gods!

"Ordained elders" (v. 23). Literally "elected by the show of hands" pastors. The organization of the early church corresponded in a general way with the Jewish synagogue, where elders or leaders were elected to serve the congregation.

Truth for today.—Effective preaching and teaching is always thoroughly suited to the situation. When Paul preached in the synagogues, he appealed to the witness of the Jewish Scripture. But among the pagans at Lystra, he pointed the hearers to the living God who created all things and called for them to turn away from the gods they had created (v. 15). So we must deal with people "where they are" and interpret the gospel in terms of their understanding.

Paul reported to the church that "God has opened the door of faith to the Gentiles" (v. 27). In Judaism, Gentiles could enter the door of circumcision, and the law, and receive the Covenant. But now, through personal faith in Jesus Christ, and without any rite, ritual, or connection with the synagogue, Gentiles could come directly to God and receive forgiveness and salvation.

Yet some today still deny that "repentance and faith in Jesus Christ" are the sole conditions of salvation. They would also require "baptism," or "receiving the sacrament" or "membership in *the* church," or "doing good works."

The Jerusalem Conference Settles Conditions of Gentile Membership (Acts 15:1–41)

The passage.—Paul leads a delegation up to Jerusalem to report how God has saved many Gentiles through faith in Christ. When a local group of converted Pharisees (Judaizers) charge Paul with heresy, Peter tells how the Holy Spirit came to believing Gentiles at Cornelius' house.

Then James speaks and the church gives unanimous expression to the view that circumcision is not necessary for Gentiles.

An official reconciling letter to this effect is drafted to the Gentile Christians in Antioch.

The issue settled, Paul and Barnabas determine to revisit the mission churches but separate over John Mark. Barnabas and Mark sail to Cyprus while Paul and Silas embark overland to visit churches in Syria and Cilicia.

Special points.—Galatians, chapter 2, amplifies what happened at the Jerusalem conference. When the Judaizers interrupted the congregational mission rally (v. 5) they created such confusion that Paul asked for a special meeting of the apostles and the elders. In the closed session, Paul declared his convictions and experiences to them (Gal. 2:2). The church leaders, James, Peter, and John, agreed with Paul.

Then followed an open church business meeting where there was much "disputing" (v. 7). In true democratic procedure, the issue was openly debated and the church heard both sides. Apparently, during the voting, the Judaizers either abstained or walked out. Church sentiment was unanimous for a free gospel.

Here is the last mention of Peter (v. 7) in the book of Acts. Peter probably worked among the churches of Asia Minor for he addressed his Epistles to them. He wrote to them from "Babylon" (1 Pet. 5:13) during the persecution of Nero. Many understand Babylon to be Rome (as in Rev. 17) and believe Peter was imprisoned and suffered martyrdom there. (See Special points on chap. 28.)

Truth for today.—Whether it is fact or fiction that Peter died in Rome, the *Quo Vadis* tradition is an inspiring story. Fleeing to escape persecution, on the Appian Way, he met Jesus. "Lord, whither goest thou?" Peter asked. "To Rome to be crucified again," Jesus answered. Ashamed of his cowardice, Peter returned to the city, and was crucified upside down, counting himself not worthy to be crucified like Jesus.

How often on a cowardly course, and running away, have we encountered the living Lord. And he has given us the strength to turn around and go back to face the battle with new courage.

God's gamblers, Paul and Barnabas, who have "hazarded" their lives for the sake of the gospel (v. 26). A gambling term, literally, "bet their lives on the line for Jesus."

The kingdom needs men today willing to put all on the line in the belief that (a) the gospel is the power of God unto salvation to everyone who will believe, (b) that love will conquer over hate, (c) that the life in Christ will triumph over death, (d) that all things material are transitory and only the spiritual abides.

Paul in Philippi (Acts 16:1–40)

The passage.—Paul and Silas visit Derbe and Lystra where a young convert, Timothy, joins them. When God steers Paul away from Ephesus and Bithynia, his purpose for Paul is revealed in a vision at Troas. Paul is called to preach the gospel in Macedonia. Luke joins the party and they come to Philippi.

Lydia, a prominent businesswoman, is converted. But when Paul cures a demon-possessed slave girl, her masters have Paul and Silas beaten and jailed. They are singing hymns and praying when God sends an earthquake. The frightened jailer and all his household are converted. The authorities learning that Paul is a Roman citizen, release them.

Luke remains in Philippi to strengthen the newly established church while Paul's party departs to visit other Macedonian cities.

Special points.—Timothy, his mother, a Jewess named Eunice, and his grandmother Lois, were probably converted on Paul's first missionary journey. Because his father was a Greek, Paul deemed it expedient that Timothy identify with the Jewish Christians by submitting to circumcision (v. 3). Timothy was Paul's constant companion and "son" in the ministry to whom he addressed two epistles. Tradition says that after Paul's death Timothy cared for the Ephesian church and suffered martyrdom when Domitian was emperor.

Lydia's conversion (vv. 14–15). As is universally true in Acts, baptism *followed* conversion. The reference to her "household" does not imply infant baptism. Other members of the household were also converted, and *then* baptized.

Truth for today.—The Philippian

jailer was a pagan, without a background in Judaism, or a knowledge of the church, the Bible, or Christian doctrine. Yet he is convicted of a deep feeling of lostness and sin and cries out, "What must I do to be saved?" (v. 30).

This is *every man's* question, at every time, in every culture! For we are made by God, for God, in the image of God. But sin has defaced that image and separated every man from God. The nameless longing in every heart is to find God and to be restored to fellowship with him.

Paul answers without qualification, "Believe on the Lord Jesus Christ, and thou shalt be saved" (v. 31). If this answer is valid for the pagan jailer, it would be valid for *anyone*. Religious ignorance, social distinctions, race, lack of culture or education, none of these are barriers to salvation. In fact there is no barrier between man and God except man's own failure to trust himself to the Lord Jesus Christ!

Paul at Thessalonica and Athens (Acts 17:1–34)

The passage.—Paul spends three sabbaths in the synagogue at Thessalonica proclaiming the crucified Christ the Messiah. When many Jews, God-fearing Gentiles and the wives of prominent men are converted, the unbelieving Jews incite a mob against Paul and Silas.

They escape by night to Berea, where openhearted Jews and Gentiles readily respond to the gospel. Later, however, Paul must flee leaving Silas and Timothy with the new converts.

In Athens Paul's preaching of a "new religion" in the synagogue and marketplace attracts the attention of the town council. At their request Paul appears before the council. Paul declares he represents the living God who created the earth and all men in it. This true God has appointed the risen Christ to judge the world. Some laugh, but one councilman, Dionysius, a woman Damaris, and others are converted.

Special points.—Thessalonica, capital of Macedonia, was 100 miles from Philippi. A thriving commercial harbor city, it was situated strategically on the main trade route. Salonika is the present-day name.

Athens was the intellectual and artistic capital of the world. It was a free city ruled by a council called the Areopagus. Obviously Paul would not call these prominent citizens "superstitious" (v. 22) or "ignorant" (v. 23). The correct translation is "very religious" and "what therefore you worship as unknown, this I proclaim to you" (RSV).

Truth for today.—They "turned the world upside down" (v. 6) was the charge of the Thessalonians against Paul. What a prophetic insight into the revolutionary dimensions of the gospel! In an ever-sinful world, the way of Christ is always opposed to man-made things as they are.

Again, at Athens, Paul demonstrates that the gospel cannot be proclaimed in a vacuum. Whether in the African bush, in a milltown, or on Mars Hill before Athenian philosophers, the effective Christian witness is familiar with the *thought world* of the lost person. In Athens, Paul uses one of their own deities (an "unknown God") for an opening illustration. He quotes their own poet, reflects an understanding of their philosophy, and brings all to focus on Jesus Christ as the fulfilment of their religious inclinations and personal need. The master preacher and teacher sets a worthy example for us today.

Corinth, Home, and Back to Galatia (Acts 18:1–28)

The passage.—Paul stays 18 months in Corinth and establishes a strong church. When unbelieving Jews bring Paul into court, the Roman governor Gallio acquits him of wrongdoing.

Turning homeward, Paul makes a brief stop in Ephesus to preach in the synagogue, visits the Jerusalem church, and returns to Antioch.

In time, the mission fields again beckon and Paul begins his third journey, first visiting the Galatian churches.

Meanwhile, in Ephesus, Apollos is preaching Jesus with a limited understanding of the gospel. Priscilla and Aquilla, who had been with Paul in Corinth, instruct him in the way "more perfectly." Then Apollos goes to Corinth to continue the work Paul has started.

Special points.—While in Corinth, Paul receives a report from the newly-formed church in Thessalonica. He writes two letters, 1 and 2 Thessalonians, commending their faith but cautioning against fanaticism concerning the second coming of Christ.

Back in Antioch, his second missionary journey completed (A.D. 49–52), Paul hears reports of legalists perverting the gospel in the Galatian churches. To correct their serious deflections from the true gospel, Paul writes the Epistle to the Galatians to be circulated to the churches of Lystra, Derbe, Iconium, and Pisidian Antioch.

Shortly thereafter he embarks on his third missionary journey (A.D. 52) following his letter with a personal visit to these churches.

Truth for today.—Corinth was a thriving commercial center. The cosmopolitan city was notorious for its immorality. Sexual lust was sanctified as a thousand priestess-prostitutes served the temple of Aphrodite. On one side of the marketplace stood the largest non-religious structure of ancient Greece, housing some 33 taverns and nightclubs.

In this profligate port city were Greeks, Romans, Jews, and adventurers from the whole Empire, gathered to transact business by day and to engage in debauchery by night. A "Corinthian" was the nickname given to a person who engaged in excessive immorality.

Into this wicked degenerate society Paul came preaching the gospel and many were converted! Even the most immoral of men are not beyond the redemptive power of the gospel! This assurance, demonstrated in Corinth and validated through 20 centuries of Christian experience, keeps the fires of evangelism and missions burning in our hearts today!

Paul in Ephesus (Acts 19:1–41)

The passage.—In Ephesus Paul finds twelve disciples of John preaching repentance. They receive Christ and are baptized. After three months preaching in the synagogue, Paul moves his headquarters to a borrowed schoolroom.

For perhaps three years Paul speaks publicly and from house to house, night and day, performing special miracles and maintaining himself by working at his trade. The pagan city is shaken to its foundations. Great numbers are converted and many burn their books of magic and renounce idolatry.

When the idol makers incite a great mob to rioting against Paul, the mayor disbands the crowd and instructs Demetrius, the chief agitator, to present the charges against Paul in court in an orderly way.

Special points.—Other sources fill in Luke's brief account of Paul's three-year ministry in Ephesus. From Ephesus Paul directed a great Asian campaign (v. 10). Churches were founded in cities for 100 miles around (v. 26). Ephesus rapidly became the leading center of the Christian world.

Here Paul met with constant and fierce opposition, perhaps was imprisoned, fought with beasts, feared for his

life (1 Cor. 15:30 ff.; 16:9; 2 Cor. 1:8 ff.). Yet with tireless energy and indomitable courage he taught and preached and dreamed of new fields to be opened, Rome (v. 21) and even Spain (Rom. 15: 24).

While in Ephesus, a messenger from Corinth brought news of disturbing conditions in the church which prompted Paul's writing two letters, both probably incorporated into our 1 Corinthians.

Truth for today.—The temple to the fertility goddess Diana (Artemis), one of the seven wonders of the world, was in Ephesus. Paul preached a gospel that challenged the idol worshipers and idol makers who paid homage to her.

The gospel always hurls a challenge to every idol worshiper whether in Africa or America. The idol may be of wood or it may be deposited in a neighborhood bank drawing interest. The idol may be an ugly image, a portfolio of stocks, or a case of personal vanity. Its worship may demand the sacrifice of a bloody chicken or the total commitment of a person's interest, time, and effort.

Like the Ephesians, we must renounce the gods we have made if we would serve the God who made us.

Paul's Farewell to Ephesus (Acts 20:1–38)

The passage.—Leaving Ephesus, Paul spent the next year visiting churches in Macedonia and Greece. He had a rendezvous in Troas with representatives from the churches bearing a collection for the poor to the Jerusalem church.

On Sunday Paul preaches in the Troas church and revives a youth who fell from the window and was taken up for dead.

Paul and the "collection delegation" embark by ship for Jerusalem. When they dock at Miletus leaders from the church at Ephesus meet Paul. After charging them to be faithful and care for the church, he bids them farewell in tears and they pray together.

Special points.—From Ephesus, Paul first went to Macedonia and wrote another letter (2 Cor.) to the church at Corinth. Then, coming to Corinth (for three winter months, 1 Cor. 16:6), he finds his letters have been effective and the church is at peace. While in Corinth, he writes the Roman epistle. During this time, Paul is promoting a collection for the Jerusalem church for the purpose not only of alleviating physical suffering but also hoping to ease the tensions between the Jewish and Gentile elements in the church.

Truth for today.—The church in Troas was meeting "on the first day of the week" (v. 7). We have no explicit command for Christians to observe the first day in place of the seventh. The early Christians celebrated Sunday as the resurrection day of the Lord.

However, Christians make a serious mistake if they understand Sunday to be a replacement of the legalistic Jewish sabbath. In Hebrews, the old sabbath is said to be a shadow, and its fulfilment is the "sabbath rest" in Christ. The life in Christ, then, is the Christian's sabbath. Thus the sabbath has been fulfilled!

Christians set aside the Lord's Day as a time to spontaneously gather for worship, witnessing, and to memorialize the resurrection of Jesus. Proper Sunday activities are determined not by legalistic prohibitions but by a personal responsibility to make the day spiritually meaningful.

To Jerusalem and Arrest (Acts 21:1–40)

The passage.—From the start of the journey Paul was warned not to go to Jerusalem. The Holy Spirit, in every city,

warned him (20:23), in Tyre (4), and in Caesarea, while at Philip's house, the warning is repeated with graphic emphasis (v. 11). Even Luke begs him not to go (v. 12) but it is settled in Paul's mind to go, even if it means death (v. 13).

In Jerusalem, the leaders of the church gladly receive Paul and rejoice in his great work among the Gentiles. But the rank and file bitterly oppose Paul as a Jewish law-nullifier. To demonstrate his sympathy with the Jewish Christians who wished to obey the law, Paul finances the Temple sacrifices of four poor men and he joins them in the ceremony of purification.

When Paul is recognized in the Temple by Jews from Asia, he is attacked by the frenzied mob. Roman soldiers quickly break up the riot and take Paul into protective custody. When the captain's suspicion that Paul is a notorious Egyptian revolutionary proves false, he is permitted to address the angry crowd from the steps of the fortress.

Special points.—His arrest in Jerusalem terminates Paul's third missionary journey (A.D. 56). In one decade, the great apostle has changed the course of history. He has borne the Christian witness to almost every major city of Asia Minor and Greece in the very heart of the then known world.

"Thousands" (v. 20) is actually "myriads" or "tens of thousands." Such had been the growth of Christianity among the Jews in Jerusalem, but note they were *"all zealous of the law."* This explains why they were not persecuted by the nonbelieving Jews. While members of the Christian sect, they were still "good" Jews, faithfully keeping the law, too. Thus both believers and nonbelievers in Jerusalem opposed Paul for preaching salvation to the Gentiles without requiring the rites of Judaism.

Paul was determined to go personally to Jerusalem hoping to bridge the schism and convert the Judaizers with a firsthand report of the work of the Holy Spirit among the Gentiles.

Truth for today.—The Judaizers charge Paul with bringing an Ephesian Gentile into the Temple (v. 29). They intend to kill him for polluting the Temple. Archaeological discoveries have established conclusively the fact that the Temple doors were shut to Gentiles. A limestone block was found in 1871 in the Temple area inscribed "Let no foreigner enter within the screen and enclosure surrounding the sanctuary. Whosoever is taken so doing will be the cause of the death that overtaketh him." Such studied bigotry was worse than the murderous hate of the mob that attacked Paul. But what of the sanctified bigotry that closes the door of church membership (and even the door of church attendance in some cases) to "Negroes," or "certain foreigners," or "that class of people" in our day?

Paul Preaches to the Mob (Acts 22:1–30)

The passage.—Standing on the steps of the fortress, Paul addresses the angry crowd. He recounts his birth and training as a loyal Jew, his zealous persecution of heretics, his conversion on the road to Damascus, and his commission from God to preach to the Gentiles.

At the one word "Gentiles" the crowd explodes in frenzied action. In the bedlam that follows, Paul is taken for safety and examination inside the tower of Antonia. As the soldiers prepare him for scourging, Paul makes known his Roman citizenship. The situation causes great embarrassment to the soldiers. The next day he is brought before the Sanhedrin.

Special points.—The Tower of Antonia. Paul may have stood on the very same steps and been imprisoned in the

same pavement area where Pilate's soldiers held Jesus the night before his crucifixion some 17 years before (John 19:13).

Verse 16 does not teach baptismal regeneration. The book of Acts, Paul's preaching, and his epistles repeatedly affirm that salvation is by grace through faith and not of any legalistic ritual or requirement (neither circumcision nor baptism). This verse is more properly translated "arising, get yourself baptized! Get your sins washed away having called upon his name." Calling upon his name washes away sin after which you are baptized!

Truth for today.—In telling of his conversion, Paul declares he was under "God's orders." His conversion, commission, and message were all of divine origin. They were not Paul's ideas. He was a "draftee," not a volunteer. Today, the call to the ministry and to the mission field must be of God, not of man. With this conviction of a divine call and mission, one can stand as did Paul, in the very face of death, without fear.

Paul in Danger of Death (Acts 23:1–35)

The passage.—The next day Paul defends himself before the Jewish court, the Sanhedrin. Knowing he will not receive a fair hearing, he skillfully divides the group into their long-standing, bitterly-quarreling factions. When the council is divided and in an uproar, Paul is returned to the fortress for safekeeping.

That night in his prison barracks Paul receives another reassuring word from God. Meanwhile, Paul's nephew warns the military of a plot to lynch Paul and he is hastily transferred under heavy guard to the provincial capital at Caesarea. With Paul goes an official letter assigning the prisoner and his case to the higher authority of the governor, Felix. He is brought under guard to Caesarea.

Special points.—The conduct of the high priest, Ananias, was in keeping with his reputation of being cruel and selfish. Summoned to Rome in A.D. 52 to give an account of mismanagement, he was later deposed and assassinated in A.D. 66. (Note Paul's prophecy, v. 3.) The gist of Paul's "not knowing" (v. 5) is scornful sarcasm, "I could not tell *from the way he acted* he was the high priest!"

Truth for today.—That night the Lord stood by Paul and said, "Take courage" (v. 11). When the whole world has tumbled in, when all human reserves have been spent, when every way seems blocked, God comes to stand by his own! Every Christian at one time or another has experienced this miracle of renewed strength. On many occasions circumstances beyond his control brought Paul to the very brink of disaster. At other times, Paul literally threw himself into danger. But because he always stood by the cross and felt the love of God, he found courage to stand without flinching. And so it will be with any Christian who in some measure shares Paul's faith and experience.

Paul Before Felix (Acts 24:1–27)

The passage.—Paul is brought to trial before Felix. The lawyer representing Ananias brings the charges: "He is a past, a revolutionary, a leader of a disturbing sect, and he has attempted to desecrate the Temple."

Paul challenges the Jews to show proof of any of the charges. He does confess to be a follower after "the way" (v. 14). But, he says, the Way is not a new religion; it is the true Judaism, the fulfillment of Jewish Scriptures.

Felix postpones the trial but returns Paul to prison to please the Jews. He also hopes to receive a bribe. Later Paul preaches to Felix and his wife of "justice and self-control and future judgment" (v. 25, RSV). Trembling, Felix dismisses Paul until a more "convenient season." In subsequent conversations, Felix' hardened heart is only entertained. Paul remains imprisoned at Caesarea for two years.

Special points.—The Roman historian, Tacitus, said of Felix, who was once a slave, that "he revelled in cruelty and lust, and wielded the power of a king with the mind of a slave." Drusilla was his third wife.

There had been rioting between Syrians and Jews in Caesarea and Felix had sent Roman troops against the *Jews,* thus incurring their ill will. Reports had reached Rome of his misgovernment and he was also in disfavor with Caesar. So now the morally weak and conscienceless politician Felix sees in the innocent man Paul, not merely an opportunity to receive a bribe, but also a chance to regain popular favor with the Jews. When Paul preached "justice, self-control, and judgment," it is little wonder that Felix trembled in deep conviction of his sinfulness!

Truth for today.—Many a man, like Felix, stands at the threshold of Christianity. A nameless longing within him makes him curious to hear more. Then comes the dilemma, the price to be paid to be a Christian. There is sin and lust that must be given up. There are compromises to maintain position or popularity that must be refused. There is the love of money that must be overcome.

So, troubled in conscience, the man comes face to face with the claims of Jesus Christ, and a decision is demanded. But the Spirit will not always strive with such a man. God spoke and Felix "trembled" but refused to repent and enter into the kingdom. As far as we know, never again did the word of God stir the heart of Felix to repentance. From that moment on, he was a walking "dead man," having sinned away his last chance for eternal life. Truly, it is a grievous sin for any man to reject the Holy Spirit of God!

Paul Appeals to Caesar (Acts 25:1–27)

The passage.—When Festus replaces Felix as governor, the high priest again presses charges against Paul. Festus advises Paul to go to Jerusalem for trial. But Paul appeals to Caesar in Rome in the firm belief that only in the Roman court can he receive a fair trial.

When King Agrippa and Bernice visit Festus, the governor tells them of Paul's case he has inherited from Felix. He is in a dilemma with a prisoner who had appealed to Caesar for trial, against whom he has no criminal charges. When King Agrippa expresses a desire to hear Paul, Festus suggests that Agrippa examine the prisoner that perchance he can uncover some basis for a charge against Paul.

Special points.—This Herod Agrippa was king of a small territory northeast of the Sea of Galilee, a petty puppet of Rome. He was son of the Herod who killed James (12:2). Bernice was his sister, a woman of rare beauty, having been married to two kings, but now living with her brother Agrippa in *incest*. Agrippa and Bernice enter the courtroom in royal apparel with Festus and an escort of notables of Caesarea. In the presence of *pomp and incest* on the throne, the *great apostle stands in chains a prisoner* (v. 29). Fortunately, heaven reverses many such earthly circumstances and evaluations.

Truth for today.—Paul appealed to Caesar. We, too, as Christians have a higher court of appeal. Above all the earthly courts and over all the judges of the world, there is the "judge eternal." How many have been misjudged! How motives have been misunderstood! How actions have been misinterpreted! How lives have been mistakenly condemned.

Let us never forget there is a higher authority in whose judgments there is no error, whose justice is tempered by love. It is before him that we ultimately stand. It is for his divine approval alone we daily strive. It is in this Judge who, in his own time will set all things aright, that *we have our life and hope!*

Paul Preaches Before Agrippa (Acts 26: 1–32)

The passage.—Before Agrippa, Paul eloquently recounts his devotion to Judaism, his conversion, his God-given commission to preach, and his obedience to his heavenly vision. Paul's zeal brings a rebuke from Festus, "Thou art mad."

But Paul, aware of Agrippa's knowledge of the Scriptures and of recent events in Palestine, appeals to the king for affirmation of the truth he speaks. Agrippa, though seemingly impressed, evades a direct answer to Paul's invitation.

The audience ended, Agrippa agrees that Paul is innocent of wrong and speculates that Paul might be freed had not the appeal to Caesar been made.

Special points.—This is an audience, not a trial, before Agrippa. Festus' purpose was to honor Agrippa and secure help in formulating a statement to Caesar.

Agrippa's reply (v. 28) "almost thou persuadest me to be a Christian" was a clever evasion. What did he mean? Many believe it was a sincere expression of interest. However, a more accurate translation of the Greek would indicate it was a frivolous rebuke made in jest— "in this short a time, do you think to make *me* a Christian?" Whether impressed by his message or not, Agrippa is convinced of his innocence.

Luke has detailed the events of the last four chapters to make a strong point for his contemporary readers and for posterity. Here is the evidence that all the Roman authorities associated with the case, Commander Lysias, Governors Felix and Festus, and King Agrippa have affirmed Paul's innocence. Neither Paul nor Christianity are to be judged guilty of any crime against the Roman Empire or the Jews!

Truth for today.—Paul "never got over" being saved! Again and again he told the story of his conversion on the Damascus road. Whatever the situation, it was an opportunity for Paul to say, "A most wonderful thing has happened to me. I have met the living Lord and been converted. What has happened to me can happen to you!"

How often we excuse our failure to witness because of "limited knowledge and training." But Christianity is basically a *personal experience with Jesus Christ to be shared,* rather than a body of fact to be taught or an argument to be won. If it has *happened* to you, you *can* share it with someone else!

Paul Shipwrecked Enroute to Rome (Acts 27:1–44)

The passage.—Paul, the prisoner, with two attendants (Luke and Aristarchus) begin the journey to Rome in custody of a centurion, Julius. At Sidon Julius grants Paul shore leave to visit friends. At Myra (southern coast of Asia Minor) they switch to a ship from Alexandria carrying a cargo of grain bound for Italy.

Enroute, the ship is driven off course in a winter storm. When all hope is abandoned, Paul tells the despondent sailors of his vision and God's promise to deliver all to safety. When the ship is wrecked on a shoal the centurion prevents the soldiers from killing Paul and other prisoners. All 276 persons aboard make it safely to shore.

Special points.—Luke was with Paul in Caesarea and accompanies him to Rome. It is believed that Luke wrote his gospel and gathered material for the first portion of Acts while in Caesarea.

The two-year sojourn in Caesarea offered opportunity to visit Jerusalem and Galilee to talk with companions of Jesus, and to collect firsthand information. Mary, the mother of Jesus, may have been still living. From her lips Luke probably heard her own story of Jesus' birth, childhood and life. This "shipwreck" chapter in Acts is prime evidence of Luke's thoroughness and competency as a historian. Luke's accuracy in the details of the voyage is one of the best descriptions of ancient seafaring that we have.

The Euroclydon (v. 14), the name of a northeast wind. Under certain conditions, typhonic winds sweep down from Crete's great mountain range (more than 7,000 feet high) to drive ships into the open sea toward North Africa.

Truth for today.—"Contrary winds," a parable of Paul's life—and ours! Paul had many advantages (a religious upbringing, Roman citizenship, good education, superior mind, etc.). He also had many personal handicaps (a thorn in the flesh, periods of physical illness, and severe mental depression, etc.). He experienced great success *and* tragic defeat. He was shipwrecked, beaten, jailed, falsely accused, and finally executed. Yet he did not groan in his infirmities, but rather gloried in them. He saw life not in pieces, but as one whole pattern of cloth. "God works all things into a design of good for his obedient child" (Rom. 8:28).

Life is not all fair weather for the Christian. There are contrary winds. For some there are periods of illness or chronic invalidism. Everyone wants a happy family, but not all will have it. All could wish for economic security, but jobs will be lost and resources depleted. But it is not what happens to us that is really significant—but *how we respond* to what happens. With Christ we can face the "contrary winds."

On to Rome (Acts 28:1–31)

The passage.—They are shipwrecked on Melita (Malta) where Paul miraculously escapes death from a viper, heals the father of the Roman official, and cures many diseases.

After three months, Paul's party sails to Puteoli, the port serving Rome. Here Paul visits a Christian congregation and then sets out for Rome. Enroute, two congregations from Rome welcome him.

In Rome, Paul is permitted to live in a private apartment though chained to a guard. He enjoys a great freedom to preach, write, and receive visitors. Immediately Paul calls the local Jewish leaders together, puts his case before them and requests a hearing of all the Jews.

When they gather Paul speaks to them all day of Jesus. As some refuse to believe, Paul condemns their blindness by quoting Isaiah. When they turn away, Paul pronounces a judgment that because of the Jews' refusal, from henceforth, God has sent salvation to the Gentiles.

While Paul waits two years for his case to be called, he preaches and teaches the gospel *unhindered*.

Special points.—Peter in Rome? If Peter had already come to Rome the Jews would not have turned to Paul for an authentic word about this "sect" (v. 22). Christianity started in Rome many years before, apparently without any apostolic leadership. Granted, it is possible that Peter *later* came to Rome after the initial persecution under Nero. But the evidence is against Peter *founding* Rome or *preceding* Paul to Rome.

To this period (A.D. 59–61) is generally assigned the writing of Philippians, Colossians, Philemon, and Ephesians.

Acts ends without recording the fate of the great apostle. What was his end? Was he found guilty and executed?

Most scholars believe that, this time, Paul was acquitted. Perhaps because the papers were lost in the shipwreck and no Jews came from Jerusalem to press charges, he was automatically freed at the end of two years. Many believed he realized his dream of evangelizing Spain. Later, he was arrested in Macedonia. This time, the conditions of his imprisonment were extremely severe (reflected in some phrases of his prison epistles). By then, Nero had unleashed his furious persecution of Christians.

Whether there were one or two imprisonments in Rome, tradition affirms that he died a martyr. As a Roman citizen, Paul's death penalty was by sword. Tradition places him in the Mamertine Prison adjacent to the Roman forum, a site that can be visited today. It is believed that Paul was executed on the Ostian Way outside the walls of Rome at a spot very near where a church, *St. Paul's Without the Walls* now stands. Paul was probably beheaded under Nero shortly after the great fire in A.D. 64.

Truth for today.—"Openly and unhindered" (v. 31, RSV) with these two words, Luke concludes Acts and thus fulfils his purpose in writing. He has shown how Christianity moved across all barriers to become universal in all dimensions. The Jews have excluded themselves by unbelief. The Judaizers have within themselves the seeds of their own destruction. The glorious gospel now offers salvation by repentance and faith in Jesus Christ to "every one that believeth" (Rom. 1:16). The book of Acts closes with Paul "preaching the kingdom of God and teaching about the Lord Jesus Christ quite openly and unhindered" (v. 31, RSV). What an epitaph for a life, whether Paul's or ours!

ROMANS

Fred L. Fisher

INTRODUCTION

If we take Paul's statement at face value, he wrote this letter to tell the church at Rome of his desire to visit them (1:10–15) and to enlist their support for his mission to Spain (15:24). But the letter is far too long for this simple purpose. We must suppose another, unstated purpose in the mind of Paul.

I think his primary purpose was to set out his missionary message in some detail. He was unknown at Rome except by a number of personal friends (chap. 16). If he were to enlist their support, he needed to reassure them about his gospel.

Consequently, this letter contains the best summary of Christian theology ever written. In it, we see the full meaning of the gospel as it was preached in the early churches.

The theme of the letter is faith-righteousness, i.e., a righteousness that comes by faith alone. The first great section (1:18—8:39) discusses the need, the reception, the ethical power, and the glory of faith-righteousness.

The second section (chaps. 9–11) discusses the place of Israel in God's redemptive purpose.

The last major section deals with the living expression of faith-righteousness in worship, in church life, in social life, and in love for weaker brethren (12:1—15:13).

The introduction is long (1:1–17) and the conclusion longer (15:14—16:27).

Scholars agree that Paul wrote the letter from Corinth in A.D. 57 or 58.

The Introduction (Rom. 1:1–17)

The passage.—Paul introduced himself and his gospel (vv. 1–7), informed the Romans of his prayers for them (vv. 8–9), spoke of his desire to come to Rome (vv. 10–15), and stated the power of the gospel message (vv. 16–17). He unconsciously revealed himself to be a man of deep love and great devotion to the cause of Christ and the gospel.

Special points.—Verses 2–4 make use of an early Christian confession, developed before Paul. It contains words that Paul did not ordinarily use, but its theology was his as well as that of earlier Christian communities. By its use, Paul sought to reassure the Romans of his orthodoxy. His faith was like theirs.

Faith was a common word with Paul. It means the believing surrender of self to Christ as *Lord*. The New Testament calls Jesus "Savior" only a few times, "Lord" hundreds of times. To have faith means to accept the lordship of Christ over all of life, to become his slave (cf. v. 1).

Righteousness and *justification* (kindred words) are often used by Paul in Romans and Galatians. To the Jews, justification was acceptance with God on the basis of good works. Paul borrowed the words. They still expressed man's acceptance with God, but the basis of that acceptance was grace acting through faith. These words meant the same thing to Paul as conversion and the new birth mean to us. God forgives the man of faith and accepts him into his fellowship. At the same time he creates in the believer a new disposition of heart. This is why we have called this righteousness, faith-righteousness.

The Gentiles' Need (Rom. 1:18–32)

The passage.—The universal need of faith-righteousness is discussed in 1:18—3:20. Both Jews and Gentiles are liable to God's judgment (3:19).

God's wrath is revealed (in the gospel) against men who persist in sin (v. 18). The Gentiles stand condemned, not because they have not heard the gospel, but because they have ignored the light they have, i.e., the light of nature (vv. 19–20) and of their own consciousness (cf. 2:14–16). Because they have light, their sin is without excuse (v. 20).

Four steps to doom are set forth in this passage. (1) Rejection of what is known about God (vv. 19–20). (2) Substitution of false gods (vv. 22–23). (3) A personal and social debasement (vv. 24–31). (4) The approval of wrong instead of the right (v. 32), i.e., spiritual blindness.

Special points.—The light which the Gentiles have is not sufficient to save; it is only sufficient to condemn. Paul believed the Gentiles were condemned because they did not live up to the light which they had.

The practice of sins is the judgment of God on *sin*. The sins which the Gentiles committed are strangely modern. Paul said this was a part of God's judgment on men who rejected him (vv. 24,26,28). There is pleasure in sin, but there is debasement and degradation as well. The man who lives a life of sin is already experiencing a foretaste of hell.

Truth for today.—Why should we preach the gospel to the heathen? Paul answered that question here. They are lost; they are doomed. Salvation comes only through Christ. The Christian's duty is to preach the gospel to the whole world.

The sins of the Gentiles were both spiritual and physical, both respectable and disreputable. Our modern tendency to limit our thought of sinful action to such things as sexual license, drunkenness, and murder stands condemned. Paul included these, but he also mentioned such personal sins as covetousness, envy, insolence, pride, boasting, and foolishness. He added such social sins as strife, deceit, spite, and slander. Sin includes any act *or* attitude which is contrary to the rulership of God in our lives.

The Case of the Jews (Rom. 2:1—3:20)

The passage.—An imaginary Jew, listening to Paul's condemnation of the Gentiles says, "Amen, Amen." This is Paul's "straw man" who often appears in this letter. Paul conducted a sort of running debate with him. Here, he replies, "You have no excuse . . . because . . . you are doing the very same things" (2:1, RSV).

How shocked the Jew must have been, yet it was true. He committed the same sins as the Gentiles, but in a more refined way. Instead of robbing men by force, he cheated them with guile. Instead of committing adultery with a harlot, he practiced serial marriage.

Paul said God is no respecter of persons (2:1–11). Not the possession of the law, but the practice of it, counts with God (vv. 11–16). The Jews, who claimed to be teachers of the law, had caused God's name to be blasphemed by their conduct (vv. 17–24). True religion is a matter of the heart (vv. 25–29).

The Jew, because he had the law, had a greater advantage, but he also had a heavier responsibility (3:1–8). The Old Testament confirms the sinfulness of the Jew (vv. 9–18).

All men stand liable to God, without excuse for their sin (v. 19). The law cannot save; it can only give a knowledge of sin (v. 20).

Special points.—Romans 2:14–15 should be read as a parenthesis. Let verse 16 follow verse 13 and the meaning will be much clearer. Paul was presenting a hypothetical case, not stating that some Gentiles actually kept the law.

Truth for today.—Religion is a matter of the inner man. This is just as true today as it was in Paul's day (cf. 2:28–29). Jesus taught that religion must come from the inside out (Matt. 20:1–15). In the eyes of God, our attitudes are more important than our actions.

The Jew incurred greater guilt for his sin because his revelation of God was superior to that of the Gentiles. What would Paul say about men in Christian lands who have access to the gospel and reject it? Surely, he would say that their condemnation was the greatest of all. Superior knowledge always brings greater responsibility.

Summary of the Gospel (Rom. 3:21–31)

The passage.—The gospel is set forth in four main points. Faith-righteousness is revealed (v. 21); it is received by faith (v. 22). It comes by grace (vv. 22b–24a); it is based on the sacrifice of Christ on the cross (vv. 24b–26).

Four things result from the gospel. (1) Boasting and self-righteousness is utterly excluded (v. 27). (2) The law of Moses as a means of approach to

God has been superseded (v. 28). (3) God is a universal God, offering salvation to the Jew and Gentile alike (vv. 29–30). (4) The ideal reign of God (i.e., "The Law") has been established (v. 31).

Special points.—Spiritual knowledge comes in a different way than other kinds of knowledge. It comes by revelation (v. 21). No amount of human study or argument can discover, verify, or disprove the gospel. It must be accepted by faith. This does not mean that the gospel is irrational, but that it is suprarational, i.e., beyond reason.

Verse 23 says that all men have come short of the "glory" of God. An attractive interpretation of "glory" is "expectation." Glory comes from a word which means "to seem" or "to appear." No man could ever achieve a glory like God's even if he did not sin. Seemingly, Paul meant that man, when he sinned, failed to measure up to what God expected of him. This is another way of saying that sin is without excuse. Whether this is correct or not, "all men" have personally sinned and this is why they stand condemned.

Verses 24b–26 speak of the cross of Christ and its meaning for all ages. His cross is "an expiation by his blood, to be received by faith" (RSV. The KJV is confusing at this point). The cross explains how a just God can accept sinners: their sins are covered by the blood of Christ. It also explains how God could forgive sinners in the past: the cross covered their sins also. We might say that God saved them on credit.

"The law" (v. 31) stands for what we might call "law and order," I think. It is God's rule in human hearts, not a system of law. Grace does not permit men to sin with impunity. It changes men so they willingly submit to the rule of God. Only grace can establish God's law.

Saved Through Faith (Rom. 4:1–25)

The passage.—Paul's "straw man" asked about Abraham (v. 1). If salvation is by faith, how was his case to be viewed? Paul answered that he was saved by faith just as all men are.

Both the Old Testament account of his justification (vv. 2–5) and the witness of the Psalms (vv. 6–8) testify to the fact that Abraham's salvation and that of all men is through faith.

Abraham was justified (cf. Gen. 15:6) before he was circumcised (cf. Gen. 17:10). This proves that he was justified by faith (vv. 9–12).

Legalistic systems of any kind are contrary to faith (vv. 13–17). The two are opposite and opposed to each other. The kind of faith that Abraham had is the kind that is now required of men who wish to be saved (vv. 18–25).

Special points.—Salvation is always by faith—the same way in all ages. The law was never meant to be a way of salvation; it demanded what man could not deliver—perfect obedience. Grace demands only that we surrender in faith.

In verse 3, it is said that Abraham's *faith* was counted for righteousness. This is the common New Testament way of speaking of justification. It is not, as many say, the transferring of Christ's righteousness to us. The Bible never says this. Our faith is counted for righteousness; it is accepted by God as if it were actually righteousness. Faith as submission of self to God is the germ of righteousness; God counts the beginning as the completed righteousness. Since faith itself is a gift of God; salvation in its entirety is still by grace.

In verses 13–17, there are a number of great words: promise, faith, right-

eousness, heirs, and grace. Opposed to them are words connected with a legalistic system: law, works, wrath, condemnation, and merit. The two systems can never be mixed. If salvation is by grace, it can never *in any degree* be by works.

"Who calleth those things that be not as though they were" (v. 17) refers to creation as the act of God. The words reflect the language of Isaiah 48:13 where the connection with creation is clear.

Abraham is a great example of faith. He believed God when there was no human basis for believing (v. 18). He did not stagger at God's promises even though his advanced age and the deadness of Sarah's womb made them seem impossible (vv. 19–20, RSV. The variant text followed by KJV would make Abraham's faith a blind faith. The text followed by the RSV is much to be preferred). He was fully persuaded that God could and would do what he had promised (v. 27).

Truth for today.—We often doubt the promises of God; they seem impossible to us. This is unchristian; God has often proved that he is able to do what he promises. Our faith should be like that of Abraham. We should consider all the reasons why God cannot fulfil his promises and then "against hope" believe. If we could see how God could fulfil his promises, there would be no need for us to have faith.

The Experiences of Life Transformed by Faith-Righteousness (Rom. 5:1–11)

The passage.—Acceptance with God brings peace, i.e., serenity and wholeness of life (v. 1). It transforms the experiences of life (vv. 2–5) and gives the Christian assurance of heart (vv. 6–11).

Special points.—A textual problem at

verse 1 influences the interpretation of verses 2–5. "We have peace" should really be "let us continue to have peace" (NEB). In the light of this, every instance of "we rejoice" should be translated, "Let us rejoice." The whole passage consists of exhortations, not statements.

The Christian should not develop a martyr complex. He should rejoice in his sufferings (vv. 3–5), but not because they are good in themselves. Rather he should rejoice because they produce spiritual growth. Knowing this, the Christian should rejoice in his sufferings, i.e., the pressures of life whether physical, mental, or spiritual.

Christian assurance comes from a consideration of the facts (vv. 6–11). God loved us enough when we were sinners to send his Son to die for us (vv. 6–8). He saved us when we were sinners and completely unworthy. "Much more" now that we are his children, he will preserve us from falling. This is one of the greatest passages on Christian assurance in the New Testament.

Truth for today.—A complaining Christian is an abomination to the Lord. We should not complain about our lot in life. Christian character can only be grown in the thick of battle. We must have struggles and difficulties, even temptations, if we are to become strong. Instead of complaining, we should rejoice in the power that gives us victory over trouble and temptation —power from God.

Cost of Salvation (Rom. 5:12–21)

The passage.—In a series of comparisons and contrasts between Adam and Christ, Paul pointed to the act of Christ on the cross as the cost of our salvation. Adam, as the instigator of human sin, acts only as the dark background against which the wonder of God's grace in Jesus Christ is presented. Paul used this comparison to show how incomparably greater is God's grace than his condemnation of man. The recurring chorus is "much more" (vv. 15, 17,20).

The primary proof of the greatness of God's grace is that the obedient death of Christ "leads to acquittal and life for all men" (v. 18b, RSV). Of course, this is true only if the sacrifice of Christ is met with personal faith.

Special points.—In verse 12, Paul began his comparison between Christ and Adam. The comparison was never finished. The dash at the end of verse 12 (RSV) indicates that Paul had more to add.

Many scholars think that Paul taught that all of Adam's descendants are held responsible for Adam's sin and condemned because of it. This is far from true. Paul had already (1:18—3:20) presented his case for the condemnation of the world. It is quite clear that each man is condemned for his own personal sin, not for the sin of Adam.

However, Adam was the first sinner. He introduced sin into the world. He polluted the stream of human life. All men sin by personal choice when they sin, but their sin is rooted in an inborn tendency to rebel against all authority, even God's. It is the tendency to sin, not sin itself, that comes from Adam.

Ethical Power of Salvation (Rom. 6:1—7:6)

The passage.—Paul had seemingly argued himself into a corner. If grace abounds where sin abounds, sin would seem to be desirable. Not so, said Paul (6:1).

The practice of sin by a Christian is ruled out by the nature of salvation (v. 2), and by the implications of baptism (vv. 3–4). The nature of salvation makes continuance in sin a spiritual absurdity (vv. 5–7). The defeat of sin by Christ has made us "dead to sin" (vv. 8–11). Therefore the Christian should not let sin reign in his life (vv. 12–14).

Again the question is raised—is grace a license to sin (v. 15)? Again the answer is, no. The meaning of life is determined by the power which rules it (vv. 16–18). Both sin and righteousness are personified as a power in this passage. The Christian life is a yielding of our whole selves to righteousness, i.e., to God (vv. 19–20). Submission to sin leads to death; submission to God leads to eternal life (vv. 21–23).

The analogy of marriage illustrates the new position of the Christian (7:1–6). Natural death ends the obligation of the woman to her husband. Spiritual death abolishes the claim of law and sin on us.

Special points.—Baptism (6:3–4) is a symbol, a symbol which portrays the death of the Christian to sin. It is a public symbol which promises and prophesies a new kind of life. To be "baptized into Jesus Christ," "into his death," and "into death" means to be baptized with reference to these things as past events. Thus baptism is a dynamic symbol which has meaning for the new Christian. It helps to strengthen his determination to live a new life. It is not essential to salvation: it is essential to a full Christian life.

"The body of Christ" (7:4) refers, I think, to the actual body of Christ, i.e., to his death on the cross. Some have taken it to refer to the church, but this does not fit this context. Paul was saying, "You Christians died to the law in the death of Christ." Our life now, because of the cross, is a life of freedom from the law's power.

Truth for today.—Living a Christian life is much more than merely avoiding sin. It is a positive yielding of ourselves to God as tools for his use. The sinlessness of Jesus was never described in negative terms in the New Testament. His sinlessness was positive. He was a man approved of God; he went about doing good. Christian righteousness must be of the same nature. When we let God use our lives in the promotion of righteousness we can be said to be living a truly Christian life.

The Futility of Legalism (Rom. 7:7–25)

The passage.—Paul used his own life as a Pharisee (seen through the eyes of a Christian) to illustrate the futility of a legalistic attempt to become righteous. Personifying sin throughout, he said that sin used the law to produce death (vv. 7–13). Indwelling sin made it impossible for him to achieve the righteousness which he desired (vv. 14–20). Life under the law led to despair, a despair from which only Christ can deliver one (vv. 21–25).

Special points.—Verse 7 tells of the passage of Paul from a state of innocence to accountability before God. Paul knew the law before it spoke directly to him. Then, one day, as he was in the act of desiring something others had, the law said, "Thou shalt not covet." For the first time, he realized he was a sinner. The law had made him to *know* sin.

Some interpreters differ, but I think it is quite clear that Paul was speaking of the struggle of the non-Christian in this chapter. His words contain a thinly veiled reference to his own futile struggle for righteousness. This is indicated by the note of despair with which the chapter ends. The Christian must also struggle against sin, but his struggle can end in victory; in Christ he has the resources of victory (cf. Gal. 5:17).

Truth for today.—All men desire a higher life, a life of acceptance with God. We must not approach the unconverted as if there were no striving for good in them. We must help men to see that Jesus is the answer to their own striving. Only then will they accept him. What man cannot achieve by his own efforts, God can bestow by his wonderful grace.

The Glory of the New Life (Rom. 8:1–39)

The passage.—This is one of the great chapters of the Bible. It begins with "no condemnation" (v. 1) and ends with "no separation" (v. 39). It defies description and needs to be read over and over until its surpassing message grips our hearts and souls. The new life is a life of liberty from the law of sin and death (vv. 1–8). It is a life of glorious hope (vv. 9–25), hope of the resurrection, hope of joint-heirship with Christ, and hope of final redemption. The new life is a life of glorious power (vv. 26–39). This power comes through spirit-led prayer and the providence of God. It enables us to face the future without fear.

Special points.—Christ has ended the tyranny of sin (vv. 3–4). The law was weak because we, with our sinful nature, could not obey it. Christ, coming in the likeness of sinful men, condemned sin. That is, he broke its power in human life; he knocked it off its perch. As a result of his work, the righteous requirements of the law are fulfilled in the Christian's life. They are fulfilled because we live by the Holy Spirit rather than depending on human resources.

How does the Holy Spirit help us in our praying (vv. 26–27)? He does not pray for us, but enters into our hearts and enables us to pray as we should and for what we should.

Verse 28 does not teach that all things are good. It teaches that God combines all life's experiences "for good" in the Christian life. The "good" is defined in verse 29; it is being "conformed to the image" of Christ (RSV). This happens only when we meet the experiences of life with love for God; it is not true automatically.

Verses 29–30 describe the sweep of salvation from eternity to eternity. It begins in eternity past with the foreknowledge and predestination of God. It continues in the present with God's calling and justification. It reaches into the eternity of the future in our glorification. All of this is spoken of dramatically as if it had already taken place. All of it is rooted in God's grace and initiative.

How can we be "more than conquerors" (v. 37)? To avoid spiritual hurt by the experiences of life is to conquer them. To use even the adverse circumstances of life for spiritual advancement is to be a superconqueror. Paul spoke from experience; he had faced the troubles he enumerated (v. 35) and used them for his own spiritual advancement.

Truth for today.—Paul looked upon himself as expendable in the service of God (v. 36). We should do the same. We often fail because we are too concerned about what will happen to us. The main thing is what will happen to the gospel; we are expendable. Only by losing our lives can we find their full meaning.

Israel's Unbelief (Rom. 9:1–29)

The passage.—Israel's unbelief was a problem to Paul and his "straw man." If Christianity was God's way of salvation, why had the Jews not accepted it?

The "straw man" felt that God owed the Jews priority over the Gentiles. Paul denied this but longed for the salvation of his own people.

The discussion of the problem goes through chapter 11. In this section, Paul asserted that the unbelief of the Jews did not mean that God had broken his promises. First, Paul asserted his own intense pain at the unbelief of the Jews (vv. 1–5) but denied that God owed the Jews anything (vv. 6–29).

God's election is by sovereign choice; it is not based on human circumstances. This was true in the case of Isaac and Ishmael (vv. 7–9), of Jacob and Esau (vv. 10–13), and of Moses and Pharaoh (vv. 14–17). Both wrath and mercy are results of God's own choice without reference to human merit or demerit (v. 18).

Paul refused to question God; God can do what he wishes with his own creatures (vv. 19–21). However, God has actually dealt with men with long-suffering (vv. 22–29).

Special points.—"Osee" (v. 25) is the archaic spelling of Hosea (cf. RSV).

In this section, Paul spoke only of man's *role in history.* Thus, it can be said that God made certain men "vessels of wrath . . . for destruction" (v. 22, RSV). The predestination of men to personal salvation is discussed in Romans 8:28–30. God never predestines any man to eternal damnation, but he does use evil men for historical purposes against their will.

Israel's Rejection (Rom. 9:30—10:21)

The passage.—Israel's rejection is due to her stubbornness. She sought salvation through legalistic works and did not submit to Christ (9:30—10:4). The law method can never work; it demands what man cannot do—perfect obedience from the cradle to the grave (v.

5). The faith method can work; man can do what it asks (vv. 8–10). The faith method makes salvation possible for all men (vv. 11–13).

Universal salvation demands universal proclamation of the gospel (vv. 14–15). Israel has indeed heard, but she hardened her heart against God (vv. 16–21). This is why she has been rejected by God.

Special points.—Paul was speaking of the Jewish nation as a whole, as a nation. Many individual Jews, among them Paul, had believed. This section explains why Israel *as a nation* was rejected of God, once and for all time. She had refused to listen to God; she was no longer a fit "vessel" for his grace.

Verses 9–10 show evidence of being a pre-Pauline formula of salvation. Paul used it because he agreed with it. Salvation demands two things which are really one. (1) Heart-belief is demanded. This is the kind of belief that makes the resurrection of Christ personal and real. (2) Confession is demanded. One must confess that "Jesus is Lord" (RSV). This confession would be primarily to the Lord, but also to men when possible. Secret discipleship is not encouraged in the New Testament. The confession would ordinarily be with words of the mouth, but it needs to be confirmed by the actions of life.

God's Rejection of Israel Is Neither Total nor Final (Rom. 11:1–36)

The passage.—Paul himself was proof that God had saved a remnant of Israel (vv. 1–6) even though the majority of the nation remained in unbelief (vv. 7–10).

God's rejection is not final. Even the salvation of the Gentiles will be used to arouse Israel to jealousy (vv. 11–16).

Under the figure of the olive tree, Paul asserted that the way was still open for Israel to return (vv. 17–24). He believed that someday God's promises would be fulfilled in the salvation of "all Israel" (vv. 25–32). (Some interpreters hold that "all Israel" here refers to Christians as "the true Israel of God." See Gal. 3:26–29; Rom. 9:6; and comments below.)

The greatness of God's grace and wisdom so filled the heart of Paul that he burst forth in a majestic doxology of praise (vv. 33–36).

Special points.—The olive tree (v. 17) represents true religion. This religion is found in Jewish heritage and tradition. With this in mind, the illustration is clear, but the horticulture bad.

The expression, "All Israel shall be saved" (v. 26) is a logical conclusion based on the rest of the chapter. The question is the meaning of "all" and of "Israel." *All* need not be given absolute meaning; it is often used in the Bible in the sense of a large portion (cf. 1 Kings 12:1; Matt. 2:3; 3:5). *Israel* could be the new Israel and mean simply "Christians." This is attractive, but the context rules it out. Paul, I think, meant that through God's redemptive purpose which included the mission to the Gentiles and the return of individual Jews, the majority of the Jews would eventually be saved by faith in Christ.

Faith-Righteousness Changes Life (Rom. 12:1–21)

The passage.—Christianity is a gospel of salvation; it is also a way of life. This chapter is a part of Paul's discussion of the living expression of faith-righteousness (12:1—15:13). It is based on the presentation of God's grace in the previous chapters and assumes that the Christian life is an obedient response to God's grace.

The first and most important response is meaningful worship (vv. 1–2). True worship consists of total self-surrender.

The second response is vital participation in church life. Christians should recognize their dependence upon one another (vv. 3–5). They should use the gifts which God has given them for the good of others (vv. 6–8). They should practice real love in all personal relationships (vv. 9–21).

Special points.—What is true worship? Paul believed it was total self-surrender to God (vv. 1–2). "Worship" (RSV) is a better translation than "service." "Spiritual" (RSV) is not a good translation of the Greek behind "reasonable." The word was meant to describe the worshiper as a rational being. The expression could be paraphrased: "This is the only kind of worship God will accept from a rational being."

What the Christian offers should be determined by what God wants—himself, his whole life ("bodies" had this meaning for Paul). His offering is a thank offering. A sin offering is not needed; Christ has already made that.

What is the proper relation between fellow Christians? Paul felt it should be one of interdependence. No Christian is an island; he must be vitally related to other Christians to give full meaning to his life (vv. 3–5). Paul used the figure of the "body" to illustrate this. The primary emphasis of the figure (in this passage) is that each church member must depend on all other members.

Verse 18 teaches that peace is an expression of love. We are to seek to live at peace with all men. If peace is not possible, we are to see to it that the fault is not ours (cf. RSV, "so far as it depends on you").

"Heap coals of fire on his head" (v. 20) does not mean to "get even" by doing good. Moffatt correctly paraphrases: "For in this way you will make him feel a burning sense of shame." The aim is to restore harmony and thus "overcome evil with good" (v. 21).

Truth for today.—What is the relation of church services to worship? If worship is giving one's whole life, going to church is certainly not all there is to it. We might think of the *essence* of worship as total self-dedication. The *expression* of worship consists of the things we do to show our dedication. The *sustenance* of worship is what is required to maintain a high level of dedication.

Going to church gives opportunity to express our dedication and should help to sustain it at a high level. There is a vital relation between church participation and the worship of God. However, we must not limit our thought of what real worship means to that. All of life must be worship if any of it is to be.

The Christian in Society (Rom. 13:1–14)

The passage.—The Christian is not only related to God and his fellow Christians; he is also a part of human society. He is related to the government of his nation and must obey and support it (vv. 1–7). Every man is his neighbor and must be loved by the Christian (vv. 8–10). The Christian lives in a sinful world and must keep separate from it; he must live his life in the light of eternity (vv. 11–14).

Special points.—Civil government (i.e., the higher powers) was evil in Paul's day; Nero was the Roman emperor. Yet, Paul regarded it as ordained of God. Bad government is better than no government. The Christian should obey its laws (if prior commitment to God permits, v. 1) and pay his taxes (v. 5).

Why? (1) The government was "from God" (RSV); to resist it is to resist God. (2) Obedience was essential to avoid the wrath of civil powers. (3) Obedience was the only way to a consciousness of doing right (v. 5).

We "owe" it to our neighbor to love him (v. 8). Love fulfils all that the law of Moses requires in human relationships. Paul suggested that we should "owe" him nothing else. Our modern "credit life" makes this difficult, but even if we cannot obey Paul's first admonition, we should obey the second.

Verse 11 states that our salvation is nearer than when we first believed. How can this be true? If one has salvation already, how can it be nearer? The answer is found in the ways in which the word "salvation" is used in the New Testament. Sometimes it refers to the beginning of salvation, conversion. Sometimes it refers to our growth in grace. Sometimes, as here, it refers to our full salvation in heaven. Paul meant that the coming of Christ was nearer. Hence, our full salvation was also nearer.

Truth for today.—Christian citizenship has a wider meaning for us than it did for Paul. He lived under an evil dictatorship; his duty was to obey and pay taxes. Of course, he obeyed only if obedience did not contradict his prior commitment to God. We, however, have the privilege of sharing in the process of government. Intelligent participation in government is our Christian duty.

Love Among Brethren (Rom. 14:1—15: 13)

The passage.—In the Roman church there was a difference of opinion about the demands of devotion to Christ. Some felt that they must be vegetarians (14:2), honor certain days above others

(v. 5), and abstain from wine (v. 21). Paul called this group "weak in faith" (v. 1).

Others ate meat, regarded all days as equally belonging to God, and drank wine. Paul was obviously on the side of these stronger Christians. However, he felt that love and respect should control Christian attitudes in such a situation.

Each group should respect the other for the devotion to Christ that led to their decisions on these matters (vv. 1–4).

Each is to be convinced in his own mind of the rightness of his decision (v. 5). All actions are to be dictated by devotion to Christ (vv. 6–9). No one is judge to another; God will judge all (vv. 10–14).

Love for the weaker brother means that nothing should be done to injure him (vv. 15–23). The strong should seek the good of the weak, not his own pleasure (15:1–2). This is the way to follow the example of Christ (vv. 3–6) and respond to the grace of God (vv. 7–13).

Special points.—The problem at Rome was not eating meat offered to idols as in Corinth. The weak could not eat meat at all without feeling condemned.

Paul was obviously on the side of those who looked on each day as alike (14:5; cf., 15:1). This does not mean that all days are to be used in the same way. Our habit of using Sunday for religious activity is good. But religion is more than religious activity. It is using the whole of life for God. Thus Monday and every other day of the week should be equally devoted to God.

There is a vital relation between being "fully persuaded" (14:5b) and "whatsoever is not of faith is sin" (14:23b). Acting without faith is acting without being convinced that what we do is right. If one believes that what he does is wrong, it is wrong to him. He is acting in a rebellious spirit.

Truth for today.—Many use 14:23b to imply that anything is right if we think it is. They say all moral decisions are relative. This is far from the thought of Paul. He was speaking of things which were not sinful in themselves. There are many things which are sinful under any circumstance—spite, envy, murder, adultery, and such things. Thinking these things are right does not make it so. Thinking something is wrong, even if it is not, makes it so however.

Reasons for Writing (Rom. 15:14–33)

The passage.—Paul said he had no intention of correcting the theology of the Romans; they did not need that (v. 14). He wrote to remind them of his own special commission and work (vv. 15–21).

Circumstances had made it possible for him to visit them and he hoped to enlist their support for a mission to Spain (vv. 22–24). He must first complete the ministry of relief for the poor at Jerusalem (vv. 25–28). The Romans were urged to become his missionary partners through intercessory prayer (vv. 29–32). Verse 33 is a second benediction (cf. 15:13).

Special points.—Paul described his ministry in sacrificial language (vv. 16–19). He was the Levite who helped to prepare the sacrifice to be offered to God. Christ, the High Priest, would make the offering after it had been sanctified (set apart) by the Holy Spirit. Paul felt it to be a great privilege to be a part of God's redemptive work.

Paul hoped to go to Rome. He did, but not in the way he had hoped. He went as a prisoner rather than as a free man. We do not know for certain that he ever achieved his dream of a mission in Spain. Some slight evidence seems to indicate that he may have.

Truth for today.—The Romans were blessed by being able to be missionary partners with Paul. We are blessed in our privilege of being partners with our missionaries. This partnership should have two dimensions: financial support and intercessory prayer. By a proper stewardship of our money and our prayer life, we can become world missionaries.

Personal Greetings (Rom. 16:1–23)

The passage.—Great leaders are needed in Christian work. The faithful labor of many unknown Christians is of equal importance. This has always been true. Paul mentioned 33 fellow laborers in this chapter. Some of them were with him; some were at Rome. Most of them are unknown to us. They are not mentioned anywhere else in the New Testament. This reminds us that many unknown Christians contributed their share to the spread of Christianity in the first century.

Truth for today.—The complimentary things that Paul said about his fellow workers are instructive: "a succourer of many" (v. 2), "my helpers" (v. 3), "risked their necks" (v. 4, RSV), "bestowed much labor on us" (v. 6), "labored in the Lord" (v. 12), "beloved" (many times). These were the kind of things Paul valued in Christians. Perhaps we need to strive for such qualities rather than for some of the things we do strive for.

Final Benediction (Rom. 16:25–27)

The passage.—This is one of the most exalted benedictions in the New Testament.

Special points.—The presence of two previous benedictions (15:13,33) has led some to think this letter was sent to various churches with different endings. Many think that 15:33 is the conclusion of the copy sent to Rome. Chapter 16 would then be the ending of the copy sent to Ephesus where some of the workers mentioned were located. Some textual evidence to support this opinion exists, but the proof is not conclusive. For all practical purposes, we can think of the letter as sent to Rome in its present form.

1 CORINTHIANS

Fred L. Fisher

INTRODUCTION

The church at Corinth, established only five years before this letter was written, was a young church with many problems. We are able, as we study, to sit in on the meetings of this infant church.

The church had written Paul about some of their problems (cf. 7:1). Paul had learned of other problems from reports by mutual friends (cf. 1:11; 5:1).

The first section of the letter (1:10—6:20) deals with the problems of which Paul had heard. They were four in number: lack of unity, laxity in church discipline, litigation between Christians in pagan courts, and the danger of sexual licentiousness.

The second major section of the letter (7:1—15:58) deals with the problems about which the church had written. They are five in number: marriage, eating meat offered to idols, proper order in church services, spiritual gifts, and the bodily resurrection of Christians.

Why so many problems in one church? One reason was the youth of the church. Most of the problems concerning which they wrote showed a lack of understanding of the ethical and religious implications of the gospel.

Another reason was the location of the church in the wicked city of Corinth. Most of the problems which Paul treated in the first section arose from this. The city was one of the most wicked in the ancient world. The Christians were influenced by the low moral standards of a pagan society. They had to be warned against compromise.

Corinth also took delight in intellectual things. They were superficially wise; they were sophists. Their delight in eloquence and wisdom influenced the church. The church tried to turn the gospel into a system of wisdom. They had to be warned against trying to compete with the world on its own terms.

Neither the Pauline authorship nor the approximate date (A.D. 55) is in question.

Introduction (1 Cor. 1:1–9)

The passage.—Paul respected a church because it belonged to Jesus Christ. In spite of all that was wrong at Corinth, he called them "the church of God," "sanctified," and "called to be saints" (v. 2). He also reminded them that they were a part of a larger fellowship of all Christians everywhere (v. 2b).

As in most of his epistles, Paul found much for which to express thanksgiving (vv. 4–9). He was grateful for their salvation (vv. 4–6) and for their spiritual enrichment (vv. 5,7–9).

Special points.—An "apostle" was a messenger, a man on a mission for another. The twelve were apostles; so were many others. Paul was an apostle; he gave his credentials of apostleship in chapter 9.

"Called" meant more to Paul than being invited. It meant that God had moved in such a way as to produce faith in man's heart. It was God's act in time by which he made effective his predestination to salvation from eternity.

Paul anticipated his discussion of spiritual gifts in chapters 12–14 by speaking of the spiritual enrichment of the Corinthians. They lacked nothing. They did not need to supplement their gifts by seeking to excel in human wisdom. The gifts which the Spirit gives are those which all Christians should desire.

"Confirm" (vv. 6,8) means to take root or be established. The Corinthians had established the truth of the gospel in their own experience of salvation. Christ would continue to confirm their salvation "unto the end."

Folly of Dissensions (1 Cor. 1:10–31)

The passage.—The church had differences of opinion ("dissensions," RSV). "Divisions" is too strong. Though Peter, Apollos, and Paul were in accord, various groups had identified their opinion with one or the other. Paul condemned the dissensions themselves, not any particular group. Dissensions implied that Christ could be divided (v. 13*a*), that each leader had a portion of truth. Or it implied that men could replace Christ (vv. 13*b*-17).

The gospel is not a system of human wisdom, but a divine power (vv. 18–25). This is why it is a riddle to a perishing world but a saving power to believers. Attempting to compete with the pseudointellectuality of Corinth would degrade the gospel itself.

Paul insisted that the membership of the church at Corinth proved his point (vv. 26–31). The scarcity of aristocrats, political leaders, and philosophers among them showed that their faith rested on the power of God, not human wisdom.

Special points.—Paul did not look down on Christian baptism. Verse 17 expresses his sense of priorities. His primary mission was to preach the gospel.

He did sometimes baptize believers. He was glad that he had not baptized many in Corinth lest they might think that he was trying to replace Christ.

"The preaching" of the cross (v. 18) means the thing preached, not the act of preaching. The gospel with the cross as its central message can be communicated in various ways.

In verse 20, "wise" is a general term. "Scribe" denotes the Jewish wise man, "debater" (RSV) the Greek wise man.

Verse 27 tells us that God used the foolish and weak (from a worldly viewpoint) to "put to shame" (RSV) the wise and mighty. In other words, when God saved the weak and foolish, he showed up the vanity of human wisdom and power. Only God's grace can bring salvation.

"Sanctification" and "redemption" are two figures of speech meaning the same thing (v. 30). Each looks on salvation from a different viewpoint. "Redemption" means that salvation is due to the price God paid on the cross. "Sanctification" means that we are made the people of God; we belong to him. Many different words are used in the New Testament to describe the one experience of salvation.

The Source of True Wisdom (1 Cor. 2:1—3:4)

The passage.—The pattern and method of Paul's ministry in Corinth had been determined by the nature of the gospel (2:1–5). He preached in plain and simple terms, refusing to use oratory and persuasive arguments. The results had been a demonstration of God's power.

Wisdom itself is not bad; God's wisdom is to be desired. The gospel is a wisdom to mature Christians (v. 6). This wisdom comes only from God (vv. 10–13) and can be understood only by

**22. Sycamore tree at Jericho
(see Luke 19:1–10)**

men who have the Holy Spirit (vv. 14–16).

This was why the Corinthians were still ignorant of the gospel as wisdom (3:1–4). They remained spiritual babes who had to be fed with milk (vv. 1–2). They still looked on things in a purely human way (vv. 3–4).

Special points.—"Mystery" (2:7) was a word Paul borrowed from pagan religions and transformed. It meant something previously hidden but now revealed to all Christians in Jesus Christ.

Chapter 2, verse 9 does not refer to heaven but to the blessings of the gospel. These blessings can only be known by revelation.

"The rulers of this age" (2:8, RSV) probably refers to Jewish and Roman rulers who combined to put Jesus to death. If spiritual rulers are meant, it is only as they used earthly rulers as instruments of their evil designs.

"Comparing spiritual things with spiritual" (v. 13) probably means combining gospel truths into a system of thought. Paul did this in words "taught" (RSV) by the Holy Spirit. The Spirit helped him choose the right words to communicate the gospel to men.

"The mind of Christ" (v. 16) is probably a synonym for the Holy Spirit. Paul meant that his message came from God.

Truth for today.—Paul's description of his ministry (vv. 1–5) should be our guide in witnessing for Christ. We often try to compete with the world on its

723

own terms. We want to be respected, recognized, and placed with the learned. It is better to use simple language to present the gospel. Witnessing is meant to lead men to Christ. Superficial eloquence, pretensions of wisdom, and efforts to be plausible often hide Christ.

Human Leaders (1 Cor. 3:5—4:5)

The passage.—Apostles and teachers are agents through whom God works to accomplish his redemption. Paul illustrated this by the relation between his work and that of Apollos (3:5–9).

However, ministers are responsible to God. If they build on the wrong foundation or use inadequate materials, they will suffer loss (vv. 10–15). If they destroy God's temple, the church, they will be destroyed (vv. 16–17).

The Corinthians should not glorify ministers. They belong to the church since their mission is to enrich the church (vv. 18–23). Christians should never think of themselves as belonging to men.

God alone can judge ministers. His commendation alone is worth having. Ministers are stewards. Faithfulness is required of them (4:1–5).

Special points.—The "reward" (3:8) of the Christian minister is participation in the joy of Christ (cf. Matt. 25:21). This happens both here and hereafter. Each servant of Christ will participate in his joy to the extent to which they have labored.

"Labourers together with God" (3:9) does not mean that Paul and God were partners. Paul and Apollos were partners; they belonged to God. "With God" should be translated as "belonging to God."

Paul preached Christ crucified (2:1–5) and so laid the foundation of the church (3:11). Every church is built upon the foundation of the work of Jesus on earth.

"Revealed by fire" (v. 13) is a symbol of the final judgment day. The adequacy of materials used by the minister will be shown by whether they burn or not.

"Saved: yet so as by fire" (v. 15) pictures a man rushing through the flames to escape a burning building. This whole discussion means that men are saved by grace but rewarded according to works.

The church—the people not the building—is God's temple (v. 16). The pagan temple contained an *image* of a god, the Jewish temple a *symbol* of God's presence, the Christian temple, *God himself.*

"Judged" (4:3) is used in the usual sense of bringing to judgment. Men may and should have opinions about the fitness of their ministers. In the final analysis, only God's judgment counts.

Truth for today.—A church is important to God. We tend to see our church's failings and fail to see its glory. We should strive to make our church what it truly is—a dwelling place for God.

In 4:5, Paul insisted that the absence of a guilty conscience did not mean that he was acquitted by God. We dare not assume that God is pleased with us just because we are pleased with ourselves.

An Appeal for Unity (1 Cor. 4:6–21)

The passage.—His argument over, Paul turned to pleading. His application of what he had said about ministers to himself and Apollos was meant to help them live as they should (vv. 6–7). Their feeling of self-sufficiency was entirely false (vv. 8–13). Paul made this clear in an ironic comparison of their imagined exaltation and his real humiliation.

As spiritual father of the church, i.e., its founder, Paul pled for unity. He admonished the church as a whole (vv. 14–17). He closed with a stern rebuke of the arrogant few who refused to follow his leadership (vv. 18–21).

Special points.—"In a figure transferred" (v. 6) means simply that Paul had applied the principles of Christian ministry to himself and Apollos (cf. RSV).

"Fools for Christ's sake" (v. 10) reminds us of 1:18. The gospel was considered to be folly by the world, the men who preached it fools. Paul was willing to be thought a fool by men for the sake of Christ.

Church Discipline Needed (1 Cor. 5:1–13)

The passage.—Sexual laxity was a mark of life in the Roman Empire of that day. It took a great deal to shock a pagan; yet, one Corinthian had done just that. He was practicing incest with his father's wife—probably his stepmother. The church, though not condoning this, refused to condemn it. Paul reprimanded them (vv. 1–2) and admonished them to excommunicate the sinful brother (vv. 3–5). Compromise here could well lead to the corruption of the whole church (vv. 6–9).

In verses 9–13, he corrected a false impression about a former letter (mentioned only here in the New Testament). He had not meant that they should avoid contact with worldly men; this was impossible. He had meant that they should discipline their own members.

Special points.—Paul had already "judged" the offender (v. 3). He felt they should discipline the man, but he did not order them to do it. This says much for the self-government of local congregations in apostolic times.

To Paul, excommunication delivered a man to Satan (v. 5). The redeemed society was under the rule of God, the unredeemed under the rule of Satan. He hoped such action by the church would lead to the destruction of the man's sinful inclination—the flesh. This, in turn, would lead to his ultimate salvation.

Truth for today.—Church discipline should be two-pronged. Our primary concern is discipline that helps people to grow to maturity in Christ. Sometimes, however, when a member's behavior becomes a public scandal, his church should exclude him. This is the only way the church can guard its reputation in the community. We promote righteousness; we should not condone evil in our midst.

Litigation Among Christians (1 Cor. 6:1–11)

The passage.—Disputes among brethren should be settled by appeal to brethren (vv. 1–6). In a series of rhetorical questions Paul made this point. Lawsuits mean spiritual defeat, no matter what the outcome (vv. 7–8).

The Corinthians were changed men in their relationship to God (vv. 9–11). They should manifest this in the way they acted in settling disputes.

Special points.—We do not know what Paul meant by saying the "saints" would "judge the world" and "angels" (vv. 2–3). It could mean that Christians would condemn them by their lives. It probably meant that Christians would share in the future reign of Christ. The Corinthians surely understood Paul; we do not.

"Least esteemed" (v. 6) means the lowliest church member. Even such a one is better qualified to judge fairly than the most esteemed in a sinful world.

Verse 7 teaches that being defrauded is better than a lawsuit with a brother. Paul did not mean to enunciate a general rule against lawsuits; what he said is usually true. The point is that we should seek settlement out of court. If such a settlement is impossible, we should forgive our brother and win him with love.

"Sanctified" and "justified" (v. 11) are two ways of saying the same thing. Sanctified means that we belong to God. Justified means we are accepted by God. Both terms describe something of what it means to become a Christian.

Sexual License (1 Cor. 6:12–20)

The passage.—What is the relation of faith to morality, of religious devotion to behavior? Paul's discussion of sexual license illustrates the relation.

The passage is difficult to analyze. Three motifs run through it. (1) Christian liberty, though real, is not license. My liberty must always be limited by my good, the good of others, and my devotion to Christ. (2) Man was made for the Lord, not immorality. He should seek those higher things that glorify God. (3) Sexual license is self-destructive. Sexual intercourse unites two people. If one belongs to the Lord, he should not unite himself to a harlot.

Special points.—"All things are lawful to me" (v. 12) was a teaching of Paul, but the Corinthians had misunderstood it. They took it to mean that liberty had no limits. He had meant that the Christian was free from the legalistic requirements of the law, especially that they could eat what they wished.

The "body" for Paul was man's total self as living in the world. Substitute "I" or "man" for "body" in this passage and you will understand it better.

Verse 18 raises many problems. Paul said that sexual license was self-destructive while other sins were not. Yet, surely murder is also self-destructive. We must limit the thought

to this context. Paul was comparing sexual license with purely physical acts such as eating. His point was that sex is more than physical.

Truth for today.—Pagans seek to control their gods; Christians seek to be controlled by God. Thus, for Christians, religion and morality are two sides of the same coin. Actions cannot be divorced from devotion. We are God's temple.

Christian Marriage (1 Cor. 7:1–40)

The passage.—Paul recognized the need for most men to marry (vv. 1–2). He gave good advice about mutual sexual relations between husband and wife (vv. 3–9). Though divorce was contrary to Christ's teaching (vv. 10–11), separation was permissible if an unbeliever (vv. 12–16).

Men should not be concerned with changing outward circumstances (vv. 17–24). The impending distress (v. 26) meant that Christians should no longer be absorbed in worldly things. They should live with full devotion to God (vv. 25–31).

To remain unmarried was better, but marriage is permissible (vv. 32–35). Fathers should arrange marriages for their daughters if it were proper (vv. 36–38). My interpretation agrees with ASV against RSV.

The Christian widow should remain unmarried; but, if she marries, it must be with a Christian (vv. 39–40). Paul insisted that all that he had said was by the Spirit of God (v. 40*b*).

Special points.—Paul was not a soured old bachelor who knew nothing of the problems of a common man (cf. related passages, Rom. 7:4; Eph. 5:21–33; 2 Cor. 11:2). He dealt with the problems of Christian marriage with sympathy and understanding. Much of what he said is dated—it pertained only to the situation at Corinth. Much is permanently valid.

He certainly thought that it was better for a Christian to remain unmarried (vv. 1,8,26,38,40). But he believed that marriage was good (vv. 2,9,38). He knew that most men and women would be tempted to sexual sin if they did not marry. For such, it was better to marry than to burn with lust (cf. v. 9).

Sometimes Paul quoted the teaching of Jesus (cf. v. 10, "Not I, but the Lord"). Sometimes he spoke without specific quotations (cf. v. 12, "I, not the Lord"). Yet, even then, he was giving Spirit-led advice (cf. vv. 25,40b). In both cases he spoke with divine authority.

Verse 14 indicates that an unbeliever is "sanctified" by a believing husband or wife. "Sanctified" means to be put aside for the Lord. Usually it refers to salvation, but not in this case. I think it means that the home is made Christian by having one Christian in it. The unbeliever in a Christian home had a privileged position; he was sanctified. He could see the power of Christ in his mate.

Truth for today.—A Christian must put Christ and his work first in his life. One way of doing this is to form no human alliances at all, to keep himself completely for Christ. Another way, the only possible way for most Christians, is to form human alliances only with those who share their dedication to Christ. When both are dedicated Christians, marriage need not interfere with full devotion to Christ. Indeed, it may very well promote and enhance it.

Love or Liberty (1 Cor. 8:1–13)

The passage.—Whether to eat meat which had first been sacrificed to idols was a real problem at Corinth. This chapter begins Paul's discussion of the problem (cf. 8:1—11:1). Most meat on pagan markets had been sacrificed when butchered. To a weak Christian, eating this meat was an act of worship directed toward the idol. Emancipated Christians saw it only as good meat; to them an idol was nothing.

This chapter contains the guiding principle—love should control Christian freedom (vv. 1–13). The welfare of the weaker brother should be the primary concern. Love is superior to knowledge (vv. 1–3). There is no sin in eating such meat (vv. 4–6). Nevertheless, brotherly love should control Christian actions (vv. 7–13).

Special points.—"Perish" (v. 11) does not mean that the weaker brother would go to hell. It means his Christian life would be shipwrecked.

Two things should be noted. (1) The action in question was not sinful in itself. Paul did not teach that a Christian was free to sin. (2) The effect on the weaker brother was to cause him to sin. By doing something he considered wrong, he acted in a spirit of rebellion. It was not a question of being criticized; it was a question of being followed. To avoid leading another into sin, personal rights should be surrendered.

Truth for today.—Each Christian is responsible for his influence on others. Loving concern for others should guide us in our actions. My freedom ends where my brother's good begins.

Love in Action (1 Cor. 9:1–27)

The passage.—Paul illustrated the demands of love by three examples in his own life. (1) Since he wanted to make the gospel free of charge (v. 18, RSV), he had not claimed his apostolic right to financial support (vv. 1–18).

(2) Since he wanted to win men to Christ, he willingly became their slave

when it was necessary (vv. 19–23). He adapted himself to the customs and tastes of others.

(3) Since he did not want to be disqualified for service to Christ, he practiced self-discipline (vv. 24–27).

Special points.—Verse 5 lists one of Paul's rights as an apostle, the "right" (RSV) to be accompanied by a Christian wife (cf. RSV). Both Paul and other apostles had this right, but Paul did not demand it.

Verse 17 means that Paul did not become an apostle by personal choice (i.e., "of my own will," RSV). He was called and commissioned by God. He deserved no credit for preaching the gospel; he had to do it (v. 16).

Paul did not expect to win "all" men (v. 22); he knew he would fail in some cases. This was why he was not discouraged by his failure to win "all."

Truth for today.—The Christian minister has a right to support from those to whom he ministers (vv. 8–14). Paul's action should not be taken to mean that all ministers should support themselves. Later, Paul apologized to the Corinthians for not demanding support (2 Cor. 12:13).

Idolatry and Wisdom (1 Cor. 10:1—11:1)

The passage.—Israel, in spite of her great privileges, was led into idolatry (vv. 1–13). This should warn the church against over self-confidence (v. 12). On this basis, Paul forbade participation in pagan religious festivals (vv. 14–21). Such action was fellowship "with devils" (v. 20) and should be avoided.

Practical wisdom should operate in ordinary social contacts (vv. 23–30). Since no sin was involved, meat which was offered could be eaten without scruple. However, if eating meat threatened the welfare of another, it should be avoided.

All things should be done for the glory of God (10:31). The Corinthians should follow Paul's example in avoiding offense to others (10:32—11:1).

Special points.—Verses 16–17 should be compared with 11:17–34 to understand Paul's doctrine of the Lord's Supper. Here, he said that participation involved a real participation in Christ. This participation, I think, is created by our faith, not by the mere act of eating.

In verse 24, "wealth" means spiritual good (cf. RSV).

First Corinthians 10:27–33 does not mean that we are to relax our opinions on such things as alcoholic beverages to avoid offense. The teaching applies only to things which are not sinful in themselves.

Truth for today.—The Christian's life should be wholly controlled by his devotion to God (10:31). Devotion does not allow us to divide our lives into segments. What we do at work, at play, and at home is just as much a part of our religion as what we do at church. All of life is religious when it is lived under the lordship of Christ.

The Veiling of Women (1 Cor. 11:2–16)

The passage.—In Paul's day, women were regarded as little more than slaves to their husbands. Only slaves and harlots went unveiled in public. Christian women were told that they were equal with men in Christ (Gal. 3:28). Perhaps they resented being forced to conform to social customs; yet, they had not rebelled (v. 2).

Paul insisted that they should conform and remain veiled in church (vv. 3–12). He based his opinion on a series of subordinations which he felt justified the social custom (he was a child of his day also). He also appealed to their sense of what was proper (vv. 13–16, RSV).

Truth for today.—Though the exact instructions of Paul no longer apply, the principles do. A Christian woman should dress sensibly and becomingly. She should avoid anything that would shock the sensibilities of society. It is more important to give a good testimony to Christ than to exercise freedom.

The Lord's Supper (1 Cor. 11:17–34)

The passage.—The Lord's Supper was often preceded by a love feast, perhaps a potluck supper. In Corinth, the rich brought food and drink and partook of it alone, even becoming drunk. The have-nots (poor men and slaves) had nothing to eat. Such behavior prevented a meaningful observance of the Lord's Supper (v. 20).

Paul condemned their selfishness and said their church meetings were harmful rather than good (vv. 17–22). He reminded them of the meaning Christ had given the Supper (vv. 23–26 is the oldest written record of its institution).

Self-examination and brotherly love should insure worthy participation in the ordinance (vv. 27–32).

Special points.—Paul received his knowledge of the Supper from the "Lord" (v. 23). This may or may not refer to a direct revelation from Christ. It probably means that Paul received his knowledge *indirectly,* through others.

"Remembrance" (v. 24) meant more to the Jews than recalling an ancient event. It meant bringing the past into the present. The Lord's Supper should be a dynamic remembrance of Christ—his death, his lordship, and his second coming. This is the meaning of participation.

"Unworthily" (v. 27) is an adverb; it describes the manner of partaking of the Supper. Many have turned this into an adjective and insisted that one must be *worthy* if he is to partake. This is not the meaning; no one is ever worthy. We can and should partake in a worthy manner.

Verse 29 insists that each Christian examine himself before partaking of the Supper. Self-examination prevents the judgment of the Lord. (Note that "judgment" is a more accurate translation than "damnation" in the KJV.) The verse has nothing to say about "open" and "closed" communion.

Verse 30 is not to be taken as a general rule. One who partakes of the Supper unworthily will not necessarily suffer sickness nor death. Paul interpreted some recent sicknesses and deaths in Corinth as judgments of the Lord. We may accept that as true without insisting that the same thing always happens elsewhere.

Truth for today.—Partaking of the Lord's Supper should be a dynamic spiritual experience. This can be true only if we act responsibly in faith. The service itself may encourage or hinder creative faith. Each church should see to it that the external arrangements of the service encourages real participation.

The Church, a Spiritual Organism (1 Cor. 12:1–31)

The passage.—The Corinthians had many spiritual gifts (cf. 1:7), but they were not using them in a Christian way. They wrote Paul for help (v. 1). This chapter is the beginning of his treatment of the subject (12:1—14:40).

Paul reminded them that they were a spiritual organism. Each member had his own function; each member depended on every other member for completeness. Boasting was excluded because the gifts were *gifts* of the Holy Spirit (vv. 4–11). The Spirit had made them one body in Christ (vv. 1–3,12–13). Each member had a different function, but his gift was to be used for the benefit of all (vv. 14–26). Mutual service, not uniformity of gifts, was what counted (vv. 27–31).

Special points.—No one can become

a Christian without the work of the Holy Spirit (v. 3). His work is both necessary and effective.

The purpose of all gifts is the "common good" (v. 7, RSV). No gift is given for one's own benefit or enjoyment.

Spiritual gifts are distributed according to the sovereign choice of the Holy Spirit (v. 11). We cannot earn them, but we can pray for them and be ready to use them when they are given.

Water baptism depends on the prior work of the Holy Spirit for its meaning (v. 13). The Spirit brings the sinner to Christ; he makes the convert one with the Christian congregation. The unity of the church as well as the conversion of the individual is publicly affirmed in baptism.

Verse 27 makes it clear that Paul called the local congregation at Corinth the "body of Christ." Paul used this vivid metaphor to teach that each church should be a reincarnation of Christ, a means by which he lives in the place where that church exists.

Truth for today.—Why do modern Christians, especially Baptists, have so little to say about spiritual gifts? (See the discussion on chapter 14 of the nature of "tongues" and "prophecy.") Perhaps we have overreacted against those who have gone to excess on the Holy Spirit. Perhaps we have become too self-reliant, depending on methods and mechanics rather than on the power of God. Neither reason is a good one. We should realize our need for spiritual power. We should pray for the gifts of the Holy Spirit. No one can serve effectively without them.

Love Is Supreme (1 Cor. 13:1–13)

The passage.—Chapter 13 continues the discussion of spiritual gifts from chapter 12. This hymn in honor of Christian love is in three stanzas. (1) Love is indispensable to the Christian

life (vv. 1–3). (2) Love is Christlike. Christian love is outgoing, self-giving, unselfish concern for others (vv. 4–7). (3) Love is the greatest of gifts (vv. 8–13). It outlives the gifts essential to service—prophecy and knowledge. It is the greatest of the three enduring gifts —faith, hope, and love.

Special points.—"Tongues of angels" (v. 1) may be the exalted language that extraordinary men spoke. It could simply point to something men cannot attain.

Imperfect things will be superseded by perfect things in the future world of fellowship with God (v. 10).

Tongues or Prophecy (1 Cor. 14:1–40)

The passage.—The gift of prophecy is superior to the gift of tongues. Prophecy ministers to all the church (vv. 1–5). Tongues minister only to the individual (vv. 6–12). Prophecy enables the "outsider" to understand; tongues only confuse him (vv. 13–19). Thus, prophecy convicts men of sin (vv. 20–23).

Church services should be orderly (vv. 26–33a). Each should be allowed to make his contribution. Each should take his turn in speaking. Each should seek the good of all.

Women should keep silence in church and seek instruction from their husbands at home (vv. 33b-40). Paul's instructions constitute a command of the Lord (vv. 37–38). Verses 39–40 summarize the chapter.

Special points.—What were the "tongues" at Corinth? What is the relation to modern glossalalia—speaking in tongues? Some passages favor the belief that the tongues were a form of ecstatic speech: only God understood them (14:2); the speaker did not understand what he said (14:14). "Tongues of angels" (13:1) may refer to the phenomenon.

Other evidence supports the theory

that "tongues" were unlearned human languages. Tongues commonly meant a human language (Rev. 5:9; 7:9). "To interpret" (12:10,30; 14:5,13,26,27,28) commonly meant to translate a foreign language (Acts 9:36; John 1:39,43; 9:7; Heb. 7:2). The discussion of tongues at Pentecost supports this idea (Acts 2:1–11). Tongues were meant as a sign for "unbelievers" (14:22) which would favor the idea that they were languages which the unbeliever could understand.

In view of the divided evidence, no one can be dogmatic. I would favor the position that the tongues were unlearned foreign languages meant to be used on the docks at Corinth to witness to the host of sailors from all over the world. In that context, they had meaning. In church services, where all spoke Greek, they were "unknown tongues."

In either case, modern "speaking in tongues" can hardly be the same as that at Corinth. Modern "speakers" usually insist that the gift is indispensable or at least superior; Paul said it was neither universal nor superior. Moderns speak in tongues only in church or in private; Paul said they were signs for unbelievers (14:22). Moderns seem unable to control their speaking; Paul said it could be controlled (14:27–28).

The gift had very limited meaning in New Testament times and none today. Paul considered it a genuine gift of the Holy Spirit (12:10), but he considered it to be the lowest of all gifts (12:10,28). It is not mentioned in other New Testament lists of spiritual gifts (cf. Rom. 12:6–8; 1 Pet. 4:10–11).

What was a Christian prophet? He was one who received his message directly from God and explained the meaning of Christ and the gospel. He differed from the modern preacher in the source of his message. The preacher interprets the Bible; the prophet spoke with direct authority. He differed from

the apostle in the content of his message. The apostle gave eyewitness testimony to the resurrection of Jesus; the prophet explained God's will and the meaning of Christ's lordship.

There is no modern equivalent to the New Testament prophet. The need for this gift vanished with the completion of the New Testament. The distinguishing mark of the prophet was a message received directly from God. False prophets could arise so the gift of distinguishing the spirits (1 Cor. 12:10) was necessary.

The admonition to silence for women (vv. 34–35) was probably due to some disorder in the church at Corinth. We do not know the background, so we are not sure of Paul's meaning. Possibly some women were insisting on speaking when they had nothing to say. I do not think this passage applies to our modern church services.

Resurrection of the Dead (1 Cor. 15:1–58)

The passage.—Bodily resurrection is a great Christian hope. Some in Corinth seemed to believe that the resurrection was spiritual only and that it happened at the death of the Christian (v. 12).

Paul gave four arguments for the fact of the resurrection. (1) It is essential to the gospel (vv. 1–11). (2) The resurrection of Christ insures that of believers (vv. 12–20). (3) It is essential to the completion of God's purpose for the world (vv. 21–26). (4) Hope for the resurrection gives meaning to Christian devotion and suffering (vv. 29–34).

One who questions the resurrection because he cannot understand the nature of the resurrection body is foolish (vv. 35–36a). The resurrection body will have continuity with our present body but will be different (vv. 36–41). It will be a spiritual, imperishable body (vv. 42–49), being victorious over sin (vv. 50–57).

The resurrection hope should inspire Christian steadfastness (v. 58).

Special points.—One of the oldest Christian confessions is found in verses 3–5. Paul quoted it as the substance of his message and the Corinthians' belief.

Christ as the "firstfruits" of the dead (v. 20) is a figure which means that his resurrection guarantees our resurrection.

The prescribed order of the resurrection (vv. 22–24) is Christ first, then believers at his coming. Paul did not mention any interval of time nor the resurrection of unbelievers. He was concerned only with Christian hope.

Many interpretations have been given to the "baptism for the dead" (v. 29). Some interpretations, such as vicarious baptism to insure the salvation of the dead, are completely unchristian. I think the best interpretation is that Christian converts were baptized with reference to their own future resurrection. This was one meaning of baptism. Paul's point was that their baptism made them subject to persecution. If their hope was vain, their action in being baptized was foolish.

Truth for today.—We are pilgrims in this present world. Our hope is for a better, future life. Every decision, every act should be made in the light of eternity as well as of time. We should be concerned about our present life and surroundings, but our concern should not be limited to these. The future hope means that our labor *now* is not in vain.

Our devotion to Christ should not waver because we do not understand all about the future life. We know enough now to meet our spiritual needs. Other things will be made clear later.

The Conclusion (1 Cor. 16:1–24)

The passage.—Paul instructed the Corinthians about their collection for the poor (vv. 1–3) and shared his plans

for the administration of the gift (vv. 3–4). Various personal notes follow (vv. 5–18), followed by various greetings (vv. 19–20). A curse is pronounced on those who do not love the Lord (v. 22). Blessings are asked for the believers (vv. 23–24).

Special points.—Paul taught proportionate and systematic giving (vv. 1–2). The tithe is not mentioned, but Paul, no doubt, had it in mind. Tithing was required of the Jews; nothing less would be worthy of Christians.

Paul spoke of the "refreshing" of his spirit through Stephanas and Fortunatus and Achaicus (v. 18). Their coming had shown Paul that the church was really concerned about him and wanted his advice. This had renewed his spirit. It had renewed his courage.

The "kiss" (v. 20) was the customary way of greeting in that day as it is in some countries today. "Holy" means that it was a Christian greeting. Peter called it the kiss of love (1 Pet. 5:14). The thought is not so much that they would kiss each other, but that one of them would kiss the rest in the name of Paul. This mode of greeting has been superseded for us by the handshake.

"Anathema" (v. 22) means to set aside as accursed, to regard as such. Lack of love for Christ showed that they were already under the curse of God. The church was to regulate its regard by reality. This malediction was directed toward the professing church members. Outsiders were already regarded thus.

"Maranatha" (v. 22) is a prayer. It means, "Lord come." Such a prayer may have been used at the Lord's Supper asking the Lord to come and bless the service. It is more likely that it was a general prayer for his final coming at the end of time (cf. Rev. 22:20). The second coming of Christ was a living hope in first-century Christianity.

2 CORINTHIANS

Fred L. Fisher

INTRODUCTION

After Paul wrote 1 Corinthians, trouble from outside arose at Corinth. Some traveling Jewish preachers, mercenaries, attempted to usurp authority over the church. They attacked Paul and accused him of being vacillating (1:17-18), a braggart (3:1), and thirsty for power (10:8).

Paul visited Corinth but failed to correct matters (2:1). He then wrote a painful letter (2:4) which Titus took as his emissary.

When Titus returned and reported that peace had been restored at Corinth, Paul wrote this letter. Unfortunately, a rebellious minority still remained in the church and refused reconciliation.

This letter has three major divisions. Chapters 1–7 is Paul's defense of his relations with the church at Corinth. Chapters 8–9 is an urgent plea for liberality in the offering for the poor in Jerusalem. Chapters 10–13 is an entreaty to the church in the light of the rebellious minority.

Is this a composite letter? Many have thought so. Arguments for the view are based on the threefold division of the letter, neither part depending on the other. The theory is that some later Christian gathered parts of three different letters and published them as one. Nothing would be lost to faith if this view were accepted.

However, no external evidence exists to support the theory. All Greek texts of the letter present it in its entirety. The diversity of subject can be explained from the background. Thus, there is an increasing number of scholars who regard the letter as a unity. I think this is the proper conclusion and my comments will be based on that belief.

Introduction (2 Cor. 1:1–11)

The passage.—Paul's salutation and blessing (vv. 1–2) is followed by a prayer of thanksgiving for God's deliverance from great peril (vv. 3–7). Paul had evidently encountered some grave peril recently in which he had despaired of his life (vv. 8–11).

Special points.—Paul called himself an *apostle* of Jesus Christ (v. 1). An apostle was a commissioned messenger. A number of disciples, other than the twelve, are called apostles in the New Testament. "Jesus Christ" identified Paul's principal. He spoke for Christ and his words were to be accepted as from Christ.

Change of Plans (2 Cor. 1:12—2:12)

The passage.—In reply to some slurs, Paul insisted that he had always been open and sincere with the Corinthians (1:12–14). His promised visit had not been made, but he reminded them that his plans were subject to God's will (1:15–22).

Further, he had determined not to come on another painful visit. He had waited for Titus to return and assure him of their reconciliation (1:23—2:4).

The admonition to forgive the sinful brother is related to the accusation that he was fickle (2:5–11). True, he had

733

urged them to punish the offender; now he wished to join them in forgiving him. In this way, Satan's designs would be thwarted (v. 11).

His premature departure from Troas was a sign of his concern for them (vv. 12–13). A great opportunity had arisen there, but Paul could find no peace of mind until he heard from Corinth. He had left Troas and gone to Macedonia to await Titus.

Special points.—"Boasting" (1:12, RSV) belongs to a group of words used 29 times in this letter. By contrast, they appear only 26 times in the rest of Paul's letters. The reason is that Paul's opponents boasted much. Their boasting was marked by pride and insincerity. Paul also boasted, but his boasting was centered in the grace of God. Thus, it was proper boasting.

To Paul, Satan was real and his designs evil (2:11). A spirit of unforgiveness would allow Satan to gain the upper hand over the church. It would put the church in his power and shipwreck its ministry.

Truth for today.—Evil gains power over us when we do wrong *and* when we fail to do right. Failure to do right is the most common sin of Christians.

Sufficiency from God (2 Cor. 2:14—3:6)

The passage.—This section opens Paul's discussion of his ministry (2:14—6:10). Paul surveyed the implications of his ministry and asked, "Who is sufficient?" (2:16b). His answer: "Our sufficiency is of God" (3:5b).

When the gospel is preached, men *must* decide; their decisions determine their destinies. Human resources are insufficient to meet the demands of the ministry (2:14–17).

Other teachers need letters of recommendation; Paul's opponents had them. He needed none. The Corinthians themselves were his commendation (3:1–3). Their salvation proved beyond doubt the divine source of his ministry.

Special points.—"Leads us in triumph" (2:14, RSV) translates a word based on the triumphal processions of conquering Roman generals. What did Paul think was his part in the triumphal procession of God? Was he a captive or a soldier? Either is possible. However, in view of his delight in calling himself a slave of Christ, it would seem that he considered himself to be the captive of God. He was not destined for execution but for service. God had made him an apostle.

Paul was a minister of a *new* covenant, new in quality and thus superior (3:6). The old (RSV wrongly adds "code") was written on stones; the new is of the Spirit. The old brought death, the new life.

Truth for today.—It is frightening to think that our witness to Christ may harm men. If they refuse Christ, our witness becomes "a fragrance from death to death" (2:16, RSV). We dare not treat our witnessing lightly. Each of us must seek the leadership and power of God.

Glory and Glory (2 Cor. 3:7–18)

The passage.—A bright car light fades to nothing when the sun rises. So also, the glory of the law fades to nothing in the presence of the gospel. Paul did not deny the glory of Moses' ministry (v. 7). He insisted that the glory of the gospel surpassed it (vv. 8–11).

The ministry of the law led to blindness; the ministry of the gospel leads to transformed lives (vv. 12–18). The object of the paragraph is to show the superiority of the Christian ministry. If Paul boasted, it was not in himself but in the gospel.

Special points.—Verse 7b is based on

a Jewish enlargement of Exodus 34:30. The Old Testament said that Moses' face, when he returned from the Mount, shown so that the people were afraid to approach him. Jewish legend had made it say that the people "could not look at Moses' face." This splendor did not last; it was fading even as the people looked. In contrast, the gospel has a permanent splendor.

In the Christian experience, the "Lord" and the "Spirit" are indistinguishable (v. 17). Paul did not mean to identify the two theologically. He meant that when one comes to the "Lord" (i.e., Jesus), he experiences the power of the Holy Spirit. They are one in their action in the human heart.

"Beholding" (v. 18) should be translated "reflecting" (RSV margin). The usual translation seems to say that our lives are transformed by contemplation of the Lord. Our translation says that our lives are transformed by reflecting the glory of the Lord. This is in harmony with the thought of Jesus; he called his disciples "the light of the world" (Matt. 5:14).

Truth for today.—Christians are often confused by those who claim to have discovered new spiritual truth. Such claims are nonsense. Jesus is the truth. The gospel is the climax of God's revelation. We may increase our knowledge of Jesus; we can never hope to go beyond him.

Saved from Despair (2 Cor. 4:1–18)

The passage.—The key words in this chapter are: "We do not lose heart" (vv. 1,16, RSV). Though Satan could blind the hearts of some, there was nothing wrong with the gospel (vv. 1–6). The gospel was contained in "earthen vessels" (i.e., human ministers), but the power of God could overcome human weakness (v. 7). Therefore, Paul's pain-

ful experiences did not lead him to despair (vv. 8–12).

The power in Paul was the same that brought Jesus from the grave (vv. 13–15). His own natural powers were fading, but the inner man was constantly renewed (v. 16). His sufferings prepared him for unseen realities (vv. 17–18).

Special points.—"The truth" (v. 2) is always the gospel in the New Testament. The inscription of the words of Jesus, "The truth shall make you free," on public school buildings is out of place. Truth may be taught there, but not *the* truth. Only where the gospel is taught is the truth proclaimed.

Hope, Faith, and Love (2 Cor. 5:1–21)

The passage.—Starting from the words of 4:18, "the things that are unseen are eternal," Paul enlarged on the idea of Christian *hope* (vv. 1–5).

This led to a discussion of the present situation of the Christian "as away from the Lord" (vv. 6–10). This life is one of "faith" (v. 7). The minister, knowing he must face the Lord's judgment, seeks only to please the Lord (v. 10).

The idea of judgment led Paul to develop the theme of the compelling *love* of Christ as the motive of ministry (vv. 11–15).

Nothing is to be judged "after the flesh" (v. 16), that is, according to external distinctions which form the basis of men's judgments. This applies to our knowledge of Christ (v. 16), to our union with Christ (v. 17), and to our ministry of reconciliation (vv. 18–21).

Special points.—Paul believed in a glorious future life (v. 1). In comparison with our present life, the future is so glorious that one should earnestly desire it (v. 2).

What did Paul mean by being "found naked" (v. 3)? A certain answer is not possible. Plato believed that when a man died, the soul, "naked of the body," lived on. Paul did not accept this; he believed the body was an essential part of man. Disembodied existence had no more appeal to him than it does to us.

Did he believe in a resurrection immediately after death? Verse 4 seems to imply this. Yet, 1 Corinthians 15:22–23 clearly places the resurrection at the time of Christ's final coming. That plain statement must guide us in our interpretation of this verse. Paul really hoped that Christ would come while he still lived. It was the further clothing that he longed for.

What about Christians who die before Christ comes? What kind of life do they now have? Paul said nothing about that here; it is doubtful that he ever speculated about it. Any answer must be speculative; the New Testament does not tell us. It does teach that Christians who die go at once to be with the Lord. Their life with him is more blessed than life on earth (Rev. 14:13).

"After the flesh" (v. 16) means according to the external distinctions which men make (RSV wrongly translates, "from a human point of view"). Paul was not thinking of subjective judgments, but of external distinctions. These distinctions of race, sex, and culture have lost their meaning to the Christian (Col. 3:11).

The point seems to be that Paul had once judged the claims of Jesus on external grounds. He thought of him as an imposter because he did not measure up to the Jewish messianic hopes. Now, since he had become a Christian, he judged Christ by spiritual standards. By these he was proved to be the Messiah indeed.

Verse 21 does not mean that Christ actually became or was treated as a sinner. It means he took upon himself the consequences of our sin. As a result,

we may receive the consequences of his righteous act, forgiveness of sins.

Truth for today.—The Christian should not view life with reference to the transitory values of life. We must view life from the standpoint of eternal realities. The standards by which we judge life will determine our response to difficulties and disappointments.

The Christian has the task of proclaiming the gospel (v. 18). In the New Testament, this *ministry* was the common task of all Christians. Not all were prophets or apostles; all were *ministers.* This concept of the ministry of all believers desperately needs to be recaptured in our modern churches.

Admonitions (2 Cor. 6:1—7:4)

The passage.—Various and unrelated materials are contained here. There is an appeal not to accept the grace of God in vain (6:1–2). They were to hold fast to the gospel against those who preached another Jesus (cf. 11:4).

Paul pleaded for them to open their heart to him (6:11–13) after further vindicating his ministry (vv. 3–10).

They were not to be "mismated with unbelievers" (6:14—7:1, RSV). This passage should be treated as a parenthesis rather than an insertion.

Related to 6:11–13 is an additional plea for the Corinthians to open their hearts to Paul (7:2–4).

A Joyous Report (2 Cor. 7:5–16)

The passage.—Paul resumed his report of his movements and emotions prior to writing this letter (cf. 2:13). He told of his longing for the arrival of Titus and his relief at the good news he had brought (vv. 5–7).

He spoke of the painful letter which he had written (vv. 8–12). Though it had caused pain, he rejoiced that it had brought reconciliation.

FON H. SCOFIELD, JR.

23. Temple of Apollo at Corinth
(see 2 Cor. 6:14–18)

Titus' report had encouraged him (vv. 13–16); he was not discouraged. His confidence in the Corinthians had been justified.

Liberality Encouraged (2 Cor. 8:1–24)

The passage.—The church in Jerusalem had more than its share of the poor. Antioch had sent relief at least once (Acts 11:29). The Jerusalem council had asked Paul and Barnabas to remember the poor (Gal. 2:10). On his third missionary journey Paul had determined to raise a fund from the Gentile churches to help relieve the need in Jerusalem.

Chapters 8–9 contain encouragements from Paul for the Corinthians to be liberal in their gifts to this fund. In this chapter, Paul cited the example of the Macedonians (vv. 1–7) and the example of Christ (vv. 8–15) to encourage them.

He also shared his plans for the administration of the fund (vv. 16–24).

Special points.—The Macedonian Christians stand as a great example of Christian giving. They gave eagerly (v. 2) beyond their means (v. 3) and begged Paul for the privilege of giving (v. 4). Dedication to God and his work accompanied their giving of money (v. 5). No wonder Paul called their giving a result of God's grace (v. 1). He urged the Corinthians to abound in this "grace" (v. 7).

The greatest example of liberality is the gift of Christ. He was rich but became poor that we might be made rich

737

through his poverty (v. 9).

Truth for today.—Paul made careful plans for the administration of the fund (v. 21). He wanted things done honorably both in the sight of the Lord and of men. Christians and churches need to be equally careful in handling the Lord's money. Safeguards must be taken to avoid any breath of suspicion.

Further Encouragements (2 Cor. 9:1–15)

The passage.—Paul's pastoral skill is revealed in verses 1–5. He said there was really no need to write about the offering (v. 1). He told them he had bragged of them in Macedonia (v. 2). His emissaries were sent to avoid his own humiliation (vv. 3–5).

Verses 6–11 seems to be an appeal to selfishness, but it is not. Giving is not sacrifice, but sowing seed from which a rich harvest will be reaped. The harvest is spiritual however; this robs the appeal of its apparent selfishness.

The final appeal is a reminder that liberal giving leads to the glorification of God (vv. 12–15). The needs of the saints would also be relieved, but the main point is that many would be led to thank God for their offering (v. 12). (This offering would also be tangible proof of God's grace among the Gentiles. It would form a spiritual bond between Jerusalem Christians and those of the Gentile world.)

Special points.—Paul said giving was a *ministry* (v. 12, "Service" in RSV and KJV). Giving is a form of ministry to God and to others in his name. We should not think of our giving as giving to the church; we should think of our gift as a gift to God.

Verse 7 says we should not give to impress others or because of pressure to give. We should give freely. The result of such giving is the blessing of God. God "loves" all men, but often the ex-

pression of his love is blocked by the selfishness of men. The cheerful ("hilarious," Greek) giver opens the way for God to express his love in countless blessings.

Hold the Gospel Fast (2 Cor. 10:1–18)

The passage.—The closing portion of the letter (10:1—13:10) begins with this chapter. This closing section contains appeals made in the light of a rebellious minority. Though invective and defense abound, Paul really sought the upbuilding of the whole church (cf. 12:19).

Paul's opponents made five accusations against him. (1) Though he wrote severe letters, he was a coward (10:1,9,10). (2) He was a worldly man (10:2; 11:11; 12:16). (3) He was a braggart (10:8). (4) He knew he was an inferior apostle (11:5; 12:11; 13:3); failure to demand support proved this (12:13–16). (5) He was an unskilled speaker and repulsive in personal appearance (11:6; 10:10).

Paul countered with accusations of his own. His opponents were servants of Satan (11:15) preying upon the Corinthians (v. 20). They delighted in argument (10:5), boasted in other men's labors (v. 15), and were false apostles (11:13).

Yet, in spite of accusation and counteraccusation, the section is primarily an appeal to the whole church. In this chapter, he appealed to them to hold fast to the gospel as he had preached it.

His reason—he did not wish to be severe with the whole church (vv. 1–6). The basis of his appeal was that his ministry had been for their good (vv. 7–12). The purpose—he wanted his field of labor to be enlarged (vv. 13–18; esp. v. 16).

Truth for today.—The weapons of

war are determined by its nature (v. 4). The Christian's warfare is spiritual, not worldly. Thus, worldly weapons are weak and ineffective. Only spiritual weapons—prayer, preaching, and dedication—will tear down worldly strongholds and capture men for God.

Self-commendation is meaningless (v. 18). It is only when the Lord commends his servants that they may know that they are accepted with him.

Do Not Be Led Astray (2 Cor. 11:1—12:13)

The passage. Is Satan real? Paul believed he was. He asked the Corinthians not to be led astray by false apostles. He feared that they might yield to the temptations of Satan as Eve had (11:1–6).

Though Paul knew that self-commendation was foolish, he was forced to it by the claims of his opponents (11:7—12:10). Though he had not permitted them to support him, he loved the Corinthians (11:7–11). He intended to undermine the claims of the servants of Satan (vv. 12–15). He admitted that he was too weak to make slaves of them as others did (vv. 16–21*a*).

Admitting his folly (v. 21*b*), he told of his Jewish background and claimed equality with his opponents in that respect (v. 22). In Christian service, especially sufferings, he claimed superiority (vv. 23–29).

He recounted his escape from Damascus (vv. 30–33) and told of visions which were superior to those of the false apostles (12:1–6). God had guarded him against too much pride by refusing to remove his "thorn in the flesh" (vv. 7–10).

Finally, he rebuked the church for their failure to commend him and apologized for refusing to burden them with his support (vv. 11–13).

Special points.—There are two ways that Christians may be led astray—in their beliefs and in their devotion. Paul feared that the Corinthians would be led to forsake a "sincere and pure devotion to Christ" (11:3, RSV). He wanted them to remain single-minded and pure.

He also feared that they might be led astray theologically (v. 4). "Another Jesus" means the same Jesus, but preached with variations which transformed it into another gospel. "Another" spirit and gospel means one of a different kind. Paul's opponents preached the same Jesus in such a different spirit that their message became a different gospel.

Verse 12 is an obscure verse with many proposed interpretations. Paul continued to refuse support from the Corinthians; in this way he hoped to undermine the claims of his opponents. They would be found "even as we" (RSV is confusing here). Paul's opponents wanted to be thought of as superior to Paul not as working on the same terms.

The whole matter rests on the matter of financial support. The opponents took it; Paul did not. The opponents said Paul refused because he knew he was an inferior apostle. This was a very thin line of attack. The Corinthians might well see that their taking money was a sign of their selfishness.

But what did Paul mean by, "they may be found even as we"? Certainly, he did not wish to grant his opponents equality in a general sense. He was an apostle of Christ; they were the servants of Satan. A guess would be that he wished to have the Corinthians judge them and himself by the same standards —on the basis of devotion to Christ.

Evil never comes in the guise of evil; it camouflages itself as good. This is no surprise. Satan disguises himself as an angel of light (v. 14). We must learn to distinguish evil from good, not by outward appearances, but by inner reality. Anything that leads us away from full devotion to Christ is evil.

Paul mentioned his visions reluctantly and as a sign of weakness. He was caught up to the "third heaven" (12:2), that is, "paradise" (v. 4). Both expressions mean the abode of God. In Jewish cosmology, the first heaven was the abode of birds, the second the place of the stars, and the third the abode of God.

There he heard unutterable utterances which it was not lawful for him to tell (v. 4). Much conjecture has centered in the content of this revelation. The only thing that can be said with certainty is that Paul received nothing which God intended for him to communicate to others.

Truth for today.—Prayers are not always answered in the way that we desire. Paul's were not (12:8–10). He prayed three times that his "thorn in the flesh" (perhaps infected eyes) might be removed. God answered the man, but not the particular prayer. He gave Paul something better—power to serve effectively in spite of his weakness—power to overcome his handicap. God always answers the one who prays; he does not always answer his prayer. He often gives us something better than we ask for. Such "failures" in prayer should not discourage us but inspire us to a continuous life of prayer.

Paul's Next Visit (2 Cor. 12:14—13:10)

The passage.—Paul planned a third visit to Corinth. He did not want to be severe with the whole church (13:10);

he pled with them to prepare for his coming. He reminded them of the loving quality of his ministry to them (12:14–18).

He warned them that he would deal harshly with the unrepentant (12:19—13:4). He feared that he might find disorder, sin, and unrepentance among them.

He called upon them to examine themselves (13:5), to prove the reality of their conversion. He hoped that he himself would meet the test and inspire them to right living (vv. 6–7). Nothing should be done contrary to the truth (v. 8). He hoped for their Christian maturity (v. 9).

Special points.—"Reprobate" (vv. 5–6) is a word based on the testing of gold to ensure its genuineness. "Counterfeit" is our nearest equivalent. Paul hoped that the Corinthians would find that they were not "counterfeit" Christians, nor he a "counterfeit" apostle.

Conclusion (2 Cor. 13:11–14)

The passage.—The conclusion fits the letter itself. A final appeal for unity (v. 11) reflects the troubles in Corinth. There are greetings of the kind with which Paul usually concluded his letters (vv. 12–13), followed by a final benediction (v. 14).

Special points.—The final benediction (v. 14) is the one most commonly used in our churches. It embodies the Christian gospel in its essence. "Grace" finds its source in our Lord, Jesus Christ. True "love" is inspired by God. Real "fellowship" is created by the Holy Spirit.

GALATIANS

W. C. Fields

INTRODUCTION

This short letter is the great manifesto of freedom for the believer in Christ. It deals with a crucial question: Should the Christian gospel be hobbled with the paraphernalia of Judaism?

The central message is that all men are justified or made right before God in the same way. For Jew and Gentile alike, salvation is by faith in Christ. Good works are insufficient. No man can ever get enough good grades for his conduct and character to earn salvation. The theme of the letter is that faith alone frees us from the penalty of sin.

Key verse: "Freedom is what we have—Christ has set us free! Stand, then, as free men, and do not allow yourselves to become slaves again" (5:1, TEV).

The purpose of the letter is to refute the Judaizers. They were Jewish Christians who were following along in Paul's tracks misleading the newly established churches. They were teaching that Gentiles as well as Jews are saved by grace, but that they must obey the Jewish law to stay in grace. Paul writes to make it clear that the accessories of Jewish law, such as circumcision, are not prerequisites to salvation.

Author: The apostle Paul.

Audience: The churches of the province of Galatia in Asia Minor. They were established by Paul on his first missionary journey.

Date: Probably around A.D. 49, either before or after the Council of Jerusalem described in Acts 15. Some scholars argue for a later date, however.

Occasion: Paul is shocked that "so soon" after leaving them he has received word that they are straying away from his teachings to follow the Judaizers (1:6).

The place of writing was probably either Antioch before leaving on his second missionary trip, or Ephesus during that trip.

The letter was a favorite of Martin Luther. It was a major source of inspiration for the Protestant Reformation in the sixteenth century. It is still a witness to the fact that the gospel of Christ leads to liberation, not bondage.

Paul's Introduction (Gal. 1:1–5)

The letter opens abruptly without the cordiality expressed in his other letters. It contains no commendation, no thanksgiving or prayer for them. Compare the introduction to Philippians. In both letters to the believers at Corinth he rejoices over them in spite of their bickering and partisanship. But not here!

Paul immediately states the two main issues: (1) his authority as a divinely appointed apostle, and (2) faith as the only basis for salvation. Apparently his enemies, the Judaizers, had attempted to undermine his teachings by telling the Galatian churches that Paul was not one of the twelve and therefore not a true apostle. At the outset he asserts his direct commission from Christ. This is an allusion to his vision on the way to Damascus and to other divinely given instructions. His call came not from human beings but from God.

Having made this important point regarding the authority of his teaching, he moves quickly to the attack. The churches in Galatia had made a grave mistake in accepting the propaganda of the Judaizers. His entirely human exasperation shows through. Paul quickly saw that some important questions were hanging in the balance. Was Christianity destined to be merely a reform movement in Judaism? Was it to be chained to Judaism and oriented to Jerusalem? Or, was it to be a forward-looking movement, outward bound into all the world?

Paul saw clearly that the first course would mean the eventual death and disappearance of the gospel of Christ. To make an impact on the pagan Gentile world, the gospel must be freed from Old Testament dietary regulation, circumcision, and the restrictive odds and ends of Jewish law. One of the most hotly debated issues of the early church was shaping up. Would Judaism capture and tame the followers of Jesus? Paul was convinced that this was not the divine intention. He could not go in person to these churches at that time, so he sends this historic letter.

Astonishment at Their Fickleness (Gal. 1:6–9)

The passage.—Paul had taught the Galatian Christians that their salvation depended solely on their faith in Jesus. This great gift was by the grace, the unmerited favor, of God. The Judaizers had come along to add another requirement: Gentile converts must become Jewish proselytes. Paul's anxiety and anger arose over the quick acceptance by these Galatian believers of this additional, unnecessary requirement. In fact, he says, this unwarranted Jewishness twists and perverts the gospel. It is a backward step. It is a retreat, a defec-

tion. Whoever preaches such a false gospel, "may he be condemned to hell!" (1:8–9, TEV). The strong language conveys his estimate of the danger of such a heresy.

Special point.—In Paul's view, the ceremonial law was a preliminary, elementary stage of religious development. It is now outdated and must be surpassed by a new way of relating to God. This new, more adequate, more mature way of relating to God is totally different. The old and the new way must not be mixed. Salvation, by God's graciousness, is now free. It comes exclusively through faith in Jesus. He says, don't clutter up free grace with the old outmoded forms of gaining favor with God through the kinds of activities which the law required.

Paul Defends His Apostolic Authority (Gal. 1:10—2:21)

The passage.—Paul reviews the events of his life to show God's authority in what he is teaching and preaching. God revealed to him that the way of faith has now replaced the requirements of Old Testament laws. This truth did not come to him from any of the apostles. It came through divine revelation. Indeed, the apostles confirmed his work among the Gentiles. They gave approval ("the right hands of fellowship") to him and his partner, Barnabas. They did not require Titus, a Greek, to be circumcised and become a Jewish proselyte.

The debate on this point indicated in chapter 2 may be the same one which occurred in Jerusalem as described in Acts 15. That discussion ended with Paul having a clear assignment to work among the Gentiles even as Peter and some of the others were to continue witnessing among the Jews.

Thus Paul claims both human and divine sanction for his teaching that Gentiles are freely saved and fully Christian without going through the motions of Jewish ceremonial law.

Special points.—When in 2:2 Paul says he went up to Jerusalem "by revelation" he indicates that God had revealed to him that his view of the Gentile converts would be vindicated. Acceptance of Titus as an equal among the believers was proof.

In 2:21 Paul clinches his argument. If a man could get right with God simply by observing the Jewish law, then Jesus died in vain. This is a pivotal statement in the letter. Life through faith in Jesus is liberation. The law stood for judgment and condemnation. Faith stands for forgiveness and freedom. The Galatian Christians, then, are free from the oppressiveness and irrelevance of Levitical law. Paul's authority in declaring this freedom for Gentile believers has been authenticated.

Paul Defends His Gospel of Faith (Gal. 3:1—4:31)

The passage.—The Christian movement faced a crisis of authority. The issue? Christ or the Jewish law. Paul appeals to history and to their own experience. He says that there were indications to Abraham and others all along that the law was a preliminary stage of religious development. But that preliminary stage is now passed. The Great Teacher has come. Follow him! You are out of elementary school now, he says. Why turn around and go back? Don't be foolish, thoughtless, and gullible!

The Galatian believers are reminded that Paul's gospel of free grace through faith has worked. They had seen it with their own eyes (3:1–5). They had received the Holy Spirit even though they had not been practicing the ceremonies and rituals of the Jewish law.

The coming of Christ illuminated many dark and obscure passages of the Old Testament. Paul cites the promise to Abraham that he would be a blessing to all nations. From the beginning God's plan anticipated an outreach to the Gentile world (3:6–29). The achievement of the gospel is to make them as Gentile believers, heirs to the promise given to Abraham (chap. 4).

Special points.—Paul's impatience with them shows through in 3:1. "Who put a spell on you?" (TEV). He says, Wake up! The Judiazers have hypnotized you. Get your senses back!

In 3:6 a bookkeeping term is used. Abraham's faith was "accounted to him for righteousness." His faith was put down on the "right" side of the ledger.

The watchcry of the Protestant Reformation was 3:11—"The just shall live by faith." Paul says flatly that there is only one way to have standing or approval with God. The law was never able to do it. Faith can.

In 3:24 the law is characterized as a temporary stage of religious development. Paul uses the figure of a Greek slave, the "pedagogue," to describe the role of the law. The pedagogue led the child to the school. There the teacher took over. Paul says the law likewise brings the searcher, the student, the disciple to Jesus, the Teacher.

Paul's "infirmity of the flesh" (4:13) is never revealed. This disability, illness, or handicap, however, was not allowed to divert attention from the message he had to deliver.

Implications of Christian Freedom (Gal. 5:1—6:10)

The passage.—The writer once more appeals to the good sense of the readers. They are free. They are not afflicted with endless ceremonies, bothersome rituals, lengthy dietary laws, and a lot of unessentials. But they do have obligations!

Circumcision is used as a symbol of the entire ceremonial law. It has no inherent spiritual or moral worth. It does not justify man before God. It is a matter of the flesh, not the spirit. This prompts Paul to illustrate the outworkings of the gospel. He lists some typical actions of the natural man, "works of the flesh" (5:17–21), and compares them to some characteristics of the redeemed man, calling these "fruit of the Spirit" (5:22–26).

The new life in Christ sets the believer free from the unproductive works of the law and turns him to works of compassion for his fellowman (6:1–10). Christian freedom must not be confused with license. We are, in a sense, under a new law, the law of love. Believers have a moral and ethical responsibility to each other in spontaneous response to God's love.

Special point—In 5:4 Paul is simply saying that there can be no salvation by the law. Those who take this route come up to the point of God's grace, up to the point of faith in Jesus Christ, but do not accept. They turn away without entering God's grace. "Those of you who try to be put right with God by obeying the Law have cut yourselves off from Christ. You are outside God's grace" (TEV).

Summary (Gal. 6:11–15)

Paul autographs his letter and calls particular attention to his distinctive signature, possibly as a warning against forgeries. He repeats the central theme of the letter that faith alone frees the believer from the penalty of sin. The thought of the conflict among the Galatian Christians on this point calls forth from him an exclamation of undying loyalty to Christ who alone is able to make men truly free.

Benediction (Gal. 6:16–18)

To all who accept the principle of faith he has outlined in his letter, to "the Israel of God" (KJV), "all God's people" (TEV), Paul wishes peace and mercy. He refers to the only glory he desires, the brandmarks of his witness to the Lord Jesus. In conclusion, he utters a prayer that would appear frequently in letters which would follow.

EPHESIANS

W. C. Fields

INTRODUCTION

This epistle is the greatest doctrinal statement among the 13 epistles of Paul in the New Testament. Galatians, Romans, and Ephesians form a trilogy of theology. In Galatians Paul defines the Christian way of salvation as being by faith, not by works. In Romans he widens his range and outlines the Christian concept of truth or righteousness. In Ephesians he gets it all together in a concise but comprehensive statement of the Christian calling. With wholeness and finality, Paul summarizes his doctrine and the reasons for his commitment.

The central message: This is the consummate statement of the glory of God as expressed in the Christian calling.

The key verse: "I urge you, then—I who am a prisoner because I serve the Lord: live a life that measures up to the standard God set when he called you" (4:1, TEV).

Purpose: to gather into one document Paul's understanding of what God is doing through Jesus Christ. Doctrines which had been discussed piecemeal in other writings of the apostle are stated here with completeness and harmony.

Author: the apostle Paul.

Audience: the churches of Asia Minor. It was probably a circular letter with copies going to the various churches. The words "at Ephesus" do not appear in some of the best ancient manuscripts. This may be the "lost" letter to the Laodiceans mentioned in Colossians 4:16. It seems to have in mind a more general audience than the church at Ephesus. It has few personal references in spite of the fact that Paul spent approximately three years there.

Date: Paul's first imprisonment at Rome, around A.D. 58–60, although some scholars argue that it was written in his second imprisonment at Rome just before 2 Timothy, the last of his epistles.

Occasion: Paul is in prison and has the time for a definitive statement about the divine purpose in history. He takes the occasion to interpret this theme in the light of what is happening in the Christian movement. Tychicus is available to deliver the letter to the churches of Ephesus and the other centers of Asia Minor.

The place of writing was Rome.

This epistle is the full Christian summary. It is the most complete statement in the New Testament of the significance of the Christian life.

Paul's Introduction (Eph. 1:1–2)

Some expressions that are characteristic of Paul occur in his opening statement of identity and salutation. "By the will of God" and "in Christ Jesus" mark the authority of the epistle. Several churches in Asia Minor probably received copies of this remarkable treatise. We have preserved for us the copy which went to the church "at Ephesus."

God's Purpose for His People and His Son (Eph. 1:1–23)

Verses 3–14 of this passage constitute one of the most complete statements of

745

Christian doctrine to be found anywhere. It is one long sentence of 268 words in the King James Version. In Greek, the original language, it is a statement of four sentences in 202 words. Paul's sentences are often long.

The section speaks of the Father (v. 3), lordship (v. 3), election (v. 4), sanctification (v. 4), foreordination (v. 5), adoption (v. 5), grace (v. 5 and other verses), redemption and atonement (v. 7), forgiveness of sin (v. 10), the dispensation of Christ and God's ultimate purpose in history (vv. 9–10). It talks about the stewardship of believers (vv. 11–12), the gospel of the good news of salvation (v. 13), the Holy Spirit (vv. 13–14), and some other subjects.

Like the entire book of Ephesians, this section is not so much a unified theme as a lot of important Christian themes strung together like beads. The central point of this recital of beliefs is verse 7. Altogether it constitutes one of the greatest doctrinal statements of all history.

The second part of chapter 1 is a prayer for knowledge and power (vv. 15–23). Paul intercedes for the church. It is a petition for spiritual insight to understand the purpose of God. Another long sentence! It is 190 words long in the King James.

Special points.—The "heavenlies" (v. 3) refers not to places but to the realm of spiritual realities where the believer's struggles and his victories are.

In verses 9 and 10 Paul reveals God's purpose for the universe. All things are brought into clearer focus through Jesus Christ. Science searches for answers as to how the universe functions. Paul expresses the Christian view as to why it functions as it does.

The New Humanity (Eph. 2:1–22)

This passage sweeps through history and into the future. It declares that there is a new family of God made up of believing Jews and Gentiles. Christ brings to man a new dimension to living: eternal life (vv. 7–10).

In verses 11–22 Paul describes the essential oneness of God's people. Race and culture separate people in the natural world. In Christ the walls of separation (v. 14) are torn down. This is the way to peace. Enmity is replaced with harmony in the fellowship of believers.

Paul makes a powerful appeal to the Gentile readers. In Christ they are no longer aliens and strangers to God's promises. As believers they are a part of "the household of God." In the church there is equality of rights and privileges. Old animosities are to be left behind. These new relationships "fitly framed together" (v. 21) make a worthy temple for the glory of God.

Special points.—In verse 2 "the prince of the power of the air" is a reference to the devil. His dominion over unregenerated humanity makes them "by nature children of wrath." They are under divine judgment.

Verses 8 and 9 are a matchless statement of salvation. You have been saved and you continue to be saved. God did it! Your faith says yes to God's action, but what happens from that point onward is through the grace, the unmerited favor, of God.

Paul's Mission (Eph. 3:1–21)

The first thirteen verses of this passage are a parenthesis. Paul begins a prayer on their behalf but pauses at the beginning to explain his relationship to this mystery of God that has unfolded in their midst. Verses 5 and 6 explain that the "mystery" of God's intentions toward the Gentiles is now cleared up. In the old days godly men knew more about this subject than they understood. But through Paul's unique mission to the

Gentiles it now has been clearly demonstrated that God's purposes of redemption always extended well beyond the Jews. In Christ, salvation is for all mankind. This all-embracing purpose of God had not been clearly recognized before. Christianity is not merely a reform movement within Judaism. The Christian mission is a worldwide mission.

Paul's prayer for the believers is resumed in verse 14. He asks that Christ might become incarnate in them (vv. 14–17). He desires for them the strength and perception to understand the vastness of God's love as revealed in Christ (vv. 17–19).

The apex of Ephesians is the magnificent doxology in verses 20–21. It states eloquently that God is able to perform his promises. The experience of salvation is personal but it is not unrelated to the "glory in the church," the fellowship of all believers.

Special point.—In 3:3 he refers to the mystery "as I wrote (before) in few words." This probably refers not to a previous epistle but to earlier references to the "mystery" in this epistle. The mystery was not the gospel itself, or in the nature of God's message, but in the destination of the gospel. It was not just for the Jews, historically a chosen people, a messenger people for God's love. The mystery had to do with God's intentions for the non-Jewish world. The followers of Christ now see that God's purpose is to redeem all who will accept salvation, Gentiles as well as Jews.

Christian Attitudes and Actions (Eph. 4:1—6:24)

The lofty concepts of the earlier chapters are now translated into practical duties for the believer. These are some guidelines for Christian thought and behavior. The Christian must "walk worthy" (4:1).

First, Paul stresses the need for unity (vv. 1–16). God's calling requires special attitudes in response, attitudes of consideration for others. He lists seven unifying factors among believers (vv. 4–6). Even the diversity of abilities should be integrated into the central purpose of the church (vv. 7–16). Each member is endowed with some capacity for service. There are no exceptions.

Right attitudes are important, but they are sterile without right actions. The new life in Christ is contrasted with the old life (vv. 17–29). A difference in character will mean a difference in conduct. The Holy Spirit is an active agent in this new quality of daily life (vv. 30–32).

Chapter 5 continues with social ethics guidelines. The subject shifts from internal relationships of the church to ethics in a society that is alien to God and hostile to God's children. In 5:1–21 Paul lists the kinds of things that should characterize the believer. They are intended to be part of a contrasting life-style to the pagan world. Paul does not call for isolation from the world, however. This would contradict the missionary imperative each believer has. But he does call for differentness in manner of life.

Marriage and home relationships should be affected by the Christian way of life. He suggests some practical outworkings of their faith in the man-wife relationships (vv. 22–32). He finds a good illustration for his purpose in the ties which bind Christ and the church.

Further fruits of Christian love should be found in household circles (6:1–9). The believer should have, as a by-product of his faith, unity and harmony in his home relationships. Parent-child behavior should reflect special qualities above and beyond the normal expectations of pagan society. Master-servant roles are to be tempered by consideration and respect not usually found in the Greco-Roman world of that time.

The kind of life Paul has outlined will not be easy. It will be a constant battle for which the beleaguered Christian minority must be equipped (vv. 10–20). Paul therefore spells out the Christian warrior's power (v. 10), his armor (v. 11), his foes (vv. 12–17), and his resources (vv. 18–20). The description is so vivid that we can visualize the prison guard Paul might have been looking at when he wrote these lines. He emphasizes the difficulties of this embattled kind of life, reminding them that he himself is an ambassador for Christ "in bonds." The victories in Christ described earlier are worthy of the struggles outlined at the close of this letter, and vice versa.

Special points.—In 4:9 reference is made to the fact that Christ "descended first into the lower parts of the earth." This is a measure of his love and his sacrifice. He came from heaven, took on the ordinary human condition, and with it he accepted death and the grave, before ascending in triumph to the Father. This is a measure of the gift of Christ to the believer.

In 6:5–9 Paul counsels bondslaves and their masters to make the best of their relationship. In the face of first-century Roman law, revolt by slaves would have been suicidal. He therefore suggests a code of behavior for the persons involved which would bring the spirit of Christ at least into the lives of the individuals involved.

Paul's Conclusion (Eph. 6:21–24)

Tychicus, who would deliver the letter to the churches of Asia Minor, is given a character reference by Paul. He would add further details of Paul's condition as a prisoner at Rome. He would amplify Paul's message to them.

The letter, which began with Paul's greeting of grace and peace, makes the full circuit and ends on the same notes. In a closing statement somewhat longer than those found in his other epistles, Paul adds the elements of love and faith. The final tone is in keeping with the exalted character of the entire letter. From beginning to end, this circular letter merits consideration as one of the greatest, if not the greatest letter ever written in the history of mankind.

PHILIPPIANS

W. C. Fields

INTRODUCTION

This is the pleasantest of Paul's letters. It is a message of love for tried and true friends. There is no censure. The word "sin" does not occur. The characteristic words are "joy" and "rejoice." The church at Philippi was not fickle like those in Galatia. It was not plagued with problems like the one in Corinth. In this sunny, bouyant little epistle Paul's warmth is lavishly given.

Philippians is a contrast to Ephesians. Ephesians is formal, carefully phrased, general in subject matter, and exalted in tone. Philippians is personal, affectionate, conversational, unsystematic, and written to one local congregation.

Author: the apostle Paul.

Audience: the church at Philippi. The city was founded and named for the father of Alexander the Great. It became a proud colony of Rome. In Paul's time it was a strategic city on a busy commercial route. Here Paul first preached the gospel in Europe (Acts 16). Lydia was the first convert. Paul and Silas were put in prison and their jailer was converted. He left a group of devoted Christians there.

On his third missionary journey (Acts 20:1) he went to Macedonia, and doubtless to Philippi. Later (Acts 20:6) he returns and leaves from Philippi to go to Jerusalem. There were many ties with this assembly of believers.

The central message: This is a thank-you note to dear friends in Christ. It is full of gratitude and affection.

Purpose: to express appreciation for the gifts they had sent by Epaphroditus and to share his own sense of victory in spite of his prison chains.

Occasion: After bringing the gifts, Epaphroditus had become sick. When he recovers Paul sends this letter to explain his long absence, to express his thanks, and to comment on his own situation and theirs.

Key verse: "For to me to live is Christ, and to die is gain" (1:21).

Date: Around A.D. 58–60, probably at the close of his first imprisonment at Rome.

This joyous epistle calls for unity and harmony in Christ. It warns against those who would mislead. It asks the church to seek the mind of Christ.

Paul's Introduction (Phil. 1:1–11)

Timothy is associated with Paul in the message of the letter (1:1). He was with Paul and Silas on their first visit to Philippi. Although Timothy is mentioned again (2:19) Paul uses the first person singular throughout the letter. His writing style is informal. Both men are characterized as "slaves" of Jesus Christ.

The church at Philippi has three identifiable groups. This indicates a development in the church structure. First, are the "saints" ("God's people," TEV). This is a title brought over from the Old Testament and from Judaism. Every Christian is a saint. The main idea in the title is not moral purity and perfection, but a consecrated, covenant people. The believer accepts as a duty the struggle toward holiness.

Second, he addresses the "bishops." These are the leaders, the overseers in the church.

Third, he singles out the deacons. *Today's English Version* translates this title as "helpers." They are mentioned in Acts (6:2) and 1 Timothy (3:8,12 f.). The word signifies those who serve.

Paul's affection surfaces immediately (1:3). He acknowledges their partnership (v. 5) and expresses thanks in advance for their continual faithfulness. Their "fellowship" (*koinonia*) in the gospel is much more than civic club comradery. It was a deep personal commitment to each other as fellow Christians.

Paul prays that they might develop mature character as a result of their discipleship (vv. 9–11). Love for God inevitably means a more understanding love for one another. He urges them to link emotion and mentality. They are to be discerning. He wants them to have the skill to be able to search among that which is good and choose the best.

News (Phil. 1:12–26)

Knowing their concern for him, he tells them news of himself. His imprisonment has resulted in spreading of the gospel through the palace guard assigned to him. Each change of the guard is a new opportunity. A further gain for the cause was the new confidence and boldness his experience inspired among the believers.

This thought leads Paul to mention that there is a mixture of motives in the witness of the Christians. Some believers agreed with his views and were sympathetic. Others were antagonistic and jealous. The latter group seems to be the Judaizers who wanted all Gentile Christians to become Jewish proselytes and be subject to the Jewish law. In Galatians Paul opposes them fiercely. Here he is much more broad-minded

toward them. Even if their understanding of the gospel is imperfect, he rejoices that at least Christ is preached by them (vv. 15–18).

Paul the prisoner shares with the Philippians his confidence that all his present circumstances will work eventually for his "salvation," his deliverance. "I shall be set free" (TEV). This thought leads him, however, to make quite clear that neither imprisonment nor death can defeat him. Life is Christ! Death is gain (v. 21). This key verse indicates Paul's sense of triumph in the midst of what some, viewing his imprisonment, would call defeat.

Paul's quandary about living or dying is the rationale which has been a guideline for persecuted Christians for centuries. Death means a release from life's inconveniences. It means freedom at last to be in the presence of the Lord. He admits to a longing for this exalted state. At the same time he has a sense of unfinished work, a feeling of obligation to his friends. Christ has given meaning and coherence to both life and death. His outlook is bright (vv. 22–26).

Humility and Unity (Phil. 1:27—2:18)

The apostle now addresses himself to the need for humility among the church members as a basis for stronger fellowship. The supreme example for this spirit is Christ himself. The letter reaches a pinnacle in 2:5–11. Christ's humiliation and exaltation are presented as cause and effect. The believers are to remember his example (2:12–16).

Special points.—"Conversation" in 1:27 should be translated "conduct" or "manner of life." Your entire pattern of living should be appropriate to a follower of Jesus! This may be an indirect reference to the Roman colonist's duty to be an example of the good citizen. When Paul urges them to "work out your own salvation with fear and trembling" (2:12) he is not suggesting that they could achieve their own salvation through the quantity or quality of their work. Rather, he is suggesting that there should be an out-working, a translation into word and deed, of the inward experience with Christ.

Plans (Phil. 2:19–30)

The subject now turns to Paul's co-workers. Timothy is given a warm tribute (vv. 19–24). Paul hopes to send him to Philippi soon. He has hopes of being freed to make the journey himself (v. 24). In the meantime, Epaphroditus is returning with Paul's letter. Paul recounts Epaphroditus' illness which was almost fatal (v. 30) and commends him for staking his life in the service of Christ.

Warnings (Phil. 3:1–21)

The "Finally, my brethren" (3:1), seems to indicate that he is about to conclude the letter. Something, however, prompts him to launch into a warning about the contentious Judaizers. He says, Forgive me for referring to this subject again, but it is very important! The tension in this section is in contrast to the other parts of the letter. Beware of these people! They would divert you from truth and freedom!

Paul reminds them of his credentials as a Hebrew of the Hebrews (vv. 4–6). This family heritage, however, he considers worthless without Christ (vv. 7–9). Christ has become the great new center for his life (vv. 10–14). This is the one worthy ambition for him now, to follow Jesus. There is a new direction to his life. Not backward, but forward!

Here, from his prison cell, the veteran missionary leader sets down some conclusions from his years of vigorous service. (1) "I count not myself to have apprehended." The battle-scarred apostle is still seeking, acquiring, trying to apprehend the greatness of God's revelation in Jesus Christ. He is still the disciple, still the student, still pursuing truth wherever it will lead him. (2) Further, he has learned to forget "those things which are behind." Past successes or failures are incidental to what God is doing now. (3) I reach forth, he says, "unto those things which are before." The set of his face is onward. The brightness of new victories is in his eyes. He refuses to rest among his souvenirs. There is more that I must see. There is more that I must do. There is more that I must be! (4) Rounding it out, he asserts, "I press toward the mark." Here is the divine discontent that propelled him into world history. And others like him! His relationship to Christ had not leveled off. He was responding to a still higher calling, an unending pilgrimage of faith and service.

Paul had earned the right to challenge the church members at Philippi to a vigorous witness. He drives home the point (vv. 15–19). Be thus minded! Have the same attitude! Don't give in to the enemies of the cross!

Special point.—In 3:20 he alludes once more to their special status as citizens in the Roman colony of Philippi. We Christians, he says, "are citizens of heaven" (TEV). The believer's relationship to Christ gives a new significance to the Roman political law even as it does to Jewish religious law! Here is the ultimate focus of all of life, "the Savior, the Lord Jesus Christ."

Challenges (Phil. 4:1–9)

After the long digression in chapter 3 in which he warns against the Judaizers, Paul returns here to the subject of dissention among the Philippians. The church which began with a woman,

Lydia, as the first convert, seems now to have its first trouble because of two women, Euodia and Syntyche. He appeals (4:3) to an unnamed colleague to help them work out their differences. One Clement is also mentioned by name. While he does not specify others, they can be assured that their names "are in the book of life."

Paul commends "the peace of God" to them (vv. 4–7). How does it come about? Rejoice! Be moderate! Don't be overanxious! Pray! Give thanks! Lay your petitions before God!

"Finally, brethren" (v. 8)—he attempts to conclude again! But exhortations pour forth. He suggests eight proper subjects for their meditation. They seem to be arranged in a descending scale. These are followed (v. 9) by proper lines of action.

Appreciation (Phil. 4:10–20)

Paul thanks them for their financial support (v. 10). He makes clear, however, (vv. 11–13) that he is not seeking such. He has learned to make do with whatever resources are at hand. He has confidence that Christ will strengthen him sufficiently for every task.

These faithful friends at Philippi had been loyal supporters of his needs. The gift they sent to him in prison by Epaphroditus (v. 18) was especially meaningful and appropriate. He expresses his confidence that in Christ all of their own needs would be supplied.

Conclusion (Phil. 4:20–23)

This epistle of love and friendship closes with a benediction. In the midst of this, however, he inserts a personal greeting to each of the members of the church. Likewise, he passes on to them the greetings of the believers in Rome. He refers to the fact that this includes Christians "that are of Caesar's household." These seem to be civil servants rather than members of Caesar's family. The concluding word is a prayer.

COLOSSIANS

W. C. Fields

INTRODUCTION

Colossae was a small, relatively unimportant city in the Lycus Valley about 100 miles east of Ephesus. It was overshadowed in Paul's time by two nearby cities, Laodicea (Rev. 3:14-19) and Hierapolis (4:15). Paul had never been there. The church was probably founded by Epaphras. In many ways the city was the least important place to which Paul wrote. The church there, however, loomed large in Paul's concern because of false teachings which were creeping into the fellowship. It is evidence of his genius that he foresaw from these small beginnings the dangers of a heresy that would shake the entire church to its foundations in the second century.

Some of the Christians at Colossae (under the influence of Gnostics) were attempting to adapt and add to the gospel a mixture of Judaism and pagan mysticism, apparently to make the Christian faith more attractive to both Jew and Gentile. Paul sensed the danger. His rebuttal to these misguided persons in a small church in a remote province of Asia Minor is sharp and clear. The letter contains his most comprehensive statement on the significance of Jesus.

Author: the apostle Paul.

Purpose: to stop the infiltration of gnostic teaching and Jewish levitical practices among Christians.

Gnosticism took on numerous forms, but it was a philosophy which viewed all matter as inherently evil. Therefore, Gnostics said, a good God could not have created matter. They then evolved a long series of intermediary powers or "emanations," the lowest of which they believed was responsible for creating earthly and fleshly things. They identified Christ with this lowest "emanation." This kind of thinking destroyed the idea of God incarnate in human flesh. One group of Gnostics said therefore that Jesus was not truly divine. Another group said that he was not truly human.

Apparently at Colossae this gnostic heresy also prompted some of the Christians to asceticism. In other places it influenced some in the opposite direction to loose, licentious living. They believed that the human body was evil and was man's prison. Release from this grip of evil comes by superior knowledge (gnosis) which is granted to the initiates. One way to conquer the evil of the flesh was to rigidly suppress the body by asceticism. This is the teaching Paul seems to be answering. Another way to conquer the body, they believed, was to ignore it as unimportant. According to this latter view, encountered elsewhere in the epistles of John and Peter, the enlightened individual is free to do whatever he pleases. The flesh and the spirit were considered separate realms.

Paul immediately saw the dangers of such alien ideas. His letter to the Colossians challenging these views centers on the person of Christ and his cosmic significance. He is not only personal Savior but also Lord of creation and head of the church.

Central message: Christ is to be exalted in the church. He is preeminent, preexistent, omnipotent, and eternal.

Key verse: "For in him dwelleth all the fulness of the Godhead bodily" (Col. 2:9).

Audience: believers at Colossae.

Occasion: Epaphras, the church leader at Colossae, apparently was not able to cope with the alien ideas being brought into the fellowship. We infer from the letter that he went to Rome to consult Paul. The apostle's insight as well as his prestige would have a bearing on the thinking of the Colossians. Tychicus was the bearer of the letter (4:7 f.). He also delivered the Ephesian letter on the same trip (Eph. 6:21 f.). Onesimus, the runaway slave, was along on the same trip (Col. 4:9) bearing a letter from Paul to Philemon, who probably lived at Colossae.

Place of writing: Rome.

Date: Paul's first Roman imprisonment would make it around A.D. 58–60.

Paul's Introduction (Col. 1:1–14)

To a people whom he had not met, Paul identifies himself as an apostle "by the will of God." He writes not as a self-appointed teacher, but as one specially chosen of God. Timothy is included in the message of greeting to them.

Paul expresses thanks for their growth in the faith. He indicates that his information came from one of their own, Epaphras. Paul identifies with Epaphras as a fellow slave of Jesus Christ.

Paul indicates that he has been praying for them continually since hearing of their situation (vv. 9–14). In all of his epistles prayer and thanksgiving are closely linked together. He gives them (v. 9) the substance of his prayers—that they might indeed be filled with "knowledge," "wisdom," and "understanding." These were in-words, catchwords of the Gnostics among them. Paul uses them deliberately, emphasizing his concern

for them achieving true knowledge, real wisdom, and "spiritual" understanding. This is his first petition to God for them.

The second petition (v. 10) is that this healthy intellectual life may produce worthy living. The third request (v. 11) is for spiritual strength. He concludes his prayer for them with thanks for their common hope (vv. 12–14).

The Nature and Work of Christ (Col. 1:15–23)

In a profound theological sequence Paul sets forth the preeminence of Jesus. Apparently the false teachers in the church had been advocating inadequate views. Paul lists seven superiorities. As translated in *Today's English Version,* Christ is (1) "the visible likeness of the invisible God" (v. 15). He is (2) the first-born Son, "superior to all created things" (v. 15). (3) "By him God created everything" (v. 16). (4) "He existed before all things" (v. 17). (5) "In union with him all things have their proper place" (v. 17). (6) He is the head and source of life for the church (v. 18). (7) He was raised from the dead (v. 18). Contrary to what the Gnostics were teaching, "It was by God's own decision that the Son has in himself the full nature of God" (v. 19). Through him God is at work reconciling all of the disharmony in his creation (vv. 20–23).

Paul's Concern (Col. 1:24—2:7)

Here the apostle inserts a statement of his credentials for presuming to correct their doctrine. His own ministry is partly one of suffering to prove as well as to proclaim God's redeeming love for the church.

The apostle ends this statement regarding his own ministry by a review of his purpose for them. It is that they may be "knit together in love," that they may have the "riches of the full assurance of understanding" (2:2), and possess "the treasures of wisdom and knowledge" (v. 3). He therefore warns them against being led astray by enticing words (vv. 4–7).

Special points.—Paul regards his own sufferings as a means to an end. "For by means of my physical sufferings I help complete what still remains of Christ's sufferings on behalf of his body, which is the church" (1:24, TEV).

"The mystery which hath been hidden" (v. 26) is phraseology taken from the Gnostics. In Paul's understanding, a mystery is a truth peculiar to Christianity not discoverable by human reason but revealed by God.

Paul's words, "Christ in you, the hope of glory" (v. 27) refer to the fact that God is visible now to the world as he appears in the lives of Christians.

Warnings Against False Teachings (Col. 2:8—3:4)

This is the main section dealing with incorrect doctrine. The so-called philosophy which was being thrust upon them was seemingly intellectual. Actually it was empty, he says. Don't go back to the "rudiments of the world," the elementary, ruling evil spirits! (2:8,20). "Fulness" was probably another of the Gnostic bywords. Paul uses it to indicate (v. 9) the essence of his entire letter, namely that Christ made the fact of deity complete. Don't turn from fulness to emptiness!

Some confusion at Colossae on the matter of circumcision leads Paul to make a positive rather than a negative statement about it. False teachers seem to have been trying to require circumcision as one more condition of salvation, as happened in the Galatian churches. In 2:11 Paul indicates the symbolic nature of this rite and declares that Christ makes circumcision unneces-

sary. In this instance, and in his references to baptism, and to other ritualistic regulations regarding food, drink, and feast days, he declares that these observances were the shadows whereas Christ is the substance (vv. 10–17). Don't confuse the symbols with the real thing! He warns also that asceticism (severe abstenance) alone is sterile (vv. 20–23).

In 3:1–4 Paul is making a transition from the earlier section on warnings against false teachings. He is about to give some practical illustrations of how the true spirit of Christ expresses itself. In the transition, however, he emphasizes the fact that the Christian life is a continual quest and that Christ is the example to follow and the goal to pursue. The new life in Christ requires a completely new mental orientation.

Special point.—Paul makes a passing reference to the second coming of Christ (3:4). It is a part of his argument. He has been stressing the close identification of the believer with Christ. The believer shares Christ's life here. He will share his glory when he comes again.

Practical Advice (Col. 3:5—4:6)

Paul lists some examples of behavior which should be shunned and some which should be adopted. Here Colossians and Ephesians resemble each other. In both, Paul regards Christian conduct as inseparable from Christian concepts. Knowing and saying the right things are important, but this mental activity is empty without the authentication of doing the right things.

In 3:5–11 he itemizes some things that are inconsistent with the Christian calling. In 3:12–17 he indicates some qualities that are desirable. In 3:17 he gives a good rule of thumb for Christian behavior: "Do all in the name of the Lord Jesus."

There follows a series of exhortations

relating to the Christian household: wives (v. 18), husbands (v. 19), children (v. 20), fathers (v. 21), servants (vv. 22–25), masters (4:1) and for the saints generally (vv. 2–6). In these instances the added dimension over common pagan practices of the time is in Paul's phrase, "as it is fit in the Lord" (3:18). Be thoroughly Christian in these relationships!

Special points.—The master-slave relationship (3:22—4:1) had many evils about it in Paul's day. It was manifestly impractical for the struggling, emerging church to try at that stage to overthrow the institution of slavery. Paul did not wait, however, to suggest some ways of changing the conditions of slavery. It was to be changed from within, by transforming both the master and the slave. This message is borne out most clearly in the epistle to Philemon. Paul is concerned with human attitudes. Christ can make a difference in these regardless of the political or social circumstances.

Personal Greetings (Col. 4:7–17)

The note about Tychicus (vv. 7–8) is almost identical with Ephesians 6:21–22 and suggests that he was the bearer of letters to both Colossae and Ephesus. Onesimus, the runaway slave, returns to Colossae with Tychicus as a believer and "brother" (4:9). The personal letter to his owner, Philemon, is also delivered at the same time.

Three Jewish brethren in Rome send greetings. Aristarchus, a "fellow pris-oner," probably is the same one who was seized by a mob in Ephesus (Acts 19:29). Only here (4:10) do we learn that Mark is the nephew to Barnabas. Paul had some harsh words to say about Mark (Acts 15:36 f.) when he dropped out of the group on the first missionary journey. Now apparently he is reconciled with him. Nothing else is known of "Jesus, who is called Justus" (4:11).

Three Gentile brethren also send greetings from Rome. Epaphras is one of their own (vv. 12–13). Luke is identified only here (v. 14) as a physician. The only other information we have on Demas is in 2 Timothy 4:10 where in Paul's final letter he says sadly that Demas had forsaken him for the "present world."

House churches, such as the one mentioned in Nymphas' house at Laodicea (v. 15), are noted several times in Paul's writings. We do not have the epistle to Laodicea mentioned in 4:16, at least by that name. Archippus (v. 17) is mentioned also in Philemon 1 and may have been standing in for the absent Epaphras as the leader of the church at Colossae.

Conclusion (Col. 4:18)

Paul closes in his own handwriting. This suggests that he may have employed an amanuensis or scribe to write the letter up to this point.

"Remember my bonds" is a touching reminder of Paul's circumstances as a prisoner in Rome.

He closes with his customary greeting, "Grace be with you."

1 THESSALONIANS

W. C. Fields

INTRODUCTION

Thessalonica was a thriving city when Paul arrived there on his second missionary journey. With him were Silas (Silvanus) and Timothy. For three successive sabbaths in the synagogue he told of Jesus of Nazareth whom he declared to be the long-awaited Messiah (Acts 17: 1–9). Some Jews, many Greeks, and some leading women of the city accepted his witness. Hostility arose and he moved into the house of one Jason. Unbelieving Jews organized some thugs ("lewd fellows of the baser sort") to drive them out of town, and they succeeded.

Shortly thereafter Timothy was sent back to check on the progress of the new church. Paul moved on south preaching in Athens, then Corinth, where he anxiously waited for Timothy to join him.

The occasion for the first epistle to the Thessalonians was Timothy's report (3:6–10). Happily, the new believers at Thessalonica were standing firm in spite of persecution. More than that, they were actively spreading the gospel. They wanted further enlightenment, however, on the second coming of Jesus.

Author: the apostle Paul.

Audience: the Greek and Jewish believers at Thessalonica.

Purpose: to express Paul's gratefulness for their stedfastness and to instruct them further on certain questions, including the return of Jesus.

The central message is reflected in a key verse (2:19) in which Paul refers to them as "our hope, our joy, and our reason for boasting of our victory in the presence of our Lord Jesus when he comes" (TEV).

The place of writing: Corinth.

Date: shortly after Paul's arrival in Corinth, around A.D. 50.

Paul's Introduction (1 Thess. 1:1)

Silvanus is the Silas of Acts 15:22 f. He joined Paul at the beginning of the second missionary journey. After the stay at Corinth we hear no more of Silas as a partner of Paul. Timothy joined the two of them when they came through his native city of Lystra on this journey (Acts 16:1 f.). He remains with Paul until Paul is executed in Rome.

Thanksgiving for the Thessalonians (1 Thess. 1:2–20)

Paul is full of gratitude. Their professions of discipleship were matched by their practice. There was ample evidence of genuine faith, love, and hope, qualities Paul looked for as authentication of a real conversion (cf. 5:8; Col. 1:4 f., 1 Cor. 13:13). "For we remember before our God and Father how you put your faith into practice, how your love made you work so hard, and how your hope in our Lord Jesus Christ is firm" (1:3, TEV).

They are truly among the elect of God (v. 4). Paul remembers that the Holy Spirit had empowered his preaching in their midst (v. 5). Their zeal in witnessing became quickly known throughout the region and beyond (vv. 6–8).

They had turned from their pagan idols. They were anticipating the return of the Lord. Truly there was reason for thanksgiving!

Special point.—God makes the conditions for election (1:4). The believer's faith enables him to enter into this glorious relationship with God. The new Christians at Thessalonica gave evidence that they had indeed met God's conditions.

Paul's Work in Thessalonica (1 Thess. 2:1–16)

There was opposition to Paul's preaching while he was in Thessalonica. After he was forced to leave, these detractors tried hard to discredit him. Itinerant pedlars of philosophy and religion were fairly common in the cities of the Roman world at that time. Some of them were greedy charlatans preying on the ignorance and credulity of the people. Paul's enemies had tried to identify him with such disreputable teachers. In this letter to the new church he left behind, he defends his conduct and that of his fellow missionaries. The brethren are asked to review the facts of his short stay.

In the first place, he points out (2:1) his ministry there added up to success for the gospel, not failure. In spite of mistreatment and insults at Philippi and opposition at Thessalonica he and his fellow missionaries spoke with the courage that comes from God (v. 2). They did not use clever tricks to win converts and they showed no impure motives (v. 3). They did not resort to flattery and sought no praise (vv. 5–6). On the contrary, they were willing even to give their lives (vv. 7–8). They had even worked—tentmaking being Paul's trade —to pay their own expenses (v. 9).

Paul reminds them that the facts are clear, that their attitudes, motives, and conduct were pure, right, and without fault (v. 10). He asks them to recall the acceptance they gave so freely then (vv. 11–12). They even suffered from their fellow citizens because of this support (v. 13), even as the believers in Judea had suffered from their own people, the Jews (v. 14). This thought evokes from Paul a bitter statement (vv. 15–16). This constant rejection of God's spokesmen by the Jews has brought (and still is bringing) God's wrath down upon them. In effect, Paul's defense says, "I stand on my record!"

Paul's Desire to Visit Them Again (1 Thess. 2:17—3:13)

The opponents of Paul in Thessalonica apparently were saying that the apostle had no real love and concern for the believers in the new, struggling church. He had not returned to comfort and counsel them in their troubles. The letter counters this notion (vv. 17–18) by asserting Paul's great desire to visit them, but he was not able to do so. "Satan hindered." Exactly what stood in Paul's way is not clear. The peace bond that Jason made with the authorities in Thessalonica may have included the provision that Paul get out of town and stay out! Whatever the cause, Paul did not view it as God's will that prevented him from visiting the Thessalonians. The adversary in some sense was Satan.

Since he could not return, he sent Timothy to strengthen and comfort the faithful (3:1–5). He was true to his pastoral calling in wanting to see how their faith was standing up under fire. Now, with Timothy's return, he knows! His joy overflows (vv. 6–13). This news generates a new longing to see them.

There is no astonishment or consternation because troubles have rained down on the new believers. Here, as elsewhere in Paul's writings, persecution was considered inevitable. Such opposition was a badge of faithful discipleship. The early disciples, including those at Thessalonica, were such a tough-minded lot that hostility and unpopularity were accepted as marks of spiritual achievement. It energized them for more daring service.

Counsel for the Future (1 Thess. 4:1—5:22)

The pagan world of the time attached little ethical or moral significance to sexual immorality. Paul reminds the believers (4:1–8) that in Christ they have chosen a higher standard of conduct than that of their neighbors, and they should live up to it.

The apostle tells them also "to live a quiet life, to mind your own business, and earn your own living" (v. 11, TEV). Excitement over the prospect of Jesus' immediate return was apparently having some irrational side effects. This practical advice introduces Paul's statement about the second coming of Christ (4:13—5:11).

The Greeks had no concept for a resurrection of the body. They believed that only the spirit was eternal. Paul here (4:13–18) explains that the believers who have died will not be left behind. On the other hand, the Jews generally believed that only those living at the advent of the Messiah's reign would share in it. Paul explains that the Christian view is different from both. Those who died as believers will be raised to take part in the coming messianic kingdom.

Another matter about Jesus' return which troubled these new disciples was, naturally, the time of his reappearing. Paul tells them clearly (5:1–11) that no one knows. He equates the Old Testament concept of "the day of the Lord" with Jesus' return. It will come suddenly and without warning. The point for the Christian is to be prepared. There is then no anxiety over the matter.

At the close of his letter, Paul packs more than a dozen bits of wise counsel into a rapid-fire finish to his message (vv. 12–25). He calls for respect for their leaders (vv. 12–13), peaceableness among the church members (v. 13), warnings again for the idle, encouragement for the timid, helpfulness for the weak, and patience on the part of everyone (v. 14). They are to avoid vindictiveness and choose instead to do good to one another (v. 15). Be joyful, pray, and be thankful (vv. 16–18)! Don't restrain the Holy Spirit and don't lightly reject strange forms of Christian expression (vv. 19–20). Don't be naive! Think! Ask questions! Analyze! "Put all things to the test: keep what is good, and avoid every kind of evil" (vv. 21–22, TEV).

Conclusion (1 Thess. 5:23–28)

The letter concludes with a challenge to holy living. He asks that they pray for him, greet the brethren, and see that the letter is read to the entire congregation. The last note is a benediction.

2 THESSALONIANS

W. C. Fields

INTRODUCTION

This follow-up letter of Paul to the Thessalonians contains his most forceful statement on the end of the world. It is akin to Jesus' statements in Matthew 24, and to the writings in 1 John and Revelation.

The central message is that for believers there are still battles to fight, but victory is assured. But don't expect victory too soon!

Occasion: The first letter had intensified their expectation of Jesus' second coming. Paul had stressed the suddenness of the Lord's return. In their excitement they misunderstood Paul's meaning. They had interpreted "suddenly" to mean "immediately." Paul writes them back to correct this idea.

Purpose: to remind the new, enthusiastic Christians at Thessalonica that the struggle with evil was not over, that it was a mistake to assume that Jesus definitely would return immediately. He writes to tell them to get on with their work and witness.

Key verse: "So then, brothers, stand firm and hold on to those truths which we taught you, both in preaching and in our letter" (2:15, TEV).

Date: shortly after 1 Thessalonians, written from Corinth around A.D. 50 or 51.

Author: the apostle Paul.

Salutation (2 Thess. 1:1–2)

The opening is almost identical to the first letter. Silas and Timothy are associated with Paul in transmitting this message also.

Thanksgiving and Judgment (2 Thess. 1:3–12)

Before dealing with their mistaken views, he commends them for what is unquestionably right and good in their midst (1:3–4). They are growing in faith and love for each other. And in spite of harassment and opposition.

Their troubles are proof that God considers them worthy of his kingdom (vv. 5–10). Justice will prevail. They will be vindicated. Their tormentors will be punished with finality. For Paul, salvation is union with God through Christ. Doom is separation from God. Salvation is the difference between being and not being, between life and death.

The return of Christ is vividly portrayed—"with his mighty angels," "in flaming fire," "taking vengeance." It will be a time of judgment, a time of retribution for the unbelievers, a time of reward for the faithful.

Therefore, in view of this awesome event. Paul prays for their spiritual progress that when it inevitably happens they may be judged worthy (vv. 11–12).

Christ and Antichrist (2 Thess. 2:1–17)

Some of the Christians at Thessalonica had concluded that "the day of the Lord," the apocalyptic events surrounding the return of Christ, had already begun (2:1–2). Paul hints that this may have been due to the influence of some false teacher or someone forging a letter in his name. In any case, this teaching is not true. "Do not let anyone fool you in any way. For the Day will not come until the final Rebellion takes place and the Wicked One appears, who is destined to hell" (v. 3, TEV).

This wicked one, "the man of sin," is graphically described as one who brazenly tries to usurp the very powers of God himself (v. 4). Paul had discussed this matter with them before (v. 5). This mysterious figure, the leader of the great eschatological (final) rebellion against God, is variously referred to in the New Testament as the antichrist, the lawless one, and the beast from the abyss (Rev. 11:7).

For the time being, Paul says (2:6) this "man of sin" is being restrained. Who was restraining him? Paul is intentionally vague in the letter, but apparently had been more explicit earlier when he was speaking personally to them in Thessalonica (vv. 5–6). This may mean that he was referring to the Roman Empire as the restraining influence of the moment. After the trouble Paul had with the Roman authorities at Thessalonica (Acts 17:6 f.), any such reference in writing to imperial power—especially a prediction of its downfall—would necessarily have to be vague for his safety and that of the church members.

Paul frequently had reason to be grateful for the Roman authorities who restrained those who were hostile to the gospel. He is saying here, however, that when this restraining influence is removed, the forces of antichrist, "the man of sin," will be free to turn their fury on the Christians. But in the end God will bring about the defeat of this creature of Satan (vv. 7–12).

Special point.—The "man of sin," the antichrist, is evil personified. He is a representative monster of wickedness bent on the destruction of God's people. Such a horror of wickedness is pictured in the book of Daniel. Jesus warned of such outbursts of ungodliness (Mark 13). This embodiment of wrong was at one time identified as the satanic ruler Antiochus Epiphanes. In the book of Revelation the antichrist is identified as imperial Rome. In the Middle Ages the Western Church applied this label to the Barbarian hordes and the Eastern Church applied it to Islam. Around the time of the Protestant Reformation the Pope was identified by some as antichrist. In the 1930's and 40's Adolf Hitler was so named. There have been others. Whatever else these passages are intended to convey, they clearly and forcefully indicate that the gospel and its adherents can always expect opposition from entrenched evil. The battle will rage, sometimes in cosmic dimensions, right up until the end of the ages.

Prayer and Obligations (2 Thess. 3:1–15)

In view of these things, Paul asks for prayer among the faithful that all may stand the test (vv. 1–5). He reprimands those who are disorderly and who shirk their responsibilities (vv. 6–15). The church is encouraged to deal firmly with such, but to admonish each one "as a brother."

Signature (2 Thess. 3:16–18)

Paul calls special attention to his signature. It authenticates any genuine letter from him. He closes with prayer that the blessings of the Lord Jesus Christ may rest upon them.

1 TIMOTHY

W. C. Fields

INTRODUCTION

This is the first of the so-called pastoral epistles of Paul. They voice the concern of Paul as a pastor-at-large for the scattered congregations of believers. They deal with church leadership, correct doctrine, and appropriate conduct. These three letters—two to Timothy and one to Titus—are the final correspondence from Paul which we have in the New Testament.

Luke's account in Acts ends with Paul serving a two-year prison term in Rome. We learn from the pastoral epistles that he was released and made a fourth missionary journey among some of the churches. Timothy and Titus were his associates in this campaign.

During the tour Titus was left to lead the work in Crete and Timothy was left in Ephesus. Paul goes on alone to Macedonia, perhaps to Philippi. From there he writes the first letter to Timothy. Later from somewhere in that region, perhaps Macedonia or Corinth, he writes to Titus. By the time he writes to Timothy the second time he has been arrested again by the Roman authorities and he knows the death penalty awaits him.

These letters are addressed to individuals, but they have strong overtones for the churches where these men served. There is urgency in them. The veteran apostle, an old man now, senses that time for him is running out and there is much work yet to do.

Author: the apostle Paul.

The audience: primarily one man, Timothy. The son of a Greek Gentile father and a strong-minded Jewish mother, Timothy joined Paul on his second missionary journey and was an associate and faithful companion to the apostle for about 15 years.

Date: uncertain, but possibly around A.D. 63 from Macedonia.

Occasion: Paul had left Timothy in charge of the work at Ephesus. The apostle knew personally of the heresies that were alive and at work there.

Purpose: to strengthen the hand and the resolve of Timothy; to reinforce his charges against the false teachers; to give suggestions for the functioning of the church; and to give personal counsel to Timothy.

Central message: stated in 3:15, "But if I delay, this letter will let you know how we should conduct ourselves in God's household, which is the church of the living God, the pillar and support of the truth" (TEV).

Salutation (1 Tim. 1:1–2)

The author uses formal tones. This is more than a personal letter. He is consciously speaking as one divinely appointed. "Apostle" means "one sent."

Paul was likely in his sixties at this writing. Timothy was younger, perhaps thirty-five. The bond between them was strong—"my own son in the faith." The early Christian leaders often worked in two's. Timothy needed additional grooming for the time when Paul would be gone. Thus this letter.

The letter stresses Timothy's responsibilities. He is an envoy (1:3) and an ordained official (4:14). He is a minister (4:6), adviser (4:13), with some authority over the church (6:17), yet he is under Paul's authority (5:21). His assignment to Ephesus seems to be temporary (4:13). He is a missionary, developing local leaders who will eventually take up the burden of responsibility.

The arduous life of both men reminds one of Martin Niemöller's statement, "God has sent me in ways that I would not have chosen and through trials I would not have dared face."

Timothy to Discipline the Church (1 Tim. 1:3–20)

Paul seems to be persuading a reluctant Timothy to stay on in Ephesus (v. 3). He is needed there to clear up the confusion caused by some misguided teachers. The heresy in Ephesus was a mixture of elements of Judaism, gnosticism (which claimed special, exclusive knowledge), and Christianity. The fondness of these teachers for "legends and long lists of names of ancestors" (v. 4, TEV) merely produced arguments. Paul says they don't know what they are talking about (vv. 5–7).

Lest some misunderstand the nature and limitations of law, Paul explains (vv. 8–11). The law makes explicit that which is wrong. It is therefore primarily for wrongdoers. It is useful because it curtails evil. It is also inadequate. The gospel lifts the believer from the negative life of avoiding wrong, to the positive life of striving for that which is right in God's sight.

Paul illustrates from his own experience (vv. 12–17). He had been a strict Pharisee and doctrinaire observer of the Levitical law. His misplaced zeal had caused him to persecute the Christians and denounce Jesus, their leader (Acts 9:4–5). Now he realizes this was blasphemy, because he was speaking evil of God. But God's grace even included him, the worst of sinners. If he could be saved and transformed, the gospel could save and transform anyone. He himself is living proof of its power.

This is the kind of gospel that is intrusted to Timothy. He should hang on to it in faith and in a good conscience (vv. 18–20). Don't deal lightly with those who could destroy it! Like Hymanaeus and Alexander, for instance. They were turned out of the church for their false teachings. This act marked the seriousness of their offense, but it was done so that they would "be taught to stop speaking evil of God" (v. 20, TEV).

Behavior in Worship (1 Tim. 2:1–15)

At this point Paul begins the discussion of some special items for Timothy's attention. Prayer is the foremost concern (2:1–8). Pray for all men. Yes, pray for kings and those in authority. Nero was emperor then (A.D. 54–68). Pray *for* him, not *to* him. This is appropriate in God's sight. Men should lead out in the prayer life of the church, but it must not be an empty performance. Their words must be matched by dedicated Christian living.

He continues the matter of appropriateness in worship with some special advice about the public role of women in the Ephesus church (vv. 9–15). The social customs of the time made it unbecoming for upright women to do public speaking or teaching. The women prominently seen and heard in public places then were generally prostitutes and others of ill repute. Paul warns Timothy to be mindful of the social realities of the time and of the circumstances of his city. The women of the congregation must not even give the appearance of evil or give the slightest excuse for their pagan neighbors to misunderstand or misconstrue the nature of the Christian fellowship.

Under these circumstances the Christian women would serve the cause of Christ better by dressing modestly and appropriately for public worship. For the same reasons, it would not be fitting for them to be teachers. Paul did not exclude women from the work of the churches and from influential roles, as seen in his mention of several by name in his epistles—Lydia, Dorcas, Priscilla, Tryphaena, Tryphosa, Persis, Julia, Euodia, and Syntyche. His appeal to the relationship of Adam and Eve (vv. 13–15) seems to be intended to remind them that this primacy of the man and the domestic role of the woman have a long history that will not easily be changed.

Special points.—The statement in 2:4 about God "who will have all men to be saved" is no ground for the idea of universal salvation. A better translation is "who wants all men to be saved" (TEV).

Jewish tradition taught that during pregnancy women were ceremonially disqualified for worship and, therefore, forfeited something in their relationship to God. Apparently in Ephesus some were speculating as to whether or not a Christian woman was "saved" during this period. Paul indicates (v. 15) that her salvation is unaffected by childbearing. The real question is: Does she persevere in faith, love, holiness, and —to pick up the subject he had been talking about—modesty? Christian obedience is the clue and key to salvation!

Church Officers (1 Tim. 3:1–16)

For Timothy and the congregation at Ephesus, Paul lays down some quali-

fications for church leaders. First, requirements for the bishop, the overseer and pastor, the guardian of souls (vv. 1–7). The qualities listed have primary reference to morality and spirituality. His manner of life is to be without fault. He must have no more than one wife. (The language does not rule out unmarried men.)

In personal conduct and in family discipline, in experience as a spiritual leader, and in reputation, he must be above reproach. He should not be a new convert (v. 16).

Standards for the deacon (vv. 8–13) are similar. He, too, must be blameless, of a good character, having his household in proper control. Inserted in this section is a requirement that wives of both classes of church officers also be exemplary Christians (v. 11).

Paul expresses the hope of visiting Timothy shortly, but in case this is impossible, these written instructions will set a course of action for the congregation at Ephesus and the other churches (v. 15). At this point Paul apparently quotes a confession or hymn of praise to Jesus, "the mystery of godliness" (KJV), "the secret of our religion" (v. 16, TEV).

False Teachers and Timothy's Growth (1 Tim. 4:1–16)

In spite of the glorious spiritual heritage to which he had just referred, some will turn away from the faith led by false and insincere teachers (vv. 1–2). He warns especially against two of their errors, forbidding marriage and the use of certain foods (vv. 3–5). Paul asserts that, contrary to the gnostic teachings of all matter being evil, the entirety of God's creation is good, if properly dedicated to him.

Paul gives Timothy some personal counsel which he is to pass on to others

(vv. 6–10). Avoid worthless legends. Keep in training with appropriate spiritual nourishment and exercise. Timothy, perhaps 30 years younger than Paul, is not to allow his lack of age to stand in his way. He must strive to be an example. He must devote himself to public reading of the Scriptures, preaching, and teaching. He is to be a diligent steward of the spiritual authority and power invested in him.

Groups in the Church (1 Tim. 5:1–25)

Timothy is advised to treat various groups in the church judiciously (5:1–2). The church's charity funds should be used carefully, especially for widows. Real need should be met, but each family must face up to responsibility for its own members (vv. 3–8). The list of widows eligible for charity should be restricted to the worthy women over sixty years of age (vv. 9–10). Younger widows should be encouraged to marry and assume responsibility for their own welfare (vv. 11–16).

Regarding church officials, Paul asks for adequate financial compensation and due care for their reputation (vv. 17–20). Timothy is to be an impartial disciplinarian, cautious in ordaining men, careful with his health, and discerning in his judgment of conduct (vv. 21–25).

Final Advice to Timothy (1 Tim. 6:1–20)

As elsewhere in his writings, Paul seeks to change the master-and-slave relationship by the gospel doing its work in the individual (vv. 1–2).

False teachers, he says, betray themselves by their inconsistency regarding the teachings of Jesus, also their pride and empty disputations (vv. 3–5).

Timothy is warned against material things as a measure of contentment (vv. 6–10). He must be aggressive both in turning away from wrong and also in turning to that which is right (vv. 11–16). He is instructed to communicate this same sense of values to the rich (vv. 17–19).

Conclusion (1 Tim. 6:20–21)

A final charge to Timothy is given. He must guard carefully the gospel which has been entrusted to his care. Paul's distinctive form of blessing closes the letter.

2 TIMOTHY

W. C. Fields

INTRODUCTION

Rome burned in July, A.D. 64. Needing a scapegoat, Emperor Nero blamed the Christians. Persecution began. From that time onward until the days of Constantine and A.D. 325, Christianity was an illegal religion. To complicate matters further, the Jewish rebellion against Rome was rising. Christianity's connection with the Jews was well known, a fact which added to the guilt of every Christian in the eyes of the imperial authorities.

Paul was known widely as a leader of the Christians. When the Christians were branded as public enemies, Paul's name would be first on the list for extermination. Nero's administration would be aware of his long prison record—in Rome, Philippi, Caesarea, and elsewhere. It would not take them long to track him down and on a charge of sedition or treason get court orders for his execution.

Occasion: Paul had expected to spend the winter at Nicopolis (Titus 3:12). His arrest may have occurred there. We do not know what the actual charge was, but this time he has no hope of release (2 Tim. 4:18). It is dangerous for anyone to be associated with him (3:11). The letter may have been written from either Nicopolis or Rome. He was executed, according to tradition, on the Ostian Way outside the walls of the city of Rome. This was his last letter.

Author: the apostle Paul.

Date: probably the fall of A.D. 64, although some scholars argue for a later time.

Purpose: He wants Timothy and John Mark to visit him as quickly as possible, before winter (4:21). In case they do not arrive in time, he has some final requests about the churches. We do not know if they saw him before his death.

Central message: "I have fought a good fight, I have finished my course, I have kept the faith . . ." (4:7–8).

Salutation (2 Tim. 1:1–2)

The affectionate greeting to Timothy as "my dearly beloved son" emphasizes the bond between them which lasted to the end.

Charge to Timothy (2 Tim. 1:3–18)

A recurring note in Paul's epistles is his remembrance of associates and friends in prayer. He prays for Timothy "night and day." In his prison cell he finds joy and gratitude in the sincere faith which a mother and grandmother had helped to instil in Timothy (vv. 3–5).

God has endowed Timothy with a special gift, a commitment. He must keep it burning at white hot heat (v. 6). He has the resources for boldness in his task (v. 7). No shame or hesitation should hamper him, not even Paul's imprisonment and apparent defeat at the hands of his enemies (v. 8). Rather on the basis of Paul's own experience of victory-in-defeat, Timothy likewise can face trouble unafraid (vv. 9–15).

The gospel has never disappointed Paul.

Some of the Christians from Asia Minor—two are named—had repudiated Paul. The stress was too much for them. But one man, Onesiphorus from Ephesus, was an exception. He went out of his way in Rome to help Paul (vv. 16–18).

Courage and Faith in Hardships (2 Tim. 2:1–13)

In both letters to him there is an inference that Timothy may be hampered by timidness. Trouble is coming for him, however. He must be strong for the task of passing on the gospel to others. They in turn will do the same thing in an endless chain of witness (vv. 1–2).

Timothy will need the discipline of a good soldier (vv. 3–4), a winning athlete (v. 5), and a successful farmer (v. 6). God's power cannot be imprisoned or destroyed, therefore Paul has found strength to endure whatever happens. He commends this kind of confidence to Timothy (vv. 7–10). Paul apparently quotes a hymn or series of familiar sayings among the Christians (vv. 11–13). They emphasize God's faithfulness in all circumstances.

An Approved Worker (2 Tim. 2:14–26)

Paul sets down seven imperatives. They are for Timothy and those whom he will train to be leaders of the church. These are important rules of conduct which he commends to them.

1. Don't fight over words. Hairsplitting discussions are unproductive (v. 14).

2. Work hard for God's approval of you. Be an accurate teacher (v. 15).

3. Avoid profane, foolish discussions. They drive people away from God (v. 16).

Paul condemns such empty, irreverent activities. They are like open sores. He cites the example of two men. They were erroneously teaching that the resurrection had already passed (vv. 16–18). But such false teachers cannot destroy the foundation God has laid. God knows who are his own (v. 19). It should come as no surprise, however, that the church, like a household, has a mixture of vessels that vary in their usefulness (v. 20). Each vessel of Christ must separate himself from defilement and strive to be a useful vessel (v. 21). He resumes his rules of conduct.

4. "Avoid the passions of youth" (v. 22, TEV).

5. "Strive for righteousness, faith, love, and peace" (v. 22, TEV).

6. Stay away from foolish, contentious arguments (v. 23).

7. Don't quarrel. Instead, be kind and gentle, a patient teacher who helps those in error to return to their senses (vv. 24–26).

Last Days (2 Tim. 3:1–9)

Timothy must not be surprised at widespread evil. The struggle will go on to the end, "the last days." Wickedness will become incarnate and show itself in many ways. Stay away from such (vv. 1–5)!

Ungodly teachers will wield strange powers over people. But like Jannes and Jambres, the Egyptian magicians who opposed Moses, they shall fail. Their depraved minds will betray them (vv. 6–9).

Last Instructions (2 Tim. 3:10—4:5)

When ungodliness is on the rampage, Timothy can take courage from his firsthand acquaintance with the experience of Paul. Timothy was an eyewitness to Paul's teaching, his conduct, and his unchanging purpose (3:10). Timothy is reminded of the bitter persecution which surrounded Paul in and near Timothy's hometown of Lystra (Acts 14:8–20). But the Lord brought Paul through it (3:11).

This kind of opposition awaits all true Christians (v. 12). Trouble will mount. Evil will degenerate men more and more (v. 13). When this happens Timothy must grasp more firmly to the truth from the Scriptures which he has been taught since childhood (vv. 14–15). The Scriptures will be his mainstay. God inspired them. They will be his instrument in teaching truth, in separating error, and in equipping men for ethical, godly living (vv. 16–17).

Paul gives a solemn charge to Timothy to be aggressive in preaching the gospel in all kinds of circumstances, whether favorable or not (4:1–2). Witness will become more difficult as men turn from truth to fiction (vv. 3–4). He must keep himself under discipline, endure suffering when it comes, but continue to declare the gospel (v. 5).

Special point.—The sacred Scriptures of the early Christians were the books of the Old Testament. They were "inspired by God." They are Godbreathed. God was involved in their authorship. Time and testing had proven them. They are "profitable" or useful (3:16). Paul contrasts the Scriptures with the teachings and writings that were not God-breathed, that were sources of error and ungodliness. They were circulating in considerable abundance in Timothy's world—the Apocrypha, writings of the so-called mystery religions of the day, the records of pagan philosphers, the views of certain

schools of thought like the Gnostics, etc. In the midst of all this literature, Paul counsels Timothy to make the Scriptures his guide. Time has proven them. God inspired them.

Later, in the midst of a massive outpouring of further written material of all kinds, the early churches became convinced that God had inspired numerous Christian writings—gospels, letters, and special accounts like Acts and Revelation. They now comprise our New Testament. They were proven by the tests of time and experience "so that the man who serves God may be fully qualified and equipped to do every kind of good work" (v. 17).

Paul's Situation (2 Tim. 4:6–18)

Paul's life is at an end. He knows this imprisonment will end in his death. But this is not defeat. It is victory (vv. 6–8). The crown of eternal life awaits him.

The remainder of chapter 4 is a touching list of personal matters. He wants Timothy to get Mark and come to him soon. Demas has forsaken him. Others are away. Only Luke is with him (vv. 9–12). He requests his cloak, his books, and parchments (v. 13). Some have abused him; others have abandoned him. But his sense of the Lord's presence is strength enough for whatever is ahead (vv. 14–18).

Farewell (2 Tim. 4:19–22)

Even in the midst of such deep emotions he pauses in closing to pass on thoughtful words about friends. There is a final plea for Timothy to come to him before winter. He concludes with a benediction.

TITUS

W. C. Fields

INTRODUCTION

This letter is akin to 1 Timothy. It expresses pastoral concerns. It deals with qualifications for church officers. It stresses sound doctrine. Ethical obligations for believers are specified. Believers are warned against false teaching.

Author: the apostle Paul.

Audience: It is addressed to Titus. He is not mentioned in Acts. In Paul's letters, however, he appears frequently as a trusted associate. A Gentile, he accompanied Paul from Antioch to Jerusalem. There Paul refused the Jews' demand that Titus be circumcised (Gal. 2:1–5). In 2 Corinthians he is repeatedly mentioned as a representative of Paul to that church. Paul had been with Titus in the island of Crete and had left him there to straighten out certain disorders in the church (1:5). Although a personal letter to Titus, this communication from the apostle has instructions which affect all of the Christians there.

Occasion: Zenas and Apollos are traveling to Crete. They seem to be the bearers of the letter (3:15). Paul has personal knowledge of the needs of the church there and takes advantage of the opportunity to respond to them.

Date: probably around A.D. 63, shortly after 1 Timothy. The place of the writing is not known, but it may have been Macedonia. It is written during Paul's fourth missionary tour, following his release from the first imprisonment at Rome.

The thirteen letters of Paul in the New Testament are not arranged chronologically, although the pastoral epistles are apparently the last ones he wrote. Rather, the sequence in the New Testament seems to be according to length, beginning with Romans, his longest, and generally diminishing in size.

Purpose: to strengthen the work of Titus, to sustain the Christians there, and to request Titus to join him before winter.

Central message: faithful leaders, sound doctrine and godly living go hand in hand in response to God's grace.

Paul's Introduction (Titus 1:1–4)

This is more than a salutation. It is a majestic statement of God's plan through the ages. Paul, "a servant of God, and an apostle of Jesus Christ," was called to advance that plan. The reference to Titus as "my true son in the faith that we share" (v. 4) may indicate that Titus was converted under Paul's preaching.

Titus' Work in Crete (Titus 1:5–16)

The first order of business for Titus is clear. He is to see that elders are duly appointed in every congregation (v. 5). "Every city" implies the existence of churches throughout the island.

Elders or presbyters and bishops or overseers are terms applied here to the same office. Paul is concerned more

769

with the good character of these officers than with an explanation of their titles (vv. 5–9). He repeats instructions previously given to Titus in person. The qualifications are the same basic requirements he sets down in 1 Timothy 3:1–7. These church leaders must be of proven character. They must be able to teach effectively and deal firmly with error.

This leads Paul to say sternly that the rebels and deceivers, some of whom are converts from Judaism, must be stopped (vv. 10–16). The people of Crete had a reputation for being an uncouth lot. Added to this tendency is the fact that some Cretan Christians were mercenary. Other believers are preoccupied with irrelevant legends. Still others are hypocritical, saying one thing and doing another. Paul says this kind of inconsistency must stop.

Proper Conduct (Titus 2:1–15)

Sound doctrine requires worthy behavior. Proper thinking cannot be separated from proper acting. Saying the right thing and doing the right thing are bound up together. All groups in the churches must conduct themselves consistently and appropriately (v. 1).

The older men are to be under self-control (v. 2). The older women are likewise to show discipline (v. 3) and influence the younger women to demonstrate moral character personally and in their homes (vv. 4–5). Titus is instructed to be a good example for the young men in word and deed (vv. 6–8). The Christian way of life is also to make a difference in the response of Christian slaves to their surroundings (vv. 9–12).

God's grace requires all believers "to live self-controlled, upright and godly lives in this world" (vv. 11–12, TEV). This manner of life is to be lived in expectation of the appearing of Christ. Note that Paul here (v. 13) applies both terms, "the great God" and "Savior," to Jesus Christ. In view of this heritage Paul gives Titus some imperatives. Teach these things! Use your full authority! Encourage and rebuke! Give no one an excuse to look down on you! (v. 15).

Godly Living (Titus 3:1–11)

Paul continues his theme that God's purpose in redemption is to achieve a higher level in human affairs. Christians are to be good citizens (v. 1). They are to relate positively and constructively to other people (v. 2). They are to rise above their own wasted, self-centered, discordant past (v. 3).

In the midst of urging Titus and the church leaders to promote a life-style of service and good works, Paul pauses with a reminder (vv. 4–7). Good works do not produce salvation! Rather, the reverse is true. Good works, a life of openness toward others and toward God, is a product of salvation. Salvation is by the grace and mercy of God. Salvation liberates one from the self-centered life. Those who think in a godly fashion will have a concern, a steady purpose to live and work in a godly fashion (v. 8).

Therefore, don't waste your time on pointless, worthless matters—"stupid arguments, long lists of names of ancestors, quarrels, and fights about the Law" (v. 9, TEV). If there are those who insist on doing these things and thereby disrupt the congregation, warn them a couple of times. If they do not stop it, have nothing more to do with them (vv. 10–11).

Personal Matters (Titus 3:12–14)

One of the purposes of the letter seems to be to request Titus to come

24. Cleopatra's arch at Tarsus

to Paul. Artemas or Tychicus, one or the other, would free Titus of his duties in Crete so that he could join Paul at Nicopolis (v. 12). Paul had decided to spend the winter there. It may have been at Nicopolis that the Roman authorities arrested Paul for the last time.

Titus is to expedite the journey of Zenas the lawyer and Apollos who probably brought the letter to Crete (v. 13). The language is not clear as to whether or not they were returning to Paul.

Once again (v. 14) Paul emphasizes the main point he has tried to make in the letter. See that the believers live lives of service in keeping with their Christian profession! "Good works" is a term used throughout the letter. It clearly refers to deeds of ethical and moral worth. Here at the close there is also an overtone which also implies that believers should get to work in some decent occupation. "They should not live useless lives" (TEV).

Conclusion (Titus 3:15)

The exchange of greetings between the believers in both places, in Paul's location and at Crete, is in the special bonds of the faith.

PHILEMON

W. C. Fields

INTRODUCTION

This is a personal letter to an old friend. It is not directed to a church. No attempts are made at doctrinal exposition. The main concern is a private matter. Paul's correspondence with Timothy and Titus includes some general matters for the churches under their care. This note is for one man, Philemon.

It is surprising that an item of such restricted nature—and such a short one—should be included in the books of the New Testament. Yet, it is a priceless example of what the gospel was doing in the pagan setting of the Graeco-Roman world. It is prime evidence of the power of the Christian gospel to break down barriers among men.

The three main personalities are an unlikely trio in the Mediterranean world of the first century. An ex-rabbi to whom non-Jews were once disdained! A Gentile of wealth who normally would have scorned a wandering Jewish teacher and who, by all standards of the time, might have been expected to deal brutally with a runaway slave! A forlorn servant and confessed thief without rights and, under ordinary circumstances, without hope of compassion! An impossible triangle for brotherhood and love. Nevertheless, the gospel of Jesus Christ turned all three in new directions and meshed their lives in a classic instance of reconciliation.

Author: the apostle Paul.

Central message: Christian love adds new dimensions to all human relationships.

Purpose: to encourage Philemon to be reconciled with Onesimus as a brother in Christ.

Audience: the aggrieved slave owner, Philemon.

Key verse: "So, if you think of me as your partner, welcome him back just as you would welcome me" (v. 17, TEV).

Occasion: Onesimus becomes a Christian under Paul's influence. He voluntarily returns to his master for restitution and recompense. He accompanies Tychicus who is also delivering Paul's letters to the Ephesians and Colossians.

Date: A.D. 58–60, during Paul's first Roman imprisonment.

Paul's Introduction (Philem. 1–3)

In addition to the appeal from personal friendship, Paul claims a hearing because of his sufferings as a prisoner for Christ. Timothy is identified with him, as in the letter to Colossae. Apphia is unknown. She may have been Philemon's wife. Archippus is mentioned in Colossians 4:17. He may have been the leader of the church which was meeting in Philemon's house, or possibly Philemon's son.

Thanksgiving for Philemon (Philem. 4–7)

Deep feelings of gratitude are expressed for the personal character of Philemon. With great tact Paul emphasizes the impact of Philemon's faith and love on the believers. We do not know what particular acts of benevolence the author has in mind. But Paul is about to

772

request him to exert these same qualities in relation to his fugitive slave. He ends this statement of gratitude by calling him "brother" (v. 7).

Plea for Onesimus (Philem. 8–22)

This part of the letter is carefully worded and full of diplomatic and subtle appeals on behalf of Onesimus. In Rome the runaway had somehow come in contact with Paul, the friend of his master. This encounter led to the conversion of Onesimus and a change in his life. The name Onesimus means "profitable" or "useful." Paul says he is now living up to his name.

Paul values him so much that he would have kept him in Rome as an assistant. But both Roman law and Christian conscience demanded that Onesimus return to his master and correct all wrongs. Apparently he had stolen something (v. 18). Paul inserts his signature as an IOU (v. 19). Paul himself will stand good for any material loss. Philemon is reminded, however, that he is in debt to Paul in a spiritual sense.

Paul expresses the confidence that Philemon will not only forgive him and receive him as a brother, but that he will go even beyond this. Paul does not spell this out. Did he mean to suggest that Philemon set Onesimus free? Or let him return to Rome to assist Paul? We do not know. He leaves it to the noble spirit of Philemon to do what seems appropriate. Paul expects to see the results for himself, however. He anticipates being freed from prison and visiting in Colossae (v. 22).

Special point.—Paul certainly was not blind to the evils of slavery. At this stage of development among the scattered churches, the most effective change the Christians could make on a slave-holding society was to witness to the transforming power of Christian love. Apparently Philemon followed Paul's suggestions regarding Onesimus. There is evidence in early church history that Onesimus became the leader of the Christian movement in Ephesus and brought together the first collection of Paul's writings.

Conclusion (Philem. 23–25)

Those joining Paul in greetings from Rome are the same persons listed at the close of Colossians (4:10 f.). Paul's customary benediction closes the letter.

HEBREWS

W. C. Fields

INTRODUCTION

This is Christianity's first major study in comparative religion. It is a carefully reasoned claim for superiority over Judaism. The style and format make it a polished literary treatise. The Greek in which it was originally written is the best in the New Testament. It resembles a sermon that sounds like it was intended to be read aloud. At the end it is a letter.

The content is systematically arranged. It is the most purely theological work in the New Testament. The author deliberately strives for rhetorical effect. He is language-conscious. The argument is designed for persuasion.

This is one of four New Testament books addressed to Jews. The others are Matthew, James, and 1 Peter. The author deals with the fact that Christ had not already returned as some expected. He also explains the significance of the rejection of Jesus as Messiah by most of the Jewish people. Gentiles now clearly have an equal claim on God's promises of redemption. In this respect, this letter is a complement to John's Gospel.

There are frequent appeals to the authority of Old Testament Scriptures. Like Isaiah 40–66, which is unlike anything in the Old Testament, this book is unique in the New Testament. Both have the same "Easter morning breath from another world." The good things of Judaism are pictured as giving way to the better things of Christianity. The moonlight of the Old Testament is replaced by the sunrise of a new era in God's dealings with men.

Author: Unknown. Various authors have been suggested since the debate on the matter began in the second century—Paul, Barnabas, Luke, Apollos, Silas, Aquilla, Priscilla, Aristion, Clement of Rome, and some others.

About the only consensus on the matter is that Paul did not write it. The style, terms, personality, and concepts of this writer differ considerably from Paul. The thirteen known letters of Paul's are all signed by him. Paul made a special point of claiming direct revelation of the gospel from Jesus Christ. This author includes himself among those who received the gospel from the original disciples.

The author, whoever he was, knew Paul well and was a friend of Timothy. He was a teacher in one of the churches. Among those suggested as author, Barnabas seems to be the most likely possibility. He was a Jew and a Levite and would have had the depth of knowledge about Jewish religious life revealed in this letter. He was from Cyprus and would be familiar with the concepts of the Greek and Roman world which are expressed here. He was a companion of Paul, a friend of Timothy, and seems to have had the respect of both Jews and Gentiles. Even so, the evidence is circumstantial and incomplete. The authorship of the letter remains uncertain. As Origen concluded at the beginning of the third century, "Only God knows."

Audience: Jewish Christians at some unknown location. They seem to be members of a particular congregation or group of believers in one locality. They are familiar with Levitical laws, Temple worship, and the Hebrew institutions. They had endured persecution and loss of property. They were now in danger of turning their backs on Christianity and returning to Judaism. The author knows them personally. Timothy, whom they know, is about to visit them (13:23). This may have been a church somewhere in Syria, Egypt, Italy, or elsewhere. The place is not known.

Date: probably around A.D. 69, before the destruction of Jerusalem by the Romans in A.D. 70. The Temple in Jerusalem seems to be still standing and functioning (10:11). There are those, however, who argue for a later date. The author is acquainted with the works of Paul. The reference to Timothy's release from prison is a factor in dating the epistle. As requested in Paul's second letter to him, Timothy may have gone to visit Paul in his final imprisonment and been arrested himself. Paul was probably arrested around A.D. 64. If these assumptions are correct, the letter to the Hebrews would fall somewhere between A.D. 64 and 70.

Occasion: These Jewish Christians were wavering in their allegiance to Jesus Christ. This letter explains why they should continue steadfastly on as disciples of Jesus.

Purpose: to encourage the Hebrew Christians to hold to their faith (3:6) and go on to maturity (6:1).

Central message: Christianity is superior to Judaism; therefore hold fast to your faith and proclaim it to others!

Introduction: Christianity Is Better! (Heb. 1:1–3)

From the first, the writer indicates literary skill. The opening sentence is a striking declaration of the significance of Jesus Christ. It is couched in language that will not offend Jews, but rather draw them on into his argument. He begins immediately to draw the contrasts which characterize the entire work. At the outset he declares the finality of the Christian faith.

The old revelation came piecemeal. In those days God's message came in scattered places and times (v. 1). The divine word came then from prophets. The new revelation has come through a Son (v. 2). God is the author of both, but the message from a Son supercedes all that went before it.

The Son's position and authority are described with beauty and power. He is not just a spokesman. God made him the agent of creation in the beginning. He will be the possessor of all things at the end of the ages (v. 2). His superiority over the prophets is indicated by the fact that he shares the glory and majesty "of God's own being" (v. 3, TEV). His mission was to make it possible for men to be clean from their sins. When the mission was completed he returned to his position beside God, the ultimate power. He is the consummation of God's revelation, supreme, and sufficient.

Christ Is a Better Mediator (Heb. 1— 2:18)

Jewish tradition held that angels were the highest messengers of revelation. The word "angel" means "messenger." They were viewed as special bearers of God's message to his people. The author speaks directly to this belief. Christ is superior to angels. Even the names indicate this difference of status. One is God's Son, the other is merely a messenger for God (1:4).

Seven quotations from the Old Testament are introduced to support the preeminence of Christ (1:5–14). Wherever the Old Testament speaks of a final and full manifestation of God in power, glory, salvation, and judgment, the author identifies this with Jesus. With the coming of Messiah, many Old Testament passages take on meanings which could not have been known or understood before.

In 2:1–4 the writer interjects the first of a series of warnings. The full light of God's revelation in Christ puts the hearers under even greater obligation than those who lived under the Mosaic law. The new revelation must not be allowed to drift past them and out of reach (v. 1). The law had its penalties and rewards (v. 2). The new revelation has to do with salvation. Its implications are so great that no one can disregard it with impunity (v. 3). This message was spoken by the Lord himself, attested to by eyewitnesses, and confirmed by miracles and gifts of the Spirit (v. 4).

The writer now anticipates a question by the Jews. How can Jesus be superior to the angels when he was a man who suffered and died? He quotes Psalm 8:4–6 to indicate that man is only temporarily "lower than the angels" (vv. 5–8). Jesus, identified with mankind and suffered temptation and death. Through his victory all men can fulfil their destiny to be crowned with glory and honor (vv. 9–18).

Better than Moses (Heb. 3:1—4:16)

The Jews respected Moses as the first and greatest of the prophets. The writer uses this important fact to further illustrate the significance of Jesus. Moses was a servant in God's house. Jesus is the Son in charge of the house (3:1–6).

The comparison between Moses and Jesus is followed by a comparison between those who followed Moses and those who follow Jesus. A generation of Israel shared in the deliverances at the Passover in Egypt and at the Red Sea, only to rebel in the wilderness and die

there (3:7–11). The Jewish Christians who have identified themselves with Christ are warned by this example not to turn back to Judaism and forfeit the spiritual maturity that Christ makes possible for them (3:12–19).

A further warning is given against retreating into Judaism. To do so would be to miss God's "rest." (4:1–13). This is a figure of speech referring to the Christian's goal or reward. It is based on the "rest" which awaited the Israelites in Canaan after their wilderness struggles (v. 8). It also has reference to God's resting on the seventh day of creation (v. 4). The Christian Jews are reminded of their ancestors who traveled to a point within sight of the Promised Land, then because of their lack of faith, they turned away from it. The exhortation here is for the congregation to help any who seem about to "come short" of God's promises in Christ. The "word of God" is the effective instrument to use in such cases (vv. 12–13). It analyzes, lays bare, reveals in their true nature and reduces to their final elements all the powers of man.

The remaining verses in chapter 4 (vv. 14–16) are a transition to the subject of the priesthood. Since Christians have a high priest, Jesus Christ, who has entered into God's rest—"into the heavens"—the Christian should do likewise (v. 14). Therefore, keep moving ahead! "Let us be brave, then, and come forward to God's throne, where there is grace" (v. 16a).

A Better High Priesthood (Heb. 5:1—8:6)

The priesthood was a central fact of Jewish tradition. Any comparison of Christianity with Judaism would have to take it into consideration. The author makes passing references to it earlier in the letter. Now he takes up the subject to show that Jesus Christ is indeed a high priest of a superior order.

Jesus possessed the qualifications for the high priesthood. He was selected to minister (5:1–3). He was appointed by God (v. 4). Furthermore, as demonstrated most dramatically in Gethsemane, he entered fully into the plight of men and could sympathize with their weakness (vv. 5–8). Through his sufferings he became the author of salvation (v. 9) and a high priest "after the order of Melchizedek" (v. 10).

Once again the author directs an appeal and a warning to his audience (5:11–14). They had been Christians long enough to be teachers themselves. Instead, they had progressed so little in the faith that they were still in the ABC stage. They were still eating baby food long after the proper time. He indicates that if they had not been so dull of mind and heart they would easily grasp the significance of a "high priest after the order of Melchizedek."

One cannot linger on with the ABC's. Or, in building a house, one cannot keep on reworking the foundation. Likewise in the faith there must be progress toward maturity (6:1–3). Some apparently were still at the elementary level, in turmoil over whether or not Jesus was actually the Messiah. The author, however, warns these wavering Jews that if anyone rejects Jesus as the true Messiah it is impossible to "renew them again to repentance" (vv. 4–6). Why? Because there will be no other Messiah or Christ. If they reject Jesus there is no hope for them.

They have had enough spiritual experience with the gospel of Jesus to make a judgment. They have glimpsed its light, tasted the heavenly gift, experienced the presence of the Holy Spirit, sensed that God's Word is good, and they have felt the powers of the coming age. If, after all of this, these Jews "fall away" and reject Jesus as the Christ, the Messiah, they are doomed.

This is not a question of falling from grace one day and getting back into grace the next day. This is addressed to first-century Jews who were trying to decide whether or not Jesus was their long-awaited Messiah. The writer agrees that this is the beginning point of the Christian experience for a Jew, but he should settle that question and move on to many other matters in the Christian faith. Those to whom he was writing had already lingered too long at this first stage of experience with Jesus. The time was overdue for progress toward maturity.

In concluding the warning, the writer gives two examples from nature (vv. 7–8). Two plots of ground both receive the same rains. One produces a worthy harvest. The other produces only thorns and briars and is rejected.

In spite of the present possibility of falling short, the author expresses confidence that they will yet go on to the full Christian experience (vv. 9–12). Even Abraham was tempted to falter on the course God had set for him. But when he continued on his way God's promise was still good (vv. 13–20).

The writer returns to the matter of Jesus being "a priest forever" after the order of Melchizedek. He continues to argue that Christ is a better high priest than the line of Levi could produce (7:1–10). Melchizedek received tithes from Abraham (Gen. 14:17–20). He was of God's original priesthood, since he preceded Levi by several hundred years. So far as the record is concerned, Melchizedek appears from nowhere and goes nowhere. The author applies this metaphor to the Son of God who is a priest continually.

The Levitic line of priesthood was

imperfect (7:11–12). It was necessary for God to draw the new priesthood from a new line, Judah from whom Jesus came (vv. 13–15). Because of his endless life, Jesus is a priest in the order of Melchizedek (vv. 16–17). Jesus is a guarantee that God will carry out his promise (vv. 18–22). The old priestly line could not fully accomplish God's redemptive purpose. However, in Christ the faithful are saved "to the uttermost" because he is consecrated high priest "for evermore" (vv. 23–28).

The author summarizes his comparison on the priesthood (8:1–6). Christ officiates in heaven. Earthly priests do work that is a copy and a shadow of the real thing which is in heaven. Then the author links the discussion on the high priesthood with the following section on the covenant. As high priest, Jesus is the mediator of a better covenant established on better promises.

A Better Covenant (Heb. 8:7–13)

Having shown that Jesus is greater than Moses and that he is also a superior high priest, he now proceeds to the argument that the new covenant in Christ supercedes the old. The old one failed (v. 7). Israel readily accepted the privileges but reluctantly took on the responsibilities of the old covenant. Jeremiah (31:31–34) proclaimed a new kind of covenant which came into being through Christ (vv. 8–9). The old one provided no assurance to sinful men of continuing under its promises. The new covenant therefore would operate by internal compulsion rather than by external restraint as in the old covenant (v. 10).

There would be no longer the need for a human priestly class, since the covenant people will know God directly in their own hearts and minds (v. 11). God will put away their sins to free the way for unhindered fellowship (v. 12).

When Jeremiah announced the coming of this kind of new covenant he automatically branded the old covenant as outmoded and to be replaced (v. 13). The Hebrew Scriptures themselves, then, announced that the old covenant would be superseded by a new one.

A Better Sanctuary (Heb. 9:1–12)

The tabernacle and its routine were symbols of the old covenant (vv. 1–5). The furniture and ceremonies were reminders of God's presence, his past dealings with them, and his will for them in the future. The purpose of all of this was to aid men to draw near to God. Only the high priest could go into the innermost part of the tabernacle, and only once a year (vv. 6–7). This annual event was to atone for his own sins as well as for those of his people.

In spite of its impressiveness, the tabernacle produced disappointing spiritual results. The author says that the forbidden holy of holies was in itself an indication that the time had not come for ordinary worshipers to enter (v. 8). The tabernacle ritual of "gifts and sacrifices" could only provide an external qualification for worship (vv. 9–10). But Christ as the high priest, by the sacrifice of his own life, removed all barriers to sinful men coming directly into God's presence (vv. 11–12).

A Better Sacrifice (Heb. 9:13—10:18)

This section is the holy of holies of the epistle to the Hebrews. It contrasts the tabernacle sacrifices of animals with the atoning sacrifice of Christ. The blood of animals qualified one ceremonially for worship (9:13). "How much more is accomplished by the blood of Christ!" (v. 14, TEV). Because of his voluntary action, Christ is the mediator of the new covenant (v. 15). His sacrifice is effective for all time.

Why did Christ have to die? The

author answers with two illustrations. The first is from secular law. A person's will becomes effective only when he dies. Christ died to put his will or testament, the new covenant, into effect (vv. 16–17). The second illustration is from divine law (vv. 18–23). A blood sacrifice of a higher order was necessary to seal the new covenant. Christ made that sacrifice with his own blood.

In contrast to the earthly high priest who entered the holy of holies annually, Christ entered once for all "to bear the sins of many" (vv. 24-28). The Old Testament sacrifices were vague images. "For the blood of bulls and goats can never take sins away" (10:1–4). Christ's death, however, was by the will of God (vv. 5–7). It was also accepted by Christ voluntarily (v. 8–14). The Holy Spirit attests to the inauguration of this new agreement between God and his people by which he says, "I will not remember their sins and wicked deeds any longer" (vv. 15–17). No other sin offering is needed. This is the full, complete, and final sacrificial act for sin. There will be no other (v. 18).

Special point.—The present tense used in 10.11 seems to indicate that the Temple in Jerusalem was still standing at the time this epistle was written. "Every Jewish priest stands and performs his services every day. . . ." If the Temple had already been destroyed by this time the author would hardly have passed this point in his argument without some reference to that enormously significant fact. This is one of the major factors in dating the epistle prior to A.D. 70 when Titus and the Roman army leveled the city, including its most famous building.

Better Promises (Heb. 10:19—11:40)

In view of all of the superiority of Jesus Christ (Jesus the Messiah) over Judaism, the author appeals to his audi-

ence to be steadfast in the open confession of the Christian hope. The promises guaranteed to them through Christ are greater than those given to their forefathers under the old agreement. But as before, the new covenant is conditional. They are promised free access to God (10:19–21). They must remain faithful, however. "Let us come near to God" (v. 22). "Let us hold on firmly to the hope we profess" (v. 23). "Let us be concerned with one another" (v. 24). "Let us not give up the habit of meeting together" (v. 25a). "Let us encourage one another" (v. 25b).

In view of all the foregoing, there seem to be only two alternatives. Either accept fully Jesus as Messiah, or deliberately reject him. The author sternly warns the wavering ones about this last course of action: destruction awaits those who oppose God (vv. 26–27). Those who opposed the Mosaic law were put to death without mercy (v. 28). Worse punishment can logically be expected for those who reject the Son of God (vv. 29–31).

The author encourages them to faith by recalling their previous faithfulness, their suffering and privations (vv. 32–34). They are exhorted to live by faith (vv. 35–39). Since faith as a life principle is the way of pleasing God, it is necessary for them to understand what faith is and how it works. "To have faith is to be sure of the things we hope for, to be certain of the things we cannot see" (11:1, TEV). This element of certainty and confidence in God's promises about living by faith, is exactly what these wishy-washy Jews needed.

Faith as a life principle is not new. From the days of the old covenant the writer uses many illustrations to signify its appropriateness and its necessity under the new covenant (vv. 2–38). These put faith to the test—Abel (v. 4), Enoch (vv. 5–6), Noah (v. 7), Abraham and Sarah (11:8–19), Isaac (v. 20), Jacob (v. 21), Joseph (v. 22), the parents of Moses (v. 23), Moses himself (vv. 24–29), Israel under Joshua (v. 30), Rahab the prostitute (v. 31), and a long list of others who crowd in on the author's limited time and space (vv. 32–38).

All of these won their victories by faith. Yet God has provided in Christ better promises, "an even better plan for us. His purpose was that they would be made perfect only with us" (vv. 39–40, TEV).

Stand Fast! (Heb. 12:1—13:19)

Proof seen in the lives of these heroes of faith under the old covenant is motivation for greater faithfulness by those who live under the new covenant (12:1). The believer's supreme example is Jesus (v. 2).

The readers of the epistle have not suffered beyond their ability to stand (vv. 3–15). Suffering is a mark of sonship. It is a discipline for maturity. Therefore face it as a challenge! Don't be like Esau and sell out your rightful blessings for nothing (vv. 16–17). They are reminded that they have come in their pilgrimage, not to fearsome Mount Sinai (vv. 18–21), but to "Mount Zion,"

to Jesus the mediator of a new and better covenant (vv. 22–24). They are warned to give attention to the message in the gospel of Jesus (vv. 25–28). The one who shook Mount Sinai will shake heaven and earth to accomplish his purpose.

The readers of the epistle are urged to maintain high standards of Christian love (13:1–3), fidelity (v. 4), generosity (vv. 5–6), and respect for the leaders of the congregation (v. 7).

The believer's allegiance is to be fixed steadily on Jesus Christ (vv. 8–19). He is unchanging and eternal. Strength for bold witness comes from God alone. The author asks for obedience to church leaders and for prayer in his own behalf "that I may be restored to you the sooner."

Conclusion (Heb. 13:20–25)

The author closes with a beautiful benediction (vv. 20–21). Then he adds a personal postscript. Listen patiently to the message of the letter (v. 22). Timothy is now out of prison and together they hope to visit them (v. 23). Greetings for all the saints and from "the brothers from Italy" (v. 24, TEV). And finally, "Grace be with you all."

JAMES

W. C. Fields

INTRODUCTION

This is the first of the seven general epistles. They are, in addition to James, the two letters of Peter, the three letters of John, and the letter of Jude. They are grouped together because they are addressed, not to individuals or particular churches, but to wider circles of believers.

The early chapters of the Acts of the Apostles describe the church when it was made up altogether of Jews. At that stage their acceptance of Christianity did not diminish their reverence for the law of Moses. They were thorough-going Jews who accepted Jesus as Messiah. They worshiped in the synagogues on the sabbath, the seventh day. Then they gathered with their Christian friends for their own special worship on Sunday, the first day of the week, the day on which Jesus arose from the grave. In those early days they continued to observe the Mosaic ritual. They merely added the Christian ordinances of baptism and the Memorial Supper. A Christian Jew's religion at that stage was Judaism plus his belief in Jesus as the Christ or Messiah. This letter comes out of that time and circumstance.

Author: He calls himself simply "James" (1:1). Four men named James are mentioned in the New Testament. James, "the brother of our Lord" (Gal. 1:18–19), fits the requirements of this letter.

This James, the son of Mary and Joseph and half-brother of Jesus, is mentioned ten times in the New Testament. He and his brothers did not accept Jesus as Messiah during his ministry (Mark 3:20; 6:1–6). James became a believer following Jesus' resurrection, but was not one of the twelve apostles. He talked with Paul in Jerusalem after Paul's conversion (Gal. 1:18–19). He is one of the church leaders in the Council of Jerusalem (Acts 15) around A.D. 49. Following Paul's third missionary journey he still appears to be head of the church at Jerusalem. Josephus, the Jewish historian, tells that James was condemned by the high priest and the Sanhedrin. He was stoned to death and buried outside the walls of the city.

Date: probably A.D. 47, which would make it the first of the 27 New Testament writings. The chief reason for this dating is that there is no mention of Gentile believers or the controversy over them which led to the Council of Jerusalem (Acts 15) in 48 or 49.

Audience: "To the twelve tribes which are scattered abroad" (1:1). It was probably written from Jerusalem to Christian Jews of the Dispersion in various parts of the Roman Empire.

Central message: "Therefore, to him that knoweth to do good, and doeth it not, to him it is sin" (4:17). A positive statement of this same theme is given in 1:22.

Purpose: practical counsel for moral and ethical Christian living.

Introduction (James 1:1)

Although the primary audience for

the letter is undoubtedly the Christian Jews, James is still a Jew speaking with a consciousness of all Jews.

How to Handle Trouble (James 1:2–18)

The practical character of the letter shows up immediately. He advises the brethren to learn to get something worthwhile even out of troubles and trials (vv. 2–4). "Count" them on the side of joy. View them as capable of being instructive. They provide a test run for your faith. Successful testing of your faith can give you confidence for anything that lies ahead.

Optimism, however, must be tempered with wisdom. He uses a banking term. If you "lack" wisdom, keep on asking God for it (vv. 5–8). God's liberality is limited only by one's faith. Faith is the essential religious attitude. Without it a man is storm-tossed, unsettled, and unstable.

Far from being unsettled, the man of faith learns to exult in life, whether he be rich or poor (vv. 9–11). He learns that worldly distinctions are transitory. He knows that the most beautiful flowers wither and die. Material things can fade away but the man of faith moves on at his own private pace.

The man of faith also is to master inward troubles, such as temptation. For this victory his crown is "life" itself (v. 13). God tempts no one (v. 14). Temptation is a moral problem which arises because of a man's own reactions (v. 15). Evil desire evolves into sin and sin into death (v. 16). God, on the other hand, is the source of unfailing good (vv. 17–18).

How to Treat God's Word (James 1:19–27)

The broad theme of the entire epistle is how to translate faith into godly action. He emphasizes human conduct throughout the message. Within this general context, he switches subjects rapidly. In this section he moves abruptly to the question of the right attitude toward God's word. The impact of his message is plain. When God tells you to do something, do it (vv. 19–21). Listen, think before you speak, don't become angry, and clean up your lives! Listening is only part of the godly man's duty. The main thing is to act on God's word (vv. 22–25). Verse 22 is a positive statement of the central message of the letter: "Be ye doers of the word."

Hot debates on theology are useless without genuine religious living (vv. 26–27). What is pure religion? He illustrates. Helping widows! Deeds of compassion and a life of godliness!

How to Deal with Partiality (James 2:1–13)

Pure religion is on the side of justice and right. But some of the believers were judging people on the wrong basis. The synagogues, where they were still meeting at the time of this epistle, were used both for worship and judicial proceedings. The Jewish courts had jurisdiction over certain religious and social matters. Some were showing partiality. The rich were being favored and the poor were pushed aside or ignored. James warns them that this is contrary to their faith in Jesus Christ (v. 1). Stop judging people on the basis of their outward appearance (vv. 2–4)!

God does not discriminate against the poor merely because they are poor. Rather, because of their sense of dependency they seem to turn more easily to him (v. 5). James reminds his readers that the rich around them are the ones who usually drag them into the courts (vv. 6–7). Again he quotes the Old Testament (v. 8). "Love thy neighbour

**25. Ruins at Ephesus
(see Rev. 2:1)**

as thyself" (Lev. 19:18).

Prejudice, showing partiality, breaks the law (vv. 9–13). To be law-abiding, you must keep all of the law, even those you do not like! Christian freedom imposes a greater responsibility to keep the spirit of the law.

How to Put Faith to Work (James 2:14–26)

This section has been viewed incorrectly by some as being in direct conflict with the teachings of Paul. Paul taught that salvation is by faith. Good works flow from this experience. James here merely has a different emphasis. He stresses the fact that genuine faith is authenticated by godly works.

"What good, is it for a man to say, 'I have faith,' if his actions do not prove it? Can that faith save him?" (v. 14, TEV). The kind of faith that is content to utter pious phrases and ignore the destitute, as one example, is "dead" (vv. 15–20).

A genuine faith is one that is actively at work. Paul said the works of the law could never save a man. James says that works of *faith* are proof of salvation. Abraham's faith was not an empty profession but a principle of action (vv. 21–24). The same is true for even a prostitute, like Rahab (vv. 25–26). Just as Abraham showed his faith by his willingness to offer Isaac, so Rahab showed her faith by aiding the spies. Faith and works cannot exist separately and alone. They must go together.

783

Special point: In verse 23 James refers to Genesis 15:6 which says that Abraham "believed in the Lord" and God "counted it" as righteousness for Abraham.

How to Control the Tongue (James 3:1–18)

Having said that words alone are not enough to show one's faith, he now warns against the misuse of words. In the synagogue and in the early churches there was considerable freedom to speak. This led to some confusion and disorder. There was widespread abuse of the teaching privilege. Some engaged in it without adequate preparation and for unworthy motives (vv. 1–2).

Be careful of your words! The tongue is like the bits in the horses' mouths, the rudder of ships, and a fire that can get out of control (vv. 3–6). Man has more difficulty taming his tongue than he does taming wild animals (vv. 7–8).

The wise man is consistent (vv. 9–18). He does not speak out of both sides of his mouth. His witness is enlightened from above. It does not produce confusion. It is pure, reasonable, and un-hypocritical.

How to Control Worldliness (James 4:1–17)

James devotes much space in his letter to what Jewish believers should do. He does not neglect to emphasize, however, what they should be. Faith must be internalized. It must become a guiding part of one's innermost self. In this section he rebukes the selfish attitudes which result in greed, strife, and disregard for others (vv. 1–3).

He warns against friendship with the forces of evil in the world (v. 4), against pride (vv. 5–10), against slander (vv. 11–12), and against false confidence in themselves (vv. 13–16). Verse 17 catches up the stern nature of this warning about the greater obligation the believer has to live a godly life. "So then, the man who does not do the good he knows he should do is guilty of sin" (TEV).

How to Get a Sense of Values (James 5:1–18)

The Christians were mostly poor. In the synagogues they attended there were rich Jews who oppressed them. James gives a scathing denunciation of such (vv. 1–6). The "Lord of sabaoth," the Lord of Hosts, will bring into judgment their materialistic, self-centered set of values.

The believers are to cultivate patience as they wait in the hope of Christ's return (vv. 7–9). The prophets and Job are held up as examples of patience for them (vv. 10–11).

James warns against exaggerated oaths. Believers are to have the habit of telling the truth, then they will have no need to resort to such things (v. 12). For the sick, he advises the believers to pray and use the best medicine available —"anointing him with oil" (vv. 13–15). In addition to these intercessory prayers, they are to pray in confession and with the confidence that prayer can have a powerful effect (v. 16). Proof? The prayers of Elijah (vv. 17–18).

Conclusion (James 5:19–20)

Like Proverbs, which this letter resembles in many respects, it comes to an abrupt close. It is practical to the very end, being concerned about the outworking of faith. Winning another to godliness is the highest work of all.

1 PETER

Curtis Vaughan

INTRODUCTION

First Peter, a brief summary of consolations and instructions for suffering Christians, was written for believers living in five different provinces of Asia Minor (1:1). There is no systematic arrangement of topics, but emphasis is placed on the privileges, obligations, and trials of the Christian life. A.D. 64 is its approximate date.

Salutation (1 Pet. 1:1–2)

The passage.—The *writer* (v. 1a) identifies himself by name (Peter) and by office (an apostle of Jesus Christ). "Apostle" (lit., one sent) meant something like "authorized ambassador." The *readers* (vv. 1b-2b) are described as to their status in the world (exiles of the Dispersion, RSV), their geographical locality (Pontus, Galatia, etc.), and their relation to God (elect, etc.). The *greeting* (v. 2c) takes the form of a prayer for "grace" (divine favor) and "peace" (spiritual well-being) to be multiplied to the readers.

Special points.—"Exiles of the Dispersion" (RSV) is used in a figurative sense. The thought is that Christians have their true home in heaven (cf. Phil. 3:20, ASV).

"Elect" is used in the Bible of those chosen out by God for a special relation to him and a special service for him. The believer's election is defined in three particulars: (1) It is "according to [on the basis of] the foreknowledge [purpose] of God" (v. 2a). (2) It is effected "through sanctification [setting apart] of [by] the Spirit" (v. 2b). (3) It is "unto [with a view to] obedience and sprinkling of the blood of Jesus Christ" (v. 2c). In Exodus 24:3–8 obedience and sprinkling of the blood are both associated with the establishment of God's covenant with Israel. Here the meaning seems to be that Christians (the new Israel) are chosen with a view to a covenant relation with God.

Thanksgiving (1 Pet. 1:3–12)

The passage.—These verses fall into three divisions, each of which contains a strand of praise to God for some particular benefit of redemption in Christ. The first strand (vv. 3–5) centers in "the privilege of the new birth" (cf. 1.23; 2:2). This birth from God, based upon his mercy, ushers believers into a new life which is represented under three figures: a "hope" (v. 3), an "inheritance" (v. 4), and a "salvation" (v. 5). "Hope," which is made possible by the resurrection of Christ, is the anticipation of sharing in the glory of God (cf. Rom. 5:2). The "inheritance" is described as something that death cannot destroy (incorruptible), evil cannot pollute (undefiled), and time cannot cause to wither away (fadeth not away). "Salvation" is the full deliverance which will be ours in glory. We have already been begotten to it and are now being "guarded" (kept safe) until we experience its full manifestation "in the last time."

The second strand of praise (vv. 6–9)

785

has to do with "the possibility of joy in present trials." The key words are "rejoice" (vv. 6,8) and "temptations" (i.e., trials, v. 6). Mention of trials, here used of afflictions borne because of one's faith, suggests that the readers were passing through a time of great stress. There was a divine necessity (if need be, v. 6) about these trials; they served the purpose of testing and bringing out the sterling quality of Christian faith (v. 7). The thought of joy, mentioned in verse 6, is expanded in verse 8. The words are very strong: "rejoice" means "exult" or even "triumph"; "unspeakable" suggests a joy "too great for words" (NEB); "full of glory" (lit., glorified) implies that the Christian's present joy is a foretaste of the joy of heaven.

The third strand of praise (vv. 10–12), intended to heighten the readers' sense of privilege, sets before them "the greatness of salvation."

First Series of Exhortations (1 Pet. 1:13—2:10)

The passage.—Verses 3–12 have recounted some of the privileges and benefits of the Christian life. The present passage discusses duties which flow from (note "wherefore," v. 13) those experiences. The principal ones are hope (v. 13), holiness (vv. 14–16), fear (vv. 17–21), love (vv. 22–25), and growth and progress (2:1–10). Everything else in the passage is subordinate to these ideas.

In the Greek of verse 13 the only imperative verb is that rendered "hope." (The word denotes joyful expectancy.) To hope "to the end" (lit., "perfectly") means to hope strongly, unwaveringly, wholeheartedly. "Grace," the object of our hope, stands here for the whole redemptive activity of God in our behalf. To experience this unwavering hope, we must "gird up the loins" of our minds and "be sober." The former term, which

reflects the customs of dress in Peter's day, suggests determined resolution. "Sober" (cf. 4:7; 5:8) suggests disciplined self-control.

A period should be placed at the end of verse 13, and verses 14–16 should be treated as a single sentence. The whole of it is a demand for holy living. Verse 14 states the matter from a negative point of view; verses 15 and 16 give the positive statement. "Be holy" (v. 15) means to be separated, dedicated, consecrated to God.

The third appeal (vv. 17–21) is for godly "fear" (i.e., reverential awe, v. 17). The practical meaning is that we are not to presume on God's favor but are to shape our lives by a healthy dread of his judgment. Peter encouraged his readers to assume this attitude by reminding them of the character of God (as Father, v. 17a, and as Judge, v. 17b), of the nature of the Christian life (a sojourning or pilgrimage through an alien world, v. 17c; cf. 1:1), and of the cost of redemption (vv. 18–21). "Vain conversation" (v. 18) denotes an aimless, empty way of life. "Precious" (v. 19) means costly, highly valued. "These last times" ("at the end of the times," ASV) points up that the coming of Christ into the world marked the climax of human history.

The fourth appeal (vv. 22–25) is for brotherly love. Verse 22 uses two different words for love. The first, "love of the brethren" (Greek, *philadelphia*), originally denoted love between blood brothers. Here it is love between brothers by grace. The second word for love (in the expression "love one another") denotes a love which counts no sacrifice too great for the one loved. "Fervently" (v. 22) suggests constancy and intensity.

The final appeal (2:1–10) of this section is for growth and progress in the

Christian life, a thought which flows naturally out of the reference to rebirth in 1:23. The imagery employed is quite diverse: the readers are represented as children in a family (vv. 1–3), as stones in a building (vv. 4–5a), as a company of priests (v. 5b), and as a chosen nation (vv. 9–10).

"Newborn babes" (v. 2) suggests that the recipients of this letter were recent converts. As such, they were urged to lay aside everything that would hinder their new life ("all malice," etc., v. 1) and to "desire" that which would promote growth ("the sincere milk of the word," v. 2). "Laying aside" (v. 1) translates a participle which probably has the force of a command (cf. RSV). "Desire" (v. 2) represents a very strong Greek word which denotes intense craving.

Verses 4–5a teach that when believers come to Christ, depicted here as "a living stone, disallowed [rejected] of men," but in God's sight "chosen" and "precious" (i.e., valuable or honored), they become "living stones" (ASV) in a great spiritual house (cf. Eph. 2:20–22). The reference to Christ as a living stone is a reminder that he is the Risen One able to impart life to his people.

Verses 6 through 8 continue the motif of Christ as "stone," but instead of "living stone" he is here thought of as "a chief corner stone, elect [choice], precious [honored]" (v. 6). The KJV rendering of verses 7 and 8 seems to contrast what Christ means to believers and what he means to unbelievers. Other translations (e.g., ASV) put more stress on the fact that one's destiny is determined by his attitude toward Christ. Those who believe in Christ, who esteem him as God does, will not be put to shame (v. 6) but will share in the preciousness (honor) which God has bestowed on Christ (v. 7a). Those who

refuse to believe in Christ will find him to be a stone over which they stumble headlong to disaster (v. 8).

In verses 9 and 10 the honor which God has accorded to Christians is enlarged upon. "Holy nation" refers to Christians as a people set apart for God's worship and work. "Peculiar people" (v. 9) means "a people claimed by God for his own" (NEB). "To shew forth the praises" (v. 9) is better translated "to proclaim the mighty deeds," i.e., the saving acts of God in behalf of his chosen ones.

Second Series of Exhortations (1 Pet. 2:11—3:12)

The passage.—The duties enjoined in the preceding section were mainly personal; those of the present section are decidedly social. Verses 11 and 12, which form a kind of introduction, base their appeal on the fact that the readers are "strangers [aliens] and pilgrims" (v. 11; cf. 1:1,17). The appeal itself is for the readers to "abstain from fleshly lusts" (v. 11) and to behave in a seemly manner among the Gentiles (v. 12).

"Having your conversation honest among the Gentiles" (v. 12) means "see that you maintain good conduct among the pagans." Peter's hope was that the goodness of his readers' lives might be the means of turning unbelievers to Christ. "The day of visitation" (v. 12) is probably a term for the day of judgment.

The believer's "civic obligations" are discussed in 2:13–17. "Submit yourselves" (v. 13) expresses the leading idea. Here the term is to be interpreted as submission to authority. In 2:18 and 3:1 it denotes a subordination of oneself to others, i.e., putting the interests of others above one's own.

In 2:18—3:7 the Christian's *domestic duties* are set forth. Three groups are charged: slaves (2:18–25), wives (3:1–6), and husbands (v. 7). It is estimated that there were 60,000,000 slaves in the Roman Empire. Included among them were laborers, domestic servants, clerks, and even the majority of teachers, doctors, and other professional people. The New Testament writers sought (as in the present passage) to give to slaves a sense of dignity in their work and to comfort them in their suffering. Moreover, they attempted to regulate the institution among their people (cf. Philem. 16; Eph. 6:9; Col. 4:1) and in so doing enunciated principles which eventually destroyed it. In the present passage "servants" (lit., house-slaves) are enjoined to "be subject" to their masters "with all fear" (v. 18; i.e., in a spirit of reverence for God). This subordination includes the meek acceptance of mistreatment at the hands of harsh masters. Two encouragements are given to the slave at this point: (1) the fact that the favor of God rests upon the man who patiently endures unjust treatment (vv. 19–20) and (2) the example of Christ (vv. 21–25). Whatever trials they must endure, they have in Christ one who knows the meaning of suffering and one who truly cares for them.

In 3:1–7 the reciprocal duties of wives and husbands are discussed. Mention of the wife's subjection to her husband (vv. 1,5) was not intended to teach that the wife is inferior to her husband. It does imply that the principle of wifely subordination is not simply a matter of convention; it is an expression of an abiding arrangement established by God in creation. "Word" is used in two different senses in verse 1. In the first instance ("obey not the word") the reference is to the gospel; in the second instance ("without a word," RSV), the reference is to the word of the wife spoken in an attempt to win her husband

to faith in Christ. Verse 2 explains that the behavior most likely to win over an unbelieving husband is that which is marked by purity ("chaste") and "fear" (i.e., reverence for God). To these qualities verse 3 and 4 add modesty and simplicity in dress (v. 3) and a gentle and gracious disposition (v. 4). Verse 3 should not be interpreted as an absolute prohibition of the wearing of jewelry and cosmetics. It is essentially a warning against a distorted sense of values.

Verse 7 shows that husbands are to be concerned about the well-being of their wives. Specifically they are to "dwell with" them "according to knowledge," and are to give "honour" to them. "Dwell with" includes all the day-to-day relations of husband and wife, but the term has special reference to sexual relations. "According to knowledge" probably means that the husband's relations with his wife are to reflect a spirit of understanding of her. "Giving honour" to the wife suggests that the husband is to show respect and chivalry toward his wife.

The series of appeals begun at 2:11 closes with a cluster of general admonitions intended for all Christians (3:8–12). Verse 8 sets forth attitudes which should mark Christians' relations with one another: unity of spirit, sympathy, "love," sensitivity to the needs of others, and humility. Verse 9 explains what their reactions to their pagan neighbors should be. Verses 10–12 assign reasons or motivations for such conduct: (1) It is the way to the highest enjoyment of life (vv. 10–11), and (2) it is the kind of life which is pleasing to God (v. 12).

Special points.—Peter (2:13–17) bases the Christian's civic duty wholly upon his relation to God, i.e., submission is rendered "for the Lord's sake" (v. 13). Question: How far are we to take our obedience? Answer: Up to the point at which obedience to civil authority involves us in disobedience to God. Higher obligations must always take precedence over the lower.

Third Series of Exhortations (1 Pet. 3:13—5:11)

The passage.—To this point the sufferings of Peter's readers have been touched upon only incidentally (cf. 1:6*b;* 2:12,15,19 ff.; 3:9). Now they loom large in all that he has to say.

Verses 13–17 describe the attitude Christians should have as they face suffering. The essential teaching is that they can and should endure suffering with courage and confidence. "Harm" (v. 13) has a special sense in this context. It does not mean that persons who do good will never suffer abuse or physical harm; the thought is that whatever disasters may befall Christians, they cannot be really harmed if they are "devoted to what is good" (v. 13, NEB). Verse 14 suggests that suffering for righteousness may be unusual, but if it should occur, the sufferer should count himself fortunate. Christians, however, are not to court martyrdom. Those who attack us for our faith are to be answered "with meekness" (i.e., gentleness, courtesy, v. 15) "and fear" (i.e., reverence for God, v. 15). Such an attitude will go far to commend the gospel to our critics.

The supreme *incentive* for the patient endurance of hardship is found in Christ's suffering and the triumph which he experiences through his suffering (3:18—4:6). This is developed chiefly in 3:18–22. The thought is that Christians, when they suffer for well-doing, are following in Christ's steps. Verse 18, however, shows that Peter saw Christ's death as much more than an example. Its main purpose was to "bring us to God," that is, to put us in a right relationship with God. Verse 22 emphasizes that Christ's death issued in complete victory.

In 4:1–6 the discussion takes a more practical turn. These verses are in essence an appeal to the readers to make Christ's sufferings a practical force in their lives, to apply to themselves the principles seen in his suffering and subsequent victory (v. 1).

Having mentioned the sufferings of Christ as an encouragement to his readers, Peter next (4:7–11) reminded them of *the nearness of the end,* at which time believers will receive their reward. In light of this four Christian duties are enjoined: (1) the leading of a disciplined and prayerful life (v. 7*b*); (2) the cultivation of love (v. 8); (3) the practice of hospitality (v. 9); and (4) ministry to one another through responsible use of spiritual gifts (vv. 10–11).

In 4:12–19 further counsel is given concerning the sufferings of believers. (1) Do not be bewildered by them (v. 12). Suffering is not foreign to faith (cf. 1 John 3:13). (2) See your sufferings as forming a bond of fellowship with Christ (vv. 13–16). In this way they become occasions for joy (v. 13) and for glorifying God (v. 16). (3) See your sufferings as a part of the process of God's judgment of the world (vv. 17–18). This judgment begins in the present time with God's own household, but in its consummation it will fall with terrifying fury upon those who disobey the gospel. (4) Understand your sufferings in relation to God's will (v. 19*a*). These sufferings, evil in themselves, are used in God's providence to bring believers into a larger share of his holiness, to make them more conformed to the image of Christ. (5) In the midst of your sufferings commit your selves to God (v. 19).

The final strand of instruction (5:1–11) has to do mainly with "responsibilities" within the church. The duties commanded are binding upon every age, but times of testing give them a special urgency.

The "elders" (pastors) were to "feed [lit., shepherd] the flock of God" (v. 2a) and to exercise "oversight" (v. 2b). This must be done "not of constraint [i.e., not because of external pressure], but willingly [i.e., with joyful and voluntary self-dedication], according to the will of God" (v. 2b, ASV). Furthermore, the elders must render their service "not for filthy lucre, but of a ready mind" (v. 2c). This statement does not forbid the desire for fair remuneration, but it does condemn the mercenary spirit which thinks only of personal profit. The "younger" believers were to "submit" themselves (i.e., show deference) to "the elder" members of the church (v. 5a).

Three duties are enjoined upon all Christians, regardless of age or rank. The first is humility (vv. 5b–7). In reference to fellow-believers this speaks of a willingness to give ourselves in service to others (v. 5b, ASV). In reference to God (vv. 6–7) the idea is that of recognizing his sovereignty and submitting to it. For Peter's readers this meant acceptance of afflictions as a part of God's discipline of their lives. The second duty has to do with sobriety and watchfulness (v. 8), an attitude especially needful in view of the vicious character of the enemy of God's people. The third duty is steadfast resistance to the devil (vv. 9–11).

Special points.—Preaching to "the spirits in prison" (3:19) is a difficult concept. After determining the identity of the "spirits," we must then ask when, how, and for what purpose the preaching was done. The traditional answer to these questions is as follows: The "spirits in prison" are the spirits of those people who lived in Noah's day and perished in the flood. They are "in prison" in the sense that they, like all unbelievers who have died, are now confined while they await the judgment of God and their consignment to eternal punishment. Christ did not preach to them in person but through Noah, while they were still alive.

The "eight souls" who "were saved by [i.e., brought safely through] water" (3:20) were of course Noah, his wife, their three sons, and their wives. Verse 21 teaches that the water of the flood has its counterpart in the water of baptism. Lest his readers should misunderstand his reference to baptism, Peter added two explanatory statements: (1) Baptism does not actually put away the filth of the flesh (v. 21b)—either literally or spiritually. It is only a symbol of cleansing. (2) Baptism is "the answer of a good conscience toward God" (v. 21c). This may be interpreted to mean "the craving for a conscience right with God" (Goodspeed) or "the appeal made to God by a good conscience" (NEB). Many see in the expression the idea of a pledge (made in baptism) to maintain a good conscience before God.

The main difficulties of 4:1–6 are in verses 1 and 6. "Arm yourselves with the same mind" (v. 1) means to have the same attitude toward sin and suffering that Christ had (cf. Phil. 2:5). The specific reference is probably to the thought that death in the flesh leads, for the Christian as for Christ, to a richer and fuller life in the spirit (cf. 3:19). "Them that are dead" (v. 6) are those who were dead at the time Peter wrote this, but were, of course, alive when they were evangelized. "Judged according to men in the flesh" (v. 6) is a reference to death as a judgment for sin which falls upon all men. The readers' pagan neighbors probably taunted them with the thought that Christians, like all other men, die and, therefore, gain nothing in their faith. Peter's answer is that though Christians are judged (i.e., experience death) in their physical nature as all men, they "live in the spirit like God" (RSV).

Conclusion (1 Pet. 5:12–14)

The passage.—The conclusion to the epistle contains a summary of the letter (v. 12), the final greetings (v. 13), a request (14a), and the benediction (v. 14b).

"Babylon" seems to have been a figurative reference to Rome.

2 PETER

Curtis Vaughan

INTRODUCTION

Second Peter, a book with special relevance for our day, was written to strengthen the hope of believers, to warn them against deadly error, and to encourage them to make progress in the Christian life. The readers appear to have been the people who earlier had received I Peter (cf. 2 Pet. 3:1). Conservative scholars generally date the book in the middle sixties of the first century, not long before Peter's martyrdom (1:14).

Salutation (2 Pet. 1:1–2)

The passage.—The author describes his readers as "them that have obtained like precious faith with us" (v. 1*b*). This was Peter's way of saying that their saving trust, "obtained" as a divine gift, was equally as valuable as his own.

The Appeal for Christian Growth (2 Pet. 1:3–11)

The passage.—Verses 3–4 set forth *God's provision for growth:* He has given us "everything we need to live a godly life" (v. 3, TEV) and has furnished us with "promises, great beyond all price" (v. 4, NEB). The former provides the power for Christian growth. The latter supplies an incentive. Verse 5*a* emphasizes our responsibility for growth; we must "make every effort" (RSV) to nurture and bring to outward expression the divine life within us (cf. Phil. 2:12–13). Verses 5*b*-7 point up the steps in Christian growth. Spiritual maturity is attained as we supply ourselves with essential Christian virtues, of which

"faith" (v. 5) is the source. "Virtue" (v. 5) means "goodness" (TEV) or moral excellence. The mention of "knowledge" (v. 5) shows the importance of the intellectual element in the Christian life. "Temperance" (v. 6) is self-control. "Patience" (v. 6) is "steadfastness" (RSV), the ability to remain unshaken by difficulty and distress. "Godliness" (v. 6) denotes a reverent awareness of God. "Brotherly kindness" (v. 7) refers to the affection we must feel toward fellow Christians. "Love" (v. 7), the crowning virtue, is that attitude which causes one to put the interests of others above his own.

Verses 8–11 teach the practical consequences of Christian growth. The first is stated in verse 8: "These are the qualities you need, and if you have them in abundance they will make you active and effective" in the knowledge of Christ (TEV). The absence of these makes a man blind to heavenly things, so shortsighted that his vision extends only to that which is earthly (v. 9). Second, by cultivating these virtues we receive confirmation and assurance of our "calling and election" (v. 10). That is, we have evidence that we are really among those whom God has called and chosen to be his own. Finally, the practice of these virtues brings a rich heavenly reward (v. 11).

The Trustworthiness of the Apostolic Message (2 Pet. 1:12–21)

The passage.—This passage was written to give the readers unwavering confidence in the Christian message.

Peter began by showing that it came from eyewitnesses (vv. 16–18). For example, Peter had been with Christ on the mount of transfiguration and had there seen Christ's majesty (vv. 16–17, RSV) and had heard the voice from heaven (v. 18a). (The transfiguration was probably singled out because the apostle was leading up to a discussion of the second coming of Christ [chap. 3], an event of which the transfiguration was a foreshadowing). In addition, Peter showed that "the Christian message is in harmony with the prophetic message of the Old Testament" (vv. 19–21). Verse 19 may teach that the word of prophecy has been fulfilled in and confirmed by the glory of Christ in the transfiguration (NEB, TEV, RSV). Or, the verse may mean that the Old Testament prophecies confirm the apostolic message (KJV, NEB). Either way, we do well to give heed to the prophetic word; it is "like a lamp shining in a murky place" (v. 19a, NEB). The dawning of the day and the arising of the morning star (v. 19b) are figures referring to the return of Christ.

Verse 20 may be interpreted in either of two ways. (1) It may be applied to the *study* of prophecy (NEB, TEV). The meaning then is that prophecy cannot be understood apart from the illumination of the Holy Spirit. (2) The verse may be applied to the *origin* of prophecy. The reference then is to the complete reliability of the Old Testament Scriptures. Either way, verse 21 offers an explanation of the statement: "It was not through any human whim that men prophesied of old; men they were, but impelled by the Holy Spirit, they spoke the words of God" (v. 21, NEB).

The Peril of False Teachers (2 Pet. 2:1–22)

The passage.—Throughout chapter two (the entire chapter should be read in a modern translation, such as RSV, NEB, or TEV) Peter opposes certain persons who by their erroneous teaching were perverting the gospel and unsettling the less stable members of the churches. The passage begins (vv. 1–3) with a warning about and a summary description of the false teachers. Note the following: (1) They smuggle in "destructive heresies" (v. 1, RSV), i.e., doctrines which are destructive to those who teach them and to those who embrace them. (2) They deny "the Lord that bought them" (v. 1). This shows that the errorists claimed to be Christians. Their conduct, however, gave the lie to their profession. (3) They "gain many adherents to their dissolute practices" (v. 2a, NEB). (4) They cause "the way of truth" (NEB, "the true way") to be slandered (v. 2b). (5) Their main motive is selfish gain (v. 3a). (6) They bring swift and certain destruction upon themselves (vv. 1c,3b). Their sentence is not idle in working itself out; indeed, "perdition waits for them with unsleeping eyes" (v. 3b, NEB).

Verses 4–10a elaborate upon the certain doom of false teachers. Three events drawn from the past are used to illustrate the matter: the condemnation of rebellious angels (v. 4), the judgment of the ungodly people of Noah's day (v. 5), and the destruction of Sodom and Gomorrah (vv. 6–9). Verse 9, which contains the conclusion of the long conditional sentence begun at verse 4 (see RSV), makes two points: God can be relied on to (1) protect his people and (2) punish the wicked. The latter are already in torment, but the full measure of their punishment cannot come until after the judgment. Verse 10a suggests that the only authority (KJV, "government") which the false teachers acknowledge is their own lust.

Verses 10b–19 describe the character and conduct of the false teachers. Mention is made of their arrogant contempt for all authority (vv. 10b–11); their irrational, beast-like impulses (vv. 12–13a, TEV); their shocking debauchery (vv. 13b–14a); their seduction of the weak (v. 14b); and their greed (v. 14c). Little wonder that Peter exclaims, "God's curse is on them!" (v. 14d, NEB). The "way of Balaam" (vv. 15–16) is the way of greed and immorality (cf. Num. 30).

"Dried-up springs" (v. 17, TEV) points up that they were wholly unsatisfying as teachers. "Mists driven by a storm" (v. 17, RSV) describes them as unstable and unreliable. Mention of their "big, empty words" (v. 18a, NEB) brings out their pretentiousness. Using "sensual lusts and debauchery" as bait, they preyed upon new converts, those who had "barely begun to escape from their heathen environment" (v. 18b, NEB). They promised freedom, though they themselves were bond-servants of corruption (v. 19).

Verses 20–22 describe the deliberate apostasy of the false teachers. They had professed to be Christians and, at least for a while, had appeared to be such. This is why Peter could speak of them as having "escaped the defilements of the world" through the knowledge of Christ (v. 20). The main thing about them, however, was that they had again become "entangled" in those defilements, showing that they never had been real Christians.

Special points.—"Dignities" (v. 10b) means persons of authority. The reference may be either to angelic beings (NEB, TEV) or to church leaders. "Suffering wrong for their wrongdoing" (v. 13a, RSV) probably means "they will be paid with suffering for the suffering they caused" (TEV). "Having eyes full of adultery" (v. 14a) vividly depicts the false teachers as unable to look at a

woman without imagining themselves in bed with her.

The Hope of the Lord's Return (2 Pet. 3:1–18a)

The passage.—Chapter 3 shows that a prominent part of the false teachers' error was their skepticism concerning the return of Christ. Verses 1–4 warn against those who deny the Lord's return. Their skepticism makes it imperative for believers to give attention to the utterances of prophets and apostles.

Verses 5–10, which contain a positive affirmation of the Lord's return, are Peter's answer to the false teachers. First, pointing to the facts of history, he showed the fallacy of their argument (vv. 5–7). They stressed a law of continuity in nature and history. Peter affirmed that this continuity was broken at the Flood and will be broken again at the day of judgment. "Standing out of the water and in the water" (v. 5) seems to mean that the earth was created out of elements contained in water and was by water (i.e., rain, etc.) sustained. Next, Peter reminded his readers that God does not reckon time as we do (v. 8; cf. Ps. 110:4). Again, the apostle asserted that what appears to be a delay in the Lord's return is really an expression of the mercy of God (v. 9). He has not forgotten his promise, nor is he powerless to bring it to fulfilment. Finally, Peter declared that "the day of the Lord" (an Old Testament concept here identified with the coming of Christ) will certainly come (v. 10a). With its arrival there will occur the dissolution of the present world order (v. 10b). "The heavens" (i.e., the sky) above us will pass away with a thunderous crash, and "the elements" (either the component parts of the physical world or the heavenly bodies) shall "melt with fervent heat." The general sense is that the world as we have known it will cease to be. Christians, however, can face the future with positive hope, for the day of the Lord will usher in the new and eternal age (v. 13).

Verses 11–18a show the practical effect of belief in the second coming of Christ. The hope of this event is a powerful incentive for dedication to God (v. 11), earnest striving for a spotless character (v. 14), steadfast adherence to the truth (v. 17), and continual growth in grace and knowledge (v. 18a).

1 JOHN

Curtis Vaughan

INTRODUCTION

First John, written in the mid-90's of the first Christian century, is, in thought, style, and vocabulary remarkably similar to the Gospel of John. The epistle was written to counteract a dangerous heresy which was threatening the fellowship of the Asian churches, apparently a form of gnosticism. Among other things, the heretics taught that righteousness is not an imperative duty of the Christian life and that Jesus is not God incarnate. Some of them appear to have denied the real humanity of Jesus. Others denied his deity. The key concepts of the Epistle are truth, love, light, knowledge, righteousness, fellowship, and birth from God.

Preface (1 John 1:1–4)

The passage.—Verses 1–3 describe "the Word of life"—his deity (v. 1*a*), his humanity (v. 1*b*), and his manifested life (v. 2). "Word" (v. 1) is a reference to Christ (cf. John 1:1), the revealer of God (cf. John 1:18). "Word of life" might mean either the "life-giving Word" or "the Word who is the Life." Verse 4 contains a statement of the purpose of the Epistle (cf. 5:13).

Fellowship with God (1 John 1:5—2:6)

The passage.—John represents the Christian life as a fellowship, both with God and with other believers. The teaching of the passage may be summed up under four leading statements:

(1) The nature of our fellowship is determined by the nature of God (1:5–7). "God is light" (v. 5); the fellowship of Christians must therefore be a fellowship in the light. Some interpret "light" as a figure for the moral perfection of God. The term may, however, mean that God is self-revealing. As it is the nature of light to communicate itself, so it is the nature of God to make himself known. To "walk in darkness" (v. 6) is therefore to live in disregard or in defiance of the revealed will of God. Conversely, to "walk in the light" (v. 7) is to live in conformity to that will. Only those who make this the pattern of their conduct can justly claim to be in fellowship with God.

(2) Fellowship makes necessary the confession of our sins and the forgiveness and cleansing which confession brings (vv. 8–10). To "say that we have no sin" (v. 8) is to claim that sin is not an inward principle of our lives. To "say that we have not sinned" (v. 10; cf. vv. 6,8) is to claim that we have never committed acts of sin.

(3) Fellowship with God is impossible apart from Christ's advocacy (2:1–2). The ideal is that we "sin not" (v. 1*b*), that is, that we may never commit a single act of sin. But "if any man sin [i.e., commit an act of sin] we have an advocate with the Father, Jesus Christ the righteous" (v. 1*c*). Christ pleads our case and assures our standing before God. His advocacy, however, is not a matter of words. It is rather the continual application of his sacrifice as the ground of our acquittal. Note the word

"propitiation" (v. 2a), which Williams renders "the atoning sacrifice for our sins." Actually Christ's sacrifice avails only for believers, but potentially he is propitiation "for the sins of the whole world" (v. 2).

(4) Fellowship with God expresses itself in obedience to his will (2:3–6). Such obedience, which involves submission to God's authority and compliance with his commands, is expressed here in terms of keeping God's commands (vv. 3–4), keeping God's word (v. 5), and living as Jesus lived (v. 6).

Contrasting Loves (1 John 2:7–17)

The passage.—The discussion is in two parts: Verses 7–11 speak of love for our brothers; this we are to practice. Verses 12–17 speak of love for the world; this we are to avoid. The command to love was "old" in the sense that John's readers had known it since they first heard the gospel. From another point of view it was "new." It was new in the experience of Christ because his life embodied and demonstrated it in a way never before known. It was new in the experience of John's readers because it was for them the expression of an entirely new way of life.

"Darkness" (v. 8c), symbolic of sin, ignorance, and the absence of God, stands for the old order. The "true light" is the light of God's self-revelation now embodied in Christ (cf. 1:5). "Hateth" (v. 9) and "loveth" (v. 10) are present tenses and speak of hatred and love as fixed principles of life. The man for whom hatred is a way of life is "in the darkness even until now" (v. 9b, ASV). This means that darkness is now, and always has been, the moral and spiritual atmosphere of his life. The man for whom brother-love is a way of life "abideth in the light" (v. 10a), which means that he lives his life within the light of divine revelation.

Verses 12–17 teach that the Christian is to avoid the spirit of the world. The substance of John's appeal is in verse 15a: "Love not the world, neither the things that are in the world." The "world" stands for unbelieving, pagan society. To "love" the world is to court its favor, follow its customs, adopt its ideals, covet its prizes, and seek its fellowship. To do this is tantamount to deserting God (cf. Jas. 4:4). "The things that are in the world" are those elements in society which stamp it as evil—its pleasures, its passions, its dominating principles. John summarizes these in verse 16 as "the lust of the flesh, and the lust of the eyes, and the vainglory of life" (ASV). Verses 12–14, which are a sort of parenthesis, give the basis for John's appeal. They show that his impulse to write did not spring from doubt of his readers' Christian experience, but rather from confidence in it. The essential qualities ascribed to them are forgiveness of sins, knowledge of God, and victory over evil.

Verses 15b–17 give two reasons for not loving the world. The first is that love for the world excludes love for God: "If any man love [habitually] the world, the love of [for] the Father is not in him" (v. 15b). The second reason for not loving the world is its transitoriness: "The world passeth [lit., is passing] away, and the lust thereof" (v. 17a). Only the man "who perseveres in doing God's will lives on forever" (v. 17b, Williams).

Counterfeit Christianity (1 John 2:18–28)

The passage.—The teaching of the passage focuses in "the last hour" (v. 18, ASV), the "many antichrists" (vv. 19–26), and the believer's security against error (vv. 20–28). In affirming that "it is the last hour" (v. 18) John may have meant that the period in which he and his readers were living was the period immediately preceding the end of the world (cf. TEV, "My children, the end is near!"). On the other hand, the last hour may be a reference to the entire Christian era (cf. 1 Pet. 1:20, NEB; Acts 2:16–17a; Heb. 1:2, NEB). A third view is that the last hour is an expression intended to characterize the Johannine period as a time of crisis, that is, as a period exhibiting the distinctive traits of the final hour.

The evidence that it was the last hour was the prevalence of opposition to Christ. In verse 18 one should note "antichrist" and "many antichrists." The singular refers to one personal embodiment of evil to be manifested at the end of the age (cf. "man of sin," 2 Thess. 2). The plural refers to those who, even as early as John's day, embodied the anti-Christian spirit and were in a sense forerunners of *the* antichrist yet to come. The "many antichrists" were the heretical teachers (Gnostics) whose activity occasioned the writing of this letter. Verse 19 suggests that they claimed to be Christians and were at one time members of the Asian churches. But although they "went out from us," explains John, they were never really "of us." Their failure to persevere was an evidence that they were not true believers. Moreover, their departure from the churches was providential (v. 19c). In this manner they came to be seen in their true character and their opportunity for damaging the churches was limited. They denied "that Jesus is the Christ" (v. 22; cf. 4:3). That is, the false teachers made a distinction between the man Jesus and the divine Christ. Jesus, to them, was a mere man, begotten as any other man and marked with the imperfections common to the race. The divine Christ, they taught,

descended upon the man Jesus at his baptism, but withdrew from him sometime before his death.

Believers have a threefold security against such error (vv. 20–28). First, they have "an anointing from the Holy One" (v. 20, ASV; cf. v. 27). "Anointing" is used figuratively of the Holy Spirit (cf. TEV). It is his presence in our lives that gives us the capacity for understanding spiritual things. "Ye know all things" (v. 20) should be read, "Ye all know." "Ye need not that any man teach you" (v. 27) means that Christians are not ultimately dependent upon human teachers.

Other sources of security for the Christian assaulted by error are his adherence to the Christian message and his union with Christ (vv. 27b–28). To "abide" in Christ is to cling to him and draw strength from him. "Confidence" (lit., freedom of speech) denotes boldness and courage.

The Children of God (1 John 2:29–3:24)

The passage.—The concept of fellowship, which has permeated much of the discussion up to this point, now gives place to that of sonship. Verse 29 introduces the new topic of discussion. In it, two truths are asserted. First, it is God who imparts spiritual life to his people. Second, the evidence of birth from God is the practice of righteousness.

In 3:1–3, John enlarges on *the wonder and glory of the believers' new relationship to God.* "That we should be called children of God" (ASV) is proof that God has bestowed his amazing love upon us. But wonderful as our present status is, our future destiny is even more so (v. 2).

In 3:4–24, John discusses two of the distinguishing marks of our relationship with God. The first is righteousness (vv. 4–10). "Everyone that doeth sin, doeth also lawlessness; and sin is lawlessness" (v. 4, ASV). That is, sin is a spirit of rebellion, and this is incompatible with birth from God. Verses 5–8 show that a life of sin is contrary to the whole purpose of Christ's incarnate ministry: "He was manifested to take away our sins" (v. 5) and to "destroy the works of the devil" (v. 8*b*). Therefore, "Whosoever abideth in him sinneth not" (v. 6*a*). This does not mean that a Christian will never commit an act of sin (cf. 1:8—2:2). It rather means that the Christian does not make sin the ruling principle of his life. Verse 9 mentions the nature of Christian experience as another reason for the believer's antagonism to sin. On the surface it seems to contradict what John asserted in 1:8—2:2, but the tenses of the verbs show that there is complete harmony between the two statements. In 2:1 "if any man sin" translates a tense which suggests occasional lapses into sin. In 3:9 "doeth" no sin, and "cannot sin" translate present tenses and denote action which is habitual and persistent. The idea is that one who is begotten of God does not, indeed, cannot, practice sin as a way of life. He may and will succumb to sin on occasion, but he does not make sin the habit of his life. This is "because his [God's] seed abideth in him." "Seed" probably stands here for the "divine nature" (RSV), or the "life principle" (Williams) given to the Christian in conversion.

A second distinguishing mark of God's children is love (vv. 11–24). This was the burden of apostolic preaching (vv. 11–12) and is the proof that Christians have passed out of death into life (vv. 13–15). Love is shown to have had its supreme revelation in the death of Christ for us (vv. 16–18). We, in turn, are under obligation "to give our lives for our brothers" (v. 16*b*, TEV). Most of us may never find it necessary actually to lay down our lives for our brothers, but verse 17 teaches that in other, less dramatic ways all of us are to demonstrate the genuineness of our love. If it is within our power to help a "brother in need" we must never refuse to do so. To fail to respond in a compassionate manner is to give evidence that there is no love for God within us.

Verses 19–24 show that the practice of loving deeds brings assurance of our standing before God. The possibility of assurance is stated in verse 19. "Hereby" (v. 19*a*) is retrospective, pointing back to the idea of loving in deed and in truth. "Heart" is used in the sense of "conscience." Verse 20 stresses the importance of assurance. Most recent interpreters see this verse as an encouragement to those who are overscrupulous. They understand the apostle to mean that if our hearts condemn us for our failures, we can appeal to God for reassurance. Our hearts, they explain, condemn us on partial knowledge, but God assesses our condition on a more reliable basis. He knows our weaknesses, our intentions, our circumstances, as well as his own provision for our sins. Other scholars take the verse to be a warning to those who are overconfident. According to them, if our hearts condemn us for our failure to practice love, God will all the more condemn us.

Verses 21–24 show that assurance of our standing before God issues in two other benefits: (1) boldness toward God (v. 21) and (2) assurance of effectiveness in prayer (v. 22).

Testing the Spirits (1 John 4:1–6)

The passage.—In this section John was dealing with people who (falsely) claimed to have the gift of inspired utterance. The passage begins with a twofold command. "Believe not every spirit" (v. 1*a*) expresses the negative side; "try the spirits" expresses the positive side. The former means that we are not to give credence to every prophetic utterance simply because the one making it claims to be speaking under divine inspiration. There is always the possibility that his inspiration comes from the spirit of evil rather than the Spirit of God. To "try the spirits" is to test them for genuineness. "False prophets" (v. 1*b*) were heretical teachers claiming to be spokesmen for God. They were, in fact, spokesmen of evil spirits.

Verses 2–3 give the test to be applied to those who claim to be God's spokesmen. No prophetic utterance is to be received as coming from God if the speaker does not acknowledge Jesus Christ as the incarnate Son of God. "Jesus Christ having come in flesh" is the very heart of the gospel. It is a truth so basic to Christianity that its denial marks one as an antichrist (cf. 2:18 ff.).

The Splendors of Love (1 John 4:7—5:3a)

The passage.—In 2:7–17 love is represented as the law for the Christian life; in 3:11–24, as one of the distinguishing traits of the children of God. Here it is treated more generally.

Verses 7–12 discuss love and its grounds. We are to love one another because "love is of God" (v. 7) and because "God is love" (v. 8*b*). The former is an affirmation that love has its origin in God. "God is love" means that love is such an integral part of God's being that it never is or can be absent from him. Verse 12 teaches that love fulfils two functions in our lives. First, it is the visible evidence that God dwells in us. The thought is that Christians, by the practice of loving deeds, become the means by which the invisible God is seen. Second, when we practice love, God's love "is perfected in us" (v. 12*b*). This means

that our love is the ripened fruit of his love.

Verses 13–16 discuss love and the indwelling of God (cf. v. 12). The idea seems to be that a life of love is the crowning evidence of the believer's union with God.

In 4:17—5:1 the thought of the perfection of love is developed. In 4:12 the perfecting of love has to do with the perfecting of *God's* love for us. Here the perfection of *our* love is discussed. "Boldness" (v. 17), which suggests fearless confidence, is represented as an evidence that our love has been perfected. "As he is, even so are we in this world" (v. 17, ASV) means that our standing before God is the same as the standing of our glorified Lord. We are accepted in him and may share in his confidence toward the Father. "Fear" (v. 18) is dread or terror, the very opposite of bold confidence. "Fear hath torment" (v. 18) means that fear (terror) is associated with punishment. Since such fear is alien to love, its presence is an evidence that perfected love is absent. Verse 19 affirms that our love is in response to God's love. Even the capacity to love comes from him. In 4:20—5:1 it is shown that love for God must express itself in love for our brothers. In 5:2 we are taught that love for one's brothers is grounded in love for God and obedience to his commands. Verse 3*a*, which is a further development of the relation of love and obedience, teaches that where there is no obedience to God, there is no love for God. The two things are inseparable.

Faith and Its Witnesses (1 John 5:3b–12)

The passage.—In verses 3*b*–5 faith is represented as a conquering power. That is to say, faith is the spiritual weapon by which temptation is met and overcome. The closing part of verse 5 indicates that faith concerns Jesus, the Son of God. The manner of statement stresses the union of humanity and deity in one person. Verse 6 gives a more precise description of Jesus: "This is he that came by water and blood, even Jesus Christ." "Water" and blood" are represented as historical events "by" which the Son of God "came." What is meant by these terms can be determined only if we keep in mind the background of the Epistle. John was combatting a heresy which differentiated between the man Jesus and the divine Christ. Its proponents held that Jesus was a mere man upon whom the divine Christ came at his baptism and from whom the divine Christ departed before he died. They insisted that Jesus was born as a man and died as a man, that only for the brief period of his ministry did the divine Christ rest upon him. This passage must be seen as a refutation of that heresy. The water and the blood should therefore be understood as references to Christ's baptism in the Jordan River and his death on the cross. John's opponents taught that the Christ came by water (the baptism) but denied that he came by blood (the death). John taught that Jesus Christ (note the joining of the human name and the divine title) came not simply with the water of baptism (as the Gnostics taught) but also with the blood of the cross (which they denied). The eternal God was incarnate Jesus not simply through a short period of his life but throughout the entire course of his human existence.

Verses 7–12 teach that our faith in Jesus is well grounded. The apostle brings forth a threefold testimony to Christ (vv. 7–8) and then affirms that this testimony is none other than the testimony of God (v. 9). (Verses 7 and 8 should be read in a modern translation, for the KJV translates a Greek text which has no ancient authority.) It is he who speaks to us in the Spirit and in the historic facts of the gospel (the water of Christ's baptism and the blood of his cross). This divine witness is then shown to be confirmed by the inner experience of the believer (v. 10). "Hath the witness in himself" (v. 10) refers to the inward witness of the Spirit. "Eternal life" (v. 11) refers not merely to endless existence. It is this, of course, but it is vastly more than this. Eternal life designates a kind of life possessed only by those who have been united to Christ through faith in Jesus Christ.

Conclusion (1 John 5:13–21)

The passage.—These verses are a recapitulation of some of the leading ideas of the Epistle. The central thought is assurance, and the key word is "know." Assurance of eternal life is mentioned first (v. 13). Though it is plainly implied that one may be a believer and yet lack assurance, the main point is that every believer may and should have this assurance. Verses 14–17 deal with assurance of answered prayer. There is a general statement about boldness in prayer (vv. 14–15) and then this is developed with special reference to intercessory prayer (vv. 16–17). Confidence of answered prayer is qualified by only one condition: our requests must be "according to his will" (v. 14). Verse 16a should be seen as a specific example of prayer which is in accord with God's will. "Sin unto death" is understood by some as a specific act of sin, such as murder, adultery, blasphemy, etc. Others interpret it as a state or habit of sin willfully chosen and persisted in. Still others interpret it in light of the background of the Epistle. "Sin unto death" is then seen as having primary reference to John's opponents, who had wilfully rejected the Spirit's witness to the person and work of Christ (cf. Luke 12:10). The thought is of a kind of sinning whose natural consequence is spiritual ruin.

Verses 18–21 are a resumé of the chief facts relating to the believer's new life—victory over sin (v. 18; cf. 3:9), birth from God (v. 19), and the knowledge of God in Christ (v. 20). Note the threefold repetition of "we know" (vv. 18–20). "He that is begotten of God" (v. 18b) is a reference to Christ who is uniquely the Son of God (see RSV). "Keepeth himself" (v. 18b) is better rendered "guards him." "Toucheth" (v. 18c) means to get a hold on. The idea is that Satan, because Christ is our guardian, is unable to grasp and keep us within his clutches.

2 JOHN

Curtis Vaughan

Second John was written by "the elder" (v. 1). Traditionally, this has been interpreted as a designation of John the apostle. Some understand the Epistle to have been written to a church, addressed by the author as "the elect lady and her children" (v. 1). It seems better to take this as a reference to a Christian woman and her family. We do not know who

they were. The letter was written about the same time as 1 John, for it reflects the same historical situation. It contains an introduction (vv. 1–4), an exhortation to love and obedience (vv. 5–6), a warning against false doctrine (vv. 7–9), counsel concerning treatment of heretical teachers (vv. 10–11), and a conclusion (vv. 12–13).

MILTON MURPHEY

26. Ruins at Pergamum (see Rev. 2:12)

3 JOHN

Curtis Vaughan

Third John is a brief pastoral note written to commend a man named Gaius for his hospitality toward Christian brethren. There is no way of knowing precisely who Gaius was. The name was very common in New Testament times (cf. Acts 19:29; 20:4; Rom. 16:23). The Epistle contains a commendation of Gaius (vv. 1–8), a warning against Diotrephes (vv. 9–11), a commendation of Demetrius (v. 12), and a conclusion (vv. 13–14).

JUDE

Curtis Vaughan

The identity of Jude cannot be definitely established, but probably he was a son of Joseph and Mary (cf. Mark 6:3) and thus the half-brother of Jesus. The Epistle, written in the third quarter of the first Christian century, was intended to counteract certain heresies which were arising within the churches. The letter is strikingly similar to the second chapter of 2 Peter.

After the initial greeting (vv. 1–2), there is a statement of the occasion and purpose of the Epistle (vv. 3–4). Jude had intended to write a more general letter discussing the salvation shared in common by all Christians. However, an emergency arose before he could carry out his plan, and he found it necessary to write this earnest appeal to contend (struggle) for the faith once for all delivered to God's people. That which created the emergency was the presence of certain ungodly persons within the churches who were distorting the grace of God to make it an excuse for immoral living. Moreover, they rejected Jesus Christ, who is our only Master and Lord. These heretical teachers are described as "certain men" who "crept in unawares" (v. 4). This means that they had secretly gained admission into the churches. TEV reads, "slipped in unnoticed"; NEB, "wormed their way in." Outwardly, they were members of those congregations, but inwardly and really, they had no living connection with it.

Verses 5–7 contain a warning of the fearful punishment in store for those who rebel against the authority of God.

Three examples are marshalled: (1) the Israelites who, after being delivered from Egypt were destroyed in the wilderness; (2) the fallen angels, "who did not stay within the limits of their proper authority" (v. 6, TEV); and (3) Sodom and Gomorrah.

Verses 8–16 contain a further description of the false brethren. They "defile the flesh, reject authority, and revile the glorious ones" (v. 8, RSV). These words speak of their immorality, their spirit of rebellion, and their slanderous talk. The "glorious ones" (RSV) are probably angelic beings (cf. 2 Pet. 2:10). The reference (v. 9) to Michael contending with the devil about the body of Moses is difficult. There is no mention of this event in the Old Testament, though Michael is mentioned in Daniel 10:13 and 12:1. It is thought that Jude drew this material from the apocryphal *Assumption of Moses*. This does not mean that he recognized this apocryphal book as canonical. It only means that he was using material in it to illustrate the point which he desired to make. Verse 11 continues the description of the false brethren: They follow "the way of Cain" and "the error of Balaam" (covetousness), and they perish in the rebellion of Korah. The prophecy of verse 14 ascribed to Enoch is apparently derived from an apocryphal work called the book of Enoch.

Verses 17–23 contain an appeal to the true believers, and the book closes (vv. 24–25) with a majestic doxology.

REVELATION

William B. Coble

INTRODUCTION

"Jesus shall reign." "Lo, I am with you alway." "Loyalty to Christ!" These three thoughts are the heartbeat of the book of Revelation. Therefore it has been a source of hope and courage to the persecuted. But to men who live in peace and security, feeling no need of its emotional charge, Revelation has been an object of much speculation.

"The revelation of Jesus Christ" (1:1) has two meanings. This book is written from, about, and for Jesus Christ. This book is also a certain kind of writing, "revelation" or apocalyptic writing. That name is given to this kind of literature because each writer claimed that he received his message by a special revelation from God.

General Characteristics

"Revelation" writing was popular with Jews and Christians for about 600 years, roughly from 300 B.C. to A.D. 300. Besides Daniel and Revelation, sixteen books of this type have been preserved. These books show us some traits of the literary form which can help us gain a better understanding of Revelation.

Each "revelation" book was written to meet a need which arose out of some particular situation. Revelation was written to strengthen Christians in Asia Minor who were being pressed to worship the Roman Emperor Domitian, who ruled during the years A.D. 81–96.

"Revelation" writing focused upon the last days. The purpose of showing men the shape of things to come was to teach them how to live in their own setting. Thus Revelation appeals to Christians to be faithful to Christ in the face of Domitian's power and cruelty.

"Revelation" writers regularly said that their message came to them in visions, that they recorded what they saw.

Much of the thought of "revelation" writing was expressed in symbols, a code language. Animals, colors, events, and numbers were most popular symbols. Each writer mixed his expressions. Some terms clearly are symbols and some clearly are literal, but often it is hard to be sure of the writer's intention. To take symbols literally twists the writer's meaning as surely as does taking literal thoughts as symbols. Therefore everyone must study Revelation humbly, seeking the Spirit's guidance and knowing that others, too, may be Spirit-led.

Most "revelation" writing was done in the name of some past hero of the faith. This act protected the author and added weight to his claims. It seems certain that the writer of Revelation was named John. Yet through the centuries men have differed over who he was. The strongest tradition says that he was the apostle, the son of Zebedee, and that he wrote Revelation between A.D. 90 and 95.

Special Characteristics of Revelation

Use of the Old Testament.—John's mind was saturated with the Old Testament, particularly Daniel and the prophets. Revelation contains more expressions and symbols drawn from the Old Testament than it has verses. Yet John interpreted these ideas and figures freely and used them as his own. He did not quote so much as one complete verse of the Old Testament. The use of a good cross-reference Bible can help you greatly in understanding Revelation.

Christology.—Jesus Christ is the center of this book, and no book pays him higher honor. Every picture and action helps develop the full meaning of Jesus as Lord of all. A most rewarding study is one which centers on who and what Christ is, what he does, and what he gives to men and expects from them.

Emotion.—John's purpose was to stir people's feelings. His readers were tormented, discouraged, and afraid; and he was trying to steel their souls. You can best feel the thrill and power of Revelation by reading it through at one time, as rapidly as possible. Only after feeling the impact of its emotion will you be ready to study its details.

Praise.—Much of the power of Revelation is in the songs of praise and thanksgiving in the heavenly visions. You need to give them particular attention. In all versions except the King James the passages stand out as poetry.

Repetition.—The main ideas of Revelation are much repeated. The thought of the book probably could be expressed in no more than eight chapters. The purpose of the repetition was to build the drama and the emotional power.

Interpreting Revelation

The existence of many views demands considerable graciousness in interpreting Revelation. You must weigh carefully two matters: (1) the way in which the message of any present interpretation could have given hope and inspiration to John's people; (2) the influence which

your approach to the whole book has on fixing the meaning of each detail.

Three primary methods of interpretation present solid possibilities.

Futurist.—The most popular method among evangelical Christians understands Revelation to be the prediction of the shape of events in the last days of human history. The first readers would have received the same message which has come to each later generation.

Poetic.—Popular with some literary groups is the idea which divorces Revelation from any period or setting in history. This approach sees Revelation as a work of pure literary art, in which John described God's conquest of every form of evil, apart from time or place.

Historical setting.—This approach has been given many titles. It assumes that Revelation was written to and for the people of that day and was meant to inspire persecuted Christians. The message is of value to later generations because it sets out eternal truths and holds out vital hopes to men in whatever conditions they have to live.

This is the approach used in this study, with the hope that it can make Revelation a source of joy and hope for you. To study the details which create much of the drama, you will have to read some more lengthy commentary.

Prologue (Rev. 1:1–20)

The first chapter sets the atmosphere for the entire book.

The setting.—The Christians of Asia Minor were under the pressure of an official drive to force all people to worship the Emperor Domitian as a god. John was a victim of this drive. Rome had determined where he was by putting him on the island of Patmos, off the coast of Asia.

John was also a slave of Jesus Christ, and he determined John's spirit and his actions. Since John was suffering for his faith and faithfulness, he could encourage his fellow sufferers.

On the Lord's Day the revelation began (v. 10).

The form of the book.—Revelation is a letter to seven churches of the province of Asia (v. 4), to be read to them publicly (v. 3). They are named in the order in which one would visit them in a circuit, going north from Ephesus and following the main roads (v. 11).

The central thought.—God is the main thought of the chapter. He is the Eternal One, "I Am" whom Moses met at the burning bush (v. 4; Ex. 3:14). He is pure, complete spirit, "seven Spirits" (v. 4). He is Jesus Christ, who was what he expects man to be, a faithful witness (v. 5). God is the A to Z, who gave all things their beginning and their purpose, and moves them toward their chosen goal (v. 8). Thus he is the standard by whom men must weigh all values and determine all their actions.

John heard a voice, like a trumpet announcing the presence of a king. The voice claimed a divine kingship, and it commanded, with the authority of a king, "Write" (v. 11).

In a vision John saw Christ, the resurrected, glorified, eternal King. In symbols John told what kind of king he is, one totally different from any Caesar. He is holy; he cannot be deceived, for he sees (knows) all; his power cannot be broken; his authority cannot be resisted; his judgment cannot be avoided; and his majesty cannot be imitated.

More important, he lives among the churches. He holds them, their leaders, and their destiny in his power.

Truths for today.—The pressures put on American Christians to conform to present standards and practices of society are not official. But they are powerful. The temptations to turn from the way, the truth, and the Life of Jesus Christ are as real as they were in A.D. 95. To turn away is still deserting him, as truly as was worshiping Caesar.

The eternal Lord is the same through the centuries. When modern men know him as John knew him, they can keep the truths of life clearly in view.

I. LIFE AMONG CHRIST'S PEOPLE (REV. 2:1—3:22)

The passage.—Each of the seven letters was to a "real, live church." Each letter showed detailed knowledge of the life of the city. This included economic, social, political, and religious conditions, as well as geography and history.

Each city was the center of a large area. So the letters, taken together, probably show the conditions of Christian life in most of the province.

The letters follow a pattern. Each is addressed to the "angel of the church."

Each letter is sent from Christ. He has some trait which was stated first in chapter 1. That trait is chosen to fit the life and needs of the church.

Each church is assured, "I know thy works," then praised for some virtue or blamed for some fault, or both. Smyrna and Philadelphia are praised. Laodicea is blamed. Ephesus, Pergamos, Thyatira, and Sardis are praised and blamed.

Each letter contains a special promise to "him that overcometh," the faithful and uncompromising disciple.

Each letter comes to a climax with the challenge for the hearer to listen.

The virtues could be found in any church: endurance and patience (Ephesus), true wealth in Christ (Smyrna), stability in suffering (Pergamos), faithfulness in love and service (Thyatira), personal purity (Sardis), and true loyalty (Philadelphia).

The faults also could be found anywhere, any time: loss of love (Ephesus), compromise with false ideas and immoral conduct (Pergamos, Thyatira, Sardis), spiritual deadness (Sardis), indifference and self-sufficiency (Laodicea).

Special points.—Why were there seven churches? Seven is one of several numbers which symbolize completeness. Probably these seven represent all the churches of the province, maybe all churches everywhere. The truths found in the letters surely would apply to all Christians. Some futurist interpreters see these churches as symbols or predictions of future or later periods of Christian history.

Doctrinal and moral compromise probably took two forms. Christians in Pergamos (2:14) and Thyatira (v. 20) compromised with paganism and society at large. They took part in local activities which gave honor to pagan gods and carried on sexual orgies. Those who did such things were following Balaam's counsel (v. 14; cf. Num. 24:14; 25:1–3).

The Nicolaitanes (2:7,15) probably believed that the body is totally evil and separate from the spirit. They felt that if one knows God, he is free to do anything with his body; so they practiced and encouraged immoral living.

"He that overcometh" is the term used to describe the true Christian. He is faithful to Christ's truth, obeys his teachings, and cannot be conquered. This person truly shares in Christ's victory over the world and its idolatry.

Each church is challenged to hear what the *Spirit* says. This fact is a reminder. In the New Testament the Holy Spirit reveals Christ's truth to men.

Truth for today.—The believer compromises his loyalty to Christ by doing anything which violates God's standards for conduct. One such act makes further compromises easier to make. Finally the "Christian" has nothing left

worth suffering for, much less worth risking his life.

Consistent resistance to the world's ways and standards finally becomes a risk of one's life. Accepting that risk is the meaning of bearing one's cross.

II. THE TRUTH OF HEAVEN (REV. 4:1—5:14)

These chapters show the vital difference between symbols and pictures. The details of these scenes are symbolic, coded ways of stating glorious truths which are the anchor of all Christian hopes. They are visions for the heart and mind, not for the eye. Efforts to paint these scenes on canvas could only veil the truth and change God's glory to hideous nonsense.

God the Creator (Rev. 4:1–11)

The passage.—The message of Revelation rests on this truth: the final key to reality and power is in heaven. On earth a Christian can see no reason for hope. But heaven gives him a hope which is alive, vibrant, and powerful.

God reigns! Every detail of this chapter highlights this truth, and every picture underscores the hymn of verse 11. Only God, the holy and eternal Creator, is worthy to rule and control man's life.

The rest of the book pictures God's control over his creation, particularly over all who try to usurp his authority.

Special points.—A throne is a sign of power to rule. The colors of God's throne show his rule to be holy, righteous, merciful, and inspiring of hope.

To Jews an elder was a ruler and a leader, one in whom all his people lived their life. Some students believe the twenty-four elders symbolize all God's people who have passed through death into God's presence in heaven. Others believe they are angelic beings who oversee the life of men on earth. Either way, the twenty-four elders are a sign of the hope which God gives men.

The sounds coming from the throne show God's wrath toward and his power over the enemies of Christ (v. 5a).

The seven lamps (lights) show that God is true and perfect spirit (v. 5b).

In heaven the crystal sea of majesty keeps man from God's direct presence, just as the sea kept John on Patmos and away from his people. But John foresaw a time when God would remove this barrier both from earth and from heaven (21:1).

The word for beast is better translated as "living being" (vv. 6–9). Some believe each of the four beings is a symbol of created life, human, wild animals, tame animals, and birds. Others think they are heavenly beings, such as were represented in the zodiac. The latter meaning seems to be more probable, because the purpose of the vision is to show God's exaltation in heaven. Their eyes probably symbolize complete knowledge of all things, and their wings show readiness and ability to act in obedience to the King.

Truth for today.—Only in submission to the eternal Creator can man of any time or any place have a real grasp of truth. To ignore or rebel against him is suicidal revolt against reality.

The Redeemer (Rev. 5:1–14)

The passage.—Man's hope rests on more than God's creative, ruling power. Equally important is his purpose. Is it gracious and restoring, or hateful and destroying? This passage gives the answer.

Christ shows us that all God's aims and methods are rooted in love.

The only way one can think rightly of Christ is shown here. He is forever the one crucified—like a sacrifice offered for

sin, resurrected, and exalted to the place of complete power and control.

Only one who in love has given himself totally for the benefit of sinful men is suited to reveal God's judgments on evil. God is love, not vengeance.

To any man the destiny of men in God's judgment is a tightly closed book. Man, unaided, cannot begin to grasp this matter. Only God can make it known clearly.

Special points.—The book (scroll) is variously interpreted. In my view, it is the written statement of God's judgments. They are so many that the scroll has writing on both sides. Seven (the number of completeness) seals show that the record is totally hidden from view.

Only an authorized person could break the seal of an official document. Who could break the seals of God's document?

The hero of Revelation is the Christ who appeared in chapter 1. Here he is described in three ways. The first two are terms for the Messiah (Christ). The Lion meant the strength and bravery of a warrior king. The Root meant he descended from David, Israel's ideal king.

The third symbol, the Lamb, is spiritual. Christ was accepted as a sacrifice offered in worship. Now he lives as one who has been offered and has risen from the death he suffered. In this way he has "overcome" all the enemy could do to him; so he is able to understand and uphold those who suffer, and reward those who overcome the enemy through suffering.

Seven horns show that he has complete power to do what he must do. Seven eyes show that he is complete spirit. This means that he is with all his people all the time and has full knowledge of all they experience.

As the King on the throne is worthy to determine man's fate, the Lamb is worthy to administer it. The praises of the Lamb show one thing clearly: although the Lamb and the one seated on the throne are not the same, they are one (vv. 9–14; cf. John 10:22–39).

Christ's redeeming work makes his followers the completion of what God purposed and began to do in Israel (v. 10; cf. Ex. 19:5–6). They are the true Israel, the true kingdom of priests. In Revelation each reference to Israel must be understood in this way. Revelation is not a Jewish book. It is a Christian book with a Jewish background.

Truth for today.—Revelation insists that behind all history is the God who revealed himself supremely in Jesus Christ. Everything he does is to redeem men from sin and its results. That fact must determine Christians' attitudes toward all Jesus did and commanded. He is more than a nice friend, whose ideas can be taken or left alone. He is our Emperor. His commands to us are absolute law.

III. PICTURES OF HOPE AND JUDGMENT (REV. 6:1—16:21)

The central theme of Revelation is God and his victorious care for his people. His judgment on evil supports and helps develop the main theme.

Behind each picture of judgment are three great beliefs: (1) on earth Christ is supreme; (2) through Christ God acts within the universe because he controls it; (3) God gives unity to all things, natural, historical, and spiritual.

The evil which God judges in Revelation is emperor worship. The judgment is introduced in three series of seven acts, then is concluded in one dramatic, final event (19:10–21).

Each of the series is a unit. The first four acts are closely related. The fifth and sixth are related to each other, but are unrelated to the first four. The sev-

enth points forward toward something which is to follow.

You need to study the three series together. They are ways of saying almost the same things. The repetition stresses the certainty of the judgments. Progress is developed by making each series more severe than the one before. The seal judgments strike one fourth of all the earth. The trumpets strike one third of all they touch. The bowls strike all who submit to the worship of Domitian.

Each judgment, like the ten plagues on Egypt, has two sides: (1) it resembles something which occurs in nature or normal human life; (2) God causes it.

Twice God's desire to cause the idolaters to repent is mentioned (9:20–21; 16:9,11). Otherwise the entire emphasis is on the punishment of wilful sin.

Opening Six Seals (Rev. 6:1—8:5)

Each horse and rider which appears after the opening of the first four seals symbolizes a form of judgment upon the Roman Empire. The first means successful military invasion. The second, civil war. The third, famine, a natural result of warfare. The fourth, pestilence or plague, a companion of famine.

The fifth seal treats the martyrs of Domitian's rage. They are "under the altar," where the blood of sacrifices was poured out. The symbol means that their deaths were self-sacrifices, acts of supreme worship and loyalty. The time for complete vengeance has not come, for more are yet to die. God will determine the time for final judgment.

The sixth seal produces complete chaos in the physical world, filling evil men with great terror.

Special points.—Historians usually trace the fall of Rome to three main causes: military invasion, corruption and strife among leaders, and physical calamities. The first four and the sixth seal judgments portrays these forces.

The white horse symbolizes the victory of the one military power which the Roman army of that time feared, Parthian cavalry. The Parthian Empire lay east of the Roman border, the Euphrates River. This force appears often in Revelation.

Some people condemn the martyrs' cry for vengeance. They who have never felt the crush of persecution do not see how Christians could express such an attitude. The answer given the martyrs does not rebuke, but assures them. They are safe now; they are not alone, and others will join them. And God will judge the guilty in his own time and way.

Protection for the Redeemed (Rev. 7:1–17)

The passage.—After the sixth judgment of each series the saints are told how God cares for them. His judgments will never touch them, although they may be killed by men. Anyone who dies for his loyalty to Christ is freed from all need, danger, or harm; since the Lamb is also the providing Shepherd of his own.

The number of God's people is limited only to those who will be faithful to Christ (v. 14). Anyone from any place can have the life which Christ gives.

Special points.—The stage is set for a climax of judgment (vv. 1–2). Then there is a delay so that God's people may be marked off, "made immune." The number is symbolic of an unlimited host. One thousand is the number of absolute completeness. It is multiplied by the number of Israel (12), then again by 12.

The tribes probably are symbolic of all nations and tongues; since all who belong to Christ are the true Israel (cf.

5:9–10). Probably the 144,000 is the great host from all nations (v. 9).

A familiar Jewish custom made the forehead the logical place for God's mark which told the world, "This man is a part of the New Israel." The Jew wore on his forehead a phylactery, a small leather pouch which contained quotations of Scripture. It marked him as a Jew.

"Great tribulation" refers to the persecution under Domitian (v. 14).

Opening the Seventh Seal (8:1–5)

The brief, dramatic pause says, "God is in no hurry. He schedules events in his own times and ways."

The incense mixed with prayers shows that God's action in judging Domitian answers his peoples' prayers for help.

Breaking the seventh seal introduces the second series of judgments.

Sounding the Six Trumpets (Rev. 8:6—9:21)

The passage.—This series of judgments is similar to the first, the seals, and is a pattern for the third, the bowls.

The first four trumpets herald judgments on the recognized divisions of the created order. First, the land. Second, the seas. Third, the fresh waters. Fourth, the heavenly bodies. One third of each of these areas is destroyed.

The fifth and sixth trumpets herald a totally different kind of judgment. Symbolic locusts from within the earth suggest torment and destruction caused by forces within the empire. The invasion of a host of Parthians on symbolic horses suggest destruction coming from outside the empire. Too, the sixth is more intense than the fifth: the locusts cause misery; the horses kill.

The special nature of the judgments of the last three trumpets is shown by describing each of them as a "woe," a source of unusual anguish and tragedy.

Special points.—The details of the locusts' appearance were intended to be repulsive. They show how Rome twisted real and natural things. Locusts which sting men and ignore grass are no more unnatural than are Rome's values and conduct. The same type of distortion is pictured by horses which kill with their breath and their tails.

In the midst of judgment God has left open a way of repentance. When evil men do not repent, the fault is theirs, not God's. Only destruction awaits them.

Truth for today.—Repentance seldom is the result of suffering alone. Men repent when they become aware of their own personal guilt and of God's gracious goodness toward them. Pain or anguish seldom produce this awareness.

Interlude of Assurance (Rev. 10:1—11:14)

Again the saints are reminded that they have no reason to fear God's judgments on the worshipers of Domitian.

The passage.—Chapter 10 has two functions. It tells of John's own feelings in declaring God's plans. God's will is recorded in a book (scroll) which is now open. His purpose is to be made known to all, as openly as thunder.

Sharing God's revelation was at first a sweet experience of fellowship. Then it became bitter because of the tragedies which had to be proclaimed.

Chapter 10 also introduces chapter 11. John's commission to proclaim God's revealed will is renewed (v. 11). The truth must go out to all peoples.

Chapter 11 is a sobering statement of triumph through suffering. God's temple shelters his people, and he provides for them. The power of their witness cannot be resisted for a while. Then for a time they are opposed, killed, and dis-

nonored. God then lifts them up again in complete victory over their enemies, who are destroyed.

Special points.—The angel in 10:1 is not one of the seven who were sounding the trumpets. He is not identified but is shown to possess earth-covering majesty. His message is for all the earth.

In 11:3, two is probably a symbolic number, rather than meaning two certain men. Two is the number of combined strength, the great power of the witness of believers united in Christ. In spreading the gospel, however, each faithful witness shares in the suffering and disgrace which lead to victory (vv. 7–12).

Three and one-half, half of seven, is the number of uncertainty. Three and one-half days is a brief period of uncertain length (v. 11). Three and one-half years is a longer period of uncertain length (v. 2).

The numbers of completeness, seven times one thousand, show that God's enemies are devastated (11:13).

Truth for today.—Power to witness is God's gift. Not all receive it; and men who do, do not receive it equally. Too, however powerful an enemy may be, or how great the suffering of the witness, God has the final word, "Victory!"

Sounding the Seventh Trumpet (11:14–19)

The passage.—The third woe is an announcement of complete victory. "Kingdoms" means "rule" or "dominion." The power of rulership on earth is taken from Domitian and given to the Lamb. To the saints this change brings the joy of reward; to rebellious nations it brings wrath, fear, and death.

Defeats of Satan (Rev. 12:1–17)

What is the origin and meaning of the conflict which demands judgment on the worship and worshipers of the emperor?

A section beginning with 12:1 and extending through 14:20 answers that question. The struggle on earth is part of a heavenly struggle.

Passage.—The accuser, the devil or Satan, is assumed to be a reality, with no effort being made to explain his origin. He suffers three defeats: (1) in efforts to destroy God's chosen ruler of the earth (vv. 1–6); (2) in being cast out of heaven (vv. 7–12); (3) in efforts to destroy God's people (vv. 13–17).

Special points.—The woman is God's people, and her child is the Christ. The resurrection defeated the attempt to destroy him on the cross.

The dragon's seven heads and ten horns probably symbolize great wisdom and unlimited power (v. 3). However, many interpreters believe they represent the line of Roman emperors (cf. 13:1).

God's people are cared for during the time of their persecution (vv. 6,13–16; cf. 11:2). Although every Christian is attacked (v. 17), there is complete victory for each one who, like Jesus, gives his life in the struggle.

The Battle Forces of Evil (Rev. 13:1–18)

The passage.—The power of the evil force seems to be too great to resist. Satan, the dragon, is the leader.

His first ally (beast) is the emperor (vv. 1–10). He has all the qualities of the three beasts described in Daniel 7: 2–6. All except those who belong to the Lamb worship him (v. 8), and he has power even to overcome the saints (v. 7).

The second ally (beast) is the group of prophets, priests, and enforcers who carry on the worship of Domitian. By performing fake miracles they make the worship appear to be proper. All who do not worship are cut off from trade and

work, and some are put to death.

Special points.—The first beast, like the dragon, has seven heads and ten horns (v. 1). The dragon gave the beast his power (vv. 2,4); so the heads and horns may mean that he has the dragon's great wisdom and power. Many feel that these also represent the line of Roman emperors (cf. 12:3).

The two lamb-like horns of the second beast indicate the power of religious appeal. This beast has the appearance of divine power; but its true character is shown by its voice, the tempting, deceiving tones of Satan.

The "mark of the beast" is a contract to the sealing of God's servants (7:3). The details are drawn from several practices. The emperor's seal had to be on every legal document, such as wills or licenses. Often this seal was not permitted to a person who did not have the official receipt for his Caesar worship during the past year. The "mark" suggests that worshiping the emperor once leaves a permanent brand on a person. The "mark" is put in places where Jews wear phylacteries. Even in public, true witnesses of Jesus do stand out in contrast to those who worship Domitian.

The number 666 is interpreted in two main ways. One is symbolic. Seven is the number of completeness or perfection. One less than seven is the symbol of evil. Three sixes together (666) means total, complete evil, like Domitian.

The other interpretation adapts a myth which was common at that time, called "Nero re-living." Some believed that Nero, recovered from his wounds, was living in Parthia, and soon would lead a Parthian army against Rome. John used this story in a Christian frame to show that Nero would become the supreme enemy of Christ. Letters of the alphabet, used alone, represented numbers. The letters of the Hebrew form of

Nero Caesar, added together, total 666. So Nero is the beast who is pictured here.

It may be that John had both these ideas in mind, for to Christians Nero was an example of complete evil.

The Battle Forces of God (Rev. 14:1–20)

Against such forces stand what looks like a pitifully weak force: the Lamb, 144,000 followers (cf. 7:4), and a sickle. While these await the battle, victory is announced from heaven. Then the punishment of the followers of the dragon and the beast is described. The saints suffer for Christ briefly, but the idolaters suffer forever.

Special points.—The 144,000 are sexually undefiled—probably a symbol of purity from idolatry, totally loyal to the Lamb, and completely dedicated to the truth. These warriors are prepared to fight the Lamb's kind of battle.

"Son of man" (v. 14) refers to Christ in his glory, power, and majesty.

A sickle was a knife used to harvest grain, and was a symbol of judgment.

Truth for today.—Christians are an essential part of God's working plan. Those who do not compromise are usable.

No word of Revelation is more fitting to people of any age than the command, "Fear God, and give glory to him" (v. 7). Verse 12 states the true meaning of being Christian—then, now, or anytime.

Glory Before Judgment (Rev. 15:1–8)

Before the last series of judgments begins there is one more glimpse of God's glory (vv. 2–4). Then he is shut off from view in a scene like that at Sinai (v. 8; cf. Ex. 19:10–25).

Pouring Out the Seven Bowls (Rev. 16:1–21)

The passage.—With slight variations these are repeats of the judgments of the trumpets. The first four bowls signal judgments on the land, the sea, the fresh waters, and the heavenly bodies. These judgments are not limited. They afflict all who bow to Domitian.

The fifth and sixth bowls are closely related and show a progression. The fifth brings great anguish and suffering, but it produces no repentance. The sixth assembles the forces of evil for death in the great battle against God.

The seventh bowl pronounces victory before the battle begins.

Special points.—The sixth bowl probably involves some form of the "Nero re-living" story. It pictures the coming of the Parthians across the border of the two empires to join the Romans in battle against the Lamb.

Anyone familiar with the Old Testament would know how often the immediate fate of God's people had been fixed by battles on the plains of Megiddo.

God's power, not man's might, crushes the enemy, Rome. This fact is shown by the city's being broken into three (the divine number) parts.

IV. THE DESTRUCTION OF ROME (REV. 17:1—20:6)

This section develops the picture which is suggested in 16:19. The focus is on the capital city of the empire.

The Great Harlot (Rev. 17:1–18)

The passage.—John begins the contrast of two women, the harlot and the bride. They are symbols of two cities, Rome and New Jerusalem.

Rome, like a harlot, uses all her beauty, charms, wealth, and power to seduce men from their loyalty to God. Fornication with her means joining in emperor worship. Yet her supreme sin is murder of the saints (v. 6). The final price which she must pay for these evils is having her "lovers" turn against her and join together to destroy her.

Special points.—Again there is use of the "Nero re-living" story, when Parthians join briefly with Rome to battle the Lamb. But he wins, for he is Lord of all lords, King of all kings (v. 14). Then the Parthians destroy Rome.

Truth for today.—God still can use even his enemies to carry out his will.

Pronouncements of Doom (Rev. 18:1–24)

This chapter is a collection of funeral dirges, not for the "helpless" sons of God, but for their "mighty" foe. They tell how Rome's pride was humbled, her power smashed, and her friends grieved.

Rejoicing of the Saints (Rev. 19:1–10)

The saints rejoice for one reason, the triumph of truth and righteousness. That triumph takes two forms, relief from oppression (vv. 2–4) and the Lamb's marriage feast (vv. 7–9).

The bride, the company of the saints, is the opposite of the harlot. She is clad in virtue and obedience to God, and is fitted to belong totally to the Lamb.

Victory in Battle (19:11—20:3)

Destruction of the beasts (19:10–21). —This is the final statement of total victory over Rome and her idolatry, the climax of the judgments of the seals, trumpets, and bowls. God's army is led by Christ, now the warrior-king, as is shown by one of his four names (v. 16; cf. 17:14). The quality of his kingship is shown by his other names. He is what he demands of men, faithfulness and truth (v. 11). He is God's message to men (v. 13). His third name is beyond understanding, because no man can comprehend all that he is (v.

12).

His army is in heaven and has the same qualities as the bride (vv. 8,14). The white horses and clothing symbolize purity and victory (v. 14).

The sword from the king's mouth wins the victory. This probably is his power of judgment, like the sickle (14:19).

The beast leads an army of those who serve and worship him (vv. 19–20).

The victory is announced before the battle (v. 17), which ends with the beast and his followers in eternal punishment (v. 20).

The dragon confined (20:1–3).—The end of Rome's two beasts is not the end of all evil. Satan, Christ's greatest enemy, is still alive and powerful. Taking away Satan's freedom is the first of two steps in his final overthrow. This figure symbolizes a spiritual concept; since Satan is a spirit being. The meaning is that he no longer can delude men into worshiping the emperor.

The 1,000 years is a symbol of a long period which perfectly fulfils its aim.

The Faithful Reigning (Rev. 20:4–6)

This passage makes a special promise *only* to those who overcome Domitian's persecution (v. 4). They are promised *only* to share in Christ's kingship, priesthood, and power to judge (vv. 4, 6). This is an appeal for total faithfulness to Christ. "The rest of the dead" (v. 5) includes all other saints.

Some take the passage out of its context and make the promise apply to all Christians. Usually they include all the blessings which Bible books promise for the Messiah's reign. Such views have led to many strange teachings and hopes.

V. GOD'S ULTIMATE VICTORY (REV. 20:7—22:5)

Evil Finally Conquered (Rev. 20:7–15)

Here the time view goes beyond Domitian. Rome is not Christ's only enemy. The total victory over evil must include all peoples. Gog and Magog symbolize all of earth's remote or barbaric nations. When he is given opportunity, Satan stirs them to rebel against God; then they, too, fall to God's judgment.

The deceiver is confined then to endless punishment, as were the two beasts.

The judgment of all men follows. One thing, their relation to the Lamb, determines their destiny. They who do not acknowledge him as Lord are put with Satan and the beasts.

The New Jerusalem (Rev. 21:1—22:5)

The passage.—God creates a new physical setting. It befits the life of the new kind of man, who lives in full fellowship with God. Men no more will be shut off from each other or from God by the great divider, the sea (21:1).

This fact frames the main thought of the passage: God now dwells with men (22:3). His presence and blessings are reserved for one kind of person, "he that overcometh" (21:7). This verse echoes the letters to the churches.

They who could not overcome, "the fearful and unbelieving," receive the same punishment as the immoral and those who give to another the worship which is due only to God (vv. 8,27).

In symbols John describes the city as the perfect dwelling place of men who live in obedient fellowship with God.

Special points.—This city is on the new earth; so the symbols which are used to describe it may be used properly to express the Christian hope of heaven.

The cube shape (v. 16) is a reminder of the holy of holies, God's dwelling place within Israel. The city is God's new, complete dwelling place among men.

The presence of God and the Lamb is the supreme reality; so the city needs no outward reminder of God, a temple (v. 22). Every need of man is provided: safety, light, worship, beauty, food, drink, and healing. What the Creator causes man to need, he provides.

Epilogue (22:6–21)

This passage is designed to end the book so that all who belong to Christ will be challenged. It is the final appeal for faithful commitment to Christ.

Two main thoughts stand out: (1) the message of this book is true (vv. 6,8–9,16); (2) Jesus Christ is coming soon to establish the things which are written (vv. 7,12–13,17). The petition, "Come," is an appeal to the Lord that he return quickly (v. 17).

The warning (vv. 18–19) means, "You must see and understand this book's true meaning, share it, and obey it!"

May the grace of Jesus Christ enable you to be a faithful and true witness

BIBLE STUDY AIDS

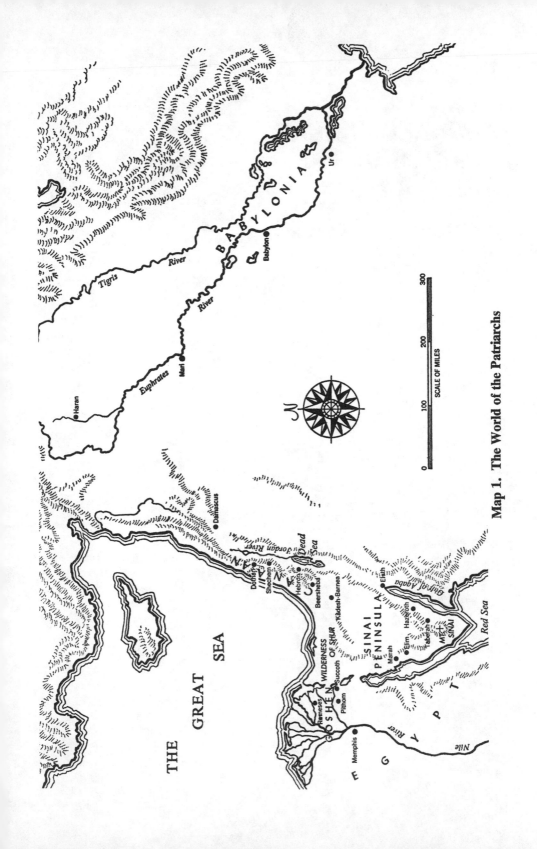

Map 1. The World of the Patriarchs

ARCHAEOLOGICAL PERIODS OF THE HOLY LAND

Kebatan Stage (food-gathering)
To 9th millennium B.C.

Natufian (incipient food-producing)
9th to early 7th millennium B.C.

Pre-Pottery Neolithic
Early 7th to late 6th millennium B.C.

Pottery Neolithic
Late 6th to end of 5th millennium B.C.

"Chalcolithic"
End of 5th to end of 4th millennium B.C.

Early Bronze I
ca 3100-2850 B.C.

Early Bronze II
ca 2900-2600 B.C.

Early Bronze IIIA
ca 2650-2500 B.C.

Early Bronze IIIB
ca 2550-2350 B.C.

Early Bronze IIIC
ca 2400-2250 B.C.

Early Bronze IV
ca 2200-2000 B.C.

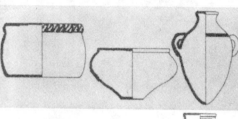

Middle Bronze I
Before 2000 to before 1800 B.C.

Middle Bronze IIA
ca 1700 B.C.

Middle Bronze IIB
ca 1600 and early 1500 B.C.

Middle Bronze IIC
ca 1575-1500 B.C.

Late Bronze I
ca 1500-1400 B.C.

Late Bronze IIA
ca 1500-1300 B.C.

Late Bronze IIB
ca 1300-1200 B.C.

Iron I or Early Iron
ca 1200-900 B.C.

Iron II or Middle Iron
ca 900-587 B.C.

Persian or Late Iron
587-330 B.C.

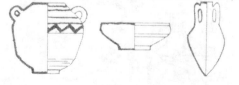

Hellenistic
330-63 B.C.

Roman
63 B.C.-A.D. 330

Byzantine
A.D. 330-638

Map 2. The Exodus

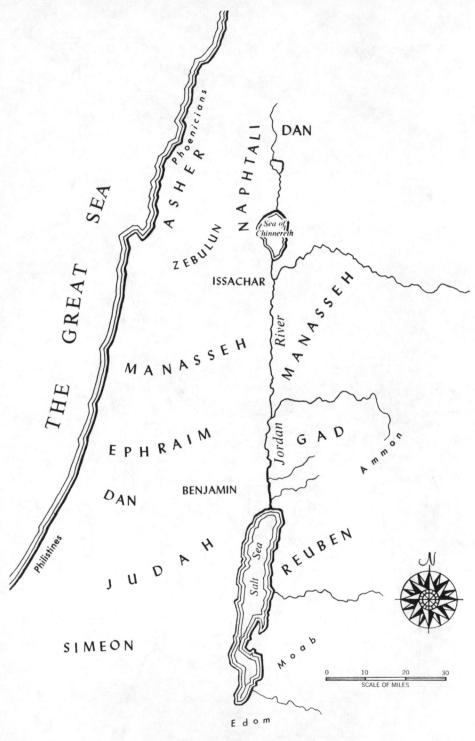

Map 3. The Time of the Judges

KINGS AND PROPHETS OF JUDAH AND ISRAEL

UNITED KINGDOM (1020-922 B.C.)	PROPHETS
SAUL, DAVID, SOLOMON	SAMUEL NATHAN

TWO KINGDOMS (922-722 B.C.)	

JUDAH	ISRAEL	
Rehoboam (922-915)	Jeroboam I (922-901)	
Abijah (915-913)	Nadab (901-900)	ELIJAH
Asa (913-873)	Baasha (900-877)	
Jehoshaphat (873-849)	Elah (877-876)	ELISHA
Jehoram (849-842)	Zimri (876)	
Ahaziah (842)	Omri (876-869)	
Athaliah (842-837)	Ahab (869-850)	
Joash (837-800)	Ahaziah (850-849)	
Amaziah (800-783)	Jehoram (849-842)	JONAH
Uzziah (783-742)	Jehu (842-815)	
Jotham (742-735)	Jehoahaz (815-801)	AMOS
	Jehoash (801-786)	
	Jeroboam II (786-746)	HOSEA
	Zachariah (746-745)	

JUDAH ALONE (722-587 B.C.)	Shallum (745)	ISAIAH
	Menahem (745-738)	
Ahaz (735-715)	Pekahiah (738-737)	MICAH
Hezekiah (715-687)	Pekah (737-732)	
Manasseh (687-642)	Hosea (732-724)	
Amon (642-640)		ZEPHANIAH
Josiah (640-609)		JEREMIAH
Jehoahaz (609)		NAHUM
Jehoiakim (609-598)		HABAKKUK
Jehoiachin (598-597)		
Zedekiah (597-587)		

EXILE AND RESTORATION (587-400 B.C.)	

DANIEL, EZEKIEL
OBADIAH, HAGGAI
ZECHARIAH, MALACHI
JOEL

SOLOMON'S TEMPLE

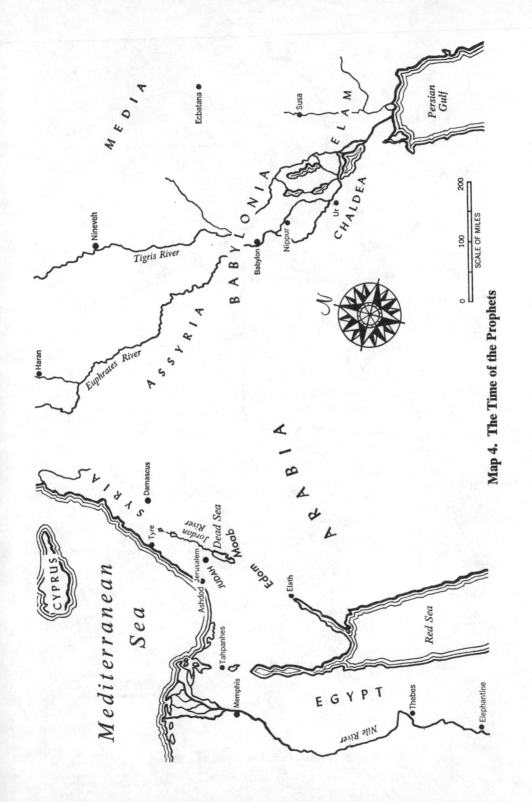

Map 4. The Time of the Prophets

Map 5. Palestine in the Time of Christ

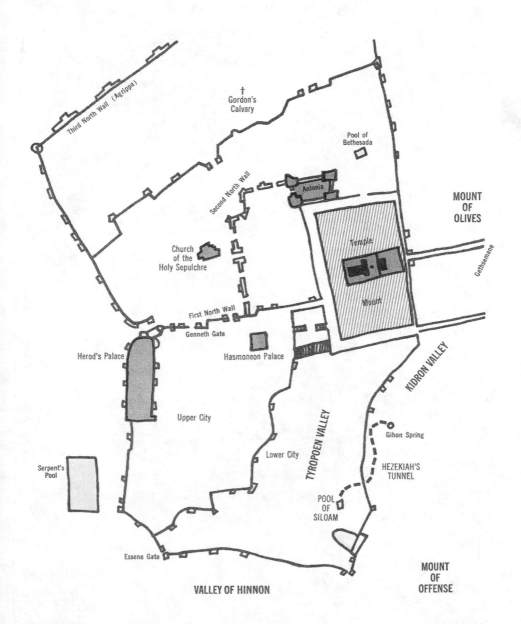

JERUSALEM IN NEW TESTAMENT TIMES

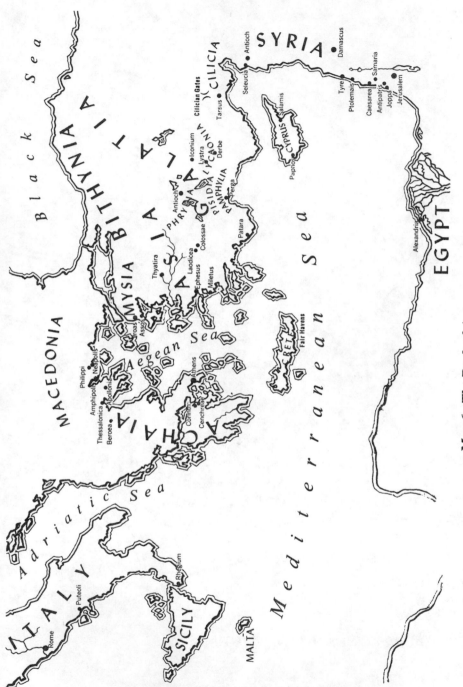

Map 6. The Book of Acts

BROADMAN